TORNADO

TORNADO

In the Eye of the Storm

JOHN NICHOL

**SIMON &
SCHUSTER**

London · New York · Sydney · Toronto · New Delhi

First published in Great Britain by Simon & Schuster UK Ltd, 2021

1 3 5 7 9 10 8 6 4 2

Simon & Schuster UK Ltd
1st Floor
222 Gray's Inn Road
London WC1X 8HB

www.simonandschuster.co.uk
www.simonandschuster.com.au
www.simonandschuster.co.in

Simon & Schuster Australia, Sydney
Simon & Schuster India, New Delhi

A CIP catalogue record for this book is available from the British Library

Hardback ISBN: 978-1-4711-8052-1
Trade Paperback ISBN: 978-1-4711-8053-8
eBook ISBN: 978-1-4711-8054-5

Typeset in Sabon by M Rules
Printed in the UK by CPI Group (UK) Ltd, Croydon, CR0 4YY

For Sophie

CONTENTS

Acknowledgements xiii

Major Characters xv

Glossary xix

Foreword 1

Prologue: Seven Seconds 9

ONE The Birth of 'The Fin' 33

TWO The Gathering Storm 52

THREE 'Everything's Changed!' 78

FOUR The Wolfpack 116

FIVE Gin-clear Skies 144

SIX 'My God, We've Lost Another One' 169

SEVEN 'The Bad Stuff' 191

EIGHT 'Please Let Him Be Dead' 211

NINE	The Mission from Hell	229
TEN	Broadcast or Die	249
ELEVEN	'Stay with It!'	271
TWELVE	A Bolshie Lady	302
THIRTEEN	'Missile Launch!'	326
FOURTEEN	Terminate the Wolfpack	351
FIFTEEN	Going Home	375
	Epilogue: 'Our Story Had Come Full Circle'	398
	In Memoriam	424
	Endnotes	427
	Bibliography	441
	Picture Credits	443
	Index	445

This book is dedicated to all the courageous, dedicated and skilled men and women involved in the liberation of Kuwait 1990–1991.
Especially those who made the ultimate sacrifice.

ACKNOWLEDGEMENTS

Many people willingly offered their valuable time and considerable expertise while I researched and wrote this book. I cannot mention every person individually but I am eternally grateful to you all.

My sincere thanks also go to:

Fellow authors Mike Napier, Ian Black and Charles Allen for their encyclopaedic knowledge of Tornado and Gulf War operations, wonderful collection of photos and access to their vast mine of Tornado-related information and interviews.

Steve Barnes and Steve Barnfield, both former Tornado Qualified Weapons Instructors, for their forensic analysis of early drafts of the book and cover image. Any remaining errors or misinterpretations of tactics or events are mine alone.

Les Hendry, the Dhahran Tornado Detachment Senior Engineering Officer, for access to his incredible database of Gulf War Tornado operations and photos. Dicky James, the IX(B) Squadron Association Historian, for his assistance with locating memoirs, documents and personnel. Matty Mathieson for his help sourcing videos and photographs. And Paul Lenihan for his assistance locating Tornado veterans.

The whole team at my fantastic publisher Simon & Schuster for their encouragement, advice and expertise, and to Thomas Harding for his time and assistance.

I am ever grateful to my friend and agent of thirty years Mark Lucas, who wields his famous red editing pen with laser-guided precision and is always a steadying source of wise counsel.

My wonderful wife Suzannah and daughter Sophie, who are always there with their unstinting love and support.

Finally, I am truly grateful to the countless serving RAF officers and veterans, and their loved ones, who told me their Tornado stories and who appear in this book. It was an incredibly emotional process at times and many tears were shed as long-buried memories were recalled. I was only able to use a fraction of the accounts I heard and it was impossible to detail every mission undertaken. Everyone involved served with courage and dignity, so I hope I have done justice to you all, and to the story of the Tornado at war in 1991.

* * *

I was assisted by many other RAF personnel, researchers, authors and historians, who offered invaluable information and contacts. It is impossible to name them all, but the following provided important leads, accounts, pictures or advice:

Spike Abbott, Colonel Cliff Acree, Colin Adair, Dave Ailano, Brian Armstrong, Vanessa Burgess, Air Commodore Al Byford, Wing Commander Gary Coleman, Gary Eason, Colonel Dave Eberly, Air Vice-Marshal Ian Gale, Paul Giverin, Group Captain Ian Hall, Lyn Hicks, Gillian Howie, Jamie Hunter, Mike Lumb, Rob McCarthy, Lawrie Marshall, Liz Merger, Dave Morris, Stuart Norris, Mark Ranger, Air Commodore Graham Pitchfork, Air Vice-Marshal Pete Rochelle, Tommy Tank, Group Captain Andy Turk, Professor Gordon Turnbull, Berry Vissers, Dame Arabella Warburton, Andy White, Simon Whittaker, Rob Woods.

MAJOR CHARACTERS

Countless Royal Air Force squadrons, units and personnel served in the region from August 1990 to March 1991 and it is impossible to list them all. Almost 200 Tornado aircrew served during the conflict itself;[1] these are just the main characters who feature in the book.

The reader should note that this book's author, John Nichol, appears as a character described in the third person in the same way as the other participants.

MUHARRAQ, BAHRAIN

Nigel Risdale (pilot)
& John Broadbent (navigator, Officer Commanding 15 Squadron[2] and Tornado Detachment Commander)

Nick Heard
& Rob Woods

Rupert Clark
& Steve Hicks

Gordon Buckley
& Paddy Teakle

Pablo Mason
& Gary Stapleton

John Peters (wife, Helen)
& John Nichol

Mark Paisey
& Mike Toft (wife, Sue)

Nigel Elsdon (Officer Commanding 27 Squadron)
& Max Collier

Dave Waddington (mother, Berenice)
& Robbie Stewart (wife, Tange; daughter, Kirsty; son, Scott)

DHAHRAN, SAUDI ARABIA

Cliff Spink, Detachment Commander

Jerry Witts (Officer Commanding 31 Squadron and Tornado Detachment Commander)
& AJ Smith

Simon (Budgie) Burgess
& Bob Ankerson (wife, Chris; son, Gareth)

Stew Gillies
& Pete Rochelle

Ivor Evans (Officer Commanding 9 Squadron)
& Dicky James

Tabuk, Saudi Arabia

Pete Batson
& Mike Heath (Officer Commanding 20 Squadron)

Trevor Roche
& Dave Bellamy

Mike Warren
& Mal Craghill

Garry Lennox (wife, Anne)
& Kevin Weeks

RAF Marham, Norfolk, UK

Jock Stirrup, Station Commander

Bill Green (Officer Commanding 27 Squadron. Wife, Jenny; son,
Jeremy; daughter, Philippa)
& Neil Anderson

GLOSSARY

AAR	Air-to-air refuelling.
ALARM	Air-Launched Anti-Radiation Missile; used to attack enemy radar systems.
AWACS	Airborne Warning and Control System; aircraft designed to provide over-watch, battlespace management and monitoring across the area of the conflict.
Boz pod	The under-wing pod carried by the Tornado which dispensed chaff to confuse radar systems, and flares to counter heat-seeking missiles.
Chaff	The strips of metallic fibre ejected from the Boz pod which reflected enemy radar signals in an effort to avoid detection or break a missile lock. Possibly used in conjunction with a missile-break manoeuvre.
CVR	Cockpit Voice Recorder; the so called 'black box' which records all intercom and radio conversation in the cockpit.

CWP   Central Warning Panel; the in-cockpit system that warns of an aircraft systems failure.

DetCo   Detachment Commander; each major RAF base had a senior officer as the overall DetCo in command of all aspects of operations and support functions. The Tornado unit on each base would have its own DetCo solely in charge of Tornado combat ops.

GLO   Ground Liaison Officer; usually an army officer attached to an RAF squadron to ensure liaison between the services.

HAS   Hardened aircraft shelter; the reinforced bunkers on airfields used to shelter aircraft from attack.

HUD   Head-up Display; a pilot's in-cockpit display which projects crucial information so that it appears in his eyeline as he looks ahead, out of the cockpit.

IFF   Identification, Friend or Foe; an electronic system that is used to tell friendly aircraft from potentially hostile ones.

IP   Initial Point; the point that marks the start of the final run-in towards the target.

LGB   Laser-guided bomb; a munition which has been converted to follow laser signals precisely onto a target.

MIA   Missing in action.

Missile break   Aggressive manoeuvres an aircraft makes in an attempt to break a missile lock. Possibly accompanied by deploying chaff or flares.

Missile lock   When an enemy SAM system targets a specific aircraft ready to launch and guide a missile in an effort to shoot it down.

MRCA   Multi-Role Combat Aircraft; the initial term by which the Tornado was known before receiving its name.

NBC   Nuclear Biological Chemical.

NVGs   Night-vision goggles.

OLF   Operational low flying; flying down to 100ft above the ground. Only allowed in very specific areas.

Pave Spike   The laser targeting pod used by the Buccaneer aircraft. Daylight only.

PBF   Pilot Briefing Facility; the reinforced building on an airfield aircrews would use to plan and brief missions.

PGM   Precision-Guided Munition; the overall term for any guided weapon.

PLB   Personal Locator Beacon; the emergency radio aircrew carry to use after ejection. When activated, it sends out a signal that can be homed in on.

PTSD   Post-traumatic stress disorder.

QWI   Qualified Weapons Instructor; aircrew who have completed an arduous course to become some of the most highly trained personnel. The role memorably portrayed in the *Top Gun* film.

RHWR   Radar Homing and Warning Receiver; the in-cockpit system that warns a crew they are being monitored or directly targeted by a potentially hostile radar system.

SAM   Surface-to-air missile.

SEAD   Suppression of Enemy Air Defences; this could include anti-radar missiles or bombs to attack sites, or jamming aircraft to confuse enemy radars.

Sky Shadow   The pod carried by the Tornado under its wing which could jam some enemy radar systems.

TFR   Terrain-Following Radar; the forward-looking radar system which, when coupled with the Tornado's autopilot, allowed the aircraft to 'fly itself', with the pilot hands-off the controls, in total darkness or bad weather.

TIALD   Thermal Imaging Airborne Laser Designator; the improved laser targeting pod rushed into service which allowed attacks by both day and night.

TOT   Time on target; the precise time bracket a formation was given to get its weapons on the target.

Triple-A   Anti-aircraft artillery, or AAA; intense cannon or machine-gun fire from the ground, using 'tracer' and explosive rounds which glowed in the darkness, giving the impression of a sparkling dome of light in the desert.

FOREWORD

The RAF Club, Piccadilly, London
20 February 2016

The marbled halls of the Royal Air Force Club in London echoed with excited chatter. Old friends greeted each other with hugs, kisses, and the occasional tear; some had not seen each other since they had fought together many years previously. Amid the grandeur of the Churchill Bar, under the renowned wartime Prime Minister's gaze, drinks were flowing, as were stories of battle, brushes with death, and friends who had made the ultimate sacrifice flying Tornados.

Upstairs, the staff prepared the grand dinner for 110 guests in the huge ballroom, with its mirrored panels and sky-painted ceiling. Polished silverware formed the centrepiece of each long table; legendary RAF aircraft, Spitfire fighters and Lancaster bombers, jostled for space with modern Tornado fast jets. Yellow ribbons, symbolising support of those MIA – missing in action – were tied around the vases. Off to one side, the Salon Orchestra of the Central Band of the RAF was rehearsing the theme tunes from suitably appropriate films – *Those Magnificent Men in Their Flying Machines* and *The Great Escape*.

A security team had already swept the building and armed police bodyguards kept a watchful eye on proceedings, and their two VIPs. The first, the United Kingdom Secretary of State for Defence, was enjoying a pre-dinner glass of champagne with the aircrew and their families. At 7pm, a teenage air cadet sounded her bugle to bring the bar to order and the second VIP, former British Prime Minister, The Right Honourable Sir John Major, stepped forward to speak. He was obviously in some pain, having undergone a hip replacement only a few weeks earlier, and was under doctor's orders to rest. But it was clear to all assembled that he felt it was his duty to attend the event, however briefly, and address those he had sent to war in the Gulf twenty-five years before:

> It is hard to believe that it is twenty-five years since the First Gulf War[1] [which] was, without doubt, a *just* war. Twenty-five years ago we celebrated a victory of freedom over oppression. Tonight's dinner is in honour of the airmen, soldiers and Special Forces who were prisoners during that conflict, which must have been a terrifying experience, especially for those who were, at the time, so young. They must have wondered what the future held, or worse – given whose hands they were in – whether they had any future at all.[2]

Although the dinner was the twenty-fifth annual reunion of the Gulf War prisoners of war, Sir John's words rang true to every single member of the large gathering, especially those who had been at the heart of the 1991 battle to liberate Kuwait from Iraqi occupation.

Some of us had indeed survived being blasted out of hostile skies, been captured, tortured, and endured endless brutality as POWs. But a greater portion of the audience were our friends and colleagues who had shown astonishing bravery and skill, flying countless missions, night after night, under truly deadly fire. They knew what fate awaited them if they too were shot down; they had seen their battered and bruised colleagues paraded as prisoners on Iraqi television. They also knew that a number of their friends had been killed. Carrying on in the face of such adversity had taken a special kind of courage. Collectively, our lives had hung by the narrowest of threads; a situation none of us had ever imagined, or were really prepared for.

* * *

Back in August 1990, when Iraqi forces had invaded neighbouring Kuwait, none of us had any concept of what the future held. Few could have accurately pointed to either country on a map. More importantly, most of us who flew out to the Gulf that year had no real concept of armed conflict. We were Cold War warriors; some at that dinner had joined the military in the 1960s, a few years after the Cuban Missile Crisis had brought the world to the brink of nuclear Armageddon. Our primary concern through the 1970s and 80s was with the threat to Europe and the West from Communism and the Soviet Union. Our training was built around the threat of mass battles, mass casualties and, ultimately, the use of the nuclear weapons. The notion of fighting a focused, regional war in a faraway desert was simply unimaginable. In 1982, as the first Tornados were just entering service, a war had been fought to liberate the Falkland Islands after the Argentinian invasion and many lives had been lost. But at the time it was regarded as perhaps an isolated incident, and, while air power had been crucial, there had not been mass attacks with hundreds of aircraft in the skies at one time.

As a young Tornado navigator in the 1980s I was part of a truly vast, 310,000-strong military machine. The RAF's Tornado force *alone*, which would eventually spearhead the defence of Saudi Arabia and subsequent attacks on Iraq, numbered around 430 bomber and fighter aircraft. The total size of the RAF was astonishing – nearly 94,000 personnel and 1,800 front-line and training aircraft.[3] To give this some context, in 2020 the RAF had around 32,000 personnel and some 570 aircraft.

Regardless of our incredible military might, I had never truly believed the Tornado force would fight any war. We trained endlessly for it, but the reality was far from my mind. Our major focus was on the deployment of nuclear weapons, and, if I had ever taken off on that mission, there would have been little to return to. We were like firefighters who had never fought a blaze, medics who had never attended to an injury.

Then, in August 1990, the brutal Iraqi dictator Saddam Hussein invaded his Gulf neighbour and everything changed. Hussein had thought the world would never intervene. His miscalculation would cost him and his nation dear. And the ramifications of the conflict he ignited still reverberate around the region, and the world, thirty years later. Within weeks of the invasion, United States President George H. W. Bush had built a near-total international coalition intent on evicting Iraq from Kuwait; hundreds of thousands of troops deployed to the region. The American and British military would be in the eye, of what would become, Operation Desert Storm.[4]

* * *

There was another group at the dinner in the RAF Club that night; the friends and relatives of those who had fought. Men and women who had sat at home, waiting for news. In many ways, theirs was the most heart-wrenching and lonely task, watching events unfold on TV, waiting to see if *their* loved one would survive. And a few listening to Sir John had received the dreaded 'knock at the door'; military officers in uniform delivering the worst news possible, as the war drew to its close. The former Prime Minister made it clear he had felt a deep responsibility to those who fought, and those who died:

I have many memories of the conflict. A few days before the war started, I visited Dhahran and when I stood on a lorry to speak to the vast array of troops and airmen gathered around, I saw how truly young so many of *you* were. I knew – though you did not – that the war would begin two or three days later, on January 16.[5] As it happens, that day was my son's sixteenth birthday and, as I looked out at the sea of faces before me, I saw many who were

barely older than him. As I spoke, my own son's face was trans-
posed on each one.

Nothing could have been a more powerful way of demonstrating – *to me* – the momentous task we were asking of *you*.
Older men and women decide on war, but it is younger men and
women who have to fight it, and risk their lives in doing so. And,
sadly, lives were lost. Mercifully few – but even *one* is too many. I
remember staying up night after night to receive reports – and this
was the hardest thing to bear – to learn which, if any, crews had
been lost. Never imagine that ministers do not share the tension
of families sitting at home. We felt every single moment; not least
since *we* were responsible for it.

His recent hip operation meant our principal guest speaker should
only have stayed at the venue for around twenty minutes, but he
spent considerable time chatting to the men and their families. He
was particularly keen to seek out those who had lost a husband,
brother, father or son and talk to them in private.[6] Over an hour
after his arrival, a bodyguard quietly reminded him he was not
meant to be standing at all.

After his departure, the drink flowed and reminiscences
became increasingly noisier. Hands were waved like wings above
the silver aircraft tableware, detailing aerial skirmishes and close
calls with death in the Iraqi skies twenty-five years before. Those
of us who had flown just a couple of missions before being shot
down (in my own case, a single op) were the target of light military ribbing by friends who had flown countless sorties in the
face of deadly fire.

Before things got too riotous, the Secretary of State for Defence,
Michael Fallon, who had come straight from a seventeen-hour flight
from the Falkland Islands, stood up to speak:

Let me start by saying, it's not simply an honour to meet you,
but humbling too. Being Defence Secretary means having to take
hard decisions that can put our people in harm's way. That's never

easy. But it's easier for *me* than it is for *you* – and *your* families. You have to carry out those political choices on the front line. And you have to face the consequences. You had to cope with something entirely new for your generation.

Since the First Gulf War, today's men and women have grown used to the idea of serving in a combat situation. But for you who took part in that seminal conflict things were *very* different. We'd just emerged from the Cold War. You were trained to guard against the hordes who might suddenly emerge from behind the Iron Curtain. You were ever on the alert for nuclear escalation. Tense and terrible though it was, it was predictable. And this shadow boxing had gone on for decades. No one really expected things to change.

And then – seemingly out of nowhere – Saddam Hussein sent 100,000 troops crashing into Kuwait. And you found yourselves part of one of the biggest conflicts of our modern era – well over half a million people assembled in the desert. It was not that you were unprepared. More that it was so unexpected; so unpredictable. That must have come as a huge shock to your system. The sudden knowledge that this wasn't a test. It was happening for real. Yet, despite all that, you remained undaunted. You adjusted. You adapted. You did us proud.

And let me make particular mention of [those] sadly no longer among your number. Their families – some I'm honoured to see here in the room tonight – need to know that we will never forget their sacrifice and service. Their names and their legacies will live on.[7]

A number of dinner guests were in tears as the Defence Secretary made his tribute to the fallen.

* * *

That reunion of colleagues who had fought above the deserts of Iraq was a momentous occasion, not least because it prompted a number of surprising realisations. As individual memories of the war, sometimes painful, often long buried, began to surface, it became obvious to me that, even after all those years, most of us still knew little of our companions' true experiences during the conflict.

Indeed, *I* had never spoken, in any detail, to my fellow prisoners of war, or even my own Tornado Squadron friends, about *their* experiences of captivity or battle; their emotions in the face of fear and possible death. And I had never spoken *at all* to the wives or children who had waited at home, praying for husbands and fathers to safely return.[8] The seeds of this book were sown.

Countless RAF, army and navy units were involved in the liberation of Kuwait and all served with courage and dedication. Nearly 50,000 British personnel deployed to the Gulf region. Of course, I can only tell the stories of a few, but I hope that their interwoven experiences will stand as a tribute to them all.

John Nichol
Hertfordshire
April 2021

PROLOGUE

SEVEN SECONDS

SATURDAY, 19 JANUARY 1991, THE GULF

Robbie Stewart stared into the hotel's polished bathroom mirror at the grey stubble that spread down his cheeks and across his jaw.

He sprayed shaving foam into his hand and saw again the yellow-white explosion of flame with its vicious red heart. Robbie's friend and fellow Tornado navigator Max Collier, and his pilot Nigel Elsdon, the Squadron Boss, had disappeared in an instant. Nigel had only been with them for a few weeks. Both had gone down on the first day of the war to liberate Kuwait from Iraqi occupation, although they were presumed dead there was no official confirmation.

Robbie's own Tornado had been travelling at 600mph, trying to escape the storm of gunfire, when the radio call came to say an aircraft had gone in. At first, he had thought one of their JP233 runway-busting munitions had exploded. Then came the sickening realisation. 'I knew immediately that the huge orange fireball was an aircraft, but there was no time to reflect, we just needed to get out of the target area.'[1] Both men had gone; their Tornado strewn across southern Iraq's desert floor.

Out of immediate danger, reality took hold. 'It was just a hollow feeling that we hadn't all made it, but there was nothing to be done or said.' At first the barrage of deadly triple-A – anti-aircraft artillery, or AAA – streaming skywards had seemed almost like a novelty. Sparkling white and yellow lights cascading over the cockpit like a firework display. Robbie, the Tornado's navigator, had felt strangely cocooned under the thick Perspex canopy. 'You could see all this happening around you, but it's calm and settled inside a Tornado with your helmet on. So quiet you feel isolated from the outside. I didn't feel any fear, I was concentrating on the job. I had one task: to release the weapon at the right point, at the exact time.'

They were now two days into the air campaign that sounded the opening salvo to drive Saddam Hussein's forces out of Kuwait, a sovereign state the Iraqi Republican Guard had invaded six months earlier. They had lost Max and Nigel on their first mission. Days later, they were about to face it all over again, now knowing beyond any doubt that death in war was real. Neither Max nor Nigel would be present at the next briefing. Nor would the grinning faces of other colleagues. The 'Two Johns', Peters and Nichol, had also been shot down earlier that first day, 17 January. All that had been heard of them was Nichol's last cry: 'We're on fire. We might have to get out!'[2] Then silence.

Four aircrew lost in the opening hours of the war.

As Robbie stood in front of the mirror, the intense triple-A barrage, the deadly, never-ending salvoes of exploding shells, the smell of sweat, the grunts, the concentration and exertion from the Tornado's high G-forces all but swamped him. The enemy gunfire had been of unimaginable intensity and volume, and yet somehow they had sailed through it untouched as they attacked the airfield. They had gone to war for the first time *ever*, with an arsenal of *real* weapons under their Tornado, against a *real* enemy who wanted them dead. Robbie's feeling was now very different from the adrenaline charge and apprehension of the first night. 'England and my family seemed a long way away and I was about to enter a hostile country where people would be trying to kill me. Again.'

Until the first jets had been lost, it had seemed they were untouchable. He sighed and slid the razor down his bronzed cheek. *Thank God for Tange*. Talking to his wife – her name was a shortened version of 'Tangerine', her childhood family nickname – the previous evening had released the pressure. The vision of her sitting on their sofa in the snug living room of their Victorian cottage in the quiet Lincolnshire village of Coleby. The bench on the green opposite their front door, the magnificent tower and steeple of All Saints Church. The low hum and familiar smell of the Tempest Arms. 'I'm safe, Tange. I'm okay,' Robbie had told her. He knew that there had been relentless television coverage of the first raids. Tange would have seen reports about Tornados going down, but said nothing. The relief and delight in her voice had made his heart soar.

Robbie had not been able to stop himself from telling her what he had seen and her sympathy was overwhelming. He had felt tears brim. It was time to go. Neither said, but both knew in their hearts that this could be their last conversation. Some of his colleagues had already had *their* final words with loved ones. Her voice had carried in his ears as he had gone back to the bar to drink to Max and Nigel's memory. The beers had the desired effect. He'd slept soundly. Only to wake up a few hours later knowing another mission loomed. Alcohol could not obliterate that. *I can't call her after every raid*. It was too much knowing that every phone call might be their last.

Robbie's young pilot Dave Waddington had also slept well, only to wake up with similar images of that first mission replaying endlessly in his head. Flying in total darkness, before the night had been lit up by the searing flames of the jet hitting the ground. *Max and Nigel gone*. 'I had looked out over my left shoulder to see a huge explosion; a fireball spreading across the desert floor. I knew it was a jet, but I couldn't quite rationalise what I was seeing.'[3] Their Tornado cockpit had been largely silent on the flight out of the combat zone. 'There wasn't much chat, there was little to say. Just a horrible, sinking realisation that we had lost our colleagues and there was nothing we could do about it. The incredible elation of getting out of danger, having done the job for the first time, for real, was quickly consumed by loss. It was really hard to accept, but you knew it had happened because you had seen it with your own eyes.'

Dave listened to the sound of Robbie's ablutions from their hotel bathroom. He was thankful to have such an experienced operator at his back. Their bond had grown over the many months they had flown together. At twenty-four, Dave Waddington was the youngest pilot on the Squadron. His navigator was forty-four, a silver-haired old hand, devoted to his wife and two teenage kids. Robbie's quiet disposition complemented Dave's flying skills, centring his focus on all that mattered – *get in, release the bombs, get out.* 'I was amazed how calm I had been as I gave a running commentary to Robbie in the back seat. All I could see was sparkling lights streaming into the sky towards us. I didn't think about there being three inches of explosive lead bullet behind it all!'

Their return to base presented them with a strange and disconcerting contrast. One moment they had been flying into furious gunfire, the next they were sitting in air-conditioned comfort amid the marbled columns of the Bahrain Sheraton Hotel, their designated quarters for the duration of the deployment in the absence of other military accommodation. They quietly drank cold beers, lancing the pain of their loss. 'When someone is killed in action, there are rituals to be observed by the survivors. It's a Royal Air Force tradition. Either fill up the guy's bar book, or drink whatever he's got in his room. It was very hard. We were drinking their beer and they weren't coming home. We were toasting lost friends, but we all knew that we would soon have to do the same thing again.'

They were in a contest now, that was for sure, where you flew through a wall of bullets and a hail of missiles. Where you either came home or you died. Despite the casualties from the first sorties, Dave pushed away such thoughts. 'I didn't allow myself to acknowledge that I might be killed. I didn't talk about it with my fiancée Claire. I didn't write a last letter. I knew death might happen, but I didn't want to acknowledge it was even a possibility for me.' If his bond with Robbie was tight in the build-up to war, that first night had cast it in steel. 'The reality of what we had been through hit us.

The loss of Max and Nige started to come to the fore in a growing realisation that in the not-too-distant future, together, we would be going again.'

Dave yawned as he dragged himself from the Sheraton's luxury bed. The frenzied conversations with other Tornado aircrew came back to him. Hearing *their* sortie descriptions. What *their* triple-A was like. What *they* had seen. Everyone was thirsting for knowledge, searching for a vital clue on how to survive what was coming next. He sat on the edge of the bed. In just a few hours he would be back up in the air. The memories of the cauldron of triple-A, the tensions and loss, resurfaced. 'A nearby target had been hit by the Americans that turned night into day in a few seconds. I remember thinking, *I can't believe we are going to get through that*. We had lost the Two Johns, Max and Nige, flown through a wall of lead and had a missile shot at us. There was no doubt in my mind the risks were very, very real and it wasn't going to get any easier.'

'Morning.'

Dave looked up as his friend and navigator flicked on the television, already pre-set to CNN 24-hour news. The American channel was the only one with reporters in Baghdad, showing the world the devastating effect of previously unseen precision attacks. It was real-time intelligence for everyone. There was something unreal about watching the reports of raids from the comfort of a hotel bedroom when they would be back over hostile territory in a matter of hours, bombing Iraq themselves.

Clean-shaven, showered and in crisply pressed flying suits, Dave and Robbie took the ten-minute bus ride to work in silence, via the causeway to the island of Muharraq and Bahrain's airfield. Forty-eight hours after the first sortie, it was clear to Robbie that there had already been a tactical rethink. The Tornados were going in for yet another attack on the massive Tallil airbase in southern Iraq. But this time, they would be on their own with just the shroud of darkness for protection; no prior 'softening up' by American bombers. Instead, the thinking went, surprise would catch the Iraqis unprepared. Robbie was unconvinced. 'To gain surprise we were not being supported by the usual myriad American aircraft suppressing surface-to-air missiles – SAMs – and radars. This way, it was hoped, we would avoid the wall-to-wall triple-A which we'd encountered on our first sortie. But I would have preferred the Americans accompanying us; to me, while the triple-A was a horrifying sight, the SAMs were the real threat.'

Instead, the eight-ship would provide their own airfield defence suppression. The first flight of four – call sign 'Belfast formation' – including Robbie and Dave, would go in and drop 20,000lb of high explosive on the gun and missile emplacements, demonstrating the immense skill that RAF crews had developed flying Tornados. A 'loft – or toss – attack' at night from low level was as dangerous as it got. Pulling up steeply from low level while the weapons aiming system calculated the exact point of release, the jet would accurately 'throw' its five 1,000lb bombs forward, towards the target. They were set to detonate over the heads of the Iraqi gunners, blasting shards of shrapnel through weapons and flesh. The hard part was then turning away from the target and manoeuvring the jet back down to low level, in total darkness and under fire.

Dave and Robbie had trained hard for this type of loft attack. *Come in fast and ultra-low, pop up, lob the bombs, get back down to low level and bugger off.* And thoroughly discourage the triple-A gunners from firing at the four-ship coming in behind with the vaunted JP233 weapons system, which would deliver surface cratering munitions and scatter anti-personnel mines to shut down Tallil's runways and deter any Iraqi repair teams.

Dave and Robbie listened in the cool of the Operations Room as the briefing moved on to Tallil's air defences. 'We knew there'd be triple-A and we knew there was a Roland missile system on the airfield. We were very apprehensive. Dave and I looked at one another. We didn't need to say much, we just looked.' There was good reason to fear the Roland SAM. Hurtling out at over 1,200mph, its 9kg warhead threw out deadly fragmentation designed to gut aircraft and crew. One of the few foreign-made SAMs purchased by the US,[4] the French-made missiles had taken down numerous Iranian jets during the earlier Iran–Iraq war. The operators in Tallil were old hands. Robbie and the others well understood its significance.

The Tornado at least had the Radar Homing and Warning Receiver. The RHWR was a key defence against any radar-guided missile attack.[5] A small green screen on the right-hand side of both cockpits, it would give an indication, a 'trace', if a radar was looking at them, and from which direction. Cleverer still, it signalled the type of enemy missile system or aircraft. If a radar locked onto the Tornado, the RHWR flashed a line across the screen, a 'strobe', and delivered a high-pitched squawk into the crew's flying helmets to warn of an imminent engagement. An even more urgent siren would sound if a missile was launched, accompanied by 'MG' flashing on the screen, indicating missile guidance. The RHWR was rightly considered a wartime 'no-go' item if it was not functioning correctly.

The intelligence briefing came to an end. Someone asked if there was any update on the Two Johns. There wasn't. Just a reminder to check their own escape and evasion kits. Robbie felt for the tube of gold sovereigns worth around £1,000[6] with which to bribe any locals, and the piece of paper – the so-called 'goolie chit' – which announced in Arabic that the bearer would receive a further £5,000 if a flier was returned to safety in one piece. In previous Middle East wars aircrew had been returned with testicles severed, and there was no indication that times had changed. Especially under the savage rule of Saddam Hussein and, more especially, given the rumours Robbie had heard of torture in Kuwait.

'Our minds were even more focused now because of the losses. I was very aware of checking and rechecking everything – we made sure all the escape kit was correctly positioned to give us the best chance if we ejected into enemy territory. We were not just concentrating on the flying side of ops. We double-checked the search-and-rescue procedures but still wondered if we were ready for the worst.' Some aircrew believed it might be better to perish quickly in the cockpit rather than slowly, at the hands of Saddam's henchmen.

The loss of comrades had really pointed up the dangers for Dave, but he couldn't let it affect him. 'I compartmentalised it, put it out of my mind and kept my focus on our own mission. There was nothing else you could do. You can't just walk away and say, "This is too dangerous." There was also the naivety of youth, probably like our Second World War RAF forebears, you just tell yourself: "It will never happen to me."'

He filed out of the briefing with another crew in their formation whose attack profile took them right over the SAM site. 'There was certainly some anxiety around; we were going very close to a Roland missile site which was a very real threat. I remember that the last thing I said to the other crew before we headed to the aircraft was, "Don't worry about the Roland, it will probably get me before it gets you."'

They all grinned. But then Dave caught Robbie's eye and saw a look of apprehension. They both knew what lay ahead. The odds might improve with the planned element of surprise, but Tallil's air defences were still a very real threat. On the first night the Iraqis seemed to just spray their triple-A randomly into the sky. Intelligence suggested they had now lowered the elevation on their gun barrels to catch the Tornados coming in at their approach height of around 200ft.

* * *

Under a mid-afternoon sun the eight pilots and eight navigators drifted out of the briefing room and headed across the tarmac towards the mess tent for some dinner. On the first night there had been a buzz of anticipation mixed with nervous laughter along the benches and tables. Not any more, reflected Robbie. 'The atmosphere was sombre. We all knew what the reality of this war now meant.'

Fliers and ground crew were all in this together. The Tornados belonged to everyone. The ground crew spent hours on them, carefully attending to every screw, bolt, cable, ramp and nozzle that held the £20 million machine together.[7] To lose an aircraft was to lose a part of themselves. To lose *their* aircrew was unbearable. And it was a very real possibility. Two sets had already been left forlornly gazing into the Arabian dawn, waiting for their jets to return, hearing only the sound of the muezzin's call to prayer. Among the engineers, the fitters, the admin staff and the logistics teams, the atmosphere was muted. Minds were focused.

Dusk was approaching as last-minute adjustments were made. Robbie found himself repeatedly checking every item of kit. The water pouches, the gold, the maps. He pulled out his small Walther PP from the leather shoulder holster and ejected the magazine, checking the eight rounds. He checked everything again then spotted his precious Ray-Bans on a table and, despite the looming darkness, stuffed them into his G-suit pants. The glare of low-level flying over the desert made them a necessity. One last time he went over the search-and-rescue procedures with Dave. Everyone else in the eight-ship was doing the same.

With their pockets bulging, G-suits tightly bound around their legs and thighs, the airmen picked up their helmets and ambled awkwardly to the waiting Tornados.

'Crews walking.' The message was sent out.

They were ready to take over the aircraft from the engineers. Robbie was pleased they were back in 'F for Foxtrot', which had carried them through the first mission unscathed. 'We said farewell to the flying-clothing boys, who wished us well with some concern showing. The jet was just 50 yards from the Operations Room but we walked out like gladiators, our kit clanking and clanging. The five 1,000-pounders already had some graffiti along the side suggesting what Saddam should do with the bombs.'

White chalk messages from the ground crew were often scrawled across the long, dark cylinders: from *One in the eye for you, Sad Man Saddam* to the endearing *Hi Sarah, Love Pete*.[8]

The aircraft loomed menacingly in the shadowed lights of the shelter. The Tornado's black nose contrasted dramatically with the desert pink of its body. Inside the sharply pointed cone was the ground-mapping radar that helped the navigator update the navigation system and identify the targets. Behind it the cockpit swept back over broad, muscular flanks. Intakes on either side of the fuselage fed air back to the powerful engine. The jet-pipes would roar, emitting yellow-blue flame from the reheat. Every fibre of its being yelled power. When the under-wing-points were harnessed with missiles, defensive pods and fuel tanks, and the belly with neatly arrayed bombs, there was no doubt what the Tornado GR1 was about. It exuded menace and meant business. The business of hitting the enemy hard. Fully armed, with its tailfin standing proud, it sent a message of dominance as it shuddered into the air. A war-fighter capable of raining fury upon its enemies, but it was graceful too.

The Tornado was neat and compact, and, for those like Robbie who had seen an aircraft or two in his twenty-five years' service, very, very effective. 'It had everything you could have dreamed of. Great navigation and targeting kit. It could fly at night, in terrible weather, at low level and hands-off. It really was superb, very modern.'

Laden with his helmet, escape equipment and G-suit, Robbie had walked past the sandbagged airfield defences, the tankers and other jets. 'Approaching the dark shape of the Tornado in the gloom, bristling with a full weapons load, ready for war, made you contemplate what you were about to do. There was a palpable sense of apprehension, hoping to God we would survive what was to come but ready for the fight. We knew the drills and were eager to get underway. This was our job, it needed to be done. We pushed all other thoughts aside.'

He mounted the steps, settled into the navigator's rear seat, which sat slightly higher than the pilot's but with instruments in front obscuring some of his forward visibility. He went through the careful ritual of strapping himself into the ejection seat, then checked his watch. Forty minutes to take-off.

Dave completed his final checks on the 30-tonne machine[9] that he was about to launch airborne under the twin thrust of its

Rolls-Royce RB199 engines. He pulled himself up on the jet-pipes to check for any loose articles, then tapped the two under-wing 2,250-litre fuel tanks. He gave the pair of Sidewinder air-to-air missiles a good shake to ensure they were properly locked on. They would be needed if Iraqi fighters showed up. He then made sure that the safety pins had been removed from each of the 1,000lb bombs, knowing his touch would be the last before they became a screaming ball of shrapnel.

Under the shadows cast by the glare of the airfield lighting he reached up to the 'Boz' self-defence pod under the right wing, checking the chaff and flare dispenser.[10]

When activated, 'chaffing' would send thousands of tiny metallic fibres – 60 per cent glass, 40 per cent aluminium, and the thickness of a human hair – into the air. They were designed to reflect and interfere with enemy radar signals, confusing both the systems and their operators. The flares would be pumped out if targeted by heat-seeking missiles; they burned off at an intense temperature, hopefully providing a more attractive target than their jet engines.

Dave examined the Sky Shadow pod on the other wing that was programmed to electronically jam enemy radar systems. They had every possible countermeasure the Tornado was designed to carry. It was reassuring for Dave to feel they were all held firmly in place if he had to throw F for Foxtrot about. 'In reality, the ground crew have already checked all this, then double-checked it, but we all did it again. Everyone had their own idiosyncrasies. I always gave the fuel tanks a tap to ensure they were full. They always were!' Everything was in order outside the aircraft. It was time to board.

Robbie fitted his oxygen pipe, intercom cable and G-suit hose into the personal equipment connector then clipped it onto the side of his seat, plugging himself into the machine's systems. He tightened the straps over his thighs and torso connected to the fastener over his stomach which held him firmly into the Martin Baker ejection seat. His hand brushed against the black and yellow-striped D-shaped ejection handles between his legs as he switched on the inertial navigation system, allowing the gyroscopes and sensors to start up their alignment process. He turned on the main computer and its monitors, and then the radios. Everything was working as advertised and the cockpit came alive with the green and red glow of the equipment. He took out the navigation cassette – the same type used to play music in a Sony Walkman – and loaded it into the main computer. It had been fed with all the information needed to navigate the route to Tallil and back, along with the precise co-ordinates of the target and aiming points.

Dave stepped back from beneath the towering fin that gave the Tornado its nickname, climbed the 9ft steps up to the cockpit and levered himself into the front seat. With his green flying helmet in place, he had the sharp, focused look of a jet pilot. It was the job he had dreamed of since he was seven. The ground crew fussed over him, pulling tight the straps on his harness. 'Give Saddam one from us, sir,' one said before climbing down and removing the steps.

Dave began his well-rehearsed start-up routine. 'There was a comfort in the well-trodden procedures. As I lowered the cockpit canopy, I felt isolated in the Tornado despite the activity outside. We had left plenty of time in case we had any problems. As I went through the checks, my nerves started to dissipate as I became part of the machinery of war. It was exactly like a training sortie, but I knew it was for real.'

Dave found the cockpit spacious compared to other jets and the ejection seat quite comfortable. He used the electric motor to raise his seat an inch, and briefly scanned the ground crew activity. He too attached his oxygen, comms and G-suit into the personal equipment connector and snapped it in place.[11] A glance at his watch told him it was thirty minutes to take-off. Plenty of time to sort out any problems. He rattled through the check list.

His cockpit was dominated by the circular moving map display right in front of him. On his left were the flight instruments, the throttles and lever to move the wings – back for low, fast flight; forward for take-off, medium-altitude flying and landing. His right hand gripped the control column – the 'stick' as it was generally known – between his legs while his left fell naturally on the throttles at mid-thigh level on the console. He paused, breathed in then looked up. The HUD – Head-up Display – dominated the cockpit front and centre. And rightly so. It was his primary flying instrument. When the Tornado was tearing along the desert floor at night, in thick fog or bright sunshine, the HUD projected speed, height, direction, weapon aiming and much more in green symbols on a glass screen.

To the left of the HUD was the Terrain-Following Radar display. TFR was the heart of the Tornado's ability to fly at night and in poor weather at very low level. A radar swept the ground ahead and gave instructions to the TFR computer system which fed the aircraft's autopilot.[12] Once activated, the pilot would remove his hands from the controls and TFR would take over; the Tornado would 'fly itself' at speeds of up to nearly 700mph and just 200ft above the ground. In total darkness or thick cloud. It was an astonishing piece of equipment.

To the right was the RHWR screen, which would warn them of incoming missiles or radar detection. Dave rapidly ran through the checks then muttered a curse. The flashing cockpit 'attention-getters' were mounted left and right of the cockpit coaming, just above the RHWR and TFR screens, and flashed red if there was a problem, attracting the pilot's attention to the Central Warning Panel (CWP) on his right. This, in turn, had more than sixty different captions which illuminated red for primary and amber for secondary-type warnings.[13] A single illuminated word on the CWP indicated the problem, such as 'FUEL', 'TFR' or 'OXY'. It was a bit like the alerts on a car dashboard, bar the fact it contained two captions that read 'L FIRE' and 'R FIRE', informing the crew their left- or right-hand engine had become an inferno. In the event of multiple failures, the CWP might 'light up like a Christmas tree'; a *really* serious problem would trigger an accompanying siren.

They were an important part of the Tornado's safety systems. Unfortunately for Dave and the engineers, F for Foxtrot's attention-getters flashed for no reason, and couldn't be cancelled.

In peacetime, they would simply 'crew out' – leave the aircraft – as it was impractical to fly with red warning lights flashing. But the spare Tornado had already been taken. And leaving F for Foxtrot meant not going on the mission. Dave was caught between a rock and a hard place. 'I knew I should really crew out of the jet; it was the correct thing to do and I certainly wouldn't be facing the dangers ahead. But what would people think of me? Say about me? What was the *right* thing to do? It was a choice, a tension between doing what was acceptable or doing what was *right*. I didn't want to let anyone down.'

The minutes to take-off were counting down. Dave felt his heart start to thud. He looked out at the engineer. 'Any suggestions?' he asked over the external intercom.

'The only thing you can do, sir, is flip up the covers and take out the bulbs.'

A big, ballsy call. Flying fast and low at night into a sky full of gunfire was already risky as hell. To not be alerted to a problem which would normally be signalled by bright lights right in front of his eyes took them a whole lot further along the hazard spectrum. Dave spoke to Robbie over the intercom. 'Shall we take the fault? The engineer said he can take out the bulbs . . .'

Robbie had his own attention-getters in the rear seat so knew they had a safety net.

'Yes,' he said. 'Take it.'

'Okay.'

Dave checked the various modes of the IFF. *Crap!* It wasn't loading up. Now this was critical. It would be suicidal flying without it. IFF – Identification, Friend or Foe – was an electronic system used by the coalition fighters and ground radar to differentiate enemy and friendly aircraft.

The ground crew loaded, re-loaded, and loaded it again. Finally, they got it working. The engineer pocketed the bulbs from the attention-getters, gave the cockpit canopy a quick wipe then closed it once again. With all the technical glitches cleared, or at least overcome, it was time to get airborne.

'Clear for engine start,' Dave said. The engineer gave a thumbs-up and Dave flicked a switch. He listened as a pleasurable low hum became a rumble.[14] The temperature gauges rose steadily from 6°C to 420°C. Even with the canopy shut and his helmet on, he could hear the powering jet engines and feel the shuddering vibration as they built to a roar.

The ground crew removed the chocks, Dave inched the throttles forward, rolled a few yards then tested the brakes by dabbing them and stopping. He taxied to the runway, feeling the heavily laden air-craft bump over the seams in the concrete. Deep blue-yellow flames glared at them from the afterburners of the other jets as they took off ahead. The Rolls-Royce engines generated 30,000lb of thrust, and burned around 600 kilos of fuel a minute at maximum power.[15] Every last ounce of it would be needed to propel the lumbering Tornado off the ground.

Their aircraft shuddered again under the turbulence as jet after jet lifted off Bahrain's friendly tarmac strip into the night sky. Dave lined up and carried out their final checks.

It was time to go.

His left hand eased forward the throttle. There was a surge of power as he pushed the engines into reheat, fully opening the jet-pipe nozzles and pumping fuel at incredible speed onto the engine's hot exhaust gas, where it ignited in a sheet of blue flame, doubling the power and making a sound like thunder.

'Engine's good,' Dave said, glancing at the gauges above his right knee. 'Captions clear.'

There was nothing on the Central Warning Panel to prevent take-off. They both felt the aircraft quiver as the engines went through maximum dry power into reheat.

He released the brakes and the Tornado's acceleration pushed him firmly back into the seat, as if a giant hand was pressing onto his chest.

'Eighty knots, 100 knots,' Dave called as they blasted down the tarmac.

The jet trembled, eager to fly, as the runway lights rushed by.

'One hundred and thirty knots,' Dave breathed. They were passing the last point at which their fully laden Tornado would be able to use its own brakes to bring them safely to a halt.

'Okay.'

The speed in the HUD rapidly increased.

'One hundred and eighty knots [207mph]. Engine's good. Captions clear. Rotating.' With the extra weight he gave himself a bit more speed then eased back the stick.

F for Foxtrot lifted off cleanly.

'Gear up.' He flicked the undercarriage handle to raise the landing gear.

'Two hundred and fifty knots. Out of reheat.'

A moment later, they were climbing through 2,000ft.

The Tornados of Belfast formation sailed through the night sky above the silent waters of the Gulf, turning northwards. Dave focused on the task ahead, a mid-air rendezvous with their tankers at 15,000ft. Air-to-air refuelling at night in total silence and near total darkness was a challenge. Before Saddam invaded Kuwait back in August, barely anyone in the Tornado bomber world had attempted to thread a probe into a swinging drogue basket in a blackout. In the hit parade of piloting skill sets, it was second only to ultra-low flying. The previous night, seven out of eight Italian Air Force Tornados had been forced to turn back from a raid after failing to hook into the tanker drogue. The pilot who had refuelled carried on alone, pelted by the flak surrounding an ammunition dump north of Kuwait City, and dropped his bombs 250ft above the deck. He was hit by triple-A gunfire forty seconds later.[16]

The aircraft had gone down at 4.30am on 18 January and the crew were MIA – missing in action. The third Tornado to be lost in the first twenty-four hours.

Dave's eyes scoured the darkness for the tanker. With a full war load the Tornado sucked up 60kg of fuel a minute in normal conditions at low level, ten times that in reheat. They carried enough fuel for perhaps two hours' flying, for a mission that would last twice that. The plan was to refuel just before entering Iraqi air space, then top up again on the way home. After six months of intense training, Dave was ready for the challenge.

'Eight miles. Heading two-seven-zero.' Robbie was the one whose skills were needed at this point. He had identified the tanker aircraft on his radar and talked down the ranges and height on the approach, plotting a course to within a few feet of the hanging basket. It was not until Dave squinted through the darkness that he could finally make out the looming belly of the tanker. They ran through the pre-tanking checks, depressurising the fuel system and extending their refuelling probe.[17]

Dave slipped the Tornado to the right, stabilising a few feet behind their target. The red light under the tanker's wing flicked off and he was cleared to join.

His concentration was all-consuming as he lined up the symbol on the HUD with the pod under the tanker's wings. His grip on the stick tightened and so did his chest with every bump as they edged forward, making tiny corrections to keep aligned. The Tornado's refuelling probe was extended to his right, but he wasn't looking at it; diverting his focus from the looming tanker could be catastrophic. Instead, he was concentrating on flying his aircraft towards a precise point on the tanker itself, knowing that as long as he was accurate the probe – almost unseen on his right – would slip effortlessly into the basket.

Robbie had a far better view of the probe and basket. With the occasional word of guidance from the back seat, Dave's concentration was only broken by the clunk of the probe engaging with the dangling fuel pipe. The feeling of satisfaction as he finally glanced to his right was strong.

But he couldn't relax. Both aircraft were travelling at nearly 350mph, with the nearest Tornado just yards away.

From now on Dave had to fly in precise formation, anticipating any jolts that might rip their connection apart. He edged the nose forward, bending the hose back to trigger the flow of high-octane fuel. The 'traffic light' on the tanker's wing turned green and Dave glanced down at the fuel gauge above his right knee. After a few minutes it showed they were once again ready for combat. He reduced power, backed away from the basket, manoeuvred to the left and joined formation with the other Tornados that had completed their own delicate night-time ballet.

For a brief moment he allowed himself to relax. He flexed his right hand, tingling and numb after gripping the stick so tightly, and fleetingly scanned the dark void below them. *Get down, get it done, go home.*

They slipped away from the tanker well short of the Iraqi border, swept the wings back and accelerated down to low level in radio silence. As they sped through the moonless sky, they completed the checks on their self-defence and attack systems. The Sky Shadow and Boz pods, and RHWR were all active. Dave set his armament safety switches to the 'live' position, ensuring their Sidewinder missiles, the 27mm Mauser cannons and the bombs were all armed and ready for instant use.[18] The fuel tanks under each wing were pre-selected for jettison just in case an emergency release was needed to evade enemy SAMs or fighters. They checked all external lights were extinguished and did a quick review of the escape and evasion. *Just in case.*

The pilots in the eight Tornados had engaged their TFR systems and removed their hands from the controls. The jets now flew themselves on autopilot through the darkness. They were on parallel track, a strategy developed when flying hands-off on TFR and autopilot in poor weather or at night. The lead Tornado and his wingman followed two separate but parallel flight paths, around 2.5 miles line abreast, as if on rail-tracks, with the second two, also line abreast, around 5 miles behind them, creating a box-shaped formation, all proceeding just 200ft above the desert floor at 7 miles per minute.[19] The crews relied on radar fixes along the route to keep the navigation systems accurate and to ensure the box remained separated.

Robbie had no way of seeing their comrades, but knew they were out there, on the same heading, bonded by the shared objectives, and shared dangers. 'We descended, lights out, into the dark

unknown, heading across the Saudi border. We were totally alone.'
He watched the moving map display tick off the distance, as they
flew in, increasing speed to over 480mph. Then they were 'sausage
side'. They had borrowed the nickname for enemy territory from the
avidly watched BBC classic *Blackadder Goes Forth*. The insanity of
the First World War trenches was beginning to echo uncomfortably
in the current conflict.

The readouts confirmed to Robbie that they were racing along at
just 200ft, the Tornado's TFR automatically adjusting their flight
path to account for every contour and obstacle, but their sensory
isolation seemed to insulate them momentarily from the hostile
world outside the warm glow of the cockpit. 'The night was pitch-
black, so the only indication of our height were the numbers on the
TV monitor. There was still no sign of any Iraqi resistance as we
approached the target. I was relatively calm, bearing in mind what
we were doing. Everything seemed to be going to plan. I had all the
weapons systems checked.'

Up front, Dave had a strong sense of the aircraft powering through
the night. His right hand rested on his lap, away from the control
column, his left hovered near the throttle. Although he was poised to
instantly take control if any problems arose, right now he was simply
monitoring the systems. 'Everyone was in the right place at the right
time. We were moving towards the target and everything was calm.
Our flight time over Iraq was about thirty minutes until we hit the
target. I was relying solely on TFR, the aircraft flying itself. There
were eight aircraft in the formation but it felt like it was just us out
there. Everything was running on rails. No triple-A. All was well.'

Robbie checked their time on target. They were a few seconds
behind schedule. Dave inched the throttles forward to increase the
speed to 630mph to pick up a little time. The HUD now told them
they'd hit Tallil precisely as planned.

In southern Iraq, it was just before 8pm on Saturday, 19
January 1991.

* * *

Back home in England it was 5pm and Robbie's wife Tange Stewart was immersed in the final scenes of the seasonal pantomime, alongside some of the children from the local Sunday school where she taught. This Saturday in mid-January offered them one last, post-Christmas treat. It had become something of a tradition. Fortunately, her teenage daughter Kirsty had been on hand to help shepherd the chirruping youngsters onto the coach for the journey to the theatre in Newark. The dame's buffoonery had the children in stitches, and their enjoyment of his saucy jokes was a welcome distraction from the terrible events unfolding some 3,500 miles to their south-east.

Earlier that day, she had penned another letter to her beloved husband after they had discussed the fateful mission where his Squadron Boss and their friend Max Collier had gone down:

> To my dearest darling,[20]
>
> It is the early hours of Saturday morning, sleep seems to elude me yet again. I am afraid last night's news of Max and The Boss was rather a shock. I will buy a card for Max's wife today and drop her a line on our behalf.
>
> It is going to be a sunny day here and Kirsty and I are going to Newark for the pantomime. She is playing in the East of England Netball Tournament next Saturday. Tonight I am going to the Heavers for dinner; I don't know that I'm very good company at present!
>
> Well, darling, all our thoughts and emotions are with you, you are never out of our mind. The kids are coping well but obviously it's difficult for them now. Keep us in your heart but do not worry about us. We have the Stewart grit.
>
> Love you loads.
>
> Tange xxx

Her thoughts drifted away from Iraq and back to the entertainment on stage. Suddenly, Tange stopped laughing. Overwhelmed by a dreadful premonition that Robbie was in terrible danger. She glanced at her watch. Nearly 5pm. She sat back and closed her eyes, trying to let it pass.

'Are you okay?' The woman in the neighbouring seat couldn't keep the anxiety out of her voice.

'Just . . . a little tired,' Tange replied.

The woman smiled and patted her on the arm, doing her best to hide her puzzlement, and failing.

Tange was in turmoil.

When they finally managed to escape the theatre, every traffic light and junction on the winding road home seemed to hold them up. She dialled the Bahrain Sheraton before removing her coat. The receptionist answered politely and put her through to Robbie's room.

No response.

Tange tried again and again, seven or eight times, with the same result.

'I'm sorry, madam,' the receptionist kept repeating. 'There's no answer.'

Tange glanced at her watch. She had a dinner date with friends across the green. On the way out she told her older son Scott to keep trying to call his father. 'Dad would love to hear from you,' were her parting words.

She hid her worries from the children, but could not ignore the dark fear inside. 'My stomach was knotting up. I knew something wasn't right.'

* * *

'Ten miles.'

The jet was still comfortably flying itself as Robbie monitored the distance to the moment when Dave would take their Tornado into the loft attack profile to toss the bombs onto the target. 'I was relatively calm, bearing in mind what we were doing. I had all the weapons systems checked and we started the attack run as planned. Our four-ship formation would complete the night attack from parallel track, lofting the 1,000lb bombs onto the triple-A sites from about 3 miles out. This should discourage the gunners from firing at the aircraft carrying the JP233 airfield denial weapons following behind us.'

In the front seat Dave was concentrating hard, his right hand ready to disengage the autopilot and take control of the jet, his left resting on the throttles, waiting to ram them forward and send the aircraft into a steep climb in order to 'throw' the bombs towards the airfield.

'Five miles,' Robbie called out over the intercom.[21]

'Five hundred and forty knots [621mph].'

They were travelling at 10.35 miles a minute 200 feet above the desert.

Robbie made a rapid calculation. *Just another thirty seconds.* They were on time and on target.

He checked the weapons systems again. No flak ahead, no hint of danger on the warning systems. All quiet. Surprise was on their side.

The Tornados of Belfast formation started their final attack procedures. 'Using the radar, I found and marked the first "offset" which updated the attack system. Suddenly, the RHWR indicated an unknown radar looking at us.'

Dave felt his chest tighten. The RHWR showed a powerful radar system searching from dead ahead, trying to acquire a lock. 'We were just coming to the "pull-up point" and starting our weapons release procedure. Almost immediately we had a missile launch indication and a siren warning screaming in our ears. A missile was in the air.'

The RHWR continued its wail.

Twelve o'clock!

Dave knew it was the worst possible direction that a missile could come from. 'Roland' flashed up on the RHWR. It couldn't be anything else. The best missile the Iraqis had was around 3 miles out, travelling towards them at a third of a mile every second.

They had just seven seconds to save their lives.

Seven seconds.

'Missile launch!' Dave said clearly and calmly. In an instant, he disconnected the autopilot from TFR and took over manual control. The green strobe on the RHWR was still pointing straight at them. Their headsets throbbed with the two-tone scream of the siren, confirming a missile was inbound.

Six seconds.

Now flying manually at over 600mph and just 200ft in total darkness, Dave snapped into a hard-left turn shouting, 'Chaff!' at his navigator. 'All I could see was a flame like a very large firework coming towards me but once I banked the aircraft left, I lost sight of it.'

The Iraqi missile operators had them locked, and the 9kg hollow charge warhead was being guided onto them with pinpoint accuracy.

The warning, like a police siren, continued relentlessly, filling their helmets. Dave's voice still sounded matter-of-fact and calm to Robbie. Their endless training had been there for a reason. It was now his pilot's job to manoeuvre them out of trouble.

Five seconds.

'Chaffing!' Robbie's right hand had moved a split second before he spoke. 'As we turned, I hit the chaff button and the Boz pod blasted out clumps of metallic strands, trying to shroud our presence from the radar-guided missile. There was no time for any fear or panic. Our reactions were hardwired.'

Four seconds.

Dave fought to turn the aircraft, hauling on the control column in the darkness, eyes fixed firmly on the HUD. His only means of knowing what height they were at, what attitude the jet was flying in, if it was climbing or descending towards the ground. 'We had a full weapons load and lots of fuel on board, so the Tornado didn't turn very quickly. It was pitch-black, we were very heavy and I was totally alert to the fact we were very, very close to the desert floor. It was all happening in seconds. It was a trade-off between being hit by a missile and hitting the ground. And the latter was 100 per cent fatal.'

Three seconds.

Dave was making the hardest possible turn, pulling the stick as tightly as he could into his stomach. The violent manoeuvre, coupled with more chaff, gave them the best chance of breaking the radar lock, causing the missile to lose guidance and fly blind.

He just needed a bit more time. A second, maybe two.

'Chaff,' Dave said again, as if toasting his companion outside a country pub.

'Okay ... chaffing ...' There was a hint of urgency in Robbie's reply as he coaxed the Boz pod to pour more metallic fibres into the sky.

Two seconds.

'Okay,' Dave responded, still trying to bury the stick in his gut.

Apart from their deep breathing, all was now silent in the cockpit. The missile was out there somewhere, but the hard turn had left them blind to its position.

One second.

Time crept by. The turn was nearly complete. Perhaps they had broken the lock?

Zero ...

Robbie felt an enormous blast rock the Tornado. 'There was a blinding orange flash as the missile exploded near the front cockpit.'

All Dave saw was searing light. 'The cockpit was consumed by an enormous flash. Everything happened in just fractions of a second. I knew I was losing consciousness and I was trying to get my hands towards the ejection handle, but I just couldn't move them.'

A secondary warning siren now kicked in. This time, a more urgent tone, like a submarine's crash dive blast, signalling multiple aircraft systems failures.

Shrapnel shattered the canopy and enveloped the underside of the Tornado, shredding hydraulic and fuel lines, causing electrical failure and a massive fireball.

The sirens then ceased as the Tornado started to disintegrate.

Dave felt a hurricane-force wind buffeting his body.

He had one final thought. *It's game over. I'm going to die.*

CHAPTER ONE

THE BIRTH OF 'THE FIN'

1960–1990

Wreckage from Waddington and Stewart's Tornado jutted out of the desert sand. F for Foxtrot's death plunge had created a crater the size of a diving pool. The chaff and flare Boz pod lay at its edge, live flares still clearly visible, chaff dispensing port still open. It had somehow survived the crash intact, but the inferno had stripped away some of the sand-coloured paint, leaving a faint hint of green – its colour a few months earlier when the camouflaged jets had blasted across northern Europe's forests and valleys.

It had now come to rest 200 miles south of Baghdad, and more than 3,000 from its natural habitat.

The Tornado had for almost a decade streaked through dark, wet nights and thick cloud, just a few hundred feet above treetops and valleys. A brainchild of the Cold War, it was able to slip below the radar, avoiding Soviet surface-to-air missiles, then suddenly materialise above an enemy airfield, ready to rain down destruction. But then, in 1989, the Berlin Wall had crumbled, and with it the great Communist alliance. The brilliance of the tactical nuclear bomber was about to be lost. The battle-winner had run out of enemies.

* * *

Robbie Stewart had joined the Royal Air Force in October 1965, six months before the birth of Dave Waddington, the pilot he would go to war with in a Tornado twenty-five years later. All it had taken for the teenage Robbie to decide where his future lay was a couple of flying lessons during the summer holidays. 'I got hooked, and that was it. My career path was set.'[1]

Three years before Robbie joined up, the Cuban Missile Crisis of 1962 had brought the world to the brink of destruction. The US 'Defense Condition' had been raised to its highest ever level: DEFCON 2. Strategic Air Command bombers were readied with nuclear weapons to 'deploy and engage' in less than six hours.[2] Britain had also stood-to its nuclear forces – including the iconic 'Vulcan' bomber that Robbie would soon serve on – at fifteen minutes' readiness. In the midst of the confrontation, an American aircraft, flying over Havana at what intelligence briefs had previously suggested should be above the range of any surface-to-air missile, had been shot down by a Soviet SA2 missile and the pilot killed. The same system had also brought down another American reconnaissance pilot, Gary Powers, two years earlier, under similar circumstances.

Disaster was averted when the Russians backed down and agreed to remove their nuclear missiles from Communist Cuba in return for America's pledge never to attempt an invasion of the island. The Western allies breathed again and lessons were learned. A hotline was established between the White House and the Kremlin for direct communication *in extremis*. And it was now clear that flying incredibly high no longer guaranteed immunity from surface-to-air missile attacks.

To stand a chance of survival, the Vulcan and its V-Force cousins had been developed to fly fast and high in order to deliver their nuclear payload uncontested. The SA2 now clearly undermined that tactic and the Delta-winged bomber was subsequently ordered to fly in beneath the detection capabilities of Soviet radar. It wasn't ideal. The 77-tonne, fully laden Vulcan was challenged by low-level flying; the forces this subjected it to induced metal fatigue, weakening its distinctive wing structure. The RAF decided that something fast, low and capable of operating in northern Europe's grim climatic conditions was required. The search for a new breed of fighter-bomber had begun.

But, in the meantime, the V-Force had to continue its role of policing the Warsaw Pact airspace. The close proximity of atomic Armageddon hadn't really featured in Robbie's youthful fantasies, but that soon changed. 'I had no notion of ever going to war when I joined up, but the reality of the Cold War became clear once I became a navigator on Vulcans. All the exercises we did, preparing for a global nuclear war, you really began to comprehend what it all meant. We all knew that if we ever took off in anger, it would probably be the end of me, my family and the world as we knew it.'

The potentially catastrophic consequences of such a conflict made Robbie and his companions hope and pray that no one would sink to such madness. But hope and prayer are rarely enough to create a place of safety in the international political cauldron. To replace the Vulcans, the RAF needed a fresh, new aircraft. An order for fifty F-111s, the latest low-level American nuclear bomber, was made then axed. Other initiatives came and went. Something custom-built was needed. And it wasn't going to be cheap. Late 1960s Britain was being pummelled by strikes, debt, loss of empire and emasculated productivity. Hobbled by its ageing bomber fleet, the RAF wanted a top-performing, cutting-edge jet that could keep the Soviet threat at bay. If Britain's moribund aircraft industry was to survive, it had to break away from the American monopoly and seek like-minded allies with whom to meet the challenges of the new era. European ones were the obvious – indeed only – option.

In March 1969, Britain entered with gusto into a partnership with
Germany and Italy, who also wanted to move away from American
dependency and enhance their own industrial base. The concept
of the tri-nation 'Multi-Role Combat Aircraft' (MRCA) was born.
Britain envisaged a twin-engine, two-man machine that would cost
around £1.6 million per airframe.[3] She would build the rear, the
Germans the middle and the Italians the wings. The RAF and the
Luftwaffe would take 420 each, the Italians 100.

The spirit of optimism surrounding the 1969 'memorandum of
understanding', its detractors said, could not possibly last. How
could you build three different components in three different
countries in which no one spoke the same language, and where
one was still using measurements in inches and feet? Then there
was the far-fetched idea of assembling all the bits and pieces like a
child's Meccano set. How were the Italians going to get their wings
to Germany when neutral Austria and Switzerland had barred all
overland transportation of military equipment?

Then the Italians insisted on the aircraft being a single-seater.
They didn't have any trained backseat navigators in the entire Regia
Aeronautica. The Germans were reluctant too, but the argument
that two pairs of eyes and hands were better than one, with the solo
pilot's workload being partly blamed for the high loss rate of the
Luftwaffe's single-seat F-104 Starfighter, won the day. By 1970 all
were on board with the idea of two engines and two seats.[4]

A highly complex and innovative design began to take shape. It
would have variable-geometry 'swing-wings'. Swept fully forward,
the wings were optimised for low-speed flight and manoeuvrability.
Swept fully back, the Tornado resembled a dart and was capable of
high-speed low-level flight carrying a heavy weapons load.

It would be truly 'fly-by-wire'; the pilot's physical inputs into his
controls would actually be sent to a computerised flying system and
then digitally on to the aircraft control surfaces. The computer systems ensured that the Tornado's handling characteristics remained
almost constant regardless of speed and wing-sweep position.
By the standards of the day, it was straightforward to fly and a

smooth, stable weapons platform.[5] In the era before the existence of composite metals, the MRCA was to be constructed from 71 per cent light alloy, 18 per cent titanium and 6 per cent steel.[6] The clear underside could carry a substantial arsenal. Its cockpit was laid out with plenty of room for the aircrew.

With success vital for all three governments, the pressure was mounting. The MRCA label also had to be dealt with. No one falls in love with an acronym. Being fast, low to the ground, nocturnal and stealth-like, *Panther* seemed a credible choice, but that was also the name given to the legendary Second World War German panzer, and a household lavatory cleaner of the time.[7] *Tornado*, on the other hand, was the same word in all three languages and created the evocative image of a force of nature that could strike with immense power and devastation.

It was an era before any form of 'night-vision goggles' (NVGs) so it would be impossible to fly the aircraft manually – visually – at low level in darkness. The key to the aircraft's success was the installation of the highly sophisticated Terrain-Following Radar system, or TFR, for low-level penetration. Originally developed by the British company Ferranti in the early 1960s, it swept the flight path ahead of a fast jet, registering the landscape and even obstacles like power lines, allowing it to fly at a near-constant altitude above whatever man or nature could throw its way.[8] The radar returns were processed to calculate the changes in the terrain, then fed into its flight computers and harnessed to the autopilot allowing the jet to fly itself, with almost no input from the crew, and maintain ground clearance at a constant height of 200ft, soaring over any terrain at high speed in pitch darkness or thick cloud. Blending into the landscape or 'terrain hugging' meant the Tornado could hide from enemy radar, reducing its vulnerability.

But the Tornado would be nothing without the power capable of complementing these other advances. On the face of it, building a jet engine was now relatively straightforward. Just get it to suck in the ambient outside air, squeeze it, heat it with ignited fuel and chuck it out of the rear pipe a great deal faster than it came in, and you could achieve remarkable thrust. The Americans were currently dominating the market, but this was a European project. It was time for the boffins at Rolls-Royce to show that Britain could still produce the innovative and the incredible. It was also a moment for the three nations to unite at the frontier of risk.

In 1970 everything depended upon Rolls-Royce's concept for the Tornado's engine. But it only existed, thus far, on paper. Each power plant had to produce 16,000lb of thrust when reheat was engaged for take-off. It had to swallow the huge influx of fuel necessary to produce the energy it took to lift a fully laden bomber. If they failed to conjure up the RB199 from scratch, the whole project would fail.[9]

Smaller than existing engines yet with more strength, it made the complex journey from the drawing board into action in four years and the RB199 demonstrated it possessed the heart of an elephant and the speed of gazelle.

* * *

Tange Webster had been warned to stay away from RAF officers. The older girls at the teacher training college in Lincoln had told her the flyboys might appear a dashing bunch in their smart uniforms and fancy jets, and, yes, they had a bit of spare cash and the whiff of heroism that came with being the vanguard against the Soviet threat, but they rarely hung about. At the student union dance in 1967, however, she actually found trainee officer Robbie Stewart pretty down-to-earth and, in his quiet way, really rather charming.

Four years later, when Tange turned twenty-four, they married and moved into the village of Coleby, with its primary school, two pubs and a church whose foundations went back to Saxon times. Robbie was flying out of RAF Scampton, a half-hour's drive away, with 27 Squadron, the unit with which he would later go to war. As the pleasantly warm summer of 1974 stretched ahead of them, Tange's walks around the village began to shorten with the breathlessness of third trimester pregnancy.

* * *

Seven hundred miles away, it was a humid afternoon on 14 August at Manching military airbase in West Germany, not far from where Messerschmitt 109s had been assembled in their thousands four decades before. Designers, engineers, mechanics and military observers now gathered to witness what they hoped would be a step change in aircraft dynamics.

The massive fin of the Tornado, in its smart red and white livery, immediately caught everyone's eye. Vital to stabilise and steer the bomber through waves of turbulent low-level air, it was as distinctive in its way as the Spitfire's elliptical wings, or the Lancaster's proud nose. For many, it would give the shiny new aircraft its nickname: 'The Fin'.

German, Italian, British and the odd American eye looked on with interest, as did the binoculars and the camera lenses of the Soviet enemy the Tornado was designed to defeat, from somewhere beyond the surrounding pine forests.

The aircraft's components had been concealed beneath tarpaulin and transported 55 miles by road from Munich. Its designers had managed to keep the prototype, P01, hidden from scrutiny, and they were determined to do so until the last moment. Given that its maiden flight was to be here in Germany, it was agreed the pilot would be British. It fell to Paul Millett, formerly of the RAF and the Fleet Air Arm, to take the controls.

After climbing the ladder to P01 and strapping himself in, Millett patiently waited as the two chase jets took off, ready to examine the newcomer at close quarters in case any issues arose mid-flight.

Under clear but muggy skies Millett taxied P01 to the runway. The sound of air molecules being ripped apart filled the deep green forests as he ignited the RB199s. The roar increased to a crescendo as fuel was poured onto the Rolls-Royce engines, throbbing with anticipation at getting airborne for the first time. The livery became a red and white blur as he powered down the runway.

Millett found the aircraft's nose eager to lift at 120 knots. Too eager. He held Po1 down, forcing it to gather more speed. The needle passed 160 knots (184mph), he eased back the stick and lifted smoothly into the air. He left the landing gear down as they climbed, in case an emergency landing was called for.[10] But all was well. Then it was time for the Tornado to look like a real combat jet. The undercarriage tucked neatly up into the broad fuselage as it powered effortlessly through the south German skies. Millett levelled off at 10,000ft then settled down to 300 knots (345mph). He was impressed. 'It flew as though this was the environment it had been built for.'[11]

There were gasps and one or two tears as the Tornado, with a chase jet at each wingtip, flew low past the spectators waiting on Manching's airstrip. The wheels liberated themselves once again from the fuselage. The handling on the approach to landing proved to be precisely as the designers had told Millett it would be. This machine flew beautifully at low level.

He took it for a low-altitude pass, then came back round. 'It feels as though it's on rails. You just sit with your hands and feet off and let the aircraft fly itself.' Thirty-three minutes after taking off, its wheels kissed the tarmac once more. 'It really felt like an aircraft that had been flying for many years. For a first flight it was something tremendous. The handling was perfect,' Millett said. 'It cannot be improved upon.'

He might have heard himself echoing the first pilot to fly the Spitfire prototype in 1936, when he said on landing: 'I don't want anything touched . . .'[12]

There was relief all round. The British aerospace and defence industry was rescued, the Germans had set the seal on their engineering prowess, and the Italians had secured a host of proper manufacturing jobs.

* * *

Robbie Stewart, like many others in the RAF, had a vague notion of the Tornado's maiden flight, but he wasn't counting his chickens. Many such projects had got this far before now, and failed. Just days before the Tornado's first flight Robbie was back in his Vulcan, 50,000ft above the North Sea, monitoring Russian maritime activity. The world felt like an unsettled place. Richard Nixon had recently resigned as US President. Willy Brandt, the West German Chancellor, had also quit over the revelation that his personal assistant had been spying for the Stasi, East Germany's intelligence service. Then the Turks invaded northern Cyprus. Spiralling oil prices were crippling the West's economy, and the Soviet Union seemed to be seizing the ascendancy in the competition for global supremacy.

Robbie still got back in time for the birth of his son in late August, and had a few weeks with Scott before he was back on duty with 27 Squadron, flying halfway round the world to Midway Island in the South Pacific, downwind of China, following a recent nuclear test by the People's Republic. The Vulcan also undertook the 'nuclear fallout detection' role – otherwise known as 'sniffing' – collecting air samples for analysis. There were upsides. The return leg home took in a refuelling stop in Hawaii. 'We had a chance to swim at Waikiki Beach; life wasn't all bad.'

His wife Tange understood the realities of service life. Robbie would be there one minute and gone the next. 'I would get the odd phone call in the middle of the night and Robbie would disappear off on exercise for days, sometimes weeks, on end. It was the middle of the Cold War and the world sometimes seemed a dangerous place; but that was all part of our lives.'

Robbie's training roster also seemed to demand an unusual number of cold-weather survival courses. 'I hope you never find yourself in the desert,' she once joked. 'You've not done the course!'

* * *

As the 1970s progressed, the Tornado began to take shape. With all three nations in harmony, the development site outside Munich grew to a workforce of almost 200 people. Three decades on from the Second World War, there had been a few stony silences in the office shared by a veteran German Luftwaffe colonel and a similarly aged RAF squadron leader.[13] Into this somewhat frosty atmosphere was thrown the snippet of information that both had been fighter pilots, one in Messerschmitts, the other Spitfires. Conversation became a touch more animated when it was discovered that each had fought in the same campaign over northern Europe in the latter stages of the conflict. Logbooks were produced, dates aligned and in no time at all the whirling, twisting and twirling hand gestures favoured by fighter pilots revealed that they had indeed shared the same airspace, though fortunately neither had been on the receiving end of the other's bullets. As one onlooker dryly observed, *they were clearly both lousy shots.*

No matter. A lifelong friendship had begun, with the Tornado at its heart. Their business now was to help develop a jet that could fly very low, and very fast. Because it had to. The Soviet defences arrayed against it were numerous and formidable. The most advanced surface-to-air missiles, anti-aircraft guns, radar and fighters. But the Tornado could dip out of sight while travelling at 600mph, 10 miles a minute, armed with the deadliest explosive device mankind had ever invented.

The Tornado project was no longer on the Cold War sidelines. The Russian spymasters in the KGB reportedly viewed it as a very serious threat. One of their top agents in West Germany, Manfred Rotsch, was also head of planning for Messerschmitt-Bölkow-Blohm, the German company building Tornado,[14] and was ordered to pass on everything he could get his hands on. The Soviets pretty much got the lot. And it didn't improve their humour. The West, the KGB discovered, was building a weapon of unsurpassed excellence. The decaying British Empire, the recently defeated Germans and even the haphazardly Communist government of Italy had formed an industrial union. It was all unfathomable to the Soviet mind. But Tornado, the Moscow comrades were told, was a problem. Even the Russian word for it – *Smerch* – suggested something subversive. The bristling defences of Eastern Europe were said to be vulnerable. And this was very serious. They had to know more.

Manfred Rotsch was put on notice. Find out everything you possibly can about *Smerch*.

* * *

In 1975, a year after the Tornado prototype took to the air, Dave Waddington also flew for the first time. His uncle owned a sharp-looking twin-engine Piper Aztec, and Dave was asked if he wanted to fly. 'YES!' was the immediate answer. His excitement grew as he was allowed to sit in the co-pilot's seat. He strapped himself in, trembling with anticipation. The feisty Lycoming piston engines roared as the Aztec sped down the runway. Dave watched the grass rush past as the wheels bounced beneath him, then the vibrations disappeared and they rose into the sky. After they had climbed to a few thousand feet, his uncle asked Dave if he wanted to take over. The 9-year-old's reply was unequivocal. *Yes please!* He reached for the control column, listening intently to the instructions. 'I was smitten. I wanted to fly. That was my dream.'[15] Dave set his heart on becoming a pilot. A fast-jet pilot.

It would be many years before he would get his hands anywhere near the Tornado, which, in the words of British Prime Minister Harold Wilson, was 'one of the wonder birds of aviation'. But his words were barely out of his mouth when the nascent bomber faced the kind of cross-examination that could cast it into the oblivion suffered by many other promising British projects.

It was 1975, and the first solely British Tornado prototype was about to take wing.[16] The gunmetal grey skies of Lancashire had cleared by the time test pilot Paul Millett eased back the control stick and felt P02, the second Tornado to be built, launch itself into the blue with familiar ease. They passed over the green fields and marshland that spread to the sandy banks of the River Ribble below.[17] The picturesque cottages of the nearby village of Fylde shrank as they climbed.

Perfect flying weather.

A blaring alarm interrupted Millett's momentary reverie. Flashing attention-getters and an illuminated caption on the Central

Warning Panel suggested a serious fault. *Low oil pressure. High temperature.* A jet of flame surged out of the right-hand engine.

There was a lengthy silence in the cockpit.

'Okay, Dave, what do you reckon?' Millett's fellow test pilot was in the back seat.

'Can't see anything wrong from here,' came the reply.

Millett waited a few seconds. The temperature continued to build. He throttled the right-hand engine all the way back to idle. The Tornado had more than enough power to fly on one. Easily enough to switch to plan B and ask the tower to check for any visual damage before making a precautionary landing. P02 slowly descended. Then there was another thump, followed by a big bang. Both sets of eyes swivelled left. Flame now blazed out of the remaining engine, which had just ingested a large seagull. More flames danced along the fuselage.

Millett immediately shut down the left engine, and slammed the right from idle straight into reheat to gain maximum power. There was an uncomfortable silence as it failed to respond and the altimeter continued to unwind. The Tornado was sinking fast towards the marshland surrounding Warton. The Ribble was no longer a ribbon. The buildings below them were rapidly increasing in size.

The altimeter passed through 500ft.

The only engine functioning was still refusing to deliver any power.

Millett scanned the gauges. *What could he do?*

Both pilots knew that their options were limited.

Prepare to eject?

And leave the second Tornado ever built, the British Tornado, to bury itself in the Lancastrian marshland?

Three hundred feet.

At least the altimeter was functioning flawlessly.

Fingers brushed the yellow and black ejection handle between their legs.

P02 was doomed.

Time to bail out.

The aircraft rocked and shuddered. Then the right-hand engine burst back into life and P02 soared skywards.

It had been a *very* close call.

The incident did much to inflame the inevitable detractors around any new aviation project. But P02, despite a few hair-raising moments which included a partial snapping of the tailfin during spin trials, soon began reaching notable landmarks, including a top speed of 809 knots (930mph).[18]

By July 1979 the first dual-control RAF Tornados rolled out of Warton, ready for instructing new pilots, though the fanfare was muted. During treacherous weather conditions a few weeks earlier, P08 had plunged into the sea 44 miles off Blackpool during a test flight involving the hazardous 'loft attack' profile. It could be dangerous work at the best of times, and was made worse in this instance by the mist and drizzle over the Irish Sea. There were no survivors.

Despite this fatal accident, the first of many, the Tornado was accepted into service three years later. And while it would certainly suffer a number of ongoing technical issues due to its cutting-edge technology, the aircrew and ground crew worked together to ensure that most tasks were completed as planned. The RAF finally had a fighter-bomber that could hit a target accurately night or day, no matter the weather.

* * *

Robbie Stewart noticed a bit of a difference going from the nuclear-armed Vulcan to the Tornado GR1. 'The Tornado had everything you could have dreamed of for the time. Computerised flying systems, navigation and targeting kit. It could fly at night, in terrible weather, at low level, hands-off. It really was superb.' One of its primary roles was as part of the nation's nuclear deterrent. For Robbie, as a navigator checking his target maps to be used if the Cold War ever turned hot, the idea was deeply unpleasant. 'You checked to see where the target was; what built-up areas it was near. That was quite a curious feeling, knowing if you ever launched, you'd be destroying a huge area. And that the world would be changing beyond recognition.' If the target was more distant, such as in western Poland, the aircraft might carry a single WE177 nuclear bomb under the left shoulder pylon and an extra, third fuel tank on the right.[19] At shorter range, the Tornado could carry two WE177s, bringing the explosive power of many Hiroshimas.

Along with its TFR, only used at night or in bad weather, the GR1's other key attribute was the crew's skill – flying manually and visually, fast and, at 100ft, far below enemy radar or, in a combat situation, even lower. No autopilot had this function so they had to become highly drilled at skimming above rugged terrain trusting their expertise to the maximum.

Fast-jet flying at 100ft and at high speed anywhere near built-up areas was forbidden across most of the UK and all of Germany, so there was no better place to practise this crucial skill than the wilds of Canada, with its deep canyons and jagged peaks. It was a real challenge and the cost in aircraft and aircrew lost bore testimony to the dangers. But those dangers had to be faced and overcome if the pilots were to fly the Tornado through the layers of Soviet air defence, beneath the searching radars, to ensure no missiles or anti-aircraft artillery (triple-A) could be guided onto them. The practice presented a real and deadly challenge, and the crews loved it.

* * *

John Peters had also had a childhood love of flying, and was now a pilot who delighted in nothing more than to be behind the controls of his Tornado. Especially when the RAF was really putting the jet through its paces, practising ultra-low-level flying, or 'operational low flying' (OLF), across the lakes and canyons of Goose Bay in north-east Canada. Usually, the only low-flying aircraft found there were the Beaver seaplanes that took sports anglers for a fortnight's holiday with some outstanding fishing in remote log cabins surrounded by millions of acres of forest, and the occasional bear. With not many souls about, it was also a fine place for some of the most breathtaking and challenging aviation.

Unrestricted by the low-level flying limits of Europe, the Tornados could tear along at ultra-low level and around 700mph in very testing conditions. A key piece of advice was not to go 'too low'. Since a lake's surface mirrored the sky, more than one pilot had become disoriented and dived straight in.[20] For pilots blessed with great vision, Goose Bay provided the clearest atmosphere they'd set eyes on. No pollution or heat haze, just 50 miles of crystalline visibility, unheard of in the Old World.

But for pilots new to Canada like John Peters, when flying over the rock, lichen and smaller and smaller trees of the northern tundra, it could be lethal. 'As the trees begin to imperceptibly decrease in height, there is a real danger of believing that you are flying too high, so you adjust the position of the aircraft lower in the sky to restore that familiar picture. If you are not careful you can find yourself being drawn closer and closer to the ground as the trees, which are normally around 50 feet high, shrink to as little as 10. It is a well-known optical illusion of low flying and everyone is made aware of the potentially fatal dangers.'[21]

The Tornado crews enjoyed some of the most exhilarating flying they ever encountered. John Peters soon discovered that one particular 15-mile-long canyon rapidly narrowed as they sped between the sheer cliff walls. It had been named 'Star Wars Valley' after Luke Skywalker's unforgettable route to the heart of the Death Star. For John, it was the ultimate challenge. 'You have to roll the Tornado onto its side and pull hard, sweeping the wings forward to increase manoeuvrability and squeeze the aircraft around the sheer walls of rock. Finally, you have to say: "No, no further," yank the stick back and pull out. It's sheer seat-of-the-pants flying.'[22]

The concentration needed was so demanding that pilots could barely look anywhere else but straight ahead and the navigator had to do the rest.[23] It took a lot of practice to have the confidence to push the aircraft down to 100ft, the height of two rugby posts. But if it came to war, to survive the Soviets' highly capable air defences in daylight, they were going to have to fly even lower.

It was exciting and exhausting work, which increased in intensity when done on the autopilot coupled to the TFR, which for those in the front seat provided the strange sensation of being on an out-of-control rollercoaster. TFR meant that night-time or low clouds no longer limited RAF attack aircraft. Britain now had the capability to attack at any time of day on any day of the year.[24]

'With the computer autopilot flying the jet, I would sit with my left hand resting on the throttle and my right lying uselessly in my lap, twitching towards the stick every time I saw a rock looming up from the ground below.'

Peters glanced intently at the tiny display screen of the TFR's 'E-scope' which showed an image of the ground in front as the radar in the Tornado's nose swept the terrain of the flight path ahead. 'As the jet soars over a ridge, prompted by the TFR, then plunges down into an unseen valley, our anti-collision lights reflect back from a solid wall of thick, grey cloud. The navigator hunches in the back with only my running commentary to brace himself for the next lurch as the jet twists, soars and swoops, following the terrain as if glued to it.'[25] The jet could continue on TFR for as long as it liked until the pilot moved the paddle bar on the stick that cuts out autopilot to get back onto manual control.

If the Tornado could fly through thick fog, over mountains and at night, it needed to have something special to deliver – other than a nuclear bomb – if it was truly going to make an impact. The new aircraft had been designed to be 'multi-role', from nuclear and conventional bombing to reconnaissance and even, in the guise of the F3 variant, interception.

* * *

In the first few hours of any Cold War conflict, the Tornado's role would be to prevent the enemy from using their airfields, and the unique JP233 'runway denial munition' was specifically designed to meet its profile for fast, below-the-radar attack. Developed during the 1970s, the JP233 was designed to render the Soviet runways built in East Germany or Poland unusable for critical operations with a barrage of cratering weapons and anti-personnel devices.[26]

Each JP233 contained thirty runway-cratering munitions weighing 57lb, designed to penetrate the surface of a runway before then exploding and causing massive 'heave distortion' to the surface area. The blast would force the tarmac upwards in a great spew of broken rubble. To discourage anyone seeking to make repairs, a further 215 anti-personnel bomblets followed on small parachutes, designed to pop up on three legs and arm themselves, detonating if disturbed. A final kicker was that a number of the munitions would continue to detonate randomly for some hours after lying dormant. It was a vicious weapon.

A Tornado could carry two of the 2.5-tonne JP233s, so a single raid by eight jets brought the potent mix of 480 cratering bombs and 3,440 anti-personnel bomblets. It was a brutal and effective method of airfield operating surface denial, with one 'slight' drawback. The scientists who developed it required the Tornado to fly straight and level down the runway, at around 200ft and 520mph, which, the aircrews observed stoically, *greatly* increased the possibility of being shot down.

And the Tornado demonstrated its versatility with other crucial tasks. The GR1A reconnaissance version could sneak behind enemy lines and record images of troop movements, defensive positions or bomb damage. It utilised a revolutionary infra-red video system which allowed image collection by both day and night. It was able to see the heat signature of aircraft on a runway or the heat trace of recently departed jets. This also meant that it was much harder for troops to conceal weapons that required engines, such as giant rocket launchers.[27]

Then there was the adapted Tornado F3, the air defence variant designed to track, intercept and, if necessary, shoot down hostile intruders. If lacking in the manoeuvrability of other, purpose-built fighters, it could still occupy a significant role as an interceptor.

* * *

Dave Waddington's passion had remained undiminished throughout his school years. He joined the RAF straight after his A-levels and by 1988 had fulfilled his dream of flying fast jets. He knew that they were Cold War warriors but felt any major conflict unlikely. 'The idea of global thermo-nuclear war didn't really enter your mind. We were certainly a deterrent, but the feeling was that if the Cold War ever turned hot, it would be so catastrophic as to be unimaginable.' Anyway, there was too much fun to be had flying, alongside a packed social life, to think about Armageddon. 'The Tornado was cutting-edge technology, I was just twenty-two and flying the RAF's most modern, capable fast-jet aircraft. Being on a frontline squadron was simply amazing – the ethos, the camaraderie, the training, the lifestyle was everything I'd hoped it would be. I was living the dream.' Part of that dream was finding himself on the front line, even with only the most distant prospect of conflict.

Nuclear war moved several steps further away one Thursday in November 1989 when the collapse of the Berlin Wall heralded the beginning of the end of the Soviet empire. There was a question mark over whether the RAF would ever be needed for combat now that its chief adversary was gone. What was the point now of the Tornado, primed to break through enemy defences that no longer existed? No one knew what the future held, except the near certainty that the 'peace dividend' would mean the military establishment faced huge cutbacks.

* * *

Seven years earlier, in 1982, Dave Bellamy had joined up after reading about the RAF's new generation of fast jets. At the age of eighteen, he went straight onto the Tornado as a navigator. 'I loved the aircraft and really enjoyed flying it, even if the prospect of any real conflict was remote.'

With the Cold War over, Bellamy could read the tea leaves. A devastating blow to the Tornado force was announced to Parliament just a week before Iraq invaded Kuwait in summer 1990.[28] The RAF was to reduce from 90,000 personnel to 75,000, with the closure of four bases in Germany and the loss of six squadrons. For Dave, 'it was a depressing possibility, so I had decided to leave the RAF early and handed in my notice'. Costs for training a navigator ran into the millions, so his contract meant he would still have to serve another two years. And take a pay cut. That was fine by him. He wanted a new challenge.

Under the government's 'Options for Change' proposals, the British Armed Forces were to be cut by almost a fifth. Gordon Buckley, one of the RAF's top five Tornado pilots in terms of hours flown, was among those who faced an uncertain future. He was based at RAF Laarbruch in northern Germany and his Squadron was in line for the chop. 'When the Iron Curtain slowly crumbled away I really wondered what our role in the RAF might be. I certainly didn't imagine we might soon be fighting a major war.'

Despite the looming cuts to RAF strength, and perhaps because of them, families like Robbie Stewart's felt that by the summer 1990 they deserved a really good holiday. Scott was now sixteen, and their aircraft-mad daughter Kirsty was about to reach her teenage years. The Bavarian foothills of Germany's highest mountain, the Zugspitze, and its forest of conifers offered the adventure-loving Stewarts the ideal location.

The Stewarts packed the car and drove from Lincoln, across Europe then down into southern Germany to camp at Garmisch. The host town of the 1936 Winter Olympics sat in a breathtaking bowl of snow-capped mountains. It was early August, the sky was deep blue and the air fresh. They took the train to the high station. Robbie was in good spirits as they clambered out of their compartment and prepared to embark on the hike to the Zugspitze's 10,000ft peak.

Then something caught his eye at the station gift shop.

In large black letters, an English newspaper headline declared:

'SADDAM INVADES KUWAIT'

CHAPTER TWO

THE GATHERING STORM

AUGUST–NOVEMBER 1990

The former British protectorate of Kuwait was a tiny oil-rich state at the head of the Gulf, sharing just two borders, one with Saudi Arabia to the south and the other with its dominant neighbour Iraq in the north. Shortly after 2am on 2 August 1990, as much of the RAF Tornado force enjoyed their summer holidays, 100,000 of Saddam Hussein's elite troops, the Republican Guard, swept south with 2,000 tanks.[1] Iraqi commandos landed by helicopter and seaborne assault. The 16,000-strong Kuwaiti army and air force put up a stiff resistance. For two days they held firm, until they ran out of ammunition. The bulk of their leadership, including their Emir, fled into the Saudi desert. The last pockets of resistance were overrun, raising their death toll to 420, while their invaders lost 300 men and 39 aircraft.

On 4 August, Kuwait ceased to exist as a state and became, instead, the 19th Governate of Iraq. Events had been set in train which would eventually cost tens of thousands of lives, and reverberate across the region, and the world, for many years to come.

* * *

A decade earlier, Saddam Hussein had made another decision with global consequences when he invaded neighbouring Iran. That war had been about border disputes, religion and Arab–Persian hegemony, and been pursued at great cost. More than half a million soldiers perished in battles frighteningly similar to the trench warfare of the First World War. Iran used human-wave attacks, sending massed infantry against barbed wire and machine-gun nests. Saddam maximised his use of chemical weapons, sending mustard gas clouds that condemned Iranian soldiers hiding in their trenches to an agonising death.

By the end, not a jot of land advantage had been gained by either side, but Iran's Ayatollah Khomeini strengthened his religious revolution and the once-prosperous Iraq was $100 billion in debt.[2] Saddam's financial weakness was compounded in 1990 after a global glut of oil led to prices plummeting. Iraq's main income was under threat because of overproduction and Kuwait was among those overproducing. The dire economic situation was a threat to the Iraqi president and his power base. There had been four assassination attempts in the previous two years. Saddam's reputation – hitherto sustained by a combination of brutality and low cunning – was tumbling as quickly as the price of oil.

Tensions rose when he accused Kuwait of stealing $2 billion by cross-drilling into Iraqi oilfields. Iraqi divisions were ordered to assemble at the border. As last-minute compromise talks were held, Iraq demanded Kuwait pay $10 billion in compensation. The Kuwaitis offered $9 billion but that just insulted Saddam's personal honour. The Kuwaitis would pay in blood and treasure. Saddam invaded and a geopolitical earthquake, with countless aftershocks, was triggered.

Margaret Thatcher was giving her full attention to President George Bush's opening address at a conference at the Aspen Institute in Colorado when news of Saddam's invasion broke. She steadied nerves by ordering the nearest Royal Navy warships to sail to the region. The British Prime Minister showed her experience as a military campaign veteran for whom the lessons of the twentieth century were clear.

The next morning, President Bush asked her: 'Margaret, what do we do?'[3]

Mrs Thatcher, who famously ordered the retaking of the Falkland Islands by military force after the Argentine invasion in 1982, replied: 'Aggression must be stopped. If an aggressor gets away with it, others will want to get away with it too. You cannot gain from your aggression.'

Saddam occupying the country with the sixth largest oil reserves on the planet was already highly troubling, and Mrs Thatcher was in no doubt about what could happen next. 'An immediate question now was whether Saddam Hussein would go over the border and seize Saudi Arabia's oilfields. If [he] were to cross the border into Saudi Arabia he could go right down the Gulf in a matter of days. He would then control 65 per cent of the world's oil reserves and could blackmail us all. Not only did we have to move to stop the aggression, therefore, we had to stop it quickly.'[4]

The prospect of Saddam's battle-hardened Republican Guard rampaging through Saudi Arabia's neatly assembled oil production facilities with its unlimited supply of 'black gold' was deeply unsettling. The land of the holiest Islamic sites of Mecca and Medina had not been invaded for more than twelve centuries. Hysteria grew among the Saudi royal court and their people. King Fahd readily agreed to an audience with senior American officers who came to ask permission to allow their troops into the kingdom for its defence. The Vietnam veteran, General Norman Schwarzkopf, who had a reputation for a short temper and great leadership, was a member of the group. 'Would strictly Islamic Saudi allow Christian soldiers onto their holy soil?' the American asked.[5]

'Yes,' came the immediate response.

Saudi's airbases and ports were immediately opened up to the military might of the world's dominant superpower. There had been little choice. Victorious Iraqi divisions were assembling on the border. The capital, Riyadh,was six hours' drive away. Saudi lay at Saddam's mercy.

* * *

Despite the arduous walks that seemed to typify their family holidays, Robbie Stewart's 12-year-old daughter Kirsty had been really enjoying the two-week break from school studies. Her dad was relaxed, there was lots of fun and laughter. There was one particularly memorable moment with him, lying in the sun by a stream before building a rock dam. But her idyll had been shattered when, ready to conquer the Zugspitze, they had seen the newspaper announcement of Saddam's invasion. Robbie Stewart had stopped, turned, and reread the first paragraph. His wife Tange glanced over his shoulder. Then their eyes met. Robbie looked like he'd been punched in the stomach. 'It hit me like a sledgehammer. I just knew how it would unfold. And I knew the Tornados I flew would be involved.'[6]

They had both been aware of the increased tensions in the Gulf but thought there had been a last-minute compromise. Both immediately understood the implications. The highway from Kuwait led straight down to Saudi Arabia and its great swathe of oilfields. One of the world's most ruthless dictators controlling half of the world's oil was a direct threat to global stability. After decades of atrocities, gassing Kurds and torturing his own, Saddam had finally crossed a line that could not be ignored.

'You know what's going to happen, don't you?' Robbie's voice was tight.

'Yes,' Tange replied quietly.

She had always known war was a *possibility*. 'But this seemed a world away from everything we knew.'[7]

'I have to call the Squadron,' Robbie said.

They took the train back to the campsite to get a stash of coins to call RAF Marham from the public phone box. There was relief on Robbie's face after the call. He'd been told to check in regularly, but they did not need to rush home early. No immediate plans had been made to deploy Tornados. The Zugspitze still loomed over them but the joy had gone out of their adventure. Every night Robbie tuned in to the news. A confrontation was looming and he was certain Tornados would be in the gathering storm. 'I wasn't really enjoying the holiday as much. Each night I read about rising tensions in the region. Both Tange and I were very aware that I might be heading that way. We had a very real sense that our lives were going to change.'

Tange had the same nagging feeling. 'We continued with our hikes around the mountains during the day, maintaining the air of a normal family holiday, but at night, when the kids had gone to sleep in their own little tent beside ours, Robbie and I would discuss the situation in whispers; the possibility Robbie might be going out there and what that might mean. There was a real sense that war was imminent.' Their quiet chatter did not go unnoticed by Kirsty. 'There were whispered conversations between Mum and Dad, staying up late at night. I had never heard of Saddam Hussein, or even Kuwait, but very soon, those words were part of my regular vocabulary. The holiday suddenly turned serious. It was really odd, because Dad was never like that, he was normally so laid-back.'[8]

Because his service life had begun in the sixties, Robbie and Tange had always known war with the Soviets was a possibility, but this was something entirely different. Fighting, flying and dealing with danger was what RAF fliers were trained to do. It was just that for Robbie the Cold War had ended, yet the prospect of dying in a real war was again staring him in the face. 'I had no doubt in my mind I would deploy and it was certainly worrying. But it was my job, what I had trained to do.'

* * *

A week after the invasion, 130,000 Iraqi troops were massed on the Saudi border itself. To the military analyst's eye, it appeared to be a 'strategic pause', a moment to rest, re-equip and rearm prior to offensive operations. It wasn't just the 1,200 tanks and regiments of heavy artillery that were unnerving the generals. The Iraq Air Force, comprising many veterans of the Iran war, was probing Saudi air space, looking for weaknesses and recording response times.[9] The strongest and quickest response the Americans had was air power. Within days of the invasion, forty-eight heavily armed F-15C Eagle fighters sounded the opening notes of the campaign to protect Saudi Arabia. The F-15s flew straight from the United States, over fourteen hours non-stop, with multiple air-to-air refuelling slots. Each fighter carried eight air-to-air missiles, and were ready to fight their way in if necessary. But the Americans needed more help.

One Tornado Squadron Commander, on leave from Germany, was pruning the roses in his garden when the house phone rang at his cottage in the east of England. 'How long will it take you to get to RAF Cottesmore?' he was asked.[10]

'Half an hour,' he replied.

When the officer pulled up at the airbase, a Tornado from his Squadron was already waiting. He took the backseat spot from the navigator and flew straight back to Germany, then on to Saudi Arabia. Royal Air Force mobilisation was taking place on a scale unparalleled since the summer of 1939.[11]

The RAF's nearest jets were in Cyprus in the eastern Mediterranean – a detachment of Tornado F3s, the interceptor or 'air defence variant' of the GR1 bomber. They were there for the good training weather as well as the odd summer beach barbecue, but were wholly unprepared for war. A few days after the invasion, the aircrew were sipping cold beers in the Mess when an 'Eyes Only' message arrived for the Squadron Boss. The twelve jets that had deployed to the British sovereign base to practise air-to-air combat were now heading to Saudi to stop, or at least slow, the impending Iraqi invasion.

'It felt as though we were going to last two or three days out there and then we'd be overrun,' one pilot said.[12] A fellow navigator described it as a 'nightmare', mainly because the Tornado F3s were only halfway through a major capability enhancement programme.

'We were deploying out to the Gulf with jets that hadn't been modernised for war. We had no chaff, no flares. We didn't have the good missiles on, we didn't have the good radars and a lot of us didn't feel we were going to come back.' Saddam's reputation for murderous chemical warfare meant preparations for Nuclear Biological Chemical (NBC) attack were also taken very seriously. 'The thing that was really worrying us was the NBC because the next time you put your respirator on it could be for nerve gas and that was you gone.'[13]

'Last letters' were written, to be delivered to loved ones if the worst happened, and wills hurriedly filled in. Then it was time to leave, just as visiting military families were arriving at the other end of the Cyprus airfield for their summer holidays on the beach. Only a week after Saddam invaded Kuwait, the twelve Tornado F3s landed at the vast, modern Dhahran airbase, on Saudi's Gulf coast. Within hours they were back in the skies again, flying four-hour combat patrols along the Iraq border, swapping shifts with their US and Saudi counterparts.

RAF Jaguars also arrived, along with shuttle loads of C130 Hercules transporters ferrying in ground crew, support staff and batteries of Rapier surface-to-air missiles. When the Hercules landed in the heat of Dhahran – 30°C at two in the morning – the loadmasters went into overdrive. 'They kicked us out of the back like there was no tomorrow and the Herc was off taxiing before we'd even put our kit down,' recalled one airman. 'At that point I suddenly thought, "My God, this is all getting a little bit tense."'[14] Very quickly the RAF had 1,000 personnel on the ground. But it wasn't enough. They were joined by 4,000 lightly armed American paratroopers rushed in from the 82nd Airborne Division as part of Operation Desert Shield, the rapid deployment of troops to protect Saudi Arabia. In response, more Iraqi divisions poured into Kuwait. At this point the horrific possibility of Saddam grabbing half the world's oil appeared to become a certainty. A few days earlier, an Iraqi officer had defected to Egypt with their invasion plans for Saudi Arabia.

An expression took hold in Saudi that seemed to capture the

allies' precarious predicament. They would be mere 'speed bumps' in an invasion, just a few battalions of lightly armed infantry who would be mercilessly rolled over by the heavy armour of the Republican Guard. The Desert Shield was in place, but reinforcements were rapidly required if it was to hold.

* * *

Feeling the Florida sunshine dry off the last droplets of pool water, Dave Waddington couldn't have been happier. He was twenty-four and a recently qualified pilot on the RAF's most advanced fast jet. The job came with a certain lifestyle that befitted his role on a frontline squadron. Camaraderie, intense training and of course some thoroughly top-notch parties. He shifted on the sunbed and glanced at his partner Claire. After a hectic day in the Florida theme parks where the G-forces were not to be sneered at but some distance from those of a Tornado, they were taking it easy at his sister's West Palm Beach home. It was early August and even after a cooling dip the heat was beginning to become uncomfortable. Somewhere in the distance, beyond the patio doors, he heard the distant ring of a telephone. He closed his eyes, shutting out the world.

'It's for you, David. Someone called Bambi Thwaites.'

He instantly sat up. Thwaites was an executive on 27 Squadron, and not one to call West Palm Beach without good reason. Dave picked up the phone in his sister's dining room and Bambi got straight to the point. He could finish his holiday, but he would be deploying to the Middle East at the end of August in support of Operation Desert Shield. He felt a rush of nervous excitement. 'I was just a Flying Officer, very young, recently qualified, and I had been picked for "the first team". There were older, more experienced hands on the Squadron but they had chosen me.'[15]

The Squadron executives clearly had a lot of faith in Dave Waddington. By 1990 the Tornado force had reached its peak of eleven frontline squadrons, including eight in Germany, and two training units, totalling nearly 230 combat jets. There were scores of other aircrew who would have readily taken his place on operations. Dave knew he was lucky. He tried to contain his exhilaration as he headed back to the pool to tell Claire he was going to war.

* * *

Life in the RAF had treated Tornado navigator Bob Ankerson well. By 1990 he had been promoted to Squadron Leader and, even though he had just turned forty, he was doing something that very few other forty-somethings did. Flying the most amazing and sophisticated aircraft in the RAF. Bob trained for war but never imagined it would happen. Service life was pleasant and he had become happily accustomed to peace. He had joined the RAF almost by accident, in 1973, a year before the Tornado took flight. He had been in Nottingham with his new wife Chris and some friends when they saw an RAF recruiting stand. Bob had recently been working in the aero-engine division of Rolls-Royce but was now between jobs. 'You could always join this lot,' one of his friends joked, pointing at the display stand. Bob had laughed but by the Monday morning had begun seriously considering the idea. Three months later he was in uniform, aged twenty-three, and heading for a career as a navigator. Like Robbie Stewart, he first flew on Vulcans equipped with nuclear weapons that, he hoped, they would never use. 'I didn't really think much about conflict. The RAF was more of a challenging lifestyle, exciting flying, something few people did.'[16]

Bob's life might not have been quite so contented if Chris had listened to her father. The couple were childhood sweethearts. They met when they were sixteen. She was educated at a convent and he at a boys' Catholic school. Chris's dad approved. As an aeronautical engineer, the clean-cut, likeable young man clearly had solid prospects. Then, five months after they were married, he was in the uniform of the RAF. His father-in-law, a Second World War veteran, made it clear to Chris that he did not approve. 'He had seen it all as a teenager and didn't want me married to anyone who might have to go to war.'

'If I had known he was going to join the RAF, he certainly would not have married you!' he admonished. But at least while the Cold War was centre stage, conflict felt unlikely.

Chris found the RAF provided a marvellous life for a young couple. The glamour of fast jets came with a social circuit of house parties and formal functions. 'War was so far from our minds. Even when Bob was on Vulcans, on 24-hour nuclear Quick Reaction Alert duty. I didn't associate any of this with going to war.'[17] And Bob was a calm, easy-going man. Not a gung-ho fighter. 'I always thought of him as a peacekeeper rather than anything else.' In early August 1990 the Ankersons were caravanning in the forests of Eifel in Belgium when they heard about Kuwait. Enjoy your holiday, Bob was told when he called his base to check if he might be needed. There was no chance of the Squadron being called up. And, anyway, 17 Squadron had a key role to play in the Battle of Britain fiftieth anniversary celebrations and flypast later that year. He could relax.

* * *

'This is Northern Fixer on Guard.'

The air traffic controller using the 'Guard' international distress frequency was rare. Gordon Buckley, instantly alert, relaxed his grip on the Tornado's control column, climbed the jet from low level, and instinctively scoured the deep blue of the summer sky above him.

'Repeat, this is Northern Fixer. Leader of Kayak formation, return to base immediately.'

More messages followed.

'Bobcat and Mallet formation, you are to RTB immediately ...' The list of all RAF units flying training sorties over northern Germany went on. Everyone was being recalled. Gordon had a strong idea what the recall was about. It was Wednesday, 8 August. Just four days earlier, Saddam had completed his conquest of Kuwait.

In the modern age, Gordon Buckley would never have been a jet pilot in the RAF. As a teenager, he had made a schoolboy pact with his best friend that as grown-ups they would become airline pilots. But Gordon's grades put paid to that. He left school with just three O-levels, but what he lacked in exam results he made up for in ambition. Aged twenty-two, Gordon was on the road to qualifying as a Post Office engineer, but his desire to fly remained. He followed his instincts and joined the RAF. Those instincts were justified. The RAF identified a naturally skilled pilot and within three years he was flying Jaguars, a fast, single-seat strike-attack aircraft. He didn't want be anywhere else. Until Tornado came along.

The air traffic controller told Gordon to divert to RAF Bruggen, home to four squadrons of Tornados and close to the West German city of Dusseldorf. His instinct about the 'Guard' call was confirmed. It wasn't going to be his last flying for that day.

Air-to-air refuelling (AAR) would be imperative in any attack plan on Iraq. With the East German border just over 200 miles away, the German-based Tornado GR1 bombers could make it to their Warsaw Pact targets and back without having to replenish their tanks. Almost none of the Germany-based crews had ever carried out AAR sorties. But if they were going deep into Iraq, that changed things. They might require at least two air-to-air refuelling slots. The idea of approaching an airborne tanker trailing a long pipe with a small drogue basket at high speed and at night had little appeal. AAR was a chore for the UK-based Tornado squadrons who would have far further to fly if the Cold War had ever turned hot. For that unimaginable conflict, the eight Tornado squadrons spread evenly between the RAF bases of Laarbruch and Bruggen, near the Dutch border, were as combat-ready as they could be. But anyone going out to the Gulf would rapidly require air-refuelling qualification. Planners scoured the records.

Squadron Leader Gordon Buckley, one of the force's most experienced Tornado pilots, was among the tiny handful of RAF aircrew in Germany qualified as an AAR instructor. Hence the call for him on the emergency frequency. 'My jet had barely come to a halt when I was ordered straight onto a Tornado with dual controls and back into the air to train another pilot.'[18] Fortunately, that pilot was a quick learner, mastering the technique that required a slow, careful

approach and a dose of confidence. One trip and he was qualified
as an instructor. They each then took another pair up, taught them
the art of AAR, and by the end of the day RAF Germany had five
new instructors.

Gordon Buckley got back to his home at RAF Laarbruch utterly
shattered, but also somewhat elated. 'I really wanted to be part of it
all; this was what we had trained to do. I didn't want to kill people
or to die, but our job on the Tornado was war and I had never
thought I might do that job for real. We were not warmongers, but
here was the possibility of being ordered to put all that training and
all those skills to the test.'

At Laarbruch's War Operations Centre, an urgent briefing had
already been given by the Station Commander. 'You need to pack
your bags tonight – we're going to war.'[19]

Iraq? Kuwait? The pilots and navigators looked puzzled. Few of
the aircrew could easily point to them on a map. Not that they had
any maps of the region to examine. The answer was provided by the
Tornado squadrons' ground liaison officers, who had photocopied
pages out of the *Times World Atlas* then taped together a mosaic
of Saudi Arabia, Kuwait and Iraq. It was the only map they had for
the entire summer.

What the intelligence officers lacked in cartography, they had
made up for in reams of information on Iraqi Air Force capabilities.
Saddam had procured a broad range of Soviet jets. He also had complex and integrated surface-to-air missile – SAM – systems, French
and Russian, plus 10,000 anti-aircraft artillery guns.

And in a somewhat surreal turnaround of events, some of the
RAF aircrews preparing for war already had experience of 'combat'
with Iraqi pilots, albeit during practice sorties while training them.
When Iraq had been viewed as 'a friend' in the region in the 1970s
and 80s, some of its air force pilots had been trained at RAF flying
schools,[20] as well as at other prestigious establishments like the
British Army's Royal Military Academy Sandhurst.[21]

Those who had worked with the Iraqis in peace knew that, if a
conflict ensued, it would not be a walkover.

For Gordon there was also the moral issue of going to war in a far-off country. 'Kuwait had been brutally invaded and we were hearing of some pretty horrific things going on over there. There was a moral question to all this. Surely it was right to help liberate an occupied country?'

* * *

Yet again the Tornado proved itself one of the airshow's top attractions. It was 8 August and the bellow and power of the Rolls-Royce RB199 engines, the muscular airframe, the reheat flames shooting out, thrilled the crowds at RAF St Mawgan in north Cornwall. Hundreds of RAF aircrew stood around their aircraft, chatting to the public, posing for pictures, keeping an eye out for girls to invite to the after-show party in the Officers' Mess.

Navigator John Nichol, a relatively new member of Gordon Buckley's 15 Squadron, had flown in from RAF Laarbruch, one of the perks of the job. 'It was a typical airshow. All your aircrew mates get together the night before, you go to the bar and have a few drinks. The form is fairly easy, all you need is a hard head and a good line in banter.' The banter took a different turn later in the day. 'I was enjoying the sunshine next to my jet, soaking up endless questions, youthful admiration and the Cornish sun when the station Tannoy system barked into life. *"The captain of the Victor tanker is to report to Station Operations immediately."* Moments later the entire tanker crew were scrambling towards their aircraft. "We're off to the Gulf," they shouted as they passed us. We just stared in disbelief, wondering what was happening.'[22]

Then the call went for another squadron's Tornado crew and thirty minutes later the Tannoy sounded again. '*15 Squadron Tornado crew is to report to Station Operations immediately!*'

After a few minutes, Nichol's pilot came back from the Operations Room.

'We're also on thirty minutes' notice to move,' he gasped. 'To the Gulf!'

'Naah, never. Don't be daft.' Nichol didn't believe a word of it.

'Yes. We've got to get this aircraft ready to go. Now.'

Order followed counter-order as rumours flew around the base. But a few hours later they were all stood down, which, after the initial tensions of the call-out, was taken as a good excuse to have a stiff drink. After a few more of those, Nichol was tearing around the bar with a tea towel on his head pretending to be Lawrence of Arabia. The 'standing down' was going very well and there was much laughter from the assembled aircrew. 'Simon Burgess, a Tornado pilot and mate of mine, called to me across the bar: *"Nichol, you might regret doing that one day!"* When we met again a few months later, in less salubrious circumstances, Simon reminded me of that night.'

* * *

To get on a war footing, Tornado training reached new heights of intensity with the emphasis on low-level flying. It came with great risks.

The weather was fine off Spurn Head on the Yorkshire coast on 14 August. No cloud below 5,000ft and visibility in excess of 6 miles. There was just a hint of summer haze, making it a bit more difficult than usual to see other aircraft in the area. The skies were busy with training sorties. One Tornado had taken off from RAF Honington in Suffolk, and was making a practice bombing run on an east coast weapons' range. Another pair of Tornados, including navigator Gordon Graham, had flown across the North Sea from RAF Laarbruch and were also practising on a nearby weapons range. Not far off Spurn Head, Graham's Tornado had just levelled off at 320ft after detecting a minor systems fault. A few seconds later he spotted a rapidly approaching aircraft dead ahead and shouted 'Break!', the command to instantly turn away. It was too late. Both aircraft were flying at the exact same height in the same place; two seconds later they collided and broke apart. Graham and his pilot ejected into the sea, but the navigator's wounds were fatal. As were the injuries to the crew of the aircraft they collided with. Graham's badly injured pilot was the only one of the four aircrew to survive the collision.[23]

*　*　*

'Fuck me, Belly, I thought you were dead!' John Nichol declared as he walked into the flat he shared with Dave Bellamy near RAF Laarbruch.

Bellamy looked up from his ironing and registered his fellow Tornado navigator's startled expression. They were barely a week into the intensive war-training. Like Gordon Buckley, Bellamy was one of the few air-to-air refuelling instructors in Germany. 'I had withdrawn my resignation so I could be part of any deployment and was then flying three or four times a day to get the rest of the Squadron AAR qualified. By mid-August, I was absolutely knackered.'[24] That 14 August, Bellamy was meant to be flying the fateful training sortie near Spurn Head, but as two of the four Tornados programmed to fly from Laarbruch had technical problems, Gordon Graham, one of the Squadron's senior officers, told him to go home.

'I was so tired, Gordon said he would lead the sortie with the Boss while I had some downtime. I was really grateful for the rest. I went back to the flat I shared with John Nichol to catch up on some chores.' That afternoon, news of the crash and deaths of three aircrew had reverberated around the Tornado force. 'There had been confusion on some of the other squadrons,' Bellamy remembered. 'The word had gone around that I had been killed in the crash. However, I knew who had been flying in my place and realised it was Gordon who'd died. It was awful.'

'You didn't serve long as fast-jet aircrew before a mate was killed,' Nichol said. 'But this crash really hit home. Gordon Graham had previously served on my Squadron and he was universally regarded as a really decent bloke and a great operator; one of life's good guys. His loss was a massive shock for my Squadron and Dave Bellamy's.'

Across the Tornado force, from RAF Marham to Laarbruch

and Bruggen, people were rushing to prepare for a war no one ever expected. It came at a cost. 'It was a real blow for 20 Squadron,' Bellamy remembered. 'We had lost the Boss, now seriously injured in hospital, and Gordon, one of our Flight Commanders, was dead. We then had Gordon's military funeral to deal with, where a number of our guys acted as pallbearers. It was an awful time.'

The short tribute, later placed in the RAF Laarbruch magazine, said it all:

As a true Officer and Gentleman, Squadron Leader Gordon Graham will be greatly missed by the members of 20 Squadron, all of whom held a deep respect for him both as a Navigator and Flight Commander. Our sympathies and hopes for the future go to his widow Gael and son Jamie.[25]

The ongoing deaths didn't make Bellamy, twenty-seven, reconsider his decision to withdraw his resignation made in the light of the looming post-Cold War cuts to the RAF. He would not duck the coming combat. Bellamy was also fast becoming the 20 Squadron expert on a brand-new missile that the RAF was rushing into service. The ALARM – Air-Launched Anti-Radiation Missile – was a clever munition. Its primary purpose was to seek out and destroy radar systems. Without them, the enemy could not see incoming jets or guide its surface-to-air missiles onto them. The ALARM was a stand-off, fire-and-forget missile that could be launched from considerable ranges, giving aircrew greater protection from groundfire. Bellamy was more than happy with that. '20 Squadron crews came to realise that they could fire a "smart" missile while avoiding the worst of any hostile defences. ALARM offered the RAF and the Tornado a radical new capability.'

* * *

Bill Green was not going to miss leading his own Squadron to war. As the Boss of 27 Squadron at RAF Marham, he had thoroughly enjoyed his time bringing the fliers and ground crew up to exceptional standards. And he was popular with aircrew and ground crew alike; a frequent visitor to the 'business end' of the Squadron engineering facilities as well as an astute planner in the Operations Room. There was something else that seemed to set him apart from the average officer. He was genuinely in love with flying. 'I would *pay* the Queen to let me fly her aircraft!' he would often quip.

He'd met his wife Jenny when they were both studying at Oxford University. They had married in Christ Church Cathedral soon after finals in 1969. In the following years they had two children and settled into RAF life. Bill and Jenny Green had dealt first hand with death in the fast-jet community on many occasions. Early on in their married life, a close RAF friend was killed in a training aircraft. The previous Sunday, they had christened his 3-month-old son. Jenny was babysitting him at their friends' home when an officer arrived to relay the terrible news. As the deceased pilot's wife was not at home, Jenny later had the crushing duty to inform the young mother that she was now a widow. 'We all understood that the possibility of our husbands dying in a flying accident was always there. You know it can happen, but you never get used to it.'[26]

That aside, RAF routine was fairly predictable. Their children grew into teenagers and squadron life was comfortable. Jenny knew her husband thoroughly enjoyed it. 'Being a Squadron Commander was a wonderful experience for Bill. He was dedicated to his men and especially to the young ground crew who he felt always gave their very best, but were not always properly recognised for their incredible efforts.'

Bill Green was regarded as a thoroughly decent and honourable man. The type whose troops would follow into battle. He also played the piano, church organ, guitar and, if the Squadron band's drummer failed to turn up for rehearsal, percussion too. Many of Bill's contemporaries thought he was destined for high command. He himself realised that the Cold War's conclusion would have significant ramifications. When the Berlin Wall came down in 1989, the countries behind the Iron Curtain experienced the first taste of freedom since Communism had been imposed on them from 1945. Bill understood that great upheaval led to turmoil. 'This is just the beginning, not the end,' he told Jenny. 'The world will now change in a very different way.' Then Saddam decided to invade Kuwait and his Squadron was one of the first to be ordered to the Gulf. Bill was told he was going to be the Detachment Commander for the Tornado bomber force. They would be deploying at the end of August. They had to prepare for war. Fast.

Bill's 17-year-old son Jeremy and 15-year-old daughter Philippa were home from boarding school as preparations ramped up. 'Living on a Tornado base meant that RAF life almost became part of family life,' said Jeremy. 'You were immersed in the day-to-day realities. Dad had known a couple of the guys killed in the crash just a few days before and we had spoken about what it all meant. We then had a conversation about what would happen if he died in any coming war. We had known some of Dad's friends killed in flying accidents over the years, so this was now a greater possibility if he was going to war. I understood those risks; for much of my life I said a nightly prayer, asking God to keep him safe when he was flying.'[27]

Jenny saw Bill take the prospect of action extremely seriously. 'On previous major detachments, there would always be a happy whistling going on as Bill put new strings on his guitar, and checked the piano accordion. None of that happened this time. This one was for real.' And the training had to be very real. As the Boss, Bill was at the forefront of the action, which included continual preparation for night-time, high-speed attack missions. As a pilot he was determined to be at the very top of his game. In the early days of August, while ensuring his Squadron was ready to deploy, he flew hour after hour, honing his flying skills to the highest level. A sortie was set for 16 August as part of the intensive pre-deployment training package. The next day the whole family would head from Norfolk to visit Bill's relatives in Northumberland to say goodbye. 'We were looking forward to spending a few days together as a family and enjoying some long walks on the beach before Bill's departure.'

That morning, Jenny had listened as he played the piano,

accompanying their daughter Philippa on the violin. Jenny had made lunch and called them to the table. 'I had to chivvy them along to eat together so we could get away in time to visit my mother over in Stamford, who was going into hospital for an operation. Bill went off to work and expected to be back around 11pm.' She spent the rest of the day with her mother and the children. Returning to their quarters exhausted, she went to bed, smiling ruefully to herself at the thought of the long johns Bill would currently be wearing under his flying suit – they had been dyed pale pink after a red T-shirt had got mixed up in the wash. At least they would go with the desert pink colour scheme of the newly painted Tornados they would be flying in the Gulf.

It was dark when Bill took off with his navigator Neil Anderson from the long tarmac strip of RAF Marham. After night-time air-to-air refuelling, they flew over the flat Norfolk landscape for TFR practice, followed by a bombing run over a range near Hull. Before returning to base, they headed out to sea, paralleling the coast. Bill decided to practise the challenging low-level loft – or toss – bombing manoeuvre that they would inevitably have to use against Iraqi airfields. They picked up a ship on the radar and chose it as the target. He flicked the control to take them out of automatic terrain following and entered a steep climb from 250 feet above the wave tops, going through a practice bomb release at around 1,200ft before commencing a recovery back to low level.[28]

*　*　*

The ringing echoed inside Jenny Green's head. It was far too early for her alarm. And there it was again. More persistent now. She opened her eyes. It was still dark. The bedside clock told her it was 1 a.m. 'The doorbell was ringing like mad. My first thought was that Bill had forgotten his key. I got out of bed and got halfway downstairs, then wondered if it was actually him, so turned back to put my dressing gown on.'

Jenny headed back downstairs. 'I got to the bottom step and

paused. If it was Bill, would he not be calling through the door to reassure me?'

Another ring. She could now sense someone standing outside. She flipped open the spyhole cover and caught her breath.

RAF Marham's Station Commander Jock Stirrup was standing outside in full dress uniform. The gold braid of his service cap glinted in the porch light. Jenny took a step back, forcing the bad news that lay on the far side of the door to remain where it was. If she did not answer, everything would still be okay.

'My life changed for ever in a split second. I instantly knew what had happened. I couldn't open the door. I just sat at the bottom of the stairs. Poor Jock had to stand outside while I composed myself.'

It had happened to others and now it had happened to her. No more would the house be filled with Bill's laughter, his music . . . his presence. She heard movement above. The children were at the top of the stairs. She couldn't delay any more. She saw her hand reach for the latch. Group Captain Stirrup spoke gently:

Bill's aircraft is missing . . . over the Wash . . . there's no hope of them being alive . . . I'm so sorry, Jenny . . .

'The rest was a blur, but the next twenty-four hours are still crystal clear, indelibly imprinted on my brain, even though it was over thirty years ago. However much you think you might know what it might be like, because you have seen *others* go through it, it is very different when it happens to you, when it is *your* life.'

Those first moments were also imprinted on Jeremy Green's teenage mind. 'I still remember it all as clear as day,' he said. 'I loved photography and Dad had arranged for me to visit his Squadron *that* night to take some pictures. But because of my grandmother's illness I put it off until another day. There was always going to be another day. If I had been there, waiting on the Squadron, as the news of the crash came in . . . it doesn't bear thinking about. Mum looked broken. We had endless visitors. We drank endless tea. At some point later the TV news showed wreckage of his aircraft being lifted from the sea. Your mind knows the worst, but you don't want to accept it.'

A Military Accident Report[29] subsequently showed that at the peak of his weapons release manoeuvre, Bill Green had rolled the aircraft into a hard bank while entering the challenging recovery phase from the loft attack; aiming to get the Tornado wings level, descending back to low level, and heading away from the target. But something had gone terribly wrong and the Tornado hit the sea at 500 knots (575mph) while still in an 18-degree dive. No attempt had been made to eject and both Bill Green and Neil Anderson were killed instantly. The report concluded that for some reason during the recovery from the loft manoeuvre, the aircraft had entered a steeper than normal dive. The crew might have been somehow distracted. But in many ways it didn't matter, another Tornado was down after just a few weeks of training for a war in the Gulf. And five aircrew were now dead.

Bill Green's body was never recovered from the North Sea and his passing was a bitter blow. He was the type of leader who cared for and loved his men, and that was reciprocated. 27 Squadron was in mourning; it would be difficult to replace 'The Boss'.

* * *

Robbie Stewart's family got back to their home in Lincolnshire on 20 August in reasonable spirits despite the interrupted Bavarian holiday. Robbie phoned his Operations Room to be told he would be deploying with his Squadron. He already knew about the horrific collision off Spurn Head which killed three crewmen on 14 August, but he hadn't heard any names. It was then that he was also given the news about his Boss, Bill Green, and friend Neil Anderson, who had died two days later. 'I just couldn't comprehend what they were saying. Bill was such a wonderful guy. I was totally floored to hear he'd died.'

Tange was in the house when Robbie made the call. As the phone hung limply in his hand, she could see his face crumple. 'Robbie looked at me but couldn't speak. He eventually managed to get out that Bill and Neil had been killed. It was such a terrible shock for all of us.'

Kirsty Stewart saw the hurt on both her parents' faces. She had turned thirteen a few days earlier and her father treated her like a grown-up. 'I still remember both Mum and Dad's reaction and how upset they were, but Dad explained about what it was like to fly at night and how difficult it could be, how you could get disorientated.' The death of close friends brought a grim focus to her father's imminent departure for war. Kirsty was growing up fast. 'There was a creeping realisation that Dad was going away, and it was really serious.'

In between sorties, Robbie had a long list of tasks, from inoculations against Saddam's biological weapons to practising pistol drills. 'We had to start preparing straight away: jabs, medicals, checking our personal weapons. I had a very real sense of what was to come, that we were heading to war. Talking to Tange and the kids was both emotional and hard. Lots of the younger guys were excited but those of us who were older, with families, were a little more realistic about what we faced.'

After long days he would get back late to their four-bedroom cottage in Coleby. Tange managed to sit him down for a few important conversations. 'We tried to sort out what we all wanted if the worst was to happen. We didn't really have much time at all as he was so busy down at Marham and we were up in Coleby. We talked about finances, the children, their education, what Robbie hoped for us all if he didn't come home. But there really wasn't much time to plan anything.'

Despite the intense preparations Robbie's pilot, Dave Waddington, found the time to visit Jenny Green and offer his condolences. 'Bill Green was a great Boss – very experienced, an old-fashioned type of officer and a lovely guy. I said goodbye to Jenny early because we were deploying and I would miss the Boss's funeral. As the youngest guy on the Squadron, there was little I could say to her. It was a very difficult moment.'

Training for war had claimed three Tornados and five lives in just a handful of summer days. The other navigator killed in the Spurn Head collision had been a close friend of Bob Ankerson, as had Neil

Anderson. 'Neil was a good operator, great company and passionate about the RAF.' His passing was a reminder to Bob that war or no war, death was the third passenger every time you flew the Tornado. 'That was the way things happened back then. There was just an acceptance. You got used to deaths in the RAF, but these were the first real friends I had lost to accidents. It highlighted the risks, but you quickly shoved any notion of death into the background, telling yourself, *It'll never happen to me* . . .'[30]

Two weeks after Gordon Graham's death his Squadron celebrated the unit's seventy-fifth anniversary. The guest of honour was 20 Squadron veteran Air Marshal Sir Victor Groom, ninety-two and a First World War ace who had flown the 120mph Bristol F2B fighters in 1918, just fifteen years after the Wright brothers' first ever powered flight. Miraculously, Groom survived the final year of the war while claiming eight 'kills'. David Bellamy was among those watching and he could not help but wonder if his own generation of Tornado aircrew might soon share the same fate as the majority of First World War pilots on the Western Front.

* * *

As the dog days of August 1990 approached, there was a last chance for a bit of family time over the bank holiday weekend. On the Friday before Robbie's departure, Tange Stewart booked a table at the local Beefeater pub in Canwick Hill for a farewell meal. Around them, others enjoyed the summer sunshine. 'It was a lovely family pub and a beautiful sunny day but the four of us were subdued and contemplating the future. I remember just thinking, *These people have no idea what is happening.* The next day my husband and my children's father was heading to war.' As Kirsty watched the other children play, she could not stop feeling uneasy. 'It was a horrible time. There was a sense that my dad was heading off on a very uncertain journey.'

After saying goodbye to them, Robbie left Marham by bus on Sunday, 26 August, heading to one of the RAF's transport bases to begin a series of long flights to the Gulf. 'As we drove off base, lots of the wives and families were standing near the exit, waving. It was sobering to see them, wondering when, or if, we would ever see them again. But there was also a real sense of excitement and anticipation on the bus. This is what we had trained to do. Then I looked out of the window to see the Norfolk countryside flashing by and realised we were heading to a warzone.'

After a two-day journey the aircrew landed at Muharraq airbase on the island of Bahrain, linked to Saudi Arabia by a causeway. In between the build-up for war, Gulf Air passenger jets were still taking off with businessmen and holidaymakers, escaping the intense August heat. Even at 5am it was over 30°C; a dry heat with no hint of any breeze. On the shimmering tarmac, Robbie could see the machinery of war was in full swing. RAF C130 Hercules transporters fought for space with civilian airliners. RAF Regiment Rapier air defence missile batteries bristled along the perimeter as countless transport aircraft flew in endless supplies and RAF tankers took off for vital air-to-air refuelling sorties. Everyone was on their toes, waiting for the enemy attack. 'The build-up at Muharraq as the machinery of war moved in was astonishing. The military had really swung into action.'

Back in Germany, the army was also gearing for war. In September it was announced that the British 7th Armoured Brigade – the Desert Rats – were deploying. The Challenger tanks and Warrior armoured fighting vehicles had turned their turrets away from the Soviet threat in the east, and shipped south to the desert. Reservists were called up. Trombones and flutes of the RAF musicians were exchanged for stretchers and bandages as they adopted their wartime role as medics. In the Gulf, the smell of war-fighting was in the air. The metallic odour of munitions mingled with the stench of aviation fuel as sweating ground crew serviced the aircraft. It was a demanding task, preparing not only for war but for a conflict in which it was clear the Tornado would play a lead role.

It was challenging too. The desert flying, Robbie and Dave agreed, *was exceptional*. No longer did they have to abide by the strict lowest-level limit of 100ft – operational low-level flying, or OLF. They flew as close to the ground as their skills and safety allowed, regularly below 100ft, ultra-low level. Something that was not strictly authorised. Looking on from the rear seat, Robbie found it thrilling. 'The desert flying was fantastic, a chance to hone our skills and practise everything at a really operational level, down at 50 feet and 540 knots [600mph]. You'd be flying across the desert at ultra-low level in gin-clear skies then suddenly a herd of camels would loom up in front of you. It was the most advanced flying we had ever done.' Very soon they were carrying full war loads, testing the Tornado to its maximum, practising air-to-air refuelling and low-level attacks. But for Robbie the excitement could not hide what they were there for. 'There was an inevitability about it all. The sense of a relentless march to war.'

Enhancements were rapidly being made to the Tornados to bring them fully onto a war footing. Radar absorbent paint was applied to try to hide them from Iraqi air defence systems.[31] HaveQuick radios, resistant to electronic jamming, were fitted, along with secure IFF systems that would easily distinguish between friendly and potentially hostile aircraft across any future battle space. Given the long combat sorties from the Gulf into Iraq, it was decided that, for many missions, the two 1,500-litre drop tanks under the wings should be replaced by the larger 2,250-litre tanks, increasing fuel load and range. The additional kit created different aerodynamics with extra drag on the aircraft, especially when carrying a full war load.

The American build-up was relentless too, and accompanied by the most sophisticated aerial weapons systems in history.[32] Western allies and Arabs were also joining the growing force. French troops and aircraft arrived, along with eight Italian Tornados, plus Egyptians, Pakistanis and Moroccans. There was even a contingent of 500 Niger soldiers to protect the holy sites of Mecca and Medina.

The build-up was a success and the immediate threat of an Iraqi invasion of Saudi Arabia subsided. The US influx had been truly astonishing. Within six weeks they had brought in the 24th Marine Expeditionary Force and the 101st Airborne Division, along with scores of Apache attack helicopters and the A-10 'tank-buster' air-craft. The Desert Shield was firmly in place. The Iraqis knew it too. Satellite photographs had shown that rather than being poised on the border, they were now digging in and waiting.

In November 1990, after three months of non-stop preparation, 27 Squadron was ordered home. It was time for others to come in and share the load. Waiting to take the flight out, Dave Waddington did not particularly mind the prospect of missing any future war. Yes, it would have been exciting, but he had been selected for the choice posting of the 'Qualified Weapons Instructor' course and the honour to become a 'Top Gun' pilot. If he passed, he was going to be the youngest Tornado QWI pilot. A big professional fillip and a career marker for greater things to come.

After the emotion of their rapid departure, Robbie Stewart was also only too happy to be home for Christmas. He was not one of the young guns, eager to be part of any upcoming war. He would do it if necessary, but Coleby, Lincolnshire, with Tange and his children, was the place he loved.

CHAPTER THREE

'EVERYTHING'S CHANGED!'

NOVEMBER 1990–15 JANUARY 1991

The intensity of training for war had drawn the individual Tornado squadrons closer together. Comprising around 130 engineers and support personnel, with some twelve jets and eighteen crews,[1] each squadron was tight-knit, with its own traditions and proud past. As they practised for war, the bonds grew deeper with the prospect that they too might make their own bit of history. The likelihood of battle was becoming an unnerving reality. They had trained hard since early August, they had taken casualties, but they were ready to face whatever lay ahead.

At RAF Laarbruch in Germany, after four months of relentless training, a good party was in order. Usually it would be the annual 'Lunch of the Year' around Christmas time, but because of the urgent deployments, this had to be brought forward. It fell to 15 Squadron's more junior crew, pilot John Peters, twenty-nine, and navigator John Nichol, twenty-seven, to organise what would be their final social event before heading to the Gulf. The 'Two Johns' had a few experienced hands to fall back on for advice. Among them was navigator Mike Toft who, with a wife and young family, was feeling the tension grow as the days to deployment counted down. The in-depth briefing on the Iraqi air defences, similar to the Soviet ones they knew only too well, had taken on a grave tone. 'We had really feared going up against them in the Cold War. The prospect now was formidable. And worrying.'[2]

That worry turned to anger in a pub one night back in England, when a couple of bikers sat down at the next table. Mike could not help but overhear the loud complaints about how tensions in the Gulf had dramatically increased petrol prices. He could barely control his anger. 'I thought, "You *bastards*! Are *you* putting *your* balls on the line to bring the prices down?" It was almost surreal. We were heading to war and those outside our bubble had not a jot of understanding about what we were going to do.'

There was at least comfort in flying the Tornado. Mike had originally been a navigator on the Canberra, the RAF's first jet bomber. It was a step change crossing over to the Tornado with its new technology and capability. 'The radar was bloody awesome at low level – really easy to use and fantastic for identifying everything from large radio masts right down to turns in fence lines. And while there were occasional issues with bits of kit not working as advertised, we all completely trusted the jet.' If Mike was going to go to war, then Tornado was the best option. After months of hard work, he was ready for a good party.

There was another wise old hand that the Two Johns could turn to for advice, and not just on hosting parties. Since joining the RAF a decade earlier, Nige Risdale had absorbed all he could about the RAF's brand-new Tornado 'electric jet' while going through training and his heart had been set on flying the aircraft. With scores of Tornados coming into service, he had been rewarded with a 'boy in a sweetshop moment' after landing at RAF Marham in late 1982, aged twenty-three. 'We were shown into one of the giant hangars and it was chock-full of brand-new, shiny Tornados. They looked amazing; a complete flying machine which really looked as though it meant business.'[3]

Nige was hooked and did not want to fly anything else. He was
not one of the hotshot pilots who favoured the single-seat Harriers
and Jaguars. He preferred the comfort of another set of hands and
eyes in the back seat, especially the 'older' experienced navigators
who could offer advice and airmanship. It was a mature quality in
a young flier, and one that over the years marked Nige Risdale out
to be one of the most trusted pilots on the Squadron. After completing the tough QWI 'Top Gun' course, he also had real experience
and knowledge. Quiet and reserved, Risdale was a hugely talented
officer, particularly respected by the younger aircrew. It was why,
at just thirty-one years old, he was the designated pilot for the
Squadron Boss, John Broadbent. Together, they would lead the
Squadron's initial combat missions. It was a job that needed a clear
head and exceptional flying ability.

The Squadron's more experienced officers were an important
source of knowledge, social and professional, to newcomers like
John Nichol. He had joined the RAF aged seventeen in 1981 as a
communications technician, and after four years had worked his
way up to the rank of Corporal.[4] An ambition took hold that perhaps he could advance further up the RAF's command ladder, so he
applied for a commission as an officer, then trained as a Tornado
navigator. The organisational skills he had learned in the ranks were
now put to good use.

The 15 Squadron 'Lunch of the Year' 1990 felt more than usually
significant. 'Even then, with war mentioned daily in the headlines, I
was still convinced it was not going to involve me,' Nichol recalled.
'I just couldn't comprehend how it would all end in battle. Surely
Saddam would see the madness of trying to take on the world's
most modern armies and air forces? And I certainly wasn't one of
those hungry for combat.' All the same, the TV reports were full
of images of the build-up in the Gulf. 'We were heading in that
direction, so John Peters and I decided to lay on a daytime version
of the "Last Supper".' They decked out the crew room in black
sheets, played mournful church recordings, had Bible readings,
then got everyone to dress in their flying suits with sandals instead

of boots. Each officer entered the crew room solemnly carrying a lit candle and walked to chairs at the end of the room where the Boss, John Broadbent, and Flight Commander Gordon Buckley ritually scrubbed their feet in a bowl of soapy water with the biggest, filthiest brushes the Two Johns could find.

There was a fair bit of drink taken and much laughter. Mike Toft demonstrated his legendary talents as a Cossack dancer. The occasional bread roll was launched, like a surface-to-air missile, across the crew room. The senior aircrew, like Nige Risdale and Gordon Buckley, looked on as though indulging recalcitrant children. It was a moment to forget both what lay ahead and those they were leaving behind. For Nichol, in among the fun was a more sobering thought that there was a chance, no matter how remote, that some of them might not be present at next year's lunch. 'People were letting off steam and most of us got a little the worse for wear. But there was a breath of something in the air, of people coming to terms with events. It was as if the religious ritual provided some sort of answer to a question we had not yet even asked ourselves.'[5]

Across the airfield, final gatherings were also taking place for Laarbruch's other squadrons selected to deploy. Nichol's flatmate and fellow Tornado navigator Dave Bellamy had finally cancelled the five-week Chilean travel adventure he had booked with his girlfriend. Instead of trekking the Atacama he would be flying over another desert. Before deploying to the Gulf, Bellamy made one last trip home. His mother's parting words were that she had been praying hard, and 'God has promised you will be safe'.

Bellamy told his pilot Trevor Roche that this divine intervention would happily extend to him, as they were in the same aircraft. Then the rest of the formation heard about 'Dave's heavenly safety'. Superstitions grew. Perhaps if they flew close to Dave and Trevor's aircraft, they too would fall under the Good Lord's umbrella? Word spread and other members of 20 Squadron asked if they could join the formation that was clearly going to be 'watched over'. While it became a bit of a standing joke, there was just a hint of seriousness behind the smiles. How *would* they survive what was coming?

It was now late November, and 20 Squadron was deploying two weeks earlier than Nichol's 15 Squadron. Bellamy was chuffed they had 'beaten' them to the punch but there was a downside: last-minute packing. He had put on a clothes wash, and with no time to dry his long johns and T-shirts, he reached for Nichol's prized microwave, trusted purveyor of so many gourmet baked bean dinners. He placed his flying long johns and T-shirts reverently inside and turned up the dial. A few minutes later there was a satisfying ping. But his delight was short-lived. 'Unfortunately, my plan hadn't worked so I stuffed the laundry, warm but still wet, in a plastic bag. The funny thing was that the process sterilised my clothes so two weeks later when my kit arrived, I had fresh but damp clothes and no mildew. John, on the other hand, had baked beans tasting of Persil Automatic.' As Bellamy threw his clothes into his kitbag he spotted handwritten notes among the unwashed crockery on the kitchen table. His flatmates had decided to write a couple of encouraging goodbye messages.

'*Bydsee bye Dave*,' Nichol had scrawled on the back of an envelope. '*Look after ya'self and check six. See ya when we collect our medals! I'll drop ya a line. All the best, John.*'

Their fellow flat-sharing navigator, who would also soon deploy to the warzone, cheerfully wrote: '*Dave, I love you dearly. Please don't leave me! Take care you twat. Luv, Glyn.*'

When Bellamy rose before dawn he tucked the notes into his trousers then proceeded to pick up his pilot from the married quarters. As Trevor Roche got into the car, his wife Katie rushed out to say a final goodbye. 'Belly, promise me you will look after him, promise me you will bring him back to me?'

'I promise,' Bellamy replied with no idea if he could honour the pledge, merely hoping against hope that his mum's conversation with God really was going to come up trumps.

* * *

Arriving at Tabuk in Saudi Arabia, Bellamy found there were washing lines for his damp kit, but little else by way of comfort, especially not microwaves. In the far north-west of the country, they were closer to the splendid reefs of the Red Sea than the arid deserts of Iraq. The enemy border lay 300 miles to the east and Baghdad another 200 miles beyond.

Tabuk was a military airbase; functional and spartan, it had a sense of purpose. There was no swimming pool or bar – nothing to distract them from the job in hand. There was little to choose from in the way of accommodation, although, as usual, the officers seemed to fare better than the airmen. It was something that was – generally – taken with good grace by the RAF rankers. The officers, after all, were the ones who went into battle. But the aircrew also understood that without the ground crew, there would be no flying; they kept the jets airworthy. Their shared mission was a mutual bond. The officers took over the little wooden villas belonging to British Aerospace (the major defence contractor – BAe) with six to a room, whereas the airmen's quarters were more basic, and twice as crowded. Dave Bellamy's formation was even luckier. There were no villas left when they arrived so they were given rooms in a single-men's block still used by BAe personnel. There was a feeling that the Saudis on the base, while generally friendly, were not overly enamoured with having a bunch of foreigners on their land. Initial co-operation had been 'difficult' at best.

The Tabuk detachment was substantial, with aircrew from a number of the RAF's UK and Germany Tornado squadrons. The base was surrounded by hundreds of miles of desert, which for the aircrew was perfect. 'The flying out there was absolutely fantastic, the best I've ever done in the air force. Most of the Saudi desert is absolutely flat but here there were fantastic valleys, mountains, volcanoes and standing stones ... and we were told we could fly as low and as fast as we needed to go.'[6] They shared the base with the resident members of the Royal Saudi and US Air Forces, which allowed the Tornados to fly mock combat sorties against the highly capable Saudi F-15s, whose pilots proved to be 'very, very good'.

Which prompted a mildly disturbing thought: *Maybe the Iraqis are just as good.*[7]

That worry was compounded by the Iraqis having the sixth largest air force in the world, with 900 jet aircraft. They would present a formidable foe.

* * *

While the earlier 'Last Supper' party had parked his troubles for one afternoon, navigator Mike Toft, still waiting at RAF Laarbruch to deploy, could not shake off the concern of leaving behind his toddler daughter and a wife who was six months pregnant. Mike was returning from his sorties to a worried partner and playful 2-year-old. *How the hell are we going to get through this?* he thought. While many of the young, single aircrew brimmed with excitement, married men like Mike were more introspective. 'It was a sense of duty that carried me through. I did not particularly *want* to go, but that's what I'd signed up to do. Was I excited? I don't think so. Was I worried? Hell yes, especially for Sue and our 1.6 kids. Leaving them behind for the unknown was damned hard.'

Mike Toft and the other 50,000 British soldiers, sailors and airmen sent to the region were under military orders. Even if it meant leaving a young family behind. The crosses being marked on the family calendar leading up to 2 December 1990 seemed to speed up as his departure date drew closer. The last forty-eight hours were the worst. 'We both knew what was going to happen and just wanted to get it over with.' To pass the time they took their daughter to a local petting zoo. It didn't help. 'It was really striking; the normality of wandering around this little park, feeding the goats and the sheep, a seemingly happy family. But amid the crowds, only Sue and I knew that I'd soon be putting my life on the line 3,000 miles away.'

Toft was flying out to replace the likes of Robbie Stewart and Dave Waddington, hurriedly spirited to the Gulf in August. He would be joining Gordon Buckley on 15 Squadron. While the prospect of war was daunting, some weight was taken off their minds when they were told their destination was Bahrain – and that they would be billeted in the five-star Sheraton in the middle of town. It had excellent rooms, air conditioning, swimming pools and, unlike Saudi Arabia, alcohol. The aircrews were told to pack their dinner jackets. When they arrived at the hotel, each pilot and navigator pair was given a room to share for the duration.

The genial expat community were eager to befriend the glamorous new arrivals and proved themselves generous hosts. During the day there was rigorous planning and preparation for war but then along came the party invitations. Gordon Buckley found it curiously unsettling. 'There was a lot of socialising with the locals joining us in the hotel bar for a drink and inviting us to their homes. It was really strange to be living the life of a businessman in a five-star hotel while preparing for war.' And he was not alone in still questioning whether there would actually be open hostilities, especially now the coalition force had grown to 800,000. 'I presumed we would threaten, have a bit of sabre-rattling and then Saddam would back down.'[8]

With the distractions of a full social life, including horse riding and windsurfing in the Gulf, interspersed with flying demanding training sorties, their surreal existence continued. Sometimes it was only the dawn chant of the muezzin calling the faithful to prayer that reminded them where they were. And why.

* * *

Nige Risdale definitely wanted to ensure that the Tornado's leading role would achieve maximum impact with the minimum risk. Only he and 15 Squadron's Boss, Wing Commander John Broadbent, who would be leading any initial attack, were given access to the US-controlled, top-secret planning. 'The missions for the first seventy-two hours of offensive operations were all to be pre-planned. The Americans controlled the show and decided that in order to keep the security lid tight, access to the raids would be limited to one crew per detachment.' Leaving behind clear-headed veterans like Gordon Buckley and Mike Toft, Nige found planning for missions that presented grave dangers a taxing and lonely affair. The Tornado was clearly among the best qualified coalition bombers to do the low-level missions and the attack plan was to use the unique runway-busting JP233 to knock the Iraqi airbases out of action – and that came with considerable risk. In any all-out war of national survival against the Soviets, high casualties had been expected and accepted. But this was a relatively parochial battle for someone else's country. Did they have to put so many lives on the line?

As one of the most qualified pilots, Nige Risdale knew better than most about the Tornado's potential. He had previously served on 20 Squadron, which had trained in dropping laser-guided bombs – LGBs – onto their targets via the Pave Spike designating pod on another very capable aircraft, the Buccaneer. Using these assets, Nige had initially thought, the Tornados could drop their 1,000lb bombs with clinical accuracy. 'I thought, *We should be using LGBs*. I'd dropped many live LGBs so I knew exactly what they were capable of. I thought we should get the Buccaneers out so we'd have precision weapons to attack the airfields.' The response to Risdale's suggestion was unambiguous. 'I was told that this was not going to happen. The sense I had got in the initial stages of deployment was that the RAF's Tornado had been "*sold*" to the Americans by "high command" as an airfield-busting force using JP233s to put airfields out of action. Which of course, was exactly the role we had trained for, so it made sense.'

In fact, while it was undoubtedly true that the RAF had been earmarked for its airfield attack capability, the idea of bringing in Buccaneers to provide precision targeting was also being discussed. And dismissed. As Air Vice-Marshal Bill Wratten, the British Air Commander, later recalled. 'Most airfields were very overcrowded, with some, such as Bahrain, particularly so. But we wanted to introduce the Buccaneer into theatre to provide ourselves with a laser target-marking capability. This led to a spirited debate in which Horner [General Chuck Horner; the overall Air Commander] made his position quite clear – the Brits simply did not need to import any more aeroplanes because the USAF could provide all the designation that might be needed.'[9]

It was decided; the JP233 would be the RAF's main contribution. It had been developed specifically for Tornados to sneak through Soviet defences then deliver their devastating ordnance via a high-speed, low-level overflight.[10] The Iraqi Air Force was able to operate from a number of very large and well-prepared bases, and the USAF lacked dedicated airfield-denial munitions, so the Americans warmly embraced the British offer of employing Tornado GR1s to complete the job.

But Nige knew that the JP233 was going to present a challenge, particularly to get enough aircraft over the target to achieve the requisite damage. The weapon had been designed to decimate Warsaw Pact runways. Punching through their thick layers built on dense northern European clay subsoil, the cratering munitions would bury themselves then explode, 'heaving' the runway surface upwards and causing massive damage. 'The tactics we had always used dictated that knocking out an 8,000ft Soviet runway on "Day One" of the Cold War going hot would require one Tornado eight-ship formation, each carrying two JP233s, attacking that single airfield. Those of us who survived that initial assault would return to base, reload, refuel and then repeat the attack about four hours later with another eight aircraft loaded with JP233s. We would have deployed thirty-two JP233s: nearly 1,000 cratering munitions and 7,000 anti-personnel bomblets. For *one single* 8,000ft runway.'

Nige was told their first target in Iraq would be the giant military airbase of Tallil, near Nasiriyah, about 150 miles north-west of Iraq's second city, Basra. It was a tough proposition. 'Tallil had *two* parallel 12,000ft runways – about the same length as Heathrow airport's – and *two* taxiways which could also be used for take-off and landing if required. Tallil effectively had *four 12,000ft* runways! There were also HAS [hardened aircraft shelter] sites in each corner of the airfield with individual access direct to the runways. During all those Cold War exercises, we never imagined we would truly have to do it for real, so the "numbers game" hadn't really mattered. That had all now changed. It was going to be a big ask.'

The old, Cold War missions had also been planned over familiar and accurately mapped terrain. Iraq was an entirely different proposition. Unlike Europe, the vast deserts were bereft of landmarks for the navigation system which fed the Tornado's main computer. The Tornado was not equipped with a 'global positioning system' – similar to a car's 'sat nav'.[11] It used an 'inertial navigation' device which was programmed with an exact 'start point' when on the ground. It then used a complex system of sensors to continuously monitor the speed, height, orientation and direction of movement of the aircraft to keep its position updated and fed into the main computer.

But inertial systems lose accuracy over time so the navigator needed to regularly update the main computer with a precise location. For the most part, they would use the ground-mapping radar to identify a prominent feature such as a radio mast, bridge or coastal outline whose exact co-ordinates had been previously fed into the system. With the point carefully identified by radar, the navigator would 'mark' its location relative to the aircraft by clicking his hand controller. In simple terms, the Tornado main computer knew exactly where the known feature was, so could precisely calculate its own position in relation to it, and the main computer would be updated with incredible accuracy.

Now, with few reliable fixing points in the Iraqi desert, and before any 'night vision' devices were widely available or in operational use on the Tornado,[12] Nige Risdale was struggling to find a way of getting the aircraft safely and accurately on target in total darkness. He sought permission to bring 15 Squadron's most experienced navigator, and his fellow Qualified Weapons Instructor, into the confidential process.

In Paddy Teakle, 15 Squadron had a highly talented and accomplished mission planner. A big, universally respected character, he had flown Victor tankers on the famous Black Buck bombing raids during the Falklands War eight years earlier. While Paddy was not easily fazed, he quickly recognised the complexity of Nige's challenges, and their need to change their Iron Curtain-centric thinking.

'The task of planning every sortie for my own Squadron would have been enough, but to plan for all of the other Muharraq-based Tornado units as well was a different challenge altogether. What exactly was our credibility with the other units? Would they understand our thought processes and the tactics we would employ? Had they undertaken the same extensive work-up training? What were their strengths and weaknesses? Unfortunately, due to the highly confidential nature of our work, these were questions that remained largely unanswered, yet they niggled away at me constantly. I tried to make the plans as simple as possible. Minimise the threat, maintain accuracy and provide an element of surprise.'[13]

Together, they began to work on how they were going to take out Tallil. In theory, they might need *hundreds* of JP233 attacks to put this single airfield out of action. 'Iraq then had countless more of these massive airbases,' said Risdale. 'We were also really concerned about our ability to produce the accuracy that we would need for these missions to be anything close to successful.'[14]

They re-examined the best maps they had of southern Iraq and saw an oil pipeline that ran along Saudi's northern border, along with a series of telecommunication masts. That was enough to give the attackers an accurate navigational fix as they crossed into enemy territory. But once inside Iraq the systems would need further radar-identifiable landmarks to feed the computer. Going back to the maps under the strip lights of the planning room at Muharraq airbase – while the rest of the squadron enjoyed nights out – Nige and Paddy saw that the Iraqis surrounded their bases with a massive metal fence whose corners provided a really useful aiming feature, easily identifiable on radar. It was a great find. But only if the 20-year-old maps were still accurate, and the Iraqis had not moved any fences.

*　*　*

The JP233 was not only unproven in battle; there was barely a Tornado pilot who had flown with one. A live drop had been undertaken during its early testing, and in 1988 two crews had flown with a fully armed and JP233-loaded aircraft to test the handling capabilities at the aircraft's maximum permissible weight,[15] but this very expensive and highly secret weapon was not authorised to be deployed for normal peacetime training. The restrictions were quickly lifted. Nige flew his first ever sortie with two live JP233s on 17 December to check how the war-laden Tornado coped with the weapons – a total of almost 5 tonnes – under its belly, at low level, before people began shooting at them for real. 'In some ways, the Tornado was a fish out of water in the desert. It had been designed for the European theatre of operations to fly at low level and in a cool climate. Now we were flying it in incredible heat, which meant the engines were less efficient.'

But the Tornado still performed well, even if it was thirsty work for its engines. As Nige and Paddy prepared the first missions of any imminent engagement, the rest of the Muharraq detachment, excluded from the secret planning, continued its training – and socialising – oblivious to what their colleagues were doing. 'I had absolutely no idea whatsoever that planning was at such an advanced stage,' remembered John Nichol. 'It was never mentioned or discussed. We simply carried on training for an event I personally thought would never take place. And, in our downtime, we continued to enjoy the nightlife of Bahrain!'

* * *

In the lead-up to war a curious cultural contrast became apparent between the British and their closest ally. American audiences exceeding 14 million, including President George Bush and the overall Allied Military Commander General Norman Schwarzkopf, had been gripped by *The Civil War,* a documentary series that captured the nation's imagination with brutal imagery of that elemental 1860s conflict. The film-makers had employed the novel technique of using the camera to slowly pan over graphic contemporary photos. Accompanied by the mournful tune of the 'Ashokan Farewell', and with a voiceover by Morgan Freeman and others, it was an instant hit when first shown on the Public Broadcasting Service that

September. A Vietnam veteran, Schwarzkopf ensured his officers watched it to better understand the nature of war. But the show was also having a negative effect on morale back home. With the prospect of mass casualties, public support for an invasion began to diminish. 'The Civil War series on TV has had a sobering effect on many,' Schwarzkopf noted.[16]

Gordon Buckley and the rest of 15 Squadron were among those from the British military who were engrossed in something entirely different. The videos of the iconic series Blackadder Goes Forth had just been released. The Two Johns, Mike Toft and, on the occasional night off from planning, Nige Risdale and Buckley's veteran navigator Paddy Teakle, gathered in a room at the Sheraton for some light relief. Laughter echoed down the corridor during the moments of blackest humour when the insanity and carnage of First World War trench warfare contrasted with trenchant comedy. But the show also had poignancy and resonance for those about to go into action. Particularly the last instalment, when Captain Blackadder, played by Rowan Atkinson, was ordered to lead his men 'over the top' – or 'sausage side' – in a doomed assault. Captain Blackadder knows 'Operation Certain Death' can only end one way. He attempts to feign madness, placing a pair of underpants on his head and pencils up his nose, telling his sidekick Baldrick to ask him questions. 'Wibble,' responds Blackadder to each in turn. The ruse doesn't work and in the final moments before leaving the trench he reflects on the insanity of war: 'Who would have noticed another madman around here?'

The whistles sound, the men go over the top, the outcome is inevitable. The final scene, shot in slow motion, is as stark and sobering as they come as the main characters are mown down by machine-gun fire.

It had a profound effect on Buckley and the watching aircrew. 'The room just fell silent at the end. It was really quite moving. It became an unwritten rule that this last episode should not be played again. The rest of them, however, were played relentlessly and most of us could recite the lines by heart. "Wibble" and "sausage side" became well-worn phrases heard while we were flying. It seemed to reflect the reality of our own approaching war.'

* * *

Not long after Gordon and his flight had arrived in the Gulf, a seismic event occurred back home that shook both the British military and their allies. During more than a decade in power Mrs Thatcher had made many enemies, not least within her own Conservative Party. Her fading political instincts failed to detect the knives now being unsheathed by her own tribe, determined to oust her at any cost. On 22 November she resigned and was replaced by John Major. The establishment was rocked and Saddam delighted. George Bush was not. The US President was handed a note during a visit to a warship in the Gulf. General Schwarzkopf noticed an instant change. 'He was stunned. Thatcher was his closest friend and staunchest ally, and had helped him the most in the early days of the Gulf crisis.'[17]

Back in Britain things weren't pretty for John Major either. Loyal to the end, he had seen his mentor brutally dispatched. But that was politics, a brutal business. The reality for Major was a tricky inheritance. Inflation was in double figures, interest rates at 14 per cent, unemployment rising by 50,000 a month and house prices falling.[18] Recession loomed as he now led Britain towards its most formidable military operation since the Second World War.

While war, diplomacy and high politics had people glued to their televisions and newspapers, at home at RAF Bruggen that November navigator Bob Ankerson got on with day-to-day tasks as a Flight Commander on 17 Squadron. Soft-spoken and avuncular, Bob was a well-liked and trusted navigator with three decades of service. So he had felt a touch put out that after so long on the Cold War front line, he was going to miss out on the real thing. He had been selected to remain on base and look after affairs while the majority of the Squadron deployed. If battle casualties started to occur as expected, a steady hand would be needed to steer the Squadron through trying times.

His wife Chris could sense his disappointment. 'He had trained all his career for this moment and didn't want to be left behind. I thought it would be tough for him, but I also felt a sense of guilt that all my friends' husbands were deploying and mine would be safe at home.' At least they could spend more time with their 12-year-old son Gareth who would soon be back from boarding school in England. In early December, Bob was back on a training course at RAF Cranwell in Lincolnshire. He was passing the delightful neo-classical main building on his way from a good lunch in the Officers' Mess when he was called to the telephone. There was little small talk. His Squadron Boss, Wing Commander Dusty Miller, got straight to the point. Another navigator had been pulled from the deployment. Family circumstances. 'You've had your last beer for a while, Bob; you're booked on a flight back to Germany first thing tomorrow. You're going out to the Gulf at the end of the month.'

'Okay, Boss.' Bob Ankerson put down the phone, told his instructors he was leaving the course immediately, went back to his room and packed his bags for war.

In their married quarters, Chris was contemplating their Christmas plans when she got the call.

'Everything's changed,' Bob told her. 'I'm deploying to the war-zone with the rest of the Squadron in a few weeks.'

For a moment she found it difficult to speak. Everything really had changed. 'But your mum and dad are coming over in a few weeks for New Year,' she said, knowing full well that family plans made no difference to war orders. Bob arrived back in Germany the next day. With so much to do, there was no time to discuss what it all meant and the implications for their future. They managed a few snatched conversations about life insurance and bank accounts, but Bob's view was everything was in order, *you'll be fine*. Chris understood. 'He was on a war footing, preparing to fly out to the Gulf. My naive thought was, *The worst won't happen to Robert; things like that don't happen to us. He'll be quite safe, do his bit, come home and we'll carry on as normal.*'

Bob's new pilot was the young but extremely likeable Simon

Burgess. In between vaccination jabs, small arms training and gathering personal kit, they managed a few sorties together. Bob quickly understood why Simon was popular. His charm on the ground was matched by smoothness in the air. Whereas most of the Squadron had had a good few months to prepare, Bob and Simon had just a few days to build their partnership. Flying low, fast, at night into enemy fire required extraordinary co-operation between pilot and navigator. Any of the usual aircrew jibes of 'talking ballast' and 'stick monkey' – navigator and pilot – were quickly parked. The pressure of flying, navigating and getting bombs on target was immense. Co-operation was everything, monitoring actions and correcting each other's mistakes. Anticipate. Communicate. They learned to work the Tornado together. 'We were flying intensively, building trust, preparing for war together; the personal relationship was going to be crucial. Although I was a Flight Commander and senior officer, once in the air, all of that was forgotten. We became a finely honed team. Developing that relationship was crucial, so that when the chips were down, we each had total trust in the other's decisions.'

* * *

Bob and Simon were training for the war while Nige Risdale and Paddy Teakle were in the midst of planning it 3,000 miles away. Standing in the Operations Room at Muharraq, arms folded, they looked over their mission planning notes, the Top Secret US Air Tasking Order, and countless charts spread across the table before them. On the area map it looked easy. Head roughly north-west and their first target, Tallil airbase, was around 500 miles from Bahrain. Perhaps sixty minutes' flight time. But you'd arrive with little fuel left in the tanks. There was no way the Tornados were going to fly from Bahrain or Dhahran directly into Iraq, or over Kuwait and its complex SAM defences. They traced a more westerly route over Saudi Arabia, along what would become known as the 'tanker trail' paralleling the border. Here, scores of jets would meet up to refuel before heading into Iraqi airspace. To attack Tallil, Nige decided on a route that began with them heading 500 miles west. 'We would have around an hour's transit from Bahrain, paralleling the Saudi border, taking on fuel, until we dropped to low level to penetrate Iraq where it was least defended. We then might have around an hour at low level to and from the target. So we also needed to refuel on the way home.' With 700 combat aircraft assembling to go into Iraq on 'Night One', at intervals timed to the nearest five seconds, the tanker rendezvous timings had to be precise.

It was all very different from what now seemed like the fairly straightforward Soviet strategy. Even the jets had changed colour from the shiny new green, grey and black Nige had seen at RAF Marham eight years earlier, to their current desert-sand. The new kit inside the Tornado, the massive new fuel tanks, the live JP233s; it had all happened very quickly. He sighed. It seemed that changes were happening so fast there was no time to absorb the impact or implications. 'Paddy and I realised we just had to ditch our Cold War mentality and re-evaluate all the tactics and procedures we had ever used in Germany. We had never really trained or prepared for the coming scenario and I had a sense of somewhat hoping for the best. We had major fuel considerations and the real possibility of less-than-accurate navigation and weapons aiming systems.'

The best they could do, Nige and Paddy concluded, was to employ the JP233 to 'harass' the Iraqi airbase's operations. 'We came up with a plan to use the JP233 to cut across the runways, access points and taxiways. Hopefully the anti-personnel mines would then hamper any repairs.' These bomblets were both vicious and cunningly designed. They would shred anyone who disturbed them. And if a bulldozer attempted their clearance, they would tip over and fire a shaped-charge slug of metal through the blade and into the driver's cab. Eight aircraft each carrying two of the 2.5-tonne devices would bring a deadly mix of cratering munitions and anti-personnel bomblets to Tallil.

Knowing that American bombers were also going to 'bomb the crap out of the airfield before we arrived', Paddy agreed that it wasn't going to be necessary to cover the entire area with JP233 munitions. 'We chose points where we could have maximum impact – taxiway and runway intersections. Break up the runway there, and you could theoretically stop aircraft entering the runway and taking off.'[19] After several submissions the plan was given the go-ahead.

While the pair spent long nights planning in secrecy, the younger officers were also hard at work ensuring the Squadron's social reputation remained intact. Indeed, on his second night in Bahrain, with senior officers missing at a meeting, John Nichol and others were ordered to take up their formal invitations to a cocktail party at the British Club. 'The club was packed out with expats eager to greet us and thank the RAF for what they were doing. From that moment on our social engagements blossomed.'

For Paddy and Nige the long nights in front of maps meant they often missed out. 'We did lots of the planning in the evenings when most of our formations were relaxing at our favourite restaurants – Señor Paco's Mexican or the Up A Tree Cup A Tea Thai. I knew Buckers was confused that I wasn't around in the evenings to socialise.' The level of secrecy imposed by the Americans had meant that even Gordon Buckley, who would actually lead a formation of Tornados with Paddy, could not be told what his navigator was doing. 'I knew Paddy was up to something, but he never told me what. He would just get up out of his bed in the morning on a day off, and say he was going to work.'

The parties and socialising were a diversion from the realities that lay ahead. If it was war then young aircrew like Peters and Nichol wanted to sharpen their skills to have a chance of surviving. That meant some of the best and most challenging training of their lives. Peters' mentor was a squadron leader who had been in the Gulf for some months. 'He briefed us on the hazards of desert flying. He made sure we took on board the ways in which the sun can deceive and disorientate, and gave us tips on how to fly low, safely, in a flat and featureless environment. It was really tricky gauging height under certain combinations of terrain and light. So we kept it careful to begin with, nothing too gung-ho. But as the days went past, and we got used to the conditions, we began winding the aircraft gradually downwards towards the deck, foot by foot, inch by inch, until we were all hammering along just above the sand, right down at 40 feet.'

On a visit to Tabuk airbase in the west of Saudi Arabia, Nichol experienced something not unlike Peters had during his *Star Wars* moments in Canada. 'We went through narrow gorges, so narrow that it seemed John Peters was continually having to roll the Tornado onto its side to squeeze through the sheer sandstone cliffs soaring high above us. We flew through the most fantastic rock formations, sculpted by sandstorms. To look at it, it was stunning. To fly through, a joy.'[20]

And flying low over Saudi Arabia, John Peters got a true sense of the scale of the assembling invasion force. 'Below us in the desert were scores of allied tanks parked in the sand along with huge piles of equipment, ammunition dumps, supply dumps and fuel bowers. On the road there was convoy after convoy of armour and supply trucks, the traffic almost continuous with vehicles chucking up huge dust plumes.'

The build-up was continuing apace.

* * *

War was far from Tange Stewart's mind. She could not hide her joy at the promise of a family festive season with her Tornado navigator husband Robbie now back home. The long, painful days and clammy August nights listening to the BBC World Service reports on the panicked reaction to Kuwait's invasion had become a memory. She was pleased, *really* pleased that Robbie had returned home after three months in the Gulf. He had been away many times before on exercises around the world but this time it had been different. Now he was back for good. Robbie was also delighted to fit back into family life with the prospect of battle banished. 'I wasn't one of those desperate to go to war. I was ready to do it if necessary, but was not hugely disappointed if not. I quickly went back to normality, enjoying family life with no thoughts of war.' In mid-December, Robbie even had time to visit Tange's village primary school to chat about the Gulf region. Dressed in his flying suit, he had chatted to the wide-eyed children about the desert geography and rock formations, although it was his videos of ultra-low flying that attracted the most attention.

Delighted with the children's reaction, he arrived back home in Coleby in good spirits. He gave his teenage daughter Kirsty a kiss and was about to get changed when the phone rang. Standing beside him as he picked up the receiver, Kirsty couldn't really hear what was said. But she didn't need to. Lowering the phone, her beloved father simply said, 'I'm going back out to the Gulf.'

'Dad's face was ashen. We knew that our lives had changed at that moment. I could see him trying to hold back tears. Not wanting to show too much emotion.'[21] It was horrible. Her dad was her idol. A constant figure of love and support. Now Kirsty only saw worry and fear. Instinctively she knew the bedrock foundation of him always being there was gone.

Tange had barely got through the front door when Kirsty and her older brother Scott fell on her. 'Dad's going back out to the Gulf . . .' The looks on their young faces confirmed her fears. 'It felt like a fist to my stomach,' Tange remembered. 'I know it was his job and his duty, but it was a real shock that after just coming home from the warzone for Christmas, he was going to have to return. As an RAF wife, I knew that in reality if anyone should be going back out, it should be him. But as a civilian wife and mother it was hard. I had to hand over my husband to the RAF again and it felt as though things were getting very, very serious.'[22] She paced the house as Robbie talked through the implications. 'I was really upset discussing it with Tange. We both had no doubt that war was just weeks away, and I was going to be part of it. It was a huge thing for the family to come to terms with. The kids were upset because they could see we were upset.' The whole family knew the reality. The Tornados would be at the forefront of the action. A small number of men would be taking immeasurable risks going into battle against a foe who would do everything they could to kill them.

The children were old enough to be told the harsh realities. Kirsty appreciated their honesty. 'It was horrible to see my parents affected like this. The people you look up to for stability, who you trust to be there for you. I could see Dad was truly concerned. There were tough conversations about what we would do if Dad was killed – how we should stay at our schools, how Mum would ensure everything would continue as normal.' Her father also explained the exact nature of a Tornado strike mission and when the war might start, that 16 January was a new moon and total darkness would cloak any potential attack. He spoke of the danger but also of the Tornado's brute strength and resilience. He explained why the RAF's job was so important. To protect as far as possible the lives of the young soldiers fighting on the ground. Robbie also arranged to meet his insurance broker friend to discuss changes to his life insurance policy. Just in case. The seeds of danger and reality which had been sown back in August were now fully grown. But 13-year-old Kirsty was grateful for being treated as an adult. 'I'm pleased we discussed it all. We could see it happening on the news and it was important we knew the reality. There was a sense we were all in this together and I would probably need to grow up a bit.'

For the Stewart family, Christmas 1990 would not be the joyous occasion they had hoped for.

* * *

David Bellamy wanted to do his best to conjure the warm feeling of Christmas back home in the flat, featureless terrain surrounding Tabuk airbase in Saudi Arabia; of lights, decorated trees and cosy carol services in village churches. The base lay 900 miles due west of Bahrain and was a similar distance in terms of comfort.[23] It had become the RAF's biggest Tornado deployment with nineteen jets and personnel from a number of squadrons. Bellamy and some of his colleagues sought solace and a moment of serenity amid the austerity. On Christmas Eve a small room converted into a chapel filled with those keen for a reminder of home and oneness with God.

To the accompaniment of a piano, they sang 'Once in Royal David's City' and a sense of Christmas enveloped the small community. The emotion of 'Silent Night', with its link to the trenches of the First World War, was followed by the uplifting 'Hark! The Herald Angels Sing', with pertinent references to 'death', 'salvation' and 'resurrection'. 'O Little Town of Bethlehem' brought the service to a close and those with families could not help thinking about children opening presents with fathers absent. Warm handshakes were exchanged as the service sheets were handed back in. Most obeying the instruction typed in bold at the top and bottom of the paper: 'NOT TO BE TAKEN AWAY'. Holding a non-Islamic religious service in Saudi Arabia was against the law.

It was now after midnight, so with formalities out of the way, the pilots and navigators retired to Bellamy's room and settled down to an alcohol-free beer. After a show of hands, it was agreed to open one of the ten-riyal (£4) presents they had bought one another from the local market. It was a curious collection. A toy Uzi machine gun, a non-leather wallet and a bottle of 'Sexy Musk Oil'. Bellamy's gift at least provided some practical use – a tape of Saudi music.

Despite its austerity, Tabuk had its own oasis. British Aerospace had built accommodation around a quadrangle with a lawn that the previous occupants had kept in good order. When the boom of Rolls-Royce Tornado engines was silent, it became a small corner of calm and relaxation. You could tread on soft, green grass, listen to the fountain and contemplate fish in the pond. A serene spot for the fliers to open their family presents on Christmas morning before heading off to the compound to serve the airmen Christmas dinner.

An old hand at the tradition of officers serving the junior ranks, Bellamy wore an unwashed flying suit for the inevitable food fight that broke out deploying Brussels sprout missiles tipped with deadly brandy sauce. After watching a football match between the RAF and a Saudi XI, the officers assembled at 7pm for their own dinner. It was a smart affair; most had packed their cummerbunds and black bow ties. The menu showed they were also in for a treat. The starter was a shrimp cocktail or French onion soup, followed by roast turkey or beef Wellington, served with the usual trimmings of baked, roasted or croquette potatoes, broccoli and, of course, Brussels sprouts.

For the fliers there was an extra treat. The BAe contractors had produced some 'altered' grape juice – homemade wine – which disappeared at an alarming rate as soon as the 'Amen' had followed the Padre's grace. The room filled with banter and goodwill, a near equal to the merriest of Christmas tables. After dessert of cake and ice-cream, and with the memories of the carol service still fresh, Bellamy felt the vocal cords stir, recording in his diary, 'I had a need to sing. Quite soon it is a riotous and joyful 20 Squadron yelling at our rivals from RAF Laarbruch, 16 Squadron. Everyone felt quite merry so we headed off to the BAe "Lightning Club" to make a night of it. Several jugs of home-brew later, our voices had turned hoarse from singing Christmas pop songs.' It was like a scene from another war, when the drink flowed and officers gathered around the Mess piano as a fire blazed during a bleak winter's day on the Western Front.

Dave Bellamy got away from the party in good order at 11pm, only to be woken up hours later by his pilot Trevor Roche crashing into their room, a good few sheets to the wind. 'This will be a short night and I bet I will be crabby tomorrow,' Bellamy noted in his diary.

* * *

For Norman Schwarzkopf, the man in charge of the effort to eject Saddam Hussein's Iraqi invaders from Kuwait, Christmas 1990 was a solitary time, contemplating the possibility that for perhaps many hundreds of young men under his command, it could be their last. The latest intelligence showed the Iraqis had built up a defensive force of 545,000 troops in and around Kuwait. In response, the coalition of the Arab world and the West had grown to 800,000 troops, one of the most powerful ground forces in history, with the very latest tanks, armoured vehicles and artillery designed to defeat the once-mighty Soviet Union.[24] General Schwarzkopf also had 2,000 combat aircraft at his disposal which would be the tip of his spear when the fighting began.

As the lights on his plastic Christmas tree twinkled and carols played from his tape machine, he drifted off to sleep. Suddenly the red telephone next to his bed gave a shrill ring. The warm voice was instantly recognisable. 'I couldn't let this day go by without calling to wish you and all the men and women under your command a Merry Christmas,' President Bush said. 'I know that you are far away from your loved ones, but I want you to know that our thoughts and prayers are with you. You now know the course we are on. Our prayers will stay with you during the coming days.'

Schwarzkopf now knew that war, and all that came with it, was imminent.

The next day he sat alone opening presents from his wife and three children. His 20-year-old daughter Cindy had written him a poem titled 'You Are My Hero'. It brought home his loneliness. 'It was the most desolate hour I had spent in Saudi Arabia. At other times I'd felt harassed, exhausted, browbeaten, burdened, now I simply missed my family.'[25]

John Major, who had only been Prime Minister for five weeks, spent the weekend before Christmas with President Bush and his wife Barbara at Camp David, discussing options for the coming battle. The President disclosed his preferred start date – the moonless night of 16 January. 'He did not glory in war or in the military might of the United States. He was a reluctant but convinced warrior.'[26] Camp David, deep in the wooded hills of Maryland, was a long way from the deserts of Iraq, and for a moment Major managed to escape his troubling thoughts. 'Work over, George and Barbara Bush gave us a delightful weekend, full of log fires, good food, Christmas songs from a small male-voice army choir and the occasional film.'

* * *

After receiving the unwelcome news of Robbie Stewart's deployment, his wife Tange had tried to keep everything as normal as possible over Christmas, visiting friends and family and outwardly maintaining the British stoicism and reserve that 'everything would be fine'. But not so far beneath the surface she was worried. 'Rob was leaving us again and that sense of the unknown hung over us all.' Only once did Robbie's mask of calm slip. Just after Christmas, the *Sunday Times* ran a huge feature on the Tornado's capabilities, weapons and potential targets the aircrews would be attacking. It included a map with all the bases in the Gulf and the type of aircraft and tactics used. He was livid. 'This is just the bloody sort of information an enemy interrogator will use against a captured airman.'

There was anger too, at the petty military officialdom facing those about to go into combat. With a wife, who was seven months pregnant, and toddler back home, Mike Toft couldn't help dwelling on the 'what ifs'.[27] Before leaving home, he'd had *the conversation* with Sue. The conversation that had happened over the centuries, when a husband going to war made provision for failing to return, usually caveated with 'should the worst happen . . .' There was one small hitch that Mike wanted to resolve before it was too late. As he was an officer on a 'Short Service Commission' contract, Sue would only be entitled to a widow's pension and a lump sum payment of around twice his salary if he was killed. But, Mike discovered, if he was on a '*Permanent* Commission' when killed, she would receive nearly *four* times his salary. It was money for nothing; Mike had always intended to stay in the RAF for life anyway, but had not yet got around to changing his short-term commission status. He quickly filled out the necessary paperwork but heard nothing in the weeks leading up to Christmas out in the Gulf. Now the deadline for war was just weeks away and still the paperwork had not been processed.

Between the ultra-low-level training sorties over the pancake-flat deserts of Saudi, Mike used his spare time to chase up the clerks. Their answer was always the same: 'It's being processed, sir.' His concern grew and he decided extreme measures were required. The

issue *had to be* resolved before he went to war. Mike stormed into
the admin Portakabin, and with the merest hint of a smile, carefully removed his pistol from its shoulder holster and placed it on
the clerk's desk. 'Is the paperwork for my Permanent Commission
sorted out yet?'

The clerk glanced from pistol to officer.

'But sir—'

'No more BUTs!' Mike firmly interjected. 'I need this to be
sorted. Now!'

'But, sir, it's Boxing Day in the UK. No one is working . . .'

For a moment there was silence, then they both laughed. Mike
holstered his pistol, his concerns somewhat dissipated. A week later
the clerk called with news. 'Congratulations, sir, you now have a
Permanent Commission!' It was just two weeks to Saddam's deadline to withdraw. Should the worst happen, Sue Toft would now
receive some reasonable compensation.

Mike Toft was not the only one considering the looming realities
of war. His pilot Mark Paisey had already taken into account what
'the worst happening' to him would mean and taken action. Paisey
was a late addition to the deployment from another squadron but
he and Mike had bonded well. 'I think it was probably much more
difficult for the married guys with kids. I was quite relaxed about
deploying to the Gulf. I'd had a bit of a rough time in the previous
months with the end of a relationship so this new phase, while it
might present dangers, was something I was quite calm about. I had
no real concerns. I had ensured all my affairs were in order and had
written a "last letter" to my mum and dad to be delivered if I was
killed, setting out my final thoughts and feelings so that they had
something from me. I sealed it in an envelope and propped it on the
desk in my room back at Laarbruch.'[28]

Knowing everything was as settled as possible, Mike and Mark
slept a little easier as the Christmas memories, good or ill, were
already fading and 1991 began.

* * *

As the fireworks detonated over the married quarters at RAF Bruggen that New Year's Eve, Chris Ankerson stared up at the bursting stars. 'I was standing outside the front door watching the fireworks, thinking, *I wonder what 1991 is going to hold in store for us all?* Another wife and I exchanged a look. We didn't say anything, but we each understood.'[29] Her neighbour's husband had already deployed. Her own husband, Bob, would soon follow. Events were now beyond their control; they had entrusted their husbands to the RAF.

Bob's parents had flown to Germany to celebrate New Year but were not told about his impending deployment. Throughout the holiday period Bob and Chris could barely conceal the strain while pretending everything was normal. Just before they left for the airport, Bob informed his parents that he was going to war. His father's eyes welled up. He too had served in combat during the Second World War and knew that the difference between death and life was measured by a hair's breadth. Bob had rarely seen his father cry. As they stood amid the civilians heading to less challenging destinations at Dusseldorf airport, tears slipped down his father's cheeks. 'Please be careful, son,' he whispered.

A few hours later, at 2am on 2 January 1991, there was another emotional farewell. This time Bob Ankerson was on the doorstep of his home, hugging and kissing Chris and his young son one last time before bidding them farewell. Her arms wrapped around his chest, the grip made awkward by the pistol carried in her husband's shoulder holster, an intrusion on the life they had built together, where war was something that had previously existed in another world.

* * *

In early January Robbie Stewart and Dave Waddington trickled back to Bahrain with other new arrivals to bolster the Tornado force, pinching themselves again at the sight of the Sheraton's marble floors, crystal chandeliers and polite receptionists. The warm welcome from both locals and expats was complemented by

the temperate climate of the Gulf. Blue skies and low humidity, ideal
for shorts, sandals and the pool, the equivalent of a perfect English
summer's day. Even when they left the hotel's comforts, the facilities
at Muharraq airbase were, in military terms, five-star. The crew
room was a fully air-conditioned Portakabin with armchairs and a
fridge crammed with cold drinks and chocolate.

Across the causeway in Saudi Arabia, the hum of aircraft engines,
the assembly of military vehicles and shouted commands to newcomers fresh into 'theatre' told Bob Ankerson and his pilot Simon
Burgess that they were very much in a new world. It was last light
on 4 January when they stepped onto the tarmac of Dhahran airbase and the RAF personnel had never seen anything quite like it.
'It was well ahead of anything we had in Europe. Seven runways,
the most modern hardened shelters, underground bunkers, all mod
cons, a very impressive set-up,' an engineer recalled.[30] Others were
also stunned by what they were witnessing. 'The first day we saw
550 helicopters all lined up. All the US Marines, the Army, the 82nd
Airborne, were coming through.' Norman Schwarzkopf's mighty
army was poised to implement the United Nations resolution to
use 'all necessary means' to restore Kuwait's sovereignty. The task
would require brute force and Saddam's invasion had been mistimed
on several counts. In the last half of the 1980s, American aerial
bombing technology had achieved astonishing advances. The US
had the most sophisticated aerial arsenal in history.[31]

At the forefront were the F-117 Nighthawk stealth fighters accompanied by B-52 bombers carrying air-launched cruise missiles, along
with advanced F-15 and F-16 fighters. Beyond the glamour of the jet
fighters the Americans had key assets such as the Airborne Warning
and Control System (AWACS), whose radars could see every aircraft flying for hundreds of miles. They also supplied countless air
tankers, critical to allowing deep strikes into Iraqi territory, and
an armada of helicopters. As the 'ally of choice', British officers in
Saudi, like Nige Risdale over in Bahrain, had already been allowed
into a highly secretive group, based at the coalition headquarters in
Riyadh, that was preparing the Master Air Attack Plan. Rigorous

A fully armed Tornado from RAF Marham during a test flight in 1988. The large JP233 runway denial weapons are clearly visible on the underside.

Looking down into the cockpit of a Tornado at low level. In the front, the pilot can be seen with his right hand on the control column and his left on the throttles. In the rear seat, the navigator has a map in his left hand and more mission notes on his knee and to his right.

Bob, Gareth and Chris Ankerson celebrate Christmas at RAF Bruggen in Germany in 1990. Tornado navigator Bob would deploy to the Gulf a few days later, it would be many months before his family saw him again.

Mike Toft and Mark Paisey swap seats in their Tornado. Navigator Toft sits in the front seat whilst his pilot takes the navigator's position.

The Tornado's twin Rolls Royce engines producing maximum power with afterburners, or reheat, engaged ready for take-off.

Navigator Dave Bellamy (left) and his pilot Trevor Roche, prepare for a mission by their Tornado armed with laser-guided bombs. Both are wearing their G-suits, and the blue leg-restraints which hold their legs against the ejection seats can also be seen. The iconic artwork began to be added to the aircraft after the first missions.

Prime Minister John Major addresses personnel at the Dhahran detachment a few days before the conflict began. The Detachment Commander, Cliff Spink, is on the left wearing his cap.

Dave Waddington, right, and Robbie Stewart, smiling, pictured in the Operations Room before their first mission on 17 January 1991. Nigel Elsdon and Max Collier would not return from this sortie.

A formation from the Muharraq detachment in Bahrain after landing from a night training sortie. All those pictured would see action just a few days later, not all survived the conflict. Left to right: Rob Woods, Nick Heard, Ricci Cobelli, 'Tommy' Tank, John Broadbent (The 'Boss'), Nige Risdale, Steve Hicks, Rupert Clark.

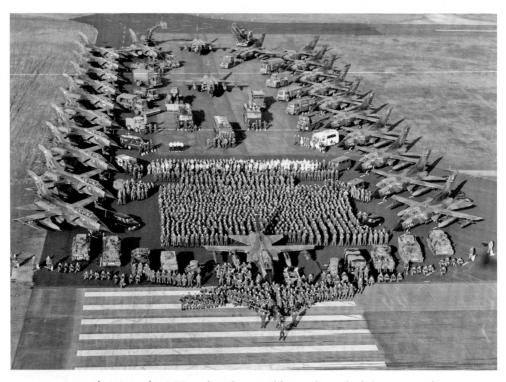

Just a fraction of RAF Laarbruch assembles at the end of the runway for a group photograph in 1989. Around half the base's Tornados are present, and perhaps a quarter of station personnel.

A pair of Tornados take on fuel from a Victor tanker during a training sortie before the commencement of hostilities.

Engineers from the 'bomb dump' at Dhahran make adjustments to live 1000lb bombs as they convert them into laser-guided bombs ready for use during the conflict.

Tornado pilot and Officer Commanding 27 Squadron Bill Green, with his wife Jenny, at the RAF Marham Officers' Mess Summer Ball in July 1990. Bill would be killed in a flying accident just a few weeks later.

Paddy Teakle, left, with his pilot Gordon Buckley prepare for a mission over Iraq. Their 'Personal Equipment Connectors', or PECs, can be seen hanging in front of them. The metal unit has connections for their G-suits, oxygen supply and communications, and clips directly onto their ejection seats.

A fully armed Tornado at the Muharraq detachment. The Boz chaff & flare pod can be seen under the wing on the far left, then an external fuel tank with a Sidewinder missile mounted above. The air-to-air refuelling probe is extended next to the open cockpit canopy. Two JP233 runway denial munitions are mounted under the fuselage. On the far right, the Sky Shadow electronic countermeasures pod, covered by a tarpaulin, is next to another under-wing fuel tank and Sidewinder.

The Navigator's cockpit of a Tornado GR1

1 Altimeter
2 Air Speed Indicator
3 Moving map and ground mapping radar display
4 TV Tabs which show navigation and target information
5 Cockpit 'attention-getters', which flash red to indicate a systems problem
6 Stores jettison selection panel
7 Undercarriage position indicator
8 Weapon selection panel
9 Radar control panel
10 Navigation mode selection panel
11 Radar Homing and Warning Receiver
12 Weapon and attack mode selection panel
13 Navigator's hand controller used for

updating navigation systems and during target attacks
14 Navigator's ejection seat
15 Ejection seat harness lap straps
16 Sky Shadow electronic countermeasures pod controls
17 Boz pod chaff and flare controls
18 Central Warning Panel which gives precise details of systems failures
19 Cassette system for navigation and target data entry
20 Main computer control panel
21 Radio and intercom controls
22 Inertial navigation system
23 Radio boxes
24 Cockpit lighting controls

The Pilot's cockpit of a Tornado GR4

1 Head Up Display
2 Autopilot selection panel
3 Cockpit 'attention-getters'
4 Late Arm switch
5 Head Up Display controls
6 Master Armament Safety Switch
7 Terrain Following Radar screen
8 Radar Homing and Warning Receiver screen
9 Flight instruments
10 Multi-Function Display
11 Engine gauges
12 Fuel gauges
13 Undercarriage lever
14 Pilot's control column
15 Central Warning Panel
16 Throttles
17 Wing sweep lever
18 Pilot weapon aiming controller
19 TFR settings control panel
20 Computerised flight systems controls
21 Radio and intercom controls
22 Mounting position for pilot's ejection seat
23 TFR system panel
24 Engine & generator control panel
25 RHWR controls
26 Cockpit lighting controls
27 Fuel temperature gauges

and detailed organisation was required to send wave after wave of aircraft into enemy airspace. The Tornados and their ultra-low-level tactics were put at the forefront of Operation Desert Storm, the plan to remove Saddam from Kuwait. Even the American fast-talking, high-fiving fighter jocks felt admiration for the Brits when it dawned on them what they *really* did. Very fast, very low at night and right over the enemy's heads. *That took balls.*

For Wing Commander John Broadbent, the Tornado Detachment Commander at Muharraq, there was no doubt about their tactics. 'I had twenty years' experience on the RAF's front line and, as far as I was concerned, nobody was seriously considering going to war in a Tornado at medium level until we had established air superiority.' If established, that dominance of the skies would negate the much-feared threat from the Iraqis' own fighters. 'Until that condition had been fulfilled, it would have been wrong, even foolhardy, to contemplate such an option. We were up against the Iraqi Air Force, powerful and battle-hardened by several years of war with Iran. We fully expected them to be ready and willing to fight and we had to judge them on their *capability*, not guess at their *intentions*.'[32]

And the Americans were not the only ones to pass comment on the dangers. Before leaving home, Gordon Buckley's wife Dawn had laid down the law. 'Whatever you do, *do not* take any risks when you are out there!' she ordered. Gordon had to take note. Dawn had previously stopped him from applying to the Red Arrows aerobatic display team because she didn't want him to take 'more risks' than he already needed to flying fast jets. But Gordon also knew the time was approaching when he would have to defy Dawn's instructions.

* * *

In those early days of January 1991, Bob Ankerson and Simon Burgess soon got down to work, trying to catch up with those who had been training for months. Nerves were certainly required. And, sometimes, it was best not to draw too heavily on one's well of courage by seeing how much was really needed. During one night

sortie, flying over the Saudi desert on autopilot at a steady 200ft
in complete darkness, Bob and Simon decided to pop one of their
high-heat anti-missile flares. 'The area around us lit up so brightly
and we could see the ground rushing past at indecently close range.
We decided not to repeat the exercise but to continue along in
darkness and blissful ignorance!' Not that they had much chance
for practice. As the 15 January deadline approached for Iraqi forces
to leave Kuwait, they managed to squeeze in only five training sorties. 'The brief was that we were cleared to 100ft but to remember
that we could be going to war any day and so to make the most of
the opportunity. We flew over the desert at 40ft, almost level with
the top of the palm trees, flashing over herds of camels out in the
bleakness. It was a truly memorable experience.'

They practised more anti-missile drills, using chaff and flares,
then spent hours on the ground reading the intelligence reports
on Iraqi SAM systems. It was a bonding experience for Simon and
Bob, thrown together just days before deploying. 'We were flying
together, working together, building up that level of trust and relationship. We both needed to know that we could rely on each other
regardless of what was thrown at us. It didn't matter what flying
we were doing, practice bombing, intense low-level TFR at night,
tanking; the important thing was that we were flying *together*.
Getting to know each other, how we worked, finding out how the
other person "thought". Building confidence before we headed into
the unknown beyond Saudi's border.'

On 8 January, exactly a week before the deadline expired, they
were told the British Prime Minister John Major would be visiting
Dhahran airbase to meet the troops. The question many asked was:
would the PM go to the effort of visiting if they weren't going to
war? Bob Ankerson and Simon Burgess could ask him personally.
They were his designated hosts on the Tornado. It was late afternoon as the pair took him through the aircraft's functions. Major
asked a few questions about the Tornado's capabilities then climbed
down from the cockpit and stood on a box as the troops gathered
round him in a large horseshoe. John Major was not a military man

and was troubled by war. 'As a non-soldier I was uneasy at sending others to war even though I had no doubt it was right to do so.'[33] His own son James was just about to turn sixteen. Many of the men before him were only a year or two older. Major knew that he would be sending some of them into a battle from which they would not return. War was all but inevitable, and he did his best to steel the soldiers and airmen. They were going to be at 'the sharp end of whatever may happen in due course'.

One senior officer present had an inkling of what was afoot. 'Something in the way he said it made me think he knew something I didn't.'[34] There were some in the crowd, and many families back home, who hoped a last-ditch meeting between US Secretary of State James Baker and Iraqi Foreign Minister Tariq Aziz might head off the possibility of conflict. That meeting, Major told them, was not about negotiation or compromise. It was to make it 'absolutely certain, beyond a shadow of a doubt, that the Iraqis understand that the allied forces are serious; that, if they do not withdraw from Kuwait and go back to Iraq, at some stage we will use the force'. That evening, Bob featured prominently on the television news and his wife Chris was overjoyed. 'I actually saw Bob on TV as he and Simon showed the Prime Minister around a Tornado. It was lovely to see him and to have that small glimpse of my husband, a tiny connection, however distant.'

As John Major left the troops he was about to send to war he was reminded again of their age. 'There is nothing impersonal about war. It is about sending young people out to fight and perhaps to die, for a cause older men decide is worthwhile.'

The odds were clearly shortening. There was quiet chatter among the troops as the gathering broke up. Beyond a miracle, fighting was now close to certain.

* * *

On 9 January 1991 the world's attention focused on Geneva's Intercontinental Hotel.

President Bush had insisted on 'going the extra mile for peace', offering the chance for Saddam to leave Kuwait without a fight. America was also facing its biggest military challenge since the humiliation and soul-searching of the Vietnam War. The US President wanted to demonstrate he was doing his best to avoid war and to reassure the public, especially those watching the graphic and bloody deaths depicted in *The Civil War* TV series.

The talks failed and at 8.55pm Tariq Aziz, Iraq's smooth-talking Foreign Minister, took to the podium to address the world's media. He spoke for thirty minutes, conveying Saddam's final threat: if America and its allies attacked, Iraq would retaliate by attacking Israel. Clearly, the dictator had not lost the cunning that had allowed him to dominate Iraq since 1968. Drawing the Jewish state into the conflict would make America's Arab coalition allies extremely uncomfortable. Aziz's final warning shot that Iraq was 'preparing for war' left little doubt about what was coming next.

The RAF aircrews in Bahrain had decided to turn in early rather than stay up till past midnight to hear news. Shortly after dawn the next day, Gordon Buckley woke up to the sound of the local newspaper being shoved under the door of his hotel room. The glum faces of Aziz and US Secretary of State James Baker staring from the front page told their own story. No compromise. No peace. 'I think we are going in, Paddy . . .' he said, dropping the paper onto his navigator Paddy Teakle's bed.

The atmosphere across the region was nervously expectant. Military hardware was everywhere. A constant reminder of Saddam's unpredictable nature were the respirators, or 'gas masks', carried by every serviceman and their proximity to their NBC – Nuclear Biological Chemical – suits. The NBC kit was there to protect against any deadly chemical or biological agents Saddam might deploy via one of his Scud missiles or air force bombers. In 1988, he had dropped a lethal cocktail of mustard gas, VX and sarin onto Iraqi Kurdistan. More than 5,000 Kurds died from a ghastly cyanide-type poisoning. Saddam had stockpiled up to 4,000 tonnes of deadly chemicals and intelligence spoke of 800 Scud B missiles with a range of 500 miles able to deliver them.[35] The press reported that chemical warfare was not only likely; it was inevitable.

John Broadbent was in no doubt about what might happen. 'We were charged with planning an air campaign to ensure that, as far as possible, Iraq's air power could not be brought to bear either on the thousands of friendly troops massing in the desert or on packed Saudi airfields and infrastructure. There was a real fear that Iraqi aircraft carrying chemical or biological weapons would attack our airfields or vulnerable ground forces.'

In fact, Saddam had been warned in private that any use of chemicals on either civilians or military would be met with the most robust response.[36] During his long meeting with Aziz, James Baker had told him: 'If conflict ensues and you use chemical or biological weapons against US forces, the American people will demand vengeance. And we have the means to exact it ... This is not a threat, it is a promise.'[37]

It was widely known that the armouries of US aircraft carriers in the region held nuclear weapons.

* * *

The preparations intensified in the remaining days before the deadline. On 13 January, a last training sortie of three Tornados flew out of Dhahran military airbase for a simulated low-level attack. There they were to test their flares against heat-seeking missiles while flying at ultra-low level, followed by one last exhilarating run through the valleys in northern Oman.[38] Soon after the flares were deployed, a radio call went out for the number four aircraft, flown by pilot Kieran Duffy and navigator Norman Dent, to check in. There was no response. Again, the call went out. Fliers began frantically scanning the skies around them. 'After several attempts with no reply and still with no sign of No 4, we spotted a large plume of black smoke several miles behind us,' the formation leader recalled. 'We immediately turned around and headed for the smoke. To our horror we found a very obvious scrape across the desert floor several kilometres long, the smoke rapidly dispersing and numerous unrecognisable items of debris scattered along the line.'[39]

There had been no Mayday call, no parachutes, no distress beacons activated and no word on the emergency frequency. Even without enemy fire, ultra-low-level – well below 100ft – flying came with extreme danger. Exactly two months earlier, Jaguar pilot Keith Collister, twenty-six, had been killed when his aircraft hit the crest of a sand dune in Saudi Arabia.[40]

The later investigation showed that during a hard left-hand turn at ultra-low level, travelling at almost 600mph, the wingtip of Kieran and Norman's Tornado brushed the sand and the air-craft cartwheeled into the desert. Pilot and navigator were killed instantly. Their Squadron Commander was deeply saddened by the loss. 'It was such a waste. That was what gave me more personal grief than anything else. They were two young lads with lots of spirit but they were gentlemen, great friends of everyone, the leading lights in the Squadron "junta"; the young men who are the Squadron personalities.'[41]

The crash was a devastating blow to morale in Dhahran, par-ticularly for close friends of the pair. 'It really knocked people who were just about to go to war themselves. Particularly the ground crew, who'll never forget that they started the aircraft up and waved goodbye as it went off.' The news of Dent and Duffy's passing had been broken to the rest of the Dhahran contingent by the Tornado Detachment Commander, Jerry Witts: 'We have sadly lost two colleagues and two friends. But we have to concentrate on the job in hand as the war may well be starting very soon. We will mourn their passing later.'[42] There was little more to be said.

Dave Waddington heard the terrible news after his own last train-ing sortie with Robbie Stewart in Bahrain. 'If you lose a friend or colleague in training like Kieran Duffy and Norman Dent, you just have to put it out of your mind. There is nothing you can do about it. There is a sorrow that someone has died, but you have to go on. You get into a Tornado full of excitement, you never think, *Crikey, I might die on this sortie*. Of course, the possibility is always there, but if you thought that way you would never go flying. Logic tells you there is a risk, but emotionally you put that aside.'[43]

News of yet another fatal training accident arrived back at the crew's home base of RAF Bruggen, where four Tornado squadrons were located. Chris Ankerson saw how the deaths affected the whole station, but she also felt something else, something possibly every other wife experienced. 'There was a terrible sense of loss and sadness, especially as they were so young, but other than expressing sympathy, there was little you could say to their friends. There was also a quite selfish notion at the back of your mind – *thank God it's not my husband*. You feel terrible about that. But it's the way things were if your husband flew fast jets.'

The two deaths brought the total in the Tornado force since August to seven, they were unlikely to be the last. No one doubted the extraordinary demands about to be asked of them.

* * *

The deaths so close to the 15 January deadline made the prospect of war and its consequences a sobering reality for the young military men. Tensions rose too. Now six weeks into the shared hotel room with John Peters, John Nichol found himself angry at his pilot's constant interruptions while he was trying to listen to the recording of messages from home his young nieces had sent along with his Christmas presents. 'I just snapped, then threw on my shorts and went for a long run along the seafront. I sat alone on a rock for an hour or so staring out to sea. It had suddenly dawned on me, in its full and horrible reality, that I was going to war. There was no turning back. It had not really hit me before then, but the message from my nieces back home had pulled the emotional trigger. After my sojourn on the rock I felt better about it, I had come to terms with it.' Peters had gone for a long run too. They had lunch together and no mention was made of the flare-up. Each understood. The time was approaching when they would be among the few in the heart of enemy territory.

The same day Duffy and Dent were killed, Mark Paisey, who would be flying alongside Peters and Nichol, sat in the Muharraq Operations Room penning his regular letter to his mother back in the UK. The light-hearted details of his formation's social life were no longer relevant. He had already told her where his 'last letter' – only to be opened if he was killed – was located and he now turned to the stark analysis of what might soon happen:

Dear Mum,

 The time is 0430 and I find myself drinking black coffee and contemplating the days ahead. All of the peace initiatives have failed and by the time you read this I expect we will be at war. It seems almost incomprehensible that, in 1991, such an undertaking is necessary. Everyone held out the hope that the fighting would never really happen. Many seem surprised it now will, and no one is prepared for the sacrifices which lie ahead.

 We are now on a shift system and I work from 0100 to 1300. Today it has rained since midnight and everywhere is flooding which seems really strange. With all the sandbags and puddles, I am reminded of the [First World War] trenches.

 Despite the immediate prospects, morale is high. Much emphasis has been placed on our training and equipment but that is all an echo of times past. Undoubtedly we are prepared, but even the best-laid plans have the habit of running amok. Let's hope the war is decisive and short, though I can't see it myself.

 Since this is probably my last letter until war breaks out, I just want to tell you that the last couple of weeks have been very happy for me. I will write whenever I can but circumstances might overtake me. Be brave yourself, I love you very much and am proud to be your son.

 Hopefully nothing will happen to me – or I will be very angry![44]

As aircrew across the region assembled for the final briefings, they were given an overview of what General Schwarzkopf wanted to achieve. The air attack plan had originally been given four phases. A doubling of aircraft strength from November meant the massive air armada could now achieve all four at once.[45]

The main objectives were to gain air superiority, destroy Saddam's Scud missile sites and chemical warfare locations and disrupt command and control. At the same time, and this was where Tornado came in, they were to suppress the Iraqi Air Force's capability which meant smashing their airfields. Everyone would then focus on going after the tanks and troops dug in around Kuwait, paving the way for the ground invasion.

In Bahrain, the Tornado crews were given an eve-of-battle pep talk by a senior officer who had flown in specially for the task. It proved less than inspiring. 15 Squadron Flight Commander Gordon Buckley, seated at the front of the briefing room, remembered that, 'the gist of it went along the lines of "how lucky you all are to be going to fight the Iraqis and how I wish I could be coming with you". But the VIP spoke so quietly that most of the audience couldn't hear him!' None of those present thought of themselves as 'lucky'. Not when going up against the world's sixth largest air force and defences bristling with multiple SAM systems. It was, thought Buckley, 'a massive prospect and I certainly did not *feel lucky* at all!' The officer, who had kept his service cap on throughout the briefing, promptly left. Few at the back of the room had actually been able to hear the not-so-rousing motivational speech.

'Why was he talking so quietly?' one asked.

'Because what he was saying was secret!' came the tart reply.

Buckley left the meeting convinced that never had a 'call-to-arms' speech done more to discourage people to fight.

As the hours ticked past, Gordon and the rest of the aircrew were now left to contemplate their immediate future. 'I began to think, *What the hell are we going up against here?*'

CHAPTER FOUR

THE WOLFPACK

16–17 JANUARY 1991

The senior officer arrived at Tabuk airbase direct from Air Headquarters in Riyadh, carrying a briefcase handcuffed to his wrist. He was waved through security and moments later entered the briefing room with the 16 and 20 Squadron formation leaders. Senior navigator Dave Bellamy watched him remove, with a flourish, a folder marked 'Top Secret' from his briefcase. 'He somewhat bigged himself up as he briefed us on the plan for the first twenty-four hours of the war. But there was no real detail on our targets or what the hell we would actually be doing.'[1] Retaining his solemn demeanour, the officer placed the secret papers back in the case, handcuffed himself to it and left.

'Dave, it's best you reserve some planning space for your formation,' one of the Flight Commanders quietly told him afterwards.

'Aha. Roger that,' Bellamy replied.

It was the morning of 16 January, the day after the UN deadline for Saddam to leave Kuwait had expired. Something was definitely on the cards for Bellamy's Squadron equipped with the ALARM anti-radar missile. The message of peace and goodwill from the Christmas service he had organised a few weeks previously was a distant memory. After breakfast the aircrew assembled in the Operations Room where maps of Iraq and Saudi lined the wall. Bellamy sensed growing excitement as the rumours of imminent operations took hold. 'Everyone was chit-chatting and laughing like little schoolboys. Some were smiling excitedly, treating it as a school outing, while still trying to acknowledge the seriousness of their situation. The Detachment Commander walked in and set it all out in simple words. Training was over, the jets were being loaded for war. It was happening.'

As lead planner for 20 Squadron, it was Bellamy's job to organise the details for the ALARM attack against their target, a major Iraqi airbase. 16 Squadron would follow in their wake with the JP233 runway-busting weapons. Al Asad lay 100 miles west of Baghdad, and a few miles from the meandering waters of the Euphrates. It was built on top of an oasis known locally as 'Abraham's Well', which was now covered with tonnes of asphalt forming two 13,000ft runways. It was a key installation housing the Iraqi Air Force fighters that protected Baghdad from a Western attack. It was strongly defended. Batteries of SA-6 SAMs, which had proven their worth against both modern Israeli jets and US fighters in Vietnam, defended the area. Each unit consisted of three missiles mounted on a tracked vehicle making it mobile as well as deadly. The SA-6 missile had a range of 15 miles, could reach 46,000ft and travel at more than 2,000mph.[2] The half-dozen launchers per battery were controlled by a single radar vehicle that could track aircraft almost 50 miles away.

The system's strength was also its weakness. To track aircraft, the radar vehicle had to emit a strong radiation signal. British defence scientists had recognised the guided SAM threat and invented something clever to counter it. The ALARM – Air-Launched Anti-Radiation Missile – could detect an enemy radar system from a range of more than 50 miles and home in on the signal. Just before impact a laser fuse would set off the high explosive warhead to demolish the equipment, and any exposed personnel.[3] While enemy SAM operators could theoretically turn off their radar to break the lock[4] of other incoming anti-radiation missiles such as the American HARM, ALARM had a clever ploy to counter the tactic. If the targeting information was lost, it would use a rocket to zoom-climb to over 50,000ft and deploy a parachute, taking up to ten minutes to descend as it waited for the ground radar site to switch on again.[5] Immediately it did so, the ALARM would update its target's position, jettison the parachute and dive down onto the target.

ALARM had been rushed into the Gulf and few had witnessed its effectiveness. Dave Bellamy knew more than most, as he had trained everyone on the system since October. 'As a stand-off, fire-and-forget missile, ALARM offered the Tornado a radical new capability. It could be launched at considerable ranges and hit any of a number of radars.' Two Tornados, each carrying three ALARMs, were to fly the 500 miles from Tabuk to Al Asad and take out the SA-6 radars guarding the airbase. If they failed, then the four Tornados from 16 Squadron following a few miles behind were going to have a rough ride delivering their JP233s onto its long runways.

Navigator Mal Craghill, twenty-two, would be one of those bombers following Bellamy's formation and hoping it had severely degraded Al Asad's defences. One of the youngest aircrew in theatre, Craghill 'had presumed Saddam would not be so stupid as to risk any sort of confrontation with the incredible forces ranged against him across the region. I thought he would back down at the last minute and we would not be required. I now knew I had been wrong.'[6] But he was now ready for the fight. 'I don't remember any real nerves at all. We were well trained and had prepared as much as possible. There was certainly a sense of trepidation; but it was more about how I might perform; not wanting to let anyone down.'

Craghill and all of the Tabuk crews were about to discover just how prepared they actually were.

* * *

Some 900 miles to the west of Tabuk, sixteen aircrew from the lead formations of 15 Squadron in Bahrain were gathering in the War

Operations Room for a similar briefing. The previous day Nige Risdale's detailed attack plan had been presented, so the crews were familiar with the task ahead. But a tight lid was kept on the precise date and timing of the attack. Early that 16 January, Gordon Buckley, leading the second half of the formation of the initial eight-ship, had detected that Wing Commander John Broadbent, the Tornado Detachment Commander and Risdale's navigator, was 'acting a bit twitchy'. Gordon was direct. 'Are we going in tonight, Boss?'[7]

Broadbent's reply was less so. 'I've heard nothing to say we aren't...'[8]

Risdale was only partway through his update when the Boss was called out of the room. A 'Top Secret' communication had just been received:

---

16 Jan 1991
From:
HQ British Forces Middle East

TO:
RAF Detachment Tabuk
RAF Detachment Dhahran
RAF Detachment Muharraq

TOP SECRET EXCLUSIVE

For Detachment Commander from Air Commander

SUBJECT: WOLFPACK EXECUTE ORDER

THIS IS THE EXECUTE ORDER

H HOUR IS DECLARED AS 0000Z 17 Jan 91

Acknowledge by FLASH Signal to Air Commander and personally by Secure Speech[9]

War was authorised and the attack start time, 'H-Hour', was set for midnight ('Zulu' or Greenwich Mean Time) that evening, 0300 local time in Baghdad. For Buckley and his companions, the impact was electric. 'It was an incredible feeling, just to look around the room and see the guys' eyes really widen. We were actually going to do it.'

Eight Tornados would be going into Tallil, each carrying two JP233s to rain down a fearsome load of runway-cratering munitions and anti-personnel mines. John Broadbent, too, was struck by the enormity of the journey they were all about to embark on: 'As I gave the brief that first night, the thing that worried me most was how I would react under fire. How would any of us feel when we saw the flak for the first time and realised that someone was actually trying to kill us? Would the training kick in and allow us to just shrug it off as of little consequence? Or would our guts turn to liquid and the urge to turn and run be irresistible? Would the fact that this was far from being the war that we'd all signed up for – to defend the "White Cliffs of Dover" – make a difference to our resolve and preparedness to make the ultimate sacrifice? I for one couldn't be sure of the answer, but we were all going to find out soon enough.'

Later, the Ground Liaison Officer (GLO), an army major, gave the final intelligence brief. This particularly popular GLO had invented a 15 Squadron tradition during Cold War exercises in Germany, in which comic lyrics he had written to the tune of 'It's a Long Way to Tipperary' were sung as any *practice* war entered its final, catastrophic nuclear phase. As their first ever *real* war mission briefing drew to a close, the GLO turned to Broadbent with a slight raising of his eyebrows: 'Squadron song, Boss?'

There was a moment's silence. Given the circumstances, it appeared an audacious question.

'Why not?' Broadbent replied.

The raucous singing was heard by navigator John Nichol as he approached the Intelligence Room for the regular evening update. He had spent the day lounging around the Sheraton's pool and marbled foyer waiting to hear news of any attack before driving to Muharraq in the late afternoon with the rest of his formation. He instantly understood what it meant. 'A tight feeling of apprehension grabbed me; I felt almost sick with anticipation. The first attack wave had their mission! I presumed we, on the second wave, would soon follow. It was a truly momentous realisation.'[10]

Unable to restrain his curiosity, Nichol knocked on the door and entered. 'I saw all my mates, in full war kit, trying very hard to deafen one another with the infamous Squadron war song. As the singing stopped, the GLO said, 'Give us twenty minutes, John, we're still briefing.' I knew then for sure, from the tone of his voice, that I had just been looking at the aircrew on the first RAF attack wave of the Gulf War.' Nichol closed the door as his pilot John Peters appeared in the corridor. 'Shit, we're really going to do this,' he said. 'It's really happening. We're going in.'

Inside the room Buckley had noticed one of the female Intelligence Officers wipe tears from her eye as the song came to an end. 'It was a strange sensation, standing there singing a ridiculous song as we were about to embark on the type of mission we had flown endlessly on Cold War exercises, but were now doing for real. Were we all going to get back okay? Was I going to be able to carry out the attack successfully?'

Buckley, and the rest of the Tornado force, would soon find out.

* * *

Similar scenes were playing out across the RAF's Gulf bases. At Dhahran, with its recent influx of GR1A recce jets, now the largest force in the region, Wing Commander Jerry Witts, the Tornado Detachment Commander, was off duty in the house he shared with other senior officers. 'We were watching CNN and chatting. I thought that now Saddam had faced-off past the deadline, he'd start to pull out. Then my phone rang.'

It was his Operations Officer. 'Can you come into work, Boss? Straight away!'

'I just grabbed my kit and drove in. I was absolutely terrified. I remember my knees were trembling, my foot was shaking on the accelerator. I was thinking, "I can't believe this! I can't believe this!" I was looking at other motorists and thinking, "I wonder if they know where I'm going?"'[11]

One of the Victor tanker pilots who would shepherd the Tornados into battle also received a phone call. 'We had particular coded messages – if the caller said, "The mail is *out*", it meant you were not needed. If the caller said, "The mail is *in*", it meant you needed to bring your crew in.' The tanker Captain's coded message was abundantly clear. 'We all came in and it suddenly dawned on everyone that we were about to do something unstoppable.'[12]

Over at Tabuk, Dave Bellamy and his pilot Trevor Roche had completed the planning for their first war mission, so returned to their room to try to relax while awaiting the phone call that would send them airborne. 'We discussed what to do if we were shot down, how we would try to get together, where we were going to keep our guns. And the circumstances where we might use them. We cut off our identity badges from our flying suits as a final act before going to war. I pondered whether to write to my girlfriend Anna, but decided not. We were both apprehensive but not scared enough to be gibbering wrecks.'

Trevor suggested they listen to some music. They put on Dire Straits' *Brothers in Arms* and for a moment were transported by the title song, written about the 1982 Falklands War, describing a soldier's need for solidarity in battle. With combat now imminent, its resonance was stark. From the haunting guitar opening to its 'fields of destruction and baptism of fire' lyrics, to the sad soldier's adieu 'let me bid you farewell', it took on a very vivid poignancy. Both men were quiet as they contemplated what lay ahead. They turned on the BBC World Service and heard Douglas Hurd, the British Foreign Secretary, suggest that there was still a chance of peace, which produced a chuckle.

Trevor shook his head. 'If there's a positive chance for peace, my cock's a kipper.'

A moment later their Squadron Boss entered the room. 'It's game on. You guys will lead the first attack. Tonight. Get some rest.'

The waiting was over.

'The show is finally on the road,' Bellamy wrote in his diary. 'Godspeed.'

* * *

Waiting was all that American General Norman Schwarzkopf, in overall command of all troops in the region, could now do. Every part of the giant military 'chessboard' he had constructed was in place, the various pieces waiting to be moved. In a few hours he was about to launch the biggest air attack ever attempted. He was ordering men into battle. He knew only too well what that meant, and nothing he could do now would change the outcome. He went to his office in the headquarters bunker in Riyadh. 'I sat down and did what soldiers going to war do. I wrote to my family, saying how much I loved them.'

> My dearest Wife and Children,
>   The war clouds have gathered on the horizon and I have already issued the terrible orders that will let the monster loose . . . we will soon be at war.[13]

After the final verse of 15 Squadron's rousing song had been belted out, the briefing room momentarily fell silent. A few glances were shared between men preparing themselves for combat. They opened the door to see the faces of the eight aircrew readying themselves for the next mission, among them the Two Johns, navigator Mike Toft and their moustachioed leader, Pablo Mason. 'Good luck!' was the chorus as they all shook hands. 'Give it to them!' Buckley led his formation into the clothing section where the safety equipment specialists kept their flying kit in pristine order. He had already taken off his wedding ring and put it in a plastic bag, remembering his wife Dawn's request for him not to take risks. He then removed all other personal effects that might compromise him if taken prisoner. It was all part of the 'sanitising' process. All the pilots and navigators now carried for personal identity was a card with their name, rank and service number, and their indestructible 'dog tags' with basic information to identify their bodies.

On the way out to the aircraft, one of the airmen took Buckley aside and passed him a hip flask. 'Here you are, sir, one for the road.'

'Thanks,' Buckley smiled. 'But I'd better not.'

Gordon checked his Walther PP in its leather shoulder holster, then the £1,000 in gold sovereigns to negotiate safe passage with local tribes if they were shot down inside Iraq. He had the 'goolie chit', appropriately enough, in his pocket.

As they left, the message 'Crews walking!' went out.

Just before 0100 on 17 January 1991, kitted up in G-suits, helmets in hand, the fliers walked purposefully to the eight waiting Tornados.

This was it – they were going to war.

Nick Heard, 15 Squadron's Qualified Flying Instructor, was in the lead four-ship of the formation, with Risdale and Broadbent. Calm, likeable and an experienced and trusted flier, the 31-year-old was a well-respected figure on the Squadron. He had sat quietly during the briefings, keeping his thoughts of the approaching danger to himself.

The intelligence had been stark. Iraq had amassed an astonishing defence network. The country was defended by 154 SAM sites and 16,000 missiles, alongside almost 10,000 anti-aircraft guns.[14] 'My stomach dropped at what we were about to do. I thought, *Bloody hell!*' Outwardly, Nick had maintained a brave face. 'But inside, I had a fatalistic view; there was a very real chance I would not come back. I never mentioned it to anyone, it just sat at the back of my mind. Regardless of how good the Tornado was, the Iraqi air defence system was also very good and we would be very vulnerable.'[15]

Now he was in the cockpit of an overladen bomber, looking across to Risdale's Tornado that was about to lead them off to war. Finally, in total radio silence, they taxied out, ready for take-off at 0200. 'I watched Nige's reheat ignite and he rolled down the runway.

Ten seconds later we followed. The Tornado was heavy with eight tonnes of fuel but we got airborne safely and I started easing in on the leader's navigation lights to take up my position on his wing. Night-time close formation had become yet another newly acquired skill in the previous few months.'

Gordon Buckley and his navigator Paddy Teakle had completed their own pre-flight checks and also started up without a hitch. As leader of the second half of the formation, they would attack Tallil one minute after Nige Risdale's assault. Gordon watched the first four Tornados roll forward in full reheat then power up into the darkness over the Arabian Gulf.[16] Buckley rumbled down to the now vacant take-off point. To his right, under the airfield lights, he saw an unforgettable tableau. 'There were people everywhere, waving, standing on the walls, on cars, anything they could climb on to see us off. It was incredibly uplifting, seeing all the troops wishing us well, in the same way the ground crews had done back in the Second World War as the bombers set off on a mission. The sense of pride was immense.' He was fully focused on getting his heavy aircraft into the air. It began to shudder and shake as he increased the power. 'It really felt as though we were doing the right thing. We were about to take off in one of the most sophisticated jets in the world to help liberate an occupied country. This is what my career in the RAF had been about. It had all led to this point.'

He waited for his number two pilot to give him the thumbs-up signalling that the rest of the formation was lined up. The digit emerged and Gordon immediately pushed the throttles through the gate into minimum reheat, all the while holding the aircraft stationary. 'When I was happy, I released the brakes and rammed the throttles open to full reheat. The aircraft roared down the runway, quickly reaching the speed that would let it take to the sky.' Just as Nige Risdale had planned, the eight-ship formed up ready to refuel before heading into Iraq via the 'back door' out to the west, and entering the fray. The thunder of aircraft taking off into the night echoed across every coalition airbase.

In the giant field hospital in Bahrain, the British medics readied themselves for the inevitable casualties. 'We were sitting outside and the noise was spectacular,' one recalled. 'I went away from everybody else and just sat and listened. It was a horrible feeling, really eerie. We all knew then that something was going to happen. Some people had a few tears.'[17] The hospital commander had equally ominous thoughts. 'Everyone was apprehensive and you could feel it. Later, there was a briefing with the Detachment Commander who said, "In five minutes' time the first aircraft will hit Baghdad. You can tell your troops." The biggest fear was, would we be able to do the job if a lot of horrible casualties came in?' All those not involved in getting jets airborne got into their NBC suits in expectation of a retaliatory Iraqi Scud attack, potentially with deadly chemicals. Some of the nurses asked the Padre to say a prayer with them. As he did so, many were in tears.[18]

Elsewhere, thousands of other fliers were readying themselves for combat. Giant B-52 bombers had already taken off from the USA on a 35-hour round trip; the longest bombing raid in history. F-18 Hornets and A-6 Intruders launched from aircraft carriers in the Gulf and Red Sea, F-117 Stealth fighters were inbound to Baghdad on a 1,000-mile flight from their southern Saudi base. It would be the first real test of their famed 'radar invisibility'. From bases all over Saudi Arabia, Oman and Bahrain, aircraft from tankers to fighters and bombers were powering into the night sky, joining a 2,000-strong armada that would descend on Iraq that first day.

Part of that armada was the Tornado force that had been given the most dangerous job: hitting Iraqi airfields from low level. As well as the squadrons from Muharraq and Tabuk, more Tornados from Dhahran were flying fast towards Mudaysis, 150 miles south-west of Baghdad. They were led into combat for the first time by their universally popular Tornado Detachment Commander, 41-year-old Wing Commander Jerry Witts. 'We were apprehensive, but there was no time to brood about it, no time to worry. We just got on with the job. I began to get quite excited; I thought it was fantastic. There were hundreds and hundreds of planes up there. We were going to stuff this bloke and he deserved it.'[19]

The Wolfpack had been unleashed.

Back in London, British Prime Minister John Major had gone to bed with mixed emotions. He knew that all the options had narrowed to this single course of action, but he was still anxious about sending young men to war. 'I wondered what would be in the minds of the young aircraft crews as, for the first time, they launched themselves into action. I found it hard to imagine, but my visit to them had convinced me that they were ready for the fight and would do their duty with distinction.'[20]

* * *

Mind firmly fixed on what lay ahead, Nick Heard climbed to 12,000ft for the first refuelling rendezvous. The fully loaded aircraft was being tested to the full, but Nick found it responding with good grace as he moved towards the right-hand hose of the VC10 tanker, unseen in the darkness ahead. 'I stabilised around 10 feet behind the basket. With a bit of power I moved in and plugged in first time; a satisfying result. Fuel flowed and we were quickly full, so we unplugged and moved to the left wing to watch the other Tornados take theirs.' As they proceeded up the 'tanker trail' paralleling the border with Iraq they were able to relax a little. Nick's navigator Rob Woods tuned one of the aircraft's radios in to the BBC World Service. The BBC was just hours away from clearing its service to become a rolling news and comment channel during the war. But for the moment, no one, bar those in the air, was aware that war was minutes away.

'It was totally surreal. We were listening to something totally innocuous like Gardeners' Question Time, waiting for the final moment when we would head over the border and start a war. At least we still had the element of surprise. Then the broadcast was interrupted to announce that there were explosions in Baghdad. We turned the radio off.' Nick then monitored all the other aircraft checking in with AWACS, the great eyes and ears in the sky. 'I knew there was a huge armada of aircraft gathering; part of the massive initial attack and it was incredible to be part of it.'

The converted Boeing 707 Airborne Warning and Control System, topped by its distinctive saucer-like radar dome, gave the coalition forces hundreds of miles of sight over the aerial battlefield. The massive fleet now approaching Iraq required four AWACS constantly in the air, spotting both enemy and friendly aircraft many miles away. If an Iraqi jet homed in on a coalition aircraft, it was up to AWACS to warn the fliers and provide them with protection.[21] If the AWACS controller broadcast the message 'picture clear', it meant there were no immediate threats at hand. It was a phrase that Tornado crews, particularly vulnerable at low level in the flat desert, were always pleased to hear.

The opening shots of the war were to be fired by Apache attack helicopters hovering over the southern Iraq desert.[22] Their task was to destroy two early-warning radars, creating a corridor down which the hundreds of aircraft could travel en route to strike airbases, power plants, communication centres and Baghdad itself. The attack was timed for 0240 local.[23] At 0239.30, the US Army pilots waited, stationary in the hover, peering into the darkness. There was no movement.

Ten seconds to go.

There was a sudden flurry of heat signatures as Iraqi personnel scurried around the buildings. The clock ticked down to 0240. The crosshairs of Apache weapons systems settled on their targets and a volley of Hellfire missiles speared away. The attack helicopters edged closer, loosing off rockets, then moved in closer still, engaging anything still standing with their 30mm cannon. Fire rose from buildings, trucks burst into flames with bodies slumped around them. During four minutes of unfettered destruction, the Apaches unleashed 27 Hellfires, 100 rockets and 4,000 cannon rounds. The Iraqi radars – and many of the personnel – were obliterated. The 'back door' had been kicked open.

A few hundred miles from Baghdad, thirty-five cruise missiles had been launched from the squadron of B-52 bombers that had flown from their base in Louisiana. Scores more cruise missiles, launched from warships in the Gulf and Red Sea, were zeroing in on the Iraqi capital. They were the opening notes in a symphony of destruction that was about to thunder through Saddam Hussein's night.[24]

The Tornados topped up with a final load of fuel before casting off and descending into enemy territory. Nick Heard was at the front of the formation. 'I felt confident as we prepared for combat. I set the weapon armament switches to live, arming the two 27mm Mauser cannon and the two AIM9L air-to-air missiles, then turned off the external lights. Rob Woods, my navigator, set up the Radar Homing and Warning Receiver, Sky Shadow electronic jamming and Boz chaff and flare dispenser pods and checked that the JP233s were correctly set up.' As they descended to 1,500ft Nick turned the TFR onto autopilot to check the system was working then reset the minimum height in stages all the way down to 200ft. 'The Tornado settled beautifully at 420 knots [480mph] over the invisible Saudi desert. On my moving map display in the cockpit, I noticed the border approaching. On one side it said "SAUDI ARABIA" and on the other "IRAQ". This was for real. I was just about to enter the airspace of a hostile, foreign country at high speed, low level and fully armed. I was about to start a war. At any point the Iraqis were now entitled to defend themselves by shooting us down. I was suddenly struck by the enormity of it all.'

A few seconds later they crossed the Iraq border. All was quiet in the desert below. They were on track and at the right speed to be over Tallil within the strict 'time-on-target' arrival of plus or minus five seconds. Despite being on autopilot, Nick concentrated hard on what lay ahead. 'I had my hands off the controls as the Tornado flew itself at around 500mph towards the target. The jet was solid as a rock. I suddenly thought, *This is amazing*, the Tornado was taking Rob and me into the heart of the Iraqi defences in total darkness and I wasn't even flying it!' Nick listened intently to the AWACS frequency and the reassuring calls of 'picture clear' from the American air controller. With ten minutes to go there were no Iraqi fighters incoming.

* * *

Far out to the west, the Tabuk formations, including Dave Bellamy and Mal Craghill, were also in the air. But problems had already started to surface. In their JP233-armed Tornado, Craghill and his 25-year-old friend and pilot Mike Warren were struggling. 'Back on the ground we'd had a failure in the weapons system which meant we shouldn't have taken off. But we decided to launch anyway; these things did happen but often cleared up once airborne. More importantly, we didn't want to be seen to be chickening out on the first ever mission. And we had no idea how quickly Saddam Hussein might capitulate – this could be our only chance to fly a war sortie!' Desperately trying to reset the system, they continued towards the border. But things got worse. 'The radar then packed up so we now had two major faults making us a liability to the other formation members. We were useless; there was no way we could continue so we left the formation and reduced weight before returning to Tabuk. I was devastated.'

David Bellamy was leading his formation of two Tornados, each carrying three ALARM anti-radar missiles to protect the three remaining bombers. After air-to-air tanking they plunged down from 10,000ft to 200ft and crossed into Iraq. Unfortunately, there was no 'picture clear' in their skies; the Iraqi Air Force had come out to defend their homeland. An AWACS air controller urgently vectored F-15s onto an Iraqi Mirage that was among the 120 enemy fighters launched to counter the initial allied attack. Within a few minutes, Dave saw what seemed like a very bright flare slowly descending from the darkness above him, which turned out to be an Iraqi fighter shot down at 30,000ft by a Sparrow air-to-air missile fired from an American F-15.

Battle had been joined.

Bellamy's formation powered through the night, allowing the TFR to do the work as they hurtled towards Al Asad. With no night-vision equipment to show the way, the only relief from the cloak of darkness they enjoyed was illuminated ground features. 'Once we were over Iraq it was all so unreal. It was mostly pitch-black but if lights were on, you could make out streets and petrol stations.'

Passing close to a brightly lit military airfield halfway to Al Asad, the crews could see Iraqi Mirage jets being hurriedly towed into hardened shelters. Sensing a potential opportunity, his pilot Trevor Roche asked, 'Shall we strafe them?'

'Nah, it's probably someone else's target,' Bellamy quickly replied. But he couldn't quite believe that the enemy appeared totally unaware that the war had started. As they dashed past the base, he knew that would soon change. Leaving the bright lights behind them, Bellamy calculated that they would be firing live weapons onto the enemy in just ten minutes. As they got closer, the sky to their right lit up as huge shock waves expanded outwards. The F-117 Stealth fighters were going to town over Baghdad, unseen by the sixty SAM sites and 3,000 triple-A cannons protecting the capital.[25] The stealth technology had worked. The Iraqis had no clue what had hit them as 2,000lb Paveway bombs, precisely guided by the F-117's infra-red and laser targeting system, plummeted from the night sky. The key objective of the first night's attack on Baghdad was to knock out the Iraqi air defence and military command and control systems so that their response to the aerial assault would be – hopefully – significantly less successful. But for Norman Schwarzkopf and his staff back at the headquarters in Riyadh, there was no way of knowing if the Stealth attacks had worked because strict radio silence had to be observed. There was, however, another way of finding out. The main target was Baghdad's International Communications Centre, which accounted for half the airwave traffic out of the capital. It was also the key transmission point for CNN's live TV stream. Soon after 0300 the CNN pictures from Baghdad went off air.[26] The BBC World Service managed some on-the-spot reports of 'flak over Baghdad' and 'bombs falling from nowhere' before their lines also went dead. Within ten minutes, all TV and radio broadcasts had ceased. There was cheering in Riyadh; the Stealth had worked, as had the countless Tomahawk cruise missiles detonating across the city. By 0400 Baghdad was plunged into near-darkness after its main power plants were struck.

Dave Bellamy's attention was drawn away from the inferno

around Baghdad as they closed on their target. He could feel the sweat run through his cropped hair, down onto his nose and cheeks. Briefly wiping it away with a gloved hand, they made their final checks. 'TFR out!' Trevor called on the final approach, switching from terrain-following mode and taking manual control in readiness for missile launch. Bellamy completed the attack routine ready for the first ever combat firing of the British-made anti-radiation missiles, their targets the SA-6 radars defending Al Asad. His formation was in exactly the right place to ensure the coverage and protection for the three Tornado bombers armed with JP233 following close behind.

'All switches confirmed live.' The missiles were ready to go.

'Stand by.'

There was one last warning Bellamy had to give before launching: 'Don't look at the flash!'

The seconds ticked down to the precise moment for launch.

'Five, four, three, two, one. Commit!'

The three missiles blasted off the Tornado's belly. A triple whoosh was followed by a huge blaze. Bellamy neglected to turn away. 'I was momentarily blinded by the rocket motors igniting.' When his vision cleared, he realised the attack had gone horribly wrong. 'I looked down to see two ALARM missiles flying out in front of the aircraft. They started to accelerate away but then immediately flew nose down and hit the desert in a flash of sparks. To say it was disappointing would be an understatement. Two failures on the first ever mission!' The third missile took off into the night, heading towards its target. But the failures raised questions which would undoubtedly need investigating.

* * *

The Tornados in Nick Heard's formation again heard the comforting AWACS 'picture clear'. In their part of Iraq there were no fighters airborne and ready to fire air-to-air missiles their overburdened aircraft would struggle to evade. In the darkness to his left, flying unseen in parallel track 4 miles away, was Nige Risdale and his navigator, John Broadbent, 'the Boss'. A few miles behind them, as if on tramlines, also unseen, were the two other Tornados. Then a minute behind them, were Gordon Buckley and Paddy Teakle, leading their four-ship in a similar box formation. Without night-vision goggles to check any positioning by sight, each crew simply presumed and trusted that the seven others were in the right place, at the right time, and at the right speed. As the eight aircraft flew themselves automatically on TFR, Buckley's thoughts were filled with the looming reality. 'None of us felt comfortable due to the war environment we were going into. But I didn't have any fear or nerves, we just didn't know what to expect. No one had ever done this before! We were the first crews ever to fly the Tornado in anger. Low-level, TFR and night-war ops. It was incredible.'

'Let me know when we're *sausage side*,' he said to Paddy Teakle, repeating the well-worn *Blackadder* phrase which would become the norm. Like Nick Heard a few miles in front, the HUD told Gordon that he was flying at 500mph, around 200ft above the vast Iraqi desert, black as velvet. There was no sight of the ground. It was like driving on a busy motorway in thick fog, at a fraction over seven times the speed limit, trusting your car's computer systems to safely navigate any obstacles ahead. At the very front of the formation, Nige Risdale peered into the impenetrable blackness, content that his plans had finally evolved into a real attack. 'I looked around, occasionally glancing in to check the cockpit indications that everything was running smoothly. The aircraft was flying itself, we were on track, on time; everything was going as planned. I wasn't nervous by that point, there was so much to be done. As the lead aircraft of eight Tornados, we were checking timings, positioning, defensive aids, speed, height and weapons selection.'[27] He also had to ensure the aircraft was serviceable, checking the fuel gauges and engine indications. Then, he noticed some bright lights on the horizon up ahead, framed against the dark. 'Someone's getting plastered in our 10 o'clock. Very impressive triple-A barrage,' he told John Broadbent in the rear seat.

'Yes, mate,' the Squadron Boss dryly replied. 'That's where we're going!'

A second later the jet turned itself left onto the final attack track, its nose pointing directly at Tallil airfield and the triple-A barrage, now in full flow.

The Tornados' 'time on target' bracket started at 0408,[28] following on from an attack by an American package of A-6 Intruders and F-18 Hornet strike aircraft. Paddy Teakle's instinct during the planning with Nige Risdale weeks earlier that the Americans would 'bomb the crap out of the airfield before we arrived' had proven correct. The US crews were targeting the Scud missile storage facilities and did not hold back.[29] The problem, Nige quickly realised, was that their attacks had 'stirred up a furious response', with the anti-aircraft cannons firing wildly into the sky. Small dots and dashes going up in spirals from small arms fire were followed by the larger and deadlier lines of triple-A explosive shells from multi-barrelled cannons.

The Tornados were 30 miles out, and in a few minutes they would hit the sphere of triple-A glowering over Tallil. 'It was obvious that it wasn't actually *aimed* at us,' John Broadbent remembered. 'Tallil's defences were not even aware of our presence yet. The guns were all firing at the Americans, thousands of feet above us. But you try telling your sphincter that! At least I was able to focus on the attack systems, so could legitimately keep my eyes in the cockpit as the white balls of fire rose up!'

Nick Heard allowed himself a brief smile. The Tornado really was superb. Here they were, directly over enemy territory, eating up a mile every seven seconds and just a few hundred feet above the ground. Then his brow furrowed briefly as he too caught sight of the staggering amount of triple-A going in his '10.30' position, just out to his left. *Glad we're not going there.* The thought had barely formed when the aircraft, still on autopilot, turned left on its next pre-programmed track. Suddenly they were heading directly towards the yellow 'inverted funnel' of fire hovering over the desert. 'It was then that the horrible truth dawned on me – that cauldron of fire *was* Tallil! I stared at the interlocking mesh of triple-A and my mouth went completely dry. A stab of fear hit me.' Nick wondered if it might be his last few minutes of flying. And living. 'There appeared no way through that gunfire, the barrage was incredible and any hit from those shells would blow us to bits. It sprayed upwards in snaking lines, a ferocious mix of coloured fire. I could see no way of getting through it unscathed. We were quite invisible in the darkness but I could not see how they could miss us with that intense barrage.'

His navigator Rob Woods was not seeing quite as much of the danger ahead as he concentrated on the attack run-in. He found and marked the target's pre-planned 'offset' positions on his ground-mapping radar, which updated the weapon-aiming computer with the exact range and bearing onto the target.[30] Racing towards the airfield Nick found himself suddenly enveloped by the gunfire. 'I was astounded to see that we were still over a minute away from weapons release. It was going to be a long minute.'

Somewhere to their left, flying just a few miles apart, Nige Risdale was similarly preoccupied. 'I thought the barrage would diminish as time went on but it just stayed the same, an intense firework display of white and red interweaving lines forming an impenetrable wall. It seemed like a solid mass.' In the rear seat, John Broadbent glanced up from his radar display. 'It was like driving through snow flurries in your car. The flakes come rushing towards you and, if you focus on one, at the last second it sweeps past the windscreen. But these exploding balls of bright light were not snowflakes!'

Gordon Buckley, one of the most experienced pilots in the entire Tornado force, felt a creeping realisation that extreme danger lay ahead. 'A truly unbelievable eruption of green and red lit up the night sky, a huge barrage.' His reactions were swift. *We're not going through that lot.* He flicked off the autopilot to try to fly around it. 'No matter where I steered the aircraft, the target pointer simply stayed on the barrage. The triple-A *was* our target! *Oh shit! We're going to have to go straight through it!*' Resigning himself to fate, he went back to autopilot. 'We were in a bloody great steam train of jets that wasn't stopping or turning around. We were going to fly into the heart of that barrage and complete the mission. No other thought entered my head.'

What had started as a small dome of light in the distance loomed ominously ahead as Nige Risdale closed on the target, ready to drop the first ever Tornado munitions in combat. For six weeks he had planned this attack, visualising what it would be like skimming over Tallil, but he had never imagined it would be like this. At 3 miles out, Nige increased engine power, throttling up to around 600mph. But he had to keep the aircraft at 'maximum dry' power, giving the fastest speed possible without engaging reheat and its long, tell-tale tongue of flame that really would draw groundfire.

'Eighteen seconds,' Broadbent called.

Nick Heard's intense concentration was momentarily broken by cannon fire blasting just past the cockpit from below and to their right, no further than 100 yards away. 'The gunfire went blindly straight up. In daylight I would have looked into the gunner's eyes, he was that close. It was an astonishing sensation. We were still a few miles from the target and the triple-A was right underneath us. But there was nothing to be done, we had to fly through the middle of it. Nothing was said in the cockpit; there wasn't the slightest thought in our minds of breaking off the attack.' Despite the intensity of the barrage, they could hear no external noise of gunfire. 'I was in a warm, quiet Tornado cockpit, yet we were surrounded by bullets. The noise around the airfield must have been astonishing but it was all quiet in our jet.'

'Ten seconds to release.' *This is it*. Nige Risdale flicked off the TFR autopilot and took manual control of the Tornado. The TFR could, if it detected an obstruction ahead such as an airfield's metal boundary fence, force the jet into a sudden pull-up, not something to be desired while dropping weapons over the target in the midst of heavy triple-A.[31] Checking his 'radalt' – radar altimeter – readings, Nige carefully nosed the Tornado down to 180ft to deliver the JP233. Gunfire was flicking past the cockpit. But he barely noticed it as they closed in on the runways.

Five seconds.

'Committing!' pilot and navigator said together, both pressing the weapons release button to give the computerised aiming system the authority to launch the munitions at the precise moment.

Four, three, two, one …

The two JP233s started spraying the airfield below. For five seconds Nige listened as the weapon rumbled while sixty runway-cratering munitions and 430 anti-personnel bomblets fell away. 'It was like driving over endless speed bumps; I could feel the whole thing rattle off right under my backside.' He was not prepared for what came next as the two huge, now empty canisters, automatically fell away. 'The jet ballooned upwards. Carrying the canisters was like flying with two huge wardrobes under the jet and the change in flying characteristics when they jettisoned was significant! I had to push quite hard to prevent ballooning too much and get back down to low level.' Nige recovered the aircraft then quickly re-engaged the TFR to allow the jet to fly itself as they streaked away from the furnace of Tallil.

Nick Heard had been coming in alongside, just out to his right. 'I noticed their JP233 munitions detonating exactly on time, slightly ahead and to our left. It was the first indication that he was there at all.' Their own Tornado flew across the runway almost parallel with Risdale's, scattering destruction onto every surface and exposed personnel before also leaping forward as the giant canisters jettisoned. 'I quickly re-engaged autopilot so I would not inadvertently fly into the ground in the excitement. I trusted the Tornado autopilot more than myself at that moment.' Seconds later they emerged from the cauldron of groundfire to the north of Tallil.

Paddy Teakle was one of the few aircrew who had previously experienced the pressure of a wartime sortie. Eight years earlier he had been a navigator on the Victor tankers that flew far over the South Atlantic, refuelling the Vulcan bombers deployed to strike the Falkland Islands' main airstrip at Port Stanley. But this was very different. People were now shooting at him, wanting him dead. As they ran towards Tallil, he calmly identified the offset marks on the radar and updated the weapons system in the main computer. They were on time and on target.

In the front seat, Gordon Buckley tripped out the TFR in case it reacted to any structure over the airbase and took manual control. It was time to go ultra-low. 'We were flying right into a huge barrage of triple-A with blue and red lines tearing past the cockpit. I had been taught right from the start of my frontline career on the Jaguar that if you encounter triple-A, go as low and as fast as you can.' Buckley did just that, descending the aircraft in darkness until the 'radalt' stopped reading out his height. He knew that it would trip off at 100ft, so he was now confident he was flying the Tornado himself in total darkness around 100ft above the ground. 'It was a very dangerous thing to do, but I had confidence in the aircraft, and our approach to the target was flat. Even at that great weight the Tornado was rock-solid because this was what it was designed to do.'

He glanced at the time to target on the HUD. They were seconds away. He climbed back up to 200ft. Right over the runway they released the JP233 which deployed with the sound of a machine gun firing. Then, like Heard and Risdale, he felt the jet shoot forward as the giant canisters fell away. Gordon did not want to hang about and poured on the power, going to maximum speed and banking hard to the right to get back down to ultra-low level and away from danger. 'The noise and response of the aircraft to the sudden release of the 5-tonne weapon load was completely unexpected. Coupled with my desire to return to ultra-low level, it felt like we were going over the edge of a large rollercoaster ride. The jet leapt forward and it really shocked me. I had to really push to get it back down to 100ft and stay at low level. It was an amazing sensation but, on reflection, manually flying back down to 100ft in darkness after an attack was not the most sensible thing to do. I didn't do it again.'

Nick Heard took a moment to look back at Tallil to see how the other crews were doing in a sky filled with gunfire and explosions. Tallil was erupting under the multiple blasts of JP233 strikes from eight Tornados in a scene of chaos, confusion and high-tech destruction. Their 480 57lb SG-357 runway-cratering devices had floated down on large parachutes. Each detonated just above the ground, firing a shaped charge that went through the tarmac, buried itself then exploded, heaving the concrete upwards and forming a large crater. On smaller parachutes the formation's 3,440 small anti-personnel mines landed without exploding, instead deploying tiny metal legs to set themselves upright, forming a giant minefield, ready to detonate and dissuade anyone from trying to repair the craters.[32]

'It had been as scary as hell,' remembered John Broadbent. 'Getting through the flak felt like trying to run through a shower without getting wet. Those few seconds it took to overfly the target were the longest of my life.' Taking a deep breath, he called for a radio check on the entire formation. '*Two*,' Nick Heard instantly responded, listening anxiously to hear if others would follow.

'*Three* ...'

'*Four* ...'

'*Five* ...'

'*Six* ...'

'*Seven* ...'

'*And eight*,' the final aircraft acknowledged.

All the Tornados made it through in one piece. Nick was delighted if not incredulous. 'The relief, not just for our own success and safety but for that of colleagues, was massive. It was incredible that we had all got through it unscathed.' Danger still lurked from above and below as they dashed across enemy terrain to the safety of Saudi Arabia. Eventually Nick's tight grip on the stick relaxed at the 'beautiful sight' of the VC10 refuelling tanker on the other side of the border 'faithfully waiting for us for a short top-up for the trip back to Bahrain'. A huge grin spread across his face as the sun came up over the Gulf. It had been a remarkable night. 'I was now a *combat* pilot! I'd done something very few pilots serving in the RAF at that time had ever done.'

Nick Heard and the other Tornado crews were among the 2,775 coalition sorties flown against Iraqi targets in the first twenty-four

hours of the war. Nineteen coalition aircraft were damaged or lost.
The Iraqi Air Force flew just 120 sorties and lost eight of its aircraft.
Countless more were destroyed in the plethora of bombing raids.[33]

The Wolfpack had been successful.

* * *

As the Tornado bombers from Jerry Witts' Dhahran formation
flew back to the safety of the border from their attack south-west
of Baghdad, it seemed like an age before the brown line marking
the international border on their moving map display approached.
'I suppressed the irrational desire to laugh as the aircraft symbol
tracked over the printed notice on the map:

> WARNING:
> FLIGHT IN IRAQ OUTSIDE
> CONTROLLED AIRSPACE
> IS STRICTLY PROHIBITED

'Just as suddenly, we were over the line. We're alive! We're safe!
My God, we've done it!' Witts performed a few 'celebratory barrel
rolls' and began dreaming of the perfect English breakfast. 'I had
never felt so high in my life.'[34]

Not everyone was feeling so joyful. Mal Craghill and his pilot
Mike Warren had had to return to Tabuk with their weapons
unused after suffering multiple technical failures. Like most complex fast jets tested to the limit on a daily basis, the Tornado did
suffer from equipment and aircraft failures. It was frustrating for
both the aircrews who had to deal with them, and the engineers
who had to fix them. But this was no comfort to Mal and Mike;
they were both devastated at not being part of that historic first raid.
'It was definitely the biggest feeling of disappointment I have ever
had,' Warren later recalled. 'Once you are there, there's nothing

worse than coming back and saying, "Yes, I was on the first night but had to turn back because of problems."[35] His young navigator Mal Craghill was unequivocal. 'I really felt a sense of letting my mates down. It had been our big chance to show what we could do and, because of equipment failure, we'd been unsuccessful. At the back of my mind, I also wondered if people might think I'd perhaps used the technical issues to avoid the challenge we faced. I was one of the most junior guys out there; what would people say about my actions? How would they judge me? Would anyone think I had bottled out?'

Like Jerry Witts, Gordon Buckley was also 'absolutely buzzing' as he headed homewards. 'If I had been taken out of the cockpit there and then and strapped to a heart monitor, the results would have been extraordinary.' As the miles grew between his Tornado and the devastation they had left behind, he turned his armament switches to the 'safe' position and began to reflect on what had happened. 'We had done an incredible job as part of the RAF's first war sorties since the Falklands War. Everything had run on rails. I thought, *Yeah, we can really do this!*' Landing back at Muharraq, Buckley and Paddy Teakle headed to the debriefing room, experiencing a massive wave of relief and satisfaction. 'We were exhilarated and our ground crews were ecstatic too,' Teakle said. 'The engineers' shifts had changed but our team refused to go home until they counted all eight of *their* jets back in. There was hugging and hand-shakes all round; a tremendous welcome!'[36]

Later that morning, the elated crews headed back to the hotel through the largely empty streets of Bahrain. The adrenaline surge from intense combat showed no sign of abating. Everything had changed from the world they had known twenty-four hours earlier, and no one was ready for bed. Gordon and Paddy invited everyone back to their room for breakfast drinks. The cold beers slipped down their throats with ease as they fed off each other's high-octane experiences. 'The banter was gushing – we were all on a high,' Gordon recalled. For Nick Heard, the reason was obvious. 'We had just taken part in the largest air operation for decades and become combat-proven crews. The change in attitude and confidence was clear.' They also knew that the Iraqi Air Force had taken a real pounding and Nick wondered if it could sustain that level of punishment for long. All three Tornado missions on the first night, from Muharraq, Dhahran and Tabuk, had succeeded without any losses.

Nige Risdale was simply content that his and Paddy's long nights of planning had come to successful fruition. But he knew, too, that alongside their hard-earned skills, a bucketful of luck had been involved.

* * *

Waiting for his friends to return to Tabuk, Mal Craghill was still worrying about his own unsuccessful sortie. 'We felt deflated, and despite there being no other decision we could have taken, Mike and I felt like we had abandoned the rest of our formation. We sat quietly in the Operations Room, waiting, talking very little, reading the technical manuals to see if there was anything we could have done differently (there wasn't), playing chess to occupy the time and wondering how our formation mates were getting on. Eventually the radio burst into life and familiar voices checked in to report a successful mission and notify the ground crew that they would be back on the ground in fifteen minutes. A feeling of enormous relief washed over us both. They had all survived. Our next thought was more selfish: when would *we* get a chance to prove ourselves in battle?'

David Bellamy landed back at Tabuk airbase after three hours and fifteen minutes of intense and gruelling excitement. 'It was a combination of high-velocity adrenaline and nerves but we survived.' The excitement finally caught up with him as they opened the cockpit canopy to the dawn sky stretching into the desert around Tabuk. Climbing down the steps he stumbled, his legs weak from the adrenaline overload. One of the ground crew helped him up, then gave him a 'glorious-tasting carton of pineapple juice'. Inside their quarters the excitement among the aircrew overflowed. 'We were chirping away like little birds. It was a joyous melee of excited schoolkids telling three different versions of that same night.' Bellamy also noticed something else from those untested aircrew who had not flown on the first missions. 'The other guys wanted to get stuck in, to get that first sortie under their belt, to prove they could do it too.'

John Nichol and John Peters, heading out to their Tornado for *their* first sortie on the second wave of attacks, had seen that same confidence of success shining in Gordon Buckley as he had walked back into the Operations Room after his first combat mission that dawn morning. 'He was showing a curious combination of excitement and slight shock. He was hyped-up from the mission, but at the same time he had seen something that had really affected him,' Peters remembered. Seeing the Two Johns staring at him, Buckley at first tried to pass it off with a quip. 'I am stirred, but not shaken,' he said dryly.[37] His navigator Paddy Teakle then loomed behind him. 'You should have seen the fucking airfield.' A cigarette shook slightly in his hands as he spoke. 'Lit up like a bloody Christmas tree. Flak everywhere. Tubes of bloody molten metal.' Paddy suddenly realised that Peters and Nichol were about to face the same thing themselves. 'Oh, but don't worry. You'll be okay.'

Buckley caught Nichol's eye. 'You'll be fine . . .' He hesitated. 'It's a piece of cake.'

'Yeah ... thanks, sir.' John Nichol had a feeling his Flight Commander was probably not telling the whole truth.

CHAPTER FIVE

GIN-CLEAR SKIES

17 JANUARY, MORNING

As Paddy Teakle's formation had headed back to the Sheraton Hotel and some post-mission beers at dawn, his wife Sonia and most of the 15 Squadron spouses were glued to the television news back at their RAF Laarbruch base in Germany. Sonia had been woken at 1.40am by an uncle calling breathlessly from Wales. 'Do you know the war has broken out?'[1] She immediately phoned a number of the other wives at Laarbruch, including Helen Peters, whose Tornado pilot husband John was preparing for his first mission. They gathered in Sonia and Paddy's married quarters for the first of endless mugs of tea and watched the hostilities unfolding on TV. Film of triple-A arcing over Baghdad abruptly switched to footage of Tornados returning to 15 Squadron's Muharraq base. The wives leaned in closer to the screen as each jet landed. The camera zoomed in as the crews clambered out of their cockpits and down onto the tarmac. Off came their helmets to reveal the sweat-plastered faces of her husband's formation. But Paddy and his pilot Gordon Buckley were missing.

Sonia's hand went to her mouth. The others looked at her with growing trepidation. Then the phone rang. Sonia snatched the receiver from its cradle. *Thank God. It's Paddy!* He'd arrived earlier than the rest of the crews and avoided the press. 'I was very relieved and said I hoped he would show his face on camera next time!'

* * *

Readying himself for his first war mission later that night, Dave Waddington, one of the youngest pilots in the region, sought out a friend from 15 Squadron, now tucking into breakfast in the Sheraton's five-star restaurant after returning from the attack on Tallil. *What had it been like?* The navigator, normally laid-back to the point of supine, was excitable. 'As he described the immense wall of triple-A they had faced, I could see it had been a hell of an experience for them, and realised that I too would soon be flying into a similar barrage.'[2]

They were joined by Dave's crewmate, Robbie Stewart, who had spent most of the previous evening writing 'last letters'. It hadn't been easy. 'How do you distil into a few paragraphs how you feel about your children and your wife? I had said our memories and love would always last, but it was really emotional to put those words on paper – even the thought that they might be opened. There was a sense of everything closing in on us.'[3] After sealing the envelopes, Robbie had asked fellow navigator Max Collier to join them for a drink, but he hadn't been in the mood. Before going to sleep, Robbie had sipped a glass of Southern Comfort and looked at pictures of Tange, Kirsty and Scott, doing his best to dismiss thoughts of what the following day might bring. Now he was finding it awkward sitting at breakfast with men who had just been in combat. He had switched on CNN first thing that morning to see the breathless reports set against the backdrop of explosions over Baghdad. 'I didn't particularly want to go to war, but it was my job; I was an RAF Officer, a professional; it was my duty and what was required of me.'

He decided to go back to his room and write another letter to his wife – one she could read immediately.

Thurs 17 Jan

My Dearest Darling,[4]

Well, it has all started as you know. I heard the Tornados go out this morning and was greatly relieved to hear that they all got back safely. I spoke to some of them this morning and they said it was like a firework display – a lot of Flak over the target but it was not directed. The TV is currently showing the results and they seem very impressive. We are waiting to go in shortly and complete our mission. I hope things will go as well for us as they have for the others. I am not sure when you will get this; not too long I hope. Look after yourself darling, I need and love you very much.

All my love,

Rob

He signed off the letter with ten kisses.

Nick Heard was also tucking into a Full English downstairs after a quick shower and change into 'civvies'. His sights were firmly fixed on the temazepam sleeping tablet he would soon take to help push away the memories of a night sky torn apart by triple-A. 'It was a surreal moment. Just a few hours earlier, my life had been on the line. Now I was enjoying bacon and eggs in the Sheraton.'[5] He really wanted to call his wife Jane, to connect with someone outside the military bubble. But she was skiing with friends in the French Alps, a long way from a phone. He smiled ruefully then swallowed the pill and headed for bed. The powerful medication had been issued by the Squadron doctor to allow aircrew to sleep soundly during the day in preparation for overnight sorties. They worked their magic in a matter of moments, so it took Nick some time to register the shrill, unrelenting ring at his bedside. With aching muscles, dry mouth and groggy head he reached for the receiver.

Jane had been in the queue for the first ski lift of the day, determined to make the most of the virgin snow, when she heard people around her talking excitedly about '*la guerre*'. She had rushed to the nearest call box and, with trembling fingers, pumped a fistful of francs into the slot. She was clearly overjoyed to hear his voice, and as Nick cleared his head, they discussed what he had done in the first few hours of the war. 'Then we chatted about how the snow was on the ski slopes and what they were all doing out in France. But the phone started bleeping and the line went dead – her money had run out!' For a moment he had been spirited away from the desert battlefield and onto the freshly pisted slopes of Val d'Isère. He blotted out the memory of the burning cone of deadly anti-aircraft fire above Tallil and slumped back into an uninterrupted sleep.

Gordon Buckley also wanted to hear his wife's voice. 'I was desperate to talk to Dawn, to let her know that all was okay. I went into our bathroom where there was a telephone and rang her in Germany, even though it was very early morning her time.'[6]

'What's the matter?' Dawn asked sleepily. Not everyone had been glued to their TV sets in the early hours. A world away from the Gulf, life was going on as normal.

'"We went in last night," I told her. We had just faced the real possibility of death, and almost certainly caused death, but no one knew what we had been doing. I began to realise the enormity of it all. Prior to that, it was all military guys doing the job we had trained to do; now I had made the person I loved most come into the picture.' He put down the handset and went back into the room he shared with Paddy, glad of its anonymity. 'I didn't want any pictures to remind me of home and normality. I just wouldn't have been able to handle the incredible contrast between what we were doing, war and death, then seeing pictures of my family smiling back home.'

He also began to understand that it was going to be 'a hellish time for the wives'. Unlike those fighting, they had little information about what was going on, except via highly colourful television accounts. He was too hyped to sleep. Even though their Squadron Boss, John Broadbent, had told them to stay in the hotel, Gordon had to get out. 'I was about to explode every time I thought of what I had done the night before.' He walked to a souk near the hotel, seeking some kind of normality, but the usual hustle and bustle was gone. He asked a shopkeeper leaning against a wall why it was so quiet. 'They went in last night to bomb Iraq,' he said. 'Didn't you know?'

* * *

Back in the Operations Room at Muharraq, navigators Mike Toft and John Nichol were finalising the plans for their own attack. It was still dark, but the 0730 take-off time was approaching. Their target was Ar Rumaylah airfield in the middle of the desert, about 50 miles west of Basra. As a Dispersed Operating Base a fraction north of the Kuwait border, its main function was to provide close air support to troops on the ground. Taking it out would mean the Iraqi Air Force had one less base from which to launch attacks against tanks and infantry when the coalition eventually invaded Kuwait. Mike Toft shared a look with his pilot Mark Paisey. *This is it; we're going to war.*[7] The pair had got to know each other well since another member of the Squadron was withdrawn from the deployment in November and Mark had stepped in as a late replacement.

Those moments before take-off are still imprinted on Paisey's mind. 'As we began the brief for the mission, the Group Captain walked in to see us. To this day, I can still hear the noise the metal legs of those orange plastic chairs made as they scraped along the floor when we all stood up. He talked to us about what was to come and ended by saying, "Extraordinary times require extraordinary men. You are all *in* the Royal Air Force, and today you *are* the Royal Air Force." His words really struck home.'[8] Mike Toft was also moved. 'Our time had come. The banter had ceased. My thoughts were with my eight-months pregnant wife and 2-year-old daughter back home. She would soon discover that war had broken out and her worrying would intensify.' He could not help wondering if he'd ever see his unborn child.

As a single man, John Nichol did not have to worry about dependants, but he was still more than a mite concerned. 'We were going on a low-level daylight raid. The first ever by a Tornado.' The bomber had been designed primarily to fly in darkness, through heavy cloud and through valleys and hills. Not in bright sunshine across a desert as flat as a billiard table. The earlier vision of hardened characters like Gordon Buckley and Paddy Teakle rocked by their experience was alarmingly fresh in his mind. Nichol could not shake off the gut-wrenching feeling that something momentous was about to happen.

That feeling showed no sign of abating as the intelligence briefer detailed the defences they would face in a few hours. He did not hold back. SA-3 and SA-6 missile sites covered Ar Rumaylah airbase, interspersed with numerous triple-A defences, including Iraqi troops armed with the latest Soviet-made handheld surface-to-air, heat-seeking missiles. In daylight, these would pose a serious threat, so it had been decided that flying straight over the runway for five long seconds dispensing the JP233 at 180ft was far too dangerous. Instead, each Tornado in the four-ship formation would use eight 1,000lb bombs to be 'thrown' in the loft manoeuvre from the safer distance of 3 miles out. The 32,000lb of explosives were to be aimed at two sets of Iraqi hardened aircraft shelters (HASs) at each end of the mile-and-a-half runway. The four aircraft would attack in a box-shaped formation, with the lead pair flying around a mile laterally apart and the next some fifteen seconds behind. They would be flying manually and visually for the entire sortie, testing their low-flying skills to the limit.

Like the mission that had just finished, the four-ship would head westwards from Muharraq, with a refuelling rendezvous in Saudi, then drop to low level before entering Iraq. Once sausage side, the route zigzagged across the desert in order to keep the enemy guessing as to their target. The small Tornado force would attack each HAS site shortly after 9.30am, a few minutes after twenty-four US Marine Corps F-18 Hornets had pummelled the SA-6 missile sites to the east of Ar Rumaylah.[9] Hopefully, this would take the edge off coming in from a flat desert framed against blue skies. And doing the loft manoeuvre in daylight did at least mean you could see your proximity to the ground more clearly in the recovery phase.

Their army Ground Liaison Officer (GLO) issued the mission

briefing, emphasising the emerging triple-A threat, then, with the same lyric sheet used ten hours earlier, they launched into the Squadron song to the tune of 'It's a Long Way to Tipperary'. John Nichol suddenly clammed up with emotion. 'There was a huge lump in my throat. Singing on exercise had been one thing, but now on the point of flying into heavily defended enemy territory, with the very real prospect of not coming back, it was entirely different. I might never see some of the men singing in that room again. Ever.'[10]

The waves of emotion surfaced for his pilot John Peters when he began 'sanitising' – removing all personal items that might give the enemy useful details of their families or personal lives if they were captured. Everything was taken from the aircrew, from lucky charms to photographs and credit cards. Removing the signet ring he'd received from his parents on his eighteenth birthday and then his wedding ring proved hardest of all. 'Thinking of Helen and the kids made me pause for a moment. Here was my life going into this little plastic bag, to be kept in case I was shot down. This was no longer make-believe; this was beginning to feel really serious.'

But it was the moment Nichol had been training for ever since he joined the RAF. 'I wanted to prove that I could do it. It was the most important day of my life. At the same time, I was only human, and the challenges seemed immense, almost insurmountable.' The need to succeed was heightened by the knowledge that people around the world were watching events unfold, scrutinising their every action. 'The expectations were massive, but the dominant pressure is the one you put on yourself. *I will not screw up. I will not let anyone down. I will be a success.*'

'Crew walking!' The announcement the ground crews had been waiting for.

Dawn was fast approaching as the eight airmen crossed the tarmac to their Tornados and carried out their final safety checks. As Mike Toft boarded to set up the navigation systems, Mark Paisey went through his fastidious scrutiny of the aircraft. Checking all around the airframe for anything out of the ordinary, levering the flaps and slats on the wings, then inspecting each 1,000lb bomb under the Tornado's belly, ensuring that all safety pins had been removed. He counted the red-flagged pins – double-checking – with the ground crew. Everything was in order, and Paisey climbed into the cockpit. The airfield was a hive of activity as the desert-pink Tornados were prepared for action. Formation leader Pablo Mason chatted with his ground crew as they made their own final checks. They were the backbone of every squadron and they cared for their aircraft like personal family heirlooms. Without the skill and dedication of the engineers, nothing would fly. 'Our ground crews were clearly nervous as we walked out to them in the half-light. Everything seemed tuned to perfection. I had walked around my aircraft and trusted her, and the men who took such loving care of her.'[11]

Beyond them, the slightly scorched jets that had just returned from war were already being prepared for Dave Waddington and Robbie Stewart's upcoming night-time operation.

* * *

First light over Baghdad revealed the consequences of Saddam Hussein's actions to the Iraqi population. Hundreds of dogs howling at the moonless sky had been the earliest hint of the potent force heading towards them; their ears pricking up at the high-pitched shriek that presaged falling bombs. Moments later the air-raid sirens had sent thousands scurrying to the shelters as the relentless barrage rained down on the capital. Emerging at dawn, the Iraqis had seen plumes of smoke by the dozen across the centre of Baghdad. The stench of burned buildings, electrical and oil fires hung in the air. The civilians crept back into their homes, fear and uncertainty fuelled by the knowledge that they were at war with the greatest military power ever known. And this was just the start. The bombing would go on until the question of Kuwait had been settled. But they kept any doubts to themselves, such was the pernicious nature of Saddam's regime and his secret police, the Mukhabarat. Few had the courage to argue against their leader's strident words. 'The great duel, the mother of all battles has begun,' Saddam declared on the early-morning broadcasts. 'The dawn of victory nears as this great showdown begins.'[12]

But dawn did not bring respite from the night-time rage. Formations of American, French and Saudi aircraft better suited to daytime fighting had been refuelling, ready to streak into Iraq at sunrise. Alongside RAF Jaguars and Tornados, the second wave was about to strike.

* * *

Amid light scattered cloud, the three Tornados of the Two Johns' formation joined up with the two Victor tankers which would shepherd them towards the Iraqi border. One Tornado had been left behind on the ground when its Sky Shadow electronic countermeasures pod malfunctioned, its crew bereft at missing their first op. The jets dropped from the tankers down into gin-clear skies and tore towards the Iraq border at around 100ft. Setting their armament switches to 'live', they streaked through the radar gap created by the Apache gunships that morning, turned east and, picking up speeds of 550mph, headed towards Ar Rumaylah.

Pablo now led the three-ship in a rough 'arrowhead formation'. Nichol and Peters followed, flying around a mile apart from Mike Toft and his pilot Mark Paisey. There was no use of autopilot or TFR; the pilots employed their ultra-low-level flying skills, tracking visually just above the desert, all in sight of each other. 'That's it then, no turning back now,' Nichol said from the back seat. 'After all the preparations and planning we were left to our own devices. From now on, the Iraqis would do everything they could to stop us. I did not really consider them the "enemy". I knew they were normal people with normal lives, with wives, children, lovers and friends. We were attacking their land and they were defending it.' In the broad expanse of the Western Desert, the three pilots instinctively took their aircraft down from 100ft to 50ft, even 30ft at times, speeding across the landscape at 9 miles a minute.

Mark Paisey, his right hand making the most minuscule of inputs on the control column, concentrated solely on the sand flashing past. Mike Toft could occasionally make out Pablo's jet tearing ahead and, looking left, Nichol and Peters roughly parallel with them. He couldn't help thinking how vulnerable they all were, canopies glinting and wings flashing in the bright sunshine. Their Tornado began bouncing hard as it was hit by the low-altitude turbulence caused by the sun beating down on the hardened desert floor. The formations of F-15 fighters, unseen high above them, provided some reassurance, ready as they were to be guided by the all-seeing eye of the AWACS onto any Iraqi aircraft attempting to repel the invaders. But still the crew could not help feeling exposed, with every Iraqi eye reporting their approach. Toft contemplated with some unease what might lie ahead. 'Heartbeats became closer together, the adrenaline pumped, and the fear of the unknown was soon to become the fear of the known. We felt exposed and very vulnerable, even at 50 feet. But we simply pressed on.'

'What the hell is that on the nose, Tofty?' Paisey asked abruptly.

Toft squinted into the haze. A large black patch that looked like an oil slick lay dead ahead. 'No idea – but it's not military.'

It mattered not; they were travelling so fast they were virtually on top of it. The 'slick' revealed itself to be a huge herd of goats shepherded by Bedouin tribesmen. As the jets tore along a few feet above their heads, the startled beasts stampeded in every direction.

Pablo Mason was relishing the rush of ultra-low-level flying, pushing the jet to 600mph around 30ft above the desert. 'I had never flown that low in my whole life. There was not much between the bottom of my jet and the ground. I could feel the rush of air through the space in between.'[13] Nichol and Peters could almost reach out and touch the faces of the Bedouin as the Tornados roared over their tented communities. It was a strange moment for Peters. 'Here we were, going to bomb the shit out of their country, and these people were looking up at us, close enough to spit.' A few minutes later, less friendly faces glared up at the three bomb-laden jets as they crossed the major north–south highway from Baghdad, only feet above a vast military convoy trundling southwards to take up defensive positions. Seeing the enemy so close suddenly made it all seem very real. The men below were there to kill them. And the reverse was also true.

'Okay. Quiet, boys,' Pablo said over the secure radio. 'Let's get to work.'

Adrenaline coursed through the airmen as the Tornados sped towards Ar Rumaylah airfield. The continued 'picture clear' calls from the American AWACS encouraged them to prepare for the daylight loft manoeuvre which would catapult their jets out of the relative safety of low level. Even though it was from 3 miles out, they would still be within range of SAMs and triple-A around the perimeter. Hopefully, the Americans were taking care of the SA-6 threat with the two dozen F-18 Hornets pummelling them hard. Hopefully.

Nichol and Peters' Tornado reached the 'Initial Point', or 'IP', a pre-selected ground feature marking the start of the target run. Peters knew that at 600mph they were just under a minute from the pull-up point, where the attack system would direct him into a steep climb. The main computer constantly fed his HUD with the aircraft's speed, height and time to the target. 'We were now flat out, at fifty feet, the desert looking close enough to touch, fizzing past like a speeded-up film.'[14] He increased speed, manoeuvring the jet further left and widening the space between them and Pablo Mason, still slightly forward and now a couple of miles away to their right, with Paisey and Toft close behind him. They would now be attacking within a matter of seconds of each other.[15]

Nichol checked the switches, preparing the aircraft for the moment the computer would direct the pull-up and calculate the exact release point to launch the bombs on their brief flight to the target. Peters made his stick-top 'live', exposing the weapon 'commit' button, and rechecked the arming and safety systems were all correctly set. Looking through the HUD, he could see all the information he required projected on the glass screen 'floating' in front of him. Their position and time on target were all good. The green, hair-thin vertical bomb-fall line and target bars showed precisely where their explosives would strike. The 'time to pull' clock was unwinding anti-clockwise. They were 8 miles out and forty-eight seconds to pull-up. Everything was in order.

Nichol was wrapped in his own routine, setting the computer into the attack profile, then head in the radar looking for the first 'offset', the topographical feature that updated the computer's navigation and aiming calculations. The three offsets were key to fixing the target exactly in space and time, relative to the aircraft, eliminating any navigational errors.[16] Once each was successfully marked it would mean the lofted bombs should land within a few metres of the target. Nichol easily found the first offset, a large metal radio mast, on the radar and marked it, clicking his hand controller to update the systems.

'Looking at offset two,' Nichol called, fixing a building halfway down the target run. 'Cancel your offset.'

'My offset is cancelled,' Peters calmly replied, thumbing the button. They had 5 miles to the pull-up point. Another thirty seconds.

The third offset was a corner of the huge metal fence the Iraqis had helpfully built around the airfield. The hard edge shone out from the radar display. Nichol marked it, giving the computer a final, precise update. It was now accurate to within a matter of feet. Peters' HUD display jumped slightly, bringing the target bars left to sit directly on where the HASs and taxiways lay unseen in the distance. He nudged the aircraft gently a few metres left to correct their track onto the updated position.

They were on time and on target.

Nichol could now see the objective clearly on radar and placed his marker in the centre of the taxiways. He then double-checked the settings for the eight 1,000lb bombs to be spread over the area in a devastating concussion of explosive power. There were no threats showing on the RHWR, and the Sky Shadow was functioning. A brief search of the burning blue skies outside the cockpit showed no enemy fighters ready to pounce.

All was set.

They were perfectly aligned for the final pull-up prior to bomb release.

Ten seconds to go.

* * *

Flying about 2 miles abeam and a few seconds ahead, Pablo began his loft manoeuvre against the hardened air shelters at the southern end of the runway. 'We were bang on target as I pressed the weapons release button, letting go of 8,000lbs of bombs. Dropping them had meant leaving the sanctuary of ultra-low level and now life started to get very interesting indeed.'[17] The Iraqi triple-A was onto them. It was daylight and the bombers presented ample targets. All hell broke loose. 'The sky suddenly changed as though someone was pulling a dark curtain across my eyes.' All around them the sky filled with exploding triple-A shells as Pablo threw the gunners off their aim by banking the Tornado hard to the right and south, and continuing the high-G turn until they were heading west, directly away from the target and back in the direction from which they had approached.

The blue horizon ahead of Peters and Nichol was abruptly torn by streaks of gunfire blazing upwards. Shells exploded around the cockpit in bursts of black and white smoke, sending shards of shrapnel spearing through the sky. Despite the maelstrom around them there was no noise inside the cockpit. John Peters had an unenviable grandstand view of the incoming threats. 'The buggers were shooting at us! Explosions were peppering up in continuous streams, right across the span of sky over the target. For every glowing tracer ball I could see, there were nine accompanying live gobbets of explosive-tipped lead that I couldn't. They looked terminally close. It was the first time we had been under fire and it was horrifying.' In the back seat, Nichol focused on the screens, the defensive aids and the switches he needed to press prior to attack, constantly firing out the metallic chaff fibres in case an enemy radar tried to lock onto them. He briefly glanced out the cockpit and spotted decoy flares spewing off Pablo's aircraft as their jet recovered from the attack. 'Happy with the target,' Nichol said, his voice calm. 'You're clear to commit.'

'Stick-top live,' Peters responded. 'Three, two, one. Pull!'

He hauled the control column into his stomach.

* * *

Flying a few seconds behind Pablo Mason, Mike Toft knew they needed to increase speed to power upwards while lugging 4 tonnes of bombs. 'We would need to use reheat which was a worry as it would provide an ideal target for any infra-red missiles out there. We made a wild guess when it would be most appropriate, the reheat kicked in and we were soon up around 630mph, ready for the pull-up. I took a quick squint at the radar and identified the aiming point.'

They were seconds away.

As they went through all the arming and firing sequences, Mike made sure all the switches were double- and triple-checked on the approach. 'This was definitely not the time to screw up as we exposed ourselves to the airfield defences.' Mark Paisey sent their Tornado soaring from 30ft into the storm. 'Out to my left I could see the decoy flares pumping out of John Nichol's jet then black puffs of smoke appeared in my peripheral vision as I concentrated on the instruments in front of me. Perhaps it was best to pretend to be in the simulator!'

Climbing through 1,300ft, the cigar-shaped green bombs were released, catapulting forwards by the jet's sharp upward trajectory. The 1,000-pounders reached the top of their gentle ballistic arc then fell to earth with increasing kinetic energy, quickly gathering speed to reach a terminal velocity that allowed them to drill several feet through concrete and tarmac. A split second later they detonated, sending an explosive ripple upwards that buckled tarmac and crippled concrete.[18]

Peters had also pulled the stick back and the Tornado's nose tipped towards the heavens. He jammed his thumb hard on the red weapons switch, and kept holding it down to launch the bombs onto the northern end of the airfield. Nichol had already begun to fire out decoy flares to confuse any incoming heat-seeking missiles.

'Committed!'

There was a pause.

Then another.

'Shit, shit, shit.'

Nothing was happening. The bombs were still glued to the Tornado's belly.

'I haven't got a package,' Peters yelled. 'I haven't got a package!'

His pilot's rising anxiety was impossible for Nichol to ignore. *But why the hell is he talking about a package?* The 'package' was the way the 1,000-pounders had been selected on the weapons system. He checked the panel indications, wondering what the hell was going on. *'Eight 1,000lb bombs at 80 metres' spacing . . .'*

Peters realised the mistake he'd made in the turmoil of combat. 'I haven't got a *pull-up*!'

The words came out strangled, and Nichol well understood why. This was horrendous. The bombs weren't coming off. They had messed up. Horribly. 'A number of weapon selection switches set up the attack sequence, and you're meant to make a final selection on the system just before you enter the loft manoeuvre. I probably hadn't hit the final button, so the computer hadn't gone into full attack mode. It was stuck in approach – not final weapons release – profile. *One small button which I'd failed to press!* Perhaps something else had gone wrong? But despite years of intense training, I knew in my heart that I'd made a straightforward, terrible mistake.'

The cockpit was filled with cursing and swearing. Although only a couple of seconds had actually passed since the pull-up point, chaos was taking hold. As Peters had waited for the bombs to come off, the Tornado soared above 1,500ft, then higher. They were now perilously exposed. Peters banked hard to the left, almost inverting them in his attempt to get back to low level. He prayed the sudden drop in height would make them harder to hit. Burdened with nearly

4 tonnes of bombs on its belly, the Tornado made heavy weather of levelling out, and was heading fast towards the desert floor.

'Recover, recover! Recover!' Nichol yelled from the back seat.

'I'm trying to!' Peters shouted, now heading away from the target. Dismay, failure and fear were taking root inside the cockpit. 'Fucking hell! What a cock-up!'

'We can't fail. Let's re-attack!' Nichol was desperate not to fail on their first ever operation. Too desperate. 'I was compounding my initial error with another. You never, ever go around for a second attack. It's a cardinal rule. Every gunslinger on the ground would be ready for us, fingers on triggers, hammering the sky. But this was the worst feeling in our lives. We were going to be the only Tornado crew who had failed! Everyone in the eight-ship on Tallil had been successful. Everyone on our formation had released. Except us. It was a major, major issue. But I also knew it would be madness to re-attack. We were in a very unhealthy situation and it was descending into chaos, confusion and panic.'

'Bugger it!' Nichol said. 'We've got to dump the bombs.' It had just gone 9.30 on the first morning of the war. There would be other opportunities. He hit the bomb jettison button and the Tornado, instantly freed of its dead weight, lurched forwards and upwards while morale plummeted in the cockpit. 'Our efforts had failure written all over them. We were already beating ourselves up hard over what other people would say. Our greatest concern was not for our lives but for our reputations.'

* * *

'Check in! Check in!' Pablo's voice broke through to the fretting aircrew. After so much time over the airfield, they were now lagging far behind their formation leader and Toft and Paisey.

'We've had a problem . . .' Nichol tried to hide the disappointment in his voice.

'Don't worry about it. Just get home.'

Mike Toft detected the sweat and fear in Nichol's response

as Paisey pushed their now substantially lighter aircraft to maximum power.

Peters also poured on more power to get away, descending again
to 30ft as the smoke from their colleagues' 16,000lb payload rose
over Ar Rumaylah. A scan around the cockpit instruments indicated everything was in order as they made good their egress from
the target area. A few miles on, he spotted a group of Iraqi soldiers
next to what looked like a communication site. He banked hard,
pulling the jet in a tight 4G turn, standing it on one wing to fly wide
of the threat.

'Suddenly there was an almighty *whump!* and my teeth rattled.
The Tornado jumped across the sky like a scalded cat.'

The stick went dead; warning sirens blared in their ears.

They'd been hit.

The right engine was on fire.

Nichol felt their jet being shoved violently sideways, like a car
shunted by an express train at a level crossing. 'It almost flipped
us over. One moment I was looking up at blue sky then, *bang,* the
aircraft was tumbling like a sycamore leaf and I was looking *up* at
brown sand. I was in a state-of-the-art £20 million jet, and a guy on
the ground with a glorified pea-shooter had just nailed us.'

The huge, juddering force of the blast knocked the wind out of
Peters. Gasping for air and hanging off the seat straps, he yelled:
'What the hell was that?'

They'd been struck by a handheld, heat-seeking missile which had
homed in on their fuel-burning engines. There had been no warning
on the RHWR. The missile, travelling at nearly twice the speed
of the Tornado, had detonated inside the RB199, blasting shrapnel in every direction. But this supreme example of Rolls-Royce
engineering was encased inside a titanium shell which, despite the
1.15kg of high-explosive that had torn it apart, might still contain
the blaze until it could be extinguished. And they had another fully
functioning engine. On full thrust, it was easily enough power to
keep them flying safely.

But their aircraft was severely wounded. With the computerised fly-by-wire system destroyed, Peters was essentially left with his control column connected to the tailplanes by metal rods, little different from those used to pilot a Second World War Lancaster bomber. 'The fly-by-wire loss sent us tumbling, the stick falling dead in my hands, a terrifying feeling for a pilot. I was pushing the controls frantically, the Tornado falling out of the sky, the ground ballooning up sickeningly in my windshield.' Nichol looked on helplessly as they wobbled towards the deck, thankful for Peters' superlative flying skills. 'We nearly hit the ground and would have been killed instantly, but John managed to recover the aircraft and get hold of it, even though it was flying like a metal bedframe.'

Peters was struggling to keep them in controlled flight. The stick was giving him nothing. 'Prepare to eject! Prepare to eject!' he shouted. 'I can't hold it.'

'Don't you bloody well eject!' Nichol rasped. 'Just get hold of it!'

He wasn't ready to give up. The Saudi border was less than 100 miles away. Every metre they made south was another metre closer to the US Special Forces Search and Rescue teams in their Black Hawk helicopters. If they could make it to a reserve airfield just over the Saudi border, or at least eject over friendly territory, they still might get home.

The Tornado staggered drunkenly, then slowly steadied. Peters nursed the stick to gain some precious altitude. If he could get a grip of the stricken jet, they might be able to limp over the border, then back to the Sheraton, some cold beers and stories that would need little embellishment. His attention was abruptly diverted to the bank of red lights glowing brightly on the Central Warning Panel at his right knee. Their Tornado was telling them something was very badly wrong. Triple-A fire hammered up towards them and struck the right-hand Sidewinder air-to-air missile, igniting its propellant as it sat on its launcher beneath the wing. Nichol watched a ray of intense flame cutting up through the metal with the intensity of a welding torch. 'Our computer-controlled environment started falling apart. We were on fire. The fly-by-wire technology was down. The live ammunition we were carrying was in danger of igniting.

The Iraqis were laying into us with a vengeance and the Sidewinder was hard at work severing the wing. An item truly crucial for flight.'

He then looked behind the cockpit and uttered a garbled expletive. 'The back of the aircraft was ablaze and the tailfin had almost disappeared. The flames were about 3 feet away and marching steadily towards where I was sitting. The engine was still burning, we had catastrophic airframe failure and we were sitting in an aircraft full of fuel and ammunition. The Tornado was nanoseconds away from blowing itself and us to smithereens. This was it. We had to get out. I shouted "We're on fire!" to JP in the front seat.'

'I know we're on fire!' Peters said, still focused on keeping the jet airborne. He hadn't had time to turn his head.

'No!' Nichol yelled. 'We've got to get out of here. Look outside!'

Now Peters could see the giant orange fireball that was rampaging down the aircraft's spine towards them. Nichol made one last call to his formation. 'We're on fire. We have to get out!' He then selected the emergency frequency monitored by all aircraft and broadcast their call sign and position. Peters pulled back on the stick to climb the jet and give them the best chance of a safe ejection. As the inferno engulfed the wing and fuselage, he shouted, 'Prepare to eject, prepare to eject . . . Three, two, one . . . Eject! Eject!'

They pulled the ejection-seat handles between their legs simultaneously.

There was a faint mechanical click, but nothing seemed to happen.

Then, just one hundredth of a second later, everything moved very quickly indeed. The straps and harness tightened around Nichol's torso and limbs, pulling him firmly against the seat. Rockets fired, the Perspex cockpit canopy above their heads was jettisoned and a giant hand seemed to reach down and yank him out of the cockpit at thirty times the force of gravity, accelerating him upwards from 0 to around 200mph in a second. The cacophony of blasting rockets was drowned by the slipstream thudding into him at 400mph and ripping through his flying suit. He tumbled, over and over, before the seat initiated the launch of a small stabilising parachute, which stopped the spinning. There was a loud crack as the main parachute then deployed leaving Nichol suspended beneath its large and comforting canopy.

The whole process, from pulling the handle, had taken a second and a half.

'I'd been catapulted from an air-conditioned, computer-controlled environment, through flames and explosions, fear and confusion. A whiplash as the parachute opens, then silence, and I was floating down.'

As he hung onto his harness straps, Nichol scanned the vast expanse of enemy desert he was descending towards. In the distance, the billowing fireball of their Tornado plunged into the desert floor, throwing up a ball of flame, followed by a column of smoke which reached for the sky. 'I knew there was something I should remember about landing. I tried to collect my thoughts, still reeling from the intensity of the attack, being hit, the fire and bailing out. I had to be quick; the ground was fast approaching.' He unlatched the 20lb survival pack attached to his harness to give him a lighter landing and just had time to bring his feet and knees together before hitting the ground. 'I landed with a bang on my backside, and the impact drove the air from my diaphragm.' The column of smoke marking the Tornado's position seemed perilously close. Nichol stood and surveyed the featureless brown terrain. 'If ejecting makes you feel out of control, it's a picnic compared to the feeling of being behind the lines, deep in enemy territory.'

* * *

'Check in!' Pablo repeated the call. He hadn't heard Nichol's final transmission. 'Check in number two.'

No reply, just the white hiss of a silent radio.

Mike Toft listened in as their formation leader then reported the loss to the AWACS crew overhead. If they had ejected and AWACS picked up their position, there was a chance they could be picked up. 'But we all knew this was unlikely. It was early morning, daylight, and, like us, the combat search-and-rescue boys also preferred to operate in the relative safety of darkness.' Every minute took them another 10 miles away from their friends, and increased their sense of devastation as the two surviving Tornados flew back to the safety of the tankers waiting across the border. Reluctantly returning his armament switches to the 'safe' setting, the thought of abandoning his men in enemy territory was unbearable for Pablo Mason. 'We wanted to turn back to help, to do whatever we could to get our two boys home, but it was hopeless. There was nothing we could do to save them.'[19] After refuelling, they sadly set course for home.

'Apart from the routine system checks, Mark and I hardly spoke,' Mike Toft remembered. 'Our thoughts were with the buddies that we had left behind in Iraq. Had they managed to eject or had they gone down with the aircraft? There was no way of knowing.' After a four-hour mission, they landed at Muharraq, relieved to make it back alive. News of Nichol and Peters' failure to return had already reached the ground crew. 'They were really distraught and were clearly asking themselves the question, *Was it something to do with us?* We could only tell them it wouldn't have been a problem with the Tornado.' Mark Paisey, too, felt their devastation. 'The overriding image I still have is the ground crew simply staring at an empty parking spot where the Two Johns' Tornado should be, refusing to leave, hoping they might eventually limp home. Our ground crew were an integral part of the overall operation; we were a family and they took the loss personally.'

The aircrew walked slowly back to the hut to sign the jets in. The Squadron Warrant Officer recognised their dejection. 'Corporal,' he called to one of his engineers, 'chairs and tea for the officers.' The war had struck the Squadron to the core. The first RAF combat losses of the war and they were two of their own; a number of men were in tears. 'We were in pieces,' remembered Mike Toft. 'They were both colourful characters and at the heart of Squadron life. It was only bloody "Day One" and we'd already lost friends. Were they dead? How the hell was this all going to pan out?'

* * *

Back in London, the Prime Minister had already received the news
of the night's events and the morning loss of a Tornado. He sat at
his desk in Number Ten Downing Street and wrote a parliamentary
address. A few hours later, he stood up before a packed House of
Commons and was granted the Speaker's permission to make a
statement.

'In the small hours of this morning, aircraft of the multinational
force began attacks on military targets in Iraq . . . the action is continuing. Attacks have been directed at Iraq's military capability,
in particular airfields, aircraft, missile sites, nuclear and chemical
facilities.' The attacks had been successful and allied losses low. He
paused. 'I regret to inform the House that one RAF Tornado from
later raids is reported missing . . .'

For those with husbands, fathers and sons flying Tornados into
battle, the final part of John Major's speech was lost in a fog of
fear and worry. The rest of the nation heard him say that Britain
had only gone to war after 'all peaceful means had failed', and in
response to Saddam's intransigence. 'We have no quarrel with the
people of Iraq,' the Prime Minister continued. 'We hope very much
for a speedy end to hostilities.' His final words resonated with those
viewers and listeners who had a serious stake in events. 'Most of
all, our thoughts go to the men and women of our forces and their
families who wait anxiously at home. They have our wholehearted
support and our prayers for a safe return home.'[20]

Tange Stewart was one of those waiting anxiously at home as
her navigator husband Robbie was preparing for his first mission.
She was on her own at the family cottage in Lincolnshire as their
children Kirsty and Scott were at boarding school. She had woken
to the news that hostilities had begun and knew that the Tornados,
and her husband, would be at the forefront of the action. Now she
felt the first tremors of anxiety. Then came the Prime Minister's
announcement. 'Suddenly it was all horrifyingly real – an RAF crew
was missing. We had all discussed what might happen, but here was

the reality writ large and it was horrendous. RAF Tornados were going down in action.' Television commentators had suggested that the aircrew might have ejected, and had gone on to discuss the possibility of them becoming prisoners of war. That scared Tange. 'We'd heard terms like that from the previous wartime generation, but it wasn't something any of us had given any real thought to. It was a terrifying prospect.'[21]

Kirsty Stewart had been woken at seven that morning in her dormitory at Stamford High School in Lincolnshire. Everyone had been hugely sympathetic to her since the beginning of the term; there were a lot of military children there, and they all knew her father was going to be close to the action. There were lots of questions about how she was feeling. 'It was a weird experience, which only served to increase my sense of apprehension. Up to then it had been a family experience, but now everyone knew what we might be facing.'[22] Shortly after the wake-up bell, the matron came in, as usual, to turn on the lights. Then she walked directly over to Kirsty's bunk bed, bent down and whispered into her ear: 'Kirsty, the war started last night.'

'It was all very surreal. I just went into classes as normal – chemistry, maths and English.' Later that day she heard about the missing Tornado. 'I knew then that things might get bad. The worst had happened. We had lost a Tornado. It was real, we were losing people, and it looked as though things were going to be as awful as we thought.'

As his daughter did her best to focus on her maths lesson, Robbie Stewart and his pilot Dave Waddington were hard at work in the Muharraq Operations Room, going over their own final calculations for their first attack. The 27 Squadron crews had arrived late morning and worked hard on the details for the raid later that night. Shaibah was an airfield south-west of Basra. It needed to be knocked out. A minute before they planned to do so, an American package of F-18 Hornets and other jets would take out an oil refinery about 4 miles away, creating enough confusion, it was hoped, for the four Tornados to unleash their JP233s undisturbed. As they pored over the maps, news came in that a Tornado had gone in with the loss of Peters and Nichol. Robbie was shocked. 'Perhaps I was naive, but I really thought that the Tornado at low level, especially TFR at night, was a pretty fabulous piece of kit. Those first ops were so well supported by defence-suppression aircraft attacking missile and radar sites, I thought we might be relatively safe. It appeared my confidence might have been misplaced.'

Dave Waddington felt his heartbeat quicken at the loss. 'Nichol and Peters had not made it home, so now we understood the nature of the task; there was a realistic threat that we might not come back.'

He took a moment, then continued preparing for his first combat sortie.

* * *

The last of the 15 Squadron wives had left Sonia Teakle's married quarters in RAF Laarbruch at 11am, after their ten-hour TV news-watching marathon. Still elated after Paddy telling her that he'd got through his first combat sortie unscathed, she went to bed, hoping to catch an hour's rest. But sleep eluded her, so she turned on the TV only to be confronted by the news that a Tornado had gone missing. Her heart began thumping as she got up and pulled the curtains aside. She saw the Station Commander's car pulling up outside Helen Peters' house across the road. 'That could only mean one thing. The Station Commander calls in full uniform for one reason only. I knew then who was missing.'[23]

The Station Commander was accompanied by the 15 Squadron Boss's wife, Maggie Broadbent. They knocked at Helen Peters' door. She knew what was coming: 'It was very bad news. Seeing them there, I immediately thought the boys were dead because that was what the arrival of the Station Commander usually meant.'[24] Helen froze as she was told that her husband was missing in action. Seeing her shock, Maggie Broadbent placed a hand on her shoulder. 'John's aircraft has failed to return. That's all we know, Helen.'

Sonia Teakle left it a few moments before crossing the street to comfort her friend. They were all fighting this war together. The television and kettle went back on. More cups of tea were called for. She also knew it would only be a matter of time before her and Paddy's young daughter Kimberly heard the news. She sat her down and delivered it herself. 'You know Mr Peters and John Nichol?' The little girl nodded. The Two Johns were at the heart of the Squadron's social activities.

'Their Tornado has crashed.'

'Are they dead?' Kimberly asked.

'I don't know. They probably managed to get out. We just have to wait and see.'

'But what about my daddy? Could something like that happen to him?'

'Of course it could,' Sonia replied. 'But we must hope it won't.'

CHAPTER SIX

'MY GOD, WE'VE LOST ANOTHER ONE'

The only landmarks in the empty desert were the black smoke rising from the downed Tornado a mile away, and the billowing white and orange parachutes. John Nichol took off his helmet, rubbed his eyes and got to his feet, grateful that, bar a stiff back and throbbing knee, he'd suffered minimal injuries after being rocketed out of a fighter-bomber travelling at 400mph a few hundred feet above the ground. He walked towards his friend John Peters, sprawled 100 yards away.

'You look bloody messy,' he said helpfully. His pilot's film star looks had taken a beating. Blood poured from a cut above his left eye.

'What are we going to do now?' Peters replied groggily.

'I don't want to worry you,' Nichol said. 'But we're in Iraq! Can you believe it?'[1]

For a moment Peters just looked at him, absorbing the curious nature of their situation. A few hours earlier, they had been among friends in the bustle of Muharraq airbase. Just a few minutes ago they had been in a multimillion-pound Tornado, ready to tick off their first combat mission. The idea of parachuting into enemy territory that morning had been a remote one. Now they were right in the middle of it, in daylight, many miles from friendly lines, each armed solely with a small pistol and eighteen rounds of ammunition. Nichol chuckled, then they both started laughing hysterically. 'Suddenly it all seemed desperately funny. We were struck by the absurdity of it all and once we had started laughing, it was difficult to stop.'

'Let's get out of here,' Nichol suggested as the feeling of merriment subsided. Their downed-aircrew combat survival drills kicked in. Nichol made a brief transmission on his Personal Locator Beacon to say they were both down but alive, and to give their bearing and distance from a pre-briefed 'search-and-rescue point'. If rescue teams were in the area, there was the faintest chance they might come running. They needed key items from the bright yellow fibreglass survival box attached to their life jackets. But getting to their water, food and extra clothing was far from straightforward. 'The way everything was packed meant we had to inflate the dinghies to get the haversacks out. We watched helplessly as the bright orange inflatables careered out of the packs. We could hardly have been more conspicuous if we'd had a Royal Marine band playing!'

After stabbing the emergency dinghies with Peters' Swiss Army penknife, they set off south, leaving behind the glaring evidence of their arrival scattered across the sand. There was nowhere to conceal them and no time to bury the equipment. They needed to run, to get away from the immediate area; any onlooker would already have seen the jet go in. The good news was Peters' status as a regular half-marathon runner; the bad was that he had torn his knee ligaments on ejection and was hobbling painfully. With haversacks on their backs and Walther pistols loaded with nine-round clips, the two hurried away from the landing site as quickly as they could. Even tramping through hot, treacle-like sand didn't completely drain Nichol of hope. 'Perhaps if we moved fast enough away from the billowing pyre, we might get lucky. It was worth a try; we certainly couldn't simply give in and wait for circumstances to overtake us!'

After a few steps, he stopped. Although they had both been 'sanitised' for sensitive and personal items before take-off, it dawned on him to double-check. He still had his route map in a pocket with the combat search-and-rescue reference points clearly marked. If the enemy found those, it could put any rescue teams in real danger. Nichol tore up the map and, as downed airmen had done in many preceding wars, stuffed it into his mouth and began chewing. The sight of his navigator eating a map was clearly a source of amusement for Peters who snorted with laughter again. They set off once more across the barren landscape.

It was approaching midday and they had been walking for more than an hour when Nichol abruptly halted again. 'I suddenly got a bad feeling. We both had this sensation down the backs of our necks that we were being watched. I could feel my scalp prickling.' Instinctively they crouched as they walked, quickening their pace. A few minutes later, the unmistakable sound of an engine cut through the desert silence. They dropped to their bellies, leopard-crawling to a dip in the sand. Peeking through a parched bush, Nichol saw movement. 'It was definitely people coming our way. We took out our pistols. I checked that we both had a round up the spout. A vehicle moved closer; clanking through the desert. Then the real horror, a group of figures shimmered on the horizon, advancing towards us.'

A red pickup truck drove past them, less than half a mile away. Then a volley of shots rang out. *What are they shooting at? Us?* Rounds zipped overhead. It was as if the searchers were trying to flush them out like game birds. Nichol's heart rate quickened. 'I remained perfectly still, my chest hammering, praying the line would turn and move away. Then there was a loud yell. We'd been spotted.'

It was the first time Nichol and Peters had experienced hostile fire outside the cockpit. The Tornado was sealed off from the outside world; even in the heaviest of triple-A, only their eyes registered the threat. It was very different on the ground. 'I'd never been shot at like this; it was very personal and there is nothing more frightening. My guts were churning. They had automatic rifles, AK-47s, the guerrilla's friend. Being torn open by one of those was not the way I wanted to go. The noise was unbelievable, endless whip cracks, a deafening *crack! crack! crack!* The clump of twigs we were lying behind was 18 inches high, but bullets were buzzing through it, swarming angrily over our heads, kicking up jets of sand around our position.' Then AK-47 rounds began puckering the ground close to Nichol's head. 'In my fear I began digging a shallow grave with my elbows, knees and face, driving my whole body down into the sand, the grains in my mouth and nose. Anything, anything to get down below the bullets, to avoid that final, shattering impact.'

A few weeks before deploying, relaxing over a beer at John and Helen Peters' comfortable home at RAF Laarbruch, the two friends had discussed – more seriously than they were prepared to admit – committing suicide rather than being captured and tortured to death. 'It all came flashing back to me,' Nichol said. 'We had joked about capture, about suicide. Saddam had promised to tear any downed aircrew "limb from limb" and we all knew the brutal way they had treated their own people. But did we really want to kill ourselves? Wouldn't that, too, amount to failure, albeit of a rather different kind? I looked at John. Now it came right down to it, could I shoot him before shooting myself? I didn't much fancy killing him. It seemed absurd; we had known each other for a long time. The moment was here – could I do it?'

Nichol turned to Peters. 'Look,' he said. 'They are going to come and get us anyway, shall we go out with a bang?

'I was suggesting we charge towards them, try to take a few of them with us before being killed ourselves; making a fight of it. Why not? It looked certain we were about to be killed anyway.'

Still dazed, Peters looked at the pistol Nichol waved towards the enemy. 'No,' he said, with surprising warmth in his voice. 'There's always hope.'

Nichol knew he was right. 'The odds were way too heavily

stacked against us. There were at least twelve of them and they had automatic rifles. There were two of us with popguns, one injured. All we could have done was stand up and loose off a couple of rounds. In return they would have split our bellies open with their AKs.' They both stood, arms raised, then immediately dropped to their bellies as gunfire erupted around them again. 'They were charging towards us, screaming, shooting wildly less than a hundred yards away. Hearts thumping, ears pounding, we tensed ourselves for the kill. This was it.'

Then the firing stopped.

Very slowly, the airmen hauled themselves upright once more, hands in the air. Another fusillade tore up the desert floor around their feet. 'They had let loose again! It was stupid, but made me realise they were as scared of us as we were of them.' Everything went quiet, apart from an Iraqi officer firing his pistol into the air. He shouted repeatedly in English, 'No, no, no, stop, give yourself up! It's okay ... up, up, up!'

Alongside him were three Bedouin trackers, including a boy aged about twelve, and a section of Iraqi Air Force personnel. 'As they got to us we expected the worst. I was rock-taut, waiting for another hail of bullets. We were both trembling.' The older, bearded Bedouin shouted dementedly at Nichol, punching him in the face. The Iraqi officer intervened again. 'We were very lucky he was there. Without him it was clear as day they would have killed us on the spot. He was shouting at them continuously in Arabic, at the top of his voice, still very worried they might kill us.'

The fliers were stripped of all their possessions, including, to the Bedouin's delight, the £1,000 tubes of gold sovereigns. The two prisoners then had their hands tied behind their backs and were prodded at gunpoint into the rear of the pickup truck. As they drove off, the young Bedouin boy brandished one of their aircrew pistols, grinned gleefully at Nichol, and drew his finger across his throat.

* * *

In the safety of his Saudi airbase, John Nichol's flatmate and fellow Tornado navigator Dave Bellamy rolled out of bed, trying to shake off the haze of nearly five hours of temazepam-induced sleep. It was approaching lunchtime at Tabuk. He had not long returned from his own first combat sortie, and his emotions were about to be challenged again.

The Detachment Commander called the aircrew into a meeting and announced that a Tornado had gone down, with the crew missing in action. He solemnly read out the names: 'John Peters and John Nichol.'[2] There was no news about whether they had ejected or been killed but everyone thought the worst. Bellamy was devastated. 'I said nothing and left the room to help plan another mission.' One of his formation, knowing Nichol was a good friend of Bellamy, came to offer his sympathies. 'I told him, as a favour, not to mention John Nichol's apparent death in my presence. I didn't want to have to deal with the extra emotion while we were already in the midst of a maelstrom. But I – unlike some of the others – would not give up hope that John had got out of his Tornado alive.'[3]

Although Bellamy was not required that night, many of his friends would be. His colleagues Squadron Leader Pete Batson and their cheerful Squadron Boss, Wing Commander Mike Heath, were preparing for their first outing. Dusk was approaching when Batson and Heath gathered the crews of their eight-ship for the briefing. The RAF was going in to strike Al Asad airbase again, following the same route as Dave Bellamy's formation a few hours earlier, targeting the home of dozens of Iraqi aircraft, including the French-made Mirage fighters. They already knew from Bellamy and the others about the heavy groundfire. The intelligence update only emphasised the growing and unexpected triple-A threat, particularly to those flying low level.

Batson had been a frontline pilot flying Vulcan nuclear bombers and Tornados since 1978, and although this was his first combat mission, he wasn't experiencing any nerves. 'I was going to do something that I had always trained for. Although it was to be in Iraq and not Eastern Europe, the only real difference between this flight and the thousands of training sorties I'd completed was that this time someone would be shooting back with heavy triple-A.'[4]

Batson and his colleagues would be part of the ongoing and relentless pummelling of Iraqi forces before the land invasion required to liberate occupied Kuwait. The air campaign was not yet twenty-four hours old, yet raids had been continuous since the first airstrikes at 2am – part of General Norman Schwarzkopf's air plan to knock out the Iraqi Air Force so there would be no threat to his fliers and ground troops from above. As part of the unremitting second wave of attacks, hundreds of aircraft were flying from dawn to dusk, and beyond. They were conducting a similar campaign to that of the Germans in 1940 – knocking out radar and communication sites while battering the air defences, airfields and air force itself into total submission. During the Battle of Britain, the Luftwaffe had failed in its mission to dominate the skies. Fifty years later, Norman Schwarzkopf was determined his air forces would prevail. And he was not holding back. Since dawn that 17 January, his F-14 Tomcats equipped with TARPS – Tactical Air Reconnaissance Pod System – had been surveying the targets hit during the night.[5] They came back with hundreds of pictures of the extensive damage caused during the first wave. But it was just the opening phase of Schwarzkopf's plan.

Batson and Heath at Tabuk in Saudi Arabia, and Robbie Stewart and his pilot David Waddington at Muharraq in Bahrain were part of that ongoing wave of destruction. Readying themselves for their first mission, Robbie and Dave went over the defensive measures they could use against groundfire threats. They had dozens of flares they could deploy as decoys for heat-seeking missiles, bundles of chaff to confuse radar guidance, plus the Sky Shadow radar-jamming system and the heavy punch of the US jets going in before them. Dave had previously been convinced the American-provided SEAD – Suppression of Enemy Air Defences – was sufficient, but now he had his doubts.

'It quickly became clear that we were in a very real fight. Before, I was not really concerned about our own attrition, but the loss of a Tornado really brought home the dangers we faced. Personally, I compartmentalised it; put it out of my mind and kept my focus on our own mission. There was nothing else to be done. You can't just walk away and say, "This is too dangerous; I'm not doing it any more." There was also a naivety of youth. You feel invincible, and, like our Second World War RAF forebears who flew the wartime bombers, you just think, *It will never happen to me.*'

Robbie had previously hoped that the Tornado force might survive the war unscathed. But that had changed within a matter of hours. 'It was a real wake-up call to hear a Tornado had gone down. It focused our minds on the reality as we prepared for our turn to continue the attack.' He collected the navigation tapes with the routing and target information recorded for the Tornado's computer, and headed off to the dining room. Dusk was settling over Bahrain as he walked alongside Wing Commander Nigel Elsdon, who had taken over 27 Squadron after Bill Green's death in August during a practice night-time loft manoeuvre.

Elsdon had less Tornado experience, but shared his predecessor's talent for calm leadership, as his immense RAF pedigree had promised. His grandfather had flown in the First World War and his father had become a Spitfire ace at the height of the Battle of Britain. 'I bet you didn't expect this a few months ago?'[6] Robbie mused as they walked into the dining tent. Elsdon smiled in acknowledgement as his avuncular, 42-year-old navigator joined them. Max Collier had smiling eyes, a fine quiff of dark hair, and two decades of flying experience. A degree of disquiet blunted Robbie's appetite, so he quickly finished his supper and left Nigel and Max talking quietly. Darkness had fallen as he and Waddington strode out to F for Foxtrot. They both felt a mixture of emotions. 'Walking out to the aircraft for that first sortie was incredible,' Waddington recalled. 'No one wants to visit death and destruction on anyone, but this was what we had always trained for, and it was going to be my ultimate professional test as a Tornado pilot.'[7]

Robbie was ready too. 'As I strapped in, ready to go, all apprehensions were forced out of my mind – we were going to work as normal. You became part of the aircraft, part of the machinery of war. You turn off any fears and worries.'

* * *

As Waddington and Stewart readied their Tornado for battle, John Nichol and John Peters' war in the air was already over. They were bundled into captivity at gunpoint, preparing for a test of their own inner strength and resolve. *These people are not going to be happy to see us,* Nichol knew. 'How would *our* ground crew treat an *Iraqi* pilot who had just dropped an awful lot of high explosive on them and killed their mates?'

The impressive array of Iraqi anti-aircraft equipment became even more hideously apparent as they were driven to a nearby airfield. 'There was triple-A everywhere. Quite literally hundreds of gun emplacements. It was staggering. There was a French-made Roland radar-guided SAM system, gun-pits with quadruple-barrelled cannons and tanks with anti-aircraft guns mounted on their turrets, alongside infantry armed with handheld missiles. Nobody on the intelligence side had foreseen this amount of triple-A, or any Roland missiles! Or if they had, we had certainly not been briefed about it. Its sheer weight of numbers meant that somebody was always going to get lucky at our expense.'[8]

The prisoners were driven around the base to great fanfare. 'Our captors paraded us, tooting and waving as if we were some sort of travelling sideshow. As they dragged us out of the vehicle we saw a huge crowd standing around waiting for us. There was loathing in their eyes, a burning intense glare of pure hatred.' Nichol remembered stories of captured aircrew in Vietnam being tortured to death and of RAF men bailing out over Germany being bludgeoned with spades. It was only when they were handed over to the officers in charge that things began to calm down. Many Iraqis had trained in Britain and spoke good English, and, with traditional Arab courtesy, they treated the pair as if they were visiting fellow fliers. They were shocked at the injury to Peters' eye. 'Who hurt you? Who hit you?' one pilot asked, assuming he had been beaten up.

Maintaining their interrogation procedures, the Two Johns did not respond. When the air-raid sirens sounded, the officers hurried them down to an underground bunker where they were introduced to the Base Commander, who proudly sported the ubiquitous Saddam moustache. 'How are they treating you? Do you want anything? Coffee?'

Again, the pair did not respond.

'Don't worry. You are safe now. Would you like some water?'

It was mid-afternoon. They had been shot down at 9.32am and were parched. Both nodded. The Iraqis brought in plates of dates, cake and oranges along with the water. Despite their hunger, Nichol and Peters refused any food, fearing it might be drugged. Moments later they heard bombs exploding in the distance. As soon as the raid ended, they were jostled into another vehicle which headed along a highway signposted to Baghdad. An hour later, they pulled into a site with a giant image of Saddam Hussein at its entrance. *This is where the fun starts*, Nichol thought as their captors became more aggressive. 'They kept banging our heads with rifles to keep them down, presumably so that we wouldn't see any aircraft or the layout of the base.' They were led down into another bunker and blindfolded. 'The atmosphere had suddenly become a lot less friendly. They kept poking us with the guns.' The questioning was more menacing, even though the interrogators were still Iraqi Air Force. 'What did you fly? Where are you from? Which base?'

The prisoners simply responded with their name, rank and number.

'You must answer our questions now or we will have to send you to the nasty people!'

Both of them knew they were referring to Saddam's Mukhabarat security service thugs. The prospect was not a pleasant one, and the outcome certain.

'We are all pilots together,' the Iraqi airmen persisted. 'Although we are at war, we have the same job to do. Talk to us, it will be better for you.'

Still they remained silent.

'If you do not tell us we will send you to Baghdad. They will hit you in Baghdad, they will put you on television, you will not like it.' That immediately struck an uncomfortable note for Nichol. 'Did that mean we were going to be paraded for propaganda purposes? Or would we be held as "human shield" hostages at a high-value target and displayed to reduce the probability of an air raid?' Saddam had no boundaries when it came to human rights. Still they remained silent. Now blindfolded and handcuffed, the pair were bundled into a station wagon and driven north for many hours, finally arriving in Baghdad.

'As the main gate of a third airfield swam up out of the inky desert blackness, there was a sudden flash of light, brilliant even through the crepe blindfold, followed by a tremendous explosion that shook the car,' Nichol recalled. 'The earth erupted around our ears, debris spattering down on the roof.' They were experiencing first hand Schwarzkopf's plan to totally destroy Iraqi military capability. Nichol could make out images in the gap under his blindfold, and in a break between bombs the station wagon sped through the gates and parked next to a concrete blast wall.

He could already hear the next wave of aircraft coming in. 'The bombs rippled across the ground, creeping towards us, crump after terrifying crump.' They were momentarily grateful to be hustled into a bunker. But seconds later, 'The noise curved across space to meet us, winding up to a furious high-pitched whistle, louder and louder as it scythed in. Everybody in the room could tell it was going to be a direct hit. Everything went deathly quiet. Then the bomb hit with a shattering roar.'

Peters and Nichol dived to the floor as the roof fell in and furniture went flying amid great clouds of dust. They could both feel the atmosphere of hostility and aggression grow. The Iraqis had in their midst two of the very enemy who were currently bringing death and destruction to their land and people. They were hauled to their feet. The barked words, the shoving; the abrupt orders increased. Nichol heard Peters being dragged out and he was alone with the guards. The room grew silent. No questions were asked. 'There was a horrible presence in the room, an aura of hatred. I could smell the sharp body odour of the surrounding guards and I could feel their enmity. I sensed a gauntlet of hostility – silent, brooding, expectant savouring of my helplessness. It was time. There was a sudden rush and they fell on me.'

* * *

If the two RAF prisoners were taking a pummelling in Baghdad, it was nothing compared to the hammering that was about to descend across Iraq for a second night. Nichol and Peters had experienced just one bombardment of the hundreds that were going in, with sorties eventually ramping up from 2,000 to 3,000 a day; a bombing raid every few minutes.[9] 'The vast majority of us thought nothing would ever equal the air power of day one,' one RAF navigator said. 'Well, it did – from day two through to day 40! If anything, it got more and more. You couldn't fly for 20 seconds without seeing at least another dozen airplanes flying past you.'[10] Some had hoped that the massive first day of airstrikes would make Saddam Hussein realise he had no hope of winning, and back down with some honour, and his military infrastructure intact. 'I thought we'd all go in on the first night, hit him for six, and he'd realise he'd bitten off more than he could chew and stop the war,' recalled Wing Commander Jerry Witts, the Tornado Commander at Dhahran airbase.

The losses were already stacking up for Saddam on the first day, with eight Iraqi fighters downed in air-to-air combat, mostly with the USAF's powerful F-15 Eagles.[11] But Saddam remained defiant, which meant Dave Waddington and Robbie Stewart's attack on Shaibah airbase would go ahead as planned. 'Time on target' was early evening, 7.30pm local time. The formation would strike after a brisk sixty-minute run, heading north from Bahrain, up through the Gulf. Shaibah was south-west of Basra and a few hundred miles south of where Nichol and Peters were being held. After taking off, all four Tornados rendezvoused with the tanker, then slipped down to low level above the warm, shallow waters of the Gulf. They headed up between the shores of Kuwait and Iran, the shortest way from Bahrain into Iraq. Moments later, the smooth ride through the darkness on TFR and autopilot was interrupted by a stream of light puncturing the sky ahead. 'Got some triple-A going out to the right,' Waddington called to Stewart in the back seat. 'I was amazed at how calm I was, as I'd never seen anything like it! It was incredible, there was so much that I was picking a route through, slaloming the aircraft at 200ft between the streaks of gunfire using the heading control dial on the autopilot. A bit like a video game.'[12]

'Speed's good at four-seven-zero. Height good, 200. Fuel fine,' Robbie said from the back seat. Few words were wasted; unlike some other crews, they kept any cockpit chat to the bare minimum. Robbie looked up from his instruments. 'The triple-A was snaking skywards, trying to hit the F-18s and A-6s which were wreaking havoc on the missile sites. You could see the odd surface-to-air missile taking off in the distance and arcing into the sky. I glanced to the port side as we swept smoothly past a triple-A site 50 yards away and could make out a moving car with its headlights on.'

Dave continued to manoeuvre the aircraft around the massed triple-A which almost had a celebratory quality, sparkling like a firework display, but one which they both knew, given Nichol and Peters' presumed capture, could have a deadly outcome. 'Left three-two-zero,' Robbie called. Dave turned the aircraft slightly to port, registering their speed at 535mph. The silence in the cockpit was punctuated by the gentle background whine of electronics and the odd 'bip-bip' made by the new HaveQuick secure radios. As they crossed from Kuwait into Iraq, Robbie could see that 200 feet below, life seemed to be going on as normal. 'It was truly surreal; we were at war and I was looking down at people on the ground as we flashed by. I actually saw one guy standing half out of his car, resting on the open door looking up at the noise of the aircraft above.'

They began the attack run, one minute out. Right on cue the

night sky to their right erupted in bright orange flames, lighting up the moonless sky. The Americans had struck home on the oil refinery in devastating fashion. 'Triple-A off to the right, just coming left now,' Dave said. The Tornado had turned onto its final approach and on a direct bearing towards the rising groundfire. 'Height good. All switches confirmed live. Three seconds from committing.'

* * *

As the Muharraq Tornados began their attack on Shaibah, Peter Batson made small talk with his Boss Mike Heath before take-off from Tabuk. 'It felt like one of our training sorties rather than the start of a war mission.'

The eight Tornados, four from 20 Squadron and four from 16 Squadron, flew to the tanker rendezvous just inside the border, then descended to low level, narrowly avoiding a flight of helicopters, fortunately a little lower and with their lights still on, heading towards Iraq on their own mission. As they crossed 'sausage side', Batson saw what he presumed was a flaming aircraft wreckage with Special Forces helicopters circling above it, firing at targets on the ground. *Perhaps a dramatic search-and-rescue mission for downed aircrew?*

As they headed west towards Al Asad airfield, something odd began to happen every time the formation crossed a highway. 'A spotlight positioned on the road would spark up. Not at us, but straight into the sky. We just couldn't understand why these searchlights were pointing upwards in the middle of the desert as we flew over.' In fact, the Iraqis had developed a simple but effective early-warning system that did not rely on the radars or electronics which were attracting hostile fire. Soldiers had been stationed at regular points across the network of desert roads, and ordered to switch on the lights whenever an aircraft passed low overhead. It had an unnerving effect on those going into battle. 'They were well spaced, giving a beam to our left and right, forming a surreal corridor; columns of light marking our progress into Iraq. It was a very basic, but very effective alert for the Iraqi gunners awaiting us!'

* * *

Dave and Robbie's Tornado heading to Shaibah was treated to a different welcome. Streams of yellow and white tracer from multiple gun systems around the airfield shot up to greet them as their formation closed on the target. Waddington took the aircraft from TFR autopilot into manual control. 'The triple-A formed a bright dome of fire; we were heading straight towards this incredible curtain of exploding lead bracketed with darkness on either side. Rationally we wanted to turn away from it, but the job was to deliver the weapons on target. I didn't say anything to Robbie, but I certainly thought, *How the hell will we get through this?*' Robbie heard the JP233 spew out its deadly contents as they crossed the runway. 'It fired like a Mauser cannon with a rapid staccato. You could hear the 57lb cratering munitions eject from the canisters then all the anti-personnel bomblets exploding out.'

'The JP233 sounded like a machine gun going off under my backside,' Dave said, 'like driving at great speed over a cobbled road.' With the weapons gone they made a hard turn 90 degrees north out of the target area. Some of the intense pressure fell away. 'I said to Robbie, "Did you see that!" It was an amazing experience. We weren't scared because we were too busy but I thought, *My God, have we just done that?*'

All four Tornados made it through the maelstrom and began their race home.

Moments later, out to Dave's left, a huge fireball erupted and spread across the desert, like a detonating bomb.

A shout came over the radio, 'Aircraft down!'

Before Dave could properly react, the tell-tale white streak of a missile leapt up towards them. 'SAM!' he yelled, immediately throttling back while simultaneously pulling a hard left turn to break any missile lock.[13] 'We were flying at just 200 feet, in total darkness, no NVGs – it was an incredibly dangerous manoeuvre.'

It was about to get a lot more dangerous. Up ahead, the formation leader also spotted another missile hunting his own jet. He broke hard right. Both Tornados were now curving in towards each other, just a few hundred feet above ground, travelling at a combined speed of almost 1,200mph in the void. Dave's aircraft suddenly bumped and bounced in heavy turbulence. It was the formation leader's Tornado hurtling unseen over their cockpit. 'We just crossed in the dark, totally blind, and had no idea how close we came to collision. It was quite disconcerting.'

As they headed to safety the formation leader called on the radio to the number three aircraft, call sign 'Charlie', crewed by the new Squadron Boss Nigel Elsdon and his navigator Max Collier:

'Charlie, are you with us?'

Silence.

'Charlie are you with us . . .?'

The calls went unanswered.

As they crossed the border and climbed towards the waiting tankers, Robbie radioed the AWACS operator for clarification. 'Can you see three or four aircraft?'

After a brief pause to check his screens, the American answered.

'There are only three.'

'The awful truth began to sink in. *My God, we've just lost another one.*'

* * *

Another Tornado had gone down, but the raids pressed on. Four hundred miles to the north-west of where Elsdon and Collier had crashed, the eight aircraft led by Pete Batson and Mike Heath were undertaking their own low-level night-time attack at Al Asad airbase. Batson lined up for the bombing run. He was the first in the stream, hoping that they might be able to get in and out before the Iraqis knew they were there. Speed was of the essence. 'The closer we got to the target the faster we went, progressing up to about 500 knots [575mph] and needing small bursts of reheat to overcome the drag effect of the JP233.' They were about 8 miles out when his attention was drawn to an astonishing sight on the horizon.

He squinted to double-check what was coming out of the darkness ahead. And no, his mind wasn't playing tricks. 'Every single airfield light was on. It was like being back home at RAF Laarbruch on a busy night of flying training. The runway lights, airfield approach lights, taxiway lights, everything, the whole place was lit up.

'We can't be going there . . .' Mike Heath said from the back seat.

But they were.

Batson did another double-take. An aircraft was flying around the airbase at about 1,000ft doing practice approaches in what appeared to be night-time training. 'It was something we had all done many times before, just not in the middle of a war. The aircraft had its red anti-collision lights flashing and, because we were so low, we were looking up at it. I really couldn't believe what I was seeing.' They were one minute away from the target. 'Mike and I rapidly discussed the threat it could be to the rest of our formation. We didn't know what it was, as we couldn't identify the type, but it could pose a very real threat if armed with missiles – so I attempted to lock my own air-to-air missile onto it, but no reassuring growl came back.' For some reason his missiles had failed to lock on. But by selecting the air-to-air combat option when they were in ground-attack mode, Batson had now cancelled the carefully crafted attack profile. 'That was a bit of a shocker. We were now about thirty seconds out with no weapon steering in the HUD.'

The Iraqis' searchlight warning system must have worked. The Tornado glittered in the bright white light of the enemy shells erupting around them. Red and orange darts speared upwards, seeking its soft belly. But the cockpit remained strangely remote from the incoming threat for these newcomers to war. 'It was totally surreal to see all the exploding, flashing light around us, but all in relative silence.' Batson now had no choice but to carry out the attack run himself, by hitting the pilot weapon aiming 'Target of Opportunity' switch. 'I now had complete control of the weapons system. Aiming wasn't going to be a problem as, with the airfield lights still on, I could see the runway quite clearly. I manually manoeuvred the aircraft to ensure the JP233 munitions would spread over it.'

Then another challenge presented itself.

'Out of the corner of my eye I spotted the aircraft that had been in the circuit, rolling down to land on the runway we were targeting.' Batson quickly brought it within the target markers in his HUD, and seconds later the JP233 delivered its cocktail of anti-personnel mines and cratering devices which detonated across both the runway and the Iraqi jet. 'Many years later, I would think back to my actions that night, but in that moment all I was thinking was that it was an enemy aircraft and at any point, now or in the future, it could pose a threat to my own forces.'[14] In the centre of the airfield the triple-A abruptly stopped. 'That moment of calm in the midst of the inferno is seared in my mind. But we still had to get out the other side and two seconds later we were back in the middle of it all!'

A missile launched dead ahead of them. With very little room for error so low to the ground, Batson hauled the Tornado into a violent turn. 'At this point, I was flying manually at about 150ft in a hard manoeuvre to the left. The missile disappeared so I returned to track and we exited the target area at high speed and raced for the border.' It had been a chaotic few minutes for a first wartime operation. 'I plugged the TFR back in and let it take control for a moment as we headed to safety. At last, I could draw a breath. Our gaggle set track to leave Iraqi airspace. Crossing the border I set the armament switches to safe and our quietly ecstatic formation climbed to medium level. I checked them in on the radio.'

All aircraft responded.

* * *

It was a very different atmosphere in Dave Waddington and Robbie Stewart's jet as their three surviving aircraft landed back at Muharraq. Those waiting watched for the second time in nine hours as another Tornado failed to return from a mission.

Dave taxied in, shut down the engines, opened the canopy and felt the warm air from the Gulf wash over him. Robbie slowly made his way down the steps where he was met by their ground crew. After handshakes and some chatter, he made his way over to the shelter where Elsdon and Collier's ground crew were waiting, their pale faces and white eyes amplified under the harsh lights. Robbie brought them into a huddle. 'We lost the Boss and Max,' he told them. 'I'm sorry.' The young engineers looked on mutely, unable to believe that they had lost another jet and its crew. Their jet. Their crew. 'The loss hit them hard and they didn't want to leave the airfield, hoping against hope we were wrong.' Robbie joined the survivors in the debriefing room inside the Operations Room. They glanced at each other, barely registering their surroundings, trying to understand what had just happened and grappling with the complex challenges of loss and survival. Some were in tears. 'It was our first bombing mission and we'd seen a crash and friends killed right in front of us. It was a very severe baptism of war.'

As news of the second loss spread, the shock waves were felt throughout the Tornado force across the three Gulf airbases, especially for those who would continue the fight. 'If you go to war, people are going to be killed,' said one navigator. 'It's one of those facts that you have to accept. So I had to get on with the job and try not to let it affect me.'[15] It was easier said than done and everyone was quiet on the bus back to the Sheraton. Then they gathered in the cellar bar to drink to the memory of the fallen. Dave Waddington felt the alcohol release the tension and pain of loss. 'It was then that the reality of what we had been through and the growing realisation of Max and Nigel's loss came to the fore. And the utter certainty that in the not-too-distant future, we would have to do it all again.'

'I had known Max for a long time,' Robbie reflected. 'He was quiet, sincere, a good operator; a really nice bloke.' He finished his beer and went to call his wife. 'Obviously, I couldn't mention anything about Max and the Boss as their next of kin may not yet have been informed. But I really needed to talk.'

* * *

Back home in Lincolnshire, Tange replaced the phone on its cradle and took a deep breath. After listening to Robbie's first experiences of war, she took out her pen.

> *Thursday 17th January*
> *To my very dearest darling,*[16]
> *Well, the waiting is over and that is a relief, but a new sort of terror drains us all. It is 11.30pm and, for the first time, the telephone has stopped ringing and I am on my own in the peace and quiet to be with you. It was lovely to hear your voice; things must be indescribable for you all out there and you are in everyone's thoughts and prayers. I spoke to the children's school boarding houses this morning and they had both been told of the outbreak of hostilities. I will collect them tomorrow as planned. Scott is having a friend over for the day on Saturday, Kirsty and I are going to the pantomime – aren't we lucky! But then I'm lucky in so many ways – I've got two lovely kids and I've got you, darling.*
> *Please come back to us safely. We will send photographs this weekend and a flight magazine will be posted with this letter.*
> *Please don't worry about us, we are coping. I just couldn't cope with losing you. Our prayers are with you.*
> *All my love,*
> *Tange xxxxxx*

Onlookers across the world were now glued to their television sets, astonished at the level of firepower being deployed over Iraq. But back at his home in Bolton, Dave Waddington's mother Berenice had decided to turn off the TV for good, to avoid hearing any more about the Tornado lost on the first morning of war. The endless reports that Peters and Nichol had gone missing were too much to bear. An interview with a retired admiral had finally made her reach for the off switch. He had shared his thoughts on how Saddam could counter the Tornado raids. 'I couldn't believe my ears! During the Second World War we had all the posters about "careless talk costs lives", yet here was this man now telling the Iraqis how best to attack our own boys!'[17] Berenice hated the thought of her son in danger. The grinning 9-year-old who had vowed to become a pilot. She gazed at his framed photograph, taken after King Hussein of Jordan had taken the salute at his graduation parade. 'We were so proud; he'd achieved so much, our little boy presented with his pilot wings – especially a lad from Bolton. When he started flying Tornados, my husband Jack and I never thought he might go to war. We were children of the Second World War and the thought of a war in the 1990s never entered our heads.

'We spent a lot of time praying David would come home safely, as I imagined lots of mothers and fathers were doing. We didn't know what the future might hold, but we knew that our sons were in grave danger after the first Tornado was lost.'

Helen Peters had already been told that her husband and his navigator John Nichol were missing in action. The following day, 18 January, the Station Commander arrived back at her front door, again in full uniform. She was enjoying more tea with a group of the other wives. 'They all looked at me in horror as he drew me gently into the kitchen. Gravely he told me the boys had probably been captured. He said intelligence sources from inside Iraq, which he was unable to discuss, had reported sighting two captured British airmen. At that point, John and John were the only two airmen missing. So it had to be them.

'At first, this seemed like the worst thing that could have happened. I knew deep down that they were both more afraid of capture than of dying. I could understand that. They were prepared for death, for the quick death; when the missile hits and the world goes white, then black. We were all as prepared for that to happen as anyone could be. They were paid to take that risk. But capture was different. We all expected the Iraqis to use their prisoners horribly. In one way, though, I was relieved. At least they hadn't carried out that mad, half-formed suicide pact. It was probably just as well, as John was never much good at DIY!

'This was the only time I cried. At least when somebody you

love dies, you know what has happened to them. You can mourn them. Now, I was facing the prospect of not knowing what had happened to John for weeks, months, perhaps for years. Perhaps never knowing...'[18]

CHAPTER SEVEN

'THE BAD STUFF'

Helen Peters remains grateful that she didn't really know what had been happening to her husband in those early hours.

Now a prisoner in Baghdad, John Peters had been isolated from his navigator John Nichol and was being led from the bunker shattered by the coalition attack a short while earlier. His next stop would be the place the friendly Iraqi Air Force officers who first questioned them had warned was where '*the bad stuff*' happened. The air was cool but he was sweating as he was shepherded into yet another concrete chamber. He barely had time to draw breath before the violence began. 'They jumped at me, initially using just boots. They laughed and joked about it, among themselves. The helplessness was a big part of it, humiliating, sordid and degrading.'

Peters steeled himself mentally. *I'm not the one degraded here.* But it was hard, especially when a boot smashed into his knee ligaments, injured while ejecting. 'I had to depend on my integrity, believe in my own worth. What were my worst fears? Suppose they

gang-raped me? Under the circumstances, it seemed only too likely.'
Through the pain he made one promise to himself: 'I'm not going
to let the bastards change me. If I come through this I'm going to
go home to Helen and my son Guy and daughter Toni. I am going
to pick up my ordinary, happy life.'[1]

The questions, and violence, continued.

As Peters suffered, so did the Iraqi people. The aerial bombardment raged on. The doubling of coalition air strength since
November allowed General Norman Schwarzkopf to pursue a
broader range of targets. By the second day he ordered the bombing of the Iraqi army on the ground, and further sites in Baghdad
itself. B-52s and A-10 tank-busters struck again and again at enemy
troops and armour in the desert.[2] Iraqi airbases like the one in which
Nichol and Peters were being held prisoner became the focus for
raids of increasing intensity. A significant number of Iraqi bombers
were destroyed on the ground, and American fighters blasted two
more of their jets out of the sky. F-111s opened a second line of
attack from Turkey, and another 200 Tomahawk cruise missiles
were launched from warships in the Gulf region. Perhaps inevitably,
the stream of US successes did not come without cost. Only two of
the six aircrew manning the three American jets downed on the
second day survived – and would now face the gruelling challenges
which currently confronted Peters and Nichol: whether to break
under interrogation and tell all they knew, or to hold their tongue
in the face of relentless torture.

While John Peters had been dragged from the crumbling bunker,
John Nichol had been left surrounded by guards. Their hostility
was as acrid as their body odour, and it quickly turned physical.
A bunched fist landed on his jaw, and was rapidly followed by
repeated kicks and punches from every quarter. 'I was trying to
hold my head down to protect my face, and my legs together to
protect my balls. They crowded around me, kicking and punching,
their blows driving in from all angles. Blood spurted from my nose,
thick and grimy on my tongue and teeth. I couldn't protect myself,
hard as I tried. They had total control. They could do anything

they damn well liked to me, and they could take as long as they liked doing it.[3]

'Only hours ago, I'd been a significant part of the biggest high-tech military offensive in history; now I was just a speck of dirt in a Third World desert, trampled underfoot, surrounded by an implacable enemy.'

Almost unbearable loneliness combined with immense pain as the savagery continued, until Nichol's aggressors finally tired and left him curled up in a corner. 'There was no sense of time. I was in an endless pitch-black vacuum.' He was not alone for long. Nichol soon found himself back alongside Peters. His blindfold was removed and he was shocked by what he saw. 'JP looked wrecked. He did not seem aware of his surroundings or appear to be taking much in, as though he had had a very thorough going-over, worse than my own.' Both were behind a long table, under bright lights, and confronted by a new Iraqi interrogator. The man was flanked by two obese thugs, 'stock villains straight out of central casting', complete with greasy hair, brown plastic shoes and, more curiously, squeezed into RAF flying suits. The interrogator waited in silence for a minute, then a tirade of questions began. What was their mission? What did they know of other missions? What aircraft were they flying?

Sticking to the standard formula, the aviators replied with name, rank and service number, and the only other approved phrase: 'I cannot answer that question.'

The questions stopped. An order was given in Arabic. One of the thugs pulled Nichol to his feet and hustled him out of the room. 'I had a horrible feeling in the pit of my stomach, that it was about to intensify. As I was dragged away I glanced back at JP, my chum of the last four years. Surrounded by the sadistic bastards, he was being re-blindfolded. I could tell they were getting ready to start on him in earnest yet again. What would they do next? Were they going to do it to me when they'd finished with him? Would I be able to hear him scream? How much could or would he take? How much could I?'

The two friends were now entering the classic routine: beating followed by questioning, followed by more beating. It would go on through the night and into the next day. Countless hours which would only stop when severe injury, death or co-operation was achieved.

Hands still cuffed behind his back, Peters was about to learn how relentless and uncompromising his captors could be. 'They grabbed me by the hair and threw my head against the wall for a few minutes. It felt terribly flat and cold, my features tried to mould themselves to whatever surface they encountered. All the time I was thinking how to protect myself, how not to give in, doubling over, twisting away from the direction of the blows.' But his captors, with many years of experience, were experts at their trade.

As the hours passed, and tiring of the exertion required, they graduated from fists and boots to sticks and lengths of hard plastic hosepipe. Violence followed by questions. Peters' eye, gashed during the ejection, became one of their favourite targets. 'It was extremely squelchy, like a wet sponge, where the face was expanding out. The more it swelled, the more they concentrated on hitting it, smashing down with some sort of pole or cane onto my eyes.' Peters hoped the swelling might at least protect his vision. But his biggest fear was letting down his service, his comrades, his friends and family, and losing his honour and integrity.

The process stretched on, the conclusion inevitable. In the short breaks between sessions, he discovered that the key was to grunt as the blows landed but never to scream. 'Once you have cried out they've got you.'

But the interrogators hadn't taken long to recognise that his badly damaged knee was his point of greatest vulnerability. They went to work on it with karate chops, heel stamps and toecaps. 'A massive arc of pain surged up through me in waves, stabbing into my armpit, jabbing up into my head, welling up through the whole side of my body.'

Then he did yelp.

'I don't know how long it went on but the kicks became more

frenzied, hammering down relentlessly onto my knee. Every time my leg gave way they wrenched me back up onto it, forcing my body weight over it, ready for the next boot heel to come smashing down onto the same spot. Over time, a question penetrated the mist. The same one I had refused to answer for the past eternity.'

'Are you a pilot or navigator?'

'Pilot . . .' Peters finally gasped.

They dropped him to the floor.

'I had broken.'

He had given in, and the effect was devastating. 'A sense of utter failure took hold of me. An overwhelming sense of shame that I had failed.'

The questions came thick and fast, now, as the interrogators pressed home their advantage. But, astonishingly, they were encyclopaedic rather than considered. They wanted to know how the Tornado operated, its bombload and their target. Nothing of major strategic significance, nothing that had not already been reported in the newspapers. Peters realised they didn't seem to understand the value of the information he could reveal. 'I knew the sequence of signals that would call in a search-and-rescue mission. These codes were good for a week. If the Iraqis had found them out, they could have invented a "rescue mission", with a good English speaker pretending to be a pilot, and simply ambushed it, shot it to pieces.'

Their failure, however, hardly consoled him. 'What mattered was having broken at all – it seemed too soon. When I was left on my own again after answering the questions the most unbearable feeling of desperation and self-loathing swept through me.'

* * *

As Peters and Nichol underwent further rounds of interrogation in Baghdad, Saddam Hussein ordered a salvo of Scuds into the night sky. The Iraqi version of the Soviet missile had been adapted to travel 375 miles carrying 330lb of explosive, which, when used against Tehran in the 1980s, had caused a level of terror that was disproportionate to its size. Most worryingly for the coalition, some variants of the weapon had been adapted to carry chemical warheads. Saddam had always promised the 'mother of all battles', as well as to 'burn half of Israel', and the threat of nerve agents was ever present.

At 3am on 18 January, surveillance systems had detected seven surface-to-surface missiles heading for Tel Aviv. It was 9pm in Washington, and primetime television was being set alight by correspondents in gas masks reporting Scud strikes in the target city. There was a collective intake of breath. Squadrons of Israeli jets prepared to take to the air for a massive strike on Iraq. It was a nightmare scenario. If the Jewish state joined the conflict, the Arab anti-Saddam coalition would quickly disintegrate.

But the Israelis were not interested in coalition sensibilities, and planned their own counterstrike. The plan would involve Israeli aircraft encroaching into Saudi airspace. General Schwarzkopf was horrified by the prospect and immediately called General Colin Powell, the Chairman of the Joint Chiefs of Staff. 'The Saudis will never buy this and you can't sneak it by them. They have people up in our AWACS and they're gonna know.'[4]

An hour later another Scud was fired from the western Iraqi desert, and hurtled towards Dhahran in eastern Saudi, another major hub for the Tornado force. Eighteen of the F3 fighter variant operated from the base's seven runways, alongside six GR1A reconnaissance Tornados and the squadron of GR1 bombers. Countless other RAF aircraft, from Hercules transporters to Chinook helicopters, and 800 RAF personnel were also deployed at the base. The troops had trained exhaustively for the much-feared possibility of a warhead packed with chemicals landing in their midst.

A Victor tanker pilot heading into Dhahran saw a massive flash on the ground below him. 'A few seconds later this yellow flare was coming up skywards and getting stronger. I said, quite loudly, that it looked like a missile and veered the plane away very, very quickly, though I'm not sure it would have done any good. It went right in front of us, rose to about 8,000ft then started to dip down. There was this massive ball of flame as it exploded.'[5] The fast-travelling flare was in fact a Patriot air defence missile, never before tested in battle. The interceptor had blasted into life and powered up to 3,000mph to meet the incoming Scud.

A Tornado F3 navigator who had just returned from a six-hour patrol stumbled from his aircraft as the ground shuddered from the outgoing blast. 'I was looking up at my pilot when there was this bang and – *whoosh* – the sudden realisation that a Patriot had been fired. It zoomed through the clouds and there was a huge flash of lightning as it hit the Scud right over our heads.' The pilot was so shocked by the explosion that he let go of the steps and tumbled down onto his navigator. And both suddenly realised the threat of fallout from the Scud's chemical warhead – if it had one. 'We were rolling round on the floor desperately trying to get our respirators on. Then we ran like hell to this pickup vehicle which had rushed to us, then over to the air-raid shelters, where we dived in absolutely scared out of our heads.'

The Al-Hussein Scud might have had an explosive only a third of the size of a Tornado's 1,000-pounder, but it carried the threat of an even more horrendous death.[6] Below the missile's ballistic arc, all service personnel were struggling into their full NBC – Nuclear Biological Chemical – kit, complete with gas masks, gloves and protective suits.

Three years earlier, Iraqi jets had saturated the Kurdish town of Halabja with mustard gas and nerve agents, massacring 5,000 adults and children. Stark images of the dead lying in the streets were flashed around the world and came to symbolise Saddam's brutality. Those who survived would never forget his latest attempt at genocide. 'I saw people lying on the ground, vomiting a green-coloured liquid, while others became hysterical, falling motionless onto the ground. Later, I smelled an aroma that reminded me of apples and I lost consciousness. When I awoke, there were hundreds of bodies scattered around me. Your loved ones, your friends; you see them walking and then falling like leaves to the ground. It is a situation that cannot be described.'[7]

The deployment of nerve agents, even anthrax and plague, had been taken very seriously by the allies. Hundreds of thousands of troops had been given vaccinations against a range of biological weapons. During the months of NBC drills, they had plenty of opportunity to dwell on the horrific possibilities of an attack. 'It may sound stupid, but I decided that if I got a whiff of it, I was going to shoot myself with the weapon I had,' one serviceman said. 'There was no way I was going to flip about on the floor like a kipper for 40 minutes.'[8] The fear was contagious. A corporal sharing a room with five other medics had woken to the scream of the air-raid sirens. 'We felt the fear and horror that war was upon us. That was the time I was thankful we'd done our ground defence training. However, what with the confusion of six bodies all jumping out of bed at once in their boxer shorts and scrabbling around, it must have taken me about 30 seconds to get my respirator and another five minutes to get my NBC suit on.'[9] With no shelter in which to take refuge, the medics put their mattresses against the window in the vain hope it might partially seal them off from the deadly fumes. They then sat around telling jokes and hoping for the best.

'NBC Black!' would be the Tannoy's coded warning for the detection of chemical agents in any warhead. The loudspeakers remained silent in Dhahran. In Tel Aviv, initial reports that the missiles had chemical warheads were quickly discredited. Following the private warning he had been given before war broke out, Saddam had grasped the fact that the Americans were not bluffing about nuclear retaliation. But the Scuds pushed the Israelis to the point where their jets were in the air, poised to attack. 'Israel has the strongest military forces of any Middle Eastern country, and has said that any attack by Iraq would bring "massive punishment",' the BBC reported. Their jets were only cajoled back down by the private pleas of General Colin Powell and a public appeal from President Bush. The Israelis remained bent on retribution; the Scud threat would have to be contained.[10]

General Schwarzkopf now came under pressure from Washington to allow Israeli officers into his Saudi headquarters to identify the best targets. His response was blunt. 'How can anybody think the Israelis have better target information than our Air Force? We've been studying that part of Iraq with the most sophisticated intelligence gathering technology ever invented.'[11] And inviting Israelis into the home of Islam was 'a dumb idea'.

But the fear of chemical attack was striking terror into both civilian and military hearts, and Schwarzkopf was under direct orders to do something about it.

* * *

Iraq's 'H3' airbase lay a few miles east of Jordan and 60 miles north of the Saudi border. US Intelligence had discovered that Saddam's chemical weapons were stored in a bunker on the old RAF airfield, ready for immediate deployment.[12] It was a priority target for the coalition, and boasted sophisticated defensive systems. F-117 Stealth fighters had attacked it in the opening hours of war and, at 11pm on 17 January, a squadron of American A-6 Intruders also launched a bombing raid on the base from a carrier in the Red Sea. As they came in, low and fast, a volley of Roland missiles rose to meet them. One struck home, forcing the pilot and weapons systems officer (the US equivalent of the navigator) to eject seconds before their jet blew apart. They would soon join Peters and Nichol under interrogation in Baghdad.

Less than twenty-four hours later, the Tornados from nearby Tabuk were tasked with shutting down its runway with JP233s. Having been forced to turn back on the first night of the war with technical failures, 22-year-old navigator Mal Craghill remained determined to notch up a combat mission, but his initial excitement was now being tempered by a more profound understanding of the consequences.

On the morning of the 18th, he had been relaxing in their shared accommodation at Tabuk with fellow aircrew, unwinding after the initial sorties, when one of their number collapsed. As Craghill rose to help him, the airman began to have a fit. 'He suddenly went stiff as a board and started having convulsions. His feet shot out, taking the leg off the coffee table. Then he went absolutely pale and lay there. I thought he was dead. My concern was that he'd swallowed his tongue. I tried to open his mouth, at which point he started lashing out at us.'[13] The medics arrived within minutes, as he was in the process of coming round. He had no recollection whatsoever of what had just happened. 'They thought it might be due to lack of food and sleep – and the stress of exposure to enemy fire'.[14] Without a clearer diagnosis, he would not be able to fly on operations again. It was a disturbing insight into the mental strains they were all experiencing. It would not be the last incident of this kind.

Craghill helped clear up the shattered coffee table then sat back down on the sofa to contemplate the mission which lay ahead that night. Try as hard as he might, he couldn't help wondering what his friend had seen that sent him over the edge. He and his pilot Mike Warren knew that H3 had rapidly garnered a tough reputation, 'heavily defended by an aggressive mixture of surface-to-air missiles and anti-aircraft artillery', and he had to fight to dismiss the image of his fellow flier convulsing on the floor. The words of the Squadron Boss before war broke out still rang in his head. 'His personal opinion was that it wouldn't be difficult convincing guys to go on the first night. It would be the second trip and thereafter that would be difficult, because then we'd all know what it was like to be fired at.'

Craghill's Boss's pre-war assessment of the effects of combat were already showing. Dean Wood was a young engineer based at Tabuk and part of his role was as the 'see-off' crew for the Tornados; helping the aircrew ready their aircraft for battle. After the first few missions, he began to notice a change in their demeanour. 'My crew were very quiet; the pilot stayed on his own while the navigator came for a smoke and a chat with us. He talked about how they'd been lucky to get back from the previous trip, how the triple-A looked like a firework display where you knew that each sparkle might kill you. It's hard to explain the feeling you get when you're talking to someone, knowing you may be one of the last to see them alive.

'What really sticks in my memory was the amount of time they now took getting into the aircraft. Previously, crews had just jumped in and were away. Now they checked everything, stood on their seats, looked around, stretching, delaying the moment that they had to go. I had never seen aircrew do this kind of thing before. It was as if they knew it might be the last time they had the chance to take in their surroundings. You don't say anything, but I was simply thinking, *God, I hope they make it back. I hope their luck stays with them.* When all the aircraft eventually taxied, everyone just stood in silence and watched them all take off, nobody said a word.'[15]

Craghill's four-ship took off into the night without incident, but one Tornado was forced to return to base almost immediately with a technical fault. The rest of his formation joined the precisely choreographed refuelling operation. 'We could see dozens of aircraft, tanking with their lights on to minimise the risk of mid-air collisions. We felt like we were part of a much bigger operation.' One by one the lights flicked out as the jets dropped down towards the border. 'Where once we had seen many, we now saw none. It felt lonely, but we knew we were far from alone and we streaked over the border at 200 feet.' H3 was only a fifteen-minute dash away, and for navigator and pilot it wasn't hard to find. 'Already we could see sporadic bursts of tracer fire. There was very little chat in the cockpit but we weren't particularly nervous. We were in a familiar environment and had trained hard for what was coming up.'

Despite the threat of anti-radiation missiles, the operators at H3 did not hesitate to employ their radars in the search for targets. The airfield defences went active. 'SAM warnings began to show on our RHWR as short "spikes" pointing in the direction of the signal's origin. Then the triple-A became more intense, forming an odd-looking light show as tracer rounds arced into the air from numerous different sites. A dome of triple-A formed over the area of H3, leaving us in no doubt where our target lay.'

Mike and Mal went through the pre-attack checks, readying the JP233s, then turned east, using the Baghdad to Jordan highway to orientate them. 'H3 was now alight with dense tracer fire up to 4,000 feet. SAM radars were searching us out.' Their RHWR was giving them warnings of the Roland, and other SAMs. Mal began dispensing chaff from the Boz pod to confuse the enemy systems. They were now heading to a target with SAM radars already tracking them, and the sky above it reverberating with gunfire. It was becoming an increasingly daunting prospect.

Eight miles ahead of them, Craghill's Tornado Squadron Boss was seconds away from his final run into H3. The defensive barrage protecting the base – a dense cloud of missile, cannon and machine-gun fire – was now truly formidable. Even at a distance, the triple-A looked impenetrable.

'Abort attack!' the formation leader ordered. 'We won't make it through that. Find a dump target.'[16]

Despite his relative youth, Craghill was well aware of the significance of what he was hearing. 'The Boss could see no way of prosecuting a successful attack due to the incredible concentration of triple-A. He clearly thought we would all be shot down. He'd seen it the night before and was able, with that very limited experience, to say that it was now very much worse. It was the best decision he could have made and took incredible courage.'

Their Boss was risking his own reputation by turning his formation away to ensure his men would live to fight another day. But he wasn't waving a magic wand. No plan had been put in place for abandoning the target run in total darkness. 'You were always expected to make it to the target, and no "abort" route was ever considered. So the "big sky" theory now came into effect! An assumption that with just three aircraft scattering at low level, we were, hopefully, unlikely to hit each other . . .'

As they turned away in the inky blackness, only fractionally above the desert floor, Craghill's radar warning alarm sounded again. 'SA-8 target tracker' was emblazoned on his screen. Another siren screeched. He ensured the Sky Shadow pod was jamming, dispensed chaff and called for Mike to roll out, heading north. Almost immediately they were 'spiked' again by the SA-8 radar. His pilot rapidly tightened the turn through another 90 degrees. 'In a sharp turn like this the radar altimeter can't be relied on, so Mike climbed slightly to ensure separation from the desert floor a few hundred feet below while I used the radar to confirm the path ahead of us was clear.' With the warning sirens and radar clear, they turned south and descended once again to 200ft. They now had no idea of the location of the other two Tornados. One of H3's secondary airstrips was now 10 miles on their nose and offered Mal and Mike an opportunity to make their first operational attack. 'We made a snap decision between us and I quickly found it on the radar, Mike lined us up, and we prepared for weapons release using a "Target of Opportunity" profile. It was certainly something we had not briefed, especially with a weapon like JP233.'

Undaunted, they scattered their munitions over the sole runway. Carrying the JP233s back to Saudi would create a real problem with fuel consumption. Mal could see lights sparkling to his right as another set of JP233s was released on an unsuspecting target.

Back at base, Craghill entered the Tabuk debrief room to hear their commander's summation. 'He was in no doubt that we would not have made it safely across the target. For a Squadron Boss to have terminated an attack sent a powerful message to all of our crews that the war was likely to be protracted and we could only fight it if we didn't unnecessarily risk our aircraft and people. In many ways, the Boss's decision was one of the best pieces of leadership I have ever seen.' The crews who had been on the very first raids were in agreement – the groundfire over H3 was 'catastrophically worse'. A frank discussion followed about their level of personal risk. 'We were all in no doubt that we would be called upon to face intense danger. Possibly to make the ultimate sacrifice, depending on the circumstances. But the war looked set to be one of attrition and there was no point in losing a lot of jets in the first few nights.'

Their Squadron Commander was right to be concerned about losses. The war was barely two days old and three Tornados, including an Italian version, had already gone down. They accounted for a third of the coalition combat aircraft losses, which included some of the very latest and most sophisticated multi-role types: the F-15E Strike Eagle and F/A-18 Hornet. Although it was yet to be officially confirmed, seven aircrew had already been killed and nine taken prisoner.

Jerry Witts, the wise Tornado Commander at Dhahran, endorsed the increasingly widely held view that the 'White Cliffs of Dover' syndrome – fliers committed to defend the gateway to their homeland with their lives – simply did not apply. 'The brief that I had been given was that we were to use our assets as efficiently as possible without losing aircraft or lives. I think our outlook was slightly different to how it would have been had we been defending British territory. We were there to do a job of work, and we were quite happy to do it. But none of us intended to die in the process.'[17]

The perils for the Tornado force were beginning to build. Several thousand sorties had already been flown by the coalition, and the RAF's GR1 – small formations flying close to the ground into devastating gunfire – was suffering the worst attrition rate. Those without a combat sortie were still eager to test their mettle, but others, like Witts, were beginning to realise that the losses they were taking during low-level attacks were unsustainable. 'We were certainly suffering a bit in the Tornado world. We'd lost three planes, which, in percentage terms, did not look very good.'

* * *

Sitting in Baghdad, and already out of that aerial fight, John Nichol was in no doubt that several of the men nearby were eager to hurt him yet again. He braced himself on a steel and vinyl chair for the next beating.

'It's okay, we don't want to know any information. Don't worry.' The voice was warm, almost gentle. The Iraqis had sent in 'Mister Nice' to extract information without the brutality enjoyed by 'Mister Nasty'. Now it was time for the wheedling appeals to logic and reason, more subtle and undermining. Nichol was offered food and drink. He declined. The questions began; simple ones about what aircraft he flew, where he came from. It was a more professional approach and every question was answered with the same stock phrase, 'I cannot answer that question.' The interrogator changed tack.

'You are dropping chemical weapons onto my country, aren't you?'

Nichol was startled by the accusation, but blocked him again with the standard, 'I cannot answer that question.'

'Okay. I know you cannot answer these questions, but you know that you will answer them . . . eventually . . . I know you will talk to me, you know, you will talk to me.'

Nichol could not disagree; it was just a question of how much longer he could hold out. *At some point I'm going to tell him what he wants.* The man now twisted the psychological knife. He did not need to ask the questions because he already knew the answers.

'I can tell you that you are a navigator.'

Shit, how does he know that? Nichol thought. It could have been a guess.

'I can tell you that you are from 15 Squadron.'

Nichol was now worried. 'He knew things about me. Where had he got them from? I had a feeling that he'd got them from John. What had they done to him to get the info? The same or worse? Worse, surely. When will I get it? What would it be like? What did they do?'

'I know you are from Bahrain.'

He could still be guessing, or have read it in the British press; his Squadron had featured heavily in pre-war coverage.

'I know that your attack did not work. I know you did not get the bombs off and that you ditched your bombs in my desert.'

Oh fuck! A cold feeling ran through Nichol; there was only one person this information could have come from. *John . . . What the hell had happened to him? Where is he, how is he?* 'I was worried about him, but even more worried about myself. Deep down I was glad that whatever had led him to talk had not yet happened to me.'

The questioning progressed, zigzagging between the cajolery of

Mr Nice and the belligerence of Mr Nasty. He was re-blindfolded
and dragged off to another room. 'I knew something very unpleasant was going to happen.' But it wasn't what he expected. Instead of
a straightforward beating he was left to contemplate the mental and
physical pain of a stress position. 'My forehead was flat against the
wall, my feet about 20 inches away from it. I was stretched right up
onto my toes. Arms handcuffed behind my back. My forehead was
supporting my entire body weight, against the cold surface.' Every
time he tried to shift position a fist slammed into him. 'I tried to
move my head. Somebody smacked it hard against the wall, a staggering blow. I tried to move my arms, manacled behind my back.
The handcuffs were of the ratchet type and, because of the beatings,
were racked up tight to the last notch, biting into my wrists, a cold
insistent metallic cutting agony.'

Every muscle in his body now screamed with the impossible effort
of maintaining the posture. It seemed to go on for hours. He could
have been struck thirty times or a thousand. Disorientated and in
torment, Nichol lost count. 'Nobody asked me anything after this.
Nothing at all. Now dazed, and stunned like a chicken before its
throat is cut, I was worried. I had lost track of how they were going
to interrogate me. This was not going by the book any more.'

A few minutes later a guard transferred Nichol to a room where
he was blindfolded and handcuffed to an iron bedstead. He could
hear other coalition prisoners being interrogated and realised more
coalition jets must have been shot down. Air raids raged overhead.
The triple-A on the roof hammered away. Bombs crumped and
rattled nearby.

The day stretched on as further interrogators loomed over him;
a kick to the ribs to get his full attention.

'Where did you come from?'

'I cannot answer that question.'

'You *will* be sorry, you know that, don't you, Nichol?'

'I cannot answer that question.'

'We will come back for you soon. You will be sorry!'

I know I'm going to be sorry! I'm already bloody sorry!

It didn't take long. As night drew in again, they came for him. He was blindfolded once more, handcuffed and taken outside, dragged around to disorientate him, then brought back into a room and pushed into the hard chair. One guard held his right arm, another gripped his left. Nichol's chest pounded. 'I knew in my heart of hearts that this was the time; it was going to get really tough now.'

'What squadron are you from?'

'I cannot answer that . . .'

A fist thudded into his face. Blood poured onto his lap, warm against his thighs. He could feel the drips through his flying suit, chemical suit and long johns. The punches went into his head, over and over. Then another question.

'I cannot . . .'

'My head rang to the blows like some kind of bell. There were brilliant lights flashing behind the blindfold. I really did see stars. I was in the middle of the Milky Way.'

Another demand, met by Nichol's stubborn response.

Somebody wrenched off his boots.

What on earth are they going to do to me now?

The interrogators then pulled out what he would learn was a favoured device. A hard plastic pipe was whacked viciously across his shins.

Again, the interrogator spoke. Again, he got the same reply.

'I cannot answer that question.'

Someone grabbed the nape of his neck and stuffed tissue paper down the back of his T-shirt. A multitude of panic-stricken questions raced through his mind. 'This was terrifying now. I'm in a darkened room in the middle of enemy territory, and somebody had just stuffed tissue paper down the back of my neck. What the hell for?'

Shit, they are going to set me on fire!

'Now I really want him to ask me another question. I want to say something. I want to tell him something, anything. But he didn't ask me a question. He just set fire to the paper.'

Nichol threw his head violently from side to side, desperate to escape the burning, to shake the tissue paper clear of his head. His aggressors continued to hammer his shins with the rubber hose as the paper burned. Mercifully, someone finally slapped out the flames.

'What squadron are you from?'

'Fifteen.'

Nichol had broken.

Like Peters, he found the simplicity of the questions curious. These were trained interrogators who could have extracted a ream of useful information, but instead the demands were simplistic. What weapons did the Tornado carry? What was the main weapon used against runways? How did they drop bombs?

'What is the countermeasures pod called?'

'Sky Shadow.'

The name seemed enough. The interrogator failed to ask what electronic countermeasures it contained, or which radars its complex electronics could defeat. After all the skill and enthusiasm they had demonstrated in the process of causing pain, it was bizarre that they were so hapless at asking questions that might yield real intelligence. They didn't know what they wanted to know. The captured aircrew were at their mercy, yet insipid queries were the best they could come up with.

'Why have you come to our country?'

'Err . . . Because we were ordered to?'

The answer, however true, provoked rage and another flurry of punches.

* * *

It was just two days into the war, but Iraq, reported *The Guardian* newspaper in London, had already 'suffered the most sustained and devastating aerial and missile bombardment in history'. It added that the White House 'insisted there would be no pause for diplomacy and the pounding would go on until Saddam Hussein left Kuwait'. The BBC reported that President Bush had told Congressional leaders at the White House: 'No one should assume the conflict will be short or easy.' The front page of the *Daily Express* screamed: 'Iraq Blitz on Israel'.

Its back pages were filled with Tottenham Hotspur's footballing woes and unsubstantiated rumours of a sale of their star midfielder, Paul Gascoigne, to an Italian club. '£8m for Gazza', the headline said, and 'Napoli bid as Spurs' chief tackles debt'. The gossip came to nothing and, away from the ferocity of battle and interrogation, life continued as normal.

Those about to undertake the continuing Tornado low-level missions would have probably welcomed the distraction of 'real world' news as they contemplated flying into the intense hail of triple-A and missiles, knowing the odds against them surviving were shortening with each raid. No one could survive that scale of fire for ever.

It was late on 18 January when Robbie Stewart managed to call his wife. Tange had had a fretful day at the school where she taught as news of the losses filtered through. 'All I could imagine was an RAF officer arriving in uniform to tell me Robbie was missing . . . or worse.' The joy of speaking to her husband diminished as he recounted their first night's attack, during which Nigel Elsdon and Max Collier had been killed. 'It was such a great shock to hear about Nigel and Max. We knew Max and his wife well and I had spent some time chatting to him before the deployment. It was all so desperately sad.'

Robbie knew the pitfalls of telephone calls home. 'I wanted to say that I was safe even though I realised the dangers of calling after each raid. I knew a call *after* a raid was also a call *before* the next one. A raid from which I might not return.'

But Tange understood. She was now painfully aware of the very real dangers Robbie confronted, had seen the increasing losses announced in the media. But she was still delighted to hear from him. 'I think we were avoiding talking about the reality of what we all faced. The kids would write him letters telling him normal things about school and I wrote every day about what was going on in the village, the weather, our plans for the future. We were trying to convince each other everything would be fine.'

Robbie found the last moments of their phone call difficult. 'We didn't say it, but we both knew in our hearts it could be our last ever conversation.'

The next day, he and his pilot Dave Waddington would embark on what would become their final mission.

CHAPTER EIGHT

'PLEASE LET HIM BE DEAD'

19 JANUARY, EVENING–20 JANUARY

A few hours before taking off on the attack that would see him blasted from Iraq's night skies, Robbie Stewart had spent a quiet moment penning another letter to his wife and children.[1]

It began, 'My Dearest Darlings, I thought I would drop you a line, though I do not know when you will get this. The initial euphoria of day one has been replaced by a more cautious mood.'

As he had during the previous night's call home, he went on to describe the crash that had claimed the lives of Nigel Elsdon and Max Collier, then finished:

We were soon clear and we both breathed easier but our thoughts were with the Boss and Max. My thoughts now are with you and the kids, darling. The nightmare continues and I just look forward to seeing you all again. I know you are brave and I am so lucky having someone with such great strength. I have told you about that sortie as I thought you would prefer [to know].

> *I love you and will do always,*
> Rob

He signed off with the usual ten kisses, little knowing what fate had in store for him, and his family.

* * *

'CHAFFING . . .!'

Robbie sprayed the sky with the metallic strands, determined to shake off the radar-guided Roland missile spearing towards them.

The fifth major wave of RAF Tornado attacks saw him and Dave Waddington targeting southern Iraq's massive Tallil airbase. Each member of their four-ship carried five 1,000lb bombs to pound its defences and pave the way for the runway-busting JP233s. This time, the Tornados were on their own, gambling that the lack of American suppressive support would not alert the Iraqi gunners, giving them the benefit of surprise. It hadn't. With F for Foxtrot only seconds from the target, running through the darkness at high speed and 200 feet, a Roland surface-to-air missile had been launched from dead ahead. Now they were banking hard, G-suits tightening, as Dave tried to break the missile lock. More chaff burst out of the Tornado's Boz pod into the night sky. A cloud of metallic confusion, striving to give the incoming weapon's radar guidance system a juicier target than the speeding Tornado. Dave was pulling the stick hard into his stomach, doing everything possible to persuade the overladen jet to turn. It wasn't enough.

Robbie watched the blinding orange flash envelop the cockpit. The exploding warhead shredded the jet and the warble of the threat warning changed instantly to the shriek of the multiple system failures siren. 'There was no time to think, only to react. I pulled the ejection handle and felt a huge detonation and a whoosh as the seat's rockets fired under my backside. That was the last thing I remember.'[2]

* * *

Am I dead?

Dave Waddington lay on a hard surface surrounded by blackness and silence. A breath of air glided across his cheek. The searing flash, the screaming sirens, the flashing warning lights, the crush of G-force were gone.

Is this what death feels like?

He tried to move his right arm, but felt a sharp jab of pain in his shoulder. He tried the same with his left. Another stab of agony shot from his elbow. 'I was concussed and completely confused. I had been in the Tornado with an absolute certainty I was going to die.'[3] He blinked, his dark brown eyes catching a star overhead and a distant memory of the missile strike. 'Everything had happened in a fraction of a second. I was losing consciousness . . . I had tried to get my hands towards the ejection handle . . . they wouldn't move . . . then an enormous wind and my last thought of, *Game over, I'm going to die*. It now appeared I hadn't!' Dave twisted painfully and glimpsed the white and orange parachute on the sand behind him. The breeze brushing his face then began to fill the canopy.

Oh God, Robbie must have ejected us!

His navigator's lightning reactions had saved their lives as the Tornado disintegrated. He turned his head to see where his friend was. There was no sign except some nearby footprints in the sand. 'I just presumed Robbie was in far better shape than me and had already started his escape and evasion while I was unconscious on the ground.' Dave tried to withdraw his Personal Locator Beacon (PLB) from its pouch in his life jacket but couldn't move his right arm. The shoulder had dislocated. Again, he tried to move his left. Pain speared up his arm. The elbow joint was sticking out at a distorted angle. The pair had ejected at around 600mph, blasted out of the cockpit to be hit by a force four times greater than the most destructive hurricane. They were lucky to be alive. Waddington rolled onto his right shoulder and it popped partially back into place. Enough to let him get up. 'I had a sense of being totally alone, wondering where Robbie was then realising that, despite my injuries, I needed to get going. Once on my feet,

I didn't feel much pain as long as I didn't move my arms; I was in total shock.'

He touched his cheeks, swollen and wet with blood. 'Although I didn't know it at the time, I had tiny bits of Roland missile warhead splattered in my face, along with pieces of my helmet's Perspex visor and other debris from the jet.' The parachute now ballooned behind him, a trembling day-glo signal in the surrounding darkness. Painfully, Dave released the harness. 'My arms were so weak I couldn't overcome the force of the canopy being inflated so just had to let it blow away across the desert. More importantly, my injuries also meant I couldn't get to my pistol or use the PLB properly either. I was in serious trouble.'

With just a small amount of water, near-useless arms, and still dazed from the missile explosion and high-speed ejection, Dave Waddington set off into the night. A few miles to the east he watched the tracer still arcing into the sky over Tallil.

* * *

Back in Lincolnshire, the bullets had just stopped flying in *Stakeout*, the Richard Dreyfuss cop comedy, when Robbie's teenage children, Kirsty and Scott, heard whistling, and a familiar sound on the front path. It was 11pm. Their mother was out with some neighbours. They were alone at their Coleby home with two friends. Kirsty recognised the sound outside all too well. It was the metallic *click, click, click* of steel-tipped shoes. Her heart sank. Military shoes. Her father had often worn them on the parade ground.

There was a knock at the door. A Wing Commander in full dress uniform. 'We looked up at him; he looked at us. I think we were all somewhat shocked. He clearly wasn't expecting to be faced with four teenagers!'

The RAF officer recovered first. 'Could you tell me where Mrs Stewart is?'

'She's having dinner with friends,' Kirsty replied, giving him directions to the house along the village lane. 'We really felt it was important he got to Mum quickly, although we had no real idea why.' The officer clicked his way back down the path, leaving young Kirsty to close the door. Wide-eyed, she leaned against the kitchen counter. 'It was surreal. We didn't really say anything, but Scott and I knew something must have happened. We just didn't want to put the words out there for fear of making them come true.'[4]

Earlier that afternoon, Tange Stewart had been overwhelmed by the sense that her beloved husband Robbie was in terrible danger. Now at dinner with her neighbours, she still couldn't shake off that feeling of dread. She did her best to hold a normal conversation with the two other couples around the table. The kids were at home, less than 150 yards away. She tried not to keep glancing out of the window. 'My stomach was really knotting up. I just knew something wasn't right.' As the main course was cleared away, the doorbell rang. Her host left the table to answer it. A moment later she returned, and leaned down to whisper in her ear. 'There's an RAF officer in the lounge, Tange.' She paused. 'He needs to speak to you.'

You couldn't be the wife of a fast-jet aviator without knowing exactly what this meant. 'Every military spouse would. There was apprehension and dread. My earlier premonitions were coming true. I had been in turmoil since the afternoon panto in Newark, so in a strange way it was a relief to have an answer. No matter how bad it was.'[5] She made her way to where a man in RAF 'blues' stood waiting. The rings on his sleeve showed his rank. Forgetting her manners, Tange didn't give him the chance to speak first. 'Tell me he's not dead,' she demanded. The Wing Commander looked her straight in the eye. 'Mrs Stewart, I'm sorry to tell you that your husband hasn't returned from his mission over Iraq tonight. There's nothing else that we know at the moment.'

Tange paced around the room, as she had done when Robbie had told her a month ago that he was going back to the warzone. Pacing was her default setting for stress and fear. The officer stood there awkwardly, unsure what to say next. 'It was all such a shock but I had the tiniest glimmer of hope, he hadn't *actually* been able to say they were dead. I held onto that. If no one could confirm Robbie was dead, surely there had to be some hope?' Suddenly, she recalled Robbie's conversation with the children just before he deployed after Christmas. *If anything happens to me, someone in full uniform will arrive at the house with the news ...*

'I have to get home and tell Kirsty and Scott!' She barely had time to register her friends' shock and concern as she ran to the door. 'Sorry for missing dessert and ruining the evening!' As she walked down the lane under the dim light of its single lamp, the crescent moon stopped her in her tracks. *Wherever you are, Robbie, my love, we are all under the same moon together.* 'I didn't know it then, but that thought would repeat itself many, many times over the coming weeks.'

There was no easy way to tell her children. 'Dad's missing ... He didn't come back from his mission.'

Kirsty struggled to take in what was being said. 'I really can't remember much about it all. It was almost like a dream, as though it was happening to someone else and I was watching it unfold.'

People started arriving at the house as the news spread. Tange's dinner-party friends came over, along with the vicar and the officer who had given her the news. They crowded into the living room, where a brass etching of an RAF Vulcan hung on the wood-panelled wall near the stone fireplace. On went the kettle, and endless pots of tea were produced from the kitchen. Tange's mothering instincts now took over. She had to protect the children. But they knew so little about what had happened to Robbie. 'I was in uncharted waters with no idea about what to do or how to react. How long would it go on for? How was I meant to cope? I quickly realised that in reality, and despite the turmoil, I would just have to.'

Kirsty's young mind was already racing. 'I loved reading Second World War and Cold War novels. I was fascinated by spy stories and people working behind enemy lines but I'd also read a lot of interrogation and torture scenes. My brain started heading down a million roads.' As other people in the living room discussed whether he was on the run or had been captured, all Kirsty could think about was her father stranded in enemy territory. She couldn't help herself, and her thoughts turned dark.

Please let him be dead ...

'It seems terrible to think back on it now, but I wanted him to be dead. I was desperately worried and just couldn't bear the thought of him being tortured and interrogated.'

Even amid her darkest fears, 13-year-old Kirsty could have had no concept of the horrors unfolding for her father and his pilot in Iraq.

* * *

The man who had shared a Tornado cockpit with Kirsty's father looked up at the night sky. He picked a star to guide his escape route and headed south towards the Iraq–Saudi border, 140 miles in the distance. Attempting another radio call, he lost his positioning so chose a new star, but a wire fence now blocked his way. With both arms dislocated, there was no way to climb over. Dazed, staggering and weakened, he followed the fence to a busy road. 'I was simply trying to put distance between me and the crash site. After four or five hours, I saw some triple-A coming from an airfield in front of me and thought, *Ah, there must be another airfield around here.*' Exhausted and in pain, he sat and took a swig from a packet of water retrieved from the only leg pocket of his G-suit that had survived the violent ejection. Dawn was approaching. *I have to get out of sight before first light.* He tried to dig a hole but his arms were useless. A sliver of sunshine appeared on the horizon. He had to find somewhere to hide. He remembered the four key words from their downed-aircrew survival course: *Protection. Location. Water. Food.*

He spotted twin 4ft-high oil pipelines nearby and crawled under them. Using his boot heels, he scraped a shallow trench, lay down and activated the emergency locator beacon, 'hoping that any guys flying overhead would hear it'. He attempted another distress call on the radio, fighting the frustration when his ineffectual hands found themselves unable to attach the aerial. Hope of rescue was diminishing. 'I had previously believed that there was the possibility of a mission being launched, helicopters coming in to get me, but when none of my calls were answered, that belief started to fade. I hadn't yet rationalised a long-term plan, only to evade capture for as long as possible.'

It was now around nine hours since they had been blasted out of the sky. Soon his family and fiancée he had recently proposed to would know they had not come back from the mission. 'The thought of my mum and Claire being told was absolutely horrendous; very, very hard for me mentally. I was alive, but they wouldn't know that. Back in England, calls would soon be being made and doors knocked on.'

After despairing at the TV coverage of the war, Dave's mother Berenice Waddington had taken to listening to the radio news at their terraced home in Bolton, a few miles north of Manchester. Late that night of 19 January, the BBC had reported that yet another Tornado had been lost. She took little notice and went to bed; it couldn't possibly be her son. A few hours later she awoke from a fitful sleep. Someone was knocking on the front door.

'Who's that?' Berenice asked her husband, Jack. Their clock told her it was 1.30am. Jack got out of bed, shrugged on his dressing gown and headed down the hall as she sat at the top of the stairs, fearful of what was about to unfold. He opened the door and she could see two RAF officers in smart light-blue uniforms.

'Are you the parents of Flight Lieutenant David Waddington?' one asked.

'Yes,' Jack responded.

'Can we come in?'

Reluctant to move, Berenice watched from her vantage point as they stepped inside. 'I just thought, *Oh no, this is bad ...*' Then she took another sharp breath. 'They had brought our parish priest! I now knew it was *very* bad news.'[6]

They all sat down in the living room. One of the officers said David was missing in action after a mission over Iraq. There was no other information, no indication if he was alive or dead. Sitting in her young son's childhood home, surrounded by pictures of Dave in his RAF uniform, Berenice found the news impossible to take in. 'I was just rocking back and forwards as if in a trance.' Someone rang their son John, a fireman on duty a few miles away, and he rushed back home. Then it dawned on them that no one had told Dave's fiancée, Claire. As they were not married, his parents were his legal 'next of kin'; the only people who could be officially informed. It had gone 2am when Dave's other brother Gerard set off for Claire's home in Cambridgeshire. In the event, a friend from Dave's Squadron at RAF Marham had also been dispatched to deliver the bad news to her.

Berenice and Jack sat staring at the photo of their son. 'There was little we could do as a family. It was like being in a dream, totally unreal. But it was all so very, very real.'

The childhood and military pictures at John Nichol's family home outside Newcastle also gazed down on parents trying to come to terms with the thought that they might never see their son again. The RAF navigator's mother and father had struggled for two days with the unreal news of having their boy 'missing in action'. They were at the centre of a media storm as speculation and comment, much of it ill-informed, raged around them. There were moments of hope. One newspaper reported that the airmen were alive behind enemy lines after a satellite had supposedly picked up their Personal Locator Beacons. It was totally untrue.

There were also moments of utter despair. In one radio broadcast, the Armed Forces Minister Archie Hamilton had all but declared their son dead. 'On the whole it is bad news if we have *not* heard anything about them, and the presumption has to be that they are *not alive*,' the politician told BBC Radio 4.[7] His crisply delivered words were met with disbelief in the Nichol council house in North Shields. John's father had kept his dignity, telling the media camped outside that all they knew was that his son was missing and 'we are keeping as calm as possible'. The headline of their local newspaper, meanwhile, proclaimed: 'NORTH AIRMAN PRESUMED DEAD'.[8]

* * *

Robbie Stewart felt the sun warm his face as it rose over the sand-coloured horizon. He had been unconscious for many hours. He blinked in the light, trying to recall the events of the previous night; the explosion, the ejection. His parachute ruffled in the wind nearby. He breathed in the fresh, early-morning air. *Thank God, I'm alive!* Then the scale of his predicament dawned on him. *Poor Tange and the kids! They've got no idea what's happened to me!* Lying spread-eagled on the desert floor, far from home, Robbie began to cry. 'I had just escaped death by the skin of my teeth and only I knew of my living state. Tears flooded down my face.'

He knew he had to move. Although his back ached badly, it was the lack of movement in his right leg that caused him most concern. He looked down. Blood was seeping through his flying suit. It didn't look good. 'The leg was numb, snapped and sticking out at right angles to my body. I couldn't feel any pain at that point, but the blood clearly indicated that the broken bone had penetrated the skin. It was a very serious problem.' He needed help. His left hand was clutching the PLB, his right the mini flares, and a packet of water was on his chest. Robbie wrongly assumed that his pilot had seen him unconscious and helped out as best he could. *Good old Dave, great lad. He's seen me lying here, put this kit out for me and then made his own escape.*

Robbie turned his head. Fifty yards away, cars and trucks carrying people to work along a busy road. The sudden movement now sent pain searing through his body and he lost consciousness again. 'I kept passing out as intense, almost unimaginable pain pulsed through me. I would later discover that I had a broken shoulder, crushed vertebrae and a leg broken in three places.'

Coming around again, he began to wonder if anyone had actually helped him, or if he had got the kit out himself, despite his appalling injuries. In reality, he had clearly done everything himself at some point during the night, including, incredibly, removing the tight-fitting G-suit. Not an easy operation at the best of times, even without a shattered leg. 'I really felt like there had been someone sitting on my shoulder helping me with the water, radio, flares and the complex task of attaching the PLB battery and aerial, all at night. I knew I couldn't escape, but it was as though God had said, "Robbie, you're going to need these." Especially as, by now, I was in no doubt that if I didn't get help I would die where I lay.'

He started transmitting on the radio but there was no reply on the distress frequencies. Blood continued to flow from his punctured leg and Robbie knew that any medical help would have to come from the very people he had been trying to kill only a few hours earlier. 'Of course, we had heard things on the news before the war about how Saddam was telling people to tear us limb from limb, but I just didn't believe it. I have an innate faith in the decency of people.'

Robbie now put that faith to the test. As a lorry approached he rapidly fired two mini flares into the air. The vehicle stopped and two Iraqi civilians got out. They indicated that the airman should raise his hands in surrender, but Robbie could barely move. The pair approached cautiously, chatting in Arabic. It appeared they were looking for weapons. Robbie painfully pointed to the Walther in its shoulder holster. One man carefully removed the pistol and threw it aside. Then both tried to lift him onto his feet. Robbie screamed in agony. 'The pain from my right leg flopping around stabbed through my body. They put me back on the ground and one guy disappeared while the other took off his head-dress and tied my legs together. Every movement now sparked unbearable bolts of pain.' The first man reappeared with a large tarpaulin and together they gently carried him to what turned out to be a cattle truck with a tailgate and wooden slatted sides. The two men lifted him carefully into the back. One took off his own jacket and eased it under Robbie's head.

The road was relatively smooth and the journey to the nearest military barracks lasted less than an hour. The tailgate dropped and Robbie was lifted down by several young conscripts clad in green uniforms, all sporting imitations of Saddam Hussein's distinctive moustache. 'They were looking on with curiosity at this British flier who was now their prisoner.' The soldiers forced him onto the back seat of a station wagon. A smirking conscript abruptly opened the door and prodded his broken leg. Robbie grimaced, fighting back a scream. 'It was a strange pain, not sharp, just constant and deep-seated. My real fear was that I was now face to face with the people we had been bombing relentlessly. All I could hope was that they wouldn't kill me. Still, there was nothing I could do about it. I certainly couldn't run away!' The conscript jabbed at his leg again. The shattered bones grated against each other. 'To his delight, I now screamed out in agony and started to vomit because of the pain.'

Grinning, the Iraqi closed the door, satisfied at his success.

They drove through the town along potholed roads. Robbie vomited again as his leg flopped and the broken bones scraped beneath the skin. An hour later, they arrived at a bunker with camouflage netting over the entrance. The Iraqis pulled him out of the car by his shoulders, allowing his shattered leg to bounce across the tarmac then kerb. He screamed again.

Robbie was blindfolded and taken to a room where another prisoner was being brutally interrogated. 'In many ways, this was worse than if it was happening to me, because your mind plays tricks. It sounded like he was being beaten half to death. It was terrible. He was saying, "Oh don't, DON'T! Stop!" It was awful to endure and my imagination ran wild. *That's going to be me next. Can I take it?*' The man was eventually removed and Robbie knew it was his turn. He was placed on a table with his feet towards the interrogator, who he could now see through the gap in his blindfold. 'He had a really thin face and, unusually, no moustache. He started asking me questions, but quickly became frustrated with me refusing to answer. So he began prodding at my broken leg, moving it around, telling me he could easily break the other leg. I was screaming in pain every time he jabbed me, desperate not to answer his questions. I knew it was going to get worse but luckily the pain became too much and I simply passed out.'

* * *

As Robbie suffered what he knew was going to be his severest test, the comrades he had left back in Bahrain underwent intense scrutiny from the press. As more Tornados were lost, the media interest had rapidly grown. With a number of bombers already confirmed missing from Muharraq, the journalists were eager to get the crews' reactions. An RAF press officer ushered a handful of reporters onto the airbase and lined up some of the airmen who had been at the forefront of the action. Without any media training, the fliers, standing in front of their Tornados, spoke freely.[9]

Pablo Mason had led the first daylight formation which attacked Ar Rumaylah airbase on the first day, when John Nichol and John Peters had been shot down. Dressed in his sand-coloured flying suit and green rollneck jumper, and sporting a tremendous 'Biggles-like' handlebar moustache, Pablo provided them with some highly charged commentary. 'There is a constant awareness that in a few seconds' time you might not exist.' Already visibly fighting to retain his composure, he went on: 'You train to control your emotions when it really matters ...' He had finally broken down in tears. 'I'm responsible for my whole crew. You feel guilty that you have survived and they haven't. We work together, play together and live together. Hopefully, we won't die together.'

Perhaps aware that emotions needed to be tempered, Nigel Risdale, the pilot who had helped plan the first missions, tried to put the aircrews' risk into perspective. 'It's equally hazardous driving around the M25 motorway every day,' he suggested. 'Thousands are killed on Britain's roads each year, but when one aircraft is lost it is news.' Risdale was one of the Squadron's most highly respected fliers, and renowned for his coolness under stress. Speaking with a sand-coloured Tornado fin visible behind him, he added: 'You've survived one sortie, but you know that calming yourself down is important so you can get to sleep, knowing that you've got another task to do in ten hours' time.'

Other aviators had also quickly parked their distress at the losses and wanted to even the score. 'Some on the Squadron were extremely angry,' recalled navigator Paddy Teakle. 'The losses motivated them. They wanted to take the fight to Saddam. This was real and they wanted payback for comrades being shot down.'[10] Mark Paisey, the pilot who had flown alongside Peters and Nichol on their mission, was also candid with his feelings after the Tornado's first ever, and never to be repeated, low-level daylight attack. 'I was in tears when I got back – we had lost our wingman and friends,' he told the journalists. 'At the moment, I'm going through the full range of emotions, from elation right down to dread and fear of dying.'

Paisey also articulated what was going through the minds of most airmen who faced a return to the battlefield. 'Next time, it's going to be harder, because you're aware it could be you . . .'

* * *

For Dave Waddington, the words 'it could be you' had become an uncomfortable reality. Badly injured and on the run in southern Iraq, he knew his chances of escape were diminishing. After scraping out a thin trench around dawn, he had managed to lie down and sleep despite the pain from his dislocated shoulder and elbow. The screech of large birds feeding from stagnant water nearby penetrated his slumber. The sound of gunfire then shook him fully awake. Bullets started pinging into the muddy sand just a few yards from where he lay. 'It was totally unreal, not something I had ever expected to encounter. It was at this point I began to realise I could very easily die.' He glanced up from his meagre cover. Two men in green military trousers and civilian coats, one young, one old, loosed off more rounds as they advanced towards him. 'As they got to within about 30 yards of my position, I really wondered if they were going to kill me.'

The Iraqis kept their distance, gesturing for him to raise his hands. With both arms dislocated it was impossible, so instead he started shouting, '*Salaam alaikum*' – 'peace be upon you'. 'It seemed odd given that I'd just been bombing their country, but it was all the Arabic I knew.'

The older Iraqi tried to soothe the younger as he yelled aggressively at the enemy invader. They gestured again for Dave to put his hands up. 'I thought, this was going to be such a stupid way to die! Just because I couldn't get my arms in the air. It was all getting very, very tense.' They eventually stopped firing and moved closer. Dave pointed to the Walther pistol in its shoulder holster which he had still been unable to reach. The younger man then began manhandling him, using the rifle butt to push him around. Again, he was calmed by the older Iraqi. Dave wondered what his fate might be. 'What was I going to go through before it ended? Being alive was a bit of a bonus as only a few hours earlier I had thought I had died. So there was still hope. At the back of the mind, however, there was also the thought that in the not-too-distant future, perhaps I might wish I really was dead.'

The pair marched Dave off at gunpoint. Astonishingly, he was soon back on the outskirts of Tallil. He now realised that during his night evasion, because of his concussion he had completed a long U-turn and ended up on the other side of the airbase. He was taken to some low buildings close to the runway he had so recently been attacking and dragged down into a pit. 'It was 7ft deep, with sides that sloped in. There were a dozen Iraqis all with rifles staring down at me. It was all very menacing. I thought, *God, what's going to happen here?*' The soldiers stepped down and searched him. 'They pretty much stripped me of everything of value and just left me with my flying suit and boots.' He was left with an older man with no teeth and a wrinkled, sunburned face who took his time searching, eventually finding the gold sovereigns the others had missed. 'His face lit up, looking like he'd won the lottery!'

As Dave was driven from the base he spotted what looked like a baked-bean can on three legs by the side of the road. It was one of the JP233 anti-personnel mines dropped by a Tornado and designed to explode if disturbed by any repair crews. *Shit! If that goes off we'll all be killed!* He pushed himself back into the seat between the two guards 'so their bodies might protect me from the blast and shrapnel if it detonated'. They pulled up at a military camp in the nearby town of Nasiriyah where a huge group of soldiers wearing red berets gathered around the vehicle. 'I was absolutely terrified. If I was going to be lynched, it was going to happen now. It felt like I was a serial killer being taken into court while an angry mob waited outside. There was a lot of noise, jostling and shouted commands. Then I was shoved back in the car and driven to a nearby medical facility.'

Dave was placed on a treatment table where a medic began digging bits of shrapnel out of his face. 'At one stage they were going to give me an anaesthetic, because my face was in absolute agony, but my military guard stopped them. I began to wonder why they might need to avoid giving me pain-suppressing drugs . . .' A medic grabbed his dislocated left arm, put his knee where the elbow was dislocated and levered it back into position. 'It was incredibly painful and I groaned loudly, but he just looked down at me and hissed, "Be a man!" It was all deeply unpleasant.'

'They cleaned up my face and plastered up my dislocated elbow. I was beginning to get really worried. I had no doubt I'd be tortured; there was an inevitability about it. The easy thing would have been to tell them what they wanted to know straight away. But doing the "right thing" was important to me. Even though I knew what that meant in reality.' As they drove towards Baghdad, Dave's arm became excruciatingly painful. The plaster cast that the Iraqi medics had put around his left elbow was so tight that it had restricted the blood flow. They stopped at another medical centre where a female doctor cut off part of the cast. Just before leaving, she edged closer to him so the guards couldn't see her, then, slipping something in his pocket, whispered quietly in his ear: 'For when you need them, Mr David.' 'I later found out it was a strip of fifteen painkillers. It was a remarkable act of kindness and really incredible bravery. She was risking her own safety to help me; I was truly indebted to her.'

* * *

The pain Robbie Stewart was enduring under interrogation had already caused him to pass out a number of times. Returning to consciousness, he squinted under his blindfold as the Iraqi interrogator began prodding his fractured leg again. Despite the intense pain, he still refused to respond.

'Mr Stewart! You're not answering our questions.' His tormentor's tone changed. 'If you continue, somebody else will come!'

The man left the room. When he returned, he spoke in a deeper voice, pretending to be a different, more threatening interrogator. But Robbie could see it was the same person through the gap in his blindfold. 'It was quite funny really; a ludicrous situation! But, unfortunately, he had also brought in his mate carrying a large pole with a ball attached.

'Now I was really scared. There was a lot of fear; a sense of anticipation about what was to come. I knew things were going to get worse, but there was nothing I could do about it. I was just waiting for it to happen. He started laying about me with this pole, repeatedly beating me across my body and legs.' As the blows rained down, Robbie fell in and out of consciousness once more. 'I was in such incredible pain from my leg I doubled up and vomited again into my hanky while trying to keep it off my uniform. Ridiculously, I was still trying to keep clean in this appalling situation! The pain was strange. It came on so quickly and was so powerful, that I simply passed out. Then when I came round they started again. I passed out so many times, it was a way of escaping.'

Despite the ordeal, in his mind Robbie continued the fight. 'I have no idea how many hours it went on for but I was still going through my options, trying to resist. I was determined to try to hold out as long as possible and not give anything away that could harm others. Of course, every time I passed out they had to stop and wait for me to come round before they could start again, which also helped prolong my resistance.

'At some point they told me with great glee that they had captured Dave. I was so relieved. Obviously, I hoped he had escaped, but hearing he was at least confirmed alive was a great boost to morale, better than any painkilling tablet they could have given me.'

The Iraqis knew Robbie had a great vulnerability and didn't waste their time. The interrogator finally wrapped his hands around the airman's shattered leg and began twisting it, grating the broken bones together. 'The pain was agonising and I began to realise that if I didn't say something, I could easily die where I lay, or at least be maimed for life.' He lapsed into grateful unconsciousness again but when he came round, Robbie was ready for the question.

'What aircraft were you flying?'

'Tornado.'

'It did not seem a big giveaway as we had just parked one in the sand next to their base! They clearly knew what we had been flying.'

More questions were pelted at him. Robbie's mind went back to the *Sunday Times* article that had infuriated him as he tried to relax back at his village home in Lincolnshire on the first Sunday of the New Year. It had only been a couple of weeks earlier, but now seemed like a lifetime ago. The article had detailed what the Tornados might be doing, aircraft numbers and basic capabilities. *That's what I'm going to give them.* He also recalled CNN naming airfields that missions had already been launched from. He gave them the same information. The Iraqis accepted it all. Plus a few fibs. 'I said we were flying very low at 500ft and that we tanked at 20,000ft.' None of the details were technical and he hoped he hadn't given the Iraqis anything they couldn't find elsewhere.

The questions finally came to an end. Exhausted and in great pain, Robbie was driven to a hospital. They cut off all his clothing while a softly spoken doctor asked some medical questions. 'He said I'd broken my collarbone, probably had a spinal compression injury as well as my obvious leg break. He directed the radiographer to take X-rays of my leg, shoulder and back.' While most fliers usually took off their wedding rings before a sortie, Robbie had kept his in place. 'Mine was part of me, so I had to wear it.' The hospital assistant gently wound a cord around its inside and began to ease it off. He saw Robbie looking at him. 'It's okay,' he said reassuringly. 'You'll be getting this back.'

Robbie was wheeled carefully into the operating theatre and told to breathe deeply into a mask.

'I slipped into unconsciousness for the second night.'

CHAPTER NINE

THE MISSION FROM HELL

20 JANUARY

The mental strain of flying nightly into the inferno, not knowing if you would come out the other side, was taking its toll across the Tornado force's three bases. The RAF now had around 150 aircraft – fighters, bombers, helicopters, tankers, transport and surveillance – in the Gulf, but the Tornado bombers were carrying out the most dangerous assignments under the most intense pressure.[1] Jerry Witts, in charge of the Dhahran Tornado detachment, believed it was plain common sense to share the stress as evenly as possible. 'It became blindingly obvious to me that we should have a plan to pace people. Also, to give the crews a chance to know when they'd be required to go, when they could psych themselves up and when they could relax as much as possible.'[2]

His thoughts were echoed by the Detachment Commander of the RAF Jaguar bombers operating alongside the Tornados from Muharraq, who recognised they could all be in it for the long haul. 'I couldn't ask my pilots to fly more than one sortie a day. And perhaps every fifth day, they should have a day off. The engineers also went on two equal shifts to fix the aircraft and to bomb them up.'[3] The Jaguars had largely been utilising medium-level dive-bomb attacks, avoiding the very worst of the low-level triple-A barrage, though they'd had some very close calls with the more powerful Iraqi systems capable of shelling at their operating heights of between 10,000 and 20,000 feet. And the Tornado F3 air defence crews, patrolling at around 25,000 feet, were also having to deal with Iraqi SAMs targeting them.

But for the Tornado bomber crews assembling at Dhahran, Tabuk and Muharraq for their next combat missions, there was an increasingly pervasive sense that some would not return. And that if they did survive *this* sortie, the odds were they'd catch it on the next one. Or the one after that.

Robbie Stewart's colleagues at Muharraq were certainly contemplating their immediate future. They had now lost three Tornados in as many days. Nige Risdale had kept his thoughts to himself when he overheard someone mention that Waddington and Stewart had gone down. *Oh no, there's another one! It's becoming like the Lancaster bombers in the Second World War! More aircraft, more friends lost every night.* He glanced around at the sixteen aviators clambering into their flight gear in preparation for the next dawn raid. 'I wondered who among our eight-ship would not come back from this trip.'

He knew he had to push away the dark thoughts as swiftly as possible. 'It was a momentary acknowledgement of what we were involved in, but with my single-minded psyche, it was quickly compartmentalised. My brain went back to what we were about to do.'[4] He glanced across at his friend and fellow pilot Nick Heard, who was also reflecting silently on the news of the recent loss. *Perhaps it might be* my *luck that runs out tonight?*[5]

But the attack plan for this latest raid had been well thought out; perfected by what the Tornado force had learned after three intense days of war. An hour before dawn on 20 January, the RAF would attack Al Jarrah, the Iraqi 'super-base' south-east of Baghdad, which housed three squadrons of Su-22 fighter-bombers and a squadron of air defence MiG-23 fighters. Gordon Buckley, one of the 15 Squadron Flight Commanders, knew they couldn't keep following the same attack profiles. 'I was struggling to sleep; the whole issue was playing on my mind. The preliminary attacks by the Americans, designed to *suppress* the Iraqi defences, were in reality stirring up a hornet's nest. It seemed crazy to be flying into that triple-A night after night. There had to be a better way. The risks were immense; there was so much fire and exploding lead being hurled into the air that the odds were against us continuing to get through unscathed.'

The Tornado force had to stop coming in at the tail-end of a mass attack that had already galvanised the enemy defences. Instead of being the *last* jets through, Buckley wanted them to be the *only* jets through. He believed a 'small, discrete formation package' would give them the best chance of getting in and out undetected. Discussing the problems with Paddy Teakle and Nige Risdale, they struck on the idea of sending two JP233 jets through as a surprise first attack, followed by four Tornados, each carrying eight 1,000-pounders, executing a loft attack, lobbing thirty-two bombs onto the triple-A positions and blasting open a corridor for the last two JP233 jets. The senior crews then presented the idea to the Tornado Detachment Commander, John Broadbent, who succeeded in getting headquarters approval.

In the small hours of the night, the eight-ship lined up on Muharraq's runway. Their target lay 100 miles south-east of the Iraqi capital, some considerable distance from Bahrain. They would have to fly more than an hour westwards, then cross the border and head north-east at low level for another hour before attacking the target. It was a four-hour, 1,600-mile round trip. Air-to-air refuelling along the tanker trail was going to be key.

The challenge of heading once again into the fiercest enemy fire was worsened by the probability of heavy cloud and severe turbulence along their route – and things began to go awry even before take-off. The crew of one Tornado at the rear of the formation had an engine problem and could not select reheat. There was no way they could get off the ground. The seven remaining aircraft climbed to 12,000ft for their rendezvous with the tankers. The meteorological wizards had not been wrong. They entered the heavy cloud to be tossed and bucked by powerful updraughts and downdraughts.

As he approached the Victor's right wing, Nick Heard fought to keep his lurching jet in position. He inched towards the mouth of the refuelling hose, snaking through the darkness a few feet ahead. 'I really felt under intense pressure. I was burning fuel, while also using up my allotted time to take on the fuel I needed.' Suddenly they entered clearer skies. He touched the throttle, propelling the Tornado's probe on the right-hand side of the cockpit towards the funnel. And then crunched straight through the flat metal plates that held the neck of the basket open and provided its aerodynamic stability. *Crap! This is really going to mess things up.* 'If you spoked the basket there was a real danger that some of the metal connections might break off and be ingested into your own engine, which could cause a catastrophic failure.'

These fragments being sucked through the blades could generate the destructive force of shrapnel, and cause the engine to self-destruct. In peacetime, 'spoking' would force an immediate return to base. But peacetime happened in another life. Nick carefully eased back the power, praying the whole basket wouldn't tear away and remain clamped on the end of his probe. Luckily, it emerged cleanly and the engine readings encouraged him to believe all was well. He manoeuvred through the darkness to the tanker's left wing, queuing behind Nige Risdale, who was experiencing his own dramas in the other JP233-armed jet.

He'd been three-quarters full when the Victor disappeared into a violent cumulonimbus thundercloud. 'It was like being on high-speed dodgems at the fairground, but on a corrugated surface rather than a nice smooth arena. And then being constantly battered from all sides by the other cars.' Nige dabbed on the reheat but couldn't keep the probe in the basket. 'The turbulence was throwing us around, the tanker around and the basket around. It was like trying to get cooked spaghetti up a jumping cat's arse as it runs away from you.' Another huge jolt pushed them away from the nozzle. With a soft hand on the stick, Nige nudged the power up and the probe towards the rim of the basket, then pushed it home. Once full, he made way for the next in line.

Having fouled up the right-wing hose, Nick Heard was keener than ever to get his tanks filled in a window of relative stability, and this time he engaged on the first attempt. But with the tanker now down to one conduit, it was going to be a struggle to cycle the other two aircraft of their formation through. His navigator was having similar concerns. 'I really don't think we can get this mission done without one of us going back to the tanker behind us to take on fuel.' Nick frowned. That wasn't a pleasant prospect. The rear tanker was 10 miles behind them, in total darkness and, odds on, in the same heavy cloud.

As lead crew for the seven remaining aircraft, Nige Risdale and John Broadbent were the refuelling priority. They had to top up again before heading into enemy territory.

Nick Heard was filling his tanks when Broadbent instructed him to go in search of the Victor at their rear. 'Bloody hell!' Nick muttered, disconnecting from his precious hose. 'I now had to turn out of the tanker trail and fly against the stream, making sure I was separated laterally from the oncoming aircraft, then try to reacquire another Victor in total darkness! Then I would have to join *their* formation and work my way around the rear Tornados to take on fuel. I was really thinking, *Things are not going well tonight.*' Without the aid of any night-vision equipment, it was a severe test. Even for the most experienced of crews.

The second Victor's situation was no easier, as Gordon Buckley was discovering. The wind was battering the hose so violently it was almost impossible to hook on. One of his formation did manage to connect, but radioed seconds later to report that fuel would not transfer. The fault could not be rectified, so returning to base was the only option. The eight-ship which had started the mission was now reduced to six.

After turning back, Nick Heard threaded his way past Gordon

Buckley's formation to the rear tanker's basket. With their runway denial munitions, his JP233-armed jet was a priority. He inched his Tornado forward, riding the turbulence, and pushed the probe home first time. 'Able to relax slightly for a brief moment, I was suddenly struck by the fact that it was a Saturday evening. Back at home, people were watching the football, enjoying a drink at the pub, and we were stuck on this tanker bouncing around in the darkness, the reward for which was being shot at in the very near future.'

In the meantime, three jets were still battling to refuel from one hose trailing behind the leading Victor. When time ran out for the third, John Broadbent reluctantly ordered it back to base. The eight-ship was now down to five. Nick Heard eventually eased away from the rear tanker with brimful tanks and dived into the black void to catch up with Risdale and the number three jet armed with 1,000lb bombs, already descending towards the border.

Gordon Buckley knew that refuelling was becoming increasingly dangerous. And the clock was ticking. His formation had to take enough fuel on board to reach the target at their allotted time. One crew was really struggling. 'The more times he tried unsuccessfully to connect with the tanker, the greater was the chance of him spoking and damaging his aircraft, perhaps fatally. I made the difficult decision to send them home.'

The eight-ship was now down to four.

Since Gordon had come up with the mission plan, he was determined to see it through. Summoning every last iota of skill he'd acquired from nearly 2,000 Tornado flying hours, he gently coaxed his aircraft through the tumult and into close formation with the giant Victor only a few feet away. A huge jolt threw him off the connection. Seconds after that, the same thing happened again. Time was running out. He knew if he didn't stay the distance, he'd be off the raid too. As the Tornado and the tanker bucked and swayed through the cloud banks, he managed to hook onto the hose for a third time.

But his relief was short-lived.

The skies suddenly cleared – to reveal the lead Victor dead ahead.

A Tornado practises the 'loft – or toss – attack' at a coastal weapons' range. With the target accurately identified by the navigator, the system releases the bombs as the aircraft climbs steeply from low-level so that they are 'thrown' forward, arcing towards the target.

Mike Toft's formation sitting on a Tornado armed with laser-guided bombs. The bomb symbols on the nose denote the tally of missions the aircraft has flown.
From left: Chris Lunt, Pablo Mason (standing), Colin Ayton, Gary Stapleton, Bob Brownlow & Jack Calder (the crew who replaced John Peters and John Nichol after they were shot down), Mike Toft, Mark Paisey.

A test drop of the JP233 runway denial weapon in 1983. The cratering munitions can be seen deploying from the large rear pod then descending by parachute. The anti-personnel mines can be seen spraying from the front pod.

RAF groundcrew training in full Nuclear Biological Chemical protective equipment in the run up to the war.

Kev Weeks, left, and his pilot Garry Lennox, centre, planning a mission at the Tabuk detachment in the run up to the conflict. They are both carrying pistols in shoulder holsters. Sadly, both would be killed during the war.

Mal Craghill, left, and his pilot Mike Warren about to head out on another mission. Mal is wearing a life jacket which contains much of his survival equipment, including his Personal Locator Beacon. Mal and Mike would eventually drop the RAF's last bombs of the war.

Anti-Aircraft fire lights up the sky over Baghdad on 17 January 1991. The triple-A over the Iraqi airfields the Tornados initially attacked was considerably more intense than this.

Mike Heath, OC 20 Squadron, at Tabuk.

Pete Batson, Mike Heath's pilot, preparing for a flight in late 1990. They would both have to eject from their Tornado in the early days of the war after a technical failure.

A smiling Steve Hicks in his navigator's seat in the Tornado he shared with Rupert Clark. Sadly, Steve would be killed during the war.

Kirsty, Tange and Scott Stewart meet Her Majesty the Queen in the Officers' Mess bar at RAF Marham in February 1990. At this point, they did not know if Robbie was alive or dead.

Chris Ankerson meets Diana, Princess of Wales, at RAF Bruggen. It was the morning after she had tearfully asked her friend, 'am I a wife or a widow?' It would be many weeks before she would know the answer.

Some of the delighted RAF POWs descend from the Red Cross aircraft on landing at Riyadh airbase in Saudi Arabia after being released from captivity. From top, John Nichol, Rupert Clark, Dave Waddington, Robbie Stewart.

John Nichol re-visits one of the cells where he was held in Baghdad during a visit in 2000 to make a TV documentary. The writing from countless previous prisoners is clearly visible on the pockmarked walls.

The site near Tallil airbase in Iraq where Dave Waddington and Robbie Stewart's Tornado hit the ground at high speed. Wreckage can be seen scattered around the crater and the Boz chaff and flare pod is clearly visible on the left edge, with live flares still primed ready for use.

John Nichol, right, next to Rupert Clark on the VC10 transport aircraft which took the newly liberated prisoners to the medical facilities in Cyprus. Bruises from the attack by guards at Abu Ghraib prison are still visible on his face. Sitting opposite from left are Gordon Buckley, Chris Lunt and Nick Heard, who were part of the team which volunteered to escort the POWs to safety.

A single Tornado races across the desert at high speed and at ultra low-level, probably below fifty feet, during a training sortie before the war.

Gordon's tanker plunged into an emergency dive to avoid collision. His probe snapped out of the basket yet again, and the Tornado was presented with a new and drastic threat. 'The one place you must never be when tanking is above the wing line because the aerodynamic flow from the huge tanker will disrupt your own airflow. Which is precisely what happened to me – the aircraft controls went completely mushy.'

Gordon pulled back the throttles, the wing dropped and the altimeter spun like a Catherine wheel. 'I had absolutely no control of my aircraft and could only watch as it rolled left and then plunged earthwards, losing about 6,000ft.' Fighting for control, he finally managed to level it out and climbed back to rejoin the Victor. 'I gave the pilot a piece of my mind and told him to keep it steady this time! I had a final stab with the probe and basket going all over the place. I don't know how, but I finally got in; it wasn't skill, just pure luck.'

With the Tornado finally latched on, the tanker crew elected to head north. It would allow them to take on more fuel before descending to the target. But it also brought the danger zone of the Iraqi border ever closer. The plan had been to devastate Al Jarrah with a series of timed strikes by eight Tornados. Now, only three aircraft – two armed with JP233s and one with 1,000-pounders – were attacking ahead. Substantially behind them, Gordon and his navigator Paddy Teakle were left contemplating whether it made sense to make a solo dash into Iraq now they no longer had any JP233 aircraft to protect. They decided to press on. 'We had a mission and we were determined to complete it. While we would not help the attackers *that* night, if we destroyed some triple-A positions with our own 1,000-pounders, it might help others visiting the same target in the future.'

Paddy Teakle agreed. 'We decided to kill some of those gun emplacements so they wouldn't have the same intense defences next time the airfield was attacked.'[6]

As they sped over the border, an AWACS operator asked them to overfly a position where it was believed a downed American crew had ejected. They didn't hesitate. Fellow coalition fliers might be in mortal danger. Good friends had been in the same boat. Burning precious fuel they could not spare, they orbited the site, eventually turning on their aircraft lights to show their presence to any downed fliers. Seconds later their RHWR warned them that an enemy radar was on to them. It was probably coincidental, but Gordon wasn't taking any chances. With no sign of the US crew, he flicked off the lights and pushed the throttles forward, speeding up to 550mph for the dash to Al Jarrah.

The three leading Tornados had already turned sharply north-east. The target was a fraction over 200 miles ahead. Their TOT was an hour before sunrise. Nick Heard hoped the front pair would get over the airfield before the enemy gunners had a chance to open fire. This was his third operational mission and the exhilaration of combat was wearing thin. Everything was quiet as they began the final run in. *Maybe our luck is in*, Nick thought, as they sped 200ft above the desert floor. They were thirty seconds from Al Jarrah when the triple-A turned night into day. 'Bollocks,' Nick muttered. The all-too-familiar barrage of multi-coloured exploding lights blossomed around the target. 'For some reason they seemed to know where we were coming from this time. Worse, the triple-A was not only intense, it was now angled downwards instead of spraying straight up. It seemed to be aimed right at us.'

The Iraqis had changed their cannon trajectory to catch aircraft attacking at low level. Had this been triggered by information gleaned during interrogation of their captured friends? For a moment Nick was struck by how much it resembled the classic sequence in the *Dam Busters* film, when Lancaster bombers flew low over the dams into the teeth of seemingly impregnable German gunfire, before dropping their 'bouncing bombs'. He had just a little sense of the fear his forebears must have faced as streams of green and red tracer fire curved towards them through the night sky. He pushed himself against his ejection seat, gripping the controls. 'Triple-A flew past our ears as we headed in, still some distance from the target. It was awful. Really bad. I just thought, *Oh BUGGER!*'

A mile or so to Heard's left, Nige Risdale's hopes of a quiet night had also been dashed. 'The air defences at Al Jarrah were more sophisticated than the other airfields and for a third time we entered a flak firestorm on a wing and a prayer. I was convinced that the barrage was better aimed and much more threatening than anything we had experienced before.' Twenty seconds out, he deselected the autopilot and manually dipped the Tornado to head in at 180ft for the JP233 release. Gunfire rattled past the cockpit as he focused on flying diagonally across the runway ahead.

Seconds later he felt the jarring reports of the runway-cratering munitions and anti-personnel mines shooting out from the giant containers beneath their feet. 'It seemed to take a long time on this one! I could feel every single submunition come out slowly, rather than the almost machine-gun rattle I recalled from the first runs.'

Nick Heard took his Tornado through the heart of the barrage, leaving a trail of gently descending but deadly parachutes. 'We popped out the other side unscathed and couldn't quite believe our luck. We had done it again and survived! But as we completed our post-target checks, Rob, my navigator, piped up that we were now below minimum fuel to get back to the tanker with enough reserves in case the problems of the inbound flight were repeated. He jettisoned the now empty external tanks, which meant that with the weapons gone too, we were in a relatively "clean" jet apart from the Boz and Sky Shadow pods and the Sidewinder missiles.' Their aircraft was now far more aerodynamic, and would burn considerably less fuel on the egress.

Gordon Buckley and Paddy Teakle were closing in for their own, now solo, attack. Their dramatic exchanges were recorded on the cockpit cassette navigation system as they headed through the darkness towards the thundering gunfire.[7]

RRRrrrRRRrrrRRRrrr.
Their RHWR radar warner screeched a warning that a SAM system was looking at them ...

Paddy: *Turning in three minutes, avoiding the SAM 3 site.*
             Heading 350.
Gordon: *Roger.*

Paddy: *Head in for the fix.*
Teakle was now head-down in the cockpit, concentrating on the
radar to update the navigation system.
AWACS: *Choctaw, picture clear.*
Using the codename of a Native American tribe, the AWACS
operator told them no enemy aircraft were in the air.

Paddy: *Crossing all those roads, railroads and rivers now.*
Gordon: *There's a lot of movement down there, do we come
            back this way?*
Paddy: *No. We go west of here.*
Gordon: *Good. Stepping the height down and speeding up.
            How's the fuel?*
Paddy: *We're running on [minimum] fuel. We'll have to punch the
            under-wing [tanks] off in about 1,000 kilos' [of fuel] time.*
They had the bare minimum to complete the mission and get
back to the tanker. They, too, would need to jettison the empty
external tanks.

Gordon: *How far away is the target now?*
Paddy: *We're hitting it in eight minutes. We're about 60
            miles south, at the moment.*
Gordon: *Good. I wonder what aircrew were down. Makes
            you wonder, doesn't it?*
Paddy: *Yep. I'm going head in for the pre-target fix. I'll use it
            as a confidence check [of the navigation system].*
AWACS: *Choctaw, picture clear.*
Paddy: *Fix is spot on.*
Gordon: *Roger.*
RRRrrrRRRrrrRRRrrr.
The SAM radar warning sounded again.

Paddy: *Target is at your 11 o'clock, 35 miles. The rest of the
            guys are approaching [the target].*
Gordon: *Setting up the escape heading of 255 degrees.*

Paddy: *Turning shortly, and pushing the speed up.*
Gordon: *When are the others on target?*
Paddy: *About thirty seconds.*
Gordon: *They're going to make the defenders really annoyed*
              before we get there!
Paddy: *Yep. Turning shortly. [Heading] 335. The fuel checks*
              at 5,200 kilos.
Gordon: *There goes the triple-A.*
Paddy: *Visual.*

'The first lot of bombs going off really did stimulate the triple-A,' Paddy recalled. 'It wasn't like the first couple of nights; it was now aimed, weaving around the heights we were flying. They were getting cleverer.'

RRRrrrRRRrrrRRRrrr.
The radar warner continued sounding its message.
Gordon   *There's the JP [JP233 weapons] going.*
Buckley could see the weapons from the Tornados ahead of them exploding.
Paddy: *Yep.*
Gordon: *There go the second lot [of JP233s]. Where are the*
              thousand-pounders?
Paddy: *In thirty seconds.*
AWACS: *Choctaw, picture clear.*
Gordon: *Boom, boom, boom!*

Coming in not far behind the third jet, Buckley had a good view of the first 1,000lb attack. 'The sight of the bombs exploding mid-air was shocking to the senses, but amazingly the gunfire did not diminish. I was expecting to see this "hole" in the triple-A as the guns were destroyed but there was nothing, no change at all. I now realised that *we* were going to have to attack into the same maelstrom.'

Paddy: *Okay, speeding up. Use your burners. Low loft*
              selected. Marking the bridge.

Teakle told Buckley to increase speed for the sharp, upward climb required before lofting the bombs. He ran through the target offsets, locating and marking them on the radar, ensuring the weapons system was as accurate as possible.

Gordon: *Switches live. Low loft light's on.*
Paddy: *Good mark on the second offset, going offset three.*
Gordon: *Speed 600 knots. Maximum dry power.*
Using the reheat well before the target, their speed was now nearing 700mph.
Gordon: *How is it on time to go?*
Paddy: *Looks good. Fifty-nine seconds to run.*
Gordon: *Looks like we're here, mate.*
Paddy: *We are not here!*

Already at the very core of the barrage of gunfire, Buckley couldn't believe the flak was so intense, so far out. 'We were at 180ft and there was triple-A coming up at us in droves, flashing lights whistling all around the canopy; it was an astonishing experience. I kept saying to Paddy, "We must be here, we need to pull up now!" He kept saying, "No, we're not there yet, keep going!" It seemed suicidal, going against everything I had trained to do in my RAF career. I was about to pull the Tornado right up into the teeth of their gunfire. At that moment I truly thought I was going to die.'

Paddy: *Forty seconds. I know the triple-A looks close.*
            You're all right. Thirty-five seconds to go.
Gordon: *Okay . . .*
Paddy: *Thirty seconds to run . . . [pause] . . . Pulling in five,*
            four, three, two, one. PULL!

The Tornado soared into the night sky. 'The barrage passed below and above us,' Teakle said. 'I could see machine-gun fire and 23mm. There was light everywhere, like we were inside a Christmas tree.' At around 1,500ft, their bombs released and began a graceful arc towards the Iraqi gun positions. The Tornado was now high and very slow. More warning sirens sounded in the cockpit. Buckley initiated the challenging loft recovery to get the aircraft back to low level.

Paddy: *Bombs all gone. It's going off all around us! There go the bombs.*

Heading away from the target, Teakle sensed the eight massive blasts over the triple-A emplacements as he monitored his instruments.

Paddy: *Height is 3,000 feet, run out heading 255. In the recovery.*

Gordon Buckley had the Tornado tipped well over on its left wing, nearly inverted, banking hard, turning and descending. Failure to recover now would lead to one thing only – the ground.

Paddy: *Jettisoning the under-wing tanks. Right, they've gone. In the descent, back down to low level, passing 1,500ft. Don't look out! Just fly the recovery.*

Pilots had to fly the recovery profile solely on their instruments, totally ignoring any potentially confusing external visual clues. Paddy was a highly experienced Qualified Weapons Instructor and had taught new pilots the drill many times. He knew how disorientating it could be. Especially at night. The manoeuvre had cost the lives of a number of Tornado aircrew. Now, in darkness and under heavy fire, Paddy felt his own aircraft plummet towards the desert floor.

Gordon: *Triple-A is still going off around us!*
Paddy: *Don't look out, mate! Just fly the plane. We're pass-ing 700 feet, and still going down. Easy, EASY!*

Audio warnings continued to fill the cockpit.

Paddy: *Start levelling off, mate! We've 300 feet to go.*

The Tornado was still heading fast towards the ground. When Teakle had yelled, 'Don't look out!' Buckley knew it was already too late. He was totally disorientated by the gunfire which now surrounded them. 'Triple-A was flying around the cockpit. Straight green lines, red flashing dots, some going straight past, some spiralling as the operators simply waved their guns blindly in the air. I felt as though I was at the heart of a firework display. I completely lost all sense of awareness of which way the jet was pointing, or where the ground was. It was like being in a sparkling kaleidoscope at night. I had no idea if I was going up or down. Luckily Paddy had taught this loft manoeuvre to students so he could talk me out of it. If I had been with someone less experienced ... well ... it simply doesn't bear thinking about ...'

Their jet bottomed out, descending through 100ft towards the desert floor, a second or two before impact.[8] Teakle's urgent warning and cool head had saved them. On the audio recording of those moments, their rapid breathing dominates the cockpit as they climb away from the ground.

Paddy: *Wings level now, 150 feet, ease the height up,*
            Buckers. That was bloody close!
Gordon: *I don't ever want to do that again. That was awful!*
Paddy: *We were right up amongst it.*
Gordon: *We don't get paid enough for this. Well done, mate.*
            Christ, triple-A is still going.
Paddy: *Yeah, it still looks close, doesn't it?*
Gordon: *I tell you, it WAS bloody close!*
Paddy: *Five's off target. Egressing.*
Teakle told the rest of the formation they were leaving the target area.

Gordon: *I can see my cold is going to get worse soon, mate!*
Buckley joked that he might report sick for the next raid. In their elation, both men couldn't resist quoting their favourite lines from *Blackadder*.
Paddy: *Captain B, my stomach's gone all squirty!*
Gordon: *My stomach's on the floor at the moment ... Oh*
            God, I think I want to die!
Paddy: *I think we almost did ...*

It was dawn on 20 January as the four Tornados that had bombed Al Jarrah, all now with their weapons systems 'switches safe', made their way back across the border. Hooking onto the tankers in daylight was straightforward. Landing at Muharraq was not. Mist cloaked the base, bringing visibility down to less than half a mile. Nick Heard couldn't believe their luck. 'Normally in conditions like this, Air Traffic Control would talk us down using their radar, or we could use another separate, airfield-based system to guide us in. But nothing was working. Was this nightmare ever going to end? Could anything else go wrong on this trip?' One by one, each navigator used his own radar to guide his aircraft down through the thick fog. Shocked into silence, Nick Heard shut down his engine. He opened the canopy and breathed in the early-morning air, feeling the warmth of the sun that was now starting to burn off the mist. 'Normally we would jump straight out, but we both just slumped back in our seats, drained and exhausted.'

One of the ground crew plugged into his jet's intercom and asked: 'Hey, sir, where's your tanks?'

Nick was not quite ready to relive the night's events. 'It's a long story . . .'

He slowly unbuckled and climbed down the ladder. 'It was the most taxing, dangerous sortie I ever flew during my whole career in aviation. I think quite a few people were affected by that raid, and some had to take a quiet moment alone to recover.'

Walking into the Operations Room, Gordon Buckley met one of the men who had carried out the loft attack with the 1,000-pounders just ahead of them, straight after Heard and Risdale's initial JP233 drop. 'He looked utterly shattered and I asked him if he was okay.'

'I'll tell you what, Buckers, I don't have too many more of those inside me,' he replied.

'He was an experienced, senior crewman and the last person I expected to hear that from.' But Buckley also knew from his own recent brush with death that a huge amount was being asked of the men who repeatedly faced the triple-A hailstorm. Reliving the mission thirty years later with the author, Buckley's memory of the experiences was crystal clear. 'I can still see my friends' haunted expressions, and it really made me assess my own feelings. At the start, there had been a certain gung-ho excitement about what we were going to do. We were trained, we were keen, we were ready; confident in our abilities to evict the Iraqi forces from Kuwait and liberate an occupied country. We were now facing death on an almost nightly basis; the realities of war were writ large.'

John Broadbent, the 15 Squadron Boss and overall Tornado Commander at Muharraq, could see how both the losses and the continued braving of triple-A were affecting his crews. 'When I looked into the faces of my colleagues during the debrief, I could see the terrible strain etched on each one of them. And bearing in mind we had just lost our third crew, I realised that some sort of change was needed.' As the crews talked through the mission, this issue came repeatedly to the fore. Buckley thought a big question mark now hung over whether they should continue with these increasingly lethal tactics. They could endeavour to further refine their low-level tactics, of course, but did they need to? Might attacking from medium level, above the triple-A, prove more effective?

Initially, Buckley had been against any move to medium-level bombing. 'All our training, tactics, weaponry, the Tornado itself, was optimised for low level.' But he was eventually persuaded that the new tactics would be more 'palatable' if the Americans could provide the suppressive support with electronic warfare jets, anti-radiation missiles and fighter escorts to defend against Iraqi SAMs and fighters.

They reached a consensus and John Broadbent discussed the situation with the overall RAF Commander at Muharraq. 'I made the point forcefully to my own Boss, and through him to HQ: it appeared to those of us flying the mission that since the Iraqi Air Force remained grounded, had we not achieved our primary task of gaining air superiority? In that case, was it really necessary to continue to attack airfields at low level as this was costing us dear? Surely it was time to take advantage of the conditions that our efforts had created to transition to the safer environment of medium level? I still go cold thinking about that sortie thirty years on and the conclusions of my subsequent Mission Report [the official document sent to HQ immediately after every operation] told the story of what I still regard as a real horror mission:

The first 2 aircraft failed to achieve surprise, suggesting that the Iraqis had developed an effective early warning system. Furthermore, the resulting defensive barrage was directed at both low and medium level indicating that the Iraqis had recognised the threat posed to them by aircraft attacking from low level. It was disappointing to note that the airburst 1000lb bombs had little apparent effect on the AAA fire. Furthermore, concern was raised that the loft manoeuvre took the aircraft, not only into the heart of the AAA barrage, but as a result, tested the considerable skills of 2 of the most able and experienced pilots on the Sqn. In the light of these facts, we have conducted a review of our tactics and have decided that there is little advantage to be gained from compression through the target. If JP233 attacks remain necessary in future, they would be better conducted as pairs of aircraft sent to the target at irregular intervals. The support afforded to our missions so far has done little to suppress what has proved to be the greatest threat – that posed by AAA barrage fire. Our preferred option would be to negate the AAA by flying above it at 20,000ft plus. However, at this altitude, 2-way contact with AWACS would be essential and fighter sweep desirable. In addition, depending upon the en-route and target area SAM threat, EF1-11 or Wild Weasel [Enemy Missile Defence Suppression assets] support might also be necessary.[9]

The casualties borne by the Tornado force in the first few days of war were not going unnoticed by Britain's American allies. When asked to comment publicly on the situation, General Norman Schwarzkopf, in overall command of the campaign, said, 'Their contribution has been absolutely superb, I am damn glad they are with us!'[10]

Lieutenant General Chuck Horner, who controlled the entire air war, was privately more frank with the overall British commander, General Sir Peter de la Billière, at the coalition headquarters in Saudi Arabia. 'Gee, Peter, I sure admire the courage of your pilots, but I'm a little concerned they ain't achieving much in relation to the risk they're taking and the effort they're putting in.' De la Billière, a former SAS commander, later recorded his reaction. 'I made some cautious reply, but from this and other comments I could tell that Chuck considered our method of operation a pretty crazy one in this environment.'[11]

The Tornado story was also gaining traction among the American press, including reporters embedded at Dhahran. Soon after Dave Waddington and Robbie Stewart had been shot down, the *Los Angeles Times* asked why the 'fabled RAF' was suffering such high losses.[12] It suggested they were the result of 'both the Royal Air Force's daring flying style and the extremely hazardous missions they have been given by allied commanders: destroying the runways that serve Iraq's air force'. This tactic, the paper continued, made the Tornados and their crews 'sitting ducks for Iraqi anti-aircraft barrages'.

What followed must have made difficult reading in certain quarters. One Tornado, it suggested, was being lost for every eighty sorties flown, whereas the Americans were flying 750 sorties per downed aircraft. But the article failed to understand – like many misinformed vocal critics at the time – that the Tornado sorties had thus far been *entirely* low level, over heavily defended airfields, and the American total included countless *relatively* safe fighter patrols plus many high- and medium-level sorties over some far more benign targets.

The piece singled out the JP233 'airfield killer' which had been used to strike Iraqi runways 'with considerable success', then made the point that Tornado aircrew knew only too well: 'The down side is that it must be delivered by pilots flying straight down the runway at extremely low altitudes – as low as 100 to 200 feet – in full range and view[13] of enemy anti-aircraft guns. Experts say the pilots cannot even take evasive action to avoid enemy fire if they want to complete their mission successfully.'

The British Air Commander tried to calm things by speaking to the press at Dhahran. 'Overall losses have been incredibly low, astonishingly low, considering the number of sorties flown and the coordination which has surrounded those sorties,' Air Vice-Marshal Bill Wratten told the media. 'I will say we have also been extremely unlucky, and bad luck does not last forever.'[14]

* * *

Back at the hotel, Nige Risdale was contemplating how any ongoing 'bad luck' might collide with his immediate future. His first mission had been a novelty, the second had seen a close call after almost colliding with another Tornado over the enemy airfield in darkness, but this latest attack was something else again. 'For me personally, that third mission was an emotional watershed. The sortie from hell, where everything that could go wrong had gone wrong.' As the Boss's pilot, Risdale felt he had to display stoicism in the face of adversity but when he got back to his room the emotions were less constrained. 'I felt totally washed out and was really worried.' He looked at the family photograph by his bed, wondering if he would get through the next mission. 'I just could not see how we would survive doing the same thing night after night. I really thought I might not see my wife and son again.'

Risdale, not known for showing much emotion even under incredible stress, felt the tears roll down his cheeks as he contemplated what lay ahead.

But he knew a phone call to Claire would straighten him out. 'She listened like the rock she has always been for me, and totally understood.' She also understood when Nige told her he couldn't call when their 2-year-old son was awake. 'I couldn't trust my emotions with him and would have broken down again. Everyone was probably suffering similar thoughts, and although most were private about their personal emotional hiccups, I don't think any of us were immune.'

Gordon Buckley was also reflecting on his own narrow escape.

'The risks were very real and people were dying. *I* had just come very close to dying. The more I relived the previous ops, the more I thought that flying through that wall of triple-A was near-suicidal.'

Their aircraft had been specifically designed for low-level bombing. It remained to be seen how much longer the Tornado force could sustain the tactic.

CHAPTER TEN

BROADCAST OR DIE

20–21 JANUARY

Gordon Buckley's reflections on his 'near-suicidal mission', and Nigel Risdale's of an 'emotional watershed', were being echoed by many members of the three Tornado detachments in the Gulf. But there was still a war to fight.

Seven hundred miles from Muharraq, the Tabuk detachment was planning another low-level sortie against H3, on Iraq's western border with Jordan. Just two nights earlier, the fierce wall of impenetrable flak around the airbase had forced Mal Craghill's formation to abort their attack. The prospect of returning was not a pleasant one. Dave Bellamy's formation planned to counter the groundfire threat with a variation on Buckley and Risdale's Al Jarrah tactics. Their first *four* jets were tasked with lofting – tossing – 1,000lb bombs to airburst over the triple-A emplacements, punching a hole in the defences through which the following four-ship would pepper the runways with their JP233s.

Nerves and bodies were beginning to fray. The pace of operations meant that Dave was on his third consecutive mission in three days. Then there was the gnawing uncertainty of whether his flatmate John Nichol was dead or alive. Perhaps dead was better. If he had survived, *what were the Iraqis doing to him?* 'This was the worst period of the war. News of the ongoing Tornado losses built up the stress, and we were all totally knackered. Our prospects did not look good.'[1]

Bellamy walked into the Operations Room late on the afternoon of Sunday, 20 January. The boyish grins and enthusiasm of the first day had long since evaporated. Four days into the war, every crew had experienced the terror of flying into intense gunfire. Now they had to contemplate doing it all again. And again. And again. Bellamy saw deep anxiety etched in the features of his fellow aviators. 'There were nerves and real fear in a few faces. A lot of the guys were suffering. The hardest part of those nightmare missions was that just as you were coming to grips with your own fear, you were then confronted with somebody else's right before your eyes. Some people went deathly quiet, others babbled on about something trivial. I managed to find some strength in silence and the inexplicable belief that I was not about to die.' Briefings over, the Squadron lined up on the runway.

The unease had already been registered by his Squadron Boss Mike Heath, who would be leading the mission. Heath had earlier told the press: 'I have a lot of youngsters here who are scared but know exactly what they have to do. I am immensely proud of them and my job is to make sure they carry out the mission successfully and return safely. I think we are absolutely right in what we are doing against Saddam and, while no one wants to go to war, we are prepared to fight until he gives up in Kuwait.'[2]

As countless Tornado aircrews prepared for their next missions, the merits and otherwise of low-level attack were being carefully scrutinised at increasingly senior levels. Tornado raids had thus far spread the payload of 106 JP233s[3] across a host of Iraqi airfields. Considerable damage had been inflicted by their 22,790 anti-personnel mines and 3,180 runway-cratering bombs. It appeared that the Iraqi Air Force had now lost their appetite – or were now unable – to fly. Group Captain Cliff Spink was the overall RAF Commander at Dhahran and, while his base had not suffered any losses so far, he was acutely aware of the pressure his crews were under. 'The risks the bombers were taking overflying heavily defended airfields, especially at the tail-end of missions when all the defences had woken up, were increasingly concerning me. Did we really need to continue to carry out operations that way? It seemed the Iraqi Air Force did not want to come out to play, so why continue to pursue incredibly dangerous ops which, for the moment, were apparently not needed?'[4]

It was time to consider moving the Tornados out of the devastating reach of triple-A and that difficult discussion was being fed rapidly up the chain of command.

* * *

Unaware of this heated high-level debate, the eight Tornado pilots at Tabuk brought their engines into reheat. Pushing his throttles fully forward, Pete Batson wondered what the night might bring. Their last raid on Al Asad had seen him drop a JP233 on a Mirage fighter as it came in to land. Its pilot would not have survived. He did his best to put the thought aside as he tore down the runway. At around 200mph he pulled back on the stick and felt the GR1 lift into the air. Seconds later, he raised the landing gear, ready to set a course for the tanker rendezvous.

'Come right,' said his navigator, Mike Heath.

Batson eased the column gently to starboard, to take up the new heading. It barely moved. Neither did the aircraft. He tried again. The control column would only shift one centimetre from the neutral position. The Tornado, like most military aircraft, was a truly complex jet with a multitude of interlinking systems and things could certainly go awry. Sometimes there was an easy solution, rather like turning a computer 'off and on again'; on other occasions, a crew could be in serious trouble.

'I can't come right,' he told Heath calmly. 'We can only go left.'

Batson's jet had a serious problem and he immediately radioed Dave Bellamy to hand over the lead of the sortie, then climbed to height, talking through the options with the Boss in the back seat. Heath could not quite believe his mission was about to be kiboshed by a technical fault. 'As a Squadron Commander leading a wartime sortie, I should not have been wondering what the hell had gone wrong with the plane I was flying!'[5]

The Tornado was relatively stable, and by careful use of the rudder Batson could force the aircraft to manoeuvre enough to go roughly where he wanted. But they needed a better solution. Gaining height away from the airfield, Batson started looking around the cockpit to see if there was anything obvious jamming the control column. His frantic efforts to scan the confined space while flying the heavy jet in pitch darkness met without success. The best option, Heath now considered, was to follow the straightforward and well-worn drill for dealing with any type of flying-controls restriction. 'We thought if we lightened the aircraft by jettisoning the bombs and a bit of fuel, we might be able to tip it upside down. If there was something jamming the controls, we would shake it out.'

They radioed Tabuk that they were going to dump the 1,000-pounders. Every base had its own designated jettison area, and Tabuk's was a nearby small weapons training range which Batson now discovered was permanently manned by safety staff. 'We received a message over the radio to say that the bloke who lived on the range was going to put the lights on in his shack. We were told to avoid jettisoning our bombs anywhere near him!' The lights were easy to find, and without the pressure of incoming hostile fire, they descended to jettison the ordnance and external fuel tanks safely. Batson took the aircraft back up to height and for the next half an hour they flew around, going inverted, left and right, manoeuvring and jostling the controls as best he could. Despite their efforts, the column still would not shift.

Mike Heath was unimpressed. 'We shook the plane around for half an hour but still we couldn't fix the problem.'

The options now narrowed considerably: land or eject.

Landing was going to be tricky, even for Batson, who had been flying RAF jets since 1976. 'The Tornado was still flying but it was agricultural flying, with me using a load of rudder to get it to slip sideways in a turn. The stick would move smoothly left, but I was fighting to then move it back right to a central position. My real concern now was that I might put in a left turn but not be able to get the stick back to neutral and the wings level again – we would lose control.'

Wary of the plethora of other aircraft around Tabuk, not least the fully armed American F-15 fighters lined up near the end of the runway on Quick Reaction Alert, Batson carefully prepared for his approach. The Tornado lost height as it headed towards the runway lights. Batson held the stick steady, keeping the aircraft on track for the centre line as best he could. Then the nose shifted left. He pushed the stick right but it still refused to move. A gust shifted them further left, so badly off course he had to abort the landing. Pouring on the power to climb away, Batson eased the jet around in a series of wide left turns before lining up for the strip again. The altimeter wound down through 1,000ft to 800, then 600. They were on target, ready to commit to touchdown. Batson felt the Tornado shudder slightly as he dropped the landing gear.

Five hundred feet.

Nose dead centre to the runway.

Then it shifted marginally to the left.

Batson poured on the power again. 'We tried various approaches to all the different runways for about an hour. But I just couldn't keep us in a position to make a landing while unable to make any "right turn" inputs on the control column. We were at risk of actually hitting other waiting aircraft. There was a dawning realisation that we were not going to get this jet on the ground. There was no particular fear; the outcome was rather inevitable.'

The options had narrowed further: from two to one.

Mike Heath's annoyance at missing the raid was now tempered by the knowledge that they had an even riskier undertaking ahead. 'We decided to throw the plane away.'

As Waddington, Stewart, Peters and Nichol had all shown, ejecting could be done instantaneously with barely a thought. But Batson and Heath now had time to dwell on the prospect of being rocketed out of a fast jet into the night sky.

Mike Heath reached for their Flight Reference Cards. The stiff, white flip-book detailed every aircraft routine from engine start-up to shut-down, then all the emergency drills, clearly presented for crews under severe pressure. After the procedures to be carried out in the event of a double engine failure or undercarriage malfunction, Heath found the ejection section. It contained fourteen basic commands to be undertaken *'if time and conditions permit'*. Unlike the other wartime aircrews that had recently banged out in a matter of seconds, Heath had time to study the check list.

'*Speed, 250 knots. Height, 9,000 feet,*' Heath told Batson, reading from the FRCs.[6]

'*Head towards unpopulated area.*'

They had to fly back to where they had just jettisoned their bombs and fuel tanks. Then:

Harness – tight and locked.

Oxygen mask – tight.

Visors – down.

Radio – call as required.

Throttles – idle.

Ejection position – assume.

'Roger,' Batson responded to each instruction, double-checking his visor and sitting firmly back in the seat.

They paused before completion.

Heath looked at the black and yellow handle between his legs, and briefly considered the multimillion-pound price-tag of the aircraft they were about to throw away. 'Even though it was a lot of money, that wasn't really on my mind. I just tightened my straps and prepared.' Air Traffic Control told them two rescue helicopters would be launched just before they bailed out. It was gone 11pm. After a brief discussion it was agreed that Mike would do a countdown from ten and then pull the handle. The Tornado's 'Command

Eject' system meant that both crew would leave the aircraft whoever initiated ejection.

There was just 900kg of fuel remaining when, now 9,000ft above the desert, Batson slowed the Tornado to the prescribed 250 knots (287mph) and moved the throttles to idle so it would head earthwards soon after the crew departed.[7]

Heath tightened his straps one final time. 'On a countdown of ten . . .'

Batson listened in nervous anticipation, waiting to be blasted from the calm confines of the cockpit.

'Seven . . .

'Six . . .'

Heath thought of his wife and two young children back home. 'I remember getting to five and thinking, *Oh, my God, I hope I've got the courage to do this.*'

Batson felt like the Boss was taking for ever. 'It was the longest ten seconds of my life and at one point I wondered if Mike had stopped counting!'

'Three . . .

'Two . . .

'One . . .'

Heath pulled the ejection handle. 'It was the hardest thing I'd done in my career.'

For Batson the whole sequence unfurled in slow motion. 'It seemed like a lifetime before anything happened.'

A split second of silence . . .

Then the detonation of a cartridge under the MK10A Martin Baker ejection seat as it unlocked from the aircraft and extended the telescopic tubes which guided it upwards.

An instant later, two more cartridges fired. Heath and Batson felt the straps around their thighs, legs and arms rapidly tighten, pulling their limbs taut against the seat for what came next.

Two small rockets blew off the canopy. The seat rocket motors fired, propelling them upwards. Their oxygen and G-suit cables detached and the emergency oxygen tanks kicked in. With barely half a second gone, each man felt a sledgehammer blow beneath his backside.

'There was an enormous bang and a flash,' Batson recalled. 'For an instant, I could see the canopy moving, then I was hit in the face by my aircrew torch, clipped to the canopy, which came loose and smashed into my visor. My head was forced into my lap, then, although it was pitch-black, there was this vast pool of white light from the flash of the ejection rocket's explosion.'

The seat rocket motor had kicked in, filling the cockpit with light and blasting them into the night with a thrust of around thirty times the force of gravity. They accelerated to around 200mph in the blink of an eye, tossed about like ragdolls in the jet's 300mph slipstream. As they somersaulted, over and over, another cartridge fired, releasing a drogue chute to slow the seat's descent and stop it from tumbling through the air.

One and a half seconds after Heath had pulled the handle, the leg and arm restraints were released, along with the personnel equipment connector linking them to the emergency oxygen supply. A vast orange and white canopy blossomed from its head box and guillotine clippers sliced through the straps fastening each man to his seat, allowing it to fall away into the night.

'The next thing I knew,' Batson said, 'I was dangling under my parachute and everything was silent.' The entire sequence had taken just 1.7 seconds.

Remembering his training, Batson wriggled from head to toe, reassuring himself that everything was intact and functioning, then looked up to check the canopy. All was well. During the six-minute descent he took a moment to enjoy the still of the night. 'It was a pleasant journey, really. I was able to see the circular irrigation fields and several small lights dotted around the area.' The ground soon came into view. He adopted the parachute landing position, feet and knees together, braced for the impact. Nothing happened. The seconds ticked by and still the desert swam below him. 'It was impossible to judge my height in the dark. I'd think, *There's still a long way to go*, then I thought the ground was rushing towards me and assume the landing position again but nothing would happen. I did that a few times then suddenly landed like a bag of spuds.'

During his ejection Mike Heath had managed to glance down briefly and watch the Tornado disappear on its final glide beneath him. His own descent was interrupted by the rescue helicopter appearing to fly straight at him. 'It was a moment of sheer fear. I was still looking up when I hit the desert and landed on solid rock. I catapulted forward, hit my head and knocked myself out. When I came to, the helicopter was a few miles away.'

After shaking himself out on landing, Batson ignored the dull ache in his knee. Rotor blades were drumming some distance away. Batson got out his mini-flare gun and fired two rounds into the air. Like Robbie Stewart the day before, he managed to immediately attract attention. But rather than Iraqis, an American rescue crew swooped down. A paramedic ran over and asked if he was okay.

'It's my leg that's really hurting,' Batson replied.

'Yeah, that's 'cos your foot is sticking out to one side!' he pronounced.

Batson had dislocated his knee on landing. The burly paramedic took a firm grip of his leg, twisted it, and popped the joint back into place.

Heath had also fired off his flares to attract a rescue helicopter's attention, and they were both flown to the field hospital at Tabuk. The first thing Batson did on arrival was admonish Heath on his ejection technique. 'For goodness sake, next time you count down to ten, pull the handle at eight and surprise me.' Heath managed a chuckle, but it was swiftly followed by a grimace. He had three badly bruised vertebrae which he knew would keep him out of the war for some weeks. 'In twenty-two years of flying with the RAF I have never been shot at and I have never had to eject,' he told the *Daily Telegraph* from his hospital bed. 'Now I've chalked up two firsts, both of which I could have done without.'

A subsequent investigation showed that a small electrical connector had probably become detached from its housing and jammed the control column. For Mike Heath and Pete Batson it didn't really matter. After only a couple of days, their war was already over.

* * *

Dave Waddington's war was definitely still ongoing, and he knew worse was to come. Suffering a double dislocation and concussion after his high-speed ejection twenty-four hours earlier, he had stumbled through the night behind enemy lines before being shot at and captured. He had already received some rough treatment, but at least the Iraqis had the decency to put a cast over his elbow. He had then been crammed into the rear footwell of a car and driven more than 200 miles north. Arriving in Baghdad in darkness, he was bundled into the interrogation centre. It was the building where Nichol and Peters had been mauled earlier, and it wasn't long before Dave was given the same welcome. He was blindfolded and shoved onto a metal stool. 'I could sense there were probably two or three guards behind me and a single interrogator in front. I knew what was coming and wondered how I'd deal with it.'[8]

The first thing they asked was his name, rank and service number. He answered truthfully as this was information he was required to give. But Dave knew it was just a formality for what was coming next.

'What aircraft do you fly?'

'I'm sorry, sir, I cannot answer that question.'

The truncheon cracked against his temple, his legs and his back, then again in the same three spots.

'What do you fly?'

Dave gave the same response: 'I can't answer that question.'

The truncheon came down again. 'There was a sort of acceptance on my part. It went past the stage where it hurt. It was just happening. I shouldn't have *had* to answer their questions and certainly didn't want to. So each time they didn't get the response they wanted, they would beat me, using sticks and fists.'

The deep abrasions Waddington had suffered to his face from

the blast when ejecting were still incredibly painful. During their early sessions, his interrogators decided to exploit that pain. 'They punched me incredibly hard a number of times in the face, huge hammer blows that rocked me sideways and sent stars spinning above my head. I remember the emotional shock as much as the physical pain. I realised I was totally helpless; completely in their hands. They could smash me around as much as they wanted. It was a worrying thought.'

The grilling continued throughout the night. Dave was knocked into unconsciousness on a number of occasions. 'I'd come round and they'd ask me another question then blows came again – head, back and legs. A couple of times they tried to hit my dislocated arm but it was in plaster so it didn't hurt that much. My thoughts were racing with a whole mix of emotions. Bouts of utter fear mixed with the strange sense of determination; not wanting to give in without a fight. I knew that fight would ultimately be pointless, and the end result the same whatever I did, but I wanted to resist for as long as possible for a couple of reasons. Firstly, and obviously, I didn't want to give away any information that would endanger my friends and colleagues. But perhaps just as importantly, I wanted to be able to say to myself, and others, "I held out for as long as possible; they really had to work to get me to talk." This was a huge player for me throughout the interrogation. I knew I couldn't sustain the brutality for ever, but I needed to feel as though I hadn't given up easily before accepting the inevitable. I suppose I just didn't want to appear weaker than others.'

During a welcome pause in the proceedings, Waddington was shoved into a corridor where he became aware of other allied prisoners of war around him. 'I could see under my blindfold that I was lying next to someone wearing American flying boots. There were eight or nine bodies lying around, crumpled up. I could hear American and British voices under interrogation, but I was drifting in and out of consciousness. They would finish with one guy then drag me back in.'

Each time the routine was the same. 'It was all standard stuff. It became a bit of a game with them asking me the same question,

"What aircraft do you fly?" and me just replying, "I cannot answer that question." They concentrated mostly on beating my back. I'd be knocked off my stool and thumped around until I lost consciousness. Drifting away, I remember feeling rather relieved. It meant I was getting a break from the violence. Then after I came round, they would start asking the same question again.'

'Why are you refusing to answer our questions? We don't need you to answer! We already have information from Peters and Nichol, so why don't you just tell us the same thing? We can bring them in here to talk to you if it helps?'

'I just replied again with my same stock phrase, "I cannot answer that question," but it was all starting to sound a bit daft by now.'

Like all the coalition POWs who underwent such violent questioning, Waddington felt much of it seemed unfocused. 'At one point they were beating the soles of my feet, but I still had my flying boots on. At times I wondered if they knew what they were doing – they seemed to have a simple, basic need to mete out physical violence.' Dave steeled himself for more stinging blows, but knew he was reaching his limits of endurance. 'There seemed to be no end to their violence. So what questions *will* I answer? What questions will I *not* answer? What am I prepared to *die* for?'

It was a key moment for Waddington. Alongside a determination to try to protect the Tornado crews still flying, he also dreaded betraying the identity of the female Iraqi doctor who had slipped a small strip of painkillers into his pocket while tending his arm. 'I'm not sure I could have lived with myself if I answered that question. It would have had truly terrible consequences for a person who had shown me such kindness.'

As the brutality continued sporadically through the night, his aggressors returned to the same question, the one that everyone knew signalled the end if they answered it. His resistance was slipping with the pain, the tiredness, the despondency, the captivity, the fear. 'I have no idea how long it went on, but you start to realise you can't go on avoiding the question for ever. These people are really out to hurt you.'

'What aircraft do you fly?'

'I cannot answer that question.'

The interrogator then lifted his blindfold and held up what Dave recognised as Flight Reference Cards. At the top it read: '*Flt Lt DJ Waddington*' then the title '*Tornado GR1*'.

'What aircraft do you fly?'

'Tornado.'

Dave had broken.

'Giving in to the interrogation and torture was the absolute bottom of the pit of the experience for me. I'd been shot down, didn't make it home. I was trying to resist, to retain some honour, but in that moment, I had failed.' He had tried his best to last as long as possible rather than giving in straight away to avoid the agony. 'I did what I thought was the right thing, right up to the far edge of my personal limit. It's something which goes right back in our military history, the principle, our heritage, our ethos to uphold. You don't want to be the one who falls short.'

Questions now came thick and fast, which Dave tried to resist. As his interrogators did not seem to truly understand what to ask, he tried to play the Iraqis at their own game, offering as little information as possible, giving misinformation where he could. He pretended that his youth, junior rank and inexperience meant he knew very little. His tactics came at considerable cost when the interrogator compared his answers about a basic Tornado tactic with those of the other POWs.

'Mister David! We know that you are lying to us. You will be sorry.'

'I really suffered when they caught me out lying about that. They seemed to lose all control and flew into a frenzy of violence. The worst beating of the nightmare so far.'

His name was also a problem.

'*David!* . . . *Joseph!* . . . Waddington, you are a Jew!'

Again and again they accused him of being an Israeli pilot, their hatred of the Jewish state fuelling their anger. 'We *know* the Israelis are flying for you!'

Dave could only tell them the truth; he knew nothing about it. But his Christian names were proving quite painful.

In Dave's mind, Robbie was still on the run, potentially on his way back home. He had no idea his friend was seriously injured and already captured. Now they wanted to know the name of his navigator. He tried his best to hold out, not wanting to hinder Robbie's escape. 'I really didn't want to give that information, but they beat it out of me too.' He waited for the moment when his courage would be tested further, when he would be forced to give away tactical intelligence that would help the Iraqis. He certainly had information on search-and-rescue procedures that could cause serious harm to others. 'Luckily, they never asked those questions, so my resolve was never tested to its limit.'

Eventually, the questions stopped and he was hopeful he had given away little of use. Battered and beaten both physically and psychologically, Dave was taken to the medical centre on the outskirts of Baghdad where, unknown to him, his navigator had just undergone a lengthy operation.

* * *

Robbie awoke in a large, comfortable hospital room with a smiling portrait of Saddam Hussein gazing benignly down on him. Judging from the bandages, the cast on his leg and minimal pain, Robbie knew that he had been well treated. He was contemplating using the pull bar above his head to move position when the door opened and a group of doctors walked in. They were led by a beaming, kindly looking man. The rest of the entourage's deference suggested that he was the senior consultant. He picked up Robbie's left hand. 'He had obviously sensed my foreboding as I'd watched my wedding ring disappear before the operation, and now, grinning with delight, he slipped it back onto my finger.'[9]

The surgeon produced Robbie's X-rays and showed him how he had fixed the bones in his leg by using two metal plates and thirteen screws. He was delighted Robbie could wiggle his toes, then explained in fluent English that he had also suffered a broken collarbone and crushed vertebrae. When they moved on, one doctor sporting the obligatory Saddam moustache stayed behind. 'You are very lucky to have been treated by this surgeon,' he said softly. 'He is the top doctor in Iraq and he was trained in a London hospital.'

Robbie had no doubt about the surgeon's concern for his well-being. The doctor left him alone with his thoughts – first and foremost, of Tange and the children. 'I imagined their dread on seeing a blue RAF uniform at the door, an image that told them without the need for any words that the worst had happened. The hot tears ran down my face again.'

He awoke from a delirious dream to find a sallow-faced medic at his bedside. The man put a thermometer in Robbie's mouth, read his blood pressure then leaned in and took his pulse. 'Me, no Iraqi, me Kurdish,' he whispered conspiratorially. Then he showed Robbie the readings as if they were top secret. 'I felt a little ray of hope that here was a man who would help me.' He drifted back to sleep, content that, in the midst of war, human kindness could still be found. When he opened his eyes, they were met with the image which would remind him that such kindness was still in short supply. 'I lay there facing this huge portrait of Saddam Hussein which hung opposite. His features had been softened by the artist to hide the fact he was a murderous tyrant who would happily kill his own people to get his own way.'

Saddam portraits and Saddam lookalikes dominated the walls and corridors of the Baghdad interrogation centre. A number of coalition prisoners were now housed there and casual brutality was the order of the day. The strike of a match and the stink of cheap tobacco in John Peters' nostrils were followed by the sharp agony of a seared wrist. Then again, on the other wrist. 'Someone was dragging on his cigarette, then carefully applying the glowing tip to my skin. He wasn't actually stubbing the cigarette out and relighting it, just touching the embers to the skin, removing it for another drag, then carefully touching it down again.'[10] Peters suddenly felt ungovernable rage. 'This was some sad, sadistic, little shit taking advantage of my complete helplessness. If I hadn't been handcuffed I would have killed that bastard.'

His navigator John Nichol was also having a tough time.

'Lieutenant Nichol, do you know that we are going to charge you with war crimes?'

The question had come with the customary kicks and slaps as Nichol lay asleep on the concrete floor of the bunker. Aching all over, stiff, bruised, flesh throbbing, he simply stared up at the Iraqi officer. 'Excuse me? I have committed no war crimes.'

'Yes, you have attacked a country you did not declare war on. You have committed war crimes. We are going to execute you.' It sounded like he meant it.

Oh well, Nichol thought.

There was a pause.

'Right,' the officer said. 'We can either execute you or put you on TV.'

Nichol contemplated his immediate future. *Broadcast or die?* The decision wasn't too difficult. 'What do you want me to say?' he eventually replied.

'I thought a TV appearance was a good deal more appealing than a death sentence, particularly since its effect would be debatable and stand a strong chance of triggering an Iraqi public relations disaster. On the other hand, I did not *want* to co-operate, or show the least willingness under any circumstances. These people were the enemy.'

'We will ask you a few questions,' the officer smiled. 'You will answer them and then you can send a message home.'

Do what you like, Nichol thought. *Shoot yourself right in the foot.*

He was taken blindfolded into a large room where a crowd swarmed around a television camera. Someone gave him a glass of water and brushed his hair. When their back was turned he ruffled it again. He wanted to look under duress. After a brief 'rehearsal' of the questions and the pre-prepared answers he was expected to give, the camera was turned on.

'How were you shot down?'

'What do you think of the war?'

Deadpan and monotone, Nichol gave the required responses. 'I was shot down by an Iraqi system. I do not know what it was. I think the war should be stopped so we can go home. I don't agree on this war with Iraq.'[11]

He hoped that by parroting the stilted English and speaking very slowly, it would be clear he was delivering words written by someone else. And by maintaining a level monotone and refusing to blink, anyone watching would know he was under duress. The Iraqis did not pick up on his charade, seemingly content to just get through the text. Then, when it was the time to give his parents a message, Nichol stared straight into the lens. 'Mum and Dad, if you're listening, everything is okay. Please pray for me. We should be home soon.'

As Nichol was led back down the corridor tears streamed down his face, soaking the crepe bandage of his blindfold. 'For me, the TV broadcasts were the lowest point; my ultimate shame. I felt as though I had let down the RAF, my Squadron and my friends. And then the thought of what my poor parents must be enduring was unbearable. I was a wreck.' In the depths of his despair, Nichol had no idea how far those TV pictures would reach, or how much they would affect his life.

* * *

Peters was also kicked awake by the guards. His blindfold was removed and an officer appeared. 'You're going on television,' he told the pilot abruptly.

'No!' Peters was not going to be used as a propaganda tool.

The slaps came in fast and hard. 'You will never see your wife and children again.' Slap.

'Is it worth it?'

Slap.

'We will kill you now.'

Slap.

One of the soldiers took his pistol out and thrust it against Peters' temple. 'You are going to die now.'

Peters was so keyed up he could almost hear the creak of the trigger mechanism. 'Okay, okay, okay,' he mumbled.

As he was dragged into the room Nichol had just vacated, Peters consoled himself that he had done his best not to co-operate. He was pushed down onto the chair and someone tried to tidy his hair. Peters knew there was little they could do with his battered face and drew comfort from the thought. 'I looked like shit and I felt shit. I was going to use that. I was going to try to refuse to say what they wanted me to say.'

As the Iraqis shouted questions and then provided the answers, Peters showed little compliance. They kept whacking him with a pistol when he refused to speak up or sit up. The pilot decided to use the injuries to his advantage. 'I wanted people to see evidence of the beatings, so turned my damaged eye towards the camera. There would be no mistaking the physical abuse.' The Iraqis cut short the questions, just demanding his name, rank and number, and confirmation that he had been shot down by missiles. Peters had done well to curtail the performance, but felt utterly humiliated. 'I hated being put on television with every fibre of every nerve. I thought I would be revealing to the world how weak I had been, how I'd given in too easily. I thought everyone would class me as a traitor. All I could think was that I was bringing disgrace to my uniform.'

As the interview drew to a close, his captors said he could send a message to his family.

'Helen, Toni and Guy, I love you . . .' A lump formed in his throat. *That's it*, Peters thought. *I've done everything they wanted. They don't need anything more out of me. I can be wasted now. I will never see my family again.* When he tried to add some words to his parents, he couldn't speak.

The interviews were broadcast on local Iraqi TV then picked up by CNN in Baghdad. Within hours, pictures of Nichol, Peters, a Kuwaiti pilot and four American POWs had been flashed around the world, prompting an unprecedented storm of global condemnation.

The harrowing images of Nichol and Peters in particular were red meat for Britain's tabloid press. The *Daily Mail* captured the public mood best. 'WHAT HAS HE DONE TO THEM?' their headline shrieked.

The Sun was less restrained: 'BASTARD OF BAGHDAD', it screamed, then demanded: 'Hang Saddam long and slow'. The faces of Nichol and Peters, its front-page opinion piece ran, 'will haunt us all for many a long day'.

Saddam could not have gifted the coalition a more perfect justification for their onslaught, especially after it was suggested that the POWs could be used as human shields at key Iraqi sites, to prevent them from being bombed. Prime Minister John Major declared the treatment of prisoners as 'inhuman, illegal and totally contrary to the third Geneva Convention'.[12] He demanded Red Cross access. 'Huge anger was aroused when captured British pilots were paraded before the camera as Iraqi propaganda,' he later recalled. 'I had met some of them in Dhahran just a few days before, and felt their plight very personally.'[13]

President George Bush echoed his words. 'If Saddam Hussein thought this brutal treatment of pilots is a way to muster world support he is dead wrong and everyone is upset about it.' Dick Cheney, the US Defense Secretary, condemned it as 'in effect a war crime'.[14]

Initially, the pictures had a positive impact on RAF morale. They now knew their comrades had not been shot out of hand by Saddam's goons. 'I am elated, now I have hope,' Dave Bellamy, Nichol's flatmate, recorded in his diary.

The news broke in Bahrain after Gordon Buckley had left the Sheraton to visit a local restaurateur he had befriended. After navigating his way through the polythene sheeting fastened across his host's front door to provide some protection from chemical attack, he was met by a beaming smile. 'They've been on the TV! They're alive and okay!'

Buckley did not have to wait long to see his fellow Muharraq fliers' beaten faces on CNN. 'It was a great relief that they were alive. Though it was obvious they were both slightly the worse for their ordeal . . .'

* * *

Helen Peters remained on tenterhooks at their home in Germany. Rolling TV coverage throughout the day had been dominated by video footage of five fliers, including John Nichol, but there was no sign of her husband. She was bathing her two young children upstairs when he finally appeared on the 5.40pm news bulletin. Fortified by a large brandy, she sat down to watch. 'It was horrible, that rush of different kinds of emotions all at once. John looked terrible. So battered; almost unrecognisable. I stood up to telephone my parents but my legs gave way.'

Although she now had confirmation that he was alive, Helen could not stop thinking that once they had forced the airmen to make the broadcast the Iraqis would have 'simply taken the boys out and shot them'.

Dave Waddington's mother Berenice was still waiting anxiously for further news of her own missing boy. She was watching TV in their neat three-bedroom, semi-detached home in Bolton when the pictures of Peters and Nichol flashed across her screen. She could not help imagining her son being similarly brutalised. 'It was horrific. They looked so terrible, so badly mistreated. Seeing them alive didn't offer us much hope.'

All that day her son John, a fireman, had used every contact he had within the RAF to try to find out more. When he finally got through to one of Dave's colleagues, his heart sank. 'An RAF officer told us that there was little chance of David or Robbie being alive because their aircraft had been seen going down in flames. No ejections had been seen. It was unlikely anyone had survived.'[15]

Berenice released a heartrending statement to the press. 'We don't know whether he is dead or has been taken prisoner. We are praying he is alive but we are prepared for the worst. All I hope is that if he has died he has done so to make a better world for our children. We believe, and he believes, that the cause he is fighting is a just one.'[16] She added that two days before hearing of his loss they had received a letter from Dave telling them not to worry. The article appeared under a banner headline: 'BLOOD AND TEARS OF COURAGE', and was accompanied by a photo of Dave and his fiancée Claire at an Officers' Mess dinner. Dave was wearing his RAF blue formal dinner jacket trimmed in silk and gold, Claire in a strapless white lace-trimmed ballgown. They looked like teenagers at a prom.

Despite the RAF officer's doleful message, Dave's sister was convinced that he must be alive. She told their mother that she would *know* if he was dead. Berenice had no idea which way to turn. 'There were so many contradictions, hope and despair. But the not knowing was the worst part; in the darkest moments it was the lack of information that was difficult to bear.'

* * *

Robbie Stewart's wife Tange was doing her best to deal with the blow of being told her own husband was missing in action. The news had reverberated around their Lincolnshire village the previous day, and the vicar had held an impromptu service. She had walked past the gravestones of All Saints into the Saxon-built tower and been startled by the packed pews within. 'There was shock and confusion on some of their faces – the whole village seemed to be moved by our situation.' They sat and listened as the vicar told the congregation of Robbie's plight. Tange held onto her son Scott and Robbie's best friend Barry as they sang 'Amazing Grace'. 'I was gripping them so tightly, coming out of the numbness of my situation and how it affected all our friends. Then I looked up into the rafters above the chancel and saw a white butterfly fluttering around freely. I wondered if it was trying to tell me something.'

Shortly after the service, RAF Marham Station Commander Jock Stirrup and his wife arrived at her house. He gave Tange a piece of advice she would not forget. 'I will only tell you information which has been *officially confirmed* by either our military, or the Red Cross.' From then on, she took everything she heard or read elsewhere as a potentially unreliable rumour. 'The thought that no one was able to confirm if they were dead kept me going. All the relatives of those missing must have held onto the same hope that their loved ones would be found alive and return to them.'

Her position was soon challenged by the flood of grainy images of Nichol and Peters. 'It was a real worry, so horrendous and so alien to everything that we had understood about life. I really hoped I wouldn't see Robbie like that.'

Then the Ministry of Defence released official pictures of Robbie and Dave which appeared alongside the other missing Tornado aircrew, Max Collier and Nigel Elsdon, in the London *Evening Standard*. The headline was sobering in the extreme: 'Be Ready for Bad News'[17] – words taken from the Prime Minister's counsel to the Commons that the nation should prepare 'to bear bad news with fortitude'.

Robbie's daughter Kirsty had gone back to board at Stamford High School. Watching the aircrew on the evening news confirmed her terrible sense of foreboding. 'It was a really horrible moment, reinforcing all the thoughts I had from the books I'd read about war, prisoners, interrogation and torture.' She could not help staring again and again at one particular image. 'John Nichol was staring at the camera and had been speaking really slowly, strangely. What was he trying to tell us? What did it mean for my dad? What would he be going through, if he was alive?'

CHAPTER ELEVEN

'STAY WITH IT!'

20 JANUARY, EVENING–24 JANUARY

Mike Toft had been on Peters and Nichol's fateful daylight raid and the outcome had continued to play on his mind. 'We were so happy to see them paraded on TV. It was clearly a terrible experience and they looked badly battered, but at least we knew they were alive. There was hope they might eventually get home. It was a real boost and it made us more determined to carry on with the job.'

Toft was now getting on with that job, in a distinctly uncomfortable and unfamiliar environment. The navigator was en route to attack an airfield 90 miles south of Baghdad. His eight-ship was about to offload 64,000lb of bombs from a height of 20,000ft. It was something he had never trained for, and it was not what the Tornado had been designed to do.[1] The mission had one unbreakable instruction from HQ: *Don't hit the mosque!* The religious site stood two and a half miles to the north of Al Najaf airbase.[2] To avoid a public relations disaster, *not even a cracked slate* would be acceptable. And an accurate strike at that height was going to be a challenge.

The Tornado weapons system was optimised for very accurate low-level attacks. Their 1,000-pounders[3] were not actually 'guided' – once they left the jet, they were on their own. But the computer aiming system had been pre-programmed to *know* precisely what the bombs' trajectory would be for the few seconds they were in the air. It also *knew* exactly where the jet was, what height it was flying at, how fast it was travelling, and what low-level winds the released bombs would be subjected to. So the computer itself would then calculate the exact moment to release the weapons.[4] The system was a huge improvement on previous versions, and on most weaponry training sorties, as long as the main computer was updated with navigational fixes, unguided bombs could be delivered to within a matter of metres of the target. And with eight of them, total destruction was almost guaranteed.

Dropping them from 20,000ft, however, posed considerable problems, not least because the aiming system was only capable of measuring wind speed and direction at the Tornado's *actual* altitude over the ground. An estimated wind speed to represent a lower altitude could be manually inputted, but the main computer still had no way of calculating how conditions would vary – and impact the flight path of the payload – during the *full* thirty or so seconds it would take to complete its journey.

Toft's formation had been told that, as their target was so vast, any dispersion due to these errors should still result in a reasonably focused spread of weapons designed to disrupt the airbase's operations. The low-level mindset had been in place since the birth of the Tornado nearly two decades before. Toft hoped he'd be able to adapt to the new environment with suitable rapidity.

Despite the lives risked and lost in pursuit of low-level excellence, old notions now had to be pushed aside. Three RAF Tornados, and one Italian version, had gone down during the execution of raids a few hundred feet above the target. But – despite misleading assertions from some sections of the media – they were not alone. The US, French, Italian and Saudi air forces had been pursuing the same low-level tactics too. Indeed, for the first few nights of the war, even the giant American B-52 strategic bombers had been flying such attacks across Iraq. One pilot remembered heading towards a chemical weapons site near Mosul, south of the Turkish border, just 50ft above the ground.[5] The B-52's wingspan was 185ft.

Now, as the losses mounted, questions were being asked across the whole coalition.

A number of American aircraft had also gone down during low-level operations, including two US Navy A-6 Intruders and two US Air Force F-15E Strike Eagles, one of the most modern combat jets in theatre. As a veteran of 500 low-level missions in Vietnam, Vice Admiral Stanley Arthur felt duty-bound to share some hard-won knowledge. From his ship in the Gulf, the Commander of the Seventh Fleet sent a carefully worded message to his senior officers. 'Gentlemen, far be it for me to dictate specific combat tactics but I must interject my early observations relative to the age-old argument of low altitude delivery versus high with a quick look at what has happened to the *multinational* [6] air forces to date. One cannot escape the fact that the current AAA environment makes low altitude delivery a non-starter.' He felt that it couldn't be successfully achieved without the benefit of surprise, and at that moment, they didn't have it. 'We learned a hard lesson in Vietnam relative to AAA,' he reminded his commanders.[7]

The French were having the same discussion. Four of their Jaguars had sustained substantial damage on an early eight-ship, low-level sortie. One pilot had a very lucky escape when a bullet from an AK-47 assault rifle passed through his helmet visor. He'd been a hair's breadth from being shot in the head, by a soldier on the ground, with a rifle.[8] Yes, it had been a lucky shot, but as the intensity of fire increased, the French decided to move their operations to 10,000ft and above. It appeared that the Iraqi Air Force may have been battered into submission during the first forty-eight hours of the air war. 'They realised fairly early on that if they were going to get airborne at all they'd be shot down,' noted an RAF planning officer in Riyadh. While the Iraqis had some truly effective jets, 'they didn't really know how to use them; their technology wasn't as good as we'd believed'.[9] In other words, perhaps the much-feared enemy fighter threat was already, largely, contained?

The growing consensus was that the risks of low-level flying now far outweighed the reward. But while all the options were still being considered, RAF Air Headquarters had ordered a mix of strategies. The Dhahran detachment would pursue a risky eight-ship night-time loft attack on Jalibah airbase, while Mike Toft and his comrades from Muharraq found themselves ordered up to more unfamiliar territory.

* * *

Instead of dropping down from the tankers, the eight Tornados felt their way gingerly up to 20,000ft. Toft contemplated their mission to Al Najaf airbase as the evening sun dipped below the horizon. It was a world away from skimming across the desert in daylight, as they had when they lost Nichol and Peters. 'The main threat to crews had been triple-A and now the aim was to fly above it. And while we knew the threat from enemy fighters had diminished, we took nothing for granted. Notwithstanding the relative safety of height, the Tornado was not designed to operate at such altitude. The primary bomb-aiming equipment was the ground-mapping radar designed for low-level operations. Now the radar was only as good as the Bomber Command radars of the Second World War.'[10]

Aircrew now had the challenge of using a radar system optimised for looking directly *at* approaching structures at low level, rather than *down* on them, and a bombing system designed to be highly accurate at 200ft, not 20,000. Mark Paisey, Toft's pilot, was also having to contend with demanding meteorological conditions. 'The weather was generally clear with little significant cloud but some ground fog was predicted to obscure features on the transit and in the target area. More importantly, there was a strong wind from the west of 70 knots at 20,000ft which would cause problems. I remember saying to Tofty that we might as well be in a Lancaster bomber because of the way we were attacking. There was very limited information for the main computer to calculate the weapons release point; especially the ever-changing winds from 20,000ft all the way down to ground level.'[11]

Leading the attack, Squadron Leader Pablo Mason was grateful for the moonless night – the shroud of darkness would provide some cover. 'We were nervous both about the sensitivity of the task and because we would be an eight-ship formation flying for the first time in a medium-level attack on the airfield. We had only ever flown out to war in the safety of low level which hid us from enemy radars.'[12] While out of range of the dreaded triple-A, they were now very much in the surface-to-air missile zone. To protect the Tornados the Americans had provided two EF-111 Raven specialist electronic jamming jets to suppress enemy radar, and two F-14 Tomcat interceptors in case any enemy fighters did manage to get off the ground.

The raid was also the first sortie for the new crew who had been sent out to replace the Two Johns. They had arrived in Bahrain direct from the UK only nineteen hours earlier. Pablo checked the time as the eight jets approached the target: 7.20pm. Ten minutes to go. 'The night was strangely quiet. My navigator gave me a final reminder that this had to be an accurate attack. If we deviated to the left by just 4km we would hit the mosque.'

A moment later their ground-mapping radar failed; they could no longer update the weapons system. Then another Tornado lost its radar too. Determined to carry on the attack, Pablo ordered an 'aerial ballet', in total darkness, and with each aircraft's external lights extinguished. He manoeuvred his own jet directly behind Toft and Paisey's. Guided only by the friendly glow of their engines just visible in the blackness, he now flew in close formation to the target. He instructed Toft to give him a precise signal when they were dropping their bombs so he could release his own manually.

The formation was now relying entirely on Mike Toft's navigation skills and the largely unpractised bomb-aiming technique. Under intense pressure to ensure the mission went smoothly, he concentrated on the green screen, trying to identify the radar offsets to feed into the main computer for an accurate drop. He became even more sceptical when the first offset – an ancient fort – had clearly disappeared 'beneath the sands of time' because nothing showed on the monitor. 'The second offset was a bend in a pylon line, an awesome aiming point from low level, but from medium level completely bloody hopeless because the pylons could not be broken out from the ground clutter.' Looking down from on high, the radar system could not differentiate between the metal structure and the ground itself. Heart racing, and only sixty seconds to target, Toft prayed that the third offset would show up. 'Without doubt, this was the most pressured I've ever been in the RAF. The first ever Tornado medium-level war mission and it all seemed to be resting solely on my shoulders.'

From the front seat, Mark Paisey could sense the tension building as his HUD counted down to weapons release. He thought a cheerful remark – 'No pressure, Tofty!' – would lighten the mood. It didn't.

The third and final offset was the nearside of a bridge over a small river. Toft peered intently at the radar screen. 'It took time to break this out from the green porridge of the display staring at me.' It finally appeared. He moved the marker over the offset and pressed the insert button, feeding the information to the main computer which registered the update. A second later the bombs fell from their aircraft.

As they made a gentle right-hand turn back towards friendly territory, Paisey counted down the seconds to impact. 'Twenty ... ten ... three, two, one ...'

The pitch-black below them turned white in an instant, then a series of orange and yellow flashes marked the detonations, the shock waves expanding out, encompassing the airbase. Secondary explosions began to show. Perhaps fuel or ammunition dumps going up. Like most aircrew, Toft had only ever dropped single 1,000-pounders on practice ranges before the conflict. Now 64,000lb of high explosive were rocking the target. 'It was a terrifying sight, and a gut-wrenching moment. I thought, *What the fuck have we just done?* It was truly terrible, almost biblical destruction, and we had most likely killed many military personnel. But you had to push that reality away from your thought process. This was war.'

As the first bombs impacted, Mark Paisey watched the sky light up with the familiar red and white streaks of gunfire. 'The bombs set off heavy triple-A, both tracer and airburst reaching up to around 18,000ft. I didn't see any SAMs launch and we had no RHWR indications. Most crews were happy with their attacks and those who were uncertain ensured they bombed to the south, thus avoiding damage to the mosque.'

All eight made it safely back to base, and the subsequent Mission Report painted a rather different picture from previous raids in terms of both bombing accuracy and threat level:

> *The accuracy of the attack was difficult to assess since the target was also the point of interest of B-52 aircraft shortly after our mission. This, together with the very slow delivery of damage assessment, made it impossible to draw out lessons for subsequent attacks. However, all crews agreed that the medium level option, with support, felt safer than low level overflight of defended targets.*[13]

* * *

Twelve-year-old Gareth Ankerson was only just starting to realise that his father Bob's role as a Tornado navigator was part of the unfolding war on television. He'd always presumed his job was pretty much like anybody else's – a driver, say, or an engineer. As the battle in the Gulf continued, the senior boys at Brandeston Hall School had been allowed to gather in the common room to watch the evening news. Gareth saw the battered faces of Nichol and Peters in the same flying suits his father wore, but he still couldn't imagine his kindly dad being in the same situation. 'I began to make the link that my dad was doing his job, he was out in the Gulf, and these things on the news all linked together, but I don't think I had a sense of how serious it all was. Not then.'[14] Gareth had been more preoccupied with his studies after arriving back for the penultimate term at his Suffolk boarding school. The possibility of Tornado pilots and navigators becoming POWs was less pressing than the poem his English teacher had set them to learn by the end of the week.

Alone at their family home at RAF Bruggen in Germany, his mother was also grappling with the unfamiliar repercussions of the conflict. When the initial Tornado losses were reported, Chris Ankerson had admonished herself for thinking *at least it's not my husband*. 'I had naively convinced myself that everyone would come home safely. Suddenly it was all very real.'[15] She became addicted to TV news. 'I started to watch all the bulletins, although many of the wives never looked at all; they didn't want live updates about what their loved ones were doing. But I drew comfort from seeing the RAF crews I knew on TV, discussing their experiences. It allowed me to feel closer to my husband.' But the bruised images of Nichol and Peters paraded as POWs had rocked her. 'Although it was a shock, I didn't know them, I had never heard of them, so I couldn't really have any other emotion than, again, *thank God it's not my husband*. It seems wrong now, of course, but I think many of us felt that way.'

The Bruggen Station Commander made sure the wives were given regular updates from the warzone. Chris would attend the briefings and then telephone Gareth at school. It felt good sharing the latest intelligence she'd received about the Tornado force and Bob's war.

The problem was, her husband's war wasn't going terribly well. On the evening of 22 January, as the newspapers were giving full vent to their outrage at Iraqi treatment of POWs, Bob and his pilot Simon Burgess entered the briefing room at Dhahran for the final time before their first war sortie – which would take them to Shaibah airfield, south-west of Basra, at medium level. Almost a week had gone by and they were grinding their teeth. 'Lots of missions had been cancelled for various reasons and I had a sense of personal frustration about not being involved in combat ops,' said Bob. 'As a Flight Commander on a frontline squadron, I felt I really needed to be doing my share of the job.'[16] There was nothing devil-may-care about his attitude, though. 'We all knew we were flying into very high-threat environments. Anyone who was surprised by the Tornados going down must have been kidding themselves.'

As they aimed for the tanker rendezvous, their Sky Shadow electronic countermeasures pod started playing up. It was a key piece of kit, jamming Iraqi radar-guided missiles, and was more important than ever now that they were operating at 20,000ft and even more exposed to SAMs. They tried turning it off and back on again, but it was still failing after they disengaged from the Victor. Bob knew they had to return to Dhahran, but was concerned that it might look like they were 'bottling out'. He attended the debrief after the rest of the formation had safely returned, 'but I felt like an interloper'. He went to his room, deeply frustrated. 'We hadn't completed the job. There was a niggling feeling that perhaps we should have pressed on regardless. By this stage of the war, most people had completed a number of ops, but we hadn't done one. It didn't sit well.' He had also just seen the newspaper reports on Nichol and Peters. 'It put some steel into me, wanting to get the job done quicker.'

* * *

The POW images continued to unleash public indignation. 'Sir, I felt angry and sick at heart for the families of those captured airmen whose photographs dominated your front page this morning,' Mrs Geraldine Peters wrote to the editor of The Times. 'What can the feeling of these families be, knowing that the suffering of their loved ones is being paraded before hundreds of thousands through the media?' She then criticised the media in general for 'proliferating Saddam's hideous propaganda'.[17]

Under the headline, 'Saddam may try to break your spirit . . . he'll never break your heart,' The Sun's letters page was packed with encouragement for the frontline fliers. 'I say a prayer for them every night and I also pray that the murderous bastard holding them prisoner will get his come-uppance soon,' Julie Staunton wrote from Torquay.[18]

And the gloves now came off against those opposing the

campaign. The actress Emma Thompson, photographed with a
'Stop War in the Gulf' placard at a London demonstration, was
given short shrift in the *Daily Express*. 'When men like that are
going through the living hell of war it makes me feel sick and
ashamed to hear the rantings of a silly actress about peace,' said one
of the paper's leading columnists. 'Could she look John Peters in the
eye in all his wretchedness and tell him he was wasting his time?
At times like this I wish the peace people would hop on a plane to
Baghdad and rant at Saddam instead.'[19]

The newspapers began arriving in the Gulf. While the front
pages featured the POWs, there were also reports about successful
Tornado missions keeping the Iraqi Air Force largely grounded.
After the recent losses at Muharraq, Nick Heard was buoyed by the
coverage. 'They were full of details about what *we*, the *Tornados*,
had been doing. It was gratifying to realise that people back home
understood the contribution we were making, the risks we were
taking, and were seemingly totally behind us.'[20]

The risks the crews were taking were great. Although some
Tornado raids were being carried out from medium level, low-level
sorties still continued, depending on the target and the degree of
strike accuracy required. A massive airbase could be attacked from
height, but a single structure or complex could not. On 22 January,
the Tabuk detachment were tasked to destroy an air defence control
station near the Jordanian border. Ar Rutbah was the location of
an Iraqi government facility for the manufacture of chemicals for
its gas attacks against Iran in the 1980s. Intelligence believed that it
may also have built three nerve-gas factories in the area.[21]

Squadron Leaders Garry Lennox and Kevin Weeks were spear-
heading the low-level eight-ship attack, each aircraft carrying five
1,000-pounders,[22] and planning to employ the loft profile to penetrate the target accurately. Three aircraft returned to base because
of technical faults but the other five pressed on through heavy
triple-A fire and rained twenty-five bombs down on the radar facility, breaching the bunker. Five seconds later, one of the crews saw a
fireball erupt in the distance. Closer inspection revealed a series of

fires on the nearby hillside. Garry, thirty-four, and 37-year-old Kev
failed to respond to radio check-ins.[23]

News of the fourth RAF Tornado going down in combat reverberated around the RAF's Gulf bases. At Tabuk, the ground crew
who had readied the jet for the mission were shattered. 'When the
crew didn't return, their see-off team refused to leave the airfield,'
said engineer Dean Wood. 'They just stayed there waiting for
news. The Boss eventually came around and told us there was little
chance they had survived. It was a terrible day and hit us ground
crew hard. We kept asking for updates, clinging onto the possibility
that they might appear.' Later that evening, Wood was again tasked
with loading weapons and readying more Tornados for take-off.
'The crews looked ever-more nervous when they arrived. The most
difficult thing was simply chatting to them. We had to appear our
normal selves, trying not to make them feel any worse than they did,
but what do you say to a man who has just lost two friends and is
flying into something that may kill him?'[24]

Dave Bellamy knew Lennox and Weeks well. He was numbed
by the loss. 'It was a very bad period of time, real stress and
intense emotional pressure. You felt a sense of personal loss even
though there was nothing you could have done. But my overriding
thought was for their wives and kids back home. What were they
going through?'

Eight months pregnant with their second child, Anne Lennox
was going through hell at her parents' home in Yorkshire. When the
Padre and an RAF officer rang the doorbell she knew immediately
what it meant. They informed her that her husband was missing in
action. There was no other news. 'My immediate reaction was anger
and rage coupled with hope. He was such a strong fighter I knew
that, if he could, he would come home. After that I felt numb.'[25]

* * *

The decision was finally made. The sortie against Ar Rutbah on 22
January would be the last Tornado low-level bombing mission of

the war.[26] 'When we stopped flying low level and went to medium level, that wasn't because we felt we couldn't take any more losses or were hurt by public opinion,' Air Vice-Marshal Sandy Wilson, the first Commander of British Forces Middle East in the build-up to war, said. 'It was a straightforward operational decision. At that stage we didn't need to go down and drop weapons at low level.'[27] The change of strategy was endorsed at the very top of government. 'Despite the Tornado losses, it was clear by 23 January that we had achieved air superiority,' wrote Prime Minister John Major. 'To reduce the risks to our aircraft we switched to operations at medium level.'[28] General Sir Peter de la Billière, the former SAS commander who had taken over from Sandy Wilson, was more forthright. 'The reason those aircraft crashed was because they were flying low level for one reason or another,' he said in a later documentary. 'And so, one said, well is this necessary? Is this a sensible thing to do? The answer was "no", and I didn't want to go on doing it.'[29]

It was a momentous change in RAF thinking. 'Our training philosophy, our aircraft, avionics systems, weapons systems, indeed our whole procurement programme had been tailored to the pursuit of the goal of perfecting low-level tactics,' Bill Wratten, the British Air Commander, said later. 'It was our chosen style of operations and we were very good at it. It was because we were so good at it, and because low level is the most difficult operating regime of all, that our crews were able to adapt so readily to less demanding ways of waging war.'[30]

To most aircrew, the move to medium-level operations made sense. 'The absolute priority to deny runway operating surfaces to the enemy was no longer compelling,' one Tornado pilot said. 'It was clearly pointless to suffer a very high casualty rate to deny the enemy a capability which he didn't appear to want to use.'[31] Jerry Witts, the Dhahran Tornado Detachment Commander, agreed. 'At this higher altitude, things seemed much more pedestrian. Triple-A was still trying its best to reach us, but now we could look down almost contemptuously on streams of tracer as they whirled about beneath us.'

Although the bombers now transitioned to medium level, the six Tornado GR1A reconnaissance jets based at Dhahran continued their solo low-level missions gathering key intelligence on Iraqi Scud launchers.

The overriding challenge was now the difficulty in establishing the effect of the medium-level use of unguided 'dumb' bombs. A few days into the tactical shift, the Tornado's success from 20,000ft was still being questioned. The Mission Report of an eight-ship attack on an oil pumping station close to Basra on 25 January was typical of the many that were winging their way up the chain of command:

Six aircraft delivered their weapons onto the target area. However, no damage assessment has yet been received on this target making it difficult to come to any conclusions. Given the ballistic errors inherent in the Tornado at medium level and the small size of the nominated target, it is likely that any direct hits would be by luck rather than design. We feel that the small size of the target required the attentions of PGMs [Precision-Guided Munitions] rather than dumb bombs, however accurately aimed.[32]

Although the writer of that Mission Report would not have known it, the ability for Tornados to deliver Precision-Guided Munitions was already on its way. Those involved with the RAF's oldest strike jet had been on the case for many months.

* * *

The twin-engine Buccaneer bomber had been in service since 1962, but it was equipped with the relatively modern Pave Spike laser-guided system, which could steer suitably equipped bombs onto their targets with incredible precision. Shortly after Saddam's Republican Guard had crossed into Kuwait the previous August, the Buccaneer force gently reminded RAF chiefs of its capability.[33] But they were turned down, mainly because there was simply not enough room at the region's airbases for more military jets. And more importantly, in the run-up to war, the Americans had already promised to provide any laser designation for Tornados if they moved to medium level. But the US air forces were increasingly preoccupied with hunting down Saddam's Scud missiles, which were presenting a real threat to coalition unity. They now had no jets to spare.

The ageing Buccaneer had its critics, but fliers loved it. 'There is nothing the Buccaneer cannot do,' recalled one pilot. 'I've flown well over 100 different types of aeroplane and to me the Buccaneer is the finest I've ever known.'[34] Armed with anti-ship missiles and conventional or tactical nuclear bombs, the jet was originally designed for maritime attacks. Powered by two Rolls-Royce engines, it could fly low and fast, over 670mph at 200ft and well below. In many ways it was the perfect partner for the Tornado. The previous November, despite the continuing belief that they would never be needed, the Station Commander of the Buccaneer base at RAF Lossiemouth in north-east Scotland had suggested it would perhaps be a good idea to review and refine the jet's use of Pave Spike at medium level. His Boss agreed. After a dozen training sorties deploying 1,000-pounders fitted with a laser-seeking head which used vanes to steer them onto target from 20,000ft, they had demonstrated that they were well capable of carrying out such attacks. A report went to the Ministry of Defence confirming their ability to 'spike' from both low and medium level. Again, the Buccaneer force offered its services in the Gulf.

The answer was an 'emphatic no'.[35]

'We were continually assured that the Buccaneer wouldn't be required but had done some planning just in case,' a senior engineer said. 'We were told that there was absolutely no way the Ministry of Defence would consider sending the Buccaneer to the Gulf. So we all relaxed, calmed down and all training ceased.'[36] Knowing they'd done their best to contribute to the liberation of Kuwait, Buccaneer pilots, navigators and ground crew enjoyed a peaceful Christmas. That relaxed atmosphere continued while the Tornados went to war. On 22 January, Buccaneer Squadron Commander Bill Cope, still eager to get out there, asked his Boss if it was wise to go ahead with his skiing holiday booked that week.

'Sorry, Bill, they do not want us,' was the response. 'Have a good holiday.'[37]

Only that morning, Lennox and Weeks had gone down in their pre-dawn raid.

Hours later, the Lossiemouth Station Commander was directed to the secure telephone at the War Operations Centre. His caller had one question: 'How long will it take you to deploy Buccaneers to the Gulf?'

Completely blindsided, he took a few moments to compose himself before responding. 'Three days.'

'*Cancel your holidays,*' the word went out to all required personnel. '*Return to base. Immediately.*'

The next day the Defence Secretary announced the imminent deployment of the Buccaneers. Why, Tom King was asked, was a 30-year-old aircraft being sent to war?

'Because we need to improve the standard of precision bombing,' he replied.[38]

* * *

While they waited for the ageing Buccaneers to provide some laser-guided accuracy, the Tornados continued the medium-level missions with their 'dumb' bombs.

On 24 January, Bob Ankerson was still waiting to complete a combat sortie. The day before, attending communion at a makeshift altar in the Padre's room, he'd had a strange premonition. 'I had the feeling that I wasn't going to get back from the sortie. No doubt I wasn't the only one who sometimes felt that way. There was no foundation for this feeling, it was just there at the back of my mind. But I drew comfort from my faith and beliefs; they provided me with a basis for coping with my subsequent experiences.'

Rested and with a clear conscience, he set about planning an attack on Ar Rumaylah, not far from the airfield where Nichol and Peters had been shot down a week earlier. The images of the POWs were still a talking point at Dhahran and one of Bob's close friends from Bruggen, Ivor Evans, was in no doubt about their effect. 'It was as we expected; we were up against someone who didn't take much interest in the Geneva Convention. But the pictures of the POWs just made us all even more determined.' As the leader of his own four-ship formation, the previous losses were also something to be considered, especially as Dhahran had – so far – not suffered any casualties. 'There was a feeling of relief and expectation – relief that we were avoiding the fatalities and expectation that it couldn't last.'

As Bob's formation prepared for a 3.50am take-off, their Tornados were each loaded with five 1,000-pounders, their mission to 'disrupt ops and destroy aircraft in the open'.[39] He went through the personal sanitisation process, but decided to keep his copy of a small New Testament Bible in his breast pocket.

By the time they got to the tanker, two of the four Tornados had turned back with technical issues. Bob and his pilot Simon Burgess were now leading the formation with the other Tornado piloted by Stew Gillies. Just before crossing the border, Bob's radar failed. Normally it would have meant an immediate return to base, but he was determined not to turn back yet again. 'I was completely happy with our navigation kit as I'd already managed to get a radar fix. My focus was on getting the mission done, not because it was hugely tactically important, but because I needed to complete it for myself. To *demonstrate* I could fly a combat sortie. Those previous feelings of not completing my first mission were really playing on my mind.' As they set their armament switches to live, the crew rationalised that, although they were already satisfied with their positioning, if they turned their radar off for a while, it might restart later.

As Stew Gillies and his navigator Pete Rochelle crossed the border, their RHWR showed an enemy Hawk missile installation had located them.[40] An American system, probably captured during the invasion of Kuwait, it remained at target acquisition status, so they pressed on. It did not take long for the Tornados to detect another hostile radar, this time from an SA-3 system – a highly effective anti-aircraft missile that had shot down an American F-16 fighter a few days earlier. Gillies was worried. 'This was more problematic. We had just started our attack run and knew this was probably real.' The crew immediately began chaffing, sending out thousands of metallic strands to confuse the potential missile track.

The two Tornados closed in on Ar Rumaylah as the early-morning pre-dawn glow appeared from the east. At 20,000 feet it was getting light, though still dark on the ground, with intermittent cloud obscuring their view. With nine minutes to go before they struck the airfield, a loud warble sounded on Bob and Simon's RHWR. Simon spoke rapidly. 'I've got a fighter showing on the nose. A Mirage.'[41]

'F-15s showing out to the right,' Bob responded. Their accompanying fighter escort went to investigate.

'Good lads!'

Five minutes from their objective, Bob had another go at fixing his equipment. 'I'm still trying the radar but getting sod all out of it,' he told his pilot. A few seconds later he added: 'Checking weapons package correct.'

They were closing fast on the target now, and the navigator was determined there were no excuses or hiccups that would end in another failure. 'The last thing we wanted was to get to the target and have the bombs not operate because of an incorrect switch selection. We had turned back the previous night, but we were going to do it right this time.'

'Switches live,' Simon announced calmly as they closed in, checking that all the weapons armament switches were made. 'Nothing on the CWP.'

The Central Warning Panel was clear.

'Roger,' Bob replied. 'We've got a minute to the turn.'

'Roger,' the pilot confirmed. 'Seventeen miles.'

They were now two minutes away.

'Fix/Attack is selected.'

The aircrew talked through the weapons system settings,

double-checking all was correct. They were closing fast as light seeped over the horizon.

'We've got a minute to run,' Bob said.

'Time to Go running down now.'

On their cockpit's audio recording, small hints of growing tension can be heard in the crew's voices.

'Okay,' Bob confirmed. 'Looking good.'

'Double-check. All switches live.' Simon was making absolutely certain everything was correct.

'Forty seconds to release . . .' Bob said above the low whine of the electronic equipment.

'Twenty seconds.'

A few miles from Ankerson, Stew Gillies' radar warner sounded the urgent siren of an SA-3 missile guidance, suggesting that a SAM had been fired at them. With ten seconds to go to the target, 'I had not seen a missile launch and my naive optimistic guess was that we had about twenty seconds before it hit us, so I decided to drop our bombs and evade the missile when we were lighter.'

Both jets pressed on with the attack.

'Ten seconds,' Bob called.

'Five, four, three, two, one . . .

'Bombs gone!'

Their five 1,000-pounders fell away.

'Okay, come left.' The words had barely left Bob Ankerson's lips when an almighty explosion shook the aircraft. On the Cockpit Voice Recorder – the 'black box' – there is a loud gasp followed by the blare of the warning siren indicating serious system failures.

As Stew Gillies released his munitions, he started an aggressive manoeuvre in maximum reheat to avoid any incoming missile. 'There was a huge orange flash and an incredibly loud, angry metallic bursting sound. The aircraft rolled violently left and pitched nose down. I thought we had been hit by the SA-3.'

'Don't eject,' he told his navigator. 'I can still fly.'

'As if!' replied Rochelle from the rear cockpit. 'We are over the Republican Guard! Fly the fucking aircraft!'

Gillies was already ahead of the game.

'My plan was to limp over to the Saudi border or at least the open desert, away from the Republican Guard, and then eject.'

Sirens screaming, Bob and Simon checked their own aircraft. 'I thought we had been hit by an SA-3 from the missile site to the south of the target. There was a feeling of total disbelief.' For a brief moment the cockpit was silent. Simon had acknowledged the warnings by cancelling the cockpit attention-getters on the coaming. The lights still flashed red but at least with the alarm silenced the crew could communicate. The captions on the CWP were indicating the urgent signal of 'L FIRE'.

'Left engine fire!' Simon called, shutting it down and hitting the fire extinguisher button. 'Stay with it,' he told Bob. He didn't want his navigator to eject. The aircraft was on fire, but at least if they were flying they had a chance of scraping home.

Stew Gillies was fighting his own battle as his Tornado lurched drunkenly across the sky. Glancing out of the cockpit he spotted multiple flashes of groundfire followed by a much bigger flash from below. *Missile launch.* 'A bright orange flame appeared to be tracking us and manoeuvring. We deployed more chaff. I broke low and the missile exploded in three flashes, well away from us.'

'Stay with it,' Simon repeated to Bob. The controls appeared to still be responding to his commands, despite the spreading flames. Then, twenty-eight seconds after bomb release, something startling caught his attention. 'Check the back!' His voice crackled with tension. 'Check the back . . .!'

Bob craned his neck around. 'The left-hand side of the aircraft was now engulfed in flames. They were spreading towards the wing root near me and grew in length to around 6 feet. I realised we would not be getting home that day.' The siren activated again, indicating further major failures. 'I told Simon we were going to have to get out of the jet *very* soon.'

'Okay, stay with it,' Simon smoothly replied, trying to get every second of flight he could before ejecting. He wanted to keep going for as long as possible to get them away from the elite Republican

Guard infantry units dug in directly below them. Like Stew, he was thinking that, if they could eject in an empty stretch of desert, there was a chance of rescue.

'Two-seven-zero.' Bob steered them due west.

They jettisoned the external fuel tanks to try to stem the fire. It made no difference to the size of the blaze.

'Stay with it,' Simon urged again.

Bob understood. 'I was closer to the flames than Simon so I was more worried, but, despite the obvious risk of an explosion, we were still flying, so it was better to stay in our cocoon.'

But not for long.

'It's burning through the wing now!' Bob stared at the flames billowing from the Tornado's left wing. Sixty-four seconds had elapsed since the explosion. 'We're going to have to go!' His tone was insistent now.

'Yes, I know.' Another alarm blared out.

'I'm losing control,' Simon yelled. The jet was no longer respond-ing to his commands. Fire was ripping through the flight control system. 'Stand by.'

'Okay, I'm ready.' Bob glanced at the altimeter: 15,000ft.

Exactly ninety seconds after they had released their bombs, the aircraft was in its death throes.

'Stand by.' Simon spoke rapidly now. 'Stand by ... eject, eject, eject!'

Both crewmen pulled their ejection handles on the third com-mand and were rocketed upwards into the breaking dawn.

The sirens burst back into life.

Then there was silence as the empty Tornado fell to earth.

* * *

As Stew Gillies powered away from what he thought was a missile exploding below, he glanced over at the other Tornado. 'I saw the canopy, front seat and backseat ejections from the aircraft of Burgess and Ankerson. We heard nothing more from them.'

In the light of the breaking dawn he watched white vapour spill over the top of his port wing, pushing past some ragged, flapping metal. He had amber warning lights on his CWP, indicating numerous failures. The Tornado was in bad shape. 'We weren't sure where we were, being without functioning navigation kit, and we needed someone to look at us from the outside. We also needed more fuel if we were fit enough to get home.'[42]

Another Tornado pulled alongside and gave Stew the bad news. 'He could see daylight through the fin and tailplane.'

Eventually, Dhahran's runway loomed ahead and they began their final approach. At 500ft Gillies flicked the undercarriage handle to lower the landing gear. Nothing happened. He then initiated the secondary, emergency system which blasted down the undercarriage. Finally, he coaxed the stricken Tornado onto the ground. In the rear seat, Pete Rochelle remembered 'holding onto the ejection handle' throughout the whole experience until the aircraft slowed to a halt. Just in case.

Shaken, they climbed out and surveyed the damage. 'There was shrapnel under Pete's seat, holes through the cockpit, the left wing, spoiler, left engine nozzle and the fin,' Gillies said. 'And a hole the size of Desperate Dan in the tailplane.' It was nothing short of a miracle that they had been able to fly at all. And an extraordinary testament to the Tornado's resilience that it had managed to carry them the 400 miles back home. Cliff Spink, the overall RAF Commander at Dhahran, was shocked by the state of the jet. 'It looked like a total wreck and it was difficult to see how it had stayed airborne. The crew did a truly incredible job to get it back to base and on the ground. It really was an astonishing achievement.'

When they'd finished scanning the devastation, the Warrant Officer in charge of the engineering ground crew turned to Stew and Pete. 'Sirs,' he said, 'I suggest you get yourselves a strong cup of tea.'

Later, a closer inspection of the airframe and overall weapons system revealed the awful truth. Both Tornados had been blown up by their own bombs. A technical issue meant that as the second bomb had fallen from each aircraft, it had immediately detonated. Stew and Pete had been extremely lucky that their jet had managed to withstand the 1,000-pounder exploding a matter of feet beneath them.

The news of Bob Ankerson's fate came as a bitter blow to his friend Ivor Evans, also flying from Dhahran. 'No matter how much we expected that it might happen, the loss of one of our aircraft was a shock – and heightened by the fact I obviously knew Bob and his wife Chris really well. But there was little time to dwell; we were all soon back into the planning and action of the war.'

Five RAF Tornados had now gone down.

* * *

After ejecting from the stricken Tornado, Bob Ankerson had sensed a great rush of air then a tumbling sensation as he was buffeted about at 15,000ft. A few seconds later and 5,000ft lower, he was abruptly jerked upwards when the parachute automatically deployed. 'It was just getting light, and looking around I could see shadows on the ground, small arms fire and triple-A. It was flat, open desert as far as the eye could see. I just thought, *What on earth am I going to do now?*'

'Bob! Bob! Are you all right?'

He glanced around to see Simon dangling beneath his parachute. 'I'm fine,' he shouted, relieved that he could see his pilot in the gathering dawn. But as they descended into cloud, Simon disappeared. It would be some time before they saw each other again.

As the sand rushed up to meet him, Bob tried to remember his parachute drills, the lessons learned from jumping off wooden benches onto green gym mats. 'I could hear, in my head, the instructor saying, "Don't anticipate the landing. Keep your elbows tucked in, knees together and legs slightly bent. Whatever you do, don't try to fend off the approaching ground!"'

He landed without injury but became immediately aware of the deep tyre tracks around him. 'It was as if I had landed on a motor-way in the desert!'

Peering into the gloom, he noticed garage-sized shapes dotted across the landscape. 'They weren't some strange topographical feature but camouflaged tank and infantry positions. I had landed in the midst of a huge military deployment of the Republican Guard!'

Bob dropped to his knees and began bundling in his parachute, ready to bury it. Seconds later, bullets cracked above his head. He looked up to see a line of a dozen soldiers heading towards him. The shots felt unnervingly close. 'There was nothing I could do. I knelt by the parachute, put my hands in the air, and waited for them to get to me.'

* * *

Three thousand miles away, his wife tried to ignore the ringing in her ears. The doorbell sounded again and she awoke with a start. It was just before 7am. 'I knew immediately what it meant. Why else would the bell ring while it was still dark?' Chris Ankerson was on her own in their comfortable married quarters at RAF Bruggen. A myriad thoughts now rushed through her mind. She put on her dressing gown and began walking down the stairs. She stopped halfway. Where the staircase turned a corner on the land-ing there was a small window. She peered out. *A black car.* Her heart raced. Every senior officer had one. 'All aircrew wives have a deep-seated fear of a black car appearing outside their house. It meant only one thing.'

She took a deep breath and made her way slowly down the remaining five steps. Wing Commander Dusty Miller, Bob's Squadron Commander, was standing on the front doorstep. Before he could utter a word, she asked one question: 'Is he dead?'

'We don't know,' Dusty solemnly responded. He then explained that Bob hadn't returned from a mission. Chris listened in shocked silence. Someone thought they 'might' have seen ejection seats coming out of their Tornado, but there was no confirmation. An hour later, Bob's great friend Allen Snowball arrived. 'Snowy' was Gareth's godfather and Bob's 'right-hand man' in case anything happened.

Her son was at boarding school in England. Chris knew she had to get a message to him. It was dawn in Suffolk and Dusty woke up Gareth's housemaster, Richard Fuller. The headmaster was immediately informed; it fell to him to deliver any important news to his pupils. He'd previously had the unenviable task of telling children a parent had died, but never of announcing to a 12-year-old boy that his father was missing in action in a hostile land.

Gareth Ankerson was having breakfast with his friends when he was told to go to the headmaster's study on a matter of 'high importance'. He tried to gauge what it was by studying Mr Fuller's face. 'I sat for a minute thinking what had I done wrong that would be so important that I would be dragged out of breakfast by my housemaster? As I walked through the dining hall my brain was racing.' For any schoolboy, a summons to the headmaster's office could mean only one thing. 'What on earth had I done to get me into so much trouble that the head wanted to see me? It was quite a scary prospect.'

He trudged through the corridors, contemplating his fate. 'The walls looked dimmer, the wooden panels suggesting they knew what the head was going to say to me. We arrived outside the headmaster's stout wooden door – it looked so evil, sucking me in.'[43]

He was told to wait as Mr Fuller went in. Sitting outside, he could hear mumbled words and the occasional mention of his name. Then the door creaked open.

'Gareth, come in please,' the headmaster said gently.

'Yessir,' he quickly replied. 'The door was laughing at me. I could hear it whispering, *You're in trouble.*'

Gareth was directed to a large, comfortable armchair, next to Mr Fuller. The head stood behind his desk. 'Gareth . . .' He paused, his brow furrowed. 'I can't tell you this standing behind here.'

What on earth could this mean? Was this a good thing, or a bad thing?

He stepped forward and perched awkwardly on the leading edge of his desk. Gareth couldn't understand why he was being so kind. *What is happening?*

'I need to tell you something very serious ...' The head paused, looking him straight in the eye. 'Gareth, your father hasn't come back from a mission ...'

He hesitated.

'He's gone ... missing ...'

'No!' Gareth screamed. 'Not my dad. This stuff does not happen to me!'

But then reality kicked in. The television reports of war in the Gulf, the newspapers, the prisoners, the conversations back home over the summer about people dying in Tornado crashes. 'At twelve years old, a light was turned on in my head and I understood what it all meant. I broke down in tears.'

The head gave him a few minutes then continued softly. 'Gareth, we received a phone call at seven this morning. I'm afraid I don't know much detail. When your father's plane was shot down it was in flames, but the aircraft next to them did see two smaller flames shoot up out of the fire. This, I would presume, would have been your father and his pilot. At this moment we are still not sure.'

Gareth instantly latched onto the words 'two flames shot up'. He knew what ejection seats did. It was a tiny glimmer of hope that he would hold onto with all his might. But he could not prevent more tears pouring down his face.

Between sobs, Gareth managed to say that he wanted one of his close friends to be told what had happened as soon as possible. 'She knew my father well and might take it quite hard as our fathers had both served together. No one ever said this, but I somehow *knew* that the RAF itself was an extension of my own family. It was the way we lived on the base when at home, the way we mixed and spoke when back at school. So I just knew it was right for her to be told separately to the rest of the school.'

The head agreed that Gareth should get some rest in Mr Fuller's flat until he was ready to see his friends.

'Are you okay?' a bunch of waiting pupils asked. Rumours must have spread fast that something had happened to his dad.

A friend handed over his treasured Sega computer game so that Gareth would have something to occupy his mind. But he couldn't stop thinking about his father. 'Why my dad? Why not someone else? I was thinking it must all be a bad dream and I'd soon wake up. The day was going very slowly and I felt as if two years had already gone by.'

Mr Fuller reappeared, asked what he wanted for lunch and handed him a letter from his dorm mates, wishing him well and asking to see him. 'I thought it was very kind, but I was just not up to speaking to people.' The housemaster then returned with some food and his close friend who had been told the news. 'We both burst into tears then chatted for a while before she had to go back to lessons.'

Gareth was summoned to the telephone. It was his mother. Chris was still in a daze but tried to be positive. 'Dad will be fine. He's trained for this. The ejection seats are wonderful. He will be fine.'

Gareth didn't buy it. 'She tried to be happy, but when she heard my voice nothing had to be said, we just cried. I asked if I was going home. My mother shouted down the phone: "Yes! Yes! Of course! You need to be here."'

* * *

The Iraqis had taken Gareth's father to a bunker just 100 yards from where he had landed. 'I could feel my knees trembling. It was such an alien situation. It was quite a terrifying prospect that someone else was calling the shots. I had gone from being an officer flying a Tornado jet and here I was shaking like a leaf. I wondered what my captors thought of me.' He was placed on a chair outside and searched. His small Bible was taken, along with his watch, then he was blindfolded and had his hands tied. An officer arrived and asked him his name and rank. As military law required, Bob supplied the details. Other questions then followed, but Bob continued the protocol of simply replying, 'I cannot answer that question.'

'They continued asking me various questions but there was no real coercion. I wondered how long that would last.' He was then driven around a series of other buried emplacements, apparently being passed up the military command chain. 'At one stage I was asked what the "C of E" engraved on my dog tags, my identification discs, meant. I explained it was my religion, Church of England, that I was a Christian. The questioner told me not to worry, that he was also a Christian, that I'd be looked after and not harmed. I wasn't convinced.' Later, at a military checkpoint, someone reached into the car and slapped him hard across the head. 'It was probably understandable; a soldier just giving vent to his feelings but with no real purpose.' As the journey continued, so did the questions, becoming increasingly threatening at each new location. 'They told me in no uncertain terms that if I didn't answer *their* questions, they would send me to someone who would *make* me answer.'

Still blindfolded, in the last ride he was aware of someone else in the car. An Iraqi voice asked, 'What is your name?'

'Bob Ankerson.'

The question was repeated. 'Simon Burgess,' came the answer. It was the first time Bob was aware that his pilot had also been caught. They were eventually taken to what appeared to be a farm court-yard. Bob was thrown to the floor in a dimly lit room.

An interrogator arrived. 'What aircraft do you fly?' he demanded.

'I cannot answer that question.' Again, Bob gave the stock reply.

The question was repeated again and again as the Iraqi made clear he was losing patience with the airman. 'There were obviously a number of people in the room. I could hear other voices and someone else was interpreting. It was curious; while there was no immediate violence, the air of menace was all-encompassing.'

The questions, and Bob's parrying of them, went on for some time as veiled threats became increasingly unveiled.

'You *will* talk to us eventually, and you *will* tell us what we want to know. You already *know* this. It is only a matter of time.'

For a few moments there was silence before the interrogator spoke again.

'You know my nickname is The Butcher?'

It was all beginning to sound deeply unpleasant and Bob's initial thought – '*It's like being in a B-movie!*' – was soon overtaken by The Butcher's final warning.

'I am going away for five minutes. When I return, I will get the answers!'

The man returned a short while later and Bob again refused to co-operate. Then began the same procedure every other prisoner of war had endured after being shot down.

'I was on the concrete floor, blindfolded and in a foetal position with my feet bent up. They started to beat me with what felt like the edge of a wooden cricket bat. Crack! I was hit on the calves and thighs. Crack! They hit my back and across the shoulder blades.' Each strike was followed by the same question. 'What aircraft did you fly?'

Bob was determined not to give anything away and to stick to the 'rules' of name, rank and number. 'But it was bloody painful and I was in no doubt that the guy meant business.' The interrogators worked as a team. One asked simple questions in clear English, another administered the beating when answers were not forthcoming. 'You have no idea if a blow is coming – but having not answered a question, you anticipate it for a very long time . . .'

The violence continued unabated, and after one of the early sessions, the interrogator left. 'I still couldn't see, but it was obvious someone was still in the room. Suddenly, I was lifted up beneath the arms and pulled across the floor. He lifted my arm onto what felt like a concrete block. This was now really terrifying and my imagination was running rampant. What was going to happen? What was this for? I presumed they were going to break my arms on the block. But then the guard just left. Looking back, I presume he was showing some basic humanity, trying to make me more comfortable in the midst of the pain, leaning me against the block. I often thought about that man over the coming hours.'

The Butcher returned and the beatings continued. 'We had been through various training scenarios, but nothing prepares you for the reality of violent interrogation and I knew that, at some point, I would have to go down a different path.'

The questions rained down, as did the cricket bat on the fleshy parts of Bob's body. Arms, thighs, back, shoulders. 'I have no idea how long it all went on. Perhaps hours? In the end I thought, *This is bloody daft, how long can I take this?* Everyone has their own personal threshold. Was it worth being permanently injured to protect what they must know already?'

Amid the blows, the same question was repeated.

'What aircraft do you fly?'

'Tornado.'

Like every person before him, whether flier or Special Forces, Bob had broken. He gave them answers that could easily be found in newspapers or on television. He took care not to make up the information, just kept it to a minimum, developing a strategy of wandering off topic into totally irrelevant areas. 'I felt that if I was talking, I was in control of what was happening. They seemed content that their interrogation was working and I was relatively happy I wasn't being asked about vital issues.'

But it was a dangerous game, because once he had started talking, he could not say 'no' to any further questions as his captors would know they had hit on something useful. Like the other POWs, Bob struggled with the notion that he had given in and was letting his friends down. 'I promised myself I wouldn't talk about Tornado operations, especially its defensive capabilities, which could put others at risk. It was daft – back at Bruggen, when we had our regular tests about the various bits of defensive kit, I always had to work really hard to remember all the facts and figures. Now, in an Iraqi dungeon, it was like the damn things were all written on a board in front of me, clear as day. I had a real fear that I could affect the safety of my colleagues and I didn't want to find myself lacking in courage.'

* * *

Chris Ankerson had also found herself in need of courage while confronted by a dizzying multitude of tasks. Bob's parents had to be told. Arrangements needed to be made for Gareth to return. She had a house full of people. The news continued to talk of coalition losses. So many cups of tea and biscuits were consumed that some-one had to get replenishments from the nearby Naafi store.[44] 'There was a lot to be done and so many people coming in and out of the quarters. Things were going on around me, Dusty making calls, friends arriving. It was all happening and I was in a daze; in fact, I was clearly in shock. I remember at one point announcing, "But it's my day to wash my hair, I need to get that done!" I realised life was going to have to go on, but at the same time, everything had changed. When Bob had graduated as an officer in 1973, I remember the reviewing officer giving the speech saying, "You will make many good acquaintances in the Royal Air Force, but only a handful of very close friends." That day, our closest friends gathered around. They were there for me and I drew such great strength and comfort from their presence.'

One of those friends was Di Evans, whose husband Ivor had been serving alongside Bob. Di had also been woken at Bruggen by a very early phone call. 'No good news comes at that hour, especially when your husband is serving in the Gulf War. I picked up the phone and the Station Commander's wife's voice immediately said, "It's not Ivor." A chill ran through my veins. *If it's not my husband, whose is it?* She then said, "It's Bob."'

As one of Chris's close friends, Di was told that the 'knock on the door' was already underway and she was to be among the next visitors to the Ankersons' home. A car would pick her up in five minutes. 'I think we were all numb and just couldn't take it all in. A huge machine of activity took over our lives as Chris's Gulf War now changed.'

And, at the back of Di's mind, an unwelcome thought was already starting to surface. 'Would that "knock on the door" be for me tomorrow?'

January 24th was the same day as the funerals of Kieran Duffy

and Norman Dent, the Tornado crew killed during low-level training in Oman eleven days earlier. Bob's close friend, Snowy, was
supposed to be taking a number of senior officers to the funeral in
England, but a more personal mission was now ordered. He was to
fly his RAF Andover transport aircraft to the UK and collect his
best friend's young son from boarding school.

As he waited in his dormitory, young Gareth knew, as the man
of the house now, it was his duty to get home. 'The most important
thing was to be with Mum, to hug her. To look after her.'

He went to bed knowing that Snowy would pick him up the next
morning. But he had a sleepless night. 'All I could see was Saddam
Hussein standing at the bottom of my bed pointing a gun at my head
saying: "It's your turn now. I have killed your father. You're next."'

CHAPTER TWELVE

A BOLSHIE LADY

25 JANUARY–4 FEBRUARY

In late January, General Norman Schwarzkopf updated the media on the progress of the war. Thirty-eight enemy airfields had been attacked. At least nine were rendered non-operational, and seventy hardened aircraft shelters had been destroyed out of a total of nearly 600.[1] 'By the last week in January the skies over Iraq belonged to the coalition. After two weeks of war, my instincts and experience told me that we'd bombed most of our strategic targets enough to accomplish our campaign objectives. It was now time, I thought, to shift most of our air power onto the army we were about to face in battle.'[2]

The weight of allied attacks now moved, with Tornados attacking ammunition and fuel dumps, and airfields from medium level. B-52 heavy bombers pummelled frontline positions day and night, causing huge destruction to armour, artillery and personnel. Their bombs were followed by millions of leaflets, encouraging the Iraqi military to desert their posts. 'If you come to us, we will treat you as an Arab brother,' they were told.[3]

Group Captain Cliff Spink was in command at Dhahran, which was at the heart of preparations for the expected land campaign. In the days before the war, his force had been bolstered by six recently modified Tornado GR1A state-of-the-art reconnaissance aircraft, though initially there was little concept of how they might be used. That changed as the first Iraqi Scud missiles hit home. 'There was a real fear of the indiscriminate nature of the Scuds,' he recalled.[4] 'The warheads that were hitting Israel were threatening to bring the Jewish state into the war and rip apart the carefully constructed alliance of Western and Arab nations.'

On a number of occasions, Spink found himself unnervingly close to the action. 'During one of the first Scud attacks, I was driving towards one of our Tornado sites on the airfield. I glanced over at the Patriot anti-missile battery about half a mile away. Suddenly there was the most enormous bang and flash as a missile launched. I could see the shock wave forming and spreading out, coming down the road towards me. I dived out of the car and buried myself as best I could in a dip by the road. Seconds later there was another huge explosion as an incoming Scud was hit and the remains fell onto the base about 300 yards from the Tornados. Then bits of Patriot missile debris started to clatter down around me. It was a pretty interesting experience.'

The attacks needed to be stopped and General Schwarzkopf was ordered to use every means at his disposal to counter the threat. But Saddam's troops had mounted the Scuds on tracked vehicles and used the sandy wastes to hide and fire them. Special Forces were covertly inserted into the Western Desert to seek out and destroy the launchers and their control systems, and a substantial proportion of coalition air assets were also diverted to the task. Cliff Spink's recce force now came to the fore.

With its revolutionary infra-red system, the GR1A could operate in total darkness. Fitted with VHS video recorders instead of the standard Mauser cannons, the Tornado Infra-Red Reconnaissance System (TIRRS) could also pick up information not visible to the naked eye, even in daylight. Images from the three infra-red sensors – one downward-looking and one on each side – produced a continuous horizon-to-horizon scan which was recorded onto video tapes. The Reconnaissance Intelligence Centre at base could review the tapes immediately after landing, even before engine shut-down. Imagery was also relayed to the navigator's display in real time.[5]

At ultra-low level and high speed, either crew member could hit a switch to highlight something of interest for later review.[6] Crucially, a unique capability of the GR1A allowed imagery to be replayed and manipulated mid-flight for a deeper analysis, perhaps during quieter parts of the sortie. The navigator's capacity to review the imagery while still en route and send results back to base not only enabled more responsive tasking of further intelligence gathering and battle-damage assessment, but even the potential to launch an immediate attack.

The system provided some startling capabilities. It could tell if aircraft on the ground had full or empty fuel tanks, if their engines had recently been used, and detect the heat trace of recently departed jets.[7] Commanders in Riyadh soon recognised that the Tornado's infra-red capability made it increasingly difficult for the Iraqis to hide their weapons. The tracks of recently moved tanks – and, more importantly now, missile launchers – were vulnerable to detection due to their heat signatures.

Using the in-cockpit review systems, one of the recce Tornados had reported a suspected Scud battery shortly after the first attacks. Navigator Gordon Walker and his pilot were tasked with confirming its presence. With no time to organise a tanker, the crew used four external tanks, one under each wing and two under the fuselage where bombs would normally be mounted; just enough to complete the mission.

'Alone, unarmed and unafraid', as their maxim had it, they took off from Dhahran at 3am and headed across the border before dropping down for a high-speed solo dash into the target area. Walker turned on the recorders and they picked up significant vehicle movement. 'We saw loads of tracks in the desert. It was like overflying Salisbury Plain [training area] seeing the army's tank tracks criss-crossing everywhere.'[8]

And sure enough, as their search continued, they located the launchers. 'We flashed over them and then headed back to friendly territory again. We thought they were firing at us, but it turned out to be the reflection of the green lights inside the cockpit on the rain outside. It was a bit spooky, though.' Travelling back to Dhahran at 670mph, Walker jettisoned all four empty tanks to lower the drag, but they still made it back with very little fuel to spare. The video tapes were rushed away for analysis. 'It appeared that we might have located as many as four Scud launchers.'

Walker was also amazed by what they could see when they played back the tape. 'It was like looking at aerial photographs of the Somme in 1915. You could see the artillery positions dug in, the zigzag of the trench patterns to the main trenches. It all looked like a classic piece of static warfare. I suppose the Iraqis fought that way because they had been fighting the Iranians for eight years and still hadn't grasped the concept of a land–air war.' The freshly analysed footage was rushed to personnel at Air HQ in Riyadh, who passed on the targeting information for immediate airstrikes.

In the first week of the war there had been thirty-five Scud attacks, then eighteen in the second. By early February they were down to one a day.[9] The recce Tornados had acquired a well-deserved reputation as 'the Scudhunters'. Despite the test of mettle, they continued their work at low level throughout the conflict, though not against heavily defended enemy airfields. In fact, an early suggestion that they should overfly airbases to assess the damage from JP233 raids was met with incredulity. *It's near-suicidal*, the planners were told. Those early low-level exploits into the heart of the triple-A fire had taken their toll on the nerves of many fliers.

One senior commander witnessed the effects for himself. 'I had gone into the crew room to grab a coffee. There were a few guys relaxing before heading off on a mission later that night. One of the aircrew was an old friend so I stopped for a chat, but his crewmate was totally unresponsive. He simply wasn't communicating, almost as though he wasn't in the room.'

The disturbed officer was clearly exhibiting *'the thousand-yard stare*', the blank, unfocused gaze of combatants who had become emotionally detached from the horrors they had witnessed. 'I was quite concerned, so asked one of my team to pop down and join me for a coffee. I didn't say why, but I asked him to look at all the crews in the room to see if he noticed anything. He immediately recognised the guy who was clearly affected by his experiences, sitting there, completely vacant. I immediately decided to take him off ops and rested him for a while.'[10]

It was not an isolated case.

* * *

John Broadbent, the Muharraq Tornado Detachment Commander, could also see the stresses building as the losses mounted. 'It was a very difficult time. Several crews were clearly feeling the strain particularly badly. This was hardly surprising – over just a few days our base had lost three crews, some presumed dead. It didn't take the brains of a rocket scientist to work out that if losses continued at that rate, you might only last a matter of weeks.'[11]

Broadbent's pilot Nige Risdale was witnessing this too. 'A few people were quietly acknowledging that they were affected by what we were doing, some more than others. On one occasion, someone asked how I could brief crews about a sortie – where we all faced the very real prospect of dying – without showing any emotion. Well, that was my job. I certainly felt those emotions, but the way I had coped was to compartmentalise them.'[12]

Not all aircrew were able to do the same.

'Frank' was a pilot who had been at the very forefront of the most dangerous low-level missions.[13] He had faced death, flying through the maelstrom to drop his JP233s over the Iraqi airfields. The triple-A had come so close that he had smelled the acrid cordite in his cockpit. He had listened to the terrified radio chatter and had to ignore the gut-wrenching effect of seeing comrades die. Frank – not his real name – had initially been able to continue on operations, somehow managing, like Risdale, to compartmentalise

his experiences. Then he had come back from another intense
low-level mission and seen the images of his friend John Peters
repeated endlessly, relentlessly, on TV. He had *seen* the bruises
on Peters' face, and *knew* they had been caused by torture rather
than ejection.

A fuse blew inside his head.

A chain of images rattled through his mind. The flak bursting
towards him, whipping over the cockpit; colleagues dying in a fireball. He felt the bile burn its way through the back of his throat at
the POWs' plight. Then he completely lost it – screaming, crying,
smashing his fists against the walls. When the medics finally got to
him, he was a sobbing wreck, barely able to function. The Senior
Medical Officer on the base could see he had suffered some sort of
breakdown and immediately evacuated him from the region.

The next day Frank arrived at the psychiatric wing of the military hospital at RAF Wroughton in Wiltshire. He was ushered
into the hands of Wing Commander Gordon Turnbull, one of the
leading military psychiatrists of his generation. Three years earlier, Turnbull's team had dealt with the fallout from the Lockerbie
bombing. Pan Am 103 had been blown up by Libyan terrorists at
30,000ft over the Scottish town, killing 270 people. RAF Mountain
Rescue teams had spent weeks combing the hillside for survivors,
and then body parts. Many had paid the price with post-traumatic
stress disorder.

PTSD – the direct consequence of a range of severe traumatic
episodes – manifested itself most commonly in disassociation,
flashbacks and nightmares. Gordon Turnbull had recently visited
America to study their treatment of Vietnam veterans, which
further fuelled his determination to assemble a team capable of
treating the inevitable psychological casualties of the Gulf conflict.
His pioneering success with Lockerbie gave him the credibility to
persuade senior commanders to allow him to lead the treatment. At
first, there was considerable resistance to this initiative from some
senior officers, who, as Turnbull put it, 'still believed that trauma
reactions were evidence of psychological frailty'. He fought hard to

enlighten them, and did not have to wait long to put his experience to good use.

Frank's official service flying record was immaculate; he was regarded as one of his cohort's best pilots. Twenty-four hours earlier he had been flying frontline operations, into the teeth of enemy fire. Now he found himself being driven in pouring rain through the front gates of a military psychiatric hospital. The car stopped and Frank stepped hesitantly onto the forecourt, looking around at the rolling hills. Supported by a nurse, he shuffled through the doors.

Waiting to greet him, Gordon Turnbull was enraged by what he saw. Someone in the Gulf medical facility had scribbled: 'Acute Melancholia with Hysterical Features' on a scrap of card and hung it around his neck on string. It bounced against Frank's olive-green RAF flying suit as he entered the hospital. 'I felt my blood boil,' Turnbull said. 'As if this poor fellow hadn't been through enough, he had flown all the way back to the UK with a diagnosis of his condition, a wrong one I was fairly sure, scrawled on a piece of cardboard for all to see. It might just as well have said "*unclean*". Forget the First and Second World Wars, I felt as if we had regressed to the Dark Ages.'[14]

The pilot barely acknowledged his new surroundings.

'I had rarely seen such a broken figure. He was hunched over and could barely walk. He looked at me, I imagine, much as he might have looked at an Iraqi interrogator. The whites of his eyes were visible above and below his irises, a sign he was producing too much adrenaline.' Turnbull well knew that 'steely-eyed pilots' could absorb a lot of stress, but, like every other human being, they had their tipping point. 'I had long suspected there was a dangerous rigidity to the highly developed defence mechanisms within pilots, one that would take a great deal to break, but when they did go, the collapse would be the equivalent of a dam bursting.'

Convinced that Frank represented the 'bow wave' of hundreds of cases from the Kuwaiti offensive, Turnbull and his psychiatrist colleague later got to work. 'Let me start, Frank, by telling you that you are perfectly safe here,' he told the pilot. 'Nothing is going to happen to you.'

Frank's eyes briefly met his. 'I'll never fly again, will I?' He started weeping. 'My career's over, isn't it?'

'We're not going to make any assumptions about what brought you here, nor do we make any assumptions about your future, Frank,' the psychiatrist said. 'We know that something traumatic happened to you. I'd like to try to understand what it was.'

'It scared the shit out of me.' The pilot faltered, wiping tears from his eyes, speaking barely above a whisper.

'What you say stays with us. I'm not taking notes.'

Sobbing and barely glancing at them, Frank said, 'Flying is everything to me. My mates are everything to me. I've never experienced anything like this. I'm not a coward. I just want to be with my mates.'

'And we want you to be back with them,' Turnbull told him. 'But the more you can tell us about it, the better.'

Frank looked at the doctor, held his gaze, then slumped back in his chair and exhaled. 'When I saw them on TV, I just snapped. John Peters and I know each other pretty well. It was the bruises around his eyes. Those weren't from any ejection. I just felt this incredible anger. And then the world started to close in on me. Thoughts, images, everything ... it just seemed to explode inside my head. I couldn't take it any more. That's when I just ... lost it.'

'It was a panic attack,' Turnbull said gently. 'It's a perfectly normal reaction, Frank, considering everything that happened.' At the word 'normal' the psychiatrist could see relief flood across Frank's face. 'Your experience was a stress reaction. Not only is it normal but it's as old as the hills. You are safe here, Frank. Nothing bad is going to happen to you.'

* * *

While Frank started his psychiatric treatment in England, the families of the prisoners of war were undergoing their own mental and emotional challenges. Chris Ankerson had no idea if Bob was alive or dead. 'How long was our ordeal going to last? Weeks, months, a year? We simply had to try our best to cope with each stage of the awful journey.'[15] Gareth Ankerson's earlier nightmare about his father's death still haunted him. 'Mum and I had to consider the worst. How would our lives change if my dad had been killed? Our only hope was that the two flames that had shot out of the fire of their jet were my father and his pilot. But how long would we have to wait to find out?'[16]

Three days after Bob was reported missing in action, his Boss, Dusty Miller, rang the doorbell again at their married quarters in RAF Bruggen. 'Chris, I need to speak to you.'

Oh no, is this it? Chris could see the grave look on Dusty's face.

It was bad news, but not of the kind she expected. 'Sorry, Chris, you're not going to believe this, but Robert's flying pay is being withdrawn.'

At first Chris had breathed deeply, thankful it wasn't the worst news, then digested the meaning of Dusty's words. The Ankersons were victims of a regulation which decreed that if an airman was missing in action, and ergo unable to do the job they were paid for, their specialist flying pay, perhaps a third of their salary, would be stopped. Chris was devastated. 'We had Gareth's boarding-school fees, bills, shopping. And a mortgage! It was simply shocking. Truly astonishing.'

But that was not the worst of it.

'Dusty then told me that Robert's salary would also cease to be paid into our joint bank account. It would now be sent directly into the RAF Bruggen administrator's care and I would be issued "an allowance" – if and when I needed cash. I was now required to present myself to a junior clerk to beg for access to our own money! I was absolutely livid. It was an archaic Second World War regulation which some faceless bureaucrat had initiated. It appeared "ladies" didn't have the financial acumen to deal with their missing husband's salary.'

Chris and Dusty spread the family financial documents across her living-room floor. 'I was furious but I needed to deal with it. After several calculations I thought, *Yes, we should be able to manage, as long as I am careful*. But I was so angry. I didn't know if my husband was alive or dead, yet they were now stopping his pay. How dare they?!'

Chris called their UK bank to explain what had happened and the manager quickly came to the phone. He was one of many who had watched the war unfold on the news. 'Mrs Ankerson, we all know what has happened to your husband,' he said. 'We are so sorry to hear about your situation. But please don't worry about anything. Be assured that I will personally ensure everything will be fine with your finances.'

It seemed that a civilian bank manager was more sympathetic to the plight of those missing in action than the military establishment that had sent them to war.

Tange Stewart faced a similar nightmare after her husband Robbie had gone missing in action on 19 January. Like Chris Ankerson, she had no idea how long her situation would last. 'I would wake up every morning and, just for a second, forget what we were going through. Then, quick as a flash, I'd be brought crashing back to reality.'

Tange had not received Robbie's payslip at the end of January, so picked up the phone. 'My bank manager said Robbie's pay had initially come through, but it had then been recalled, so he presumed I'd be receiving Robbie's pay by some other means. I was speechless; really annoyed and worried. How was I meant to cope without any money? More calls were made, voices were raised. Messages were sent flying up the military chain of command and, eventually, I received Robbie's pay.'

It seemed the issue had been resolved until she received a letter from Archie Hamilton – the Armed Forces Minister who had announced in a radio interview that Nichol and Peters were probably dead. It stated that she would only be paid Robbie's salary for thirteen weeks, after which she would get a certificate to claim a pension and life insurance. 'I said no one would be giving me any such *certificate* until they could prove my husband was dead!'

The bureaucratic short-sightedness forced Tange to confront

the possibility of Robbie never returning. 'It was really difficult to cope. As the days dragged by, I began to think years into the future. How to get the children through their education, then perhaps I could travel out to Iraq to find out what had happened to Robbie, if he was still alive? I just didn't know how to think or react.'[17]

Chris Ankerson went one step further. She had been told that the head of the RAF, Air Chief Marshal Sir Peter Harding, would visit RAF Bruggen. 'I'd had enough and requested a personal meeting with him. I had decided not to take any more of this nonsense. I was going to become *"the bolshie lady"*.'

The Chief of the Air Staff was not having a good day. He arrived late for their meeting in the Officers' Mess after the ground crews' wives had given him a piece of their mind over the Gulf airmen's working conditions and financial allowances. Chris was not in the mood to take any prisoners. 'I poked him in the chest and said: "How dare you take my husband's money from me!" This wasn't something you normally did to the RAF's most senior officer, but I was so angry with "the system". I had always toed the party line, been meek and mild, but I just flipped and told him exactly what I thought.'

Harding exploded. 'What do you mean? Who told you this?' He already knew about the archaic rules and had specifically told his staff that they should be ignored.

'Hearing me tell him that, despite his orders, they had been implemented was clearly a shock. A ripple seemed to go through his waiting Staff Officers. Sir Peter turned to them and said, rather forcefully, "Sort this all out. Now!" There was quite a bit of scurrying around and the matter was quickly resolved.' But not entirely. Bob's full salary would still have to be paid into the care of the RAF Bruggen administration team and *then* issued to Chris on request. It appeared that wives of those missing in action still could not be *completely* trusted to manage their own affairs.

* * *

As Harding tried to keep up morale on the home front, the spirits of the Tornado force were lifted by the move to higher altitudes, albeit with questionable effectiveness. On 26 January an eight-ship attacked an ammunition dump 170 miles south of Baghdad. While the munitions had rained down on the general target area it had not been a great success. Yet again, the Mission Report told a familiar story:

> A majority of bombs had impacted between the sheds. Indeed, only one of the [190] storage sheds was clearly seen to have been destroyed. It was disappointing to see such an apparently small amount of damage for the effort involved.[18]

That disappointment, it was hoped, would soon be reversed. On the same day as the ammunition dump attack, the first two Buccaneers carrying Pave Spike laser targeting pods set off to join the Tornados in the Gulf, fulfilling the Defence Minister's promise to 'improve the standard of precision bombing'. With the desert camouflage paint still drying on their airframes, they left RAF Lossiemouth in Scotland for the nine-hour, non-stop journey – honouring their Station Commander's commitment to be ready to go to war within three days.

The force's 140 personnel had been inoculated, equipped with chemical warfare suits, issued personal weapons and asked to make wills. Bill Cope, the Squadron Boss, departed with his most experienced crew at 4 a.m. arriving at Muharraq later that day. Their arrival was somewhat underwhelming. 'If we had expected a welcome for bringing a much-needed additional capability to the RAF element in-theatre we were to be disappointed,' Cope later said.[19] That night he went for a drink with the Jaguar Detachment Commander in the top-floor bar of the Sheraton Hotel, where they were quartered. What was the drill for a Scud attack? Cope asked. Do we go down to the basement?

'Not really,' his friend replied. 'If a Scud hits the hotel it will be coming vertically downwards at about Mach 5 and will probably pass through all floors before ending up in the basement. So most people rush up here for a beer while watching the Patriot missiles launching from Dhahran across the causeway.'

Cope considered the advice carefully while sipping his beer.

With the Buccaneers in place, the Tornados from Pablo Mason's formation at Muharraq were pulled off war sorties for a rapid training programme. The navigator who had released the bombs on the Tornado's first ever medium-level mission now formed part of the team for the first precision strike. Mike Toft had mixed feelings. 'I was a bit miffed that we were not continuing to "do our bit" as the war went on around us. But on the other hand, I was slightly relieved that we wouldn't be putting our pink bodies in harm's way for a few days.'[20]

As the end of January approached, the ageing Buccaneers and the Tornados flew a number of practice missions, establishing the best way to operate in concert. Using its Pave Spike targeting pod, the Buccaneer navigator identified the target on a small cockpit TV screen and the system then focused a laser beam on the target. The Tornados carried standard 1,000lb bombs fitted with a special nose attachment consisting of a 'seeker head' linked to guidance vanes, or 'wings'. The head could 'see' the Buccaneer's laser spot on the target and when the bombs were released, their seekers could track the laser and send signals to the small canard 'wings' which moved, allowing the bomb to 'fly' precisely towards the laser spot placed on the target.[21]

By early February, the Tornados had a precision targeting capability.

* * *

While Tornado pilot Frank's comrades were flying to war, Wing Commander Gordon Turnbull was attempting to reconnect him to the world he had known before his collapse. He used the same formal psychological debriefing he had utilised after the Lockerbie disaster, ensuring the pilot talked in detail about his experiences.

Frank was told that all his conversations with the psychiatric team were in total confidence. He had the freedom to say exactly what he was feeling because nothing was on the record. He had been allowed to call his wife at his home base and to let her know that he was safe and would be coming to see her and their child very soon.

The key for the psychiatrists was to understand exactly what had happened to Frank in the lead-up to his breakdown. The pilot had to recall and recognise the specific events in what they called the 'cognitive domain phase'. 'To give us all the information we needed to help him, Frank had to respond to our simple *"who, what, why, where, when questions"* in order to establish a timeline.'

Frank talked about the night-time raids and the unbelievable stress that aircrew faced flying into the triple-A. Turnbull was shocked and began to realise that the JP233 sorties were nothing like the sanitised attacks he had seen on TV. Frank went on to tell them about the high attrition rate in the Tornado force and how it had affected some of the aircrew. He talked about the fears and feelings he experienced during the combat missions. He had been able to handle the stress of war until the 'trigger moment' occurred – his utter distress and revulsion at the television pictures of the brutalised POWs, which also made him terrified of what would happen to his wife and child if he was shot down. 'Frank had been constantly reliving the missions, seeing the flak, seeing the explosions, replaying the movie again and again in his head. We were into classic flashback territory.'[22]

'We told him that the flashbacks were "unprocessed memories" with his mind presenting them again and again as a way of trying to find an explanation for events that defied reason.' Turnbull also explained his 'Pint Pot' theory where levels of stress grew inside until it 'overflowed with a physical force of enough power to knock somebody off their feet'. Frank's particular 'Pint Pot', they explained, had already been filled to the brim by his previous experiences. 'To anyone else, the sight of Peters and Nichol on TV, although distressing, would not have had the same impact. That it had done so with Frank was down to the fact that he knew them so well.'

The key for the pilot was to understand what had happened to him, to 'demystify the event' and hasten his recovery. Turnbull was amazed at how quickly he got it. 'As soon as he started to understand that it was his personal emotional connection to Peters and Nichol that had caused the fuse to blow, Frank made a remarkably swift recovery.' The flashbacks and nightmares formed the cornerstones of his PTSD; without either of these symptoms the condition began to diminish.

Within days his state had improved considerably. Turnbull now had an even greater ambition: to help fulfil Frank's earlier wish to get back to his Squadron. 'This had been his number one priority. To the best of my knowledge there had never before been a case of an RAF pilot returning to flying duties in the wake of a breakdown during combat operations.'

Turnbull now needed to convince his own Boss that Frank was ready to return to duty. After examining the pilot, the senior medic concluded, 'Well, this is remarkable. He appears to be fixed.'

Frank was sent back to his home base for re-evaluation flying the Tornado, before a return to normal duties. Perhaps even in the warzone.

* * *

With her husband missing in action and her only son back at boarding school, Chris Ankerson allowed herself to be absorbed by the news; reading the papers, watching television or listening to the radio. The daylight hours were usually fine, as friends visited regularly. But darkness brought the most troubling thoughts, and, one night, the pent-up emotions eventually spilled over. 'I lost all control. It wasn't one particular incident, just everything tumbling down on top of me.'

It was 3am, and there was only one thing for it. She phoned her friend Di Evans.

Di's husband, Ivor, was also serving in the Gulf, and she had stayed with Chris for the first few days of her ordeal. 'This huge machine of activity took over our lives and the news played constantly on TV. Chris had slept like a baby every night and I kept going into her room to see if she was okay. I was wide awake and unable to even have a nap. I eventually went home to sleep in my own bed. A few days later, the phone rang again in the middle of the night. I obviously thought it was now my turn for the "knock on the door". But Chris's teary voice just said, "What am I, Di – am I a widow or a wife? What am I?" I told her to come around immediately.'[23]

As Chris walked over, she bumped into two armed RAF policemen.

'Morning, Mrs Ankerson,' they said. 'Is everything okay?'

Everyone on base was very aware of her circumstances.

'I'm fine, I'm fine, thank you,' Chris said between sobs. 'I'm just going to Mrs Evans' house.'

'Do you need us to escort you there?'

'No, I'll be fine. Thank you.' She continued on her way. 'It was those tiny human touches which made such a difference.'

Di knew that Chris had arrived. 'I didn't need to worry where she was; I could hear the terrible crying as it got nearer to my front door.'

They chatted through the early hours until they both remembered that Princess Diana was visiting Bruggen that afternoon on a morale-boosting trip and they were both scheduled to meet her. They snatched some sleep then dressed for the visit. 'Princess Diana was so delightful,' Chris said. 'So kind and understanding. It was important to us that people outside our military bubble understood what was happening. It wasn't just our husbands at war. We were part of it all, too.'

Fluctuating emotions were also assailing Tange Stewart. With no reports of an ejection from Robbie's aircraft, in her darkest moments she feared he had perished along with Dave Waddington. Then the *Daily Express* splashed a story saying two Iraqi 'peasants' had overpowered the navigator and 'sold' him to the authorities for £15,000; the bounty that Saddam had put on captured airmen.[24]

The piece also quoted an 'RAF source' speculating that Robbie might have been injured and unable to defend himself. Although the story appeared to be based on conjecture, it contained some curiously accurate details, though Tange could never have known that at the time.

The next day the press pack appeared in her small village, eager for more information. Tange refused to give any interviews. Fortunately, her teenage children Kirsty and Scott were at home when the story broke. 'The phone went crazy and all the press kept knocking at the front door,' Kirsty said.[25] 'There were TV cameras, with lights shining on our house. The press intrusion was really difficult. We were a very private family and the notion of us being on the front pages was really difficult.'

Kirsty's young mind was turning once more to darker thoughts. 'I was thinking of all those spy novels again. I eventually told Mum that I didn't want Dad to be alive and suffering. I would rather he was dead and at peace and I was now more scared than ever. If he was alive, he could be being terribly tortured and I couldn't bear that thought.'

With no idea how close to the truth she had been, Kirsty returned to boarding school wearing her father's old jumper as a reminder of his touch, 'and I clumped around in a pair of his flying boots trying to feel closer to him'.

School was a helpful diversion, although she struggled in some lessons. 'My mind drifted but the teachers were so understanding. In one English class, we were meant to be writing an essay about *Macbeth* but I just stared out of the window. The teacher saw me and quietly suggested I write about how I was feeling instead. I wrote a poem about missing Dad. Which really helped.'

Amid the emotional and financial turmoil, the Queen stepped forward and requested a meeting with some of the families of the missing aircrew. Berenice Waddington was still struggling with the uncertainty of whether her son David was alive or dead. 'I spent most of my time simply hoping and praying, and little else. Then our liaison officer rang to say the Queen would like to meet us. At first,

I said, 'No, I'm not really up to it. But they eventually persuaded me, promising to make all the arrangements.'[26]

Uniformed drivers collected the families from across the UK and drove them to RAF Marham in Norfolk. Berenice and her husband Jack were spirited down from Bolton, while another RAF car wound its way through the icy Lincolnshire lanes with the Stewarts. The day before, Kirsty had been taken to buy new clothes; a maroon skirt, cream tights and red velvet shoes. She was now finding the journey a great challenge. The Officers' Mess had informed them they would provide a packed lunch. They wanted to make the occasion as special as possible. 'As a 13-year-old, I thought a packed lunch meant a sandwich, a KitKat and a can of Coke. But the Mess, trying to be really kind to us, had provided an expansive finger buffet on huge platters covered by silver cloches! We were eating in the back of the car while trying to avoid the gourmet smoked salmon, asparagus spears and prawns spilling onto our posh new clothes.'

Tange picked at the food while eyeing the frost-covered hedgerows and ploughed fields. 'Everywhere was white and icy, and as the scenery flashed by I thought, *That view is exactly how I feel inside.*'

Jock Stirrup, RAF Marham's Station Commander, escorted the families around the base. To help them understand what the airmen had been doing, they were shown the planning areas and the aircrews' flying kit in the locker rooms. Berenice Waddington had a difficult moment. 'We saw David's peg where his flying suit would hang. It was empty. There was just his name pinned to the wood. That really hit us both hard. It spoke volumes about our situation.'

Aside from the Waddingtons and the Stewarts, the base also hosted the families of the first Tornado crew to go down – Nigel Elsdon's parents and Max Collier's wife Molly with their three sons. With no official confirmation that any downed aircrew were dead or alive, all the airmen were currently listed as MIA. Berenice found it strange. 'We met a lot of the other families, which was very moving, but it was an unusual gathering of people. None of us knew if our loved ones were alive or dead.'

It would be many weeks until they each found out the truth, but the awkwardness of not knowing was forgotten when the Queen entered the Officers' Mess bar, where the families had assembled.

Primed with the knowledge that Her Majesty always made the running in any small talk, Scott Stewart had decided to help her and prepared his own discussion beforehand. Drawing confidence from being dressed in his missing father's new, light-grey pinstripe suit, the 16-year-old schoolboy bowed then launched into a ten-minute speech about the support they had received from the people of Coleby and how they were coping. Her Majesty listened intently. Tange thought she looked pleased having someone actually talk to her. 'I was very proud of Scott. The whole day was a huge boost to our morale. Taking us out of ourselves; a real relief from our ongoing worries. The Queen was simply wonderful, so friendly and approachable.'

Kirsty found it a strange experience going from their 'Stewart bubble' into a group suffering the same emotions. 'I realised that many other people were affected by the Gulf War and my child's world was a lot larger than I knew.' Dressed in her smart new outfit, Kirsty curtsied gracefully as the Queen approached. 'She was really lovely and we chatted about my netball at school and how she cheered Prince Charles on when he had played sport. It was all very surreal.'

* * *

While it was cold and frosty in Lincolnshire, the clear weather in the Gulf had been assisting the planning for the first laser-guided bomb (LGB) attack. The Pave Spike system could only be used in daylight and clear skies. Night-time bombing was out as the target could not be identified, and any changing cloud cover could mean that the laser beam would not reach the target nor perhaps be spotted by the seeker head. On 2 February, it was time to see if the

Tornado could become the first RAF jet to drop a Precision-Guided Munition in war. The target was a bridge that spanned the River Euphrates halfway between Baghdad and Basra, just north of the town of Samawah.

Four Tornados, each equipped with three 1,000lb LGBs, were given the task of destroying the bridge. A pair of jets would fly with a Buccaneer that would laser-designate for both. After the short break in combat operations, Mike Toft readied himself for the sortie. 'It was time to go sausage side again. The bridge was on Highway 8; one of the key supply routes. In preparation for the ground war, we needed to take out the bridges to hamper the Iraqi capability to get reinforcements down to their front lines. It was my third mission and yet again there was a huge change in tactics. We were now going to war at medium level, *and* in broad daylight. It was not a comfortable feeling.'[27]

With clear weather now forecast over Samawah, they were given the final go-ahead after breakfast. Faced with their first operational sortie, nerves were evident among the Buccaneer force. 'It was a tense moment for all of us because the crews that came out [to theatre] were very scared,' said the Buccaneers' senior engineering officer. 'No one had been in combat before or knew what to expect. Some had false bonhomie and others snapped at the ground crew. The ground crew understood the tension the aircrew felt and handled them like eggs. We all knew that success or failure of the Buccaneer would depend on how well the aircrew did.'[28]

There was a great deal at stake. Thanks to the Pave Spike's recording system, there was no hiding place. 'These videos would be used to demonstrate to the world that this was indeed pinpoint bombing designed to minimise loss of life,' said one officer. 'Accuracy was a political necessity.'[29]

Nearly every member of the Buccaneer detachment headed out to see off the first raid. 'It was quite emotional,' one airman remembered. 'You get very attached to the aircrew because you work with them day in and day out. You get to know their little habits and what they like and don't like. They picked up their helmets and walked out to the aircraft. We were so nervous we just sat there and didn't know whether to speak to them. Always in the back of your head was, *please let them come back*.'[30]

It had been a tumultuous week for Bill Cope. Only a few days before he had been packing his salopettes to go skiing with his wife; now he was holstering a loaded pistol ready to lead his Buccaneers on their first raid. 'I believe most Squadron Commanders have a mental image of how they think they will go into battle for the first time. Typically, it will be to lead the crews we have trained with for months or even years. On my first mission the reality was rather different. As we transited over Iraq, heading for the bridge, I wasn't leading at all, the Tornados were. We were at high level not low level and over land, not over sea.'[31]

Like the Tornado crews, the Buccaneer airmen now found themselves in uncharted territory. Some way from their target they met dense cloud. With their antiquated navigation equipment, it was vital that they stayed with each other. If they got lost, the mission would fail. 'Visitors always assume that the Middle East is in burning sunshine,' said Cope. 'Not so. I was in cloud staring at a Tornado's wingtip. I listened to lots of Soviet radar systems just as I had in the simulator at home, but these were real signals coming back from real enemy radars. The thought running through my mind was, *It's not supposed to be like this*.'

With 50 miles to go, the cloud suddenly gave way to open skies and the jets, in arrow formation, found themselves in broad daylight, directly over enemy territory, a brown landscape under flat grey light. With a minute to go, the flak opened up below them, but there was no time for fear; the Buccaneer crews needed to positively identify the target. Amid the incredible concentration of fire, the navigators picked up the bridge over the Euphrates and set their individual target designators on either end. Heavy traffic continued across, unaware of what was about to happen. Satisfied with the target acquisition, they signalled to Pablo and his number two. Six 1,000-pounders sailed towards the target, the canard wings on the munitions guiding them towards the laser spot.

After a nerve-racking wait, a huge blast billowed from one end of the bridge, completely enveloping an Iraqi lorry. Another detonation then hit the opposite end. Pablo was delighted. 'The Buccaneers had done the fine-tuning and our bombs did the work. It was pure weapons aiming to perfection. We blasted our target.'

Within hours, the results of the sortie were being signalled up the chain of command. Group Captain Cliff Spink was at a meeting at Air Headquarters in Riyadh. 'I was in Air Vice-Marshal Wratten's office when one of his team burst into the room. The Boss looked up to see what was so important. His Staff Officer produced a communication detailing the immediate results of the first LGB attack – the bridge had been dropped exactly as planned. The Buccaneers' Pave Spike system operating alongside the Tornados had worked perfectly. There was utter delight in the room. And a real sense of relief. We had demonstrated that this new bombing technique, something the Tornados had never really trained for, was a great success on its very first outing.'

The film of the strike was also shown to the personnel back at Muharraq. 'They were amazed at the video and the results, but the biggest reaction of all was when we showed it to the Tornado guys at the debrief,' recalled the lead Buccaneer navigator. 'They had no idea until then what they had done, how effective it had been. It was fantastic to actually see the results. It was a big lift for them.'[32]

The ground crew were also amazed. 'That really brought it home. Good Lord, we were actually killing people, and a lot of guys grew up,' said one.[33] 'Seeing it on the television screen made me painfully aware that people were going to die because of what we were doing. As engineers we were responsible to the aircrew who pushed the buttons. I found that difficult, but eventually accepted that the bridges were crucial. And we saw the effect that knocking those bridges down was having on Iraqi soldiers in Kuwait. Supplies weren't reaching them.'

The next morning the *Daily Telegraph* ran the headline: 'Buccaneers Claim Laser Bomb Success'. 'The other good news, at least in our minds,' Mike Toft thought after reading the piece, 'was that we had not lost a Tornado for the last ten days.'

The mission was the advent of precision weaponeering for the Tornado. This was not good news for the Iraqi leader, who, according to the *Daily Express*, was taking tranquillisers to get over the headaches from the relentless aerial bombardment. 'Sinking Saddam Is Under Sedation,' the front page read on 4 February.[34]

But there was also an unforeseen psychological impact on the Tornado crews who now began dropping bombs with clinical accuracy. During an attack on another bridge across the Euphrates, Gordon Buckley rolled the jet to look for his bombs' strike. 'A lorry drove onto the bridge and I actually felt a bit sick. In an aircraft, you feel isolated from the mayhem you cause. I thought, *God, I've just killed him*. The bomb exploded right on target and seconds later the truck drove out of the smoke and debris. I was pleased he had survived – that was one lucky Iraqi.'[35]

Buckley's concerns about killing others were brought back to the fore after bombing an airbase. 'You need to see this film, it's amazing,' the Intelligence Officer had said on his return. The black and white footage showed the laser marker hovering over the roof of the base's Pilot Briefing Facility – the reinforced concrete bunker where aircrew could plan operations in what was previously believed to have been relative safety. 'There was a flash of light outside the PBF; I was told this was someone opening then closing a car door,' recalled Buckley. 'Although you couldn't see a person, you could then see a door opening and closing at the side of the PBF as they walked in. I was watching someone like me – probably aircrew – walk into their PBF as I had done many thousands of times back home. Then all four walls simply exploded outwards as our bombs hit home. Whatever, whoever, was in that PBF was instantly obliterated. That really affected me. There was a war to be fought and the targets were legitimate, but it really brought home the reality of what we were doing.'

* * *

Still facing his own very personal consequences of war, Robbie Stewart was recuperating in an Iraqi military hospital. A fortnight into his stay, he told one of the doctors treating his shattered leg that he was feeling much better. It was a huge mistake. He was bundled into a truck along with his crutches and thrown into the grim Mukhabarat prison complex, where, unbeknown to him, all the other POWs were now being held by the much-feared Iraqi Intelligence Service, the 'secret police'.

His welcome here was rather different to that of the smiling London-trained surgeon he had woken up to after his surgery. A guard threw him over his shoulder, carried him to a cold dank cell, flung two blankets on the floor, and dropped Robbie to the ground. He then grabbed him by the neck and pulled his face close. 'My child,' he hissed, drawing his index finger across his throat and pointing at Robbie. 'You!'

The metal door clanged shut, echoing down the corridor. A bar was pulled across, then chains, and finally a key turned in the lock. 'The closed door had shut out all the light. I thought of Tange and how she would have hated to be enclosed like this. The floor was cold and hard and I could not get warm with the two blankets they had given me. I pulled them up to my nose and dropped into a very unsettled sleep, dreaming that I was back at home with my family.'[36]

Robbie steeled himself for the coming days.

CHAPTER THIRTEEN

'MISSILE LAUNCH!'

By early February, 22-year-old Mal Craghill, the Tornado force's youngest navigator, was a veteran of the conflict. He had flown a number of raids, witnessed the mental distress of some of his companions, and lost friends in battle. Now, Mal and the Tabuk aircrew were waiting for the next major development in their Tornado's warfighting capability: the Thermal Imaging Airborne Laser Designator.

The TIALD pods were the up-to-the-minute version of the ageing Buccaneer's Pave Spike. In late 1990, it had still been in the research-and-development stage. Only two prototype pods existed. But with the imminent onset of war in the Gulf, the RAF had ordered Ferranti to speed up production in case precision targeting became necessary. It had done.

In the third week of January, four Tornado crews had arrived to undertake trials at the Aeroplane and Armament Experimental Establishment at RAF Boscombe Down in Wiltshire. On 2 February they made the inaugural drop of a laser-guided bomb targeted by a British-built laser pod.[1] Four days later, the two prototype pods were flown out to Tabuk. With its infra-red capability, unlike Pave Spike, it enabled laser targeting at night. Tornado crews would soon deploy laser-guided bombs under cover of darkness.

In the meantime, those without Buccaneer Pave Spike support continued with the Tornado's bombing system, optimised for low-level operations, for the ongoing medium-level attacks. On 6 February, Craghill and his pilot Mike Warren prepared to hit an airfield south of Baghdad. Its proximity to the capital meant they would be entering what was solemnly referred to as the 'Super MEZ' – the Missile Engagement Zone. Saddam had sited a host of SAM batteries around the capital, including the battle-proven SA-3 and the giant SA-2 which had knocked Gary Powers' U2 reconnaissance jet out of the sky at 70,000ft over the Soviet Union in 1960. It may have been ancient, but it was still effective. To help smooth the way, Craghill's formation was accompanied by two Tornados equipped with ALARM anti-radar missiles and American EF-111 aircraft armed with powerful radar jammers.

The night was still and clear as their eight-ship refuelled at the border then pushed on towards Baghdad. Craghill's pre-war training had focused on the visual characteristics of the Iraqi SAMs as well as their technical capabilities. 'Knowing the colour of the missile's rocket flame, and the typical salvos fired, meant we might be able to identify what was being launched. Two missiles in quick succession with a short-burning blueish flame would probably be an SA-8, two missiles a few seconds apart with a longer-burning yellow flame were likely SA-6.'[2] To control the missile, a radar ground station locked on or 'illuminated' the aircraft, working out its precise position, and updated the missile while in flight, guiding it close enough to the target for the proximity fuse to detonate the warhead with its lethal shards of shrapnel.

Approaching the Super MEZ, Craghill now watched in amazement as salvos of SA-8, SA-3 and SA-6 missiles were fired off without any guidance. 'The Iraqis wanted to be seen to be doing something, but didn't want to attract the attention of the anti-radar missiles and get themselves killed in the process.' Some of the SAM operators would not be so timid. Seconds later, his RHWR showed 'SA-2 TA' – Target Acquisition.[3]

'This was not necessarily a big deal. "Target Acquisition" had become relatively common and I continued to prosecute the attack while monitoring the RHWR screen.'

Then an audio alarm sounded and the display switched to 'SA-2 TT' – Target Tracking. This was a major escalation. The Iraqi operator was clearly unaffected, or unconcerned, by the presence of jammers and anti-radar missiles. He was using his own radar to track their aircraft, updating his target information in preparation for a launch. The bearing indication flashed on Mal's display, showing the direction of the threat. Craghill dispensed chaff and confirmed to Mike that the jamming pod was responding correctly. 'We both assumed that was as far as it would go. We now had only a few miles to run to weapons release; less than ten seconds. Then, the unthinkable happened.'

The alarm switched abruptly to a ferocious warble. Craghill saw 'SA-2 MG' – Missile Guidance – on his RHWR. The Iraqi operator had locked his system onto their aircraft and was about to launch. 'I looked out of the cockpit in the direction the RHWR showed the threat was coming from. A fraction of a second later I saw an almighty flash as a massive missile came off its launcher. It was a gloriously clear night and I could now see that an SA-2 was on its way up to us.'

The deadly 35ft-long SA-2 Guideline missile was accelerating to its maximum speed of Mach 3.5 (2,685mph). Craghill made a snap decision to complete the bombing run then defend against it without the extra weight of their weapons.

'Press on with the attack,' he said quickly. 'The pod is jamming.'

He felt Mike weigh up the advice – albeit for a microsecond.

'Roger.'

'With just a couple of seconds until bomb release, everything now happened very rapidly. Our actions were completed on instinct, with no time to register any emotion.' Craghill made a rapid radio call to say they were defending against an SA-2, broadcasting their location to cue their radar jamming support. 'Although there was nothing they could do to protect us from *this* missile, they could begin jamming the appropriate radar frequencies so that if we defeated the SA-2, it was less likely that we would be engaged in a follow-up attack.' They monitored the burning rocket plume throughout its flight. 'It was a curious feeling watching this huge missile track towards us. I wasn't particularly scared over those three or four seconds; I just knew we had to defeat it. The consequences of not doing so were unthinkable.'

Two seconds later, their five 1,000lb bombs released and Mike pulled the jet into a violent right-hand turn. Blind to the other seven aircraft in their formation, and relying again on the 'big sky' theory, they plunged down through the darkness towards the missile. 'When the shit hits the fan, your response has been hardwired after years of training. We did the drills instinctively, without thinking. Mike manoeuvred as hard as possible to make it harder for the missile to follow our flight path, while I called out the heights, checked our Sky Shadow pod was jamming, and kept dispensing chaff, hoping to break the missile's lock.'

There was a bright flash as the SA-2's 195kg fragmentation warhead detonated behind them and its shrapnel blossomed. Craghill felt the shock wave rock their Tornado. Although seemingly unscathed, they were still in real danger. 'The manoeuvre had taken us from 20,000ft down to 13,000ft. This close to Baghdad, it put us within reach of an awful lot of triple-A systems. Mike put the jet into a climb on full afterburner, uncomfortably highlighting our position in the darkness, but essential to regain height and momentum in case of another attack.'

Later, safely back on the ground, they discussed whether prosecuting the attack had been the right thing to do. 'We decided it was. What saved us was our training and that we trusted each other to do what was required. That, and probably a huge dose of luck. But it had been a close call and we had come pretty close to being shot down. Or worse. There was little time to dwell on it; there was a war to be fought and we were back on a mission the following day.'

* * *

Just a few miles from where Mal Craghill and Mike Warren had almost been shot down, the coalition prisoners of war had been gathered in one of the most feared locations in Iraq. The Mukhabarat prison in Baghdad, run by Saddam's secret police, was relentlessly cold, dark and depressing. From floor to ceiling, the cell's ice-cold chocolate-brown tiles numbed the brain and turned the stomach. In some crude designer joke, the tiles matched the only thing that broke up the prison's rectangular boxes – the 'toilet'. Embedded within its dark, noxious hole was a mass of ancient darkish-brown excrement. There was no furniture in the cells, not even a piece of foam to lie on, just two thin blankets which provided little respite from the chill.

Robbie Stewart had been transported to the prison from his hospital bed. 'The floor was freezing and rock hard. I thought the draught on my face was from an open window, but soon realised that the breeze was actually cold air falling from the freezing tiles on the walls.' His cell boasted two plastic bowls, one for water and one for food. Very little of either was forthcoming. The only light came from a narrow window covered by an iron grille high above him which cast criss-cross shadows over the floor and walls. Robbie was clearly just the latest in a long line of tortured souls who had inhabited this space. A series of strokes had been scratched onto the brown tiles, batches of six struck through with a single diagonal line – the classic record of time endured there by its previous inhabitants. Robbie was in no doubt that for the many thousands of Iraqis incarcerated here over the years, there would have been no happy ending.

The passing hours turned into passing days. Robbie's stomach would rumble as he waited for any sign of human contact. As the shadows blurred, the hatch in the heavy steel door would be drawn back and flatbread and something masquerading as soup thrust through. 'We got a single miserly meal per day. The liquid was very hot but extremely thin, with streaks of fat; it was reasonably salty and edible. I sipped it slowly, letting it warm me as the heat reached my stomach.'[4] Time passed more quickly if you savoured every scrap.

There was little to hear, bar the occasional sound of footsteps in the corridor and the rattle of a key in a lock. He found a piece of old soap in a corner and used it to write Tange's name on the wall. 'I had no picture, but these few letters projected her image whenever I looked at them.' He would fall asleep beneath the thin blanket, dreaming of his wife. 'Tange was making tea. I was dressed in my yellow prison suit. We would be chatting then I'd turn to leave. "Where are you going?" she'd ask. "I have to be back in Baghdad," I'd reply, then I'd wake up and, depressingly, I was back in my cell.'

The same surreal dream, of being back among loved ones while still dressed in yellow prison garb, was shared by almost all of the POWs during their ordeal.

Robbie was unaware of it at the time, but his friend and navigator was only a few metres away, separated by thick prison walls and solid steel doors. Their captors, perhaps still convinced that David Joseph Waddington had to be an Israeli pilot, had thrown him into what appeared to be a 'punishment cell'. 'There was a metal grille at the end of the cell on the outside wall, but it was covered over so no light could enter. When they first threw me in, I looked at the single electric light and thought, *If they turn that off, I'll be in real trouble*. After a couple of hours, I was plunged into darkness as the light went out. It rarely came on again over the next three weeks.'

Dave nonetheless managed to measure his area of confinement – around 5ft wide and 12ft long. On the couple of occasions when the dim light flickered on, it revealed a dank chamber with a foetid hole in one corner that passed for a lavatory. As the weeks ground by, Waddington began to struggle with the darkness. 'It was horrendous. The intense boredom was made infinitely worse by the fact that I couldn't see a thing. I became very concerned for my state of mind. How long could I survive like this?'

As well as the coalition prisoners, the Iraqis also kept some of their own in the cells. 'One of the worst aspects was the terrible noises people made,' John Nichol said. 'You could hear the pitiful screams of other prisoners enduring God knew what torment. One night I woke up to hear an Arab man being dragged past my cell. He was screaming for mercy as they beat him over and over again. It sounded like the Iraqis wanted to punch and kick him to death. In between the prisoner's pleas, I could hear the guards' threats and curses. His pitiful mewling was fuelled with the anguish of total mental breakdown.'

During one particularly suffocating stretch, Dave Waddington found himself drawn away from his internal battles by those yells and screams outside his steel door. He was momentarily sustained by the reminder that he wasn't the only one struggling. But it did not take long for him to descend once again into the echoing void. 'It was miserable, worse than the broken arms, worse than the torture. All that pain was fleeting but the darkness was interminable.'[5]

The guards took great pleasure in making Waddington's life as miserable as possible. After being treated for his injuries at the previous hospital, he had arrived at the prison in bare feet, wearing only a surgical gown and his underwear. After asking for another blanket two guards opened his door, letting in some precious light. They dropped a blanket to the floor then both urinated on it before kicking it inside his cell. 'I tried to air it as best I could and it eventually dried out a bit. I managed to get a screw off the grille and used it as a basic needle to help fashion a pair of rather fetching moccasins for my freezing feet.'

Bob Ankerson had decided that the best way to get through his POW ordeal was to become the 'grey man', anonymous and undemanding. 'I avoided aggravating the guards and tended to be ignored in terms of some of the bad treatment others were clearly enduring.'

As days turned to weeks, the night-time tedium was broken by the endless coalition bombing raids on the capital. Through the tiny gaps in the metal grilles, most of the POWs could see the green and red flashes of triple-A fire soaring into the sky, alongside the blazing orange of exploding ordnance. Bob was constantly uplifted by the allied offensive. 'To my ever-present question of how or when victory might happen, there was no answer. So part of my defence mechanism to cope with this extreme, unknown and potentially violent situation was to deal with it moment by moment. My immediate future was measured in minutes and hours. Not days. In fact, I didn't know what the future held. Or, if I had any future at all.'

Bob, too, had no contact with other prisoners, and little idea of what was happening outside his cell. For the most part, the doors rarely opened, and the prisoners languished in their own squalor and their solitary journey to starvation. But he wasn't so desperate for company that he wished the footsteps coming down the corridor would stop outside his door. The sound of the key being turned in his lock was the last thing he wanted to hear. 'Were you going to be taken away to be interrogated or beaten? You'd hear another cell door being opened then sounds of people crying out in pain. Then you thought, *Is it my turn next?* It was a terrible existence.'

The Iraqis appeared obsessed with their belief that Israeli pilots were bombing them from American and British jets. As Dave Waddington knew all too well, any hint of Jewish blood was ruthlessly challenged. The Mukhabarat seemed increasingly intent on following the unappealing example of the German Gestapo, starting with a demeaning physical examination. One by one the POWs were dragged out of their cells. Bob was taken to a brightly lit room and ordered to drop his trousers. 'It was a really disturbing experience; your mind races as you have no idea what is about to happen. But it became clear that they just wanted to check for circumcision; looking to see if any of us were Jewish.'[6]

Blindfolded and still wearing his hospital pyjamas, Robbie Stewart was subjected to an even more intimidating experience. Two burly guards lifted him out of his cell and dragged him along the corridor to the basement. 'Suddenly I felt my pyjamas pulled down together with my underpants. What were they going to do? I was truly petrified.'

He could feel people staring at his exposed genitals for several minutes before his clothes were replaced and he was frogmarched back the way he'd come. 'I was actually pleased to be back in my cell. It sounds really strange to say now, but I felt more secure locked away from the guards.' But they could still strike fear into their charges. One who had taken a particular dislike to Robbie would stand outside his door shrieking. He would order Robbie to get to his feet, then lie back down again, knowing the airman had a shattered leg. And yet he was also capable of moments of haunting lyricism. 'He had a wonderful, melodic voice, singing mournful and haunting Arabic songs long into the night. In the morning, he would revert to his spiteful self.'

After his own circumcision check, Dave Waddington was catapulted back into his ongoing nightmare. 'At one stage, I don't think I saw any light for a couple of weeks. I began developing a "strobing" behind my eyes, whether they were open or closed. It would drive me crazy. Sometimes I'd hammer on the door just so the guards would open the hatch to see what was wrong, even though I knew they'd go mad and punch me in the face. It was worth it just to see something other than blackness.' Like most of the POWs, regardless of their prior beliefs, Dave found himself turning to God for comfort. 'I'm not a particularly religious person, but I prayed an awful lot. I even returned to my Catholic upbringing, making rosary beads out of wool torn from my blanket. When I was really down, when I couldn't stand it any more, something would happen to boost my spirits, like the light coming on for a minute or a guard coming round with an extra piece of bread.'

There was always hope.

A few days into his incarceration, Robbie was taken to another part of the prison to have his broken leg re-plastered. The doctor was accompanied by a guard in a smart green suit. Robbie held the man's gaze for a moment. 'That was a mistake; his eyes narrowed and the muscles around his jaw went taut.' Robbie recognised him as the jailer who went out of his way to make his life a misery. It did not bode well.

The doctor removed some thick bandages from a brown case. His sidekick leered and drew a long-bladed knife from his jacket pocket. Robbie felt the touch of cold steel against his cheek, then the blade slide down towards his neck. Desperate not to catch the guard's eye again, Robbie focused on the doctor plastering his leg. The blade disappeared back into the suit. Only to be replaced by a pistol, which he held inches away from Robbie's face, and loaded with a theatrical flourish. Robbie felt the cold, hard muzzle against his forehead then the unmistakable sound of the weapon being cocked. 'The doctor seemed oblivious to the nutter with the gun. For all he was concerned, this man could have been a nurse wiping my brow.'

'I am going to shoot you,' the Iraqi rasped.

Robbie stared down at his fresh cast, refusing to believe that they would go to the trouble of fitting it if he was about to be executed. He closed his eyes and waited. The muzzle was removed, then the butt crashed into the side of his head. He looked up in time to register the guard pulling back his arm, preparing to deliver another punishing blow. 'The scene became somewhat surreal as the guard continued to pistol-whip me, while the doctor continued to plaster my leg.'

Eventually the guard grew bored and the doctor completed his task. Robbie was thrown back into his cell, with a throbbing skull and the smell of drying gypsum. 'Later, I slipped into my dreams, escaping to the hills of Scotland where Tange and I had enjoyed so many walking holidays.'

* * *

While the POWs battled with cold, hunger and despondency, their colleagues at Muharraq spent their time between missions in the comfort of the Sheraton Hotel. It was a bizarre existence. 'The contrasts of living in a five-star hotel and flying war missions really were stark,' Gordon Buckley recalled. 'One moment, we were flying ops over enemy territory, dropping sophisticated weapons, destroying infrastructure, killing people, then a few hours later we would be by the pool ordering a club sandwich and a beer. It was difficult to reconcile at times. Especially when the worst happened. You never knew when reality would hit.'

The crews were also living cheek by jowl with the press. Most of the aircrew were relatively happy with the set-up. Nick Heard enjoyed the company of people who offered a very different perspective from military life. 'The media guys became friends and generally played a fair game, respecting when to talk to us, when to give us space, especially if we had lost a jet. Our socialising meant things were said over a beer we would never want to appear in print, but they rarely crossed that line, and on the odd occasion one of them did, it was the rest of the media guys who brought them up sharp.'

After one incident where an off-the-cuff remark appeared in a newspaper, the Detachment Commander warned the press pool in no uncertain terms that if boundaries were not respected, they would be evicted from the base and have no access to any crews. Mike Toft remembers a slightly different version of events. 'One of the newspaper reporters overstepped the mark and he found himself thrown, fully clothed, into the hotel swimming pool by some very angry aircrew. He deserved it, and the matter was resolved.'[7]

By mid-February, with no aircraft from Muharraq lost in more than three weeks, things had settled into a routine, underpinned by the Pave Spike-enabled precision bombing. 'We gained confidence in what we were doing,' Heard said. 'Working from the Sheraton was surreal at times, but I enjoyed the contrast between ops and then having the ability to unwind with a beer or do some exercise.'

One of the TV reporters, Tony Birtley, enjoyed both the exercise and the drinks with the RAF fliers. Tornado pilot Rupert Clark, now a veteran of fourteen missions,[8] was renowned for his mathematical skills and his prowess on the squash court. Birtley challenged him to endless games, and emerged from most encounters with only a sweat-drenched shirt and drooping shoulders to show for it. John Broadbent, the Tornado Detachment Commander, was also on Clark's hit list. 'Rupert was a lot better player than me,' he said. 'But he was generous enough of spirit not to destroy my morale too comprehensively. Our matches became an important way for me to relax.'[9]

Clark's sporting expertise and brainpower were coupled with tremendous talent as a marksman. The Cambridge University graduate, fondly referred to as 'Posh Git' by his Squadron mates, had represented Great Britain Under-18s in the international rifle championships.[10] Neither that nor his successes with a squash racquet ever went to his head. The press corps found him down-to-earth, and he would often share a beer in the small hours with Birtley and his fellow reporters.[11]

Clark was in a good place. He had married before deploying on operations and his wife was expecting their first child. He shared a hotel room and a Tornado with his affable navigator Steve Hicks, who, with two young children of his own, had a few tips about fatherhood ready to pass on.

Hicks, twenty-nine, was a popular member of the Squadron and a good friend of navigator Mike Toft. They lived within spitting distance of each other in the RAF Laarbruch married quarters. Deployed for three months in the Gulf, they had shared long chats and many cigarettes outside the Squadron's buildings as they contemplated how the war was progressing. Steve had previously served as an Air Electronics Operator on Nimrod maritime patrol aircraft and was affectionately known as 'Diddley-dit' because of his Morse Code skills.

* * *

Operations continued apace and, on 10 February, a Dhahran crew dropped the base's 1,000th 1,000lb bomb. The final unguided weapons were dropped two days later.[12] While laser-guided bombing greatly improved targeting results, the system was certainly not infallible. Weapons could veer off course if there was a technical fault, perhaps with the seeker system, or if sudden cloud cover obscured the target, and hence the laser beam. And because some attacks were now on bridges near population centres, occasional tragedies did occur. During one early LGB attack on the Euphrates river crossing in Falluja west of Baghdad, a 1,000lb bomb failed to guide and hit the crowded marketplace causing terrible devastation, and as many as 130 deaths.[13]

It later transpired that perhaps three bombs had failed to guide. Pre-attack planning had taken that possibility into consideration so the approach track was along the river in the hope that any errant munitions falling short would land in the water.[14] Two had, but the third veered into the built-up area where the cost borne by civilians, as is so often the case, was horrendous.

Hamid Mehsan, a Falluja merchant, lost his son, brother and nephew in the incident. He later described what he saw to a British journalist: 'A bomb hit just over there and as soon as it exploded, the old buildings fell down. The people were buried, and I saw the men digging with their shovels to bring out the dead. I saw people without their throats. Some they did not find: my son Omar was never found, we found only his head.'[15]

Although it would be of no comfort to those whose lives had already been shattered, precision bombing now allowed the allied air forces to prepare the battlespace for the approaching invasion. The Tornados were ordered to focus on taking out the enemy airfields, and especially their hardened aircraft shelters as intelligence had suggested that when the ground war began, the Iraqis might launch kamikaze-style attacks using aircraft loaded with Saddam's chemical weapons.[16] The bombers were tasked with ensuring the remnants of the Iraqi Air Force remained firmly grounded.

While the RAF continued its attacks on airfields, other allied forces were targeting Iraqi military 'command and control' facilities, but horrific tragedies involving civilians still occurred. At 0430 on 13 February, two American F-117 Stealth bombers each dropped a huge 2,000lb laser-guided bomb on what was believed to be an Iraqi military command bunker in the Amiriyah district of Baghdad. It was actually sheltering hundreds of civilians. The bombs cut through 10 feet of reinforced concrete before detonating. The destruction was catastrophic. Reports vary, but it is estimated that around 400 people – mostly women and children – were killed. It was a stark reminder of the brutality of war, and how it was the innocent who often suffered most.

As preparations for the ground war continued, the scale of RAF attacks rose from six to twelve aircraft: eight Tornados, each armed with two 1,000lb LGBs, supported by four Buccaneers. Shortly before dawn on 14 February, the jets took off for Al Taqaddum airbase, 40 miles west of Baghdad. As they would be entering the area of the Baghdad 'Super MEZ', they had USAF Wild Weasel and EF-111 aircraft on hand, specifically designed to deal with the threat posed by enemy radar systems.[17] American F-15 fighters also patrolled the area.

There had been much discussion about tactics, so the lead navigator who planned it had sought John Broadbent's advice. With the enemy fighter threat eliminated, support from accompanying US anti-missile aircraft, and their own jamming pods, the Squadron Boss was content the SAM threat could be dealt with. 'Attack directions sometimes had to be compromised by the overriding requirement to ensure accurate identification of weapons release points. Al Taqaddum offered featureless approaches from all but one direction. By this stage of the war, we had been delivering LGBs from medium level for almost two weeks in a relatively benign environment, so when the navigator came to me to discuss his choice of attack direction, his reasoning was perfectly sound.'[18]

Two hours and twenty minutes into the mission, the airfield's two parallel 12,000ft runways came into view. Pablo Mason was first over the objective, scoring a direct hit on the selected HAS. With their RHWRs untroubled by missile threats, the rest of his formation followed, sending their laser-guided bombs down onto the aircraft shelters. A few minutes later, the next four bombers and two laser-designator Buccaneers began their final run in.

Nigel Risdale was leading, with John Broadbent in the navigator's seat. They were halfway down the delivery run when their accompanying Buccaneer crew reported that cloud cover made it impossible to identify the target. Risdale pulled out of the stream.

Nick Heard was next, coming in from the west with the early-morning sun on his face. 'We were wary as we knew the target would be hot territory inside the Super MEZ. As we approached at height, the airfield disappeared under our nose so you lost sight of the target. It didn't matter as the Buccaneer's laser pod would be guiding our bombs. There was a *bump, bump* as the bombs came off and descended into the HAS.'

Heard pulled away to the north and the rest of the attack followed in.[19]

Rupert Clark and Steve Hicks were experienced operators. The morning sun was glinting off the ribbon of the Euphrates far below as the pair prepared to release their munitions. The clock had just passed 8.42am when the Al Taqaddum runways appeared. Their target was a HAS on the south-east corner of the airfield. Five seconds before dropping, Rupert noticed a brief burst of signals from an enemy radar on his RHWR.[20] He glanced quickly outside then back at the screen. There was no visible sign of any missile launch or further indication of radar activity. They pressed on.

Just after weapons release,[21] an urgent shout rang out over the radio. 'Missile launch! Missile launch!'[22]

Their attention was immediately diverted from the attack.

'Two missiles airborne. Heading for the formation.' The frantic warning came from one of the accompanying Buccaneer crews who had seen the initial blasts from the ground as the missiles left their rails.[23]

Clark and Hicks instantly scanned the ground, looking for the rocket flame and smoke trail of an attacking SAM. Nick Heard dipped his wings in turn. 'I was looking down, searching to see if I could see anything coming our way. We had no idea who was being targeted.'

All eyes were on stalks. 'The words "missile launch" really got our attention,' said John Broadbent, now some distance from the target. 'Everyone was heads up, looking out of the cockpit, searching for the incoming missiles.'

'SAM! SAM! SAM!' A split second later a sharp-eyed American

fighter spotted what everyone was looking for: two plumes gunning skywards.

Pablo Mason saw them streaking up towards a Tornado. 'I saw two puffs of black smoke just off my port wing as I was running south, and the last of our team was running onto the target.'

Rupert Clark hadn't initially seen the missiles heading towards his aircraft. But suddenly his RHWR screamed a warning: 'Missile Guidance'! His heartbeat quickened. Powered by solid-fuel rocket motors, the pair of SA-3 missiles had already reached their maximum speed of 2,300mph.

'Break left!' Hicks shouted while releasing chaff. Clark was already ramming the throttles into full power, lowering the Tornado's manoeuvring flaps and throwing them into a tight turn. But the missile was too fast. 'We were going through north, when there was this huge explosion and I felt the blast wave hit the aircraft.'[24]

The first missile exploded a few feet off the port side of the Tornado and fragmentation from the 60kg warhead peppered the fuselage.

'You okay?' Clark shouted back to Hicks. He didn't have time to register the lack of response. 'I saw the second missile coming up at us vertically, waggling as it guided onto me. I pulled on the stick as hard as I could. There was nothing else I could do. The missile disappeared from view, going behind and to the right of the aircraft. Then there was another explosion.'[25]

A smudge of smoke appeared as the second SA-3 detonated, sending more shards of shrapnel into the jet. 'When the second missile hit, the whole cockpit was shattered. The instruments were gone, as were both engines.'[26]

Pablo Mason had a clear view of what had happened. 'I saw the SA-3 missile explode on the other side of their jet. I could see the aircraft was still intact as it came out of the second blast, and was still flying.' The jet dived northwards looking 'strangely graceful' as it faded further into enemy territory. Descending, now with no power, Clark attempted to glide as far as he could, away from the danger area. He again called Hicks. There was still no reply.

Nick Heard searched the sky for further SAMs. 'I could see the trails of where the two missiles had come up from the ground intersecting with the trail of smoke from a jet heading gently down. We didn't know who it was. I just kept manoeuvring my jet to check if anything else was heading towards us, but also so I could keep an eye on the descending aircraft to see if anyone ejected.'

Clark's secure HaveQuick radios were down so he could not communicate with Heard or anyone else in the formation. He watched the altimeter unwind as the Tornado descended through 15,000ft. He knew ejection was inevitable but delayed as long as possible, increasing the distance from the launch site.[27] The aircraft became less and less responsive to his inputs until eventually there was nothing more he could do.

'Steve, are you okay?'

There was still no reply from his navigator.

Clark pulled the handle, ejecting them both. 'I got a massive kick up the backside as my seat fired. I was fully conscious and remember thinking, *When are all these explosions going to stop?* Suddenly there was dead silence, no noise at all, and I was hanging from my parachute in clear blue skies. The trouble was, it's Iraq below you.'[28]

When Pablo Mason called the entire formation to check in, it was clear to navigator Mike Toft who was missing. '*Fuck!* All I knew was that Rupert and Steve were in serious trouble. I was immediately thinking, *Are they alive? What's happened?* This latest loss really hit us hard, especially as we had been incident-free for so long.'

The downed aircraft's approximate position was relayed to the AWACS as the surviving crews reluctantly turned south for home. Nick Heard could still see the consequences of the missile attack. 'We just watched the smoke trail of the descending Tornado, still desperately hoping to see some ejections. There was nothing.' It was another ominously quiet transit back to Muharraq. 'I had joined the RAF with Rupert and we'd gone through officer training together. Hicksy lived a few doors away from me on the married patch. I was friends with them both. I now presumed I'd just seen both killed.'

Nige Risdale and the Boss also shared a silent flight home. 'The only thing we could hope for was that they had managed to eject. It may sound cold now, but there was nothing else to do, apart from hope.' John Broadbent was also numb. 'The journey back to base seemed interminable. It was our first loss since 20 January, and all the more shocking for that.'

When the formation arrived at Muharraq, Heard and a close friend of Hicks were sent to the Sheraton to pack up the aircrew's personal belongings. 'It was a sad task,' Heard said. 'Sorting through all their kit – shirts, family pictures, books, socks – to be sent home to their loved ones. I was reminded of how many times it must have happened during the Second World War to the men in Bomber Command.'

The military personnel were not alone in being devastated by the loss. The journalistic contingent shared their distress. Some had become trusted listeners to the men going into battle. Among them was Ian Henry of the *Sunday Express*, who had spent long hours chatting and drinking with Clark. 'Rupert was a man of obvious dedication to his chosen career,' Henry wrote three days after the incident. 'He was anxious not to give away any details which might help the enemy, but also anxious to help readers understand the risks he and his colleagues undertook. Their faces will be two more that will be sorely missed. It leaves a real gap in the banter around the poolside bar.' He then added: 'As professional fliers the brave crews of the RAF may be steeled to the acceptance of losses, even the loss of close friends. I knew Flight Lieutenant Clark only fleetingly, but I find it hard to bear that his smiling face is absent.'[29]

Clark's regular squash partner Tony Birtley was distraught. With tears in his eyes, he sought out one of 15 Squadron's Flight Commanders, Gordon Buckley. It was Buckley's day off, so he was enjoying his regular club sandwich and a beer by the pool. 'Rupert and Steve have been shot down,' Birtley sobbed. 'The rest of the formation saw their aircraft get hit by a SAM and they didn't eject.'[30]

Buckley was shattered. 'It hit us all really hard. We had thought we were over the worst of the air threat, but now it appeared that two more mates had been killed. The morale took a real downturn

and it was a harsh wake-up call. The risks were still very real every
time we crossed that border.' Before the war had started, Buckley
had snapped a picture of Steve Hicks sitting at the hotel bar. 'It was
a great photo. Hicksy was grinning the way I always remember him;
he had a really infectious smile . . . That image remains emblazoned
on my memory thirty years on.'

* * *

The next day, 15 February, at 2.30pm, Baghdad Radio announced
that Iraq would leave Kuwait. The capital's streets filled with
crowds celebrating the end of the war. 'Air-raid sirens wailed, and
Baghdadis fired rifles into the air,' the *Los Angeles Times* reported.
'People gathered in excited groups to discuss the news.'[31]

Saddam said he would abide by the UN resolution for uncon-
ditional withdrawal of his troops. But then came his conditions:
all allied forces would withdraw from the region, war reparations
would be made to Iraq, and the Kuwaiti royal family would be
replaced by a new government. In addition, Israel would pull out of
the occupied Arab territories. It was, said President George Bush, a
'cruel hoax'. The American leader went on to say: 'Until a massive
withdrawal begins, with those troops visibly leaving Kuwait, there
will be no let-up in the offensive.'[32]

The streets of Baghdad fell silent again as the next raids came in.

Indeed, the bombings grew in intensity. It was becoming clear
that the ground assault was near. A flurry of further diplomatic
activity began with Tariq Aziz, the Iraqi Foreign Minister, flying to
Moscow for peace talks on 21 February. Saddam also considered it
an appropriate moment to make a bellicose speech. 'The mother of
battles will be our battle of victory and martyrdom,' he said over
the airwaves. 'They want us to surrender, but of course they will
be disappointed.'[33]

On this occasion, President Bush did not feel obliged to respond
in person. Instead, the White House issued a statement: 'Our forces
remain on a steadfast course. The liberation of Kuwait continues.'[34]

Ground attacks against Iraqi tank, artillery and infantry positions intensified. In response, Saddam ordered his troops to set fire to more than 300 Kuwait oil wells. A dark, noxious cloud hovered over the looming battlefield.[35]

* * *

For the prisoners in Baghdad, the days of confinement rolled on. The marks etched on their walls showed they were now deep into February. They had learned to live with the stench of their own sweat and excrement, the dirt under their nails, matted hair, body lice and the interminable cold. And the chocolate-brown tiles. The monotony was broken only by the nightly bombing of Baghdad. 'Lying on my favourite spot on the cell floor, I could see up through the window bars and into the night sky,' John Nichol recalled. 'It never really occurred to me that this might prove any danger to us. I could see the tracer arcing into the sky and the detonations of the coalition bombs. I came to rely on the bombing as a sign that I was not alone. It was comforting, the way a train passing in the night was comforting when I was a young boy, tucked up safely in bed. I was starving and must have lost a couple of stone, I lived in fear of the footsteps stopping outside my steel door, and I was terrified by the screams of pain and suffering of those around me. But I wasn't alone. My friends were in the skies above us, continuing the fight.'

Dave Waddington's weight had also plummeted; he was always last in line for his measly helping of food. Nearly three weeks into his nocturnal existence, the guards dished out boiled rice instead of the usual slimy soup. It was the prisoners' first solid food since arriving at the Mukhabarat jail. Dave waited anxiously as he heard the helpings gratefully received in the other cells. 'By the time they got to me they'd run out. All I got was a tiny piece of pitta bread. I was devastated and almost burst into tears. I was trying to work out how long it would be before I starved to death.'

Dave's mind slipped into oblivion during the long hours of gloom.

'I remember praying, "Wouldn't it be good if this building was hit by the coalition bombing so the Iraqis had to move us?"'

He was about to be granted his wish.

As he lay on his blankets in the pitch darkness, Robbie Stewart also prayed for the war to finish. It was 23 February and the night was unusually quiet.

'Suddenly, there was a low moaning rush followed by an unbelievable roar like some demented banshee screaming with toothache,' he recalled. 'I could hear the crackling of sound waves and then an enormous explosion. The walls shook, the ceiling fell in and the flap on the steel door was blasted open. I could see flames through the small window as I cleared my ears from the impact pressure.'

Terrified of instant obliteration, Robbie put his plastic water bowl on his head and shouted, 'Incoming!' 'There was a short period just before each explosion when I wondered if my name was on that particular bomb.'

As each one fell, the air parted. It sounded like a high-speed train thundering through a station. The explosions reverberated through the building, undermining the walls and shaking free the brown tiles. In the middle of the attack, Dave Waddington realised with some irony that his prayers had been answered. 'I was absolutely scared stiff. It was much worse than being shot down; you could hear each bomb a fraction of a second before it hit. I didn't know whether I was going to be alive or dead in the next few seconds. I just lay there thinking, hoping, *Please let me survive.* There was absolutely nothing I could do; it was truly terrifying.' Another explosion bowed his steel prison door inwards. Like his navigator, Dave sat in the corner with his plastic water bowl over his head.

As he listened to the screaming detonations and felt the shock waves resonate through the building, John Nichol also grabbed his plastic bowl. He had used it to save some water for his first wash in four weeks, and readied it now in case a fire broke out. With around half a pint of water, it was unlikely to provide much protection, so he quickly tore a square out of his tattered blanket, padded the inside of his larger food bowl and placed it on his head. Given his

A Victor tanker trails its hoses ready for a Tornado armed with laser-guided bombs and its accompanying Buccaneer 'Pave Spike' targeting aircraft to refuel before crossing the border into Iraq.

At the end of the war, Steve Hicks' friends carry his coffin to an awaiting aircraft for his final journey home. From left, Pablo Mason, John Broadbent (OC 15 Squadron) Nige Risdale, Steve Barnes, Dave Cockerill.

Former prisoners John Nichol and Rupert Clark face the media after being reunited with their families at RAF Laarbruch.

Dave Waddington and Robbie Stewart are finally reunited with their families at RAF Marham after seven weeks of captivity. From right: Kirsty, Robbie, Tange and Scott Stewart; Dave Waddington and his fiancée Claire.

John Peters and John Nichol take a Tornado airborne again for a first flight together after their release from captivity.

Jerry Witts enjoys his first beer in the 31 Squadron crewroom on landing back at RAF Bruggen after flying some of the Tornados home from Dhahran.

Robbie Stewart, left, and Dave Waddington plan their first Tornado sortie together after returning from captivity.

John Broadbent at Kuwait
international airport after the
ceasefire with some of the captured
Iraqi weapons.

General Sir Peter de la Billière (right),
the UK forces' commander, alongside
General Norman Schwarzkopf,
the overall coalition commander,
arriving at Heathrow Airport in 1991
following the end of the war.

Three Tornados from the Muharraq detachment in late 1990 armed with JP233 runway denial weapons. Very few Tornado aircrew had actually flown the jet loaded with this weapon prior to the build-up to the conflict.

Simon Burgess, left, and Bob Ankerson prepare for a training sortie together after the war. Sadly, Simon would be killed in a flying accident a few years later.

John Nichol presents former Prime Minister Sir John Major with a signed Tornado print as thanks for being the Guest Of Honour at the 25th anniversary reunion of the Gulf War POWs in 2016.

Philippa and Jeremy Green, whose father Bill was killed in a Tornado accident before the war started, with the trophy the family presented to 27 Squadron in his, and his navigator Neil Anderson's memory.

Kirsty Stewart about to go flying with her father Robbie during a Tornado training sortie.

A 'Diamond Nine' formation of Tornados pictured during the final days of the Tornado's RAF service in February 2019.

The RAF POWs during their annual reunion and celebration in 2019; most are looking older, greyer, balder, rounder and wiser. From left: Dave Waddington, Rupert Clark, Robbie Stewart, John Peters, John Nichol, Bob Ankerson.

A post-war formation of the RAF's major combat aircraft involved in Operation Desert Storm. From top, Tornado F3, Buccaneer, Tornado GR1, Jaguar.

Two Tornados taxi out ready for an early evening take-off from RAF Marham in 2018.

paltry resources, it was the best protection available; he was grateful
for anything in the maelstrom. 'The whole building was shaking.
I could hear rubble falling and I thought the floor was going to
collapse. Everybody was yelling at the tops of their voices to be let
out. I was petrified, waiting for the fourth bomb to hit the bullseye.
I resigned myself to the notion I was about to die.'[36]

Bob Ankerson was also cowering in his cell. 'We were the "target
for tonight" and it was a curious experience. I actually felt quite
tranquil. I put my trust in the hands of God, simply thinking, *Thy
will be done*. My faith had provided me with comfort through
the ordeal so far; I could only wait to see what transpired next.
But as I curled up in a ball on the floor, I had the biggest knot in
my stomach.'

The last of the four bombs exploded almost on top of the POW
block, blowing in walls, ceilings and doors, freeing some of the
prisoners from their weeks of isolation. Rapid, disjointed and manic
chatter broke out through the shattered prison, between comrades
rendered incommunicado for the previous weeks.

Nichol recognised Rupert Clark's distinctive public-school
accent, amazed to hear someone from his own Squadron. Clark
had been captured a few minutes after ejecting and sent to the
Mukhabarat jail after some truly horrific beatings, during which his
leg had been broken.[37] It had taken four American 2,000-pounders
to discover he was with his RAF comrades.

'Rupert! Good to hear you, mate!' Nichol shouted.

'John Nichol,' he replied. 'How are you? We thought you
were dead!'

'How's Steve Hicks?' Nichol asked.

After an emotionally charged silence, Rupert replied: 'Steve's dead.'

Clark described how they had been shot down nine days earlier,
and that Hicks had been killed in the initial blast. Nichol listened
with a heavy heart. He and Steve Hicks had both served in the
ranks before being commissioned as officers. They shared an
unspoken bond.

Nichol then remembered he had seen his old friend Simon

Burgess, Bob Ankerson's pilot, in one of the courtyards of a previous prison. 'Budgie Burgess,' he called. 'Are you in here?'

'John Nichol,' Burgess shouted back. 'How are you, mate? I haven't seen you since you were pissed at that airshow last August, running around with a tea towel on your head. I bet you regret that now!'

Laughter echoed among the dust and debris.

Bob Ankerson heard his pilot's voice for the first time since the day they ejected. 'Are you all right, Simon?'

'Yes, I'm okay.'

Bob was delighted. 'We were both still alive and in it together.'

Robbie Stewart listened to everyone 'talking excitedly as if they were in their back gardens leaning over the fence'. Then, through the chatter, he heard a voice that brought tears to his eyes. 'Has anybody seen Robbie Stewart?'

'Hi Dave, I'm here!' Robbie replied, overjoyed. 'The thin Bolton accent floated up through the chaos. Dave Waddington was just down the corridor. It felt fantastic knowing that he was alive.'

Dave experienced conflicting emotions. 'Joy that Robbie was alive, happiness that we were still together, but sadness that he hadn't got away.'

The Iraqi guards had now recovered from the shock of the bombing and used crowbars to open some of the cell doors. Prisoners were dragged downstairs and out of the ruined building. Eventually one of them unlocked Bob Ankerson's door and he was led over the piles of rubble and pools of water veined with leaking kerosene. He was pushed onto a bus crammed with other evacuated prisoners in their drab yellow suits with 'POW' emblazoned on the front. All the seats had been removed but it was still crowded. Bob spotted a tiny gap. 'As I flopped down, my hands went to the floor and touched the hands of the POW next to me. For just a few seconds we gripped hands and both had a moment of human comfort. It was an immense morale boost. He was a complete stranger but we were both in it together. I was back among friends. No longer isolated.'

Being less mobile than most, Robbie was delighted to get out of his cell. A diminutive Iraqi guard entered, pulled the navigator's arms over his head and carried him out in a fireman's lift, over chunks of masonry and down stairwells dripping from the ruptured water pipes. Robbie was thrust at two brawny guards who grabbed an arm each and started running him across a stretch of concrete covered in rubble. With his broken leg still held together by plates inserted five weeks earlier, Robbie gritted his teeth through the excruciating agony. 'Just when I thought I would collapse from pain and lack of breath, they stopped and pointed to the incredible destruction.'

'This is what your American friends have done,' one guard hissed, pushing Robbie up against a wall. The guards moved back, then unslung their AK-47 rifles. 'I had the terrible feeling that this was how it was all going to end,' Robbie said. 'They raised their rifles. I was suddenly very calm and unafraid. I had talked to Tange about the prospect of me not returning, about the kids' education and their lives after my death. I was a Christian and now facing two AK-47s. I looked to God for extra strength and found it as I stood waiting for the bullets.'

Robbie stared at the gun barrels aimed at his chest, bracing himself. The seconds ticked by. The guards lowered their rifles and hustled him towards the bus. A few yards from the open door, they let go of him and stood back. Without his crutches, Robbie tottered towards the open door. The bus moved forward a few yards, just beyond his reach. Robbie swivelled right and hobbled after it. Just as he was about to get on, the driver put the vehicle in reverse. The guards laughed uproariously at the infantile game. Finally, Robbie lunged for the doorway and was pulled inside. 'Collapsing on the floor, I felt the hands of the person next to me. He touched my fingers then squeezed them, giving me a wonderful feeling of companionship in this dreadful predicament. I returned the squeeze.'

There was a clatter at his feet. His crutches. Followed by the unmistakable sound of a body being thrown down next to him. A Kuwaiti pilot who had been shot down in the early stages of the war. The Iraqis hated him intensely, blaming him for Iraq's predicament.

Robbie listened as they proceeded to beat him ferociously. 'It was an awful sound, a deep groan spilled out as they kicked and punched him. Then I made out the noise of my crutch hitting his body as he screamed in pain. We sat there, unable to move, as they pounded him until I heard a crack as my crutch snapped in two. The beating stopped and the guards muttered contentedly and left.'

The bus doors finally closed and it headed away, taking the prisoners to another unknown destination, and an uncertain future.

* * *

The menacing cloud from the oil-well fires over Kuwait spread like a gathering storm across the horizon. From the shoreline of the Gulf, all the way along the border to the Western Desert, great holes were blasted through the Iraqis' defensive sand berms to create gaps for the armoured assault force. At 4am on 24 February, in driving rain, the first US Marines crossed the border into Kuwait under the covering fire of 155mm howitzers. Their progress was fast and the resistance minimal.[38]

Not far from the Marines, the Challenger tanks of the British 1st Armoured Division also advanced into battle. Three hundred miles to their west, a French light division and the US 101st Airborne pushed through the open desert as part of the surprise 'left hook', to come in behind the heavy Iraqi troop concentrations. Across Saudi Arabia 150,000 troops and 1,500 tanks began their advance, heralding the start of the ground war to retake Kuwait.

At 10pm local time in Washington, 6am in Iraq, President Bush appeared on television. 'The liberation of Kuwait has now entered the final phase. I have total confidence in the ability of the coalition forces, swiftly and decisively, to accomplish their mission.'[39]

CHAPTER FOURTEEN

TERMINATE THE WOLFPACK

24 FEBRUARY–5 MARCH

As lives were lost on the battlefield, life outside the region continued as normal.

Sue Toft was heavily pregnant with their second child when her navigator husband Mike had been summoned to war. They both knew he would not be there for the birth. 'I could never have left the theatre of ops,' he said. 'I had a duty to my friends, my pilot, Mark, my Squadron; we had a mission to complete. It might sound cold, but I was more use with them than back in Germany with Sue. More importantly, there was absolutely no suggestion from Sue that I should return.'

As February dragged on, Sue was moved to the military hospital in Germany in preparation for the birth. Returning safely from each raid, Toft would call the ward for an update. Then, just before the ground war started, 'We were in a Japanese restaurant by the hotel. A few hours earlier, we had been on combat ops. I was now enjoying a beer and a fantastic meal. It was surreal. In another few hours I would head back out on ops and perhaps put my life on the line. I was living in truly strange times.'

Leaving his noodles and beer, Mike headed once more for the telephone, armed with a fistful of coins. 'After the previous false starts, my tired wife was brought to the phone with our new daughter in her arms.' A sharp gurgle and an indignant squeal suddenly echoed down the line. 'The midwife had pinched the baby's toe to make her cry so I could hear! It was a wonderful moment and quite a contrast to the reality of war.'[1]

Toft went to bed a happy man. The next morning, he was assigned a mission near the Super MEZ in Baghdad. The Muharraq Detachment Commander was waiting in the Operations Room to congratulate him on his new arrival. With a broad grin, Toft handed the DetCo an official 'Leave Pass' requesting six days' compassionate absence, starting immediately. 'When we returned from our mission, the Leave Pass was in my locker annotated with the single word "Refused".'

But there was also a handwritten note taped to a chilled bottle of Moët & Chandon champagne:

Sorry about the leave, Tofty. Perhaps the attached will help wet your new daughter's head. Many congratulations and best wishes. Dave Henderson. Muharraq DetCo.

There was also a promise that, once the war was over, Toft would be one of the first to return home. After debriefing, his formation retired to the bar to raise a toast. As they clinked beers, his pilot Mark Paisey looked him in the eye. 'Tofty, we now have all the more reason to get back safely!'

It was a sentiment echoed across the region as the conflict entered its final, decisive phase. There was still a deep-seated fear that Iraq would use chemical weapons against allied ground troops. Satellite imagery had shown Su-25 Frogfoot ground-attack aircraft at Shaibah airbase, only a few miles north of the Kuwaiti border. The Frogfoot was more than capable of delivering chemical munitions. Precision bombing was required to destroy its runway, and the Tornados were once again called into action.

The two prototype Thermal Imaging Airborne Laser Designator (TIALD) pods had been rushed into service and were now based with the Tabuk detachment. Their superior night-time targeting capability had quickly been battle-proven. Ten Tabuk crews were rapidly trained on the new equipment and round-the-clock operations were now available to mission planners.[2]

Dave Bellamy led his TIALD-equipped formation towards Shaibah airfield 700 miles east of Tabuk. He was initially puzzled by an unexpectedly early sunrise. 'As we got closer, the glow became a red pinprick of fire. That single fire became two or three, then ten or twenty. It was countless oil-well fires, and it looked like hell on earth.'

Bellamy then noticed streaks of light rising from the desert out to his right – the launch of hundreds of rockets targeting Iraqi troop positions. The rockets arced out in front of them before descending away to his left where the desert sparkled as the munitions exploded. The ground attacks were clearly intensifying. Five minutes out, Bellamy heard a Texan drawl issuing orders over the radio as further targets were identified. 'Then the ground bubbled up in red flame, like jam bubbling in a pan. It was giant B-52 bombers, unseen in the darkness, each dropping eighty-odd 1,000lb bombs.'[3]

Minutes later, the Tornados sent their TIALD-guided bombs into Shaibah, blasting huge craters at each intersection of the runway and taxiways. The Frogfoots would no longer be able to take off, and the threat of imminent chemical attack was diminished.

Bellamy's formation's egress took them north along the border. 'On one side we saw street lights and neon strips at petrol stations in Iran, while on the other, the landscape burned with bomb blasts and fires around Basra. It was an apocalyptic vision, like watching a movie with no soundtrack. An astonishing, silent image of war.'

After landing, Bellamy recorded his memories in his diary: 'It was a rare trip and those images of the battlefield are fixed in my mind for ever.'

And, as the war neared its denouement, more personnel were entering the fray.

* * *

It was with a sense of foreboding that Wing Commander Gordon Turnbull had dropped off his young sons. 'I watched all three walk into school with a lump in my throat, then headed to RAF Brize Norton for my flight to the Gulf.'[4]

He only had himself to blame. A few days earlier, his Boss had called about the Tornado pilot Gordon had treated after his breakdown in the early days of the war. 'Frank has just successfully carried out his first operational mission back in the Gulf.'

Before the psychiatrist could express his delight, his Boss went on, 'Of course, Turnbull, you realise what this means, don't you?'

'I told him I reckoned I did. I was to visit the main bases with an eye firmly looking out for signs of underlying combat-stress reactions.' At the RAF's main transport base in Oxfordshire, Turnbull boarded a huge Tristar capable of carrying over 300 passengers. 'There were only fifteen of us. The jet was loaded from floor to ceiling with ordnance. Shells wrapped in plastic like flat-packs of giant soup cans. Their pointed noses stretched from the cockpit to the tail.' He squeezed between the shells and into a seat, wondering what the future might hold.

His first port of call was Frank's Tornado base. He was anxious to see how he'd readapted to combat operations. Turnbull was met by the Squadron's Commanding Officer, who told him that the Tornados were about to go 'downtown'. They walked between the austere bunkers to the operation's briefing. 'I was keen to see how the crews dealt with the pressure of imminent combat. But having a shrink sit in on a pre-mission brief was huge. I tried to imagine how my presence would have gone down at a pre-mission briefing of a Bomber Command squadron during the Second World War.'

'How's Frank getting on?' he asked the CO.

'You can see for yourself.' They stepped into the concrete interior of the air-conditioned facility. 'We're here.'

The pair stood at the back as Turnbull learned that the formation was to strike a command and control bunker close to Baghdad.

He noticed considerable tension in the room, few questions asked and 'brief flashes of humour'. He also spotted Frank at the front, scribbling notes.

Turnbull counted the jets taking off, then, ninety minutes later, counted them all back without loss. He uttered a quiet prayer of thanks. Afterwards, 'the atmosphere had changed completely. The debriefing was characterised by noise and full, highly detailed descriptions of the mission. This was not just a technical download but a psychological one too, in which the Tornado crews were ventilating emotions. They were processing the information of the shared experience they had just been through. This was all good, healthy stuff.' He stepped outside the bunker with the CO, who lit a cigarette.

'Did you find what you expected?'

'I don't really know what I expected,' Turnbull replied. 'But I'm amazed.'

'In what way?'

'At their ability to switch emotions on and off,' he said. 'It's like a cloak they slip on and off. Remarkable.'

Turnbull heard the heavy bunker door clank open behind him.

'Good to see you looking so well,' Turnbull said as he and Frank shook hands.

'I am well,' Frank replied, smiling at his therapist. 'I just wanted to thank you for everything you did.'

'I didn't do anything,' Turnbull said. 'It was really all down to you.'

There was nothing else to say. With a hesitant smile, Frank thanked him again and left, a very different person to the broken man who had come through Turnbull's door three weeks earlier.

He knew that senior RAF officers still remained deeply sceptical about allowing psychiatrists onto bases. 'I concluded my visit would be a one-off, but it had been invaluable nonetheless. Far from being ostracised by the crews, I felt in a quiet kind of way that I'd been made welcome. With the ground offensive underway, we could all now hope for a swift conclusion to the conflict. With any luck there would be no need to deploy large numbers of psychiatrists to the front line.'

Turnbull now concentrated on his next mission. The missing RAF prisoners of war. Although it was still not known who was alive or dead, Turnbull had been adamant that any captured aircrew would need thorough psychological debriefing when freed. 'Going home immediately, I warned, would almost certainly prove disastrous. These people needed to decompress.'

The RAF eventually agreed, and as the prisoners' ordeal continued, Gordon prepared for any repatriations.

* * *

When the ground war began, the POWs had been evacuated from the shattered Mukhabarat prison and driven through the devastated streets of Baghdad. Their new destination was the notorious Abu Ghraib prison, run by the Ba'ath Party and home to countless thousands of political prisoners and criminals. Spread over a vast site, it had a well-deserved reputation for torture and extrajudicial killings.

The POWs were led in silence through its long, cold corridors, carpeted with bird droppings, and past hundreds of barred cells. Hobbling now on his one remaining crutch, Robbie Stewart was hustled into a freezing cell measuring 10 feet by 6. Piling in behind him came Dave Waddington, Bob Ankerson, John Nichol, Rupert Clark, an Italian Tornado pilot and the Kuwaiti pilot battered with Robbie's other crutch. After weeks of solitary existence, and despite the threat of what future Abu Ghraib might hold, the prisoners were overjoyed to be in each other's company. 'It was bliss,' said John Nichol. 'This was the first time I had really been with any friends since being shot down. It was like being at a very small, very crowded party.'[5]

Nichol helped Robbie to the floor then sat down himself, placing Robbie's broken legs over his own to provide some relief from the cold. Robbie immediately felt the body warmth and shared spirit.

'It was so uplifting all being together, it soon deteriorated into schoolboy gabble. We were excited, cracking jokes and forgetting our dire predicament.'[6]

The stories poured out, from being shot down to torture. It was a healing moment. The aircrew were bursting to share their bottled emotions – the humiliation, fear and pain of interrogation. 'Sitting in solitary confinement, everyone had reached the same conclusion,' said Nichol. 'That they had given in too readily.' But it soon became clear that every one of them had broken at pretty much the same time. The cold cell walls and floor became momentarily forgotten as the men chatted in hushed voices through the dark hours of the night.

Bob Ankerson was among those who felt the burden of self-reproach and guilt begin to lift. 'It was an amazing night. The joy and relief of being together, able to talk, just to be alongside a friendly face was incredible.'[7]

Nichol too was delighted. 'We were in prison, beaten to shit, we still didn't know if we were going to survive, but we were on a fantastic high.'

They had barely snatched twenty minutes' sleep before Abu Ghraib came to life. The chatter of its many thousands of prisoners, punctuated by the angry bark of guards, warming up for the day ahead. For weeks the POWs had grown used to meagre helpings of cold, slimy food, but when their door now clattered open, a guard appeared with a steaming washing-up bowl filled with leek soup, another with dark, sweet tea, and some flatbread. 'We had the most extraordinary scene of seven starving men standing in a circle passing the bowl around, each offering it to his neighbour, very politely saying "after you",' said Robbie. 'Small sips were taken, though each of us actually wanted to guzzle the lot. The bowl was then passed on, with another "after you".'

Later that morning, all the POWs were moved into the central courtyard to sit in the blazing sun, cross-legged and heads down. To help pass the time, the guards wandered around casually punching or whipping a POW across the head or back with their regulation lengths of hard-rubber hose. Throughout the day, each prisoner was taken for further interrogation.

With the invasion underway, their captors' questions had become increasingly focused. 'What can you tell us about the ground offensive? Where will the main allied thrust come? Will there be a seaborne invasion or a frontal assault on Kuwait City? Where would paratroopers be used?'

The airmen were clearly ill-equipped to answer, but the Iraqis were undeterred.

'I am giving you one chance to save your life,' Nichol was told as he sat once again in front of an interrogator. 'Tell me something about the ground offensive so I can save your life.'

'I was really trying very hard to come up with *anything* I could tell him since he seemed perfectly calm and serious. But I had nothing to give. My ignorance must have been obvious as he eventually let me go.'

At the end of an eventful day, the POWs were marched to yet another section of the prison and locked in solitary confinement once more.

* * *

There was one man who knew precisely how the ground war was progressing, and what was planned for the coming hours. From the basement of his command bunker in Riyadh, General Norman Schwarzkopf listened to a flurry of incoming reports. Major assaults had been preceded by thirty-minute artillery barrages which saw 10,000 shells and half a million bomblets rain down on the enemy front line. M1A1 Abrams main battle tanks equipped with mine ploughs smashed through their defensive positions, sometimes burying Iraqi soldiers alive in their own trenches. Following units streamed north towards Kuwait City. American armour also pushed into the desert from the west in surprise attacks on the Iraqi flank. One of Schwarzkopf's key objectives, aside from retaking Kuwait, was now to inflict such damage on the Republican Guard that they would never again pose a threat to their Arab neighbours.

He was woken later to be told that radio intercepts suggested that Iraqi troops were being ordered to abandon Kuwait City. The US Marines were attacking Kuwait International Airport and were within 10 miles of the capital. Fearful that the Republican Guard might slip through his grasp, Schwarzkopf urged his commanders to push forward hard, especially the heavy divisions coming in from the west in the 'left hook' through the desert. By nightfall, a massive armoured force was arrayed against the largely unsuspecting Republican Guard, who, seven months earlier, had been at the spearhead of the Kuwait invasion force. Schwarzkopf was content with their progress.[8]

Saddam Hussein realised his options were now severely limited. The only effective offensive weapon left in his arsenal were Scuds. One was fired on the morning of 25 February at Dhahran, where a substantial part of the Tornado force was based alongside thousands of allied forces. It was intercepted by a Patriot missile. That evening, another Scud was picked up heading towards the base, but its trajectory suggested it would land just beyond the Patriots' protective umbrella. It hit the periphery; coming down on a US accommodation block, killing twenty-eight and injuring eighty-nine. It was the worst single coalition loss of life during the entire war.[9]

* * *

Life inside Abu Ghraib was as grim as any of the other Iraqi jails the POWs had experienced. Dave Waddington had lost his homemade blanket moccasins in the violent evacuation from the Mukhabarat prison. Luckily, he had found some plastic bags in his cell to wrap around his feet. They served a dual purpose. 'On the few occasions we were allowed out of the cell to use the "toilet", they protected my feet from the overflowing pits of urine and faeces. And when they wouldn't let us out, I could pee in one of the bags, tip it out of the window, then turn it inside out and pop it back on my foot.'

Isolated in their cells, the prisoners could hear the misery. One evening, the guards targeted an Iraqi civilian and did not relent for eight hours. 'His screams echoed and rolled around the prison,' Nichol said. 'The cries were unearthly – lingering, agonised, banshee wails interspersed with sharp yelps of pain. Because the noise was rasping, playing continually on the edge of our nerves, it was impossible to sleep.'

The next morning, Robbie Stewart saw the prisoner tied to a post in the courtyard below their cells, as the guards set about him again with their rubber hoses. He watched as the man's skin became streaked with livid red welts. 'His cries grew weaker and I wondered how much longer he could last. I was also wondering how long the war would last and if we would ever be released.'

The POWs were eventually paired up in cells and Nichol was partnered with Larry Slade, a US Navy F-14 Tomcat backseater. Their cell also overlooked the courtyard where many of the beatings took place. Three Arab inmates waved up at them from their window opposite. Nichol and Slade waved back. A surreal handsignal conversation took place: the inmates mimed dropping bombs from an aircraft and gave the two airmen a thumbs-up. There were suddenly angry shouts from below and guards pointing furiously at the POWs' windows.

'Shit,' said Slade. 'They're coming to get us.'

A minute later, in a nearby cell, Robbie heard aggressive voices and boots pounding up the stairs. His cell door burst open, framing two huge Iraqi guards who demanded to know if they had been communicating with the Arab prisoners. 'We shook our heads and backed slowly to the wall. They slammed the door and went to the next cell.'

Bursting in on Nichol and Slade next, the guard screamed, 'Were you looking out the window?'

'No, no. Not us,' the pair replied in unison.

The guards thundered on.

A few minutes later they were back. With menace. They started on Slade first, punching him to the ground as Nichol looked on. 'It was as bad, if not worse, than anything in the interrogation. They were kicking the shit out of him. I was watching from the corner, frozen with horror. It was a concerted, merciless avalanche of furious blows and thudding kicks. There was no escape.'

Nichol knew with some dread that he would be next. The assault on Slade went on and on until the screams died out and he lay motionless. The Iraqis gave him a couple more kicks, then advanced towards Nichol. 'They punched and kicked me until I fell, then started kicking me in the face. I could feel the blood streaming down my cheeks and mouth in a hot torrent. I remember lying there, watching the bright red drops spattering down onto the dull grey concrete.'

Barely conscious, Nichol was pulled upright. As the blows continued, he raised his arms to protect his head.

'Keep your hands down!' a guard screamed. 'I'm going to break your face.' The Iraqi laid in with another frenzied attack.

'What were you signalling?' he demanded.

'We were just waving,' Slade mumbled through his broken lips.

'Right,' the guard said. 'You're dead.' He took out a pistol and pulled back the slide to load a round.

'You two, stand together.'

Nichol was shoved up next to the American.

'You are now going to die,' he said.

Both airmen looked down the barrel of the loaded weapon. 'For a number of seconds, the Iraqi stood quivering with rage, knuckles white, the slack taken up on the trigger. We were a heartbeat away from death. He pulled the trigger. *Click*.'

There were no rounds in the pistol. The guard had removed the magazine. He sneered at the POWs' petrified faces, then walked away.

The Iraqis returned later that evening with their rubber hoses, smacking them against the wall, demanding to know which cell the POWs had communicated with. The two airmen caved in. 'We felt terrible. With a burning sense of shame we told them.'

Ten minutes later, screams echoed from the opposite side of the courtyard.

'That was a very low time for us, Larry and me. We were responsible for those screams. But we had had enough for one day.'

* * *

Unknown to the POWs, Norman Schwarzkopf's ground troops were giving the Iraqi army an even more vigorous pummelling. Feeling the weight of the allied force arrayed against him and the inevitability of defeat, Saddam played his last card. On 26 February he publicly stated that Kuwait was no longer the 19th Governate of Iraq, and that his forces were going to leave the Emirate 'by the end of the day', thus fulfilling the UN diktat.

But the Americans paid little heed.

Schwarzkopf knew that the hour of reckoning was upon the Republican Guard and urged his troops forward. 'The Iraqi retreat was disintegrating into chaos. Large units were all trying to make it to Basra but were finding the Euphrates bridges down, and, as we'd anticipated, convoys were bunching up in the extreme south-east corner of Iraq.'[10] As the general had envisaged, the enemy was being driven into a small pocket where they could be decimated. 'Until we destroyed the Republican Guard, our job was only half done.'

By 27 February the retreating enemy columns tearing north up the eight-lane highway out of Kuwait were being hit non-stop, both by the tanks coming in from the west and the US Marines from the south. Once the airborne assets joined the fray, the road was quickly dubbed the 'Highway of Death' as the shattered vehicles and bodies piled up. 'The road out of Kuwait to Basra was an awful sight,' recalled a Tornado F3 navigator patrolling overhead. 'There was no way they could get off it to do anything, they were just slaughtered. It was better they died on that road than our boys, we were all acutely aware of that. But it didn't reduce the horror of what we saw.'[11]

The Americans set about the task of inflicting such pain on Iraq's armed forces that they would be permanently crippled. The coalition stacked up its air power, rotating eight fresh aircraft to attack every fifteen minutes, relentless in their destruction of as many Iraqi Republican Guard units as they could place in their gunsights.[12]

In between these attacks, Black Hawk helicopters equipped with loudspeakers flew over the battlefield, telling the Iraqis: 'Get out of your vehicles. Leave them behind and you will not die. We will let you go home.' A great many Iraqis had already abandoned their positions and thousands of POWs were being taken. After just four days of fighting, 3,000 of Iraq's 4,300 tanks had been destroyed, as well as 2,140 of its 3,100 artillery pieces.[13] The press was quickly onto the scent of victory. 'Saddam's outgunned elite smashed in armoured duel',[14] the *Daily Express*'s headline ran.

Like the Iraqis on the road to Basra, the POWs in Abu Ghraib felt the war had reached an apocalyptic moment on the night of 27 February. The sonic boom of jets was a constant overhead as the final air attacks went in. Nichol hunkered down in his cell, huddled up with Larry Slade, still dazed and covered in dried blood from their beatings. 'Explosion after explosion thundered incessantly nearby, until the air itself felt exhausted. It was terrifying. The bomb blasts seemed to be getting closer and closer. There was no way this prison would withstand a direct hit, or even a near miss.'

The pandemonium went on throughout the night, with little sound of opposition from the Iraqi triple-A. The enemy, it seemed, had lost the will to fight.

* * *

That same night, the Tornado TIALD force was again ordered up to hit Iraqi airbases. Now well versed in laser bombing, Mal Craghill and his pilot Mike Warren were told to strike the Al Habbaniyah helicopter hangars, west of Baghdad. They flew 500 miles north-east, destroyed the target and returned to Tabuk, two hours and fifteen minutes after taking off. After so many weeks at war, it had been a largely unremarkable mission.

'We had just got back to our accommodation after the debrief and put the BBC World Service on the radio,' Craghill recalled.

'Suddenly the newsreader announced that it was all over, a ceasefire had been agreed. I was bloody delighted; it appeared that Kuwait had been liberated and we had survived! Mike and I had dropped the last RAF bombs of the war.'

The ceasefire codeword was broadcast across all coalition aircraft radios:

'*Terminate Wolfpack. Terminate Wolfpack.*'[15]

It was approaching 5am in Iraq when President George Bush made his announcement from the White House. 'Exactly 100 hours since ground operations commenced, and six weeks since the start of Operation Desert Storm, all United States and coalition forces will suspend offensive combat operations. Iraq's army is defeated. Our military objectives are met. Kuwait is once more in the hands of Kuwaitis.'[16]

Jerry Witts, the Tornado Boss at Dhahran, woke up to find that one of his rival Squadron Commanders had pinned a note to his door: '*Bush declares cessation of offensive action. Last one back to Bruggen is a cissy!*'[17] Like the many servicemen in Saudi Arabia, Witts immediately headed off in search of illicit alcohol to celebrate the victory.

Over in more liberal Bahrain, the morning briefing at Muharraq airbase was laced with booze. A Buccaneer pilot was having breakfast when he spotted his navigator. 'He had the glazed look in his eyes he has when he's pissed; it was a look I knew very well. "It's all over," he said. It was Guinness and Macallan whisky at nine o'clock in the morning. By eleven I was out of my tree.'[18]

Mike Toft was delighted with the news, especially as he had been promised a spot on one of the first flights home once the war ended. 'There was a real sense of relief. It was a strange sensation as we had been living on the edge for six weeks. But ultimately it was simply a case of, *Thank God it's all over.*' Toft went in search of the clerk to book himself on the next transport aircraft out. He had an appointment to meet his new daughter.

At Tabuk, Dave Bellamy and his pilot Trevor Roche were woken at 5.20am as the Tannoy blared, 'Ceasefire declared. All missions now on a two-hour standby.' Minutes later a friend entered their room with a bottle of Johnnie Walker Red Label whisky. Soon the whole detachment had wind of the ceasefire and the pre-dawn merriment began.

Bawdy singing and boozy cheers greeted Bellamy at the Lightning Club. 'It was hearty handshakes, smile after smile, and a time to see everyone happy again. It was good to see the guys throw off the shackles of fear and uncertainty.' At some point the celebratory photographs took on a wintry aura when a foam fire extinguisher was discharged into the throng. The sun was beating down as Bellamy led a gaggle of merry airmen across the tarmac to breakfast. They no longer had to force down food, worrying about what might lie ahead over enemy skies. On the way they passed one of the base's most senior officers, 'pissed as a fart, in flying suit and moccasins, trying to pour out a glass of home-brew while balancing the plastic container on his head'.

There were more photos, a bonfire, drinking. 'A barbecue went ahead in scorching sun. Lots of people wanted pictures of the aircrew. I was unsure if we deserved it and felt like a prize poodle on show.' Eventually Bellamy slipped back to his quarters. 'I didn't feel like celebrating with full vigour while my flatmate John Nichol was still captive. I was sunburned, exhausted and emotional. I lay down with tears rolling down my cheeks and slept the sleep of paupers, content to be alone.'

When he awoke a few hours before midnight on 28 February, the base had fallen silent, no jets taking to the air, just the muffled sound of contented men snoring behind closed doors. Bellamy called his girlfriend. 'My conversation was stilted and tired. It had been so long since we had last spoken that I had forgotten how to communicate. We didn't really know what to talk about, we had been living such different lives for six weeks.' He finished the call then went to find the Intelligence Officer.

'Have they released the POWs yet?' Bellamy asked.

'Hopefully over the next forty-eight hours,' he was told.

'I truly hope he is safe,' Bellamy wrote in his diary. 'The war won't truly be over until I know what has happened to John.'

In the meantime, the British newspapers trumpeted the news of the victory. 'Surrender!' or 'Victory!' ran the headlines in almost every edition.

'It has been a very remarkable military campaign,' Prime Minister John Major told a press conference. 'I doubt there have ever been any campaigns better organised by the military than this one; it has been a supreme success for them.'[19] He too, had not forgotten about the British prisoners of war. 'We want them back immediately,' he said. 'There is no question of any delay.'

February 28th was a terrifying day for the families of all the missing airmen. Only now would they discover whether their loved ones had survived. Chris Ankerson had become used to 'living in the limbo' of not knowing whether Bob had ejected or gone down in his Tornado. 'The end of the war meant I'd soon receive the news. Good or bad. It was a terrible prospect.'[20]

The feeling of dread gripped Tange Stewart. Ever since the RAF liaison officer had appeared at her friends' dinner party, she had clung to the fact that Robbie had not been *confirmed* dead. It had been reported that the Iraqis would hand over prisoners or the remains of the deceased once ceasefire negotiations had concluded. 'They were the most truly horrendous days of the whole experience.'[21]

Berenice Waddington felt the same. 'The wait was so tense. Was David alive and a POW, or had he died in the Tornado crash?'[22]

For 12-year-old Gareth Ankerson, the weeks at boarding school without any new information had led him to a very dark place, and as February came to an end he was struggling. 'My confidence in my father being alive had been totally destroyed. I lost faith that I would ever see him again. I kept thinking how I said goodbye with just a hug, telling myself, *That's no way to say goodbye to someone who is going to die.*'[23]

* * *

The night of heavy bombing over Abu Ghraib had merged seamlessly into a cacophony of small arms fire and explosions on the morning of 28 February. Hunkered in their cell, John Nichol turned to Larry Slade and asked: 'What the hell's going on?'

'One of three things,' Slade replied. 'One of our guys has been shot down close by, they've got hold of him and they're celebrating. Or, there's a battle going on outside and some of our Special Forces are coming to get us. Or ... the war is over ...'

Moments later the prisoners were bundled out of Abu Ghraib and onto a bus. An air of menace accompanied the diminutive guard with his Saddam moustache who patrolled the aisle. Robbie Stewart again made the mistake of catching a guard's eye. The man knelt beside his seat, stroked the back of his neck, then grabbed a clump of hair and ripped it out. Fighting back the pain, Robbie kept his head bowed. 'He strutted off, then returned to stroke my hair once more, then karate-chopped me across the back of my neck.'

The man strolled around the bus looking for more victims. 'On his next return, I glanced at Bob Ankerson across the aisle, who was bent over with a lovely tuft of hair ripe for pulling. I thought to myself that the guard should go for Bob this time and give me a break.' He pulled out yet more of Robbie's hair. 'My hair was long but this was not the way to cut it. I whimpered in pain then suddenly realised what he was after. I shouted out louder and moaned, holding my head. This seemed enough to satisfy the sadist who wandered away.'

The bus eventually moved off. 'If you had been standing a little distance from that bus,' John Nichol said, 'you would have seen the prayers coming out of it, wraithlike, rising up to the heavens.'

A few hours later the POWs arrived at yet another prison on the outskirts of Baghdad. After being forced to run yet another gauntlet of yelling, punching, kicking soldiers, they were shoved back into solitary confinement in tiny, dank cells. Nichol counted 750 ticks on the wall marking the days endured by a previous occupant. His spirits drooped again.

However, despite the occasional screams that echoed around the stone corridors, the POWs soon began to detect a calmer atmosphere. Robbie Stewart dared to hope that the war might be over.

'There was no bombing and I knew something had changed. The guards talked with excitement in their voices.' Later in the day a bowl brimming with food was pushed onto the floor and the delicious aroma of lamb filled his cell. 'Something had definitely changed. I could make out rice, vegetables, slivers of meat and a bone. With great deliberation and utter pleasure, I slowly scoffed the lot. Using my tongue I delved into the core of the bone and retrieved the delicious marrow. I certainly slept well that night.'

As Robbie listened to allied jets coming in over Baghdad, like the rest of the POWs he still had no idea that a ceasefire had been ordered. 'The bangs I heard were not from bombs but supersonic booms. Was this a new tactic? Or were some of the lads having a bit of fun. Whatever the reason, I was desperate not to let my hopes rise.'

A few days later, on Sunday, 3 March, there was a tangible change in the guards' demeanour. For the first time in six weeks, the airmen were allowed to wash, albeit using the same barrel filled with warm water and the accumulation of the previous users' dirt. 'The scum didn't matter,' said John Peters. 'It was a marvellous feeling after weeks of grime just to feel the warm water coursing down my body.'[24] Robbie took the opportunity to wash his underpants, 'which had been worn back to front, inside out and upside down'. He was given a new yellow suit with 'PW' stitched on the front and doused with a can of perfume. 'Hope was in the air and it was a tremendous lift to think about home, the notion that the ordeal might soon be over.'

On 4 March, John Peters was given laces for his plimsolls which he hoped could only mean one thing: he was going to be released. He heard a group of Iraqi officers touring the building.

One entered Peters' cell and simply said, 'The war is over, you are going home in ten minutes.' Peters could not quite believe what he was hearing. He had been convinced that he would never see his wife and two young children again. 'It was the first confirmation I'd had of the secretly hoped-for fact. They had said it, it was undeniable. And it was tremendous. A rush of emotion and relief ran through me. I had no thoughts of whether we had won or lost, only the thought of going home.' He was taken outside and joined a group of nine Americans to eat some pitta bread, cheese and tomatoes. But there was no sign of his navigator John Nichol or any other RAF POWs.

The ten men were handed over to the International Red Cross and spirited out of Baghdad to the Jordanian border, then passed to British and American embassy officials under the glare of television camera lights and a barrage of media questions. Their ordeal was over. More importantly, Peters could now pass on the names of all the POWs he had seen or heard in the various prisons. Sadly, he could also confirm those who were not being held. Although details could still not be officially confirmed, the list was quickly flashed back to the UK and German Tornado bases. Family liaison officers were dispatched to pass on what little news was available, good and bad.

* * *

Mike Toft was also on his way home. His Detachment Commander had fulfilled the promise he made after the birth of Mike's daughter and the navigator was offered a seat on one of the first VC10 passenger jets flying out of the region after the ceasefire. He boarded with the bottle of Moët & Chandon safely stashed in his kit. As they flew over Greece, Toft was asked if he would like to go to the cockpit, where he was handed the radio headphones. The VC10 captain had been told the reason for his early return and arranged a telephone-patch over the RAF's high-frequency radio monitoring system, straight to Mike's married quarters. It was a very expensive method of communication and the captain had used his own credit card to book the call.

Mike's eyes welled up and his words caught in his throat. Finally, he managed a simple, 'Hi, babe, I'm in the air, on my way home, see you when I land.' He went back to his seat a contented man. A few hours later, he was on the ground. 'It was an incredible experience to land on home soil, back from war. Sue had driven down to meet me. It was simply fabulous, quite indescribable. As I stepped down onto the airfield, there were my girls.' Reliving the events thirty years later with the author, Tofty's voice again cracks at the memories. 'I had survived. I was home to my family. I had all three of them in my arms. The war was over.'

* * *

Like John Peters, Bob Ankerson had been given plimsolls with shoe-laces and 'for the first time in the whole ordeal, I allowed myself to believe it might be nearing the end'. But Ankerson and the remaining POWs had to wait one more night before they too were taken out to a waiting bus.

Robbie limped towards it using his single crutch and was finally reunited with his pilot, Dave Waddington. The elation of release was still tempered by worry. Waddington was not yet ready to believe it was all over. 'I hoped that the guards were telling the truth, but we simply did not know for sure. This was Iraq and the brutal regime of Saddam and his sons. Another ending was possible. We could just as easily be lined up in Baghdad's main square and be shot to show that Saddam was still in charge. One thing was certain, this was going to be the end, one way or another.' Robbie gripped his friend's hand, trying to convince him that in fact they were being freed.

After what they had all suffered, Dave remained unconvinced. 'I thought Robbie was actually trying to tell me, *If I don't see you again, if this is it mate, good luck* ... I was still very nervous.'

Directly in front of them sat John Nichol, whose face was still badly bruised from the beating in Abu Ghraib. As they passed through the bombed streets, Robbie watched the navigator stare out of the window like a child in a sweet shop. 'Nichol could not contain himself any longer and blurted out, "Cor, look at all that damage!" as we passed the clinical destruction of buildings across Baghdad.' The guards started to give him a few hostile stares so Robbie told him to pipe down. 'We then drove in silence through the streets, marvelling at the accuracy of the missiles until we stopped at our destination.' They had arrived at the Baghdad Novotel and the care of the International Red Cross.

The POWs had been freed so quickly because of Norman Schwarzkopf's ceasefire demands. 'Number one was the immediate release of all prisoners of war as well as a complete exchange of information on troops listed as missing in action and the return of any remains. It was essential that I account for everyone. There was no way I wanted a repetition of the POW and MIA agony of the Vietnam War.'[25]

In the days following the ceasefire, Tange had devoured the newspapers and watched television in the hope of discovering something about Robbie. Newspaper reports suggested that some POWs were dead. The *Evening Chronicle*, Nichol's local paper in the North East where his parents lived, splashed, 'Have They Murdered John?' Then added: 'Reports Claim British Aircrew Tortured and Killed'.[26] The line was followed up the next day in a *News of the World* piece headlined: 'Stormin' [Norman] Battles to Get Pilots Back'. The report contained the paragraph: *'Military intelligence sources have been told two airmen, probably British, have been tortured to death by Saddam's brutal interrogators. Their identities are not known.'*[27]

The words began to gnaw at Tange Stewart. 'We simply didn't know what to believe. It was a very bad time for everyone. A lot of POW names had already been released. And the worry of not knowing was simply impossible to bear.'

John Peters' list of the airmen he had heard in the prisons had been examined and some details were being passed on. Of course, Peters had only seen a few prisoners, so without definitive confirmation – which meant the release of bodies – it was impossible to be sure who had survived. It was a dire situation for all concerned. In desperation, Tange called the RAF Marham Station Commander, Jock Stirrup. He was in a meeting but his assistant took him the phone. 'Are you leaving us until last to tell because Robbie and Dave are dead?' Tange demanded. Stirrup told her there was still no

further news. 'I feel so bad about that now,' Tange said, remembering the events thirty years on. 'The poor man had so much on his
plate and he would obviously have already told us what he knew.
But I was simply beside myself with worry.'

It was now 5 March, and later that day she saw their RAF liaison
officer walk past her kitchen window. He was in full uniform and
carrying a briefcase. 'I immediately realised that Robbie must be
dead and he was bringing official paperwork that I needed to sign.'
Tange ushered him in and waited. He opened the briefcase and
pulled out a bottle of champagne. 'He's alive!'

'It was an utterly wonderful, wonderful feeling. Tears flowed. It
was such an incredible release from the ordeal.'

Waiting at school, Kirsty Stewart had slumped into a bean bag
watching the news in her common room when the house matron
appeared. 'Kirsty, come with me please, I have someone to see you.'

Kirsty felt her chest tighten as she entered the room and saw
Lesley Norris, a trusted family friend. 'She was the person I had
chosen to give me any news, good or bad. Now she was standing
there, looking at me. I just stopped in my tracks. I presumed she was
going to tell me my dad was dead. She took hold of me and gave me
a huge hug. But it felt like the "wrong type" of hug for bad news.'

'Is Dad dead?' the schoolgirl asked.

'No! He's alive,' Mrs Norris said. 'I've come to tell you your
dad's alive.'

Kirsty broke down in tears.

Within an hour she was back in Coleby, reunited with her mother
and brother. Villagers armed with champagne arrived and a huge
celebration began. Once again, the community assembled in the All
Saints Church, beneath the ringing bells.

In Bolton, Dave Waddington's mother had not strayed far from
home since the ceasefire had been called. The phone rang.

'I grabbed it and our liaison officer said, "Are you sitting down?"'

'Oh my gosh. We all looked at each other. Which way was the
news going to go?

'He said, "Your son is alive!"'

'Well! We just screamed our heads off. We were overjoyed, and overcome with relief. At last we knew. We were dancing around, shouting, hugging each other.

'I then heard the liaison officer say, "I tell you this, Mrs Waddington, there are grown men in the room with me crying their eyes out."

'So we all cried together. It was simply marvellous – David was alive. It was the best moment of our lives. Nothing will ever surpass that.'

At around the same time, Chris Ankerson heard the doorbell ring at their home in Germany. '*Oh, oh*, I thought, heading downstairs, just as I'd done six weeks before. The Station Commander's wife stood outside. She had a huge grin on her face and just shouted, "Bob's alive!" I was overjoyed. But I knew that, at the same time, other families across the Tornado force were receiving the worst news possible.'

* * *

Very few of the POWs in the second batch got much sleep during their first night of freedom at the Novotel. After a breakfast of hot croissants, coffee, honey, jam and boiled eggs, the POWs were hustled through the scrum of waiting press and onto a bus. They arrived at Baghdad's Saddam Hussein International Airport to find the gates bolted. There was an interminable wait before they opened and hundreds of former Iraqi POWs poured out. Only then were the airmen allowed to board a Swiss Air passenger aircraft chartered by the Red Cross.

Nichol looked out of the window and realised that leaving was not going to be straightforward. 'As we began taxiing out, the Iraqi soldiers who had been loitering around ran towards their gun emplacements and trained the barrels of their weapons directly at our civilian airliner. It may have been no more than an empty gesture of defiance but a graveyard hush settled over the interior of the aircraft. We were very, very vulnerable.'

'No, they wouldn't dare . . .' one of the POWs muttered.

'They can't be . . .' another said.

'But what have they got to lose?'

As the jet rolled down the runway, the long gun barrels tracked it until the wheels left the tarmac. Finally, a tremendous cheer went up.

The jet was still in Iraqi airspace when two American F-15 fighters approached, pulling victory rolls before coming in close, firing off brilliant infra-red flares in celebration. One of the pilots lowered his mask, punching the air in celebration. Moments later two Tornado F3s joined the passenger jet on the other wing. Nichol grinned as this time, in more restrained fashion, the RAF fliers gave a gentle wave to their comrades. 'Somehow the sight of those friendly aircraft, shepherding us home, brought our freedom into sharp focus. The four fighters escorted us into Saudi airspace and as we crossed the border another huge cheer went up. We were finally liberated.'

Looking out of the windows as they taxied in at Riyadh's enormous military airbase, the POWs could see a huge reception lined up on the tarmac. There were thousands of American troops waving, clapping and cheering at the return of their jailed comrades. Several of the British airmen had tears in their eyes when they saw their fellow RAF personnel formed up in uniform, standing rigidly to attention in the 30°C heat. 'That brought a lump to my throat all right,' recalled Nichol. 'But it was important not to let rip the waterworks just yet; there was too large an audience.'

Standing at the top of the steps Robbie Stewart gratefully stepped through the cabin door into brilliant sunshine. Below him stood General Schwarzkopf, at the head of a long line of VIPs including the British Ambassador, the RAF's most senior officer Air Vice-Marshal Bill Wratten, and the Prince Regent of Saudi Arabia. 'It was a truly amazing spectacle,' Robbie said. 'Certainly not what I had expected.'

As the former POWs reached the bottom of the steps, General Schwarzkopf gave each a crunching handshake. 'Welcome home, you guys,' he said. 'You've done a great job.'[28]

CHAPTER FIFTEEN

GOING HOME

MARCH–APRIL 1991

After shaking hands with General Schwarzkopf, the returning POWs were quickly ushered onto a waiting RAF Hercules and whisked away to a nearby military airfield where a group of RAF 'minders' had assembled to look after survivors.

Despite the fact that it was now known that a number of the missing aircrew were *definitely* alive, there was still no formal confirmation of those who were dead. Every eventuality had to be catered for. John Nichol's Flight Commander Gordon Buckley was among those standing in the mid-afternoon heat. 'We thought that each POW would need a "minder", a friend, who could identify with him, help him through the early stages of getting back to freedom and readjusting to normal life. I was there for John, but, sadly, we still didn't have full details of who was coming out of the prisons. So all those still listed as MIA had someone on the tarmac. It was just a matter of us all waiting.'[1]

Nick Heard stood alongside his fellow Tornado aircrew, wondering if *his* charge would arrive. He had last seen his friend Rupert Clark and his navigator Steve Hicks moments before their Tornado was shot down on 14 February. 'The Iraqis had never released any comprehensive information about prisoners, so I was asked to be Rupert's prospective minder – even though I truly believed I'd seen him die. And no one had told us who was on the Hercules, so we just waited to see who would walk off the back. We presumed that not all of the missing crews we were sent to meet would be coming home.'

As the British POWs settled into the Hercules' uncomfortable mesh seats for the ten-minute flight, a crew member handed John Nichol a British newspaper. 'You probably need to see this,' he said. A few days old, one story reported his parents being battened down at their home in the North East. A second suggested he had been tortured to death alongside John Peters. For Nichol, totally unaware of the worldwide coverage *their* war had garnered, the news was shattering. 'It was appalling. I pictured my parents sitting in a darkened house, shuttered up like a bunker, while the press prowled about outside. It was more than I could take. I found it hard to control myself.' He threw the paper aside as the noise of the Hercules' engines dropped in pitch and it lurched into its descent.

Heard and Buckley watched the wide-bellied aircraft bounce onto the runway and taxi in. The minders smoothed their green flying suits as the rear hydraulic ramp descended. All eyes were fixed on their colleagues stepping down onto the shimmering tarmac.

Buckley spotted John Nichol and ran over. 'It was a truly warming sight to see our friends, still in their yellow prison overalls, walk out to freedom.' He gave Nichol a big hug then stepped back. 'You stink! And you need to get rid of that prison garb too.' Despite the ribbing, Nichol was delighted. 'It was incredible to see so many of my friends standing there. And, in Buckers, I could not have wished for a better escort home.'

Heart racing, Nick Heard peered into the group. Another familiar figure limped towards him with a huge smile lighting up his distinctive, angular face. 'When Rupert walked out of that aircraft in Saudi, with John Nichol and the others, I was simply gobsmacked. I had been convinced he'd not survived that missile strike. I rushed over, grabbed hold of him and simply hugged him. Bloody hell, it was amazing!'

Dave Waddington, Robbie Stewart, Bob Ankerson and his pilot Simon Burgess were also collected by their waiting friends. As the survivors filed out, five other RAF officers remained stationary, looking on. Steve Hicks, Garry Lennox, Kevin Weeks, Nigel Elsdon and Max Collier were not coming home. Their bodies would be repatriated on a later Red Cross flight. 'It was at that moment we finally discovered who had not made it,' Buckley said. 'So, sadly, their five minders, now unneeded, departed back to their bases.'

The survivors boarded the VC10 for the three-hour flight from Riyadh to the British military base on Cyprus. As Buckley chatted to Nichol, he realised that the navigator 'had absolutely no idea how the war had been fought, the cost, the results, or how his Squadron at Muharraq had fared'. In the meantime, he and his fellow minders had more pressing questions. 'As military aircrew, we wanted to know what they had endured in captivity. What the Iraqis had done to them.'

Nichol suddenly had other matters of importance to focus on – his favourite dish, chicken tikka masala, and a lot of chocolate, all washed down with gin and tonic. 'The transition from the hideous nightmare of imprisonment to the absolute normality of crew-room banter with my mates had happened in a handful of hours. Even then, I did not completely relax until we touched down at RAF Akrotiri.'[2]

They were driven the three miles to the five-storey, 200-bed military hospital on the southern Cyprus peninsula. Robbie Stewart and the others were light-headed with their newfound freedom. 'We felt like schoolboys set free for the first time, giggling on the bus, making jokes about anything that entered our heads.'[3]

Ushered into a reception room, they were greeted by Gordon Turnbull, who had rapidly set up a facility for psychiatric treatment and medical checks. Turnbull had staked his career on the issue when he made the case with his superior just after the ceasefire. 'I told him we needed to debrief the POWs. That whatever happened, our unit needed to get to the POWs first. If we could take care of them immediately, there was a good chance we could help them come to terms with their experiences early enough to prevent the imprint from causing long-term problems.'

'How do you know it will work?' his Boss asked.

'I don't know,' Turnbull replied. 'But you saw what we achieved with one Tornado pilot. With the right support we can help others too.' He then handed over his proposal for treating the airmen. 'The bottom line is, if they go back to the UK, if we succumb to the public relations imperative to reunite them with their families, then we've lost them.' His Boss had agreed, and Turnbull got to work.

'What do you guys want?' Turnbull asked as he greeted the men. Nichol had an immediate request. 'The thought that my parents might still be wondering if I was truly alive, and were worrying themselves sick, was consuming me.' He was taken to a phone and, after a few failed attempts, got through. 'The first sound of my dear mother's voice pushed my long-suppressed emotions over the edge. It was the sound of freedom at last. I simply broke down. Tears streaked down my face.'

Robbie Stewart was also ushered to a phone and dialled his home in Lincolnshire. After a couple of rings, a familiar voice answered. 'Hello . . .?'

Robbie could hardly get his words out before he too broke down in tears. 'Just to hear Tange was all I needed. It was out of this world. I could hardly believe that I had got through it all, I was alive, albeit injured, but at last I was now free.'

For the first time in six weeks, Tange no longer had to worry. 'Hearing his voice was just so overwhelming. We were all sobbing. The reality of what we had been through hit hard; it was such a wonderful sensation. I no longer had to live each day wondering if my husband was alive or dead.' Amid the tears, she told Robbie how supportive the villagers of Coleby had been, and about the family's meeting with the Queen. 'He simply couldn't understand why we'd seen her and was just flabbergasted to hear he had been national news.'

The shock of realising that their POW story had received global coverage was something they would all have to come to terms with. 'Incarcerated in a cell, alone, isolated,' Robbie remembered, 'I simply had no idea of the coverage, the publicity, and the horror that our captivity had aroused.'[4]

The early March weather in Cyprus brought warm sunshine and blossoming flowers. Robbie was just surfacing from a blissful night's sleep between crisp, clean sheets, when a smiling nurse dressed in an immaculate military uniform brought him breakfast. 'It was quite a contrast to the previous six weeks. I realised I had quite a bit of adjusting to do.' He strolled onto the balcony, luxuriating in the glorious weather. Breathing in the rich Mediterranean air, relishing its distinct saltiness, his thoughts turned to the family he longed to see. But he knew there was work to be done first.

Gordon Turnbull led the former prisoners through the process he had designed to help them deal with their experiences. 'Their brains had done whatever was needed to survive their interrogation and captivity. Now that those survival skills were no longer needed, I explained that they had to de-orbit.'

The POWs were going to have to relive their experiences, and be open about how they were affected. Not everyone was happy at the prospect, nor about being detained for five days by a 'shrink', John Nichol foremost among them. 'The only reason I'm going along with this,' he said, his face barely an inch from Turnbull's, 'is because you're a senior officer and we've been ordered to. I want you to know that my colleagues and I think this scheme of yours is a shite idea and it won't work. I just want to get home, to be with my family. We all do. Sir!'[5]

Nichol's words were a challenge to Turnbull. He'd had success with Tornado pilot Frank, managing to get him back on combat operations, but what if that was a one-off fluke? *Do I have the wherewithal to re-equip them for normal life?* The last thing he wanted was a confrontation, so he spoke to the navigator in a soft voice. 'Please, John, just watch this space.'

Nichol stormed off.

Turnbull had got the message. The task of rehabilitating the POWs was not going to be an easy one.

* * *

While the ex-POWs were coming to terms with life away from captivity, those still on duty in the Gulf remained deeply suspicious of Saddam Hussein's intentions. Combat air patrols continued to be flown, ever vigilant for a resurgence of aggression. And respirators were still carried in case the dictator was foolish enough to deploy any of the chemical weapons he retained. 'For those who were flying, it was a case of everybody being on their best behaviour,' said a Tornado F3 pilot. 'We had to be very careful because people were fatigued and the last thing we wanted at that stage was to lose an aircraft through aircrew error.'[6]

John Broadbent, the Muharraq Tornado Detachment Commander, certainly noticed the change in attitude. 'We took a break from flying for a few days, but it soon became obvious that we should get back into the air, if for no other reason than to keep ourselves current. I found it quite remarkable how reluctant some crews were to undertake anything particularly demanding, especially if it involved low flying. Having survived combat operations, they didn't want to risk themselves unduly in peacetime.' It was a sentiment that most aircrew could identify with.

After the ceasefire, teams of army engineers began clearing the battlefield and inspecting the damage. Nigel Risdale and John Broadbent were offered the chance to join them in an RAF Chinook helicopter. 'We flew up the coastal strip of Saudi and into Kuwait,' said Risdale. 'The oilfields were still burning furiously and the rolling black smoke created a massive, ugly blanket over a huge area, creating a truly horrific picture. Putting aside the obvious environmental damage, it seemed to underline the spiteful nature of the regime.'

'We headed a short way up the "Highway of Death" at low level,' Broadbent recalled. 'It was a very sobering experience. I'd seen some images on TV but wasn't fully prepared for the reality. Mile after mile of destroyed vehicles stretched to the horizon, some still smouldering, plenty of civilian cars and trucks in the mix, presumably looted by the fleeing Iraqi ground forces. If I'd had any doubts about the effectiveness of air power and conversely the vulnerability of ground forces in a permissive environment before that short flight, I certainly didn't afterwards.'

The journey became an education for the Tornado fliers, who would never normally see the results of their 'handiwork'. Inspecting the hardened aircraft shelters they had bombed, almost identical to the ones housing his own squadron of Tornados back at RAF Laarbruch, was a revelation to Broadbent. 'The damage was nothing short of devastating. We had fitted our LGBs with post-impact delay fuses so that they would penetrate the roof of the HAS before exploding inside. The blast of a 1,000lb bomb in a confined space was enough to utterly destroy the contents of the HAS and often blow off the giant steel – supposedly blast-proof – doors. It must have been absolutely terrifying to be on the receiving end of our bombs.'

They also had the chance to inspect some of the damage the initial JP233 raids had caused. The results they saw at one area of an airbase were inconclusive; there was minimal evidence of the mass destruction to the runways and taxiways they could get to. It appeared some of the cratering munitions may have punched straight through the surfaces, the subsequent explosions absorbed by the sand rather than causing the huge 'upheave' expected on the European soil and clay substructure they were designed to be used against. Of course, it was not known what repairs had been carried out, or how the anti-personnel mines had disrupted those operations. All that was known for sure was that the Iraqi Air Force had effectively been grounded in the first few days of the war.

'We also managed to crawl over a multitude of Soviet-era military hardware,' said Broadbent. 'Not surprisingly, I was particularly interested in the triple-A pieces and SAMs that had engaged us during our missions. I couldn't help wondering what the operators had thought as we thundered overhead in our Tornados, whether they'd been as scared of us as we were of them.'

The level of deliberate devastation caused by the Iraqis was shocking at every level. A female RAF officer on another battle-zone flight over the suburbs of Kuwait City stared in disbelief. 'Imagine seeing a house that's been burned out, with a car turned over in the drive and a swimming pool that's black and has pieces of furniture floating in it. Then try to imagine a whole city like that.'[7] Worse, the occupation had seen numerous acts of rape and torture, and the killing of more than 1,000 Kuwaitis.[8] Saddam's secret police, the Mukhabarat, who had taken such pleasure in their work on the POWs, had been deployed to Kuwait with brutal intent. An American woman married to a Kuwaiti described random acts of violence that included shooting people just to steal their car. 'Rape became commonplace, with soldiers breaking into houses to violate women. Suspected resistance fighters endured inconceivable barbarity at the hands of skilled Iraqi interrogators who used electric drills, acid and knives to obtain confessions. Often, innocent people, having survived such depravity, would be taken home and shot in front of their families as a warning to others.'[9]

* * *

Tucked away from the destruction in the eastern corner of Saudi Arabia, a calmer existence had returned to Tabuk. Mal Craghill had completed 22 operational missions, dropped 89 bombs, including 17 laser-guided, and two JP233s. 'In just a few short months the Tornado force had undergone a massive transformation, from a Cold War, low-level, primarily nuclear strike force, to a highly accurate, medium-level laser-guided bomber and one of the most experienced combat forces in the world.'[10]

Craghill and his pilot Mike Warren had been part of an astonishing air armada deployed to the Gulf. At the start of the conflict, 2,430 allied aircraft had been based in the region, or close enough to project air power into it. The RAF initially contributed 135 aircraft: 18 Tornado F3 fighters, 46 Tornado GR1/1A attack and recce aircraft, 12 Jaguars, 17 tankers, three Nimrods, 31 Chinook and Puma helicopters, seven Hercules and one HS125 transport aircraft. Countless other transport and supply aircraft flew missions in and out of the region. By the start of the land war, a further twelve Buccaneers and more Tornado GR1s had flown into theatre to support the precision-guided bombing attacks. Around 3,000 RAF personnel were deployed across the Gulf.[11] When the ceasefire came into effect, the allied forces had flown 110,000 sorties, of which the RAF flew over 6,100 – the largest number of any nation except the US.[12]

After sixty hours of operational flying, Craghill and Warren decided they had earned some post-war relaxation. 'The time was spent panic tanning,' said Warren. 'Everybody was concerned that they should be as bronzed as possible when they returned home. Others were very busy packing up equipment. People said they were bored and couldn't wait to get home, but I think it was a good idea that we had that period at the end of the war. It gave you a chance to settle yourself, wind down, relax a bit and get a few of the war stories out of your system.'[13]

A week after the war ended, Craghill and Warren said goodbye to the aircraft that had served them so well. 'For me, the Tornado had performed wonderfully. It never let me and Mike down when we needed it most. The losses, although all traumatic, were lower than we probably expected considering the dangerous nature of the missions we undertook. I had always felt "solid" in the Tornado. If one can ever feel so; it was a reasonable environment to go to war in.'

Mal's Squadron boarded a transport aircraft for the journey back to RAF Laarbruch. 'There was an enormous cheer as we got airborne. It was a six-hour flight and the big surprise was that the RAF presented everybody with a small bottle of red wine to drink with the meal. I thought I was dreaming ...'

* * *

The returning troops' flight path took them over the RAF hospital in Cyprus where Gordon Turnbull was still searching for a break-through moment with his reluctant patients. He brought all seven POWs together for a group debrief. Since the standard military mind-set was to bottle up emotions, it was always going to be a gamble.

He removed his Wing Commander rank tabs and placed them on the floor. There were a couple of approving nods from the men sitting on hard plastic chairs arranged in a semi-circle in the airy hospital room overlooking the sea. Turnbull gave a brief history of post-traumatic stress disorder, arriving at his experiences with the RAF Search and Rescue teams following the Pan Am 103 bombing over Lockerbie which had killed 270 people a few years earlier, scattering bodies across the countryside. 'I was able to describe how men I knew, men renowned for *not* cracking under pressure, had cracked in a number of cases. Given that the Mountain Rescue teams were known to be uniformly tough, this seemed to impress the aircrew.' Then Turnbull told them that PTSD was categorically not about flaws in the character of men who went into battle. He also described how their Tornado colleague Frank had gone 'back into the fight' after his rehabilitation programme.

The sound of lapping waves filled the silence; Frank's story was shocking news to the POWs. They had no idea that some of their fellow fliers, some of their close friends, had suffered such debilitat-ing mental assaults. There was a murmur of approval as they began to comprehend the complexity of their situation.

At their next session, Turnbull noticed that one of the POWs was silent and withdrawn as the others discussed what had happened to them in the interrogation centre. A tear trickled down his cheek. One of the group put a hand on his shoulder. 'What's wrong, mate?'

At first the airman refused to say, but then admitted, 'I feel guilty.'

'Guilty about what?' the man next to him asked.

'Guilty about giving in to the interrogation. I told them more than my name, rank and service number. I told them a lot. Nothing that would have compromised operational security ... I don't think ...' he said, weeping openly now. 'But I just feel so bloody guilty.'

Recognising a breakthrough, Turnbull remained silent, allowing their stories to unfold. 'What happened next was amazing. One by one, all the others confessed to feeling exactly the same way. I was totally spellbound. What, I wondered, would have happened if this hadn't come out? This man, all of them, would have been living a lie, and it would have eaten away at them.'

The psychiatrist listened as the men began discussing the reality of their interrogation and beatings – that they all knew they would break at some point. How they had all felt a 'need' to suffer before the inevitable happened. Militarily, it was a mostly pointless gesture. But from the perspective of personal honour and integrity, it had been crucial to them all that they had endured as much violence as individually bearable before giving in.

As he watched the excited and impassioned discussion, Turnbull also noticed something wonderful begin to happen. 'A voice I'd not heard since we'd started the debriefings was now animatedly engaged. A voice with a strong Geordie accent. I looked up and caught John Nichol's eye, and this time he gave me an almost imperceptible nod. I realised that if I could win over sceptics like John Nichol, the guys on the front line who really mattered, then there was every chance the therapy could work on anyone.'

Despite his complaints, Nichol had listened carefully to the psychiatrist's words, that there was 'nothing unmanly' about PTSD. 'He told us the most important thing was to talk about our experience and not to bottle it up or ignore the feelings. Being military aircrew, we were sceptical about baring our souls, but, in retrospect, everyone agreed that the whole process was necessary.'

Robbie Stewart found the group debriefings tremendously helpful, especially listening to others' experiences. 'I had no real problems mentally; although I was beaten, I wasn't really tortured. But unknown to us, Gordon Turnbull led the POWs back into the world we had left the previous August. His gentle probing and sympathetic manner opened the closed doors in my mind and released pent-up feelings. All this was done without me realising at the time.

Only years later could I look back and see the help which prevented me from suffering from any PTSD.'

The POWs had been well cared for; emotionally, psychologically and medically. The same could not be said for every soldier, sailor and airman who fought in the Gulf. It was a time before 'mental health' was openly discussed in the military, and the vast majority of the forces would return to their homes and loved ones with no decompression or debriefing at all.

After a few days in hospital and the mentally draining psychological debrief, everyone was suffering from cabin fever. Nichol and Rupert Clark decided to organise an 'Escape Committee' in order to have a proper drink. They persuaded a medic to covertly transport them the 3 miles to the Officers' Mess on the other side of Akrotiri airbase, 'only for one quiet beer', they promised. The pilots, navigators and minders walked into the long bar, which was overflowing with fellow fliers – crews of RAF passenger jets, tankers and transport aircraft using Cyprus as a hub to supply the Gulf. Given the former POWs' international press coverage, they were instantly recognised. A huge cheer went up, followed by clapping and back-slapping as they waded into the gathering.[14] 'I shall never forget the moment we walked into that bar,' said Buckley. 'The sea of green flying suits was overwhelming and the camaraderie was intoxicating. As were the pints of Cypriot beer.' Those drinks flowed even more freely when the President of the Mess invited the new arrivals to drink at the Mess's expense. They needed no second bidding, and 'one quiet beer' was rapidly followed by a dozen considerably louder ones.

In the increasingly convivial atmosphere, Nick Heard felt the constant pressure of operations ebb. 'It was simply awesome to be part of that gathering with so many crews in the bar from other aircraft. The party just got bigger and bigger. We could not wait to get home, but before then, many brandy sours needed to be sunk. It was an incredible night.'

The Tornado crews met friends they had trained with. The reunions required further drink to be taken. 'What could be better therapy, we asked ourselves, than to be back in an RAF bar with your mates, a few beers and a fair sprinkling of attractive women,' Nichol said. Unfortunately, the POWs' 'Escape Committee' had not fully comprehended their sensitive status on base amid the ongoing terrorist threat. During a shift change at the hospital, their absence was discovered, triggering a huge security alert. Searches were launched, but no one thought that the first place to look should be the Officers' Mess bar. 'We returned to the hospital rather the worse for wear,' Nichol admitted. 'And a bit ashamed at having caused the people who were looking after us so much trouble. It was a good night, though.' As one of those responsible for the POWs, Nick Heard was given a dressing-down by a senior officer. 'She was decidedly peeved that most of her POWs were missing and told the minders we were going to be in a lot of trouble for being part of it. We decided that we could easily accept any bollocking, bearing in mind the risks we'd all been taking in the skies of Iraq over the previous six weeks at war.'

The former POWs completed five days of therapy before flights home were arranged. Some were allocated RAF HS125 VIP jets. Looking down on the snow-capped Alps, Robbie Stewart knew he was in the lucky group. 'There was something surreal about sitting comfortably in a business jet, sipping a drink, cruising past Italy and then over France when only a week earlier we had been prisoners in Baghdad, fearing for our lives.'

On a damp, misty Norfolk afternoon, Tange, Kirsty and Scott Stewart were driven to the 27 Squadron HQ and ushered quietly into the Wing Commander's office. Kirsty stared out as the HS125 came in to land. 'It taxied towards the Squadron site and finally the door opened and the steps came down.'

Waiting to step down onto home soil, Robbie was bemused by the reception. 'Most of our ground crew were lined up waving, and I could see our Station Commander, Jock Stirrup, and other senior officers waiting to greet us.'

He hauled himself out of his seat and made his way awkwardly towards the open door.

Remembering the moment thirty years on, Tange Stewart begins to weep. 'I watched my darling husband hobble down those steps and I was utterly shocked. When he left us he had been fit and tanned. Now here he was, his hand resting on his minder's shoulder for balance, looking pale, drawn and weak.'[15]

The image is also fixed in Kirsty's mind, who was also in tears reliving the events. 'It was agonising to watch my dad limp out of the aircraft. He was really thin, almost wizened, struggling to walk. I was horrified. For much of the experience I felt I had been living in a surreal nightmare. Now it was all shockingly real.'[16]

Robbie limped slowly down the path to the HQ building, still holding onto his friend for support. When he reached the entrance, he was pointed towards the office where his family were waiting.

'The door opened and Dad hobbled in,' said Kirsty. 'He took one step forward then tried to "run" – unsuccessfully – towards us. We all fell into each other's arms and hugged. It was the most amazing, wonderful moment of my life. At last I knew he was alive.'

Recalling the reunion, Robbie – and the author – also descend into floods of tears. 'This was the moment I had been dreaming about and will treasure always. To see their faces, so relieved to see me but still unsure of my wellbeing. Few words were spoken, we just cried and hugged. Just being able to touch each other was all we wanted. The kids hung on so tightly, as if determined never to lose me again. Tange looked beautiful but had a weariness in her eyes. She had coped with so much trauma alone.'

Tange gripped her family tightly. 'We were all in tears, but back together again. It was all over.' A few miles away in their Coleby village, the bells of All Saints Church rang out once more. This time in celebration.

* * *

As operations in the Gulf wound down, the battle-scarred Tornados arrived back at their bases in dribs and drabs. Their once pristine, sand-coloured livery was now stained with the heat and smoke of intense, wartime flying. A small patch could be seen on a few, covering the hole of a triple-A strike. Four Tornados had been lost in training before the war, another with a technical malfunction at Tabuk, and six went down over enemy territory.

There had clearly been some issues with equipment failures. Like all military aircraft, the Tornado was a complex mix of electronics, computerised systems, hydraulics, flying controls and all manner of military hardware crammed into a small airframe which could fly, under fire, at over 700mph in rain, sleet, snow or desert conditions. Some missions had certainly been lost to technical problems, but the incredible teams of dedicated engineers had fought tirelessly to keep the aircraft ready for battle and, despite some challenges, the force had carried out more than 1,800 war sorties delivering over 100 JP233s, 123 ALARM missiles, along with 4,200 'dumb', and nearly 1,000 laser-guided, bombs.[17] It had been an incredible achievement by all involved, on the ground and in the air.

Seven Tornado aircrew had died during training for the conflict, and five in battle. A total of forty-seven British servicemen lost their lives during the war to liberate Kuwait. John Broadbent had presided over some of their final journeys home.

'The war had been over a few weeks and most of the British forces had returned to their peacetime locations, leaving my detachment one of the last in theatre. As one of the few senior officers in the region, it fell to me to oversee the remaining coffins onto their RAF transport aircraft for repatriation to the UK. One of the dead from my own Squadron, Steve Hicks, was among them. I'll never forget waiting with our small bearer party that was to carry Steve onto the RAF Hercules. We stood there staring at the coffins all neatly lined up and covered in Union Jacks. I have never felt so humbled. Or so sad.'

* * *

As the cost was still being counted, things moved on apace for the survivors. Whether arriving home via RAF transport, or in a Tornado, each returning squadron was welcomed back to its base by joyous crowds, VIPs and emotional families.

On arrival at RAF Laarbruch, Mal Craghill was presented with a drink, and a challenge. 'Before I reached the bottom of the steps, I had a bottle of champagne in one hand and a bottle of beer in the other. I was then faced with the conundrum of how to shake hands with the Chief of the Air Staff!'[18]

Jerry Witts, who had commanded the Tornados in Dhahran, was also confused by all the attention. 'It was a beautiful day flying across the snow-covered Alps, then the green fields; all the lovely things you don't see in the desert. We'd had a tip-off there would be a reception, but I didn't expect the RAF Germany Band and half the station personnel waving flags. It was all a bit over the top, really. I remember standing up in the Tornado and saying to Adie, my navigator, "God I'm embarrassed. What do I do now?" He told me I should just try getting out.'[19]

John Peters arrived back at RAF Laarbruch in style on another RAF business jet. He had already spoken to his wife Helen at length by phone, and been through Gordon Turnbull's full psychological debrief. *I'll be fine*, he told himself.

Walking towards the HQ building, he saw Helen holding their daughter Toni in her arms. 'The ground began to quiver and dissolve. Guy came toddling out from behind her, down the stairs towards me, his thick mop of hair shining. "Daddy!" he shouted. I gathered him into my arms, hugged him in a long, long hug. I had worried so much in prison that he might have forgotten me, it was fantastic that he still recognised me. I was overwhelmed. Then Helen was in my arms and we held one another long and close. It felt like for ever since we had parted. Toni had only been two months old when I left, a little baby. Now she looked completely different; a diminutive grown-up, her character emerging. Completely adorable and pretty. My happiness at being with them again was almost unbearable.'[20]

Most of the reunions were continued with vigour in the various bars which dotted each RAF station. After an emotional reunion with his wife, Nick Heard headed to the Officers' Mess. 'It was a wonderful, memorable time, but at the back of my mind the occasion was marred by the thought that we had lost a number of friends and there would be no homecoming celebrations for their families. So there was a striking contrast to the happiness in the bar that day. There was joy, laughter and celebration for some of us, while not far away in the married quarters, there was incredible grief and sadness. That was the reality of our war. I was one of the lucky ones; I was back home with my wife. Not everyone who had flown the Tornado to war was that lucky.'

* * *

While the survivors enjoyed reunions with loved ones, and the bereaved began to make arrangements for funerals. In the UK and across the Atlantic, questions began to be asked as to why the coalition's victorious army had not continued along the road to Baghdad and knocked out Saddam Hussein while the allies had him on the ropes. The clamour from armchair-generals and analysts calling for the dictator's destruction grew.

James Baker, the Secretary of State, later explained precisely why he thought it was a terrible idea. 'Removing him from power might well have plunged Iraq into civil war, sucking US forces in to preserve order,' he told the *Los Angeles Times*. 'Had we elected to march on Baghdad, our forces might still be there.' He also cautioned that an American occupation would lead to Iraq fracturing along ethnic and religious lines, with the majority Shia taking over from Saddam's Sunni-led regime and the Kurds in the north seeking autonomy. More importantly, it would play directly into the hands of the fundamentalist Shia-dominated Iranian theocracy. 'The mullahs could export their brand of Islamic fundamentalism with the help of Iraq's Shiites and quickly transform themselves into the dominant regional power.'[21]

General Norman Schwarzkopf also dealt fulsomely with the concept of 'regime change' after the war to liberate Kuwait which had worldwide support, and nine UN resolutions authorising the coalition's actions. 'The resolutions that provided the legal basis for our military operations in the Gulf were clear in their intent: kick the Iraqi force out of Kuwait. We had authority to take whatever actions were necessary to accomplish that mission, including attacks into Iraq. We had no authority to invade Iraq for the purpose of capturing the entire country or its capital.'[22] Like Baker, he knew that the costs of governing and security would be prohibitive. With some prescience, Schwarzkopf then said: 'I am certain that had we taken all of Iraq we would have been like the dinosaur in the tar pit, we would still be there. We, not the United Nations, would be bearing the costs of our occupation. This is a burden I am sure the beleaguered American taxpayer would not have been happy to take on.'

Although no one knew it then, Baker and Schwarzkopf were offering a remarkably accurate vision of the future – when the idea of regime change was revisited in 2003.

The British Prime Minister also had to fend off criticism that Saddam was still in situ, arguing that the war had severely weakened the dictator. 'It put the world on notice of his potential to do harm,' John Major said. 'It set a pattern for peacekeeping and allowed the United Nations to begin a weapons inspection programme which did much to limit Iraq's chemical and nuclear weapons capability. And above all, although it may be unfashionable to think in such terms, it was morally the right thing to do. It gave a signal that the world expected certain standards in international behaviour and would act to enforce them.'[23]

Within days of the war ending, the lights had returned to Baghdad for the first time in two months. Iraqi television came back on air, schools opened and the water supply was restored. But with no sightings of Saddam since the ceasefire, rumours abounded of his death or that he had fled to Algeria seeking asylum. Then, on the evening of Sunday, 3 March, a familiar face appeared on Iraqi television: 'a 45-second videotape of smiling Hussein meeting his aides', the LA Times reported. 'The message was clear. Someone is running Iraq and that someone is Saddam Hussein.'[24]

Despite the firepower arrayed against him, Saddam had survived. As he would for more than a decade longer.

* * *

Saddam Hussein's immediate future was of no interest to the Tornado crews who had hastened his forces' eviction from Kuwait. It was back to business as usual. At least that was the plan. But it was difficult for those who had been at the heart of the action. And, for those who had not.

'The bonding had been so strong, it took me three or four weeks to get over not being with my people,' one of the medics from Muharraq remembered. 'It was difficult readjusting. You found that people who were out there talked together in huddles. It was a shared experience. There's a divide between us and people who were not out there.'[25]

Tornado engineer Dean Wood had spent the war at Tabuk. He too hankered after the action. 'It was so wonderful to be home safely with my wife and young children. To put it all behind me,' he said. 'But I quickly realised I was really missing all those fellas I'd been with. We had lived and worked side by side amid a war; every hour of every day together. We'd had colleagues killed. Lots of things remained unsaid between us, but we all felt the same emotions. And we instinctively knew how the others felt. I missed the bond we had shared, the camaraderie of war. We missed it so much that just a couple of days after we returned, we all arranged to go out together for a bit of a drinking session. Our wives were not too happy about that! But it was difficult for those who had not been there to understand what we had gone through.'[26]

What Dean Wood and those Gulf War veterans could never have imagined as they enjoyed their drinks, and the initial days of peace in March 1991, was that they, and their Tornados, would return to combat operations in the Gulf region on countless further occasions over the following decades.

'The dust created by the turmoil of the Gulf War soon settled as everyone returned from their post-war holiday and the Squadron tried to return to some sense of normality,' Gordon Buckley said. 'In hindsight that was never going to happen. Too much had gone on in people's personal lives and wartime experiences. I often thought about the bombs we dropped; I can still see that Pilot Briefing Facility exploding, annihilating everyone inside. You don't want to kill anyone but that's what happens when you go to war. It's what needs to be done. Part of being a Tornado crew is destruction and killing.'

That destruction and killing would eventually continue through the whole operational life of the Tornado.

Nigel Risdale shared Buckley's perspective. 'When I was training in 1982 and had first seen those shiny new Tornados in a hangar, ready for the possibility of a nuclear war, I could never have conceived we would fight a regional, limited conflict in the desert. Yet in truly trying circumstances the Tornado force had done an incredible job of adapting to constantly changing requirements, carrying out missions the vast majority of people had never trained for, or perhaps even heard of before. But we adapted quickly to the new tactics and weapons. That's what the RAF had always been about and it was truly gratifying to be part of it. And the Tornado itself performed magnificently too. To have a machine that was so flexible, adaptable, becoming more capable with each new development, was just astonishing. It was a great aircraft and proved itself in an environment it was never designed for.'

Risdale had been among the many aircrew who had flown straight home to an emotional reunion with his family. 'I was really proud to have been part of those early Tornado war operations but, now, life had to go on.'

A few weeks after returning, he was back in the UK visiting friends and family. 'I was walking through a bright, modern shopping centre in Northampton with my wife and young son. We were just passing the time, browsing the shop windows, when the most bizarre and curious feeling washed over me. I looked around at all these people rushing about, living their "normal" lives; shopping, eating, going to and from work. It dawned on me that my own life had changed irrevocably. These people had no idea what I – and more importantly my family – had gone through just a few weeks before.

'When you have been through an experience like war, life-threatening and life-defining, it concentrates the mind and you realise what is important. And what is not. I had faced death and survived, some of my friends had not. At that moment, looking at the crowds rushing by, I suddenly realised what was important in my own life – holding hands with my wife and son. Nothing else mattered.'[27]

* * *

Not every child was able to hold a much-loved father's hand. On 27 March 1991, an RAF VC10 flew the officers and airmen from Steve Hicks' Squadron to Cornwall for his funeral. All wore full dress uniform and black armbands. Steve had left final instructions that if anything were to happen to him, he was to be buried in the area he considered home after his time based there on Nimrod maritime patrol aircraft. He had also requested he be laid to rest in sight of the sea.

Steve's Squadron Commander, John Broadbent, was among those waiting at the Norman church of St Eval near Padstow. With its strong connections to the RAF in the region going back to the Second World War, and only a mile from the coast, it would be the perfect resting place.[28]

Thirty years after leading his Squadron to war, the experience still plays on Broadbent's mind. 'Not many days go by that I don't think about that time. Steve's death in particular still haunts me. He and Rupert Clark were number four in my own four-ship formation, so I saw it as very much part of *my* job to do the best I could to keep *them* safe. In that, I failed. I still wonder: if only . . . if only . . .? As his Boss, what could I have done differently? What *should* I have done differently?

'I asked his Flight Commander, Gordon Buckley, if he'd give the eulogy. It should really have been me, but I was afraid that my emotions would get the better of me and I'd break down. I felt Steve deserved more dignity than that. I was very relieved and grateful when Buckers agreed to take on that heavy responsibility.'

The mist was hanging on the wooded landscape and a stillness had settled in the air as the hearse, carrying the casket draped in a Union flag, passed through the discreet security cordon and stopped outside the church. The uniformed pallbearers, all RAF friends of Steve, moved forward to lift the coffin onto their shoulders, then slow-marched down the aisle past the countless memorials to the many others who had already given their lives in the service of their country. Coming to a smart halt, they lowered the coffin, stationing their comrade's body in front of the altar.

Gordon Buckley had arrived early, to sit at the front. He kept his eyes straight ahead as the others filed in. When the time came, he walked to the lectern and turned to face the congregation. 'I couldn't believe it – the church was packed to overflowing. People crammed, standing and sitting, in every space. It was very hard; I thought, *How the hell am I going to do this?* Then I looked down and into Steve's widow's eyes. I knew I had to do it for her, and his two young sons. At that moment, I realised the true enormity of what we had all been through. There were now wives without husbands, children without fathers.'

Tears and moments of laughter filled the deep-vaulted ceiling as Buckley spoke warmly about the man who had gone from being a sergeant and Air Electronics Operator on Nimrod maritime surveillance aircraft, to an officer and fast-jet navigator. They heard about his humour, his caring nature and his devotion to his family.

A later obituary expanded on his contribution to the RAF:

Steve was a worker, a man who could be relied upon to complete any task well. He was not slow in voicing his opinions or prodding someone's shoulder in defence of others. He was a successful ingredient in the formula that is XV Squadron. In the Gulf, his contribution was exemplary. He was generous to a fault and a loyal person, devoted to the Squadron; a man of principles, of truth. We pray that he may rest in peace, and we extend our love and friendship to his wife and two children.[29]

The last hymn was sung, then Steve's friends gently lifted him back onto their shoulders for his final journey. He was buried in the churchyard, overlooking the sea, as an RAF bugler sounded the 'Last Post'.

At 3.25pm a Nimrod aircraft roared overhead, then the howl of Rolls-Royce RB199 engines was heard as four Tornados approached through the thinning mist. Directly over the cemetery the lead aircraft pulled up vertically in full reheat, soaring away from the remaining three jets, signifying a missing man; a departed comrade. It climbed upwards, the orange flames of its afterburners lighting up the grey sky.

A hush fell over the mourners as the thunder of engines slowly ebbed into the distance. The long moment of silence passed, then John Broadbent marched up to the grave, saluted, paused, about-turned and walked away. Each officer followed in turn, saluting their fallen comrade. After bidding a final farewell, they left Steve in sight of the crashing ocean. Just as he had wanted.

EPILOGUE

'OUR STORY HAD COME FULL CIRCLE'

1991–2020

The Tornado had proved itself in war, and those who had flown it in combat now presumed they would enjoy the peace. The following decades would show their presumptions were sorely misplaced, and many would deploy on countless more military operations.

'I think that because the Gulf War, and the use of air power, had been so successful, there was a sense that this was the new world order. Perhaps this was our role from now on?' said Gordon Buckley. 'Politicians must have looked at the incredible military power they controlled, thinking that we could be deployed around the globe to police trouble spots and ensure a more stable world. Of course, it didn't work out like that . . .'[1]

For nearly thirty years, the Tornado would be an integral part of Britain's military operations, from Iraq, to Kosovo, Afghanistan, Libya, Syria and back to Iraq again. Wherever there was a need for combat air support, a Tornado would normally be found nearby.

Sadly, not all those who had been bloodied in the jet's first battles in 1991 would survive to see the aircraft eventually retire in 2019.

* * *

The Tornado force had initially returned to the routine training designed to counter the Cold War threat. But that threat no longer existed. The continuing demise of the Soviet Union had brought with it the demolition of the massive standing armies of the Communist era. The British government, in turn, embarked on a grand cost-cutting defence review as part of the so-called 'peace dividend'. Personnel would be reduced by around 18 per cent across the Armed Forces. The RAF was about to lose around 20,000 people; the nine squadrons of the Tornado force would be reduced to six, and its bases in Germany from four to two.

It would be the end of an era.

Only months after returning from captivity, John Peters and John Nichol made their final flight together as three of RAF Laarbruch's four Tornado squadrons were disbanded. 'In the whole of our professional lifetime, a squadron had never been decommissioned, yet now, in the space of a few days, three of them disappeared,' said Nichol. 'It was an emotional time, as though most of your family was emigrating to Australia.'

The family might have been splitting up, but not before a drink-fuelled final dinner.

Nichol had been tasked with ensuring the evening went with a bang. He took his duty seriously. 'I'd ordered thousands of pounds' worth of fireworks. Rockets the size of champagne bottles took off like surface-to-air missiles. The sky lit up like those Iraqi airfields on the first night of the war. Our Squadron's war trophy had been set up outside the Officers' Mess for the grand finale. We loaded the four-barrelled Iraqi triple-A gun with some serious pyrotechnics. It brought back quite a few memories to those watching when they blasted off.'

The Two Johns then set off for a ski trip in Garmisch, the delightful German town in the foothills of the Zugspitze where Robbie Stewart's family had learned of Iraq's invasion of Kuwait. The pair spent a week enjoying the slopes, raising the odd glass to absent friends, and reminiscing before heading off to their new bases, Nichol's in England and Peters to RAF Bruggen in Germany.

Snow flurries rode along the bus's headlight beams as it pulled to a halt outside Peters' new station. Nichol helped his pilot unload his kit. 'That's it then, that's the end of us,' he said as Peters scooped the skis onto his shoulder. They shook hands, slightly awkwardly, then hugged. 'As the bus pulled away I looked back and could see JP standing in a pool of light, with the snow falling around him. We would never share a cockpit again.'[2]

Jenny Green had said her goodbyes to the RAF before the Gulf War started. Her husband Bill had been killed flying a Tornado training mission a fortnight after Iraq's invasion of Kuwait in 1990 and his body was never recovered from the North Sea. The following January, from her new civilian home, she had watched the first mission take off from Muharraq, the same airbase from which Bill should have led his Squadron to war. When the first losses were reported, Jenny knew exactly what their loved ones would be facing. 'It was a very poignant time, seeing all the Tornados, wondering what might have been. The worst had already happened to me, but I knew other people were now going through what I had. Everything changes. In the words of many widows, you feel excommunicated; a bad omen. My security pass was taken away and I was required to move out of our married quarters. I don't think they wanted to be cruel, but the RAF needed to move on quickly. Other people were waiting to take over our house.'

For Jenny and Bill's 17-year-old son, Jeremy, it was a time of intense change. 'After Dad died, and as a teenager heading into adulthood, you have to grow up,' he said. 'You have been exposed to the harsh realities of life. It was a very difficult time for us all and you lose a little bit of your youth but, in reality, we had to carry on, get back to a new "normality" and focus on what really mattered. We had lost a father and husband so, in a way, you feel the need to become "the man of the house". But at the same time you are still a kid who has lost his dad and you feel guilty about moving on. And I could see that Mum really suffered with a lot of the archaic rules in the aftermath of Dad's death. She had to deal with all the financial aspects, the funeral, the social aspects. She had been a military wife all her married life. Now, she was out of that community.'[3]

'There was a sense that we were no longer wanted,' said Jenny. 'No one *set out* to be hurtful, it was just the way it was. After twenty-three years as an RAF wife, I was simply no longer part of that structure.' Within two months, the family was out of their military home, forced to start anew when they hadn't really had a moment to mourn. 'It is a time when you hardly feel able to put one foot in front of the other, yet you have to uproot your children and move.'[4]

As the war went on, Jenny was struck by the lack of central co-ordination to help and support those at their lowest ebb. Shortly after the ceasefire, she wrote to every RAF widow she knew asking if they wanted to get together to discuss a plan to help the next generation. 'Thank goodness someone is finally doing something about this,' was the universal response.

At the first meeting, a year after the war ended, twenty-six of them gathered, passionately determined to help formulate a new policy. 'There were huge gaps in the way the RAF dealt with widows at that time, in terms of housing, information, pensions and the immediate aftermath of bereavement. The military just didn't realise how let down we widows felt. No one had ever told them. I think the RAF really wanted to get this right, but did not know *how* to truly help.' Jenny set up the RAF Widows' Association and the group began designing training sessions for the officers nominated to liaise with any next of kin, and bereavement packages for widows explaining their rights. 'We provided comfort, friendship and someone to talk to who knew what the new widow was going through. Sadly, we had a unique understanding.'

Anne Lennox's husband Garry had been killed alongside his navigator Kevin Weeks when their Tornado had crashed during the last low-level attack of the war. She was heavily pregnant with their second child when she was eventually given the news that Garry had not survived. 'I'd hoped beyond hope that he would come home. I knew that if he possibly could, he would get through it. And it all seemed to no avail. Then I just began to feel a bit numb.' Surrounded by pictures of her family and late husband, Anne talked about how the imminent birth of her son, and protecting her young daughter, took over her life. 'I had to be strong for the children. Someone once said to me, they didn't know how I survived, given that I'd had a bereavement, I had to move home, and have a baby. But I managed it.'[5]

Although it was too late for Anne Lennox, the RAF Widows' Association began to address a number of lingering issues. 'One of the first problems we dealt with,' said Jenny Green, 'was that rather than having to leave your home within a few weeks or months of your husband's death, widows can now stay in their married quarters for two years if needed.'

*　*　*

Not long after the first three squadrons disbanded, the Tornado was back on operations over Iraq. Given Saddam Hussein's previous history, it should not have come as a surprise.

Shortly after the 1991 conflict ended, the Kurds in northern Iraq and the Shias in the south, encouraged by American promises, had rebelled against the dictator, seeking secession. They were brutally suppressed. Although the West once again drew back from direct involvement, 'safe havens' were created, enforced by British and American aircraft policing 'no-fly zones'. They provided little security. Under the ceasefire agreement, Saddam was not allowed to use fixed-wing aircraft above the 36th parallel in the north or below the 32nd parallel in the south. But he was still free to use his helicopters and troops. Yet again, he attacked his own people with breathtaking savagery. Many thousands were killed, tens of thousands displaced.

In August 1992, two years since the first F3s had arrived to deter Saddam from invading Saudi Arabia, a detachment of six Tornado

GR1s returned to Dhahran, tasked with overseeing the no-fly zones. 'We had all assumed that Iraq was consigned to the *"been there, done that"* pile,' Mal Craghill said as his Squadron deployed. 'But the reality was that less than two years later I was back, conducting Operation Southern Watch sorties, trying to prevent Saddam Hussein from persecuting his own people. In reality, little was being achieved. We saw troop movements, fires burning and reported them back. But nothing was really done. Basically, the Iraqi army was burning the Marsh Arabs out of their homes so they could massacre them. We certainly felt helpless at first.'[6]

Monitoring operations soon turned into direct action, and in early 1993 100 coalition aircraft attacked Iraq's rebuilt air defence systems which had been targeting them in the skies of southern Iraq. Mal Craghill found himself over enemy airspace once again, dropping bombs on the same facilities he had pulverised two years earlier.

He would go on to serve another seven tours in the region over the following years.

While Craghill had returned to the fight, others were training the next generation of fliers. Among them was Simon Burgess who, alongside Bob Ankerson, had fought in vain to keep his Tornado airborne after a bomb had detonated prematurely. After ejecting, both men had spent the rest of the war as prisoners. Five years on, Simon was still flying fast jets, but now using his experience to teach trainee pilots at RAF Valley in Wales.

On 13 February 1996 he was programmed to fly a routine sortie to assess local weather conditions.[7] He powered down the runway and the Hawk jet lifted off, then, due to an engineering fault, almost immediately became uncontrollable, rolling towards the ground. Simon ejected but sadly it was outside the ejection seat parameters and he was killed. He was twenty-eight.

Simon was buried with full military honours in Humberston, Lincolnshire. Many Gulf veterans were among the 200 who filled the church. The service was relayed to as many again who were standing outside.[8] Shots from the firing party rang out as his coffin was lowered into the ground, and as the 'Last Post' faded a flypast of two Tornados

followed by four Hawks roared overhead. In time-honoured tradition, one of the Hawks pulled vertically out of the formation in the
'missing man' salute.

A number of the mourners were former Second World War RAF
prisoners of war. 'We old veterans have a great respect and regard
for our new Gulf War friends,' one said. 'We share their sense of loss
at the death of this young pilot. It was very obvious that the wider
family of the Royal Air Force were also mourning the loss of a highly
respected and popular officer.'[9]

The sound of the jet engines soon faded, but the words etched on
Simon Burgess's headstone speak of what he left behind:

> BELOVED HUSBAND, SON & BROTHER
> LOVED & REMEMBERED ALWAYS
> FLY HIGH AND FLY FREE

While some from the 1991 Gulf War Tornado community decided
to stay on and make a career out of the service, others decided to
try something new. When navigator David Bellamy's Squadron was
disbanded as part of the defence cuts, he decided to resurrect his idea
of pursuing a career as a civilian Electronic Warfare Instructor for
a major defence contractor. 'I resumed my studies with a summer
school in 1991 at Norwich University. We had a guest presenter for
one section – a British-Iraqi lecturer. He proceeded to give a speech
about the war, accusing the coalition pilots of revelling in the bombing, wearing mirrored sunglasses, and cheering as they killed people.
He could not have been more wrong.

'The war to liberate Kuwait was a just war and I was proud to have
flown the Tornado as part of it. It was a cornerstone of my life. It took
me a few years to "come down" from the war-fighter I had become
in 1991. In fact, I don't think I really calmed down until the birth of
my daughter three years later.'

Shortly after the war Bellamy had married, and asked his wartime
pilot Trevor Roche to be in the guard of honour and to give a reading.
His friend happily obliged.

While Dave had been working in 'civvy street', Roche had furthered his credentials as one of the RAF's outstanding pilots when he took on several flying jobs that culminated in serving as a test pilot for the newest generation of combat aircraft which would eventually replace the Tornado. Trevor left the RAF in 1998, joining British Airways and eventually captaining one of the huge Airbus A320 passenger jets. But he also continued piloting vintage aircraft for a civilian display company. He would go on to fly thirty-seven different types, from a 1909 Blériot monoplane, the oldest airworthy flying machine in Britain, to Spitfires and Hurricanes.[10] Roche loved the sound of engines and the freedom of flight.

* * *

During school holidays in the 1980s, Robbie Stewart's young daughter Kirsty had frequently accompanied her father into the planning room at RAF Marham, poring over maps and listening to the Tornado aircrew discuss tactics. 'Dad really enjoyed planning his sorties and some of that certainly rubbed off on me. I loved the notion of aviation; the sights and the smells. And I loved spending time with Dad and his friends on the Squadron.'[11]

It was perhaps unsurprising that only a few years after Robbie's return from captivity, she announced that she wanted to join the RAF. Furthermore, she wanted to become a fast-jet pilot. They took her seriously. In the years before what is now known as the 'First Gulf War', the RAF had egregiously banned women from becoming pilots or navigators. But attitudes had rightly changed, and in 1994, after qualifying on Tornados, Jo Salter had become the first RAF female fast-jet pilot. Kirsty followed in her footsteps four years later. She was coming towards the end of her training when Al Qaeda terrorists flew hijacked passenger jets into the Twin Towers of the World Trade Center and the Pentagon during the 9/11 attacks in 2001. She had no doubt that the Tornado would spearhead the conflict which would surely follow this devastating strike at the heart of America.

Gordon Buckley's navigator Paddy Teakle had also remained on in 2003 was commanding a Tornado squadron monitoring the no-fly zones. By then, his Tornado transformed into the superior GR4 with advanced and navigation capabilities. The conversion was the ng of a series of significant enhancements that would give the aft the ability to fire Brimstone anti-armour precision missiles and drop advanced precision-guided bombs, as well as incredible reconnaissance and targeting capabilities with the new RAPTOR and Litening pods.[12]

It was quite a change from hurtling towards enemy fire at ultra-low level in the pitch darkness, which came as a relief to Teakle and the crews now facing another war. 'The Tornado had truly become the multi-role combat aircraft it had originally been conceived to be.'[13]

Teakle was crewed with a young pilot who had been in his teens when Paddy was dropping JP233s on Iraqi airbases from 200ft. As they crossed the border into Iraq on a 'familiarisation' mission early in January 2003, twelve years after Teakle had first entered the country, an order came to attack an air defence facility near Tallil airbase in response to an infringement of the no-fly zone. 'So within minutes of the very first operational sortie of his life, my young pilot found himself dropping two laser-guided bombs onto an Iraqi bunker, and I found myself attacking facilities at an airfield back where it had all begun for me in 1991.'

President George W. Bush, the son of George H. W. Bush, was intent on achieving what his father had chosen not to do after Kuwait had been liberated during the First Gulf War. There was unfinished business to be dealt with. Teakle began to witness another massive build-up of forces in the Gulf, and was given command of the Tornado Combat Air Wing in the coming conflict.

There were many who had warned of the dangers of 'regime change' in Iraq in the wake of the first conflict. But others still lamented the lack of ambition in 1991. Among them was Margaret Thatcher, the Prime Minister who had been dramatically ousted from power two months before the conflict.

In the following years, she showed no reluctance in expressing her ongoing disapproval of the way the First Gulf War had ended, telling one documentary maker, 'When you are dealing with a dictator, he has got not only to be well and truly defeated, but has got to be seen to be defeated *by his own people*.'[14] She went further during a later victory celebration in Kuwait, openly lamenting the failure of Britain and America to wipe out Saddam Hussein. 'I only wish that I had stayed on to finish the job properly. Perhaps then we wouldn't be where we are today, with this cruel and terrible man securely in power.'[15]

The scene was set for the Second Gulf War.

Paddy Teakle and the Tornados went to war in Iraq again on 20 March 2003. 'The fear of the unknown for me was entirely missing: this was now familiar ground. Among the team, however, things were different, as for many this was their first taste of combat. I could feel their excitement and trepidation.'

The first three days of the war went well; the combat novices quickly showed their mettle. But on 23 March tragedy struck. An American Patriot missile battery mistook a Tornado returning to Kuwait as an enemy aircraft. Flight Lieutenants Kev Main and Dave Williams were killed instantly when the 90kg warhead detonated, bringing down their aircraft. As the Tornado Detachment Commander, Teakle had to lead from the front. 'I visited aircrew and ground crew in their workplaces and encountered a wide raft of emotions: shock, disbelief, anger even, but what shone through above everything was resilience, stoicism and resolve. The team had taken a heavy hit but it had come out fighting and more united and determined than ever before.'

Main and Williams would be the last Tornado combat deaths, but not the last deaths in the conflict. Norman Schwarzkopf and James Baker's previous words of warning soon proved prophetic. An invasion, they had said, would end in America occupying a disunited country with unresolved enmities, and, in the ensuing chaos, there would be civil war at great human and economic cost. They were right.

Kirsty Stewart was among those in the Tornado force who had heard the news about the tragic 'blue-on-blue' with dismay during her training. In 2006, she joined her first squadron, walking into the very same office at RAF Marham where fifteen years earlier the family had waited for Robbie's return to freedom. 'It felt as though things were coming full circle. When I'd been on the site in the late 1980s, helping Dad on the Squadron, the trees surrounding the hardened aircraft shelters were just saplings, now they were enormous firs, dominating the landscape. The image really struck home. Time had marched on.'

The 2003 invasion and 'regime change' had indeed heralded long-term occupation. The capture and execution of Saddam Hussein only seemed to spur on the insurgency. And Tornados were once more at the heart of the action when Kirsty Stewart deployed on operations in 2006.

Supporting coalition troops from medium level, she knew her operational tour would be very different to her father's war of ultra-low flying into a storm of triple-A and SAMs. But the first time she entered hostile territory, she experienced a strong connection with the past. 'Not long after crossing the border, I glanced down at my moving map display and saw the word "*Tallil*". I suddenly realised the significance of where I was. It was a surreal moment. It was a clear day and I could see the whole airfield. I realised that below, still buried in the sand, was my dad's mangled Tornado GR1. Somewhere down there he had regained consciousness after his traumatic ejection at 600mph. He had been lying on the sand weeping, looking up to where I was now flying, worrying about me as a young girl and his family back home. On that patch of earth he had realised that his injuries were so bad, that his only option was to attract the enemy's attention and deal with the terrible consequences. That part of our family's personal story had come full circle and I felt really close to Dad in that moment. But it was astonishing to think that I was still fighting an ongoing conflict; a conflict he had nearly died in *sixteen* years earlier. It was all rather sad.'

Around the same time, Pete Batson was also finding his wartime experiences coming into sharper focus. The former Tornado pilot was now teaching new aircrew at RAF Cranwell in Lincolnshire.

A few years after Saddam Hussein had been eventually defeated in the second Gulf conflict, and as part of the peace dividend, young Iraqi military pilots began to arrive in Britain for training. It was a curious turn of events. 'When I was an instructor in the 1980s, we had taught Iraqi student pilots when their country had been our friend in the region,' Batson recalled. 'They would sometimes come to my house for dinner or a drink and I never gave it a second thought. But I then went on to fight against them in 1991.'

Now, Iraq was once again an ally and the next generation of Iraqis were already back in the British training system.

A framed map of Batson and Mike Heath's raid on Al Asad airbase – when Batson had instinctively bombed an Iraqi Mirage as it came in to land – hung in the student headquarters. Examining the target map of their homeland, the new intake asked Batson about his memories of the 1991 war. 'The young Iraqis were all very pro-British, which was strange given that I and some of their other instructors had been attacking their country. Some of their relatives had been pilots, one had actually been the senior officer in charge of the air defence system around Al Asad, so he would certainly have been trying to kill me. This gave me pause for thought about what war actually meant. The deaths and suffering. My mind turned to the Iraqi Mirage I'd dropped the JP233 on. It was entirely possible that I might have killed one of my students' relatives. It had been war, it was what was required, but it certainly felt surreal talking to them about it all. It was curious how it all turned out, and I wondered what the future might bring for this latest batch of Iraqi aircrew, and their country.'

Pete Batson was soon to be reminded of the slender thread by which life hung. His own Gulf War had come to a frustrating end when a technical fault meant he'd had to eject from his Tornado with his Squadron Boss, Mike Heath. While Mike managed to return to Tabuk to shepherd his men through their last few war sorties, Batson's injuries meant he did not recover in time to fly into battle again. Heath's leadership qualities saw him pass up the ranks, rising to Air Vice-Marshal. But his military service had been interrupted by a number of skirmishes with cancer. He had fought it off successfully on each occasion, until it returned with a vengeance when he was working at the United States Central Command in Florida.[16] He decided to return to the UK and retire, but on 17 November 2007, while preparing to leave, he was struck by a massive heart attack and died. He was fifty-seven.[17]

'He was very highly regarded,' a post on a military website read. 'One of the most friendly and approachable senior officers I have ever been privileged to meet. Always keen to chat in the bar – and liberal with the use of his bar book!'[18]

Mike Warren was another Tornado pilot who utilised his hard-won spurs to teach the next generation of aircrew. He and his navigator Mal Craghill had dropped the last RAF bombs of the war in 1991. After returning, their Squadron was disbanded and Mike eventually moved on to instructing duties.[19] He finally left the RAF and became an airline pilot, building a new life at the family home in Ormskirk, Lancashire, with his wife, 7-year-old daughter and 4-year-old son.

On 24 February 2008, a cold front had come in from the Atlantic, bringing rain to Manchester, no doubt making the 156 passengers who boarded Mike's Airbus A320 shortly after lunch even more delighted with the promise of warmer temperatures in Cyprus. As co-pilot, Warren offered the holidaymakers comforting words of welcome as they departed. For two hours they cruised over Europe in skies he was all too familiar with after his Tornado days. They had crossed the Alps and were heading down to southern Europe when Mike suffered a heart attack. The Purser rushed to the cockpit to administer first aid, frantically trying to keep him alive while the Captain diverted to Istanbul airport. They made an emergency landing just after 8pm and waiting paramedics immediately came on board. There was nothing they could do to save the 43-year-old former RAF aviator. He was already dead, just days before his little boy's fifth birthday.[20]

Thirty years after they flew into battle together, Mal Craghill still has the fondest memories of him. 'I feel genuinely privileged to have been crewed with Mike. Not only was he a very good pilot and a great friend, he was one of life's truly lovely people. I never met anyone with a bad word to say about him. We certainly had our share of "*holy shit!"* moments during the war, but I never worried that we wouldn't come out the other side because I trusted him completely. His cheeky grin is sadly missed at our annual Tornado reunions.'[21]

* * *

The Tornado that Mike and Mal had flown continued to perform peerlessly in its GR4 upgrade, demonstrating its adaptability as one of the most capable ground-attack aircraft and flying combat operations in a number of different theatres of war.

In Iraq, the invasion and occupation had come at a tremendous cost. From 2003 to 2011, 4,431 US personnel were killed,[22] thirty times more than the 1991 war. By the time the Tornado and British ground forces withdrew from Iraq operations in 2009, 179 UK service personnel had lost their lives.[23] The plight of the Iraqi people was harder to quantify; estimates of civilian deaths range from around 100,000 to nearly half a million.[24]

And after the post-9/11 war to expel Al Qaeda and the Taliban from Afghanistan, the Tornado had entered the fray in 2009 in support of the 10,000 British troops deployed to contain the resulting insurgency in Helmand Province. Then, in 2011, it also deployed over Libya in the battle to oust Muammar Gaddafi. The 3,000-mile return trips from RAF Marham to the southern Mediterranean were the first attack missions flown from UK soil since the Second World War.

But the new breed of Tornado did not just excel on the battlefield. In 2014, its reconnaissance capabilities were employed to provide imagery for those tasked with countering the floods which had devastated areas of the UK. Then in August that year, three GR4s were deployed to Chad to help track down the 276 schoolgirls kidnapped by the Islamic terror group Boko Haram in northern Nigeria.

It was all very different from 1991, hurtling along, only feet above the desert floor. The aircraft designed amid the threat of Cold War nuclear Armageddon now wore a coat of many colours.

* * *

Dave Bellamy had flown his last Tornado sortie with Trevor Roche in August 1991, just days before he left the RAF. 'I asked the Boss if I could swap pilots so that I could fly one final time with Trev,' he said. 'The Boss replied, "There's no keeping you two apart!"

'Trev did a high-speed fly-by over the Squadron HQ, then the champagne was broken out after we landed. There were smiles and laughter, but also a sinking feeling of knowing that something important was over.' Trevor had also eventually left the RAF to be an airline and civilian display pilot. Dave's subsequent work as an Electronic Warfare Instructor took him the length and breadth of the Middle East.

On 1 July 2012, he was instructing clients in Abu Dhabi in the complexities of radar jamming. Returning to his hotel suite, he made a drink and tuned in to BBC Radio 2 via the internet. At the turn of the hour the news came on. Only half listening, he heard the news-reader announce that a Gulf War veteran had been killed flying a vintage aircraft. 'Immediately the hairs went up on the back of my neck. There were only a few people that this could be. The more they said, the closer it got. And then they said his name.'

Trevor Roche had been one of the star attractions at a summer aircraft display in Bedfordshire, piloting a 1923 de Havilland DH53 Humming Bird monoplane. After taking off in blustery condi-tions, he was making a level turn close to a copse of fir trees when the classic machine plummeted to the ground. Trevor was killed instantly. The subsequent Air Accident Investigations Branch report concluded, 'It seems likely that the loss of control was the result of a combination of the challenging operating and handling charac-teristics of the DH53, the turbulent effect of the trees and the gusty wind conditions.'[25]

As the news sank in, Bellamy paced his room. 'I was furious and ended up smashing up a dining chair in my hotel suite. After everything we had done together, I could not accept his death with-out anger. Foolishly, you think if you had been there, things would be different. Losing Trevor was monumental, it really knocked me sideways for some time. After all that truly life-threatening danger in the war, he died in a peacetime accident, flying a vintage air-craft. That is when I cracked and my world collapsed around me. I finally understood what many others had been through losing a loved one.'[26]

Trevor's wife Katie had made Bellamy promise to keep her husband safe during the war and now asked him to deliver his friend's eulogy. Dave readily accepted. 'Trevor was my "other brother", my brother in arms. I was devastated. But he died doing the thing he loved: flying. That's all I can hold onto.'

The first line of his obituary in the *Telegraph* said it all:

Squadron Leader Trevor Roche, who has died aged 52, was a former RAF fighter pilot and flew so many types of aircraft, from pre-First World War monoplanes to Airbus airliners, that his career aloft encompassed almost the entire history of aviation.[27]

With the RAF's last Tornado training fatality occurring in 2012, forty-five aircrew had been lost – seven on wartime operations and thirty-eight in training.[28] By the early 1990s, the RAF had been losing around ten aircrew a year in accidents away from the battlefield.[29]

Inevitably, it meant that the RAF Widows' Association's numbers increased. And so did Jenny Green's awareness of the archaic injust-ices of the military system, particularly the rules governing military pensions for the surviving spouse, which legislated against any remar-riage or committed relationship. 'It all seemed terribly unfair,' Jenny said. 'If you found love again, and remarried or cohabited, then you lost your late husband's Armed Forces Pension, and, if you had one, your own War Widows Pension. But having a different lover each week was deemed to be okay! It was totally ridiculous; old-fashioned and insulting.'

Furthermore, the rules changed depending on when and how your husband had actually died. Baffled by the discrimination, Jenny, by then also the chairwoman of the War Widows' Association, and her colleagues threw all their energy into upending the legislation. 'Our groups had significant support for the campaigns because we occupied the moral high ground. I confess I loved the political challenge and the fight to rectify a wrong. Together, we continued chipping away at the many anomalies in the rules and gradually managed to get a lot changed.'

Enlisting the support of the national press, the various groups mounted an energetic campaign to heap pressure on the then Prime Minister David Cameron to revise the system. In 2014, as Tornado crews risked their lives against ISIS in Syria and Iraq, Jenny and the War Widows' Association succeeded in overturning the injustice. Just before Remembrance Sunday, *The Times* reported that all widows in receipt of their military pension would be allowed to keep it, whatever their personal circumstances: 'The landmark move, which will affect up to 300,000 current and future widows over the next four decades, followed almost ten years of lobbying and campaigning by the War Widows' Association.'[30]

Sadly, the new legislation did not apply to all, and the association is still campaigning on behalf of the 300 or so who had remarried *before* the change came into force. Having already chosen to surrender their pensions to pursue love, they have not had them reinstated and are still left out in the cold.

Another battle won, Jenny could give more attention to her own family. 'At the time of a loved one's death, you can't believe you can rebuild your life. But you have no choice other than "to cope", to move on. I have been lucky enough to rebuild a good and useful life. I am also enormously proud of my children; they coped with everything so well and were very helpful to other children who tragically found themselves in the similar situation of losing a father.'

Her grandson William Green, named after his Tornado pilot grandfather, has inherited his love of aviation. 'He looks so much like Bill; it is so very special to spend time with him. I took him to see the Harrier jets at RAF Wittering carrying out training flights. He was really taken by the sights and the sounds, asking if he could learn to fly too. I said he probably needed to ask his mum and dad ...'

* * *

Like Bill Green, Jerry Witts was a truly inspirational leader. As the Tornado Detachment Commander, his empathy and charisma helped carry the Tornado force in Dhahran through difficult times. He later reflected on all that had passed in the 'blur' of the six-week war:

'Twenty-one Scud attacks and as many false alarms. The losses, the POWs. The hits and, not too often, the misses. The fatigue, frustration and fear. The exhilaration and excitement. Mission by mission, target by target, we were part of an unstoppable force. Old myths were dispelled and new tactics evolved. Through it all, the ups and the downs – and there were plenty of both – there was a constant feeling of massive support from home. It was very gratifying, not to say humbling, to know that people cared for us all. My own [memories] will always include the simple bravery and fortitude of our families back at home. The sheer guts of the [engineers] loading bombs as bits of Scud rained down. Watching young, inexperienced aircrew grow so quickly into seasoned campaigners. Most of all, the feeling of immense personal privilege to have shared such company and commanded such people.'[31]

The pictures of Witts at the annual Gulf War reunions show a smiling, contented man surrounded by his friends and fellow aircrew. Those at the British Embassy in Washington also welcomed his affability during his later posting as Air Attaché in the United States. During a ceremony on the White House lawn, he gave a sideways nod to his humble Wiltshire roots when he was heard to murmur, 'Not bad for a ploughman's grandson!'[32]

Then, aged sixty-one, Jerry was diagnosed with corticobasal degeneration. In his habitually indomitable style, he helped raise funds for much-needed research into the brain disease, even as his own health deteriorated. In later years he became totally immobile, and his only movement was the blink of an eye.

In 2020, as the world became gripped by the coronavirus pandemic, his wife contracted Covid-19 and Jerry had to be taken into a nursing home. On 3 June, aged sixty-nine, the Squadron Commander who had done so much to care for his men died of pneumonia. Isolated because of the Covid restrictions, he was far from the bosom of his friends and family.

After his death, one of his officers from the Dhahran days told *The Times* obituarist: 'Throughout all the troubles, Jerry stood tall, taking a pragmatic view at all times. His leadership was outstanding and I do not know any one of the 400 of us out there who would not follow him anywhere.'

In normal circumstances, many hundreds of his military friends would have flocked to pay their respects at his funeral. Because of the ongoing constraints, only one was able to do so.

Alongside just a handful of his immediate family, his Gulf War navigator, AJ Smith, read Second World War fighter pilot John Gillespie Magee's poem, 'High Flight'. All those who had flown the Tornado to war with Witts could fully relate to the words:

Oh! I have slipped the surly bonds of Earth
And danced the skies on laughter-silvered wings;
Sunward I've climbed, and joined the tumbling mirth
of sun-split clouds, and done a hundred things
You have not dreamed of .[33]

Most American forces had left Iraq in 2011, but when Islamic State took over huge swathes of the country three years later, they were forced to return. RAF Tornados joined them, back in the skies where it had all begun twenty-three years earlier.

Flying out of Cyprus from 2014, the jets were striking ISIS units that at one point had threatened Baghdad itself. Their bombs and missiles now targeted lone gunmen, terrorists planting roadside IEDs, bomb factories and even small barges transporting weapons and personnel across rivers. Over the following five years ISIS was gradually pushed back to a final redoubt in north-east Syria.

But the Tornado's legendary status as a battle-proven machine eventually proved no match for ongoing defence cuts. It was time to finally stand down. It was announced that the remaining squadrons were to be disbanded, the jets broken up, sold for scrap and spare parts.

On 26 January 2019, two Tornados flying from Cyprus carried out the aircraft's final strike missions. Armed with Brimstone missiles and

500lb Paveway II bombs, the pair hit Islamic State positions in Syria.[34] In the previous five years, the Tornado had been responsible for a third of the 4,315 casualties inflicted on the ISIS extremists by the RAF.[35]

Among those carrying out the final operations was 27-year-old Nathan Shawyer. Nathan had not been born during the first Tornado attacks in Iraq in 1991. He flew home from Cyprus with the retiring aircraft in February 2019. 'I'm the last ever Tornado pilot to be trained by the RAF. After everything that's come before, it's quite a thrill, quite an honour,' he said. 'It was an absolutely awesome machine to fly. The Tornado has given us [countless] years of fantastic service, been all over the world and done a lot of things for the United Kingdom.'[36]

James Heeps was one of the Squadron Commanders of the final detachment to take to the skies over Iraq. He had been a young boy glued to the television news reports of those first strikes in 1991. 'I never dreamed that nearly thirty years later I'd be one of the last Squadron Commanders taking the Tornado out of service on operations,' he said on his return to RAF Marham. 'For over a third of the Royal Air Force's existence, this aircraft has been the backbone of its ground-attack fleet. We've grown up seeing it, now we've served on it, and taken it to war; there's an emotional connection. As I shut the engines down today there was a little bit of sadness as well.'[37]

The jet was not going to pass into history without an appropriate farewell, and on 14 March 2019 many hundreds of personnel associated with the Tornado, ranging in age from eighteen to over eighty, descended on RAF Marham to send it off in style.

The day began with a formal parade in front of Sir Stephen Hillier, the Chief of the Air Staff. A Tornado pilot himself, Hillier had been rushed out to Dhahran in late January 1991 as a 'battle casualty replacement' after Bob Ankerson and Simon Burgess had been brought down by their own bombs and captured by the Iraqis. He went on to fly fifteen combat sorties during the First Gulf War, then deployed on countless other operations across the region over the following years, eventually rising to the highest position in the RAF.

After the parade, a lone Tornado took off to perform one final display. Breaking a few minor aviation rules, the crew made a number of low-level passes over the cheering crowd, culminating in a screaming flypast at around 100ft and some 600mph – exactly as it would have done during the first missions of the Gulf War in 1991. Despite many of the crowd ducking, and the constant shriek of car alarms prompted by the blast of high-speed turbulence, no one complained.

'If my eyes are just a little bit glassy, it's not just down to the wind that's blowing today here at Marham ...' Air Chief Marshal Hillier told a television news crew.[38]

Later that evening, in one of the RAF's newest hangars built to house its very latest acquisition, the F35 Lightning, hundreds of Tornado men and women gathered for dinner. At one end stood a brightly lit Tornado GR4, repainted in the grey and green 1980s Cold War camouflage, and surrounded by many of the weapons it had carried over the course of its incredible lifetime. The volume of chatter among those who had served on the jet grew in direct proportion to the amount of alcohol consumed as they relived their tales of war and peace.

As the formalities drew to a close, Sir Stephen rose to his feet. He recounted his own final flight a few days earlier, when he had flown a series of flypasts over iconic Tornado sites. As he led the last formation over Tain Air Weapons Range in Scotland, the Range Safety Officer's voice could be heard on the radio.

'Tornado flight, are you ready for a message?'

'Go ahead,' Hillier replied.

'Tornado, as you depart Tain Range for the last time, can I just say what an honour and privilege it has been to serve the Tornado force over the past decades.'

The Range Officer then continued with his regulation weapons safety check.

'So Tornado – for the *final* time – I ask you to confirm you are all now *switches safe*.'

There may have been a slight crack in the Chief of the Air Staff's voice as he told the story.

'In that time-honoured way which we all know so well, the radio calls rippled up through the formation.'

'Three, switches safe.'

'Two, switches safe.'

'One, switches safe. Thank you, Tain. Tornado is en route.'

Everyone in the audience, many with tears in their eyes, knew this was the last goodbye for the faithful aircraft that had flown an astonishing 186,000 hours on combat operations.

'So tonight, at this splendid dinner,' Hillier continued, 'and in front of the Tornado force present and past, I conclude simply by echoing those words from that final flight.

'For the very last time, and for the whole Tornado force, I say, *Tornado, we are switches safe, and we are going en route.*'

Hundreds of chairs scraped back as the audience rose as one to give a lengthy standing ovation to 'The Boss', and to the aircraft they loved.

* * *

For those who have experienced the dangers, excitement, fear and loss of combat, there is a shared, inner understanding. A sense of comradeship and conviction.

This book began with an account of the twenty-fifth annual reunion of the Gulf War POWs, their colleagues, and some of the loved ones of those who had not returned. After being contacted by the author, President George H. W. Bush, the man who had set the liberation of Kuwait in motion in 1991, sent the group a personal letter:

It is with humility and pride that I send warmest greetings to all those gathered. I wish I could be with you to convey my personal respects and my gratitude; I hope you know I have never forgotten the important role you played in this multinational effort.

Too often it is said we have no heroes. Not so! We do have heroes and each one of you – aviators and soldiers of clear purpose who put service ahead of self – is a hero in the truest sense of the word. Your service and gallantry will long be remembered, and all freedom-loving peoples owe you a lasting debt of gratitude.

This United States Navy man and former Commander-in-Chief salutes you and sends you best wishes for a memorable gathering to celebrate duty, honor, and liberty.[39]

A Second World War pilot who had seen action himself, President Bush's words were warmly received. 'I would never take anything away from those who went after me,' Nick Heard said. 'But I doubt there is much to compare to that first week of the war in 1991. Night low-level operations, into the heart of incredibly heavily defended airfields. Those intense images of the domes of the triple-A we had to fly into are still imprinted on my brain.'

Coming home relatively unscathed, Mal Craghill admitted to 'enjoying' the war. 'That's not to say I don't recognise the suffering, and the loss of some close friends, but we were doing the job we were trained to do, the job we wanted to do. We were given the chance to put our hard-earned skills to the test. We did *exactly* what was asked of us – Kuwait had been liberated from enemy occupation. That was the task; that's what was done.'

Images of the war frequently appear in Gordon Buckley's mind. 'I lost some great friends and the memories are still very fresh. The guys waving us off on the first night, a Tornado on the runway in front of me going into full reheat. The incredible triple-A. Some images bring a smile to my face too, as I remember the camaraderie and excitement. Others bring sadness as the sense of loss takes over. I find that Steve Hicks' smiling face flashes up ever more regularly.'

Thirty years after the war ended, navigator Mike Toft has his own reflections on the conflict. 'What makes military people serve, fight, risk their lives? It's certainly not the money or the glory. It's not really Queen or country. In the end it's your mates, standing – flying – on your left and right. They rely on you, and you on them. We fight together, we celebrate together, and sometimes some of us die together. Being part of a unit with a combined purpose was incredible. I was part of a great force, with some exceptional friends and colleagues; a solid team flying a solid aircraft. I was very, very proud to have served alongside everyone on the Tornado.'

* * *

The legendary Tornado developed exponentially from its original design during the Cold War as a conventional and nuclear bomber to be deployed in extremis against Soviet targets. Its inventors built a machine that may not have been blessed with the beauty of the Spitfire or the rugged, imposing presence of the Lancaster, but it did have something else: stoicism, endurance and the ability to adapt to the challenges of the times, whether against a heavily defended enemy airbase filled with fighter jets, or a lone suicide bomber hiding in a mudbrick compound.

Yet the men and women who built and serviced the jet, and those who took it into the skies in peace and war, outshone its myriad technological advancements. While always part of a vast team, each was an individual – a father, son, mother or daughter prepared to give their lives for each other, and in the service of their country.

When Bill Green was killed in a Tornado accident in the build-up to the Gulf War in the summer of 1990, his son Jeremy was just a teenager. Voice cracking at times, Jeremy relived his experiences when talking with the author. 'Thirty years on, the memories of my dad are still strong. In the years after he died, I would think of him every single day. Then, late one night, I suddenly realised he hadn't come into my mind. And, as time went on, I began to realise, *I haven't thought about Dad for a couple of days now*. It was a painful, perhaps guilty, realisation that I was moving on.[40]

'For years afterwards, my sister Philippa and I would see friends enjoying time with their fathers. Perhaps learning to drive, moving home, helping with DIY. We didn't have any of that. We missed out on an important part of life's experience. On one tragic day in August 1990, everything had changed. But wherever we are in the world, the family always makes contact on the anniversary of his death to remember him, to raise a glass in celebration of a good life.

'I knew a girl at university whose father had also been killed in an RAF flying accident when she was only two years old. We had a ridiculous argument about the worst time to lose a parent. She thought *my* situation was worse as I had grown up with my dad; he was an integral part of my life when he was killed. But I thought *she* had had it far worse than me, as she had never really known her own father. She'd never experienced the love I had. I had been lucky to spend time with this amazing person; a wonderful, kind, family man. And even though our time together was cut short, I cherish every moment.

'Growing up on a Tornado base, the RAF becomes part of your life, part of your family. I knew all the jet's capabilities and its role; it was a truly amazing aircraft and I was fascinated by it as a machine. But for me, the son of a Tornado pilot and Squadron Boss, I was staggered by what the crews themselves did; their manifest love of flying, their incredible skill and expertise. Their unique bravery flying the Tornado in war – and while training during peace – was truly astonishing.

'A year after my father died, his Squadron arranged for me to have a flight in a Tornado. I think they wanted me to have a sense of what Dad's job had been; to feel a part of his life. A memory of him to hold onto. It was a truly wonderful experience and it gave me a connection to Dad; a very real sense of the excitement and exhilaration of fast-jet flying.

'In those brief moments aloft, flashing over the countryside at high speed and low level, I began to understand why my father had loved such a dangerous job, why he loved being part of a team. Why he truly loved flying the Tornado.'

Bill Green's body was never recovered after the accident, but the much-admired Squadron Commander's legacy lives on in the hearts of all who served with him. However, as Jeremy quietly made clear, the full consequences of military service affect no one more than the beloved of the fallen. 'My son William knows what his grandfather did, that he flew Tornados; that he died in a flying accident. We didn't really talk about the circumstances that much, but he obviously picked up on some of the family conversations. A few years ago, when he was around six or seven, someone asked him what he wanted for Christmas. William said he wanted a submarine, so he could go to the bottom of the North Sea to find his missing grandad.'

IN MEMORIAM 1979–2019

Pilot: Flight Lieutenant (Retd)
Russ Pengelly (BAe)
Navigator: Squadron Leader John Gray
12 June 1979 – Irish Sea
XX950 – Panavia MRCA

Pilot: Squadron Leader
Michael Stephens
27 September 1983 – Norfolk, UK
ZA586 – Tornado GR1

Pilot: Flight Lieutenant Ian Dixon
28 October 1983 – Norfolk, UK
ZA558 – Tornado GR1

Pilot: Flight Lieutenant Michael Barnard
Navigator: Flight Lieutenant John Sheen
12 December 1985 – North Sea
ZA610 – Tornado GR1

Pilot: Flight Lieutenant Steven Wright
Navigator: Flight Lieutenant John O'Shea
10 May 1988 – Berge, Germany
ZD808 – Tornado GR1

Pilot: Flight Lieutenant Colin Oliver
Navigator: Flight Lieutenant
Anthony Cook
9 August 1988 – Cumbria, UK
ZA593 – Tornado GR1

Pilot: Flight Lieutenant John Watts
Navigator: Lieutenant Ulrich Sayer GAF
9 August 1988 – Cumbria, UK
ZA329 – Tornado GR1

Pilot: Flight Lieutenant Mike Smith
Navigator: Flight Lieutenant
Alan Grieve
13 January 1989 – Wiesmoor, Germany
ZD891 – Tornado GR1

Pilot: Flight Lieutenant Stephen
'Alfie' Moir
21 July 1989 – North Sea
ZE833 – Tornado F3

Pilot: Major Dennis Wise USAF
Navigator: Flight Lieutenant
John 'Stan' Bowles
14 August 1990 – North Sea
ZA545 – Tornado GR1

Navigator: Squadron Leader
Gordon Graham
14 August 1990 – North Sea
ZA464 – Tornado GR1

Pilot: Group Captain William Green
Navigator: Squadron Leader
Neil Anderson
16 August 1990 – North Sea
ZA561 – Tornado GR1

Pilot: Flight Lieutenant Kieran Duffy
Navigator: Flight Lieutenant
Norman Dent
13 January 1991 – Masirah, Oman
ZD718 – Tornado GR1

Pilot: Wing Commander Nigel Elsdon
Navigator: Flight Lieutenant
Max Collier
17 January 1991 – Talil AFB, Iraq
ZA392 – Tornado GR1

Pilot: Squadron Leader Gary Lennox
Navigator: Squadron Leader
Adrian 'Kev' Weeks
22 January 1991 – Ar Rutbah, Iraq
ZA467 – Tornado GR1

Navigator: Flight Lieutenant
Stephen Hicks
14 February 1991 – Al Taqaddum AFB,
Iraq
ZD717 – Tornado GR1

Pilot: Flight Lieutenant Stuart Walker
Navigator: Flight Lieutenant
Nigel 'Norm' Orme
8 July 1994 – Akrotiri, Cyprus
ZH558 – Tornado F3

Pilot: Flight Lieutenant Peter Mosley
Navigator: Flight Lieutenant
Patrick Harrison
1 September 1994 – Perthshire, UK
ZG708 – Tornado GR1A

Navigator: Flight Lieutenant
Martin 'Jesse' Owens
10 March 1995 – North Sea
ZE789 – Tornado F3

Pilot: Squadron Leader
William Vivian
Navigator: Flight Lieutenant
Derek Lacey
15 June 1998 – North Sea
ZE732 – Tornado F3

Instructor Pilot: Flight Lieutenant
Greg Hurst
Student Pilot: 2 Lieutenant
Matteo Di Carlo ITAF
21 January 1999 – Nottinghamshire, UK
ZA330 – Tornado GR1

Pilot: Flight Lieutenant
Richard 'Dicky' Wright
Navigator: Flight Lieutenant
Sean Casabayo
14 October 1999 – Northumberland, UK
ZD809 – Tornado GR1

Pilot: Flight Lieutenant Kevin Main
Navigator: Flight Lieutenant
David Williams
23 March 2003 – Ali Al Salem AFB, Kuwait
ZA710 – Tornado GR4A

Navigator: Flight Lieutenant (Retd)
Mike 'Wolfie' Harland (BAe)
14 November 2007 – Norfolk, UK
ZA554 – Tornado GR4

Pilot: Flight Lieutenant
Kenneth Thompson
Navigator: Flight Lieutenant
Nigel Morton
2 July 2009 – Argyll and Bute, UK
ZE982 – Tornado F3

Pilot: Flight Lieutenant Hywel Poole
3 July 2012 – Moray Firth
ZD812 – Tornado GR4

Pilot: Flight Lieutenant Adam Sanders
Navigator: Squadron Leader
Samuel Bailey
3 July 2012 – Moray Firth
ZD743 – Tornado GR4

ENDNOTES

Major Characters

1 Data provided by Les Hendry, 31 Sqn Senior Engineering Officer.
2 Many squadrons are actually designated by Roman numerals. They are presented throughout the book in this way for ease of understanding.

Foreword

1 There had obviously been many other conflicts in the region, perhaps most notable between Iraq and Iran. But this phraseology is regularly used in the media.
2 The extracts have been edited and abridged from Sir John Major's full speech delivered that night.
3 'Defence Estimates' 1989; some of the total number included new aircraft replacing those being phased out so the actual figure of aircraft at the time was around 2,000.
4 Operation Desert Storm was the international codename for the

mission. The British codename was 'Operation Granby'.
5 The date of the start of the conflict is variously described as both 16 and 17 January. When the first attacks commenced in the early hours of what was 17 January in the region, it was still 16 January in America. Hence the disparity.
6 There were two female American POWs but they were not at the reunion.
7 The extracts have been edited and abridged from Michael Fallon's full speech at the dinner.
8 At the time, the RAF had no female aircrew on combat operations.

Prologue: Seven Seconds

1 Robbie Stewart, private diary and John Nichol interview.
2 Pablo Mason, *Pablo's War* (Bloomsbury, 1992).
3 Dave Waddington, John Nichol interview.
4 National Defense University Washington DC Research

Directorate; Daniel K. Malone, 'Roland: A Case For or Against NATO Standardization?' (May 1980).

5 John Peters and John Nichol, *Team Tornado* (Michael Joseph, 1994).

6 Memories about the exact value and number of the sovereigns vary.

7 John Peters and John Nichol, *Team Tornado* (Michael Joseph, 1994).

8 Charles Allen, *Thunder and Lightning* (HMSO, 1991).

9 The figure for the wartime maximum-all-up weight of the aircraft varies between publications and individual memories.

10 John Peters and John Nichol, *Tornado Down* (Michael Joseph, 1992).

11 Michael Napier, *Tornado Over the Tigris* (Pen and Sword, 2015).

12 Ibid.

13 Michael Napier, *Tornado GR1: An Operational History* (Pen and Sword, 2017).

14 Peters and Nichol, *Team Tornado*, op. cit.

15 Ibid.

16 Aeronautica Difesa (Iraq 1990).

17 Napier, *Tornado Over the Tigris*, op. cit.

18 *Air Power Review: First Gulf War 25th Anniversary* (RAF, 2016).

19 Although 'parallel track' formations were meant to be standard across the Tornado force, differing separations were used depending on the mission or individual squadron tactics. These distances and timings are approximate.

20 Tange Stewart's letter is edited for brevity and clarity.

21 Events reconstructed from Stewart/ Waddington personal accounts and the Tornado Cockpit Voice Recorder recovered from their crash site.

Chapter One: The Birth of 'The Fin'

1 Robbie Stewart, private diary and John Nichol interview.

2 *Department of Defense Dictionary of Military and Associated Terms* (2001).

3 Ian Black, *RAF Tornado: Owners' Workshop Manual* (Haynes, 2014).

4 Ibid.

5 Napier, *Tornado GR1*, op. cit.

6 Black, *Owners' Workshop Manual*, op. cit.

7 Ibid.

8 Ian Hall, *Tornado Boys* (Grub Street, 2016).

9 Black, *Owners' Workshop Manual*, op. cit.

10 Ibid.

11 BAE Systems Tornado First Flight 1974: https://www.youtube.com/watch?v=yIFul_xyP38

12 Jeffrey Quill, *Spitfire: A Test Pilot's Story* (Crecy Classic, 1983).

13 Hall, *Tornado Boys*, op. cit.

14 United Press International report, October 1984.

15 Dave Waddington, John Nichol interview.

16 *Superjet: Secrets of the Tornado*, Forces TV, 2019.

17 Black, *Owners' Workshop Manual*, op. cit.

18 Ibid.

19 Napier, *Tornado GR1*, op. cit.

20 Peters and Nichol, *Team Tornado*, op. cit.

21 Ibid.

22 Ibid.

23 Napier, *Tornado Over the Tigris*, op. cit.

24 Ibid.

25 Peters and Nichol, *Team Tornado*, op. cit.

26 Napier, *Tornado GR1*, op. cit.

27 Black, *Owners' Workshop Manual*, op. cit.

28 *Hansard*, House of Commons, 25 July 1990.

Chapter Two: The Gathering Storm

1 Alastair Finlan, *The Gulf War 1991* (Osprey Publishing, 2003).
2 Ibid.
3 Margaret Thatcher Foundation: https://www.margaretthatcher.org/
4 Ibid.
5 Norman Schwarzkopf, *It Doesn't Take a Hero* (Bantam, 1992).
6 Robbie Stewart, private diary and John Nichol interview.
7 Tange Stewart, John Nichol interview.
8 Kirsty Murphy (née Stewart), John Nichol interview.
9 Stan Morse, *Gulf Air War Debrief* (Aerospace Publishing, 1991).
10 Allen, *Thunder and Lightning*, op. cit.
11 Ibid.
12 Ibid.
13 Ibid.
14 Ibid.
15 Dave Waddington, John Nichol interview.
16 Bob Ankerson, personal account and John Nichol interview.
17 Chris Ankerson, John Nichol interview.
18 Gordon Buckley, personal account and John Nichol interview.
19 Mike Toft, personal account and John Nichol interview.
20 Pete Batson, John Nichol interview.
21 https://assets.publishing. service.gov.uk/government/ uploads/system/uploads/ attachment_data/file/530766/ Army_FOI_2016_77154___ Number_of_Iraqi_cadets_ trained_in_Britain_from_1992_ to_1988_plus_5_Iraqi_officers_ staff_training_1970_and_1980.pdf
22 Peters and Nichol, *Tornado Down*, op. cit.
23 Military Aircraft Accident Summary, 1990: http://www. ukserials.com/pdflosses/ maas_19900814_za464_za545.pdf
24 David Bellamy, private diary and John Nichol interview.
25 RAF Laarbruch Station Magazine, September 1990. Edited for clarity.
26 Jenny Green, John Nichol interview.
27 Jeremy Green, John Nichol interview.
28 Military Aircraft Accident Report: http://www.tornado-data.com/ Production/MAAS%20Reports/ ZA561.pdf
29 Ibid.
30 Bob Ankerson, personal account and John Nichol interview.
31 Black, *Owners' Workshop Manual*, op. cit.
32 Finlan, *The Gulf War 1991*, op. cit.

Chapter Three: 'Everything's Changed'

1 Precise numbers varied across the squadrons.
2 Mike Toft, personal account and John Nichol interview.
3 Nigel Risdale, personal account and John Nichol interview.
4 Peters and Nichol, *Tornado Down*, op. cit.
5 Ibid.
6 Allen, *Thunder and Lightning*, op. cit.
7 Ibid.
8 Gordon Buckley, personal account and John Nichol interview.
9 *Royal Air Force Historical Society Journal 32* (MOD, 2004).
10 *Air Power Review*, op. cit.
11 Some very basic handheld GPS systems were available but they were not integrated into the Tornado navigation system.
12 Some NVGs (night-vision goggles) were in theatre by this time. But no crews were properly trained on

them and, in general, they were not compatible with the cockpit lighting, or with the ejection seat system and low-level combat operations. Some pilots did have a set but they were not in operational use.

13 Paddy Teakle, correspondence with John Nichol and his personal account, edited for clarity.

14 Nigel Risdale, personal diary and John Nichol interview.

15 Information supplied by Rob McCarthy, who took part in the flight.

16 Schwarzkopf, *It Doesn't Take a Hero*, op. cit.

17 Ibid.

18 John Major, *The Autobiography* (HarperCollins, 1999).

19 Ed Herlik, *Separated by War: An Oral History by Desert Storm Fliers and Their Families* (Tab Aero, 1994).

20 Peters and Nichol, *Tornado Down*, op. cit.

21 Kirsty Murphy (née Stewart), John Nichol interview.

22 Tange Stewart, John Nichol interview.

23 Napier, *Tornado GR1*, op. cit.

24 Finlan, *The Gulf War 1991*, op. cit.

25 Schwarzkopf, *It Doesn't Take a Hero*, op. cit.

26 Major, *The Autobiography*, op. cit.

27 Mike Toft, John Nichol interview.

28 Mark Paisey, personal diary and John Nichol interview.

29 Chris Ankerson, John Nichol interview.

30 Allen, *Thunder and Lightning*, op. cit.

31 Finlan, *The Gulf War 1991*, op. cit.

32 John Broadbent, personal account and correspondence with John Nichol.

33 Major, *The Autobiography*, op. cit.

34 Allen, *Thunder and Lightning*, op. cit.

35 Finlan, *The Gulf War 1991*, op. cit.

36 Major, *The Autobiography*, op. cit.

37 Opening Statement, James A. Baker, Senate Foreign Relations Committee, 19 May 2010.

38 Napier, *Tornado GR1*, op. cit.

39 Michael Napier, *Blue Diamonds* (Pen and Sword, 2015).

40 Allen, *Thunder and Lightning*, op. cit.

41 Napier, *Blue Diamonds*, op. cit.

42 Allen, *Thunder and Lightning*, op. cit.

43 John Nichol interview.

44 Letter from Mark Paisey to his mother dated 13 January. Edited for brevity and clarity.

45 Morse, *Gulf Air War Debrief*, op. cit.

Chapter Four: The Wolfpack

1 David Bellamy, personal diary and John Nichol interview.

2 These official figures vary according to sources.

3 Gordon Buckley, personal account and John Nichol interview.

4 Not all these missiles 'locked' – this term is used for ease of reading.

5 Morse, *Gulf Air War Debrief*, op. cit.

6 Mal Craghill, personal account and John Nichol interview.

7 Gordon Buckley, personal account and John Nichol interview.

8 Ibid.

9 This is an edited and condensed version of the actual signal (supplied by 9 Sqn Historian, Sqn Ldr Dicky James) to ensure it is more easily understood.

10 Peters and Nichol, *Tornado Down*, op. cit.

11 Jerry Witts' account is constructed and edited from: *Thunder and Lightning* (Allen), the *RAF Yearbook Special: Air War in the*

Gulf (IAT Publishing, 1991) and *Tornado GR1* (Napier). There are some discrepancies in the various accounts; resolved here as far as possible.

12 Allen, *Thunder and Lightning*, edited for brevity.

13 Schwarzkopf, *It Doesn't Take a Hero*, op. cit.

14 The Operations Room: Desert Storm – The Air War Day One (2020): https://www.youtube.com/watch?v=zxRgfBXn6Mg&feature=youtu.be

15 Nick Heard, personal account and John Nichol interview.

16 *Air Power Review*, op. cit.

17 Allen, *Thunder and Lightning*, op. cit.

18 Ibid.

19 Jerry Witts.

20 Major, *The Autobiography*, op. cit.

21 Morse, *Gulf Air War Debrief*, op. cit.

22 The Operations Room: Desert Storm – The Air War Day One, op. cit.

23 This is a slightly different time to the 'H-Hour' which is when the mass attacks occurred, and is cited by Norman Schwarzkopf as the opening shots of the war.

24 The Operations Room: Desert Storm – The Air War Day One, op. cit.

25 Morse, *Gulf Air War Debrief*, op. cit.

26 The Operations Room: Desert Storm – The Air War Day One, op. cit.

27 Nigel Risdale, personal account and John Nichol interview.

28 Mission Report, supplied by John Broadbent.

29 Paddy Teakle, John Nichol interview.

30 Napier, *Tornado Over the Tigris*, op. cit.

31 There were also a couple of reports by crews who attacked in TFR mode that, when the canisters jettisoned, they experienced a TFR pull-up over the target.

32 Allen, *Thunder and Lightning*, op. cit.

33 The Operations Room: Desert Storm – The Air War Day One, op. cit.

34 Jerry Witts.

35 Mike Warren, quoted in Allen, *Thunder and Lightning*, op cit.

36 Paddy Teakle's account is collated from *Separated by War* (Herlik), correspondence with John Nichol, and Forces TV documentary *Air War in the Gulf.*

37 Peters and Nichol, *Tornado Down*, op. cit.

Chapter Five: Gin-clear Skies

1 Herlik, *Separated by War*, op. cit.

2 Dave Waddington, John Nichol interview.

3 Robbie Stewart, private diary and John Nichol interview.

4 The full text of the letter has been edited and abbreviated for clarity.

5 Nick Heard, personal account and John Nichol interview.

6 Gordon Buckley, John Nichol interview.

7 Mike Toft, personal account and John Nichol interview.

8 Mark Paisey, personal diary and John Nichol interview.

9 *Air Power Review*, op. cit.

10 Peters and Nichol, *Tornado Down*, op. cit. Some detail has been edited for clarity and continuity. Some further reflections have been added by John Nichol.

11 Mason, *Pablo's War*, op. cit. Some detail edited and abridged for clarity.

12 Morse, *Gulf Air War Debrief*, op. cit.
13 Mason, *Pablo's War*, op. cit.
14 Peters and Nichol, *Tornado Down*, op. cit.
15 Individual recollections of the final moments of attack differ slightly. Resolved as far as possible here.
16 Peters and Nichol, *Tornado Down*, op. cit.
17 Mason, *Pablo's War*, op. cit.
18 Peters and Nichol, *Tornado Down*, op. cit.
19 Mason, *Pablo's War*, op. cit.
20 *Hansard*, House of Commons, 1991.
21 Tange Stewart, John Nichol interview.
22 Kirsty Murphy (née Stewart), John Nichol interview and personal notes.
23 Herlik, *Separated by War*, op. cit.
24 Peters and Nichol, *Tornado Down*, op. cit.

Chapter Six: 'My God, We've Lost Another One'

1 Peters and Nichol, *Tornado Down*, op. cit.
2 The DetCo had actually used Nichol's correct name 'Adrian' but, for ease of explanation, 'John' is used in the text.
3 David Bellamy, private diary and John Nichol interview.
4 Pete Batson, personal account and John Nichol interview.
5 Morse, *Gulf Air War Debrief*, op. cit.
6 Robbie Stewart, private diary and John Nichol interview.
7 Dave Waddington, John Nichol interview.
8 Peters and Nichol, *Tornado Down*, op. cit.
9 Allen, *Thunder and Lightning*, op. cit.
10 Ibid.
11 Morse, *Gulf Air War Debrief*, op. cit.
12 Allen, *Thunder and Lightning*, op. cit.
13 It was not clear what this missile was – but every possibility had to be countered.
14 Batson was given information later that it was a Mirage F1EQ multi-role jet, optimised for both ground-attack and air defence operations.
15 Allen, *Thunder and Lightning*, op. cit.
16 This is an edited and abbreviated version of the full letter.
17 Berenice Waddington, John Nichol interview.
18 Peters and Nichol, *Tornado Down*, op. cit.

Chapter Seven: 'The Bad Stuff'

1 Peters and Nichol, *Tornado Down*, op. cit. Some quotes edited for brevity and this is a condensed account of their interrogation.
2 Morse, *Gulf Air War Debrief*, op. cit.
3 Peters and Nichol, *Tornado Down*, op. cit.
4 Schwarzkopf, *It Doesn't Take a Hero*, op. cit.
5 Allen, *Thunder and Lightning*, op. cit. Some quotes edited for brevity.
6 Morse, *Gulf Air War Debrief*, op. cit.
7 'Halabja: Survivors talk about horror of attack, continuing ordeal', *Ekurd Daily*, 2008 – edited for brevity.
8 Allen, *Thunder and Lightning*, op. cit.
9 Ibid.
10 Schwarzkopf, *It Doesn't Take a Hero*, op. cit.
11 Ibid.

12 Jim Corrigan, *Desert Storm Air War: The Aerial Campaign Against Saddam's Iraq in the 1991 Gulf War* (Rowman & Littlefield, 2017).

13 Mal Craghill, personal account and John Nichol interview.

14 It later transpired that the airman had suffered from a tonic-clonic seizure – a form of epileptic fit.

15 Dean Wood, private diary and John Nichol interview.

16 There are differing accounts of the exact words. This is Craghill's version.

17 Allen, *Thunder and Lightning*, op. cit.

Chapter Eight: 'Please Let Him Be Dead'

1 Letter abbreviated and edited for clarity.

2 Robbie Stewart, personal account and John Nichol interview.

3 Dave Waddington, John Nichol interview.

4 Kirsty Murphy (née Stewart), John Nichol interview.

5 Tange Stewart, John Nichol interview.

6 Berenice Waddington, John Nichol interview.

7 Reported in the *Evening Chronicle*, 19 January 1991.

8 Ibid.

9 TV News Pool report from 19 January.

10 *We Were There – Tornado Force*, Forces TV, 2015.

Chapter Nine: The Mission from Hell

1 *Royal Air Force Historical Society Journal 32*, op. cit.

2 Allen, *Thunder and Lightning*, op. cit. Some quotes edited for clarity.

3 Ibid.

4 Nigel Risdale, personal account and John Nichol interview.

5 Nick Heard, personal account and John Nichol interview.

6 Herlik, *Separated by War*, op. cit.

7 Transcript of Teakle's tape reproduced in Herlik, *Separated by War*. Dialogue edited here for clarity.

8 The cockpit recording of the attack showed that the radalt had 'unlocked' which happens at 100ft – it is unclear what height the crew actually bottomed out at.

9 'Attack on Ubaydah Bin Al Jarrah Airfield – 20 Jan 91', Mission Report, supplied by John Broadbent.

10 *RAF Yearbook Special: Air War in the Gulf*, op. cit.

11 General Sir Peter de la Billière, *Storm Command: A Personal Account of the Gulf War* (Harper Collins, 1992).

12 'British Fliers Suffering Higher Rate of Losses', Kim Murphy and Douglas Frantz, *Los Angeles Times*, 1991.

13 Clearly, in darkness, the Iraqi gunners could not actually 'see' the Tornados.

14 *Los Angeles Times*, op. cit.

Chapter Ten: Broadcast or Die

1 David Bellamy, private diary and John Nichol interview.

2 Con Coughlin, *Daily Telegraph*, January 1991.

3 *Royal Air Force Historical Society Journal 32*, op. cit.

4 Cliff Spink, John Nichol interview.

5 Mike Heath's account was retrieved from: http://www.ejectorseats.co.uk/tornado_down.html in June 2019. The website is no longer active.

6 Tornado FRC Ejection card – edited for brevity and clarity.

7 Report on the Engineering Investigation into the Accident of Tornado GR1 ZD893, Ministry of Defence, 1991. Supplied by Pete Batson.

8 Dave Waddington, John Nichol interview.

9 Robbie Stewart, private diary and John Nichol interview.

10 Peters and Nichol, *Tornado Down*, op. cit. Edited for brevity.

11 Interview is an edited account of the full version.

12 *Financial Times*, January 1991.

13 Major, *The Autobiography*, op. cit.

14 *Financial Times*, January 1991

15 Berenice Waddington, John Nichol interview.

16 *Daily Record*, January 1991.

17 *Evening Standard*, January 1991.

Chapter Eleven: 'Stay With It!'

1 Some personnel had practised 'level' bombing techniques from medium altitude, but they were few and far between. The Tornado could actually perform 'dive bombing' from that height which could be remarkably accurate and a few missions were conducted. But a heavily laden jet, rapidly descending into heavy triple-A, was not something many wanted to try.

2 The name of this target appears differently in some documents.

3 The Tornado had a couple of other weapons at its disposal, but none were suitable for this environment. There was a proposal to use cluster bombs against some targets but plans did not evolve.

4 This is a very basic explanation of the Tornado weapons system.

5 Herlik, *Separated by War*, op. cit.

6 Author's italics.

7 Corrigan, *Desert Storm Air War*, op. cit.

8 http://aviateurs.e-monsite.com/pages/1946-et-annees-suivantes/premiere-mission-jaguar-sur-le-koweit.html

9 Allen, *Thunder and Lightning*, op. cit.

10 Mike Toft, personal account and John Nichol interview.

11 Mark Paisey, personal account.

12 Mason, *Pablo's War*, op. cit. Some quotes edited for brevity.

13 Mission Report, supplied by John Broadbent.

14 Gareth Ankerson, personal account and John Nichol interview.

15 Chris Ankerson, John Nichol interview.

16 Bob Ankerson, personal account and John Nichol interview.

17 *The Times*, January 1991.

18 *The Sun*, January 1991.

19 *Daily Express*, January 1991.

20 Nick Heard, personal account and John Nichol interview.

21 Anthony Cordesman, *Iraq and the War of Sanctions: Conventional Threats and Weapons of Mass Destruction* (Praeger, 1999).

22 Napier, *Tornado GR1*, op. cit.

23 'Statement on the Loss of RAF Tornado Aircraft in Combat during the Conduct of Air Operations against Iraq'. This was the official brief given by the RAF in 1991.

24 Dean Wood, private diary and John Nichol interview.

25 John Nichol interview, *BBC Breakfast*, 2001.

26 The 20 Squadron official Gulf War history: https://sites.google.com/site/raflaarbruch/home/laarbruch-squadrons/no-20-squadron/20-sqn-history-whilst-at-laarbruch

27 Allen, *Thunder and Lightning*, op. cit.

28 Major, *The Autobiography*, op. cit.

29 *The Gulf War*, BBC, 1996.

30 *Royal Air Force Historical Society Journal 32*, op. cit.

31 Al Byford, personal account.

32 Mission Report, supplied by John Broadbent.

33 Graham Pitchfork, *The Buccaneer Boys* (Grub Street, 2013).

34 Allen, *Thunder and Lightning*, op. cit.

35 Pitchfork, *The Buccaneer Boys*, op. cit.

36 Allen, *Thunder and Lightning*, op. cit.

37 Pitchfork, *The Buccaneer Boys*, op. cit.

38 Ibid.

39 The account of this mission is constructed from: Bob Ankerson's private account and John Nichol interview; RAFC Cranwell 20th Anniversary of Operation Granby commemorative brochure; Ankerson/Burgess Cockpit Voice Recorder tape; Gordon Thorburn, *A Century of Air Warfare with Nine (IX) Squadron, RAF* (Pen and Sword, 2014).

40 Ibid.

41 Dialogue constructed from the recovered 'black box' Cockpit Voice Recorder from their aircraft and from Ankerson's personal testimony.

42 Thorburn, *A Century of Air Warfare*, op. cit.

43 Gareth's account is constructed from a school essay he later wrote about his experiences, and his interview with John Nichol.

44 The on-base 'supermarket', the Navy Army and Air Force Institution.

Chapter Twelve: A Bolshie Lady

1 Morse, *Gulf Air War Debrief*, op. cit.

2 Schwarzkopf, *It Doesn't Take a Hero*, op. cit.

3 *Los Angeles Times*, January 1991.

4 Cliff Spink, John Nichol interview.

5 This is a very basic explanation of a very complex and technologically advanced process.

6 The actual phrase used was 'event'.

7 Black, *Owners' Workshop Manual*, op. cit.

8 John Godden, *Shield and Storm* (Brassey's, 1994). Some quotes edited for clarity.

9 Schwarzkopf, *It Doesn't Take a Hero*, op. cit.

10 The senior commander asked not to be named, or the base identified, in order to protect the person involved.

11 John Broadbent, correspondence and interviews with John Nichol.

12 Nigel Risdale, personal account and John Nichol interview.

13 Professor Gordon Turnbull, *Trauma* (Corgi, 2011). Frank's account is constructed from Turnbull's writings on the case. Some details have been edited and disguised.

14 Ibid. Some quotes edited for clarity.

15 Chris Ankerson, John Nichol interview.

16 Gareth Ankerson, personal account and John Nichol interview.

17 Tange Stewart, personal account and John Nichol interview.

18 *Air Power Review*, op. cit.

19 Pitchfork, *The Buccaneer Boys*, op. cit. Some quotes edited for clarity.

20 Mike Toft, John Nichol interview.

21 This is a very simplified explanation of laser-guided bombing – the actual practice was far more complex and required close co-ordination.

22 Turnbull, *Trauma*, op. cit. Quotes edited for clarity and brevity.

23 Di Evans, correspondence with

John Nichol – quotes edited for clarity.

24 *Daily Express*, January 1991.
25 Kirsty Murphy (née Stewart), John Nichol interview.
26 Berenice Waddington, John Nichol interview.
27 Mike Toft, personal account and John Nichol interview.
28 Allen, *Thunder and Lightning*, op. cit. Some quotes edited for clarity.
29 Ibid.
30 Ibid.
31 Pitchfork, *The Buccaneer Boys*, op. cit.
32 Allen, *Thunder and Lightning*, op. cit.
33 Ibid.
34 *Daily Express*, February 1991.
35 Gordon Buckley, personal account and John Nichol interview.
36 Robbie Stewart, private diary and John Nichol interview.

Chapter Thirteen: 'Missile Launch!'

1 Napier, *Tornado GR1*, op. cit.
2 Mal Craghill, personal account and John Nichol interview.
3 This is just a précis of the various indications on the RHWR.
4 Robbie Stewart, private diary and John Nichol interview.
5 Dave Waddington, John Nichol interview.
6 Bob Ankerson, personal account and John Nichol interview.
7 Mike Toft, personal account and interview with John Nichol.
8 Allen, *Thunder and Lightning*, op. cit.
9 John Broadbent, correspondence and interview with John Nichol.
10 Tony Gallagher, *Daily Mail*, February 1991.
11 Ian Henry, *Sunday Express*, and Allen, *Thunder and Lightning*, op. cit.

12 Napier, *Tornado GR1*, op. cit.
13 It was never completely established which Tornado formation, if any, might have been involved; indeed, there had been suggestions that some incidents like this might have been caused by failed Iraqi ground-to-air missile systems, though this seems unlikely. Information on this incident gathered from various crews in the region and from: https://www.hrw.org/reports/1991/gulfwar/CHAP3.htm#P141_23985. There are conflicting reports about the exact date and the number of casualties. There is no doubt an incident occurred.
14 Again, there are conflicting accounts and memories. There is little doubt that at least one bomb could have hit the marketplace.
15 Ed Vulliamy, 'Limbs and lives blasted away by allied bombs,' *The Guardian*, 3 May 1991.
16 Morse, *Gulf Air War Debrief*, op. cit.
17 Mason, *Pablo's War*, op. cit.
18 John Broadbent, John Nichol interview.
19 Nick Heard, personal account and John Nichol interview.
20 Martin Bowman, *Jet Wars in the Nuclear Age: 1972 to the Present Day* (Pen and Sword Aviation, 2016). Some quotes edited for clarity. This account is constructed from various sources.
21 One 1,000lb LGB had actually remained stuck on the rail.
22 Nick Heard, personal account and John Nichol interview.
23 Mason, *Pablo's War*, op. cit.
24 Bowman, *Jet Wars in the Nuclear Age*, op. cit.
25 Ibid.
26 'Pilot tells of escape from Tornado blaze', *Daily Telegraph*, 11 March 1991.
27 Ibid.

28 Ibid, and Bowman, *Jet Wars in the Nuclear Age*, op. cit.
29 Ian Henry, *Sunday Express*, 17 February 1991 – edited for brevity.
30 Gordon Buckley, personal account and John Nichol interview.
31 *Los Angeles Times*, February 1991.
32 Ibid.
33 Ibid.
34 Ibid.
35 Morse, *Gulf Air War Debrief*, op. cit.
36 Peters and Nichol, *Tornado Down*, op. cit.
37 *Sunday Express*, 5 January 1992
38 Schwarzkopf, *It Doesn't Take a Hero*, op. cit.
39 United Press International, February 1991.

Chapter Fourteen: Terminate the Wolfpack

1 Mike Toft, personal account and John Nichol interview.
2 Napier, *Tornado GR1*, op. cit.
3 David Bellamy, private diary and John Nichol interview.
4 Turnbull, *Trauma*, op. cit. Some passages edited for brevity.
5 Peters and Nichol, *Tornado Down*, op. cit.
6 Robbie Stewart, private diary and John Nichol interview.
7 Bob Ankerson, RAF Police interview 1993, and John Nichol interview.
8 Schwarzkopf, *It Doesn't Take a Hero*, op. cit.
9 Morse, *Gulf Air War Debrief*, op. cit.
10 Schwarzkopf, *It Doesn't Take a Hero*, op. cit.
11 Allen, *Thunder and Lightning*, op. cit.
12 Morse, *Gulf Air War Debrief*, op. cit.
13 Ibid.

14 *Daily Express*, February 1991.
15 20 Squadron official Gulf War history, op. cit.
16 *New York Times*, March 1991.
17 *RAF Yearbook Special: Air War in the Gulf*, op. cit.
18 Allen, *Thunder and Lightning*, op. cit. – edited for clarity.
19 John Major Archives: www.johnmajorarchive.org.uk
20 Chris Ankerson, John Nichol interview.
21 Tange Stewart, John Nichol interview.
22 Berenice Waddington, John Nichol interview.
23 Gareth Ankerson, personal account and John Nichol interview.
24 Peters and Nichol, *Tornado Down*, op. cit.
25 Schwarzkopf, *It Doesn't Take a Hero*, op. cit.
26 *Evening Chronicle*, March 1991. The newspaper actually used Nichol's Christian name 'Adrian'.
27 *News of the World*, March 1991.
28 Peters and Nichol, *Tornado Down*, op. cit.

Chapter Fifteen: Going Home

1 Gordon Buckley, personal account and John Nichol interview.
2 Peters and Nichol, *Team Tornado*, op. cit.
3 Robbie Stewart, private diary and John Nichol interview.
4 Ibid.
5 Turnbull, *Trauma*, op. cit.
6 Allen, *Thunder and Lightning*, op. cit.
7 Ibid.
8 Eric V. Larson, *Misfortunes of War: Press and Public Reactions to Civilian Deaths in Wartime* (Rand Corporation, 2007).
9 Finlan, *The Gulf War 1991*, op. cit.

Edited quotes. Using her American passport, Dina actually managed to escape Kuwait before the war started.

10 Mal Craghill, personal account and John Nichol interview.

11 Around 7,000 in total served in the region during the crisis.

12 *RAF Yearbook Special: Air War in the Gulf*, op. cit. Slightly different figures appear in other publications.

13 Allen, *Thunder and Lightning*, op. cit. Edited quote.

14 Peters and Nichol, *Tornado Down*, op. cit.

15 Tange Stewart, John Nichol interview.

16 Kirsty Murphy (née Stewart), John Nichol interview.

17 Figures vary depending on the publication consulted. These are amalgamated from the *RAF Yearbook Special* (1991) and *Gulf Air War Debrief* (Morse).

18 Allen, *Thunder and Lightning*, op. cit.

19 Ibid. Edited quote.

20 Peters and Nichol, *Tornado Down*, op. cit.

21 James Baker III, *Los Angeles Times*, 1996.

22 Schwarzkopf, *It Doesn't Take a Hero*, op. cit.

23 Major, *The Autobiography*, op. cit.

24 *Los Angeles Times*, 4 March 1991.

25 Allen, *Thunder and Lightning*, op. cit. Edited for clarity.

26 Dean Wood, private diary and John Nichol interview.

27 Nigel Risdale, personal account and John Nichol interview.

28 http://www.lannpydar.org.uk/steval/raf%20links.html

29 *Laarbruch Listener* Magazine, May 1991 – edited for brevity and clarity.

Epilogue: 'Our Story Had Come Full Circle'

1 Gordon Buckley, personal account and John Nichol interview.

2 Peters and Nichol, *Team Tornado*, op. cit.

3 Jeremy Green, John Nichol interview.

4 Jenny Green, private diary and John Nichol interview.

5 Anne Lennox, John Nichol interview, 'Gulf War, Changed Lives', *BBC Breakfast*, 2000. Edited quotes.

6 Mal Craghill, personal account and John Nichol interview.

7 Military Air Accident Summary, 14 May 1998.

8 RAF Ex-POW Association Newsletter No. 60, 1996.

9 Ibid. Edited quote.

10 *Daily Telegraph* obituary, 24 July 2012.

11 Kirsty Murphy (née Stewart), John Nichol interview.

12 Black, *Owners' Workshop Manual*, op. cit.

13 Paddy Teakle, 'No Ordinary Job: A Personal Perspective', published in *Air Power Review* (RAF, 2018). Edited quotes.

14 *The Gulf War*, BBC, 1996 (author's italics).

15 *The Guardian*, 6 March 2001.

16 https://www.justgiving.com/fundraising/heathy

17 https://www.pprune.org/military-aviation/366836-5-marathons-5-days-memory-late-avm-mike-heath.html

18 Ibid.

19 https://www.pprune.org/military-aviation/315261-co-pilot-michael-warren-dies-during-plane-flight.html

20 *Daily Mail*, 25 February 2008.

21 Mal Craghill, correspondence with John Nichol.

22 US Department of Defense: www.
    defense.gov/casualty.pdf
23 Ministry of Defence: www.gov.uk/
    government/fields-of-operation/iraq
24 https://www.bbc.co.uk/news/
    world-middle-east-11107739
25 BBC News, March 2013.
26 Dave Bellamy, personal account and
    John Nichol interview.
27 *Daily Telegraph* obituary, 24 July
    2012.
28 'Tornado: In Memoriam 1979–
    2019', document produced by Wing
    Commander Gary Coleman.
29 John Nichol – Flying Authorisers
    Course, 1994.
30 Deborah Haynes and Sam Coates,
    The Times, November 1991.
31 *RAF Yearbook Special*, op. cit.
    Edited quotes.
32 This section constructed from the
    Telegraph and *Times* obituaries,
    July 2020.
33 John Gillespie Magee Jr (1922–
    1941), August 1941.
34 *Daily Telegraph*, 5 February 2019.
35 Craig Hoyle, FlightGlobal,
    November 2014, and: https://

www.edrmagazine.eu/
the-end-of-tornado-gr-4-role-in-
op-shader-tornado-gr-4-retirement-
its-effect-on-the-air-war-on-terror.
There are some conflictions
regarding the precise numbers of
casualties and dates of final strikes.
RAF Typhoons and Reaper UAVs
were responsible for the other
deaths.
36 BBC News, January 2019.
37 Forces TV, Ministry of Defence,
    2019.
38 Sir Stephen Hillier, correspondence
    with John Nichol.
39 Letter to John Nichol from
    President George H. W. Bush.
    Edited contents.
40 Jeremy Green, John Nichol
    interview.

In Memoriam

1 Information taken from 'Tornado:
   In Memoriam 1979–2019',
   document produced by Wing
   Commander Gary Coleman.

BIBLIOGRAPHY

BOOKS

Allen, Charles, *Thunder and Lightning* (HMSO, 1991)

Black, Ian, *RAF Tornado: Owners' Workshop Manual* (Haynes, 2014)

Bowman, Martin, *Jet Wars in the Nuclear Age: 1972 to the Present Day* (Pen and Sword Aviation, 2016)

Cordesman, Anthony, *Iraq and the War of Sanctions: Conventional Threats and Weapons of Mass Destruction* (Praeger, 1999)

Corrigan, Jim, *Desert Storm Air War: The Aerial Campaign Against Saddam's Iraq in the 1991 Gulf War* (Rowman & Littlefield, 2017)

Crawford, Neta, *Costs of War* (Brown University's Watson Institute for International and Public Affairs, 2001)

de la Billière, General Sir Peter, *Storm Command: A Personal Account of the Gulf War* (HarperCollins, 1992)

Finlan, Alastair, *The Gulf War 1991* (Osprey Publishing, 2003)

GEC Ferranti, *TIALD – The Gulf War* (GEC Ferranti Defence Systems Ltd, 1991)

Godden, John, *Shield and Storm* (Brassey's, 1994)

Hall, Ian, *Tornado Boys* (Grub Street, 2016)

Herlik, Edward C., *Separated by War: An Oral History by Desert Storm Fliers and Their Families* (Tab Aero, 1994)

Herriot, David, *The Tornado Years* (Pen and Sword, 2019)

Larson, Eric V., *Misfortunes of War: Press and Public Reactions to Civilian Deaths in Wartime* (Rand Corporation, 2007)

Major, John, *The Autobiography* (HarperCollins, 1999)

Mason, Pablo, *Pablo's War* (Bloomsbury, 1992)

Morse, Stan, *Gulf Air War Debrief* (Aerospace Publishing, 1991)

Napier, Michael, *Blue Diamonds* (Pen and Sword, 2015)

Napier, Michael, *Tornado Over the Tigris* (Pen and Sword, 2015)

Napier, Michael, *Tornado GR1: An Operational History* (Pen and Sword, 2017)

Peters, John and Nichol, John, *Tornado Down* (Michael Joseph, 1992)

Peters, John and Nichol, John, *Team Tornado* (Michael Joseph, 1994)

Pitchfork, Graham, *Buccaneer Boys* (Grub Street, 2013)

Quill, Jeffrey, *Spitfire: A Test Pilot's Story* (Crecy Classic, 1983)

Schwarzkopf, Norman, *It Doesn't Take a Hero* (Bantam, 1992)

Thorburn, Gordon, *A Century of Air Warfare with Nine (IX) Squadron RAF* (Pen and Sword, 2014)

Turnbull, Professor Gordon, *Trauma* (Corgi, 2011)

MAGAZINES

Air Power Review: First Gulf War 25th Anniversary (RAF, 2016)

RAF Yearbook Special: Air War in the Gulf (IAT Publishing, 1991)

Tornado GR 1974–2019 (Air Media Centre, HQ Air Command, 2019)

PICTURE CREDITS

4. Murharraq formation: John Broadbent; RAF Laarbruch: John Nichol
5. Refuelling: Wilbur Wilson via Les Hendry Dhahran archive; engineers: Andy White
6. Bill and Jenny Green: Jenny Green; Teakle and Buckley: Gordon Buckley
7. Rear cockpit: Tommy Tank
8. Front cockpit © Ian Black
9. Tornado formation: Mike Toft
10. Groundcrew in NBC © Ian Black
11. Weeks and Lennox: Tabuk photo archive via Matty Mathieson; Craghill and Warren: Mal Craghill
12. Anti-Aircraft fire © Patrick de Noirment / REUTERS; Heath: Tabuk photo archive via Matty Mathieson; Batson: Pete Batson
13. Hicks: Rupert Clark; Stewarts and HM Queen Elizabeth II: Robbie Stewart
14. Chris Ankerson and Princess Diana: Bob Ankerson; crash site: Robbie Stewart
15. Nichol in former cell © Mike Moore / *Daily Mirror*
16. Nichol and Clark on aircraft: John Nichol; low-level flying: Dave Bellamy
17. Hicks' coffin: John Broadbent
18. Nichol and Clark and the media: John Nichol; Waddington and Stewart reunion: Robbie Stewart
19. Peters and Nichol: John Nichol; Witts in crewroom: Jerry Witts via Les Hendry Dhahran archive; Stewart and Waddington: Robbie Stewart
20. Broadbent: Nige Risdale; De la Billière and Schwarzkopf © Dennis Stone / Shutterstock
21. Three Tornados © Mike Lumb; Burgess and Ankerson: Bob Ankerson
22. Major and Nichol: John Nichol; Robbie and Kirsty Stewart: Robbie Stewart; Philippa and Jeremy Green: Jenny Green
23. Diamond Nine formation © Stuart Norris; POW reunion: John Nichol
24. Post-war formation © Ian Black; Tornados at sunset © Mark Ranger

INDEX

Abu Ghraib prison, Baghdad 356–8, 359–62, 363, 366–7, 370
Afghanistan 398, 411
AIM9L air-to-air missile 129
air-to-air refuelling (AAR) xix, 24–5, 57, 62–3, 64, 66, 70, 75, 76, 87, 88, 94, 95, 122, 125, 127, 130, 137, 139, 149, 152, 164, 181, 196, 201, 231–5, 279, 286, 327
ALARM (Air-Launched Anti-Radiation Missile) xix, 67, 116–18, 130, 132, 327, 389
Al Asad airbase, Iraq 117, 118, 130–2, 174, 182–6, 251, 409
Al Habbaniyah helicopter hangars, Iraq 363
Al Jarrah 'super-base', Iraq 230–1, 235–45, 249
Al Najaf airbase, Iraq 271–2, 274–7
Al Qaeda 405, 411
Al Taqaddum airbase, Iraq 339–42
Anderson, Neil xvii, 70, 72, 73–4
Ankerson, Bob xvi
    Ar Rumaylah attack sortie 285–6, 287–8, 289, 290, 292–3, 403, 417
    deployed to Gulf 61, 92–3, 105, 106

desert flying training 107–8
family reaction to shooting down of 293–6, 300, 309–12, 316–17, 366, 373
Neil Anderson, on 73–4
POW/captivity in Iraq 296–301, 332–3, 347, 348, 356, 357, 367
RAF, joins 60
release from Iraqi captivity/end of war and 366, 370, 373, 377
Shaibah airfield attack sortie 277–9
wife, meets and marries 60–1. See also Ankerson, Chris
Ankerson, Chris xvi, 60, 61, 92–3, 105, 109, 113, 278, 292, 293–4, 296, 300, 309–11, 312, 316–17, 366, 373
Ankerson, Gareth xvi, 93, 277–8, 294–6, 300, 301, 310, 366
anti-aircraft artillery (AAA) (Triple-A) xxii, 10, 46, 131, 154, 172, 181, 200, 217, 230, 249, 274, 305, 315, 329, 363, 381–2, 399
Apache attack helicopter 77, 128, 152
Ar Rumaylah airfield, Iraq 148, 149, 152–65, 223
Ar Rutbah, Iraq 280–3, 286

Arthur, Vice Admiral Stanley 273
A-6 Intruder 126, 134, 181, 199, 273
A-10 tank buster aircraft 77, 192
AWACS (Airborne Warning and
    Control System) xix, 106, 127–8,
    129, 130, 132, 153, 154, 164, 184,
    196, 235, 238, 239, 245, 342
Aziz, Tariq 109, 110, 111, 344

Ba'ath Party 356
Bahrain Sheraton Hotel 12, 13, 29,
    85, 91, 105–6, 120, 144, 145,
    146, 161, 187, 267, 313–14, 335,
    336, 343
Baker, James 109, 110, 111, 391,
    392, 407
Batson, Pete xvii, 174–5, 182, 184,
    185–6, 251–8, 408–9
Battle of Britain (1940) 61, 175, 176
Bellamy, Dave xvii
    air-to-air refuelling instructor
        66–7
    Al Asad attack sortie 116–17, 118,
        122–3, 130–2, 142–3, 174
    deployed to Gulf 74, 81–3, 99–101
    Electronic Warfare Instructor
        404, 412
    end of Gulf War and 364–5
    final Tornado sortie 412
    Gordon Graham death and 66–7,
        74
    H3 attack sortie and 249–50,
        252
    Lennox and Weeks loss, on 281
    marries 404–5
    Peters and Nichol MIA, reaction
        to news of 174
    POW TV broadcasts and 267
    RAF, joins 50–1
    Roche death and 412–13
    Shaibah airfield attack sortie 353
Berlin Wall 33, 50, 68
B-52 bomber 106, 126, 128, 192,
    273, 277, 302, 353
Billière, General Sir Peter de la 246,
    282
Birtley, Tony 336–7, 343

Blackadder Goes Forth 27, 91, 133,
    242
Black Buck bombing raids,
    Falklands War (1982) 88
Black Hawk helicopter 161, 363
Boko Haram 411
Bomber Command 274, 343, 354
Brimstone anti-armour precision
    missile 406, 416–18
British Aerospace (Bae) 83, 100, 101
British Army:
    Royal Military Academy
        Sandhurst 63
    7th Armoured Brigade (the
        Desert Rats) 75
British Forces Middle East 119, 282
Broadbent, John xv, 147
    Al Jarrah sortie 231, 233, 234, 244
    Al Taqaddum sortie 339, 340,
        342–3
    commencement of Gulf War,
        apprehension on 119–20, 121
    deployment to Gulf 80, 81
    Hicks funeral and 395, 397
    'Highway of Death', observes
        380–1
    Iraqi air defences, observes 381–2
    planning of RAF sorties 85, 107,
        111
    repatriation of dead and 389
    Rupert Clarke and 336–7
    stresses building within unit as
        losses mount, observes 306
    Tallil attack sortie 124, 133–4,
        135, 136, 139, 147
Broadbent, Maggie 167, 168
Buccaneer bomber xxi, 86, 283–5,
    313, 314, 321–4, 326, 327, 339,
    340, 364, 383
Buckley, Dawn 107, 123, 147
Buckley, Gordon xvi, 51, 96, 107,
    110, 405, 420
    air-to-air refuelling instructor
        62–3
    Al Jarrah attack sortie and
        231, 233–5, 237–42, 243–4,
        247–8, 249

Blackadder Goes Forth and 91
Clark and Hicks shooting down, reaction to 343–4
concerns about killing others 324
deployment to Gulf 61, 62–4, 81, 84, 85, 92
Gulf War, on effect upon use of Tornado in subsequent conflicts 398
Hicks funeral and 395, 396
John Nichol release and 375, 376, 377, 386
POW TV broadcasts, reaction to 267
RAF, joins 61–2
returns home from Gulf 393–4
Sheraton Hotel, on contrast of time between missions in comfort of 335–6
Tallil attack/first war sortie 119–20, 121, 123–4, 125, 133, 135–6, 138, 141, 143, 144, 147–8, 149
Burgess, Simon xvi, 65, 93–4, 106
Al Shaibah airfield attack sortie 278–9, 286, 287, 288, 289–90, 292–3, 403, 417
death 403–4
desert flying training 107–8
POW/captivity 297, 347–8
returns home from Gulf War 377
Bush, George H. W. 4, 53, 54, 90, 92, 102, 110, 198, 208–9, 267, 344, 350, 364, 406, 419–20
Bush, George W. 406

Cameron, David 414
Canada, Tornado low-level flying training in 46–8, 97
Canberra bomber 79
Chad 411
chaff (strips of metallic fibre ejected from Boz pod) xix, xx, 19, 58, 108, 129, 157, 175, 212, 287, 328, 341
chemical weapons xxi, 53, 58, 110–11, 115, 126, 165, 196,

197–9, 205, 207, 267, 273, 280, 313, 338, 352–3, 380, 392
Cheney, Dick 267
Chinook helicopter 196, 380, 383
Clark, Rupert xvi, 336–7, 340–4, 347, 356, 375–7, 386, 395
Civil War, The (documentary series) 90–1, 110
CNN 13, 121, 131, 145, 228, 266, 267
Cold War (1947–91) 3, 6, 33, 35, 41, 42, 45, 48, 50, 56, 61, 62, 67, 68, 79, 87, 88, 92, 95, 120, 121, 216, 382, 399, 411, 418, 421
Collier, Max xvi, 9–12, 28, 145, 176, 184, 186–7, 209, 211, 270, 319, 377
Collister, Keith 112
combat-stress reactions xxi, 306–9, 314–16, 354–6, 377–8, 379–80, 384–6, 390. See also PTSD (Post-traumatic stress disorder)
C130 Hercules transporters 58, 75, 196
Cope, Bill 285, 313, 314, 322
Craghill, Mal xvii, 118, 130, 140, 141, 142, 199–203, 249, 326, 327, 328–9, 330, 363–4, 382–3, 390, 403, 410–11, 420
cruise missiles 106, 128–9, 131, 192
Cuban Missile Crisis (1962) 3, 34
CVR (Cockpit Voice Recorder) ('black box') xix, 288
CWP (Central Warning Panel) xx, 21, 23, 43, 161, 287, 289, 291
Cyprus 41, 57, 58, 377, 379–80, 384–7, 410, 416, 417

Daily Express 209, 280, 317, 324, 363
Daily Mail 266–7
Daily Telegraph 257, 323–4, 414
Dent, Norman 111–12, 114, 301
Desert Shield, Operation (2 August 1990 – 17 January 1991) 53–127

Desert Storm, Operation (17
    January 1991 – 28 February
    1991) 4, 107, 127–364
allied air armada deployed to the
    Gulf 115, 382–3
Baghdad, decision not to
    continue coalition attack to
    391–2, 393, 406–7
begins/first wave of air sorties
    116–68
ceasefire 364–71, 372, 377, 380,
    383, 392, 401, 402
civilian casualties 338–9
coalition air strength, doubling
    of 192
coalition combat aircraft losses
    203–4
ground war 321, 338, 339, 350,
    351, 356, 358–9, 362–4
Iraqi forces retreat and defeat
    362, 364, 380–1
Dharan, Saudi Arabia xvi–xvii, 4–5,
    58, 94, 106, 108, 111, 112, 119,
    121, 126, 140, 142, 180, 196–7,
    198, 204, 229, 230, 246, 247,
    251, 267, 274, 278, 279, 282,
    283, 286, 291, 292, 302, 304,
    305, 314, 337, 359, 364, 390,
    402, 415, 416, 417
Diana, Princess 317
dog tags 124, 297
Duffy, Kieran 111–12, 114, 300–1

EF-111 Raven 245, 275, 327, 339
82nd Airborne Division, US 58, 106
ejection seat, Martin Baker 18,
    19–20, 32, 162–3, 213, 236,
    254–5, 288, 290, 293, 295 296,
    403
Elizabeth II, Queen 318–19, 320,
    378
Elsdon, Nigel xvi, 9–12, 176, 184,
    186–7, 209, 211, 270, 319, 377
Evans, Di 300, 316–17
Evans, Ivor xvii, 286, 292, 300
Evening Standard 270

Fahd, King of Saudi Arabia 54
Falklands War (1982) 3, 5, 54, 88,
    122, 137, 141
Fallon, Michael 2, 5–6
Falluja, Iraq 338
F-18 Hornet 126, 134, 149, 154, 167,
    181, 204
Ferranti 37, 326
F-15 57, 83, 106, 153, 130, 180, 204,
    253, 273, 287, 339, 374
F-14 Tomcat 175, 275, 360
F-111 35, 192
F-104 Starfighter 36
F-117 Nighthawk 106, 126, 131, 199,
    338
'Frank' (combat stress case) 306–9,
    314–16, 354, 355, 379, 384
F-16 106, 287
F-35 Lightning 418
Fuller, Richard 294–6

Gaddafi, Muammar 411
Garmisch, Germany 51, 399–400
Geneva Convention 267, 286
Gillies, Stew xvii, 286, 287, 288,
    289, 290–1, 292
'goolie chit' 15, 124
Goose Bay, Canada 46–8, 97
Graham, Gordon 65–7, 74
Green, Bill xvii, 67–74, 176, 400–1,
    413–15, 421–2
Green, Jenny xvii, 68, 69–71, 73,
    400, 401, 402, 413–14, 421
Green, Jeremy xvii, 69, 71, 400–1,
    421, 422
Green, Philippa xvii, 69, 70, 421–2
Green, William 414, 422
Groom, Air Marshal Sir Victor 74
ground crew 16–17, 19, 20, 22, 23,
    45, 58, 67–8, 75, 83, 112, 125,
    141, 142, 150, 151, 164, 177,
    187, 243, 281, 284, 291, 312,
    321, 323, 387, 407
Ground Liaison Officer (GLO) xx,
    63, 120, 121, 150
G-suits 17, 19, 20, 124, 212, 217,
    220, 255

Gulf War, First. *See* Desert Shield, Operation and Desert Storm, Operation
Gulf War, Second. *See* Iraq War

Halabja, Iraq 197
Hamilton, Archie 219, 311
Harding, Air Chief Marshal Sir Peter 312, 313
HARM (anti-radiation missiles) 118
HAS (hardened aircraft shelter) sites xx, 87, 149, 155, 339, 340, 381
Heard, Jane 146–7
Heard, Nick xvi, 420
    Al Jarrah attack and 230, 232, 233–4, 236, 237, 243
    Al Taqaddum attack and 340, 342, 343
    Clark release and 375–7, 386, 387
    media and 280, 336
    return home 390–1
    Tallil attack and 124, 127, 129, 132–3, 134–5, 136, 137, 138, 139–40, 141–2, 146
Heath, Mike xvii, 174, 175, 182, 184, 185, 250, 251–8, 409–11
Heeps, James 417
Hellfire missile 128
Henderson, Dave 352
Henry, Ian 343
Hicks, Steve xvi, 337, 340, 341, 342–4, 347, 376, 377, 389, 395–7, 420
'Highway of Death', Iraq 362, 380–1
Hillier, Sir Stephen 417, 418–19
Horner, General Chuck 86–7, 246
HS125 transport aircraft 383, 387
H3 airbase, Iraq 199, 200, 201–3, 249
HUD (Head-up Display) xx, 21, 24, 25, 27, 31, 133, 138, 154, 155, 185, 186, 276
Hurd, Douglas 122
Hussein, Saddam 17, 101, 107, 178, 180, 188, 208, 224, 324
    capture and execution of 408
    chemical weapons and 58, 73, 110–11, 115, 197, 198, 199, 338, 402

    coalition forces failure to overthrow during First Gulf War 391–2, 393
    Desert Storm ground war and 359, 362
    Iran-Iraq war (1980–8) and 53
    Iraqi Air Force capabilities and 63
    Kuwait invasion and 4, 6, 10, 24, 51, 52, 53, 55, 58, 61, 69, 80, 85, 106, 283
    Kuwait, Iraqi forces withdrawal from and 344, 362
    'no-fly zones' within Iraq and 402–3, 405–6
    oil wells, orders troops to set fire to Kuwaiti 345, 350
    POW/captured aircrew threat 15, 172, 221, 267, 279, 317
    SAM batteries and 327
    start of Gulf War and 121, 129, 130, 151, 152, 165, 180
    Thatcher resignation and 92
    UN deadline for Iraqi forces to leave Kuwait and 104, 116, 118, 121

IFF (Identification, Friend or Foe) xx, 22, 76
'Initial Point' (IP) xx, 154
International Communications Centre, Baghdad 131
Iran 181, 280, 353, 391
Iran-Iraq war (1980–8) 14–15, 53, 57, 107, 280, 305
Iraq:
    chemical weapons attacks on civilians within 110, 197
    coalition forces decision not to invade 391–2, 393
    ground war with coalition forces in Kuwait 321, 338, 339, 350, 351, 356, 358–9, 362–4, 382
    invasion of Kuwait 1–3, 4, 6, 24, 50, 51, 52–5, 56–7, 58, 61, 63, 64, 69, 97, 101, 283, 286, 400
    Iran-Iraq war (1980–8) 14–15, 53, 57, 107, 280

'no-fly zones' in 402–3, 405–6
Operation Desert Storm and
    127–364
retreat from Kuwait 362, 380–1
searchlight warning system,
    improvised 182–3, 185, 245
UN deadline for forces to leave
    Kuwait 104, 108, 109, 110,
    111, 113, 116, 121
Iraq Air Force 57, 63, 83–4, 87, 107,
    115, 117, 130, 140, 142, 148,
    173, 175, 178, 180, 191, 244,
    250–1, 273–4, 280, 338, 381
Iraq War (Second Gulf War) (2003–
    11) 406–9, 411
Islamic State (ISIS) 414, 416, 417
Israel 110, 117, 196, 198–9, 209, 261,
    303, 331, 333, 344
Italian Air Force Tornados 24, 76,
    203, 272, 356

Jaguar, SEPECAT 58, 62, 80, 112,
    138, 152, 229–30, 273, 313, 383
Jalibah airbase, Iraq 274
JP233 (runway-busting munitions)
    9, 48–9, 89–90, 95, 117, 129,
    138–9, 149, 167, 183, 201, 225,
    231, 249, 305, 315, 381, 382, 389

Khomeini, Ayatollah 53
King, Tom 285
Kurdistan, Iraqi 110, 197
Kurds 55, 110, 197, 263, 391, 402
Kuwait ix, 2, 7, 9, 10, 15, 94, 106, 107
    coalition forces invasion of 148,
        175, 350, 358–9, 359, 362–3,
        364, 382, 389, 391, 392, 393
    deadline for Iraqi forces to leave
        116
    Iraqi invasion of 52–5
    liberated by coalition forces 364,
        382, 420
    oil wells set on fire 345, 350
    pilots in Iraqi captivity 266, 349,
        356
Kuwait City 24, 358, 359, 382

Lancaster bombers 1, 39, 161, 230,
    236, 274, 421
laser-guided bomb (LGB) xiii, xx,
    86, 283, 320–3, 326, 337, 338,
    339, 381, 382, 389, 406
'last letter' 12, 58, 104, 114, 145
Lennox, Anne xvii, 281, 401–2
Lennox, Garry xvii, 280–1, 285,
    377, 401–2
Libya 307, 398, 411
Lockerbie bombing 307, 314–15,
    384
'loft attack' 14, 29, 45, 72, 231, 243,
    274
Los Angeles Times 246, 344, 391
low-altitude/level flying 14, 17, 18,
    21, 24, 26, 35, 36, 37, 39, 40, 45,
    46–7, 65, 70, 76, 79, 86, 90, 95,
    103–4, 107, 108, 111, 112, 126,
    128, 129, 133, 137, 138, 149,
    152, 153, 154, 156, 159, 167, 174,
    181, 184, 202, 204, 209, 224,
    230, 231, 236, 241, 244, 245,
    246, 248, 249, 250, 272–4, 275,
    276, 277, 280, 281–2, 283, 301,
    304, 305, 306, 307, 322, 327,
    328, 380, 382, 401, 406, 418,
    422
Luftwaffe 36, 41, 175
Lycoming piston engine 43

Magee, John Gillespie: 'High
    Flight' 416
Main, Kev 407
Major, James 109
Major, Sir John 2, 4–5, 92, 102,
    108–9, 127, 165, 267, 282, 366,
    392
Mason, Pablo xvi, 123, 151, 152,
    153, 154, 156, 157, 159–60,
    163–4, 223, 275, 314, 322, 323,
    339, 341, 342
Master Air Attack Plan, coalition
    forces 106–7, 115, 175
medium-altitude/level sorties 20,
    107, 186, 230, 244–5, 246,
    274–6, 277, 278, 280, 282, 283,

284, 285, 302, 314, 321, 327,
339, 382, 408
Mehsan, Hamid 338
Messerschmitt 42, 39
Messerschmitt-Bölkow-Blohm 42
MIA (Missing in Action) xx, 1, 24,
319, 371, 375
MiG-23 231
Miller, Dusty 93, 293, 294, 300,
310–11
Millett, Paul 39–40, 43–4
Ministry of Defence, UK 270, 284
Mirage 130, 131, 174, 251, 287, 409
missile break/missile lock xix, xx,
31, 183, 212
mission planning (RAF) 85–90, 91,
94–6, 106–7, 111, 115, 116, 117,
119, 125, 133, 134, 135, 136,
142, 320, 339, 353
M1A1 Abrams main battle tank 358
Muharraq, Bahrain xv–xvi, 13, 75,
·106, 336, 400
Mukhabarat (Iraqi secret police)
152, 178, 325, 330, 333, 345,
347, 356, 359, 382
Mukhabarat prison, Baghdad 325,
330–5, 345–50, 356, 359
Multi-Role Combat Aircraft
(MRCA) xxi, 36–7, 406
mustard gas 53, 110, 197

Nasiriyah, Iraq 87, 225–6
Nichol, John xvi
    Abu Ghraib prison, captivity in
        356–7, 358, 360–2, 363, 365,
        367, 370
    Ar Rumaylah airfield attack
        sortie/shot down 10, 13, 15,
        143, 148, 149, 150, 152–65,
        167, 168, 224, 254, 286
    captured by Iraqis 169–73
    deployment to Gulf 64–5, 78–9,
        80–2, 90
    desert flying training 96–7
    disbandment of RAF Laarbruch's
        Tornado squadrons and
        399–400

Gordon Graham and 66–7
Gulf War commencement,
    apprehension on 113, 120–1,
    123
Mukhabarat prison, Baghdad,
    captivity in 345, 346–8
POW/captivity 173–4, 177–80, 181,
    188, 189, 191, 192–5, 204–8,
    219, 223, 250, 258, 260, 264–5,
    266–8, 270, 271, 274, 275, 311,
    332, 345, 346–8, 356–7, 358,
    360–2, 363, 365, 367, 369, 370
POW TV broadcasts and 264–5,
    266–8, 270, 271, 277, 278,
    279, 286, 307, 315, 316
RAF, joins 80
release from captivity/end of war
    and 369, 370–1, 373–4, 375,
    376, 377
Tornado navigator training 80
Turnbull rehabilitation and 378,
    379, 385, 386, 387
night flying/attacks xxii, 11, 14, 18,
    21, 22, 24, 26, 27, 29–30, 37, 45,
    46, 48, 49, 62, 73, 88, 94, 107,
    108, 130–42, 176, 184–5, 233,
    241, 320, 327, 353, 363, 406, 420
'night-vision goggles' (NVGs) xxi,
    37, 133, 183
Nimrod maritime patrol aircraft
    337, 383, 395, 396, 397
9/11 405, 411
Nixon, Richard 41
Norris, Lesley 372
Nuclear Biological Chemical (NBC)
    attack xxi, 58, 197, 198
suits 110, 126, 197, 198, 313
'nuclear fallout detection' role
    ('sniffing') 41
nuclear weapons xxi, 3–4, 6, 34–5,
    41, 45–6, 48, 50, 58, 60, 61, 110,
    111, 120, 165, 174, 197, 198,
    284, 382, 392, 394, 411, 421

Oman 111, 126, 301
101st Airborne Division, US 76–7,
    350

operational low flying (OLF) xxi,
    46–7, 76

Paisey, Mark xvi, 104, 114, 148, 151,
    152, 153, 154, 157, 159, 160,
    164, 224, 274, 276, 277, 352
Patriot air defence missile 197, 303,
    314, 359, 407
Pave Spike (laser-guided targeting
    pod used by Buccaneer
    aircraft) xxi, 86, 283–4, 313,
    314, 320–1, 323, 326, 327, 336
Paveway bombs 131, 417
Personal Locator Beacon 170, 213,
    214, 220, 221
Peters, Geraldine 279
Peters, Helen xvi, 144, 150, 167–8,
    172, 189–90, 191, 192, 266,
    268, 390
Peters, John xvi, 10, 13, 15
    Ar Rumaylah airfield attack sortie/
        shot down 10, 13, 15, 143, 144,
        150, 152, 153–65, 167–8, 174,
        224, 254, 271, 274, 286
    Canada, low-level Tornado
        training in 46–7, 48
    captured by Iraqis 169–73
    deployment to Gulf 78–9, 80–1
    desert flying training 96–7
    disbandment of RAF Laarbruch's
        Tornado squadrons and
        399–400
    Gulf War commencement,
        apprehension on 113, 114,
        121, 123
    POW/captivity 177–80, 181, 188,
        189–90, 191–2, 193–5, 205,
        208, 223, 258, 260, 263–4,
        265–8, 270, 275, 309, 311,
        368–9
    POW TV broadcasts and 265–8,
        270, 271, 277, 278, 279, 280,
        286, 307, 309, 315, 316
    release from captivity/end of war
        and 368–9, 370, 371, 376
    returns home after war 390
    Turnbull rehabilitation and 390

'picture clear' 128, 130, 132, 154,
    238, 239
Pilot Briefing Facility (PBF) xxi,
    324, 394
Powell, General Colin 196, 198
Powers, Gary 34, 327
Precision-Guided Munition (PGM)
    xxi, 321
PTSD (post-traumatic stress
    disorder) xxi, 306–9, 314–16,
    354–6, 384–6
pull-up point 30, 154, 155, 158

QWI (Qualified Weapons
    Instructor) xxi, 77, 80, 88, 124,
    241

radar altimeter ('radalt') 136, 138,
    203
Radar Homing and Warning
    Receiver (RHWR) xxi, 15, 21,
    26, 30, 31, 129, 156, 160, 201,
    202, 236, 237, 277, 286, 287,
    328, 340, 341
RAF Akrotiri 377, 384–6
RAF Brize Norton 354
RAF Boscombe Down, Aeroplane
    and Armament Experimental
    Establishment 326–7
RAF Bruggen 62, 66–7, 92, 105, 113,
    278, 286, 293, 299, 300, 310,
    312, 317, 364, 400
RAF Cranwell 93, 408
RAF Honington 65
RAF Laarbruch 51, 62, 63, 64, 65,
    66–7, 78–9, 81, 84, 101, 104,
    144–5, 167–8, 172, 185, 337,
    381, 383, 390–1, 399
RAF Lossiemouth 284, 285, 313
RAF Marham xvii–xviii, 55–6,
    66–8, 70, 73, 74, 79, 95, 219,
    269, 319, 371, 405, 408, 411,
    417, 418
    send off for retiring Tornado at
        417–18
RAF Scampton 38
RAF St Mawgan 64

RAF Wroughton 307
Rapier surface–to air missiles 58, 75
RAPTOR pod 406
Red Cross 267, 269, 369, 371, 373, 377
Regia Aeronautica 36
Republican Guard, Iraqi 10, 52, 54, 59, 283, 288, 289–90, 293, 359, 362, 363
respirators ('gas masks') 58, 110, 196, 197, 198
Risdale, Nigel xv
   Al Jarrah attack and 231, 232–3, 236–7, 243, 247, 249
   Al Taqaddum attack and 339, 342–3
   Blackadder Goes Forth and 91
   deployment to Gulf 81
   'Highway of Death', observes 380–1
   mounting losses, reaction to 223, 230
   planning, air attack 85–90, 94–5, 106–7, 119, 142
   QWI 'Top Gun' course 80
   returns home from Gulf 394–5
   stresses building as losses mount, observes 306–7
   Tallil attack/first war sortie 124–5, 133, 134, 135, 136, 137, 138, 142
   Tornado training 79–80
Roche, Trevor xvii, 81, 82, 101, 122, 131, 132, 364–5, 404–5, 412–14
Rochelle, Pete xvii, 286, 288, 291, 292
Roland missile 14, 16, 30, 177, 199, 202, 212, 214
Rolls-Royce 19, 23, 38, 39, 60, 64, 100, 160, 284, 397
Rotsch, Manfred 42–3
Royal Air Force (RAF) xv
   aircrew losses per year in accidents away from the battlefield 413
   Air Headquarters, Riyadh 116, 274, 323
   mobilisation for Kuwait conflict 57–8
   morale within 112, 114, 227, 267, 305–6, 313, 317, 320, 336–7, 343–4
   'Options for Change' proposals (1990) and 50–1
   'peace dividend' cost-cutting defence review and 50, 399
   salary rules for families of missing or lost airmen 103, 310–13
   size of 3
   specialist flying pay 310
   Tornado force reaches peak of eleven frontline squadrons 59–60
Royal Air Force Club, London 1–7
Royal Saudi Air Force 83, 152, 272

Salter, Jo 405
SAM (surface-to-air missile system) xx, xxi, 14–15, 16, 26, 63, 94, 108, 115, 124, 131, 201, 230, 237, 238, 245, 277, 279, 339, 343, 381–2, 407
   Hawk surface-to-air missile 286–7
   SA-2 327, 328–9
   SA-3 149, 287, 288, 289, 327, 341
   SA-6 117–18, 132, 149, 154, 177, 183, 327
   SA-8 202–3, 327
Samawah, Iraq 321
'sanitising' process (before war missions) 123–4, 150
SA2 missile 34, 35
Saudi Arabia:
   coalition forces launch Kuwait attack from 350
   Iraqi threatens to invade 3, 52, 54–5, 56–9, 76, 402
Schwarzkopf, Norman 54, 90–1, 92, 101–2, 106, 115, 123, 131, 175, 192, 196, 198–9, 245, 302, 303, 358–9, 362, 371, 374, 375, 391–2, 407

Scud missile 110–11, 115, 126, 134,
    195–6, 197, 198, 283, 284, 303,
    304, 305, 313–14, 359, 415
SEAD (Suppression of Enemy Air
    Defences) xxii, 175
search-and-rescue procedures 15, 17,
    164, 170, 171, 182, 195, 262
searchlight warning system, Iraqi
    improvised 182–3, 185, 245
Second World War (1939–45) 16, 37,
    41, 60, 92, 105, 125, 161, 176,
    188, 189, 216, 230, 274, 310, 343,
    354, 395, 404, 411, 416, 420
Shaibah airbase, Iraq 166, 180–2,
    183–4, 278–9, 352, 353
Shawyer, Nathan 417
Short Service Commission contract
    103
Sidewinder air-to-air missiles 19, 26,
    161–2, 237
Sky Shadow pod xxii, 19, 26, 129,
    152, 156, 175, 202, 208, 237, 279,
    329
Slade, Larry 360–3, 367
Smith, AJ xvi, 416
Snowball, Allen 'Snowy' 294, 301
Southern Watch, Operation 402–3,
    406
Soviet Union 3, 38, 39, 41, 42, 46, 48,
    50, 75, 87, 95, 149, 327, 399
Sparrow air-to-air missile 130
Spink, Group Captain Cliff xvi, 251,
    291, 302–3, 323
Spurn Head 65–6, 72, 73–4
Squadrons (RAF):
    15 Squadron xv–xvi, 64–5, 78–89,
        91, 115, 118–21, 123–6, 144,
        145, 167, 205, 231, 244, 343
    16 Squadron 101, 117, 118, 182
    17 Squadron 61, 92
    20 Squadron xvii, 67, 74, 81–2, 86,
        101, 116, 117, 182
    27 Squadron xvi, xvii, 38, 49, 51,
        67–8, 72, 77, 166–8, 176, 387
    31 Squadron xvi
    Stewart, Kirsty xvi, 28, 51, 55, 56,
        73, 74, 98–9, 145, 165, 166, 188,

    214–15, 216–17, 270, 318, 319,
        320, 372, 387, 388, 405, 407–8
Stewart, Robbie xvi, 9–11, 12,
    13–14, 15, 16, 17, 18, 22, 25,
    26–7, 28–30, 257, 366
    Abu Ghraib prison, Baghdad,
        captivity in 356–7, 360, 367
    daughter's RAF career and 405,
        408
    deployment to Gulf 55–6, 72–3,
        74–5, 98, 99, 103, 105–6
    desert flying training 75–6, 112
    Elsdon and Collier deaths and
        9–11, 184, 186–7, 209, 211
    Green and Anderson deaths and
        72–3
    Iraqis capture 220–2, 257, 317, 318
    Kuwait invasion, first hears of
        55–6
    'last letters' 145
    Mukhabarat prison, Baghdad,
        captivity in 325, 330, 331,
        333–5, 346, 348
    'operational low flying' (OLF)
        training 46–7, 76
    ordered home from Gulf 76, 84,
        97–8, 99
    POW/captivity in Iraq 222, 223,
        226–8, 262–3, 268, 269, 270,
        311, 317, 318, 325, 330, 331,
        333–5, 346, 348–50, 356–7,
        360, 366, 367, 368
    RAF, joins 34, 35
    release from captivity/end of war
        and 367–8, 370–1, 372, 374,
        377
    return home from Gulf War
        387–8, 408
    salary changes made by RAF
        during time as POW 310–13
    Shaibah attack sortie 9–11, 12,
        145–6, 151, 165, 166–7, 175,
        176–7, 180–2, 183–4, 186–7,
        188
    Tallil attack sortie/shot down
        13–32, 33, 210, 211–17, 246,
        408

Tornado, first flies 45–6
Tornado maiden flight and 40–1
Turnbull rehabilitation and 377,
    378, 379, 385
Vulcan bomber, flies 34–5, 40–1,
    45, 60
wife, meets 38
Zugspitze holiday/first hears of
    Gulf War 51, 55–6, 72, 400
Stewart, Scott xvi, 29, 41, 51, 98–9,
    145, 165, 188, 214, 215, 216,
    269, 318, 320, 387
Stewart, Tange xvi, 11, 28–9, 51,
    72, 145
    deployment of husband (Robbie
        Stewart) to Gulf and 55, 56,
        73, 74, 77, 97–8, 103
    fears for husband on outbreak of
        war 165–6, 188, 209, 325
    first meets husband 38
    Queen, meets 320
    realities of service life,
        understanding of 41
    release of husband from captivity
        and 371–2, 378
    return home of husband and 387–8
    shooting down and captivity of
        husband and 214–17, 220,
        263, 269, 311, 317–18, 319,
        320, 325, 331, 335, 349, 366
Stirrup, Jock xvii, 71, 269, 319, 371,
    387
Strategic Air Command, US 34
Sun 267, 279
Sunday Express 343
Sunday Times 103, 228
Super MEZ (Missile Engagement
    Zone), Baghdad 327–8, 339,
    340, 352
Su-25 Frogfoot 352, 353
Su-22 fighter-bombers 230–1
Syria 398, 414, 416–17

Tabuk, Saudi Arabia xvii, 82–3,
    99–100
Tactical Air Reconnaissance Pod
    System (TARPS) 175

Taliban 411
Tallil airbase, Iraq 13–16, 20, 27–8,
    87–8, 94–5, 120, 125, 129–30,
    134–9, 145, 147, 159, 212, 214,
    225, 406, 408
Teakle, Kimberly 168
Teakle, Paddy xvi
    Al Jarrah attack sortie 235, 237–42
    commands Tornado squadron in
        Kuwait, monitoring 'no-fly
        zones' 405–6
    Iraq War (Second Gulf War) and
        407
    losses of Tornados as motivation
        for air crew, on 223–4
    mission planning 88–9, 90, 91,
        94–6, 142, 231, 235
    outbreak of Gulf War and 110
    Tallil attack sortie 125, 133, 134,
        137–8, 141, 142, 143, 144–5,
        147, 149, 167, 168
Teakle, Sonia 144–5, 167, 168
Tel Aviv, Israel 196, 198
Terrain-Following Radar (TFR)
    xxii, 21, 26, 27, 31, 37, 46,
    47–8, 70, 108, 129, 130, 132,
    133, 136, 137, 138, 152, 167, 181,
    183, 186
Thatcher, Baroness Margaret 53–4,
    92, 406–7
Thermal Imaging Airborne Laser
    Designator (TIALD) xxii,
    326–7, 353, 363
Toft, Mike xvi
    Al Najaf airbase attack sortie and
        271–2, 274–7
    Al Taqaddum airbase attack
        sortie and 337, 342
    Ar Rumaylah airfield attack
        sortie and 123, 148, 151, 152,
        153, 154, 157–8, 160, 163–5
    birth of second child during
        deployment to Gulf 351–2
    ceasefire announcement/end of
        war and 364, 369
    deployment to Gulf War 84–5,
        91

Toft, Mike – *continued*
  Hicks and 337, 342
  laser-guided bomb (LGB)
    attacks, first 314, 321, 324
  'Last Supper' party before
    deployment and 78–9, 81
  media, on relations with 336
  Permanent Commission, secures
    before deployment to Gulf
    103–4
  returns home from Gulf 362, 364,
    369–70
  Tornado, on trust in 79
Toft, Sue xvi, 84, 103, 104, 148, 351,
  369–70
Tomahawk cruise missile 131, 192
Tornado, Panavia:
  AIM9L air-to-air missile 129
  aircrew losses flying, total 413
  autopilot xxii, 21, 26, 30, 31, 37,
    46, 47–8, 108, 129, 134, 135,
    136, 137, 152, 181, 183, 237
  Boz pod xix, 19, 26, 31, 32, 33,
    129, 202, 212, 237
  Brimstone anti-armour precision
    missile and 406, 416–17
  chaff xix, xx, 19, 31, 32, 33, 58,
    108, 129, 157, 175, 202, 212,
    287, 289, 328, 329, 341
  cockpit 15, 18, 20–1, 37, 160,
    162–3, 213, 237, 240–1, 304,
    305
  cost of 17, 160, 236
  decommissioned 416–18
  dual-control 45
  engine, Rolls-Royce RB199 18,
    19, 23, 37–8, 39, 44, 64, 90,
    100, 136, 160–1, 162, 231,
    232, 251, 254, 289, 304, 341,
    397, 417
  final strike missions 416–17
  first enters service 3
  flares 19, 33, 129
  Flight Reference Cards 254, 261
  fly-by-wire system 36, 161, 162
  fuel tanks 18, 19, 24–5, 26, 46, 76,
    95, 252, 254, 290, 304

G-suit and 17, 19, 20, 124, 212,
  217, 220, 255
GR4 406, 411, 418
HaveQuick radios 76, 181, 342
HUD (Head-up Display) xx, 21,
  24, 25, 27, 31, 133, 138, 154,
  185, 186, 276
IFF (Identification, Friend or Foe)
  xx, 22, 76
laser-guided bomb (LGB) attacks
  xiii, xx, 86, 283, 320–4, 326,
  337–8, 339, 381, 382, 389,
  406
Litening pods 406
maiden flight 39, 40, 43
map display, circular moving 20,
  27, 129, 140, 408
Mauser cannons, 27mm 26, 129,
  183, 303
Multi-Role Combat Aircraft
  (MRCA) xxi, 36–7, 48–9,
  406
named 37
navigation systems 3, 18, 20, 26,
  45, 88, 89, 95, 125, 151, 155,
  176, 237, 238, 272, 286, 291,
  406
nickname 'The Fin' 20, 39
'offset' positions, radar 30, 135,
  137–8, 155, 240, 275–6
1,000lb bombs 14, 19, 30, 86, 149,
  151, 155, 158, 212, 234, 239,
  249, 314, 321, 329, 337, 338,
  339, 353, 381
operations see individual
  operation and place name
Precision-Guided Munitions,
  capability to deliver 283–4,
  321–4, 326–8
prototypes 39–40, 43–5
RAF peak of eleven frontline
  squadrons 59–60
RAF service, accepted into 45
RAPTOR pod 406
retires (2019) 399, 417–18
Sidewinder air-to-air missile 19,
  26, 161–2, 237

Sky Shadow pod xxii, 19, 26, 129,
152, 156, 175, 202, 208, 237,
279, 329
swing-wings 36
'Target of Opportunity' switch
185, 203
technical malfunctions 130, 132,
140–1, 152, 162, 199, 251–8,
275, 279, 286, 288, 289,
291–2, 389
throttles 20, 21, 23, 27, 30, 44, 48,
125, 232, 235, 236, 251, 254,
255, 341
'time to pull' clock 155
Tornado Infra-Red
Reconnaissance System
(TIRRS) 303–4
weight of 18–19
weather, flying in bad 18, 21, 26,
45, 46
WE177 nuclear bomb and 46
Tornado F3 (air defence variant) 49,
57–8, 196, 197, 230, 362, 374,
380, 383, 402
Tornado GR1A (reconnaissance
version) 49, 121, 196, 283,
303–4, 383, 402
Turnbull, Gordon 307–8, 309,
314–16, 354–6, 377–8, 379–80,
384–5, 390

United Nations (UN) 106, 116–17,
344, 362, 391–2
US Air Force (USAF) 83, 86–7, 180,
273, 284, 339
US Army: 82nd Airborne Division
58, 106
101st Airborne Division 76–7, 350
Strategic Air Command 34
US Marines 106, 350, 359, 362
24th Marine Expeditionary Force
76–7
U2 reconnaissance jet 327

VC10 refuelling tanker 127, 139
Victor tanker 64, 88, 122, 137, 152,
196, 232, 233, 234, 235, 279

Vietnam War (1955–75) 54, 90, 110,
117, 177, 273, 307, 371
Vulcan bomber 34–5, 40–1, 45, 60,
61, 137, 174, 216

Waddington, Berenice xvi, 188–9,
218, 219, 268–9, 318–20, 366,
372–3
Waddington, Dave xvi, 34
Abu Ghraib prison, captivity in
356, 359
Bill Green and 73
deployment to Gulf 59–60, 76,
84, 105–6
desert flying training 75–6,
112–13
flies for first time 43
Iraqis capture 224–6, 317
'operational low flying' (OLF)
training 46–7, 76
POW/captivity in Iraq 258–62,
268–9, 270, 317, 318–19, 331,
332, 333, 334, 345–6, 348,
356, 359, 366
'Qualified Weapons Instructor'
course 77
RAF, decides to leave 50–1
RAF, joins 49–50
release from captivity/end of war
and 370, 372–3
return home from Gulf War 377
Shaibah attack sortie 11–12,
13, 145, 151, 166–7, 175–7,
180–2, 183–4, 186–7
Tallil attack sortie/shot down
11–32, 33, 34, 210, 212–14,
217–19, 224–6, 230, 246, 254
Waddington, Jack 189, 218, 219, 319
Walker, Gordon 304–5
Walther PP 17, 124, 170, 221, 225
Warren, Mike xvii, 130, 140–1, 200,
201–3, 327, 330, 363, 382, 383,
410
War Widows' Association, RAF
401, 402, 413–14
War Widows Pension, RAF 413
WE177 nuclear bomb 46

Weeks, Kevin xvii, 280–1, 285, 377,
    401
Wild Weasel 245, 327, 339
Williams, Dave 407
Wilson, Air Vice-Marshal Sandy
    282
Wilson, Harold 43

Witts, Jerry xvi, 112, 121–2, 126,
    140, 141, 180, 204, 229, 282,
    364, 390, 415–17
Wood, Dean 200, 281, 393
Woods, Rob xvi, 127, 129, 135
Wratten, Air Vice-Marshal Bill
    86–7, 247, 282, 323, 374

Read on for an extract from
John Nichol's previous book

LANCASTER

LANCASTER –
The Forging of a Very British Legend

CHAPTER 1: *'I've got a strange feeling about this bloody Munich job'*

Late afternoon, Sunday 7 January 1945. The leaden skies spread from horizon to horizon. Ground crews had been working the snow ploughs all day to keep the runways clear.

Now, at last, the snow had abated and the job was on.

Dusk was falling fast as the drab green Fordson crew-bus took the seven men out to their giant Lancaster bomber: one of sixteen from their base scheduled to be part of this operation, scattered at their dispersal points around RAF Metheringham, 12 miles south-east of Lincoln.

Metheringham was a new, purpose-built affair, which had risen from the flat, windswept Lincolnshire farmlands and become operational a year earlier. It was a nondescript place, playing host to bleak Nissen huts and a concrete block of a control tower – one of hundreds of such bases dotted across eastern and southern England. Lincolnshire – 'bomber county' – had the lion's share, being the best-placed platform for taking the war to the enemy.

The Fordson's engine stuttered in the cold as it reached its destination. Jettisoning their last cigarettes, nerves taut, the aircrew disembarked, the oldest of them twenty-six, the two youngest still only nineteen. Breath pluming in the frigid air, they stamped their feet and rubbed their hands, glancing at one another, waiting for nerves to settle, focusing on the task ahead. They did their best to echo their driver's cheery smile as she waved goodbye and walked the short distance to the looming beast that lay in wait for them.

In service since 1942, before many of the crew had joined the Royal Air Force, their four-engined Lancaster bomber was just one of 7,377 built to serve in Bomber Command. What the crew could never have known was that over half – an astonishing 3,736 – would be lost during the course of the war. Towering on its undercarriage over 20ft above them, the Lancaster was the spearhead of the British assault into the heart of Nazi Germany; its upper surfaces were coated with camouflage greens and browns, and matt black on its lower flanks, belly and the undersides of its wings. The ghostly attire of the night bomber.

They each climbed the short ladder through the square door on the starboard side of the Lancaster, just aft of the wing: Jim Scott, twenty-three, the pilot and captain; Bob Dunlop, also twenty-three, the bomb-aimer who doubled as front gunner; Ken Darke, twenty-one, the navigator; Harry Stunell, the wireless operator, also twenty-one; Les Knapman, the flight engineer and 'old man' of the crew at twenty-six, whose responsibility was to ensure the smooth running of the aircraft, as well as covering for the pilot.

The mid-upper gunner, Jack Elson, was one of the 19-year-olds. The other gunner, and the 'baby' of the crew, was Ron Needle. He held the loneliest position of all, far from the rest of his friends in the rear gun turret at the back end of the aircraft, hence his nickname of 'Tail-End Charlie' or, more colourfully, 'Tail-Arse Charlie'.

They boarded in silence and without ceremony. Many crews had long-established rituals from which they dared not deviate – relieving themselves on the rear wheel of the aircraft, perhaps. Their ground crews complained that this rotted the rubber, but toilet facilities were minimal once airborne. Others would give voice to a particular song before embarking. The Andrews Sisters' 'Shrine of St Cecilia' was particularly popular; its lyrics spoke to the souls of all bomber crews.

> *I kneel in my solitude, and silently pray*
> *That heaven will protect you, dear, and there'll come a day*
> *The storm will be over and we'll all meet again*
> *At the Shrine of St Cecilia.*

On a night such as this, their voices – some quivering, some firm – could ring out with the resonance of a choral mass.

Many carried mascots or talismans, some personal, some for the entire aircraft, and woe betide them if by chance they left their lucky charm behind.

But that wasn't the way things worked on this Lancaster.

Ron Needle, in particular, had no time for superstitions. 'I've always accepted life as it is. What will be will be.' It was a good philosophy for a young man who had to face death on a near-nightly basis. In the job they'd volunteered for, boys had to grow up fast.

The down-to-earth Brummie had volunteered for the RAF eighteen months earlier, as soon as he'd reached the age of eighteen.

> I saw my first enemy aircraft one Wednesday afternoon whilst
> in the back garden at home. The Luftwaffe bombed the Royal
> Orthopaedic Hospital in Northfield on 23 November, 1940. I
> was around 100 yards away as it unfolded. That was the point I
> decided to join the RAF and fight back against the Germans. Boy,
> I was angry! I really wanted to take the war back to Germany.

Ron was going to get his wish. He exchanged a quick, tight grin with his friend, wireless operator Harry Stunell, whom he'd got to know well over the months they'd been together, dubbing him 'a gentleman with a great sense of humour'. Humour was a great weapon against fear, as long as you always treated fear with respect.

It was a short climb into the Lancaster, a brisk prelude to a long and dangerous journey, in which evasion in a crisis was far from straightforward. For Ron, the Lanc would always remain an 'elegant and very beautiful aircraft'. For some of his older colleagues, the fact that it wasn't easy to get out of the Lanc in an emergency counterbalanced its other undoubted virtues. Apart from the main door, the only exit (other than a sea-ditching hatch roughly midships on the top of the fuselage, not designed for a parachute escape) was the tiny forward hatch, just 22 inches by 26, tucked under the padding where the bomb-aimer lay in the nose of the aircraft when dispatching his deadly payload.

At least Ron, as rear-gunner, had the possibility of rotating his turret to one side in an emergency and bailing out backwards from his Perspex bubble. *If* all went well. *If* he had time to firstly open the doors behind him and reach into the aircraft for his parachute (it was too bulky to wear in the turret), stowed on the bulkhead. *If* he could then connect it to his harness, in the midst of the chaos and confusion. There were a lot of *if*s for the men flying Lancasters in Bomber Command.

This was his crew's eleventh sortie. They'd scraped through their tenth only forty-eight hours earlier. On a night run against a pocket of enemy troops near Bordeaux, all hell had broken loose. They'd been caught in anti-aircraft fire. Their first bombing run had been aborted, so they'd had to go again, their Lancaster shuddering as the flak hammered and burst around it, far too close for comfort, buffeting the men so violently that Ron Needle's only thought had been, *Let's get the hell out of here.*

At last, the payload had gone, and, relieved of its weight, the Lanc had leapt skywards, leaving the airmen's stomachs hollow. The thought of being shot at while carrying fourteen 1,000lb high-explosive bombs – a typical load for such a target – wasn't a comfortable one for any of them. However often you flew, you knew that every time could be the last. Each sortie was like 'going over the top' for the troops in the trenches in the First World War. You could never leave anything to chance – but, at the same time, you knew that so much was entirely out of your hands.

They'd got home safely – no injuries, no damage to the aircraft – but very shaken. They all knew that, in their line of business, survival was never something to be taken for granted. Never far from their minds was the thought that, whenever they lifted off from the runway, death was 'the eighth passenger' in their Lancaster.

* * *

The briefing room that afternoon had been blue with cigarette smoke. Everyone had groaned when the briefing officer drew back the security curtain that covered the map, and revealed the red cotton line marking their route.

Munich.

A long run; four hours or so there, another four back.

Though they didn't know it yet, this was to be the last major aerial assault of the war on the heart of a city already pulverised by over seventy raids during the previous five years. The Western Allies, having achieved near-total dominance in the air by this stage in the conflict, were pushing their point home, softening up the Germans to facilitate the Russians' westward advance.

Ken Darke, along with the other navigators, made notes on routing and heights; pilots paid close attention to the route and other elements of the attacking formation. They were all familiar with the routine. 'It was a totally normal day,' Ron recalled. 'We'd had breakfast. We had such good food as aircrew; bacon, real eggs, not the powdered variety! Tea, toast and jam. We really were well looked after. Then we would just wait to see what the day would hold. It was just another day in Bomber Command.'

The briefing over, the time had hung heavily. There were checks to be run, the ground crews busy about their cherished aircraft, night-flying tests to be completed. However often you did it, your nerves tingled and you longed for the moment of takeoff. After checking the guns and ammunition, rear-gunner Ron could only wait. 'We would just hang around and chat. But you never really talked about what we were going to do, what we might face. I suppose no one wanted to really acknowledge what we might be feeling. Even if you felt it, you could never admit to being afraid.'

Once aboard their Lancaster, Ron turned left – all the others turned right – and clambered aft through the narrowing fuselage, past the Elsan, a bucket-like toilet, slotted into its place midships and fitted with a lid that, in theory at least, stayed clamped down on its contents when not in use. For the duration of the flight, Ron was separated from the rest of the crew, firstly by a set of double swing doors on the fuselage, and then by the sliding doors of his capsule. All communication would be by intercom. Squeezing himself into the turret protruding from the tail, his back was now to the rest of the aircraft and he would face outwards, without the advantage of knowing what he was flying into, until the crew – hopefully – landed back at base, over eight hours later. It was the loneliest spot on earth. And one of the most cramped.

With its 102ft wingspan and four mighty Merlin engines, each as big as a car, the Lancaster's 69ft-long fuselage was essentially built around its giant 33ft-long bomb bay. The interior of the aircraft, barely 6ft across, and 6ft high at best, was traversed near the centre by the twin steel spars, to which the wings were attached. These spars narrowed the gap between floor and ceiling to just a couple of feet, creating a letterbox-like space the crew had to clamber through when moving forward or aft. To compound their difficulties, they had to squeeze in between the equipment racks and crew stations, which narrowed the interior further, taking care that their heads and bodies didn't connect with jutting metalwork.

You might be secure enough in your confined crew position, but moving around was hard enough in normal circumstances. Moving around in flight, in darkness – and the Lancaster was a night worker first and foremost – and wearing a bulky flying suit, was much tougher, even when you were accustomed to it, as these young men were. Moving around while under attack or on fire – well, that was something else again.

Ron's role was one of the most vital to the safety of the Lancaster. Sitting on a leather padded seat, knees bunched up, in an area about the size of an oil-drum, exposed to the night sky on all sides through his flimsy Perspex turret, his job was to scan it ceaselessly for danger. His gloved fingers were never far from the triggers of his four 0.303-inch Browning machine guns. The Lancaster wasn't built for comfort, but Ron's electrically heated flying suit kept the worst of the chill at bay – if it worked. Sometimes one side was burning hot, the other bone cold. But that was the kind of thing you got used to. Cold was always a problem in a Lancaster.

Ron waited for his pilot to go through the cockpit checks. Everything had to be in perfect order before takeoff. The pilot was the boss, the 'skipper', even if other crewmen outranked him. On Ron's Lancaster, his pilot Jim Scott was a flying officer, while the navigator Ken Darke was a more senior flight lieutenant. None of that mattered now. Ken would take orders from Jim for the duration of the flight. Everyone would watch everyone else's backs. That was the way to survive, unless survival was taken out of your hands by German anti-aircraft guns or by the deadly fire of Messerschmitt or Junkers fighters.

Once all the checks were completed to the skipper and flight engineer's satisfaction, Ron heard the low growl of the four Merlin engines as they each burst into life, finally giving vent to a deep-throated roar as the huge aircraft lumbered towards the runway. Through his turret, he could see about twenty well-wishers who'd gathered to wave them off.

The squadron commander was there, the ground crew who looked after the aircraft on the base and all but mothered it, and a group of WAAFs [members of the Women's Auxiliary Air Force] who worked round the base, as radio operators, parachute packers, drivers and debriefing officers.

I always drew comfort from seeing them – there was a sense of us all being in it together. They knew what we were facing; they'd seen so many eager young crews set out on an op and fail to return home. As we sped down the runway, all I could see was the blackness of the concrete, a slight glow from the snow, and all those people waving, disappearing from view.

Ron hadn't felt any sense of foreboding before taking off that day, beyond the usual nerves and adrenaline rush that came no matter how often you flew. That apprehension almost always disappeared, if you were lucky, the minute you set your mind to the task in hand. But his mate, the wireless operator, 21-year-old Harry Stunell, couldn't suppress an obscure sense of foreboding. Each Lancaster crew was a tight-knit bunch, seldom fraternising seriously with other crews. The ever-present threat of death made men chary of close friendships. But Harry did have a friend in a fellow wireless operator, and, in the crew room before the flight that afternoon, as they stood by the kit lockers, he confided, 'Bill, I've got a strange feeling about this bloody Munich job.'

Bill Winter had already noticed that his buddy, normally so cheerful, had been a bit long in the face that day, and now did his best to reassure him. It was Harry's father's birthday, wasn't it? Maybe Harry was just desperate to be celebrating with his dad in a pub at home in Brighton. Bill, the calm, good-natured son of a policeman, patted his friend on the back. 'We all get these feelings sometimes. You'll be okay.'

'Tonight feels different. I don't feel happy at all,' Harry replied.

But he had to keep his feelings to himself. The unspoken golden rule was that you never let on misgivings to your crewmates. And the rest of them, like Ron, seemed to feel this was just another operation: dangerous, of course – they all were – but routine. They'd spent the time before boarding chatting idly about what they'd do when it was over, whether to go to the pub for a few pints of weak wartime beer, or have a drink in the mess, or, if there was time, visit friends or family away from the base. There was still a life to be lived, away from the war in the skies over Germany.

Harry quietly took his place a short way aft of the navigator's station, exchanging a grin with Ken Darke, who'd already squeezed his 6ft 2 frame into position.

Ken was twenty-two years old and a London bank clerk in civvy street. Fair-haired and handsome, but also bookish and reserved, he was the brainbox of his family, and dearly loved by them. He had settled down in the RAF, found his niche, and made friends quickly with fellow airmen and WAAFs. As the war progressed, the backgrounds of air crews had broadened: initially, the RAF had looked to the middle classes and the public schools for its ideal recruits. Now, everyone mixed in, more or less happily. Harry had been an upholsterer before joining up; Ron, a butcher from Birmingham. Nobody cared about backgrounds or schooling. Least of all the senior echelons of Bomber Command, for, as casualties mounted to unprecedented levels, they could no longer pick and choose who would fly their aircraft to war.

Ken drew the curtains round his cubby-hole to shut in the light from his desk-lamp and spread out his charts. At 6ft 2, he was lucky to have the luxury of the navigator's space. There were rear-gunners even taller than he was, but their knees must have been jammed under their chin.

Jim powered up the engines, waiting for the takeoff signal as their roar reached a crescendo. Then the green light flashed and he released the brakes. Ron's chest pushed against the controls of his Browning machine guns as the craft thundered down the runway. He felt the tail-wheel lift beneath him first, which always gave him a curious sense of elation, then the main wheels left the ground, as the Lanc lifted into the night sky, soaring with a lightness that belied its size.

RAF Metheringham grew tiny beneath them as they set course to join the rest of the 50-mile-long bomber stream, bound for the Bavarian capital.

It grew colder as they climbed, dropping around 2 degrees for every 1,000ft. As they crossed the French coast at about 7.45 p.m., the temperature at 19,000ft was bitter. The men in front could benefit from the Lancaster's heating system, which was at its most efficient there, but Ron Needle, exposed to the freezing outside air in his Perspex turret, was grateful for his heated flying suit and thick gloves.

Time passed both too slowly and too fast; suddenly, it was only forty-five minutes to target. As they drew closer, Jim urged them all to keep a look out for enemy fighters. Ron kept his eyes even more strictly peeled for enemy aircraft – Messerschmitt 110s and Junkers 88s, whose cannon were more powerful and had a longer range than his machine guns. To his relief, none came. If they had, the Lancaster's wonderful manoeuvrability might just have kept them out of trouble, but he was glad they didn't need to put that to the test right now. Their experience two days previously, when attacked by a German fighter, had been bad enough. Hopefully, tonight would be different.

Light sparkled off the sheen of the upper surface of the wings and their aircraft jolted and shook in the turbulence of the bomber stream. The full attacking formation they were part of that night comprised nine Mosquitos and 645 Lancaster bombers. The black skies around them were crowded and dangerous. Stunell recalled that 'tension was at concert pitch, reaction speeds intensified. Young lads who had not long ago feared our strict headmasters, were now flying into the Third Reich, which was presided over by one of the biggest bullies of all time'.[8]

Ron could hear the voice of the bomb-aimer over the intercom: 'Route markers ahead, Skipper.' Though he was aware of the glow in the sky, he couldn't see what Bob Dunlop could: the brightly coloured red, green and yellow indicator flares dropped by the Pathfinder Force that had preceded them to mark the route and the target itself. He didn't look directly at the glowing sky. Gunners never did. 'Bright lights affect night vision. It takes about ten minutes for eyes to adjust to the dark.'

The skies above Munich began to glow as the fiery rain of bombs from the aircraft at the head of attack force began to fall. Harry Stunell pushed any forebodings to one side, moving up to look out from the cockpit onto what he remembered as a huge boiling sea of flame, an Impressionist landscape daubed with lurid orange and red brushstrokes. Beneath him, Pathfinder aircraft were swooping down to replenish burnt-out target flares, in order to ensure subsequent bombs were concentrated on the heart of the city. Munich was ablaze.

Near him, the pilot kept a watchful eye out for other Lancasters in the stream, jostling for position to commence their attack runs. Collisions happened at moments like this, or, worse, you could be on the receiving end of bombs falling from a Lanc above you. Some would drop their payload out of sequence, some too early. The darkness was bursting into a maelstrom of noise and flame, and, coupled with the roar of the engines and the stabbing brightness of the searchlights, you could never be sure of anything. Stunell decided he didn't want to see the horrors unfolding below and returned to his station.

Their Lancaster was approaching the target. Bob's voice, striving to be calm, talking to Jim, crackled in Ron's intercom, too: 'Steady ... steady ... right a bit ... steady ... correct left a tad ... steady ...'

Ron prayed it wouldn't be a dummy run again.

'Keep her there. Right!'

A moment's silence, then: 'Bombs gone!'

The Lancaster's load, a massive 4,000lb 'Blockbuster' bomb, escorted by 954 4lb incendiaries, hurtled towards the stricken city. The Blockbuster, as the name suggested, was designed to blast structures apart, leaving them exposed to the incendiaries that would ignite the exposed and shattered interiors. War from the air was a brutal business.

Released of its burden, the pilot had to control the aircraft as it leapt upwards – another instance of potential risk if someone was flying above you.

Then came the moment they all loathed.

'Hold her for the photo.'

It meant keeping straight and steady for a few seconds while the camera behind the bomb-aimer took automatic flash shots of their run through its own small porthole on the floor. How the crewmen hated those few seconds, vulnerable to attack and unable to manoeuvre. The pictures were vital, mandatory. Analysed back home, they served a dual purpose: proof that the Lancaster had done its job; and material to assess the success of the raid. But those brief moments seemed like the longest of the entire flight.

It was then that disaster struck.

A bomber stream should fly to its target on one course, and return home by another. No marker lights showed on any aircraft, and, apart from the blazing target and the pale glow of the moon, it was dark – too dark to see fast-moving allies close by.

Ron had heard the 'bombs gone' announcement, and was thinking, *Good, now we can go home.* Jim Scott, holding the Lancaster steady for the photo-run, had suddenly caught sight of something out of the corner of his eye. A giant, dark shape, heading straight for them. He grappled with the controls to avoid the collision, but it was too late. With a roar, their aircraft was flipped out of control and, engines screaming in protest, started to plummet earthwards, towards the burning city they had just bombed.

Harry Stunell's foreboding hadn't been misplaced.

Ron's only thought was: *What the hell is going on?*

Endnotes

1 See *In the Middle of Nowhere* by Richard Bailey.
2 Bombers were scattered at individual 'dispersal points' around the main runway – this made it impossible for an enemy fighter or bomber to destroy several aircrafts at once.
3 The Andrews Sisters were a hugely popular close-harmony girl band of the war years. 'The Shrine of St Cecilia' dates from 1942, and its lyrics, dealing with a town ravaged by an undefined storm 'from up above', which has miraculously spared the Shrine of St Cecilia, would have had direct appeal to bomber crews. St Cecilia is the patron saint of music.
4 Ron Needle, *Saved by the Bell*, and John Nichol interview.
5 Miles Tripp, *The Eighth Passenger*; and see John Nichol and Tony Rennell, *Tail-End Charlies*.
6 Mel Rolfe, *To Hell and Back*.
7 Information from Lincolnshire Aviation Heritage Centre, East Kirkby.
8 Quoted in Rolfe, op. cit.

CONTENTS

Acknowledgements   6

Foreword   7

Introduction   8

1   The Mists of Antiquity   10

2   Getting Serious   17

3   Hambledon   29

4   Lord's   42

5   Roundarm   61

6   Towards Saturation   80

7   Across the Wider Seas   96

8   A Mountain Called Grace   108

9   Test Cricket   125

10 The Roaring Nineties   166

11 Age of Gods   199

12 Death of an Age   256

13 The Halcyon Twenties   271

14 Bradman   305

15 Bodyline   323

16 The Second Long Dark Night   361

17 Reawakening   375

18 The New Formula   461

19 Bastions Fall   512

20 Packer and Beyond   554

Index   636

Acknowledgements

THE AUTHOR gratefully records his thanks to the following people and publications for helping to make *Pageant of Cricket* what it is. The largest single suppliers of pictures were The Photo Source (whose Dave McLoughlin and Chris Shuff were most considerate), Patrick Eagar, and Adrian Murrell (All-Sport). Of all the numerous books consulted, the most helpful have been Sir Jeremiah Colman's *The Noble Game of Cricket*, Robin Simon and Alastair Smart's *The Art of Cricket*, and *The Noblest Game* by Neville Cardus and John Arlott. My debt to little John Wisden is great, for not only have the Almanacks that bear his name been a constant source of information, but the *Wisden Book of Test Cricket 1877–1984* and the *Wisden Book of Obituaries* proved a huge convenience among reference books. Jack Pollard's mighty *Pictorial History of Australian Cricket* and Hugh Barty-King's *Quilt Winders and Pod Shavers* were other major sources.

Special gratitude is extended to my old friend Richard Smart, and to Adam Sisman, Robert Updegraff and Tracy Florance, all of Macmillan, for their encouragement at a crucial time; to Sir Donald Bradman for kindly consenting to write the foreword; to Roger Marsh for brilliantly interpreting an idea for the dust-jacket; to Chris Barker for his skilled photography of precious old pictures; and to Steven Lynch for casting an eye over the final proofs. For their contributions, ranging from considerable to notable, appreciation goes to the following: David Allan, David Rayvern Allen, Chris Aspin, *Australian Cricket* magazine, Australian National Library, Australian News Bureau, Australian War Museum, *Barbados Advocate*, *Barbados Daily News*, Charles Barnett, Brian Bassano, Mrs Anne Bowen, Robert Brooke, E.K. Brown, J.F. Burrell, Peter Bush, Dr Richard Cashman, Dennis Castle, *Cricketer* (Australia), Clive Crickmer, *Daily Express*, Timothy d'Arch Smith, Phil Derriman, Dixson Gallery (Sydney), *Evening Standard*, R.C. Fine, Ric Finlay, Clive Finn, Peter Frith, Alric Gaskin, Matthew Gilbert, Peter Goodall, Guildford Muniment Room, Chris Harte, B. Harwood (Wadhurst Cricket Club), Murray Hedgcock, *The Hindu*, Hong Kong Cricket Association, Gerald Howat, *Indian Cricket Annual*, Ken Kelly, Mrs Lilly Laker, Mark Leech, *Mail on Sunday*, *Manchester Evening News*, *Melbourne Age*, Melbourne Cricket Club, Robert Missen, Mitchell Library (Sydney), Graham Morris, David Munden, *The Nation* (Barbados), Don Neely, H.A. Osborne (Sussex County Cricket Club), *Pakistan Cricketer*, J.E. Peckover, Alan Phillips, Gordon Phillips, Ken Piesse, *Protea Cricket Annual of South Africa*, *Punch*, *Rand Daily Mail*, Raymond's News Agency, Miss Netta Rheinberg, Jack Robertson, Brian Rowe, Hugh Sackville-West, Salisbury Museum, Headley Samuel (Dellmarr Studios, Jamaica), Stephen Saunders, Srenik Sett, Ms Ilsa Sharp, Singapore Cricket Club, Bill Smith, Mike Smith, Ric Smith, John Snow, *South African Cricketer*, Southern Newspapers, Garry Sparke, Richard Spiller, Sport & General, the *Sun*, Surrey County Cricket Club (Ian Scott-Browne and Mrs Anne Bickerstaff), *Sydney Morning Herald*, Bob Thomas, W.W. Timms, Jan Traylen, W.A. Walton (Chichester Priory Cricket Club), Bob Warburton (Lancashire County Cricket Club), Andy Watts, Professor Derek West, *West Indies Cricket Annual*, Harold Wolfe, Tony Woodhouse, Peter Wynne-Thomas, *Yorkshire Post*, and Zafar Ahmed. Wherever possible owners of copyright have been consulted and acknowledged. Any oversight will have been inadvertent, and the author will examine any further claims which might arise.

FOREWORD

ANDREW LANG wrote once that 'no-one invented cricket – it evolved.' Despite the diligent research of historians, the origin of cricket remains a mystery, though there are many clues suggesting its evolution from primitive games and pastimes as far back as the 13th Century.

The earliest description of a cricket match appears to have been written in 1706, though clearly it was played in some form or other ages before. From that time on we have a reasonable picture of its development. In the early days it was predominantly, probably exclusively, played in England, and there are fascinating pictures of the early days in Kent and Sussex and at Hambledon. This last, in Hampshire, is popularly referred to as the cradle of cricket, though it was certainly not the birthplace.

Much as we are indebted to these early references and to the men who collated them – men of the stature of Joseph Strutt, John Nyren and the Rev. James Pycroft – my own belief is that cricket came of age only when overarm bowling was legalised. I cannot imagine the sport having any real crowd appeal or public support in the 20th century with underarm bowling. Just one delivery of the latter type not so long ago brought forth a most caustic rebuke from no less a person than a Prime Minister.

At least in those early days they didn't have to worry about legislation to control bumpers. There were undoubtedly enjoyable moments, as may be deduced from an old club minute which read: 'a wet day, only three members present, nine bottles of wine.'

Fortunately the legacy of dedicated historians has been, and is being, emulated in the modern era, and this is one of the great fascinations of cricket. No other sport compares with it in providing literature to gladden and inspire the hearts of the followers in so many parts of the world who now embrace cricket – the game at which the late Sir Frederick Toone said you could 'exhaust yourself but never your subject'. My own love of cricket and my enjoyment of it has been enriched enormously through reading works by writers such as Sir Neville Cardus, H.S. Altham, E.W. Swanton, David Frith, A.A. Thomson, J.M. Kilburn, Ronald Mason, Ray Robinson and many others. My great regret is that I didn't have more time to read before my playing days were over.

A marvellous picture of the legendary batsman Victor Trumper in action, still proudly displayed in pavilions, club rooms and private homes in many parts of the world, whets our appetites. The sight of his flowing cover-drive was sadly never captured by movie film. Now television and modern colour photographs produce vivid action pictures of today's star players, making us regret all the more that we are denied forever the opportunity of comparing, say, the bowling actions of Kortright and Lillee, simply because the former lived in the pre-movie age. But perhaps it is as well that we don't know who was the fastest bowler of all time: if we knew the answer, the joy of debate would be at an end.

Now David Frith has searched the archives and libraries of the world to produce for the enjoyment of cricket-lovers an illustrated history which goes closer to providing us with a complete picture of the past than anyone else has been able to achieve. I know it was done at the expense of untold hours of work at all times of the day and night. Thank goodness the cricket world has always thrown up men like David Frith, who seems to regard a contribution to cricket history as a duty to mankind. His thanks will be the gratitude and enjoyment of his readers.

SIR DONALD BRADMAN, AC
Adelaide
January 1987

INTRODUCTION

THIS IS the realisation of an old, old dream. In the absence of a superheavyweight illustrated history of cricket, I have produced one for myself. Being a slave to the game, its history and its marvellous personalities and legends, I am also one of those unimaginative souls for whom words are not usually enough – though there are over 120,000 of them sprinkled among this mammoth medley of pictures. Over two unforgettably hectic years, *Pageant of Cricket* took several thousand hours to compile; but the labours were gladly endured, and through the fatigue there is a shaft of delight, for the finished product, the picture cavalcade, may now be shared.

Even 2000 pictures – many more than have ever been collected into any of cricket's 10,000-plus previous publications – may not be enough for the insatiable perfectionist. But it needs to be understood that the selection had to be sweated down through successive levels. It began with the examination of well over half-a-million illustrations. After this came the indexing of over 50,000 picture references – a task complicated by the necessity to see through numerous misidentifications in original captions – and to provide some where none existed previously. Then, as if I had chipped tons of oysters away and tossed them into a vast container, I was faced with the huge and daunting task of making the final selection of pearls. Swimming about in this boundless ocean left me short of oxygen and wondering where the strength to swim a further stroke might come from. And yet all this was only a start. The final selection had to be sized, balanced, laid on the page, and described. This last stage was where I discovered my true endurance level – and became a most anti-social person, working through the day and much of the night for weeks on end, praying that my labours would be completed before my mood of self-denial exhausted itself.

I am not among those who believe in letting others do their research for them. The best helping hand remains, I think, at the end of one's arm: though there were lonely moments in the small hours when doubt crept in. All the same, I stand four-square responsible for any defects there may be.

The pictures, on the whole, are meant to speak for themselves, though some needed a little prompting. Rarity value, chronology, balance and historical significance were the keynotes. The need to exclude pictures which have been grossly over-used was weighed against the desirability of including such masterpieces as the 1928 Hammond cover-drive and the 1950 Miller square-cut. Old favourites are in, but the majority of the illustrations will be completely new to modern eyes, being either unpublished or first published many years ago.

Although it has been hinted that a predilection for pictures is a betrayal of the craft of words, I prefer to believe that the reality of a good photograph surpasses beyond calculation even man's most distinguished attempts at verbal description. How could it be otherwise? I sometimes feel, in any case, that the beloved game is much oversubscribed with words.

Why is the fascination of a pictorial image a source of such sublime comfort? Perhaps it is because Time is usually our greatest adversary in life: one is either so busy day by day that there is simply insufficient time to do all one needs and wants to do, or, when old age comes, there is not enough time left. Thus a good picture, a vivid and innocent link with the past, reaches back and cheats Time, an utterly priceless experience.

A comprehensive sweep was the aim. Some photographs – those of Lord Sheffield, W.F.E. Marx, Frank O'Keeffe and Rowland Bowen come to mind – were extremely difficult to locate, and were not among the half-million originally trawled. But they're here now, thanks to friends. To them, and to others who have helped to make this volume what it is, thanks are tendered elsewhere.

The roots of the 'pageant' hold somewhere in the mists of the game's antiquity, while its final growths are suspended in the hectic, shifting second half of the 1980s. If international cricket seems to dominate the last section, that is no less than a faithful reflection of the trend in cricket. The game's spread has been astounding. The financial foundations, now soaked in sponsorship, are spectacular: anathema to some; the means of a good living, even small fortunes, to others. Yet little is new. Threads run back well into cricket history. In the game's Middle Ages sponsorship/patronage was heavy. Intimidation by fast bowlers is nothing new: Daft used head protection when he batted in 1870, and Hendren in 1933. There were rumblings when Middlesex signed overseas players in the 1890s. Pitches have been cursed at since batsmen had to face Lumpy's fast underhand stuff on his chosen abomination of turf in the 18th Century and their successors picked pebbles from the unrolled Lord's strip in Dickens' time. Stoddart's players of 1894–95 in Australia were accused of drinking too much. Indeed, the continuity of the game as it keeps pace with the life around it is one of its more appealing fascinations.

A phenomenon which seems strictly modern is the moneyspinning, crowd-pulling, one-day, limited-overs variety of cricket, but even this is not entirely new, in that the one-day formula is as old as the game itself. Many of the early illustrations were created during matches of one day's duration, though there were neither over limits nor presentations of banking-house or tobacco-company cheques on the balcony of Lord's or at Canterbury before the beady eye of a television camera.

Television itself has changed the game's image markedly. Only a few thousand once watched a day's play in an important match, the remainder having to make do with their newspaper reports or with a glimpse of action at the newsreel theatre. Now the action is beamed 'live' and non-stop, sometimes across conti-nents, in colour, into the homes of millions. The players respond with positive and sometimes theatrical cricket, particularly in fielding. And the game thrives as never before, in spite of the almost ceaseless murmur of discontent.

Test cricket is no longer the sole preserve of the three founder members of the Imperial Cricket Conference. Political agitation now wields a power infinitely greater even than that of Lord Harris, whose thin, authoritative voice from Lord's – before the Great War slammed shut one of the most golden of eras, and for a few years afterwards – was as the proclamation of an Almighty.

Cricket's outstanding glory today is its very inter-nationalism. West Indies apart, any country seems to have the beating of any other. If cricket's gradual 200-year sophistication process is reflected from this festival of graphic illustration, then so too is the spread of the game throughout the world. The price has been a deterioration in conduct, so that it retains for the most part only the most fragile of links with the exemplary pursuit enjoyed by its founding fathers. Nonetheless, a stage for art and drama, chicanery and vaudeville humour, and for endlessly unexpected happenings, cricket is revered by millions, and will last in some shape or form forever.

This book aims to enlighten a little, entertain a lot, and, if the world's leaders should ever mess things up completely, perhaps one day, should a future civilisation uncover it, it might serve to 'tell it in pictures' and even help to get the game restarted – two-stump wicket, hockey-style bat, tricorn hat and all.

DAVID FRITH
Guildford
January 1987

THE MISTS OF ANTIQUITY

SOME sports know who their forebears were. Cricket's heritage is too ancient for that. The tossing of stones or pieces of wood or balls of wool and hide must have come naturally to bored shepherds and their sons, or to villagers in playful mood, just as self-protection against the missile, or even aggressive intent, would almost as certainly have been born in man as he selected a 'bat' of suitable 'feel' – if not with the fastidiousness of a Geoffrey Boycott. The earliest brands of cricket would be almost, but not quite, unrecognisable to modern eyes. And yet the basic principle remains unaltered. The bowler wishes to do something clever or intimidating with the ball; the batsman – unless he be a Bradman or a Botham – gives first thought to survival, and then seeks to make the bowler his slave.

The Frenchman thinks of his early love affairs;
the American gloats over his most successful speculation;
the Hindu contemplates his previous existence;
and the happy Englishman dreams of cricket.

SIR JOHN SIMON

Ancient Britons at play: an interpretation by Donald McDonald in Surrey and England cricketer W. W. Read's book Annals of Cricket *(1896).*

Above: *King Edward I, probably the first father known to have indulged his son in the matter of cricket clothing or equipment. The 'Hammer of the Scots' reimbursed Prince Edward's chaplain and chamberlain £6 in 1300 for the lad's playing at 'creag' and other games at Westminster and in Newenden, Kent, 'creag' almost certainly being an ancestral form of cricket. If it was, it did little for the Prince of Wales, for, in contrast to his mighty father, he was feckless, effeminate and feeble.*

Top left: *A recently-discovered mid-13th-century psalter bears this historiated initial, decorating Psalm 53: 'the fool hath said in his heart there is no God', a lament often echoed by unlucky cricketers down the ages. If the figure is partaking of a crude form of cricket, the allusion to the fool is an early example of the stigma which has often attached to those who pursue such useless pastimes.*

Left: *If this monk and nun are not playing a game closely related to cricket, then there is a stunning element of coincidence about this illustration from the border of* The Romance of Alexander, *written and illustrated about 1340, and now housed in the Bodleian Library, Oxford.*

11

Illustrations from Joseph Strutt's Sports and Pastimes of the People of England *indicate, from old manuscripts, how the people filled spare moments and rid themselves of excess energy –* top and bottom: *club-ball in the 13th and 14th centuries;* centre: *trap-ball in the 14th century, a relative of cricket which has been preserved by enthusiasts.*

Cricket in Guildford, Surrey in the mid-1500s, an artist's impression of John Derrick at play. Derrick is immortalised in the Guildford court records, having testified in 1598, when he was about 59, that he played cricket on a disputed parcel of land by the North Town ditch when he was a pupil at the 'free Schoole of Guldeford'. The land had also been used for bear-baiting and as a timber yard. Below: *The extract from the Court Book shows the word cricket – or 'creckett' (third-last line) – the earliest surviving example of the word, though there are those who prefer to believe that 'criquet', discovered in a 1478 document in the French Archives, refers to the game which the English and the British Empire took to their hearts while the people of St Omer and beyond rejected it.*

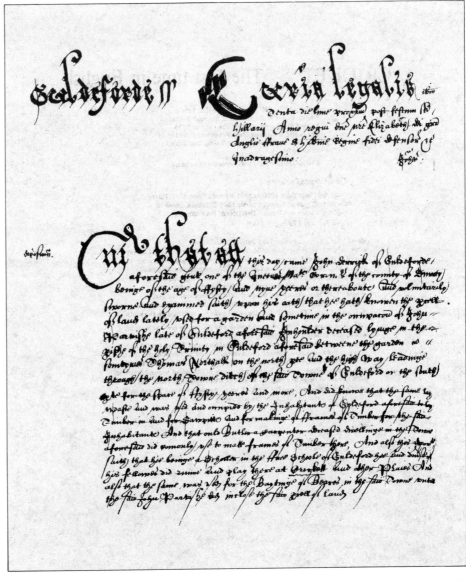

A game of cricket in the time of Queen Elizabeth (1558–1603), a rendition in oils presumably owing much to imagination. Left: *Leonard Hagety's interpretation of cricket in rudimentary times has a convincing tone about it.*

Hampshire's enduring involvement with cricket goes back at least as far as 'Good Bishop' Thomas Ken, famous hymnist, who wrote of playing the game in 1651 while a pupil at Winchester.

CRICKET developed throughout the 17th century, though its associations were still principally with frivolity, even decadence, and its conduct then presented physical dangers unfamiliar to players of the late 20th century. Hitting the ball twice was probably within the rules of the game, and participants were killed as a result. In 1624 Jaspar Vinall was killed in Horsted Keynes, Sussex as a batsman swung at the ball a second time in an attempt to avoid being caught. Henry Brand of Selsey died from a similar injury to the head in 1647, a year after the first specific cricket match of which record survives: at Coxheath, Kent. It was here that the first evidence of betting emerged. Churchyards were favoured venues for playing, though such antics were disapproved of by the church authorities. In 1622 six respectable parishioners of Boxgrove, Sussex were prosecuted for playing cricket on consecrated ground, three charges being levelled at them: that they offended 'the 7th article' relating to the sanctity of churchyards, that the church windows were threatened with what presumably was a hard ball, and that 'a little childe had like to have her braynes beaten out with a cricket batt'. There were other similar instances. Some cricketers in Maidstone were found guilty of playing on a Sunday in 1640, and seven parishioners of Eltham were fined for playing cricket on the Lord's day in 1654. Edward Bound of Shere, Surrey was similarly charged in 1671, but exonerated by general pardon. From it all emerged one distinct pointer to the future: William Bedle, who was to become the first person ever named as being a pre-eminent cricketer, was born in 1679.

Carefree meadow cricket around the time of William and Mary, competitive edge evident, clothing suitable for a chill spring contest if not for flaming June.

4   I was invited to dinner by Mr. Trench, where were 12 Englishmen more, where wee had entertaynment for princes.

5   After dinner at our Consull's I was invited to a collotion at Assera, that is at 4 a clock, to Mr. Sheapheard's, kin to Mr. Raulins, of Stratford; where also wee had most noble accommodation.

6   This morning early (as it is the custom all summer longe) at the least 40 of the English, with his worship the Consull, rod out of the cytty about 4 miles to the Greene Platt, a fine vally by a river syde, to recreate them selves.   Where a princely tent was pitched; and wee had severall pastimes and sports, as duck-hunting, fishing, shooting, handball, krickett, scrofilo; and then a noble dinner brought thither, with greate plenty of all sorts of wines, punch, and lemonads; and at 6 wee returne all home in good order, but soundly tyred and weary.

      And here I cannot omitt the sight wee mett as wee rod from the cytty to this Greene Platt.   The

The first-known reference to cricket outside Great Britain: the Rev. Henry Teonge's diary records play near Aleppo, Syria, in 1676. In 1709 William Byrd was playing cricket with friends in Virginia. Right: *Title page of William Goldwin's* Musæ Juveniles *(1706), which contains the first description of a cricket match (In Certamen Pilae).*

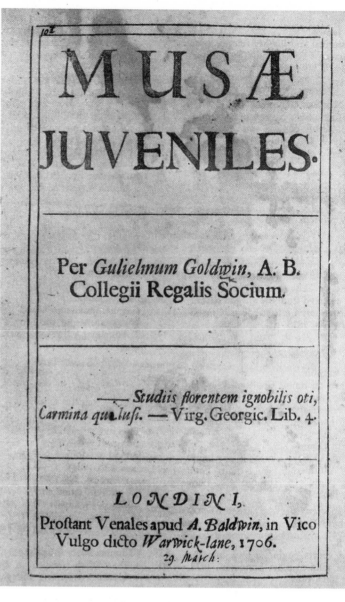

MUSÆ
JUVENILES.

Per *Gulielmum Goldwin*, A. B.
Collegii Regalis Socium.

——— *Studiis florentem ignobilis oti,*
Carmina qui lusi. ——— Virg. Georgic. Lib. 4.

L O N D I N I,
Proftant Venales apud *A. Baldwin*, in Vico
Vulgo dicto *Warwick-lane*, 1706.
29. *March:*

The *Sabbath-Breakers;* Or, *Young-Man's*
Dreadful Warning-Piece.

Being a very difmal Account of four Young-Men, who made a Match to Play at Cricket, on *Sunday* the 6th of this Inftant *July* 1712. in a Meadow near *Maiden Head Thicket*; and as they were at Play, there rofe out of the Ground, a Man in Black with a Cloven-Foot, which put them in a great Confternation; but as they ftood in this Frighted Condition, the Devil flew up in the Air, in a Dark Cloud with Flafhes of Fire, and in his Room he left a very Beautiful Woman, and *Robert Yates* and *Richard Moore* haftily ftepping up to her, being Charm'd with her Beauty went to Kifs her, but in the Attempt they inftantly fell down Dead.

The other two, *Simon Jackson* and *George Grantham*, feeing this Tragical Sight, ran home to *Maiden-Head*, where they now lye in a Diftracted Condition.

Alfo the Minifter of *Maiden-Head* Pray'd with them frequently his Prayer is here at Large, and likewife his Sermon which he Preach'd the Sunday following, the Text is *Remember the Sabbath-Day, to Keep it Holy.* Exod. 20. ver. 8.

Left: *Further dire consequences for cricket-playing breakers of the Sabbath. Messrs Yates, Moore, Jackson and Grantham of Maidenhead may well have been drinking to have known such hallucinatory reprisal.* Below: *Possibly the earliest woodcut of a cricket match, c.1720, a charming item once owned by the prominent collector Charles Pratt Green.*

The agreement between the 2nd Duke of Richmond and Alan Brodrick before their matches in 1727.

GETTING SERIOUS

THE earliest-known county match, Kent v Surrey at Dartford in June 1709, was undoubtedly played to a set of rules and conditions, but the oldest-known are in the form of an agreement between the Duke of Richmond, one of the great early patrons, and Mr Brodrick of Pepperharowe, Surrey, for home and away matches in 1727. Later codes of the Laws of Cricket started from this prototype.

The game was spreading, thanks to wealthy enthusiasts such as these, and foreign territories were now feeling the impact, notably in India, where mariners of the East India Company were known to be playing in 1721, at first for their own amusement before the bewildered gaze of the locals, and gradually enticing those onlookers to sample this peculiarly English and esoteric recreation.

At home, cricket was tendering its roots into the soil of Cambridge and then Oxford during the first few years of the 18th century, initiating yet another tradition which was to flourish during the centuries ahead.

The 2nd Duke of Richmond. His team, playing in the Sussex village of Slindon, near the family seat at Goodwood, were led by Richard Newland, whose nephew, Richard Nyren, became a leading light in the great Hambledon era.

17

Cricket on the Artillery Ground, Finsbury, 1743, by or after Francis Hayman, RA, painted for the decoration of Vauxhall Gardens, and frequently reproduced since. The batsman, with curved bat, defends his twin-stump wicket against a white ball 234 years before the world was stunned by Kerry Packer's 'innovation'. The scorer cuts his notches, and the wicketkeeper was thought to have been Hogarth, the satirist, a friend of Hayman's. Left: Mary Turner defined many a cricket-lover's passion when she wrote, in 1739, of Dr Phillip's father as wishing he 'had not annything else to do he could play at cricket all his life'. Below: The earliest bat now known to survive. It belonged to James Chitty of Knaphill, Surrey, and is housed at The Oval.

Dr Phillip   Easthoadly September 2th 1739

According to my promis have sent you one Peice of Nankeen and a few Peares which I hope will Com safe to hand, last Munday youre father was at Mr Payns and pbaid at Cricket and came home please anuf for he strouck the best ball in the game and whished he had not annything else to do he ould play at Cricket all his life (Tuesday I Brusil, to see David wich broght us word he was like to live and this morning youre father set of for Brightling but hope whe shall have a more favourable account at his return Dr Phillip I hope you will be very carful in the choice of youre aqaintance for youth are soone drawn into errors for there is many desineing people that ly in wait to take in the unwarry therefore I must bag you will be carfull and surcumspect in all youre actions and put youre trust in your Maker ho hath promised to deliver all thos ho callupon him

Peggy H & J joine in love to you

From youre Affet

Mother Mary Turner

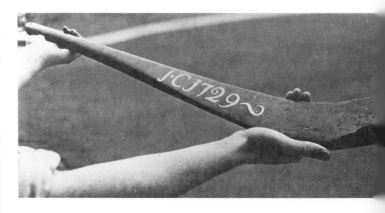

The earliest book illustration of cricket being played, by Hubert Gravelot, 1739. It decorated the Arms of Shrewsbury.

A characteristic painting of the 1740s: Sir William Benett of Fareham, Hants, a lifelong cricket devotee who eventually became Hambledon CC's president. Edward Penny, RA, painted him when he was 12.

19

An engraving of Frenchman Louis Boitard's popular drawing entitled grandly An Exact Representation of the Game of Cricket – Inscribed to all Gentlemen Lovers of that Diversion *and published in 1743.*

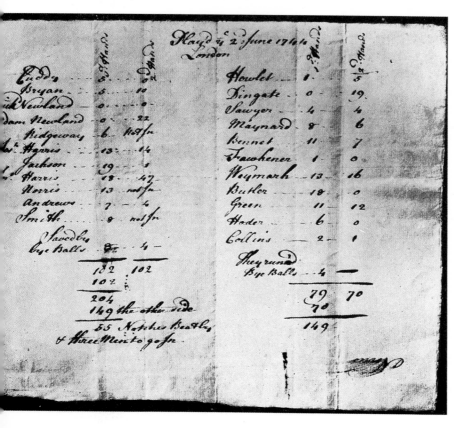

Above: *Cricket at Eton in 1742, by E. F. Burney, illustrating Thomas Gray's* Ode on a Distant Prospect of Eton. Left: *The earliest full scorecard to survive from an important match: Kent v All-England, 1744, at the Artillery Ground (where cricket is still played). The contest was celebrated by James Love (Dance) in* Cricket: An Heroic Poem.

First mention of Norfolk cricket in the Norwich newspapers, May 1745. The game is proudly referred to as a 'manly diversion'. Right: Manly or not, it was not a pastime to entice the Rev. Henry Venn once he had been ordained. After his last match before entering the Church, in 1747, he tossed his bat down, inviting any of his friends to have it. 'I will never have it said of me, ''Well struck, Parson!'' ' he boomed.

Left: William Rice, posed in the fashion of the day, with an oversize bat: painting by Robert Scaddon. Below: Master Rice would have needed a match ticket like this to gain entry to an important match in 1744, the year in which admission charges are first recorded.

21

A coloured engraving of 'a cricket match in Mary-le-Bone Fields' by Charles Grignion after Francis Hayman, published in 1748. Below: John Stedman's House and School, a watercolour by artist unknown, shows youngsters testing their skills in the playground, a spreading practice until the last quarter of the 20th century.

A haunting painting, thought to be by Paul Sandby, c.1743, part of Sir Jeremiah Colman's magnificent former collection, most of which was presented to MCC in 1947. The setting is thought to be the Yorkshire moors. Below: Cricket at Brading, Isle of Wight, now thought to be a later copy of an earlier work, but still enchanting.

23

Cricket's most notable casualty remains Frederick Louis, Prince of Wales, son of George II. A keen patron of the game, especially in Surrey, he became, through his enthusiasm and generosity, the 'head and right arm' of cricket in that county during the 1730s and 1740s. But cruelly the game cost him his life. Hit in the side while playing on the lawn of his Buckinghamshire residence, Cliefden House, he died some months later, in March 1751, when the resultant internal abscess burst.

His Royal Highness Prince Frederick &c.

In this historic little workshop the Duke family manufactured cricket balls from 1760 until 1841, when the firm moved. The photograph comes from Hugh Barty-King's informative Quilt Winders and Pod Shavers: the History of Cricket Bat and Ball Manufacture.

Semi-casual cricket within sight of Windsor Castle, about 1761, an engraving by Benjamin Green after a drawing by Samuel Wale. *Right: Reaching into the future and back again, bats spanning 200 years: mid-18th century, early straight bat (1793), a woodwormed Fuller Pilch bat, one of the many used by W. G. Grace, and the blade used by Bradman on his final tour of England (1948). This imposing array forms part of MCC's massive collection at Lord's.*

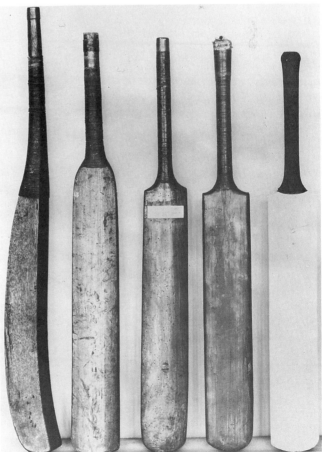

For children the instinctive thing has so often and for so long been the implementation of a bat-and-ball game.

Far left: *Canterbury is a district rich in cricket history. This oil by Henry Hodgins recreates some action from around 1761.* Far lower left: *Cricket equipment serves again as fashionable prop for a charming study of children in the 1760s: the Sondes children, painted by Zoffany.*

Left: *Sir Thomas Hudson's painting, c.1760,* The Boy with the Bat *(Walter Ramsden Beaumont Hawkesworth, a distant relative of Guy Fawkes), with Newark's old castle beyond. The lad is also holding the two stumps still standard to the game. A dozen years or so hence the third stump was introduced.* Below left: *A more renowned study of cricket-minded youth: Lewis Cage, by Francis Cotes. The painting was shown at the Royal Academy's inaugural exhibition in 1769, and was described by Horace Walpole as 'very pretty'.*

Below: *Receipt to the Duke of Dorset for 11 cricket bats and two cricket balls – total charge by William Pett of Sevenoaks in 1766: £1-14-6.*

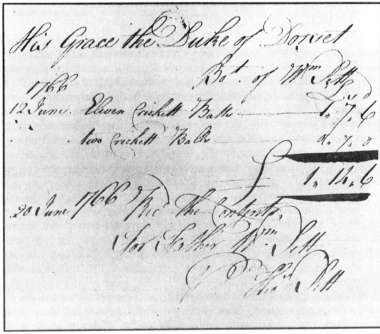

Harrow pupils at play in 1765. The public schools were to become a cornerstone of the English game, providing well-drilled young amateurs – usually batsmen – to county teams and the national XI. Below: *Kent v Sussex at Sevenoaks Vine, 1773. Lord Sackville gave the ground by deed of trust 'to be a cricket ground forever'.*

A Village Called Hambledon

HAMBLEDON, the Hampshire village nestling a few miles from Petersfield, has long taken on a signal meaning, for it was here – or more exactly up on the exposed Broadhalfpenny Down two miles away – that cricket grew in stature with massive significance. The right men happened to be available at this particular time, chief among them being Richard Nyren, left-hander, landlord of the Bat and Ball Inn, and 'General' of this mighty team which beat sides labelled Surrey, Kent and even England, home and away. Hambledon's grand period dates from approximately 1770 until the decline hastened by the formation of MCC in 1787, and into that period were crammed deeds galore which had the crowds roaring with excitement. William Beldham had much early success with Hambledon, but the heroes of the club's great days were yeomen such as Tom Sueter, architect, chorister, wicketkeeper, batsman; James Aylward, farmer and high-scoring batsman (his 167 for Hambledon against England at Sevenoaks in 1777 was regarded as near-miraculous); publican Thomas Taylor; shoemakers Edward Aburrow and Noah Mann; fast (underhand) bowler Thomas Brett and his longstop George Leer, a brewer; the accurate William Barber, shoemaker and publican/caterer; William Hogsflesh, one of the best of bowlers; blacksmith Richard Purchase; the highly self-esteemed 'Buck' Stewart; the 4th Earl of Tankerville, patron and good player; and the mighty John Small, supreme among batsmen for many years. Later, with Beldham, came grocer Tom Walker, 'Old Everlasting', high-scoring plodder and early (still illegal) roundarm bowler; and his brother Harry; and John Wells, Beldham's brother-in-law; and David Harris, the potter from Crondall, who was the best bowler in England. Through those golden years the Hambledon men played and drank hard, won hearts and established pride in an unlikely pocket of England from which, without too fanciful a calculation, it may be seen that the game we now know has sprung.

The length of the pitch in regulated matches seems always to have been 22 yards (an agricultural chain), but the evolution of the bat's width reached a warm-tempered point in 1771 when Thomas 'Shock' White of Reigate used a bat wider than the stumps. The Hambledon chiefs soon fixed a maximum width of 4¼ inches.

The renowned Bat and Ball Inn, by Broadhalfpenny Down, Hambledon, sacred landmarks for cricket-lovers of all nations, and (left) the parlour within, where the walls hold fast the stirring conversations of Nyren, Small, Beldham and Sueter as they debated with urgency the match to come or the match just finished – or toasted the mysterious 'Madge'.

Below: E. H. Shepard's delicate impression of the Hambledon men at play was accompanied by some E. V. Lucas verse: 'The daisies lost their pretty heads, when David Harris bowled'.

Belanger's painting of the Kent v Hampshire fixture of 1774 at Sir Horace Mann's ground at Bishopsbourne, Kent. John Frederick Sackville, 3rd Duke of Dorset, is about to seal Kent's victory by catching Hampshire's last man, while 'Lumpy' Stevens, the celebrated bowler, is standing as umpire. One of the fielders is John Minshull, who scored the first century of which there is record: 107 for the Duke's XI v Wrotham in 1769 (34 singles, 15 twos, nine threes, and four fours, all run). It may have been after the match depicted above that the Duke of Dorset, overcome with admiration for Small's batsmanship, presented him with a beautiful violin. The cricketer reciprocated with the gift of one of his finely-carved cricket bats.

Right: *A poignant picture of the Rev. Robert Waugh as a boy, painted around 1777 by Robert Edge Pine.*

'Lords and Gentlemen of Surrey and Kent' playing at Knole Park, Kent, seat of the Duke of Dorset, on August 6, 1775. Below: In 1774 some gentlemen and noblemen of Kent sat at the Star & Garter in Pall Mall and settled on a new set of 'Articles', one clause of which specified a third stump to the wicket (which would be fixed where the visiting team chose, so long as it was within 30 yards of a point selected by the home side).

An emblematical Representation of the Game of Cricket.

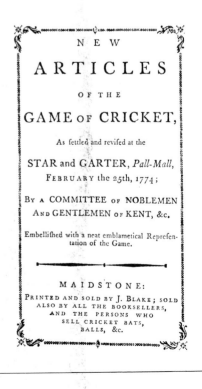

NEW
ARTICLES
OF THE
GAME OF CRICKET,
As settled and revised at the
STAR and GARTER, *Pall-Mall,*
FEBRUARY the 25th, 1774;
BY A COMMITTEE OF NOBLEMEN
AND GENTLEMEN OF KENT, &c.
Embellished with a neat emblematical Representation of the Game.

MAIDSTONE:
PRINTED AND SOLD BY J. BLAKE; SOLD
ALSO BY ALL THE BOOKSELLERS,
AND THE PERSONS WHO
SELL CRICKET BATS,
BALLS, &c.

Sir William Draper, who chaired the committee which revised the Laws in 1774. He played for Eton, but was 'better remembered for having captured Manila'. Right: The 2nd Earl of Northington, Hambledon CC president in 1778. Below: A match at Maidstone around 1780.

A familiar and favourite colour plate, once labelled **Hambledon 1777**. But now doubt has been cast on that title. Sevenoaks has been suggested. No-one can be sure of venue or year.

The boy with the dreamy eyes of a David Gower and the uncomfortable posture was painted around 1780 by Joseph Wright, the eminent artist from Derby.

34

Cricket was regarded in some circles as a pursuit only for men – and certain types of men at that – but such paintings as this one of the Countess of Derby and friends at The Oaks, Surrey in 1779 presented a more graceful image, encouraging women to take part. The first-known women's match had taken place in Bramley, Surrey as long ago as 1745.

'Miss Wicket' could hardly expect to keep her elaborate hat on in going for a quick single, but she and her equally emancipated friend 'Miss Trigger' present a healthy and happy picture in John Collet's 1778 work.

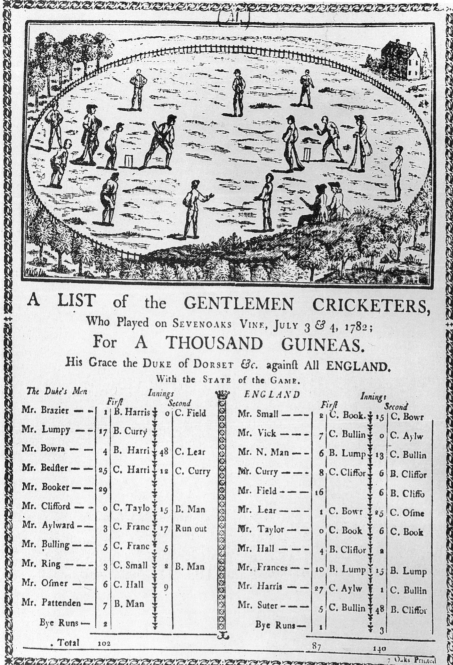

Scorecard of a match at Sevenoaks Vine in 1782, with the huge sum of 1000 guineas at stake. The Duke's Men (Kent) won on the second day by four wickets. The bowler had yet to secure credit for a wicket, unless he bowled the batsman out.

A LIST of the GENTLEMEN CRICKETERS,

Who Played on SEVENOAKS VINE, JULY 3 & 4, 1782;

For A THOUSAND GUINEAS.

His Grace the DUKE of DORSET &c. against All ENGLAND.

With the STATE of the GAME.

The Duke's Men	First Innings		Second		ENGLAND	First Innings		Second	
Mr. Brazier — —	1	B. Harris	0	C. Field	Mr. Small — — —	2	C. Book.	15	C. Bowr
Mr. Lumpy — —	17	B. Curry			Mr. Vick — — —	7	C. Bullin	0	C. Aylw
Mr. Bowra — —	4	B. Harri	48	C. Lear	Mr. N. Man — —	6	B. Lump	13	C. Bullin
Mr. Bedster — —	25	C. Harri	12	C. Curry	Mr. Curry — — —	8	C. Cliffor	6	B. Cliffor
Mr. Booker — —	29				Mr. Field — — —	16		6	B. Cliffo
Mr. Clifford — -	0	C. Taylo	15	B. Man	Mr. Lear — — —	1	C. Bowr	25	C. Osme
Mr. Aylward — —	3	C. Franc	17	Run out	Mr. Taylor — —	0	C. Book	6	C. Book
Mr. Bulling — —	5	C. Franc	5		Mr. Hall — — -	4	B. Cliffor	2	
Mr. Ring — — —	3	C. Small	2	B. Man	Mr. Frances — —	10	B. Lump	15	B. Lump
Mr. Osmer — —	6	C. Hall	9		Mr. Harris — —	27	C. Aylw	1	C. Bullin
Mr. Pattenden —	7	B. Man			Mr. Suter — — -	5	C. Bullin	48	B. Cliffor
Bye Runs —	2				Bye Runs —	1		3	
Total	102					87		140	

7 Oaks Printed

Although cricket was not as firmly established in the North in 1780, it was popular enough for the promoter to include The Cricketers, a dance on stage at The Theatre, Leeds.

36

Not without a passing resemblance to latterday cricket fan Mick Jagger, Richard Heber poses, with cricket accessories, for American artist John Singleton Copley. Heber in later life built up an enormous collection of books (almost 150,000), though very few could have been concerned with cricket. The spectacular swelling of the cricket publishing industry did not occur until the 1970s.

Below: *David Harris, Hampshire-born, and the best bowler of the 1780s and 1790s. Releasing the ball from near his armpit, he made it lift and was fast enough to worry even the best of batsmen. Tom Walker was once able to take only one run off him from 170 consecutive balls. Harris, a bachelor, practised unendingly, until gout slowed him down.*

Sir Horatio Mann, MP, owner of several estates in Kent, and a genial patron of cricket, with grounds of his own, and skilled players on his payroll. 'His life was rather dedicated to pleasure than business,' according to the Gentleman's Magazine, *and bankruptcy interfered with his indulgences.*

Cricket at Moulsey Hurst, Surrey, around 1780. Actor David Garrick's house is on the far bank.

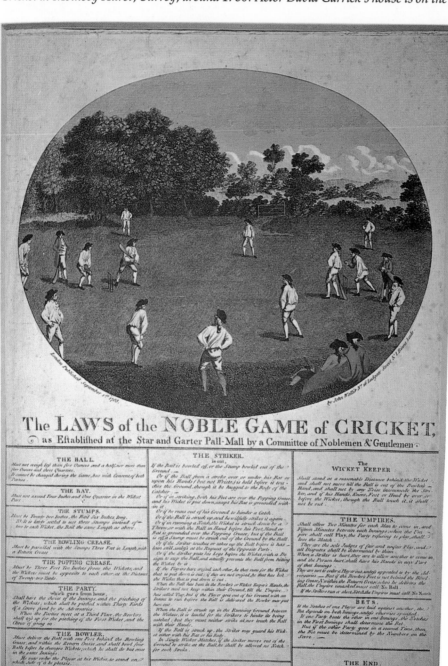

The first broadsheet edition of the Laws of Cricket, published by John Wallis of London and L. Binns of Leeds, with a new version of a favourite scene on the headpiece.

Right: Edward 'Lumpy' Stevens (1735–1819), whose merciless underhand bowling earned him literally countless wickets in the years before proper records were kept. He it was who prompted legislation to add a middle stump after beating John Small again and again, only to see the ball race through the space between the twin stumps. He once won his employer, the Earl of Tankerville, £100 by pitching four consecutive balls on a feather. This portrait, painted by Almond, hangs at Knole House, Sevenoaks, and is probably the earliest of a professional cricketer.

BOOK 12

Six PRINTS of MANLY RECREATION, as practised in PUBLIC PLACES in and about LONDON.

Printed for & Sold by Bowles & Carver

N.º 69 St. Paul's Church Yard, London.

CRICKET, Played by the Gentlemen's Club, White Conduit House, Islington.

Robert Dighton's Cricket Played by the Gentlemen's Club, White Conduit House, Islington, *one of six engravings of British sports, 1784. Some of these gentlemen, in their wigs and fashionable garb, members of the Star and Garter Club, were soon to form MCC.*

The Cathcart family in 1785, painted by David Allan. The match beyond, played at Schaw Park, Alloa, was for 1000 guineas, and is thought to be the earliest-known depiction of a cricket match in Scotland. The land is now trodden by golfers.

The warmth of the summer sun and the smell of the grass may almost be experienced first-hand from Tomkins's View of Caversham through the Gateway, *1791.*

John Frederick Sackville, 3rd Duke of Dorset – by Gainsborough – a pleasure-loving and influential patron of cricket in the 18th century.

Right: *Tom Walker, 'Old Everlasting', a dour batsman and 'unadulterated rustic' according to Nyren, who recalled his 'wilted applejohn face, long spider legs, as thick at the ankles as at the hips'. His knuckles were often chipped as he batted, 'but he never showed blood'. His value was as great to Hambledon as, say, Bill Lawry's was to Australia in the 1960s.*

The Duke of Dorset's appointment in 1784 as British Ambassador in Paris evoked some satirical responses, given that he tended to be preoccupied with cricket and women. A cricket tour to Paris in 1789 had to be aborted at Dover when news of the French Revolution came through.

An early charity match: Gloucestershire against Oxfordshire in 1787, with proceeds going to Tewkesbury Abbey Fund. The Abbey is seen beyond. Painting by Joseph Farington.

THOMAS LORD

YORKSHIRE-BORN and Norfolk-educated Thomas Lord (1755–1832) was employed by the White Conduit Club when some of the club's members decided to found Marylebone Cricket Club. As Lord set about laying the pitch and attending to facilities in Dorset Square he can little have realised that he was establishing the most famous ground in the world of cricket – after an enforced move in 1809 and another in 1813–14 to the present site. MCC became the power in the land, and no deeds on the field could be more satisfying than those performed at Lord's.

Thomas Lord, businessman, fast underhand bowler, and groundsman. Portrait by George Morland. A hardworking man of vision, Lord has his ground as a memorial, and as part of English culture.

The 8th Earl of Winchilsea, Lord's principal backer and chief founder of MCC, even though he happened also to be president of Hambledon. He raised a regiment to fight in the American War of Independence.

MCC v White Conduit on Lord's first ground in Dorset Fields, 1788. Below: Charles Lennox, 4th Duke of Richmond, the third important figure in the founding of MCC. He duelled with the Duke of York, and died in Quebec in 1819 after being bitten by a pet fox. Right: The Wood Children, *a charming study by Joseph Wright in 1789.*

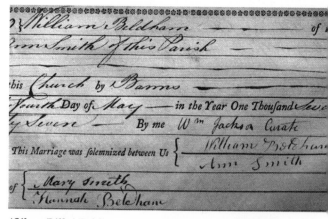

'Silver Billy' Beldham (1766–1862) was for years the premier batsman in England – and therefore the world. He gave much thought to his game, and was a genuine allrounder. But it was his glorious batsmanship which earned him immortality. The photograph (left) was taken when he was 91, five years after he had walked the seven miles from his home in Tilford, Surrey to watch Godalming play England. The sketch, by George Shepheard, shows him in his pomp. The rare example of his signature (above) comes from his marriage certificate.

An admission ticket from 1787.

Another 1000-guineas contest: the Earl of Darnley's team against the Earl of Winchilsea's at Lord's, the latter side (who won) with three given men (Beldham, Walker and Wells). Below: The Masters Foster, off to a compelling match of their own in 1792: painting by Henri-Pierre Danloux.

Primitive cricket as played at Stonyhurst College, Lancashire returned in 1794 after having been 'preserved' in France for about 200 years. Below: The Marquess Cornwallis, a Kentish cricket patron who had the misfortune to sign the British surrender to the Americans at Yorktown in 1781.

The breathtaking beauty of J. M. W. Turner's painting of Wells Cathedral might distract attention from the casual cricket being played in the forecourt. **Left:** *Anglo-Dutchman Thomas Hope, a cultured individual, signalled his Englishness by adopting cricket props as J. F. Sablet painted him during his Grand Tour of Europe.*

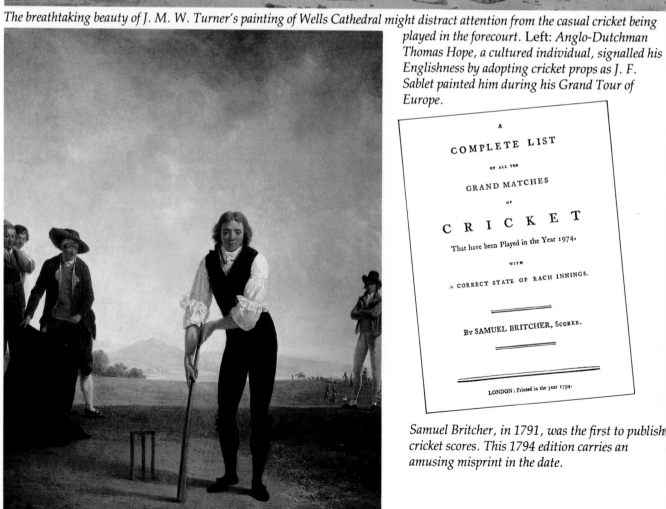

A

COMPLETE LIST

OF ALL THE

GRAND MATCHES

OF

C R I C K E T

That have been Played in the Year 1974,

WITH

A CORRECT STATE OF EACH INNINGS.

By SAMUEL BRITCHER, Scorer.

LONDON: Printed in the year 1794.

Samuel Britcher, in 1791, was the first to publish cricket scores. This 1794 edition carries an amusing misprint in the date.

John Nyren of Hambledon Born 1764.

Frank Reynolds' dreamlike watercolour has John Nyren reflecting on the fading glory of Hambledon as the 18th century drew to a close. The cries of 'Tich and turn!' had died and the large crowds were no more. In old age this son of Richard Nyren would at last put the memories down on paper.

The girls to their marbles and the boys to their cricket, even if they lack the appropriate manly clothing: a stipple engraving by Birchall after Mrs Trewineau, 1795.

Below: The match between Greenwich pensioners with one arm and with one leg – 1000 guineas the stakemoney – drew a big crowd to Montpelier Gardens, Walworth in 1796. Crowd overflow led to a riot and many were bruised in the disarray and confusion.

y 1805, the
ear of the
attle of
rafalgar,
p-hats were
e
ricketer's
hosen
eadgear.

hurſday a game of cricket was played
urſt, the gentlemen of that town and
, againſt thoſe of the Eaſtern part of
ty, which terminated in favour of
as under :

TE OF THE GAME.
WADHURST AND MAYFIELD.

INNINGS.		SECOND INNINGS.	
c. T. Martin	2	b. J. Marchant	2
b. J. Reed	11	run out	3
R. Marchant	7	b. R. Marchant	3
ditto	4	c. T. Martin	0
ne, b. J. Reed	0	c. M. Ades	11
b. R. Marchant	3	b. R. Marchant	6
rd, c J. Tyrrell	4	b. J. Marchant	1
n, not out	19	b. ditto -	3
ck, c. M. Ades	3	c. ditto -	0
b. J. Reed	0	not out	0
b. ditto ,	0	b. J. Marchant	2
Byes	2	Byes	2
	55		33

EASTERN DIVISION.

INNINGS.		SECOND INNINGS.	
b. W. Baldock	1	not out	4
, b. J. Cooper	16	c. I. Birt	5
dſon, b. ditto	11	b. W. Baldock	7
c. H. Day	7	c. J. Cooper	3
run out	4		
ant, b. I. Birt	2	not out	7
n, not out	9	c. R O. Stone	9
nden, c. R. Stone	1	ſhambled out	1
rd, b. I. Birt	0	c. R. Smith	1
c. ditto	0		
ant, b. ditto	0		
Byes	1	Byes	0
	52		37

return match, we underſtand, is to be
at Mountfield, on Saturday the 30th

The first-recorded leg-before-wicket
decision was in 1795, but here, a year
later, in a match in Wadhurst, Sussex,
a man named Cruttenden was
'shambled out'. Whether he was lbw,
run out while daydreaming, or
'shamming' when he knew he was out is
likely to remain a mystery for all time.

This young chap, though dressed in the style of his elders and betters, looks rather
too pensive to be a killer of all but the best bowling. Pencil and watercolour by
Henry Edridge.

Lord Frederick Beauclerk did not always dress like this, though the uncompromising expression conveys a hint of his notoriously impatient nature. A fine batsman, he averaged 61 in 1803, an astonishing performance for that time, even allowing that the wicket has gradually grown in size over the years. In 1797 he had taken 66 wickets, a record for major cricket until 1813. Though a man of the Church, he often let himself down with his fiery temper and rough language, especially in some of his important single-wicket contests. Beauclerk, a descendant of King Charles II, became an autocratic figure at Lord's, which he frequented for well over half a century.

Below: *A match at Chatham between sailors and soldiers or marines, 1802.*

Youthful determination radiates from the pint-size batsman – the spirit that kept foes at bay and built an Empire. Left: Lord James Hay, who grew up to become a soldier, and was shot dead from his horse while serving at Waterloo with the Brigade of Guards.

The first book of cricket instruction was published by Thomas Boxall, a skilful bowler, in 1801. Left: Although cricket was in slump in 1805, the churchyard, like this one in Warfield, Berks, continued to attract, probably for its tranquillity and flat ground.

51

Edward Hayward Budd, benign old man with his gun and his dog, once, when he was 23, amazed the cricket world by hitting a ball clean out of Lord's with his 3 lb bat. A vigorous player – as a bowler and fielder too – he often seemed intent on deciding a match with a few swift blows. Twice he made hits for nine in the days before boundaries were introduced. Born in Buckinghamshire, Budd eventually moved back to the country, dying in Wroughton, Wilts in 1875, aged 90. He scored the first century on the present Lord's ground.

An end-of-season contest between women of Surrey and Hampshire offered huge prizemoney.

Lord George Byron played in the first recognised Eton v Harrow match at Lord's in 1805, scoring 7 and 2 for Harrow (or 11 and 7 by his own account), 'together joined in cricket's manly toil' as he put it in Hours of Idleness. His club-foot made recreation difficult.

Advertising another grand cricket match at Lord's, 1816, with the invitation to buy equipment from Mr Lord's house, which was in Upper Gloucester Street, just past Marylebone workhouse.

The kinship that cricket can breed: James Warren Childe's 1817 painting gives the lad an undersize bat.

The Duke of Wellington, who watched his troops play cricket near Brussels just before the Battle of Waterloo, is alleged to have said that the battle was really won on the playing fields of Eton. Many a patriotic cartoonist dwelt on this, Wellington dispatching Napoleon with all kinds of delivery.

1 Long Stop	5 Umpire	9 Middle Wicket	13 Umpire
2 Long Slip	6 Hitter	10 Hitter	14 Long Field off
3 Wicket Keeper	7 Point	11 Scorers	15 Bowler
4 Short Slip	8 to cover Point & Middle Wicket	12 Legg	16 Long Field on

CRICKETING.

Cricket at Lewes, Sussex: the frontispiece to William Lambert's Instructions and Rules for Playing the Noble Game of Cricket (1816).

RURAL SPORTS OR A CRICKET MATCH EXTRAORDINARY.

nesday October 5 1811. A Singular Cricket Match took place at Balls Pond Newington. The Players on both sides were 22 Women 11 Hampshire against 11 Surrey. The Match was made between ... Noblemen of the respective ... for 500 Guineas ... The Performers in the Contest were of all Ages and Sizes.

The treatment that female cricket enthusiasts dread: Rowlandson ridicules the women of Hampshire and Surrey as they play for 500 guineas at Ball's Pond, Newington in October.1811. Below: Oxford Gentlemen take on a United England XI in Oxford around 1820.

William Lambert was regarded as the best batsman in England – one of a long, distinguished line of succession. But he was banished from big cricket in disgrace, deemed guilty of having 'sold' the England v Nottingham match in 1818. Heavy betting and rigging of matches were fairly common at this time. In 1817, the powerfully-built Surrey-born Lambert crowned a great career by becoming the first to score two centuries in a match (Sussex v Epsom at Lord's). This was also the first time 1000 runs had been recorded in a match. He averaged 63.57 that season, a record until W. G. Grace beat it in 1871. Lambert died in 1851, aged 72.

Rugby School, 1816. The boys had good coaches and the best facilities, and while they were inculcated with the moral virtues of cricket, they, like the pupils of a dozen or more other public schools, carried their talents into the Universities, counties and even into the England XI.

Charterhouse, 1816. The school was eventually moved from ever-swelling London to the quiet and blissful greenery of Godalming, Surrey in 1872. Peter May remains Charterhouse's greatest cricketing product.

Thomas Beagley, scorer of the first century in the Gentlemen v Players match at Lord's (113 not out in 1821, 15 years after the first of these great encounters). A powerful Hampshireman, he was also a fine long-stop.

Benjamin Aislabie (1774–1842) was the first MCC secretary, serving from 1822 until his death. A near-useless cricketer himself, and weighing 20 stone at the end, he was a popular, good-humoured administrator, described variously as 'quasi king of the MCC' and 'a hippopotamus among greyhounds'.

John Willes (on leading horse), from Kent, saw the possibilities of bowling roundarm when he saw his sister bowling it. (She had no option, with her hooped skirts.) For 15 years he bowled roundarm, and was unpopular. Then, on July 15, 1822, at Lord's, he was no-balled. He hurled the ball down in disgust and rode off, never to play in another important match. But evolution was on the march.

The spread of cricket reached grotesque lengths when sailors from HM battleships Fury and Hecla pitched wickets at Igloolik in the frozen north. Drawing by Captain Lyons, RN, c.1822.

George 'Squire' Osbaldeston, a short, dashing and strongly-built allround sportsman, was a frenzied fast underhand bowler and aggressive batsman, proud of his prowess to such an extent that when beaten at single-wicket by Brown of Brighton in 1818 he scratched his name from the MCC members' list.

William Ward, MP, scored 278 for MCC v Norfolk at Lord's in 1820 (his bat weighing over 4 lbs), a ground record until 1925. His place in history is made even more secure for his role in saving Lord's from the builders in 1825, when Thomas Lord was in financial difficulty. Ward bought his interest for £5000.

The Cricket Match, *a popular work by* *James Pollard, published 1824.*

Left: *Stirrings in faraway Australia. In* *1821 the New South Wales Governor,* *Lachlan Macquarie, orders through his* *storekeeper some cricket bats and balls* *for scholars at the local academy. More* *seeds of the game are thus planted.*

Below: *The village of Benenden, Kent* *overflowed with cricket talent, and of* *the Mills brotherhood Richard was* *outstanding. Left-handed, he was 'a* *severe punisher'.*

Rural St John's Wood, at Lord's ground, was as delightful a place as any to visit in the immediate post-Regency period.

Left: *Future Prime Minister Benjamin Disraeli, a painting completed in 1824 while he was staying with his publisher as his first novel neared completion.*

Below: *The pride of Yorkshire cricket in the late 1820s was the Darnall ground, near Sheffield, where there was seating for 8000. Here, in 1826, local left-hander Tom Marsden hit 227 in a big match; but his talent was dissipated before he was 30. In 1827 the first 'experimental match' was played here to test roundarm bowling, which was legalised soon afterwards. Darnall fell from favour because the rival Hyde Park ground was nearer to Sheffield.*

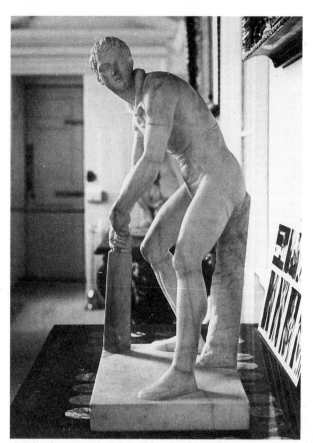

Cricket began to inspire all kinds of worship as it took a hold on public imagination. The imposing marble statue by Henri Rossi was completed in 1825, and a year later Dagley's Death's Doings *appeared, a book of defiant, wry prose and verse, stating – almost for the first time – that* Life's Like the Game of Cricket. *Below:* Not much of a crowd, but Lord's, whose pavilion burned down in 1825, was a restful haven.

ROUNDARM REVOLUTION

WALKER and Willes had toyed extensively with roundarm bowling – in which the arm swung through almost or entirely horizontally – only to face persistent and understandable disapproval. But batting had come to dominate bowling, and the tide of opinion strengthened towards legalisation. The chief protagonists by 1827 were the Sussex pair, F. W. Lillywhite and James Broadbridge, and it was decided that year to have three trial matches, Sussex v All-England. Sussex won at Sheffield and Lord's, at which point some of the England players refused to play the third match 'unless the Sussex bowlers bowl fair, that is, abstain from throwing'. Some withdrew, others played, and at Brighton, All-England won the third contest, thus helping the cause. The 'March of Intellect' style of bowling gained wider acceptance. Lillywhite, in his top-hat and cotton braces, and his colleague, Jem Broadbridge, had won the day. The revolution might not have been accomplished so quickly had not G. T. Knight (who bowled roundarm in the 'England' team) written a series of influential letters on the subject to the *Sporting Magazine*. He demolished the notion that a roundarm delivery was a 'throw'. The continued resistance of William Ward and Thomas Lord, John Nyren and player–journalist William Denison could not prevent a modification by MCC to Rule 10 in the spring of 1828. The bowler could now raise his arm to the level of the elbow; bowlers went on bowling through at shoulder height; the umpires did nothing about it; and in 1835 the arm was permitted to be swung through horizontally. For a few years it became a bowler's game once again – though wides, much more numerous in roundarm bowling, were now penalised for the first time.

George Thomas Knight, the one pioneer of roundarm who was effective in the campaign of words. His letters to the Sporting Magazine *pointed the way to cricket's 'growing up', leaving bowlers of the next generation to ponder over the possibilities of raising the arm further still: to complete overarm. Knight, a gentleman of Kent and Hampshire, who later lived abroad, was a nephew of novelist Jane Austen.*

A bat gauge dated 1827, reminder of a further duty for the umpires, in addition to watching the level of a bowler's arm.

Right: *William Lillywhite of Brighton, 'The Nonpareil', a cunning, mature bowler who, in 1837, became the first to take 100 wickets in a season in 'big' cricket. His skill and his role in forcing the acceptance of roundarm bowling placed him prominently in cricket's ranks of the immortals.*

Below: *Mr Ireland's Royal Gardens, Brighton, where the third experimental roundarm match was played in 1827.*

An Army–Navy cricket match of an unusual kind: Chelsea Hospital Pensioners (red coats) take on the naval veterans from Greenwich, missing limbs proving little bar to enthusiasm and effort. The watercolour was created by Henry Alken junior in 1825.

An early ancestor of the county match as known today. A Nottingham XI play host to a team from Leicestershire around 1829.

Betting on cricket – and even fixing, or trying to fix, the result – was still rife, even at Lord's, the conduct not always as wholesome as suggested by Leonard Hagety's sketch. The idyll of pre-Victorian cricket is assumed (below) in Ernest Prater's picture, an impression of 'our forefathers' at play on the village green.

'Short, fat, plain' Mary Russell Mitford lauded village cricket at the expense of the 'first-class' game. People 'degrade it into an affair of betting and hedgings and cheatings', she wrote. Her book Our Village, published in 1832, gives a warm insight into the humble version of the game during Georgian times. Miss Mitford died in Swallowfield, Berks in 1855, aged 68.

Fuller Pilch, photographed in Abe
Lincoln pose, was the finest batsman in
England between the Hambledon era
and W. G. Grace. Tall and erect, his bat
straight, he perfected forward play.
Born in Norfolk, he earned national
admiration, especially in 1834 when he
set a new season's aggregate record of
811. He was lured to Kent in 1836, at
the height of his career, for £100 per
annum, and eventually took over the
Saracen's Head Inn in Canterbury,
having seen his adopted county to much
success through his high-class batting
and shrewd generalship.

Pilch (1803–1870): lithograph by G. F. Watts.

Left: *'Honest Will' Caldecourt, an exemplary figure in the annals of the game. For
40 seasons he was engaged as a practice bowler at Lord's. He was also an
outstanding umpire, and coach at Harrow and Cambridge. And in a minor match,
Watford v Herts, he once hit six sixes off a six-ball over, over a century before Sobers
and Shastri performed the feat.*

The Duke of Wellington, leader of the Tories, succumbs to a full-toss from King William IV, lithographer C. J. Grant's comment on the dissolution of Parliament over the first Reform Bill of 1831.

Nyren's 1833 classic The Young Cricketer's Tutor and the Cricketers of My Time, *which owed much to Charles Cowden Clarke's literary skills, was fronted by Robert Seymour's delicate engraving of Lord's.*

Below: *On the banks of the Severn, by Fretherne Park, Gloucestershire, An XI of England (with Lillywhite) bowl to XX Gentlemen of Gloucestershire.*

Cricket before Stonehenge, *a watercolour painted in 1831 by J. Brown as a mark of respect to the Gentlemen of the Stonehenge Club.*

Below: *Rain, or something worse, seems about to halt the day's play, but William Davies, as painted by Thomas Henwood, stays cheerfully at his scorer's table, with scoring-book, clay pipe, and bottle of port . . . or two.*

A page, basic as could be, in William Davies' scorebook for 1832.

Early settlers in Australia ride away for temporary respite from the deprivations, a game of cricket being a reminder of home. Left: The Rev. J. H. 'Wacky' Kirwan, a mellow-looking gentleman, made history in his younger days by bowling down all 10 of MCC's wickets when they played Eton in 1835. Though a low roundarmer in action, he could bowl with fearsome speed.

NEW LAWS of the GAME of CRICKET, 183

INSTRUCTIONS FOR PLAYERS.

PITCHING THE WICKETS.—After the ground is agreed upon, which should be smooth and level turf, and the wickets pitched according to the following laws, let the party who are furthest from their home have the choice of innings, and pitching first wicket.

UMPIRES.—Let the one at the bowler's wicket stand exactly behind it, to mark the direction of the ball. His opponent also behind, but a little on one side of the opposite wicket.

BOWLERS.—Let the best hands be chosen without partiality or favour, as success depends greatly upon them. A slow bowler should deliver the ball so as to ground about three yards and a half before the wicket, and in fast bowling about five yards before it. If the ball be directed to the off stump, it will frequently be struck up, and cause a catch; if to the near stump, the striker will be likely to get some runs. The bowler should practise a particular turn of the wrist, which makes the ball twist in rising to the wicket, as it often puts the striker out. He should avoid letting the ball touch the ground more than once; and should use himself to either side of his wicket. He should deliver the ball in an upright posture, with the hand below the elbow, and keep his eye upon his wicket, so that if the bat's-man leave it before the ball is out of hand, he may be put out.

THE STRIKER should stand just behind the popping crease, keeping his legs clear of the wicket. The bat in guarding the wicket should be held upright, with the handle inclined a little forward before the middle stump, raising it a little as the ball is delivered, and marking with the eye where the ball pitches, in order to a good stroke. He should never think the ball will miss from its apparent direction, but always play as if he were certain it would hit. Let the face of the bat be held exactly even and parallel with the stumps. If the ball ground about four yards in front of the wicket, let him make a moderate stride forward with his left foot, keeping his right foot steady; by which means he will meet the ball before it can twist much; but if it ground at a greater distance, it may be safer ¬ke behi⌐ ⌐rease, takin⌐ ⌐o knock ⌐ If ⌐

stand before the popping crease ready to run, but mind the ball is fairly gone from the bo or he will be put out. Let each keep his bat on the outside of his partner, and be carefu against one another.

THE WICKET-KEEPER must see that the players are in their proper places, and give h by signs rather than by words, watching every opportunity to put the striker out, if he ground to run while the ball is in play. He should relieve the bowlers as much as i tossing the ball home to them.

FIRST SHORT-SLIP should stand so as to reach within two feet of the wicket-keeper hand, and must be an active player. He should run behind the wicket-keeper when the ba in, or take his place if he run after a ball. Sometimes a second short-slip is placed player and THE POINT.

THE POINT should be in a line with the popping crease, about seven yards from the by keeping his eye on the ball as it grounds, form his judgment whether the striker will hit

MIDDLE-WICKET OFF should stand not far from the bowler's wicket, and on the o throwing in the ball, he must not do it harder than necessary, and at about the same he bail. Should the bowler leave his place, this man should take it till he returns.

LEG OR HIP should stand a little farther back than the popping crease, and about si from the wicket.

LONG-STOP.—His station is behind the wicket-keeper, and he must be active in stop bowl, as well as catching one tipped with the edge of the bat. He must throw in well how he backs up.

TO COVER POINT AND MIDDLE WICKET.—Place a man between these two, but fu ⌐han they ⌐ ball whi⌐ ⌐ miss.

A new set of the Laws, with a good, grainy woodcut for decoration. Law 14 stated that a bowler may now raise his hand or arm in delivery as high as the elbow but no higher.

Lord's was often referred to as 'Dark's' during the years (1835–1864) of James Henry Dark's proprietorship of the ground. A keen player since the age of 10, and later an umpire in important matches, Dark bought the lease of Lord's from William Ward, and earned the gratitude of cricket-lovers by caring seriously for the ground and resisting all temptations to allow development on the land.

Fuller Pilch, playing in the 1837 Gentlemen v Players match at Lord's, is out 'hat knocked on wicket'. The four stumps were part of an experiment to even the balance, but the amateurs still lost by an innings.

Sheep kept the grass low at Lord's, though the cut would not have been very even.

69

Another bright morning at Lord's, with more players than spectators.

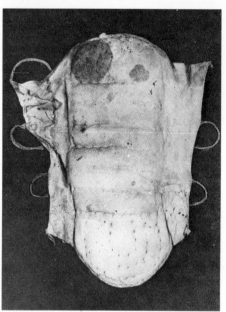

Right: *Edward Gower Wenman performed the exacting task of keeping wicket to Alfred Mynn with skill and bravery. From Benenden, Kent, Wenman later developed buckskin leg-guards (left).*

Left: *Commemorative handkerchief to mark the MCC 50th Anniversary match in July 1837, in which the South beat the North (with Box and Cobbett) on the second day.*

Right: *The elegant Ladies of Rochester in the process of beating the Ladies of Maidstone in Brown's Meadow in 1838.*

The mighty Alfred Mynn, huge of frame, warm of heart. Born in 1807, the 'Lion of Kent' was coached by the rebellious Willes, and after wild beginnings with his fast roundarm, he became more accurate, still swift, and too much for most of the batsmen who querulously faced him. The earth 'seemed to tremble' under his impressive six-pace approach, and the ball shot towards the batsman 'as if propelled from a Whitworth gun'. A second long-stop once spat blood for a fortnight after being hit by a Mynn delivery. He was a principal figure – with the bat too – for Kent and for the Gentlemen for two decades. In 1836 he was hit on the ankle during a North v South match at Leicester, and went on to make a century while in agony from the swelling. Tied to the roof of a stagecoach, he endured a bumpy 100-mile ride to London and there came close to having the leg amputated. As he prayed, the doctors changed their minds. The great days returned, especially as national single-wicket champion, but he knew the debtors' prison. He died in 1861, aged 54, much mourned.

William Clarke (1798–1855), a scheming slow bowler who learned from Lambert, was born near Nottingham and ended up founding Trent Bridge as a prospering venue for big matches (having married widow Chapman, who ran the Trent Bridge Inn – seen above in the late 1830s). Clarke, a former bricklayer, with only one eye since youth, moved to London at the age of 47, and became a practice bowler at Lord's. Suddenly, he was organising an 'All-England XI', and soon he had some of the finest cricketers in the land playing for him in 'evangelical' (and certainly profitable) matches all over the country as the railway networks sprang up, easing accessibility.

Entitled An Early Match on a Natural Pitch, this delicate sketch serves as a reminder of the rough surfaces upon which batsmen had to survive before pitch-care became an art. Right: The rotund Harry Sampson was one of the best early batsmen to come out of Yorkshire. A Sheffield publican, he held the record for the highest score on ice: 162. More impressively, he beat Tom Marsden at single-wicket in 1841.

All is style at Eton College: one of a set of 12 prints by Canon George Winter, published by Ryman about 1840.

74

Left: *The widening world of cricket – top, Northumberland Cricket Club's ground in Newcastle-upon-Tyne, long since built over; middle, a match in Melbourne, the costume of a different kind, in 1841, three years after the foundation of Melbourne Cricket Club; and bottom, an Army v Navy match at Portsmouth around 1840, the sailors in the field.*

Below: *Musical tribute (1839) to 'Honest' Baxter of Surrey as he prepared for his last match, on Richmond Green. Laudatory and joyful throughout, the composer felt the need to end with a reference to the spectre of Death: 'It's vain to block, your score of runs is full'.*

James Cobbett, Surrey-born, was one of the earliest of great spin bowlers: 'his fingers seemingly unglued, joint by joint, till the ball quitted the tips of them at last, just as you would spin a top'. He died of consumption at 38.
Below: *Robert James's much-loved* Tossing for Innings, *depicting local Nottingham chimney-sweeps.*

Sussex beating MCC (with Pilch and Martingell) at Tom Box's ground, Brighton in August 1844. C. G. Taylor (below) made, as the Illustrated London News put it, 'the very extraordinary number of 100 runs'. Taylor was described as the 'most finished batsman of the day', possessed of unflinching courage, science and activity.

Left: William Hillyer in 1845 became the first bowler to take 200 'first-class' wickets in a season. A Kent team-mate of Mynn's, he bowled at a brisk pace from a pleasing action, and cut the ball from leg. He was also a good slip fieldsman.

Aquila Clapshaw (1801–1860), a fourth-generation member of a bat-manufacturing family which carried on its business into the 1970s.

The Horns Tavern (since demolished), where Surrey County Cricket Club was inaugurated in 1845, at a dinner presided over by the Hon. Frederick Ponsonby (later the Earl of Bessborough).

Australian-born William Tunks, businessman, politician, cricket fanatic, who saw to it that the first challenge from Melbourne cricketers was taken up by those of Sydney in 1856. He was also instrumental in finding a proper ground in Sydney for important cricket, and was the NSWCA's first honorary treasurer. In 1845 he made the first century in Sydney of which record still exists.

What has come to be accepted as the first international cricket match was staged on September 24 and 25, 1844, between USA and Canada, in Harlem, New York, and this depiction, now in that city's museum, is thought to be of that site, St George's Cricket Ground, with 'The Red House' beyond. Canada won the match by 33 runs, and with it the $1000 stakemoney.

Hyde Park, Sydney, 1842. Now a park in the centre of a bustling city, the area was the setting for early matches of moment.

Left: *The 4th King's Own Regiment at play in Sydney, the barracks being adjacent to the land where eventually was built the Sydney Cricket Ground.*

Below: *Kent v All-England at Canterbury, 1845, on the old Beverley ground.*

CLARK'S TRENT-BRIDGE CRICKET GROUND.—NOTTINGHAM, AUGUST 22, 23, 24.

William Clarke's Trent Bridge ground in Nottingham, the scene of many a great performance in the years ahead, hosts a Nottingham v All-England match in 1842, Pilch, Mynn, Lillywhite & Co. proving far too strong for the locals.

CRICKET.—NOTTINGHAM *v.* ALL ENGLAND.—Final close of the game on Wednesday.

...D—First Innings.		Second Innings.			NOTTINGHAM—First Innings.		Second Innings.	
... by Barker	3				Butler Parr, c by Pilch	6	c by Wenman	2
... Noyes	0				Barker, c by Ponsonby	17	c by Dorrington	3
...edgate	11				Clark, b by Hillyer	18	b by Mynn	26
...itto	60				Guy, c by Box	8	b by Mynn	3
...Clark	61				S. Parr, b by Lillywhite	15	b by Mynn	5
... by Guy	21				Butler, c by Ponsonby	12	c by Ponsonby	24
... Guy	33				Good, c by Lillywhite	3	c by Pilch	1ι
...aby, c by Parr	7				Oscroft, run out	6	b by Lillywhite	5
... by Clark	12				Noyes, b by Dean	12	c by Hillyer	8
...Noyes	7	not out	1		Chapman, b by Mynn	11	not out	1
... not out	0	not out	3		Redgate, not out	8	b by Mynn	8
	13	Bye	1		Byes, &c.	6	Byes, &c.	9
	228		5			122		110

Sir Spencer Ponsonby Fane, J. L. Baldwin and Lord Bessborough, founders, in 1845, of I Zingari, a club for amateurs, its aim being to promote cricket in its 'finest' sense. The oldest of wandering clubs, it enjoyed an imposing fixture list last century, and now lists over a dozen England captains in its ranks over the years.

Left: *George Whieldon, who played for Derbyshire, with his recently-developed spliced bat, with the Lord's pavilion behind him, c.1845.*

79

TOWARDS SATURATION

CRICKET, regarded in many minds as the game for gentlemen, received a substantial injection of democracy when Clarke, with moneymaking in his mind, got together his All-England XI in 1846. They travelled to Cornwall and Lancashire and Ireland and Cambridgeshire, playing in unmanicured fields against eager and overawed town and village combinations often of 22 players, Clarke pocketing high percentages of the takings. The game was on the move. Fenner's was opened in 1846, and that season saw a telegraph scoreboard and scorecards being sold at Lord's for the first time. It was the year of the last great single-wicket championship. Cricket was being played in all parts of the British Empire. Calcutta Cricket Club was already an old club, and now Madras Cricket Club was formed. And, lest it be thought to have been a universally tranquil game, Canada and the USA suspended annual competition after a Canadian batsman charged bodily into the bowler as he was about to make a catch.

Harvey Fellows, pictured in the dignity of old age, was the fastest bowler yet seen when, in 1848, at the age of 22, he bowled with a speed described as 'electric' and 'terrific' – and all underhand. Even Pilch sometimes played him 'with his head turned away'.

The mighty Mynn with his talented little adversary Nicholas Felix (real name Wanostrocht) before their single-wicket challenge at Bromley, Kent in 1846. In two such matches that summer, both lost, the left-hander managed only four runs off the bat from 518 balls sent down by his gargantuan adversary.

George Nixon Duck, the least-appropriately named of batsmen, provides one of the earliest pictures (1848) of a protected species, even if he boasts only one leg-guard to go with his pair of batting gloves. Bristol-born, he played in Yorkshire and Scotland before settling in Surrey, where he became a vice-president of Beddington CC.

The Rev. Walter Marcon, like Fellows, a product of Eton, was just as fast as his contemporary, and had just as brief a career. He broke a batsman's leg at Oxford, and usually had three long-stops in addition to a wicketkeeper. All this with an underhand action.

The year 1848 was loaded with destiny in that it saw the birth of W. G. Grace at Downend, Bristol on July 18. Of all cricket's giants he remains the most towering figure for his dominance over a protracted period and for his immense influence on the game. His presence cast a lasting spell over the nation. Right is Downend House, where he was born; below is the actual room; below right is the family orchard, his cricketing nursery.

Clarke's moneymaking 'missionaries' of the All-England XI, 1847: Joseph Guy, George Parr, William Martingell, Alfred Mynn, William Denison (the first eminent cricket reporter), James Dean, William Clarke, Felix, Oliver Pell, William Hillyer, William Lillywhite, William Dorrington, Fuller Pilch, Thomas Sewell. Dorrington was to die the following year, victim of the cold, damp conditions often experienced by the travelling cricketers.

This charming painting of a match at Wittersham, Kent 'circa 1840–50' was once in the collection of Sir Jeremiah Colman, but in 1983 was considered a fake by Robin Simon, head of the Institute of European Studies in London, who suggested that the scoreboard featured was decades before its time.

Durham en fête *for the match against the star-studded All-England XI in May 1849. 'Old Clarke's' band won a low-scoring match, making 91 and 69 to the local XX's 67 and 51, only one Durham man reaching double figures.* **Below:** *A reasonably good crowd at The Oval in 1848, St Mark's Church towering in the background. Watercolour by C. J. Basébe.*

The Rev. James Pycroft, whose classic The Cricket Field *was first published in 1851. It was rich in detail of 18th- and early 19th-century cricket, and featured an engaging interview with Beldham.* Top right: *Main entrance to The Oval, c.1850, spectators arriving by coach.* Right: *The dawn of cricketana: Staffordshire figures and fairings decorated mantelpieces – and fetched big prices at auction a century and a half later.*

Wherever they went the English took tea and cricket. German artist Carl Werner painted these enthusiasts in Rome in 1850.

It didn't even need to be dry. In 1854 (others have tried it since) these adventurers landed on the Goodwin Sands at 5 pm and played till almost sunset. 'This awfully melancholy place,' a reporter called it: 'Here thousands of gallant fellows have been entombed – here millions of property have been engulfed'.

Disabled Greenwich pensioners – 'these worn-out sons of the ocean' – took the field, in 1848, to the band's blaring rendition of Rule Britannia, *but soon had the crowd 'in an almost continued roar of laughter by the grotesque figures the poor old veterans made'.*

The Cricket Ground, Harrow, from which have sprung University, county and Test players. This strongly textured work is by Nathaniel Whittock. Below: The Town and University of Cambridge (1847) bears the unmistakable touch of N. Felix, and became one of the rarest of cricket lithographs.

Lipschitz's pirated version of A Cricket Match between Sussex and Kent, originally engraved by Phillips after portraits by Drummond and Basébe and published by W. H. Mason. The imaginary gathering of great figures of the 1840s is set in Ireland's Royal Gardens, Brighton, with Pilch facing Lillywhite, Wenman the non-striker, Tom Box keeping wicket, and Caldecourt umpiring at this end.

Strokes of the day: illustrative guide for the batsman of 1845 who wished to improve his game: based on Felix's work.

PLAY

THE DRAW

HOME BLOCK

FORWARD

THE CUT

LEG HALF VOLLEY

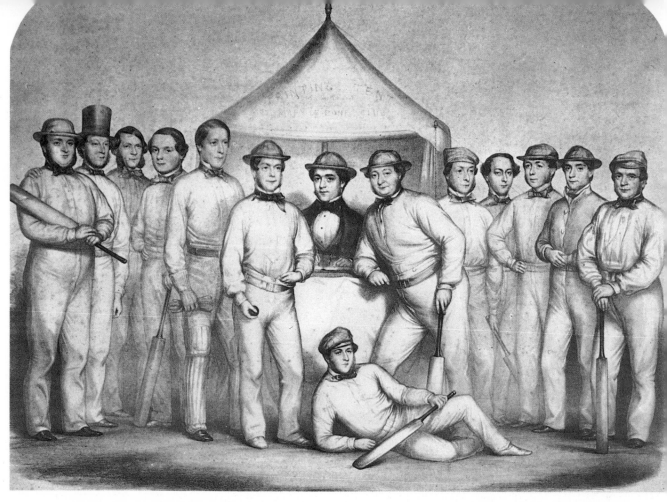

The United England XI, a breakaway touring band of professionals, set up in 1852 by John Wisden and Jemmy Dean out of discontent at Clarke's greed and dictatorial attitude. Those lined up in J. C. Anderson's lithograph of the mid-1850s are, from left: Hunt, Wright, Adams, Mortlock, Lockyer, Wisden, Frederick Lillywhite, John Lillywhite (reclining in front), Dean, Caffyn, Grundy, Martingell, Sherman, and Sampson. Fred Lillywhite, positioned in his printing tent, printed scorecards, fed the Press with scores, and published his now rare Guide to Cricketers *from 1849 to 1866. The United XI and the All-England XI eventually sank their differences and played 'grand' matches against each other for the players' charity.*
Below: *Actors v Merchants at Lord's, mid-1850s: more revenue for the ground's proprietor.*

Probably the oldest surviving photograph of a cricket match: Roger Fenton's exposure of the 1857 match between Hunsdonbury and the Royal Artillery.

Left: *Run-diggers rather than gold-diggers – the USA team which met Canada at Hoboken, New Jersey in 1856, in the seventh match in this oldest of international series.*

Alarm at the prospect of injury from fast bowling is nothing new. Punch had something to say in 1854. Right: Thomas Hughes's influential period classic Tom Brown's School Days *first appeared in 1857.*

Cricket was played in Holland in the middle of the 19th century — though here there seems danger of play being stopped by a burst dyke. The Dutch — some of them — have remained keen on the game, and have boasted victories over modern Test teams on their matting pitches.

John Corbet Anderson's lithograph of four famous Surrey cricketers of the 1850s and 1860s: Tom Sherman, fast bowler and daring batsman; Julius Caesar, aggressive batsman; William Caffyn, fine batsman who coached in Australia; and Tom Lockyer, who succeeded Box as the best wicketkeeper in England.

Cricket on the Padang, Singapore in 1851, a year before the Singapore Cricket Club was founded. There were then fewer than 500 whites resident in the colony, and as in so many corners of Empire, the game meant a comforting link with the routines and flavours of 'home'.

A garrison cricket match on the Esplanade in Corfu, 1853. The Greek island was then a British protectorate, and cricket of an idiosyncratic kind has been played there ever since.

'Felix' (Nicholas Wanostrocht) (1804–1876), cricketer, schoolmaster, artist, inventor of a bowling machine and tubular India-rubber batting gloves, and author of another of cricket's classics, the instructional Felix on the Bat, *first edition published 1845.*

Tom Box (1808–1876), Sussex-born, was the leading wicketkeeper of his day, working in partnership with the immaculate bowler Lillywhite.

One of the world's great grounds new-born: Old Trafford, Manchester kicked off with a match between Manchester and Liverpool in 1857.

Left: *Free Foresters in 1859, three years after the club's foundation. They played against county teams and fielded some famous names, though a Rugby schoolboy observed that 'all of 'em have got grey hair except three, and they've none at all'.*

Right: *V. E. 'Teddy' Walker, perhaps the best allrounder in the world in 1860, took all 10 Surrey wickets for England at The Oval in 1859 and then scored a century.*

G. MARSHALL   F.F. MORRES   W. HAMMERSLEY   A. BURCHETT   B. GRINDROD   G. ELLIOTT   J. BRYANT
T. WILLS   J.B. THOMPSON   JOE RHODES   W. FAIRFAX   THORNTON   E.H. WHITLOW

This Victoria team beat New South Wales at Sydney in 1859 by two wickets in the big match of the season.

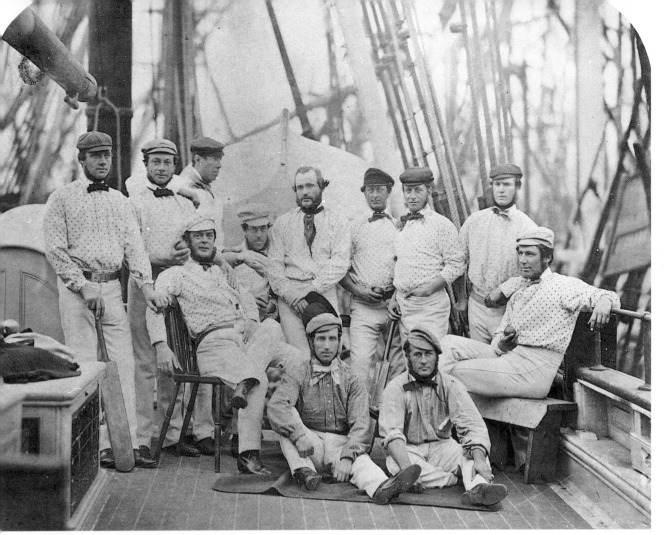

The first overseas touring team: George Parr's English side which sailed from Liverpool to North America on September 7, 1859. Managed by Fred Lillywhite, whose account of the tour initiated a prolific genre, the side won all five matches (against odds of 22) in Montreal, Hoboken, Philadelphia, Hamilton and Rochester. Pictured are John Wisden on the kitchen chair, John Jackson on the bench, Alfred Diver and John Lillywhite in front, and, standing, Robert Carpenter, William Caffyn, Tom Lockyer, H. H. Stephenson (crouching), Parr, James Grundy, Julius Caesar and Tom Hayward. The opposition on this pioneer tour was poor. Wisden had bowling figures of 8 for 39, 14 for 24, 16 for 17, and 13 for 43.

The Englishmen's voyage across the Atlantic was a nightmare of icebergs and tossing seas, prompting Wisden's celebrated remark that the briny was in need of the roller. The players were lucky to survive the journey – and were then delivered late when the captain of Nova Scotia missed the Gulf of St Lawrence at the first time of asking. Life was not all that much more comfortable (right) while travelling through North America, and though subsequent touring teams have had hardships of other kinds while visiting farflung parts, seldom have players had to play in muffs and greatcoats, as happened in Rochester.

John Ritchie's cherished Village Cricket, *evocative as an old cricket painting could ever be*. Left: Youth and Old Age, *or* A Game of Cricket, *by Alexander Hohenlohe Burr portrays a poignant and eternal theme.*

George Parr (1826–1891), 'the Lion of the North', Clarke's successor as leader of Notts and All-England, batsman supreme after the age of Pilch, and pioneer of overseas tours. Left: Bowled by a shooter, no uncommon occurrence on the poorly-prepared pitches of the day

Grand National Cricket Match, English-born goldfields artist S. T. Gill's view of the NSW v Victoria match on Sydney's Outer Domain in January 1857, with the townsfolk, merchants, businessmen, militia and pedlars all in attendance. The home team won by 65 runs, making 80 and 86 to Victoria's 63 and 38 in this second match in the series.

Boy Playing Cricket, *a study of an Aboriginal by J. M. Crossland, completed at the Poominindie Mission, South Australia.*

elow: The intercolonial rivalry continues between Victoria and NSW, this 858 match in Melbourne, only a couple of years after the establishment of the Melbourne Cricket Ground, being won by Victoria by 171 runs (59 and 238 to 7 and 69). Two of W. G. Grace's cousins played in the match, George Gilbert or NSW and William Rees for Victoria. This lithograph by Henry S. Glover ow hangs in the MCG Museum.

ACROSS THE WIDER SEAS

ENGLAND's first tour, to North America in 1859, hazardous though it was, could only be but a dress rehearsal for the greatest venture of all, to the awakening continent, and developing community, of Australia. The Melbourne catering firm of Spiers & Pond got Anglo-Australian cricket competition under way by sponsoring the venture – though it should be pointed out that the cricket tour was only their second choice: Charles Dickens had turned down a lecture tour. After several top players had declined, a team of 12 was gathered, the nucleus being Surrey men, and they sailed from Liverpool on October 20, 1861, aboard SS *Great Britain*, bound for Melbourne via the Cape of Good Hope. Arriving on Christmas Eve, to a tumultuous reception, H. H. Stephenson and his team were at practice at a secret location next day, Christmas Day, and were in good fettle for the inaugural match, against a Victorian 18, or more exactly an 18 of Melbourne and suburban clubs, at Melbourne Cricket Ground on New Year's Day 1862. In all they won six matches, drew four, and lost to 22 of Castlemaine and 22 of NSW & Victoria. The pattern for numerous absorbing England v Australia encounters to come was set, with Yorkshireman Roger Iddison commenting, not altogether prophetically, at the end of this first tour: 'Ah doan't think mooch to their play, boot they're a woonderful lot o'drinkin' men!'

The long voyage behind them, Stephenson's team reach the haven of their Melbourne hotel, the Cafe de Paris in Bourke Street. Their arrival was an excellent Christmas present for some of the more awe-struck and eager locals.

The first English team to tour Australia, 1861–62: William Mortlock (Surrey), William Mudie (Surrey), George Bennett (Kent), Charles Lawrence (Surrey), Heathfield Harman Stephenson (captain, Surrey), W. B. Hallam (Spiers & Pond's agent), William Caffyn (Surrey), George Griffith (Surrey), Tom Hearne (Middlesex), Roger Iddison (Yorkshire), Tom Sewell jnr (Surrey), Edward Stephenson (Yorkshire). Missing from this pre-voyage group is George 'Tiny' Wells (Sussex), who sailed ahead with his wife.

This and the two pictures following, all believed to be unpublished previously, are the earliest photographs of an international cricket match. All were taken by C. Nettleton of Melbourne, and this one shows the Eighteen of Victoria in the field against the first English team in their opening match.

The crowd was estimated at 15,000 (with others looking in) on the opening day of England's Melbourne match, which lasted four days. England won by an innings and 96 runs. Above: Griffith, a left-hander, is taking strike for England. Below: England in the field, the wicketkeeper probably H. H. Stephenson.

Right: At Sydney the English side played before another large crowd, as S. T. Gill's watercolour testifies.

The era of the photographer had arrived, though the size and weight of his equipment were for some years to be a handicap. So too was the necessarily slow shutter speed, as shown in this group of cricketers from Annesley, Notts as long ago as 1860.

Right: *Joseph Wells, father of H. G. Wells, the novelist. In 1862 he became the first to take four wickets in four balls, playing for Kent v Sussex at Box's ground in Brighton.*

Edgar Willsher (1828–1875).

By 1860 the British residents of Hong Kong had a cricket ground, the Government having allocated some harbourside land, which was used for over 100 years. A mat-shed became the first clubhouse.

100

A scene from the historic Surrey v All-England match at The Oval late in August 1862, in which All-England raised the first total of 500, most of the runs coming from Grundy (95), Carpenter (94) and Hayward (117). It remains a match of great moment, however, for what happened on the second evening. Edgar Willsher (pictured left) walked quickly and quietly up to the crease to bowl his left-arm fastish ball to the Surrey opener. For years there had been dissatisfaction at the height of the bowling arms of Willsher and others. Now, umpire John Lillywhite, at the bowler's end, called 'no-ball' – again and again. Eventually Willsher, a tall, slim Kentish man with a faraway look in his eyes and only one lung, stalked off the field, his players following. Lillywhite, ironically the son of the bowler who forced roundarm acceptance, was asked by the Surrey committee to relent, refused, and was replaced. The match continued, to be drawn after three days – 'though with a little less waste of time it might have been [finished]' according to a contemporary report. Willsher, the best bowler in England at that time, continued to play, and in 1864 MCC rewrote Law 10, permitting bowlers to bring the arm through at any height.

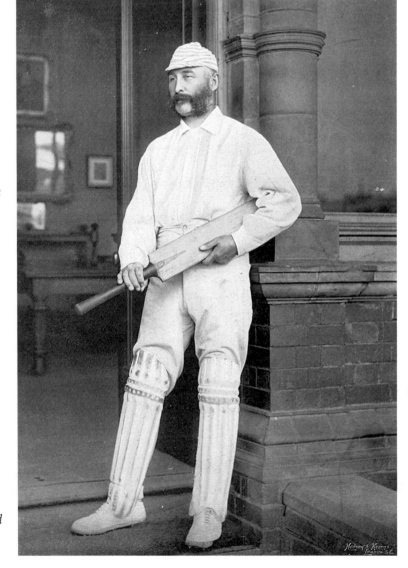

Right: E. M. Grace, 'The Coroner', elder brother of 'WG'. In 1862 he took 5 for 77 and 10 for 69 and scored 192 not out for MCC v Gentlemen of England at Canterbury.

Nottinghamshire 1862, one of the strongest combinations of Victorian times. Standing: Richard Daft, James Grundy, George Parr, George Anderson (umpire), John Jackson, Charles Brampton, A. E. Bateman, John Johnson (hon. sec.), George Wootton, Alfred Clarke (son of William); in front: Cris Tinley, Charles Daft, Sam Biddulph. 'Foghorn' Jackson weighed 14 stone and generated fierce pace from a run-up of only four yards. He was accurate by roundarm standards, pitching in the occasional head-high full-toss, and took 671 wickets in important matches between 1857 and 1863. He died in a Liverpool workhouse in 1901 and had a pauper's burial. Tinley, in contrast, switched from fast to slow underhand bowling with great success. Tinley and Jackson: 'a corkscrew at one end and a thunderbolt at the other'. Below: Parker's Piece, Cambridge, with the gaol in the distance, and straw boaters now in vogue. Many a talent was fostered here, including that of the young Jack Hobbs.

The All-England XI play the breakaway United All-England XI at Lord's in May 1863, proceeds going to the Cricketers' Fund Benefit Society (for whose support there was dire need). Takings over the two days, with 11,158 attending the match, were £303.12.0, £116 of which had to be paid out to the players engaged in the contest.

Below: Tom Hayward and Robert Carpenter, two of the best professional batsmen in the land in the 1860s. Both from Cambridgeshire, which county enjoyed a few years of glory through their heavy scoring, they served rival travelling teams, but came together as a powerful force for the Players v the Gentlemen.

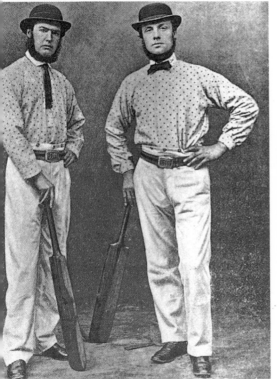

The Adelphi Hotel, Sheffield, birthplace of Yorkshire County Cricket Club in January 1863. Mine host was Harry Sampson, and Michael Ellison was elected president by the group of enthusiasts.

Slindon Cricket Club, in Sussex, traces its history back to this group of 1863 and beyond. They played on the village common.

England's second tour of Australia took place in 1863–64, and the team are seen here playing on Sydney's Domain, where they met 22 of NSW in three matches. The opposition was feeble, their 106 wickets (the second match was drawn owing to bad weather) falling for only 443 runs. Parr's English team broke off their Australian tour halfway and crossed the Tasman Sea to play some matches in New Zealand.

The Albert Ground, in Redfern, an inner suburb of Sydney, where major matches were played. Some famous players, Spofforth among them, sprang from the Albert Club, which established its ground in 1864 and had visions of attaining the eminence of the Melbourne Cricket Club. Problems with rent and friction with the NSWCA brought about the ground's demise.

The second English team to Australia, photographed at Lord's before the voyage: Robert Carpenter, Julius Caesar, R. C. Tinley, Alfred Clarke, George Tarrant, E. M. Grace, George Parr (captain), Tom Lockyer, John Jackson, Tom Hayward, George Anderson, William Caffyn, the only player who had been on the first tour. He stayed in Australia for seven years as a coach, as had Charles Lawrence of the 1861–62 team.

Team groups of 1863, each of a varying background. Here confidently sit the Eton XI, with Alfred Lubbock, on the third seat from the left, one of the most talented young batsmen in England. Next year, when captain, he scored 174 not out against Winchester, and though available only occasionally in ensuing years of first-class cricket, he revealed a special batting skill, almost rivalling W. G. Grace.

Residents of Yokohama, Japan make a team to play against the British Fleet when it called. The game was never to catch on in the land of the rising sun.

Chichester Priory CC, 1863, before a dining-room which still exists. Seated with bat is James Dean, and next to him, arm on rest, James Lillywhite jnr, who led the first English Test tour of Australia. The full-length figure on the left, in bowler hat, one hand in pocket, is Henry Foster, who fathered the famous Worcestershire brotherhood, and in the centre of the photograph, bareheaded, is Archibald Lewis Smith, who became MCC president in 1899.

Above: *New Year's Day 1864, and the English team start their Australian tour with a fixture against 22 of Victoria before a large crowd at Melbourne.*

Left: *George Parr, the English captain, seen as cricket missionary in the bush.*

Above: *Tom Humphrey and Harry Jupp, two prolific batsmen for Surrey. In 1864 the former became the first to reach 1000 runs in a first-class season.*

Left: *Young America 1864, containing four members of the amazing Newhall family. The Civil War did little to help cricket's survival across the Atlantic, although Philadelphia remained a stronghold for some years yet.*

Wisden Cricketers' Almanack: *the first edition 1864. The 'bible' for cricket-lovers saw off all competition, including the Lillywhite publications, to become the premier annual reference book.* Right: *The founder, John Wisden (1826–1884), 'The Little Wonder' from Brighton. A tiny man, he was still a fast roundarm bowler, and took all 10 wickets, bowled, for North v South at Lord's in 1850. Next season he took 455 wickets in all matches. He was a fair bat, too, scoring 148 in the first match at Bramall Lane, in 1855. His name lives on with the Almanack and the monthly magazine.*

Below: *A joyous celebration of youthful triumph: Henry Garland's* Winner of the Match: Excelsior Cricket Club, Islington.

A Mountain Called Grace

CRICKET has seen a number of truly great players, and some who justify the description 'phenomenal', for they improved techniques and altered attitudes, and drew towards the game such attention as it had not usually known. Of these, William Gilbert Grace, born near Bristol on July 18, 1848, retains pride of place for several reasons. He was so much better than his contemporaries that probably only Bradman has ever matched him in this respect; he set so many new records that it seemed almost unfair that such a giant should be permitted to roam among pigmies; and everything about him was associated with magnitude – size of scores, aggregates of runs, centuries and wickets, physical bulk (especially when the superb athletic shape of early years gave way to a paunch), length of career (an astonishing 44 seasons), and not least his overbearing presence, which alone crushed his more timid opponents. Paradoxically he had a shrill, high-pitched voice, and, far from fearing him, his close friends adored him. Much of his gamesmanship was at the expense of weaker personalities. He graduated as a doctor of medicine, but still cricket came first. He was always listed as an amateur, yet he made heaps of money out of tour and match fees and testimonials. He and Gladstone were the most easily recognisable men in England in the last quarter of the 19th century, and it seems evident that the fame – and bearded face – of 'WG', 'The Old Man', 'The Doctor', 'The Champion', will always be synonymous with cricket, the game he changed, by his wonderful batting, from a 'one-stringed instrument into a many-chorded lyre'.

Young Grace, a champion athlete as well as a prodigious cricketer. He announced his arrival in big cricket with scores of 170 and 56 not out for South Wales v Gentlemen of Sussex at Hove in July 1864. He turned 16 two days after the match.

The Sussex team of 1864, in front of the Royal Brunswick pavilion.

English Civil Service XI in a French field, Paris Cricket Club batting.
Below: HMS Britannia's team takes time off from ruling the waves.

Rawdon Lee and William Akerigg, stalwarts of Kendal Cricket Club, Cumberland: an 1865 studio photograph.

Annandale sports ground, lying below Simla, India, in 1865. When British soldiers played here during the Second World War the pitch was pointing across the field, and the Himalayas far to the left formed a sightscreen 'at the Tibet end'.

Cricket on the Barbados Garrison Savannah around 1865: a modern impression by Kathleen Hawkins. That year Barbados and British Guiana (now Guyana) played 'home and home' matches for the first time, Guyana's all-out 22 remaining an unsavoury record.

Left: *The I Zingari team which played Gentlemen of Norfolk at Sandringham in 1866. The Prince of Wales (future King Edward VII) sits left of centre.*

Below: *The stylish pavilion at Lord's, built to replace the one destroyed by fire in 1825, and enlarged during the winter of 1865–66.*

An 1866 allusion to the professional cricketer's dependence on the game's patrons: an unchanging factor.

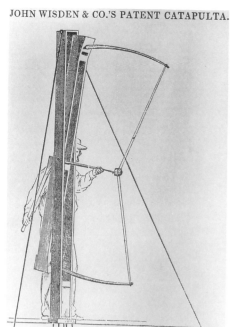

JOHN WISDEN & CO.'S PATENT CATAPULTA.

The principle of working the Catapulta will be shown at 2, New Coventry Street, Leicester Square, London, W.

Perhaps owing something to the Agincourt tradition, Wisden's Catapulta was advertised in 1867.

Five brothers Grace sit with the West Gloucestershire team at Knole Park, Bristol in July 1866: WG, almost beardless, is extreme left; brother Henry, in a striped shirt, is next to him, with EM and Alfred (in cap) next to him; GF (Fred) sits in front of Alfred. The father of the clan, Dr H. M. Grace, is in a top-hat, centre of back row; and there are two cousins (Pocock) in the group. West Gloucs won – as was their custom – by an innings.

Left: *William Nicholson, another who 'saved Lord's'. He advanced over £18,000 in 1866 to ensure that MCC would secure the freehold.*

Comfort for the patrons of Lord's cricket ground came with the new grandstand in 1867, purchased for £1435 by a consortium of MCC members who sold it to the club in 1869 for £1703. In 1867 the Press were granted special facilities at Lord's for the first time.

The Tasmanian team – or some of it – which played Victoria in 1867. A year later the Tasmanians were dismissed for 18 by Victoria in Melbourne. It was to be over 100 years before the 'Apple Isle' was to be accepted into the Sheffield Shield competition.

Right: Edmund Ferdinando Sutton Tylecote, wicketkeeper and batsman, of Oxford, Kent, the Gentlemen, and England, who scored 404 not out in a Clifton College house match in 1868, the first quadruple-century ever recorded.

Keen and cheerful Yorkshire pro Tom Emmett, a fast left-arm bowler, took 16 wickets in a day against Cambridgeshire at Hunslet in 1869. About this time he and George Freeman (fast right-arm) were a formidable combination on pitches that were generally substandard. Emmett, nonetheless, put plenty of work on the ball, and was never short of a wry comment in his thick dialect. He played in England's first Test match and returned twice more to Australia, and toured America, later becoming coach at Rugby School, but dying in 1904 in straitened circumstances.

A naval dockyard team, Sheerness, 1867, well-dressed, fit-looking, and unchanging forever through the magic of the new photographic process.

C. I. Thornton, a hitter of vast distances, raced to 107 off 29 scoring strokes in 70 minutes at Scarborough in 1866, for the Gentlemen of England v I Zingari. He played for Eton, Cambridge, Kent, Middlesex and assorted other teams, and was chief founder of the Scarborough Festival. He could drive a cricket ball over 150 yards, and at Canterbury he once hit all four balls of an over from V. E. Walker out of the ground.

William Midwinter, the only man to play Test cricket for England v Australia and vice versa. Born in the Forest of Dean, Gloucestershire in 1851, in 1869 he scored the first-known double-century in Australia, 256 for Bendigo v Sandhurst. The deaths of a son, wife and daughter within a year destroyed him. He died a year later in an asylum.

Some of the 1868 English team seem to be gaining little enjoyment from their visit to Niagara Falls, though the need to 'freeze' for the camera may account for their expressions. They won five and drew the other of their six matches, and never did the opposition look like totalling 100 runs in an innings.

THE NATIVE THAT CANNOT BE BOWLED OUT.

The Native that Cannot be Bowled Out: *Benjamin Disraeli, Prime Minister, at the crease, autumn 1868; wicketkeeper W. E. Gladstone soon about to displace him for the first of his four terms.*

113

Charles Dickens had a soft spot for cricket, and is portrayed here getting a charity match under way in front of his Kent home, Gadshill Place, with an underhand delivery, while the players – the batsman excepted – give him a cheer. The oil painting is thought to have been executed around 1868.

An exceptionally rare photograph of Lord's, possibly around 1870, and probably showing an Eton v Harrow match, to judge from the abundance of top-hats and crinolines. The newish Tavern (built 1868) is clearly visible on the far side.

The Aboriginal team at Melbourne in 1866. In 1868 some of these brought unusual entertainment, if scant cricketing talent, to England – Johnny Mullagh apart, for he was a player of rare skill. Mullagh scored 1698 runs and took 245 wickets on the tour. Cuzens, too, did the double, but apart from Charles Lawrence, the former Surrey player, who led them, the performances of the rest were poor, understandably when the strange climate and conditions are taken into account. Before the tour the team played in Australia, under the guidance of Tom Wills, a Victorian player (some of whose family were killed by Aborigines). The group pictured are: standing at the back – Tarpot, T. W. Wills, Mullagh; front – King Cole, Dick-a-Dick, Jellico, Peter, Red Cap, Harry Rose, Bullocky, Cuzens. King Cole died in London during the tour, having contracted pneumonia. Many English spectators were left with thrilling memories of the demonstrations of boomerang-throwing and other native skills.

As J. T. Wilson saw the main entrance to The Oval in 1870.

Left: Ted Pooley, Surrey wicketkeeper, who set a record by making 12 dismissals in a match, Surrey v Sussex, at The Oval in 1868. He would have played in the first of all Test matches, except that he was still in custody in Christchurch, NZ after trying to cheat a local. Pooley finished up in Lambeth workhouse.

115

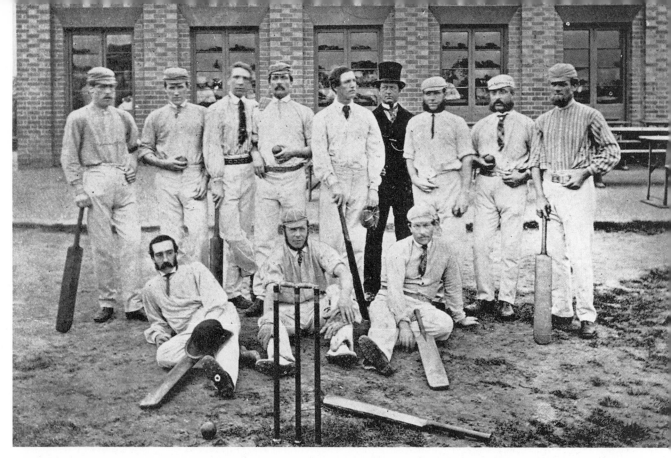

George Summers (reclining left) in 1870 became the first player to be killed in a first-class cricket match. Batting for Notts against MCC at Lord's, he was struck on the head by a ball from fast bowler John Platts of Derbyshire. The ball may have hit a pebble upon pitching. Summers 'reeled like a teetotum and fell' and W. G. Grace (who made a century and a duck in the match) rendered what assistance he could. But Summers, unwisely undertaking a bumpy train ride back to Nottingham, died four days later. The strong Notts XI of 1869, above, is: standing – Fred Wild, William McIntyre, William Oscroft, Jemmy Shaw, Richard Daft, Jemmy Grundy (umpire), George Wootton, Alfred Shaw, Walter Price; front – Summers, Sam Biddulph, Tom Bignall. Daft went in to bat with a towel and scarf wrapped round his head after Summers had been removed from the field.

William Yardley, who was keeping wicket when Summers fell (if the batsman had ducked Yardley would have 'got it between the eyes'). Yardley scored the first century this year (1870) in the long series of Varsity matches.

George 'Tear'em' Tarrant died in 1870, aged only 31. He was part of the Cambridgeshire strength, and second in speed to only John Jackson: 'all over the place like a flash of lightning' said WG. When he toured Australia in 1863–64 he inspired the boy Spofforth.

Yorkshire's George Freeman, an auctioneer, took over as the best fast bowler in England after Jackson's decline. He bruised WG at Lord's in 1870, the great man claiming in afteryears that Freeman troubled him most in his younger days.

Another rare photo of Lord's ground, probably shot from where the Warner Stand is now situated.

At the opposite end of the Universe things were starting to stir: a semi-casual game on Nelson Square, Picton. After years of international struggle New Zealand were destined to enjoy succulent fruits of success at long last in the 1980s.

Blackballing a Member was the caption to this entry in Percy Cruikshank's Comic Almanack for 1869. It remains unclear at which age group the humour was directed.

In 1870 James Southerton raised the record with 210 first-class wickets in a season. A cunning roundarm offspinner, he played for three counties in one season, but settled for Surrey when county qualifications were introduced in 1873. He played in the first Test match, his age then being 49 years 119 days. He was landlord of The Cricketers pub in Mitcham for some years.

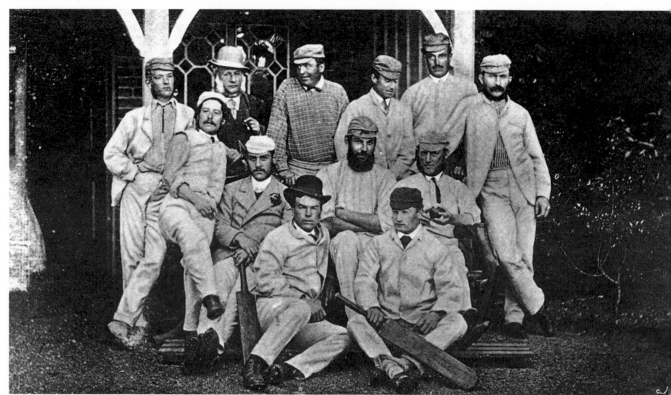

W. G. Grace had a triumphant season in 1871, becoming the first to reach 2000 runs and to hit 10 centuries in a season, and 1000 runs in a month. Here he sits with an unusually animated United South of England XI: back – Pooley, John Lillywhite, Griffith, Tom Humphrey, Silcock, James Lillywhite jnr; seated – Charlwood, G. F. Grace, WG, Southerton; front – Jupp, Richard Humphrey.

F. C. Cobden, a fast roundarm bowler, was one of those rare cricketers to have had his name bestowed on a match. He won the 1870 Varsity match at Lord's by dismissing the last three Oxford batsmen in three balls, Cambridge winning by two runs.

Left: 'Out!' but it's not the end of the world.

Below: *The East Melbourne XI which beat Melbourne in the 'Lost Ball' match of 1871. A hit through the railed fence was chased by an East Melbourne fielder, who fell heavily in vaulting the railing. 'Lost ball' was called, six runs were awarded, but when the batting side eventually lost by two runs it was claimed that the batsmen had run eight before the cry of 'Lost ball'. The decision stood.*

Left: *After three tours of North A[merica]
by English professional combinat[ions],
in 1872 an amateur side venture[d],
playing before variably-sized cro[wds],
swamping the opposition (top sc[ore]
against them: 31) and returning
undefeated. WG scored 142 in To[...]
From the left: A. Lubbock, R. A.
Fitzgerald (MCC secretary), A.
Appleby, W. H. Hadow, C. J. O[...]
W. G. Grace, W. M. Rose, A. N.
Hornby, Hon. George (later Lor[d]
Harris, F. P. U. Pickering, C. K.
Francis, E. Lubbock. Fitzgerald,
leader, wrote an amusing book on
expedition, Wickets in the Wes[t]
which disclosed the absurd brevit[y]
WG's speeches.*

Below: *Arthur Appleby holds a [...]
New Jersey.*

Left: *Richard Humphrey, younger brother of Tom, also of Surrey[,]
turned from plumbing to professional cricket and was a stylish, c[...]
batsman, who had a highly successful season in 1872, when he m[ade a]
superb 96 for Players v Gentlemen at Lord's and two seventies for
Surrey in their match against Yorkshire (with Emmett and Hill) [...]
Oval. Thereafter Dick Humphrey's form slumped, and he turned [to]
umpiring in 1881, and coached at Clifton College. His body was
recovered from the Thames in February 1906.*

*Clifton Cricket Club,
Bristol, playing on the
Downs, near Hollybush Lane,
probably in the early 1870s.*

The cricketers of HMS Britannia at play in 1873, probably at Hambledon.

In 1873, W. G. Grace scaled another virgin peak in achieving the 2000 runs/100 wickets double. He also hit the first century before lunch (for Gentlemen of the South v Players of the South at The Oval). 'The early part of the season was very wet,' he later wrote, 'and batting generally was not up to the standard of previous years.' He was married this year.

Amateur batsmen were now dominating the game, and only two professionals could rank with them in 1873: Harry Jupp of Surrey and Richard Daft (above), the Notts captain after George Parr, who excelled at back play against the fast bowlers. He made his highest score in 1873: 161 v Yorkshire.

Arthur Haygarth (1825–1903), to whom students of cricket history owe an incalculable debt. Self-effacing and meticulous, he began gathering material at 16, while at Harrow. All 14 volumes of Scores & Biographies were his work, and provide a mass of detail from 1744 to 1878.

Prince's Ground, West London, was an important venue for cricket matches until the early 1880s, when development – bricks and mortar – squeezed it out of existence. It had survived this 1874 American baseball sortie, and had seen some thrilling performances with bat and ball, including the first-ever score of 600 (by Oxford), in 1876.

Harry Phillips of Sussex made a substantial contribution to the game's improvement when, in the match against Gloucestershire in 1873, he dispensed with his long-stop and took full responsibility for his wicketkeeping. In time, especially as keepers became less brave and stood back to fast bowlers, long-stops were scoffed at altogether.

Left: Brown boots suited the Yorkshiremen in 1875. There were some mighty players here. At back: G. Martin (umpire), John Thewlis snr; standing: George Pinder, George Ulyett, Tom Armitage, Joe Rowbotham, Allen Hill, Andrew Greenwood; seated: Tom Emmett, John Hicks, Ephraim Lockwood, Charles Ullathorne. They were all professionals, not unfamiliar with the taste of ale.

A hot day in Zanzibar in 1875, but cricket is irresistible to the Jack Tars – and their hardy spectators.

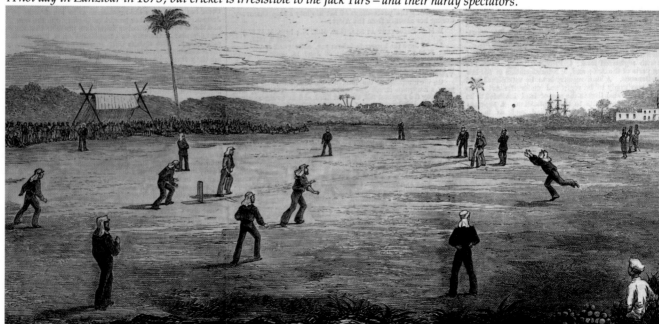

Above: *The pride in being portrayed, in 1874, in front of the Lord's pavilion is almost tangible.*

Aborigines amuse themselves on the Point Macleay Mission, South Australia, in the early 1870s. Very few black Australians have had the inclination, backed by the necessary skill, to reach first-class cricket.

Left: *Gloucestershire 1874, county champions this year and in 1876 and 1877. Standing: C. K. Pullin (umpire), T. G. Matthews, F. J. Crooke, J. A. Bush, R. E. Bush, E. M. Grace, E. M. Knapp; seated: E. C. B. Ford, F. Townsend, W. G. Grace, G. F. Grace, R. F. Miles. In contrast to Yorkshire, these were all amateurs.*

'What a jolly wicketkeeper he would make!' muses the scion of the grand house, in this charming engraving in The Graphic of June 12, 1875, after a painting by J. Ballantyne.

English club cricket continued to expand as a convivial exercise, an antidote to social barriers (up to a point), and a chance to prove one's manhood. This game is under way at Balls Park, Hertford around 1875.

THE BIRTH OF TEST CRICKET

AFTER the two tours of Australia in the 1860s, a third was organised in 1873–74, this one giving Australia the chance to see the great WG – who used the trip as a well-paid honeymoon. Colonial reception was a mixture of awe, gratitude and occasional mockery. Still the local opposition came in the form of odds – 22 players in a team being the norm – and conditions of grounds and of travelling facilities tested the Englishmen's fortitude and patience. However, another tour was inevitable, and James Lillywhite jnr of Sussex sailed, with 11 other professionals, from Southampton in the P&O steamship *Poonah* on September 21, 1876. They played in Australia and then New Zealand before returning to Melbourne to play a Combined Australian team, this time on even terms, 11 a side. The match began on March 15, 1877, and came to be regarded as the first Test match.

Lillywhite and his pioneer Test players at Priory Park, Chichester a few days before they sailed. Standing: Harry Jupp, Tom Emmett, Arthur Hobgen, a club member, who financed the tour, Allen Hill, Tom Armitage; sitting: Ted Pooley, James Southerton, James Lillywhite jnr, Alfred Shaw, George Ulyett, Andrew Greenwood; in front: Harry Charlwood, Jack Selby.

The developing Melbourne Cricket Ground prepares for the great contest, which was to last into the fourth day.

MELBOURNE CRICKET GROUND
1877

The articles of agreement by which James Lillywhite jnr secured the 1876–77 English trip to Australia, and thus became the first Test captain of England.

Left: *Charles Bannerman, born in Woolwich, who faced the first ball in Test cricket, and went on to make a glorious 165 before retiring with a broken finger. It was the first century ever by an Australian off a touring English team. Next-highest score for Australia in this inaugural Test was Tom Horan's 20.*

Nottinghamshire's Alfred Shaw, a cool and scheming slow-medium bowler in the Clarke/Lillywhite tradition. He bowled the first ball in Test cricket, and took 5 for 38 in Australia's second innings.

Tom Kendall, left-arm bowler, also English-born, took 7 for 55 in the England second innings, to bring an opening 45-run victory to Australia.

Dave Gregory, who resembled Ned Kelly, led Australia to victory in the first of all Test matches.

Above: W. G. Grace did not go on the 1876–77 Australian tour, thus leaving it anything but the best that England could field. But he had a glorious 1876 season, making the first triple-century in first-class cricket (344, MCC v Kent, Canterbury). This was followed by 177 against Notts and 318 not out against Yorkshire. In a 'minor' match at Grimsby he hit 400 not out.

Above left: Edwin Evans cheered in at the Albert after batting well against Lillywhite's Englishmen.

Left: While in New Zealand, some of the English team almost came to grief crossing the Otira Gorge in flood. They slept by the fire that night before pushing on to Christchurch.

This rare photo of a match between the Army and Melbourne Cricket Club at the MCG suggests that even in 1878 Australian batsmen were good at playing off their pads.

Right: *Four great Australian Test pioneers: Fred Spofforth, Tom Horan, Jack Blackham and Harry Boyle. 'Demon' Spofforth, who took the first Test hat-trick, struck terror into batsmen's hearts. Horan became a fine writer on the game. Blackham was the best of the early Test wicketkeepers. Boyle, a top medium-pacer, first exploited the 'suicide' fielding position.*

Mostly gentlemen: the Kent team of 1876. Standing: E. Henty, G. G. Hearne, H. S. Thomson, W. B. Pattisson, W. Foord-Kelcey, F. Penn, F. A. MacKinnon, V. K. Shaw; seated: W. Yardley, Lord Harris, C. A. Absolom, Major J. Fellowes. Major Fellowes founded the Devon Dumplings and the Hampshire Hogs.

Ten years after the Aboriginals' tour came the first full-scale Australian invasion of England's cricket fields, the team led by Dave Gregory, and numbering only 12, which left little room for injury or illness. Received with no excessive enthusiasm, they quickly shook the cricket world by defeating MCC on a sodden Lord's ground in a single day. The attendance of 500 at the start swelled to 5000 as news spread across London. The Australians, for the second time in 15 months, had sounded warning that they could play the game. The team pictured is: standing – F. R. Spofforth, J. Conway (manager), F. E. Allan; middle row – G. H. Bailey, T. P. Horan, T. W. Garrett, D. W. Gregory, A. C. Bannerman, H. F. Boyle; front – C. Bannerman, W. L. Murdoch, J. M. Blackham. Midwinter joined the team.

Above: *A somewhat distorted impression of the Australians' match against C. I. Thornton's XI at the Orleans Club, Twickenham. 'Demon' Spofforth must here be bowling one of his well-concealed slower balls.*

The Surrey team of 1877, with few names that lasted: standing – J. Carmichael, S. H. Akroyd, A. Chandler, W. Abbott, R. Humphrey, J. Street (umpire); seated – E. Barratt, G. G. Jones, G. Strachan (captain), G. F. Elliott, J. Southerton, H. Jupp.

Passions scarcely stir, peace prevails, in Queen Victoria's England of 1878. John R. Reid's A Country Cricket Match, Sussex, from which this engraving was taken, was exhibited at the Royal Academy. Below: Carshalton Park, Surrey, September 1878: Sir Jeremiah Colman's XI – S. W. Scott (Middx), J. Thompson, E. Pooley (Surrey), W. C. Wheeler, R. I'Anson, J. Southerton (Surrey), S. Smith, Sir J. Colman, H. B. Burnell, H. Gabbatiss (umpire); in front – S. A. Jones, G. Burton (Middx).

In 1878–79, Kent captain and MCC luminary Lord Harris took a team, predominantly of amateurs, to Australia, where they played – and lost by 10 wickets – a Test match at Melbourne. The tour became notable for an ugly crowd demonstration during a match at Sydney. Umpire Coulthard was set upon after giving local hero Murdoch run-out, and Harris, Hornby and the big Yorkshireman Ulyett were involved in some rough handling. The other umpire, who was unscathed, was Edmund Barton, who became Australia's first Prime Minister.

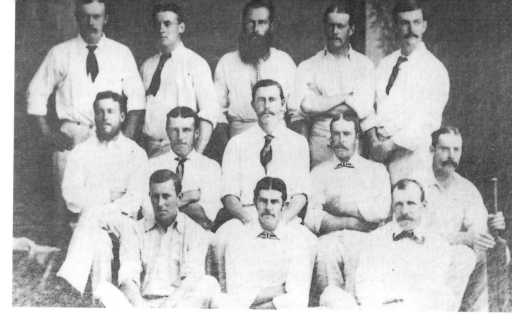

The 1878–79 touring English team: back row – F. Penn, A. J. Webbe, C. A. Absolom, S. S. Schultz, L. Hone; seated – F. A. MacKinnon, A. N. Hornby, Lord Harris, H. C. Maul, G. Ulyett; front – A. P. Lucas, V. P. F. A. Royle, T. Emmett. Leland Hone, an Irishman, kept wicket. The batting was fairly strong but the bowling was thin. All the same, they enjoyed the adventure to a man.

The Melbourne Cricket Club received their English guests in some style. The menu for the banquet in honour of the team was no ordinary printing job.

Right: John McCarthy Blackham, from Victoria, visited England with the first eight Australian touring teams, and captained his country. Brave and quick, he set new standards for wicketkeeping, seldom retreating from the stumps to even the fastest bowling. His gauntlets are to be seen in Melbourne Cricket Club's museum.

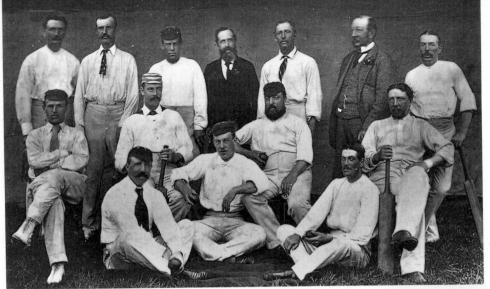

'Whether cricket tours have been overdone or not is a subject that would give rise possibly to considerable diversity of opinion,' stated *Lillywhite's Annual* in its coverage of the undefeated 1879 tour of North America. The team was: standing – G. Pinder, W. Barnes, E. Lockwood, J. P. Ford (promoter), R. Daft (captain), Captain Holden (Notts secretary), J. Selby; seated – A. Shrewsbury, G. Ulyett, A. Shaw, W. Oscroft; front – T. Emmett, W. Bates, F. Morley. All were from either Notts or Yorkshire.

W. G. Grace and Harry Jupp, of Dorking, Surrey, had at least one thing in common: they were dramatically reluctant to leave the wicket, even sometimes when there could be little doubt about the dismissal. Just before Arthur Shrewsbury came on the scene, 'Juppy' was probably the best of the professional batsmen.

Admission ticket (signed) to James Southerton's benefit match, North v South at The Oval, 1879.

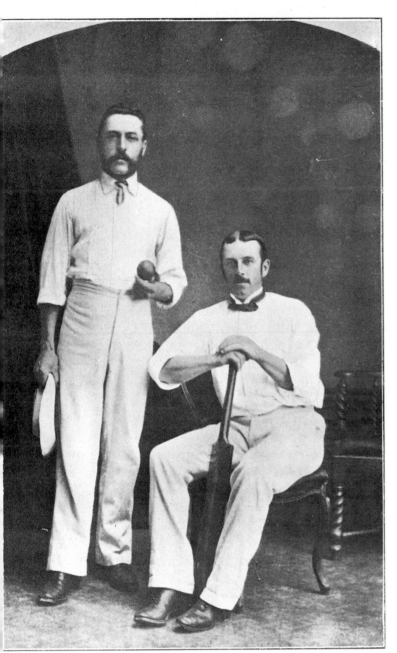

Francis Thompson (1859–1907), the anguished drug addict, rescued from degradation in London, but never able to forget the beloved Lancashire of his birth. His poem At Lord's is the one most often quoted to this day, concluding 'O my Hornby and my Barlow long ago.' That pair (left), R. G. Barlow, a stonewall batsman and left-arm bowler (standing), and Albert Neilson Hornby, who captained England in the historic Ashes Test of 1882 and at rugby, gave, with wicketkeeper Dick Pilling, great pride and strength to the Red Rose county. 'And I look through my tears on a silent-clapping host as the run-stealers flicker to and fro. . . .'

The Aborigines at play, around 1880, on the Coranderrk Aboriginal Station, Healesville, Victoria have a small audience, even including the batting side in waiting. They even seem to have their own version of W. G. Grace at extra cover. Photograph by Fred Kruger, 'gold medallist of Geelong'.

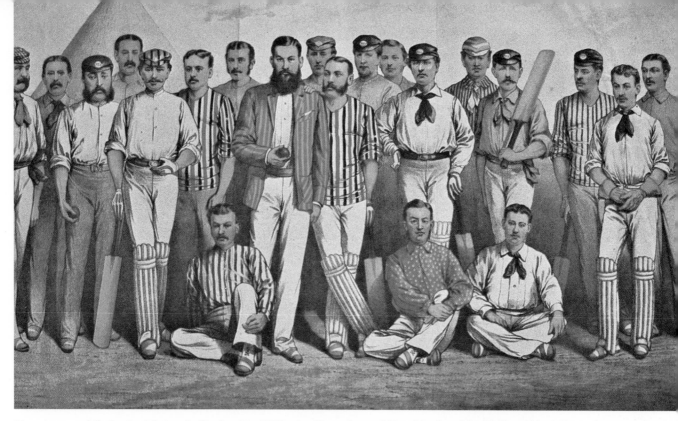

Twenty-one of the best cricketers in England in 1880: standing – James Lillywhite jnr, John Selby, Alfred Shaw, George Ulyett, Lord Harris, W. R. Gilbert, A. N. Hornby, W. G. Grace, A. P. Lucas, G. F. Grace, William Oscroft, A. G. Steel, Richard Daft, A. J. Webbe, Tom Emmett, Ephraim Lockwood, Richard Pilling, Fred Morley; front – Harry Jupp, Ted Pooley, Billy Bates. Seven of these played in the first Test on English soil, at The Oval in September 1880, though G. F. (Fred) Grace, WG's young brother, who registered two ducks in the match but held a skyscraping catch at the Vauxhall end off the giant Bonnor, died a fortnight later from pneumonia, having slept in a damp bed.

C. W. Alcock, secretary of Surrey CCC (and of the Football Association), was instrumental in arranging the first Test match in England. A popular and genial administrator, he also wrote on the game, and was one of those whom history marks down as having devoted a lifetime to cricket's promotion and well-being.

Robert Thoms, a highly respected umpire, who stood in England's first home Test. White 'dentist's' coats were still in the future.

The 1880 Australians, the first team to play a Test match on English soil. Standing: G. E. Palmer, W. H. Moule, G. J. Bonnor, G. Alexander (manager), T. U. Groube; seated: F. R. Spofforth, H. F. Boyle, W. L. Murdoch (captain), P. S. McDonnell, A. C. Bannerman; front: A. H. Jarvis, J. Slight, J. M. Blackham. They lost the Test, by five wickets, but won 21 and drew four of their 37 matches. London-born McDonnell, only 21, topped the batting averages, and 'Joey' Palmer, a brilliant spinner, only 20, took most first-class wickets: 76 at 11 each. Spofforth sustained a hand injury and was a crucial absentee from the Test match.

Billy Murdoch topped W. G. Grace's 152 in the Oval Test of 1880 by one run. Australia's leading batsman for some years, with an innings of 321 for NSW to his credit, he eventually joined Sussex, as an amateur.

Below: Lord Harris cuts off a boundary in the 1880 Test; and the crowd gives vent to its excitement at the end, the home victory atoning for the 1877 upset in distant Melbourne.

Queen Victoria and the Prince Consort, with some of their children, spend a while at a cricket match at Balmoral, the visiting team for this match in the autumn of 1881 being Abergeldie. **Below:** *A new infirmary was opened in Marylebone in the summer of 1881, perhaps timely in view of the recent smallpox epidemic in London. These indivertible cricketers must have felt sanitised against the contagion.*

William Nicholas Roe, who became the world record-holder in July 1881 with a score of 415 not out in a Long Vacation match at Cambridge. His innings for Emmanuel v Caius, in 90° heat, lasted five hours – and would have been extended had not the Caius LVC players called the match off after the second day.

The first team to sail to Australia and New Zealand as part of the Shaw/Shrewsbury/Lillywhite enterprise. This 1881–82 combination, all-professional, consisted of: standing – G. Ulyett, R. Pilling, James Lillywhite jnr, J. Conway (local manager), W. E. Midwinter, W. Bates; seated – A. Shrewsbury, A. Shaw (captain), T. Emmett, E. Peate; front – R. G. Barlow, W. H. Scotton, J. Selby. This was the first touring side to be the subject of serious scandal allegations: fisticuffs, heavy betting on matches, late champagne-drinking sessions.

Tom Garrett, at 18 the youngest to play in the inaugural Test – and the last survivor at the time of his death in 1943. A fast-medium bowler, he took 18 wickets in three Tests in 1881–82.

Left: George Giffen, who became the dominant allrounder in Australian cricket for a dozen years, and (seated) George Eugene Palmer, who took 20 wickets in the two Sydney Tests of the 1881–82 series to help Australia to the only two victories in the four-match series.

C. T. B. Turner was only 19 when the English cricketers came to his hometown of Bathurst, NSW to play 22 of the local cricketers. Turner, who had always been an assiduous practiser, was let loose with his well-controlled medium-pace offcutters – and took all 10 English wickets. The world would soon be hearing a lot more of 'Terror' Turner, who was to finish, in 1894, with a rare 101 Test wickets at 16.53 in only 17 matches. **Middle:** Percy McDonnell, a strong hitter, who blasted 147 for Australia at Sydney in the third Test of 1881–82, adding 199 with Alec Bannerman (right), who made a valuable but typically laborious 70. McDonnell's score included a hit off Bates over the pavilion, four missed catches, and 16 fours. It was his first first-class hundred. This season Bannerman, brother of Charlie, became the first to hit twin centuries in a match in Australia.

The St Peter's College XI, Adelaide, the cricket bloom such as was beginning to appear in the public schools around Australia. Good sportsmanship was the essence, but hard competition, in keeping with life in a young country, was readily embodied into the attitudes of young sportsmen.

W. H. Cooper, who spun his legbreaks vast distances, took nine wickets for 200 runs in the opening Test at Melbourne in 1881–82.

In Affectionate Remembrance
OF
ENGLISH CRICKET,
WHICH DIED AT THE OVAL
ON
29th AUGUST, 1882,
Deeply lamented by a large circle of sorrowing
friends and acquaintances.

R.I.P.

N.B.—The body will be cremated and the
ashes taken to Australia.

The 1882 Australians sent shockwaves through England by beating England at The Oval, a 'tragedy' that prompted the 'Ashes' announcement in the Sporting Times. *The colonial conquerors are: S. P. Jones, A. C. Bannerman, G. J. Bonnor, F. R. Spofforth, J. M. Blackham, W. L. Murdoch, G. E. Palmer, G. Giffen, H. F. Boyle, T. W. Garrett, H. H. Massie, P. S. McDonnell, T. P. Horan.* Below: *Back to the school/club/village match, where naïveté always has a place.*

"CRICKETING INTELLIGENCE."

Sporting Old Parson (to Professional Player). "WHY IS A BALL LIKE THAT CALLED A 'YORKER,' SIR?"
Professional Player. "A 'YORKER,' SIR! OH, WHEN THE BALL'S PITCHED RIGHT UP TO THE BLOCK——"
Sporting Parson. "YES, YES—I DIDN'T ASK YOU WHAT A 'YORKER' WAS"—(*with dignity*)—"I KNOW THAT AS WELL AS YOU DO.
BUT WHY IS IT CALLED A 'YORKER'?"
Professional Player. "WELL, I CAN'T SAY, SIR. I DON'T KNOW WHAT ELSE YOU COULD CALL IT!"

The first 'clear' photograph of a Test match: England v Australia at The Oval, August 1882 – with a few of the players moving too fast for the camera shutter. **Left:** As modern artist Roger Marsh saw the contest between Hornby and Spofforth. The Australian's contribution was decisive: 7 for 46 and 7 for 44. England (101 and 77) were overthrown by Australia (63 and 122) chiefly through 'The Demon's' efforts and a smashing 55 from Hugh Massie.

Left: The Ashes, which materialised from the mournful announcement in the newspaper following England's shock seven-run defeat at The Oval. When the Hon. Ivo Bligh took an English team to Australia, some Melbourne ladies presented him with the little urn containing the ashes of a stump . . . or bail . . . or ball. Generations of English and Australians have battled for the precious trophy, which remains at Lord's irrespective of who is 'in possession'.

The launching of Cricket, a twopenny weekly, in 1882 was well timed. Its 17th edition recorded the 'Ashes match'. The journal ran for 32 years.

Ted Peate, the droll Yorkshire slow left-arm bowler (who set a new record with 214 wickets in 1882), would have been one of England's heroes in the Oval Test with his eight wickets – had it not been for his miserable plight in being last man out with England eight runs from victory. 'Ah couldn't troost Maister Stood!' he said. C. T. Studd had scored two centuries off the Australians that summer, but it was observed that he was in a very agitated state in the closing stages of the Oval Test. Studd (right), flanked by brothers J. E. K. and G. B., was a brilliant batsman and good medium-pacer, playing for Cambridge and Middlesex before embarking on missionary work. He died in the Belgian Congo in 1931.

May 1882, at Fenner's, Cambridge, with the young undergraduates facing the bowling of the Australian team. C. T. Studd scored 114, he and his two brothers making 297 runs in a match won by the University by six wickets.

The English team which went to Australia in 1882–83 and won back the no-longer-mythical Ashes by winning the second and third Tests. Australia levelled at 2–2 by winning a fourth Test, but no-one seemed to care, for English honour had been restored. Standing: F. Morley, Martin Cobbett (author and reporter), G. F. Vernon, G. B. Studd, W. W. Read, R. G. Barlow; seated: C. F. H. Leslie, E. F. S. Tylecote, Hon. Ivo Bligh (captain), C. T. Studd; front: W. Barnes, W. Bates, A. G. Steel. Steel made 135 not out (aided by three misses) at Sydney in the fourth Test, and himself dropped Bonnor four times while he hit 87. The huge Australian was missed eight times in all. In 1886, Barnes missed a punch at Australia's McDonnell and hit a wall instead.

Steam-trams and horse-drawn carriages take patrons to the Sydney Cricket Ground, probably during the 1882–83 Test series, play already under way. Such building has taken place on the ground in the ensuing years as to render it almost unrecognisable.

Spofforth had all the requisites of a great bowler: a keen brain, athleticism, stamina and a fiery temperament. Right: Later in life – not as fast but still crafty.

142

George Giffen, who would have bowled from both ends if the Laws had allowed, took the first 'all-ten' in Australian first-class cricket with 10 for 66 for the 4th Australian XI v The Rest at Sydney in 1883–84. The South Australian grew in stature and influence season by season.

Right: *The enchanting* Captain of the Eleven, *completed by Philip Calderon in 1882.*

Below: *Native cricketers, Madras. Indian cricket was still seen – not totally without justification – as a joke, but the joke was to be avenged inside 100 years.*

143

Billy Bates (right) was an ebullient Yorkshireman, a snappy dresser, known as 'The Duke'. A roundarm offbreak bowler and good-looking batsman, he toured Australia five times in the 1880s, and played all 15 of his Tests there. His fielding and catching were unreliable and kept him out of home Tests. However, his great moments of glory came at Melbourne on the 1882–83 tour, in the second Test, when he scored 55 and took 7 for 28 and 7 for 74 to bring England the first innings victory in Test cricket. In the first innings he took the first England Test hat-trick, dismissing the powerful trio McDonnell, Giffen and Bonnor. But tragedy stalked. Five years later, in Melbourne, he was hit in the eye . . .

Ettwell Street
Moldgreen
Huddersfield
April 8 / 1888

Dear Sir

I hope you will excuse me for not answering you letter sooner as Mrs Bates is not able to write much & she never does much writing & I can assure you that I have not had much time to do anything since I came home & the Dr told me I was neather to write no read very little sow I have done very little at all since I arrived. & & can assure you that I have had notthing but but trouble for this last 2 years as Mrs Bates as not been at all well for the last 2 years allways been under the Docters & it still sow

Home threar was more for me as our little boy W. Edrick was all but dead & Mrs Bates had been for seven nights & days with him & I can assure you that I have not slept in bed yet since I arrived Home & we have had the house nearly full of Drs nearly all the time but I tham most to enform you that he is a little better now & I think he will get over it now as we have begin to have a little rests with him now but he has suffered forfull as he been suffering from Sparams & croup & inflamaction in the wind pipe & not only that he as an apciss on his throut yet So now I must conclude I Remain

I will drop you another line or two in a few more days

Yours Truly
Willie Bates

. . . and almost lost the sight of it. His career was effectively over. Melancholy followed (he tried to end it all on the voyage home), and troubles mounted. His son (who became a county cricketer) was ill, and in 1891 his wife died. At the height of his sorrows Bates wrote the above letter. He died in 1900, aged 44, two months before fellow Yorkshireman Ted Peate.

Left: *Another Yorkshire tragedy: Albert Luty, playing in a club match at Yeadon, near Leeds, in August 1883, was hit on the head by a ball from Merritt Preston, a fast bowler who later played for Yorkshire. Luty died from the blow, and was buried in Yeadon churchyard – where Preston was also laid to rest in 1890, having succumbed to a chill. He was 36. Luty, 29, had been married for nine days.*

144

Though sharing the montage of *Some Famous Living Cricketers* in **The Graphic** in 1883 *with a lord, two future lords, a clergyman and a future Lord Mayor of London, there is no mistaking the paramount position of W. G. Grace in his solitary, bearded splendour. His own social standing had been enhanced in 1879 when he qualified as a doctor of medicine.*

Below: *Yorkshire's Ephraim Lockwood, who burst on the scene in 1868, made his only double-century, 208, against Kent at Gravesend in 1883, when he was 38. Oddly, his form left him thereafter.*

Nottinghamshire were England's strength in 1883, '84, '85 and '86, when they were county champions. Standing: W. Barnes, F. Brown (secretary), A. Shrewsbury, E. Mills, W. H. Scotton, J. Selby; seated: W. Wright, W. Attewell, A. Shaw, W. Gunn; front: M. Sherwin, W. Flowers.

145

Left: The Batsman of the Future, *a painting of some warmth by James Hayllar.* Above: *A batsman of the past. In 1884 the Hon. Robert Grimston passed into the Great Pavilion in the Sky, while still president of MCC. As a young man he earned admiration at the way he played Mynn's fierce attack. An Harrovian, he stayed close to his old school in cricket, and at Lord's he was among the more extreme reactionaries, preferring sheep to keep the grass down rather than new-fangled machinery.*

Smokers and Non-Smokers (close examination will reveal the one type against the other) at Lord's at the end of the 1884 season, when some of the touring Australians joined the match. Bannerman, Spofforth, Giffen and Palmer are in the back row, Scott, Murdoch and Bonnor in the middle, and McDonnell in the front. Bonnor hit 124 for the Non-Smokers (WG only 10), punishing fellowcountryman Spofforth as was seldom seen. The abstainers won by nine wickets, and £561 was raised for the Cricketers' Fund.

A good, controlled stroke on Peckham Rye in 1884, a sketch by 14-year-old Charlie Hammond a year before he set off for Australasia, artist's equipment in his baggage. The graphic diary of his wanderings was published by Oxford University Press in 1980.

Left: **Three Young Cricketers** *by George Elgar Hicks, 1883, a preliminary oil sketch for Earl Dudley, the subjects being his sons. The Earl died before the main commission was started upon, and no major work eventuated.*

The Philadelphians finally felt themselves ready for a tour of England by 1884. A committee raised the money – covering bare expenses – and an itinerary, strictly against amateur teams only, such as Gentlemen of MCC and Gentlemen of Derbyshire, was agreed. The Americans went home happy, having won eight, drawn five and lost five of their games. Better was to come on future tours, until the game went into decline just before the First World War. Standing: J. B. Thayer jnr, W. Brockie jnr, E. W. Clark jnr, C. A. Newhall, H. McNutt, J. A. Scott, W. C. Lowry; front: W. C. Morgan jnr, R. S. Newhall (captain), F. E. Brewster, H. Brown, S. Law, D. P. Stoever, T. Robins jnr (scorer). Thayer was drowned when Titanic went down in 1912.

147

The England XI at Lord's, Australian Test match 1884. Standing: C. K. Pullin (umpire), E. Peate, A. P. Lucas, Hon. A. Lyttelton, A. Shrewsbury, F. H. Farrands (umpire); seated: A. G. Steel, Lord Harris (captain), W. G. Grace, W. W. Read, G. Ulyett; front: S. Christopherson, R. G. Barlow. Peate took 6 for 85 in Australia's first innings, Ulyett 7 for 36 in the second, rivalling Spofforth for speed and accuracy on a 'bald-headed' pitch. Steel, a Lancastrian amateur allrounder, made a wonderful 148 in England's innings of 379.

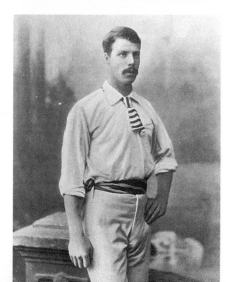

W. L. Murdoch, Australia's captain, scored 211 in his side's 551 in the Oval Test of 1884, the first Test double-century.

Above left: *Walter Read, who scored 117, going in at No. 10 for England in the Oval Test, belting his century in 113 minutes. William Scotton (above) had opened and scored 90 in 5¾ hours. Their ninth-wicket stand was a record 151. Harry 'Tup' Scott (left) had made 102 for Australia, putting on 207 with Murdoch, a Test record at the time. All 11 Englishmen bowled, including wicketkeeper Lyttelton with underarm lobs.*

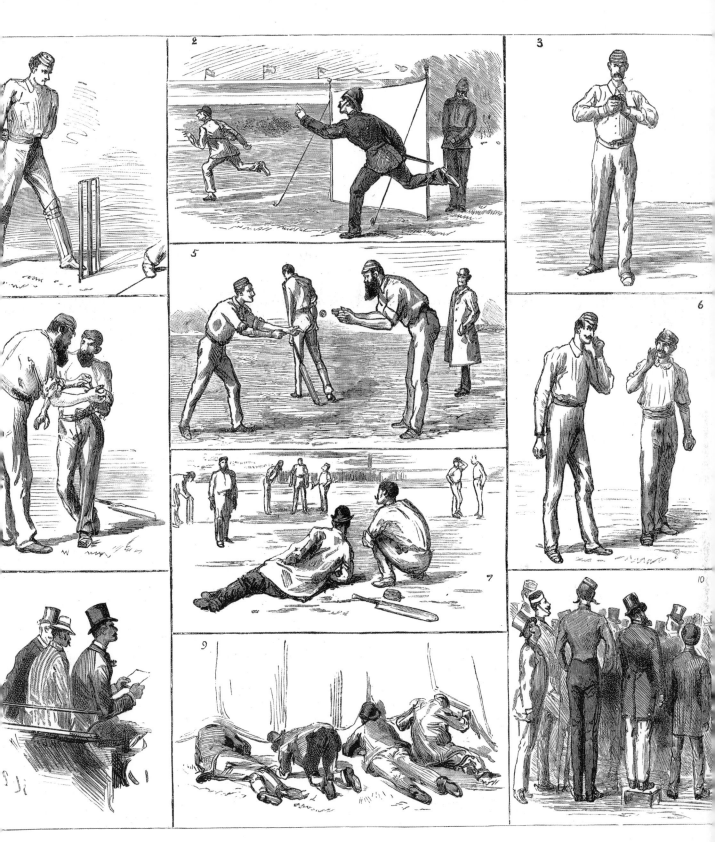

The first Test match to be played at Lord's, in July 1884, brought England a comfortingly comprehensive victory by an innings and five runs over Australia, starting an era of great joy for England, who won 14 and lost only three Tests to Australia between 1884 and 1890. The drawings show: 1. England wicketkeeper the Hon. Alfred Lyttelton 'waiting for a rise'; 2. a Bobby chasing a pickpocket; 3. Spofforth, the 'Demon'; 4. WG advising the injured Blackham not to play any more; 5. WG and A. G. Steel practising catching after Spofforth was dismissed; 6. Spofforth to team-mate: 'How shall I manage Barlow?' 'Put on the pace'; 7. a 'well-earned repose'; 8. Lord Harris's carriage; 9. behind the screen; 10. a soldier 'bigger than the giant Bonnor'.

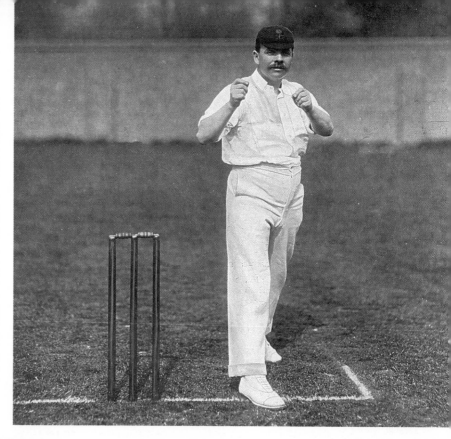

In Adelaide's first Test, the opening match of the five-Test 1884–85 series, Billy Barnes hit 134 for England.

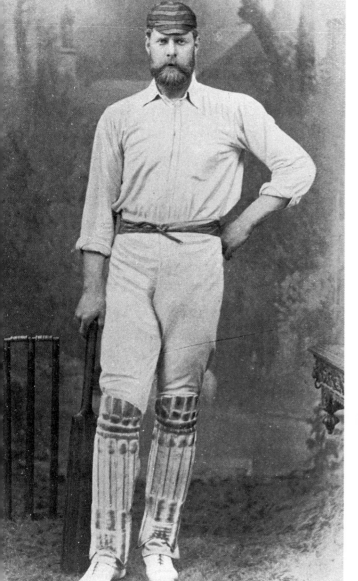

Johnny Briggs, the bubbly little Lancashire player, hit a two-hour century in the second Test, at Melbourne, though Australia fielded a weakened and completely new XI from that in the first Test, those players having demanded 50% of the gatemoney. Briggs won fame, and 118 cheap Test wickets, as a shrewd left-arm spinner. He was also a brilliant fieldsman.

Wilfred Flowers, a reliable pro from Notts, scored 56 and took 5 for 46 in the third Test, at Sydney, where Australia pulled back to 1–2 with a six-run victory.

Left: Mighty George Bonnor set up Australia's win in the fourth Test, also at Sydney, with a muscular century in 100 minutes out of 131 scored while he was in. England won the deciding fifth Test by an innings at Melbourne, Shrewsbury making 105 not out.

Eleven of England's premier cricketers in 1885. They never did all play in the same Test team, but each left his mark on the international as well as domestic game.

The almost all-professional Yorkshire team of 1885, second in strength only to Notts, whom they managed to beat at Trent Bridge. Standing: G. Ulyett, R. Peel, W. H. Woodhouse, Turner (scorer), J. Hunter; seated: W. Bates, E. Peate, L. Hall (captain), T. Emmett, F. Lee; front: J. M. Preston, J. Grimshaw. Louis Hall, an ascetic lay preacher and dour batsman, carried his bat through the innings 17 times. Preston was the bowler whose delivery killed Albert Luty in 1883.

The innocence of unadulterated grass-roots cricket: 'colts' at play in a Surrey village, a drawing by John White, 1885.

Below: Prince Alfred College XI, Adelaide, 1885, with one of Australia's best batsmen ever, Joe Darling, standing extreme right. This year, aged 14, he scored 252 in six hours against rivals St Peter's. Blood ran down his fingers, which were frayed by the twine on the bat.

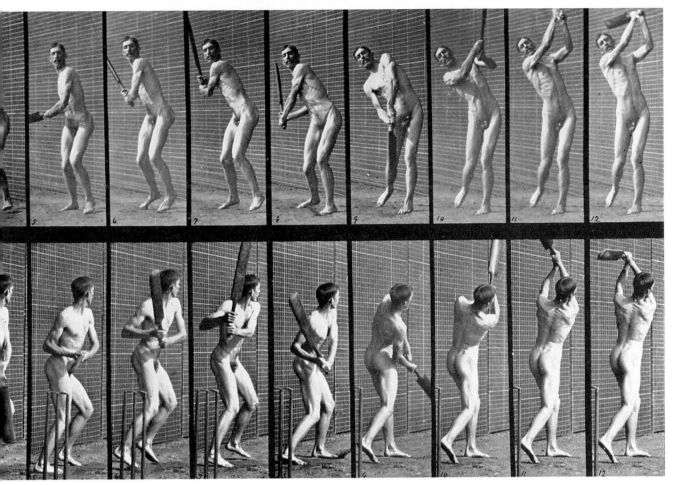

Pioneer of moving pictures, Eadweard Muybridge, was born in Kingston-upon-Thames, Surrey in 1830, and spent some time in the USA, where he experimented with multiple cameras worked by trip-wires. Later came electronically-controlled shutters. These photographs are from Muybridge's folio volumes Animal Locomotion, published in 1887, and constitute the earliest of all genuine cricket action close-ups. His model was 'the best allround cricketer in the University of Pennsylvania'.

Johnny Crossland of Lancashire, thought by many to be the fastest bowler in England, though he seemed to throw his paciest ball. Lord Harris cancelled (and forfeited) Kent's return match against Lancashire in 1885 in protest – but got Crossland in the end on a technicality: he was living outside the Lancashire boundaries.

An old theme with a modern echo: following the financial demands of the 1884 Australian team it was apparent that some cricketers were no longer impelled by the purest of desires.

James Stewart Carrick appropriated the world individual record for Scotland when he made 419 not out for West of Scotland against Priory Park, Chichester in July 1885. A left-hander, he batted for over 11 hours, and James Lillywhite jnr played for the host team. The second day's play was extended by a few minutes for Carrick to beat Roe's 415.

153

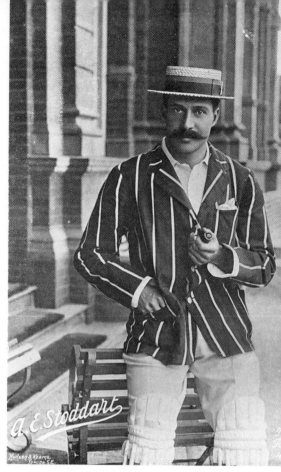

A. E. Stoddart, future England captain, pushed the individual world record higher still, a year after J. S. Carrick's tour de force, with an innings of 485 for Hampstead against Stoics in August 1886. He had played cards till dawn before the one-day match, batted almost through Hampstead's innings of 813, then played tennis, went to the theatre, and turned in at 3 am. No declarations were then permitted, and Stoics did not bat.

Above left: An I Zingari player of the 1880s, from a watercolour by the Earl of Ypres.

Left: The Parsee cricket team which toured England in 1886, blazing a trail for others from the subcontinent. The Parsees were the first race in India seriously to take up the game, but these enthusiasts, who paid their own way, were doomed to disappointment, winning only one and losing 19 of their 28 matches. Another team visited England two years later and did appreciably better.

William Gilbert Grace scored a century and took all 10 wickets in an innings in MCC's match against Oxford University at Oxford in 1886. That same summer he scored 170 against Australia in the Oval Test match, having been missed several times. Scotton was his usual slow self, and WG's century came out of 129. WG thus reclaimed the individual Test record, Shrewsbury (164) having held it for one match.

Right: W. E. Roller scored 204 for Surrey v Sussex at The Oval in 1885, and performed the hat-trick. This commemorative painting hangs at The Oval.

Below: A vision of a Test match at Lord's, c.1886, by G. H. Barrable and R. Ponsonby Staples. Garrett of Australia, in Melbourne CC colours, fields the ball, and the Prince of Wales stands by the boundary with Princess Alexandra. Lillie Langtry, a friend of the Prince, looks out of the picture, the huge original of which hangs in the Memorial Gallery at Lord's.

The 1886 Australian team in England, the first to tour under other than its own private enterprise. This team was chosen and organised by Melbourne Cricket Club. Standing: R. A. Thoms (umpire), J. McIlwraith, J. W. Trumble, A. H. Jarvis, W. Bruce, S. P. Jones, G. E. Palmer, F. R. Spofforth; seated: B. J. Wardill (manager), J. M. Blackham, E. Evans, H. J. H. Scott (captain), G. J. Bonnor, T. W. Garrett, G. Giffen, F. H. Farrands (umpire). Not the happiest blend of cricketers, they lacked the presence of Bannerman, McDonnell and Murdoch, and were defeated in all three Tests. In all, 39 tour matches were played that damp summer, of which nine were won, eight lost and 22 drawn. Injuries, particularly to Spofforth, worsened their plight, though Giffen performed so consistently well that he achieved the double (1424 runs and 154 wickets); and Palmer came close.

Sammy Jones, whose 87 at Old Trafford in the first Test of 1886 was Australia's highest score in the series. In the 1882 Test W. G. Grace had run him out when he went to pat the pitch, and on the 1888 tour he suffered an even greater misfortune when he contracted smallpox.

The wounded and weary 1886 Australians return: how Phil May saw it in The Bulletin. Spofforth (inset) had flown away to matrimony.

156

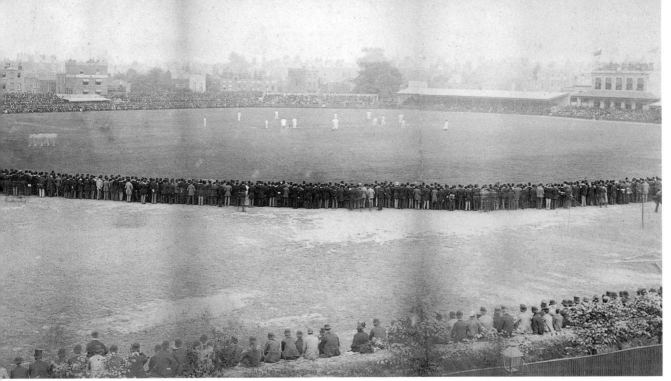

Standing room only for most of the 'public' spectators at the 1886 Oval Test, which England won by an innings on the third day. WG made 170, W. W. Read 94, and Australia were bowled out for 68 and 149.

George Lohmann, a genius among medium-pacers. The fair-headed Surrey man took 112 wickets (35 against South Africa) at the paltry cost of 10 each in only 18 Tests. He took 12 for 104 in the 1886 Oval Test. He died from TB in 1901, aged 36. **Right:** *Arthur Shrewsbury, the little Nottinghamshire master. He scored 164 in the Lord's Test of 1886 on an evil, rain-affected pitch, an innings which crowned his reputation as the finest of the professional batsmen, or perhaps of them all. Extremely patient and careful in his strokeplay, he brought negative pad-play to a fine art.*

Over-ambition, rivalry and obstinacy resulted in two English teams touring Australia at the same time in 1887–88, Shaw and Shrewsbury's sponsored by Melbourne CC and Hawke's by the Sydney Association. A year earlier an English side led by Shrewsbury had won both Tests in Australia, despite being bowled out for 45 at Sydney on the first day. The 1887–88 parties combined for one Test, at Sydney, won by England, for whom Lohmann took nine wickets and Peel 10. Australia made only 42 and 82 on a brute of a pitch, which was wet, and in poor light.

Left: One of the English touring teams, Shaw and Shrewsbury's: standing: G. Brann, L. C. Docker, James Lillywhite jnr, J. M. Read, A. D. Pougher; seated: G. Ulyett, R. Pilling, C. A. Smith (captain), A. Shrewsbury, G. A. Lohmann; front: J. M. Preston, J. Briggs, W. Newham. C. Aubrey Smith, of Cambridge and Sussex (and later Transvaal), was an eminent actor who later became a Hollywood film star.

Left: The other 1887–88 English team in Australia: standing: J. T. Rawlin, M. P. Bowden, G. F. Vernon, Sir T. C. O'Brien, J. Beaumont; seated: A. E. Newton, W. Bates, Hon. M. B. Hawke (captain), W. Attewell, R. Peel; front: R. Abel, W. W. Read, A. E. Stoddart. Hawke returned to England when his father died, and Vernon took over the captaincy. Stoddart, who hit 285 against 18 Melbourne Juniors, was an England rugby player as well, and stayed on with Shrewsbury's football team.

Inappropriate costume matters less when everyone's the same: this group of worthies turned out for Weaverham, Cheshire in 1886.

Charles Thomas Biass Turner, Australia's 'Terror', born in Bathurst, NSW, in 1862. During the 1887–88 season he took 106 wickets in 12 matches, the only time a bowler has ever reached 100 in an Australian season. Even allowing for the fact that pitches were not protected from the weather, it was a wonderful performance. This is the only known action photograph of Turner.

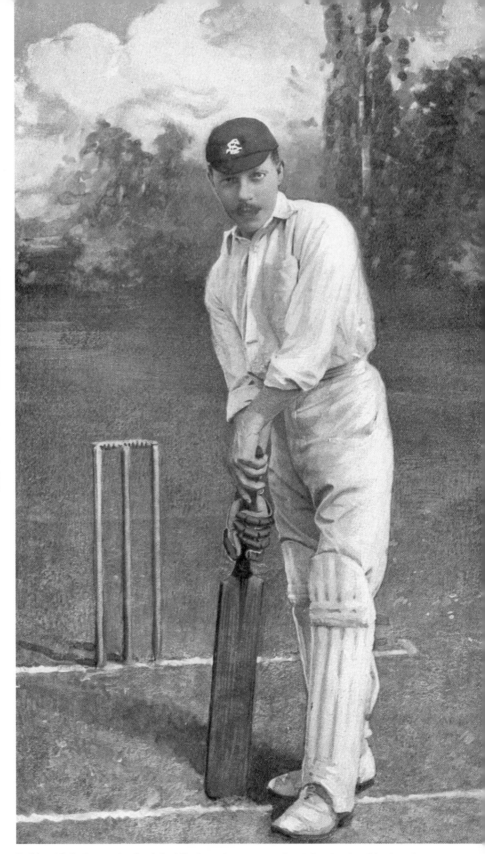

Bobby Abel, Surrey's cherished little cockney, scored 120 for England in South Africa's first Test series, in the second Test, at the newly-opened Newlands, Cape Town, in 1888–89. It was the first first-class century scored in South Africa. Abel's career was long, and took many seasons to bring its rewards. Then, in his late thirties, 'The Guv'nor' began to make over 2000 runs a season with regularity, despite allegedly poor eyesight and a noticeable apprehension when facing the fast bowlers, even on the beautiful Oval pitches.

Left: Dr L. O. S. Poidevin, Australian Davis Cup tennis player, NSW and Lancashire allrounder, and cricket-writer. In 1887–88, when aged 11, he scored 271 not out and took 19 of his opponents' 20 wickets.

The Australians of 1888, who won the Lord's Test, but lost the Oval and Old Trafford Tests each by an innings. In all they won 19 matches, lost 14, and drew seven, another sorry tale caused by the paucity of solid batting and reliable fielding to back up the penetrative bowling of Turner and Ferris. Standing: J. J. Ferris, S. P. Jones, A. H. Jarvis, J. Worrall, C. W. Beal (manager), J. J. Lyons, J. M. Blackham, H. F. Boyle, J. D. Edwards; seated: G. J. Bonnor, C. T. B. Turner, P. S. McDonnell (captain), G. H. S. Trott, A. C. Bannerman. The presence of Jones and Lyons in the picture had to be faked.

The 1888 tour opened at Norbury Park with a two-day fixture against C. I. Thornton's XI. W. G. Grace, here facing the bowling, and in his 40th year, was lbw to Turner for 10 and stumped by Blackham off Ferris for 4. The Australians won by six wickets.

Two brilliant colonial boys: Jack Ferris (standing), a left-arm medium-pacer from Sydney, who took 385 wickets altogether on the 1888 and 1890 England tours, and Charlie Turner, another NSW cricketer, who bagged 462 wickets on those two tours. Bowling into each other's footmarks, they were accurate and lethal, and for a few years Australia's attack was this pair.

Above: *Bobby Peel of Yorkshire and England, who, like all the top-class bowlers of the period, took advantage of the uncovered pitches. He destroyed Australia at Manchester in 1888 with 11 wickets. All told he took 102 Test wickets at 16.81.*

Below: *A little tension but mostly contentment and pleasure radiate from a group of Free Foresters and Rugby School boys before their match in 1888. Cobden, hero of the 1870 Varsity match, smokes a pipe.*

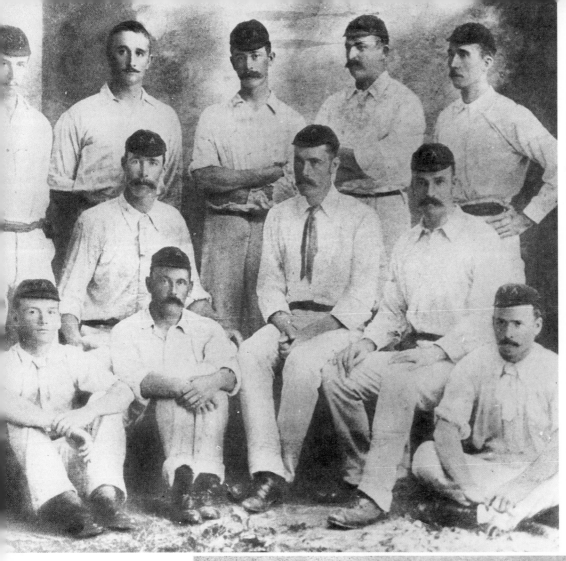

The first South African Test XI, Port Elizabeth, March 1889. They scored 84 and 129 and lost by eight wickets against a less-than-full-strength England team. Worse followed at Cape Town, where they were skittled for 47 and 43 against England's 292 (W. H. Ashley 7 for 95 in his only Test). Back row: A. Rose-Innes, A. B. Tancred, C. E. Finlason, C. H. Vintcent, F. W. Smith; seated: P. Hutchinson, O. R. Dunell (captain), W. H. Milton; front: A. E. Ochse, R. B. Stewart, G. A. Kempis. In the Cape Town Test, Tancred became the first batsman to carry his bat through an innings in Test cricket: 26 not out as South Africa collapsed for 47.

Right: *The 1888–89 English team prepares to sail to South Africa, where the two Test matches played hardly warranted the designation. The impeccably-dressed party is: standing – B. A. F. Grieve, A. C. Skinner, A. J. Fothergill, J. M. Read, R. Abel; seated – C. A. Smith, Major Warton (manager), Hon. C. J. Coventry, J. E. P. McMaster, M. P. Bowden; front – J. H. Roberts, H. Wood; insets: J. Briggs, G. Ulyett, F. Hearne. Bowden, at 23 years 144 days, is the youngest man to captain England. He stayed in Africa and died there four years later.*

The Magpies and Jesus teams, Cambridge, 1889, with two conspicuous sportsmen in their midst: S. M. J. Woods (seated third from left) and Gregor MacGregor (seated third from right). Australian-born Sammy Woods was a rampaging rugby forward who played for England, and was called up to help the 1888 Australian touring cricket team. He became a legendary fast bowler, hard hitter and bold captain for Somerset. MacGregor played rugby for Scotland and kept wicket for Middlesex and England. Seated extreme left is Cyril Foley, who played for Middlesex and Worcestershire, and took part in the Jameson Raid.

Johnny Briggs, the tragic clown, had incredible figures in the Cape Town Test of 1888–89: 7 for 17 and 8 for 11. All 15 wickets were bowled except one, which was lbw. Briggs made his highest score, 186 for Lancashire v Surrey at Liverpool in 1885, two days after his wedding. He toured Australia six times, but had a severe epileptic seizure in a theatre in Leeds during a Test match in 1899. His twin sons were among hundreds who mourned him intimately when he died in Cheadle Asylum in 1902.

Right: The groundstaff at Kennington Oval in 1889. Much rolling and human sweat went into pitch-preparation. Staffs in modern times have been reduced drastically.

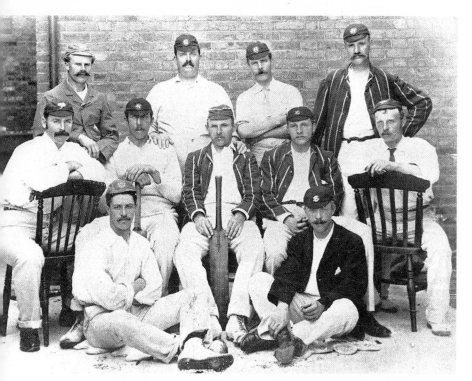

The Players XI at The Oval, 1889. After years of reversal at the hands of WG and the Gentlemen, the professionals were now mounting a much sterner resistance. This match was won by nine wickets. Standing: Walter Wright, Mordecai Sherwin, Henry Richardson, Billy Barnes; seated: George Ulyett, William Gunn, Arthur Shrewsbury (captain), George Lohmann, Bobby Peel; front: Walter Quaife, Bobby Abel. The tall Gunn scored 61 and 98 not out, and Barnes made 90 before being adjudged run-out – 'through an umpire's mistake'.

Mitcham Green: the ancient patch of Surrey land has seen cricket for several centuries, and many notable players have sprung from its grassy triangle, including Tom Richardson, Herbert Strudwick, Andy Sandham.

In Australia there was cricket English-elite-club style for the 'better class of chap' with I Zingari Australia, founded in 1888 (as the Iona Cricket Club).

The Original English Lady Cricketers, who toured the land for some years, playing under assumed names. It paid well until the manager disappeared with the profits, at which point disbandment was unavoidable.

Left: *Dr John Barrett, a left-hander, carried his bat for 67 not out through Australia's second innings of 176 in the 1890 Test match at Lord's. WG was out second ball, but saw England home with a splendid 75 not out.*

Left: *Fred 'Nutty' Martin of Kent, who was given his chance for England in 1890 when a few Test regulars were unavailable. He took 12 Australian wickets for 102, but never played in an Ashes Test again. He was deadly on the rain-affected pitches that abounded.*

Kenny Burn, from Tasmania, is remembered as the player chosen as wicketkeeper for the 1890 Australian tour of England, though he had had no experience behind the stumps. Yet 'The Scotsman' was a considerable batsman, making 41 centuries at home, including two beyond 350. At the time of his death in 1956, at 92 he was the oldest surviving Test cricketer.

THE ROARING NINETIES

THE GAME had grown up. There was a County Championship, suitably financed, thanks to low wage bills, moderate costs, large attendances and generous private patronage. Test cricket was well established between England and Australia, and there were hopes for South Africa. Club cricket thrived, and in 1890 the North-East Lancashire League was formed, a pointer to the future. The four-ball over had given way to five (six in Australia), and umpires began to look the part in their white coats. Records were being broken, and the public imagination captured. The people had their favourites, and the newspapers fed their appetite. Old WG was 41 as the 1890s dawned, and was surely just about finished, but there was the exceedingly reliable Shrewsbury with his beanpole ally Billy Gunn from Notts, and the tough lads from Yorkshire, the admirable Abel and Lohmann at The Oval, and the brilliant and dapper 'Stoddy' from Middlesex. Partisanship was sometimes parochial to the degree that Yorkshire claimed Ulyett and Peel, and Stoddart preferred to play for Middlesex, when England played Australia at The Oval in 1890. But cricket was being case-hardened for the 20th century as a national obsession, a pastime/industry of unshakeable importance. The most golden of ages was about to unfold.

Dr W. G. Grace, forever the game's figurehead, leads the charge in Punch's *imagined response to the threat of major disruption at Lord's in 1890 as Sir Edward Watkin proposes to construct a railway which would have crossed the cherished old cricket ground.*

Blandford Fletcher's warm evening colours convey blissful country peacefulness, the village lads imitating their heroes, their little stomachs turning at the realisation that they are actually being watched.

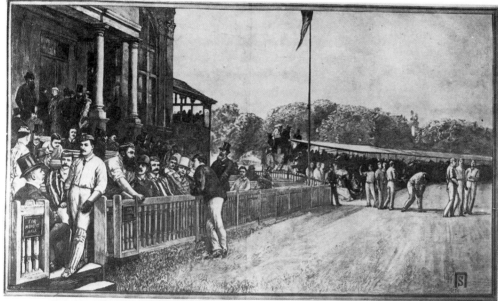

The new pavilion at Lord's transcends in grandeur all that ever preceded it, and in 1891 the Gentlemen's opening batsmen wait for the Players to take the field – from a separate dressing-room and gate, of course.

Right: *Little old Somerset became a first-class county in 1891, joining Gloucestershire, Kent, Lancashire, Middlesex, Nottinghamshire, Surrey, Sussex and Yorkshire. Crushed by Surrey at The Oval (out for 37 in both innings, Lohmann 11 for 40), they avenged the defeat in August and also beat Kent, Yorkshire and neighbouring Gloucestershire (twice). Back row: E. J. Tyler, G. Fowler, Rev. A. P. Wickham, R. C. N. Palairet, J. B. Challen; middle row: S. M. J. Woods, L. C. H. Palairet, V. T. Hill, C. J. Robinson; front: H. Murray-Anderdon (secretary), W. N. Roe, H. T. Hewett (captain), A. E. Newton, G. B. Nichols.*

A revealing panorama of the Sydney Cricket Ground during the Australia–England Test match of 1891–92.

So now it was Lord Sheffield's turn to take a team to Australia, the biggest (and far from cheap) signing being W. G. Grace, who led the expedition. Standing: R. Carpenter (umpire), W. Attewell, G. A. Lohmann, J. M. Read, G. Bean, J. W. Sharpe, R. A. Thoms (umpire); seated: J. Briggs, G. MacGregor, W. G. Grace, R. Peel, A. E. Stoddart, R. Abel. Missing from the group are H. Philipson and O. G. Radcliffe. Alfred Shaw was manager. Australia won at Melbourne and Sydney, but England won by an innings at Adelaide, a victory set up by Stoddart's 134 and Peel's 83, and sealed by Briggs's six wickets in each innings.

The gigantic Bonnor was no longer part of the Australian team, but the diminutive Alec Bannerman was, and made runs at a turgid pace that still were precious to his team's run-bank in the two Tests won, especially the 91 at Sydney, when Australia had trailed by 162 on first innings. Bannerman batted for 7½ hours, usually surrounded by close fielders, and hit only three boundaries.

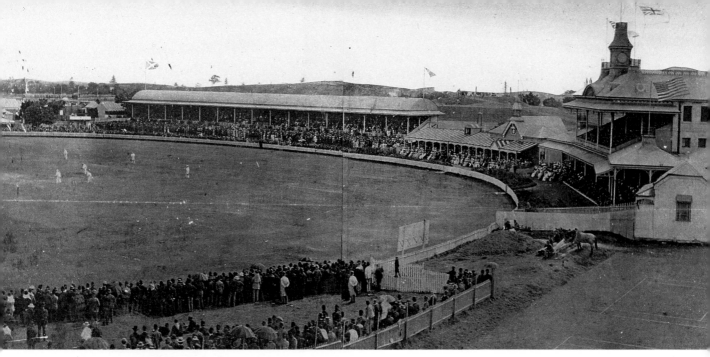

Left: *Burly South Australian Jack Lyons hit a blitzing 134 on the third day of the Sydney Test, while Bannerman pottered about. He got his runs in only 2¾ hours, with hits to the scoreboard and on top of the ladies' pavilion off Briggs.* **Below left:** *Bobby Abel carried his bat for 132 through England's first innings at Sydney, a feat rarely emulated in Ashes Tests since.*

George Giffen took 10 wickets in the Sydney Test but otherwise had a quiet 1891–92 series. For South Australia against Victoria at Adelaide, however, he somewhat dominated the match with an innings of 271 and bowling figures of 9 for 96 and 7 for 70, exertions that might well turn a man's hair prematurely white.

Henry North Holroyd, third Earl of Sheffield, Viscount Pevensey, Baron Sheffield of Dunsmore, Meath, Baron Sheffield of Roscommon, in Ireland, and Baron Sheffield of Sheffield, Yorkshire (1832–1909), with His Majesty King Edward VII.

THE LATE
LORD SHEFFIELD & KING EDWARD

Lord Sheffield, of whom surviving likenesses are difficult to come by, was a great benefactor of Sussex cricket. And his generosity was extended to Australia. At the end of the 1891–92 tour, which left him heavily out of pocket, he donated £150 for a trophy, to be contested by the colonies of New South Wales, Victoria and South Australia. The Sheffield Shield thus came into being, Victoria winning the first series in 1892–93.

ENGLAND V VICTORIA NOV. 1891
W G.GRACE BATTING   G.RUDD PHOTO

W. G. Grace sets off for a run at Melbourne during the English team's match against Victoria, the second engagement of the 1891–92 tour. He scored 159 not out, carrying his bat through the innings of 284. By April, Australian fans will have been reflecting with mixed emotions that this was the Champion's only hundred on the tour – though he came out at the head of the batting averages, where he belonged.

On October 10, 1892, the P&O steamship **Bokhara** (2940 tons) was wrecked in a gale off Sand Island, in the Pescadores, Formosa, two days out of Shanghai. Many of the cricketers pictured perished. They had taken part in the Interports match in Shanghai. Players from Hong Kong and Shanghai are in the group. The Hong Kong players were victims of the disaster on the voyage home. The most eminent player lost was John Dunn (seated, with moustache and ringed cap). Born in Hobart in 1862, he was educated at Harrow and played four matches for Surrey in 1881. He toured North America with the Gentlemen of Ireland, and once made six centuries in a week in Dublin. His runmaking continued after his posting to Hong Kong, where he became known as 'the Grace of the East'.

Lord Hawke and his mixed team take time off from their tour of North America in the cold autumn of 1891 to see Niagara Falls, where Captain Webb ('so foolish and so rash') had lost his life in the rapids. Sammy Woods (right, back row) was too fast for most of the American and Canadian batsmen, though the team did manage to lose the opening fixture, against the Philadelphians, on the imposing Germantown CC ground.

The English team which visited South Africa in 1891–92 had two unexpected faces in its mids – Australian players Murdoch and Ferris, who joined the short list of those who have played Test cricket for two countries. Standing: J. Leaney (umpire), E. Leaney, F. Martin, G. W. Ayres, A. D. Pougher, W. Chatterton, E. Ash (manager); seated: H. Wood, G. G. Hearne, J. T. Hearne, W. W. Read (captain), J. J. Ferris, W. L. Murdoch; front: W. Brockwell, G. Brann, V. A. Barton, A. Hearne. England won the sole Test, at Cape Town, by an innings. Harry Wood, the Surrey wicketkeeper, made 134 not out, and Ferris took 13 for 91.

Hardly cricket weather in Manchester in August 1892.

ADMISSION 6ᵈ EACH

EVERY ONE ENTERING TAKES HIS OWN RISK OF THE WEATHER. NO MONEY RETURNED

The crowd outside the Entrance to the Old Trafford Ground, on Monday last.

Adelaide Oval remained unpretentious in the 1890s – when this district match was played and when Lord Sheffield's team called – just as it does, in its charming way, today.

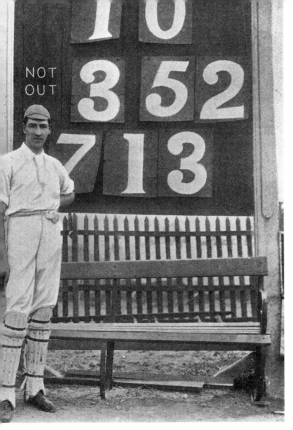

Frank Laver, a Test player and tour manager of the future, stirred Australia's reviving interest further as the 1890s unfurled with an innings of 352 not out for East Melbourne against St Kilda. Right: The newly-promoted Somerset took delight and inspiration from the unexpectedly huge opening stand by L. C. H. Palairet (left) and H. T. Hewett, who posted a record 346 for the first wicket against Yorkshire at Taunton in 1892 before Hewett was out for 201.

The Last Match of the Season, *a whiff of romance as the 1892 English season draws to a close.*

The Australasian Cricket Council was formed in 1892, but had dissolved by 1898, having had no power without money. The players wished to control their own affairs, as they were to demonstrate generation after generation.

Surrey 1892, premier team in the land: champions in 1887, 1888, 1889, 1890, 1891, 1892 and 1894 and 1895, a run of success unmatched until the 1950s. Heavy scoring by Abel, Walter Read and John Shuter, the fast bowling of Tom Richardson and Bill Lockwood, backed by Lohmann's rare skill, and the allround play of Maurice Read made them one of the most powerful combinations ever seen. Standing: T. Richardson, E. C. Streatfeild, K. J. Key, J. M. Read, F. Boyington (scorer); seated: H. Wood, G. A. Lohmann, J. Shuter (captain), W. W. Read, W. H. Lockwood; front: R. Abel, R. Henderson.

Below: *Shrewsbury's 8½-hour innings of 212 comes to an end in Nottinghamshire's match at Lord's against Middlesex in 1892 His team (466) won by an innings. The bowler is 'Turkey' Rawlin and the catcher Jim Phillips, who later became an eminent umpire.*

Intense rather than angelic, the small boys of S. Anselm's School team in 1893 exude a sense of responsibility appropriate to cricketers who formed the new Derbyshire prep school's first cricket team.

Spectator participation at Lord's, 1893, as a gentleman interrupts his small talk to hold a 'ripping' catch.

C. L. Townsend (left), a brilliant young legspinner and left-hand batsman, performed the unique feat, in 1893, of a hat-trick in which all the victims were stumped. His wicketkeeper accomplice in this oddity – for Gloucestershire against Somerset at Cheltenham – was W. H. Brain (right).

175

Madras v Bombay, May 1893, with European faces only. Some distinguished English cricketers played regularly in India (R. M. Poore is in this group, seated extreme left), where the game was still organised on a separate communal basis.

Australia's traditional weaning process has been one of barefoot boys, kerosene cans, and no obvious frills.

On their 1893 tour of England, the Australians lost the Ashes, losing at The Oval and drawing the other two Tests. Among their triumphs, though, was an innings of 843 against Oxford & Cambridge Past & Present at the United Services Ground, Portsmouth. The total was a new world record. Alec Bannerman scored 133, Billy Bruce 191, and Hugh Trumble 105 as the tourists batted into the third day. The Universities side, labelled unashamedly as 'very weak', used 10 bowlers, one of whom was a young man named Ranjitsinhji.

The Hon. F. S. Jackson of Cambridge and Yorkshire hit 91 against Australia at Lord's on his Test debut in 1893, and 103 at The Oval in the next Test, which England won by an innings.

That victory was set up by W. G. Grace and A. E. Stoddart, drawn (right) as they came in for lunch on the first day with 134 on the scoreboard without loss – their third successive century stand that summer against the Australians. Grace (68) and Stoddart (83) were both out at 151, the latter having enjoyed even more escapes than his bulky partner as catches were grassed off Turner, Giffen and McLeod.

The lbw Law then allowed padding away all but the straight ball.

Right: Harry Graham, 'The Little Dasher', achieved the unique feat of scoring a century in his maiden innings in a Test in England (Lord's, 1893) and also in Australia (Sydney, 1894–95). Born in Melbourne in 1870, he later suffered mental instability, and died in an asylum in Dunedin, New Zealand in 1911.

177

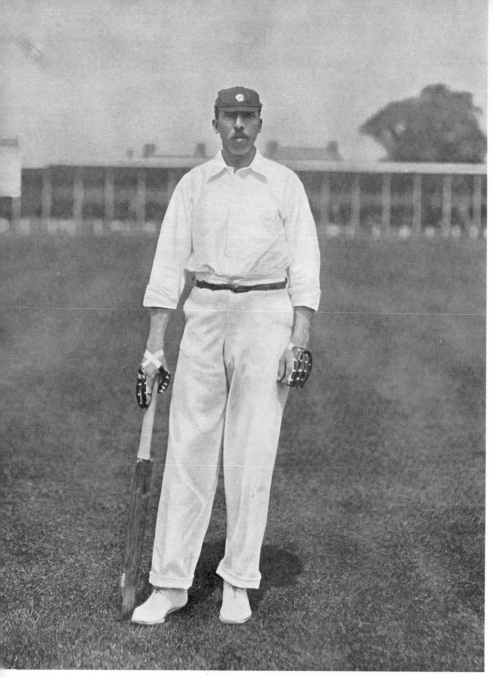

Catches in the outfield have been matters of anxiety ever since serious cricket began.
Left: William Gunn of Notts, who scored his only Test century, 102 not out, at Old Trafford in 1893. Exceptionally tall, he used his great reach to advantage, and applied his disciplined technique with elegance and style. A founder of Gunn & Moore, he died, in 1921, a rich man. His famous Notts partner, Arthur Shrewsbury, made 1893 a good year for them both by scoring 106 in the Lord's Test.

Although his field setting, as depicted, is far from aggressive, Tom Richardson was a great-hearted and lethal fast bowler, whose best – and frequent – delivery was a ball which cut back from the off at lightning speed. Here the killer ball gets Giffen in the Australians' match against Surrey, won by the county.

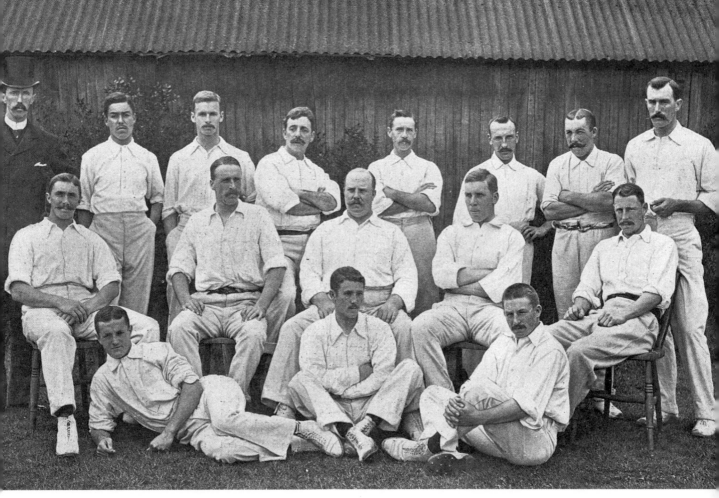

The first South African team to tour England. 'Krom' Hendricks, a brilliant fast bowler of Malay extraction, was included in the 1894 party, but then withdrawn upon 'the greatest pressure by those in high authority in the Cape Colony'. Standing: W. V. Simkins (manager), C. O. H. Sewell, G. S. Kempis, D. C. Davey, F. Hearne, C. H. Mills, J. Middleton, A. W. Seccull; seated: T. W. Routledge, G. Cripps, H. H. Castens (captain), C. L. Johnson, E. A. Halliwell; front: G. A. Rowe, D. C. Parkin, G. K. Glover. Cripps was born in India, Johnson in County Kildare, and eight of the others were English-born. They won half their 24 fixtures, none of which was first-class.

No unseemly dives and lunges were expected of outfielders in Victorian times. The days when green knees were an essential badge of commitment lay far in the future.

All seems lost for Yorkshire with their score 19 for 9 at Headingley in 1894. But Hirst and Hunter pulled the total up to 61, leaving Gloucestershire to make 78 for victory. It was too much for them.

Eyesight is crucial not only to batsmanship but to fielding. Here Abel holds a catch safely some distance from the bat in 1894. It was believed to have been during the Gentlemen of the South v Players of the South match at Lord's, with Hewett, the Somerset left-hander, the batsman whose time thus expired.

Andrew Ernest Stoddart took two English teams to Australia, the first, in 1894–95, here sailing in Ophir from Tilbury. They contested a thrilling, action-packed series of five Tests which saw Test cricket really come of age in terms of public interest and newspaper coverage. Lining the rail, in their official straw boaters, are F. G. J. Ford, L. H. Gay, J. T. Brown, A. C. MacLaren, R. Peel, A. Ward, W. Brockwell, Stoddart, W. A. Humphreys. Humphreys, 45, was a Sussex underhand lob bowler. He played in none of the Test matches, but was a companionable tourist – and carved the Christmas turkey.

Bobby Peel bowls for the English team of 1894–95 at Melbourne, probably in the match against Victoria. It was Peel's pleasure to take the final wicket in the first-Test victory at Sydney, also at Melbourne in the second, and to hit the winning run at Melbourne in the fifth.

Tom Richardson taking all 10 wickets against Essex at The Oval in 1894. On the Australian tour he bowled with great fire and courage.

Syd 'Tich' Gregory (right) came good at last with 201 in the opening Test – which Australia sensationally lost by 10 runs after England had followed on. Frank Iredale (left) made an important 140 at Adelaide, where Australia won.

181

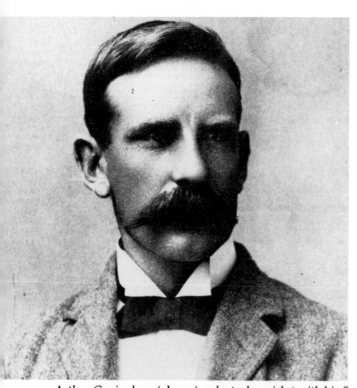

Arthur Coningham (above), who took a wicket with his first ball in Test cricket for Australia, Melbourne 1894, his only appearance. A wild man, he conducted his own divorce proceedings in 1900, revolver at his hip, against an eminent Sydney priest whom he accused of being 'the other man'. **Above right:** *Albert Ward of Lancashire, whose 75 and 117 helped England win the amazing opening Test at Sydney.*

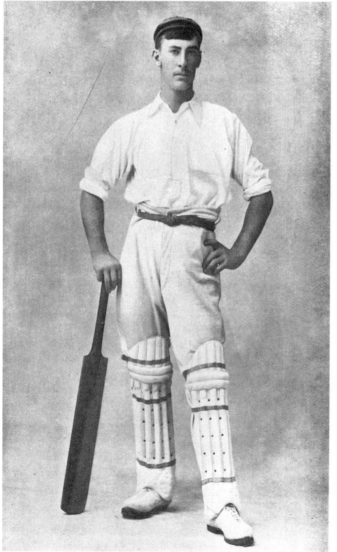

Australian newspaper cartoon suggesting England's loss of the third Test was caused by excessive drinking. **Left:** *The major cause was Albert Trott, 21, who scored 38 not out and 72 not out and took 8 for 35 at Adelaide on his Test debut. A bowler of numerous varieties, and a strong hitter as a batsman, he seemed to be Australia's discovery of the age; but he was not chosen for the next tour of England, in 1896, when his brother Harry was captain. Instead, he went to England and qualified for Middlesex, serving them wondrously well for some years.*

Left: J. T. Brown, who won the Ashes for England with a rollicking 140 in the final Test, at Melbourne (where Stoddart had made 173 in the second Test, the highest by an England captain in Australia until 1974–75). Set 297 for victory in the fifth Test, England were 28 for 2 when Jack Brown joined Ward. Brown reached 50 in a record 28 minutes, and the pair put on a record 210. England went on to win by six wickets, and Giffen's 475 runs and 34 wickets in the series had not been enough.

Honest Tom Richardson bowled his heart out under the broiling Australian sun, taking 32 wickets in the five Tests. Back home in 1895, he took the staggering total of 290 wickets, and in the four seasons 1894 to 1897 this kindly, tough toiler actually took 1005. Left: The first English team in West Indies, early 1895, pictured with opponents in St Kitts. All amateurs, under R. S. Lucas, they regarded it as a social tour, but still won 10 of their 16 matches. Over 6000 spectators watched the first day's play in Barbados.

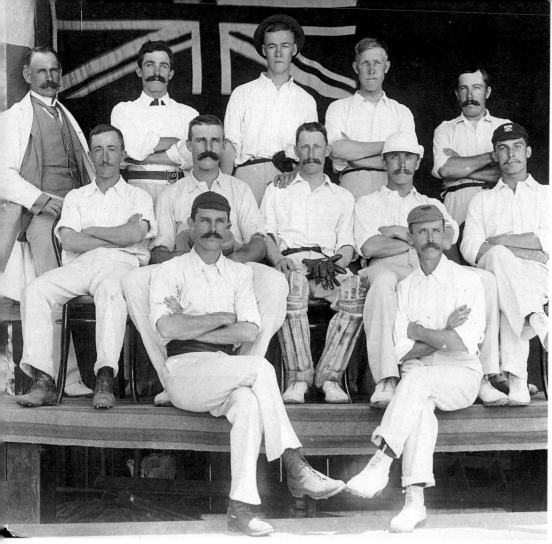

The South African team which faced England at Port Elizabeth in the first of the three 1895–96 Test matches – all won resoundingly by England, for whom Lohmann was next to unplayable. In this Test he took 7 for 38 and 8 for 7, finishing with a hat-trick, and at Johannesburg he returned 9 for 28 and 3 for 43. He wrapped up the series at Cape Town with 7 for 42 and 1 for 45. His perhaps slightly apprehensive opponents pictured are: standing – umpire, C. G. Fichardt, J. H. Sinclair, J. T. Willoughby, J. Middleton; seated – R. A. Gleeson or F. J. Cook, R. M. Poore, E. A. Halliwell (captain), T. W. Routledge, F. J. Cook or R. A. Gleeson; front – C. F. W. Hime, F. Hearne.

Charles Kortright bowls to H. W. Bainbridge at Edgbaston in 1895. This is the only surviving photograph of the Essex express bowler in action. Regarded by batsmen of the time as being the fastest bowler yet seen, it is impossible to place him accurately a century later. The testimony of contemporaries needs to be respected. A man of means, 'Korty' hardly ever worked, but his seriousness about propelling a cricket ball was never in doubt. Stumps were knocked yards, with batsmen still waving their bats airily. He did not always manage to control a short temper.

C. J. Kortright (1871–1952), who was kept out of the England XI by Tom Richardson. When his chance did come, in 1899, he was injured.

Australian Test player Jack Worrall registered the first quadruple-century in Australia when he made 417 not out for Carlton v Melbourne University in 1895–96. Carlton's total of 922 was a new world record for all cricket. High scoring was the order of the day, for East Melbourne totalled 876 against Richmond and Melbourne made 683 against St Kilda – all on the same day. In Sydney club cricket that season there were five centuries in Paddington's innings against Burwood. It all followed the pattern set in 1895 by W. G. Grace and A. C. MacLaren, and Capt. W. C. Oates and Pte F. Fitzgerald, who made an unbroken second-wicket stand of 623 in an Army match at the Curragh in Ireland.

Wormwood Scrubs railway station, awash with club cricketers on a Saturday afternoon in 1895.

No radio or television, but the newspapers kept the scores updated. Here Mr Higgins, the electrician of the Exchange Telegraph, is reading the tape as a description of a game at Lord's is tapped out.

The summer of 1895 saw W. G. Grace, then 47, batting more successfully than at any time since the 1870s. He became the first batsman to score 1000 runs in May, the product of 10 innings, one of which was his 100th first-class century: a small matter of 288 against Somerset before a large crowd at Bristol. Woods, unusually nervous, bowled a helpful full-toss to an untypically flustered WG for the 100th run. He then went to 200, at which point a jeroboam of champagne was sent out. He had made every ball bowled to him look ridiculously easy. Although the bulky champion was now claiming that 'I can bat but I can't bend', he had reasserted himself as cricket's Colossus.

WG's amazing summer inspired waves of tangible affection in the shape of testimonials from the **Daily Telegraph**, the Sportsman, MCC and Gloucestershire, the sum total reaching £9073 8s 3d. The cartoon has the editor of the Telegraph handing over the cheque with the remark 'Don't mention it, Doctor; and thank you for what you have done for my circulation'.

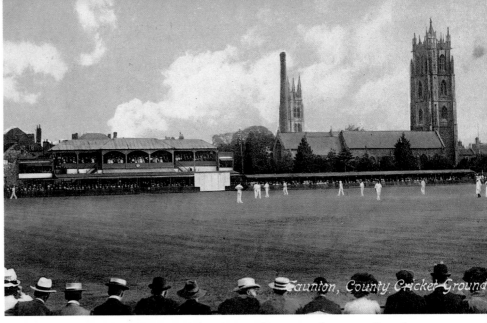

Taunton, where Archie MacLaren (left) of Lancashire stormed to a new first-class record individual score of 424 in July 1895, passing WG's 344, made in 1876. The Somerset bowlers had just conceded 692 to Essex, and now Lancashire piled up 801. MacLaren, having scored 120 in the deciding Test at Melbourne last winter, raised his reputation still further with this 470-minute showpiece, hitting 62 fours and a six. He and A. G. Paul put on 363 in 190 minutes for Lancashire's second wicket, only 35 short of Shrewsbury and Gunn's world record.

"On the Free List at the Oval."

Hansom cabs and omnibuses: ways and means of a free peek at The Oval, 1895.

Walter Mead of Essex, a bowler of offbreaks and legbreaks. Against Hampshire at Southampton in 1895 he captured 17 wickets for 119; but Essex lost, Harry Baldwin taking 13 for 78 for the home side.

Not the most suitable of conditions, but cricket is cricket, even in Kohat, near Peshawar, in what is now Pakistan. Photograph from 1896.

Over !

George Davidson might have become a name to conjure with had he not played for struggling Derbyshire. He did the 'double' in 1895, and next summer he scored 274 against Lancashire at Old Trafford, a Derbyshire record still 90 years later. Davidson contracted pneumonia and died in February 1899. He was only 32, and left a widow and six small children, for whom a fund was set up.

Left: Surrey v Derbyshire at The Oval, 1895: another damp pitch and more patting down after each over.

A. D. 'Dick' Pougher (pron. Puffer) of Leicestershire, whose greatest moment came when he took five Australian wickets for no runs with offspin for MCC at Lord's in 1896. The tourists were out for 18. Their problem was that this jug-eared bowler kept the ball low and turned it less than was threatened by his finger and wrist action.

Cricketers, dreaming perhaps of past or future triumphs, were among those who forgetfully consigned their bats to the Great Eastern Railway Company's lost-property office at Liverpool Street station.

G. H. S. Trott, leader of the 1896 Australian team in England. His 143 at Lord's was a remarkable innings, his stand of 221 with Syd Gregory (103) being a new Test record.

Left: If there was one thing that would rankle with a Yorkshireman it was the knowledge that Lancashire's 801 in 1895 was a world record. This was put right in 1896 with Yorkshire's 887 at Birmingham.

189

Hugh Trumble, on his third tour of England, took 148 wickets in 1896, including 12 in the Oval Test. By the end of his Test career, in 1903–04, the tall Victorian had taken 141 wickets in Ashes Tests, a record until beaten by Lillee.

Left: *Kumar Shri Ranjitsinhji, the languid Cambridge-educated Indian, who played for Sussex over a 25-year span from 1895, burst on the Test scene with an enchanting, wristy 154 not out in England's second innings at Old Trafford, having scored 62 in the first. Australia won a thriller by three wickets, holding out against the gallant marathon of Richardson (13 for 244 in the match). MCC had not seen fit to select 'Ranji' for the previous Test, at Lord's, but the Lancashire club had no such qualms. His aggregate of 2780 for the season took the record from WG.*

Left: *The Nottinghamshire CCC membership ticket produced mixed viewing: the county finished sixth in 1896, Lord Hawke's Yorkshire taking the title. The ticket for the Gloucestershire v Australians match at Bristol brought nothing sensational compared to the county's return match with the tourists at Cheltenham, where Gloucestershire were bowled out by Trumble and McKibbin for 17 in the second innings, WG scoring 9.*

Ernie Jones, the bronco fast bowler from South Australia. He bounced one through WG's beard, and gave the Australian attack more fire than it had ever known, except in the early years of Spofforth. The bowling actions of Jones and spinner Tom McKibbin, however, were called into question in 1896, and during the 1897–98 Tests Jones was 'called' for throwing. A down-to-earth character, when asked by the Prince of Wales if he had gone to Adelaide's Prince Alfred College, he replied: 'Yeah, I drive the dust-cart there'.

Gilbert Laird Jessop (1874–1955), the greatest consistent hitter the game had seen until the coming of Botham. In days when a hit over the boundary counted five runs, and the batsman lost the strike, he hit 53 fast hundreds, 15 of them inside an hour. He was a fiery fast bowler too in his younger days, and a brilliant cover fieldsman. The fastest of 'The Croucher's' centuries came in Gloucestershire's match at Sheffield in 1897: 40 minutes.

Right: When five England professionals went 'on strike' for more pay before the 1896 Oval Test, Punch pleaded for 'Fair Play, Fair Pay, and Friendliness'. Abel, Hayward and Richardson relented, but Gunn and Lohmann never played for England again.

Eton, from the Royal Library, Windsor Castle, showing the Town of Windsor cricket field, a painting exhibited at the Royal Academy by Frederick Goodall in 1897.

Below: *P. F. Warner's English team watch their fellows bat against a mainly English-born team at Staten Island, New York in September 1897. The visiting 'batters' made enough runs on a powdery pitch to win the match.*

Henry Perkins, a ginger-haired former Cambridgeshire player, became MCC secretary in 1876, succeeding R. A. Fitzgerald, and retired in 1897. He presided over many events of profound significance, and was one of those men who 'lived for cricket'. 'He had his foibles,' stated Wisden upon his death in 1916. In other words, he drank rather a lot.

Stoddart's second team (1897–98) had a much more difficult time of it in Australia than the first. Australia were resurgent and the English combination did not enjoy the best of fortunes on or off the field. Standing: J. T. Hearne, A. C. MacLaren, T. W. Hayward, J. Briggs, G. H. Hirst, A. E. Stoddart, A. Priestley (friend), N. F. Druce, E. Wainwright, J. R. Mason, W. Storer; front: a host, J. H. Board, K. S. Ranjitsinhji, a host, Major B. J. Wardill (Melbourne Cricket Club), T. Richardson.

Joe Darling, the chunky South Australian left-hander, became the first batsman to make 500 runs in a Test series. His scores in the 1897–98 series included 101 at Sydney in the first Test, 178 at Adelaide in the third, and 160 at Sydney in the fifth, when he rattled to three figures in a mere 91 minutes.

Not much fun when a chap's ball drops into the water: casual play interrupted at Hockley Brook, Birmingham, 1897.

An historic picture of Ranjitsinhji trotting from the field at Sydney at the end of his 175 in the first Test of the 1897–98 series. The players wore black armbands out of respect to their captain, Drewy Stoddart, whose mother had died in England a few days before the match, and who was too distraught to play in either of the first two Tests. Ranji would not have played had the start not been delayed by three days because of rain. His throat infection clearing, he batted at No. 7, and his magnificent innings, following MacLaren's cultured 109, lifted England beyond 500 for the first time in a Test match. England went on to win by nine wickets, but lost the remaining four Tests by wide margins.

Charlie McLeod (facing) and Clem Hill during their second-wicket stand of 124 in the second Test of 1897–98, at Melbourne, which Australia (520) won by an innings.

Clem Hill, a future Australian captain, had scores of 96, 58, 81 and 188 in the first four Tests of 1897–98. A solidly-built and game left-hander, he was only 20 at the time. His Test career ended in 1911–12, midst controversy, but his last innings for South Australia did not come until 1922–23. In 1900–01 he scored 365 not out against NSW at Adelaide, beating Murdoch's Australian record.

Left: *John Thomas Hearne, the complete medium-pacer. He served Middlesex regularly and faithfully from 1890 until the First World War, and finished with over 3000 first-class wickets, three times passing 200 in a season. A yeoman professional, born in Buckinghamshire in 1867, he took nine wickets in an innings on eight occasions, and his toils on the 1897–98 tour of Australia, in the most adverse conditions he ever encountered, were rewarded with 20 Test wickets.*

OVAL, 1898.

Another summer, another cricket season, with no international cricket to disturb the domestic scene.

F. E. (later Sir Francis) Lacey took office as MCC secretary in 1898, an amateur cricketer of some eminence who played for Hampshire, scoring 323 not out against Norfolk at Southampton in 1887. A barrister and disciplinarian, stern and over 6 ft tall, he brought a new efficiency to the administration at Lord's.

Tom Hayward, Surrey's prolific Cambridge-born batsman, by the scoreboard recording his 315 not out against Lancashire at The Oval in 1898. When he heard that Yorkshire had given J. T. Brown a bonus for his triple-century the same day, he said he'd get out at 100 in future – a pledge he broke repeatedly.

Lord Hawke's English team of 1898–99, which played and won two Tests in South Africa. Albert Trott was wanted by England even if Australia had ignored him. He took 17 wickets in the two Tests. P. F. 'Plum' Warner carried his bat for 132 at Johannesburg in his maiden Test. Standing: G. A. Lohmann (manager), W. R. Cuttell, F. Mitchell, F. W. Milligan, A. G. Archer, A. A. White (umpire); seated: S. Haigh, H. R. Bromley-Davenport, Lord Hawke (captain), A. E. Trott, J. H. Board; front: J. T. Tyldesley, C. E. M. Wilson, P. F. Warner.

Lord's has ever been more than a cricket ground. It has been a social headquarters, and never more so than when Oxford met Cambridge, when the luncheon interval – as here in 1898 – was for 'parading' as much as taking refreshment. Jessop and Bosanquet played in this match, and R. E. Foster had just been dismissed for 57, to the regret of all who appreciated classical batsmanship.

Some of the earliest moving film was shot at Lord's in 1898 when the Gentlemen v Players match was dedicated to W. G. Grace's 50th birthday (July 18). Shrewsbury and WG led the parade past the cine-camera, which was positioned near where the Warner Stand is now situated. The tall William Gunn may be seen ahead of the players following.

J. T. Brown (300), the hero of the 1895 Melbourne Test, and his tall partner John Tunnicliffe (243) enjoy the fruits of their labours as recorded by the scoreboard at Chesterfield: a world record opening stand of 554 for Yorkshire (champions in 1898) against Derbyshire, who went down by an innings.

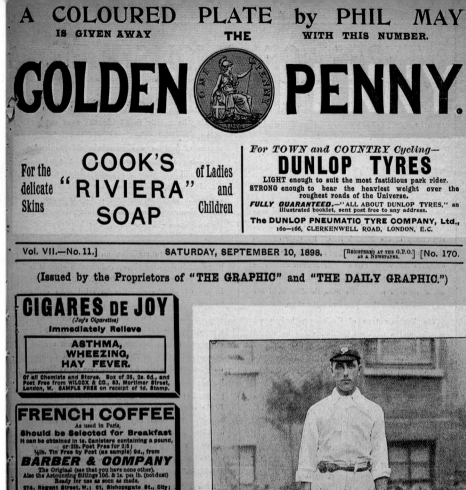

Photograph by E. Hawkins & Co., Brighton.
THE YOUNG BOWLER OF THE YEAR.
Rhodes, the new Yorkshire Professional Bowler, who, in his first year of County Cricket has headed the first-class bowling averages during most of the season.

Arthur E. J. Collins, 13, a pupil at Clifton College, scored 628 not out in a house match in June 1899, a score higher than any in an organised match before or since. He and his two brothers were killed in the First World War.

Young Bowler of the Year indeed. Wilfred Rhodes was only 20, in his first season with Yorkshire, a quiet left-arm bowler and right-hand batsman – though he didn't bat much then – from the village of Kirkheaton in the West Riding. He practised a lot and thought about the game ceaselessly, and by the time he was finished, after the 1930 season, when he was 52, his cunning and persistence had won him a world record total of 4187 wickets, having taken five or more in an innings on 286 occasions. Never bored by cricket, he took as much pleasure from his final wicket as from his first. In his first season he bowled to WG and in his last he bowled to Bradman. His batting developed and he rose up the order, and it was a particular source of pride to him that he shared in England's first- and tenth-wicket records against Australia. For years the Yorkshire team was built around him and George Hirst, and when, as the system dictated, various amateurs came to captain Yorkshire, the real strategist was 'old Wilfred'. He died in 1973, aged 95, having been blind for the last 20 years.

AGE OF GODS

THE GOLDEN AGE which had begun in the 1890s gathered a glorious richness in the season of 1899. Not only did the lyrical Ranjitsinhji, silk sleeves fluttering, become the first to score as many as 3000 runs in a season, but a young man came from Australia and showed English cricket-lovers batsmanship of such dash and genius that there seemed little point in trying to compare him with past masters. This was Victor Trumper, who had been lucky to get on the tour on half-share terms. After the 1899 visit the fans longed for him to return. Batsmen were now running the game. Sussex had Ranji and Fry, Surrey Abel and Hayward (who made 448 together for the fourth wicket against Yorkshire), Gloucestershire had Jessop and Townsend, though no WG any more. He had left in a huff after all those years and had set himself up at Crystal Palace with the new London County team. MacLaren and Tyldesley packed them in at Old Trafford, and even humble Hampshire had some high-scorers in Major Poore and Captain Wynyard. Trott broke new ground with Middlesex, becoming the first to put 1000 runs and 200 wickets in the book in one season. The Foster brotherhood flourished with Worcestershire, little Quaife did his bit for Warwickshire, and Shrewsbury and Gunn were still to be seen grinding out their hundreds for Notts, joined now by the talented A. O. Jones. Somerset were at least colourful and unpredictable, and Yorkshire were, as ever, nothing flashy, but deeply stocked with skill and grit. Cricket was stronger than it had ever been: still developing, not always for the better, and as much a part of people's hearts as it could ever be.

Victor Thomas Trumper, on England tour at 21 in 1899, scored over 1500 runs, with an amazing 300 not out against Sussex and a lovely Test century at Lord's.

Left: *Captain E. G. Wynyard, who helped Major Poore to put on 411 for Hampshire's sixth wicket at Taunton, an English record. Highly versatile in sport, he took 5 for 38 with lobs in this 1899 match.*

199

Australia retained the Ashes in 1899 by winning the second Test at Lord's. The other four were drawn. Standing: J. J. Kelly, M. A. Noble, H. Trumble, C. E. McLeod, Major B. J. Wardill (manager); seated: E. Jones, F. Laver, J. Darling (captain), S. E. Gregory, A. E. Johns, W. P. Howell; front: C. Hill, V. T. Trumper, F. A. Iredale.

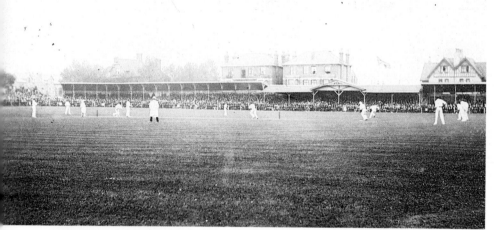

Play in Trent Bridge, Nottingham's first Test match, 1899, which marked the end of W. G. Grace's Test career. He leads England off (below) with Ranjitsinhji and wicketkeeper Storer.

A more sensational debut in England than Bill Howell's in 1899 could hardly be imagined. He took 10 for 28 for the Australians against Surrey. He gave the ball a lot of offspin.

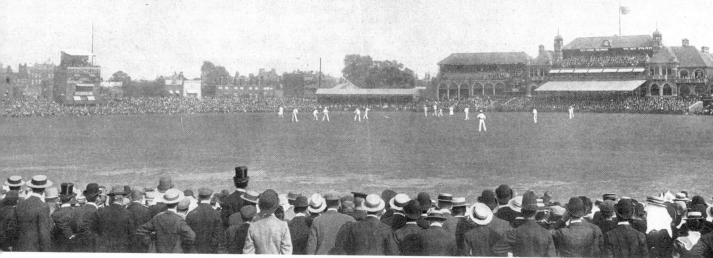

Full house at The Oval on the opening day of the final Test of 1899 as England try to level the series. Openers F. S. Jackson and Tom Hayward are batting, and were not separated until 185 was on the board. England made 576 and Australia, with 352, had to follow on, but forced a draw.

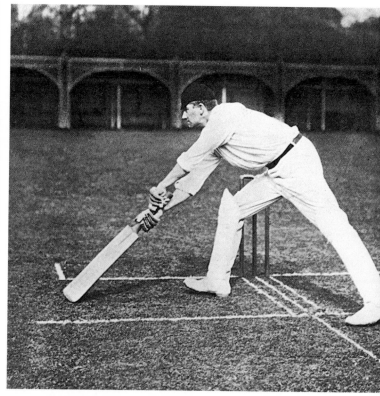

Trumble prepares to slip his sweater back on as the Australians leave the field for lunch in the Oval Test. They had little to cheer them for England went on to score their highest total yet against Australia, 576, something to gladden the hearts of immigrants from the Old Country far away in the New.

Above right: Montague Alfred Noble, an intellectual cricketer who became one of Australia's best captains. He didn't quite emulate Trumble in doing the double on this trip, but his vital contributions were numerous.

Right: Albert Trott climbs over the experimental netting used at Lord's for a short time. In 1899 the Australian 'exile' lifted a ball from Noble, during the MCC match, right over the Lord's pavilion, a gigantic hit which did his game little good in the long run as he almost forgot defence entirely. A victim of dropsy and booze, Trott shot himself at his Willesden lodgings in 1914.

Kent v Sussex at Tonbridge, Newham (facing) and Ranji in, Alec Hearne bowling. Hearne was one of the most skilful bowlers in England, bowling leg- and offspin, and was a handsome batsman. Unluckily he never played in a Test.

w long will he keep his end up?"

Trouble in South Africa inevitably brought the Boer leader, Paul Kruger, into sporting cartoons.
Right: Major R. M. Poore, exceptionally tall and much-travelled sportsman. He came home to Hampshire and hit 1551 runs at 91 in 1899, with seven centuries, including 304 against Somerset. Then he went to the USA to buy mules for the British Government before going to the conflict in the Cape.

202

Playing out Time in an Awkward Light sends a tingle down the spine of anyone who has ever batted in such a situation. The original, by Frank Batson, hangs in the pavilion at Trent Bridge.

THE LITTLE WONDER.

MIRING TRIO: They will want him at Leeds.

Bobby Abel continued to make runs galore, including a Surrey record of 357 not out against Somerset at The Oval, but 'Rip's' call for him to rejoin England was unanswered. Right: Reginald and Wilfrid Foster, brothers who made two centuries each in Worcestershire's match against Hampshire at Worcester in 1899: then a unique feat.

THE season of 1900 saw further high scoring. Abel made 12 centuries, beating WG's record of 10, and Hayward scored 1074 runs before the end of May in this first English summer of the six-ball over. The first West Indies tour of England took place – captained by Aucher Warner, brother of 'Plum', they started at WG's Crystal Palace ground and picked up to win five of their 17 matches – and Devon County Wanderers won the cricket section at the Paris Olympic Games. There was much about which to reminisce during the winter of 1900–01: the Players scored 502 to beat the Gentlemen by two wickets at Lord's (Abel 98, Hayward 111, Brown 163), R. E. Foster having charmed two centuries in the match for the amateurs. For the first time in 35 years WG was not chosen for this great fixture – which might have been as well for the 52-year-old champion, since the weather was 'tropical'. Ranji performed another miracle by passing 3000 runs again, and Trott reached 1000 runs and 200 wickets for the second season. The follow-on was now, sensibly, made optional upon a 150-run deficit, and the campaign to stamp out 'throwing and dubious bowling' began with Jim Phillips' no-balling of Lancashire fast bowler Mold and Somerset slow left-armer Tyler. But for the Boer War, Lord's would have seen South Africa playing West Indies, an encounter that politicians rendered impossible until the clandestine fixtures of the 1980s. New South Wales raised the world-record total to 918 in their match against South Australia at Sydney, while Yorkshire's match against Worcestershire at Bradford in 1900 was all over in a day. Cricket then, as now, as ever, was fun.

The best day of the school week: cricket afternoon! Right: *Dr W. G. Grace rejoices as his new club, London County, is awarded first-class status.*

" Ha, Ha ! "

Left: *Albert Trott, the bowler of offcutters, swervers, legspinners, thunderous fast yorkers, tantalisingly-hung slow balls. In 1900, for the second season running, the hard-drinking Middlesex Aussie took 200 wickets and scored 1000 runs.*

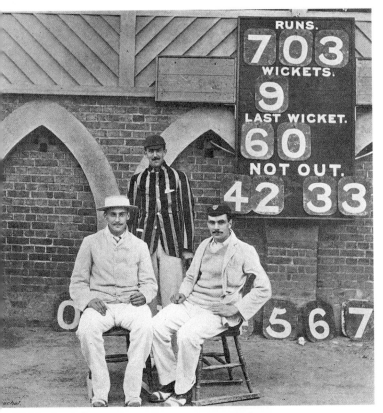

Arthur Mold was a penetrative fast bowler for Lancashire – and in three Test matches – until called for throwing. Thereafter he considered his career to have been worthless. Umpire Phillips no-balled him 16 times in the home game against Somerset in 1901.

Another big score, this one by Cambridge University v Sussex, 1900: 703 for 9, the centurions being C. P. Foley (standing), F. G. J. Ford and Gregor MacGregor.

Dan Leno, music-hall comic and singer, practises in his back garden. He had a team of 'eccentric' cricketers who played in charity matches.

Left: C. B. Fry, Englishman of vast sporting and intellectual accomplishment. International cricketer, soccer player, world long-jump record-holder, scholar, author, conversationalist, he batted with acute brainpower, and was prolific if not necessarily beautiful to behold. In 1901 he scored 13 centuries, six of them in succession, his record until equalled by Bradman and later Procter. Fry made 94 centuries in all.

Yorkshire, under Lord Hawke's firm leadership, were county champions three years running from 1900 to 1902, and were unbeaten between August 1899 and July 1901. Standing: E. Wainwright, Lees Whitehead, W. Rhodes, D. Hunter; seated: G. H. Hirst, E. Smith, Lord Hawke, F. Mitchell, J. Tunnicliffe; front: D. Denton, T. L. Taylor, J. T. Brown. Smith, Mitchell, Taylor and the captain were all amateurs. David Hunter, the wicketkeeper, made 914 catches and 351 stumpings in a distinguished career which extended from 1888 to 1909.

Above left: *Tom Straw, Worcestershire's wicketkeeper, who was out 'obstructing the field' in 1899 and again in 1901, both times against Warwickshire, once at home and then away.*

Left: *Ungainly but effective: how Abel dealt with some testing deliveries during his long career, in which he amassed over 33,000 runs. This parry was made in Surrey's match against Sussex at Hove in 1901, when The Guv'nor's 44 and 47 helped set Surrey up . . . until Fry (65) and Ranji (100 not out) saw Sussex to safety. This season Abel took Ranji's aggregate record by making 3309 runs.*

Staffordshire-born Sydney Francis Barnes (1873–1967) was chosen by Archie MacLaren for his Australian tour in 1901–02 when he was barely known outside the North-West. But the stern-faced, uncompromising Barnes was a worldbeater. He took six wickets in his first Test, 13 in the second, and then injury put him out. By the end of an intermittent Test career he had taken 189 wickets at 16.43 in only 27 Tests, spinning the ball with immensely strong fingers at a rasping pace, backing it all with an overbearing personality. Some judges still regard Barnes as the best bowler the world has seen.

Clem Hill played a big part in Australia's 1901–02 success with the rare sequence of 99, 98 and 97. Reg Duff (below), from NSW, went in at No. 10 in the second innings of his maiden Test, at Melbourne, and scored 104, adding 120 for the 10th wicket with Armstrong, who was also on debut.

Sydneysiders gather outside the *Herald* building as scores from the 1901–02 Adelaide Test come through. They were to be delighted.

The 1901–02 English tourists knew of the dangerous reputation of Jack Marsh (above), the Aboriginal fast bowler, and asked for him to be omitted from a country team they were due to play in Bathurst. He played on and off for NSW, his action 'gazelle-like', his pace hot. But his action was suspicious. He tried to clear himself by bowling with a hidden wooden splint on his right arm, but he was called for throwing 19 times in February 1901, and drifted from the game. A colourful dresser, he began to drink heavily, and in 1916 he was killed in a street brawl in Orange, NSW.

Above left: *Len Braund of Somerset was of great value to England in his first series of Tests, 1901–02, bowling legspin (often taking the new ball, as was still the custom), making runs (a century at Adelaide), and proving to be a remarkable slip fieldsman. A long career brought him nearly 18,000 runs (HS 257 not out) and over 1100 wickets (9 for 41 best). Later he umpired; lost both his legs; and was bombed out several times in the Second World War.*

Left: *Charles Eady, the Tasmanian giant, beside the evidence of his colossal score for Break-of-Day against Wellington in March/April 1902: his 566 stretched over four Saturdays (with Easter intervening) and contained 13 hits over the boundary (worth five) and 68 fours. It lasted 477 minutes and remains the highest score ever made by an adult. His team totalled 911. Eady, 31 at the time, had played twice for Australia without success, a month previously at Melbourne, and at Lord's in 1896.*

Within weeks of the end of the 1901–02 Anglo-Australian Test series it was England's turn to see the triumphant Australian side first hand; and a thrilling series the 1902 rubber turned out to be, Australia being bowled out for 36 in the drawn Edgbaston Test (Birmingham's first), winning by three runs in the famous Old Trafford Test, and losing by one wicket at The Oval (Jessop's match). Standing: W. P. Howell, H. Trumble, J. V. Saunders, W. W. Armstrong, A. J. Y. Hopkins; seated: V. T. Trumper, J. J. Kelly, R. A. Duff, J. Darling (captain), M. A. Noble, C. Hill; front: S. E. Gregory, H. Carter. E. Jones is missing.

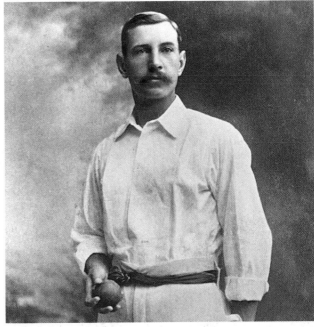

Bill Lockwood of Surrey, one of the best cricketers in the world in 1902, and the fabled Richardson's 'other half'. In the Old Trafford Test Lockwood's pace and variations brought him 11 wickets, followed by 5 for 45 at The Oval.

Left: 'Tell yer wot! You be England and I'll be Victor Trumpet!' – the ultimate tribute to the great Australian batsman, whose name the urchin almost got right.

The 11th Australian touring team reached England in the spring of 1902, and were soon busy finding their land legs in the nets at Lord's, the customary objects of much local curiosity. One of the strongest teams of all time, they won 23 of their 39 matches and lost only to England (by one wicket) and Yorkshire.

Below: Jessop, whose name, like Trumper's, is stamped on the 1902 Test series. At The Oval he hit a century in only 75 minutes to swing a lost cause England's way. Hirst and Rhodes completed a one-wicket victory.

Long before he was carried to his grave at the tragically early age of 37, Victor Trumper was considered the most naturally skilful batsman there had ever been, with the possible exception only of Ranji; and much of that reputation was established on the 1902 tour, when Trumper overcame difficult, damp conditions to make 11 centuries – the highest only 128, for he usually considered his duty to be done when he had made a century and there were others waiting to bat. His aggregate of 2570 was supreme for an Australian in England until Bradman stormed the Old Country.

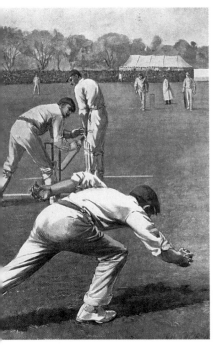

One of Test history's inspired catches: Hill has turned Hirst fine down the leg side and Braund has darted across to make the catch: Australia 10 for two wickets in the first Test ever at Edgbaston, soon to be 36 all out, Trumper 18 of them, the only double-figure score.

Below: The England XI still widely regarded as the best of all time. At Edgbaston they scored 376 (Tyldesley 138) and bowled Australia out for 36 before rain and bad light forced a draw. Standing: G. H. Hirst, A. F. A. Lilley, W. H. Lockwood, L. C. Braund, W. Rhodes; front: C. B. Fry, Hon. F. S. Jackson, A. C. MacLaren (captain), K. S. Ranjitsinhji, G. L. Jessop, J. T. Tyldesley (on arm of seat).

Advertisers soon caught on to cricket's sweet and clean image.

Duff and Trumper open for Australia in Bramall Lane, Sheffield's only Test match. Australia won it to go one-up in the 1902 series with two to play. Hill scored 119 and Noble took 11 wickets. The return of the rangy Trumble (left), whose hand was injured in the pre-tour nets at Lord's, brought the tourists to full strength. He took 10 wickets in the Old Trafford Test and 12 at The Oval. The fourth Test, at Old Trafford, ended when Fred Tate (below left) was bowled with England four runs from victory. Earlier he had missed a vital outfield catch, and was inconsolable after this his only Test appearance. He was not to know that his small son, Maurice, was to atone for his mistakes in the 1920s. Below: Jack Saunders, the penetrative Victorian spinner, took 18 wickets in the series, including the vital one of Tate.

Abel and the tall Somerset amateur Lionel Palairet open for England at Old Trafford in 1902. They contributed little to their side's 262 and 120, Jackson saving England's pride with 128. Australia's 299 and 86 gave them a supremacy at the end of three runs. Right: The strong figure of Hirst beside his longtime Yorkshire and England colleague and friend Rhodes. Hirst (58) and Rhodes (6) saw England home by one wicket in the Oval Test, not getting them in singles, as romantic legend has it, but scoring the 15 needed with the help of a four and a two. Rhodes took the winning single off Trumble. They had been responsible for humiliating Australia for 36 at Edgbaston (Hirst 3 for 15, Rhodes 7 for 17), and in the tourists' next match, against Yorkshire at Headingley, Hirst (5 for 9) and Jackson (5 for 12) got them out for 23. 'Bah goom,' said a local, 'they did bat bad'.

Jimmy Sinclair, who hit South Africa's fastest Test century (80 minutes) at Cape Town against the 1902 Australians on their way home. Left: Arthur Shrewsbury scored two centuries in a match for the first time in his career in Notts' match against Gloucestershire at his beloved Trent Bridge in July 1902. He was 46, and batting as well as ever. But declining health and melancholia overshadowed his soul, and in the following May he shot himself.

E. G. Arnold, a trusty Worcestershire allrounder, enjoyed the delight of a wicket with his first ball in Test cricket – enhanced by the fact that it was Trumper's – Sydney, December 1903. Left: MacLaren (in cap) and R. H. Spooner after their opening stand of 368 against Gloucestershire at Liverpool in 1903. This pair of graceful, spirited amateurs caught the imagination of the young local would-be writer Neville Cardus, who passed on that spirit down the ages.

In 1903–04 the first English team under MCC auspices toured Australia: a contented blend if Hayward's overt affection for Tyldesley is any indication. They won the first, second and fourth Tests, and lost the other two, thus regaining the Ashes, under 'Plum' Warner's leadership, despite the unavailability of such as MacLaren, Fry and Jackson. Trumper was in brilliant form for Australia, and Noble seemed to be the world's best allrounder, but Rhodes bowled beautifully (15 for 124 on Melbourne's sticky – on another of which he bowled Victoria out for 15), and the novelty of Bosanquet's googlies won the fourth Test, at Sydney. All the batsmen played major innings. From left: A. E. Knight, G. H. Hirst, T. W. Hayward, J. T. Tyldesley, W. Rhodes, B. J. T. Bosanquet, E. G. Arnold, L. C. Braund, A. F. A. Lilley, P. F. Warner, R. E. Foster. Absent from group: A. E. Relf, H. Strudwick, A. Fielder.

Melbourne Cricket Ground is an impressive sight as England take the field for the fifth Test, already having regained the Ashes. Braund was about to take 8 for 81, but after rain England were skittled out for 61, Cotter, the young tearaway, making his first real impact on Test cricket with 6 for 40. In the second innings Trumble took his second Test hat-trick and finished a glorious career with 7 for 28.

'Dick' Lilley of Warwickshire, whose Test career stretched from 1896 to 1909, made 17 dismissals in the 1903–04 series – and had fun 'picking' Bosanquet. Left: R. E. 'Tip' Foster, who made a massive and magnificent 287 at Sydney in the opening Test in his maiden innings. A prime luminary of the Golden Age, he captained England against South Africa in 1907, and played soccer for his country. He died in 1914, aged 36, a victim of diabetes.

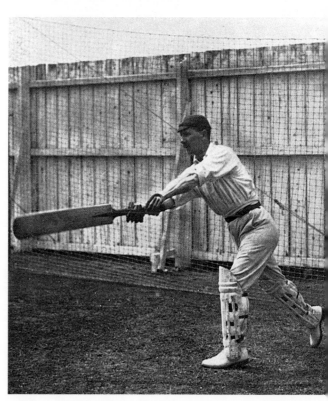

Albert Relf (top) of Sussex kept a diary on the 1903–04 tour of Australia. Entries were brief, but give an insight into the pleasures and pressures of touring in an age when man was just starting to motor around – and, across the Pacific, in Kittyhawk, to fly.

Johnny Tyldesley, an expert wet-wicket batsman, was a master at dropping his wrists and killing the spiteful kicker, or of hitting 'on the up' with power and precision. The diminutive Lancastrian played very valuable innings in the first two Tests of the showpiece 1903–04 Ashes series. By the end of his long career he had made over 37,000 runs, with 86 centuries.

As candid a picture as could ever emerge from a dressing-room in Edwardian times: the England professionals at Adelaide, Lilley seated on the left, Braund shirtless on the right. The full-length nude is unidentified. Right: Albert Knight, the Leicestershire professional, made a welcome 70 not out in the fourth Test, at Sydney. Known to pray about his cricket, he may well be asking for guidance here as he buckles on his pads.

The 1904 South Africans on their way to England. They won 13 of their 26 matches, lost only three, and tied with Middlesex. Still no Test matches in England were granted. That came next tour, three years hence. Standing: S. J. Snooke, C. M. H. Hathorn, S. E. Horwood, J. H. Sinclair, G. H. Shepstone, W. A. Shalders, J. J. Kotze, F. Mitchell (captain); seated: R. O. Schwarz, L. J. Tancred; front: J. Middleton, B. Wallach, G. C. White, E. A. Halliwell. C. B. Llewellyn, who was playing league cricket, played in six matches.

For MCC, Bosanquet took 9 for 107, thus inspiring Schwarz to bowl the new googly himself. Kotze, an express bowler, took 104 wickets and often forced Halliwell, a first-class wicketkeeper, reluctantly to stand back to him, in 'the prevailing fashion'. The tour, financed by Sir Abe Bailey, the South African industrialist, was a success other than in the matter of meeting costs. It fell £2000 short.

A good crowd for Church's league match against Accrington. Cricket in the North of England showed the way in competitive club cricket, where sets of rules brought a discipline lacking in the casual Southern variety. League cricket was still a few generations away in the Home Counties.
Below: G. W. Beldam, whose close-up action photographs took cricket's documentation a huge illustrative step forward, following the earlier important studio work of Hawkins of Brighton. His photographs, with C. B. Fry's commentary, in 1905 and 1907 were turned into two of cricket's most precious books.

Left: Herbert Jenner-Fust, who died in 1904 at the age of 98 (his son lived to 99). He was the last survivor of the 1827 Oxford v Cambridge match, and a fine wicketkeeper. President of MCC in 1833, it was said that one of his quirks was that he never bothered to watch WG play.

A little bit of fun from Sussex players Relf, Seymour, Vine and Killick, who pretend to dig up the pitch before Surrey's second innings at Hove in 1904. The cricket world was still buzzing at the news from Harrogate a fortnight earlier when the Yorkshire v Kent match was declared void after an infringement of the Laws: the effects of wear and tear on the pitch had been made good overnight. Bad luck for Yorkshire's Schofield Haigh, for he had performed a hat-trick.

'Peter' Perrin comes in at Chesterfield, having hit an unbeaten 343 for Essex against Derbyshire, still a record for the county. His innings, in July 1904, lasted 5¾ hours and included 68 fours, also still a (world) record. Essex totalled 597, and if there was one thing more remarkable than Perrin's innings it was the fact that his side lost the match on the third day. Derbyshire replied with 548 (Ollivierre, a West Indian, 229), bowled Essex out a second time for 97 (500 fewer) and knocked off the 147 for victory by nine wickets (Ollivierre 92 not out). Perrin, a long-serving amateur who made 66 centuries and reached 1000 in 18 seasons, later became an England Test selector, though he never won a cap himself.

WG and his Anglicised Australian friend Billy Murdoch, known as 'Mother' and 'Father' during their association with WG's London County team, for which so many star players – and promising youngsters – were invited to play. Photograph taken in 1904.

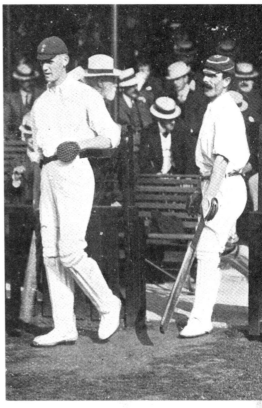

Arnold Warren (Derbyshire) (left) and George Thompson (Northants), two loyal county professionals, resume their innings for the Players against the Gentlemen at The Oval in 1905. Both fast-medium bowlers, they each took eight wickets in the match, won by 128 runs, though the amateur opposition could have been a lot stronger.

The Hon. F. S. Jackson, who had an exceptional Test series against the Australians in 1905. He won all five tosses, led his team to victory at Trent Bridge and Old Trafford, made most runs (492) on either side, at the highest average (70.29), scored centuries on his home ground, Headingley, and at Old Trafford, and topped the bowling (13 wickets at 15.46).

Below: Canterbury Week, August 1905, Alex Kermode, Lancashire's Australian fast bowler, coming in to Kent left-hander Dillon, in Fred Huish's benefit match. Kent lost by eight wickets.

THE PRINCES ARRIVE ON THE CRICKET GROUND

PRINCE EDWARD WINS THE TOSS

VIEW OF THE GROUND SHEWING THE NEW PAVILION

PRINCE EDWARD SCORES OFF HIS FIRST BALL

PRINCE ALBERT IS QUITE A STYL

The King's sons played with teams of Eton schoolboys at Home Park, Windsor in the summer of 1905. Prince Edward of Wales, the future Edward VIII, was then 11, and scored 17 not out in a total of 104. The younger Prince Albert, who became George VI upon the abdication of his brother in 1936, scored 9 out of 92, and revealed himself as 'quite a stylist'. When King George VI died in 1952, Wisden remarked: 'A left-handed batsman and bowler, the King bowled King Edward VII, King George V and the present Duke of Windsor in three consecutive balls, thus proving himself the best Royal cricketer since Frederick, Prince of Wales, in 1715.' Did the young prince switch from right-hand to left-hand?

The 1905
Australian team
submitted to
more than the odd
Kodak still
camera. The
movie film taken
here and at the
Trent Bridge Test
still survives.

Left: *David
Denton of
Yorkshire, whose
2405 runs in
1905 set an
aggregate peak
for the county
unsurpassed
until 1925, when
Herbert Sutcliffe
exceeded it.*

Right: *Bosanquet
and the smaller
Tyldesley pass a
bobby as they
resume after
lunch in the
Trent Bridge
Test. The latter
scored 56 and 61,
while 'Bosie'
completed
England's victory
with 8 for 107.*

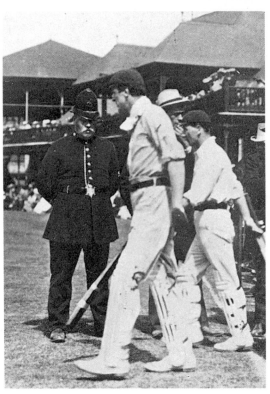

More emulation
of heroes,
assertion of
manliness, or
just plain fun on
Wimbledon
Common,
c.1905, the girls
less interested
than they ought
to be.

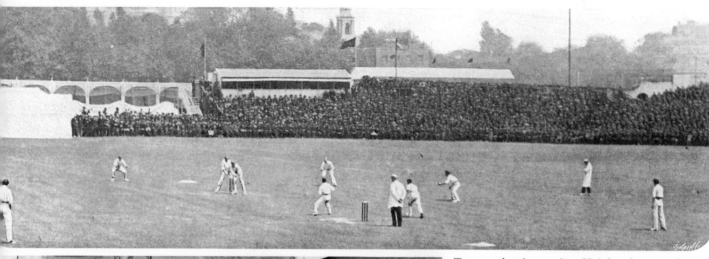

Trumper batting against Haigh, who opened England's bowling with fellow Yorkshireman Rhodes in this Lord's Test. Replying to England's 282, Trumper and Duff began belligerently, making 57 in 33 minutes. Rain, which washed out the third (final) day, spoiled a promising match – in which no out-and-out fast bowler played.

Take a public swimming bath, like this at London's St Bride's Institute, cover it over, lay down some felt and coconut mat, and lease it out for cricket practice: some evenings for the men, and some for the girls.

Bosanquet, who turned the ball from the off when it ought to have spun from leg: perhaps the sensation of the Edwardian age.

Left: Heroes of the Oval Test: Australian fast bowler 'Tibby' Cotter, who finished with 7 for 148, followed by C. B. Fry, 50 not out, to be extended to 144, his only Test hundred against Australia.

Some illustrious names are gathered in brotherly communion here at The Oval in 1905. The Australians' names are not in italics: back row – E. G. Arnold, P. M. Newland, A. J. Y. Hopkins, W. P. Howell, W. W. Armstrong; standing – W. Rhodes, A. O. Jones, V. T. Trumper, T. W. Hayward, C. E. McLeod, W. Brearley, F. Laver, A. F. A. Lilley, D. R. A. Gehrs; seated – C. B. Fry, M. A. Noble, Hon. F. S. Jackson (captain), J. Darling (captain), A. C. MacLaren, C. Hill; front – A. Cotter, R. H. Spooner, J. J. Kelly, J. T. Tyldesley, G. H. Hirst, S. E. Gregory. Missing: R. A. Duff. Jones, Newland, Howell, and Gehrs did not play in the Test.

Those sunny summers of yore? Lord's unplayable after a storm in 1905.

Right: *George Herbert Hirst stands alone as the only man to score 2000 runs and take 200 wickets in a season. He did this in 1906, having scored a Yorkshire record 341 the previous year, at Leicester. Rosy-cheeked, solid as an oak-tree, modest and honest, he was a credit to Yorkshire, England and cricket.*

Below: *Walter Brearley, amateur fast bowler for Lancashire and, on four occasions, England. He had shoulder-generated pace, stamina and no shortage of self-confidence. Against Somerset at Old Trafford in 1905 he took 17 for 137. His relations with the Lancashire committee were as stormy as in S. F. Barnes's case. When watching new young fast bowlers in later years Brearley would exclaim that he could throw his hat faster.*

Warwick Windridge Armstrong (1879–1947), a Goliath of a cricketer who weighed around 21 stone on his fourth and final tour of England in 1921. On the 1905 tour he hammered Somerset for 303 not out at Bath, and a few months later he made the first triple-century in New Zealand. In a district match in Melbourne in 1903–04 he piled up 438 for Melbourne against University. The appetite for runs was apparent, but he also liked long spells of bowling, legbreaks, some rolled, some wristy, sometimes attacking, but often negatively, down the leg side. An overbearing giant, he led with great force – even, or especially, when it came to taking on authority, as in the Australian players' revolt against the Board of Control in 1911–12.

Below: *Hampshire v Worcestershire, Portsmouth, 1906, Burrows (Worcs) having just bowled E. M. Sprot.*

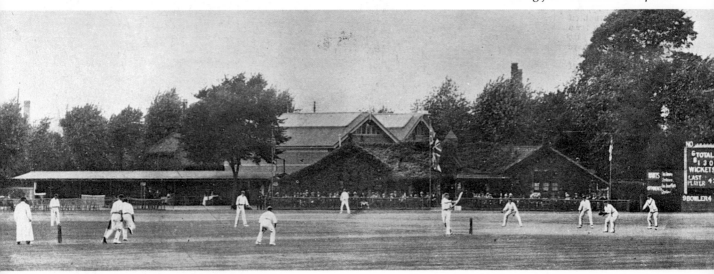

James Rainey Munro ('Sunny Jim') Mackay, a brilliant Australian batsman in the Trumper mould, who reeled off scores of 203, 90, 194, 105, 102 not out and 136 in matches for NSW in 1905–06. He also scored six centuries for his club. A charming country boy, he inadvisedly signed a disapproved contract with Melbourne CC, with others, and was suspended. He went to South Africa, where they were soon regarding him as the world's best batsman, but his eyesight was damaged when a motorbike knocked him down, thus ending a brief but dazzling career.

J. B. King, greatest of Philadelphian cricketers. He might have got into a World XI around the turn of the century for his extraordinary ability to swing a ball to a perfect plan. He demolished county teams, and made runs too. Against Surrey in 1903 he scored 98 and 113 not out, and having made the first triple-century by an American, 315 for Belmont v Germantown, 1905, he raised the record to 344 not out a year later. In 1909 he took 10 for 33 against All-Ireland, having bowled the not-out batsman with a no-ball. He died in 1965, aged 92.

Right: P. W. Sherwell, South Africa's captain, with P. F. Warner before the Test which brought South Africa's first victory – by one wicket, Johannesburg, January 4, 1906. Left: E. Hawkins' photographic shop in Brighton, where delightful pictures of cricketers could be bought for a few pence.

The 1906 West Indians, the first to play a first-class match in England. They did better than in some quarters was expected, winning seven and losing 10 of their 19 matches. Smith did the double, and three others made centuries. Standing: R. A. Ollivierre, C. S. Morrison, L. S. Constantine, G. Challenor, J. E. Parker, W. J. Burton, O. H. Layne, C. B. Cumberbatch; seated: A. E. Harragin, H. B. G. Austin (captain), P. A. Goodman, G. C. Learmond; front: C. K. Bancroft, S. G. Smith. Constantine was the father of the great between-wars player.

Lancashire v Kent, Old Trafford, June 1906: E. W. Dillon facing Frank Harry, who took 6 for 26 and 9 for 44 for Lancashire against Warwickshire here a month earlier. Dillon made 76 and 34 for the eventual county champions, but they were beaten by 10 wickets, Tyldesley's 295 not out having boosted Lancashire to 531. A young left-hander named Frank Woolley made his debut for Kent in this match, and received a kindly word from Tyldesley after being bowled for nought. Woolley scored 64 in the second innings.

A. Chevallier Tayler's imposing painting commemorates Kent's first Championship, earned in 1906. Colin Blythe, the brilliant but highly-strung slow left-arm bowler sends one down to Lancashire's Johnny Tyldesley at Canterbury (where the large canvas now hangs in the pavilion) in a match won by Kent by an innings. It was the sixth of 11 consecutive victories as they stormed to the title, Yorkshire stumbling at the end by losing to Gloucestershire by one run at Bristol. 'Punter' Humphreys is portrayed at silly mid-on, R. N. R. Blaker mid-off, C. H. B. Marsham, the captain, at extra cover, C. J. Burnup at cover, Arthur Fielder silly point, J. R. Mason slip, and Jim Seymour at gully. The wicketkeeper is Fred Huish. At straight-hit is E. W. Dillon, while K. L. Hutchings, who scored a typically breathtaking 176, is at wide long-off. The non-striking batsman is Billy Findlay, who substituted for the artist in the absence of MacLaren, who was in India in the winter of 1906–07. Tyldesley scored only 19 and 4 in this match, having made 295 not out, his highest score, in the Old Trafford match earlier.

Arthur Fielder's fast bowling accounted for 158 wickets in Kent's 1906 Championship summer, to which he added an amazing 10 for 90 for the Players at Lord's. His second tour of Australia, 1907–08, was more successful than the first.

Queenslander Alan Marshal scored 4350 runs and took 210 wickets in all cricket in 1906, and was signed up by Surrey for 1907. He fell out with the committee in 1910, and died in Malta in 1915.

Oxford and Somerset wicketkeeper Harry Martyn was Test class, but never capped. The brave and efficient manner in which he stood up at the stumps to the fire of Brearley and Knox for the Gentlemen at Lord's in 1906 was talked about for years afterwards.

The heyday of county cricket: 80,000 people watched this Surrey v Yorkshire match during its three days in July 1906. This is a record, but the metropolitan grounds in particular were all drawing big attendances. Walter Lees was the lucky beneficiary of this Oval match, won by Surrey, who were looking like potential champions. Lees pocketed £2120, but his county fell away later in the season and finished third.

Left: *For Tom Hayward, 1906 was one long purple patch. The Surrey and England opener, now opening for the county with a young man named Hobbs, broke the season-aggregate record with 3518 runs (this stood until 1947), equalled Fry's 13 centuries in a season, and in six days he scored two centuries at Trent Bridge and two more at Leicester.*

Right: *J. H. King, a bulwark of Leicestershire, forgot himself in 1906 by getting out 'handled the ball' at The Oval. He did the double in 1912, and 11 years later, when 52, scored his second double-century.*

A not-overstrong MCC team toured New Zealand in 1906–07, via South Africa, but they won 10 and lost only two of their 16 matches. An unpleasant moment among the days of blissful adventure came when one of the horses hauling their heavily-laden coach on the way to Otira collapsed and died from exhaustion. One of the English cricketers next received a painful flick in the eye from the tip of the coachman's whip. New Zealand's Plunket Shield was inaugurated this year.

The telegraph boy was a fairly familiar sight, dashing onto the field. The messages were seldom of much moment, and the players, especially the amateurs, were usually disposed to stuff the telegram nonchalantly into the pocket.

Below: Nottinghamshire, led by A. O. Jones, county champions in 1907, for the first time since the great days of the 1880s.

South Africa managed to survive their first Test match in England, at Lord's in 1907, when Braund made 104 and Jessop blitzed 93 in England's 428. Ted Arnold (5 for 37) shot South Africa out for 140 and they followed on; but the third day was washed out. Here Fry turns chest-on to the Boer fast bowler Kotze. England took the three-match series with a victory at Headingley.

Colin 'Charlie' Blythe, a lovable Londoner, took over 2500 wickets, most of them for Kent in a 20-year career, but also 100 for England, including 15 for 99 in his country's victory over South Africa at Leeds in 1907. An epileptic, he was greatly stressed by the long spells of concentration and tension inherent in a slow left-arm bowler's daily campaigns, but he was in Rhodes's class – some thought Blythe had the edge – and his 17 for 48 (all in a day) at Northampton in 1907 was the supreme set of match figures until Laker's in 1956.

Trooper Holland, 11th Hussars, veteran of Balaclava (1854), plays against Nottingham Ladies at Trent Bridge a few weeks after Notts' Championship triumph.

Charles Crombie's whimsical explanations of the Laws were published in conjunction with Perrier in 1907.

WICKET KEEPER.
42 – If the wicket-keeper incommode the striker by any noise or commotion the striker shall not be put out.
Copyright of "Perrier" Water.

Left: *Alf Vogler, considered by England captain R. E. Foster in 1907 to have been the best bowler in the world. He swung the new ball then bowled offbreaks and legbreaks, with the odd googly. In the Lord's Test his 7 for 128 included some top-class batsmen. The South African googly quartet of Vogler, Schwarz, White and Faulkner took almost all of England's wickets in the 1907 series – and were lying in wait at home two years later.*

Right: *The magnificent Ranji in his magnificent robes as the Jam Saheb of Nawanagar. He was installed in 1907, having left county cricket with Sussex after the 1904 season. He had had to fight for succession of the title, and ruled an initially impoverished State; but hard work and dedication bore fruit, and, blessedly for followers of county cricket, Sussex had not seen the last of him.*

Although 1907 was remembered for such oddities as Northamptonshire's dismissal for 12 at Gloucester, the lowest ever in a county match, and for the wretched Trott's ruining of his own benefit match with four wickets in four balls and then a hat-trick, and for the four century opening stands in a week by Hobbs and Hayward, all this was trivia for men of Nottinghamshire. Their team had won the title, and here, completing an unbeaten season, they march to an innings victory over Lancashire at Liverpool, Wass bowling to A. H. Hornby.

Australia emphatically regained the Ashes in 1907–08, winning four Tests and losing only the second, in Melbourne, by one wicket. A bright spot for England was the Test debut of George Gunn (above, hatless), who made 119 and 74 at Sydney. His partner in the photo, Jack Hobbs, also launched one of the greatest Test careers with 83 in the second Test. Below: Clem Hill and Roger Hartigan (116 on debut) after their eighth-wicket record stand of 243 at Adelaide in furnace heat had turned the match. Hill battled against sickness, but it was the bowlers who wilted.

Above: *Kenneth Hutchings, the clean-hitting Kent amateur whose two-hour century lit up the second Test, at Melbourne, which England won by a solitary wicket, thanks to Barnes and Fielder* (below), *who made the 39 needed – though Hazlitt's wild throw at the end precluded a tie.*

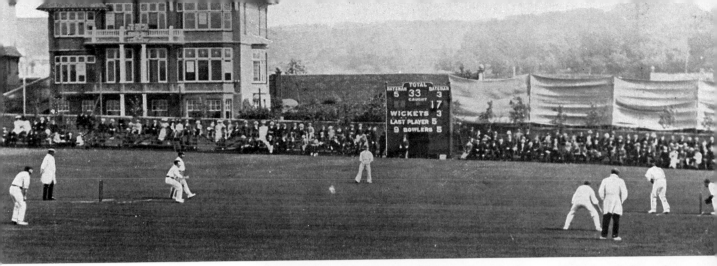

Still a chance to see the legendary Ranji bat in August 1908. Here he copes with the difficulties imposed by Yorkshire's Scofie Haigh at Hove – none too successfully. He was bowled for a duck. Rain spoilt the game, which, as was then the pattern, started on a Thursday and finished on a Saturday.

Right: *The smiles on the faces of the Northamptonshire players would soon be fading. In their first encounter with Yorkshire since elevation to the Championship three years earlier, in 1905, they fielded out to a total of 356 for 8 and then caved in for 27 and 15, Hirst taking 12 for 19 and Haigh 6 for 19. G. J. Thompson, unable to bat because of lumbago, might have put a slightly better face on matters.*

Two remarkable feats in minor cricket: H. R. Nicoll (left) took 10 for 29 for Kobe against Yokohama in October 1909, and thus became known as the 'demon bowler in Japan'.

Right: *J. A. Prout scored 459 for Wesley College, Melbourne against Geelong College in 1908–09, a record for an Australian public school. The disheartened opposition had to field out to a total of 710.*

1909: another Australian year, and the tourists await their English breakfasts at the London headquarters, the Inns of Court Hotel. From the left: 'Barlow' Carkeek, Vernon Ransford, Roger Hartigan, Frank Laver, 'Sammy' Carter, Jack O'Connor.

In July 1909 the man known with great affection as 'The Surrey Poet', Albert Craig, died, aged 59. A Post Office clerk in Huddersfield, he had ventured south in the hope that his versifying ability would earn him a living. Soon his penny rhymes and essays on the players, never notable for any literary quality, were selling rapidly at cricket and football matches, promoted by the creator himself in a jocular and, where need be, diplomatic fashion. Here, at The Oval, he was a special favourite – even more so when the rain was falling and he responded to the need for entertainment. He eventually came to refer to himself as the 'Captain of the Spectators'. He was never more exhilarated than when he ran, puffing, from the dressing-room to announce that Surrey had won the toss. 'For though of football for five months I've sung, I'm mighty glad now spring has sprung'.

Below: Surrey batting against Kent in 1909 in the traditional Blackheath fixture. Woolley and A. P. Day made attractive centuries and 'Mossy' Spring hit 97 for Surrey, who lost by an innings.

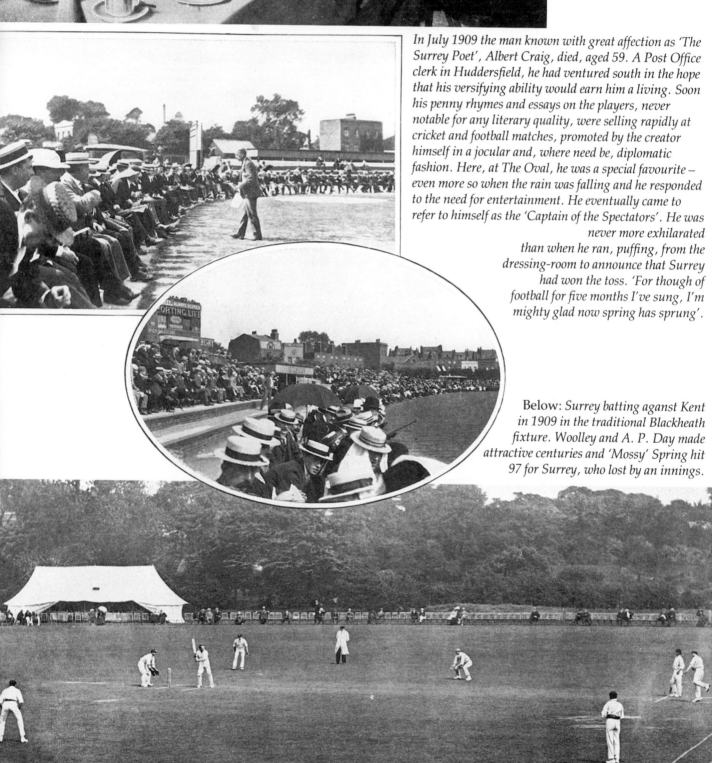

For Nottinghamshire lads Shrewsbury and Gunn were now heroes of the past. Today, as they had their own disorganised contests on the Parade Ground, Nottingham Forest, it was George Gunn and Tom Wass and big Alletson and little Hardstaff whom they worshipped and strove to emulate.

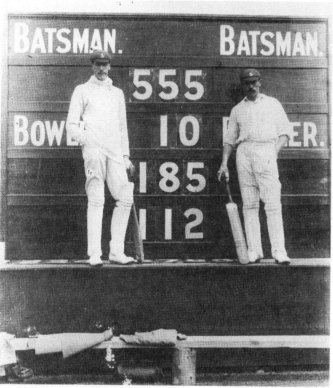

M. A. Noble and S. E. Gregory, Sydney men of somewhat contrasting stature, go out after lunch in the Australians' match against Oxford University. Noble made 107, Gregory 51, and for the undergraduates medium-pacer H. A. 'Barmy' Gilbert took 8 for 71, which got him into the England squad for the first Test, though he did not play in the end – ever.

Above left: *The willowy Frank Woolley and Kent's No. 11, Arthur Fielder, after their record last-wicket stand of 235 against Worcestershire at Stourbridge in 1909. Woolley made 185, Fielder 112 not out, and the match was won by an innings. They came together when Kent were still 40 behind Worcestershire's 360, and raised the total to 555. Woolley had earlier retired for a while after being hit in the mouth by a ball from Ted Arnold.*

Left: *Blythe's benefit match in August 1909 was Kent's match against Hampshire, at Canterbury, and was won by the home side. Here, Fry and Llewellyn, the South African left-hander, resume for Hampshire. They made most of the runs, Fry 63 and 94, his partner 79 and 0 (bowled by the beneficiary). Llewellyn played in 15 Tests for South Africa, and was in England's 14 at Edgbaston in 1902, but did not play.*

Nightmare memories of 1902 returned as Australia again collapsed in the Test at Edgbaston, this time for 74. Macartney has just been caught by MacLaren off Blythe. Jack Hobbs showed how to bat on a wet pitch, his 62 seeing England home by 10 wickets. Below: Australia pulled level at Lord's, Ransford making 143 not out and Armstrong taking 6 for 35. Noble leads Australia out, having put England in to bat, then regarded as a daring thing to do.

Australia won at Headingley to go ahead in the series, and drew the remaining two Tests of 1909. Here, at Old Trafford, Macartney makes the first breakthrough, bowling Warner. Carter is the wicketkeeper. Frank Laver then ran through England, swinging the ball in the breeze and snapping it back from the off, to finish with 8 for 31.

Kent: county champions 1909. Standing: A. Fielder, F. H. Huish, F. E. Woolley, W. Hearne (scorer), W. J. Fairservice, C. Blythe; seated: S. H. Day, J. R. Mason, E. W. Dillon (captain), K. L. Hutchings, D. W. Carr; front: E. Humphreys, J. Seymour. Hutchings and Humphreys made over 1000 Championship runs, while Blythe took 178 wickets.

Left: *D. W. Carr, a club cricketer of 37 who had been fascinated by the googly as bowled by Bosanquet and the South Africans, played for Kent in 1909, and found himself in the England XI at The Oval. He had immediate success but was overbowled. His sole Test appearance yielded 7 for 282.*

Right: *Warren Bardsley, the NSW left-hander, scored 136 and 130 at The Oval, the first instance of twin centuries in a Test. He toured England four times, and each tour was productive. A keen practiser, patient and correct of method, he made 53 centuries.*

In 1909–10 another MCC team set sail for South Africa, H. D. G. Leveson Gower as captain. By the time Hobbs (facing Dave Nourse, above) and Rhodes put on a record 221 for the first wicket as a platform for an England victory at Newlands in the fifth Test, South Africa were already 3–1 up. Blythe (7 for 46 and 3 for 58) completed the execution here, but legspin/googly bowling dominated the series, the ball bouncing chest-high off the matting. Vogler took 36 wickets and Faulkner 29, the latter also scoring 545 runs. Schwarz, now past his best, and White bowled little. For England, lob bowler Simpson-Hayward took 6 for 43 in the first Test, seven wickets in the second, and 5 for 69 in the third.

Laurie Quinlan, who hit a century in 18 minutes in a club match in Australia in February 1910. Playing for Cairns club Trinity against Mercantile, he smote eight sixes and eight fours between 4.41 and 4.59 in the afternoon. Russell Penny equalled this Australian record in Charters Towers in 1985–86, though Don Bradman's century off three eight-ball overs in 1931–32 may have equalled or even beaten this time.

Interest throughout South Africa during the Tests against England in 1909–10 was intense, and shopkeepers did their best to keep the scores going.

TRAFALGAR SQUARE, A.D. 1910.

OLD LADY FROM THE PROVINCES: "And 'oo's this 'ere gentleman, Mr. Policeman?"

POLICEMAN (*who often has to answer this question, as if reciting a task*): "The above statue represents the only gent cricketer what don't write about cricket. The statue was erected as a token of gratitood and esteem by the workin' journalists of London—now then, you boys, pass along there, pass along!'"

William Charles Smith of Surrey, known as 'Razor' because of his frail physique, had one sensational season, 1910, in which he captured 247 wickets, having added a fast, kicking legbreak to his usual sharp offspinner. Bill Hitch stood bravely very close at short leg to pick up many a catch. In the Oval match against Northants, Smith took 14 for 29.

Cricketers who like to write about the game – and pick up a few pounds for their efforts – were already being seen as a problem.

R. St L. Fowler (left) goes out to bat for Eton against Harrow at Lord's in 1910 in a match he made all his own. He top-scored with 21 and with 64 in the follow-on and then bowled

Harrow out for 45, taking 8 for 23 with offspin as his opponents hopped around nervously. 'Fowler's match' became a conversation piece of the first magnitude.

Phil Mead had made his debut for Hampshire at 18 in 1905. By his retirement in 1936 he had passed 1000 runs in a season 27 times, and scored over 55,000 runs, with 153 centuries, fourth in both all-time lists. He was unlucky to win only 17 Test caps. Here, in 1910, he is bowled by Tom Wass in the MCC v Notts match.

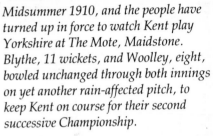

Midsummer 1910, and the people have turned up in force to watch Kent play Yorkshire at The Mote, Maidstone. Blythe, 11 wickets, and Woolley, eight, bowled unchanged through both innings on yet another rain-affected pitch, to keep Kent on course for their second successive Championship.

Taunton, August 1910, and lowly Somerset (played 18, won 0, lost 15) manage another Worcestershire wicket as Newton catches W. W. Lowe off Robson. The visitors twice passed 300 to win by 295 runs.

Right: *Philip Ridgeway Le Couteur, another who appropriated an entire match at Lord's. Playing for Oxford in the 1910 Varsity match, this 24-year-old Australian slammed 160 and then took 6 for 20 and 5 for 46 with legspin to send the Dark Blues to their champagne with a victory by an innings and 126 runs.*

Trumper plays to backward point and sets off for his 100th run in the second Test of 1910–11 against South Africa at Melbourne. His double-century in the next Test, at Adelaide, was one of the greatest innings of the many played by this genius. The series was high-scoring, particularly for Australia, who won 4–1.

One of the South Africans demonstrates the googly to locals and his team-mates Vogler and Stricker at Melbourne. In the fourth Test of 1910–11 Australia brought in their own googly man, H. V. Hordern.

G. A. Faulkner had a stupendous series in Australia, scoring 732 runs (204 at Melbourne, 115 at Adelaide), taking 10 wickets as well.

An old man remembers: Ted Alletson, many years on, lovingly holds the bat with which he slaughtered the Sussex bowling when Notts played at Hove (pictured above), in May 1911. Going in again with a first-innings deficit of 176, Notts were only nine runs ahead with three wickets left when Alletson went to the crease. A big man (refer Notts group on page 229), he thumped 50 runs in 47 minutes before lunch was taken with no special expectancy. But what came afterwards was simply phenomenal: a further 142 runs off that bat, out of 152 for the last wicket, in a mere 40 minutes. Killick went for 34 off one over with two no-balls, and in all Alletson hit eight sixes and 23 fours in his 189, his last 89 having come in a quarter of an hour. Sussex had insufficient time now to score the runs for victory. Alletson could never reasonably have been expected to make a habit of this.

Below: Fred Huish of Kent honoured fellow wicketkeeper Herbert Strudwick in the Surrey man's benefit at The Oval in 1911 by stumping nine batsmen in the match. Here E. C. Kirk pays the price of overstepping, D. W. Carr the bowler.

The first All-India team toured England in 1911 – some of them are seen here with their Sussex opponents – and were rated as a disaster. They won only two and lost 10 of their first-class matches. Matters might have improved had K. M. Mistri played more than six innings (188 runs), but his duties 'kept him in close attendance on the Maharajah of Patiala', who led the party. Left: The best bowler for the Indians was Palwankar Baloo, a left-arm spinner who was a mainstay for the Hindus in the Quadrangular. An Untouchable, he took 114 wickets in all tour matches. Right: R. D. Burrows of Worcestershire, who sent a bail flying 67 yards 6 inches when he bowled Lancashire's Huddleston at Old Trafford in 1911 – a world record. Below: Reggie Spooner, who went on to 190, plays safe as C. B. Fry hits to mid-on in the Gentlemen v Players match at The Oval.

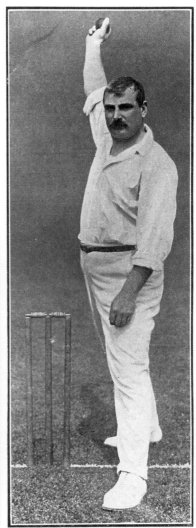

Warwickshire won their first Championship in 1911, led by the brilliant but eccentric young Frank Foster. Fourteenth in the table of 16 counties in 1910, they leapt dramatically. Points for first-innings supremacy in drawn matches now counted; but Warwickshire did not play Essex, Kent, Middlesex or Notts. Still, it was refreshing to see one of the 'smaller' counties taking the palm. Standing: C. Charlesworth, C. S. Baker, S. H. Bates, E. F. Field, J. H. Parsons, S. Santall, E. J. Smith; seated: W. G. Quaife, F. G. Stephens, F. R. Foster, G. W. Stephens, W. C. Hands.

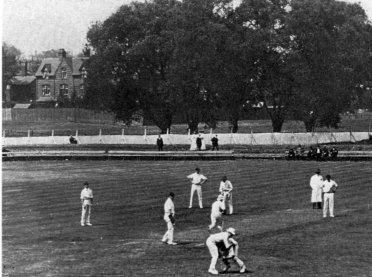

Warwickshire v Northants, Edgbaston, 1911, and Quaife, all 5½ feet of him, nudges through slip on his way to 113, leaving two fielders to sort themselves out.

Left: C. J. B. Wood of Leicestershire, who carried his bat through both innings against Yorkshire at Bradford, scoring 107 and 117. He carried his bat on another 13 occasions. A coal merchant, he captained his county, his career spanning 27 years to 1923.

The handing back and forth of the Ashes continued when a strong MCC team went to Australia in 1911–12 and beat a star-studded team in the remaining four Tests after losing the first. Foster, fast left-arm, and Barnes controlled the series, sharing 66 wickets, while Hobbs, Rhodes and Woolley made centuries, Hobbs and Rhodes having opening stands of 147 at Adelaide and a record 323 at Melbourne in the next Test. Woolley also hit 305 not out (in 205 minutes) against Tasmania. But the feat which always tends to stand out is S. F. Barnes's thrustful opening spell at Melbourne in the second Test, when he dismissed Bardsley, Kelleway, Hill and Armstrong for three runs – having felt unwell for some hours. Later the crowd barracked him as he deliberated over his field setting, so he threw the ball down and refused to continue until they quietened. Back row: S. P. Kinneir, E. J. Smith, F. E. Woolley, S. F. Barnes, J. Iremonger, R. C. Campbell (not a team member), J. Vine, H. Strudwick; seated: W. Rhodes, J. W. H. T. Douglas, P. F. Warner (captain), F. R. Foster, T. Pawley (manager), J. B. Hobbs, G. Gunn; front: J. W. Hearne, J. W. Hitch; inset: C. P. Mead. Johnny Douglas took over the captaincy when Warner fell ill after the first match.

A. O. Jones, the Notts captain, shows that the 'dog stroke' is not obsolete, even if it was seen less often.

Dr H. V. Hordern took 12 wickets on his debut in Ashes Tests, at Sydney in 1911–12, and finished with 32 wickets in a losing series. Hill had to employ him as a stock bowler, and the strain told. He believed that England's top batsmen had his googly worked out towards the end of the series. Hordern toured with the Philadelphians, and later played for WG's London County. Like all true spin bowlers, he simply 'loved to bowl'.

S. F. Barnes takes a wicket in the opening Test of the 1911–12 series, at Sydney, the only match won by Australia. Fast bowler Cotter, who loved to hit sixes, was caught in two minds and gave a return catch to the bowler. At 426 for 8, Australia could hardly have begun a series more promisingly . . . and yet.

In the red corner:
Clem Hill.

In the blue corner:
Peter McAlister.

The historic cable which led to a brawl in 1912. Clem Hill and Peter McAlister, both Australian Test selectors, had been at loggerheads over selection and tactics. They met, with Frank Iredale, the other selector, and Syd Smith, at the NSWCA offices in Martin Place, and soon McAlister's remarks proved too provocative for Hill, who told him he had been 'looking for a bloody punch in the jaw all night', and gave him one. The two wrestled, and McAlister came close to toppling out of the window before they were separated. Hill resigned. They were turbulent times for the Australian Board, for a dispute over who should manage the team to England in 1912 went on for weeks, with passions running high. Eventually six major players refused to tour. The absence of Armstrong, Carter, Cotter, Hill, Ransford and Trumper left it one of the weakest ever to tour.

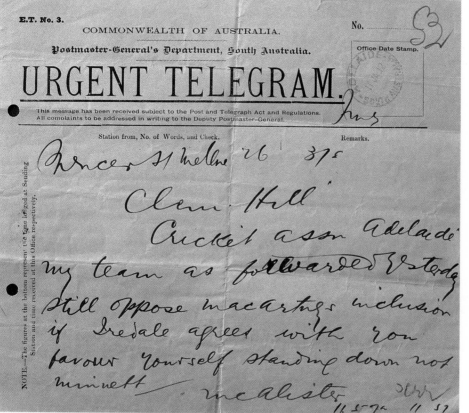

MCC playing members took their jolly flag to the Argentine in 1912 – here they field against Southern Railways at Talleres – playing three so-called 'Tests' under Lord Hawke, or his deputy, A. C. MacLaren, winning two and losing one, and covering distances of unfamiliar length.

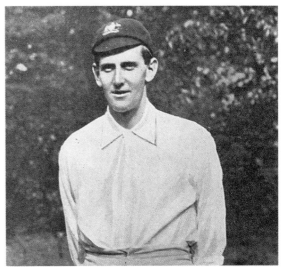

Gervys Hazlitt, who took 7 for 25 for Australia against England at The Oval in 1912, bowling brisk offbreaks on a drying pitch. Australia were then bowled to defeat: 65 all out. Hazlitt had a weak heart, and died in 1915. Left: A Yorkshireman, a Sussex man and an Aussie: Frank Mitchell (South Africa), Charles Fry (England) and Syd Gregory (Australia), captains in the 1912 Triangular Tournament.

247

A PERFECT UNDERSTANDING BETWEEN HOBBS AND RHODES RESULTS IN MANY STOLEN RUNS

GREGORY, WHO IS CELEBRATING HIS FIFTIETH INTERNATIONAL MATCH.

WHITTY.

THE ENGLISH CAPTAIN STUDYING JUNE IN ENGLAND.

HAZLITT.

TUESDAY (FOR THE MOST PART)

SPOONER WELL TAKEN AT FORWARD SHORT LEG BY BARDSLEY.

JENNINGS A WORTHY SUCCESSOR TO NOBLE AT POINT.

SAUVE QUI PEUT! MOST OF THE AUSTRALIAN BOWLERS ARE INCONSISTENT AS TO LENGTH BUT EMERY IS THE CHIEF OF THE ERRATICS

AT 5·30

STREET AND MOSS COME OUT TO SEE IF PLAY IS POSSIBLE. SHOUTS (BY THOSE WHO SHOULD KNOW BETTER) "PUT YOUR COATS ON!"

Action from the third of the nine Triangular matches in 1912, England v Australia at Lord's, when rain spoilt matters, though Hobbs scored 107 and Macartney 99. King George V had visited Lord's during the Australia v South Africa match, the first instance of a reigning monarch watching Test cricket.

There were several ways and means of going to the cricket in 1912, and those who went to Northampton in July found themselves somewhat surprisingly following Northants as a joint Championship leader with Yorkshire. The match was drawn, and by the end of the season the northern county were supreme again, with Northants in a dizzy second place.

Left: Jimmy Matthews, the slight Victorian spinner, who took two Test hat-tricks on the same day: May 28, 1912, at Old Trafford, as Australia crushed South Africa by an innings. His 'straight breaks' accounted for Beaumont, Pegler (did he get a touch before the ball hit his pad?) and Ward. The small crowd then saw Herby Taylor, Schwarz and Ward, again, all out in three balls a couple of hours later.

Right: D. R. A. (Algie) Gehrs, whose scarcely-recognised 50-minute century for South Australia v Western Australia at Adelaide in 1912–13 was the fastest in Australian first-class cricket until David Hookes's 34-minute hundred in 1982–83.

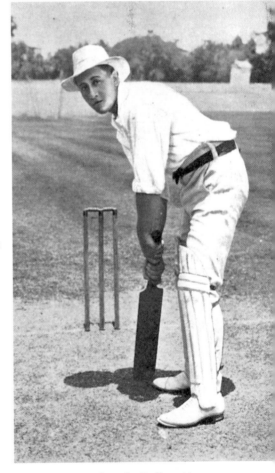

In April 1913, when the Suffragette movement was at its peak, a target for the 'feminists' was the pavilion at Tunbridge Wells Cricket Club. Valuable records were lost, the cause did nothing to further its aims, and a new pavilion was built in nine weeks, the funds raised by public subscription.

Tom Hayward in 1913 became the second batsman to score 100 centuries, and as he reached the milestone at the best of all places for him, The Oval, many in the crowd of 5000 must have reflected that in 1895, when WG did it, it was widely held that nobody could possibly emulate The Doctor in this awesome accomplishment. Hayward earned this hundred as hard as any, being hit often. A true professional in every way, he brought lustre to the paid man's ranks. His young partner, Jack Hobbs, was now ready to take over completely.

J. Hayward (Surrey)

Right: *Shock for Warwickshire at Tonbridge in June 1913: bowled out for 16 on a pitch 'distinctly queer'* Below right: *In 1913–14 Arthur Sims took a strong side to New Zealand, and in the first match he (184 not out) and Trumper put on 433 against Canterbury at Christchurch. Their three-hour onslaught remains easily a world eighth-wicket record. (The scoreboard is one run out in the photograph.)*

Left: *Slow scoring has been an irritation on and off for many years. This is how the complaint was aired in 1913.*

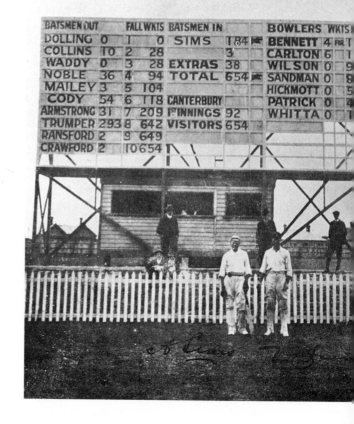

BATSMEN OUT		FALL WKTS	BATSMEN IN		BOWLERS	WKTS	
DOLLING	0	1 0	SIMS	184	BENNETT	4	
COLLINS	10	2 28		3	CARLTON	6	1
WADDY	0	3 28	EXTRAS	38	WILSON	0	9
NOBLE	36	4 94	TOTAL	654	SANDMAN	0	8
MAILEY	3	5 104			HICKMOTT	0	5
CODY	54	6 118	CANTERBURY		PATRICK	0	4
ARMSTRONG	31	7 209	1st INNINGS	92	WHITTA	0	1
TRUMPER	293	8 642	VISITORS	654			
RANSFORD	2	9 649					
CRAWFORD	2	10 654					

Left: *H. W. Taylor, South Africa's master batsman, and captain in the 1913–14 series against England, when he stood alone – so skilful at back-play on matting surfaces – in resisting S. F. Barnes. Herby Taylor scored 508 runs in that series, averaging 50.80. In his 42 Tests between 1912 and 1932 he made 2936 runs for South Africa at 40.78, with seven centuries.*

Right: *If ever a bowler was next to unplayable it was S. F. Barnes in South Africa in 1913–14, when he took 49 wickets in four Tests (missing the fifth through a dispute). Taking in the 1912 Tests, he had felled 83 Springboks in only seven Tests.*

J. N. Crawford, a brilliant allrounder, who twice did the double before falling out with Surrey. He took 30 wickets for England on the 1907–08 Australian tour, and in a minor match on the Sims tour of New Zealand he slammed 354 against South Canterbury at Temuka, with 14 sixes and 45 fours, putting on 298 in only 69 minutes with Trumper, in a total of 922 for 9.

Norman Rippon and Tom Patton almost exceeded belief with a partnership of 641 for Buffalo River's third wicket against Whorouly at Gapstead, Victoria in March 1914, in the grand final. Patton (408) was killed in the Great War, while Rippon (321) married the scorer.

251

Confusing as well as uncommon: two sets of twins in the same match. W. H. and J. S. Denton (in striped blazers) played for Northamptonshire and A. D. E. and A. E. S. Rippon for Somerset. At this time also Warwickshire had the Stephens twins playing for them.

A. P. Day seems to have been guilty of poor footwork in the Gentlemen's innings against the Players in the last such encounter at Lord's before the First World War. Hitch bowled him for 1, but the amateurs went on to win, with J. W. H. T. Douglas, swerving around off stump, taking 9 for 105 and 4 for 67 in long spells.

Sam Coe batted chancelessly for four hours to make 252 not out against Northants at Leicester in 1914, a Leicestershire record destined to last beyond 70 years. An ancestor of the county's 1980s bowler Les Taylor, Coe's other distinction was that he was the first of Bosanquet's googly victims.

Kent's C. E. Hatfeild in difficulties in Kent's match against Essex at Tunbridge Wells, July 1914. The score was already 400 for 5, Seymour having made 214 and Jennings 106. Kent won by an innings.

Another Eton–Harrow match is over, this in 1914, and the top-hatted Etonians rush to congratulate their batsmen, who have seen them home by four wickets.

Six weeks after the death of his beloved father, Frank Foster drove and pulled for 260 minutes against Worcestershire at Dudley in June 1914, finishing with 305 not out as he declared. Future Test umpire Frank Chester was one of the suffering bowlers. In a short but productive career Foster did the double twice and returned some spectacular bowling and batting performances. His bowling was based on a swerving left-arm attack on the pads and outside. A motorbike accident ended his career, and he had all kinds of troubles in later life. Left: Flaming June, 1914, Eastbourne: as good a place as any to while away the hours as Oxford University strive to stay on terms with Mr H. D. G. Leveson Gower's XI.

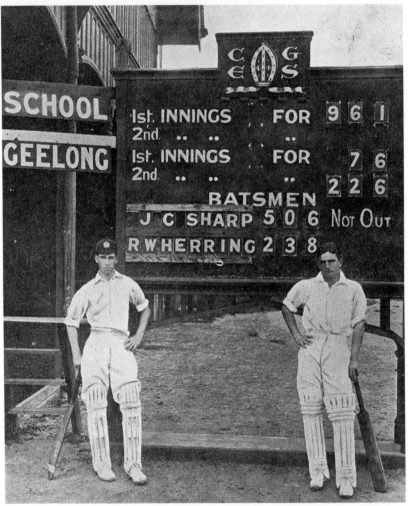

More records topple as J. C. Sharp (left) of Melbourne Grammar School is displayed before his enormous score of 506 not out against Geelong College in the Australian season of 1914–15. His partner, R. W. Herring, made 238, and the School's total was 961. The Geelong boys were dispatched for 76 and 226 in reply.

War had already been declared as Kent fought out their match against Warwickshire at Gravesend in the last week of August 1914 (Charlesworth facing and Kinneir his partner). Surrey called off their last two matches, without forfeiting their position at the top of the table, and thus won their first Championship since 1899.

Sydney Gordon Smith, Northants' Trinidad-born captain in 1914, did the double for the third time, having done so also on the 1906 West Indian tour. A most accomplished left-hander, he moved on to New Zealand.

Right: *The centenary of Lord's current ground was marked in June 1914 with a match between the MCC side which had toured South Africa (Barnes pulled out on the morning of the match with an injury, though there were rumbles that – again – he was dissatisfied with the offered fee) and The Rest. The most capricious of all factors, the weather, took a hand, as so often happened, and the touring team replied to The Rest's 467, made on a hard pitch, with 94 and 184 (Hitch 12 for 93) on a wet one. MCC held a centenary dinner on the second evening, attended by a great galaxy of famous cricketers, Lord Hawke presiding. C. E. Green, Lord Harris, W. G. Grace, F. S. Jackson and C. B. Fry also spoke. WG, about to enter the last year of his life, was given an overwhelming ovation. So many great chapters were ending.*

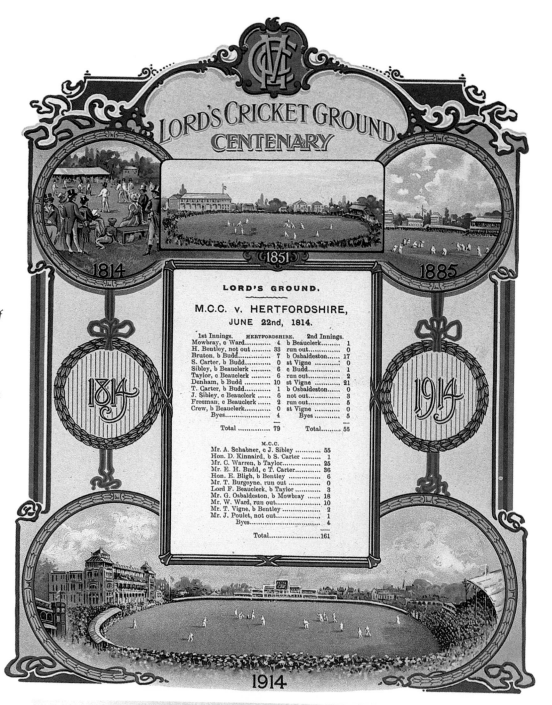

LORD'S CRICKET GROUND CENTENARY

1814 · 1851 · 1885 · 1814 · 1914 · 1914

LORD'S GROUND.

M.C.C. v. HERTFORDSHIRE,
JUNE 22nd, 1814.

1st Innings.	HERTFORDSHIRE.	2nd Innings.	
Mowbray, c Ward	4	b Beauclerk	1
H. Bentley, not out	33	run out	0
Bruton, b Budd	7	b Osbaldeston	17
S. Carter, b Budd	0	st Vigne	0
Sibley, b Beauclerk	6	c Budd	1
Taylor, c Beauclerk	6	run out	2
Denham, b Budd	10	st Vigne	21
T. Carter, b Budd	1	b Osbaldeston	0
J. Sibley, c Beauclerk	6	not out	3
Freeman, c Beauclerk	2	run out	5
Crew, b Beauclerk	0	st Vigne	0
Byes	4	Byes	5
Total	79	Total	55

M.C.C.

Mr. A. Schabner, c J. Sibley	55
Hon. D. Kinnaird, b S. Carter	1
Mr. C. Warren, b Taylor	25
Mr. E. H. Budd, c T. Carter	36
Hon. E. Bligh, b Bentley	6
Mr. T. Burgoyne, run out	0
Lord F. Beauclerk, b Taylor	3
Mr. G. Osbaldeston, b Mowbray	18
Mr. W. Ward, run out	10
Mr. T. Vigne, b Bentley	2
Mr. J. Poulet, not out	1
Byes	4
Total	161

Cricket's Dilemma encapsulated the problem neatly, and with the likes of WG exhorting cricketers everywhere to enlist, batsmen, bowlers and wicketkeepers rushed to don uniform. Many would never tread a cricket field again.

255

DEATH OF AN AGE

THE GAIETY and innocence of spirit of cricket in the Edwardian years was not lost without trace after the horror of the Kaiser's War, but the vestiges that survived had been shaken severely and came out rather misshapen. The world had changed: it was shocked, heavily depleted, and now prone to bouts of cynicism. Cricket therefore automatically reflected this. Post-war cricket embodied that sense of relief that showed in players' eagerness to get back onto the turf and spectators' keenness to push through the gate to watch them. But these were all either avoiding or absorbing a disillusionment that was inevitable when the dark years of 1914 to 1918 had not, after all, preceded days of ease and wealth fitting to a victorious nation. So the bereaved went to the cricket, and a rebirth took place, the game slightly changed in conduct and appearance, as was the world that housed it.

For Surrey and England in every sense: Ernie Hayes, Bill Hitch and Andy Sandham have enlisted in the Sportsman's Battalion of the Royal Fusiliers and begin their training in Hornchurch.

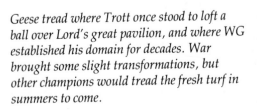

Geese tread where Trott once stood to loft a ball over Lord's great pavilion, and where WG established his domain for decades. War brought some slight transformations, but other champions would tread the fresh turf in summers to come.

FIELDING

BOWLING

UMPIRING

OUT!

BATTING

J.H.DOWD·15

STUMPING

The enemy would seem to have no sense of fair play whatsoever, leaving those who contemplated J. H. Dowd's The Kaiser's Cricket to wonder what chance cleancut cricketers had at the Front.

Anzac soldiers play cricket under shellfire on 'Shell Green', Gallipoli in December 1915. Australia, a Federal entity since 1901, had proud battle honours from the field of Test cricket. Now this young country was earning honours for gallantry in conflicts of infinitely deeper meaning.

Surrey's perky little wicketkeeper Herbert Strudwick does his bit in a South London munitions factory. Team-mate 'Razor' Smith worked at the same establishment.

The greatest of attacking batsmen turns his attention to the German enemy: Captain G. L. Jessop of the 14th Service Battalion, Manchester Regiment calls for recruits in a speech in Albert Square, Manchester.

Cricket keeps the Royal Navy men happy 'somewhere in the tropics' early in 1915. An officer, in a letter home, gave an assurance that the ship was ready for action despite the air of relaxation. C. M. Padday's drawing shows the negligible risk of the loss of the spun-yarn ball, while the bucket wickets appear impregnable.

Tommy Atkins takes time off from his war.

Harry Lee (bareheaded), the Middlesex batsman, was reported as killed in action in May 1915, but turned up some weeks later, badly wounded, having been captured but later repatriated by the Germans.

Sadness was everywhere. W. G. Grace died on October 23, 1915, aged 67, having suffered a stroke. He resented the Zeppelins floating sinisterly across the South London sky above his home. He shook his fist and bawled shrill reproval. 'But you didn't allow Ernie Jones's thunderbolts to upset you!' a friend comforted. 'But I could see him!' WG retorted. The death of The Greatest Cricketer touched everyone who had the slightest contact with the game. They had been just as deeply affected at the news from Australia in June when Victor Trumper, the batsman and man without blemish, had died in hospital. His funeral (above) stopped Sydney. Reports of sportsmen among the missing in France came flooding in. And following the loss of R. E. Foster, A. G. Steel, A. E. Trott, A. E. J. Collins and A. O. Jones in 1914 came news of Stoddart's suicide in April 1915. Sadness was everywhere.

Wounded soldiers watch and chat and watch and chat as the boys of Eton play the visiting Winchester boys on Agar's Plough in the troubled summer of 1916.

An 'English' XII take the field at Bombay Gymkhana, December 1915, for a war relief funds game. J. G. Greig scored 216 and Frank Tarrant took 9 for 35 as 40,000 watched.

There were rays of sunlight: Surrey and England fast bowler Neville Knox joins the uniformed bridegrooms. He took time off as a private in the Public Schools Battalion to marry Miss Olive Palmer at Oxted.

The British Government advised citizens in 1916 to take gas-masks everywhere – just in case. The Germans had used poison mustard gas at Ypres in April 1915, ending and ruining many lives. Essex player and journalist E. H. D. Sewell was not going to be 'caught' at the crease.

Killed in action, July 1916: Second Lieut. W. B. Burns of the Worcestershire Regiment, aged 32. Fine batsman for the county: 196 in a stand of 393 with Arnold at Edgbaston, 1909. Ferocious bowler for several years, though there was doubt about his action.

Killed in action, September 1916: Lieut. K. L. Hutchings of the King's Liverpool Regiment, attached to the Welsh Regiment. The Kent and England batsman was blown apart by an exploding shell. He was 33.

Killed in action, July 1916: Percy Jeeves of the Royal Warwickshire Regiment, aged 28. A most likable Yorkshireman, he bowled fast for Warwickshire, and seemed England material. P. G. Wodehouse's fictional manservant was named after him.

Killed in action: left – *Second Lieut. M. W. Booth of the West Yorkshire Regiment, July 1916, aged 29. A quality allrounder, he and Alonzo Drake had bowled unchanged through consecutive matches in August 1914 for Yorkshire in the West Country.* Centre: *Lieut. H. G. Garnett of the South Wales Borders, December 1917, aged 38. A brilliant left-hander, he hit 1758 attractive runs for Lancashire in 1901, toured Australia unsuccessfully that winter, pursued business in the Argentine, returned to establish a fresh reputation as a wicketkeeper, and was among the first to volunteer in 1914. Above right: Second Lieut. W. W. Odell, MC, of the Sherwood Foresters, October 1917, aged 31. A fine Leicestershire medium-pacer, he twice took eight wickets in an innings.*

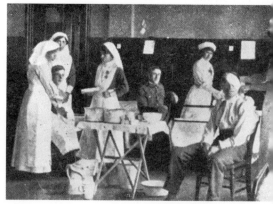

The pavilion at Old Trafford was transformed into a Red Cross hospital for the military during the First World War. In four years 1800 patients were treated, the beds occupying every spare section of floorspace, even in corridors and on landings.

According to Punch *the Germans would never comprehend cricket, even in wartime. The 'Hun airman's' report supposedly read: 'We dropped bombs on a British formation, causing the troops to disperse and run about in a panic-stricken manner'.*

Killed in action: Albert 'Tibby' Cotter of the Australian 12th Light Horse, October 1917, aged 32. Before his last action he tossed up a ball of mud and said to a mate, 'That's my last bowl, Blue. Something's going to happen.' He had had a premonition that a Turk would get him. One of the great early Test match fast bowlers, he was inclined to be indifferent as to whether he split a stump or a batsman's rib. Right: Sergeant Colin Blythe of the Kent Fortress Engineers, killed near Passchendaele, November 1917, aged 38. Enrolled despite his epileptic condition, this taker of 2500 wickets was mourned especially deeply. His shrapnel-punctured wallet rests in the museum at Kent's St Lawrence ground, Canterbury.

Keeping the home fires burning: Miss Jose Collins takes a rest from the stresses of being leading lady in The Maid of the Mountains at Daly's Theatre.

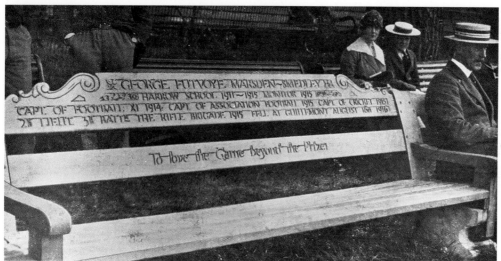

Fund-raising at Lord's: George Robey, the 'Prime Minister of Mirth', greatest of front-cloth comics, auctions bats, including some used by WG, proceeds going to St Dunstan's Hostel for Blind Servicemen. Right: Frank Chester, who later became a much-respected umpire. His promising playing career was shattered when he lost his right arm in the fighting around Salonika, Greece, in the summer of 1917.

Memorial seat overlooking Harrow School's cricket ground: for George Marsden-Smedley, 1st XI captain 1915, killed in action August 1916. Below: The Australian Imperial Forces take the field against an English Army XI at Lord's, July 1917. E. P. Barbour, C. T. Docker and C. G. Macartney lead the parade, with Kelleway behind, hand on chest.

This group of cricketers pictured at Lord's during the war includes an England captain, a Middlesex player, and one of the outstanding Australian prospects. P. F. Warner was, by now, 'Mr Cricket' at Lord's – though he still needs a towel to dry off, like ordinary mortals. On his left, in striped blazer, is Nigel Haig, nephew of Lord Harris, and a future England player and Middlesex captain. The tall figure is R. J. A. Massie, a dangerous fast left-arm bowler, son of H. H. Massie, the old Australian Test batsman. Sadly for son Jack – and for cricket – he was badly wounded – as well as decorated for 'conspicuous ability, initiative, resourcefulness, and devotion to duty' – and was never able to claim that promised place in the Australian Test XI. Johnny Moyes considered him the finest left-arm bowler he had ever seen.

Strange things happen in wartime, so there should have been little surprise at the staging of a baseball match at Lord's. A Canadian team played an American team, proceeds going to the Canadian Widows and Orphans Fund. Over 10,000 watched, and E. H. D. Sewell found that not only was the noise – as symbolised by the soldier's megaphone – undesirable but the game was inferior to cricket.

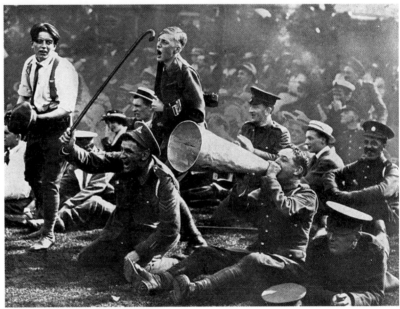

Lord Harris, captain of England in the first English Test match, in 1880, transcends the years to take part in the match between Captain P. F. Warner's XI and Public Schools at Lord's in 1918. His Lordship was then 67 years of age. Having survived this attempt to stump him, he was run out for 11.

265

The hefty Maharajah of Patiala on his way to a 'Jessopian' 83 in a Famine Relief Fund match in Bombay in November 1918. C. K. Nayudu made a century, and Ranji, back from France, was a distinguished spectator.

With the war all but won, His Majesty King George V watches the England v Dominions match at Lord's in 1918, flanked by Lord Hawke, in straw boater, and Walter Long, Harrow XI 1873, Wiltshire, Devonshire, MCC president 1906, Member of Parliament, future First Lord of the Admiralty.

P. F. Warner, in Harlequins cap, drives wristily in the England XI innings against the Dominions at Lord's in July 1918.

Tragically late casualties in the Great War were two of the phenomenal South African googly quartet: Gordon White (above), who died in Palestine in October 1918 from wounds. He was 36. Reggie Schwarz (above right) died in France on November 18, seven days after the Armistice, from influenza, having survived two wounds. He was 43, a major in the KRRC, and had been awarded the Military Cross.

Representative of the thousands of cricketers who perished at the war front and whose promise was thus never to be fulfilled was Lieut. G. W. E. Whitehead. Captain of the Clifton College XI in 1913 and 1914, he had made 259 not out against Liverpool, and was regarded as 'the perfect flower of the public schools'. He was 'as happy with a good book as when he was scoring centuries'. He was so modest that 'strangers sometimes failed to realise his worth'. He was killed one month before the end of hostilities while serving with the Royal Flying Corps.

Alfred Hartley's first-class career was over when the war started. He had made useful runs for Lancashire, his highest score being 234 against Somerset at Old Trafford in 1910, his best season. He was killed in France in October 1918.

267

Some of the unexpected things that war brings are actually touched by magic. The conflict brought together batting geniuses from Australia and South Africa in the shapes of Charlie Macartney (right) and Herby Taylor, who batted for Dominions against the English XI at Lord's in August 1918, the South African wearing leg-guards from the past, Macartney's from the new era.

County club secretaries meet at Lord's to draw up the fixtures for the first peacetime season, 1919, in which it was decided to play two-day Championship matches – an experiment soon abandoned. P. F. Warner is nearest camera, facing Capt. F. C. Toone, who was to manage several MCC tours. MCC secretary Francis Lacey stands at the head of the table.

Left: J. C. 'Farmer' White was one of legions of cricketers who lost four prime years to the Great War, but he stretched his career (he was an amateur) to 1937, when he was 46. A slow left-arm bowler of great accuracy and patience, he took over 2300 wickets, including 16 for 38 in a day for Somerset v Worcestershire at Bath in 1919.

Right: G. T. S. Stevens lit a torch of hope with an innings of 466 not out for Beta v Lambda in a house match at UCS. He was 18 and had an Oxford, Middlesex and England career ahead of him.

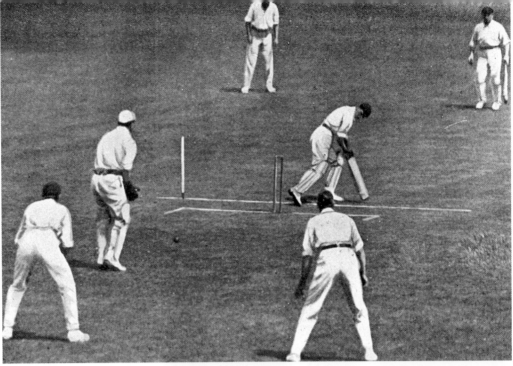

Essex v Lancashire, Leyton, 1919: Ernest Tyldesley bowled for a duck by Johnny Douglas as the southerners, through their mustard-keen captain and fellow fast bowler G. M. Louden, fired their way to victory. They shared 17 wickets.

Right: *Middlesex v Lancashire, Lord's, 1919: Johnny Tyldesley scampers home as Murrell takes the throw. The spectator is Patsy Hendren.*

Below right: *Yorkshire were 1919 champions, but they didn't quite rule the world. A strong Rest of England XI beat them at The Oval by 10 wickets at the season's end. Roy Kilner is caught on the rebound by Woolley. Strudwick keeps wicket, Mead at slip, Douglas at midwicket.*

Alonzo Drake, who died, after long-term heart trouble, in February 1919, aged 34. A left-hander, he had taken all 10 wickets for Yorkshire v Somerset at Weston in 1914, 15 for 51 in the match.

269

Cricket was resumed with gusto at every level, and South Shields CC, County Durham, happily assembled before their imaginatively designed pavilion in 1919.

Above: 1919 saw the death of one of the grand old figures, William Caffyn, at his Reigate home, at the age of 91. Throughout the 1850s he was one of the premier allrounders, and he went with both of England's teams to Australia in the early 1860s, staying to coach. A fine cutter, he preferred hard, true pitches to a noticeable degree, though he did resist John Jackson's intimidatory bowling more than once on a poor pitch at Lord's.

We can't all be obsessed with cricket. There are other things in life. Harold Earnshaw called his drawing Caught.

270

THE HALCYON TWENTIES

A COMPARTMENT had been shut tight, and new rooms of history were about to be entered. Children emerged from the puzzling years of war and grew into county, state, province and Test cricketers. The seniors, such as Hobbs and Woolley and Macartney, continued their stream of achievements, but the new names had to, and did, come through. Bowlers' footholds and batsmen's standing ground could now be covered against the weather, which helped the former more than the latter, as the eternal quest for the perfect balance between bat and ball was sustained. Australia now had eight balls to the over, and soon (1927) the ball would be reduced in size. It was as eventful a decade as most. Huge and humiliating scores were recorded; Glamorgan became the 17th first-class county in 1921; the first wireless commentaries on cricket were heard; matches stretched into seven and eight days in Australia; Barbados chalked up scores of 700-plus; West Indies and New Zealand became Test sides; the Women's Cricket Association was formed; the Sheffield Shield was expanded by Queensland's entry; the first Test triple-century was scored (April 1930). And whatever images of the 1920s subsist – jazz, flappers, Chicago gangsters, Lindbergh, Baldwin, and Ramsay MacDonald – for cricket people it will always remain the era of Hobbs, Hendren and Hallows, Freeman, Woolley and Hammond, Ames, Fender and Sutcliffe, Macartney, Mailey, and McDonald, Gregory, Ponsford and a formidable young man named Bradman who emerged in 1928.

J. W. Zulch in 1919–20 became the first South African to make two centuries in a match, for Transvaal v OFS at Bloemfontein. That season Dave Nourse scored the first South African triple-century.

Right: P. H. 'Tim' Tarilton, who turned the first double-century scored in West Indies immediately into a triple-century. His 304 not out in Barbados's 623 came off Trinidad bowling at Bridgetown early in 1920.

His Highness 'Ranji' plays his final game for Sussex, at Hastings, August 1920. Now 47, heavier, and minus one eye through a shooting accident, he was bound still to thrill everyone by his presence, even if his great skills had faded. He made almost 25,000 runs at 56.37, with 72 centuries, though this magician's place is estimated by the speed of his movement and the suppleness of his wrists. Generous and gentle, yet he was a man apart, as in this last photograph. R. A. Young is the wicketkeeper, with Arthur Gilligan beside him, Vallance Jupp with hands in pockets, and bareheaded Maurice Tate at the rear.

Herbert Sutcliffe (left) and Percy Holmes at Portsmouth in August 1920, when they posted 347 for the first wicket against a strong Hampshire attack. Sutcliffe made 131 and Holmes went on to 302 not out.

Their technique was probably found wanting, but the enjoyment factor must have been every bit as rich as for Test or county cricketers: a farmhouse team at Nedging Tye, near Ipswich, 1920.

Right: Emmott Robinson, a workaday Yorkshire medium-pacer who grew to become the personification of the county: shrewd, mean, obdurate. As captain, he ran a kind of council of war with the equally shrewd Rhodes, and the pair gave Cardus many a tale to write or adapt in his inimitable style during the 1920s. 'Our Emmott' later became an umpire, as do so many cricketers who cannot stay away from the game just because the joints have started to creak.

James Seymour during his benefit match, Kent v Hampshire, Canterbury, 1920. The event had weighty consequences, for Inland Revenue used it as a test case, which eventually went to the House of Lords, which found in favour of the cricketer. Since then professionals' benefits and testimonials have remained tax-free. Seymour's loyal service ought not to be overlooked. He reached 1000 in 16 seasons and made 53 centuries, three of them double-centuries.

Percy George Herbert Fender (1892–1985) was a highly individualistic cricketer: tall, thin, bespectacled, with an exceptionally long sweater and a Chaplin moustache. He led Surrey in lively, questing fashion throughout the 1920s, flogging runs lower in the order . . . to order . . . and bowling a strange mixture of legbreaks, swervers, offbreaks, slower balls and whatever else came into his head. The Test selectors were never convinced about him for more than a match or two at a time – he was capped only 13 times by England – and, largely through Lord Harris's influence, his captaincy flair was never tested at Test level. Yet he made 19,000 runs in carefree style, took almost 1900 wickets, and held 600 catches, mostly at slip and many quite wonderful. He is remembered, though, for one brief innings, at Northampton in 1920, when he crucified the Northants bowlers to make a century in 35 minutes, the fastest in first-class cricket in terms of time, equalled under artificial conditions by Steve O'Shaughnessy in 1983. And in 1927 the amazing 'Percy George' took six wickets in 11 balls (five in seven) for Surrey v Middlesex at Lord's. An interesting cricketer, one might say.

George Brown of Hampshire made his highest score against Yorkshire at Leeds, 232 not out in 1920.

Below: *The Australian team at Sydney for the first Test of the 1920–21 series, when the post-war resumption of Ashes Test cricket saw the first 5–0 whitewash – to be extended, to England's horror, to eight Australian victories in a row as the countries continued their unequal struggle in England in 1921. Standing: W. A. S. Oldfield, E. R. Mayne (12th man), C. Kelleway, J. M. Gregory, J. Ryder, A. A. Mailey, J. M. Taylor; seated: H. L. Collins, W. Bardsley, W. W. Armstrong (captain), C. G. Macartney, C. E. Pellew. Six of them were centurymakers in the series, while Mailey spun out 36 batsmen in the four Tests in which he bowled, with 9 for 121 in England's second innings at Melbourne in the fourth Test. Jack Gregory's fast bowling accounted for 23 wickets.*

Farewell to Middlesex: captain P. F. Warner acknowledges the cheers after his side's victory over Surrey at Lord's had secured the Championship for 1920.

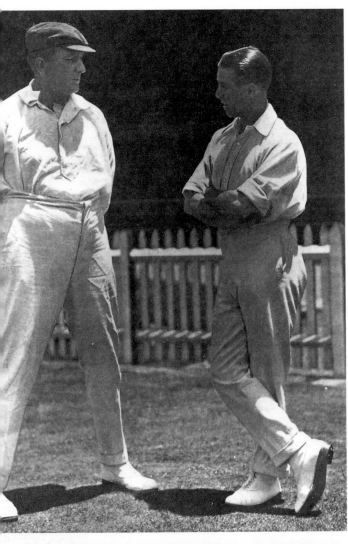

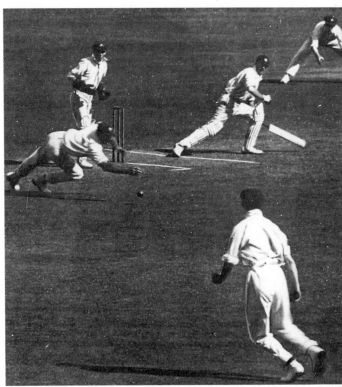

Rhodes nudges past Gregory in the opening Test, won by Australia by 377 runs. Collins scored 70 and 104 on his Test debut, and Armstrong made 158 in Australia's second innings of 581, the first of his three centuries in the series. Left: *The heavyweight and the middleweight: the bulky Warwick Armstrong looms intimidatingly over his English opposing skipper, Johnny Douglas, who was Olympic middleweight boxing champion in 1908: first Test, Sydney, 1920–21.*

Collins has some luck at the start of the second Test, at Melbourne, as Rhodes puts down a catch before he had scored. Harry Howell was the unlucky bowler. Collins made 64, Australia 499, and England lost by an innings. Below: *And the Melbourne spectators naturally loved every minute.*

Jack Hobbs, in trilby hat, falls to an excellent catch by Australian wicketkeeper Carter off McDonald for 27 in the fourth Test, at Melbourne, February 1921. Hobbs's partner, 39-year-old Harry Makepeace of Lancashire, went on to make 117, but England suffered another heavy defeat, this time by eight wickets.

Jack Gregory was the beau idéal of an allrounder in the 1920–21 Tests. 'Found' in Australia's Army ranks, the tall, strong Sydney man made a century, a 93, and three seventies, to average 73, and to his 23 wickets he added a record 15 catches, his reflexes at slip being exceptional. He, above all, was the darling of Australian crowds – and soon of English too.

The highest score by a batsman in his first innings in first-class cricket is W. F. E. Marx's 240 for Transvaal against Griqualand West at Johannesburg in 1920–21.

Cecil Tyson, a 32-year-old left-hander, made a sensational debut for Yorkshire at Southampton in May 1921, scoring 100 not out and 80 not out off a good Hampshire attack. He followed with 29 against the Australians, and 0 and 23, but difficulties over employment terms stopped him from playing further.

Australia recorded consecutive victory No. 6 when battle was resumed in England in 1921. Armstrong leads his men out in the first Test, at Trent Bridge, where England (112 and 147) went down by 10 wickets. The other tourists clearly visible are Gregory, Taylor, Collins, Pellew, wicketkeeper Carter, and Andrews.

Left: *The opening Test of the 1921 series, the 100th between England and Australia, was marked by some unusually frequent and ugly bouncers from Gregory and McDonald, who took eight wickets each. One of Gregory's lifters hit Ernest Tyldesley in the face, the ball falling onto the stumps, and the batsman being helped off in distress.*

Right: *Warren Bardsley, who made 106 in the Australians' match with MCC at Lord's, dextrously hops over his wicket in avoiding a short ball from Jack Durston. Durston laid out Armstrong in this match with a bouncer to the head. Ill-feeling pervaded the match, Armstrong having insisted on shorter hours of play.*

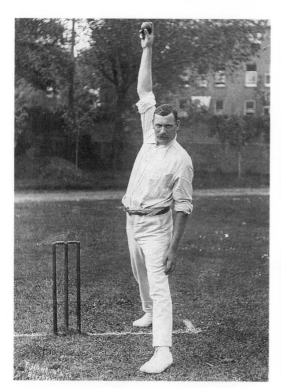

Bill Bestwick of Derbyshire took all 10 Glamorgan wickets at Cardiff on June 20, 1921. On the same day Jack White also took all 10 for Somerset at Worcester. Early in July, Rushby of Surrey also took all 10 against Somerset, and later that month Charlie Parker did so for Gloucestershire.

Glamorgan, newly-elevated, leave the field in jubilation after the best launch imaginable, a victory over Sussex at Cardiff on May 20, 1921. The margin was only 23 runs, Bowley's 146 all but having carried the southerners to victory. Glamorgan captain N. V. H. Riches is the bald player in the group on the right. The encouraging start was a deception. Only one more victory was achieved, among 14 defeats, and the Welsh side finished bottom of the Championship.

Future Prime Minister Lord Dunglass (later Lord Home) (right) goes to bat for Eton v Harrow at Lord's in 1921. His partner is the Hon. D. F. Brand (later Lord Hampden).

Left: J. W. H. T. Douglas achieved his best-ever figures with 9 for 47 for Essex v Derbyshire at Leyton in 1921. He characteristically polishes the ball on his arm.

Right: Arthur Mailey, the carefree little Australian legspin/googly bowler, took 10 for 66 against Gloucestershire at Cheltenham, and later incorporated the analysis into the title of his hilarious and touching autobiography.

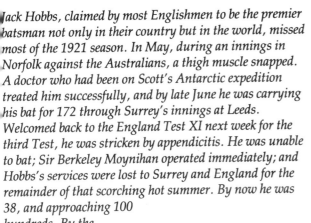

Jack Hobbs, claimed by most Englishmen to be the premier batsman not only in their country but in the world, missed most of the 1921 season. In May, during an innings in Norfolk against the Australians, a thigh muscle snapped. A doctor who had been on Scott's Antarctic expedition treated him successfully, and by late June he was carrying his bat for 172 through Surrey's innings at Leeds. Welcomed back to the England Test XI next week for the third Test, he was stricken by appendicitis. He was unable to bat; Sir Berkeley Moynihan operated immediately; and Hobbs's services were lost to Surrey and England for the remainder of that scorching hot summer. By now he was 38, and approaching 100 hundreds. By the time he did hang up his boots, after the 1934 season, he had 197 centuries (or 199 according to another reputable source) and 61,237 runs, both performances without equal. And his admirers have always said that he could have made numerous runs and centuries more had he not been so often happy to toss his wicket away.

J.B. HOBBS
ENGLAND'S PREMIER BATSMAN

An oddity of the 1921 Test series was that only one century was hit by the all-conquering Australians – Macartney's 115 at Headingley – while three were made for England: Jack Russell's 101 at Old Trafford and 102 not out at The Oval, and Phil Mead's then-home-record 182 not out at The Oval. But Frank Woolley came close twice in the Lord's Test. Here he swings Mailey away for four during his 95 (he was stumped by Carter off Mailey), which was followed by an equally splendid 93. The Hon. Lionel Tennyson also batted courageously in this match, scoring 74 not out and finishing 'black and blue all over'.

Charlie Macartney had bundles of confidence and the good eye, strong wrists and magical gift of instant assessment and rapid execution that make a master batsman. His slow left-arm bowling gradually gave way to batting, and on the 1921 tour he hammered dramatic notice as to what he could do by taking 345 off Notts within a day, with 51 boundaries. Some way through his assault he called for a heavier bat. He made over 2000 runs on this tour, as he had done in 1912, getting down low over his slashing drives and always looking for the pull against anything short of a length. Short, squarely-built, audacious, clean-living, he remains one of the greatest of Australian batsmen of any era.

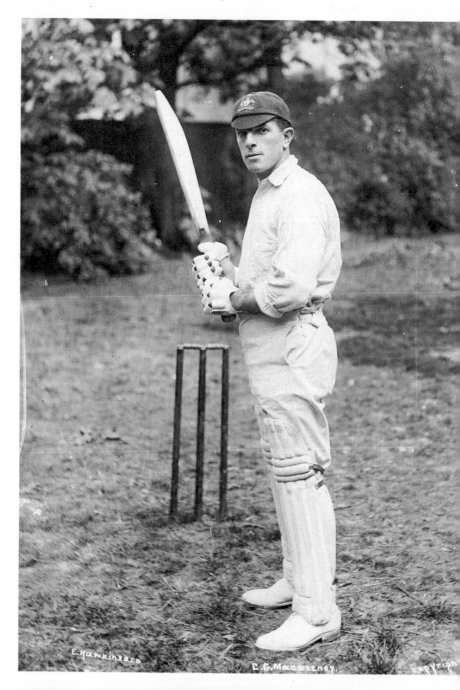

A. C. (now known as C. A. G.) 'Jack' Russell reaches England's first ce of the 1921 series, Old Trafford, fourth Test. H. S. T. L. Hendry is at wicketkeeper Carter. **Left**: Hendry bowled by Parkin for 0 in the third T Headingley. Parkin (16 wickets) had been England's best bowler in Aus bowling seam and spin.

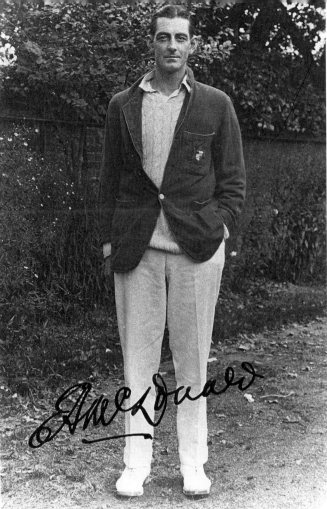

The first of the great opening pairs of fast bowlers brought Australia much success in the 11 Tests in which they functioned together. Jack Gregory (left), 6 ft 3½ ins, bounded in and bowled after what was known not entirely fondly as a 'kangaroo leap'. His speed was very considerable and his hostility blatant, overt, but so much a bowling force was he that his left-handed batting (he usually shunned gloves) was sometimes overlooked. Yet he made the fastest of all Test centuries, in 70 minutes, at Johannesburg on the way home from the 1921 England tour. His comrade-in-arms with the new ball was Ted McDonald (above right), who glided to the wicket with poise and menace. He later joined Lancashire, and in 1925 he took 205 wickets. In the 1921 series, when stricken England used 30 players, McDonald took 27 wickets to Gregory's 19.

Left: *George Hirst, 50, Yorkshire's great servant, bids farewell to his adoring fans at Scarborough in 1921 (though his final first-class match was not until 1929). T. L. Taylor is with him.*

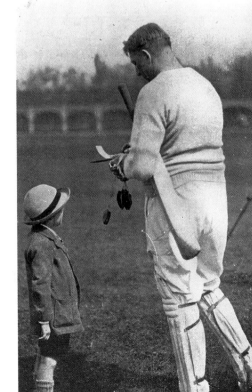

Right: *Lucky not to have been trodden on, the little man is privileged to obtain Armstrong's autograph.*

281

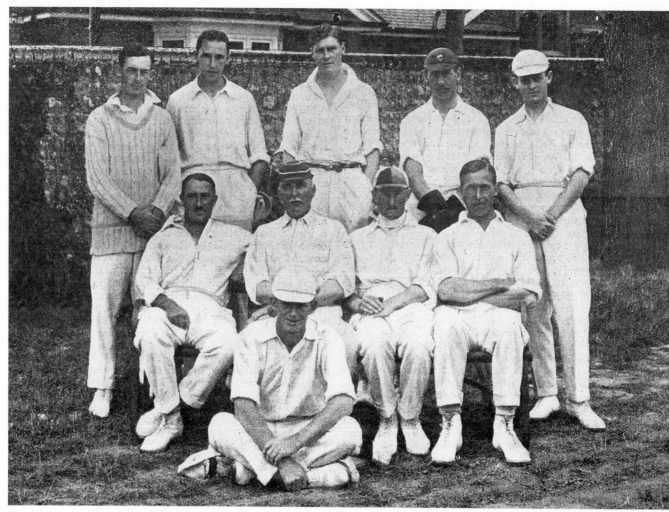

The demoralised English cricket public were given a tonic in late August 1921, just when it seemed that Armstrong's mighty band of Australians would go through their tour undefeated. All through the summer Archie MacLaren, 49, had been saying he could find an eleven to beat them, and at Eastbourne he had his chance. His team were bowled out for 43 by McDonald and Armstrong! Michael Falcon of Norfolk and Aubrey Faulkner then dismissed the Australians for 174, and Faulkner made 153 and Hubert Ashton 75 in the second innings of 326, which left a target of 196. Clem Gibson (6 for 64) bowled them out for 167. The heroes were: H. Ashton, C. H. Gibson, A. P. F. Chapman, G. E. C. Wood, G. Ashton; seated: G. A. Faulkner, A. C. MacLaren (captain), G. N. Foster, M. Falcon; front: C. T. Ashton. W. Brearley was absent. The Australians promptly lost the final tour match too, against C. I. Thornton's XI.

Right: Wilfrid Timms, only 18, scored 154 not out against Essex in 1921 in his second match for Northants, and was carried shoulder-high from the field by his schoolfriends.

Below: Kaffirs lay the matting pitch at Johannesburg before the Test match in which Jack Gregory smote a record 70-minute century.

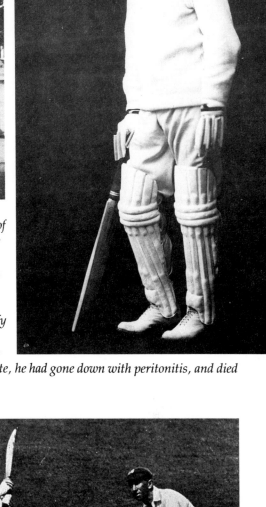

In 1922, seven years after his death, W. G. Grace was remembered in the erection of the Grace Gates at Lord's, through which legions of great and lesser cricketers have since walked – or been driven. **Right:** Frank O'Keeffe made headlines in 1921–22 when, having moved from Sydney, he made 87 and 79 for Victoria against his own State, 180 against South Australia, and, most impressively, 177 and 144 for The Rest against Armstrong's returning touring team. A good slow bowler too, O'Keeffe was snapped up by Lancashire League club Church, and planned to qualify for the county. A thinking cricketer, he had been credited in Melbourne with innovating the practice of fieldsmen walking in as the bowler ran in. Suddenly this brilliant and popular sportsman was no more. Never fully well in England's climate, he had gone down with peritonitis, and died in a Hampstead hospital in March 1924. He was 27.

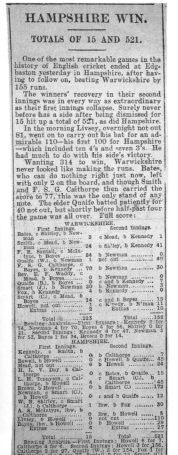

HAMPSHIRE WIN.

TOTALS OF 15 AND 521.

One of the most remarkable games in the history of English cricket ended at Edgbaston yesterday in Hampshire, after having to follow on, beating Warwickshire by 155 runs.

The winners' recovery in their second innings was in every way as extraordinary as their first innings collapse. Surely never before has a side after being dismissed for 15 hit up a total of 521, as did Hampshire.

In the morning Livsey, overnight not out 81, went on to carry out his bat for an admirable 110—his first 100 for Hampshire—which included ten 4's and seven 3's. He had much to do with his side's victory.

Wanting 314 to win, Warwickshire never looked like making the runs. Bates, who can do nothing right just now, left with only 2 on the board, and though Smith and F. S. G. Calthorpe then carried the score to 77, this was the only stand of any note. The elder Quaife batted patiently for 40 not out, but shortly before half-past four the game was all over. Full score:

WARWICKSHIRE.

First Innings.		Second Innings.	
Bates, c Shirley, b Newman	3	c Mead, b Kennedy	1
Smith, b Newman	24	c Shirley, b Kennedy	41
F. R. Santall, c McIntyre, b Boyes	84	b Newman	0
Quaife (W.J.) b Newman	1	not out	40
F. S. G. Calthorpe, c Boyes, b Kennedy	70	b Newman	30
Rev. E. F. Waddy, c Mead, b Boyes	0	b Newman	0
Quaife (B.J.) b Boyes	0	c and b Kennedy	7
Smart (J.) b Newman	20	b Newman	3
Fox, b Kennedy	4	b Kennedy	0
Smart (C.) c Mead, b Boyes	14	c and b Boyes	15
Howell, not out	1	c K'nedy, b N'man	11
Extras	2	Extras	10
Total	223	Total	158

Bowling Analysis.—First Innings: Kennedy 2 for 74, Newman 4 for 70, Boyes 4 for 56, Shirley 0 for 21. Second Innings: Kennedy 4 for 47, Newman 5 for 53, Boyes 1 for 34, Brown 0 for 14.

HAMPSHIRE.

First Innings.		Second Innings.	
Kennedy, c Smith, b Calthorpe	0	b Calthorpe	7
Bowell, b Howell	0	c Howell, b Quaife	45
Mead, not out	6	b Howell	24
H. L. V. Day, b Calthorpe	0	c Bates, b Quaife	15
L. H. Tennyson, c Calthorpe, b Howell	4	c Smart (C.), b Calthorpe	45
Brown, b Howell	0	b Smart (C.)	172
Newman, c Smart (C.), b Howell	0	c and b Quaife	12
W. R. Shirley, c Smart (J.), b Calthorpe	1	lbw, b Fox	30
A. S. McIntyre, lbw, b Calthorpe	0	lbw, b Howell	5
Livsey, b Howell	0	not out	110
Boyes, lbw, b Howell	0	b Howell	29
Extras	4	Extras	27
Total	15	Total	521

Bowling Analysis.—First Innings: Howell 6 for 7, Calthorpe 4 for 4. Second Innings: Howell 3 for 156, Calthorpe 2 for 97, Quaife (W.) 3 for 154, Fox 1 for 70, Smart (J.) 0 for 37, Santall 0 for 15, Smart (C.) 2 for 5.

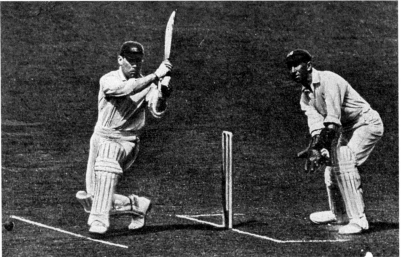

Patsy Hendren gradually emerged as a major run-scorer in the 1920s, and was to finish second only to Hobbs in the list of hundreds with 170 when he retired in 1938 at the age of 49. Here he plays a favourite stroke in his innings of 277 not out for Middlesex v Kent at Lord's in 1922. The wicketkeeper is Hubble.

There never has been a match quite to compare with this one at Edgbaston in June 1922. In reply to Warwickshire's 223, Hampshire were bowled out by Harry Howell and the Hon. F. S. G. Calthorpe for 15. In the follow-on, George Brown made 172 and Walter Livsey earned a maiden hundred. Hampshire's 521 put them 313 ahead, a startling turnabout, and Warwickshire, bowled out by Kennedy and Newman, fell 155 short.

283

Bernard Quaife (left) and his father, William (of Warwickshire and England), who played for the county together. For 10 remarkable minutes in 1922 they batted against Billy Bestwick and his son in a Championship match at Derby.

An old England captain makes a return to Lord's: in an Actors v Variety Artists match C. Aubrey Smith, 59, thespian and fast bowler for Cambridge, Sussex, Transvaal and England, makes a fatal stroke after notching 19 runs.

Left: The ever-restless allround gentleman C. B. Fry tries his hand at politics, autumn 1922. He canvasses in Brighton, in which town he and Ranji had played so many long innings. Gladstone sent him a goodwill telegram on behalf of all Liberals, though Fry insisted he was an Independent. He won 22,059 votes, only 4785 fewer than the Tory candidate. He later fought the Banbury seat, and lost by only 224, and Oxford, where he was again narrowly defeated.

Below: England had a pulsating 2–1 victory in South Africa in 1922–23, losing the first Test, winning the next (below) at Cape Town by one wicket, and winning the fifth at Durban, where Russell hit two centuries in what was his final Test.

Third Test, Durban, 1922–23, and Phil Mead has just been caught by Dave Nourse off Blanckenberg for 181, made in 7½ hours, the first Test hundred on the new Kingsmead ground. England, led by F. T. Mann, made 428, and the match was drawn. Mann's 84 was his highest Test score. Herby Taylor scored hundreds for South Africa in the first, fourth and fifth Tests.

The first thousand-run total: Victoria's 1059 against Tasmania at Melbourne in February 1923. The Victorian XI, virtually a 2nd team, included a 22-year-old bank clerk, Bill Ponsford (in strapped pads), who had been trying to impress the State selectors. He made his point with a 477-minute innings of 429 (42 fours) in which he had the honour of hitting the 1000th run. He overtook MacLaren's world individual record by five runs, although a body of opinion was opposed to first-class status for the match. In the next season Ponsford and Edgar Mayne posted 456 for Victoria's first wicket against Queensland, an overall Australian record until overtaken by David Hookes and Wayne Phillips in 1987 (462 unbroken in five hours, SA v Tasmania, Adelaide).

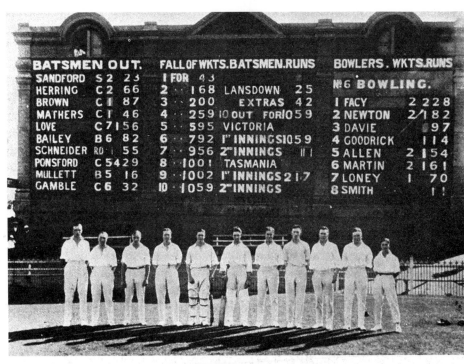

Right: *The jumbo roller does its stuff on the Hove pitch, spring 1923, pushed by Maurice Tate (in blazer), who was to emulate Trott and Alec Kennedy this summer by scoring 1000 runs and taking 200 wickets. Arthur Gilligan is to Tate's left, Cornford, the wicketkeeper, and George Cox snr right of picture.*

The camera lens was now getting closer to the action. This 'Long Jimmy' came to Lord's in 1923.

All through foul winter they dream of cricket, and summer's warmth. And in June this is what they find. Wry observation by Frank Reynolds in Punch. And the spring of 1923 brought chill conditions, these Surrey players (below) huddling around the fireplace at The Oval. Hitch sits cross-legged. They went on to beat Gloucestershire, Peach taking 7 for 15.

Alfred D. Taylor, who died in 1923, left the largest collection of cricket books yet seen, having written some valuable books of his own, some concerned with Sussex cricket, and notably a catalogue of cricket literature which for years was a key source of reference. His researches led to his being called 'The Cricketologist'.

286

In 1923 a West Indies side toured England, winning six and losing seven first-class matches, often in cold, damp conditions alien to them. George Challenor impressed greatly with six centuries, and George Francis, another Barbados player (seen above during his 41 against Surrey – he took five wickets in each innings as the tourists forged a 10-wicket victory), was highly-regarded for his 'old-fashioned' (i.e. at the wicket rather than 'off theory') fast bowling.

Right: Jack Hobbs reached his 100th century in Surrey's match against Somerset at Bath in May 1923, unusually hitting three sixes in his unbeaten 116. The operation in 1921 seemed to have taken a lot out of him – he was now 40 – and he had a few unlucky dismissals. But he made 2087 runs in 59 innings. There was still a lot more Hobbs to come.

Hendren (13 centuries) topped 3000 runs in 1923, but the graceful Woolley was also in rich form. Here he watches as Kent partner G. J. Bryan scores against Middlesex at Canterbury. Woolley made 270 in this innings of 445 – though Kent lost.

Yorkshire were the power in the land between the First and Second World Wars, winning the County Championship in 1919, 1922, 1923, 1924, 1925 and seven times in the 1930s. Their cricket was utterly uncompromising, and performances against them were taken as the ultimate test at county level. This 1923 team won 25 of their 32 Championship matches, with Rhodes and Roy Kilner doing the double in these matches alone, and four others passing 1000 runs and Macaulay the third to get 100 wickets. Standing: Maurice Leyland, George Macaulay, Abe Waddington, Norman Kilner, Herbert Sutcliffe, Billy Ringrose (scorer); seated: Arthur Dolphin, Wilfred Rhodes, E. R. Wilson, G. Wilson (captain), Emmott Robinson, Percy Holmes; front: Edgar Oldroyd, Roy Kilner.

Major the Hon. L. H. Tennyson was by nature a hitter, and here goes a six off J. W. Hearne as Hampshire move towards their first-ever win at Lord's over Middlesex. Mead's plodding, unobtrusive 145 and Newman's eight wickets had much to do with it.

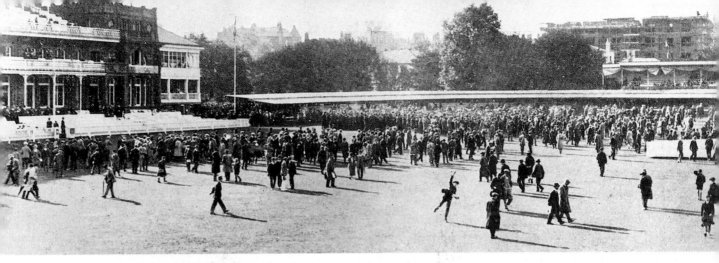

Demonstration at Lord's, only a mild one, but the crowd's patience was stretched during the 'Test trial' in August 1923 (there were no Tests due until the following season) when damp conditions held up play. In a match of dropped catches, Tate had a spell of five wickets without cost, and Hendren and Mead, the season's heaviest scorers, made one run between them in four innings.

Left: *Alec Kennedy (left) and Jack Newman carried Hampshire's attack for many seasons, both bowling fast-medium, Kennedy employing an awkward inswinger: he took 10 for 37 for the Players against the Gentlemen at The Oval in 1927. They both achieved the double in five seasons, and in 1921 and 1923 they bowled together throughout a match unchanged. Kennedy played five times for England on the 1922–23 tour of South Africa, but Newman was uncapped. In 1922, though, he was sent from the field by Tennyson after kicking down the stumps in a fit of pique at Trent Bridge. His captain ticked him off, made him apologise, and gave him £1.*

Surrey captain P. G. H. Fender and his monocled bride, Frinton-on-Sea, 1924.

T. G. Grinter scored his 100th century in club cricket when he made 141 for Wanstead against Woodford Wells in 1924. Handicapped by a war wound to his left arm, he was given eight matches by Essex, for whose Club & Ground side he once scored 245.

Midsummer 1924 saw the reunion of survivors of the great Cambridge University side of 1878. Six of them are in the group, including the Hon. and Rev. E. Lyttelton, at the head of the table, and the Hon. Ivo Bligh (now the Earl of Darnley) to the right of him (with beard). Oxford Blue and Middlesex and England batsman A. J. Webbe is second from the right.

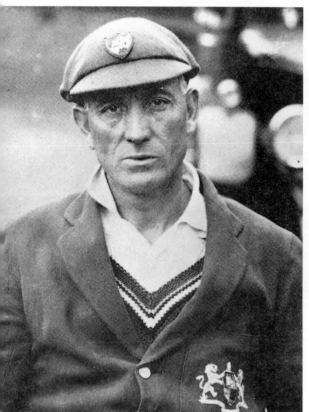

In July 1924, in the Gentlemen v Players match at The Oval, Arthur Gilligan was hit over the heart by a ball from Fred Pearson. It was a serious blow, but he went in to bat next day and hit a brisk hundred. The injury had a long-term effect, however, and he was never quite the threat as a bowler as he had been before. Nonetheless, he led England to Australia that winter, and proved to be as popular and considerate a captain as his country has ever known.

Charlie Parker, a good enough slow left-arm bowler to have won many more than his one England cap (he was rather too outspoken and independently-minded for the authorities), took a hat-trick in each Middlesex innings for Gloucestershire at Bristol in 1924 after his side had been swept away for 31. The innings of the season, Hammond's 174 not out, helped Gloucester to victory. Parker was 41, Hammond 21. Right: For the second Test, at Lord's, of their 1924 tour, South Africa brought in Aubrey Faulkner, now 42, and resident in England since 1911. He made 25 and 12 (here he plays Dick Tyldesley, with George Wood the wicketkeeper) and took 0 for 87 in England's innings of 531 for 2 dec (Hobbs 211, Sutcliffe 122, Woolley 134 not out).

A. E. R. Gilligan and Maurice Tate for a brief period formed the best pair of opening bowlers in England, and early in 1924 they bowled Surrey out for 53 and Middlesex for 104 and 41 in consecutive matches. Then came the Edgbaston Test, where they bowled South Africa out for 30, Gilligan taking 6 for 7, Tate 4 for 12, including a wicket with his first ball in Tests. They shared nine wickets in the second innings (Deane was run out).

Above: 46-year-old Dave Nourse gets tangled up during his innings of 37 in the 1924 Oval Test, his 45th and last. Soon the tough left-hander's son, Dudley, was to start out on a career quite as distinguished as his father's. The wicketkeeper is Strudwick.

Left: Meintjes, the South African, is finely caught by Bill Hitch in the tourists' match against Surrey. Hitch was a speedy bowler and dangerous hitter in the lower order, and he often stood much closer than this at short leg.

Left: *Herby Taylor's admirable back play is demonstrated during his innings for South Africa at The Oval in 1924.*

Right: *Maurice Tate, the laughing giant from Sussex, manfully bowls on in Australia during the 1924–25 series, when he broke Mailey's record with 38 wickets. It took him 2528 balls, every one bowled with heart, off a short run-up, and fizzing off the pitch almost as if gathering pace.*

Replete with famous names, the 1924–25 MCC team lost four Tests in Australia, but won by an innings at Melbourne in the fourth Test the only time Gilligan won the toss, their first Ashes win for 12 years. England actually scored eight centuries to Australia's six, but too much depended on Tate as a bowler. The first three Tests each finished on the seventh day, and public enthusiasm was at a rare pitch. This season saw the first eight-ball overs in Tests – as well as the first wireless commentary. Standing: H. Howell, R. K. Tyldesley, A. P. F. Chapman, F. C. Toone (manager), M. W. Tate, W. W. Whysall, J. L. Bryan; seated: F. E. Woolley, J. W. Hearne, J. W. H. T. Douglas, A. E. R. Gilligan (captain), J. B. Hobbs, E. H. Hendren, H. Strudwick; front: R. Kilner, A. P. Freeman, H. Sutcliffe, A. Sandham.

Sydney, December 1924, and Herbert Sutcliffe tucks another ball away for runs during his excellent Ashes debut, which brought him 59 and 115. He followed this at Melbourne in the next Test with 176 and 127, and made 143 there in the fourth Test. In the series he scored 734 runs at 81.56. Below: Sutcliffe and Hobbs during their memorable all-day stand of 283 at Melbourne in reply to Australia's mammoth 600.

Collins, Kelleway, Mailey and Ryder watch in amazement as the elegant Australian wicketkeeper Bert Oldfield glides across to leg – no vulgar diving or sprawling – to catch Hobbs off Gregory at Sydney before England had scored a run in the fifth and concluding Test of the happy 1924–25 series. The congregation on the Hill has yet to absorb it. The eruption is still to come. A new name entered the Test match lists here: Clarrie Grimmett, the New Zealand-born spinner, who took 11 wickets.

Surrey v Warwickshire, The Oval, May 1925: the old firm of Hobbs and Sandham have put 232 on the board for the first wicket, but now Alf Jeacocke has got an edge to Parsons, and E. J. 'Tiger' Smith brings off a good, wide catch. Smith, who won 11 Test caps, was spared until 1979 – when he died in his 94th year – to tell his tales and dispense his unembellished advice.

Jack Hobbs started the 1925 season needing 13 centuries to equal W. G. Grace's record number of 126. By July 20 he had made 12 of them; but then for almost a month he could not reach three figures, to the chagrin not only of himself but of hordes of reporters and photographers and spectators. The Star's photographer caught him napping on August 11, and the newspaper's artist did the rest: Hobbs dreaming of that elusive century. Six days later he was out of his agony . . .

294

At last! On Monday, August 17, 1925, after spending a reasonably relaxed Sunday 91 not out, Jack Hobbs drew level with W. G. Grace. The Somerset–Surrey match at Taunton briefly came to a standstill as Hobbs smiled characteristically and broadly, and Fender, his captain, took him out a drink – thought to have been ginger ale. Hobbs's young amateur partner, Douglas Jardine, seems less than uncontrollably excited. Next day, when the cameras had left, Surrey went after 183 for victory and Hobbs made 101 not out, thus standing alone in the centuries table. He has stood there ever since.

An MCC team toured the Caribbean in 1925–26, the most profound effect being that Wally Hammond contracted an illness that almost took his life. The players gathered around Trinidad-born Lord Harris on his 75th birthday: back row: P. Holmes, F. B. Watson, E. J. Smith, L. G. Crawley, R. Kilner; standing: C. T. Bennett, G. C. Collins, H. L. Dales, W. R. Hammond, T. O. Jameson, C. F. Root; seated: H. D. Swan, G. Challenor (West Indies), Hon. F. S. G. Calthorpe (captain), Lord Harris, H. B. G. Austin (West Indies), Lord Tennyson; front: T. H. C. Levick (manager), W. Williams, W. E. Astill.

Percy Holmes pulls Hearne during his innings of 315 not out for Yorkshire v Middlesex at Lord's in June 1925. It was the first triple-century at Lord's, but was a ground record for only a year, Hobbs adding one run to it in 1926. Left: Harry Surtees Altham first published his erudite book A History of Cricket in 1926. Schoolmaster, Oxford Blue, Surrey and Hampshire batsman, coach, Test selector, MCC president and a decorated soldier, he was as enthusiastic and kindly as a cricket person could be.

Ernest Tyldesley, Lancashire's high-scoring batsman of quiet charm, with a magnificent drive and hook, and tight defence, achieved a run of 10 successive scores of 50 or more in 1926, something without precedent, and equalled since only by Bradman. The younger brother of J. T. Tyldesley, he passed 3000 runs in 1928, and in 1934, when 45, he notched his 100th century.

Charlie Macartney, now 40, blazes his way towards a century before lunch at Headingley in 1926, thus emulating his compatriot Trumper, who did so at Old Trafford in 1902. Macartney was dropped fourth ball, and was 112 at lunch. He finished with 151, having made 133 not out at Lord's; and he scored 109 in the next Test.

The undergraduates of Oxford University learned a thing or two in the course of three days in June 1926 when Hobbs and Sandham put on 428 for the first wicket at The Oval, a Surrey record. Sandham made 183 and Hobbs went on to 261.

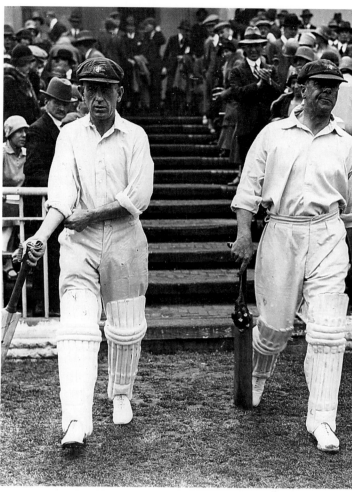

Another great opening pair, Herby Collins and Warren Bardsley of NSW and Australia. They scarcely functioned as a pair in the 1926 Tests, rain and Collins' ill-health interfering. Bardsley, having carried his bat for 193 in the Lord's Test, stood in for Collins as captain in the next two.

With four Tests drawn, England's chances of winning back the Ashes rested on their fortunes in the final Test, at The Oval. Young Percy Chapman replaced Arthur Carr as captain, and Rhodes, 48, and Larwood, 21, were called up. When Hobbs (above) was bowled by a full-toss from Mailey for 37 English hopes drooped — and the bowler chuckled.

The dignified gentleman presiding over his prize blooms is F. R. Spofforth, Australia's 'Demon' of the 1870s and 1880s, who settled in England and became wealthy as head of the Star Tea Company. Pictured on his Surrey spread shortly before his death, Spofforth expired on June 4, 1926, aged 72. Within 11 weeks Australia had lost the Ashes which had been as much his creation as anybody's.

England take the field for the decisive Oval Test 1926. Chapman, Hobbs and Greville Stevens are seen in the forward group, followed by wicketkeeper Strudwick, Woolley, Geary, Tate, and, coming through the gate, fast bowler Harold Larwood, whose second Test appearance this was.

Collins pushes Rhodes away. Woolley is at slip, Tate leg slip, Larwood gully, Sutcliffe silly mid-off, Chapman short leg. Hobbs and Sutcliffe's centuries set up an England triumph, Australia (302 and 125) losing by 289 runs.

298

Right: George Reuben Cox had first played for Sussex in 1895, but his best performance did not come until 1926, when his crafty slow left-arm bowling reaped in 17 wickets for 106 in the match against Warwickshire at Horsham. He was then 52. His last match came two years later, by which time he had taken over 1800 wickets and was about to see his brilliant son, 'George junior', launched on a batting career with Sussex which took him very close to an England cap. This animated oil of 'George senior' hangs in the Sussex CCC committee-room at Hove.

Below right: The second innings of 1000. Victoria have pushed their record up to 1107 in their match against NSW at Melbourne in 1926–27. Ponsford considered himself unlucky to play on for 352, while Ryder's 295 came after he claimed to be trying to throw his wicket away after reaching three figures. Ponsford and Woodfull had started things off with a first-wicket partnership of 375. Victoria won by an innings and 656 runs, but, without most of their star players, were bowled out for 35 in the return match at Sydney a month later, McNamee taking 7 for 21 on a pitch which deteriorated after NSW had made 469 (Kippax 217 not out).

Below: The urchin's scepticism might be justified if he were to overlook Hobbs's many thousands of runs and brooded instead on the full-toss dismissal at the hands of the mischievous Mailey.

BATSMEN	OUT.	FALL OF WKTS.	BATSMEN.	RUNS.	BOWLERS.	WKTS	RUNS
WOODFULL	C 7 133	1 FOR 375	ELLIS	63	5 BOWLING		
HENDRY	C 3 100	2 " 594	BLACKIE	27			
PONSFORD	B 6 352	3 " 614	EXTRAS	27	1 M̠cNAMEE		124
LOVE	S 3 .6	4 " 631	9 OUT 1107		2 M̠cGUIRK	1	130
KING	S 3 7	5 " 657	VICTORIA		3 MAILEY	4	362
HARTKOPF	C 3 61	6 " 834	1ST INNINGS		4 CAMPBELL		89
LIDDICUT	B 2 36	7 " 915	2ND INNINGS		5 PHILLIPS		64
RYDER	C 7 295	8 " 1043	N.S.W.		6 MORGAN	1	137
MORTON	RO 0	9 " 1046	1ST INNINGS 221		7 ANDREWS	2	148
		10 "	2ND INNINGS		8 KIPPAX		26

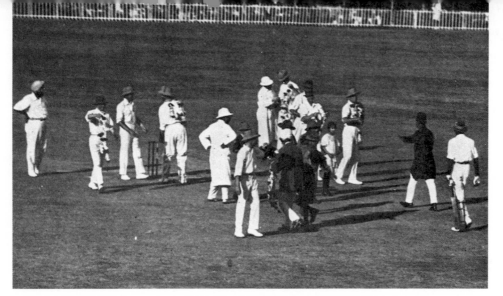

The first MCC tour of India took place in 1926–27, a long and arduous odyssey which also took in Burma and Ceylon (where R. E. S. Wyatt scored a century and took a hat-trick in the same match). Tate performed the double on the tour, which acknowledged the development of Indian cricket as it approached its first Test match. In the picture, the MCC players are having garlands bestowed upon them. On the left is the Maharajah of Patiala, who hosted them and played in a few matches.

C. K. Nayudu, who hit 11 sixes in an innings of 153 for Hindus against MCC, was to lead India in their first Test match, at Lord's in 1932. A brave, proud soldier–batsman, he had a first-class career extending from 1916–17 to 1956–57 (when he was 61), and his highest score, 200, was made when he was 50. Hugely respected, almost deified by large sections of the Indian cricket community, Colonel Nayudu became a Test selector and a vice-president of the Board of Control for Cricket in India.

Walter Hammond celebrated his recovery from illness by making 1042 runs within the month of May in 1927. The 1000th came only 22 days after the first, and he thus equalled the feat of WG in 1895. Hammond scored five centuries and a 99 in that cycle, and finished with 2969 runs that season, the highest runscorer. Punch was prophetically accurate in linking the young Gloucestershire batsman with the shades of WG.

300

The first New Zealand team to tour England arrived in 1927 and left in September with a record of 38 matches played, 13 won (seven first-class) and five lost. No Tests were played, but many friends were made by this modest and cheery band, and the somewhat condescending conclusion was made by Wisden that they would probably hold their own in the County Championship. Legspinner Merritt took 107 first-class wickets and six batsmen reached 1000 runs. The captain, Tom Lowry, a Cambridge Blue, is absent from this group of New Zealanders and their Durham hosts.

In August the New Zealanders played Surrey, and the first wicket to fall was Stewart Dempster's, to a snap catch at slip by E. R. T. Holmes, for 6. Dempster, who later played for Leicestershire, made a century in the second innings and finished the tour with over 2000 runs in all matches, as did Roger Blunt. Jack Mills made 103 in this innings, which totalled 313, but Surrey passed it, launched by the 40th century opening stand made by Hobbs and Sandham for Surrey.

The first wireless broadcast of a cricket match in England took place in May 1927, when Essex played the New Zealanders. Canon F. H. Gillingham (in hat), a noted Essex amateur batsman himself, gave the commentary – and unwittingly dented the BBC's charter by describing some of the visible advertisements during a rainy interval.

Right: *Bill Ponsford, the comfortably-built Australian with the 2 lb 10 oz bat and an endless appetite for runs. In 1927–28 he raised his world record to 437 in Victoria's match against Queensland at Melbourne, and thus became the only man to score two quadruple-centuries. Then, with 202 and 38 against NSW and 336 against South Australia, he proceeded to pile up over 1000 runs in four consecutive innings, all at Melbourne. His preceding innings had been 133 at Adelaide. Cricket had never envisaged such a plethora.*

Ponsford, the Record-breaker

L. E. G. AMES

WILLS'S CIGARETTES.

A. P. FREEMAN.

Three great Kent cricketers who had sensational seasons in 1928 – Leslie Ames, Frank Woolley, and 'Tich' Freeman – and yet only two of them were chosen for the 1928–29 MCC tour of Australia, and neither of them played in a Test. Woolley scored 3352 runs (60.95), more than anyone else (Tyldesley, Sutcliffe, Mead and Hendren all passed 3000), but missed the tour, the team having been selected piecemeal during the summer. Leslie Ames, on figures the most successful of all wicketkeeper–batsmen, became the first to do the double with 1919 runs and 121 dismissals, a feat he repeated in 1929 and 1932. Most of Ames's victims came off the tossed-up legspin/googly bowling of the dwarflike Alfred Percy Freeman, who bagged an alltime record of 304 wickets in 1928. His wicket-taking reached phenomenal proportions in the years to follow. From 1928 to 1935 – eight seasons – he took 2090 wickets, almost reaching 300 again (298) in 1933.

Left: The funeral of Yorkshire and England left-handed allrounder Roy Kilner (inset), at Wombwell in April 1928. There were over 100,000 people in the streets to pay respects to a much-loved cricketer who died at 37 from enteric fever contracted during a coaching engagement in India.

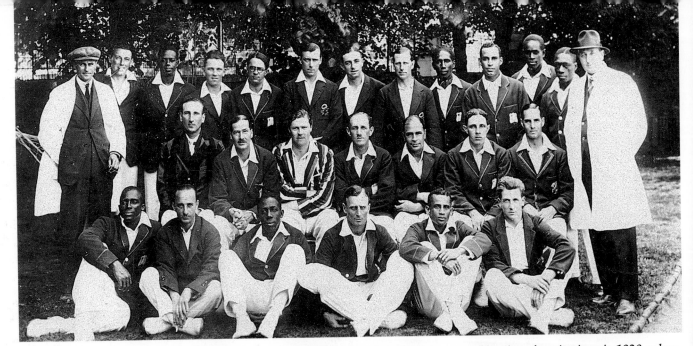

West Indies became the fourth Test nation – or 'entity' in their case, since they were a combination of territories – in 1928, when they played England at Lord's, Old Trafford and The Oval, losing by an innings each time. This led to the predictable conclusion that their elevation had been a mistake; but the progress hoped for came in due course, and just over half-a-century on, they were to rule the cricket world. One of the prices paid, however, is that the companionable intermixing of this Lord's group seems no longer possible. *Standing:* F. Chester (umpire), M. W. Tate, C. R. Browne, M. Leyland (12th man), C. V. Wight (12th man), C. Hallows, W. R. Hammond, G. E. Tyldesley, C. A. Roach, F. R. Martin, J. A. Small, G. N. Francis, L. C. Braund (umpire); *seated:* D. R. Jardine, G. Challenor, A. P. F. Chapman (captain), R. K. Nunes (captain), V. W. C. Jupp, M. P. Fernandes, H. Sutcliffe; *front:* H. C. Griffith, A. P. Freeman, L. N. Constantine, H. Smith, W. H. St Hill, H. Larwood (West Indies names not in italics). *Tyldesley scored 122 in this match, and Freeman took 22 wickets in the three Tests.*

Right: Lancashire left-hander Charlie Hallows (wearing dark belt, with his faithful partner Harry Makepeace), a year after Hammond, joined the select list of those who have scored 1000 runs in May when, having made five centuries already in 1928, he needed 232 more runs on May 30 . . . and made exactly that score against Sussex at Old Trafford, being 190 not out at the start of the last day in May. He played only twice for England in those years of batting wealth.

The star attraction of the 1928 West Indies team was Learie Constantine (seen here giving his standard treatment to Essex at Leyton, where he hit 130 in 90 minutes). He did the double on the tour, and showed miraculous fielding ability that had him dubbed 'Electric Heels'. He was to bring great honour to his race in the years ahead, both on the cricket field and off, becoming a barrister, a government minister, and finally a member of the House of Lords.

304

BRADMAN

DONALD GEORGE BRADMAN was born in Cootamundra, NSW on August 27, 1908, a day which rivals Australia Day itself in its significance to the nation, for the baby became a boy batsman of exceptional promise, and he became a young man who tore the book of existing batting records to ribbons. There have been batsmen with reflexes to match his, and others with comparable powers of concentration. Some have had his kind of disdainful attitude towards the bowling fraternity. Some have shown the same kind of stamina, run-greed, wrist-power, range of strokes, even the innate sense of authority. But never have all these commodities been endowed so prodigally upon one man. He possessed an unswerving determination to succeed, and no bowler was able to stop him long-term. His figures are the most powerful proof of his supremacy, a dominance that would have exerted itself in any era, but the testimony of his contemporaries, players and spectators alike, in Australia and England, renders the debate conclusive – this side of sentimentality and patriotism. Grace, Ranji, Trumper, Hobbs, Hammond, Hutton, Sobers, either of the Richardses, or the Chappells, or Gavaskar. None came within sight of 'Our Don's' record of a century every second match, or third innings, 37 of them double-, triple- or quadruple-centuries. None got near his first-class average of 95.14 and Test average of 99.94. Since winning cricket matches comes from making runs in sufficient quantity, the argument ends there, without the need to examine individually the many fat, fast and fine innings with which Bradman destroyed the opposition's bowling and morale.

A rare photograph of Don Bradman batting in his first Test match, December 1928. He made only 18 and 1, the second innings on a 'sticky dog', at Brisbane Exhibition Ground, Australia (122 and 66) going down by 675 runs, a margin no-one involved, least of all the 20-year-old who was now dropped for a match, would ever forget.

One of cricket'
famous
photographs:
Herbert
Fishwick's
study of
Hammond
during his
innings of
225 for MCC
v NSW,
November
1928, the
epitome of
poise and powe
Hammond's
scores in the
Tests were
44, 28, 251,
200, 32, 119
not out, 177,
38 and 16, a

total of 905, a new record. He
made 1553 runs on the tour,
another record: but
Bradman's total for the
1928–29 first-class season
was 1690, an overall record.
New marks were being made
everywhere: Hammond had
just come from an English
season in which he had taken
78 catches, 10 of them in a
match against Surrey in
which he also hit two
centuries.

Chapman's Englishmen at the nets at Adelaide Oval. Tyldesley is on the left, Freeman
prepares to bowl, Ames sits padding up, Hammond and Jardine bowl, with Leyland between
them, and the skipper is beyond.

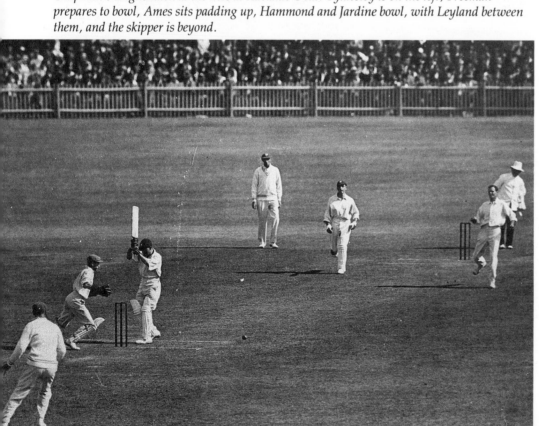

During his partnership of 333
with Hammond in the match
against NSW, Patsy
Hendren missed an attempted
hook at Kelleway. Oldfield,
the wicketkeeper, makes to
retrieve, and Hooker is at
mid-on. Hendren finished
with 167, Jardine had made
140, and MCC declared at
734 for 7. Bradman,
however, scored 87 and 132
not out, adding an unfinished
249 with Kippax, his captain,
who made 136 not out.
Kelleway took ill in the first
Test, and Gregory's knee
gave way. Neither played for
Australia again.

Don Blackie was in his 47th year when called up to play for Australia for the first time in the second Test of the 1928–29 series, at Sydney, where he took 4 for 148 off 59 six-ball overs. A swerving offspinner, with bow-legs, he did even better in the next Test, in his hometown, Melbourne. Here he took 6 for 94, and finished with 14 wickets in his three Tests at only 31.71 in this high-scoring series.

Leicestershire's George Geary toiled manfully through 81 overs in Australia's innings of 491 in the fifth Test, at Melbourne, taking 5 for 105. He finished atop the England averages with 19 wickets at 25.11. J. C. White took 25.

Australian captain Jack Ryder is lbw to Geary for 25 in the second Test. Duckworth seals the dismissal with his customary wail.

Clarrie Grimmett, who turned 37 during the 1928–29 series, was Australia's leading wicket-taker with 23, reward for his nagging persistence and control, his spin variations giving the Englishmen no peace. And there was still a lot of cricket left in 'The Gnome'.

Archie Jackson was only 18 when he made two centuries in a match for NSW. Australia blooded him in the Adelaide Test of 1928–29, when he was only 19, and he scored a beautiful 164 and 36. England won the first four Tests, but by the fifth Jackson was a member of a victorious Australian side. But his shadow was not meant to touch the ground for long. He died from tuberculosis in 1933, at the age of 23. There was to be no lasting second coming of Trumper after all.

Alan Kippax (left) and his No. 11 partner Hal Hooker resume their last-wicket stand for NSW v Victoria at Melbourne at Christmas 1928. The partnership realised 307, a world record. Hooker then took four wickets in four balls in the return match at Sydney, where NSW took first-innings points with their 713 for 6 (Bradman 340 not out) and thus won the Sheffield Shield. Kippax, who scored 260 in the Melbourne match, was a most charming stylist and also a very heavy scorer. His omission from the 1926 Australian tour of England, at a time when he was at his peak, remains one of the mysteries of Australian cricket.

A question of which is the more lunatic: riding with hounds straight across a cricket ground, or playing cricket on New Year's Day, as these gentlemen are doing on Broadhalfpenny Down, Hambledon, on January 1, 1929.

Below: *Percy Chapman opens the Venetian Fete in Hythe. Since leading England to an outstanding victory in Australia in 1928–29 he had played little cricket, and J. C. White and A. W. Carr led England against South Africa in 1929.*

The wonderful George Gunn scored 164 not out at Worcester on his 50th birthday, June 13, 1929. He often achieved whatever he set his heart on doing.

G. O. 'Gubby' Allen, who took all 10 Lancashire wickets for 40 (eight bowled) when they played Middlesex at Lord's in June 1929. Another fine amateur career was now unfolding.

The old firm of Hobbs and Sutcliffe was back in business in the fifth Test against South Africa in 1929, Sutcliffe having opened with E. T. Killick and Ted Bowley in the earlier Tests, when the 46-year-old Hobbs was injured or ill. Here, at The Oval, Sutcliffe (left) made a hundred in each innings for the second time in a Test, and Hobbs (right), cap sometimes askew, scored 10 and 52.

M. J. C. Allom made New Zealand's maiden Test match memorable by taking four wickets in five balls, including the hat-trick. Playing in his first Test, the large Surrey fast bowler took 5 for 38 and 3 for 17 to hasten England's victory at Christchurch, the margin eight wickets.

Harold Larwood was making a reputation for himself as a bowler of furious speed, and Notts' and England's opponents acknowledged him as the most dangerous around. In the 1929 Lord's Test match, in fading light, he hit South Africa's wicketkeeper 'Jock' Cameron on the head, and he was carried off for treatment. It was seven tour matches later that Cameron was well enough to resume playing.

Above left: *Don Bradman, merciless as ever on anything even slightly short, adds more runs towards his eventual 452 not out for NSW v Queensland at Sydney in January 1930, an innings which displaced Bill Ponsford from the world record. Still only 21, Bradman was on the highest pedestal already. As the Queenslanders carried him off in triumph (above) the world wondered what came next.*

The young champion, fresh from his triumph (and the Queenslanders really did think he looked sprightly enough to make another 452), meets Charlie Bannerman, 78, scorer of Australia's first Test Century.

In 1929–30, for the only time ever, a country played two concurrent Test series. While England played in New Zealand, another side played in West Indies, and are here taking the field in the Barbados Test: L. E. G. Ames, E. H. Hendren, A. Sandham, W. Rhodes, R. E. S. Wyatt, Hon. F. S. G. Calthorpe (captain), J. O'Connor, W. E. Astill, N. E. Haig, G. Gunn, W. Voce. Hendren, who was 40, made 1765 runs on the tour, and won the West Indian spectators' hearts. Rhodes was 52, Gunn 50, Haig 42, and Astill 41. Sandham, now 39, scored 325 in the Kingston Test – the first Test triple-century – in England's 849. George Headley made 223 for West Indies in this match, having scored two centuries in the previous Test, at Georgetown.

A somewhat uncommon sight: Notts fielding in civvies against Hampshire at Southampton in May 1930. The home side still needed one run for a five-wicket victory when the extra half-hour ended on the second evening. Notts captain A. W. Carr refused to play on, took his team onto the field next morning in lounge suits (Barratt and Voce wore overcoats) and off Carr's second ball Kennedy hit the winner.

In the first 100 years of Test cricket only 10 bowlers struck successfully with their first ball. One was Matt Henderson, a left-arm fast-medium bowler, who dismissed England's E. W. Dawson at Christchurch in January 1930 with his first delivery It was also the first wicket to be claimed by New Zealand in a Test match.

Lancashire, county champions in 1926, 1927 and 1928, won back the title in 1930, winning 10 of their 28 Championship matches, losing none, and gaining first-innings points in eight. Dick Tyldesley and Ted McDonald took over 100 wickets, while Ernest Tyldesley, Frank Watson and Jack Iddon passed 1000 runs. Standing: G. Duckworth, F. B. Watson, J. L. Hopwood, J. Iddon, F. M. Sibbles, M. L. Taylor, E. Paynter; seated: C. Hallows, E. A. McDonald, P. T. Eckersley (captain), G. E. Tyldesley, R. K. Tyldesley.

Don Bradman took England by storm on his first visit, in 1930, from the first innings, 236 at Worcester, to the last, 96 at Scarborough. Here he goes out with Ponsford (in cap) at Southampton to complete 1000 runs in May. He finished the tour with 2960 runs at an average of 98.67.

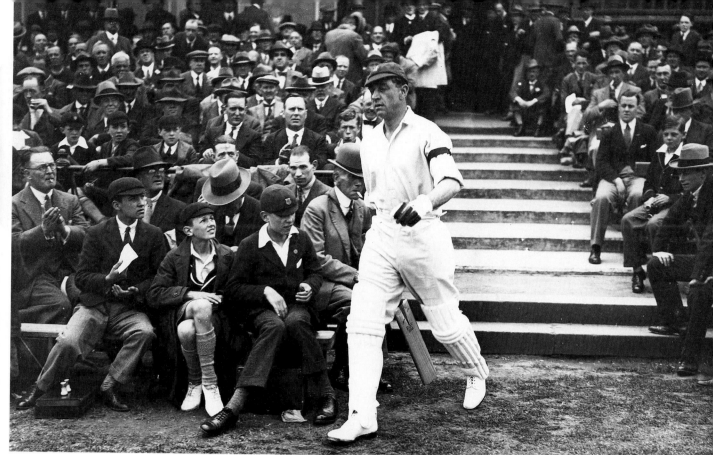

The paramount hero of the 1928–29 tour of Australia, Wally Hammond, strides out to resume battle in the opening Test of 1930, at Trent Bridge. But he was destined to follow his 905 runs in Australia with no more than 306 in this series. Grimmett got him out five times, and finished with a record and crucial 29 wickets.

Syd Copley, a Notts groundstaff player, came on as 13th man for England and held a very impressive catch at mid-on to dismiss McCabe on the last day of the 1930 Trent Bridge Test. The course of the match was altered, and England went on to a 93-run victory.

When Surrey played Middlesex at The Oval in August 1930 there was some confusion as to whether Hobbs needed 16 or 26 to pass WG's record career aggregate of 54,896. Here he reaches 16 and doffs his cap to the applause. He finished with 40. Nigel Haig (in cap) is the bowler and Ian Peebles (bareheaded) is at short leg.

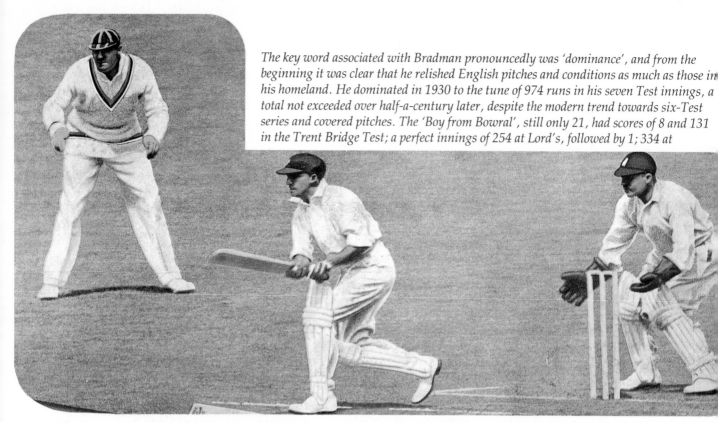

The key word associated with Bradman pronouncedly was 'dominance', and from the beginning it was clear that he relished English pitches and conditions as much as those in his homeland. He dominated in 1930 to the tune of 974 runs in his seven Test innings, a total not exceeded over half-a-century later, despite the modern trend towards six-Test series and covered pitches. The 'Boy from Bowral', still only 21, had scores of 8 and 131 in the Trent Bridge Test; a perfect innings of 254 at Lord's, followed by 1; 334 at

Headingley (he is seen above during his Leeds 'slaughter'); 14 at Old Trafford, where a Peebles googly undid him; and 232 at The Oval, where his fourth-wicket stand of 243 with Jackson (73) turned the match Australia's way. Victory here by an innings (Hornibrook 7 for 92 in England's second innings) gave Australia the Ashes back – and also, it has been suggested, gave certain Englishmen the first clue as to the best method of subduing the little master batsman. On a pitch freshened up by light rain he was noticeably uncomfortable against the lifting ball in line with his body. Perhaps Bradman was human after all?

Harold Larwood fires one down to McCabe in the 1930 Headingley Test. The ball is almost on the young Australian batsman. Larwood's pace was unquestionable, but he managed only four Test wickets in 1930.

Bradman comes in at Headingley after his extraordinary innings of 334. Going in on the first morning in the second over, he reached 105 by lunch, 220 by tea, and 309 at the close, Chapman having stuck to attacking fields much of the day. Bradman's dismissal next morning ended a 448-ball masterpiece which had lasted less than seven hours and contained 46 fours, 34 of them in front of the wicket. He now owned the England–Australia Test record, having topped R. E. Foster's 287, and was £1000 better off, thanks to a benefactor. Hammond later made 113 in 5½ hours, and rain eventually saved England.

Ian Peebles, England's young Scottish-born googly bowler, goes through his paces before the learned eyes of Arthur Mailey (nearest camera), Ranji and Duleep at Jodrell Hall, Cheshire. The Australian manager took Mailey to task for advising Peebles, but was put in his place with the good-natured retort that 'bowling is an art, and as such international'. The pensive Duleepsinhji already knew something about bowling, overcoming that of Northants at Hove in 1930 with a Sussex record innings of 333.

K. S. Duleepsinhji, here batting in the Old Trafford Test, had made a beautiful 173 at Lord's a month earlier on his Test debut. He was all grace, with a touch of his uncle Ranji's obvious genius.

315

Left: *England played five Tests in South Africa in 1930–31, and here, in the first, at the Old Wanderer ground, Johannesburg, as England pursued 240 for victory, Maurice Turnbull (61) is bowled by E. P. Nupen, who was a great cutter of the ball on matting surfaces. He followed his five wickets in the first innings with six in the second, and England lost by 28 runs. The remaining four Tests were drawn.*

Herman Griffith, who caused a sensation when he inflicted on Don Bradman his first duck in Test cricket (below), bowling him round his legs. Griffith was one of West Indies' best fast bowlers in the early days of their Test cricket, although he was already in his late thirties. His name is remembered in the gates to Kensington Oval, Bridgetown, Barbados.

Left: *Archie Jackson tries to swing a ball from Constantine and is lbw for 13 in the NSW v West Indians match.*

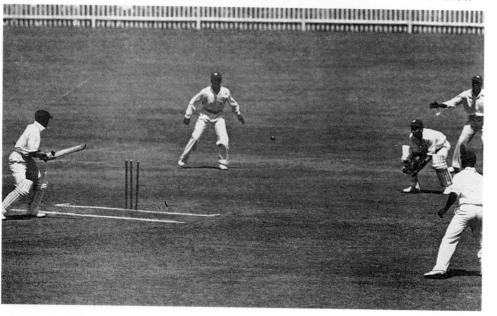

Bradman's duck in the fifth Test, Sydney, 1930–31. He had contributed 223 and 152 to two of Australia's four victories, but the jubilant West Indians won this fifth Test by 30 runs, Headley having made his second century of the series, and F. R. Martin 123 not out.

Part of the charm of county cricket has always been the variety of venues, and the refreshing departure from the headquarters grounds. Here, in rural Sussex, the county entertain Surrey in Horsham's cricket week in June 1931. Hobbs, now 48, became the first to 1000 in the season in this match, and Tate took nine wickets for Sussex, Ted Sheffield, a medium-pacer, 5 for 35 in Sussex's first innings. Surrey won an entertaining contest by 12 runs with less than five minutes remaining.

Roger Blunt, who scored 96, cuts Peebles in the Lord's Test of 1931, New Zealand's first in England. His partner, M. L. 'Curly' Page, made 104, and Dempster 120 in a total of 469 for 9 dec, which persuaded the authorities to grant the New Zealanders two more Tests (one lost, the other rain-ruined). Blunt made the first triple-century in New Zealand (for Otago) upon his return home. Right: Jack Mills, a tall left-hander, who scored 117 at Wellington on Test debut, and C. S. Dempster, who helped him put on 276 then, had a successful 1931 England tour.

Formula for frustration: Fred Root's notorious leg trap in action against Essex at Leyton in May 1931. He took five wickets in each innings, and finished with 123 in the Championship this year. C. F. Walters is at forward short leg Maurice Nichol, who died in 1934 is the second leg slip.

H. G. Vivian plays his maiden Test innings for New Zealand against England at The Oval, 1931. Only 18, 'Giff' Vivian scored 3 (one of Gubby Allen's five wickets for 14) and a top-score 51. In 1965 his son played for New Zealand at only 19 in a Test match in Calcutta which was also his maiden first-class match.

Glory shared: in the Varsity match of 1931, Alan Ratcliffe (right) scored 201 for Cambridge, the first double-century in the series. Next day, however, the Nawab of Pataudi (left) scored 238 not out, putting on 174 in only 95 minutes with H. G. Owen-Smith, who had made a superb 129 for South Africa at Leeds in 1929.

Some of the South Africans – Eric Dalton, Len Brown, Jimmy Christy, Neville Quinn, Quintin McMillan, Herby Taylor and Bruce Mitchell – work out on deck on the voyage to Australia, late 1931. A grim fate awaited them: defeat in all five Tests, three of them by an innings, humiliation in the last, and innings by Bradman of 226, 112, 167 and 299 not out.

George Gunn and his son G. V. Gunn (right) both scored centuries in Notts' innings against Warwickshire at Edgbaston in 1931, thanks to an extension of a couple of overs which brought George junior his hundred. The inimitable George senior, now 52, received a serious head injury in 1932 from a full-toss from Alf Gover. This prompted his retirement.

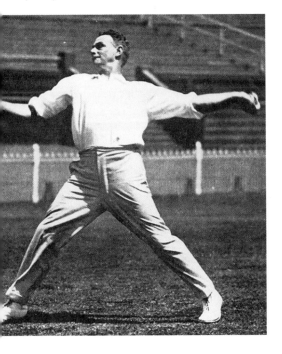

Herbert 'Dainty' Ironmonger, in his 50th year, spun out 31 South Africans in four Tests in 1931–32, 11 at Melbourne on a hopeless sticky, their totals being 36 and 45. Right: Eddie Gilbert was no-balled for throwing during this season. He played on, his pace furious, once knocking Bradman's bat from his hands.

The Players XI at Lord's, 1932, 11 names that echo richly down the years: standing: Eddie Paynter, George Duckworth, Bill Voce, Frank Woolley, Maurice Tate, Harold Larwood; seated: Herbert Sutcliffe, Patsy Hendren, Jack Hobbs (captain), Walter Hammond, Tich Freeman. The last two are in danger of burning their fingers. Hobbs made his 16th century in G v P fixtures, and Hammond, Duleepsinhji and Pataudi also made hundreds.

A. H. Bakewell is dropped by J. W. Hearne in Northants' match at Lord's in 1932. Fred Price is the Middlesex wicketkeeper. Fred Bakewell was an unorthodox and prolific batsman and clever short-leg fieldsman, who scored 107 for England v West Indies at The Oval in 1933. His career was ended in 1936 by severe injury in a car crash – hours after he had scored 241 not out.

Still probably the most renowned 'firm' of opening batsmen: Jack Hobbs and Herbert Sutcliffe, one from the South, one from the North. Their partnerships for England became the stuff of legends.

On July 12, 1932, Hedley Verity of Yorkshire spun for himself the best analysis ever recorded in a first-class innings: 10 for 10, including a hat-trick, in 19.4 overs (16 maidens), against hapless Notts on a damp Headingley pitch. It was the second time he had taken all 10. In a splendid career, Verity took 1956 wickets at a mere 14.90, 144 of them in 40 Tests.

F. S. Ashley-Cooper, the eminent historian, died on January 31, 1932, aged 54. His authority was unrivalled and unchallenged, and his output was heavy. For five years he edited Cricket, and was once Notts' secretary. He built up a large book and picture collection, which was sold to Sir Julien Cahn.

Trouble brews at Leyton: in August 1932, Harold Larwood experimented with fast 'leg theory' in Notts' match against Essex. Dudley Pope, utterly inconvenienced, has poked a catch up for Keeton. Two days earlier, Larwood, his bowling partner Voce, their captain Carr, Percy Fender and D. R. Jardine had met to discuss the likelihood of this kind of bowling being successful in the forthcoming tour of Australia.

To their great joy, India became a Test cricket nation in June 1932 when they played England at Lord's. They had a good first morning, Nissar bowling Holmes and Sutcliffe, while Woolley was run out, to make it 19 for 3. Jardine (79) carried the score to decency, and is here seen (in Harlequin rather than England cap) cutting his opposing captain, C. K. Nayudu. His partner is Hammond. Jardine was 85 not out in the second innings when he declared, and India, needing 346 to win, were bowled out for 187.

June 16, 1932, and a new world record for a first-wicket stand has just been established. Percy Holmes (224 not out, having been dropped at 3) and Herbert Sutcliffe (right), who threw his wicket away for 313, put on 555 in 445 minutes for Yorkshire (eventual champions) against Essex at Leyton, beating fellow Yorkshiremen Brown and Tunnicliffe's mark of 554. There was a ripple of panic when the total was adjusted to 554, but a 'no-ball' was found and the final score put back to 555 for 1 dec. Bowes and Verity then bowled Essex out for 78 and 164.

BODYLINE

CRICKET had a rough passage to ride in the early 1930s when England attacked Australia with fast short-pitched bowling in line with batsmen's heads and throats. The prime target was the phenomenal Bradman, whose average for the series crashed to 56.57, which would have brought a thin smile of satisfaction to the lips of the 'mastermind', England's captain, D. R. Jardine, of Winchester, Oxford and Surrey. He had prepared his campaign meticulously, consulting with F. R. Foster (who was later horrified to read of the purpose to which formerly non-intimidatory leg-theory bowling had been applied) and Arthur Carr, the Notts captain, whose fast men, Harold Larwood and Bill Voce (left-arm), were to be Jardine's twin spearhead. Australian batsmen weaved and ducked, took their chances with the hook, were pummelled around the body (especially Ponsford), caught in the teeming ranks of short-leg vultures off feeble parries, and fought to hide their despair. Miraculously, nobody was killed, though at Adelaide, Woodfull was hit sickeningly over the heart by Larwood as he bowled to a conventional field (Jardine instantly switched to the Bodyline field), and Oldfield top-edged the same bowler into his temple, which was cracked. Larwood took 33 wickets at 19.52 in the five Tests, Voce 15 at 27.13, and Gubby Allen, who flatly refused to employ Bodyline, 21 at 28.24. Jardine's team won the series 4–1 (Bradman's sole century aided victory for Australia at Melbourne in the second Test), though exchanges of cables halfway through almost saw the tour called off: MCC did not like accusations of 'unsportsmanlike' tactics, while the Australian Board could not face with equanimity the loss of further gatemoney. The wider evil was the inevitable experimentation with Bodyline by club and school cricketers. It was a day of merciful salvation when restrictions were placed on field-settings, and Bodyline as it was observed in 1932–33 became illegal. The 50th anniversary of that stormy series coincided with the 1982–83 Ashes series, during which interest was rekindled, and new theories took wing concerning alleged sinister political conspiracies. What truly mattered to cricket-lovers was that intimidation was still rife, and the authorities were a great distance away from solving the problem. The Bodyline series, viewed over half-a-century on, was described by W. F. Deedes as 'cricket's Hiroshima'.

Bodyline was tangible well before the 1932–33 MCC tour of Australia. Larwood and Voce had tried it out with Notts, and here, at The Oval, in August 1932, Jack Hobbs remonstrates against the persistent short bowling of Yorkshire's Bill Bowes. Hobbs's England partner Sutcliffe (hands on hips) lends an ear, while 15 yards away the tall fair-haired Bowes talks matters over with his skipper Brian Sellers, Leyland, and Verity (bareheaded). Within months Hobbs was writing surprisingly blandly about the acrimonious Bodyline Ashes series, and P. F. Warner, who had condemned Bowes's tactics at The Oval, found himself as manager of Jardine's England team but powerless to restrain him from using Bodyline.

Above: *Stan McCabe played a daring, brave and brilliant innings of 187 not out for Australia in the first Test, at Sydney, hooking and pulling Larwood, Voce and Allen with thrilling audacity and the necessary measure of luck. Vic Richardson later claimed that had he not got out for 49, when they had added 129 for the fifth wicket, Bodyline might have been stifled at birth.*

Above: *Jardine watches Bill Woodfull toss before the opening Test. Australia won, batted, made 360, thanks to McCabe, but conceded 524 to England as Sutcliffe, Hammond and Pataudi (on debut) made centuries. They then collapsed before Larwood (5 for 28) in the second innings for 164 and lost by 10 wickets.*

Jack Fingleton manages to get the ball away through the leg-trap in the Sydney Test. He made a courageous century for NSW against the legside bouncer blitz and a gutsy 83 at Melbourne before his luck ran out in the shape of a 'pair' at Adelaide. His book Cricket Crisis *remains a vivid and prime source book.*

Left: *The famous 'Yabba' (Stephen Harold Gascoigne), whose stentorian barracking from the Hill at Sydney, essentially good-humoured, was often more entertaining than the cricket. His comments were invariably corny but boomed out in style, and he unquestionably knew the game. Jack Hobbs asked to meet him when he walked round the ground on his final visit there.*

Sutcliffe, his highest Test score of 194 behind him at Sydney, where he survived playing on to O'Reilly at 43, has no such luck in the next Test, at Melbourne, where the same bowler hits his stumps for 33 as England aim for 251 for victory after Bradman had atoned for his first-ball dismissal with a second-innings 103 not out. O'Reilly (5 for 66, 10 wickets in the match) bowled them out for 139. In the series the tall, balding, medium-pace legspin-googly bowler from a NSW bush town took 27 wickets, and was to extend his bag of English wickets to a remarkable 102 in four series, establishing a reputation for hostility and skill that matched that of S. F. Barnes.

Right: Bradman's hopes of survival and runmaking rested principally on stepping swiftly to leg and hitting through the near-empty off side. Here at Adelaide he managed 66 in the second innings, in which Woodfull valiantly carried his bat for 73 not out.

Below: The archetypal photograph of Bodyline clearly shows the menacing inner ring of fielders at Brisbane as Larwood bounces the ducking Woodfull at approximately 95 mph.

Above: *Eddie Paynter's tonsillitis forced him into hospital during the Brisbane Test, but the little left-hander emerged in England's hour of need, still suffering, and scored 83, to keep his side in the match. In the second innings he had the pleasure of hitting a six to win the match.* Left: *By the grace of God, Ruth Oldfield and daughters have their husband and father, Bertie, back after the blow sustained at Adelaide.*

Vic Richardson (left) batted with typical resolution against Bodyline and was almost the only Australian who passed the time of day with the Englishmen, so low had relations sunk. Tim Wall (right) was Australia's only effective fast bowler, and finished with 16 wickets at 25.56. He also took all 10 NSW wickets for 36 in South Australia's match at Sydney that season.

The main English 'villains', the captain apart: Bill Voce (left) and Harold Larwood. His labours left Larwood with a damaged foot, so he missed the New Zealand leg of the tour.

Types of records: **above:** *Harold Larwood's remarks endeavoured to justify the method of attack used in the 1932–33 Tests. He refused to apologise when the English authorities realised how deep was the rift created by Bodyline, and never played for England again. On the other side of the Columbia '78' Frank Foster expresses his disappointment at being implicated in the 'plot'. Left: Hammond made more cricket records when the team went on to New Zealand. In the Christchurch Test he hit 227, and at Auckland 336 not out in 318 minutes, with 10 sixes and 34 fours, the third century coming in only 47 minutes. It took the Englishman past Bradman's world Test record score, and in his last four Test innings Hammond had now made 739 runs, twice out.*

Phil Mead, at 46, was still piling up the runs in 1933, and was second in the national averages, behind Hammond, with 2576 runs at 67.79 – each bonus for a fifty 'another sack of coal for the winter'.

Right: C. S. 'Father' Marriott, a clever legspin-googly bowler, played once for England, at The Oval in 1933, and took 11 wickets for 96. His reward was an MCC tour place that winter to India. A master at Dulwich College, he played for Kent, having learnt to play in Ireland, and having played first for Lancashire.

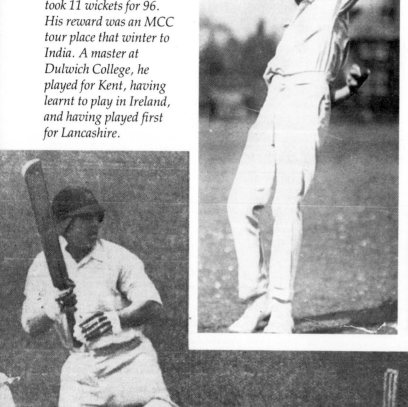

Above: Manny Martindale, from Barbados, was West Indies' best bowler on the 1933 tour of England, taking 103 wickets, 14 in the three Tests. At Old Trafford he cut Hammond's chin open, and he and Constantine gave Jardine a sustained dose of Bodyline. The England captain made a courageous 127. Left: Patsy Hendren had a big year in 1933: over 3000 runs, 11 centuries, including 301 not out for Middlesex v Worcestershire at Dudley, and two in the match against Kent. And just to be on the safe side against all this bumper bowling, his wife sewed some extra peaks on his cap. Below: The North London Girls' Cricket Team get themselves ready for the season.

Above: *Tich Freeman continued to weave his spell in the sunny, high-scoring summer of 1933. He took 298 wickets at 15.27 with his buzzing, hovering spinners.* Above right: *John Langridge, who served Sussex from 1928 to 1955. At Hove in 1933 he and Ted Bowley made 490 for the first wicket against Middlesex, the third-highest such stand thus far. Langridge, also a sound slip fielder, scored over 34,000 runs, with 76 centuries, but never played for England.* Right: *Brian Sellers, Yorkshire's new captain, leads his gladiators out in 1933, when they completed another hat-trick of Championships. They took the title also in 1935, 1937, 1938 and 1939. Behind the no-nonsense Sellers is Percy Holmes, in his final season, his century stands with Sutcliffe numbering 69, and behind him are Wilf Barber (bareheaded), Maurice Leyland, then Hedley Verity (who took 190 cheap wickets, including 17 in a day at Leyton) and wicketkeeper Arthur Wood.*

The ultimate amateurism: English womanhood on Clacton beach.

Bob Crisp, the South African Test bowler, took four wickets in four balls in 1933–34 for the second time. This time Natal were the victims, at Durban, while in 1931–32 Western Province had been playing Griqualand West at Johannesburg.

England won two and drew one of the three Tests in India in 1933–34. The first Test ever in India was here at Bombay's Gymkhana ground, and Les Townsend, the Derbyshire allrounder, is hooking Nissar. Townsend's partner, B. H. Valentine of Kent, went on to make 136 in his maiden Test innings. England won by nine wickets, Morris Nichols taking 3 for 53 and 5 for 55, and giving – with E. W. 'Nobby' Clark – much short stuff to the Indian batsmen. The solar topees served as much as protection against bouncers as against the scorching sun. Lala Amarnath, in the second innings, scored 118, India's first Test century.

Yorkshire's Arthur Mitchell (left) and C. F. Walters go to bat for MCC against the Viceroy's XI at Delhi. Walters had just made a record nine centuries for Worcestershire in 1933.

The Indian and England players, third Test 1933–34, Madras. Standing at rear: Major E. W. C. Ricketts, Dilawar Hussain,
A. H. Bakewell, A. Mitchell; standing: J. W. Hitch (umpire), C. J. Barnett, L. Amar Singh, E. W. Clark, M. J. Gopalan (12th
man), L. F. Townsend, C. S. Nayudu, L. Amarnath, V. M. Merchant, James Langridge, J. B. Higgins (umpire); seated: M. S.
Nichols, Naoomal Jeoomal, C. F. Walters, Yuvraja of Patiala, D. R. Jardine (England captain), C. K. Nayudu (India captain),
H. Elliott, S. Wazir Ali, H. Verity, S. Nazir Ali; front: S. Mushtaq Ali, R. J. Gregory (12th man). Jeoomal's head is bandaged
after a blow from a Clark bouncer, which he top-edged. He retired hurt and was unable to bat in the second innings.

Permission was given to Miss Miers of
Melbourne YWCA to wear a mask when
keeping wicket. 'Facial disfigurement,'
stated The Australian Cricketer, 'would
be very serious for a lady'.

Victorian batsmen often capitalised on moderate Tasmanian bowling, but in
1933–34 I. S. Lee (258) and S. O. Quin (210) indulged themselves to the
extent of 424 for the fourth wicket. Ian Lee, a left-hander, was only 19, while
Stan Quin kept wicket: both had successful careers for Victoria.

Big Bill Bowes was an awkward bowler, with fair pace and sharp lift allied to movement. In 1934 he took 147 first-class wickets, and dismissed Bradman in his last three Test innings of the summer . . . for 304, 244 and 77. Frank Chester is the umpire pictured, and the batsman is Andrew Sandham, who scored 219 for Surrey against the Australians. It was his great partner Hobbs's final season – he played little – and henceforth it was to seem rather strange and lonely for his faithful aide, now 44.

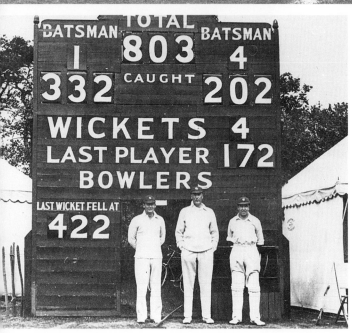

One of Kent's great 'fun' days came in 1934 at Brentwood when they ran up 803 for 4 dec against Essex, Bill Ashdown (left) scoring 332 (he made another triple-century against Derbyshire at Dover next season), Frank Woolley (centre) 172, and Leslie Ames (right) 202 not out. The total took seven hours, 623 runs coming on the first day.

Right: Day of shock: during Essex's previous home match, at Chelmsford, one of the visiting players, 29-year-old Worcestershire batsman Maurice Nichol, who had a highest score of 262 not out, had died during the night, having played golf on the rest day. 'Horseplay' was denied – he was known to have a heart weakness – and a bruise on him was attributed to a blow by a cricket ball. He had enjoyed a couple of quiet drinks before retiring to bed with a pipe and a book. He was engaged to be married. A minute's silence was observed on the Monday, and the players wore black armbands. C. F. Walters, Nichol's captain, then moved quietly and elegantly to a score of 178.

Hit Century as Colleague Lay Dead

CROWD'S CHEERS HID TRAGEDY

From Our Special Correspondent
K. C. SPIERS

CHELMSFORD (Essex),
Monday.

C. F. WALTERS, the Worcest captain, batted for himself and for a dead colleague to-day.

He put up one of the best scor of his life—172—but through it there was never a smile on h face.

Even when the gay crowd at t Essex County Ground burst in cheers he gave no sign that he hear

For at an hotel not far away colleague, Maurice Nichol, one of E land's most promising young cricket was lying dead.

A chambermaid who had gone to ro Nichol got no reply to her knocks. S called the manager, and the 28-year-batsman was found dead in bed.

WHAT DID IT MEAN?

He had apparently had a heart seizu for ever since pneumonia attacked h two years ago he had been a doom man . . . .

The vast crowd of holiday-mak knew nothing of the tragedy when game began to-day. The town w gay with bunting and flags; the s was shining.

Then the players came on the fi wearing black armlets. What did mean?

The first over, a sign from Walt

d. May 21 1934 age 29

No Horse-play Before Cricketer's Death

AN indignant denial of a "disgusting suggestion" that horse-play preceded the death of

Hendren, the only professional among nine Misters and a Reverend in the MCC XI playing the 1934 Australians, dashes from the separate dressing-room, exchanging pleasantries with Mrs A. P. F. Chapman, the captain's wife. Popular Patsy scored 135, but Ponsford made 281 not out.

Never too late to learn: James Oldis, 102, with young friends in Eastville Park, Bristol, midsummer 1934. The veteran was still walking seven miles a day.

Left: Cricket books have enjoyed a boom in the 1970s and 1980s, but at Hudson's Bookshop in Birmingham in 1934 there was a reasonable display, including titles by Bradman, Tate, Grimmett, Peebles, Macartney, Constantine, Mailey, Larwood, Sammy Woods, etc, prices around half-a-crown to seven-and-six.

Below: A costume re-enactment in 1934 to celebrate the bicentenary of Sevenoaks Vine Cricket Club drew large support. Lord Sackville and Lord Gage, descendants of the captains – or 'generals' – in the 1734 match, led the Gentlemen of Kent and of Sussex respectively.

Tom Goddard, of the giant hands, whips down another offspinner for Gloucestershire at The Oval in 1934. His career was long (1922–52) and fruitful (2979 wickets), and four times he reached 200 wickets in a season. He took all 10 against Worcestershire in 1937, and eight times took nine wickets in an innings. Capped only eight times by England, he did the hat-trick at Johannesburg in the 1938–39 series.

Below: R. W. V. Robins, 'down the track', is missed by Ben Barnett in the Gentlemen's match against the Australians. Robins, who played 19 times for England, was a lively batsman and vigorous spinner of legbreaks and googlies.

Above: England take the field at Trent Bridge at the start of the 1934 series. Australia won by 238 runs to go one-up in the delicate first post-Bodyline rubber. Chipperfield of NSW was out for 99 in his maiden Test innings. From left: M. Leyland, H. Sutcliffe, W. R. Hammond, L. E. G. Ames, H. Verity, K. Farnes, T. B. Mitchell, C. F. Walters (captain), Nawab of Pataudi.

Mabel Bryant, captain of the England women's team, shows her girls how at the Liverpool college where she taught physical culture. Left: Hammond, who had a dismal 1934 series against Australia, falls to an Oldfield stumping at Trent Bridge, for only 16. Grimmett, the bowler, took 25 wickets in the five Tests, and O'Reilly 28. No other Australian took more than six.

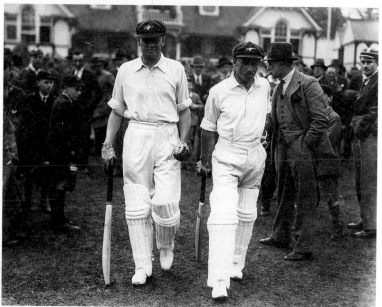

Bill Woodfull (left) and Don Bradman at Worcester, where The Don started the 1934 summer with a double-century, as he had done four years earlier on his first English tour. He made 2020 runs (758 in the Tests), with seven centuries. Stan McCabe scored eight, his aggregate being 2078. English crowds saw for themselves the heralded brilliance of his footwork and strokeplay.

England complete a rare Lord's Test victory over Australia, Hendren having dived smartly forward to catch Wall and give Verity his 15th wicket of the match, 14th of the day. Caught on a damp pitch, Woodfull's men failed to avoid the follow-on, and the Yorkshire left-armer (7 for 61 and 8 for 43) completed his job efficiently and modestly.

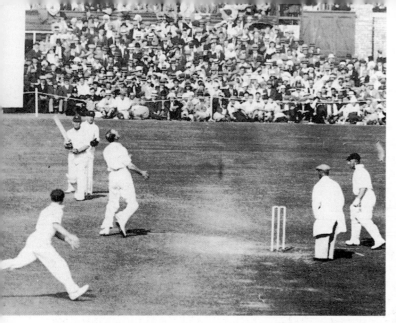

At Old Trafford, after O'Reilly had dismissed Walters, Wyatt and Hammond in four balls, Hendren (132) and Leyland (153) rescued England, their stand of 191 for the fifth wicket, in heatwave conditions, ending as O'Reilly caught-and-bowled Hendren. England totalled 627, but McCabe's 137 led Australia out of danger. Right: *The heaviest-scoring pair of all, Bradman and Ponsford, resume their stand of 451 for Australia's second wicket at The Oval, where the total was 701 and eventual victory came by 562 runs. Ponsford made 266 in what was his final Test, and Bradman 244. In the previous Test, at Headingley, Bradman (304) and Ponsford (181) put on 388 for the fourth wicket.*

The spectre of Bodyline materialised insensitively during the Australians' 1934 tour when Voce reverted to it, and took 8 for 66 for Notts. Woodfull discreetly expressed his feelings, and on the last day Voce was absent with a 'leg injury'. Leg theory was seen in the Tests, chiefly from England's Clark, but to little avail.

Below: *Sabina Park, Jamaica, during the 1934–35 West Indies v England series, where the home team took the rubber in this fourth Test, Headley making 270 not out. Three years earlier the 'black Bradman' had hit 344 not out for Jamaica against Tennyson's team.*

Sydney grade cricket matches drew large crowds – even when Bradman wasn't playing. Here, in 1934–35, Western Suburbs play Mosman at Pratten Park.

Left: Myrtle Maclagan of England reaches the first-ever century in a women's Test match: January 7, 1935.

Below: Essex and England allrounder Morris Stanley Nichols. Against Yorkshire at Huddersfield in 1935 he scored 146 and took 11 for 54. A right-arm fast bowler and left-hand batsman, he did the double eight times, but found himself in the England XI only 14 times. He kept goal for QPR.

Left: Harold Gimblett, when only 20, thrashed Essex for a 63-minute century at Frome in 1935. Up from his village, he was playing his first first-class match. Arthur Wellard, the big man with him, was a hearty fast bowler and thumper of sixes, also for Somerset, and in 1935 he set a record of 66 sixes, which lasted for 50 years, until another Somerset player, Ian Botham, beat it.

337

The scenic Stinchcombe Stragglers ground, Dursley, where several Gloucestershire benefit matches were played in the 1930s.

Joe Hardstaff jnr, playing for Notts against the 1935 South Africans, saves his skin by a deft piece of batwork when 85. He went on to 154, and earned his first England cap that summer. One of the most elegant of batsmen, golden-haired, always eager to grasp the initiative, in a career interrupted by the Second World War he registered 83 centuries, 10 of them doubles.

Just the right amount of footwork, a flowing arm movement, and Frank Woolley has a six off Bob Gregory in Kent's match against Surrey at The Oval. Woolley, now 48, cruised to 229, and again made over 2000 this year. By his retirement in 1938 his figures were awesome: 58,959 runs, 145 centuries, 2066 wickets, 1018 catches.

Five Kent amateurs, with man-size dog: W. H. V. Levett, F. G. H. Chalk, J. G. W. Davies, A. P. F. Chapman, B. H. Valentine.

Below: *The doughty Yorkshire left-hander Maurice Leyland batting in the 1935 Lord's Test, which saw South Africa win on English soil for the first time. Leyland came good in the Oval Test with 161.*

Below: *R. E. S. Wyatt drives South Africa's Bell in the Lord's Test. Having made 149 in the Trent Bridge Test, Wyatt now presided over England's first home defeat by the Springboks.* Right: *Cigarette-makers were suggesting that a few puffs helped.*

339

Jack Siedle of South Africa plays Bowes in the 1935 Oval Test, which was one of the four unfinished that summer. His partner is Bruce Mitchell, who made 128, having scored a decisive 164 in the Lord's Test, which Crisp, Langton and Balaskas then converted to an historic 157-run victory. Bakewell is bareheaded at forward short leg. Wicketkeeper Ames scored 148 not out for England.

Left: Eric Dalton, who went in at No. 8, made 117 for South Africa at The Oval, and put on 137 with A. B. C. Langton for the ninth wicket. He is seen hooking J. C. Clay, a fine Glamorgan offspinner who was unlucky only ever to have won this one England cap.

No ball: no game. The cricket-ball industry has always flourished, of necessity, and these artisans are at work in the factory in Teston, a village in Kent. In modern times vast quantities of equipment have been imported from India and Pakistan.

340

James Langridge, slow left-arm bowler and left-hand batsman, did the double for the fifth time in 1935. He won a few England caps, unlike unlucky brother John, and captained Sussex after the war.

The last photograph taken of H. B. 'Jock' Cameron – here with his wife. A neat and efficient wicketkeeper and ebullient batsman (he hit 90 in 105 minutes in the 1935 Lord's Test for South Africa, having punished Verity for 30 off an over in the Yorkshire match at Sheffield), he died of enteric fever soon after returning from the UK tour. He was 30. **Below:** William Capel, aged 103, on his day out, June 1935. He and fellow inmates of the Central Homes, Stratford, were taken to Loughton. He was considered by doctors to be 'a marvel for his age'.

There has been no greater pair of spin bowlers than Bill O'Reilly and Clarrie Grimmett, pictured here just after the war. Their last campaign together for Australia was in South Africa in 1935–36, after which the 44-year-old Grimmett was dumped. In that South African series he took 44 wickets, becoming the first bowler to take 200 Test wickets. Australia won the first Test by nine wickets, drew the second (in which two glorious innings were played: Nourse 231, McCabe 189 not out), and won the last three by an innings. In these, Grimmett took 10, 10 and 13 wickets. O'Reilly took 27 in the series, and both bowlers were well supported by wicketkeeper Oldfield and skilful close fielders, notably Fingleton and Vic Richardson, the captain (Bradman having been unavailable).

Left: *Jack Mercer, who took over 1500 wickets in a long career, principally with Glamorgan, took all 10 wickets of Worcestershire for 51 at Worcester in 1936. A member of the Magic Circle, this genial fast bowler later coached Northants and became the county's scorer, serving until well into old age.*

THIS SPARROW WAS KILLED AT LORD'S BY A BALL
BOWLED BY JEHANGIR KHAN (CAMBRIDGE UNIVERSITY)
TO T. N. PEARCE (M.C.C.)
ON JULY 3RD 1936.

Arthur Fagg of Kent obliges some Southampton schoolboys just after scoring 257 against their county in early summer 1936. Two years later he performed a unique feat in scoring two double-centuries in a match, Kent v Essex at Colchester.

The dangers of flying low at Lord's: this innocent sparrow was killed instantly by the ball which is now its headstone in the Museum at Lord's. It was bowled by Jehangir Khan (father of Majid) of Cambridge to T. N. Pearce of MCC in July 1936.

May 1936, and summer, as so often, is a long time coming. Hot tea was served to the Surrey fielders, umpires and Somerset batsmen at The Oval. Frank Lee, whose 69 was the highest score for Somerset in an innings defeat (Alf Gover five wickets in each innings), has his bat tucked under his arm.

One of cricket's alltime greats struggles in difficult conditions in only his second county match: Denis Compton, 18, batting at No. 8 for Middlesex against Notts at Lord's in June 1936, eludes G. F. H. Heane's grasp at gully as wicketkeeper Ben Lilley watches. Compton made 26 not out, and was lbw to Larwood in the second innings for 14. (Since 1935 a batsman could be out if the ball pitched outside off stump.) Jim Smith and Laurie Gray then bowled Notts out for 41.

The cavalier cricketer–golfer Leonard Crawley plays a big nine-iron in his innings of 63 for Essex against Kent at Southend in M. S. Nichols' benefit match in August 1936. Nichols himself and Jack O'Connor made centuries in Essex's 465, and Kent were then shot out for 151 and 98, the fiery Ken Farnes taking 6 for 69.

The England XI which played India at Old Trafford in 1936. It contains some non-regular faces: five in the back row, Hardstaff excepted, played only 25 times for England between them. Standing: H. Gimblett, A. E. Fagg, J. Hardstaff, A. R. Gover, T. S. Worthington, L. B. Fishlock; seated: H. Verity, R. W. V. Robins, G. O. B. Allen (captain), W. R. Hammond, G. Duckworth. A record 588 runs were scored on the second day, India ending it 190 for 0.

V. M. Merchant and Mushtaq Ali, two of India's greatest batsmen, open at Old Trafford, where they both made centuries, and posted 203, second innings.

Lala Amarnath, who had made India's first Test century, was sent home for 'indiscipline' during the 1936 tour, in which 22 Indian players featured.

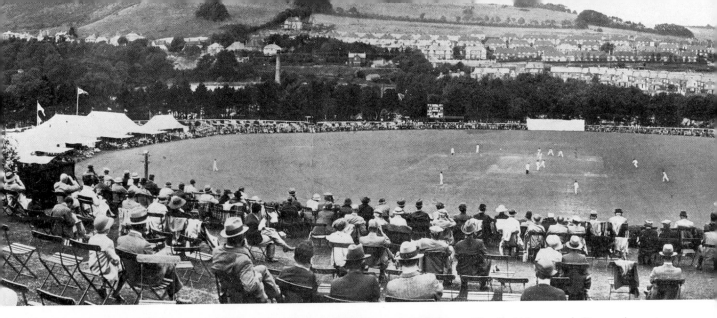

The Crabble ground, Dover, August 1936, and Kent are completely outplaying Yorkshire, whose hopes of retaining the County Championship evaporated with this reversal. Ames scored 120 for the home side, whose 406 was the highest by any side against Yorkshire since 1934, and Kent openers Les Todd and Colin Cole took eight wickets each.

Left: *Notts v Surrey, Trent Bridge, June 1936, and Surrey wicketkeeper Ted Brooks catches Arthur Staples off Alf Gover, making Notts 24 for 4. Rain prevented a conclusion, but Surrey took first-innings points. Gover, whose pace was as brisk as his action was untidy, took 200 wickets this and the following year, an admirable achievement on the heartless Oval pitches of the day.*

Preston's first county match – Lancashire v Gloucestershire, July 1936 – saw 40 wickets fall for only 529 on a drying surface. There were 13 lbws. Here the masterly Wally Hammond plays Sibbles during his match top-score of 65.

345

Derbyshire, so long a Cinderella county, became champions in 1936, winning 13 of their 28 matches outright and five on the first innings. Standing: H. Elliott, L. F. Townsend, W. H. Copson, H. Parker (scorer), A. V. Pope, D. Smith, C. S. Elliott; seated: H. Storer, T. S. Worthington, A. W. Richardson (captain), T. B. Mitchell, A. E. Alderman. Worthington, Townsend, Smith and Alderman all passed 1000 runs, and Copson and Mitchell took 100 wickets, and Alf Pope 94. Charlie Elliott later became a Test umpire and selector.

Right: With MCC off to Australia in the autumn of 1936, six weeks of relaxation had to be tempered with fitness levels. Verity and Wyatt play quoits on the deck of Orion.

Below: Mohammad Idris Yusuf, who scored 412 not out in Salisbury in the 1936–37 season, the highest score known in Southern Africa.

Below right: W. N. Carson (left) and P. E. Whitelaw after their world record stand of 445 for Auckland's third wicket against Otago at Dunedin on December 31, 1936. Bill Carson, a left-hander, played cricket (though not in Tests) and rugby for New Zealand, while Paul Whitelaw played twice against England in 1932–33.

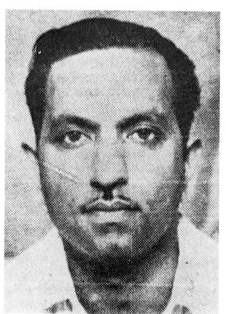

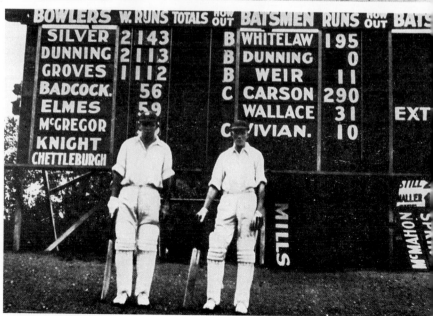

So much depended on the toss – and upon D. G. Bradman – during the Test series of 1936–37. There was much luck floating around in the matters of injury and who happened to be batting after pitches were splashed by rain. England, helped by rain, won by 322 runs at Brisbane and an innings at Sydney, where Hammond scored 231 not out. Voce took 17 wickets in these two matches. Then Bradman came into his own. Holding himself back at Melbourne, he added a record 346 for the sixth wicket with Fingleton (136), and followed with 212 at Adelaide, where his team drew level. He, McCabe and Badcock then scored hundreds at Melbourne, where Australia piled up 604 and won by an innings to take the series 3–2.

THE MAN OF
A CENTURY

Left: *How do you get this man out? Hammond and Ames might be asking as Bradman piles up 270 in the third Test.*

Right: *Bradman seems to be offering a comforting arm to his friend and opposing skipper Gubby Allen as they return from an inspection after a shower at Melbourne in the third Test. The overall attendance was 350,534, a match record.*

Yorkshire won the Championship again in 1937, but it didn't put these Lancashire lasses off their game as they had their own 'hard-fought' contest on Blackpool beach. Right: *R. H. Moore, who set a new individual Hampshire record with a 380-minute 316 against Warwickshire at Bournemouth. He hit 43 fours and three sixes, and gave not a single chance.*

Left: *Boy prodigy Tony Pawson batted his intrepid way to a schoolboy record innings at Lord's of 237, for Lord's Schools Under-16s in 1937. He became a Kent batsman, England soccer amateur, writer, and top fly-fisherman.*

Below: *England v New Zealand, Old Trafford, 1937, and Walter Hadlee, later to father the great Richard and his brothers, crashes into his stumps when only seven short of a century. Freddie Brown is at second slip, the unemotional Hammond at first, with Ames the rather perplexed wicketkeeper. Wellard was the bowler.*

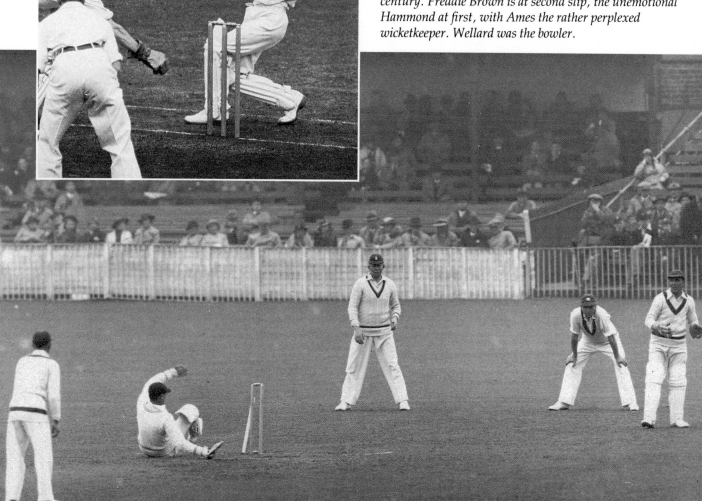

New Zealand fast bowler Jack Cowie completes figures of 6 for 67 (10 in the match) by catching Jim Smith off his own bowling. This left New Zealand needing 265 to win the 1937 Old Trafford Test, but Tom Goddard (6 for 29) bowled them out for 134. The other two Tests were drawn.

At 48, Patsy Hendren decided to call it a day. No more big cricket for him after 30 years of it. Always a nervous motor passenger, he enjoyed this carriage ride to the Scarborough ground during the last few days of his final season, 1937.

Charles Barnett, the dashing Gloucestershire opener (left), escorts 21-year-old Len Hutton to the middle in the 1937 Oval Test between England and New Zealand. The young Yorkshireman had started his Test career with 0 and 1 at Lord's, followed by a century at Old Trafford, and great things lay ahead. In 1938 Barnett was 98 not out at lunch on the first day against Australia at Trent Bridge; when he and Hutton went on to centuries, putting on 219 towards England's eventual 658 for 8 dec.

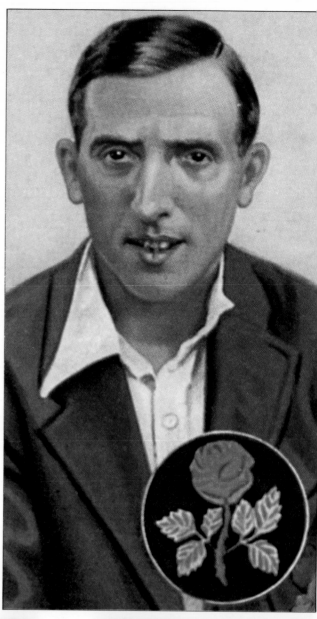

Right: *On the same day in 1937 that Dick Moore scored 316, Eddie Paynter scored a five-hour 322 for Lancashire against Sussex at Hove, after an overnight sleeper journey from the Manchester Test. Paynter put on 268 in 155 minutes with Washbrook. That night he celebrated at Brighton's Ice Palace.*

The Dowager Countess of Darnley, widow of Ivo Bligh, of Ashes renown, talks with Hugh de Selincourt, author of classics The Game of the Season *and* The Cricket Match. *The occasion was the launching, at Great Comp, Kent, of the Australian Women's first tour of England, in 1937.*

England's team for the first Test against Australia, played at Northampton in June 1937, and won by the visitors by 31 runs. Myrtle Maclagan, Molly Hide and Betty Snowball are the central three.

Jim Minter, who hit a century in only 34 minutes for Sydney club Balmain against Manly in 1937–38.

Lord Tennyson, whose tour it was, and the promising young W. J. Edrich go out to bat against Sind. The tour was arranged when projected South African and West Indian tours of India fell through, but illness and injury hampered the side, who won eight and lost five of the 24 fixtures. A 'gold' presentation bat given to His Lordship by a Bombay brewery turned out to be made of iron 'valued at seventeen shillings and sixpence'.

Back to basics, and true innocence. No bouncers here, no unbearable nervous tension – though there is always scope for a little cheating, perhaps, and petulance. Drawing by J. H. Dowd.

J. H. Parks ascended a pedestal in 1937 which he might always occupy alone: the Sussex allrounder scored 3000 runs and took 100 wickets with inswingers and offcutters. He was capped once for England that summer.

'Now I'll tell you something about old WG!' Ernie Jones, Australian fast bowler on the 1896, 1899 and 1902 tours of England, has his say at a gathering of the generations in Adelaide to bid farewell to the 1938 Australian team, bound for England. His enthralled fellow diner is Jack Fingleton. **Right:** At the same function, Walter Giffen, who toured in 1893, sits with C. L. 'Jack' Badcock, a brilliant prospect who had scored 325 at 21 for South Australia v Victoria, but who was destined for excruciating failure in the 1938 Tests.

Don Bradman, off to England in 1938: at the fancy-dress ball (left); saluting in Gibraltar with General Harington (it was remarked that he ought not to have saluted hatless) (below left); and greeted by the Mayor of Southampton when Orontes docked (below right). Soon he was visiting Sir Douglas Shields, renewing thanks for steering him through serious illness at the end of the 1934 tour.

Above: *The 1938 Australians enter the Temple of Apollo, Pompeii.*

Above: *Having found his land legs, Bradman opened the tour with 258 against Worcestershire, his third double-century against that county. Here he takes a quick breather, having reached 150. Jack Badcock contributed 67 to a fourth-wicket stand of 277.*

Left: *Ernie McCormick, the one fast bowler in the Australian side, bowls yet another no-ball in the opening match at Worcester. He was called 19 times by umpire Harry Baldwin in his first three overs, for dragging his back foot over the crease, and 35 times in all in the two innings. Charlie Bull, who was killed in a car crash a year later, suffered a nasty facial injury in trying to hook one of McCormick's no-balls.*

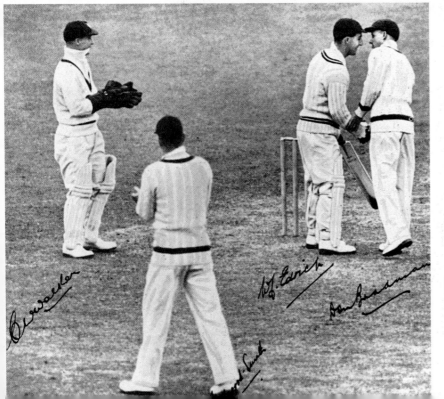

Bill Edrich, 22, is congratulated by Don Bradman upon reaching 1000 runs before June 1, 1938. He did it in 15 innings (four centuries), and every run was scored at Lord's, his home ground. Bradman gave him the chance to collect the 10 runs needed by declaring in the closing stages of the match.

353

Wisden *wore a new dress in the spring of 1938. The 75th edition carried the now-famous woodcut (by Eric Ravilious) for the first time, and among the rearrangements was the bringing of the county reports into alphabetical order.*

Jack Fingleton (left) and W. A. (Bill) Brown walk confidently out to reply for Australia to England's 658 for 8 dec at Trent Bridge in 1938. Hutton, Barnett, Paynter (216 not out) and Compton had already made centuries, and there were to be three for Australia: McCabe's glorious 232, and in the follow-on, hundreds by Brown and Bradman. The Fingleton–Brown combination had meant opening stands for Australia on the 1935–36 South African tour of 93, 105, 233, 99 and 162, with Fingleton extending his three centuries in the last three Tests to four in four innings when Australia had faced England at Brisbane in December 1936.

Stan McCabe reaches 100 at Trent Bridge with a single off Doug Wright. His amazing onslaught began soon after he had reached his half-century. A hooked six off Farnes was followed by uninhibited hooks and cuts and drives, until he was 160 at the fall of the ninth wicket. He then hit 72 of 77 added for the tenth, finishing with 232 (22 fours in his last 80 minutes), one of the greatest innings ever.

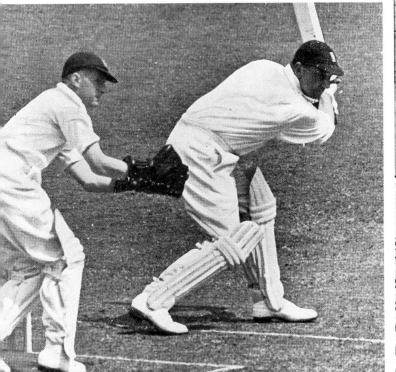

RECEIVED TELEGRAM.
URGENT RATE PREPAID

ATEST, SYDNEY

AUSTRALIAN BROADCASTING COMMISSION
SYDNEY

BRIGHTENING FLEETWOOD HAMMOND FIRSTLY FULL 2 HASSETT SECONDLY FULL
4 STRAIGHT UNCHANCE BOWLER THIRDLY NOBALL FULL 2 OFFDRIVEN RUNAPPEAL
HUTTON FOURTHLY 4 SWEPT BOWLER KEEPER OFFPUSHED

10-26 PM WB

Message	Over	Bowler
46	34	Fleetwood Smith

Ball	Batsman	Where Hit	Fielded	Score	Comments
1	Hammond	full toss off drive-Hassett		2	Chasing fields brilliantly
2	"	full toss-uppish straight drive		4	Almost a catch to bowler
3	"	full toss-NO BALL-off drive-Hassett		2	appeal for run out against Hutton at bowler's wicket
4	"	swept past James on fence		4	at deep square leg
5	"	back to bowler		–	
6	"	keeper			
7	"	played slowly to cover-McCabe		–	

REMARKS:

Hammond's 240 in the 1938 Lord's Test, starting midst the ruins of 31 for 3, was practically on a par with McCabe's magnificent Trent Bridge double-century. He saw off the dangerous McCormick and established command over the Australian bowling, even over the persistent menace of O'Reilly and the unpredictable but potentially lethal left-arm spin of Fleetwood-Smith. The series of distinguished innings was extended by Bill Brown, who carried his bat for an elegant 206 not out, and Don Bradman, who saved Australia with a second-innings hundred. Below: The first two Tests having been drawn, and Old Trafford rained off completely, Australia retained the Ashes by winning the Headingley Test. Bradman scored a century, O'Reilly took 10 wickets and Fleetwood-Smith seven. Spectators afterwards surveyed the scene of the 'crime'.

During the 1934 and 1938 tours, Australian wireless listeners were treated to often realistic synthetic broadcasts, based on cables such as this. Experts in the studio interpreted the ball-by-ball messages and gave 'commentary', with sound effects, through the cold winter nights. An Aborigine, listening to Hutton's 364 at The Oval, is supposed to have asked: 'How many'd this plurry fella make if he was batting in daytime?'

Hugh Bartlett, who hit a century in only 57 minutes for Sussex against the 1938 Australians.

355

How to make a perfect pitch: 'Bosser' Martin oversees his men at The Oval as the great roller goes up and down, up and down, up and down . . . In August 1938, Len Hutton, 22, and his England colleagues took full advantage of the pluperfect surface, and the enforced absence of McCormick from Australia's attack. England ground out a world Test record of 903 for 7 dec, Hutton 364, Leyland 187, Hardstaff 169 not out.

Right: *At last, after batting for 12¼ hours, Hutton square-cuts a four off Fleetwood-Smith to reach 335 and pass Bradman's England–Australia record of 334. Somewhere in the packed Oval a man played* Rule Britannia *on a trombone. Bradman was the first to congratulate the young Yorkshireman, who went on to make 364 in 13 hours 17 minutes, having hit 35 fours.*

Below: *Bradman chipped an ankle bone while bowling in the Oval Test, and played no further part in the match. Thus ended his country's hopes that he might match Hutton run for run. Fingleton was also injured, so that Australia batted two short.*

Hutton still has enough strength to grapple with Fleetwood-Smith for souvenir stumps at the end of the Oval epic. England won by an innings and 579 runs, the nine men of Australia subsiding for 201 and 123, Bowes (in picture) taking seven wickets and Farnes five.

Hammond shakes hands with Australia's deputy captain, McCabe, after the four-day match. Neither had been at the forefront of the run gluttony at The Oval, but both had played innings of imperishable glory earlier in the series. Stan McCabe, still only 28, had very little cricket left, foot trouble prompting early retirement.

Don Tallon, considered unlucky, like Oldfield, to have missed the 1938 tour, equalled the world wicketkeeping record in 1938–39 by making 12 dismissals (9c, 3st) for Queensland v NSW at Sydney.

Paul Gibb's Test debut was delayed when the Manchester Test of 1938 was washed out, but at Johannesburg a few months later the Yorkshire amateur fashioned a worthy and careful double of 93 and 106 on debut.

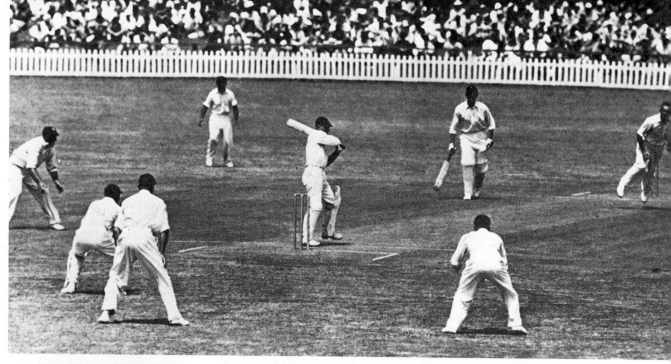

The 1938–39 South Africa v England Tests turned out to be another run-feast. Home batsmen recorded six centuries, England 11, including Paynter's 117 and 100 in the first Test and 243 in the third, at Durban. When the teams returned to Durban for the fifth Test, it was decided to play it to a finish, England being 1–0 ahead. It was left as a draw after 10 days' play (none on the eighth). The England players could delay embarkation no longer. Needing 696 to win, they were 654 for 5, Gibb 120, Hammond 140, and Edrich, after a long string of failures, 219. A record 1981 runs had been scored – Nourse (above) claims four of them – and the concept of 'timeless Tests' was stifled.

Left: Emrys Davies, Glamorgan's stalwart left-handed allrounder, scored 287 not out against Gloucestershire at Newport in 1939, a county record. In 1935 he had become the first Glamorgan player to achieve the double. He later became a Test match umpire.

Below: The three Tests between England and West Indies in 1939 were the last before the Second World War (though an MCC team for India, 1939–40, had been selected in anticipation). At Lord's, Hutton and Compton, the bright new generation, had made hundreds, and here at Old Trafford, Hammond hits out at googly bowler C. B. Clarke, who had him stumped by Derek Sealy in the first innings. Compton is his partner. In this match, a low-scoring draw, Hammond became the first fielder to hold 100 Test catches.

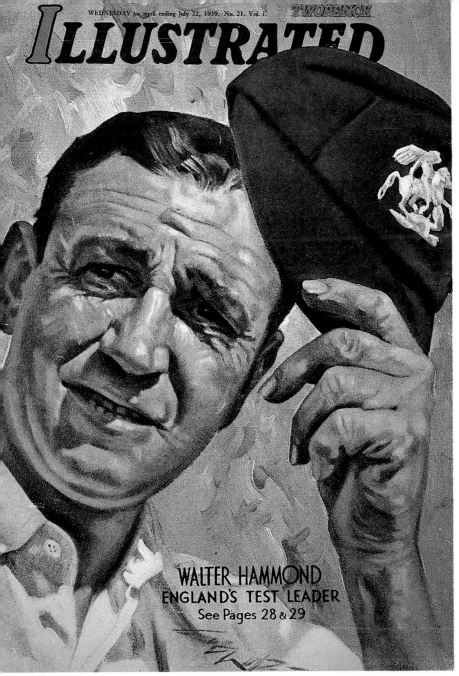

ILLUSTRATED

**WALTER HAMMOND
ENGLAND'S TEST LEADER**
See Pages 28 & 29

Hutton and Walter Keeton (right) of Notts open against West Indies at The Oval. Keeton, who had scored 312 not out against Middlesex a month earlier, played on to Tyrell Johnson's first ball in Test cricket. Left: English cricket's father figure, Wally Hammond. Below left: Hammond catches Sealy off Bowes in the Old Trafford Test. Below: Jamaica's Leslie Hylton, a fast bowler who took 16 wickets in his six Tests. In 1955 he was hanged for the murder of his wife, whom he shot after discovering she had been unfaithful.

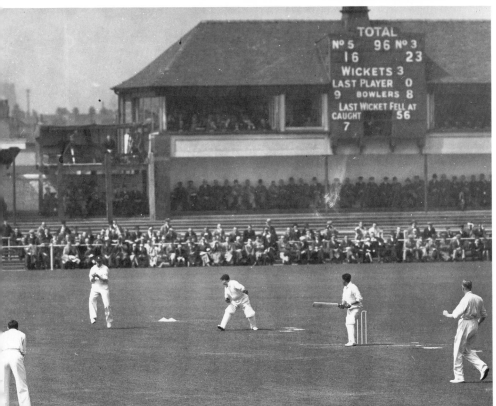

359

Not quite the all-mod-cons accommodation enjoyed by the modern cricketer on tour, but the West Indians seem happy enough in their 'hi-de-oh-dah' conga in Derek Sealy's bedroom. Victor Stollmeyer and his brother Jeff lead the line, followed by Gerry Gomez, Bertie Clarke, Ken 'Bam Bam' Weekes (who blazed to 137 in the Oval Test), and unidentified. Soon they were hurrying home, their last seven matches unplayed. War was looming in Europe.

Right: *Eric Rowan, who made almost 2000 runs during South Africa's 1935 tour of England, scored 306 not out for Transvaal v Natal at Johannesburg in 1939–40, a new South African record.*

Left: *George Headley gives rough treatment to Verity in the 1939 Lord's Test, in which he repeated his 1930 feat of a century in each innings. Unlike Bradman, he was not surrounded by batsmen of high quality. So often he carried West Indies alone, and the record of this nimble and inventive craftsman (small of stature, like Bradman) should be seen in that context: 10 centuries in 40 Test innings, average 60.83.*

The somewhat overweight former Lancashire and England cricketer giving advice to the Cheshire county women's team is Cecil Parkin, the 'cricket comedian' himself, whose qualifications were high: he could spin a ball every conceivable way – and did so during his stormy first-class career in the 1920s. Here, at Winnington Park, Northwich, in the summer of 1939, the girls were probably unaware that Mr Parkin used to experiment in the nets with his wife as the batsman, often sending her home with chipped fingers and bruised thighs.

THE SECOND LONG DARK NIGHT

ON SEPTEMBER 3, 1939, all of the deeds of Bradman and Hammond and Headley, of Verity, Constantine and O'Reilly, froze into museum exhibits, for Britain and the Commonwealth were in a full state of war against German tyranny. Sport and other frivolities were put in their place – perhaps where they truly belong – strictly as devices for amusing those under strain and restoring the troubled soul. After the period of 'phoney war', first-class cricket almost ceased to exist. Cricketers, as in the First World War, donned – and died in – uniform in the Second. The season of 1939, which had seen the eight-ball over introduced into English cricket, and a widening of the wicket from 8 ins to 9 ins in an attempt to restore the balance between bat and ball, was to be the last for so many. Old England, 'peace-loving and ill-prepared as she was', as Churchill put it, had firstly to survive, and then win through. What came next was worse than Bodyline.

Cricket's wholesome code may not be enough in the face of the evil that threatened in the late 1930s, suggests David Low's Evening Standard cartoon. Neville Chamberlain offers a straight bat to Hitler, Franco and Mussolini.

Part of the Yorkshire response to war: Capt. Hedley Verity, Sgt-Major Frank Smailes, Capt. Herbert Sutcliffe, Sgt Maurice Leyland, and Sgt-Instructor Len Hutton. Hutton sustained a serious injury to his left forearm when he fell in a gymnasium in York. Bone-grafts left the arm shorter and his future as a Test match batsman in some doubt.

Left: *The British lion bats for freedom in Tom Webster's cartoon, erected on the frontage of London's Gaiety Theatre to help the drive for War Savings. German bombs exploded all around, but the lion played an unbeaten innings.*

Above: *Not all peacetime production was diverted to martial necessities. Surridge 'Herbert Sutcliffe autograph' bats were being produced in the winter of 1939–40 in the hope and belief that cricket would continue, and that the war would be a short one anyway.*

Left: *Denis Compton, Fred Price and Leslie Compton, together with most of the Middlesex team, soon became special constables at the police station near Lord's. The young England batsman then joined the Army, was posted to India, and found himself scoring 249 not out for Holkar v Bombay in the final of the Ranji Trophy in 1944–45 – when future England batsman Reg Simpson made his first-class debut for Sind.*

Lieut. P. T. Eckersley, RNVR, MP; killed in a flying accident in August 1940, aged 36. A middle-order batsman of less than first-class standard, and a fine fieldsman, he led Lancashire to the Championship in 1934 – and in 1935 arranged for his team to fly from their Cardiff match to their next at Southampton, the first team to travel thus.

Second Lieut. R. P. Nelson, Royal Marines; killed in October 1940, aged 28. Cambridge Blue in 1936, he had played a few matches for Middlesex before joining Northants, whom he captained in 1938 and 1939. In that final year he had the slight and amusing satisfaction of seeing the county move up one place after five years at 17th.

Lieut. G. B. Legge, RNVR, Fleet Air Arm; killed in November 1940, aged 37. A former Kent captain, having been an Oxford Blue 1925–26, he toured South Africa and Australasia, and played in five Tests. At Auckland, on the 1929–30 tour, he hammered 196 in the fourth Test. He was also a reliable slip fieldsman.

Below: One of the numerous gatherings of cricketers of varying skills who played for war relief funds. This group of British Empire XI players and Capt. J. W. A. Stephenson's XI includes six current or future Test cricketers. In the front row are Ken Farnes, the Essex and England fast bowler; Desmond Donnelly, a future MP; J. W. A. Stephenson of Essex; Hugh Bartlett of Sussex; and Alec Kennedy of Hampshire and England. Standing (second from left) are Bertie Clarke of West Indies and later Northants and Essex; E. D. R. Eagar (seventh from left), a future Hampshire captain and secretary; and Tom Goddard (third from right) of Gloucestershire and England. At the back are George Emmett (second from left), Gloucestershire batsman who was awarded a Test cap in 1948, and Charlie Barnett (third from left), the Gloucestershire and England player. The match was played at Cheltenham in September 1940.

Pilot Officer G. G. Macaulay; 'died on active service' in December 1940, aged 43. He was among the best bowlers ever produced by Yorkshire, bowling good-length medium-pace offspin, capable of spells such as 7 for 9 in 14 overs against Northants at Kettering in 1933. He played eight times for England, taking a wicket at Cape Town in the 1922–23 series with his first ball in Test cricket, and later hitting the winning run in England's one-wicket victory.

Cricket had to learn to live with distortions and liberties during the war years. Because of a shortage of clothing coupons, these Canadian soldiers, based somewhere in England, had to play in pyjamas.

Cpl W. M. Wallace, in uniform, who played for New Zealand before and after the war, prepares to toss with G. L. 'Dad' Weir (who played in the two 'Hammond matches' of 1932–33) in an Army match at Eden Park, Auckland in November 1941.

A great batsman emerged in Australia's second season of wartime cricket: Arthur Morris, still only 18, scored 148 and 111 in his debut match for NSW against Queensland at Sydney immediately after Christmas 1940.

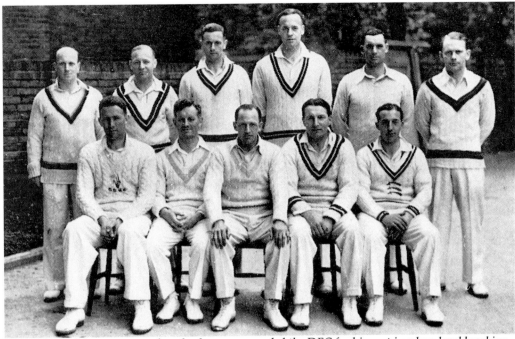

More top cricketers in – and temporarily out of – uniform: an RAF team which played at Lord's in June 1941: standing: Sgt R. J. Gregory (Surrey), Sgt G. S. Mobey (Surrey), Cpl W. E. Phillipson (Lancs), Sgt J. F. Parker (Surrey), Cpl L. J. Todd (Kent), Sgt C. Washbrook (Lancs and England); seated: P/O A. D. G. Matthews (Glamorgan and England), F/Lt C. T. Ashton (Essex), F/Lt R. W. V. Robins (Middx and England) (captain), F/O C. J. Barnett (Gloucs and England), P/O W. J. Edrich (Middx and England). Shortly after this match Bill Edrich, now a squadron leader, was awarded the DFC for his part in a low-level bombing raid on Cologne. In the following year Claude Ashton, one of the famous Cambridge University brotherhood, was killed over Caernarvon when his aeroplane collided with one piloted by R. de W. K. Winlaw (Cambridge and Surrey), who also perished.

Left: Capt. A. W. 'Doolie' Briscoe, MC; killed in Abyssinia in April 1941, aged 30. A fine batsman for Transvaal, he was not seen at his best in his two Tests for South Africa, one against Australia, one against England.

Right: Flight Lieut. D. F. Walker, RAFVR; killed over Holland in June 1941, aged 28. A left-hand batsman, Donald Walker had had three successful years as a professional with Hampshire, scoring four centuries, and averaging 26.

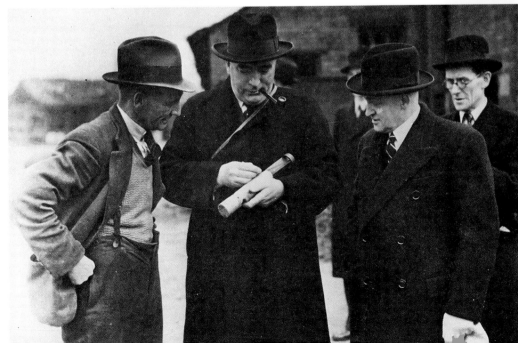

Australia's Prime Minister, R. G. Menzies, a staunch cricket-lover, autographs an unexploded incendiary bomb which the Luftwaffe dropped on Old Trafford – with scant respect for the ground where MacLaren once ruled, and Trumper scored a Test century before lunch. With Menzies are the groundsman and the chairman of the ground committee.

365

Destruction during the 1939–45 war knew no bounds, and many a cricket club had its square involuntarily dug up, either for food production or by enemy action. Pavilions were damaged too, leading to many proud recoveries and animated prolixities in afteryears. Here, at Wallasey, Cheshire, a parachute mine in 1941 rendered cricket difficult if not impossible.

Pilot Officer Kenneth Farnes; killed in a plane crash, October 1941, while flying with the RAF, over Northamptonshire. He was 30. A man of culture, and standing well over 6 ft, Ken Farnes had conspicuous success at Cambridge, his pace being exceptional, with difficult bounce. He played for Essex as an amateur throughout the 1930s, setting up many victories with his hostility, and made his Test debut at Trent Bridge in 1934, when he took 10 wickets. He toured West Indies, Australia and South Africa – and wrote a book on his experiences – and in 15 Tests he took 60 wickets at just under 30, admirable in a high-scoring era. His fast-bowling successes were frequent, not least for the Gentlemen, for whom his 8 for 43 in 1938 brought only their second victory over the Players at Lord's since the First World War. His was an especially grievous loss to English cricket.

Thirteen-year-olds Eric Innocent and Ron Curtis of the London Boys' Brigade find themselves going out to bat in the exalted environment of Agar's Plough in 1942. Eton's headmaster had allowed 800 of the boys to camp there, far from the horrors of the Blitz.

Sgt Observer R. G. Gregory, RAAF; killed June 1942 while flying over Assam, India. A brilliant young cricketer, he had played for Victoria while still at school, and Australia, against England in 1936–37, when only 20, scoring 80 in the Ashes-deciding Melbourne Test. A legspinner too, he had been unlucky to miss the 1938 tour of England.

Flight Lieut. A. B. C. 'Chud' Langton; killed November 1942 while flying over Accra, Gold Coast. On the South African tour of England in 1935 he took 115 wickets, and made important contributions with bat and ball (he was a fast-medium bowler) to his country's first Test victory in England. He played for Transvaal for 10 years.

Andrew Ducat, the Surrey and England batsman and England footballer, collapsed at the wicket at Lord's and died instantly on July 23, 1942 while batting for Surrey Home Guard against Sussex Home Guard. The match was abandoned, and his score was entered as 'not out 29'. He was 56. A quiet and popular man, Ducat made 52 centuries in his career of a quarter-century, the highest 306 not out against Oxford at The Oval in 1919. Two years later he hit 290 not out against Essex at Leyton, having led Aston Villa to victory in the FA Cup in the meantime. Later he was coach at Eton.

A Royal Air Force XI, Lord's, September 1942. They drew an exciting one-day match against the Army before 14,000 spectators, £153 being raised for Army and RAF benevolent funds. Standing: Sgt C. Washbrook (Lancs and England), Cpl E. P. Robinson (Yorks), F/O R. W. G. Emery (Auckland – and later New Zealand), Sgt L. J. Todd (Kent), Sgt L. G. Berry (Leics), Sgt H. S. Squires (Surrey), F/O R. E. S. Wyatt (Warwicks and England), P/O C. W. Walker (South Australia); seated: F/Lt A. D. G. Matthews (Northants, Glamorgan and England), Wing Cdr W. S. Dailey, S/Ldr W. J. Edrich (Middx and England), F/Lt L. E. G. Ames (Kent and England). Charlie Walker, who toured England with the 1930 and 1938 Australian teams as second wicketkeeper, was killed during a flight over Germany in December 1942. He never played in a Test match, but made 320 dismissals in 109 first-class matches, including 149 stumpings, many off Clarrie Grimmett.

Bill Bowes, the Yorkshire and England fast bowler, now a lieutenant in the Royal Artillery, was captured by the Italians at Tobruk in June 1942. He organised sport for 1700 fellow prisoners during captivity in Italy and Germany, until freed by the Americans in April 1945.

A wartime group at Lord's, containing some famous names. On the extremities of the back row are S. C. Griffith of Sussex and Len Hutton; centre back row are R. W. V. Robins and G. O. B. Allen; and the front row consists of G. F. H. Heane (Notts), B. H. Valentine (Kent), F. R. Brown (Surrey), and Learie Constantine. Freddie Brown was a prisoner-of-war, in the same camp as Bill Bowes, but emerged to start a second cricket career as captain of Northamptonshire and England. G. T. S. Stevens is next to Billy Griffith.

Flight Lieut. F. G. H. Chalk, DFC; missing over the English Channel, February 1943, later presumed killed, aged 32. Oxford captain in 1934, he scored 108 in the Varsity match, and captained Kent in 1938 and 1939, in which summer he made his highest score, 198 against Sussex at Tonbridge. Within a week of the outbreak of war Gerry Chalk carried his bat for 115 against Yorkshire at Dover and then made 94 against Lancashire. He was a considerable allround sportsman, and is remembered by Kent for his batsmanship, fielding and dynamic captaincy. A rear gunner, he won the DFC by fighting off an Me-110, then transferred to a Spitfire squadron.

Another highly-gifted batsman, Frank Worrell, makes an early impact on the game. Seated, left, in the striped blazer, Worrell, then only 19, scored 308 not out for Barbados v Trinidad at Bridgetown in 1943–44, putting on an unbeaten 502 for the fourth wicket with John Goddard (seated far right, also in pads). Two years later, Clyde Walcott (third from left, standing) scored 314 not out for Barbados v Trinidad at Port-of-Spain, adding an unfinished 574 for the fourth wicket with Worrell (255 not out). All three, particularly Worrell and Walcott, were destined to play major roles in establishing West Indies cricket in the post-war period.

Lieut. D. A. R. Moloney; died from wounds while a prisoner-of-war, July 1942, after capture at El Alamein, aged 31. He played for Otago, Wellington and Canterbury, and toured England with New Zealand in 1937, making 64 at Lord's on Test debut. On the tour he scored 1463 runs and took 57 wickets.

The second major England cricketer to lose his life in the Second World War was Hedley Verity, the matchwinning Yorkshire and England slow left-arm bowler, pictured here (right) for the last time in cricket flannels, alongside Yorkshire allrounder and future England captain Norman Yardley. They were playing in Omagh, Northern Ireland in September 1941, and Verity took 8 for 55. He had taken 7 for 9 in his final county match, at Hove in 1939, as Sussex were skittled for 33 on a wet pitch under early-September sun. From Britain, Verity went with his regiment, the Green Howards, to India, where he was a bad dysentery case, then to the Middle East, and finally to Sicily. On the plain of Catania, surrounded by Germans as he and his men made through a cornfield, Captain Hedley Verity, the cricketer with the best figures ever recorded, 10 for 10, was revealed by flares and

burning vegetation almost as clearly as if it were a bright summer's afternoon at Headingley. He was hit severely in the chest, captured with his Lancastrian batman, and ferried to Reggio, across waters he had once sailed as a member of MCC teams Australia-bound. In Naples, Verity's condition worsened, and several days after an operation, he died on the last day of July 1943, and was buried in Caserta. He was 38.

Pte Jack Lee; killed in Normandy, July 1944, while serving with the Pioneers. He was 42. Brother of Harry and Frank Lee, he served Somerset well as an opening batsman and legspinner, and played soccer for Arsenal and other clubs.

This 'Northern Cricket XI' contained some big names: Charlie Hallows, George Pope, Manny Martindale, Ellis Achong, Bill Andrews and George Cox jnr stand in the back row, and in the front are Bill Farrimond, Eddie Paynter, Charles Leatherbarrow, Winston Place, and Edwin St Hill. They played a fund-raiser in Burton-on-Trent in August 1943.

The Oval, requisitioned by the authorities, is almost unrecognisable as the conversion to a prisoner-of-war camp is completed. The 'cage', as it happened, never contained foreign captives. Much reconversion and development had to be undertaken when the war ended.

The latest German evil in 1944 was the V1, the flying bomb, contemptuously known as the 'doodlebug'. Pilotless, it was filled with high explosive, and careered to earth when its fuel supply was exhausted, to wreak appalling devastation. On July 29, 1944, a V1's guttural sound suddenly ceased over St John's Wood. It seemed that Lord's, having withstood the thunderbolts of Kortright and Cotter, Gregory and Larwood, and the bombardments of Trott and Jessop and Wellard, was about to be disembowelled by one of Hermann Goering's lethal playthings. Taking the only evasive action possible are batsman Jack Robertson (Middx) of the Army XI, wicketkeeper Andy Wilson (Gloucs) of the RAF XI, and Squadron Ldr Bill Edrich at slip and F/Lt Austin Matthews at gully. They were spared, and Robertson celebrated immediately with a six.

Right: C. S. Nayudu, the young googly bowler, who sent down a record 917 balls for Holkar against Bombay in the final of the 1943–44 Ranji Trophy tournament. His opponents scored 462 and 764, and he was bowling and fielding for 18½ hours. The match total of 2078 (Compton 249 not out in the last innings) was a world record.

370

Capt. G. D. Kemp-Welch, Grenadier Guards; killed when the Guards' Chapel was bombed, June 1944. He was 36. Son-in-law of former Prime Minister Stanley Baldwin, he was a Cambridge captain and successful Warwickshire batsman and medium-pacer, and made centuries on Tennyson's Jamaica tour in 1932.

W. N. Carson, New Zealand world record-holder (refer p.346), and his bride, Auckland, 1940. He sailed to war later that year, and in 1941 was mentioned in despatches during the Battle of Crete. In 1943 he was awarded the Military Cross, but was hit by shrapnel in Crete and then extensively wounded in Italy in 1944, and died on the hospital ship bound for New Zealand. Major Carson was 28. Left: Rusi Modi, who strung together seven centuries in seven matches, finishing with a run of 1008 runs in seven innings (av. 201.60) in the 1944–45 Ranji Trophy. His figures on India's 1946 tour of England were moderate. Right: Having hit Rommel for six out of Africa, Field-Marshal Viscount Montgomery of Alamein visits Lord's during an England–Australia 'Victory Test'. With him is 'Plum' Warner. As a St Paul's schoolboy, 'Monty' had once acquitted himself well against old WG's bowling. The words of Australia's Prime Minister John Curtin echoed: 'Australians will always fight for those 22 yards. Lord's and its traditions belong to Australia just as much as to England'.

Major M. J. L. Turnbull, Welsh Guards; killed by a sniper in Normandy two months after the D-Day landings, 1944. He was 38. Maurice Turnbull, Cardiff-born, played cricket for England and rugby and hockey for Wales. A superb batsman, he led Glamorgan throughout the 1930s, and was the club's secretary. He also became a Test selector, and was co-author of two tour books. A greatly respected man.

371

Down with the barbed wire. The war is over, and The Oval can be rededicated to cricket, lovely cricket all summer long . . .

. . . and up with the nets so war-weary men can find a length and get the cover-drive working again. The Australian Services team, under Lindsay Hassett, prepare for action at the Saffrons ground, Eastbourne, spring 1945.

Below: *The Australian Services side, having won two and lost two of the five 'Victory Tests' in England in 1945, stop over in India on their way home. Skipper Hassett stands seventh from the left, and three further along is Keith Miller, the exciting fast-bowling, big-hitting discovery. Standing from left, are R. S. Whitington, K. O. E. Johnson, Bob Cristofani, and Jack Pettiford. On Miller's left is Cec Pepper. Third from the left in front is Keith Carmody; second from right Stan Sismey.*

The bombs have stopped raining down on London, St Paul's has survived – and so has the desire to knock a ball around, as demonstrated by these Blackfriars office workers in their lunch-hour.

Below left: *The Oval was used as a furniture repository during the Blitz. Now it's time to get it all back to surviving owners, and to let the Surrey CCC members have their entrance and Long Room back.*

Above: *Japanese prisoners are forced to make themselves useful in the Singapore they had so callously occupied by filling in the eyesore trenches they had dug on the Cricket Club's Padang ground.*

Left: *The Alamein Club, Cairo provides British troops with relaxation now that the real fighting is over. In a match in Cairo in 1942 between a South African XI and Military Police, Dudley Nourse hit nine successive balls for six, and 11 in 12, a world record.*

373

Above: *VE Day was May 8, 1945, and within three weeks normality had returned well and truly at Frenchay, Gloucestershire, for the club was playing Stapleton, with BBC commentary by the legendary Test match broadcaster Howard Marshall.*

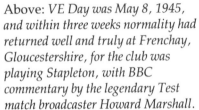

Left: *Test cricket was under way within a year of the end of the war, Australia going to New Zealand to play their first-ever Test against their neighbours. At Wellington, Australia won by an innings, New Zealand being bowled out for 42 (O'Reilly 5 for 14 in his final Test) and 54 on a rain-affected pitch. This spectacular catch by Verdun Scott got rid of Tallon (left) in Australia's innings. The other batsman is Ian Johnson. It was two years before the match was granted Test status – and 28 years before Australia again played New Zealand.*

Left: *Surrey had to postpone their centenary a year because of the war, and here, in May 1946, at the battered ground, Old England meet the King. From the right: Sandham, Allom, Ted Brooks (Surrey), Sutcliffe, Freeman (shaking hands), D. J. Knight, Woolley, Hendren, Fender (with His Majesty) and Jardine (head only visible). A restoration appeal was under way to raise funds to repair the bomb-damaged pavilion.*

REAWAKENING

LIVES had been lost, souls had been scarred. Now life had to go on as normal, if only most people could remember what 'normal' was. The skies were now clear, the martial sounds had died away. Uniforms were being exchanged for serge 'demob' suits. Air-raid shelters were dismantled. Anxiety levels dropped. Once the exhilaration of victory had settled, exhaustion became apparent. There had to be a restoration of entertainment. The lights were back on in London and elsewhere. Now it was up to sport to provide an escape as never before in this period of drab austerity and rationing. The questions no longer were 'How near are our boys to Berlin?' and 'When will Japan give in?' Instead, it was: 'Can Hutton play on with that arm injury?' and 'Will Bradman continue playing?'

The Germans seemed to have been fascinated by cricket pavilions: the Old Trafford structure suffered. But the game went on as soon as peace was restored. Below: The England and India teams for the first post-war Test in England, at Lord's. Hardstaff scored 205 not out, Alec Bedser took 11 wickets on debut, and England won by 10 wickets. Bedser took another 11 wickets in the next Test, at Old Trafford.

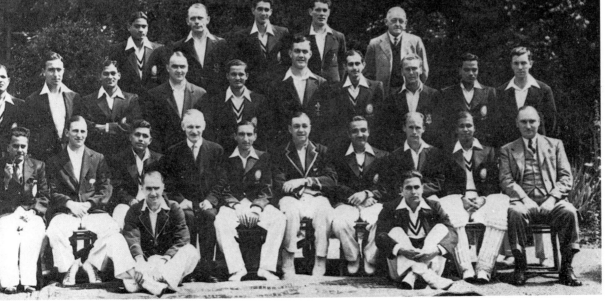

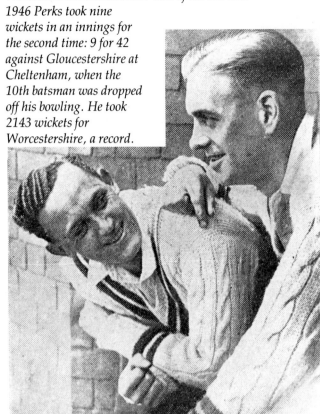

Below: *Reg Perks (left) and Dick Howorth, pillars of Worcestershire cricket either side of the war. In 1946 Perks took nine wickets in an innings for the second time: 9 for 42 against Gloucestershire at Cheltenham, when the 10th batsman was dropped off his bowling. He took 2143 wickets for Worcestershire, a record.*

Eric Hollies trundled away for Warwickshire from 1932 to 1957, trapping 2323 batsmen in first-class cricket with his rolled legbreaks and well-disguised googlies. In 1946, he took 184 wickets at 15.60, with the remarkable achievement of an 'all 10' (against Notts at Edgbaston) without assistance from the field: seven bowled, three lbw.

A form of indoor cricket was pioneered in Australia after the war, played here by returned soldiers. Netting protected the spectators, and an umpire sat up on a tennis-style perch. The version was revived in the 1980s, with modifications.

In their third match of the 1946 tour, the Indians were 205 for 9 against Surrey when C. T. Sarwate (left) and Shute Banerjee came together, Nos 10 and 11, and both made centuries. Their 10th-wicket stand of 249 was a record for that wicket in England, passing Woolley and Fielder's 235 in 1909.

Here he comes! The speculation was about to end as Bradman faced English bowling for the first time in eight years. MCC had made 506 for 5 dec (Hutton and Washbrook laborious centuries), and Bradman now batted tentatively for 2½ hours, looking 'rather frail', for a top-score 76 in South Australia's total. His son John (right) watched play with England's new bowling king Alec Bedser.

Every Saturday night on tour the MCC players compulsorily wore their bow-ties at the Saturday Night Club gathering. About to enjoy the sort of meal forgotten in England since pre-war times are Norman Yardley, T. P. B. (Peter) Smith, Bill Voce and Dick Pollard. Right: One thing has never changed: a man's game can improve only through constant practice. George Tribe, a talented spinner from Victoria, who played in three Tests against England in 1946–47 with dismal luck, develops his mystery balls on a concrete pitch laid across adjoining backyards of neighbours in Maribyrnong.

Most of these young spectators eager to see the opening Test of the 1946–47 series were only toddlers when Brisbane saw its last Test match. In 1936–37 rain helped England. Now, 10 years on, an incredible deluge left the Gabba pitch unplayable – after Australia had made 645, Bradman, now securely back in the saddle, 187, Hassett 128 and newcomer Colin McCool 95. Bradman was thought by English fieldsmen to have been caught at slip by Ikin off Voce when 28, but the umpire did not agree.

Top: On a gluepot, with Miller (7 for 60) and left-arm medium-pacer Toshack (3 for 17 and 6 for 82) making the ball kick off a length, England's survival depended as much as anything upon keeping the bat (and the facial features) out of trouble. Hammond's 32 was a masterly display of batsmanship on a damaged pitch. Above: Hammond strikes Toshack for six, Sid Barnes, at forward short leg, no doubt admiring the shot. England, 141 and 172, had resumed Ashes cricket in the worst manner conceivable. The crushing victory at The Oval in 1938 – the previous contest – had been paid for in large part.

Left: Radio listeners in those pre-television days depended on the ball-by-ball descriptions of Arthur Gilligan, Alan McGilvray and Vic Richardson, former captains respectively of England, NSW and Australia. Their friendly, informative commentary won them an affectionate following throughout Australia and – through the early-morning crackling – the United Kingdom.

Australia won again by an innings at Sydney in the second Test, Bradman and Barnes each scoring 234 and adding 405 for the fifth wicket. Then, in the third Test, at Melbourne, first-innings parity came at last: Australia 365 (McCool 104 not out), England 361. Morris then scored 155, Tallon a swift 92 and Ray Lindwall 100, and England needed 551 to win. Washbrook, here being bowled for 112 by Dooland, set up a platform for the draw. **Below:** Hammond becomes a distinguished early Test wicket for Lindwall, whose pace is exceptional. McCool stands to attention at slip, seemingly in reverence.

Keith Miller, RAAF hero, Australian allrounder, was endowed with film-star looks and a larger-than-life personality that expressed itself in storming attacking innings, mind-blowing bowling spells of bouncers, yorkers and googlies, and inspired catches at slip. A toss of the long black hair, a cheeky grin, and all within view were reminded that cricket was, first and foremost, a sport. A thrustful captain of NSW (he transferred from Victoria), he was too unpredictable for the likes of Australia's Test selectors when it seemed his turn to take over the national XI.

With Australia still two Tests up in the 1946–47 series, the fourth Test, at
Adelaide, was also drawn after some high scoring. Compton hit a century in each
innings, Hutton made 94 and 76, and Godfrey Evans, when England needed time,
was 95 minutes in opening his score. For Australia, Morris also scored twin
centuries, Miller made his first in Tests, and Bradman was bowled by Bedser for
nought with a tremendous inswinging legcutter. Earlier, Bedser himself (above)
was bowled by Lindwall, the first of his three bowled victims in four balls. Australia
won the last Test, at Sydney, by five wickets after Hutton had scored 122 retired ill
(and unable to bat a second time) and Doug Wright's pacey legspinners and googlies
had brought him 7 for 105 in the first innings.

'Can I see the English cricketers?' The
boy was lucky. The doorman of the
Hotel Windsor in Melbourne directed
him to the lounge, where some of the
MCC players ignored the ban on giving
autographs.

The Empire Cricket-Writers' Club was formed during the 1946–47 tour, and some distinguished player/journalists partook of a
game in Perth. Seated are Bill Bowes, Jack Fingleton and Arthur Mailey, and (third from right) George Duckworth, and in the
back row are E. M. Wellings, J. M. Kilburn, R. S. Whitington, E. W. Swanton and Vivian Jenkins.

Some of South Africa's most cherished cricket history lost its tangibility late in 1946 when the Old Wanderers ground in Johannesburg was demolished to make way for the expansion of the railway. The old ground had seen Johannesburg grow from a mining camp to a large city. The new ground at Illovo was staging a Test match 10 years later, Ellis Park having served in the meantime.

Vijay Hazare (left) and Gul Mahomed (right) put together a world record partnership of 577 for the fourth wicket when they batted for just on nine hours (Hazare batted for 10½) for Baroda against Holkar in the final of the Ranji Trophy at Baroda in March 1947. Hazare, one of the current breed of patient, run-hungry Indian batsmen, with two double-centuries to his credit, scored 288, and Gul Mahomed, a dashing left-hander, finished with 319 in Baroda's total of 784. They won by an innings and 409 runs as an era of grotesquely high scoring got well into its gargantuan stride.

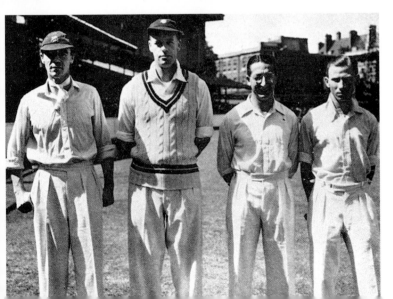

Left: When Nottinghamshire scored 401 against Surrey at Trent Bridge in May 1947, the visiting batsmen strapped their pads on with extra determination . . . and made 706 for 4 dec. Surrey's four centurymakers were: E. R. T. Holmes (122 not out), Jack Parker (108 not out), Stan Squires (154), and David Fletcher, in only his second match (194). A beautiful pitch defied the best efforts of Notts bowlers Butler, Jepson, Voce and five others.

381

Above: *Willie Watson batting for Yorkshire in the Roses match at Bramall Lane in August 1947. As always, the fixture drew many spectators from both sides of the Pennines. Around 22,000 attended on the Saturday, 12,000 on Monday, 15,000 Tuesday.*

The Test matches were well attended too, by a cricket-hungry nation who revelled in a warm summer in which England won three and drew two Tests in a happy series with South Africa. Alan Melville (above), the elegant Springbok captain and former Oxford and Sussex player, made two centuries in the opening Test at Trent Bridge, and another here at Lord's, giving him four in a row, since he had made 103 in the 'timeless Test' before the war. Right: *By bowling V. I. Smith, England allrounder Ken Cranston completed an over in which he had taken four wickets to wrap up South Africa's second innings at Headingley.*

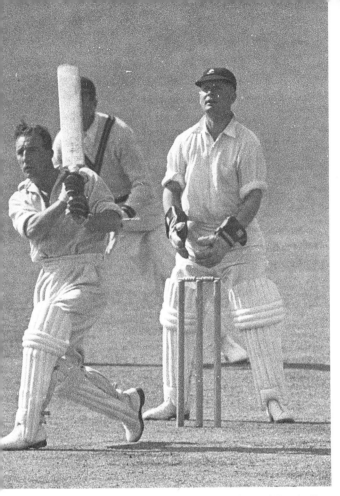

The summer of '47 belonged to Bill Edrich (left) and Denis Compton (right), who both passed Hayward's record of 3518 runs in a season (1906). Edrich made 3539, with a dozen centuries, average 80.43, Compton 3816, average 90.86, his 18 centuries surpassing Hobbs's record 16 (1925). The 'Middlesex twins' slaughtered the South African attack, Compton shaping 1187 runs from it, Edrich 869. In the Tests, they had partnerships of 370 at Lord's and 228 at Old Trafford, and their seemingly unstoppable runmaking, backed by Jack Robertson's 2214 runs and Syd Brown's 1709, brought Middlesex the Championship, Jack Young, Jim Sims, Laurie Gray, and Compton and Edrich themselves taking most of the wickets. And if these two laughing cavaliers were to go on for some years yet, making a record 424 unbeaten for the third wicket against Somerset at Lord's the following season, the greatest source of pride would always be to say, 'I saw them in 1947'.

The heavy South African runmaking tended to be overshadowed by the exploits of Compton and Edrich, but Bruce Mitchell (right) scored 120 and 189 not out in the Oval Test, and by the time he had played in his last Test (making 99) two years hence, his aggregate of 3471 (48.89) was, and still is, a South African record. In this 1947 series, Dudley Nourse's skill was evident also. He made two centuries, a 97, and four other half-centuries.

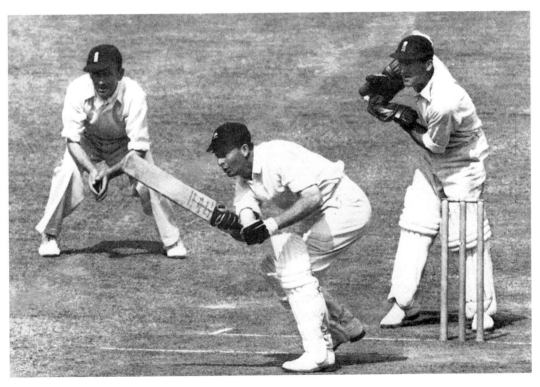

383

While Middlesex beat Gloucestershire on a spinner's paradise at Cheltenham – despite Goddard's 15 wickets – to place one hand on the Championship, England and South Africa fought it out in the fifth Test, at The Oval. The visitors, by Yardley's closure, were left to get 451 in seven hours. They finished gallantly with 423 for 7. Here Ken Viljoen cuts Howorth past Hutton at gully, while Yardley jumps anxiously and Evans, the wicketkeeper, watches. Mitchell, who finished 189 not out, is Viljoen's partner. This was Dick Howorth's first Test, and he had Dyer caught off his first ball.

In the first week of September 1947 Denis Compton sailed – not without some uneasy moments – past Hayward's aggregate of 3518, and here acknowledges the applause with some relief. He made 87 not out and 86 for South of England v Sir Pelham Warner's XI at Hastings. The wicketkeeper is S. C. 'Billy' Griffith.

Left: Yorkshire left-hander Gerald Smithson, a conscript – 'Bevin Boy' – in the coalmines in 1947, had to be cleared of his duties by the British Government before he was able to tour West Indies with MCC in 1947–48. He scored 0 on debut, and 35 in each innings of his other Test. He later played for Leicestershire.

Right: Bombay's K. C. Ibrahim had a huge appetite for runs. During 1947–48 he made 709 between dismissals, a world record. Seven years earlier, when brought in late after having been chosen as 12th man against Western India, he made the best of his opportunity by scoring 230 not out. He played in four Tests for India in the 1948–49 series against West Indies, scoring 85 and 44 on debut but then reaching double figures only once in six innings.

Another of cricket's magic moments: Don Bradman scampers the run which completed his 100th first-class century. The Indians were the delighted opposition, in their match against An Australian XI at Sydney in November 1947. The tourists went on to victory by 47 runs (Mankad 8 for 84), one of only two successes on the tour. Bradman's 100th hundred, his 'most exhilarating moment', came in only his 295th innings, and was cheered by a Saturday-afternoon crowd of over 32,000. Now 39, he was enjoying the same sort of rejuvenation as WG in 1895. In his only Test series against India he had scores of 185 at Brisbane, 132 and 127 not out at Melbourne (his only twin Test centuries), and 201 at Adelaide (where he had lived since 1935). (Hazare scored two centuries in the Adelaide Test.) In 12 innings this season Bradman hit eight centuries, 1296 runs.

George Headley becomes the first black man to captain West Indies: Bridgetown, January 1948. The England captain is Lancashire dentist Ken Cranston, standing in for the injured Gubby Allen. England, plagued by injuries and generally outplayed, lost the series 0–2, and won none of the other matches. MCC lived to regret sending a side lacking Compton, Edrich, Bedser, Wright, Yardley and, till the seventh match, Hutton. Below: Andy Ganteaume, 27, of Trinidad, who scored 112 in his only innings in Test cricket, Port-of-Spain, February 1948. In this match S. C. Griffith scored 140 for England, his maiden hundred in first-class cricket.

In 1947–48 Western Australia became the fifth Sheffield Shield team, admitted on a limited basis. They promptly won two of their four matches outright and another on first innings to average 65% and take the trophy. Keith Carmody (front left), an ex-PoW, was skipper and coach – as well as innovator of the 'umbrella field'.

385

The 1948 Australians land in England. Their record was to be superior to that of any other touring team: won 25, drawn nine, lost none. They won four of the Tests, and were dismissed only once in a day, and that was for 721 by Essex at Southend! There was talent in this side – such as Brown's batting and Ring and McCool's legspin – which never needed to be exploited fully. Bradman made 2428 runs and six others passed 1000. Seven bowlers took 50 or more wickets. It was a fittingly glorious farewell for The Don.

The changed England that Bradman, Hassett, Barnes and Brown encountered: it would be years before the wreckage of the Hitler war became unobtrusive. Young clerks on a bomb-site in the City of London do their Compton and Bedser impressions.

The centenary of W. G. Grace's birth fell on July 18, 1948, and Gloucestershire marked it by fixing a memorial to the gates of the Bristol ground he dominated.

Stuck in the Adelaide bank, Bruce Dooland missed selection for the 1948 tour. But not stuck for long. He took his rare spinning skill to the English leagues and then signed for Notts, for whom he took 770 wickets in five seasons.

One who went: Neil Harvey, a left-hander in the pedigree line of Hill, Darling and Bardsley, first played for Australia at 19, and scored 153 in his second Test, against India at Melbourne, his home ground. He was a certainty for England, and got into the Test side for the fourth Test, when he scored 112. This was the amazing match at Headingley in which Australia scored 404 for 3 for victory on the final day, Morris and Bradman putting on 301. Harvey's brothers (all of whom played State cricket) and parents share his delight at tour selection.

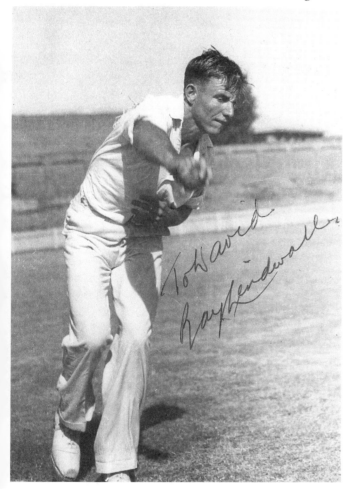

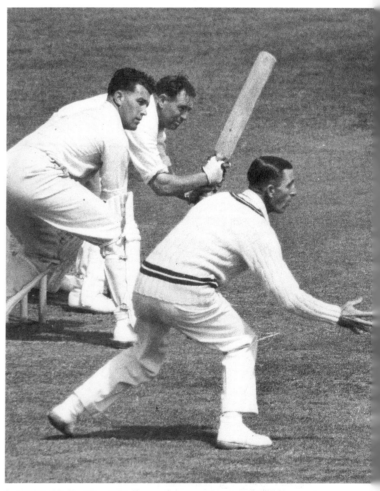

England now saw first-hand what a devastating fast bowler Ray Lindwall was, and how beautifully smooth his rolling action could be. The threat he posed with the new ball even prompted A. P. Herbert to write some verse on the subject.

In 1948, H. E. 'Tom' Dollery – here cutting while Leslie Compton and Jack Robertson watch – became Warwickshire's first professional captain. A prolific county batsman, he was unable to take full advantage of his four Test appearances.

387

The unmistakable cover-drive of Len Hutton, leaning low into the shot against Toshack (who took 7 for 81) in Yorkshire's second match against the 1948 Australians, at Bramall Lane. The nation was stunned when Hutton was dropped from the England team for the third Test. **Right:** Denis Compton made a stirring 184 in the Trent Bridge Test, often withstanding Miller and Lindwall in dreadful light. Eventually, in taking evasive action, he toppled into the stumps. Morris, Johnson and Tallon are close witnesses. The Nottingham crowd, with memories of the pillorying of their own Larwood and Voce, booed vigorously.

The earnest search for young talent went on throughout England. Middlesex trawled 36 local schools, and at the nets at Chiswick the likely lads were joined by 18-year-old legspinner Ian Bedford, who had made a successful county debut in 1947. Alec Thompson watches him. Bedford's early promise was not sustained, though Middlesex called him back as captain in 1961. He collapsed and died while playing in a club match in 1966.

Two Tests down, England were soon in trouble in the third, at Old Trafford: 119 for 5, and Compton retired with a gashed brow. But after a few stitches and a stiff brandy, he returned to make an heroic 145 not out, though Lindwall greeted him with a hot blast. Bedser accompanies him after an interval, a tailender who was developing his own runmaking ability: in the next Test, at Headingley, he went in as nightwatchman and scored 79.

The 1948 Manchester Test had more than the average ration of violence. Sid Barnes was also seriously hurt when fielding in his customary silly-leg position to Dick Pollard, whose big heave at a slow ball gave Barnes no chance. He came back from the infirmary and tried to bat, but collapsed from the pain. He had a bruise the size of a dinner-plate over his kidney region. It was an eventful series for him: in the Lord's Test he had scored 0 and 141.

The monarch of the crease with the monarch of the realm, Balmoral 1948.

Bournemouth, August 1948, and the Glamorgan players rejoice in having won the Championship, never having finished higher than sixth. The tallest figures are captain Wilf Wooller and Johnny Clay, to whom the county owed more than could ever adequately be expressed.

How could it happen? England had been bowled out at The Oval for 52 in the final Test, and Australia were 117 for 1 as Don Bradman came in for what would almost certainly be his final innings at this level. He had scored 6996 runs for 69 dismissals. Four runs would have left him with a Test career average of 100. The Englishmen cheered him at the wicket, and Hollies bowled him second ball for 0 with a googly. Arthur Morris, at the other end, went on to 196, and would gladly have given his captain four of those runs to alleviate the general sadness. The greatest of all Test careers had ended. A knighthood awaited Bradman, who still had much to give the game as administrator, selector, advisor, writer. Future generations would gaze upon his record in disbelief.

B. B. Nimbalkar (right) came within 10 runs of overtaking Bradman's world record 452 not out when he made 443 not out for Maharashtra against Kathiawar at Poona in December 1948. With the total 826 for 4 at a lunch interval, Maharashtra discovered that their opponents had conceded this Ranji Trophy match, thus leaving Nimbalkar in second place in the exalted list.

Left: Len Hutton, having top-scored with 30 in England's disastrous 52 at The Oval, is caught behind off Miller for 64, again top score, in the second innings.

Sid Barnes, Australia's most notorious rebel, takes guard with a miniature bat in the Bradman testimonial match in Melbourne, to Don Tallon's amusement. The authorities seldom found 'Bagga's' antics amusing, and having filmed the Royal family at Lord's, jumped a turnstile, and taken out the drinks as 12th man in a lounge-suit, he was omitted from the Test team for reasons outside cricket. He sued and vindicated himself.

Everton Weekes, the West Indian with the savage, catlike approach of Bradman, set a fresh record of five consecutive Test centuries when, to his 141 at Kingston in the last Test against England in March 1948, he added 128, 194, 162 and 101 later that year on the tour of India. In his next Test innings, at Madras, he was run out – a very close decision – for 90.

Right: F. G. Mann, captaining England in his first Test series, as did his father, tosses with Dudley Nourse (right) before the third Test of the 1948–49 series, at Cape Town. England won an exciting opening contest at Durban by two wickets, thanks to Cliff Gladwin's famous scurried leg-bye.

Dudley Nourse, a first-innings centurymaker with Bruce Mitchell, is stumped by Godfrey Evans off Roly Jenkins in the Cape Town Test, New Year 1949. Spinners took most of the wickets in this drawn Test, Compton taking five wickets for the only time in a Test. The jack-in-a-box Evans was proving to be a great asset for England behind and sometimes in front of the stumps.

Hutton and Washbrook, with their record opening stand of 359 at Johannesburg, stole much of England's early batting limelight, but Gloucestershire left-hander Jack Crapp batted steadily, his 56 at Johannesburg being followed here by 35 and 54, another half-century in the next Test, and 49 in the last, when England won on the bell by three wickets, Crapp hitting 'Tufty' Mann, the probing slow left-arm bowler, for 10 off three balls.

South Africa's innings at Johannesburg began disastrously, and they were 19 for 3 before Nourse (129) and Billy Wade (54) rescued them. Here Viljoen is run out after some slick fielding by Jenkins. To the right of the picture are Alec Bedser (in sunhat), Eric Rowan (Viljoen's partner), and Cliff Gladwin.

In May 1949 the English second-wicket record was transferred from Shrewsbury and Gunn to the young Cambridge undergraduates John Dewes and Hubert Doggart, who both made double-centuries in a stand of 429 against Essex at Fenner's. They told their captain they had no desire to go on for a further 27 runs to beat the recent world record set by Nimbalkar and Bhandarkar. Doggart had made history in 1948 by scoring 215 not out on his first-class debut.

F. S. Trueman, Yorkshire's new 18-year-old bowler, beats and bowls the Oxford captain, C. B. Van Ryneveld. Trueman took four University wickets for 31.

Another bright new name in 1949 was F. S. Trueman, 18, who picked up a few wickets for Yorkshire at Oxford (where the county lost to the University), including Clive van Ryneveld, the South African.

Horace Hazell, 39, Somerset's successful and jolly slow left-armer, bowled 105 consecutive balls against Gloucestershire at Taunton in 1949 (mostly to Tom Graveney) without conceding a run. In helpful conditions he finished with 8 for 27.

Left: Mild-mannered D. V. P. Wright of Kent took his seventh hat-trick in 1949, placing himself at the top of a rare table. Doug Wright's fastish legspinners and googlies, sometimes devastating, sometimes erratic and horribly costly, brought him over 2000 wickets between 1932 and 1957, 108 of them for England.

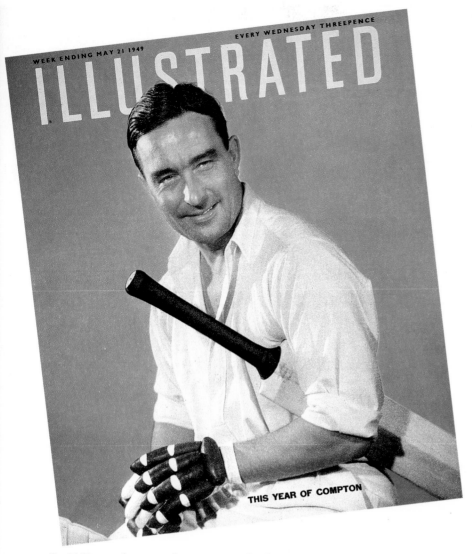

WEEK ENDING MAY 21 1949

EVERY WEDNESDAY THREEPENCE

ILLUSTRATED

THIS YEAR OF COMPTON

By 1949 most boys – and men – wanted to be Denis Compton – at least those in the South of England. And for women everywhere he was the smiling heart-throb of the cricket field. Glamorously associated with Brylcreem, he was also Britain's Sportsman of the Year in 1949.

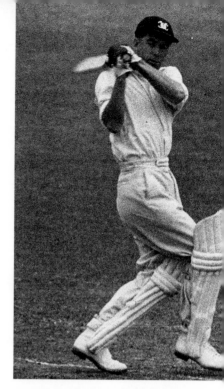

Martin Donnelly, a polished New Zealand left-hander, scored 206 in the Lord's Test in 1949, when his country, strong in batting, made its point with four honourable draws in the three-day Tests. Donnelly, who passed 2000 runs on this tour (he first toured as a 19-year-old in 1937), emulated A. P. F. Chapman in scoring hundreds at Lord's for the Gentlemen and in a Varsity match and Test match. He also played rugby for England.

HRH the Duke of Edinburgh, MCC president in 1949, opens new nets at Woodford Green, Essex with the sound of clattering timber. He batted, in lounge-suit, for 15 minutes in the net, which was financed by the National Playing Fields Association, and lamented that there were not enough playing fields in Britain.

In July 1949 Middlesex's elegant Jack Robertson scored 331 not out at Worcester, the most runs scored in a post-war day's play in England. Then, in the car park, he found his tyres let down.

394

Len Hutton was still England's – the world's – outstanding classical batsman, and in June 1949 he scored 1294 runs, the most ever in a month – and this despite three consecutive ducks.

New Zealand boasted two left-handers of extraordinary talent on the 1949 tour. Besides Donnelly there was Bert Sutcliffe (reaching his century in the Oval Test), who made 2627 runs on the tour, and went home to score 355 for Otago v Auckland. Three years later he scored 385 against Canterbury, the highest score by a left-hander.

Wilfred Rhodes sends down what was probably his last ball. He opened a new school ground near Wakefield in 1949, when he was 71. Soon blindness was to engulf him as he lived on to within five years of his century.

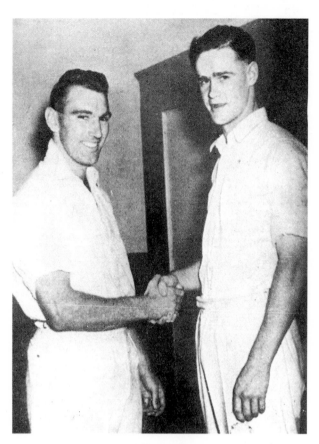

Two young lions entered the arena in 1949, John Reid of New Zealand (left), who turned 21 during the tour, and Brian Close, who did the double in this his first year with Yorkshire, and also became England's youngest-ever Test player at 18 years 149 days. Both had towering careers before them.

Waiting batsman Tom Graveney in conversation with the man who remoulded cricket commentary, John Arlott, already, with his distinctive Hampshire tone and grand use of words, the 'voice of cricket'.

An unlikely but happy sequel to Bodyline was the emigration to Sydney of Harold Larwood (left) and his wife and daughters. Larwood was greeted by former adversary Jack Fingleton, who had encouraged the move.

Left: The eternal comfort of a cup of tea and a tray of sandwiches – here in the clubhouse of Littlewick Green, near Maidenhead – a scene repeated in several thousand parts of England every Saturday afternoon.

Keith Miller was a shock omission from Australia's team to tour South Africa in 1949–50, but joined them in time for the first Test when Bill Johnston was injured. Here, at Cape Town, Miller hits Nourse with a bouncer. Australia won 4–0, with Neil Harvey making four centuries, the most brilliant being his 151 not out at Durban to bring Australia home by five wickets after Tayfield (7 for 23) had bowled them out for 75 in the first innings. Moroney scored two centuries at Johannesburg in the fourth Test.

Surrey offspinner Jim Laker went back to his native Bradford in May 1950 for a Test trial match, and recorded the astonishing figures of 8 for 2 off 14 overs, The Rest disintegrating on a drying pitch for 27. Here P. B. H. May involuntarily pushes his third ball from Laker into the safe hands of Hutton in the leg trap. In time, Laker's name came to be associated with freakish bowling figures.

Peter May, by 1950, had already been spoken of for some years as a prospective Test batsman, but in 1950, at Lord's, M. C. Cowdrey of Tonbridge School batted like a young Hammond to score 126 not out and 55 for Public Schools v Combined Services. Only 17, to May's 20, Cowdrey gave English cricket-lovers further cause to hope that the post-war generation of cricketers would in time match their forebears.

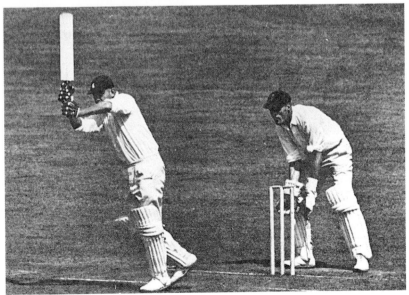

The 1950 West Indies team shook England by winning a Test for the first time on English soil. The Lord's victory saw wild (restrained by later standards) scenes of jubilation, but West Indian success became something of a habit as they won at Trent Bridge and The Oval too. Standing: W. H. Ferguson (scorer), A. L. Valentine, C. L. Walcott, H. H. H. Johnson, L. R. Pierre, A. F. Rae, R. E. Marshall, C. B. Williams; seated: E. D. Weekes, R. J. Christiani, J. B. Stollmeyer, J. D. C. Goddard (captain), J. M. Kidney (manager), G. E. Gomez, P. E. Jones, F. M. M. Worrell; front: S. Ramadhin, K. B. Trestrail.

The '3 Ws' headed the West Indian batting on the 1950 tour, sharing 20 centuries and almost 6000 runs. The most graceful of the Barbadians, Worrell, scored 261 in the Trent Bridge Test and 138 at The Oval, while the largest, Walcott, hit 168 not out in the Lord's Test. Everton Weekes also scored a Test century at Trent Bridge, but his biggest innings (below) was 304 not out against Cambridge at Fenner's in his side's 730 for 3. Dewes and Sheppard had shown the way, rather more sedately, with an opening stand of 343 for the University. Weekes had just scored 232 against Surrey.

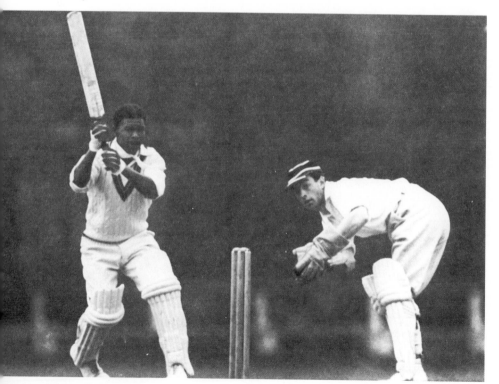

Sonny Ramadhin (Trinidad) and Alf Valentine (Jamaica), ingenuous young men with hardly any big cricket behind them, overran England in 1950, 'Ram' taking 135 wickets (26 in the Tests) with right-arm 'mystery' bowling and 'Val' taking 123 (33 in the Tests, including 8 for 104 at Old Trafford on his debut). Little Ramadhin took 11 in the historic victory at Lord's.

During the war the English learned a lot about patience and discipline, virtues displayed here on the Saturday morning of the 1950 Test at The Oval, when queues stretched round the ground.

Below: Jeff Stollmeyer, a veteran of the 1939 tour, and Allan Rae gave West Indies some solid starts during the 1950 Test series. Rae, a left-hander, made two centuries.

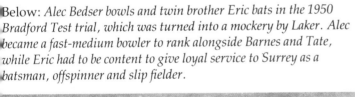

Below: Alec Bedser bowls and twin brother Eric bats in the 1950 Bradford Test trial, which was turned into a mockery by Laker. Alec became a fast-medium bowler to rank alongside Barnes and Tate, while Eric had to be content to give loyal service to Surrey as a batsman, offspinner and slip fielder.

John Warr, one of the young 1950–51
MCC players, shows how not to catch.

Jack Iverson and family. The Victorian, 35, had not seen a Test match before the
first one he played in, at Brisbane in December 1950. His puzzling spinners were
generated by a flick of his large middle finger, and though it seemed his stock ball
was the offbreak, few of England's batsmen played him with conviction. He
demolished them with 6 for 27 in the third Test, at Sydney.

England skipper Freddie Brown is caught by Loxton off Iverson in the Brisbane
Test. He made 17, the only double-figure score apart from the masterly 62 not out
by Hutton (far end), who was stranded. On a rain-wrecked pitch, England had
declared at 64 for 7, Australia (three down for 0 at one point) at 32 for 7.

Left: An unhappy Denis Compton leaves the Melbourne Cricket Ground after
being ruled out of the second Test with his familiar knee trouble. He had a ghastly
series, averaging 7.57 from eight innings in the Tests.

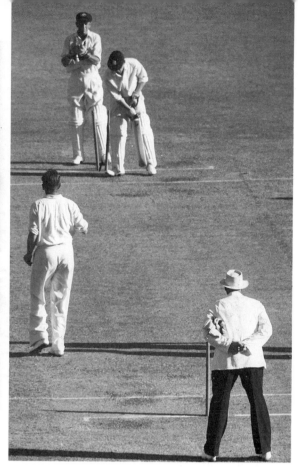

With beercans still some way in the future, Melbourne fans were content with their 'pots' or 'ponies'. This Boxing Day gathering saw Australia moving on towards a narrower victory than that at Brisbane: this one by only 28 runs. Left: Cyril Washbrook was probably the England batsman least comfortable with Iverson, who bowls him for 8 to make the first inroad into the innings when the tourists needed only 179 for their first post-war victory in an Ashes Test.

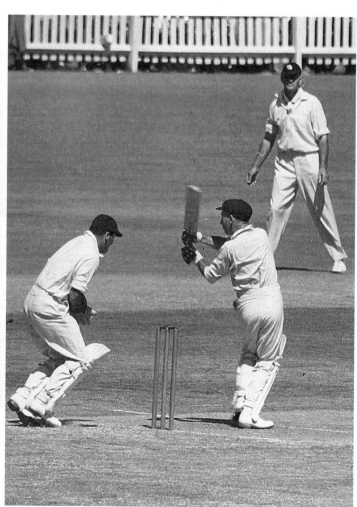

Australian captain Lindsay Hassett, pocket-sized and dapper, gets Wright away to leg in the Adelaide Test of 1950–51.

England's valuable allrounder Trevor Bailey had his thumb broken by Lindwall in the Sydney Test, and could not bowl.

Neil Harvey was noted for his poise and balance, even when he failed to connect, as here at Adelaide. He had a quiet but steady 1950–51 series.

A rather weary Len Hutton withdraws to the shelter of the Adelaide dressing-room under the admiring gaze of the Australians, having carried his bat for 156 through England's innings of 272, in reply to Australia's 371 (Morris 206). Miller, who had scored 145 not out at Sydney to set up an innings victory, now made 99, while Jim Burke worked his way to 101 not out on debut. Australia went four-up.

Victory at long last for England. Their first post-war win against Australia came in the 15th Test, at Melbourne, where Reg Simpson's 156 not out, made in part on his 31st birthday, set up the eventual triumph. Here Ian Johnson drops him off Miller. A vital last-wicket stand of 74 by Simpson and Roy Tattersall (10) put their side onto the path to victory. Hutton, who averaged 88.83, was there at the end, the other principal hero being Bedser with 30 wickets.

Unusual incident at Lancaster Park, Christchurch, where England played a Test after the 1950–51 series in Australia. Washbrook has been given out lbw to Fenwick Cresswell, but was recalled and continued his innings after New Zealand's captain Walter Hadlee had told the umpire that Washbrook had got a touch with the bat.

Peter Heine, later to have a ferocious reputation as a fast bowler for South Africa, smashed 123 not out in 22 minutes in a senior club match in Pretoria in 1950–51. Below: J. E. Pothecary, who was to tour England with the 1960 South Africans, took all 20 wickets in a club match in Cape Town in 1950–51, when he was only 16.

John Dewes, back from an unspectacular English tour of Australia, had scored 1262 runs for Cambridge at 78.88 and 739 for Middlesex at 61.58 in 1950. This boundary as Surrey's Tony Lock erred in length helped Dewes towards a total of 483 runs in only nine innings for Middlesex in 1951. Keeping wicket is the most capable Arthur McIntyre.

Len Hutton leaves the field at The Oval in July 1951, having become the 13th batsman to score 100 first-class centuries. Applauding him in are Surrey players O. J. Wait (off whom Hutton scored his 100th run), Jim Laker, Tom Clark, Tony Lock, Jack Parker, Arthur McIntyre, Alec Bedser and Laurie Fishlock, with Hutton's partner Vic Wilson following him in.

Left: *The find of the 1951 season was Bob Appleyard, who took 169 Championship wickets for Yorkshire at 13.93, and 200 in all in his first full season, at the age of 27. Norman Yardley presented him with his cap in August during the Essex match at Bradford, when he took 12 for 43 with sharply-spun and beautifully-controlled offspinners and cutters. Tuberculosis was to interrupt his career, but he came back to win nine Test caps and tour Australia. Fred Trueman, also newly-capped, is on the left of picture.*

Below: *South Africa's Jack Cheetham sweeps a ball from Laker during the 1951 Oval Test. England's wicketkeeper is Don Brennan, and the leg-trap (still unrestricted) is inhabited by Tattersall, Hutton and, in cap, England captain F. R. Brown.*

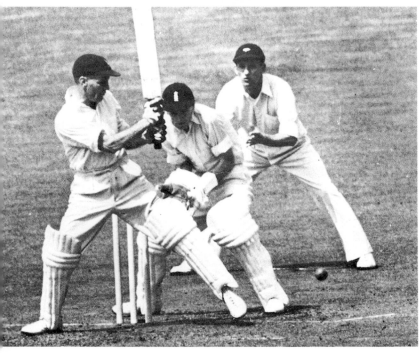

Top: *The 'incident' of 1951: Len Hutton 'obstructing the field' in the Oval Test. He waved his bat at the ball as it fell from his forearm, and distracted the wicketkeeper, Endean: a strange way for England's champion to end his 100th Test innings.* Above left: *Worcestershire's Hugo Yarnold is caught at slip to give Warwickshire victory with four minutes to spare. In this season Yarnold set a wicketkeeping record by stumping six (and catching another) against Scotland at Dundee.* Above: *Roy Tattersall, the Lancashire and England offspinner (second from right) shows his Young Cricketer of the Year trophy (the first such) to the South Africans and Denis Compton.* Left: *Eric Rowan during his 550-minute South African record innings of 236 in the 1951 Headingley Test. At 42 he was the oldest Test double-centurymaker. South Africa lost the series 1–3.*

India's first-ever Test victory over England came with an innings victory at the Chepauk, Madras in February 1952. Roy and Umrigar made hundreds for India, and Vinoo Mankad took 8 for 55 and 4 for 53. Five of his wickets came from stumpings by Sen. Here Mushtaq Ali hooks Statham. The players wore black armbands in memory of King George VI, who died on February 6.

West Indies' advance was checked when they toured Australia in 1951–52. They lost four Tests and won one. Australia's pace attack of Lindwall, Miller and Johnston held the initiative, indulging in lengthy spells of short-pitched bowling which the victims never forgot. The West Indian spinners were still always likely to strike, and Hassett has just become Ramadhin's first scalp.

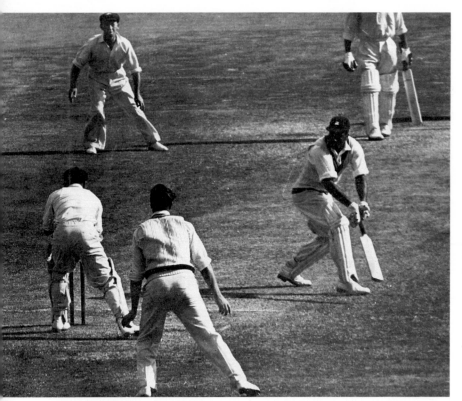

The mighty 3Ws were temporarily eclipsed in Australia, West Indies' only two centuries coming from Worrell and Stollmeyer. Walcott was comfortably stumped by Langley off Ian Johnson in the second Test, at Sydney, for 10, following his 60 in the first innings.

Right: A long way from where Lindwall's ball hit his pads, West Indies captain John Goddard is adjudged lbw in the thrilling fourth Test at Melbourne, making West Indies 0 for two wickets. Langley, Miller and Johnson seem only mildly interested.

406

Australia's one-wicket victory at Melbourne was only the fifth by such a narrow margin in Test history, and came after West Indies (272 and 203) had left the home side a target of 260. Hassett's 102 got them into position, though at 192 for 6 it was either side's match. When Bill Johnston joined Doug Ring at the fall of the ninth wicket, 38 runs were still required. And as West Indies fell apart in the field, the two merry Victorians tapped and swung until the scores were level . . . when Johnston turned Worrell to leg for the winning run.

While in Sydney, the 1951–52 West Indies players visited the grave of Victor Trumper, in Waverley Cemetery, which overlooks the Pacific Ocean. Looking on as John Goddard places a wreath are Prior Jones, John Trim, Alf Valentine, Cyril Merry (manager), 'Sammy' Guillen, Wilf Ferguson, Denis Atkinson and Robert Christiani.

Len Hutton leads England onto the Old Trafford turf and into a revolutionary new era. The first professional to captain England in the 20th century, Hutton contributed a century in this match to help towards a third successive victory over India. He scored 150 in the previous Test, at Lord's. Following him out in this third Test are Laker, Evans, Ikin, Watkins, Sheppard, Graveney and Bedser.

Young Yorkshire fast bowler Fred Trueman burst dramatically on the Test scene in 1952, taking seven Indian wickets at Headingley on debut, including the obstinate Manjrekar (above), one of four batsmen to fall before a run had been scored in the second innings. Later in the series Trueman took 8 for 31 at Old Trafford.

Reg Simpson (right), pictured with Bill Edrich at Scarborough, scored the last of his 10 double-centuries in Notts' match against Warwickshire at Trent Bridge. A cool and technically sound opener, he would have won many more than his 27 Test caps had his career not coincided with those of Hutton and Washbrook.

Above: *Cuan McCarthy, a fast bowler who had toured England with South Africa the previous year, was no-balled for throwing in Cambridge University's match at Worcester in 1952.*

Jack Walsh, an Australian left-arm wrist-spinner in the skilful line of Fleetwood-Smith, played for Sir Julien Cahn's XI and then joined Leicestershire, picking up wickets seemingly at will in many matches. In 1952 he did the double.

Left: *Jack Young, the Middlesex and England slow left-arm bowler, took 1361 wickets at under 20, but was confessedly no great batsman. Grove of Warwickshire was not content to knock out merely one stump at Lord's in 1952.*

They may not have known it, but Surrey, as they celebrated winning the 1952 County Championship, were launching a habit that was to last seven seasons. Skipper Stuart Surridge (under the Surrey crest) was a bold, forceful leader, who mustered the short legs to Laker's bowling, and, as the seasons unfurled, had at his disposal such other world-class bowlers as Tony Lock, Alec Bedser and Peter Loader and batsmen Peter May, Micky Stewart and Ken Barrington. McIntyre was a Test wicketkeeper, and the supporting players, though often undersung, were of above-average quality. Early declarations hastened victory after victory for this powerful side, the Warwickshire match of 1953 being won in a single day. After Surridge's five Championships, May took over and added two more.

Left: *Denis Compton's favourite pull shot brings him very special runs against Northants at Lord's, June 11, 1952. The runs took him to his 100th century, and it was only his 552nd innings. Only Bradman (295) has got there faster.*

Jack Hobbs, the master batsman and gentleman professional, receives 70th birthday congratulations in his shop in Fleet Street, on December 16, 1952. He was knighted the following year, and died in 1963 at the age of 81.

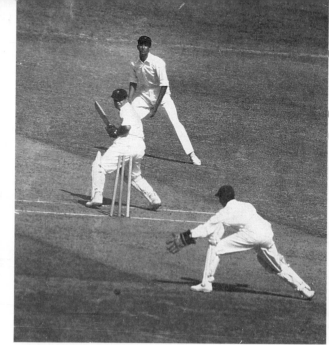

Pakistan claim their first wicket in Test cricket as India's Pankaj Roy is bowled by Khan Mohammad in the inaugural Test at Delhi in October 1952. **Below:** *Hazare goes for 76, bowled by Amir Elahi. The wicketkeeper is Hanif Mohammad.*

Godfrey Evans scored 98 before lunch for England v India at Lord's in 1952, and might have reached his century had not the opposition deliberately slowed things down. His jaunty 104 helped lift England to 537. He is remembered most of all for his athletic and unquenchably enthusiastic wicketkeeping, which brought him a one-time Test record tally of 219 dismissals in 91 Tests.

A second early strike for Pakistan as the great Indian allrounder Mankad is bowled by Khan Mohammad for 11. But after India had totalled 372 Mankad made the game his own, his slow left-arm cunning bringing him 8 for 52 and 5 for 79 in an innings victory.

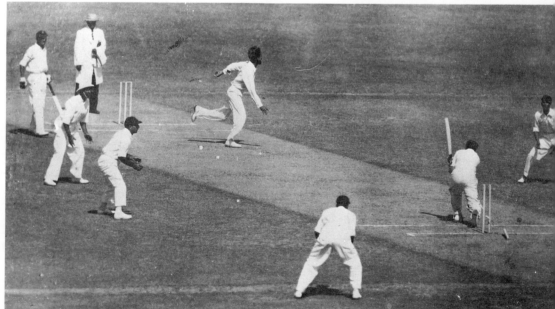

410

Another of cricket's innovations shows itself in Australia as South Africa's calculating offspinner Hugh Tayfield bowls (in the Queensland match: Ken Mackay is the non-striker) with two silly mid-offs and two silly mid-ons (one is out of picture). Tayfield bowled indefatigably to take 30 wickets in the five Tests and 84 on the tour.

Australia led South Africa 2–1 as the final Test began. Jack Cheetham's unfancied young Springbok team had surprised thus far, as much as anything by their wondrous fielding – and Russell Endean's matchwinning 162 not out in the second Test, at Melbourne. Back on that ground for the fifth Test, Australia seemed safe with 520 on the board, but the tourists replied with 435 – during which this scramble between bowler Benaud and batsman Anton Murray (Geoff Noblet running to the stumps) gave the crowd something further to squeal about . . .

. . . then Australia scored only 209, Neil Harvey's rich run coming to an end with only 7, giving him 834 runs for the series. Here 17-year-old Ian Craig, who had scored 213 not out for NSW against the South Africans, survives a quick single and lands at the feet of Endean. Craig, on Test debut, made 53 and 47.

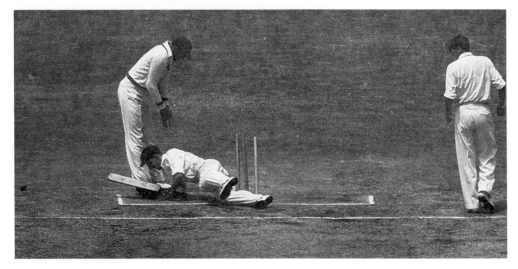

411

Needing 295 to beat Australia at Melbourne in the fifth Test of 1952–53, South Africa were 191 for 4 when Headley Keith was joined by Roy McLean. The pair romped to victory, McLean (nearest camera) hitting an unbeaten 76 to go with his first-innings 81.

Another triumphant return: South Africa went on to New Zealand, and at Wellington their opener, Jackie McGlew (in front), scored 255 not out, then South Africa's record score. With Murray (also pictured), who made 109, McGlew put on a record 246 for the seventh wicket.

Freddie Trueman, the fast bowler England had been praying for all through the years of hardship against Lindwall and Miller, earned the Young Cricketer of the Year trophy for his deeds in 1952, the presentation taking place the following year, with Australia's captain, Lindsay Hassett (right), in attendance. Trueman's progress was not uninterrupted – he played (successfully) only in the final Test of the 1953 Ashes series – nor was he ever to be in the England team – for various reasons – for long, unbroken spells.

At the other end of the age scale: S. F. Barnes, England's demon of the pre-First War period, rolled his arm over for a complete over at the age of 80, getting his testimonial match at Stafford under way in the spring of 1953. Batsman Cyril Washbrook seems happy to stay at umpire Chester's end.

Not merely a couple of reporters in the Headingley Press-box for the Ashes Test of 1953, but Sir Donald Bradman and D. R. Jardine, arch-opponents in the Bodyline series, when few if any words were exchanged, and now unlikely to add to the conversation, in spite of somebody's comic sense of seating arrangements.

Hutton and Hassett toss at Old Trafford, 1953. The Australian captain won all five tosses, but bad weather, Willie Watson at Lord's, and Trevor Bailey almost everywhere preserved a no-decision series up to the final Test at The Oval.

Left: Some great Australians were in town for the opening of the Memorial Gallery at Lord's in 1953. Bill O'Reilly, Arthur Mailey and Bert Oldfield contribute some dry observations to make the Duke of Edinburgh smile. Behind HRH is MCC president, the Duke of Beaufort.

413

Sensing that England might now, at last, be strong enough to beat Australia, the optimistic spectators turned up in their thousands, this crowd waiting to get in at Lord's following in some early birds who had been waiting outside for 22½ hours. And this was for the Monday's play. Keith Miller's 109, following first-innings centuries by Hassett and Hutton, put the pressure on England, who lost three for 12 that evening. Then on the final day Watson (109) and Bailey (71 in 4¼ hours) fought one of the great rearguard actions to save England.

As successful a trio as any county has ever produced: Alec Bedser, Tony Lock and Jim Laker of Surrey, waiting for their train to Leeds for the fourth Test. Bedser took 39 wickets in the series (14 for 99 at Trent Bridge), beating Tate's 1924–25 record, and Laker and Lock were to be instrumental in winning the all-important Oval Test, taking 4 for 75 and 5 for 45 respectively in Australia's second innings of 162.

Peter May did not survive the first Test of 1953, but a batsman of such obvious class was soon going to be recalled, and at The Oval he scored an important 39 and 37 from the No. 3 berth. His first innings ended with Ron Archer's catch at leg slip.

414

National heroes all: the England team which regained the Ashes in 1953, Australia having held them for 19 years. Standing: T. E. Bailey, P. B. H. May, T. W. Graveney, J. C. Laker, G. A. R. Lock, J. H. Wardle (12th man), F. S. Trueman; seated: W. J. Edrich, A. V. Bedser, L. Hutton (captain), D. C. S. Compton, T. G. Evans.

Compton made only 16 in England's first innings at The Oval, which owed most to Hutton's 82 and Bailey's 64, but this meaty hook was a rehearsal for the stroke with which Compton was to finish the match on the fourth day, bringing back the Ashes, his loyal partner Edrich in with him at the end, 55 not out.

Alan Davidson, one of several young but immature Australian allrounders on the 1953 tour, is castled by Lock for 21. Archer top-scored with a gallant 49.

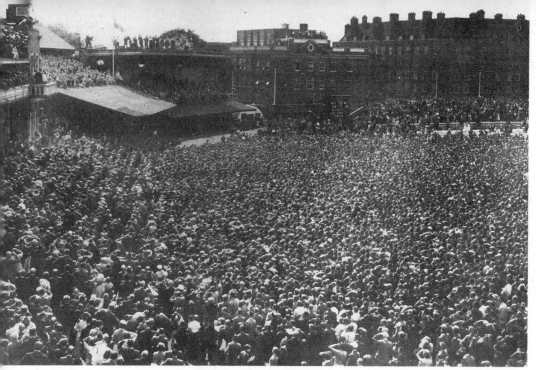

An experience that would last each of these jubilant spectators a lifetime: the Ashes have been won back by England in Coronation Year, an event to rank with the conquering of Everest in the hearts of local cricket-lovers.

Right: *A young coloured player in South Africa, Basil D'Oliveira, about whom much would be heard a dozen years on, was doing incredible things with bat and ball in the primitive cricket environs of Cape Town. In a match in 1953–54 he hit 225 in 65 minutes, with 28 sixes and 10 fours.*

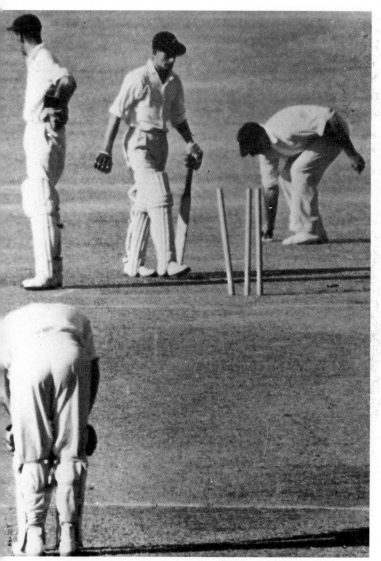

Left: *New Zealand toured South Africa in 1953–54 and had a hard time of it, losing the Test series 0–4. In the third Test, at Cape Town, John Beck of New Zealand was run out for 99. His partner, Eric Dempster, bows in distress. This was the closest Beck would ever get to a Test century.*

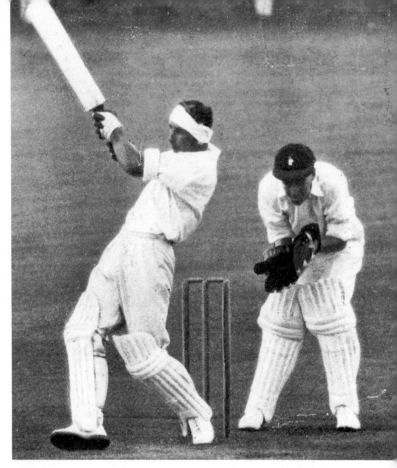

There had been murmurs about Tony Lock's action, particularly when he fired in his fast ball, for several seasons, and now, in Barbados, in MCC's match against the Island, there is an unreality about the scene as Lock has bowled a 17-year-old named Garry Sobers, only for umpire Harold Walcott at square leg to no-ball him for throwing. The somewhat chilling moment has been preserved through the alertness of the *Barbados Advocate's* photographer.

Above: *Tragedy stalked the South Africa v New Zealand Test at Ellis Park, Johannesburg over Christmas 1953. Bert Sutcliffe was badly hit by a ball from Neil Adcock, as was Laurie Miller. Then Bob Blair received news of his fiancée's death in a train disaster in New Zealand. Sutcliffe (above) returned to smash 80 not out, in which he hoisted seven sixes. Blair also batted, and hit Tayfield for four sixes in an over. In their second innings New Zealand collapsed against Adcock (5 for 43) to be out for 100 and lose by 132 runs.*

Left: *Trouble in Georgetown, 1954. England have just taken a wicket and the West Indian crowd don't like it. Hutton, who had scored 169, refused to take his team off, saying he wanted more wickets. England went on to win by nine wickets to keep the series alive.*

Left: *Willie Watson swings at Gerry Gomez during the opening Test in Jamaica. The Yorkshire left-hander, having scored a century in his first Test against Australia, now made 116 in his first against West Indies.*

If the 1953 Ashes victory was Len Hutton's finest hour, the ensuing Caribbean tour was imbued with brave endurance on his part which retrieved an apparently lost cause. Having lost the first two Tests (Walcott 220 and Holt 166 at Bridgetown), England won at Georgetown (Hutton is seen hooking Gomez during his 169), drew at Port-of-Spain after West Indies had amassed 681 for 8 (Weekes 206, Worrell 167, Walcott 124) and won at Kingston, where Hutton batted for almost nine hours for 205 after Bailey had taken 7 for 34.

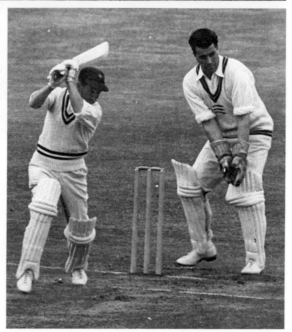

Left: Jock Livingston, a compact left-hander from Sydney, served Northamptonshire nobly from 1950 to 1957, three times reaching 2000 runs. He made two double-centuries in 1951 and two in 1954.

Left: Compton was on the rampage in the Trent Bridge Test against newcomers Pakistan in July 1954, making 278 (165 in 105 minutes while Bailey was with him) in his 100th innings for England. It ended when he was bowled by 16-year-old Khalid Hassan.

Hanif Mohammad, 19, getting the feel of things with a brief knock against Indian Gymkhana, made over 1600 runs on the 1954 English tour. The Little Master, 5 ft 3½ ins and 8 stone, was still developing, but was soon to annex the world's longest and biggest innings, bringing immeasurable pride to his young nation, Pakistan.

Left: Fazal Mahmood precedes his captain, A. H. Kardar, from the field of triumph after bowling Pakistan to a stunning 24-run victory with six wickets in each innings at The Oval with Bedser-type bowling. Bedser and Bailey had been rested by England, a decision subsequently regretted.

Not much of a tour for Frank Tyson: 1 for 160 at Brisbane when Australia piled up 601 for 8 dec and won by an innings, and now, at Sydney in the second Test, knocked senseless by Lindwall. He went off eventually with a huge lump on the back of his head. But Tyson would be back . . .

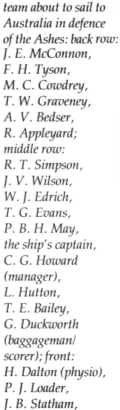

The 1954–55 MCC team about to sail to Australia in defence of the Ashes: back row: J. E. McConnon, F. H. Tyson, M. C. Cowdrey, T. W. Graveney, A. V. Bedser, R. Appleyard; middle row: R. T. Simpson, J. V. Wilson, W. J. Edrich, T. G. Evans, P. B. H. May, the ship's captain, C. G. Howard (manager), L. Hutton, T. E. Bailey, G. Duckworth (baggageman/scorer); front: H. Dalton (physio), P. J. Loader, J. B. Statham, K. V. Andrew, J. H. Wardle.

England got determinedly back into the 1954–55 series with a narrow victory in the second Test at Sydney, Wardle lifting England with a swishing top-score 35. Here Johnston gets a ball past him. Statham, his partner, helped add vital runs – 43 and 46 – for the 10th wicket in both innings, first with Wardle, then Appleyard.

Arthur Morris was always a batsman the opposition were anxious to dismiss. He scored 153 in Australia's 601 at Brisbane, but now, in the evening at Sydney as he and Favell tried to see Australia quietly to the close, Bailey got one to lift and brush the glove, and captain Hutton was ready for the catch.

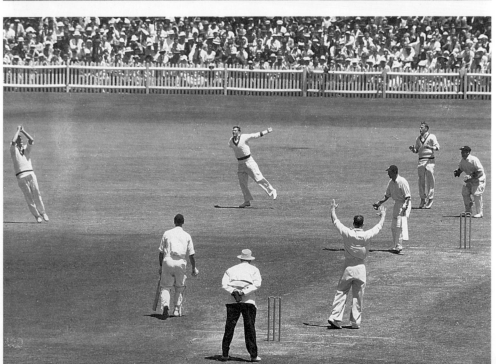

England went in again at Sydney 74 in arrears, and were soon 55 for 3. Hutton fell to a gully catch by Benaud off Johnston. May and Cowdrey (in his first Test series) then added 116, and Australia were set 223 to win. Tyson (6 for 85) bowled them out with Statham (3 for 45 into the breeze) for 184. Australia no longer appeared absolute certainties to regain the Ashes.

Above: *The action that won a series. Tyson, Northants' Lancashire-born bowler, shortened his run-up after Brisbane and bowled probably as fast as man has ever bowled. He was 24, strong, intelligent, willing, and he took 28 wickets in the series at 20.82, including 7 for 27 on a broken surface at Melbourne.*

Left: *England in more trouble in the third Test, at Melbourne, as Miller has Hutton caught by Hole at slip; but Cowdrey, 102 out of 191, saved them initially and May's 91 after Statham had taken 5 for 60 set the stage for Tyson. Another win at Adelaide meant the Ashes were safe.*

Right: *Clyde Walcott pounded five centuries against Australia on his home pitches in 1955, avenging his failures on the 1951–52 tour.*

Below: *Caribbean Press-box during the Australians' tour. The respected Ray Robinson has his binoculars raised. Ernest Eytle is next to him, with Keith Butler and Percy Beames in front. The journalist standing on the right, Jack Anderson, was murdered in 1978 by an intruder in his Jamaica home.*

Keith Miller's swashbuckling career was nearing its end. His back gave him continued discomfort, and he was in his 36th year when he was a member of Australia's first touring team in West Indies early in 1955. He took few wickets, but made three centuries in the Tests, the last at Kingston, where McDonald, Harvey (204), Archer and Benaud (78 minutes) also reached three figures in Australia's 758 for 8 dec. Miller took 6 for 107 too in West Indies' first innings. Despite Walcott, Ian Johnson's men won 3–0.

Below: Yorkshire and Bombay have often enough been their countries' champions, but New South Wales's record of nine consecutive Sheffield Shields from 1953–54 is quite respectable. This 1954 team is: standing: J. W. Burke, E. K. Cotton, B. C. Booth, W. P. A. Crawford, A. K. Davidson, R. B. Simpson; seated: R. E. Briggs, O. Lambert, A. R. Morris (captain), J. E. Norton (manager), R. Benaud, J. H. de Courcy, J. C. Treanor.

A sickening sight for New Zealand eyes: Auckland, March 1955, and England have cast the home team aside for 26, the lowest Test score ever, to win by an innings. Bert Sutcliffe made 11 of the runs. Tyson took 2 for 10, Statham 3 for 9, Appleyard 4 for 7, Wardle 1 for 0. The sadness from England's point of view – though not immediately – was that this was Hutton's last Test. He scored 53, batting at No. 5.

BOWLER	WKTS	RUNS	ENGLAND		BATSMEN OUT			FALL	WKTS
TYSON	2	10	1st INNINGS	246	LEGGATT	1	1		6
STATHAM	2	9			POORE	0	2		8
BAILEY			NEW ZEALAND		REID	1	3		9
APPLEYARD	4	7	1st INNINGS	200	SUTCLIFFE	11	4		14
WARDLE	1	0			McGREGOR	1	5		14
GRAVENEY			TOTAL 8	26	CAVE	5	6		22
MAY			BATSMEN IN		McGIBBON	0	7		22
SIMPSON					COLQUHOUN	0	8		22
COWDREY			MOIR		RABONE	7	9		26
HUTTON			SUNDRIES						

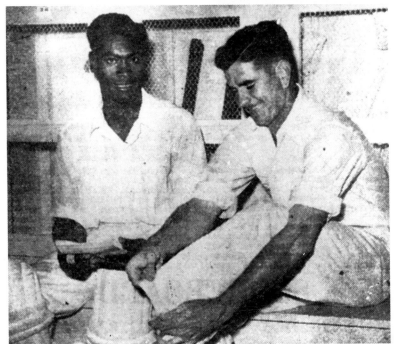

One of the weirdest and at the same time most praiseworthy stands in Test cricket came from Clairemonte Depeiza (left) and Denis Atkinson, who came together in the 1955 Barbados Test when West Indies were 147 for 6 in reply to Australia's 668 (Miller 137, Lindwall 118, Archer 98). They put on a world Test record 347, Depeiza scoring 122, Atkinson 219. Atkinson, West Indies' captain in this match, uniquely then added a five-wicket haul to his double-century. The match was drawn.

Left: *Derek Shackleton, Hampshire's Todmorden-born medium-pacer with the silky action and perfect length, took 8 for 4 against Somerset at Weston in 1955. From 1949 to 1968 he took 100 wickets in a season – a string of 20 seasons, a record.*

Alec Bedser was brought back for one more Test in 1955, at Old Trafford, and had John Waite caught on the drive by Don Kenyon for 113.

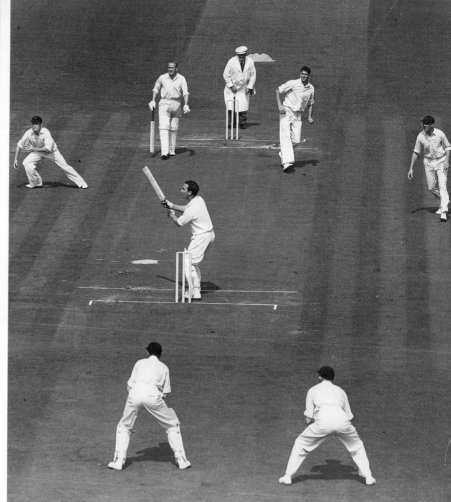

An unusual sight: two left-handers open for England. Brian Close and Jack Ikin faced the new ball against South Africa at The Oval, where the two countries squared up to each other for the fifth time in 1955, having won two Tests each. England won by 92 runs, May easily top-scoring with 89 not out, and Laker and Lock taking 15 wickets. Compton (right), hooking Heine (who took 21 wickets in four Tests), scored 30 in each innings. His partner is Watson, and South Africa's captain, Cheetham, is at silly mid-off, McGlew at silly mid-on.

The MCC 'A' team take the field in Pakistan, 1955–56, led by D. B. Carr. The aim of the tour was to maintain interest in areas where international cricket was seen only infrequently, but this venture turned sour when some of the English players' high spirits exceeded normal bounds: they ducked local umpire Idris Begh in water, and a diplomatic crisis took some time to soothe. Wisden commented that 'some of the players did not realise that the type of humour generally accepted by most people in Britain might not be understood in other parts of the world'.

MCC 'A' players, from the left: Peter Richardson, Harold Stephenson (obscured), Mike Cowan, Brian Close, Allan Watkins, Billy Sutcliffe, Jim Parks (obscured), and Donald Carr.

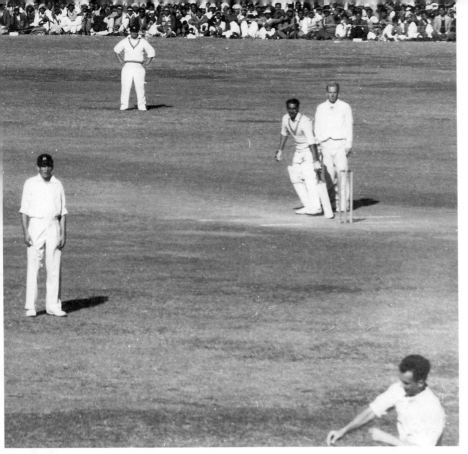

In the first representative match, Pakistan v MCC, in 1955–56, at Lahore, Tony Lock toiled through 77 overs to take 3 for 99. The bowler and captain Carr watch numbed as Alan Moss misses a catch from Kardar, who is already at the bowler's end.

Alimuddin and Hanif Mohammad were Pakistan's established opening pair for some years, not, perhaps, putting big first-wicket scores into the book with the regularity of Hobbs and Sutcliffe, but contributing much, nonetheless, to the new nation's credibility.

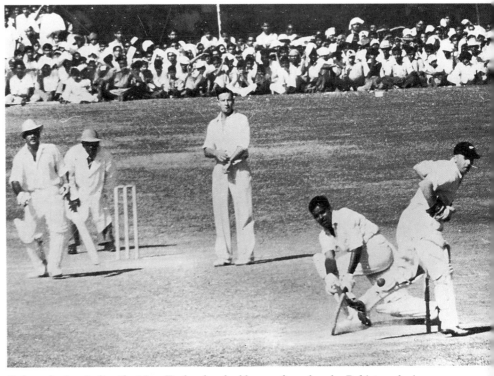

New Zealand conceded heaps of runs on their 1955–56 tour of Pakistan and India (2557 in six innings, average 65.56 per wicket). The scoring orgy peaked in the fifth Test, at Madras, when Mankad (left) and Roy opened with 413, a world Test record.

Before playing India, the New Zealanders had been softened up by Pakistan, losing by an innings at Karachi, where Zulfiqar Ahmed spun 11 out with offspin on a matting surface. At Lahore things looked better for the visitors, who made 348 and had Pakistan 111 for 6. Imtiaz Ahmed, the wicketkeeper, then joined Waqar Hassan, and they added 308 for the seventh wicket. Waqar finished with 189 and Imtiaz (seen sweeping Moir during the colossal stand) made 209 in an 11¼-hour marathon.

The VIP enclosure at the Bagh-e-Jinnah ground at Lahore is graced by the presence of Lord Home, a cricketer and cricket-lover since his days with Eton, Oxford, MCC and Middlesex, and soon to become Britain's Prime Minister. He was a guest of the Governor of West Bengal during the second Pakistan v New Zealand Test of 1955–56.

Some 'firsts' are sweet and some are nothing less than ecstatic. New Zealand had played 45 Tests over 26 years without a victory. Now, at Auckland, on March 13, 1956, scoring 255 and 157, they left West Indies 268 to win. Cave, Beard and Alabaster cut right through the batting, reducing the visitors to 16 for 4, 22 for 6, and at long last, 77 all out, to win by 190 runs. Oddly, the two in pads, nearest camera, are Valentine (right), the last man out, and Guillen, the ex-West Indies player, who stumped him.

Jim Laker leaves the scene of his imagination-defying feat in the Old Trafford Test of 1956. On a responsive pitch he bowled with clinical perfection, stamina and the utmost coolness to take 9 for 37 and 10 for 53, carrying England to an Ashes-winning victory by an innings and himself onto a pedestal. He felt he had bowled better in taking 5 for 88 off 65 overs in Bombay on a Commonwealth XI tour, on a perfect surface and against very strong opposition. But this 1956 performance had a stunning effect not only on the floundering Australian batsmen but on the cricket world generally. In the five Tests Laker's offspin harvested 46 wickets at 9.61. Only Barnes, with 49 wickets in 1913–14, stands above him in the overall Test table. Even Laker's team-mates seem not to have absorbed the full significance of his deed as he walks casually, shyly off.

Above: *Harvey b Laker 0. He can hardly ever have bowled a better ball. Like Mackay, Harvey suffered the indignity of a 'pair'. Left: The second-innings rout continues as Miller is bowled for a duck by Laker.*

Peter May captained England to a 2–1 victory over Australia to retain the Ashes in 1956 and was also a part of Surrey's sixth successive Championship combination. Life was good.

The 'grand old man', C. B. Fry, died in September 1956, a compulsive conversationalist to the end: Cardus said he stopped talking only for two minutes (and then reluctantly) for the Armistice Day ceremony while covering the 1936–37 Australian tour. He survived bouts of mental instability which found him waltzing with an invisible partner and trotting naked along Brighton beach. He met Hitler and some of his thugs, and was broadminded about them. A most gifted and fascinating gentleman.

Above: Alan Walker, from Sydney, took a hat-trick for Notts in 1956, the wickets falling to the first three balls of Leicestershire's second innings, at Leicester. It was then realised he had finished off the first innings, and had thus taken a rare 'four in four'. A brisk, slinging left-armer, Walker could not force a way past Lindwall and Miller into the Australian team, but was capped by his country at rugby and scored a 70-yard try at Twickenham on the 1947–48 Wallabies tour.

MCC toured South Africa in 1956–57, and had another tight series. It finished 2–2, with one draw. There was some dogged batting by both sides, and tight bowling especially from Tayfield (here having Compton caught on a broken pitch at Pretoria), who bowled a record 137 scoreless balls in succession in the Durban Test.

428

England's 1956–57 South African tour saw Johnny Wardle come into his own, bowling wrist-spin such as tended to be frowned upon as frivolous back in Yorkshire. In the second Test, at Cape Town, he helped place England two-up by spinning out 12 South Africans for 89, including John Waite (above left), who has edged Wardle into the safe hands of Cowdrey at slip. It was a sensational innings in that South Africa were bowled out for 72, but the talking point for a long time to come was Russell Endean's dismissal (above right). He padded Laker away, and when the ball bounced towards him he used his hand to push it away. He became the first 'handled the ball' victim in a Test.

May goes in the second Test, c Waite b Tayfield 8, one of the offspinner's 37 wickets in the series (he had innings analyses of 8 for 69 at Durban and 9 for 113 at Johannesburg). May had a nightmare run in the Tests: 153 runs in 10 innings. And yet he was able to stroke 1270 runs in all first-class matches (55.22), topping the list.

South Africa had to win the fifth Test, at Port Elizabeth, to level the series. The mean Heine, having broken Bailey's hand at Durban, now bowls him, though he had scored 41, top score in England's miserable 110 on a suspect pitch. South Africa, their first-innings 164 the highest total of the match, won by 58 runs.

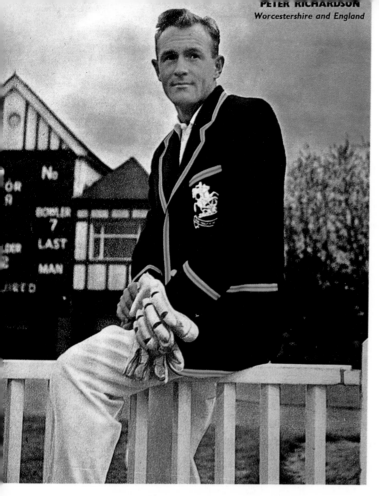

PETER RICHARDSON
Worcestershire and England

Left: Peter Richardson, who made the slowest Test century (his record lasted only a year) when he took 488 minutes to get to 100 in England's opening Test, at Johannesburg, of the 1956–57 South African tour. The slightly-built Worcestershire (and later Kent) left-hander scored over 2000 runs in his 34 Tests, with five centuries. There were some strange entries going into the book of batting records around this time. In the Pakistan v Australia Test at Karachi in October 1956 a mere 95 runs were ground out in a full day's play; and yet the first innings past 600 was recorded in Pakistan as Karachi Whites amassed 762. In India, C. L. Malhotra scored 502 not out in a college match in Patiala, following it with 360 and 144: 1006 in three innings. Unique. There was something about these subcontinental junior matches: in 1953–54 S. V. Patker had hit a world record 83 fours in an innings of 431 not out in a Bombay schools match. At a slightly higher level, Joe Solomon, later a West Indies Test batsman, made a century in each of his first three first-class innings, spread over three matches in 1956–57 and 1957–58. And in England, in 1957, Lancashire (166 for 0 dec and 66 for 0) beat Leicestershire without losing a wicket.

Right: Worrell, Weekes, Ramadhin and Walcott have a relaxing cocktail before the heavier duties of the West Indians' 1957 tour of England present themselves. It looked a strong side, but three Tests were lost and two drawn against a rampant England XI. Below: Worrell plays Moss in the tour curtainraiser at Eastbourne. The wicketkeeper is S. C. Griffith, and Micky Stewart is a decent distance away at short leg.

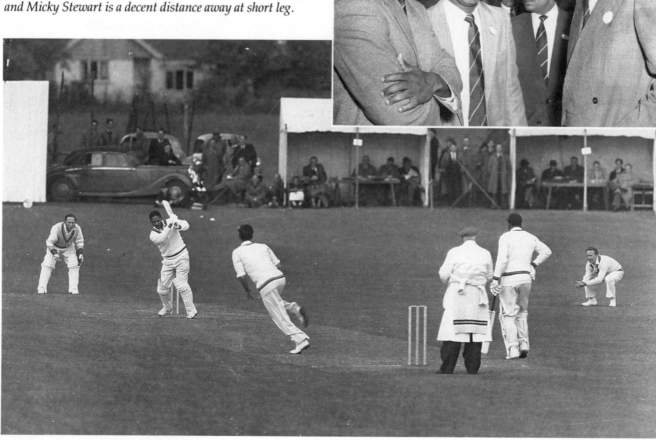

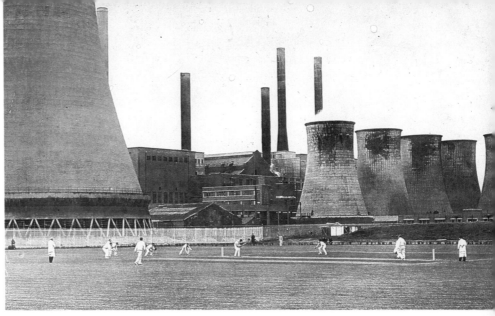

The variety of venues remains a major fascination. Cricket under the cooling towers at Aylestone Road, Leicester was the fate of some county 2nd XI players in the mid-1950s. **Below:** The six survivors of the 1911–12 MCC side in Australia sit with R. G. Menzies (third from left) at the 1957 Lord's Test: George Gunn, Frank Woolley, Sir Pelham Warner, Wilfred Rhodes, S. F. Barnes, Phil Mead.

John Murray of Middlesex, a future Test player and world-record-holder, emulated Leslie Ames in 1957 by scoring 1000 runs and completing 100 wicketkeeping dismissals in a season.

Below: O. G. 'Collie' Smith, here caught by Preston of Essex, scored 104 against Australia in his maiden Test and 161 at Edgbaston in his first against England. A brilliant prospect, he had come from Kingston, Jamaica, from Boys' Town, and was a fair offspinner too. Tragically, he was killed in a road accident in England in 1959.

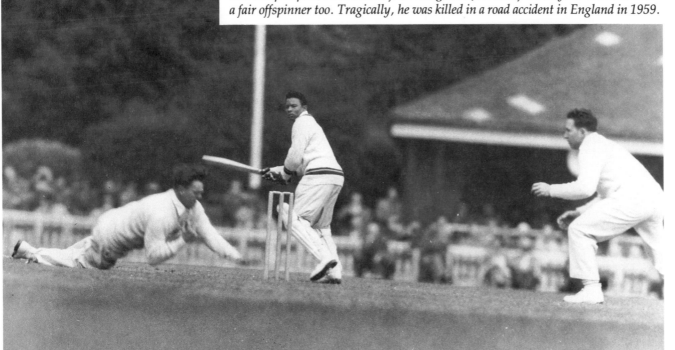

The 1957 Test series will forever be remembered for the fourth-wicket stand of 411 between May (above facing Ramadhin) and Cowdrey. Batting again 288 in arrears at Edgbaston, May (285 not out) and his partner (154) shut out Ramadhin (7 for 49 in the first innings) and his fellow bowlers. The little spinner sent down 98 exasperated overs. Right: In the Trent Bridge Test Trueman bowls Weekes. Worrell carried his bat for 191 not out. Below: Loader completes England's first Test hat-trick at home since 1899, bowling Gilchrist at Headingley.

David Sheppard, who had captained England in Len Hutton's absence in two Tests in 1954, and who later became Bishop of Woolwich and of Liverpool, runs Sobers past Walcott at slip during the 1957 Oval Test. The wicketkeeper is West Indies captain Gerry Alexander.

Tom Graveney seized his chance when recalled by England in 1957. Here, at The Oval, Alexander and Sobers watch a ball heading for the boundary during Graveney's 164. At Trent Bridge he had made 258, which was to remain the highest of his 11 Test centuries.

In the Oval Test, England made 412, though Bailey contributed nothing, being run out (his 7 for 44 at Lord's had helped England towards a three-day victory). At The Oval they won for the third time that year inside three days, Lock (11 for 48) and Laker spinning West Indies out for 89 and 86 (captain Goddard absent with 'flu) on an underprepared pitch.

433

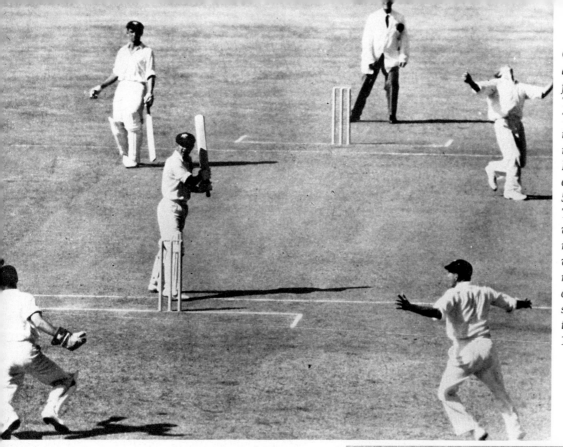

Colin McDonald watches aghast as Waite catches him for 99 off Eddie Fuller at Cape Town. Australia won this Test by an innings, and took the last two as well, finishing unbeaten in any match. Benaud took 30 wickets (106 on the tour) and averaged 54.83 with the bat in the Tests, and Davidson took 25 wickets. Wally Grout took a record six catches behind the wicket at Johannesburg in his maiden Test. McDonald's opening partner, Jim Burke, scored 189 in 578 minutes in this Cape Town Test of 1957–58.

Right: Australian left-arm spinner Lindsay Kline polishes off South Africa's second innings for 99 at Newlands, Cape Town for the innings victory by completing a hat-trick, Neil Adcock being caught by the nimble Bob Simpson at slip. Trevor Goddard thus carried his bat for 56 not out. Australia's 22-year-old captain Ian Craig leaps at silly mid-off.

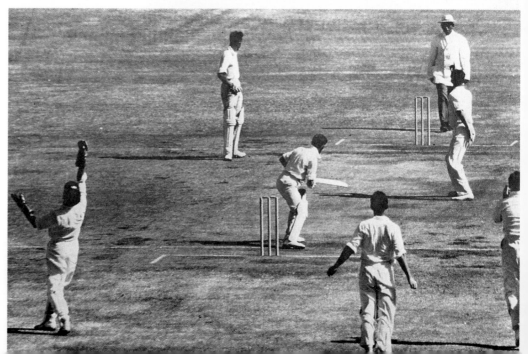

The slowest Test century transferred from Peter Richardson to South Africa's Jackie McGlew at Durban. He took 545 minutes to reach three figures – and now falls to Gaunt, caught by Grout, half-an-hour later.

434

Some astonishing innings were played during the 1957–58 series between West Indies and Pakistan. Left: Hanif Mohammad comes in after the longest innings ever played. His 337 at Bridgetown, made when Pakistan followed on 473 behind, extended through 16 hours and 10 minutes. He and his partners had century stands for the first four wickets, and his side eventually made a token declaration at 657 for 8. Right: Conrad Hunte (in ringed cap) and Garry Sobers resume their stand in the third Test, at Kingston, which amounted to 446 for the second wicket. Hunte was run out for 260, but Sobers went on to set a new Test record, passing Hutton by one run to finish 365 not out in a total of 790 for 3 dec. Pakistan's bowling was depleted by injury to Mahmood Hussain, and Fazal Mahmood laboured through 85.2 overs to finish with 2 for 247, Khan Mohammad being less successful with figures of 54–5–259–0. Sobers, now the giant of world batsmanship, stroked two centuries in the next Test.

Left: At a moment like this, in an age when the TV slow-motion replay was still only a future vision, it paid not to avert one's eyes: Peter Philpott (NSW) holds a peach of a catch at Sydney from the bat of Western Australia's Lawrie Sawle, who later became a Test selector.

Hampshire's West Indian import, the prolific Roy Marshall, cuts Terry Spencer of Leicestershire at Grace Road in May 1958. Later in the match, Shackleton's bowling was described yet again as 'almost unplayable'. Marshall's opening partner is Peter Sainsbury.

Above: *Les Jackson (left) and Harold Rhodes, who bowled Hampshire (the eventual runners-up in the Championship) all out for 23 at Burton in August 1958. Jackson had a fabulously successful season, taking 143 wickets at 10.99, the lowest average since 1894. At Kidderminster, against Worcestershire, he did the hat-trick, all his victims being caught by wicketkeeper George Dawkes.*
Right: *New Zealand were on their knees all season in their five Tests in England in 1958, losing four, five times failing to reach 100. Here Cowdrey catches Petrie off Lock at Headingley.*
Right: *Some of the county captains who met in 1957 to discuss 'brighter cricket': May, Wooller, Eagar, Emmett, Washbrook, Brookes, Tremlett, Insole. The wettest season in memory followed in 1958.*

436

Subhash 'Fergie' Gupte, an Indian legspin/googly bowler of the highest class, took 9 for 102 on Kanpur's matting wicket in 1958–59 against West Indies. He played in 36 Tests and earned 149 wickets. His fieldsmen cost him many more.

Above: *Sydney blond giant Gordon Rorke was even more fearsome from the batsman's end, his stride taking him feet beyond the batting crease. In 1958–59 he took eight England wickets for 165 in two Tests, and at times it seemed he was impossible to score from.*

Left: *Albert Lightfoot and Raman Subba Row after their sixth-wicket stand of 376 for Northants at The Oval in June 1958. Lightfoot's maiden century took 383 minutes, and Subba Row's 300 (566 minutes, 42 fours) against his old county, Surrey, was a record for his new one.*

Left: *Freddie Trueman made it to Australia at last in 1958–59, having surprisingly been omitted (as was Lock) from the previous tour four years earlier. He managed only nine wickets in the three Tests in which he played, and Lock, who tended to push the ball through too fast, took only five wickets at 75 in four Tests.*

Below: *Mushtaq Mohammad, who is accepted as the youngest Test player, though details in Pakistan remain unconfirmed. At 15 years 124 days he emulated his brothers Hanif and Wazir in playing for his country. The opposition was West Indies, at Lahore. He did little of note, but treated it as just another match. The full realisation came later.*

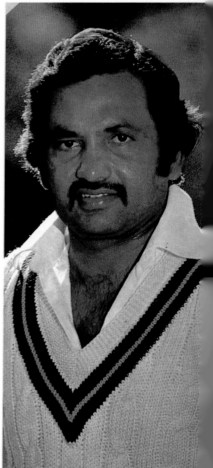

Left: *Roy Gilchrist, a ferocious little fast bowler from Jamaica, who specialised in bouncers and beamers, was sent home by West Indies' management on disciplinary grounds from the 1958–59 tour of India and Pakistan. A compensation was the emergence of Wes Hall, who took 46 wickets in the eight Tests.*

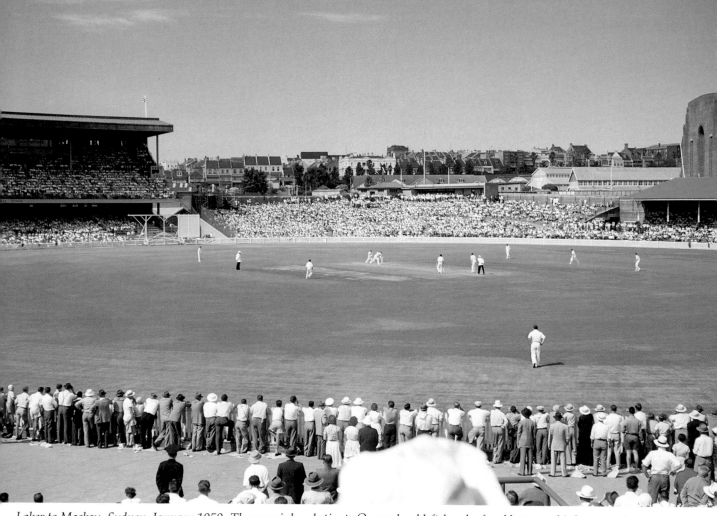

Laker to Mackay, Sydney, January 1959. The ungainly, obstinate Queensland left-hander fared better on his home pitches, having been powerless to resist the great England offspinner in 1956. Laker was anything but a failure on his only Australian tour, taking 15 wickets at 21.20 in four Test matches.

The first fatality in first-class cricket since Summers's death in 1870 occurred when Abdul Aziz, only 17, died in hospital soon after being hit over the heart by a slowish delivery while batting for Karachi against Services in the final of the Qaid-e-Azam Trophy in January 1959.

In January 1959, Hanif Mohammad overtook Bradman's record 452 not out with a marathon 499 (run out) for Karachi v Bahawalpur, at Karachi. He placed 64 fours, and lost his eyelashes in the heat.

As his captain, May, runs for a single, Graveney is signalled out lbw to Davidson for 22 at Sydney in the third Test of 1958–59. Australia's new captain, Richie Benaud, launches into applause. England, now 64 for 3 in the second innings and still 74 behind, seem to be headed for a third defeat, but May went on to 92 and Cowdrey made a six-hour century. This was the only draw among four Australian victories, a new, enthusiastic spirit having developed in the home camp. It had seemed that May's side was one of the very strongest ever to have left England. Their defeat was made harder to bear in that the bowling actions of Meckiff, Rorke, Slater and Burke all came under suspicion, though none was called by the umpires.

Left: *Laker was forced to miss the Adelaide Test because of a sore spinning finger, but came back for the fifth Test, at Melbourne, and took 4 for 93 off 30.5 eight-ball overs, including Colin McDonald, caught by Cowdrey for 133, his second consecutive century.*

Left: *Richardson and Cowdrey pay tribute to Ray Lindwall as he comes off at Melbourne with the Australian bowling record under his belt. In his 57th Test he had exceeded Grimmett's 216 wickets. Lindwall was now 37, and thoughtfully referred to by purists as the last of Australia's straight-armed bowlers.*

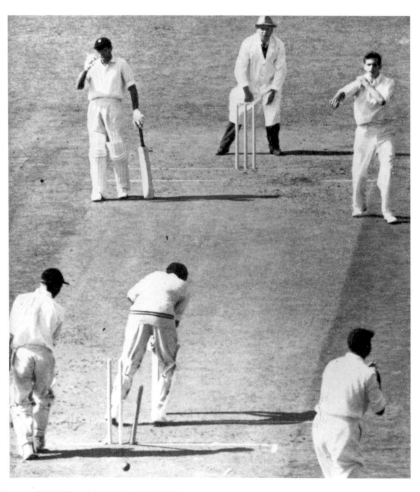

Jim Stewart of Warwickshire hit 17 sixes in the match against Lancashire at Blackpool in July 1959. He hit 10 of them in his first innings of 155 and seven more in his 125 in an unsuccessful run-chase.

Right: *The perfect legbreak. Lancashire's Tommy Greenhough bowls Ghorpade of India in the Oval Test, where England completed a heavy 5–0 whitewash which served as some compensation for their recent thrashing in Australia.*

A neat fingertip catch by Leicestershire's Jack van Geloven spells the end for Warwickshire's Norman Horner at Edgbaston in July 1959. The keeper who either couldn't quite reach the snick or sensibly left it to the fieldsman is Ray Julian.

Surrey, so used to being county champions since 1952, had to make do with third place in 1959 behind Yorkshire and Gloucestershire (the latter having more bonus points, though they each finished with 186 altogether). Surrey began well against Sussex at Guildford – Loader makes a caught-and-bowled off Ken Suttle, to the approval of Swetman, Barrington and May – and won by nine wickets, Laker taking 10 in the match.

441

Jasu Patel, 35, spun India to their first-ever victory over Australia when he took 9 for 69 and 5 for 55 with his jerkily-spun offbreaks at Kanpur in December 1959.

Wally Grout, whose progress was delayed by fellow Queenslander Don Tallon, made up for lost time when given his chance. In 1959–60 he set a new world wicketkeeping record with eight catches in Western Australia's innings at Brisbane. 'The Griz' won his first Test cap at 30, and caught 163 and stumped 24 in his 51 Tests. He died, at 41, in 1968, having secretly nursed a heart condition for some years.

Right: A quick bit of thinking gains NSW a wicket in their Sheffield Shield match against South Australia at Sydney in January 1960. Leon Hill has missed a no-ball from Misson, which brushed his arm. Unsighted, he set off for a run, but was sent back. Johnny Martin at slip gathered the ball and threw a stump down. Ray Flockton, the other slip fielder, scored 264 not out in this match after a long sequence as NSW's 12th man.

New Zealand's Gary Bartlett had an action that disturbed not only by its awkward mechanism but by the questionable arm movement. He also dragged persistently, as in this delivery against Craig's 1959–60 Australians.

In 1959, S. J. Reddy produced an annual covering non-white cricket in South Africa. The leading player, Basil D'Oliveira, was on the front cover. The issue previewed a visit by a West Indies team under Worrell – a tour that was never to be.

President Dwight D. Eisenhower became the first president of the USA to watch a Test match when he attended the fourth day – a very slow day's play – of the Pakistan v Australia Test at Karachi on December 8, 1959. Wearing a Pakistan blazer, he sits next to President Ayub Khan.

A worrying feature of West Indies' bowling in the 1959–60 series against England was the amount of short-pitched bowling. Here Hall bounces Cowdrey (who made 114 and 97) in the Jamaica Test. Right: Norman O'Neill, the powerful Sydney batsman. He hit three centuries in the Tests during Australia's 1959–60 tour of Pakistan and India, and a career-best 284 at Ahmedabad against the President's XI.

England must have felt that another wicket would never come when Sobers and Worrell came together at 102 for 3 and batted for 9½ hours before Sobers was bowled by Trueman, operating around the wicket, for 226. Worrell went on to 197 not out in this first Test of the 1959–60 series, at Bridgetown, when Alexander declared, with little time remaining, with West Indies 563 for 8 in reply to England's 482. Sobers batted for 647 minutes, Worrell 682.

The second Test, in Trinidad, won by England, saw the only positive outcome of the series, and was marred by serious crowd disturbances after Charran Singh was run out (Swetman breaks the wicket while Dexter appeals). Barrington made his second courageous century of the series here, and M. J. K. Smith scored 108. England's other batsmen responded to the challenge, with hundreds coming from Dexter (2), Cowdrey (2), Subba Row and Parks during the series.

Left: England captain May sees Hall splinter a stump in the Kingston Test. His 45 was his last innings of the series. An abscess which refused to heal caused his repatriation, and Cowdrey took over the captaincy for the last two Tests.

Below: Later in the innings Trueman is lbw to Chester Watson, one of six leg-before victims in the innings. Umpire Burke is signalling the batsman out with May's broken stump.

Anti-apartheid demonstrations, an increasingly familiar sight in the years ahead, were staged during South Africa's 1960 tour of England. They hadn't the weight of later protests, but this one at Edgbaston before the first Test lacked nothing in conviction.

Above: *Mike Smith lbw to Trevor Goddard without scoring in the third Test of 1960, between England and South Africa at Trent Bridge. O'Linn is the Springboks' substitute keeper, Waite having hurt himself.*

The discontent over bowlers with dubious actions was stretched further when Geoff Griffin arrived in England with the 1960 South Africans. The climax came in the Lord's Test, where he is being scrutinised by umpire Syd Buller. Griffin took South Africa's first Test hat-trick, but was later called for throwing by umpire Frank Lee. Griffin was called again in the exhibition match which followed the early finish of the Test – and then again for not notifying the umpire that he was switching to underhand. Griffin played no further Test cricket and did not bowl again on the tour.

Right: *In a heart-stopping instant Syd O'Linn's fine innings of 98 in the Trent Bridge Test ends as the juggling produces a catch for Colin Cowdrey (left) off Moss's bowling.*

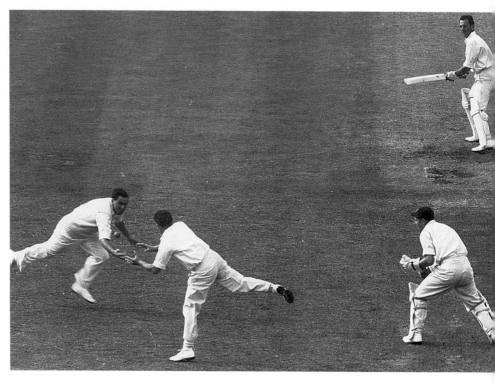

445

O'Linn, the former Kent player and Charlton Athletic footballer, throws himself over in the effort of hitting England offspinner David Allen for six in the Old Trafford Test. The bowler, Trueman and Parks watch the flight of the ball with understandable interest. With this drawn match, England had now gone 16 Tests without being defeated.

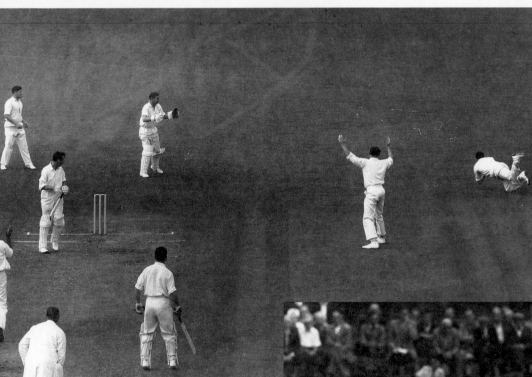

John Waite is caught spectacularly by Trueman off Dexter for 87 at The Oval. Goddard made 99, and with South Africa leading 419 to 155 on first innings, England were in dire jeopardy. Cowdrey and Pullar then put on 290 for the first wicket – Waite stumping Pullar to complete 100 dismissals – and England floated to safety.

Tony Lock, whose mop of ginger hair gave way to an intimidating bald dome, dominated the short-leg region for years, petrifying batsmen with snap catches – and fielding like this in Surrey's match at Blackheath in 1960, when Kent batsman Stuart Leary had his foot safely anchored. Lock's flick seems even to have taken Swetman by surprise.

If international cricket was sagging by the late 1950s, the 1960–61 West Indies tour of Australia was just the shot in the arm it needed: a tie, a thrilling draw, and, when it was all to play for in the fifth Test, a two-wicket victory, all five Tests being played to a positive tune. At Brisbane (above) O'Neill made an impressive 181 for Australia, many of his runs coming from muscular hooks like this off Sobers. The most wonderful of all the five innings in this opening encounter, however, came from Garfield Sobers (above right), who stroked 132, his 10th Test century, as if the Australian bowling came from mere boys. In the final innings Australia needed 233 to win. At 49 for 4 and 92 for 6 they were facing defeat. Davidson (80) and Benaud (52) then swung the match, only for both to lose their wickets. In the frenzy of Hall's final over, which began with Australia six short with three wickets left, Benaud, the last major batsman, was caught behind, Grout was missed by Hall off a skyed caught-and-bowled and then was run out, and in trying for the winning run, Meckiff was beaten by Solomon's side-on throw. It was Test cricket's first tie.

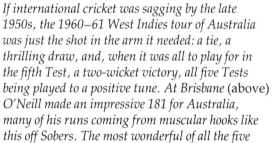

The people of Melbourne needed no prompting when, with the nation still buzzing over the tied Test in Brisbane, the Australia–West Indies circus moved south for the second Test. The MCG was well-attended as Australia won by seven wickets. By the time the fifth Test came round, Melbourne did itself proud with a world record attendance of 90,800 on the second day.

Above: *In the second Test, at Melbourne, left-arm spinner Johnny Martin, in his maiden Test, took three highly distinguished West Indies wickets in four balls: Kanhai, Sobers, and Worrell, seen being caught by Simpson. Hunte, the non-striker, scored 110. Above right: West Indies drew level at Sydney, Sobers scoring another beautiful century at high speed, and Alexander making 108 at No. 8. McDonald, Australia's sturdy opener, is shown surviving a return catch to the off-balance Valentine. Right: The Adelaide Test, the fourth, was drawn, but featured some attractive cricket. Rohan Kanhai finishes in the dust again as he canes a loose ball from Kline. Kanhai scored 117 and 115.*

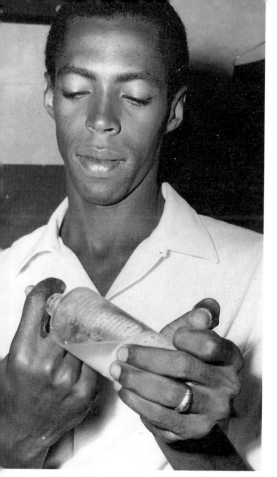

Lance Gibbs, West Indies' tall, thin offspinner, treats his recurringly sore spinning finger during the Adelaide Test, a match also remembered for the hat-trick he took in Australia's first innings.

The Adelaide Test had a drawn-out tension at the end that tore the nerves more savagely than the Brisbane tie, where everything happened so fast in the last quarter-hour. The Adelaide Test of 1960–61 saw West Indies needing one more wicket (runs were of no account) in the final 110 minutes. Ken Mackay (left) thrived on such a situation, but Lindsay Kline, his fellow left-hander, batted at No. 11 only because there was no No. 12. Even so, Wes Hall chivalrously refrained from 'bouncing' him. The overs ticked by, and at one point the West Indians were convinced they had Mackay caught. Heroically the pair stood firm through hastily-delivered overs as the clock hands seemed barely to be moving. Finally Hall bowled the last ball of the match. It lifted. Mackay let it hit him on the chest. Australia had survived.

Right: Wally Grout studies a photo of the incident which caused a hiccup in the final stages of the deciding Test at Melbourne. A bail came off, but the umpires, unable to explain it, allowed Grout to carry on batting. Australia won by two wickets – and the adored West Indians had a ticker-tape farewell through Melbourne's streets.

Left: Frank Worrell and Richie Benaud, opposing captains in the great 1960–61 series, found themselves playing for a new Australia–West Indies trophy – the Worrell Trophy – a concept dreamt up by the Australian Board, whose Sir Donald Bradman made the official presentation in Melbourne.

Above: *Bill Alley, the down-to-earth, 42-year-old Australian, survived this early-season run-out attempt by Kent's Derek Ufton to lay a foundation for an amazing season's aggregate of 3019 runs in his 64 innings in 1961. The laughing, non-stop-talking, competitive Somerset left-hander made 11 centuries, two of them satisfyingly against the Australian touring team. A quarter of a century later, because of the incursions of non-first-class limited-overs cricket, no batsman since Alley had made 3000 runs in a season.*

Graham McKenzie turned 20 during his first Test appearance for Australia, at Lord's in 1961. Gentle of nature, but a heavyweight, with a powerful, vigorous action, he took 5 for 37 in England's second innings, and in the years ahead captured his 100th, 150th and 200th Test wickets at the earliest ages then known. He later played for Leicestershire.

The first Ashes Test of 1961, at Edgbaston, found England in deep trouble, all out for 195, and conceding 516 for 9 dec to Australia. In the second innings, however, Subba Row made 112 (on his Ashes debut) and the lordly Ted Dexter (above driving Mackay) made an assertive 180.

Maurice Hallam, who in 1961 scored 203 and 143, both not out, in Leicestershire's match against Sussex at Worthing. He had scored a century and a double-century in another match two years previously, and not until Zaheer Abbas did any batsman match Hallam in this considerable feat.

With Benaud absent with a shoulder injury, Neil Harvey led Australia in the 1961 Lord's Test, in which batsmen had to cope with a 'ridge' in the pitch. Needing only 69 to win, Australia had to struggle. Harvey is caught at the wicket off Trueman. But Burge, his partner, saw the tourists home with 37 not out.

Below: Hampshire, under A. C. D. Ingleby-Mackenzie's swashbuckling captaincy, became county champions in 1961 for the first time. From the left: Peter Sainsbury, Leo Harrison, Henry Horton, Colin Ingleby-Mackenzie, Jimmy Gray, Danny Livingstone, Roy Marshall (obscured), 'Butch' White, Mike Barnard, Alan Wassell, Derek Shackleton.

451

A wealth of cricket history assembled at Lord's in 1961, the gathering organised by Rothmans. All England players, the 23 veterans played in a total of 449 Test matches between 1899 and 1957. Standing: Laurie Fishlock, Len Hopwood, George Geary, Arthur Wellard, E. W. 'Nobby' Clark, Bill Voce, Jack Durston, Bob Appleyard, George Brown, Peter Smith, E. J. 'Tiger' Smith, George Duckworth, Eric Hollies; seated: Denis Compton, Tom Goddard, Bill Hitch, J. N. Crawford, Frank Woolley, Sir Jack Hobbs, Wilfred Rhodes, S. F. Barnes, John Gunn, H. I. 'Sailor' Young.

Left: In Bill Lawry, Australia unearthed a true Test match cricketer. He scored over 2000 runs on his first tour of England, in 1961, and ground out centuries in the Tests at Lord's and Old Trafford which were the foundations upon which Australia built the two victories which ensured retention of the Ashes. As Lawry acknowledges the applause for his hundred at Old Trafford, wicketkeeper Murray and short leg Trueman join in. In the previous Test, at Headingley, on a poor pitch, Trueman's 11 wickets, including a spell of 5 for 0 with cutters at reduced pace, had brought England a levelling victory . . .

. . . but Lawry's Old Trafford century and Benaud's 6 for 70 won a match that had seemed lost. Operating round the wicket, Benaud bowled May (below) round his legs, out of the rough, for a famous duck.

Above: *Polly Umrigar played the last of his 59 Tests for India in April 1962, having compiled a record (at the time) 3631 runs for his country, with 12 centuries.*

Above: *Tragedy at Bridgetown as India's captain, Nari Contractor, is hit on the back of the skull by a bouncer from Barbados bowler Charlie Griffith in March 1962. There was a fracture, and he bled from the nose. Surgeons fought to save him, and Frank Worrell was among those who gave blood. Contractor survived but was finished with cricket as a player. The Nawab of Pataudi jnr took over as captain, the youngest ever in a Test at 21 years 77 days. Griffith was no-balled for throwing later in the fateful match. West Indies trampled all over a demoralised India, winning all five Tests, though Umrigar made a then-record 172 not out and Durani 104 in Trinidad in the fourth Test.*

Bob Barber, a batsman who switched from a stodgy style to all-out attack, sweeps during England's tour of India, who won 2–0. In Pakistan, however, England won one and drew the other two Tests, Barber (86) and Pullar (165) posting 198 for the first wicket at Dacca.

453

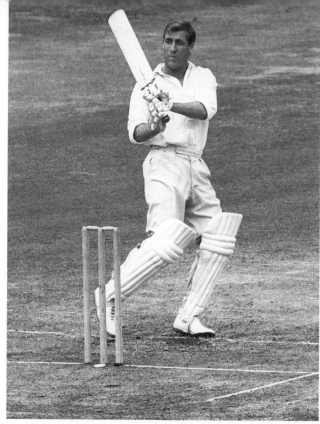

Above: *Middlesex's Norfolk-born left-hander Peter Parfitt struck a rich vein of runs soon after his Test baptism, scoring seven centuries for England between 1961–62 and 1964–65, including three in four Tests against the 1962 Pakistan team in England.*

Left: *John Reid would have been given a place in a World XI in the early 1960s. On the 1961–62 tour of South Africa, 1915 runs flowed from his bat (a South African record), and back in New Zealand in 1962–63 he belted 15 sixes, a world record, in an innings of 296 for Wellington against Northern Districts at Wellington.*

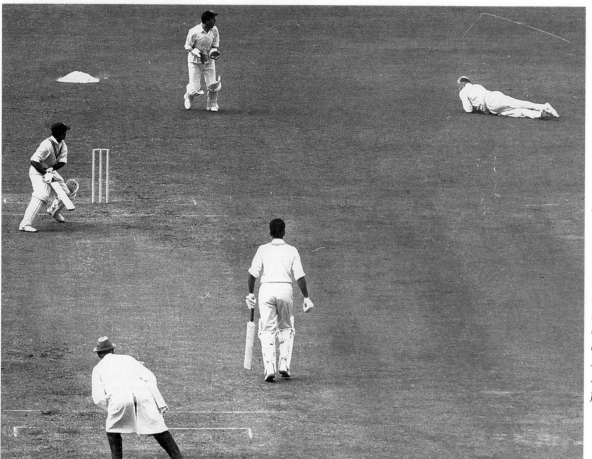

England swamped Pakistan 4–0 in the 1962 Tests. Cowdrey, Graveney, Parfitt and Dexter all scored heavily. England's fast men did the damage. At Trent Bridge Lock brought off one of his special catches to dismiss Mushtaq Mohammad for 55.

Mr and Mrs Ted Dexter, England captain and wife, in Australia, 1962–63. Susan did some modelling while her husband led England in a stalemated 1–1 series which fell some way short of what the Australian public had come to expect after the 1960–61 Australia–West Indies series.

Naturally the 1962–63 tour by MCC produced memorable moments, such as this huge hit out of the Melbourne confines by Dexter off Australian XI bowler Veivers. Dexter's partner, Cowdrey, later gave the Adelaide crowd a treat during the South Australia game by stroking 307, a new highest score for an English touring team in Australia, passing Woolley's 305 not out against Tasmania at Hobart in 1911–12.

Red faces at Perth: the 1962–63 MCC side took the field thinking that Barry Shepherd, captain of the Combined XI, would bat upon winning the toss. He didn't. He put MCC in and got them out for 157. Lock, who had missed selection for the tour, joined Western Australia, and took 3 for 36. Combined XI won by 10 wickets, Bob Simpson scoring 109 and 66 not out, useful additions to a personal aggregate that was to touch 1000 by December 22, the earliest date ever in an Australian season.

Left: *Nineteen-year-old Ian Chappell hits his wicket in trying to evade a short one from Brian Statham in South Australia's match against MCC in 1962–63. Neil Hawke is the other batsman.*

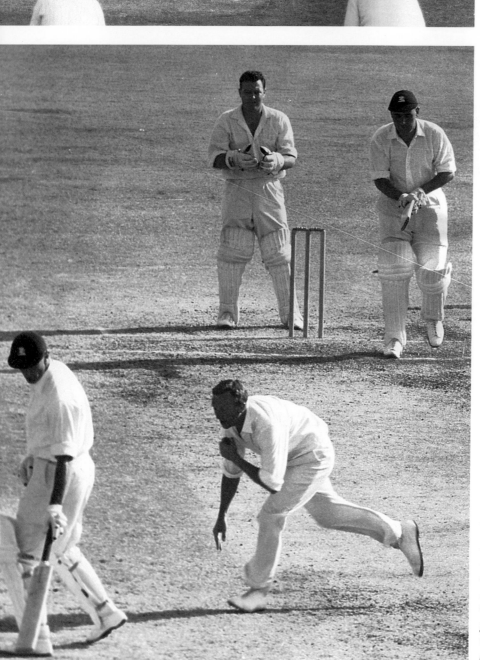

Two old ladies at the cricket. But their names are redolent of immortality. On the left is Anne, longtime widow of Victor Trumper, and her companion is Clara, sister of Charlie Macartney, and the last survivor of the family.

Left: *Cowdrey caught-and-bowled by Benaud for 9 in the first Test of the 1962–63 series, at Brisbane, and England have to be careful to get a draw out of it. Dexter (this end) got 99, and the match was inconclusive. Australia's grip on the game was earned by Brian Booth, who made a century here and in the next Test, and Lawry (98), Mackay (86 not out), with half-centuries from Simpson, O'Neill, Harvey, Burge and Benaud.*

One hundred and one years on, the first English tour match is jocularly re-enacted on the same Melbourne ground where the H. H. Stephenson's XI v XVIII of Victoria match was staged in January 1862: much had changed and much had stayed the same.

Left: *England won the second Test, at Melbourne, to go one up, and this seemed to be the winning run. David Sheppard (113) puts his head down and charges past Cowdrey. But Lawry at backward point threw straight, and 'The Reverend' left the field alone, the winning runs coming right afterwards.*

John Murray, given his chance behind the stumps for England in the third Test, at Sydney, damaged his shoulder in catching Lawry

down the leg side. There was nothing for it but to catch up on some reading in the motel, though he bravely batted in the second innings, surviving painfully for 100 minutes (above) and somehow making 3 not out. Titmus, Murray's Middlesex team-mate, offspun his way to the best figures of the match (7 for 79), but Australia won by eight wickets.

457

Right: *In the Adelaide Test of 1962–63, the faithful fast man Brian Statham overhauled Alec Bedser's world Test record of 236 wickets. His captain, Dexter, and colleague-in-arms Fred Trueman know full well how much toil and effort went into the achievement.*

Left: *Neil Harvey, in his last series, hit 154 at Adelaide, though twice in two balls he was missed off Illingworth (here by Cowdrey) and again soon afterwards. He put on 194 with O'Neill, and ended his shining career with 6149 Test runs and 21 centuries.*

Below: *Dexter is caught by the tumbling Simpson wide at slip off Benaud, and England are in jeopardy on the last afternoon at Adelaide. But Barrington (132 not out) and Graveney saw their side safely to the draw.*

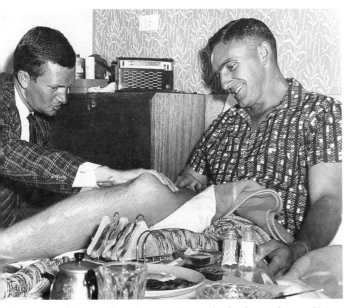

A concerned Australian skipper, Benaud, checks on the condition of his prime allrounder, Alan Davidson, after an injury had prevented him from bowling after a few overs in the 1962–63 Adelaide Test. Davidson (24 wickets at 20) was Australia's best bowler in this as in so many other series, but Benaud had often to cajole the fast left-armer for 'just one more big effort'. Right: Sir Donald Bradman, now 54, came out of retirement to lead the Prime Minister's XI against MCC at Canberra on February 6, 1963. He played-on to a ball from Statham for only 4, to huge widespread disappointment. Sir Donald went through the formality of a toss with Dexter.

A little goodwill never did any harm: MCC players Tom Graveney and Alan Smith join in an informal match with some Melbourne youngsters. Smith, of the peculiar wicketkeeping gait, played in four Tests in Australia and two in New Zealand afterwards, featuring in a stand of 163 (unbroken) with Cowdrey at Wellington, a then-world record in Tests for the ninth wicket. Right: Australia had only to draw the final Test of 1962–63, at Sydney, and duly did so. Davidson was back to his fiery best, here troubling Ray Illingworth in the first innings. The Yorkshireman was drafted as an opener in the second.

Ken Barrington cuts McKenzie during the last Test of 1962–63. He made 101 and 94 at Sydney, batting with bulldog determination and awesome concentration. Barrington had become the rock upon which English batting existed in the early 1960s.

A. G. 'Johnny' Moyes at the ABC microphone with Ray Lindwall. Moyes, a fine batsman at Sheffield Shield level before the First World War, became an authoritative voice on radio, and wrote a number of books on the game. He died suddenly in January 1963, aged 70.

Major Rowland Bowen, who started The Cricket Quarterly in January 1963, later described it as 'the only scholarly, literary, artistic, historical and statistical magazine on any sport or game, save chess'. Unquestionably erudite, it ran for seven years. Bowen then produced a revolutionary history of cricket's development, one of its predictions being that the game would dwindle to a juvenile pastime.

THE NEW FORMULA

IN 1963, Sir Pelham Warner died in January, Sir Jack Hobbs in December, both having lived long enough to hear of the abolition, after the 1962 Gentlemen v Players match, of the distinction between amateurs and professionals. Henceforth all English cricketers would be 'players', with none having his initials appended to a different side of his name to another. The practical needs of the wage-earner in the second half of the 20th century had at last been acknowledged. Overnight the 'shamateur', the Varsity type who was given a sinecure to maintain his amateur status, ceased to exist. It was hoped that more young players might be attracted to the English first-class game, which now, against the wishes of traditionalists, allowed the appendage of limited-overs one-day county cricket to be attached. With all its new rhythms and demands, the new, truncated game perplexed many, but did at least delight those who fostered it by attracting sizable crowds and, most convincingly, drawing a sellout at Lord's for the first Gillette Cup final, on September 7, 1963. In the year of the 100th edition of *Wisden Cricketers' Almanack* and a knighthood for Frank Worrell (New Year Honours 1964), the game of old had suddenly been pushed some distance forward, and hurriedly. The front-foot no-ball Law was to keep bowlers a proper distance from the batsmen, but fast men like Hall and Griffith were still lethal with no sightscreens behind them. If this shortcoming was a throwback to the 19th century, a feature of the old game which was dying before cricket's very eyes was the part entertainingly played by the legspinner. With regulation 75-yard boundaries and dead pitches, he became an anachronism – most markedly in the 'new' game, the one-day match which brought in lifesaving cash through sponsorship and transfusions at the turnstiles.

Frank Woolley presents a Gillette Cup Man of the Match award (one of many new concepts cricket needed to accept) to Northants batsman Roger Prideaux after his side's victory over Warwickshire in the first-ever full round of matches, May 22, 1963.

C. L. R. James, the Trinidadian political and cricket writer, published Beyond a Boundary *in 1963, a book of some profundity which gives a legitimate insight into West Indian cricket, and places the game in general into perspective.*

Lord's is many things, one of its functions being to serve from time to time as a laboratory for experiment. When Lindwall bowled with a smaller ball and swung it like a boomerang the conclusion was obvious. Now, the famous Trevor Bailey forward defensive is being used in the experiment, in 1963, with four stumps and the old lbw Law whereby a ball needed to have pitched between wicket and wicket. Derek Shackleton was the ideal 'pinpoint' bowler.

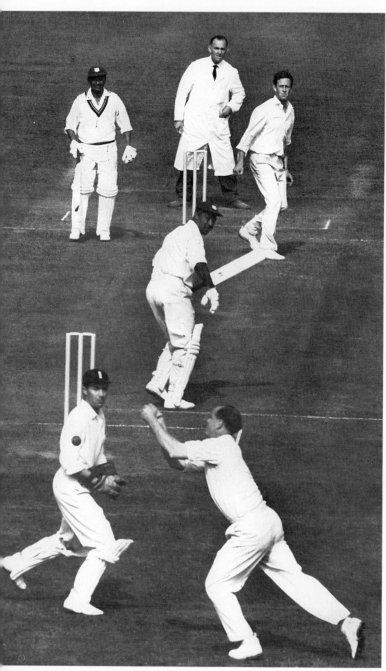

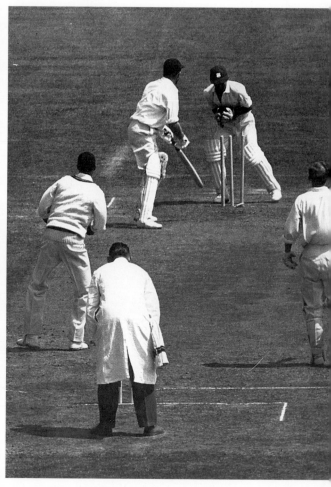

Above: *Ken Barrington has been bowled by West Indies offspinner Lance Gibbs in the opening Test of 1963, at Old Trafford, and England edge nearer to an innings defeat. The other batsman is Micky Stewart, who top-scored for England with 87. Left: Frank Worrell, West Indies' captain, made 74 not out in his side's 501 for 6 dec (Hunte 182, Kanhai 90) and here enjoys a let-off from Close off Statham. The non-striker is Solomon, hero of the Brisbane tied Test, and England's wicketkeeper is Keith Andrew.*

The Nawab of Pataudi, India's young captain, dons his Sussex sweater and hits Lancashire's Ken Higgs through the covers at Hove. 'Tiger' Pataudi, captain of Oxford this season of 1963, scored 153 for the University against his father's old county, Worcestershire, showing little reaction to the loss of sight in one eye in a car crash.

Right: Colin Cowdrey's forearm is broken by a ball from Wes Hall in the dramatic Lord's Test of 1963. He returned, arm in plaster, with Hall to bowl the last two balls to David Allen, and with England six runs from victory. Not for the first time, Worrell found himself yelling above the crowd's din to warn Hall not to bowl a no-ball . . .

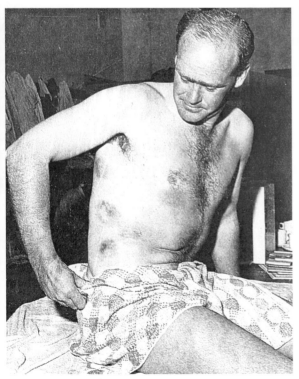

. . . but this time there was to be no tie. Allen survived, and the contest ended in a thrilling draw, a result not possible in the new limited-overs variety of the game. Left: Brian Close, with a bold, charging 70, had taken England to the threshold of victory, his price a tender selection of bruises as Griffith and Hall hit him yards down the pitch. Dexter had also played a remarkable innings, his first-innings 70 being a flashing exhibition of strokeplay against fierce bowling.

463

Stewart lbw Sobers 39, Edgbaston 1963. The supreme allrounder could be lethal with the swinging new ball. England drew level here, Trueman following his 11 for 152 at Lord's with 12 for 119. But West Indies found their touch again at Headingley, making runs (Sobers 102) and Griffith and Gibbs bagging 16 of the wickets.

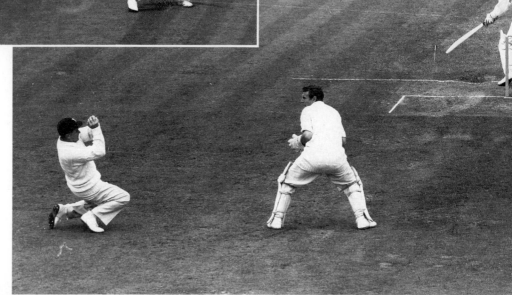

Right: *Phil Sharpe of Yorkshire, one of the safest of slip catchers, holds a fast one from Sobers at Edgbaston, where West Indies were dispatched for 186 and 91 in a moist atmosphere.*

There must be some sort of future in this game! And there was for Harold 'Dickie' Bird, whose middle stump is sent cartwheeling by Sobers in the West Indians' match at Leicester. From Yorkshire and then Leicestershire as a player, Bird became the best-known of Test umpires.

Three promising Yorkshire lads pose proudly for the Yorkshire Post *after being awarded their county caps in 1963: Geoffrey Boycott, future England batsman, Tony Nicholson, seam bowler, and John Hampshire, whose batting won him eight Test caps that might have been so many more.*

Tex Dexter is caught behind off Sobers in the final Test at The Oval, wicketkeeper Deryck Murray moving nearer to an impressive 24 dismissals in his maiden Test series. England failed to hold West Indies when they set out to get 253 for victory. Kanhai made 77 and Conrad Hunte's unbeaten 108 saw them home. **Above right:** When it was all over, the captains, Dexter and Worrell, were interviewed by Peter West on BBC TV's Sportsview. It could now be seen that the fatherly and shrewd Worrell – who was to die from leukaemia only 3½ years later – had moulded a powerful West Indies team together, free of the old interterritorial infighting and jealousy, and strong on motivation.

Dexter's consolation for losing the Test series 1–3 was Sussex's winning of the first Gillette Cup when they beat Worcestershire at Lord's by 14 runs. (And they then beat the West Indians in a one-day challenge match.) From the left: Les Lenham, Jim Parks, Alan Oakman, Graham Cooper, Dexter, Richard Langridge, Ken Suttle, Tony Buss (obscured), Ian Thomson, Don Bates, John Snow. .

R. G. Nadkarni bowled 131 balls without conceding a run in India's match against England at Madras, when the visitors were reduced by illness, and fighting to occupy the crease. The slow left-armer finished with figures of 32–27–5–0, and actually headed India's batting for the series with 98.00, thanks to a century and five not-out innings. The series ended in five drawn Tests, India scoring seven centuries to England's four. Titmus's skill brought him 27 wickets. Below: Salim Durani aims a sweep at England slow left-arm bowler Don Wilson during his innings of 90 at Bombay, when he put on 153 with Borde for India's seventh wicket.

Bob Simpson, back with NSW after five high-scoring seasons with Western Australia, continued to realise his teenage promise at Shield level, scoring 359 for NSW against Queensland at Brisbane in 10½ hours, and 247 not out against Western Australia at Sydney in the next match, and 135 against Victoria at Melbourne at Christmas, all in the season of 1963–64. But at 28 he had yet to score a Test century. The barrier was to be broken down with a vengeance in England in 1964.

The world well beyond the cricket field was shocked and disfigured by the killing of US President John F. Kennedy on November 22, 1963. The South Africans were playing NSW when the news came through just after dawn on the second day, and both teams lined up in grief and respect before play began.

The cricket world was stunned in its own fashion when Australian fast bowler Ian Meckiff was no-balled for throwing in the first Test against South Africa, at Brisbane in December 1963. Umpire Colin Egar (seen below with police escort after he had received threats) called Meckiff four times, and he bowled no further, leaving big cricket, aggrieved and perplexed.

Below left: In the third Test, at Sydney, the big right arm of Graham McKenzie is in evidence again as he bowls John Waite comprehensively. In this Test, South African Graeme Pollock, not yet 20, scored a lovely 122.

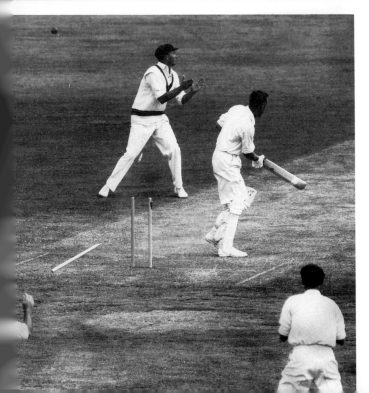

467

Above: *Richie Benaud leaves the Test field for the last time, Sydney, February 1964, having established a reputation for shrewd and driving captaincy matched by few. He had handed over the leadership to Simpson in the second Test. Benaud's spin bowling had set an Australian record of 248 Test wickets, alongside which went 2201 runs and 65 catches.*

Top left: *Brian Booth, a batsman of near-classical method, scored a century in the first and fifth Tests against South Africa, but fell at Adelaide to wicketkeeper Lindsay for 58.*
Middle left: *In catching Tony Pithey at Adelaide, Grout overtook Oldfield's Australian record of 130 dismissals.*
Left: *The Adelaide Test saw a wonderful stand of 341 between Eddie Barlow (201) (in cap) and Graeme Pollock (second from right), who made 175. Barlow's double-century made him only the third South African to top that mark against Australia. Trevor Goddard (left), the captain, and Peter van der Merwe help the tired but exhilarated young men commemorate the stand, which enabled the Springboks to draw the series.*

Trent Bridge, Old Clarke's ground from way back, almost full in 1964, the England v Australia series under way.

Above: *Early in the match, Neil Hawke, the Australian bowler, accidentally knocked Fred Titmus, England's makeshift opener, off his feet. Boycott, in his maiden Test innings, was safe, but Titmus would have been run out had not Grout chivalrously held the ball when it came to him.* **Left:** *Tense moments early in the Australian innings as Flavell has hit Lawry's pad and Barrington gathers the rebound. Rain spoiled the match, as it did the next at Lord's.*

Right: *Modern microphones set into the turf might have enlightened the audience as to Phil Sharpe's comment as he inadvertently pops the ball back to Australia's Tom Veivers in the 1964 Trent Bridge Test. Umpire Syd Buller remains as expressionless as ever.* Below: *Veivers in the action again as he hooks Flavell straight into the safe hands of fearless Fred Trueman. While this was not one of the most distinguished Ashes series, it had its moments.*

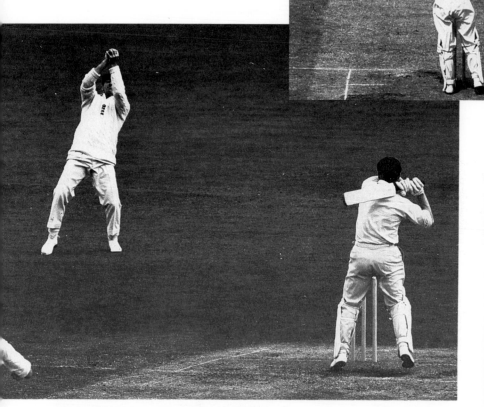

Below: *At Lord's, John Edrich scored 120 in his maiden Ashes Test innings. Peter Burge extends a warm handshake.*

Arnold Long became the first wicketkeeper to hold 11 catches in a match (seven in the first innings) when he achieved this for Surrey against Sussex at Hove in 1964.

Australia broke the deadlock at Headingley, Burge hitting a McCabe-like 160, with many strokes like this, particularly off Trueman's short stuff. Titmus took 6 for 94 in the match off 77 overs, and Dexter was flayed for taking him off at 187 for 7 and calling for the new ball. Aided by Hawke and Grout, Burge doubled the score, and England lost control of the match thereafter. Australia won by seven wickets.

The luck without which no cricketer can go too far: Bob Simpson is run out, but given not out, in the Old Trafford Test, and his opening stand with Lawry can continue. It reached 201, a new Australian record against England, and Simpson made sure of his first Test century with a score of 311 in 762 minutes. His side made 656 for 8 dec, and the Ashes were safe. England's reply contained 256 from Barrington – his 10th Test century but first at home – and 174 from Dexter. Veivers toiled through 95.1 overs.

Continental cricket goes on keenly: Holland are playing Denmark at Aalborg in 1964. When the Australians called in at The Hague they were beaten, to the amazement of the outside world.

The Oval, Saturday, August 15, 1964, and Trueman's quest for his 300th Test wicket is over at last. He had Hawke cheerfully caught by Cowdrey, and in his 65th Test the controversial Yorkshireman with the mop of jet-black hair had broken through cricket's equivalent of the four-minute mile.

Left: Nineteen-year-old Derek Underwood receives his county cap from his Kent captain, Colin Cowdrey. The phenomenal left-arm spinner took 9 for 28 at Hastings this summer, and had 1000 wickets at the age of 25.

Further celebrations, this time at Worcester, August 25, 1964. For the first time in their history Worcestershire have become county champions. Captain Don Kenyon (right) scored a century in this clinching match (he made 74 in his career), and Graveney (in towel) scored 2271 runs in the Championship, as well as his 100th hundred.

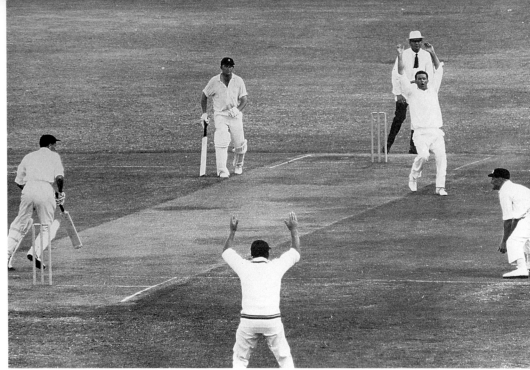

In 1964–65 England toured South Africa – for the last time before political isolation descended on cricket in that country. England won the first Test at Durban, and drew the other four. In the opening contest, in which Barrington and Parks made centuries for England, captain caught captain (above), Trevor Goddard having played Price to Mike Smith at short leg.

Left: *Possibly a world record for altitude: M. L. Jaisimha of India has lost his grip, and Australia's wicketkeeper, Jarman, watches the orbiting bat with some trepidation. India won this Bombay Test in October 1964 by two wickets to share the three-match series.*

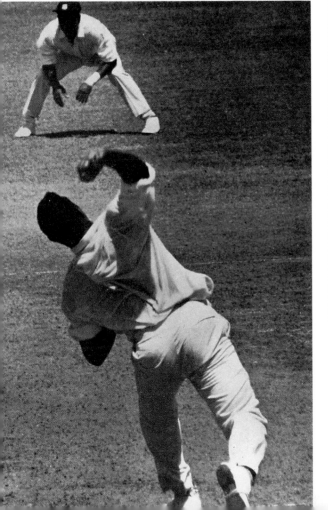

Above: *West Indies batsman Jackie Hendriks has been seriously hurt by a McKenzie bouncer to the head, Bridgetown 1965. The irony was that Griffith of West Indies (and the suspect action – see left) had been the fast bowler causing most concern. Several Australian players branded him as a 'chucker', which made Simpson and Lawry's stand here of 382 the more meritorious.*

Not much left of Lancashire's Geoff Pullar's wicket after Ron Hooker of Middlesex had finished with it in the Championship match in 1965.

Rohan Kanhai (121) gets under a pull off Philpott in the last West Indies v Australia Test of 1965. It came as a surprise when the tourists, two down, pulled one back, bowling West Indies out for 131 (Hunte carrying his bat for 60) and going on to win by 10 wickets.

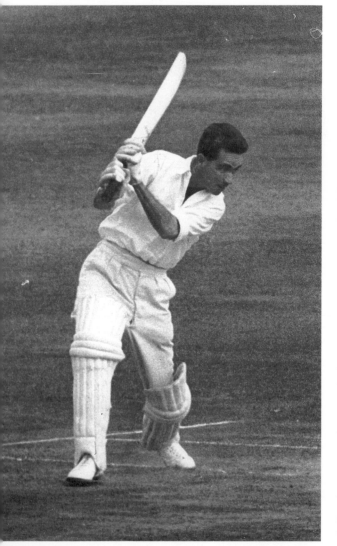

Above: Herbert Sutcliffe (second from left), now 70, scorer of 16 centuries for England and with the high Test average of 60.73, sees commemorative gates in his name at Headingley being officially opened in 1965 by his former Yorkshire captain Sir William Worsley (left). Sutcliffe scored 149 centuries in a first-class career which spanned the between-the-wars period. He died in 1978, aged 83.

Left: Leicestershire's Ceylon-born Clive Inman, who hit a half-century in the world record time of eight minutes at Trent Bridge in 1965. Notts were bowling for a declaration, rendering this entry less than serious.

There has never been a better fieldsman than Colin Bland, a Rhodesian who played in 21 Tests for South Africa, averaging 49.09 with the bat, with three centuries, and not only running out many opponents but saving countless runs by his very lethal presence in the field. He actually had lengthy regular fielding practice sessions, and could hit a stump with astonishing frequency. In 1964–65 he became the first South African to score 1000 runs in a home season. Rothmans' calendar photograph conveys some of Bland's athleticism.

Northants captain and wicketkeeper Keith Andrew effects a characteristically neat and balanced – if unusual – catch to dismiss Bob White of Middlesex in 1965. Andrew would have played for England many more times than twice, but, as they never tired of saying, 'he couldn't bat'.

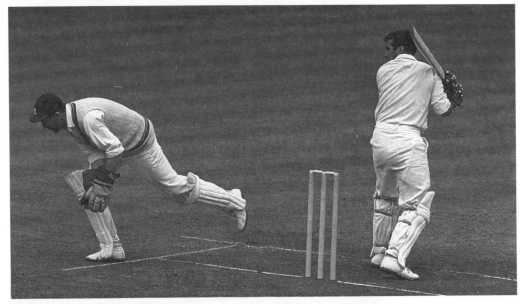

Bespectacled Geoff Boycott cast aside his stodgy image in the 1965 Gillette Cup final, scoring 146 with an array of strokes. Yorkshire tore 317 runs out of the Surrey bowling in 60 overs, and won the cup. This batting outburst by Boycott was often referred to in later years.

475

John Edrich drives New Zealand's Brian Yuile at Headingley in 1965. He finished with 310 not out, having hit the highest number of boundaries (57) ever in a Test innings. The closure is imminent, and Parfitt, another of Norfolk birth, is with him. Earlier Edrich had put on 369 for the second wicket with Ken Barrington (163), who had been dropped after the Edgbaston Test for taking so long over his 137 (437 minutes), going scoreless at one stage through 20 overs.

Left: *Little room for manoeuvre as the slash is played just over ace Glamorgan fielder Peter Walker's sun-hat. Wicketkeeper is future Test umpire David Evans.*

Below: *Never forgetting the little 'uns: the lads of a Cricklewood and a Shoreditch school battle out the final of the Middlesex CCC Junior Cup on Lord's sacred turf.*

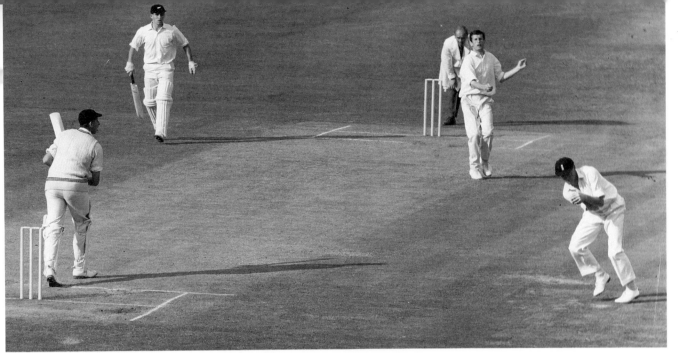

M. J. K. Smith missed very little at short leg, and here he bags New Zealander Bruce Taylor's wicket for Sussex fast bowler John Snow, playing at Lord's in his first Test, June 1965. Vic Pollard is the non-striker.

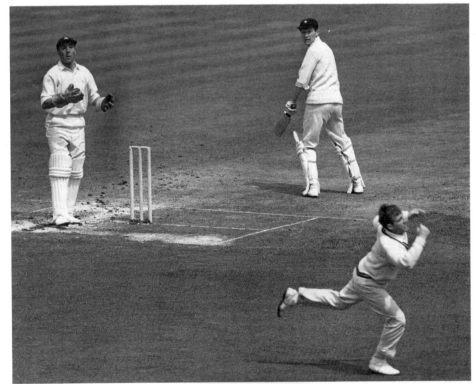

Peter Parfitt made a name for himself as an agile fieldsman who missed next to nothing. With this unexpected catch he got rid of Kent's Mike Denness for Middlesex while his wicketkeeper and conversation companion, John Murray, looks on knowing he will not be disappointed.

Lord's had never known cricket on a Sunday until one Sabbath in 1965, when MCC permitted a charity match between Middlesex and the Lord's Taverners, proceeds going to the Middlesex Centenary Youth Trust and the National Playing Fields Association.

477

R. C. Robertson-Glasgow, who died by his own hand in March 1965, was a fast bowler for Oxford and Somerset who once took 9 for 38 at Lord's for his county. He wrote about cricket with an instinctive insight into technique and personality, and much good humour.

Having dispatched New Zealand in all three Tests in 1965, England found South Africa a stronger proposition in this first summer of twin tours.
Above: Boycott beaten by slow left-arm bowler McKinnon at Trent Bridge. England lost by 94 runs.

South Africa have won at Trent Bridge, and happy skipper van der Merwe leads his men off to the celebrations. Behind him are Ali Bacher, Jackie Botten, Atholl McKinnon, Colin Bland, Richard Dumbrill, Graeme Pollock and Denis Lindsay. Pollock's 125 off 145 balls was considered one of the finest innings ever seen on this ground. His brother, fast bowler Peter, contributed just as strongly with match figures of 10 for 87.

The chorus looks positive, and Eddie Barlow is out, lbw to the recalled Statham at The Oval in the final Test of the 1965 summer. England, desperate to draw level in the series, shot South Africa out for 208, Graeme Pollock this time giving no trouble, being deceived by Titmus (below) for 12. Peter Pollock (5 for 43) then got rid of England for 202. Bland now made a vital century, and time and the weather frustrated England (308 for 4) at the end.

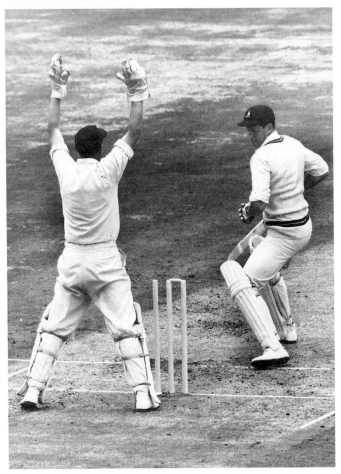

David Brown, England's new fast bowler from Warwickshire, gets one through Lindsay in the Oval Test. Bacher can scarcely believe what he has seen. But soon the South Africans were free to celebrate only their second series victory in England, the first having been 30 years previously. And now the political door was about to shut on the cricketers from the Cape as far as tours to and from England were concerned.

Hong Kong Cricket Club, 1965, with skyscrapers all around and the harbour beyond. Ten years later the inevitable came to pass: development of the site and a move to Wongneichong.

Peter Allan, Queensland fast bowler, played only once for Australia, against England at Brisbane in December 1965, but showed the selectors what they were missing by taking all 10 of Victoria's wickets at Melbourne for 61 early in January. He failed to take a wicket in the second innings, Victoria making 387 for 7 to win after an opening stand of 213 by Redpath and Watson.

There were seven totals beyond 400 in the 1965–66 Ashes series, four by Australia, for whom Bill Lawry always seemed to be batting. At Melbourne, in the second Test, the Australian opener touched one round the corner for Mike Smith, England's captain, to hold the catch mantis-like. Lawry's partner, Burge, went on to make 120, and the bowler, Bob Barber, had an exceptional innings coming up in the next Test, at Sydney – 185 off 272 balls, putting on 234 with Boycott.

Bob Cowper shattered many records in scoring 307 for Australia at Melbourne in the final Test. It was the first Test triple-century in Australia, and the longest innings played in Australia (727 minutes). It made the Ashes safe for his side, shutting England out after they had made 485 for 9 dec. Behind Cowper, who later became a highly successful businessman, comes John Edrich, who scored two hundreds for England in the series.

Doug Walters (second from right) became almost as famous for his card-playing as his gifted batting. When play was held up through rain in the fifth Test of 1965–66, at Melbourne, Walters could look back on an exceptional introduction to Test cricket, having scored 155 at Brisbane and 115 at Melbourne in his first two Tests. His first century was scored at 19 years 357 days: only Harvey and Jackson among Australians had been younger. Walters' companions at the card table are Veivers, Burge and Ian Chappell.

Ted English, who played for Hampshire at the turn of the century, celebrates his 102nd birthday on January 1, 1966. Already he had passed his best first-class score: 98. He died eight months later.

Ted Clark of Middlesex snicks Somerset's Fred Rumsey past desperately diving Terry Barwell, June 1966. Clark's 95 not out saw his side home by six wickets. Rumsey took 100 wickets this season.

The shy young giant from New Zealand is Bruce Taylor, who has raced to a century on his first Test appearance. The left-hander made 105 at Calcutta in March 1965, and took five Indian wickets in their first innings. Bert Sutcliffe, who scored 151 not out, leads the applause.

Below: Harold Rhodes, the Derbyshire fast bowler, who had played twice for England in 1959, bowls at Lord's before an MCC 'jury', who also saw films and heard medical evidence during a four-hour enquiry in March 1966. Rhodes's basic action was considered fair, but he was deemed to be 'occasionally suspect'. He carried on bowling for Derbyshire, but never played Test cricket again.

Conrad Hunte brought welcome stability to the top of West Indies' batting order, averaging 45 in his 44 Tests. He got the 1966 campaign in England off to a good start with 135 at Old Trafford, here hooking Welshman Jeff Jones.

Jones drops another one short, and West Indies captain Garry Sobers is quickly onto it, hitting it for four, nearer to his final 161 which launched a sequence of four truly marvellous Tests for him in which further scores of 163 not out, 94 and 174, all from the No. 6 berth, set up three West Indies victories and turned the Lord's Test into a draw from seemingly certain defeat. He also took 17 wickets in these four matches – and held some fine short-leg catches.

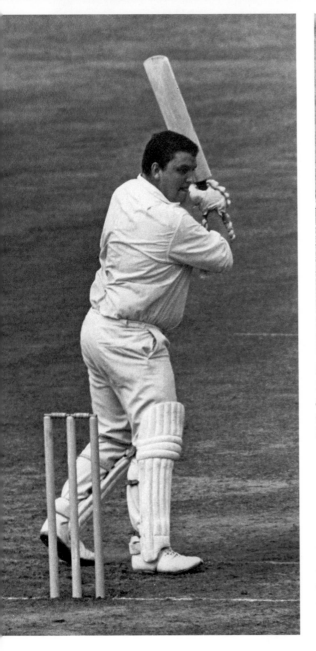

Boycott ducks from trouble in the Lord's Test against West Indies, 1966, a wise reaction to Hall's bouncers if one can get down fast enough and the ball kicks high as expected. Hall's fast-bowling ally Griffith waits threateningly at short leg. Boycott went on to 60, and England to a promising first-innings lead of 86.

Left: Colin 'Ollie' Milburn had a good start in Test cricket, making 94 on debut at Old Trafford after having been smilingly run out for a duck. Then, at Lord's, the hefty Northants opener saw England to safety in the fourth innings with a hearty unbeaten 126 full of thumping drives and hooks. His advent as a Test batsman was the most refreshing thing for an age.

Sobers applauds his cousin David Holford in at Lord's after the 1966 Test had been snatched back from England by this pair. In their second innings West Indies were 95 for 5, nine runs ahead, when Holford, in his second Test match, joined Sobers (who had been missed early at slip). No further wicket fell. They had added 274 when Sobers declared, and England – mainly Milburn – played out the draw.

Right: *Basil D'Oliveira, the underprivileged Cape Coloured who, in cricketing middle age, climbed through English league and county cricket, won an England place in 1966, and brought strong middle-order batsmanship and steady medium-pace bowling to the side.*

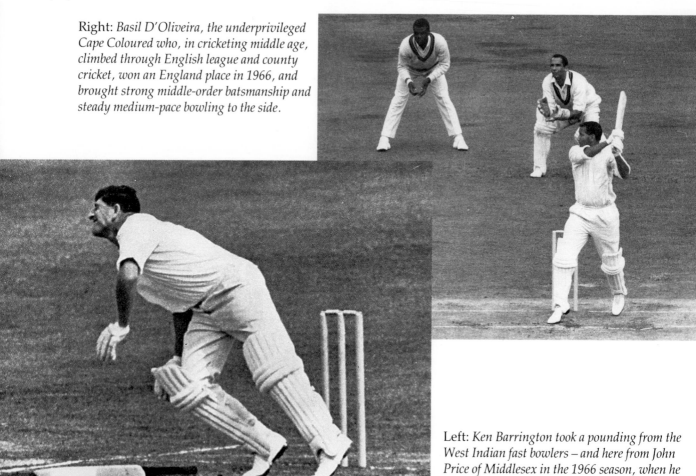

Left: *Ken Barrington took a pounding from the West Indian fast bowlers – and here from John Price of Middlesex in the 1966 season, when he was left out of the Test team after two matches because physical and mental strain had caught up with him.*

484

Derek Underwood, England's No. 11, collapses after being hit in the teeth by a short one from Griffith, and wicketkeeper Hendriks, himself recently so seriously injured, can scarcely look. West Indies needed one wicket for victory, duly obtained, with well over 100 runs between the two sides. Underwood recovered – and made a 'pair' in the next Test.

The rapacious Rohan Kanhai hooks Snow at Headingley, where West Indies went 3–0 ahead with an innings victory. They were no fun to bowl to: Nurse and Sobers made centuries here; Basil Butcher had made 209 not out at Trent Bridge; and Kanhai was to score 104 at The Oval.

Goodbye to a beloved landmark: the old Tavern and clocktower at Lord's are demolished in the autumn of 1966. The new Tavern, by the Grace Gates, was opened in June 1967 and the ambitious new Tavern stand a year later.

Snow and Higgs after their tenth-wicket stand of 128 in the Oval Test. Officials hastily replaced the beer-glasses with teacups, fearful lest cricket be seen in the wrong light.

England found her Messiah in Brian Close, who replaced Cowdrey as captain for the 1966 Oval Test. Sobers won his fifth toss, but West Indies made only 268. England responded with 527, Graveney scoring 165, Murray 112, Higgs (No. 10) 63, and Snow (No. 11) 59 not out. The last three England wickets added 361. Close then managed his bowling skilfully again – and caught Sobers close-in first ball off Snow – to complete an innings victory which did much to wipe away the humiliating memories of '66.

Bacher smartly catches Cowper in the Transvaal v Australians match of 1966–67, the first-ever Australian match to be lost on South African soil.

Cricket pictures don't come much uglier than this. During West Indies' tour of India in 1966–67, the Calcutta authorities oversold the seated accommodation, and on the second day disgruntled spectators, also suspecting forged tickets, took to stoning the police, setting fire to awnings and gouging the pitch. The West Indians fled the ground. They were coaxed into resuming play on the third day, the Indians rendered willing by a bonus offer.

486

Left: *The highest score by a woman was recorded by Jan Molyneaux, who made 298 for Olympic v Northcote in Melbourne's A grade final in 1967.*

Right: *Denis Lindsay played a big part in South Africa's 3–1 home victory over Australia, scoring 606 runs (three centuries) and taking 24 catches behind the stumps. Pollock hit two centuries, one a double, and Procter made a successful Test debut.*

Right: *India's first shared tour of England was a sad experience for them as they lost all three Tests. At Headingley, Boycott made a tedious 246 not out and was subsequently dropped, and Pataudi made 64 and a charming 148. But the Indian captain's luck did not hold at Lord's, where Murray held him off Brown for 5, one of the keeper's six catches in the innings.*

An exotic variation of cricket is played by the women of New Caledonia, where there are subtle differences, though the principles and aims are similar to those of the mainstream game. The missionaries brought cricket here, as to so many outposts.

487

Some of them looking like soldiers out of uniform, some perhaps even revealing a touch of boredom, a committeeroomful of county cricketers sits listening to the findings of the Clark Report at Lord's in the spring of 1967. The report examined the structure of the county game and made recommendations. But on the whole its findings were ignored. This year the Cricketers' Association was formed, giving the players, in effect, their own union. And soon overseas players would be allowed to sign for counties – on an unrestricted basis.

Pakistan fared little better than India in England in 1967, losing two Tests and drawing the first, at Lord's. Hanif Mohammad batted for nine hours for 187 not out, some of the runs coming from boundaries – 21 of them – and some from pushes such as this past England skipper Brian Close.

Pakistan soon in trouble again at the start of the second Test: Javed Burki lbw to Arnold for 1 at Trent Bridge, where England won by 10 wickets. New wicketkeeper Alan Knott seems pleased.

He's done it again: Barrington comes home for another Test century, this one at Trent Bridge being one of three by him in the three Tests against Pakistan in 1967. The bowler is Ibadulla, the keeper Wasim Bari.

England won the Oval Test, but Pakistan somehow took the honours. Sixty-five for 8 in their second innings, and still 159 behind, they eventually made 255, Intikhab Alam (left) scoring 51 and Asif Iqbal a dazzling 146. They put on a record 190 for the ninth wicket.

Yorkshire were in the middle of another hat-trick of Championships. They leave the field at Harrogate at the end of 1967 with the title safe: Fred Trueman, Don Wilson, Brian Close, Ray Illingworth, Phil Sharpe, Doug Padgett, Ken Taylor. Note the plaster on Close's brave forehead.

489

A batsman of patent class toured England with the 1967 Pakistan team. Majid Khan, son of pre-war Indian player Jehangir Khan, attracted extra attention with an innings against Glamorgan (which county he joined the following year) of 147 which included 13 sixes, second only to John Reid's 15. In a long and varied career Majid made over 27,000 runs, with 73 centuries, one of them before lunch in a Test.

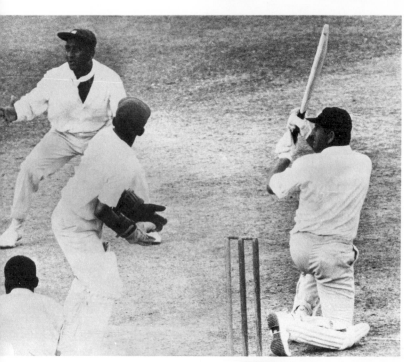

Above: Ken Barrington made 143 in the opening Test of the 1967–68 West Indies v England series, at Port-of-Spain, his fourth century in four Tests. West Indies hung on for a draw. Above right: Sobers lbw to Snow (a shooter) first ball, and West Indies in deep trouble again in the second Test, at Kingston. Right: And then, on the fourth day, trouble of a different kind. England captain Cowdrey goes to try to quell the crowd demonstration.

Cowdrey and Sobers could do little in the face of an angry Sabina Park crowd, whose disappointment at Butcher's dismissal expressed itself in violence. The police tried to end it with teargas, but forgot to check the wind direction. John Snow's photograph from within the England dressing-room shows the gas clouds coming. When play was eventually resumed, England had lost their momentum, Sobers made a superlative century, and in an extra 75 minutes' play tacked on as a sixth day, England found themselves having to hang on.

Left: *Graveney strokes his way towards 55 in the third Test, yet another draw. He had made a century in the first Test. Here at Bridgetown, Edrich made 146. The one result came in the fourth Test, at Port-of-Spain, after Sobers declared with little to gain, and paid the price. Cowdrey, who made 148 and 71, was leading England because the 1967 Test captain, Brian Close, had been found guilty of time-wasting in a county match at Edgbaston, and characteristically had refused to apologise.*

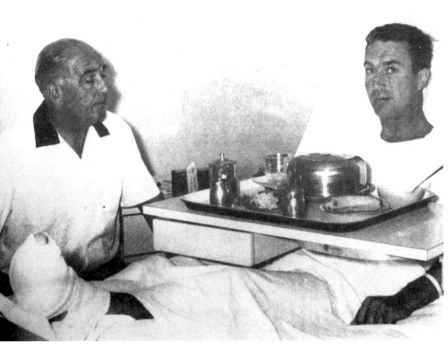

Left: *England vice-captain Fred Titmus hospitalised in Barbados after losing four toes in a boating accident before the third Test. MCC manager Les Ames is at the bedside. Tony Lock was flown in from Western Australia as replacement.*

Australia won all four Tests when India visited in 1967–68, Cowper and Simpson each scoring two centuries, Ian Chappell and Lawry one each, and Walters averaging 127 for 254 runs. Jaisimha scored India's only hundred, though Wadekar (above) came close with 99 at Melbourne. He has just edged Renneberg between Jarman and skipper Simpson (who advanced his Test aggregate past 4000 in this match).

Left: *Basil Butcher and Clive Lloyd (in cap) have just had a big partnership for Guyana against Jamaica at Georgetown in the Shell Shield in 1967, the second year of the sponsored competition. Lloyd was now a Test player, and made his first Test century in the 1967–68 series against England. A career of rare distinction lay ahead of him.*

He's done it! The cry rang out across the St Helen's ground and into the TV microphone as Garry Sobers, now, in 1968, the captain of Notts, hits the sixth ball of Glamorgan left-armer Malcolm Nash's over for six – as he had done with the preceding five balls. For the first time in a first-class match the maximum off a six-ball over had been achieved.

Graham Dowling, New Zealand's captain, scored 239 against India at Christchurch in February 1968, the highest score until then for New Zealand. His innings lasted 9¼ hours.

Planning the next campaign: Colin Cowdrey, during one of his terms as England captain, watches a county match at Lord's early in the 1968 season with former Essex captain and England batsman Doug Insole, now chairman of the panel of Test selectors.

When Australia landed in England in 1968, Johnny Gleeson was the object of special interest, his middle-finger action causing him to be regarded as a 'mystery' bowler. Arthur Fagg is the umpire.

The setting could easily be in one of a score of cricketing countries, but the somewhat unlikely identification is Staten Island. In the summer of 1968 the cricketers play on Walker Field, a nickel ferry ride from Lower Manhattan, as had previous generations for almost a century: surface of matting, outfield of long grass, and enthusiasm bubbling high.

Lawry's Australians won the first 1968 Test, at Old Trafford, but ran into trouble at Lord's, being bowled (and caught) out for 78. Knight's horizontal catch to get Walters (top-scorer with 26) was one of several special efforts.

The principal cause of the Australian collapse was a hailstorm on the first day which interrupted England's innings, which was highlighted by a rollicking 83 from Milburn. Australia followed on, but winter still hovered and they were able to escape.

With a perfect sense of occasion, Cowdrey scored a century as he became the first to play in 100 Tests. His innings in the drawn Edgbaston Test was hampered by a leg injury, and he had a runner in the latter stages.

Barry Richards, the 23-year-old batsman from South Africa, joined Hampshire for the 1968 season and scored 2395 runs (47.90), more than any other. Runs flowed from his usually immaculately straight bat with a calm fluidity, and in the 10 years ahead boredom was his greatest enemy.

If ever a washout presented itself it was the Oval scene on the final day of the 1968 series, with Australia one up and 85 for 5 at lunch when the storm came. But volunteers (below) helped the groundstaff mop up and play miraculously resumed with 75 minutes remaining.

It was attack all the way when England got out onto the field at The Oval with a chance to snatch five Australian wickets and so level the Ashes series. The breakthrough was slow in coming, but then Underwood began to exploit his favourite conditions. McKenzie (pictured) was the eighth wicket to fall, caught by Brown, and Inverarity, first in, was last out with only about four minutes remaining. Underwood finished with 7 for 50.

Right: Basil D'Oliveira, the coloured South African who earned a place in the England XI, became the central figure in a world-shaking crisis at the end of the 1968 season. Having scored 158 in the Oval Test, he found himself left out of the MCC team to tour South Africa. Then, when Tom Cartwright withdrew because of injury, D'Oliveira was selected. But when South Africa's Prime Minister Jon Vorster said D'Oliveira would not be welcome, MCC cancelled the tour. A series of events had been set in train that would culminate in South African cricket's rejection by the world's control bodies.

Bob Connolly of the Rand Daily Mail instantly struck the thematic chord when in 1968 apartheid smeared international cricket. The D'Oliveira affair had crippling effects on the game in South Africa – and complicated matters elsewhere as cricket people and outside protestors took a deeper interest in the situation in the Republic.

The first meeting of the Test and County Cricket Board, December 1968, under the chairmanship of C. G. A. Paris. The new structure placed the Cricket Council as the supreme body, the TCCB running the first-class game, the NCA minor levels, with MCC reverting to private, albeit influential, status.

Below: *Ken Barrington and wife Ann return from Australia late in 1968 after he had suffered a heart attack during a double-wicket match.*

Tom Cartwright of Warwickshire (later Somerset and Glamorgan) took his 1000th wicket during the 1968 season. A peculiarly English medium-pacer, accurate, persistent, doing a little something with each ball, he was chosen for five Tests – and once scored 210, at Nuneaton.

Right: *West Indies toured Australia in 1968–69 and, starting to fade, lost the series 1–3. Some high scores were recorded, though none by stylish Paul Sheahan (right), with whom the Australian selectors persevered throughout.*

497

NSW and Australian wicketkeeper Brian Taber on his way to a world record-equalling 12 dismissals (9 c, 3 st) in the State match against South Australia at Adelaide in 1968–69.

Right: Doug Walters was in Bradman-like form against West Indies in 1968–69, totting up 699 runs in six innings, with 242 and 103 on his home patch at Sydney in the final Test, the first instance of a double-century and century in the same Test.

When England's tour of South Africa was cancelled, they went instead to Pakistan, drawing the Tests in Lahore and Dacca, and putting a sizable total on the board at Karachi (502 for 7, Milburn 139, Graveney 105, Knott 96 not out, on the verge of his first Test century) when all was pandemonium as rioting spectators invaded the field. Knott and Brown fled, followed by the Pakistan fielders, and the tour was abandoned forthwith.

Opinion was divided when Ian Redpath was run out while backing up, West Indian Charlie Griffith being the executioner at Adelaide in January 1969. (The other three run-outs in the innings were conventional.) This form of dismissal was associated with India's Mankad, who twice got Bill Brown out in this fashion in 1947–48.

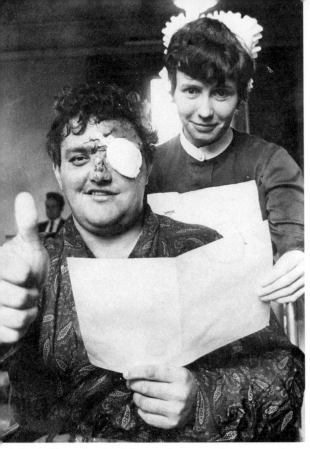

Colin Milburn lost his left eye after a multiple car crash at Moulton, near Northampton, in May 1969. The tragedy was intensified by the fact that of all its entertainers, the 18-stone, 27-year-old Geordie was the one cricket could least afford to lose. Milburn tried hard to make a comeback, and scored a fifty for Northants at Guildford, but the task was too great, and he was forced to retire.

Seymour Nurse, the dapper Barbadian, said a spectacular farewell to Test cricket with a final innings for West Indies of 258 in 476 minutes against New Zealand at Christchurch in March 1969.

Below: John Hampshire gave English cricket fresh heart by scoring a debut century at Lord's against West Indies in 1969. His career at the top was to be erratic, but when in command he was as good to watch as any contemporary. He has edged Sobers wide of Lloyd. England won the Test series 2–0.

The Lancashire lads loosen up for season 1969, when the winning of the John Player 40-overs Sunday League, the first of two in a row, also presaged a run of success in the 60-overs Gillette Cup, when Lancashire supporters, grown in number and in vocal support, cheered them to victory in the finals at Lord's in 1970, 1971, 1972 and 1975. Pictured are Barry Wood, Jackie Bond (captain), Ken Shuttleworth, David Lloyd, Farokh Engineer (at the steering-wheel), Peter Gooch, David Hughes, Jack Simmons.

Ray Illingworth, after 18 seasons with Yorkshire, finds himself in new colours after leaving his native county after the 1968 season. Leicestershire's secretary–manager Mike Turner snapped him up, and at the age of 36 the wily offspinner became captain of the Midlands club. When Colin Cowdrey suffered an achilles tendon injury in 1969, 'Illy' was the selectors' surprise choice as captain of England, a role he occupied successfully until 1973, taking wickets, scoring two centuries, and winning a reputation as a shrewd strategist. In 1979 he became Yorkshire's manager, and in 1982, aged 50, he captained his old county.

The Irish and West Indian players at Sion Mills, Londonderry in July 1969, when there would have seemed to be only one likely winner. And yet Ireland won by nine wickets, having bowled the West Indians out for only 25 on an 'emerald green' pitch. Derek Goodwin, Ireland's captain (centre of front row), took 5 for 6 and Tony O'Riordan (third from right, standing) 4 for 18.

Younis Ahmed of Surrey (and later Worcestershire and Glamorgan) is spectacularly run out in the Gillette Cup match against Hampshire, whose Bob Cottam appeals to umpire 'Lofty' Herman.

Phil Sharpe of Yorkshire holds a smart catch off the edge of Derbyshire's David Smith's bat in a 1969 Championship match at Chesterfield, watched by Smith's partner Peter Gibbs and Yorkshire's wicketkeeper Jimmy Binks, who in 1960 had held 96 catches, the most ever recorded in a season (Murray held 95 that season).

Right: Young Somerset batsman Greg Chappell, a few days short of his 21st birthday, plays the smooth on-drive against Middlesex that was to become the hallmark of this great batsman. On June 15, 1969 he scored the first hundred in the John Player League.

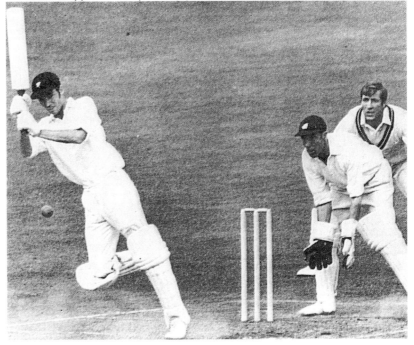

Left: *The slight figure of Glenn Turner sadly leaves Lord's after tenaciously carrying his bat through New Zealand's second innings of 131 for 43 not out, England having won by 230 runs. Turner was already on Worcestershire's staff and was playing in only his fourth Test. His strictly defensive game gave way in time to complete mastery at the crease, and a highly creditable 103 centuries.*

Right: *A staggering caught-and-bowled by New Zealand pace bowler Dayle Hadlee ends Alan Knott's brief innings in the Lord's Test and hastens England's dismissal for only 190. Ward, Underwood and Illingworth then dispatched the visitors for 169, John Edrich made a second-innings century, and it was the old story for the Kiwis.*

Right: *England's Phil Sharpe, who made 111 at Trent Bridge in the second Test of 1969, falls lbw to Dick Motz at The Oval, making the burly pace bowler the first to take 100 Test wickets for New Zealand.*

There are all sorts of ways of making a living, and in 1969, Fred Trueman, who had earned a crust bowling fast swingers, bouncers and yorkers for Yorkshire and England, taking 2304 wickets, a record 307 of them in 67 Test matches, took to the stage. Telling jokes of varying quality, he trod the boards of a number of Northern working-men's clubs and entertainment centres, invariably receiving an affectionate reception. Later came radio commentary and countless other unpredictable activities.

Ambar Roy splendidly caught-and-bowled by Hedley Howarth, something of a specialist at this, in New Zealand's series-levelling victory over India at Nagpur in October 1969. Left-hander Roy had hit the ball towards Dowling (hands raised), who deflected it wide of Howarth. **Below:** The New Zealanders were often dissatisfied with the umpiring in India, and Bruce Murray's lbw (to Prasanna) in the drawn Hyderabad Test was felt to be one of the most debatable.

Les Favell leads South Australia out for the last time. At 40, this aggressive little opener had made more runs for South Australia – a final aggregate of 9656 (38.17), with 23 centuries – than any other batsman, and had played in 19 Tests.

During the 1969–70 season the NSW team were told by the administrators to cease wearing rubber-soled spiked footwear, since it had, in their opinion, a detrimental effect on their mobility. The players thus dumped their cast-off shoes outside the dressing-room – apart from John Benaud, whose defiance cost him the captaincy.

Right: *Australia's 1969–70 visit to India was marred by several severe crowd disturbances, this one at the Brabourne Stadium, Bombay, when the crowd rioted after a decision against Venkataraghavan. Fires were started on the terraces and some of the rioters later besieged the Australians in their dressing-room, having sinister designs on captain Bill Lawry in particular. Doug Walters' suggestion that Lawry be handed over to the demonstrators so the players could get on with the victory celebrations was overruled by manager Fred Bennett.*

From India, where they won 3–1 (and endured a further, minor riot at Calcutta) Australia went on to the contrasting environment of South Africa, where they were to be thrashed in all four Tests. In the second, at Durban, Graeme Pollock (right) made the highest score ever made for South Africa, 274, in seven hours, with 43 fours and a five. Here he plays a ball from Alan Connolly. Barry Richards scored a 116-ball century, and the total of 622 for 9 dec was their highest ever in Tests.

504

Barry Richards leans into a drive against Laurie Mayne in the fourth South Africa v Australia Test of 1969–70, at Port Elizabeth. He scored 126, his second century of his only Test series, which netted 508 runs at 72.57. Below: The South Africans, having completed a 4–0 clean sweep over Australia, leave the field and enter what was to become a long period of exclusion from legitimate international cricket. Procter, having just taken 6 for 73, leads off, with captain Ali Bacher and keeper Lindsay behind him.

Walters made 74 when Australia followed on at Durban in the second Test, but Procter and Peter Pollock often made life difficult with short lifters. Walters' improvised reaction, jumping with face turning away, gave way to an equally alarming ducking with bat left up, periscope-style.

South Africa were due to tour England in 1970, but the swell of protest grew to such proportions that, although the cricket administrators fought to protect it, even to reducing the itinerary and planning extra protection at grounds, the anti-apartheid lobby and the more specific 'Stop the Seventy Tour' group forced the British Government to take an interest in the controversy, as much on safety as moral grounds. This group outside the Grace Gates at Lord's represented one of the smaller, quieter demonstrations.

505

The 1970 tour of England by South Africa having been cancelled upon 'advice' from the Home Secretary, the Cricket Council hastily arranged a series between England and a strong Rest of the World team, sponsored by Guinness. Although, by their very nature, the matches could not be regarded as Test matches, some persisted in referring to them as such for several years afterwards. The announcement came at a Press conference addressed by Raman Subba Row, S. C. Griffith and J. A. Bailey.

The ghost of Lord Hawke would have contemplated barbed wire on the square at Headingley with some puzzlement and anguish. Such battle preparations were withdrawn when the South African tour was cancelled and the threat of damage by demonstrators receded.

It is unlikely that a stronger cricket team ever took the field than the 1970 Rest of the World side. Rohan Kanhai, Mike Procter, Barry Richards, Graeme Pollock and Intikhab Alam prepare for action, and in addition England faced Garry Sobers, Clive Lloyd, Eddie Barlow, Mushtaq Mohammad, Farokh Engineer, Deryck Murray, Graham McKenzie, Peter Pollock, and Lance Gibbs. Future generations were left to wonder how England managed to win one of the five matches, the Trent Bridge contest, where D'Oliveira and Greig (both South Africans) shared 14 wickets, Illingworth scored 97, and Luckhurst 113 not out.

Above: *The end of a great career: Tom Graveney leaves the first-class field forever (apart from a few matches for Queensland), having scored nearly 48,000 runs, with 122 centuries, in a two-county career for Gloucestershire and then Worcestershire between 1948 and 1970. He averaged 44.38 in 79 Tests for England. The Warwickshire players complete the guard of honour at Worcester.*

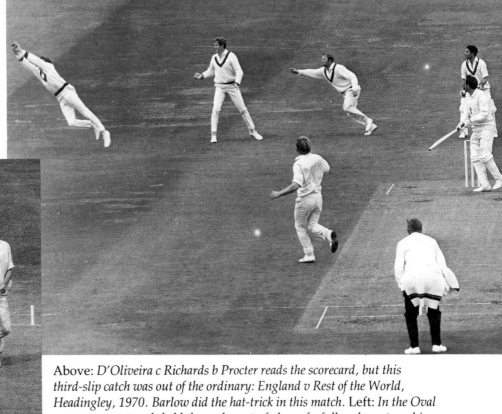

Above: *D'Oliveira c Richards b Procter reads the scorecard, but this third-slip catch was out of the ordinary: England v Rest of the World, Headingley, 1970. Barlow did the hat-trick in this match. Left: In the Oval contest, spectators beheld the undreamt-of glory of a full-scale partnership between Sobers and Pollock, the West Indian finally becoming one of Peter Lever's seven wickets. Lever's 7 for 83 earned him a place on MCC's winter tour of Australasia.*

Left: *Barry Richards became associated with a third country – Australia – as the political furore began to rage around his native land. For South Australia against Western Australia at Perth in 1970–71 he made an amazing 356, scoring 325 in a day. Few challenged the claim that he was the best batsman – right-handed, at least – in the world.* Above: *Back in South Africa, some of the cricketers carried on from within the fight to have cricket in South Africa free and open to players of all races. Peter and Graeme Pollock walked off after one ball of a match at Cape Town and handed a protest to the SACA against the omission of two non-white cricketers from the team chosen to tour Australia in 1971–72.*

Right: *It was becoming clearer by the day that cricket and politics were inextricably meshed together. Guyana's President Forbes Burnham makes a presentation to Garry Sobers at Georgetown, watched by Everton Weekes, Lance Gibbs and Rohan Kanhai. But things had not always been so amicable between the politician and the cricket star. When Sobers innocently went to Rhodesia for a double-wicket tournament he was strongly castigated, and Burnham demanded a public apology.*

The opening Test of the 1970–71 series, at Brisbane, was going well for Australia, with Stackpole scoring 207 and Walters 112, when Illingworth suddenly flung himself to catch Redpath, and a collapse ensued. From 372 for 2 at one point, Australia were out for 433. The match was drawn, as was the next, at Perth.

Bob Willis, a 21-year-old Surrey novice fast bowler, leaves for Australia as a replacement for the injured Alan Ward in the MCC party. He did not let the side down in his four Test appearances, but anyone who had predicted that here was a future England captain who would overcome several knee operations to finish with 325 wickets in 90 Tests would have been mocked or ignored.

Illingworth and Lawry shelter from the persistent rain at Melbourne which eventually saw the abandonment of the Test. Left: Brian Luckhurst faces Alan 'Froggy' Thomson at Brisbane, where he made 74 and 20 not out on Test debut. Boycott is his partner. Luckhurst scored two plucky hundreds in the series with damaged hands.

The cancellation of the third Test led to the staging of the first-ever one-day limited-overs international, enough top officials from both countries being on hand in Melbourne to sanction the event ad hoc. *They could little have foreseen that the truncated form of international would become, in a relatively short time, a serious rival to its senior, Test cricket, and that one-day internationals would even be escalated to a World Cup format.* **Above left:** *McKenzie bowls Knott for 24. Australia, 191 for 5, won this inaugural one-day international by five wickets.* **Above right:** *When England moved on to New Zealand, Derek Underwood took both his 1000th first-class and 100th Test wicket in the Christchurch Test. He was still only 25.*

Down in front of the Paddington Hill at the Sydney Cricket Ground in February 1971 an unsober spectator makes a grab at England fast bowler John Snow, who had hit Australian tailender Jenner on the head with a short ball. Defending the 1–0 lead they earned in the earlier Sydney Test, when Snow was irresistible with 7 for 40, England fought their way through this additional ('seventh', i.e. sixth) Test – through a torrent of beer-cans which prompted Illingworth to lead them off the field, and through umpires' warnings about intimidation, and the loss of Snow with a damaged hand – to win by 62 runs, thus regaining the Ashes.

510

Sunil Gavaskar made an awesome debut in Test cricket during India's 1970–71 tour of West Indies, won by the visitors 1–0. Hooking Dowe in the fourth Test, at Bridgetown, where he scored 117 not out, he totalled 774 runs in his eight innings, average 154.80, crowning his achievement with 124 and 220 in the final Test, at Port-of-Spain, where West Indies, 166 ahead on first innings, were eventually shut out. India owed much also to Dilip Sardesai, who had scores of 212, 112, 150 and 75 in the series.

Right: *In the second Test of 1970–71, at Port-of-Spain, Trinidad's Jack Noreiga, 34, took 9 for 95 in India's first innings in only his second Test for West Indies. His offspinners went unrewarded in the second innings, when India sailed to a seven-wicket victory. As he is congratulated afterwards it seems that opposing captain, Wadekar, whom he dismissed for nought, still cannot believe it.*

Left: *Paul Dunkels, who played once for Warwickshire in 1971 and once for Sussex the following year, stood 6 ft 10 ins, about 15 ins taller than Kallicharran. Probably the tallest first-class cricketer of all, Dunkels was not the first to show that size is not everything. His fast-medium bowling proved ineffective at top level.*

Right: *King Hussain of Jordan, who, like Dunkels, was educated at Harrow, played for the Jordanian Royal Amman Cricket Club in 1971 against a British Embassy team. Jordan won.*

BASTIONS FALL

TO THOSE living through it, the decade of the 1970s seemed to be bringing change on a larger, faster scale than ever before. Even before the 'Packer Revolution' of 1977, older followers had had to cope with the new one-day form of cricket, which ran to three county competitions alongside the Championship by 1972, and had been adopted with enthusiasm – and vital financial benefit – in the other major cricketing countries. Those same long-term devotees were still trying to come to terms with an English game not only no longer governed by MCC but 'democratised' by the cessation of the amateur/professional distinction, the chief disadvantage of which became apparent in the general no-risks attitude among the all-professional captains. At the highest level, though, dwelt the most unfamiliar realities: that with India's defeat of England in 1971, the flag had been lowered on home soil to all the other countries bar New Zealand; that India indeed might be considered Test champions of the world, having just beaten West Indies; and that world cricket dominance, like the County Championship itself, was healthily open to many more candidates than once was the case. This was proof that the global game was stronger allround, but by its very shape, the organisation of its finances and presentation was due for drastic reshaping.

Old warriors don't fade away – they switch counties. Brian Close, 40, after playing for Yorkshire since he was 18, found his services dispensed with, and so signed for Somerset in 1971, secretary A. K. James seeing to it that he did not change his mind.

Head injury not only to batsmen but close-in fielders has been a constant source of anxiety, and would eventually see players resorting to protective helmets, but in 1971 it was still at the fanciful-experiment stage. This unsightly but effective grille version was tried out by Lancashire's David Lloyd.

Geoff Boycott, newly appointed as Yorkshire's captain in 1971, stands unwittingly a prophetic distance apart from his men. Though he continued to grind out thousands of runs at his own careful pace (indeed this year, recovered from the arm fracture in Australia, was his best: 2503 runs, average 100.12) Yorkshire had their worst-ever season in 1971, and continued to struggle. Boycott had communication problems with his players, and was relieved of the captaincy after eight seasons.

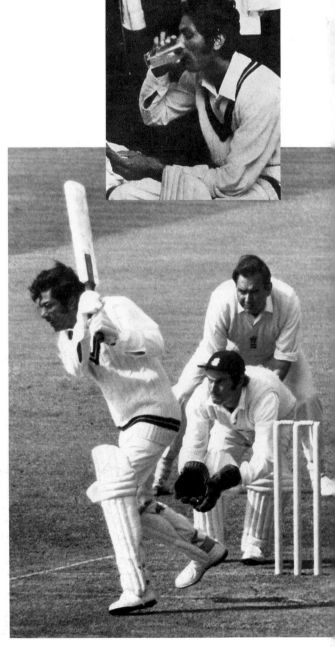

In the 1971 England v India Test at Lord's fast bowler John Snow semi-playfully impeded Sunil Gavaskar as he went for a run, and sent him flying. Snow's penalty was a one-Test suspension.

Right: Pakistan's Zaheer Abbas, making his first Test appearance against England, drives for more runs in his 274 at Edgbaston in June 1971. He added a record 291 for the second wicket with Mushtaq Mohammad, and Pakistan declared at 608 for 7. Knott, England's wicketkeeper, scored 116, but England followed on and needed rain as well as Luckhurst's century to see them to safety. Inset: Zaheer refreshes himself after his epic innings and opens the first of the congratulatory telegrams. England stole victory at Headingley to take the series 1–0.

513

As the England team lined up to be presented to The Queen during the India Test at Lord's in 1971, a mischievous wiseacre in the Press-box conjectured as to who would bow to whom when Her Majesty reached Geoff Boycott. The Yorkshire captain, of course, was fully conversant with Royal etiquette. Following The Queen and Ray Illingworth is Sir Cyril Hawker, president of MCC, and the umpire is Arthur Fagg.

Above: *The Indians were given a rapturous welcome home in Bombay after beating England in England for the first time. Wadekar, the captain, was paramount among the heroes. When later he presided over an Indian defeat, his house was stoned by angry mobs.*

India's historic Oval victory in 1971 came when they bowled England out for 101 and left themselves a target of only 173. Medium-pace wrist-spinner Chandrasekhar (6 for 38) destroyed England. He bowled Edrich (above) for 0.

514

David Hughes of Lancashire pours 24 glasses of champagne, one for every run he took off an over from Gloucestershire's John Mortimore in the late-evening gloom at Old Trafford in the Gillette Cup semi-final of 1971. The match, televised, ended at 8.50 pm, and Hughes's calculated late assault swung the match when Procter's fast bowling in particular had seemed to have sewn it up for Gloucestershire. Lancashire went on to win the final at Lord's by 24 runs, though Asif Iqbal (above right, changing direction as John Shepherd finishes up at his end) nearly won the cup for Kent with a fine innings of 89, ended by a leaping catch at cover by Jack Bond.

Garry Sobers, proud father of seven-month-old Matthew, arrives in Australia to captain a Rest of the World team in a substitute series for the politically-cancelled tour by South Africa. Goaded by the Press for apparently playing too much golf, Sobers unleashed a merciless assault on the Australian bowling at Melbourne in the third of the five-day contests, finishing with 254, one of those innings that give those who witness them a feeling of joyous gratitude and even a superior air.

Soon after Sobers's matchless double-century, Australian batsman Graeme Watson found himself facing a fast full-toss from Tony Greig. He swung at it, missed, and was struck a fearful blow in the face. Intikhab, Greig, Engineer, umpire Max O'Connell and Sobers carried Watson to the treatment room, and in hospital he remained on the critical list for several days. He had heart massage and 40 pints of blood transfusion. As he slowly recovered, he was warned against playing again, but he did return, won a place on the tour of England a few months later, and played in two Tests. At Southampton, Watson (176) and Stackpole (119 not out) posted 301 for the first wicket against Hampshire.

In the second Australia v Rest of the World match of 1971–72, at Perth, a raw tearaway bowler named Lillee, who had taken 5 for 84 a season earlier on his Test debut, against England, tore through the World XI to finish with 8 for 29. There were to be triumphant exits such as this without number in the years ahead. **Above right:** *Another rare talent was being polished in Perth at the same time. Wicketkeeper Rodney Marsh was shaking off the 'Iron Gloves' tag, and with Lillee as his chief ally he was to go on to world Test records. Redpath is his legside victim in Perth.*

The next surprise on the international circuit came when New Zealand held West Indies to five draws in the Caribbean in 1971–72. In the first Test, at Kingston, Lawrence Rowe, on his home ground, made a most remarkable entry into Test cricket with 214 in the first innings and 100 not out in the second. New Zealand's wicketkeeper is the late Ken Wadsworth. **Above right:** *Glenn Turner in action in the fourth Test, at Georgetown, where he followed his innings of 259 against Guyana with an identical score against West Indies, making 387 for the first wicket with Terry Jarvis (182). Turner made four double-centuries on the tour, two of them in Tests, and apart from him and Jarvis, Congdon (2), Hastings and Burgess all made Test hundreds. Sobers, though he took the world Test aggregate record from Cowdrey, was restricted to one Test century, but Kallicharran made a debut hundred and another, and Charlie Davis and Fredericks reached three figures.*

Gambling returns to Lord's in 1972 over a century after bookmakers of another, unwanted kind were banished. The new system was strictly controlled, with cricketers, like jockeys, not permitted to bet, and odds laid only against team rather than direct individual performances. This time the ghost to smile would have been that of old William Lambert.

The best cricketer in the world in the early 1970s, if it was not Sobers, was Mike Procter, who had a hat-trick of lbws besides a century in Gloucestershire's match against Essex at Westcliff in 1972. In 1970–71 he had equalled the record of Fry and Bradman in scoring six centuries in consecutive innings.

Surrey offspinner Pat Pocock recorded figures in the match against Sussex at Eastbourne in 1972 that were beyond compare: seven wickets in 11 balls. In his last over he began with a hat-trick, took his seventh wicket with the fifth ball, and Joshi was run out off the sixth.

The third limited-overs county competition, the 55-overs Benson & Hedges Cup, began in 1972, and provided Leicestershire (under Illingworth) with their first trophy in their 93 years' existence. Now that the drought was broken, other honours would follow. Yorkshire's John Hampshire has lost his bat after a scrambled single. His side's 136 for 9 (McKenzie 3 for 22) was never enough. Leicester's Yorkshireman Balderstone (41 not out) won the Gold Award.

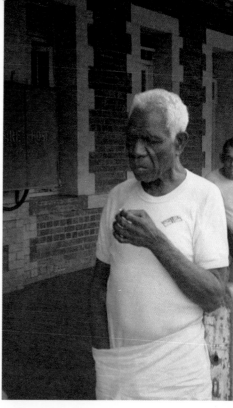

Eddie Gilbert, the Aboriginal fast bowler who terrified Australian batsmen in the 1930s, was found languishing in an institution in 1972, unable or pathologically unwilling to communicate. He had been in care since 1949, and died in 1978.

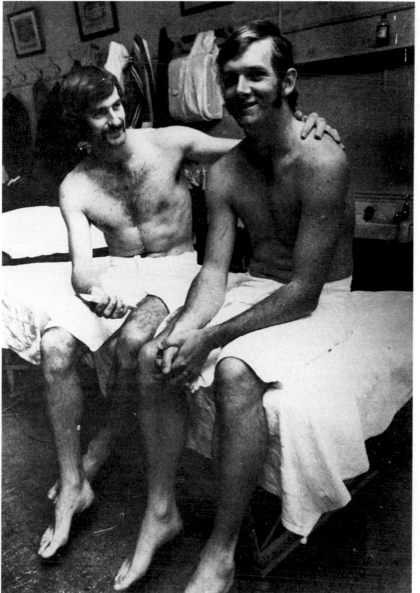

Dennis Lillee and Bob Massie unwind after Australia had won the Lord's Test to level the 1972 series 1–1. Massie, in his first Test, bowled sensationally to return 16 for 137, eight wickets in each innings, swinging the ball late and sharply, often from an unusual angle from around the wicket. Lillee took the other four, leaving England to wonder how the Western Australian pair could be controlled if not overcome.

'That's Massie. Wait till you meet Lillee, mate!' This was Australian cartoonist Rigby's exultant reaction to the 'Massiecre' at Lord's in that crazy week in June 1972.

Midst Massie's assault, Lillee took four wickets of much importance: Edrich, Luckhurst (twice), and Boycott, who not only had to suffer the disappointment of being out, but, as was customary, had to face the amateur dramatics of his executioner at close range.

Keith Stackpole, Australia's answer to Milburn, made 114 in the third Test of 1972, at Trent Bridge – and was glad of a quiet rest afterwards. Ross Edwards' 170 not out in the second innings put a lot of pressure on England, but Luckhurst, with England's highest score of the series, 96, held out, mainly with Parfitt and D'Oliveira, for a draw.

519

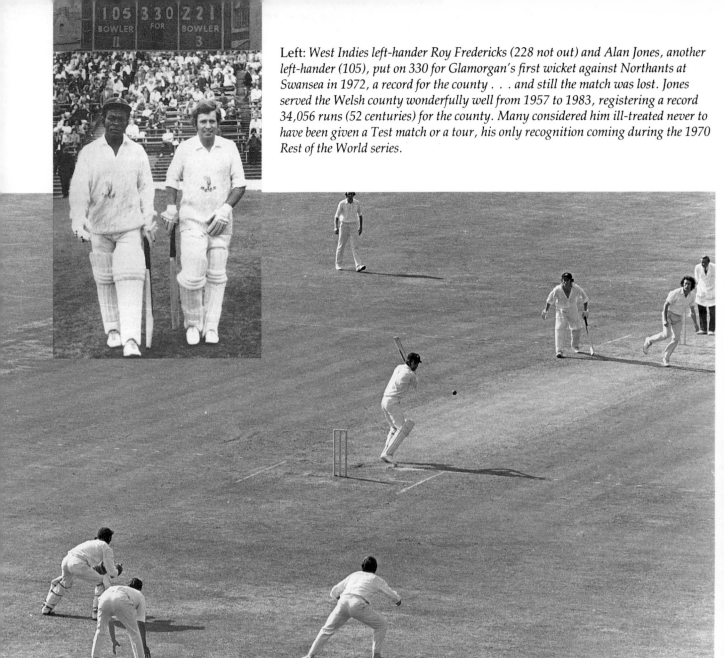

Left: *West Indies left-hander Roy Fredericks (228 not out) and Alan Jones, another left-hander (105), put on 330 for Glamorgan's first wicket against Northants at Swansea in 1972, a record for the county . . . and still the match was lost. Jones served the Welsh county wonderfully well from 1957 to 1983, registering a record 34,056 runs (52 centuries) for the county. Many considered him ill-treated never to have been given a Test match or a tour, his only recognition coming during the 1970 Rest of the World series.*

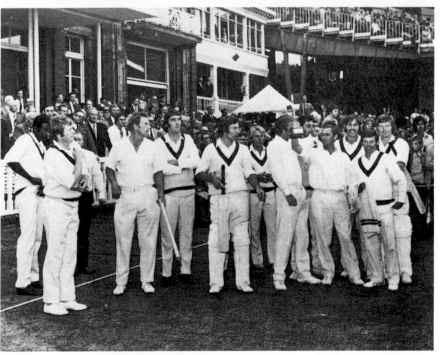

Above: *Having lost the Headingley Test on a deplorable pitch, Australia needed to win the Oval Test to square the series. Their cause was helped by centuries from Greg Chappell – seen cutting a ball from Snow – and his brother Ian. Lillee took his wicket tally to 31, a new record, and the 242 for victory were hit off for the loss of five wickets, Ian Chappell's young side showing much character and promise.*

Left: *Lancashire, having completed a hat-trick of Gillette Cups, group calmly in the gathering gloom of September at Lord's, 1972, as if it is all becoming rather routine.*

Essex, who finished fifth, and Leicestershire, who came sixth in 1972 (Warwickshire took the Championship), battled out a late-season match in August at Leyton, Leicestershire holding out for a draw. Keith Boyce, Essex's West Indian allrounder, took nine wickets in the match plus two catches, one of them 'around the corner' to dismiss John Steele for 51 off Ray East's bowling. Captain/wicketkeeper Brian Taylor watches tensely.

India played enthusiastic hosts to England in 1972–73 and won the series 2–1, mainly through their spin bowling. Superb close catching played a part too, as exemplified by Solkar's diving effort to get Knott (above left) at Delhi, where England won by six wickets. India won at Calcutta and Madras, in the latter Test the former Indian captain, Pataudi, matching Greig's humour by removing his sunhat as he dived in to field. Greig himself knew how to play to the gallery. One of his acts consisted of picking up Viswanath (left) and cradling the little Indian lovingly when he reached his century in the last Test, at Bombay. This and Engineer's 121 in the same innings were the only centuries conceded by Tony Lewis's side in the series, though only Lewis himself, Fletcher and Greig scored hundreds for England.

Four spin wizards who took India to the top: Chandrasekhar, Venkataraghavan, Bishan Bedi and Eripalli Prasanna, who respectively snared 242, 156, 266 and 189 Test wickets for India in this golden age of spin. Chandra's fizzing legbreaks and googlies took 35 wickets in the 1972–73 series against England, Bedi's classica. slow left-arm 25. Venka and the flightier Prasanna often vied for the offspinner's place in the side.

The Adelaide spin twins, Ashley Mallett (offspin) and Terry Jenner (high-tossed legspin). Jenner's style made him a luxury at Test level, but Mallett was tight and clever, and finished, in 1980, with 132 wickets in 38 Tests. His best figures, 8 for 59, came at Adelaide in December 1972, against Pakistan.

Majid Khan, having scored his first Test century at last in the first innings, becomes one of the growing number of c Marsh b Lillee victims in the second innings, having made 47. Australia won all three Tests, their only worry being Lillee's back injury, which he bravely defied in the last Test. Marsh became the first Australian wicketkeeper to make a Test hundred when he scored 118 at Adelaide.

Doug Walters during one of the showpiece Test centuries of modern times. He hit a century between lunch and tea on the first day of the Port-of-Spain Test in March 1973, on a pitch which encouraged bowlers. Australia went on to win by 44 runs.

Late in the match Keith Stackpole (above) was hit while fielding close, and after rushing to the boundary to tell jeering spectators what he thought of them, he was persuaded by Redpath to go off for treatment. Ian Chappell and Kerry O'Keeffe are behind. Chappell's tough band did well to win the series 2–0, though Lillee's breakdown was offset by the unavailability of Sobers after 85 consecutive Tests.

Mushtaq Mohammad moves towards 201 for Pakistan against New Zealand at Dunedin, February 1973, when he and Asif Iqbal (175) added 350. Mushtaq then took 5 for 49.

Brian Hastings bowled for 110 at Auckland, and thus ends a world Test record 10th-wicket stand of 151. Collinge was 68 not out.

Rodney Redmond scored 107 and 56 on his Test debut, joining Jack Mills and Bruce Taylor in that distinction – left-handers all three. The difference was that this match against Pakistan at Auckland in February 1973 was Redmond's one and only Test, even though he toured England later that year.

Back from West Indies with stress fractures of the lower spine, Dennis Lillee seemed to have meagre prospects of extending his thunderous but brief career. And yet, with his courage and determination, recovery came inside two years.

Right: *Derek Underwood was a batsman's assassin on a rain-affected pitch, getting lift and sharp movement at a brisk pace. In May 1973, at Hastings, he took 5 for 43, and then, after Kent players had helped the Fire Brigade to mop up after torrential rain, he ran through Sussex with an analysis of 8 for 9. His nickname of 'Deadly' was never more apposite.*

524

Bevan Congdon, New Zealand's 1973 tour captain, copes with an awkward ball from John Snow in the Trent Bridge Test, where he made a gritty 176 in his side's 440, which left them only 39 from victory. In the next Test, at Lord's, Congdon made 175 in a New Zealand record total of 551 for 9 dec. Only two missed chances late in the match stopped New Zealand from achieving their first victory over England.

Left: *Asif Iqbal eyes his Kent partner Colin Cowdrey in awe and admiration as the Englishman comes off at Maidstone in July 1973 having scored 100 not out against Surrey, his 100th century in first-class cricket.*

Brian Lander (right) *and his Durham team follow up their victory over Yorkshire in the 1973 Gillette Cup in the only sensible fashion. Lander took 5 for 15 as Yorkshire were bowled out for 135 at Harrogate, a total Durham overtook for the loss of five wickets to become the first Minor County side to humble a first-class county.*

Keith Fletcher saved England at Lord's in 1973 when New Zealand were pushing towards victory. The Essex man dug in and made 178, which, with 92 from Boycott, half-centuries from Amiss and Roope, and a valuable 23 not out by Arnold (a stand of 92 for the ninth wicket with Fletcher) held the tourists at bay.

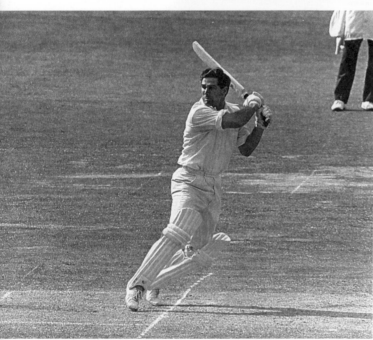

Above: *Lancashire-born Vic Pollard carved out laudable centuries for New Zealand in the Trent Bridge and Lord's Tests of 1973, and made 62 at Headingley. His offspin also served his side well. At Lord's, Mark Burgess also reached a century, providing New Zealand with three in a Test innings (Congdon 175) for the first time.*

Above right: *Rachael Heyhoe Flint has just been presented with the first Women's World Cup by HRH Princess Anne after England had beaten Australia in the final of the limited-overs tournament at Edgbaston in 1973. Mrs Flint scored 64 and Enid Bakewell a fast 117.*

Right: *Ken Kelly's award-winning photograph of Worcestershire's Ron Headley losing his grip in a limited-overs match against Gloucestershire in 1973. He had recently been called into the West Indies Test team, his name now proudly listed with his father's.*

The first Test against West Indies in 1973, at The Oval, was lost by England, but the setback was softened by the century by fair-haired Lancastrian Frank Hayes. Unfortunately for Hayes and his country, he played in only nine Tests over the next three years, all against West Indies, but was unable to get settled. His Test career average was a mere 15.

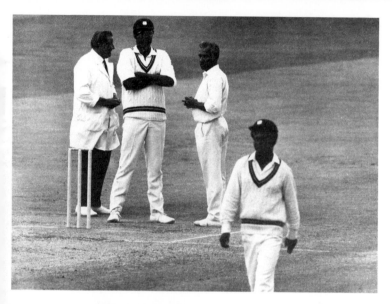

Above left: Trouble at Edgbaston as West Indies captain Kanhai (with the taller Clive Lloyd) stands near the umpire, Arthur Fagg, who had taken exception to Kanhai's remarks and walked out of the game on the second evening, returning later. Above: Kanhai feels better for having banged Chris Old straight back for four in his second-innings 54. Left: Saturday afternoon in the 1973 Lord's Test, the stands evacuated for a bomb alert, and umpire Bird dutifully guards the pitch.

The countdown is over, and New Zealander Glenn Turner has reached 1000 runs before the end of May 1973. The scene in the Northampton dressing-room is aptly tinged with relief and jubilation: Dayle Hadlee, Richard Hadlee, Turner, Bruce Taylor, Rodney Redmond, Brian Hastings.

Above: Garfield Sobers plays with distinctive ease in his final Test appearance in England – Lord's 1973 – and the last of his 26 Test centuries, 150 not out in West Indies' 652 for 8 dec. At 37 he was having fitness problems. The crowd sensed they were seeing the modest Muhammad Ali of cricket for the last time, and acknowledged him with special affection. Left: Intikhab Alam, the accurate Surrey and Pakistan legspinner (here watched by umpire Tom Spencer), in 1973, at Guildford, became the first from his country to take 1000 first-class wickets.

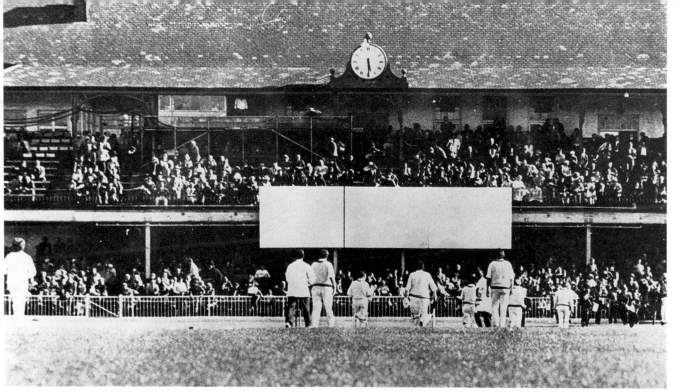

Off to an endless sunset: players leave the Bramall Lane turf forever on August 7, 1973, the ground thereafter being built upon in the interests of Sheffield United Football Club. This last Yorkshire–Lancashire match at the 118-year-old venue appropriately ended in a draw, and the turf was sold to cricket fans, who were able to take their own few square-feet of history away and lay it in their gardens.

Right: England's cricketers find Rolling Stone Mick Jagger a source of cheer and support during their 1973–74 tour of West Indies.

Aftab Baloch, who scored 428 for Sind (951 for 7 dec) v Baluchistan at Karachi in 1973–74. When he toured England with Pakistan a few months later he was thoughtfully allocated Room 428 in the team's headquarters hotel.

In November 1973, Queensland's Sam Trimble, 39, scored his 26th century and went on to pass 8000 runs in Sheffield Shield cricket, joining only Bradman and Favell. Australia never chose Trimble for a Test match.

529

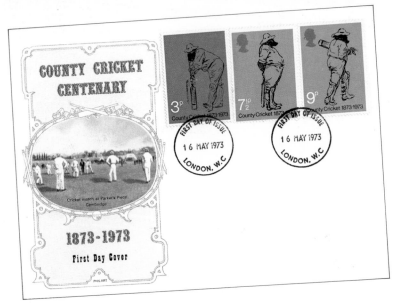

The British Post Office marked the centenary of the County Championship in 1973 with a set of stamps, the subject chosen being the still-recognisable W. G. Grace, the illustrations being taken from Harry Furniss's work of 1896. The issue was not free of argument, for although the first strict qualifications rules for county cricket were introduced in 1873, champion counties had been recognised since 1864, albeit on Press opinion.

Above: England's brawny, uninhibited John Jameson goes immediately for the hook against Andy Roberts, West Indies' new fast bowler from Antigua, and is dropped on the boundary in the third Test, Bridgetown, March 1974.

Left: Dennis Amiss, having scored 174 at Port-of-Spain in the first Test (soured by Greig's 'running out' of Kallicharran as the umpires were preparing to call time), went further at Kingston in the next Test with a 570-minute 262 not out when England went in again 230 behind. The 30-year-old Warwickshire batsman hit 40 fours and a six – and consumed many salt tablets.

Greg Chappell working his way towards a special Test record. In the Wellington Test of March 1974 he became the fourth batsman to score a double-century and a century in the same Test: further, his 247 not out and 133 gave him more runs in a Test than any other batsman (Sandham's 375 runs, Kingston, 1930 was the previous highest). Chappell's brother Ian also scored twin centuries in this match, the first fraternal double in Test history.

Although Amiss made three worthy centuries in the 1973–74 West Indies v England series, and Greig made two, Fletcher one, and Boycott finished with 99 and 112 at Port-of-Spain (where England squared the series, Greig's offspinners claiming 13 wickets), Jamaica's Lawrence Rowe made an imperishable mark on this set of Test matches, scoring 120 at Kingston, 302 at Bridgetown (see picture), and 123 in the final Test. He and Kallicharran (two centuries) dominated the West Indian batting, though Sobers added another jewel to his crown by becoming the first batsman to reach 8000 runs in Test cricket.

Not to be outdone, Glenn Turner scored a pair of centuries in the next Test, at Christchurch, the first such instance for New Zealand. A cut forward of point off a Dymock no-ball brought up the second hundred, and soon New Zealand had their first-ever victory over Australia, a triumph made sweeter in that the series had not been free of acrimony.

Left: *The future of West Indies cricket: small risk that the game will wilt in the sunny islands so long as West Indies keep winning and so long as boys like him continue to see cricket as a means of having fun – and perhaps in time even of making good money.*

Andy Roberts, the first Antiguan to play for West Indies, was carving a trail of wickets and physical hardship through cricket with his cold, silent, extra-fast bowling. Here, operating for Hampshire at Basingstoke in May 1974, he has beaten the veteran Cowdrey on the hook stroke and knocked him out cold. To worsen Cowdrey's plight, he was out hit-wicket. Greenidge attends Cowdrey, Richard Lewis bends down, and Roberts stands on the right.

Will Taylor, 90 (left), receives an illuminated address in 1974 from Derbyshire's president, the Duke of Devonshire, to mark his 70 years' service to the club as player, secretary (1908–59), committeeman and vice-president.

Above: *An 18-year-old whose name few knew how to pronounce – Ian Botham – shakes his head after being hit in the mouth by Roberts in the Somerset–Hampshire Benson & Hedges quarter-final at Taunton in June 1974. Sainsbury assists him. Somerset's cause seemed lost, but Botham set about the bowling, hit 45 not out, and got Somerset home by one wicket.*

Left: *Earlier in the match, Hampshire's Mike Taylor was caught by his twin brother Derek off Hallam Moseley.*

David Lloyd of Lancashire made his England debut in 1974 against India at Lord's and scored 46, three of his colleagues making centuries towards an innings victory. Then, at Edgbaston (above), he stood centrestage with 214 not out, handling three of India's master spinners with relative ease.

In the Lord's Test, India were bowled out for a pitiful 42 in their second innings, Chris Old (above) taking 5 for 21, Geoff Arnold 4 for 19 in the humid conditions. Also pictured is Eknath Solkar, who top-scored with 18 not out. Below: When Pakistan came to Lord's they fared little better. Underwood – here getting Zaheer caught by Greig – took 13 wickets after rain seeped under the covers.

Sir Donald Bradman made his final visit to England in May 1974, speaking at a Lord's Taverners gala charity dinner at the Anglo–American Sporting Club in London. Having methodically autographed all 1000 menus the day before, he delivered a response to Lord Home's speech which was as well-prepared and entertaining as any of his greatest innings. Later, at the sports auction, Sir Don's 1936–37 Australian blazer fetched £750.

John Jameson and Rohan Kanhai after their world record second-wicket partnership of 465 unbroken for Warwickshire v Gloucestershire (without Procter) at Edgbaston in July 1974. Jameson made 240, Kanhai 213, both not out.

Kent have won the 1974 Gillette Cup, beating Lancashire (118) by five wickets on a Monday, the Saturday having been washed out. Beneath Mike Denness are John Shepherd, Norman Graham, Colin Cowdrey, Bob Woolmer, Graham Johnson, Derek Underwood and Brian Luckhurst, and crouching are Dave Nicholls, Alan Knott, Alan Ealham and James Graham-Brown. Kent won 10 titles during the 1970s.

Zaheer Abbas made another double-century on his second tour of England, avenging his scores of 1 and 1 in the farcical Lord's Test by shaping a nine-hour innings of 240 at The Oval. His first hundred came with this edge off Old.

There were two big surprises awaiting England in Australia in 1974–75: the first that Lillee had overcome his crippling back injury . . . and this was the other: Jeff Thomson from Sydney, who slung the ball down at a sizzling pace, getting dangerous lift off a length, and not worrying overmuch where the ball landed. He took 33 wickets in 4½ Tests before injuring his shoulder, and Lillee took 25 in 5½, injuring a foot in the sixth Test, where England took advantage of the terror twins' absence to pull back to 1–4.

Lillee bounces Cowdrey at Perth, December 1974. The 42-year-old maestro had flown in as a reinforcement for injury-hit England. Australia had the artillery to win the Ashes in emphatic manner, the slips cordon holding anything that moved, and the pitches being less than batting paradises.

Throughout the 1974–75 series in Australia, England's batsmen were in a state of siege against the pummelling of the Australian attack. At Perth, Fletcher, who had scored the slowest first-class century in English cricket less than four months ago (in the Oval Test against Pakistan), could scarcely find a run: this went for the whole series until the fifth and sixth Tests. The bowler is Jeff Thomson, the other batsman Tony Greig, who took the battle to the enemy, smashing 110 at Brisbane.

Left: Doug Walters was at his attacking best in the Perth Test, hitting a century between tea and the close on the second day, reaching the mark with a six off Willis off the final ball. With Ross Edwards' century and Greg Chappell's seven catches, Walters hastened Australia's victory by nine wickets to go two up.

The Hill at the Sydney Cricket Ground, once the territory of good humour, bonhomie and banter, had now turned into a seething, stinking gathering-place for loud-mouthed drunks. The number of beer-cans cleared away after each day's play was astronomical.

Australia, under Ian Chappell's no-nonsense leadership, recaptured the Ashes by winning the fourth Test, at Sydney, in January 1975. Marsh imitates Nureyev as Geoff Arnold ruefully ungloves, having fallen to Mallett with only 35 balls remaining. John Edrich was left 33 not out, having returned with a broken rib after being hit by Lillee. Edrich led England in this Test, Denness having dropped himself.

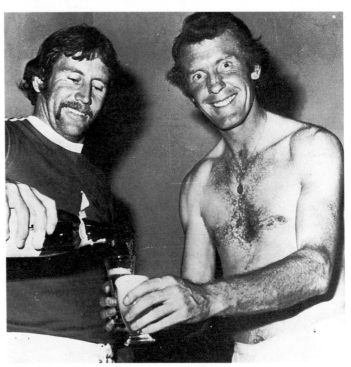

Above left: *Here come the umpires . . .? A reminder that there is always room for a chuckle in cricket: these spectators simply dressed up at Melbourne during a bad-light stoppage and 'sold the crowd a pup'.*

Above: *Ian Chappell and Mike Denness toast the '74–75 series, made a little less lopsided by England's innings victory in the sixth Test, when Australia were shorn of their Lillee–Thomson cutting edge, workhorse Max Walker taking 8 for 143 and Denness and Fletcher scoring big centuries.*

Left: *As usual, there was Test cricket going on in several parts of the world. Clive Lloyd (sweeping Prasanna) hit 163 at Bangalore in the first India v West Indies Test of 1974–75.*

India and West Indies went to Bombay in late January locked 2–2 in the series. Here the Indian spinners and left-arm seam attack were tamed to the tune of 604 for 6 dec, Lloyd making 242 not out, Fredericks 104, Kallicharran 98 and Murray 91. By the sixth day India were at last forced to submit, by 201 runs, and Viv Richards, who had scored 192 not out at Delhi in his second Test, grabs a souvenir stump. Gordon Greenidge had also been launched successfully with 93 and 107 in his maiden Test, at Bangalore.

Bombay players smile in relief as much as triumph after winning the Ranji Trophy in 1974–75 under the captaincy of Ashok Mankad (far right, with hand on shoulder of team-mate). After winning India's premier trophy for 15 consecutive years, nothing less than a continuation of that success was expected of them. Then in 1973–74 Karnataka won for the first time. Bombay pessimists felt it would be years before their team got back on top. But a year later they won the Ranji again – beating Karnataka in the final.

Pakistan was developing a reputation for producing teenaged prodigies, and Javed Miandad was the best of them in the 1970s. At 17, in the 1974–75 season, he scored 311 for Karachi Whites against National Bank at Karachi, and two years later he made his Test debut at Lahore and scored 163 against New Zealand in his first innings, and 206 and 85 at Karachi in his third Test, becoming the youngest, at 19 years 141 days, to make a Test double-century. A career of much brilliance and turbulence was unfolding.

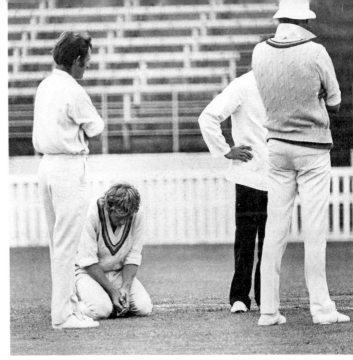

Auckland, Tuesday, February 25, 1975. Day of dread. Impatient at the delay in claiming the last New Zealand wicket for an innings victory, England fast bowler Peter Lever dug in a bouncer to the No. 11, Ewen Chatfield, who had scored 13. Unable to deal with it, he was struck on the temple. He collapsed, moaning, legs twitching, face blue. His heart stopped for several seconds. MCC's physio and a St John's Ambulance officer raced out and began working on the stricken batsman, administering mouth-to-mouth resuscitation and heart massage, while Lever (top right) slumped to the turf, weeping and believing he had killed Chatfield. At last the 24-year-old Wellington player was taken off (right) and rushed to hospital, where a hairline fracture was detected. He eventually made a complete recovery, and was still playing Test cricket 11 years later. The irony of this brush with death was in the fact that England's own batsmen had just escaped it daily throughout the Australian tour.

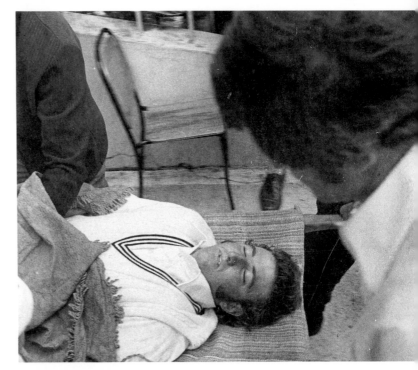

Left: *The Asian Cricket Conference sits in Lahore in December 1974, the aim of delegates being to promote cricket not only in and between Pakistan, India and Sri Lanka but in Malaysia, Singapore, Burma and Hong Kong. President was A. H. Kardar of Pakistan (second from right).*

At Barbados's Garrison Savannah, on February 19, 1975, Garfield Sobers is knighted by Her Majesty before his adoring people and the mother who raised him not a mile away. Not only was he honoured as perhaps the greatest allround cricketer the world has seen, but as an exemplary sportsman whose natural charm shamed many of his prima donna contemporaries around the world. It was not entirely inappropriate that the investiture took place by the nearby racetrack.

Below: Snow stops play, Buxton, June 2, 1975, and Lancashire players Peter Lever, Clive Lloyd, Frank Hayes and David Lloyd, with 477 for 5 on the board, can feel smug. Umpire Bird seems apprehensive: justifiably: Derbyshire were bowled out for 42 and 87 after the thaw.

Sir Neville Cardus, who had become a kind of patron saint of cricket-writing, died on February 27, 1975, aged 86. His romantic newspaper and magazine reports and essays captured the imagination of several generations, transporting the game and its players from the ordinary to the rarefied.

In 1975 cricket at last staged a World Cup, England playing host, with six Test-playing countries – England, Australia, West Indies, New Zealand, India and Pakistan – and two ICC associate members, Sri Lanka and East Africa, participating. Prudential Assurance provided £100,000 in sponsorship. A most successful tournament, blessed by good weather and crowd support, got under way after a gathering of players and officials at Buckingham Palace, where they were presented to The Queen Prince Philip and Prince Charles.

The epic 1975 Prudential World Cup final at Lord's saw Australia chasing West Indies' 291 for 8 (60 overs: Lloyd 102, Kanhai 55), and becoming panicky in their running between wickets. Five of them were run out in their total of 274, including last man Thomson, who had added 41 thrilling runs with Lillee for the last wicket. Above: Opener Alan Turner gets home too late to beat Viv Richards's direct hit. His 40 and Ian Chappell's 62 were top scores for the runners-up.

Right: Gary Gilmour took 5 for 48 for Australia in his 12 overs in the final, having shattered England with an amazing exhibition of left-arm swing bowling in the semi-final at Headingley three days earlier, finishing with 6 for 14. It seemed successor to Alan Davidson had been found, but the easy-going Gilmour never did realise the expectations.

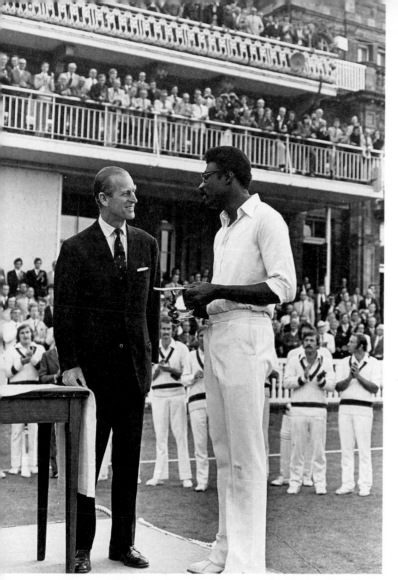

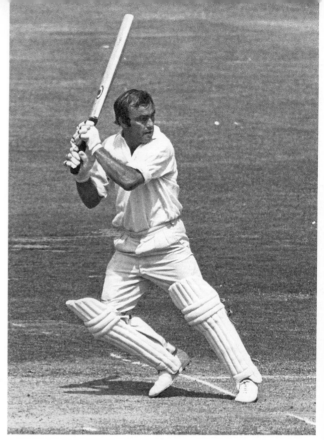

Ashes battle recommenced in 1975 after the World Cup, and John Edrich scored a doughty 175 at Lord's, one of the three drawn Tests of the summer. Tony Greig had scored 96 after taking over from Denness as captain following the English disaster of Edgbaston, where Australia were put in, made 359, and then rolled England over for 101 and 173 after rain, Lillee, Thomson and Walker all having five-wicket hauls, and Gooch bagging a pair on his England debut. The Australians, as the line-abreast formation (below) suggests, oozed aggression and confidence.

In the trembling afterglow of a long, tense day, Prince Philip, Duke of Edinburgh, MCC president, hands West Indies captain Clive Lloyd the Man of the Match prize, a personal memento to go with the World Cup.

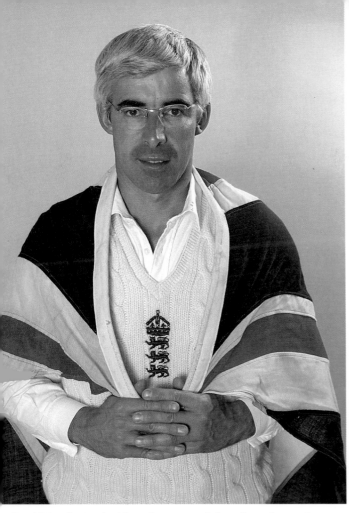

David Steele, 33, had long been regarded as the archetypal county pro, with no higher potential. His selection for England in 1975 in their hour of need thus captured the nation's imagination, especially when the grey-haired, bespectacled, waddling Northants man batted gutsily for 50 and 45 against Lillee and Thomson at Lord's on his debut. His other scores in the series were 73, 92, 39 and 66, and next season he started with 106 against West Indies. He was sent back to county cricket after eight Tests for his beloved England, averaging 42. Above right: Gordon Greenidge, the athletic Hampshire-raised West Indian, crashed 13 sixes in an innings of 259 for his county against Sussex in 1975, having hit 13 a year earlier in an assault on the Pakistanis for Derrick Robins' XI at Eastbourne. When in the mood and with his luck running, Greenidge was the complete killer at the crease, and at one stage held the highest score in all three county limited-overs competitions.

'Streaking' became a craze among the inebriated and uninhibited in the mid-1970s, and Lord's first streaker descended during the Test match. Turner, Knott and umpire Spencer could only smile, but the magistrate fined the young gentleman a sum equal to his winning bet.

The Headingley Test of 1975 was nicely poised by the fourth evening, Australia being 220 for 3 and in need of a further 225 for victory, both Chappells out, but McCosker 95 not out and Walters 25 not out and perhaps ready at last to turn on one of his special displays for an English audience. But there was to be no final-day's play, for supporters of the imprisoned George Davis crawled under the pitch-covers during the night and dug the turf and poured sump-oil on it. Their demonstration was aimed at drawing attention to their friend's alleged innocence. The match was abandoned. Rain would have taken away much of the fifth day in any case.

Bob Woolmer of Kent made a couple of thirties and had Ross Edwards lbw for 99 at Lord's on his Test debut in 1975, missed the next Test, and then made a marathon 149 when England followed on at The Oval. His time to 100 (396 minutes) was then the slowest in England–Australia Tests.

Australian captain Ian Chappell leaves the South Australian Cricket Association office at Adelaide after a hearing over his behaviour in 1975–76. A brilliant batsman, believed by some to have had even more talent than younger brother Greg, he was also a good legspinner, a slips catcher in the Simpson class (this season he became the first Australian to hold 100 Test catches), but most notably a captain who never missed a trick, who would die for his men, as they would for him, and who seemed to despise opponents and administrators.

Left: *Having moved from South Australia to Queensland and, in 1975–76, taken over the Australian captaincy from his brother, Greg Chappell wrote another record by making two hundreds in his first Test as leader, against West Indies at Brisbane, where he also hit the winning run.*

Right: *A truly remarkable innings came from the flashing bat of Roy Fredericks in the Perth Test, his century coming off a mere 71 balls, in only 116 minutes. Here he canes a short ball from Gilmour. Fredericks finished with 169, Lloyd, his fellow Guyanese, 149, West Indies with 585, and an innings victory, Roberts finishing Australia off with 7 for 54 on the fast WACA pitch. Below: West Indies' slim offspinner Lance Gibbs, playing in his 79th and final Test, is congratulated on passing Trueman's Test record of 307 wickets (67 Tests). Gibbs finished with 309, having propelled 27,115 balls.*

Above: *Streaking becomes an international sport. This invader successfully jumped the stumps, holding up play in the Perth Australia–West Indies Test. Some of the Australian players took to playing a square-cut or two across the buttocks of intruders.*

India scored 406 for 4 to win the third Test of the 1975–76 series, at Port-of-Spain, and level the series in astonishing fashion after Viv Richards had made his third century in as many Tests. Gavaskar and Viswanath made centuries and Amarnath a crucial 85 in the fourth innings. India paid the price in the next Test, however, the West Indies fast bowlers blitzing them at Sabina Park. Three Indian batsmen were badly injured while batting and two bowlers were hurt while fielding, so that five out was all out (for 97) in the second innings. As ever, the cartoonists were ready, pens poised, to give their own interpretation.

Bishan Singh Bedi needed all his philosophical strength in the Caribbean after his team's courageous performances all came to nothing in the final Test. During this injury-strewn match, with Holding, Daniel, Julien and Holder an extremely difficult proposition on a dubious pitch, India used all 17 tour players as their need for substitutes grew. One of them, Surinder Amarnath, went down with appendicitis on the fourth day.

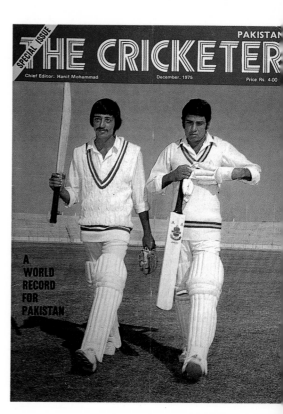

Right: Pakistan batsmen continued to attack the record book. In 1969–70, Arshad Parvez (396 not out) and Usman (236 not out) had put on 599 unbroken for the third wicket in a non-first-class college game. Now, Khalid Irtiza (left) (290) and Azlam Ali (236) stole the Whitelaw–Carson world third-wicket record by adding 456 for United Bank in their BCCP Patron's Trophy quarter-final against Multan at Karachi, a feat honoured on the front cover of the national cricket magazine.

Richard Hadlee's first great field day came at Christchurch in 1974 when his 7 for 130 in the match helped New Zealand to their first victory over Australia, but here at Wellington in February 1976 he leads off having taken 7 for 23 against India, the best figures ever to date for New Zealand (11 for 58 in the match). Few could have foretold that 10 years hence he would be an even greater menace to batsmen with his clever, well-organised seam variations.

Above: No respecter of persons, Dennis Lillee pounds in a bumper to Graeme Pollock during an International Cavaliers' tour of South Africa. Though his country was now outlawed, Pollock managed to serve up spasmodic reminders of his greatness as the years passed.

Right: Viv Richards made 1710 Test runs in 1976, a record, and 829 of them came in the four Tests he played in England. Here, in the first, at Trent Bridge, he hit four cannonball sixes and 31 fours in an innings of 232. Experience with Somerset had advanced the Antiguan's game, but it was clear that here was a huge natural talent.

At long last the ladies are welcomed onto the sacred Lord's turf. In 1976, in the Golden Jubilee year of the Women's Cricket Association, England and Australia played a one-day international before an enthusiastic gathering. Rachael Heyhoe Flint leads England, the eventual winners, into the field. Enid Bakewell (centre) later scored 50 and Chris Watmough (second from left) 50 not out. Australia's top-scorer was Sharon Tredrea with 54. Mrs Flint batted for 8½ hours for 179 to save the Oval Test, one of three draws.

A much uglier version of cricket: Brian Close, aged 45, ducks one of a succession of vicious bouncers from West Indies bowler Michael Holding (known on the circuit as 'Whispering Death') in the Old Trafford Test of 1976. Close and his 39-year-old partner John Edrich had to withstand a brutal assault on the third evening, when England went in needing 552 in 13¼ hours. Roberts, Holding and Daniel seemed intent on frightening England's two tough veterans, and Holding was eventually warned by umpire Alley for intimidation . West Indies captain Clive Lloyd admitted later that 'our fellows got carried away'. England were out for 126, an improvement on their first-innings 71, and lost by the huge margin of 425 runs. Greenidge made very fine hundreds in both innings, but his feat was overshadowed by the unsavoury over-aggression that was now becoming a key feature of West Indian cricket.

West Indies won the 1976 series
against England 3–0, taking the
Oval Test conclusively, Holding
bowling fast and beautifully to take
14 wickets (12 bowled or lbw). But
Amiss (above), with his modified
stance – a squarer shuffle –
compiled an heroic 203, his second
double-century off West Indies Test
bowling.
Right: Viv Richards went a stage
further, falling only nine runs short
of a triple-century. When England's
keeper, Knott, stumped Rowe he
became Test cricket's top performer,
passing Evans's 219 dismissals.
Marsh later overtook him.

ort **OKAY, SO I'M
OVELLING NOW!**

Greig cheered as
he goes on
his knees

Gerry's
header
gives
Spurs
a lift

Pledge
5p for
Chelsea!

DING **READY TO PUT**
SCREWS ON

Left: England's tall,
blond, South African
captain Tony Greig
inflamed the West
Indians by saying he
planned to make them
'grovel'. He could
laugh at himself by the
gruelling last day or
so of the series.

Right: Another world
record from Pakistan:
Waheed Mirza (324)
(left) and Mansoor
Akhtar (224 not out)
with 'Little Master'
Hanif after their stand
of 561 for Karachi
Whites' first wicket
against Quetta.

549

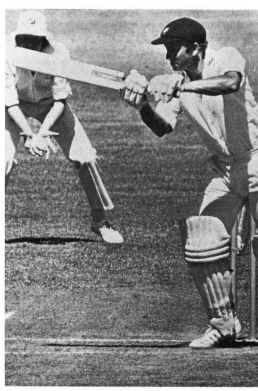

Above: *Doug Walters made the highest of his 14 Test centuries in his 62nd Test, a 6½-hour 250 against New Zealand at Christchurch in February 1977. He and Gilmour (101) added 217 in little more than three hours.*

Above left: *Clive Lloyd, the big, loose-limbed West Indian left-hander, equalled Jessop's record speed for a double-century, reaching 200 in only 120 minutes in the tourists' match against Glamorgan at the St Helens ground, Swansea in August 1976. There have been few more destructive hitters than Lloyd, whose heavy bat, with multiple rubber grips on the handle, swung through a sweeping arc.*

Left: *Zaheer Abbas, the Pakistani with an exceptional hunger for runs, twice in the 1976 season scored a double-century and a century (all not-out) for Gloucestershire: against Surrey at The Oval in June and Kent at Canterbury in August, a feat all his own. A batsman of some style, he consciously sought high achievement, and was firmly on course to register a century of centuries.*

Above: *Final over of the drawn Test at Christchurch, with Lillee bowling to a field seldom seen and even less often photographed, nine men in the slips cordon. It is believed that one of the players arranged the crescent with a dust-jacket for his forthcoming book in mind.*

'Doctor' Lillee discusses Jeff Thomson's X-ray with the patient. 'Thommo' suffered a severe injury to his right shoulder when he and Alan Turner collided in the field in the Adelaide Test between Australia and Pakistan in December 1976. Thomson was indisposed for the rest of the season.

Right: *Last ball of a tense Currie Cup match between Western Province and Transvaal at Cape Town, and Clive Rice has shot the ball through Rob Drummond, and Transvaal have won by four runs. WP were despondent, but still went on to win the Currie Cup in 1974–75, with Transvaal, for the moment, left to dwell on their 21 previous triumphs to Natal's 18.*

Above: *A sight to tease English eyes as their persecutor, Viv Richards, in a Queensland cap, is bowled by Lillee for a duck in a Gillette semi-final at Perth, when the home side, out for 77, knocked Queensland over for 62.* Left: *Bob Willis tests an Indian batsman in the 1976–77 Calcutta Test. England won the first three Tests, and the fast man took 20 wickets in the series.* Below: *John Lever, who took 7 for 46 at Delhi (and scored 53) on Test debut, has an lbw shout against Mohinder Amarnath at Madras, where the Essex left-armer took seven wickets but was accused by Bedi of applying vaseline to the ball to aid its swinging powers.*

England captain Greig pads the ball away with his own special brand of theatricality in the Calcutta Test, when he reached his century in 415 minutes, a grand piece of application considering he was far from well throughout. In this match he became the first to 3000 Test runs and 100 wickets for England.

Above: *Peter Petherick completes a hat-trick at Lahore in October 1976 in his first Test for New Zealand. The offspinner has had Intikhab taken by a slick catch by Geoff Howarth. Pakistan won the series 2–0, with one match drawn.*

Left: *Ian Brayshaw, Dennis Lillee and Rodney Marsh savour the proud pleasure of having won the Sheffield Shield and the Gillette Cup in 1976–77. Western Australia had now all but buried the memory of the long cinderella period.*

Packer and Beyond

LOOKING BACK on it, it can so easily seem that big cricket was ripe for the revolution which swept through it in 1977. Many of the major players, particularly the Australians, were disgruntled at their relatively poor pay when compared with the rewards as opposed to obligations of champion golfers and tennis players. The catalyst came in an unlikely shape. Kerry Packer, an Australian second-generation media baron, tried to overcome his frustration at not being allowed exclusive television rights of Test cricket by setting up his own series of matches featuring dozens of the world's best players, all of whom had been signed for large sums of money and granted comforts previously unfamiliar to them. The established authorities, deeply dismayed, did their best to offset the loss and undermine the success of World Series Cricket (a success which was a long time in materialising), and soon a state of war existed in international cricket. Families were split over the rights and wrongs, and friendships were shattered as the traditional and rebel organisations sweated at their tug-of-war. It was a sectarian matter. And the sadness of the situation was magnified in that it was all happening so soon after cricket's greatest birthday party, the Centenary Test match of March 1977, in Melbourne. Blissfully ignorant of the secret plans that were being laid for the breakaway movement, the majority of the players, ex-players and followers sat back, champagne glass in hand, and revelled in a classic five-day match and the ocean of nostalgia in which it floated.

Most of them went to Australia in their playing days by sea. Now, early in March 1977, this large group of England Ashes Test cricket veterans prepares to fly to the sun for the grand celebration in Melbourne of 100 years of Test matches. The elderly gentleman with the stick is P. G. H. Fender, at 84 the oldest to undertake the long journey. He was almost blind, and took his grandson with him: 'He is my eyes'.

The highlight on the field in the Centenary Test, from England's point of view, was Derek Randall's brave stroke-filled innings of 174. It was his first Ashes Test, and like all his team-mates, he had failed in the first innings, when England crashed for 95 (Lillee 6 for 26, Walker 4 for 54) in reply to Australia's equally jittery first-day 138. Australia settled down in the second innings, Marsh scoring 110 not out, Ian Davis 68, Walters 66, and debutant David Hookes 56 (including five fours off consecutive balls from Greig). England's remote target was 463, and Randall, with help from Mike Brearley (in picture), Amiss, Greig and Knott, almost reached it. Australia's winning margin, 45 runs, was the same as in the first of all Tests, on the same ground, 100 years less two days before.

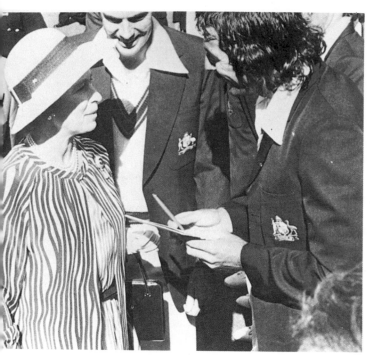

Australia's resurrected bowling hero Dennis Lillee, whose 11 wickets failed to win him the Centenary Test Man of the Match award (Randall edged him out), had the effrontery to ask The Queen for her autograph when Her Majesty met the teams. The gracious lady later sent him a signed photograph.

Right: *Australian opener Rick McCosker, his jaw broken by a bouncer from Bob Willis, batted at No. 10 in the second innings – and hooked a Lever bouncer for four, to the roars of appreciation of a huge MCG crowd. McCosker's 25 was extremely useful, viewed against the eventual narrow margin of victory.*

No photograph expresses better the spirit of camaraderie – even forgiveness – in which the Melbourne Centenary Test of 1977 was bathed. Sir Donald Bradman, whose head was constantly having to be withdrawn from the flying fast stuff sent down by Harold Larwood in the 1932–33 'Bodyline' series, is seen conversing with his old tormentor, a situation patently unlikely back in the days of hot combat. Larwood (right) may have been picturing his four dismissals of The Don in that series, while the greatest of batsmen could have been thinking of the hundreds of runs he scored in all Tests against the Notts express. Lillee is a fascinated listener.

Ray Illingworth, 45, and Ken Higgs, 40, wise old heads, put on 228 for Leicestershire's 10th wicket against Northants in 1977, after their side had collapsed to 45 for 9. Higgs was run out for 98, leaving 'Illy' 119 not out.

Left: He's back home! Derek Randall, irrepressible clown, hero of the Centenary Test, seems glad to be back in England, a country whose cricket he was to serve so well but which in turn maltreated him with erratic selection. Some followers felt he was worth a permanent place in the Test XI for his high spirits and electric fielding alone.

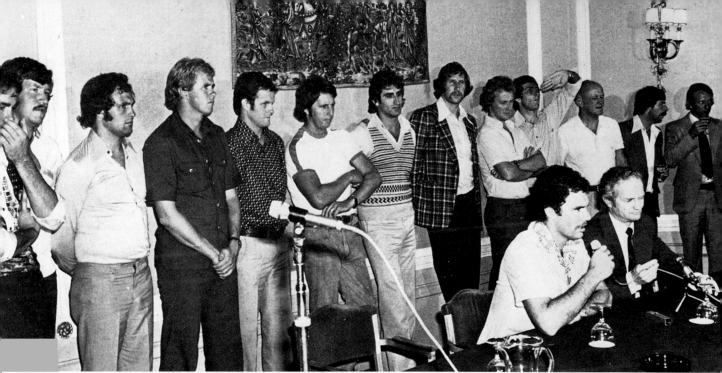

The 'Ugly Australians', the rebellious, 'uncouth' image established under Ian Chappell's captaincy, lingered still over Greg Chappell's 1977 team in England, a less than cohesive side, particularly after the camp split with the revelation in May that the majority had signed to play in the disapproved Packer World Series. Lillee did not tour.

Left: Mike Brearley courageously pioneered a protective skullcap in 1977, brushing mockery aside with the assertion that he valued the part of his anatomy under it as Thomson and Pascoe flung down their bouncers.

Below: Tony Greig, a prime figure in the setting-up of World Series, lost the England captaincy as a result (Brearley getting it), but continued to play a big part in the 1977 Tests. At Old Trafford, where he made 76, the umpire had no sight of a faint touch to Marsh. Marsh did.

The front-page story on August 12, 1977 was Geoff Boycott's 100th century. He was the 18th batsman to achieve this (John Edrich had done so a month before) but the first to do so in a Test match – and before his adoring Yorkshire crowd at Headingley. There had been an inevitability about it from the moment this determined man took strike. 'Magic!' he repeated as he sipped champagne at the close. He had emerged from self-imposed Test exile in the previous match, at Trent Bridge, with a tedious 107.

The summer of 1977 saw England reclaim the Ashes with a resounding 3–0 victory, but it was a summer of distraction and manoeuvrings in the face of the Australian rebellion which touched other countries too as players signed for Packer and consequently became unavailable for Test cricket. The International Cricket Conference thus sat at Lord's in July with more worries than usual on its plate.

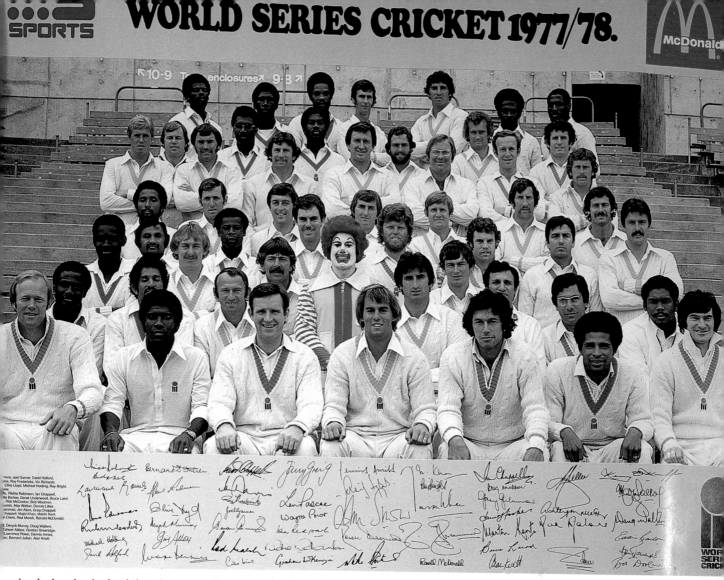

Anybody who doubted that the cream of world cricket had signed for Kerry Packer had only to gather the evidence as portrayed on a bright poster readily available in hamburger bars around Australia.

Left: *Greg Chappell completes Australia's victory in pouring rain in the one-day international at The Oval in June 1977. He finished 125 not out. Some said the skies wept for the costly mess in which cricket now found itself.*

Right: *Kerry Packer seemed a fearsome adversary, physically and financially, to the established game. Law and Fluck saw him as Genghis Khan: 'He wasn't very lovable,' said Packer, 'but he was bloody efficient.' Most of the rebel players felt that was something the old administrators were not.*

559

One of many amazing revolutionary features of World Series Cricket was the laying of pitches grown in concrete tubs in greenhouses. They were craned into position at VFL Park, Melbourne (the MCG being positively unavailable), and played better than the opposition had hoped and expected, though not with any great life.

Below: Australia, depleted by the mass defection to World Series Cricket, played five Tests against India, capping 12 new players in the series, which was full of suspense, Australia winning 3–2. The visiting captain was the affable B. S. Bedi, who was very seldom seen without one of his colourful patkas on his head.

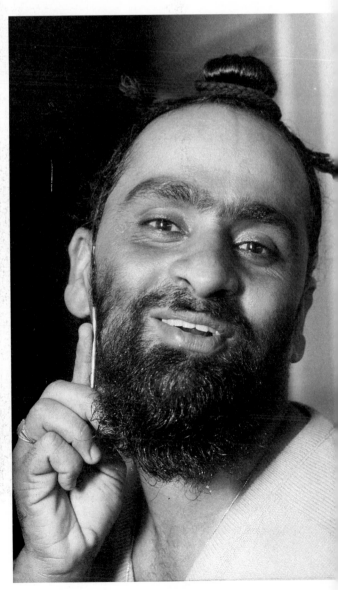

Night cricket was World Series' greatest innovation, and the first such game, at VFL Park on December 14, 1977, was a fateful happening, for although crowds for a time were so meagre as to be an embarrassment to the organisers, these noisy nocturnal offerings – coloured clothing, white balls, black sightscreens and all – became big, brash, moneyspinning occasions.

The full-strength West Indies side crushed Simpson's inexperienced Australians at Port-of-Spain (where Peter Toohey edged a Roberts bouncer into his face) and Bridgetown. The West Indian Packer players then fell out with the Board, and six newcomers came in, and lost to Australia by three wickets. West Indies won the fourth Test and the fifth was drawn, Toohey scoring 122 and 97.

Bob Simpson, now 41, was recalled by Australia in their hour of need, having retired from Test cricket 10 years earlier. He took charge of the 'legitimate' Test side for five home Tests against India, scoring 176 in 6½ hours at Perth (and needing to cool his feet) and 100 at Adelaide.

Another helmet appears: Australia's Graham Yallop ducks to Colin Croft (8 for 29 a year earlier in his second Test) at Bridgetown.

Right: *In South Africa a huge advance was made in the setting-up of the multiracial South African Cricket Union, the hopes of the new body being that it would bring the end of isolation. Standing: S. B. Myers (WP), F. B. Gouws (OFS), M. Henning (Tvl), N. E. Markham (Natal), F. Brache (WP), D. J. Lewis (Rhodesia); seated: D. V. Dyer (Natal), M. R. Varachia (Tvl) (president), B. Wallace (WP), J. L. Pamensky (Tvl) (hon. treasurer).*

Hassan Howa, president of the 'non-racial' South African Cricket Board, has vigorously opposed anything in the slightest suggestive of compromise, even refusing large sums of sponsorship offered to his organisation. 'You cannot have normal cricket in an abnormal society' has been his battle-cry.

Above left: Mudassar Nazar. Son of a Test player, he made the slowest Test – and first-class – century when, against England at Lahore in December 1977, he stayed put for nine hours and 17 minutes. It was only his second Test match, and fears were felt that the tempo of his marathon innings might become the norm and even be contagious. But Mudassar was to strengthen his game, rather as Glenn Turner had done, and he built an admirable career.

All three 1977–78 Pakistan–England Tests were drawn, Haroon Rashid making two centuries. In the third Test, at Karachi, when Boycott captained England after Brearley's arm was broken, Abdul Qadir (above bowling to Roope) followed his 6 for 44 at Hyderabad with 4 for 81. Phil Edmonds (right) took 7 for 66 at Karachi, then the best figures for either side in these Tests.

When 'Thommo' bowled them, he really bowled them. In the fourth Test, 1977–78, at Sydney, he showed that that great right shoulder of his had healed properly. India's Viswanath had made 79.

World Series Cricket was tailored for television, right down to the vividly-coloured caps. Kerry Packer's Channel 9 now had its own cricket, and it gave it heavy promotion and saturation coverage, with more cameras and more angles and more tricks of presentation than had ever before been envisaged. Ian Chappell, having forsaken Australia's traditional baggy green cap, bats in WSC gold, with World XI players Greig, Procter and Knott in close attendance.

At last New Zealand's day has come: their first victory over the Mother Country, at Wellington, February 15, 1978. Richard Hadlee, holding sweater, took 4 for 74 and 6 for 26, and shakes his captain Mark Burgess's hand. Others are Dick Collinge, who took his 100th Test wicket here, wicketkeeper Warren Lees, Geoff Howarth and Dayle Hadlee. England levelled the series at Christchurch, where Ian Botham made his first Test century.

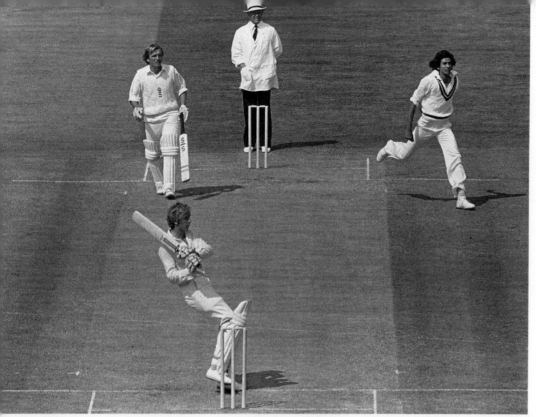

Another golden talent steps onto the Test match stage in 1978: David Gower swivels round and takes four runs in his first Test innings, at Edgbaston, Pakistan's Sikander Bakht the bowler, Clive Radley (making his second Test century) Gower's partner. Gower's incomparable ease of strokeplay and elegant, unruffled style were to prove an invaluable enhancement to the game in an era of recurring violence and ugliness.

England won at Edgbaston in 1978 by an innings, Chris Old having wrecked Pakistan's first innings with 7 for 50, including four wickets in one over. But in the second innings, when tailender Iqbal Qasim had been in for a while as nightwatchman, Willis let him have a bouncer, which badly lacerated Qasim's mouth, to general condemnation.

Ian Botham, escorted by Geoff Miller, Clive Radley, David Gower and Bob Taylor, walks off at Lord's after bowling England to another innings victory over Pakistan in 1978. His 8 for 34, achieved with clever variations and late swing, went with his century (his second in succession) to make a match contribution unique in Test history. Many other unique performances followed.

Having seen Pakistan off, in the first half of the 1978 summer, England, under Brearley, went one better against New Zealand, winning all three Tests. Geoff Howarth, though, made 94 at The Oval and 123 here at Lord's, where bowler Botham's agony was assuaged in the second innings when he (5 for 39) and Willis (4 for 16) demolished the Kiwis for 67.

Imran Khan, who first toured England in 1971 as an 18-year-old swing bowler with little control, was now an allrounder of world class for Pakistan. He hits lustily in a Gillette match against Lancashire in 1978, when Sussex went on to beat Somerset in the final at Lord's.

There were 14 centuries scored during the 1978–79 series between India and West Indies (India won 1–0), four of them by Gavaskar. But the highest was Faoud Bacchus's 250 at Kanpur, where he was garlanded upon reaching three figures.

That same season, India and Pakistan played each other for the first time for 18 years, political tensions having eased. Zaheer, having made 176 in the drawn first Test, now scored 235 not out at Lahore, where Pakistan won.

Sunil Gavaskar and Dilip Vengsarkar resume their colossal stand of 344 (unbroken) against West Indies at Calcutta over New Year 1979. Lacking their World Series players, West Indies had an attack consisting of Sylvester Clarke, Norbert Phillip, Malcolm Marshall, Derick Parry and Vanburn Holder, none of whom could make much impression on a good pitch. Gavaskar, who had now made twin centuries in a Test three times, declared to set the visitors 335 in 365 minutes, and they clung on for a draw at 197 for 9 when bad light forced an end 11 balls early. Shivnarine, 36 not out in two hours, pulled away often as spectators moved behind the bowler's arm. His effort, a dropped catch, and India's surprisingly casual over rate saved his side.

Sarfraz Nawaz, the big, awkward Pakistan fast-medium bowler, had the best of many good Test match days at Melbourne in March 1979, when he took 9 for 86 in Australia's second innings, claiming the last seven wickets for one only run.

Australian WSC players Thomson, Wessels, McCosker and Pascoe are under siege in the Georgetown dressing-room after disgruntled West Indian fans had rioted. The helmets were worn seriously and bats brandished for self-defence. They were later able to escape quietly.

566

VFL Park, Melbourne during the second year of World Series Cricket. The four-day 'Supertest' began at 2 pm and went through till 10 pm, floodlights having been turned on before dusk. After the dinner break the temperature sometimes dropped uncomfortably. Then, the crowds built up, with coffee flasks and blankets necessities. Apart from the limited-overs matches, these games drew poor attendances, and as the traditional Tests and Sheffield Shield matches suffered as well, with many cricket-lovers too confused to go to any cricket match at all, it was abundantly clear that cricket's great split had to be resolved – quickly.

The Englishmen, South Africans and Pakistanis were content in their blue costume, the Australians in their wattle gold (not yellow), but the West Indians were none too comfortable in pink – the homosexual's colour in the Caribbean.

When World Series finally gained access to the Sydney Cricket Ground, 'establishment' cricket-followers were dismayed. The invasion of the old game by the Americanised new concept seemed complete. On the century-old SCG visiting players' balcony are World XI players Mike Denness (manager), Dennis Amiss, Bruce Francis (consultant), Asif Iqbal, Bob Woolmer, Eddie Barlow, Mike Procter (in doorway), Barry Richards, and Zaheer Abbas.

567

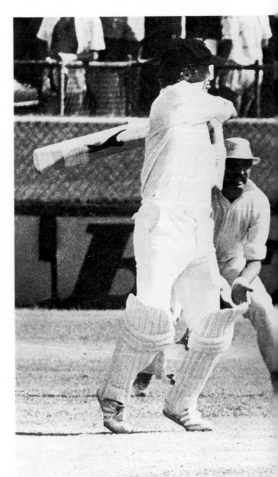

Left: *Lillee was a star attraction with World Series, his name chanted by the crowds as he ran in to bowl, and his response duly theatrical. The umpire is Douglas Sang Hue, imported from West Indies and adding to the international flavour.*

Kim Hughes, promising for several years, was one who got his Test chance with the Packer players unavailable. At Brisbane he scored 129 against England, his 369-minute century being then the slowest for Australia in Tests.

Above: *Gower's 102 at Perth was one of only two centuries for England in the six Tests of 1978–79, a series won 5–1 against a Packer-depleted Australian side. In conditions which helped bowlers, this was a sterling innings. Rodney Hogg, the sprawling bowler, took five wickets in each innings, and a record 41 in the series, bowling mercilessly at the off stump and moving the ball predominantly in to the bat.*

Right: *A pall of gloom descended over the last weeks of the 1978–79 Ashes series when news came through that the companionable Jimmy Burke had taken his own life. A dogged and valuable opening batsman, he had made a century in his first Test, in 1950–51, and two others in his 24-Test career for Australia. For some years he had been a popular radio commentator.*

Above: *Lancashire's captain Jack Simmons spent several northern winters in Tasmania, and led them, to huge local acclaim, to their first major success, the 1978–79 Gillette Cup.*

Left: *Geoff Boycott, while ever the studious craftsman, had a grim '78–79 tour, averaging only 21.92 in the Tests, with a highest score of 77. Here he plays Hogg in the Melbourne Test, where Australia drew back to 1–2, Graeme Wood scoring 100 and Hogg again taking five wickets in each innings.*

In the fourth Test, at Sydney, Randall played an innings to rank with his 174 in the Centenary Test: 150 in almost 10 hours when England went in again 142 in arrears. With massive self-discipline he and Brearley, the captain, slowly turned the match round. Hendrick, Emburey and Miller then bowled Australia out for 111 for a 93-run victory that ensured retention of the Ashes. Behind Randall are Hughes and wicketkeeper John Maclean.

There was great anxiety during the Adelaide Test of 1978–79 when Australian opener Rick Darling collapsed after being hit in the chest by a ball from Willis. After being tended by the pitch – Emburey released his tongue blockage – the dashing young local man was taken to hospital. Some hours later he returned to the Oval and resumed his innings. Australian captain Graham Yallop, who scored superb hundreds in the first and sixth Tests, put England in here, and Botham's 74 saved a total English disaster. But Australia then crashed for 164 (five behind), saw Bob Taylor score 97 to lift England to 360, and then subsided themselves for 160 to lose by 205 runs. It was a series all Australians wished to forget, and which prompted everyone to pray for a reconciliation which would see the likes of Lillee, Chappell and Marsh back in the Test team.

Right: *Flashback to the High Court hearing, with Kerry Packer and his principal spokesman, deposed England captain Tony Greig. In November 1977 Mr Justice Slade found for WSC on all nine points at issue, and the TCCB and ICC were prevented from banning WSC players: this would have been 'restraint of trade'. The bitter feud went on, both sides losing large sums. Then, in April 1979, the war ended. Channel 9 got the coveted TV rights in Australia and their marketing arm, PBL, became the Australian Cricket Board's promotion agents.*

Derek Randall remained the most fascinating player on view, and averaged 47 in 1979. But the Test selectors never backed him consistently.

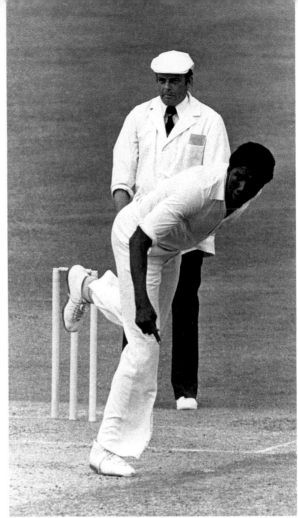

West Indies retained the Prudential World Cup in 1979, beating England in the final at Lord's by 92 runs. Viv Richards (above left) made a splendid 138 not out, but Collis King, his partner, scored an 86 that made sure of things. Boycott and Brearley began with 129, but it took too long, and in the gathering darkness the 6 ft 8 ins Joel Garner (above right) crashed through to finish with 5 for 38.

Right: Runs flowed in a torrent from Glenn Turner's bat, and when he scored 109 against Lancashire at Southport in 1979 he completed the unique set of centuries against all 17 counties, MCC, Oxford and Cambridge Universities, and four Test countries.

Left: *The boyish David Gower came of age as a Test player during the 1978–79 tour of Australia, but any followers back home in England who were still unconvinced had their proof in the opening Test against India at Edgbaston in 1979. Gower stroked 200 not out, Boycott made 155, England 633 for 5 dec, and Willis, Botham, Hendrick and Edmonds then bowled England to an innings win.*

Below: *India's little master, Gavaskar, continued to treat the batting crease as his God-given domain, irrespective of venue or opposition, and in 1979, when India needed 438 to beat England at The Oval, he almost piloted them to victory with a 490-minute 221, his 20th Test century. India finished on 429 for 8 and the match was drawn.*

Above: *Mike Procter receives the Lawrence Trophy for the fastest hundred of 1979 (57 minutes, Gloucestershire v Northants, Bristol). Jim Laker, now a shrewd TV commentator, holds the microphone while former Hampshire skipper Colin Ingleby-Mackenzie makes the jokily hearty speech.*

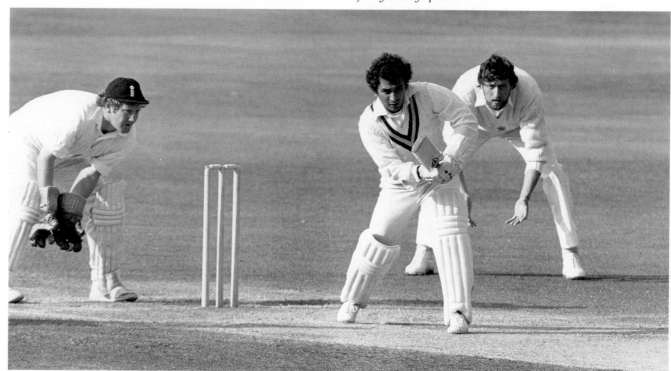

Ian Botham receives the Man of the Match medallion from adjudicator John Edrich at the end of the 1979 Oval Test, having taken seven wickets on a plumb pitch – and passed 1000 Test runs in his 21st match, which gave him the fastest 1000 runs/100 wickets double, two matches fewer than Vinoo Mankad. Cornhill Insurance were now sponsoring English Test cricket, a valuable biproduct of the Packer revolution which made top players wealthier and the game more securely based financially.

Essex had never won a thing before 1979, but that season this happy and talented band, under Keith Fletcher's smart but unfussy captaincy, won the Benson & Hedges Cup and the Championship. The Daily Express gave Essex their Team of the Year award. In the 1980s, trophies became a regular matter. With Fletcher are John Lever, Stuart Turner, Neil Smith, Brian Hardie, Ray East, Graham Gooch and Mike Denness.

Jim Parks snr, who did the unique 3000 runs/100 wickets double in 1937, poses with his son Jim, who played in 46 Tests for England, and grandson Bobby, Hampshire's wicketkeeper in the 1980s, who acted as England's substitute wicketkeeper at Lord's in 1986 when Bruce French was injured. The Parks family, genial men all, were one of cricket's great dynasties. Jim senior died in 1980 at the age of 77.

India beat Australia 2–0 in the six Tests of 1979–80, even though Geoff Dymock took 12 wickets at Kanpur – dismissing every Indian batsman in one innings or the other. Pictured is Kim Hughes in the first Test, at Madras, driving Dilip Doshi during his century. Hughes added 222 with Border (162). Doshi, a cunning slow left-arm bowler, took 6 for 103 in his first Test innings, and went on to take over 100 Test wickets although he was 31 when he started in Tests.

Cricket would never be the same again after the disruption and eventual reshaping of the international game following the advent of World Series. The new formula for 1979–80 in Australia was to invite England and West Indies for three Tests each and an extensive limited-overs tournament. Mike Brearley, the England captain, was the target of regular abuse from the crowd – and of this Holding bouncer with the white ball at Sydney. Australians seemed to regard Brearley as standing for all that offended them about the English character.

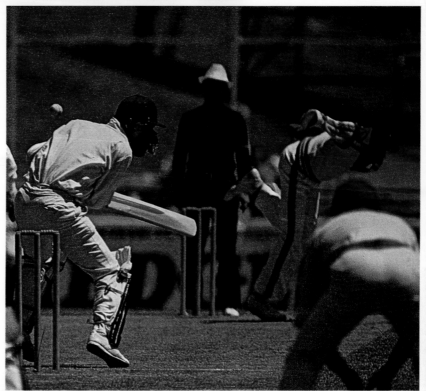

Lillee (in helmet) caused a stir in the Perth Test by using a bat made of aluminium. He had an interest in the firm manufacturing them. Brearley objected, since the ball was being scarred, and a long, angry discussion ensued. Lillee eventually hurled the metal bat away in frustration. The incident tended later to overshadow several milestones: Lillee's 100th wicket against England and Boycott's carrying his bat for 99 not out.

Greg Chappell, back in charge of Australia (having missed the Indian tour, when Kim Hughes was captain), led his side to victory in all three Tests of 1979–80 against England – and to defeat twice against West Indies. At Sydney his 98 not out saw Australia home by six wickets.

Below: Yorkshiremen Graham Stevenson and David Bairstow depart the floodlit Sydney ground in triumph after a helterskelter partnership that turned a lost cause in a limited-overs international against Australia. 'Nice night for it!' Stevenson had chortled on his arrival in the crisis.

Missing a century by a foot: Graham Gooch gambles on Hughes's throw and is run out for 99 in the Melbourne Test. Gooch's maiden Test century came four months later, against West Indies at Lord's.

Joel Garner, Colin Croft and Michael Holding, whose hostile bowling took almost all of the wickets for West Indies on the '79–80 tour, as was the case generally as the side, under Clive Lloyd's firm control, won match after match.

575

On the way back from Australia, England called in to play a special Test match in Bombay to celebrate the golden jubilee of the Board of Control for Cricket in India, such is the frantic calendar and expediency of transportation of modern international cricket. The occasion provided Botham with another chance to create a record: this time a century and 10 wickets (he took 13) in the same Test. England's classy 38-year-old wicketkeeper, Bob Taylor, also carved a special niche: he equalled Wasim Bari's record of seven catches in a Test innings, and became the first to hold 10 in a match. He caught Shivlal Yadav (above) in both innings. Eight of his catches were off Botham's vibrant bowling.

The New Zealanders were toasting victory with an increasing frequency, but this one, at Dunedin in February 1980, was extra special in that they had vanquished the mighty West Indies – by one wicket. Gary Troup, Peter Webb, Bruce Edgar, Richard Hadlee, Jeremy Coney, John Wright and John Parker savour the TV replays. For their part the West Indians felt aggrieved at the umpiring.

Ian Botham (centre) found himself captain of England in 1980, at the age of 24, with 25 Tests behind him. The opposition, for the next 10 scheduled Tests, unfortunately for him, was West Indies. Here he sets Peter Willey's field at Lord's, watched by Desmond Haynes, who scored 184, the highest for West Indies on that ground. Willey (100 not out) and Willis (24 not out) put on 117 for the 10th wicket to save England (who were 92 for 9) in the Oval Test.

West Indies captain Clive Lloyd, on his 'home' ground, Old Trafford, moves to a face-saving century – and past 5000 Test runs. His side won by two wickets at Trent Bridge, but were somehow held to draws in the other four Tests.

Kim Hughes had free-flowing, imaginative innings of 117 and 84 in the Centenary Test at Lord's – rekindling Trumper's spirit, as Jack Fingleton put it.

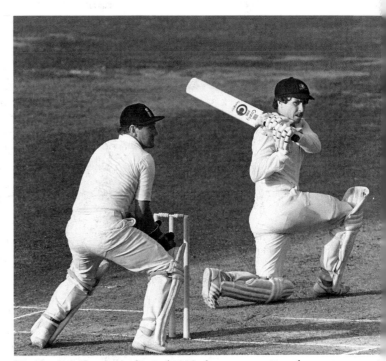

The English Centenary Test of 1980 also saw a century from Australian opener Graeme Wood, his third in Tests. Australia declared at 385 for 5, and Pascoe (5 for 59) and Lillee (4 for 43) bowled England out for 205; but rain blighted the match.

If the rain and the unwillingness of the umpires to get the show on the road (they were manhandled by frustrated MCC members) did nothing to help the 1980 Centenary Test, at least the great gathering of former players from England and Australia ensured that the event would be just as nostalgically convivial as its 1977 Melbourne counterpart. The front row alone includes a bright galaxy of Ashes Test heroes: O'Reilly, Darling, a'Beckett, Ponsford, Sandham, Ray Steele (ACB treasurer), May, Greg Chappell, S. C. Griffith (MCC president), Botham, Bob Parish (ACB chairman), F. G. Mann (TCCB chairman), Hendry, Allen, Wyatt and Fender.

John Arlott, for 35 years the voice of cricket on radio, bade farewell after the Centenary Test. Players and crowd showed their affection. Right: Boycott during his 128 not out, which ensured an unenterprising draw.

Intimidation is a long-term problem, and few attempts have been made to curb it. Umpire Bailhache tried at Melbourne in 1980 when Lance Cairns bounced one at No. 11 Jim Higgs, who was caught off his glove as he ducked. No-ball was called against the New Zealander.

Roland Butcher, Middlesex player, was chosen to tour West Indies with England in 1980–81, and when he made his Test debut in his native land, Barbados, he became the first black West Indian to play for England. He had lived in London since he was 13. The local newspaper expressed the prevalent feeling of ambivalence about Butcher: 'Our boy, their bat'.

The love–hate relationship – with not a great deal of the love – between trans-Tasman cousins New Zealand and Australia was fanned at Melbourne on February 1, 1981 when Trevor Chappell was instructed by brother Greg, Australia's captain, to bowl the final ball of a limited-overs international along the ground to ensure that New Zealand batsman Brian McKechnie had no chance of hitting the six needed for victory. The Chappells had few supporters in the indignant wave of outrage which followed, although it was observed in some cynical quarters that they were only exploiting an existing loophole (which was then swiftly blocked up), their decision having been guided by the large sums of prizemoney demanded by the players and now freely allocated by administrators and their sponsors.

Michael Holding bowled probably as probingly as a fast bowler ever could during the 1980–81 series against England, particularly at Bridgetown, where he gave Boycott the full treatment before getting him for 0 and 1. Gooch, also in the picture, made a valiant 116 in the forlorn second England innings.

Robin Jackman, 35, the chirpy little Surrey seam bowler, was deported from Guyana, a hard-line anti-apartheid territory, because of his strong South African playing and coaching links. With him went the England team, which meant cancellation of the Georgetown Test. The team waited in Barbados while other Caribbean territories debated the matter, and the tour eventually proceeded. Politics – not noticeably soaked in rationality – had once more pushed sport around, this time the cricket-lovers of Guyana being the losers. Below: Jackman was eventually capped by England in the Bridgetown Test, and took Greenidge's wicket with his fifth ball. It was safe enough for him to field on the boundary in this friendliest of islands.

Graham Dilley congratulates a shy, tired but satisfied Peter Willey on making a century which saved England's first innings at Antigua, late March 1981. West Indies had steamrollered to victory in the first two Tests, but centuries here by Willey and Boycott, together with brave marathon innings past 150 by Gooch and Gower at Kingston in the final Test, stopped the rot.

A century by Vivian Richards seemed preordained in Antigua's first-ever Test match. The island's greatest sporting son, recently married, hit 90 of his 114 runs in boundaries. It was his sixth century in 12 Tests against England (who now preferred Downton to Bairstow as their wicketkeeper).

Below: Boycott about to reach his 20th Test century. The 40-year-old's latest feat of endurance ensured a draw at St John's, Antigua.

Of all the setbacks endured by England in West Indies early in 1981 – the repatriation of Willis through injury, the Jackman rumpus, the heavy defeats – nothing compared with the sudden tragic death of team coach, assistant manager and former Test battler Ken Barrington. Cheery, unfailingly polite, modest, conscientious almost to a fault, and cricket-wise, he was respected – even adored – by his players, and his death on March 14, 1981 after a heart attack in the team's Barbados hotel caused universal grief. He was 50. This photograph was taken at Kensington Oval on his last morning.

Protective helmets were being worn by most batsmen – and, with dubious morality, by infielders – as the 1980s unfolded. This model, worn by Victorian and sometime Australian and WSC player Richie Robinson, resembled a Nazi helmet stumbled upon in an army relics disposal shop.

Left: John Emburey, flushed and fatigued after a long spell of offspinning under a scorching West Indian sun, brought much-needed classical guile and cool nerve to the international scene when he was not employed by Middlesex in their successful quest for trophies under Brearley and his 1983 successor Mike Gatting.

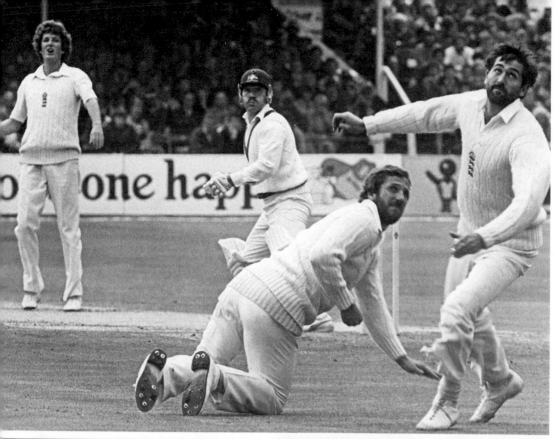

England picked themselves up after the West Indies setback, and with Willis recovered, faced Australia again. The visitors won at Trent Bridge – the first English Test to include Sunday play – with Allan Border, here edging Willis past Botham and Gooch, making match top score of 63. Willis took his 200th Test wicket in this match, and Marsh went to the top of the Test wicketkeeping catches list.

Geoff Lawson took 7 for 81 in the Lord's Test, which was drawn. Only Massie (1972) had returned better figures there for Australia. This was Boycott's 100th Test, and he equalled Cowdrey's record of 60 half-centuries. Right: Botham in one of the greatest match-turning innings ever. At Headingley, England followed on 227 runs behind, and lost their seventh wicket at 135. Having relinquished the captaincy after the Lord's Test, Botham assaulted the Australian bowling like a man with nothing to lose. Supported by Dilley (56), Old (29) and Willis (2), he scored 149 not out . . .

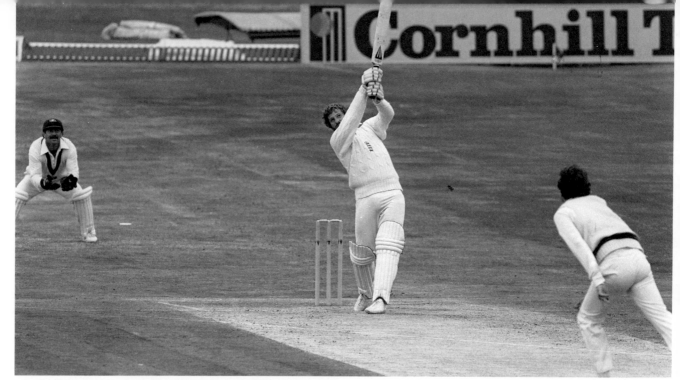

. . . Botham was unstoppable, it seemed, at Headingley, crashing an 87-minute century (here Alderman goes for a six) and taking England to an unexpected lead of 129 as he punished Lillee, Alderman and Lawson, spinner Bright getting only four overs: an incredible turnaround, but England's task still seemed too great.

Australian captain Kim Hughes is hit by the tornado named Willis as the England fast bowler, eyes blazing, tried to complete the miracle hinted as possible by Botham's astonishing assault with the bat. The big man stormed in and had Trevor Chappell, Hughes and Yallop caught just before the lunch interval. Old took Border's important wicket, Willis got first-innings centurymaker Dyson, and Marsh, caught off the hook (Marsh had passed Knott's Test record of 263 dismissals in this match).

The next to go was Lawson (right), beaten by sheer speed, and Australia were 75 for 8, still 55 short of victory. Lillee (who had broken Trumble's Ashes record of 141 wickets in this Test) then swung the odds back Australia's way, adding 35 with Bright in only four overs. Willis finally had Lillee caught at mid-on, which left Bright and Alderman. The latter twice edged Botham to Old . . . and was dropped. But then Willis finished the job, bowling Bright for an England victory by 18 runs and personal figures of 8 for 43.

Botham's exploits in the 1981 Tests tended to overshadow everything else, including the skill and persistence of Terry Alderman, whose seam bowling brought Australia 42 wickets in the six Tests, a record against England. His senior partner, fellow Western Australian Dennis Lillee (shown passing on a tip), took 39 wickets: a curious situation that a pair should take 81 wickets in a series and still finish on the losing side. Lillee, now 32, and reduced by a viral ailment, was still as clever and demanding as a Spofforth.

The question remains: who was the making of whom? Did ex-captain Botham turn the 1981 series round because recalled skipper Brearley knew how to get the best out of this erratic buccaneer? Or did Botham's great innings at Headingley (and Old Trafford: an 86-ball hundred) and bowling at Edgbaston (5 for 1 to steal a 29-run victory) elevate Brearley's reputation as a shrewd leader to that of pure genius?

Left: *Dirk Wellham, who scored a century on his first-class debut for NSW, now does so in his first Test, The Oval 1981.*
Right: *Yallop swings at Willis in the Edgbaston Test. In the next, at Old Trafford, he made a 114 full of flair, and with Border making 123 not out (the slowest hundred for Australia) they reached 402: 104 short of victory.*

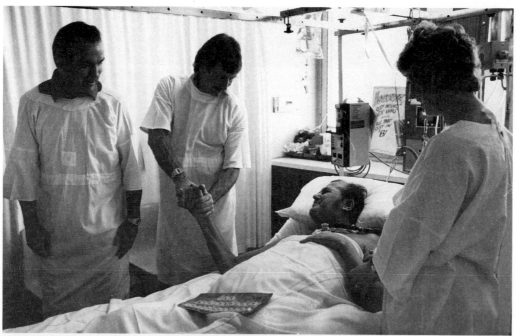

One of Australia's strong men of the 1960s, the burly Neil Hawke, fought a titanic struggle for his life during 1980–81 following complications to an operation. His obituary was written in readiness for the Adelaide newspapers, as his heart needed reactivating 12 times. As the fight went on against septicaemia, gangrene, liver and kidney failure, he lost weight and could not speak. Communication with former team-mates Bob Simpson and Ian Chappell later became possible with Scrabble letters. With his wife-to-be constantly by his bedside, Hawke eventually made an heroic recovery.

Left: *The County Championship returns to Nottinghamshire after 52 years. Clive Rice and his men, Richard Hadlee (105 wickets and 745 runs) and Derek Randall (1093 runs) chief among them, take the salute at Trent Bridge. Rice led from the front with 1462 runs (56.23) and 65 wickets.*

Seen by the Yorkshire Post's cameraman from the outside world, Geoff Boycott, his solicitor Duncan Mutch, and Yorkshire secretary Joe Lister discuss the crisis which now, and for some years yet, was clutching at the heart of Yorkshire cricket. In the season just ended, 1981, Yorkshire used four captains, but the relegated Boycott was not one of them. He was still a heavy rungetter, having averaged over 100 again in the 1979 season, but no longer required as captain. His feud with manager Illingworth now led to the setting-up of a 'troubleshooting' committee.

Sunil Gavaskar, captaining Bombay against Karnataka (led by his brother-in-law Viswanath) in a Ranji Trophy semi-final at Bangalore in March 1982, decides out of boredom – some said petulance – to bat out the second innings left-handed. Batting low in the order, he made 18 not out as Bombay finished on 200 for 9. A fortnight earlier, Gavaskar had scored 340 against Bengal, putting on 421 with Parkar (156) for the first wicket.

Geoff Boycott became top Test runmaker when he passed Sobers's 8032 in the Delhi Test of 1981–82, when he also passed 40,000 first-class runs. He played only one more Test, returning to England a fortnight later with a viral infection and having experienced difficulties with the management.

In India, massive attendances fix their attention on every ball, anxious to perceive and enjoy the nuances. These Bangalore fans were more tolerant of Chris Tavaré's somnolent batting than spectators in his homeland. In the next Test, at Delhi, he made 149, his first Test century. In August 1981, the Kent batsman had made the slowest fifty in English cricket (306 minutes) in the Old Trafford Test against Australia.

England captain Keith Fletcher taps the stumps down in exasperation after being adjudged caught behind in the second Test of 1981–82, at Bangalore. It was an unhappy and frustrating series for him and his team, who lost the opening Test, at Bombay (Doshi, Kapil Dev and Madan Lal all having five-wicket returns), and could not get back into the series in the face of delaying tactics in the field and obdurate batting by India. In this Test, Gavaskar's 172 lasted 708 minutes, an Indian record. **Above right:** *Gundappa Viswanath reaches 200 in the Madras Test, when his record 222 (638 minutes) together with Vengsarkar's 71 retired hurt and Yashpal Sharma's 140 (490 minutes) saw 415 runs scored between the fall of the second and third wickets.*

Film-star treatment awaits all who tour India. The Calcutta Test attracted almost 400,000 people, but even away from the Test grounds the clamour to touch, to make a gift, to obtain an autograph, is neverending. John Emburey is about to make a young man's day with a handshake.

A hideous Test incident: Dennis Lillee has kicked Pakistan captain Javed Miandad, who threatens to club the fast bowler with his bat. Umpire Crafter intervenes. Lillee, who claimed he had been provoked, was fined $200 and suspended for two one-day internationals.

OWZAT?

310

Lillee was reinstated quickly as a national hero. Three Tests later, at Melbourne, he passed Lance Gibbs's world Test record in the course of taking 7 for 83 against West Indies. His 3 for 44 in the second innings helped inflict a rare defeat on Clive Lloyd and his men – avenged a month later at Adelaide.

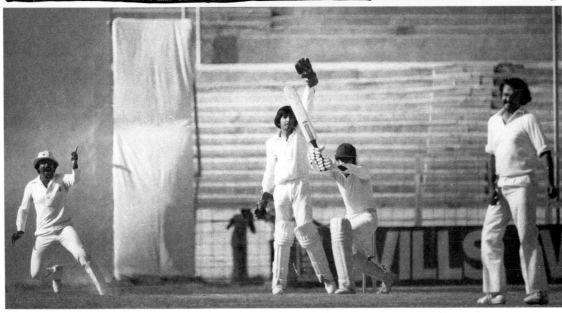

Roy Dias of Sri Lanka, playing in his country's second Test match, is lbw to Iqbal Qasim at Karachi for 53. A fine strokemaker, Dias scored 98 in the next Test and 109 in the one after that. Qasim took his 100th wicket for Pakistan in the next Test.

Left: *Sri Lanka, having won the ICC Trophy for non-Test countries in 1979, had pursued their claims for Test status, supported by India and Pakistan. The great day came on February 17, 1982, when Bandula Warnapura led his team against Fletcher's England, and was well on the way to victory until Emburey took 6 for 33 and Sri Lanka's last seven wickets fell for eight.*

Gladstone Small, Warwickshire's Barbados-born fast bowler, needed 18 deliveries to complete an over against Middlesex at Edgbaston in 1982. Umpire Alley called 11 no-balls and a wide.

Below: *Quality international cricket again at Newlands, Cape Town, as South Africa play an English XI of Test players who had gathered secretly and against the general advice of the TCCB. The tour fee was large enough to brook few refusals.*

Above: *A close shave for SAB English XI batsman Graham Gooch as Vintcent van der Bijl, the clever South African giant, gets one through him at Cape Town.* Left: *Boycott, in unfamiliar beard, and Gooch lead out the 'rebel' English team at the Wanderers ground, Johannesburg.*

The South African national team of 1981–82 included three players who had played in the last Test match 12 years ago. This combination won the first four-day match and drew the other two. Standing: Jimmy Cook, Ray Jennings, Steve Jefferies, Alan Kourie, Kevin McKenzie, Garth Le Roux; seated: Peter Kirsten, Barry Richards, Graeme Pollock, Mike Procter (captain), Ronnie Ericson (manager), Clive Rice, Vintcent van der Bijl.

TCCB chairman F. G. Mann announces a three-year Test ban on the 15 English players who toured South Africa. The decision was made primarily to satisfy other Test countries whom England would soon be entertaining or touring. **Right:** Glenn Turner refreshes during his grand innings of 311 not out for Worcestershire v Warwickshire at Worcester in 1982. It was his 100th century, and his early mentor, Billy Ibadulla, was on hand to serve him. Amiss seems fascinated.

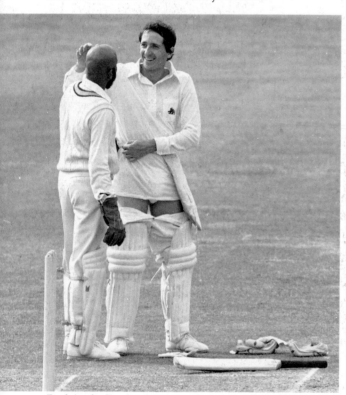

Back in the England XI, Randall made 126 at Lord's against India in 1982 – and paused during costume adjustments to admire Kirmani's hairstyle.

It was obvious that the brisk, steady runmaking of Allan Lamb of Northants would earn an England place as soon as he was qualified: he was South African-born but his parents were British. In 1982 he made 99 against India in a one-day match and 107 in his third Test.

Ray Illingworth, aged 50, leads Yorkshire out, having taken over as captain from Chris Old (following him out) midway through 1982. He had first played for the county 31 years earlier. Although his return to the helm did little to improve Yorkshire's position, it demonstrated that his experience was of more use out in the middle than from the manager's position in the dressing-room. David Bairstow (behind Old) took over in 1984, and was sacked in 1986.

Ian Botham employs the reverse sweep during his rampaging 208 against India at The Oval, July 1982. His double-century came off only 220 balls, possibly the lowest number ever in a Test. When he was eventually caught by Viswanath, hopping across from slip, as Botham played the reverse sweep against Doshi, those who disapproved of this irreverent, disturbing stroke said 'Told you so'.

Imran Khan, now Pakistan's captain, receives the felicitations of his men during the 1982 Edgbaston Test, when he took 7 for 52 in the first innings. Tahir Naqqash took 5 for 40 in the second, but Randall's 105 and a Taylor–Willis last-wicket stand of 79 saved England, who went on to victory by 113 runs. They won at Headingley too, but in between Pakistan won at Lord's, Mudassar surprising with 6 for 32 with honest seamers.

Mohsin Khan, the Pakistan opening batsman, set up the Lord's success with an 8¼-hour 200, the first Lord's Test double-century since Martin Donnelly's in 1949.

Warwickshire's Alvin Kallicharran and Geoff Humpage
return from a partnership of 470 against Lancashire at
Southport in July 1982. 'Kalli' made 230 not out,
Humpage 254 (with 13 sixes), and the massive stand, an
English fourth-wicket record, took only 293 minutes. Still
Warwickshire managed to lose by 10 wickets, Graeme
Fowler making two centuries for the home team, using a
runner almost throughout.

Above: *Bob Willis, England's
long, lean fast bowler, has a
shout against Imran. Drafted in
as England captain when
Fletcher's services were
dispensed with in 1982, the
Warwickshire captain was
awarded the MBE this year, and
soldiered onward to 1984, when
he retired with an England Test
record of 325 wickets.*

Left: *Australian cricket-writer
Ray Robinson, who died in July
1982, two days before his 77th
birthday, was a gentle,
knowledgeable and popular man
whose books,* Between Wickets
and From the Boundary *in
particular, had the same sort of
influence on Australian readers
as Cardus had on English. As a
young sub-editor, 'Robbie' had
had a hand in coining the word
'Bodyline'.*

Above: *Pakistan contested another tense series in 1982–83 against the visiting Indians, winning the six-Test rubber 3–0. Zaheer scored his 100th century at Lahore, and the series was high-scoring all round. The picture shows Mohinder Amarnath, who made three centuries in the series, playing Imran Khan, who took 40 wickets.* Left: *Mudassar Nazar (231) and Javed Miandad (280 not out) during a break in their huge stand of 451 in 533 minutes for Pakistan's third wicket at Hyderabad. This equalled the Ponsford–Bradman second-wicket stand at The Oval in 1934 as the highest in Test cricket.*

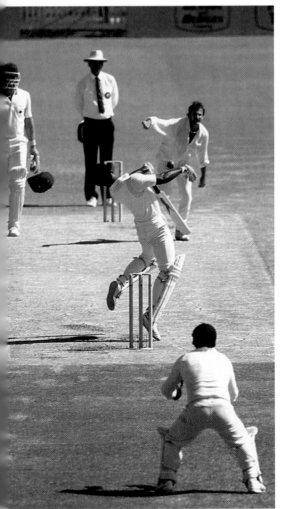

Above: *Viv Richards, batting in the Shell Shield for Leeward Islands, is bowled first ball by Wayne Daniel of Barbados at Bridgetown. It seems that West Indies batsmen have the same problems against the wide array of fast bowlers in domestic cricket as foreign batsmen do in Test matches and one-day internationals against West Indies. In the first 20 seasons of the Shell Shield, Barbados won it 12 times.*

Left: *Lillee rips a short ball past England tailender Norman Cowans's nose in the 1982–83 Ashes series, when the hot blast of Australian pace was often too much for Willis's England team. Fast bowlers worldwide were now indulging themselves in this way against inept late-order batsmen.*

The Perth Test, the first of the 1982–83 Ashes series, was overshadowed by an invasion of the field by spectators, mostly drunk and some festooned with Union Jacks. When Terry Alderman tried to tackle one who had struck him on the head, he fell and seriously damaged his shoulder. Stretchered from the ground, he was unable to play again that season.

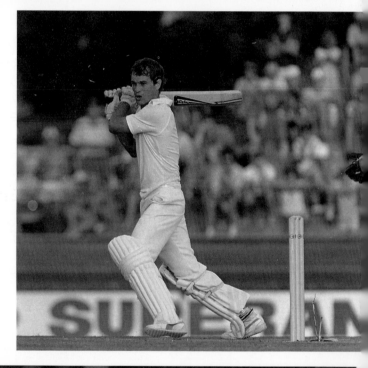

Above: *Marsh has just held his 300th catch in Test cricket, a dizzy statistic never before touched. In this Brisbane Test he held nine catches, six in the second innings, Thomson and Lawson the fast bowlers to benefit.*
Above right: *South African-born Kepler Wessels on his way to a Test debut 162 and 46, his aggregate beating Archie Jackson's 200 on his Australian debut 54 years earlier. Australia won at Brisbane, and forged ahead at Adelaide, where Willis misguidedly put them in.* Right: *At Melbourne, English spirits rose again in a more tightly contested issue. Cowans took 6 for 77, and his team-mates approved.*

THE AUSTRALIAN

NUMBER 5718   MONDAY JANUARY 3 1983   30 CENTS* FREIGHT EXTRA

'In or out' riddle opens Ashes decider

By PHIL WILKINS

AUSTRALIAN opener John Dyson will continue batting at 34 today after surviving a dramatic first-over run out controversy before he had scored in the Ashes-deciding fifth Test against England at the Sydney Cricket Ground.

Australia's leading umpire, Mel Johnson, standing in his fourth Test of the series, ruled Dyson had safely made his ground after England's captain, Bob Willis, hurled down the wicket.

Repeated replays of the incident indicated Dyson was out of his ground.

Umpire Johnson said last night: "I could only give it as I saw it. I thought it was only six inches in or six inches out, and I thought it close enough not to give him out."

Match Report – Page 16

The England team maintained its season-long policy of refusing to discuss umpiring issues. The team manager, Mr Doug Insole, would make no comment.

By stumps on a rain-disrupted first day of the crucial Test, Dyson had batted for 196 minutes for his chanceless half-century in Australia's first innings of 3-138 to put Australia well on the way to winning back the Ashes.

The Dyson controversy brought back memories of umpire Lou Rowan's equally contentious decision in the 1970-71 Ashes series when Geoff Boycott threw down the wicket of Keith Blackpole at 38 in the first Test in Brisbane.

THE cause of the uproar ... video film from Channel Nine's coverage of yesterday's fifth Test shows Dyson well short

DYSON cuts the English captain, B. cordon for a single n his way to

Above: *The final Test, at Sydney, began with Australia leading 2–1, and England needing to win to retain the Ashes, but an air of distraction blanketed the game after Australian opener John Dyson was run out by some distance in the first over, but given not-out. He stayed in for five hours to make 79. This important decision showed up the folly of not utilising television replays to help umpires. This umpire, relying on fallible senses, was seen as a fool by millions of viewers who saw the truth distinctly.*

To screams of excitement England win the Melbourne Test by three runs as a last-wicket stand of 70 by Border and Thomson is broken. Botham, who completed the 1000 runs/100 wickets double against Australia in this match, found the edge of Thomson's bat; Tavaré at slip failed to hold the catch; and Geoff Miller skipped behind him to secure the ball inches from the turf. England (284 and 294) and Australia (287 and 288) had completed a near-perfect contest to mark their 250th Test match. Over 15,000 went on the last day to see what might easily have been only one ball.

England's second piece of bad luck at Sydney saw them shut out finally from any real chance of winning. Kim Hughes hit a ball onto his boot when 17 and Geoff Cook dived to catch it. Given not-out, Hughes went on to a six-hour 137. A fan gave Greg Chappell some 'new Ashes' afterwards, christened 'Urnie'.

597

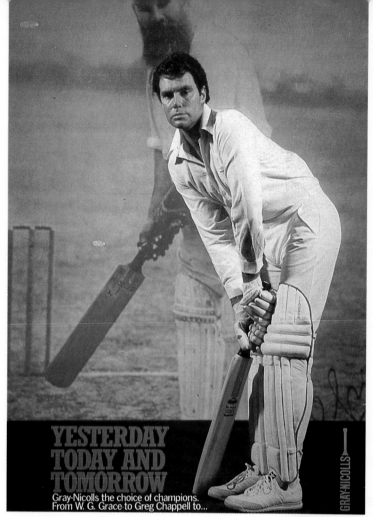

YESTERDAY
TODAY AND
TOMORROW
Gray-Nicolls the choice of champions.
From W. G. Grace to Greg Chappell to...

GRAY-NICOLLS

Another image of man extending an old limit on the cricket field: England's Bob Taylor, in stumping Queensland's Wayne Broad in October 1982, becomes the leading wicketkeeper with 1528 dismissals, one more than John Murray.

Above: *Gregory Stephen Chappell finished the 1982–83 Ashes Test series with 22 centuries and recognised status of at least the best white batsman in the world. A serious man, he strove for rectitude in strokeplay and dignity in all that he did. Off the field, too, his shrewdness in investment was already pointing to millionaire status.*

Right: *David Hookes blasting towards the fastest hundred ever in terms of balls faced. Irate at Victoria's tall challenge to South Australia to score 272 in about 30 overs, Hookes slammed his red cap on and went out to open the innings. In 43 minutes he reached his century, off only 34 balls. Adelaide Oval had often been his playground, but never quite to this degree. His 107 out of 128 in 55 minutes included 17 fours and three sixes. Wickets then fell, the light faded, and a memorable match was drawn.*

598

The Indians lost 0–2 in West Indies in 1982–83, the local fast bowlers continuing to hold sway. The local batsmen, too, supped well, taking eight centuries off the Indian bowling. The visitors, however, made five, the gallant, adaptable Amarnath two of them. Here Vengsarkar hangs on at Bridgetown.

Below: The seemingly impossible happened when a West Indies team visited South Africa in January and February 1983 in the wake of a Sri Lanka team. In the face of world disapproval the South African Cricket Union had managed to lure enough good cricketers to be able to present an international bill of fare for cricket-lovers from Cape Town to Johannesburg. At Newlands, Peter Kirsten, the Springboks' captain, tosses with Lawrence Rowe, the rebels' leader.

Above: Colin Croft, Sylvester Clarke and Collis King (on haunches) bring Caribbean sparkle to Johannesburg. The West Indies XI and South Africa won one 'Test' each, and South Africa won the one-day internationals 4–2, but the visitors gave a great fillip to the game. For their trouble they were banned for life by the West Indies Board.

599

Prior to the West Indians' tour of South Africa, a Sri Lankan combination had made a two-month tour. It was conceived in Holland, arrived at after flights out of Hong Kong and Taipeh, and gave little satisfaction all round. The tourists, who were banned for life for defying the Sri Lankan Board, lost 11 and drew the other three of their matches. In that short time, though, most of them earned the equivalent of a lifetime's pay, which helped ease the burden of ostracism when they returned home. Woutersz is seen padding away the leading legspinner Denys Hobson in the last match, at Newlands, where the South Africans gorged their way to 663 for 6 dec, Pollock 197, Seeff 188 and Cook 112 (his fourth hundred against them).

Essex and England fast bowler Neil Foster displays the steel plates which were inserted alongside cracked vertebrae. The treatment worked.

Right: Rick McCosker, in blazer, the New South Wales captain, brings home the Sheffield Shield – with the help of Geoff Lawson – after NSW had won the first final, against Western Australia in March 1983. It was the State's 37th Shield success.

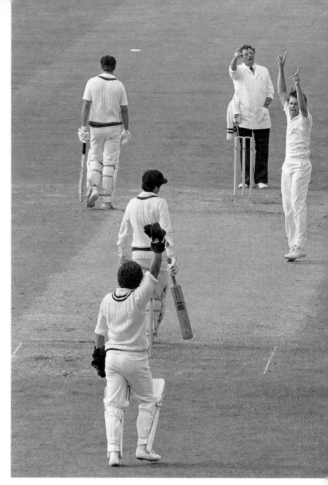

Steve O'Shaughnessy, 22, having equalled Percy Fender's record 35-minute century, is taken down south by the Manchester Evening News to meet the grand old Surrey and England cricketer, now 91. O'Shaughnessy raced to his century in farcical circumstances, Lancashire being fed long-hops and full-tosses by Leicestershire in the hope of a declaration at Old Trafford in the last match of the 1983 season. He hit five sixes and 17 fours, and put on 201 with Graeme Fowler (100 in 46 minutes) in only 43 minutes. Fowler took 10 sixes and five fours.

The first shock in the 1983 World Cup (the third to be staged in England) was Australia's defeat by Zimbabwe at Trent Bridge (here Wood is caught behind by Houghton off captain Fletcher).

The second 1983 World Cup shock came from these men, the Indians, who beat West Indies at Old Trafford. Sri Lanka later upset New Zealand, but the greatest surprise came when India (183) beat West Indies (140) in the final. Players standing: Yashpal Sharma, Kris Srikkanth, B. S. Sandhu, Ravi Shastri, Sandeep Patil, Roger Binny, Kirti Azad, Sunil Valson; front: Dilip Vengsarkar, Syed Kirmani, Kapil Dev (captain), Mohinder Amarnath, Sunil Gavaskar, S. Madan Lal.

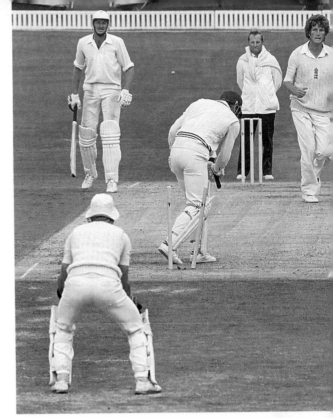

Above: *England v New Zealand, Headingley, August 1, 1983, Jeff Crowe's wicket shattered to give Bob Willis his 300th wicket in his 81st Test.*

Left: *Indian captain Kapil Dev playing the outstanding innings of the 1983 World Cup, a bold blitz of 175 not out against Zimbabwe at Tunbridge Wells. India were 17 for 5, but Kapil sailed into the bowling, hitting six sixes and 16 fours. India, from the edge of elimination, went on to win by 31 runs, to beat Australia, then England in the semi-final, and mighty West Indies in the final.*

Below: *Graeme Fowler making his first Test century, against New Zealand at The Oval, July 1983. Tavaré also made a hundred, their stand amounting to 223.*

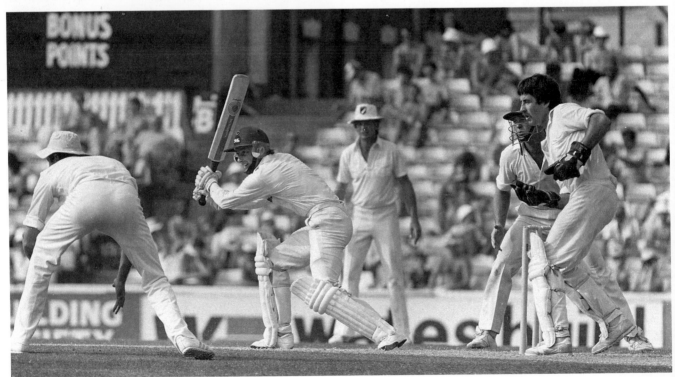

The 1980s were showing New Zealand to be anything but the pushovers of old, and at Headingley in 1983, on their ninth Test tour of England (29th Test), they beat the Old Country on English soil at last, and by skilful seam bowling, traditionally England's own strength. Soaking up the champagne are (back) John Bracewell, Martin Crowe, Ewen Chatfield, Jeff Crowe, Ian Smith, Trevor Franklin; standing: Evan Gray; front: Warren Lees, Sir Allan Wright (manager), John Wright, Geoff Howarth, Lance Cairns, Richard Hadlee, Jeremy Coney, Bruce Edgar, Martin Snedden. Below left: Howarth's runs and cool captaincy were a weighty factor in New Zealand's successes, another being the development of those who had played county cricket.

England successfully introduced Leicestershire slow left-armer Nick Cook in 1983, and he gathered 17 wickets in his first two Tests and 11 in a Karachi Test before luck and form ran out.

Anshuman Gaekwad, son of Test player D. K. Gaekwad, showed an almost superhuman patience and power of endurance in batting for 652 minutes for his double-century for India against Pakistan at Jullundur in September 1983. It was the slowest double-century ever, surpassing the Nawab of Pataudi junior's effort 16 years earlier, 622 minutes. Gaekwad's 201 lasted 671 minutes in all. Only six longer innings had been played in Test cricket. Kuruppu of Sri Lanka stretched the record further in 1987 with 201 not out in 778 minutes against New Zealand at Colombo in his maiden Test innings.

Left: Desmond Haynes joins Endean, Hilditch and Mohsin Khan in the curious little list of those who have been given out 'handled the ball' in a Test. The West Indian's aberration occurred at Bombay in the fourth Test of the 1983–84 series, won 3–0 by the tourists. A ball from Kapil Dev hit bat and pad and rolled towards the stumps. Haynes flicked it away with his gloves.

Below: Gordon Greenidge applies his famed shoulder power to hit Indian medium-pacer Binny in the Calcutta Test. Clive Lloyd (161 not out) set up the innings victory here. Greenidge, having made 194 at Kanpur in the opening Test, had one of his poorest series.

Gavaskar beats Bradman's record 29 Test centuries. The Indian reached his 30th century at Madras in December 1983, against West Indies, in his 99th Test (174th innings). He batted this time for 644 minutes for 236 not out, impressively his 13th 'ton' against West Indies.

Top: *New Zealand went on turning the screw against England on their home pitches. The tall Coney has reached his first Test hundred.* Above: *Martin Crowe also made a century at Wellington, shutting England right out.* Left: *The West Indies stormtroopers – Eldine Baptiste, Wayne Daniel, Andy Roberts, Malcolm Marshall, Michael Holding, Winston Davis – who took 97 Test wickets on the 1983–84 tour of India (Marshall 33 and Holding 30).*

605

England's 1983–84 winter tour of New Zealand and Pakistan was best forgotten by several of the major tourists. Newspapers subsequently published allegations of scandalous goings-on, including the smoking of cannabis – all vehemently denied. England's on-field performances, after a worthy 463 (Botham 138, Randall 164) at Wellington, were dismal. At Christchurch, Richard Hadlee (left) smote 99 vigorous runs off 81 balls on a pitch which raised suspicion, and then took 3 for 16 and 5 for 28 as England were rushed out for 82 and 93, hanging their heads in shame at an innings defeat inside 12 hours of playing time. Botham (left) goes first ball in the second innings, caught by Martin Crowe off Stephen Boock, the slow left-armer, who took 3 for 25.

At Auckland, New Zealand protected their winning lead by piling up 496 for 9 dec (John Wright, Jeff Crowe and Ian Smith all making centuries). England then lost Fowler first ball, but Chris Smith (left), the South African-born Hampshire batsman, dug in for over 7½ hours for 91. Randall made another century, and England too reached 400-plus. But the draw ensured New Zealand's first series win over England.

Allan Border, 98 not out in the first innings, reaches 100 not out in the second, having held West Indies out at Port-of-Spain in March 1984. Below: Wayne Phillips, batting No. 8, reached a brave and brisk century at Bridgetown, where Australia went down to the first of three heavy defeats.

In Pakistan, where England lost for the first time, Bob Willis returned to England because of illness. David Gower then took over (above) and scored 152 at Faisalabad and 173 not out at Lahore, both Tests drawn.

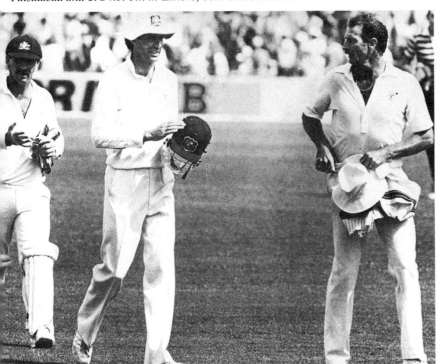

Sydney, January 1984, and three giants of the game all leave the field for the last time, a triple retirement from which Australia would take a long time to recover. Rod Marsh closed his career with a record 355 dismissals (95 catches off Lillee) in 96 Tests. Greg Chappell, with 182 against Pakistan in his final innings, finished top Australian rungetter (7110) and fieldsman (122 catches, a world record). Dennis Lillee, who had defied potentially crippling injury, had 355 Test wickets, a record that would last 2½ years.

Above: *The first Asia Cup is held on high by Gavaskar, whose turn it was to captain India again. The trophy was contested in limited-overs matches with Pakistan and Sri Lanka in the green cricket oasis built in Sharjah by Sheikh Abdulrahman Bukhatir, and the winners took $US50,000 in prizemoney. The venue was to stage many lucrative benefit matches for Indian and Pakistani players.* Left: *Clive Lloyd with a silver salver to mark his 100th Test appearance, Jamaica, 1984. The genial giant retired a year later with a peerless Test captaincy record: 74 matches, 36 victories, 26 draws, and only 12 losses.*

One of the most serious injuries inflicted by the West Indian fast brigade was a hairline fracture near Andy Lloyd's eye in the Edgbaston Test of 1984. The England opener, hit by a short ball from Marshall, was wearing a helmet. Double-vision kept him out of cricket for some time. In the Old Trafford Test six weeks later Paul Terry's arm was broken by a ball from Winston Davis. Terry came back and tried to bat with his arm in a sling.

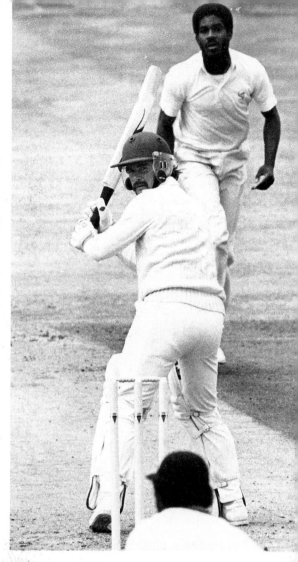

Malcolm Marshall, probably the fastest bowler in the world, added 24 more scalps to his belt during the 1984 Tests in England, when West Indies made a clean 5–0 sweep of the series. With a damaged left hand bound in plaster, he took 7 for 53, his best Test figures, in the Headingley Test. **Right:** Allan Lamb swam stoically through the sea of West Indian success in scoring three centuries in the series – and adding another in the end-of-season Test against Sri Lanka at Lord's.

Gordon Greenidge (in cap) engineers an astonishing win for West Indies at Lord's (where Botham had taken 8 for 103), scoring 214 not out in West Indies' 344 for 1 to win on the fifth day. With Gomes (92 not out) he added 287.

An old-fashioned pose marks a unique occurrence as two batsmen glow with satisfaction after both making a century on first-class debut: Keith Medlycott (117 not out at No. 9) and Nick Falkner (101 not out at No. 6) performed the feat for Surrey against a moderate Cambridge University XI at Banstead in June 1984.

609

Botham's 300th Test wicket: Dujon touches one off the lively Oval pitch into Tavaré's safe hands, yet another auspicious landmark for the England allrounder, who now had over 3000 Test runs as well.

Below: The unbeatables – or so it seemed in 1984, when West Indies went through the English tour with only one reversal, in the one-day international at Trent Bridge. Roger Harper was, as an offspinner, almost an alien; Garner took 29 Test wickets; and Lloyd and Richards were as effective a pair of batsmen as any in the world.

England's tortures went on into late August in 1984 when Sri Lanka played their first Test match at Lord's. Their captain, Duleep Mendis (pictured), hit 111 and 94, Wettimuny 190, Ranatunga 84, and, in the second innings, Amal Silva, the wicketkeeper, 102 not out. Gower's pained expression lasted all season.

Below: In August 1984, G. Neville Weston, the leading authority on W. G. Grace, died. He filled his home with an extraordinary collection of pictures, scrapbooks, chinaware, letters, scorecards and other relics of cricket's Grand Old Man.

Above: *Autumn 1984, and a charity dinner for Bill Edrich and Denis Compton (right) is enhanced by the surprise appearance of Keith Miller (centre).*

Left: *Sidath Wettimuny grows tired towards the end of his monumental 190 for Sri Lanka, the longest innings (10 hours 36 minutes) ever played at Lord's. His and his colleagues' application and correctness showed up their English opponents.*

Below: *Middlesex 1984, with captain Mike Gatting and seven other recent England caps. The county won the NatWest Trophy this season, and six other titles between 1980 and 1986.*

They were due to be there for only six weeks, but when the New Zealanders embarked on their tour of Pakistan late in 1984 they were determined not to be stuck for entertainment. They thus armed themselves with 40 movies on video, the stocks being in the safe hands of the much-travelled Evan Gray, Jeremy Coney and Ewen Chatfield.

Cricket remains many things, the most precious being an innocent, pleasure-giving pastime for the young, as for Afghan refugee children near the Khyber Pass, finding sanctuary from the Russian occupiers, or the five-year-old little chap from Ipswich, Queensland who has won a bat in a newspaper competition, and must be hoping to grow big enough one day to use it.

The Hyderabad Test between Pakistan and New Zealand in November 1984 was the 1000th Test match, and Javed Miandad rendered it special by scoring his 12th and 13th Test centuries. Pakistan won the short series 2–0, which suggested that the videos were not helping the Kiwis. (In fact, Coney the captain and the team manager complained strongly about the standard of umpiring.) New Zealand reversed the result in the return series soon afterwards.

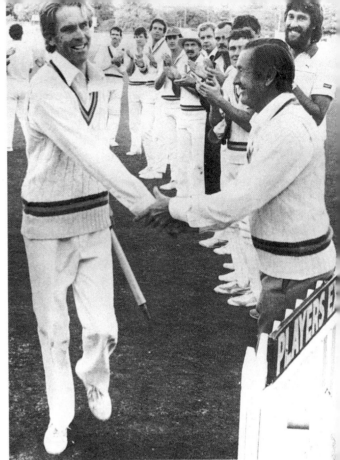

In January 1985 Ravi Shastri emulated Garry Sobers by hitting all six balls of an over for six. The Hindu *assembled a kind of montage. Batting for Bombay against Baroda at the Wankhede Stadium, Shastri also took possession of the fastest double-century in first-class cricket: 113 minutes. The 36 runs came off Tilak Raj.*

John Inverarity says farewell to a highly creditable career which left him top of the Sheffield Shield aggregates. Having played for and captained Western Australia with considerable success between 1962–63 and 1978–79, he switched to South Australia in 1979–80 when a teaching appointment took him to Adelaide. He won six Australian caps. In this final match, in March 1985, Inverarity took 7 for 68 with left-arm spin, his best figures, scored 55 in the first innings, and held a good catch to end Queensland's innings and give South Australia a 12-run victory.

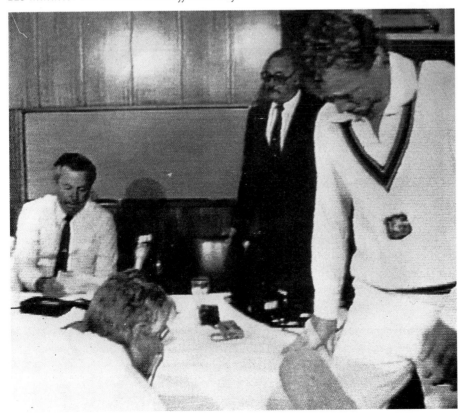

Left: *Farewell of a different kind. Kim Hughes, overcome, leaves a Press conference in Brisbane after announcing his resignation from the Australian captaincy. He had spoken of 'constant criticism, speculation and innuendo by former players and a section of the media over the past four or five years'. His captaincy had never seemed as cool and methodical as Greg Chappell's, but his batting sometimes bordered on genius. In the next two Tests against West Indies, however, he made 0, 2, 0 and 0. Omitted from the England tour, he threw in his lot with the rebel team to South Africa.*

The big discovery of India's 1984–85 series against Gower's England team was Mohammad Azharuddin, a wristy 'natural' player, who uniquely scored a century in each of his first three Test matches.

Top: Chris Cowdrey is given out caught at slip at Delhi, off Shivaramakrishnan. Above: Edmonds and Pocock (four wickets each) come off after spinning India out. England then levelled the series.

Mike Gatting trots his 200th run in the 1984–85 Madras Test, where England pulled ahead 2–1, holding their superiority in the fifth Test. England made 652 for 7 dec at Madras, and Fowler had already scored 201. Neil Foster's admirable seam bowling in great heat and humidity earned him 11 wickets, and the spinners, Pocock and Edmonds, stuck to their marathon task. England won by nine wickets.

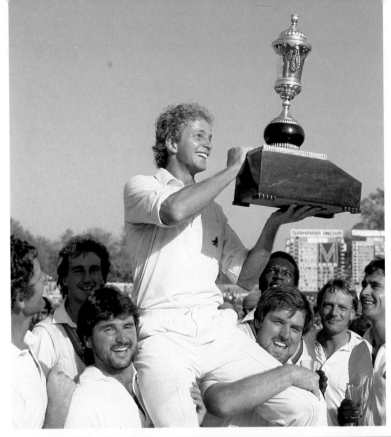

Left: *David Gower, England's captain, relishes a touch of the de Mello Trophy from his heavenly perch after England had sealed their series victory in India at Kanpur in February 1985. After India had made over 500, Gower himself played an important innings of 78 which led his side out of the danger of a follow-on. England's win was all the more meritorious in that they had lost the opening Test.*

Below: *The Australians augment their ecstasy with a few cans after beating the mighty West Indies at Sydney in January 1985. On a responsive pitch legspinner Bob Holland took 10 for 144 off 55 overs in the match, with slow left-armer Murray Bennett in valuable support. It was West Indies' first Test defeat in 27 matches.*

Bottom: *West Indies still beat Australia 3–1, and then they beat New Zealand 2–0 in the Caribbean, where ducking and weaving remained batsmen's essentials. Wright sways from Marshall at Bridgetown. At Kingston, where things got really nasty, Coney had his forearm broken by Garner.*

Dazed at the announcement telling of the assassination of India's Prime Minister Mrs Indira Gandhi, the crowd at Sialkot, scene of the one-day international between Pakistan and India, disperses after the instant abandonment of the match. Vengsarkar was 94 not out. The killing happened as the England team were settling in upon arrival in Delhi on October 31, 1984, and their tour was thrown into doubt. They went to Sri Lanka while confusion reigned, and then resumed the tour proper on November 13. Tragedy struck again just before the first Test when the British Deputy High Commissioner, Percy Norris, was gunned down in Bombay shortly after hosting a party for the England team. Manager Tony Brown, after lengthy discussions with the TCCB and the Foreign Office, let the tour continue, a decision which turned out to be the right one.

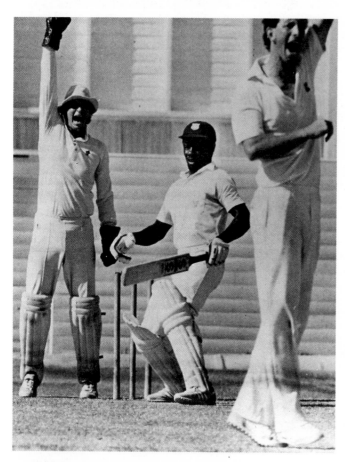

Richie Richardson, the Antiguan with a touch of Weekes about him, survives a caught-behind shout against New Zealand's Boock at Georgetown when 98. He went on to 185.

Eighteen-year-old legspinner Laxman Shivaramakrishnan took 12 wickets at Bombay, to help India beat England in the opening Test of the 1984–85 series. The tourists handled him better subsequently.

Tim Robinson of Notts, a perceptive choice for the Indian tour, was unlucky with umpiring decisions in the first Test, but showed his worth at Delhi, setting his side up with an innings of 160 in almost nine hours of unruffled defence and well-judged strokeplay. He later made 74 at Madras and 96 at Kanpur

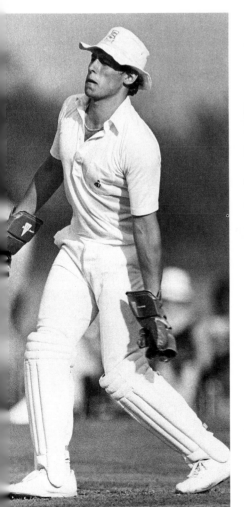

India's spirits were lifted soon after their home Test series defeat by England when they won the World Championship of Cricket, a seven-nation limited-overs tournament promoted by the Victorian Cricket Association as part of the State's 150th anniversary celebrations. Beating Pakistan with comfort in the final at Melbourne, India thus added another trophy to previous successes in the game's shortened version, such as the World Cup and the Asia Cup. Late that night, with the elixir of victory, they did a lap of honour in Shastri's car, a prize for being 'champion of champions' in the three-week event.

Left: David East, Essex's reliable wicketkeeper, equalled Wally Grout's record of eight catches in an innings when he accepted the offerings of the first eight Somerset batsmen to fall at Taunton on July 27, 1984, East's 26th birthday. The next batsman was bowled, and Botham (152) then declared at 363 for 9.

Sri Lanka thought they had done well to make 479 on an admittedly 'flat' pitch at Faisalabad against Pakistan in October 1985, the talented young Aravinda de Silva scoring 122 in 510 minutes, having reached his century with a six off Imran. But Qasim Omar (*here batting against India*) made 206 and his captain, Javed Miandad, was 203 when he declared, closing a dead match. Their stand for the third wicket was a towering 397.

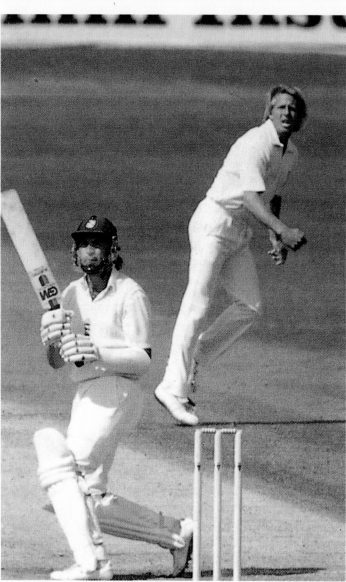

England captain David Gower swivels easily into a hook against Craig McDermott in the third Test, at Trent Bridge. The 20-year-old Queensland fast bowler took 30 wickets at 30 in the series, including 8 for 141 off 36 overs at Old Trafford, and displayed immense promise. Unfortunately he had to be asked to shoulder too much work, and suffered a reaction. Geoff Lawson's poor health proved a handicap to Australia, who used legspinner Bob Holland more as a stock bowler in four Tests. Gower was in tremendous form, making 86 at Lord's, 166 at Trent Bridge, 47 at Old Trafford, 215 at Edgbaston and 157 at The Oval. His aggregate of 732 (81.33) had only twice been exceeded (by Hammond and Sutcliffe) in a series for England against Australia.

England's campaign to regain the Ashes in 1985 began well with a five-wicket victory at Headingley. Robinson, who scored an impressive 175 on Ashes debut, hooks Thomson, who took his 200th Test wicket at Edgbaston.

Above: *Australian skipper Allan Border, cap rammed on head, a mass of concentration, carried on his heavy runmaking of the previous tour, his 196 in the 1985 Lord's Test setting up an eventual four-wicket victory to level the series with four to play.*

Right: *Graeme Wood, out of form, grafted a worthy 172 in 10 hours at Trent Bridge, his eighth Test century. Greg Ritchie made an attractive century in Australia's 539, which ensured a draw. Wood's partner, Wessels, was contained by England throughout, a factor which had a significant influence on the series.*

A touch of 'Flower Power' came into the game in 1985 when Tim Hudson (in stetson) staged celebrity matches on his private ground in Cheshire. David Hookes, Ian Botham, Brian Close and Viv Richards were among those who played.

Mike Gatting's long-term promise began to be fulfilled in India, and now, at Old Trafford, he made a businesslike 160. This was followed by 100 not out at Edgbaston, and he topped the 1985 Test averages with 87.83.

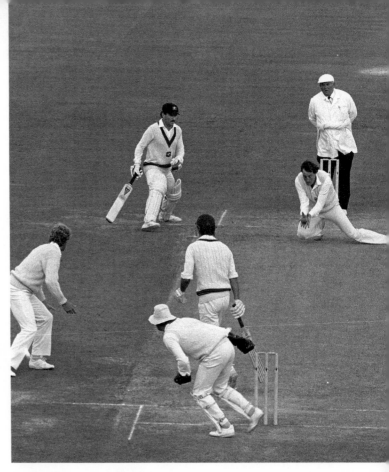

Kepler Wessels is prised out again, this time by Emburey with a return catch. The Australian opener, now batting at No. 3, had made 50, and his partner, Border, went on to 146 not out as Australia batted out the draw at Old Trafford: still 1–1, with two to play.

Hardly having raised a sweat, Viv Richards comes in at Taunton in June 1985 having slaughtered Warwickshire with a 258-ball innings of 322, with 42 fours and eight sixes.

Ian Botham came in at 572 for 4 in the Edgbaston Test and smacked his first ball, from McDermott, for six, one of 80 sixes from his clubbing bat in 1985, a new record, passing old Somerset player Arthur Wellard's 66 in 1935.

With this ball Australia's fight to hold the Ashes in 1985 collapsed. On the last evening at Edgbaston in the fifth Test, after further play had seemed impossible during the wet morning, Australia in the form of Ritchie and Phillips were holding out with some comfort. Wayne Phillips then played his favoured cut against Edmonds down towards the dancing Allan Lamb. The ball lobbed up, Gower caught it, and the umpires ruled the batsman out. Dispirited collapse followed, and England went 2–1 up with one Test remaining.

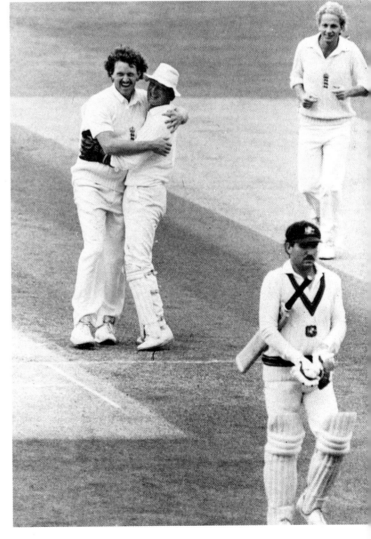

Above: Gooch made sure of his first century against Australia with a blistering 196 at The Oval, and Gower joined him in a memorable second-wicket stand of 351 off 75 overs. A crushing innings victory won England the Ashes. Right: Border, Australia's backbone, goes for 58 in the Oval shambles, the bowler, Richard Ellison, heading for a 5 for 46 return. His 17 wickets at 10.88 put him top of England's bowling averages.

Mike Gatting, England's vice-captain, was an early serious casualty on the tour of West Indies in 1986 when a bouncer from Marshall eluded his attempted hook and smashed the bridge of his nose. A player found a splinter of bone in the ball. Gatting was repatriated for a series of operations, returned, and had his thumb broken.

Joy unconfined on the England balcony at The Oval on September 2, 1985, the cocktail one of the penalties of success. Soon the mood would alter drastically as England ventured to West Indies. **Right:** *Clive Rice, South Africa's captain, and Kim Hughes, leader of the rebel Australian touring team of 1985–86. The Australians were banned from Tests for three years, a grievous loss.*

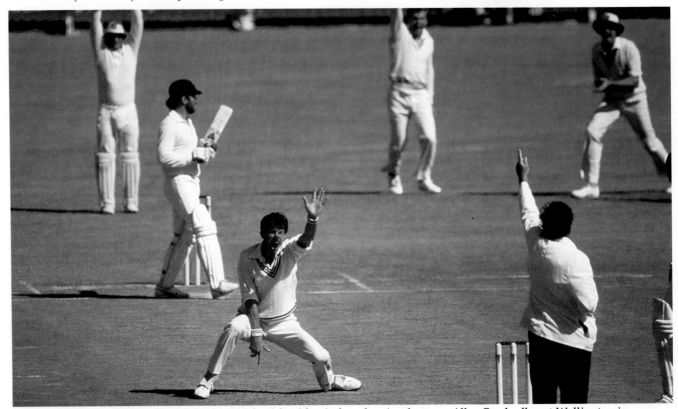

Richard Hadlee, in his 61st Test, takes his 300th wicket (the sixth to do so) as he traps Allan Border lbw at Wellington in February 1986. New Zealand won this series, as they had just done in Australia.

Seldom in modern times have West Indies' opponents dished it out to them, but Greg Thomas, England's fastest bowler, whistled the odd bouncer through. Richie Richardson evaded this one at Bridgetown, and made his second century.

Malcolm Marshall, a terror bowler whether operating for Barbados, Hampshire or West Indies, made life perilous for England's batsmen again in the 1985–86 series, and took 27 wickets, as did Garner. England were expected to do better this time, but another 0–5 humiliation occurred.

Patrick Patterson, a Jamaican and sometime Lancashire and Tasmania fast bowler, was the surprise packet in the series against England, taking seven wickets in a lethal attack on a shaky pitch in the opening Test, at Kingston.

Patterson – bow-legged, and you could balance a cup and saucer on his backside, according to one observer – strikes at Kingston, Jamaica, having debutant David Smith caught behind. West Indies' pace quartet blasted England out for 159 and 152. Graham Gooch, the non-striker, was given a rough passage, especially in Antigua, by the hardline anti-apartheid lobby, who felt, among other things, that his ban for touring South Africa should have been much longer than three years.

The price of life against this phenomenal and non-stop West Indies pace attack was cheap. Captain Gower rode his luck at Kingston, opening with a six.

Gower's Leicestershire vice-captain, Peter Willey, made a typically gritty 71 at Kingston, top score for either side in the match.

It had to happen: in the helterskelter world of one-day internationals, 'handled the ball' was always a possibility. The first to succumb was Mohinder 'Jimmy' Amarnath, who seems unable to decide whether to laugh or weep after offending in India's WSC final against Australia at Melbourne in 1986.

Ray Lindwall reckoned that if he couldn't get lower-order batsmen out without bowling bouncers at them he ought to hand his Australian blazer back where it came from. Such chivalry had long since perished by the 1980s. Marshall habitually bounced tailenders from the moment they came in. Here Emburey is helpless at Port-of-Spain in April 1986.

An emotional scene at the Sara Stadium, Colombo on September 11, 1985 as Sri Lanka win their first Test match. In their 14th Test they beat India by 149 runs. Amal Silva made 111, and Dias, Madugalle, Mendis and Aravinda de Silva all made runs. Rumesh Ratnayake took a decisive 9 for 125 in the match.

Two thunderclaps hit the cricket world in 1986: Viv Richards (above) hit the fastest Test century, and his England opponent and Somerset colleague and friend Ian Botham (top right) wrote a confession, for a newspaper, that he had once smoked cannabis. He was banned from first-class cricket for two months for 'bringing the game into disrepute'. Richards, on his home ground of Antigua, expedited West Indies' 5–0 'blackwash' by hammering a century off only 56 balls – he is shown 'crossing the finishing line' – in 81 minutes, with seven sixes and seven fours altogether in his breathtaking 110 not out. It was his 20th Test century in his 82nd Test. Jack Gregory's 70-minute century (67 balls) remained the fastest in Tests in terms of time.

Norman Gifford, wheeling away at 46 after 26 years in county cricket, took his 2000th wicket during the 1986 season, when he captained Warwickshire. He switched counties in 1983 after 23 years with Worcestershire.

Above: *Saleem Malik began scoring Test centuries for Pakistan at the age of 18, and by 1985, when he was 22, he had five in the book, a product of the batting conveyor-belt in his fervent country.*

Above: *Kapil Dev was back in charge for India's 1986 tour of England, one of the world's four great allrounders, with Botham, Hadlee and Imran. Kapil, still some way short of 30, was soon to take his 300th Test wicket, having passed 3000 runs. Though his personal contributions were moderate, he had the sublime satisfaction of leading India to a 2–0 series victory in England.*

Right: *Sunil Gavaskar, at 36 still one of the world's great batsmen, if subject to moods, did little in the three Tests in England in 1986 – judged on his own rarefied standards – though he played in his 115th Test – a new record – and three months later, at home against Australia, he made his 33rd Test century.*

Dilip Vengsarkar batted his way to a special place of honour by making his third hundred in a Lord's Test match, his 126 not out leading India to a 47-run first-innings advantage in the 1986 encounter which was converted to an eventual five-wicket victory that lit the millions at home in India with deep delight. Vengsarkar, tall and smooth in strokeplay, was never a headline-maker but was a major contributor to India's successes in Test matches and one-day internationals. Here, as at Headingley in the next Test, Vengsarkar was in the nineties when last man Maninder Singh went to the wicket. Both times the young Sikh held out for his senior partner to reach his goal.

In the tradition of Trumper, Macartney and Milburn, Krishnamachari Srikkanth felt from the moment he took strike at the start of an innings that the new ball should be battered into old age without delay. Patrons kept their eyes fixed on the play when this bat-swinger was at the crease. In England in 1986, he got going only once, in a one-day international.

Left: July 29, 1986, Edgbaston, Warwickshire's match against Lancashire gently dying on the third day, and Dennis Amiss chops the ball away to bring up his 100th century, an agonising six weeks after the 99th. He was the 21st batsman to enter the Hall of Century Centurions, having taken more innings (1081) than any apart from W. G. Grace (1113).

Below: *Viv Richards, who had played for Somerset since 1974, and Joel Garner (right), who joined the county in 1977, were both refused contract renewals by the club at the end of the 1986 season, the committee's strategy being based on building for the future in view of Somerset's poor showing in recent seasons.*

New Zealander Martin Crowe was the major new signing. Ian Botham, expressing fury at the decision and loyalty to his West Indian friends, announced he would leave the club too. A meeting called by dissident members failed to oust the committee or reverse what could only be seen as a brave decision.

Martin Crowe, one of the young lions of world cricket in the mid-1980s, toured England with New Zealand in 1986 with certain ambitions, the most burning of which was to score a Test hundred at Lord's. When it came, after he had to lunch on 99 on the third day, he was realising a dream which had been in his mind since he was eight years old.

Bill Athey, with a classy 142 not out against New Zealand in a one-day international at Old Trafford, regained a place in the England Test team, and Martyn Moxon at last got his first Test chance (he scored 74) in the Lord's Test against New Zealand. Two Yorkshiremen batting for England had now become a rare sight.

Bob Taylor, 45, came hurriedly out of retirement during the 1986 Lord's Test after England wicketkeeper Bruce French was hit on the head by a Hadlee bouncer. Taylor, who was doing public-relations work for sponsors Cornhill, kept immaculately through much of the New Zealand innings until substitute Bobby Parks arrived.

The old master and the new: Geoff Boycott (above) and Graeme Hick (right). Boycott, 45, made his 150th first-class century in the 1986 season, still batting with all the famed caution and concentration. But at the end of the season the Yorkshire committee refused to renew his contract. He had reached the end of the road with his native county. There was no members' revolt this time. And after 23 seasons in which he had passed 1000 runs, he fell eight runs short this time. If there was to be a playing future it would have to be with another county. Hick became the youngest batsman to make 2000 runs in a season when he did so in 1986 at the age of 20. Born in Zimbabwe (formerly Rhodesia), he had already scored 50 centuries in all cricket, crowning his 50th with a score of 309 in a club match. Already a big asset for Worcestershire, Hick decided to qualify for England, which would entail waiting a further seven years.

Above: John Bracewell, New Zealand's offspinner, sprang a surprise in the 1986 Trent Bridge Test by hitting 110 at No. 8 to lift his side to 413, a lead of 157. Hadlee's 10 wickets in the match saw New Zealand storming to an eight-wicket victory. Above right: David Gower, deposed as England captain after the first Test against India, made a glorious 131 in the Oval Test against New Zealand. With him is the new captain, Mike Gatting, who made 121. Below: Botham's back – and showing what England were missing during his two-month ban. He had Edgar caught off his first ball, drawing level with Lillee's Test record of 355 wickets, and trapped Jeff Crowe lbw next over to become top man.

The New Zealanders enjoy the first series victory in England, persistent rain having blocked a result at The Oval after Botham had smashed 59 not out in 55 minutes to top off the Gower and Gatting centuries. Tasting the celebratory nectar are, back row, Bruce Edgar, Brian Barrett, John Bracewell, John Wright, Derek Stirling, Willie Watson, Trevor Franklin; front: Martin and Jeff Crowe, Jeremy Coney (captain), Evan Gray. Richard Hadlee, who took 19 wickets in the three Tests and was a perpetual menace, is among those missing.

Sir Donald Bradman, now 78, leaves his last committee meeting of the South Australian Cricket Association, having gradually wound down his commitments after almost 60 years of playing and helping to run the first-class game.

A surprise tailpiece to the New Zealanders' tour came with Ken Rutherford's 317 at Scarborough against Brian Close's XI. The 20-year-old from Otago batted only 230 minutes and hit eight sixes and 45 fours off a strongish attack.

Test cricket's second tie comes to pass at Madras on September 22, 1986, Maninder Singh, protesting loudly, having been adjudged lbw by umpire Vikram Raju to Greg Matthews's spin. Border, Australia's captain, has his hands aloft, wicketkeeper Tim Zoehrer picks up the ball, the tall Bruce Reid throws his hands up, and Geoff Marsh, sunhat in hand, leads the charge to the refreshments. The series – a tie and two draws – was played in an ill-tempered atmosphere. The first tied Test, at Brisbane 26 years before, was in the 498th Test match. This was the 1052nd.

In October 1986, West Indies were beaten for only the second time in their last 37 Tests, confounded at Faisalabad by Imran Khan and Abdul Qadir for a pathetic 53 all out, their lowest-ever Test total. Here Richards is caught by Rameez Raja for 0 off Qadir (6 for 16).

Above: Bruce Reid, Australia's tallest player at 6 ft 8 ins, was their major bowling discovery of the mid-1980s, though his left-arm fast-medium bowling was largely unsupported.

Left: Dean Jones, a tall, stylish Victorian, emerged as a Test-class batsman with 210 against India in the tied Test. The gaps left in the Australian line-up were slow to fill, but Jones, Boon and Geoff Marsh kept hopes alive.

Allan Border, as he entered the top 10 of Test match runmakers, saw the Ashes comfortably retained by England with their victories at Brisbane and Melbourne in late 1986. The man who scored the millionth Test run (Bombay, October 1986) had his gratification reduced by Australia's longest-ever sequence without a Test victory, broken at Sydney in January 1987 with a thrilling win over England.

West Indies' reversal at Faisalabad was swiftly avenged at Lahore, and with a continuing supply of fast bowlers such as Courtney Walsh (above) the world champions were looking ahead with awesome confidence. Right: Chris Broad, brought back by England for the 1986–87 tour of Australia, was resoundingly successful, making centuries in the Perth, Adelaide and Melbourne Tests.

England, with three lost series in 1986 and no victory in 11 Tests, were awash with jubilation and relief after beating Australia in 1986–87. Mike Gatting and his men, winners of the three international competitions – the 'Grand Slam' – experienced the same kind of satisfaction known by their touring predecessors throughout over a century of overseas cricket tours.

INDEX

Abbott, W. 129
Abdul Aziz 439
Abdul Qadir 562, 634
Abdulrahman, Sheikh Bukhatir 608
a'Beckett, E. L. 578
Abel, R. 159, 162, 164, 166, 169, 174, 180, 191, 199, 203, 204, 206, 213
Absolom, C. A. 128, 131
Aburrow, E. 29
Achong, E. E. 369
Adams, T. 88
Adcock, N. A. T. 417, 434
Aftab Baloch 529
Aislabie, B. 56
Akerigg, W. 109
Akroyd, S. H. 129
Alabaster, J. C. 426
Albert, Prince 136
Alcock, C. W. 134
Alderman, A. E. 346
Alderman, T. M. 584, 585, 596
Alexander, F. C. M. 433, 444, 448
Alexander, G. 135
Alexandra, Princess 155
Alimuddin 425
Alken, H., jnr 63
Allan, David 39
Allan, F. E. 129
Allan, P. J. 480
Allen, D. A. 446, 463
Allen, G. O. B. 309, 318, 323, 324, 344, 347, 368, 385, 578
Alletson, E. B. 235, 242
Alley, W. E. 450, 548, 590
Allom, M. J. C. 310, 374
Almond 38
Altham, H. S. 7, 296
Amarnath, L. 330, 331, 344
Amarnath, M. B. 546, 552, 595, 599, 601, 625
Amarnath, S. B. 546
Amar Singh, L. 331
Ames, L. E. G. 271, 303, 306, 311, 332, 334, 340, 345, 347, 348, 367, 431, 491
Amir Elahi 410
Amiss, D. L. 526, 530, 531, 549, 555, 567, 592, 629
Anderson, G. 102, 105
Anderson, J. 421
Anderson, J. C. 88, 90
Andrew, K. V. 419, 462, 475
Andrews, T. J. E. 277
Andrews, W. H. R. 369
Anne, Princess 526
Appleby, A. 120
Appleyard, R. 404, 419, 420, 423, 452
Archer, A. G. 196
Archer, R. G. 414, 415, 422, 423
Arlott, John 396, 578
Armitage, T. 122, 125
Armstrong, W. W. 207, 209, 223, 224, 236, 245, 246, 274, 275, 277, 281, 282, 283
Arnold, E. G. 214, 223, 230, 235, 261
Arnold, G. G. 489, 526, 533, 537
Arshad Parvez 546
Ash, E. 172
Ashdown, W. H. 332
Ashley, W. H. 162
Ashley-Cooper, F. S. 321
Ashton, C. T. 282, 365
Ashton, G. 282
Ashton, H. 282
Asif Iqbal 489, 515, 523, 525, 567
Astill, W. E. 295, 311
Athey, C. W. J. 630
Atkinson, D. S. 407, 423
Attewell, W. 145, 158, 168
Austen, Jane 61
Austin, H. B. G. 226, 295
Aylward, J. 29
Ayres, G. W. 172

Ayub Khan, President 443
Azharuddin, M. 614
Azlam Ali 546

Bacchus, S. F. A. 565
Bacher, A. 478, 479, 486, 505
Badcock, C. L. 347, 352, 353
Bailey, Sir Abe 217
Bailey, G. H. 129
Bailey, J. A. 506
Bailey, T. E. 401, 413, 414, 415, 418, 419, 420, 429, 433, 462
Bailhache, R. C. 579
Bainbridge, H. W. 184
Bairstow, D. L. 575, 581, 593
Baker, C. S. 244
Bakewell, A. H. 320, 331, 340
Bakewell, Enid 526, 548
Balaskas, X. C. 340
Balderstone, J. C. 518
Baldwin, H. 187, 353
Baldwin, J. L. 79
Baldwin, Stanley 271, 371
Ballantyne, J. 124
Baloo, P. 243
Bancroft, C. K. 226
Banerjee, S. 376
Bannerman, A. C. 129, 135, 138, 139, 146, 156, 160, 168, 169, 176
Bannerman, C. 126, 129, 138, 311
Baptiste, E. A. E. 605
Barber, R. W. 453, 480
Barber, Wilfred 329
Barber, William 29
Barbour, E. P. 264
Bardsley, W. 237, 245, 274, 277, 297, 387
Barlow, E. J. 468, 479, 506, 507, 567
Barlow, R. G. 133, 137, 142, 148, 149, 151
Barnard, H. M. 451
Barnes, S. F. 207, 224, 232, 245, 246, 251, 255, 325, 399, 412, 427, 431, 452
Barnes, S. G. 378, 379, 386, 389, 391
Barnes, W. 132, 142, 145, 150, 151, 164
Barnett, B. A. 334
Barnett, C. J. 331, 349, 354, 363, 365
Barrable, G. H. 155
Barratt, E. 129
Barratt, F. 312
Barrett, B. J. 633
Barrett, J. E. 165
Barrington, K. F. 409, 441, 444, 458, 460, 462, 469, 471, 473, 476, 484, 489, 490, 497, 582
Bartlett, G. A. 442
Bartlett, H. T. 355, 363
Barton, Edmund 131
Barton, V. A. 172
Barty-King, H. 24
Barwell, T. I. 481
Basébe, C. J. 83, 87
Bateman, A. E. 102
Bates, D. L. 465
Bates, S. H. 244
Bates, W. 132, 134, 137, 142, 144, 151, 152, 158
Batson, F. 203
Baxter, 'Honest' 75
Beagley, T. 56
Beal, C. W. 160
Beames, P. J. 421
Bean, G. 168
Beard, D. D. 426
Beauclerk, F. 50
Beaufort, Duke of 413
Beaumont, J. 158
Beaumont, R. 249
Beck, J. E. F. 416
Bedford, P. I. 388
Bedi, B. S. 522, 546, 552, 560
Bedle, W. 15
Bedser, A. V. 375, 377, 380, 385, 386, 389, 392, 399, 402, 404, 407, 409, 414, 415, 419, 423, 458
Bedser, E. A. 399
Bélanger, L. T. 31

Beldam, G. W. 217
Beldham, W. 29, 30, 44, 45, 84
Bell, A. J. 339
Benaud, J. 504
Benaud, R. 411, 420, 422, 434, 440, 447, 449, 451, 452, 456, 458, 459, 468
Benett, Sir William 19
Bennett, C. T. 295
Bennett, F. W. 504
Bennett, G. 97
Bennett, M. J. 615
Berry, L. G. 367
Bestwick, W. 278, 284
Bhandarkar, K. V. 383
Biddulph, S. 102, 116
Bignall, T. 116
Binks, J. G. 501
Binny, R. M. H. 601, 604
Binns, L. 38
Birchall 48
Bird, H. D. 464, 527, 540
Blackham, J. M. 128, 129, 131, 135, 139, 149, 156, 160
Blackie, D. D. 307
Blair, R. W. 417
Blaker, R. N. R. 227
Blanckenberg, J. M. 285
Bland, K. C. 475, 478, 479
Bligh, Hon. Ivo 140, 142, 290, 350
Blunt, R. C. 301, 317
Blythe, C. 227, 230, 235, 236, 237, 238, 240, 263
Board, J. H. 193, 196
Boitard, L. P. 20
Bond, J. D. 500, 515
Bonnor, G. J. 134, 135, 139, 142, 144, 146, 149, 150, 156, 160, 168
Boock, S. L. 606, 616
Boon, D. C. 634
Booth, B. C. 422, 456, 468
Booth, M. W. 262
Borde, C. G. 465
Border, A. R. 574, 583, 584, 585, 597, 607, 619, 620, 621, 622, 634, 635
Bosanquet, B. J. T. 197, 214, 215, 217, 221, 222, 237, 252
Botham, I. T. 190, 191, 337, 532, 563, 564, 565, 570, 572, 573, 576, 577, 578, 583, 584, 585, 593, 597, 606, 609, 610, 617, 619, 620, 626, 627, 629, 632, 633
Botten, J. T. 478
Bound, E. 15
Bowden, M. P. 158, 162
Bowen, Rowland 8, 460
Bowes, W. E. 322, 323, 332, 340, 357, 359, 367, 368, 380
Bowley, E. H. 278, 310, 329
Box, T. 70, 76, 87, 90, 91
Boxall, T. 51
Boyce, K. D. 521
Boycott, G. 10, 464, 469, 475, 478, 480, 483, 487, 509, 513, 514, 519, 526, 531, 558, 562, 569, 571, 572, 574, 578, 580, 581, 583, 586, 587, 591, 631
Boyington, F. 174
Boyle, H. F. 128, 129, 135, 139, 160
Bracewell, J. G. 603, 632, 633
Brache, F. 561
Bradman, D. G. 10, 25, 108, 198, 205, 210, 238, 271, 296, 305, 306, 308, 311, 312, 314, 315, 316, 319, 323, 325, 327, 332, 333, 335, 336, 337, 342, 347, 352, 353, 354, 355, 356, 360, 361, 375, 377, 378, 379, 380, 385, 386, 387, 389, 390, 391, 409, 413, 439, 449, 459, 498, 517, 529, 534, 556, 595, 605, 633
Bradman, John 377
Brain, W. H. 175
Brampton, C. 102
Brand, D. F. 278
Brand, H. 15

Brann, G. 158, 172
Braund, L. C. 208, 211, 214, 215, 216, 230, 304
Brayshaw, I. J. 492, 553
Brearley, J. M. 555, 557, 562, 565, 569, 571, 574, 582, 585
Brearley, W. 223, 224, 227
Brennan, D. V. 404
Brett, T. 29
Brewster, F. E. 147
Briggs, J. 150, 158, 162, 163, 168, 169, 193
Briggs, R. E. 422
Bright, R. J. 584
Briscoe, A. W. 365
Britcher, S. 46
Broad, B. C. 635
Broad, W. R. 598
Broadbridge, J. 61
Brockie, W., jnr 147
Brockwell, W. 172, 180
Brodrick, A. 17
Bromley-Davenport, H. R. 196
Brookes, D. 436
Brooks, E. W. J. 345, 374
Brown, A. S. 616
Brown, D. J. 479, 487, 496, 498
Brown, F. 145
Brown, F. R. 348, 368, 400, 404
Brown, G. 273, 283, 452
Brown, 'George of Brighton' 57
Brown, H. 147
Brown, J. 67
Brown, J. T. 180, 183, 196, 197, 204, 206, 322
Brown, L. S. 319
Brown, S. M. 383
Brown, W. A. 354, 355, 386, 498
Browne, C. R. 304
Bruce, W. 156, 176
Bryan, G. J. 287
Bryan, J. L. 292
Bryant, Mabel 335
Budd, E. H. 52
Bull, C. H. 353
Buller, J. S. 445, 470
Bullocky 115
Burge, P. J. P. 451, 456, 470, 471, 480, 481
Burgess, M. G. 516, 526, 563
Burke, J. W. 402, 422, 434, 440, 568
Burke, P. 444
Burn, E. J. K. 165
Burnell, H. B. 130
Burney, E. F. 20
Burnham, Forbes 508
Burns, W. B. 261
Burnup, C. J. 227
Burr, A. H. 94
Burrows, R. D. 224, 243
Burton, G. 130
Burton, W. J. 226
Bush, J. A. 123
Bush, R. E. 123
Buss, A. 465
Butcher, B. F. 485, 492
Butcher, R. O. 579
Butler, H. J. 381
Butler, K. 421
Byrd, W. 16
Byron, Lord George 52

Caesar, J. 90, 93, 105
Caffyn, W. 88, 90, 93, 97, 105, 270
Cahn, Sir Julien 321, 408
Cairns, B. L. 579, 603
Caldecourt, W. 65, 87
Calderon, P. H. 143
Calthorpe, F. S. G. 283, 295, 311
Cameron, H. B. 310, 341
Campbell, R. C. 245
Capel, W. 341
Cardus, Neville 7, 214, 428, 540, 594
Carkeek, W. B. 234
Carmichael, J. 129
Carmody, D. K. 372, 385
Carpenter, R. 93, 101, 103, 105, 168
Carr, A. W. 297, 309, 312, 321, 323
Carr, D. B. 424, 425
Carr, D. W. 237, 242

Carrick, J. S. 153, 154
Carson, W. N. 346, 371, 546
Carter, H. 209, 234, 246, 276, 277, 279, 280
Cartwright, T. W. 496, 497
Castens, H. H. 179
Cathcart family 39
Cave, H. B. 426
Chalk, F. G. H. 339, 368
Challen, J. B. 167
Challenor, G. 226, 287, 295, 304
Chamberlain, Neville 361
Chandler, A. 129
Chandrasekhar, B. S. 514, 522
Chaplin, Charlie 273
Chapman, A. P. F. 282, 292, 297, 298, 304, 306, 309, 315, 333, 339, 394
Chappell, G. S. 305, 501, 520, 531, 536, 544, 545, 557, 559, 570, 575, 578, 579, 597, 598, 607
Chappell, I. M. 305, 456, 481, 492, 520, 523, 531, 537, 541, 544, 557, 563, 586
Chappell, T. M. 579, 584
Charles II, King 50
Charles, Prince 541
Charlesworth, C. 244, 254
Charlwood, H. R. J. 118, 125
Charran Singh 444
Chatfield, E. J. 539, 603, 612
Chatterton, W. 172
Cheetham, J. E. 404, 411, 424
Chester, F. 253, 264, 304, 332, 412
Childe, J. W. 53
Chipperfield, A. G. 334
Chitty, J. 18
Christiani, R. J. 398, 407
Christopherson, S. 148
Christy, J. A. J. 319
Churchill, Winston 361
Clapshaw, A. 77
Clark, E. A. 481
Clark, E. W. 330, 331, 336, 452
Clark, E. W., jnr 147
Clark, T. H. 404
Clarke, A. 102, 105
Clarke, C. B. 358, 360, 363
Clarke, C. C. 66
Clarke, S. T. 566, 599
Clarke, William 72, 79, 80, 82, 83, 88, 94, 102, 126, 469
Clay, J. C. 340, 389
Close, D. B. 396, 424, 462, 486, 488, 489, 491, 512, 548, 619, 633
Cobbett, J. 70, 75
Cobbett, M. 142
Cobden, F. C. 119, 161
Coe, S. 252
Cole, C. G. 345
Collet, J. 35
Collinge, R. O. 523, 563
Collins, A. E. J. 198, 260
Collins, C. 295
Collins, H. L. 274, 275, 277, 294, 297, 298
Collins, Jose 263
Colman, Jeremiah 23, 82, 130
Compton, D. C. S. 343, 354, 358, 362, 370, 380, 383, 384, 385, 386, 388, 389, 392, 394, 400, 405, 409, 415, 418, 424, 428, 452, 611
Compton, L. H. 362, 387
Coney, J. V. 576, 603, 605, 612, 615, 633
Congdon, B. E. 516, 525, 526
Coningham, A. 182
Connolly, A. N. 504
Connolly, Bob 496
Constantine, L. N. 304, 316, 328, 333, 361, 368
Constantine, L. S. 226
Contractor, N. J. 453
Conway, J. 129, 137
Cook, F. J. 184

Cook, G. 597
Cook, N. G. B. 603
Cook, S. J. 591, 600
Cooper, G. C. 465
Cooper, W. H. 138
Copley, J. S. 37
Copley, S. H. 313
Copson, W. H. 346
Cornford, W. L. 285
Cornwallis, Marquess 45
Cotes, F. 27
Cottam, R. M. H. 501
Cotter, A. 215, 222, 223, 236, 246, 263, 370
Cotton, E. K. 422
Coulthard, G. 131
Coventry, Hon. C. J. 162
Cowan, M. J. 424
Cowans, N. G. 595, 596
Cowdrey, C. S. 614
Cowdrey, M. C. 397, 419, 420, 421, 429, 432, 436, 440, 443, 444, 445, 446, 454, 455, 456, 457, 458, 459, 463, 472, 486, 490, 491, 493, 495, 500, 516, 525, 532, 534, 535, 583
Cowie, J. 349
Cowper, R. M. 481, 486, 492
Cox, G., jnr 299, 369
Cox, G. R. 285, 299
Crafter, A. R. 589
Craig, A. 234
Craig, I. D. 411, 434, 442
Cranston, K. 382, 385
Crapp, J. F. 392
Crawford, J. N. 251, 452
Crawford, W. P. A. 422
Crawley, L. G. 295, 343
Cresswell, G. F. 403
Cripps, G. 179
Crisp, R. J. 330, 340
Cristofani, D. R. 372
Croft, C. E. H. 561, 575, 599
Crombie, C. 230
Crooke, F. J. 123
Crossland, J. 153
Crossland, J. M. 95
Crowe, J. J. 602, 603, 606, 632, 633
Crowe, M. D. 603, 605, 606, 629, 630, 633
Cruttenden 49
Cumberbatch, C. B. 226
Curtin, John 371
Curtis, A. 366
Cuttell, W. R. 196
Cuzens 115

Daft, C. 102
Daft, R. 9, 102, 116, 121, 132, 134
Dagley, R. 60
Dailey, W. S. 367
Dales, H. L. 295
Dalton, E. L. 319, 340
Dalton, H. 419
Daniel, W. W. 546, 548, 595, 605
Danloux, J.-P. 45
Dark, J. H. 69
Darling, J. 152, 193, 200, 209, 223, 387
Darling, L. S. 578
Darling, W. M. 570
Darnley, Dowager Countess 350
Darnley, 4th Earl 45
Davey, D. C. 179
Davidson, A. K. 415, 422, 434, 440, 447, 459, 541
Davidson, G. 188
Davies, D. Emrys 358
Davies, J. G. W. 339
Davies, William 67
Davis, C. A. 516
Davis, George 544
Davis, I. C. 555
Davis, W. W. 605, 608
Dawkes, G. O. 436
Dawson, E. W. 312
Day, A. P. 234, 252
Day, S. H. 237
Dean, J. 82, 88, 105
Deane, H. G. 291
de Courcy, J. H. 422
Deedes, W. F. 323
Dempster, C. S. 301, 317
Dempster, E. W. 416
Denison, W. 61, 82
Denness, M. H. 477,

534, 537, 542, 567, 573
Denton, D. 206, 221
Denton, J. S. 252
Denton, W. H. 252
Derby, Countess of 35
Derrick, J. 13
Depeiza, C. C. 423
de Selincourt, H. 350
de Silva, P. A. 618, 625
Devonshire, Duke of 532
Dewes, J. G. 393, 398, 403
Dexter, E. R. 444, 446, 450, 454, 455, 456, 458, 459, 463, 465, 471
Dias, R. L. 589, 625
Dick-a-Dick 115
Dickens, Charles 9, 96, 114
Dighton, R. 39
Dilawar Hussain 331
Dilley, G. R. 581, 583
Dillon, E. W. 219, 226, 227, 237
Disraeli, Benjamin 59, 113
Diver, A. 93
Docker, C. T. 264
Docker, L. C. 158
Doggart, G. H. G. 393
D'Oliveira, B. L. 416, 443, 484, 496, 506, 507, 519
Dollery, H. E. 387
Dolphin, A. 288
Donnelly, Desmond 363
Donnelly, M. P. 394, 395, 593
Dooland, B. 379, 380
Dorrington, W. 82
Dorset, Duke of 27, 31, 32, 36, 41
Doshi, D. R. 574, 588, 593
Douglas, J. W. H. T. 245, 252, 269, 275, 278, 292
Douglas-Home, Sir Alec 278, 426, 534
Dowd, T. H. 257, 351
Dowe, U. G. 511
Dowling, G. T. 493, 503
Downton, P. R. 581
Drake, A. 262, 269
Draper, Sir William 33
Druce, N. F. 193
Drummond, R. A. 551
Ducat, A. 367
Duck, G. N. 81
Duckworth, G. 307, 312, 320, 344, 380, 419, 452
Dudley, Earl 147
Duff, R. A. 207, 209, 212, 222, 223
Dujon, P. J. L. 610
Duke family 24
Duleepsinhji, K. S. 315, 320
Dumbrill, R. 478
Dunell, O. R. 162
Dunkels, P. R. 511
Dunn, J. 171
Durani, S. A. 453, 466
Durston, F. J. 277, 452
Dyer, D. V. 384, 561
Dymock, G. 531, 574
Dyson, J. 584, 597

Eady, C. J. 208
Eagar, E. D. R. 363, 436
Ealham, A. G. E. 534
Earnshaw, H. 270
East, D. E. 617
East, R. E. 521, 573
Eckersley, P. T. 312, 363
Edgar, B. A. 576, 603, 632, 633
Edinburgh, Duke of 394, 413, 541, 542
Edmonds, P. H. 562, 572, 614, 621
Edrich, J. H. 470, 476, 481, 491, 502, 514, 519, 537, 542, 548, 558, 573
Edrich, W. J. 351, 353, 358, 365, 367, 370, 383, 385, 408, 415, 419, 611
Edridge, H. 49
Edward I, King 11
Edward VII, King 110, 155, 170, 191, 220
Edward VIII, King 220
Edward, Prince 11
Edwards, J. D. 160
Edwards, R. 519, 536, 544
Egar, C. J. 467

Eisenhower, President D. D. 443
Elizabeth I, Queen 14
Elizabeth II, Queen 514, 540, 541, 555
Elliott, C. S. 346
Elliott, G. F. 129
Elliott, H. 331, 346
Ellison, M. 103
Ellison, R. M. 621
Emburey, J. E. 569, 570, 582, 588, 590, 620, 625
Emery, R. W. G. 367
Emmett, G. M. 363, 436
Emmett, T. 112, 120, 122, 125, 131, 132, 134, 137, 152
Endean, W. R. 411, 429, 604
Engineer, F. M. 500, 506, 515, 521
English, E. A. 481
Ericson, R. 591
Evans, D. G. L. 476
Evans, E. 127, 156
Evans, T. G. 380, 384, 392, 407, 410, 415, 419, 549
Eytle, E. 421

Fagg, A. E. 342, 344, 493, 514, 527
Fairservice, W. J. 237
Falcon, M. 282
Falkner, N. J. 609
Farington, J. 41
Farnes, K. 334, 343, 354, 357, 363, 366
Farrands, F. H. 148, 156
Farrimond, W. 369
Faulkner, G. A. 231, 238, 282, 290
Favell, L. E. 420, 503, 529
Fazal Mahmood 419, 435
Felix (N. Wanostrocht) 80, 82, 86, 87, 91
Fellows, J. 128
Fellows, H. 80, 81
Fender, P. G. H. 271, 273, 289, 295, 321, 374, 554, 578, 601
Fenton, Roger 89
Ferguson, W. 407
Ferguson, W. H. 398
Fernandes, M. P. 304
Ferris, J. J. 160, 161, 172
Fichardt, C. G. 184
Field, E. F. 244
Fielder, A. 214, 227, 232, 235, 237, 376
Findlay, W. 227
Fingleton, J. H. W. 324, 342, 347, 352, 354, 356, 380, 396, 577
Finlason, C. E. 162
Fishlock, L. B. 344, 404, 452
Fishwick, Herbert 306
Fitzgerald, F. 185
Fitzgerald, R. A. 120, 192
Flavell, J. A. 469, 470
Fleetwood-Smith, L. O'B. 355, 356, 357, 408
Fletcher, Blandford 167
Fletcher, D. A. G. 601
Fletcher, D. G. W. 381
Fletcher, K. W. R. 521, 526, 531, 536, 537, 573, 588, 590, 594
Flint, Rachael Heyhoe 526, 548
Flockton, R. G. 442
Flowers, W. 145, 150
Fluck, Peter 559
Foley, C. P. 163, 205
Foord-Kelcey, W. 128
Ford, E. C. B. 123
Ford, F. G. J. 180, 205
Ford, J. P. 132
Foster boys 45
Foster, F. R. 244, 245, 253, 323, 327
Foster, G. N. 282
Foster, N. A. 600, 614
Foster, R. E. 197, 199, 203, 204, 214, 215, 231, 260, 315
Foster, W. L. 203
Fothergill, A. J. 162
Fowler, G. (Som) 167
Fowler, G. (Lancs) 594, 601, 602, 606, 614
Fowler, R. St L. 239

Francis, B. C. 567
Francis, C. K. 120
Francis, G. N. 287, 304
Franco, General 361
Franklin, T. J. 603, 633
Frederick Louis, Prince of Wales 24, 220
Fredericks, R. C. 516, 520, 538, 545
Freeman, A. P. 271, 292, 303, 304, 306, 320, 329, 374
Freeman, G. 112, 116
French, B. N. 573, 630
Fry, C. B. 199, 205, 206, 211, 214, 21 , 222, 223, 228, 230, 235, 243, 247, 255, 284, 428, 517
Fuller, E. R. H. 434
Furniss, Harry 530

Gabbatiss, H. 130
Gaekwad, A. D. 604
Gaekwad, D. K. 604
Gage, Lord 333
Gandhi, Mrs Indira 616
Ganteaume, A. G. 385
Garland, H. 107
Garner, J. 571, 575, 610, 615, 623, 629
Garnett, H. G. 262
Garrett, T. W. 129, 137, 139, 155, 156
Garrick, David 38
Gatting, M. W. 582, 611, 614, 620, 622, 632, 633, 635
Gaunt, R. A. 434
Gavaskar, S. M. 305, 511, 513, 546, 565, 566, 572, 587, 588, 601, 605, 608, 627
Gay, L. H. 180
Geary, G. 298, 307, 452
Gehrs, D. R. A. 223, 249
Genghis Khan 5 9
George II, King 1
George V, King 220, 248, 266
George VI, King 220, 374, 389, 406
Ghorpade, J. M. 441
Gibb, P. A. 357
Gibbs, L. R. 449, 462, 464, 506, 508, 545, 589
Gibbs, P. J. K. 501
Gibson, C. H. 282
Giffen, G. 137, 139, 143, 144, 146, 156, 169, 177, 178, 183
Giffen, W. F. 352
Gifford, N. 626
Gilbert, E. 319, 518
Gilbert, G. H. B. 95
Gilbert, H. A. 235
Gilbert, W. R. 134
Gilchrist, R. 432, 438
Gill, S. 95, 99
Gilligan, A. E. R. 272, 285, 290, 291, 292, 378
Gillingham, F. H. 302
Gilmour, P. J. 541, 545, 550
Gimblett, H. 337, 344
Gladstone, W. E. 108, 113, 284
Gladwin, C. 391, 392
Gleeson, J. W. 493
Gleeson, R. A. 184
Glover, G. K. 179
Glover, H. S. 95
Goddard, J. D. C. 368, 398, 406, 433
Goddard, T. L. 434, 445, 446, 468, 473
Goddard, T. W. J. 334, 349, 363, 384, 452
Goering, Hermann 370
Goldwin, W. 16
Gomes, H. A. 609
Gomez, G. E. 360, 398, 417, 418
Gooch, G. A. 542, 573, 575, 580, 581, 583, 591, 621, 624
Gooch, P. A. 500
Goodall, F. 192
Goodman, P. A. 226
Goodwin, D. E. 501
Gopalan, M. J. 331
Gouws, F. B. 561
Gover, A. R. 319, 343, 344, 345
Gower, D. I. 34, 564, 568, 572, 581, 607, 610, 2 3

614, 615, 618, 621, 624, 632, 633
Grace, A. 111
Grace, E. M. 101, 105, 111, 123
Grace, G. F. 111, 118, 123, 134
Grace, Henry 111
Grace, H. M. 111
Grace, W. G. 25, 55, 65, 81, 95, 101, 105, 108, 111, 116, 118, 120, 121, 123, 125, 127, 132, 133, 134, 135, 145, 146, 148, 149, 151, 155, 156, 157, 160, 164, 165, 166, 168, 170, 171, 177, 185, 186, 187, 190, 191, 197, 198, 199, 200, 204, 217, 218, 245, 250, 255, 256, 260, 264, 283, 294, 295, 300, 305, 313, 352, 371, 385, 386, 530, 610, 629
Graham, H. 177
Graham, J. N. 534
Graham-Brown, J. M. H. 534
Grant, C. J. 66
Gravelot, H. 19
Graveney, T. W. 393, 396, 407, 415, 419, 433, 440, 454, 458, 459, 472, 486, 491, 498, 507
Gray, E. J. 603, 612, 633
Gray, J. R. 451
Gray, L. H. 343, 383
Gray, Thomas 20
Green, Benjamin 25
Green, C. E. 255
Greenhough, T. 441
Greenidge, C. G. 532, 538, 543, 548, 580, 604, 609
Greenwood, A. 122, 125
Gregory, D. W. 127, 129
Gregory, J. M. 271, 274, 275, 276, 277, 281, 282, 294, 306, 370, 626
Gregory, R. G. 367
Gregory, R. J. 331, 338, 365
Gregory, S. E. 181, 189, 200, 209, 223, 235, 247
Greig, A. W. 506, 515, 521, 530, 531, 533, 536, 542, 549, 553, 555, 557, 563, 570
Greig, J. G. 260
Grieve, B. A. F. 162
Griffin, G. M. 445
Griffith, C. C. 453, 461, 463, 464, 473, 483, 485, 498
Griffith, G. 97, 98, 118
Griffith, H. C. 304, 316
Griffith, S. C. 368, 384, 385, 430, 506, 578
Grignion, C. 22
Grimmett, C. V. 294, 308, 313, 333, 335, 342, 367, 440
Grimshaw, J. 152
Grimston, R. 146
Grinter, T. G. 289
Groube, T. U. 135
Grout, A. T. W. 434, 442, 447, 449, 468, 469, 471, 617
Grove, C. W. 408
Grundy, J. 88, 93, 101, 102, 116
Guillen, S. C. 407, 426
Gul Mahomed 381
Gunn, G. 232, 235, 245, 309, 311, 319, 431
Gunn, G. V. 319
Gunn, J. R. 452
Gunn, W. 145, 151, 164, 166, 178, 187, 191, 197, 199, 235, 393
Gupte, S. P. 437
Guy, J. 82

Hadlee, D. R. 502, 528, 563
Hadlee, R. J. 348, 528, 547, 563, 576, 586, 603, 606, 622, 627, 630, 632, 633
Hadlee, W. A. 348, 403
Hadow, W. H. 120
Hagety, L. 14, 64
Haig, N. E. 265, 311, 313
Haigh, S. 196, 218, 222, 233

Hall, L. 152
Hall, W. W. 438, 443, 444, 447, 449, 461, 463, 483
Hallam, M. R. 451
Hallam, W. B. 97
Halliwell, E. A. 179, 184, 217
Hallows, C. 271, 304, 312, 369
Hammond, Charlie 147
Hammond, W. R. 8, 271, 290, 295, 300, 304, 305, 306, 313, 315, 320, 322, 324, 327, 328, 334, 335, 336, 344, 345, 347, 348, 355, 357, 358, 359, 361, 364, 378, 379, 397, 618
Hampshire, J. H. 464, 499, 518
Hands, W. C. 244
Hanif Mohammad 410, 418, 425, 435, 438, 439, 488, 549
Hardie, B. R. 573
Hardstaff, J., jnr 338, 344, 356, 375
Hardstaff, J., snr 235
Harington, General 352
Haroon Rashid 562
Harper, R. A. 610
Harragin, A. E. 226
Harris, D. 29, 30, 37
Harris, Lord 9, 120, 128, 131, 134, 135, 148, 149, 153, 255, 265, 273, 295
Harrison, L. 451
Harry, F. 226
Hartigan, R. J. 232, 234
Hartley, A. 267
Harvey, R. N. 387, 397, 402, 411, 422, 427, 451, 456, 458, 481
Hassett, A. L. 372, 378, 386, 401, 406, 407, 412, 413, 414
Hastings, B. F. 516, 523, 528
Hatfeild, C. E. 253
Hathorn, C. M. H. 217
Hawke, Lord 158, 171, 190, 196, 206, 247, 255, 266, 506
Hawke, N. J. N. 456, 469, 471, 472, 586
Hawker, Sir Cyril 514
Hawkesworth, W. R. B. 27
Hawkins, E. 217, 225
Hawkins, Kathleen 110
Hay, Lord 51
Hayes, E. G. 256
Hayes, F. C. 527, 540
Haygarth, A. 121
Hayllar, J. 146
Hayman, Francis 18, 22
Haynes, D. L. 577, 604
Hayward, T., snr 93, 101, 103, 105
Hayward, T. W. 191, 193, 196, 199, 201, 204, 214, 223, 228, 231, 250, 383, 384
Hazare, V. S. 381, 385, 410
Hazell, H. 393
Hazlitt, G. R. 232, 247
Headley, G. A. 311, 336, 360, 361, 385
Headley, R. G. A. 526
Heane, G. F. H. 343, 368
Hearne, A. 172, 202
Hearne, F. 162, 179, 184
Hearne, G. G. 128, 172
Hearne, J. T. 172, 193, 195
Hearne, J. W. 245, 292, 296, 320
Hearne, T. 97
Hearne, W. 237
Heber, R. 37
Heine, P. S. 403, 424, 429
Henderson, M. 312
Henderson, R. 174
Hendren, E. H. 9, 269, 271, 283, 287, 289, 292, 303, 306, 311, 320, 328, 333, 335, 336, 349, 374
Hendrick, M. 569, 572
Hendricks, K. 179
Hendriks, J. L. 473, 485
Hendry, H. S. T. L. 280, 578
Henning, M. 561

Henty, E. 128
Henwood, T. 67
Herbert, A. P. 387
Herman, O. W. 501
Herring, R. W. 254
Hewett, H. T. 167, 173, 180
Hick, G. A. 631
Hicks, G. E. 147
Hicks, J. 122
Hide, Molly 350
Higgins, J. B. 331
Higgs, J. D. 579
Higgs, K. 463, 486, 556
Hilditch, A. M. J. 604
Hill, A. 120, 122, 125
Hill, C. 194, 195, 200, 207, 209, 211, 212, 223, 232, 245, 246, 387
Hill, L. T. 442
Hill, V. T. 167
Hillyer, W. 76, 82
Hime, C. F. W. 184
Hirst, G. H. 179, 193, 198, 206, 210, 211, 213, 214, 223, 233, 281
Hitch, J. W. 239, 245, 252, 255, 256, 286, 291, 331, 452
Hitler, Adolf 361, 386, 428
Hobbs, J. B. 102, 228, 231, 232, 236, 238, 245, 248, 250, 271, 276, 279, 283, 287, 290, 292, 293, 294, 295, 296, 297, 298, 299, 301, 305, 310, 313, 317, 320, 321, 323, 324, 332, 383, 409, 425, 452, 461
Hobgen, A. 125
Hobson, D. L. 600
Hodgkins, H. 27
Hogarth, William 18
Hogg, R. M. 568, 569
Hogsflesh, W. 29
Holden, Captain 132
Holder, V. A. 546, 566
Holding, M. A. 546, 548, 549, 574, 575, 580, 605
Hole, G. B. 421
Holford, D. A. J. 484
Holland, R. G. 615, 618
Holland, Trooper 230
Hollies, W. E. 376, 390, 452
Holmes, E. R. T. 301, 381
Holmes, P. 272, 288, 295, 296, 322, 329
Holt, J. K., jnr 418
Hone, L. 131
Hooker, J. E. H. 306, 308
Hooker, R. W. 474
Hookes, D. W. 249, 285, 555, 598, 619
Hope, Thomas 46
Hopkins, A. J. Y. 209, 223
Hopwood, J. L. 312, 452
Horan, T. P. 126, 128, 129, 139
Hordern, H. V. 241, 245
Hornby, A. H. 231
Hornby, A. N. 120, 131, 133, 134, 140
Horner, N. F. 441
Hornibrook, P. M. 314
Horton, H. 451
Horwood, S. E. 217
Houghton, D. L. 601
Howa, H. 562
Howard, C. G. 419
Howarth, P. G. 553, 563, 565, 603
Howarth, H. J. 503
Howell, H. 275, 283, 292
Howell, W. P. 200, 209, 223
Howorth, R. 376, 384
Hubble, J. C. 283
Huddleston, W. 243
Hudson, Sir Thomas 27
Hudson, Tim 619
Hughes, D. P. 500, 515
Hughes, K. J. 568, 569, 574, 575, 577, 584, 597, 613, 622
Hughes, Thomas 89
Huish, F. H. 219, 227, 237, 242
Humpage, G. W. 594
Humphrey, R. 118, 120, 129

637

Humphrey, T. 106, 118, 120
Humphreys, E. 227, 237
Humphreys, W. A. 180
Hunt, T. 88
Hunte, C. C. 435, 448, 462, 465, 474, 482
Hunter, D. 179, 206
Hunter, J. 152
Hussain, King of Jordan 511
Hutchings, K. L. 227, 232, 237, 261
Hutchinson, P. 162
Hutton, L. 305, 349, 354, 355, 356, 357, 358, 359, 362, 368, 375, 377, 380, 384, 385, 388, 390, 392, 395, 397, 400, 402, 404, 405, 407, 408, 413, 414, 415, 417, 418, 419, 421, 423, 433, 435
Hylton, L. G. 359

I'Anson, R. 130
Ibadulla, K. 489, 592
Ibrahim, K. C. 384
Iddison, R. 96, 97
Iddon, J. 312
Idris Begh 424
Ikin, J. T. 378, 407, 424
Illingworth, R. 458, 459, 489, 500, 502, 506, 509, 510, 514, 518, 556, 586, 593
Imran Khan 593, 594, 595, 618, 627, 634
Imtiaz Ahmed 425
Ingleby-Mackenzie, A. C. D. 451, 572
Inman, C. C. 474
Innocent, E. 366
Insole, D. J. 436, 493
Intikhab Alam 489, 506, 515, 528, 553
Inverarity, R. J. 496, 613
Iqbal Qasim 564, 589
Iredale, F. A. 181, 200, 246
Iremonger, J. 245
Ironmonger, H. 319
Iverson, J. B. 400, 401

Jackman, R. D. 580, 582
Jackson, A. A. 308, 314, 316, 481, 596
Jackson, F. S. 177, 201, 211, 213, 214, 219, 223, 255
Jackson, H. L. 436
Jackson, J. 93, 102, 105, 116, 270
Jagger, Mick 37, 529
Jaisimha, M. L. 473, 492
James, A. K. 512
James, C. L. R. 461
James, Robert 75
Jameson, J. A. 530, 534
Jameson, T. O. 295
Jardine, D. R. 295, 304, 306, 321, 322, 323, 324, 328, 331, 374, 413
Jarman, B. N. 473, 492
Jarvis, A. H. 135, 156, 160
Jarvis, T. W. 516
Javed Burki 489
Javed Miandad 538, 589, 595, 612, 618
Jeacocke, A. 294
Jeeves, P. 261
Jefferies, S. T. 591
Jehangir Khan, M. 342, 490
Jellico 115
Jenkins, R. O. 392
Jenkins, V. G. J. 380
Jenner, T. J. 510, 522
Jenner-Fust, H., snr 217
Jennings, D. W. 253
Jennings, R. V. 591
Jepson, A. 381
Jessop, G. L. 191, 197, 199, 209, 210, 211, 230, 258, 266, 370, 550
Johns, A. E. 200
Johnson, C. L. 179
Johnson, G. W. 534
Johnson, H. H. H. 398
Johnson, I. W. 374, 388, 402, 406, 422
Johnson, John 102
Johnson, K. O. E. 372
Johnson, T. F. 359
Johnston, W. A. 397,

406, 407, 420
Jones, A. 520
Jones, A. O. 199, 223, 229, 245, 260
Jones, D. M. 634
Jones, E. 191, 200, 209, 260, 352
Jones, G. G. 129
Jones, I. J. 482, 483
Jones, P. E. 398, 407
Jones, S. A. 130
Jones, S. P. 139, 156, 160
Joshi, U. C. 517
Julian, R. 441
Julien, B. D. 546
Jupp, H. 106, 118, 121, 125, 129, 132, 134
Jupp, V. W. C. 272, 304

Kaiser Wilhelm 256, 257
Kallicharran, A. I. 511, 516, 530, 531, 538, 594
Kanhai, R. B. 448, 462, 465, 474, 485, 506, 508, 527, 534, 541
Kapil Dev 588, 601, 602, 604, 627
Kardar, A. H. 419, 425, 539
Keeton, W. W. 321, 359
Keith, H. J. 412
Kelleway, C. 245, 264, 274, 294, 306
Kelly, J. J. 200, 209, 223
Kelly, K. 526
Kelly, Ned 127
Kempis, G. A. 162
Kempis, G. S. 179
Kemp-Welch, G. D. 371
Ken, Bishop Thomas 14
Kendall, T. 126
Kennedy, A. S. 283, 285, 289, 312, 363
Kennedy, President J. F. 467
Kenyon, D. 423, 472
Kermode, A. 219
Key, K. J. 174
Khalid Hassan 418
Khalid Irtiza 546
Khan Mohammad 410, 435
Kidney, J. M. 398
Kilburn, J. M. 7, 380
Killick, E. H. 218, 242
Killick, E. T. 310
Kilner, N. 288
Kilner, R. 269, 288, 292, 295, 303
King, C. L. 571, 599
King, J. B. 225
King, J. H. 228
King Cole 115
Kinneir, S. P. 245, 254
Kippax, A. F. 299, 306, 308
Kirk, E. C. 242
Kirmani, S. M. H. 592, 601
Kirsten, P. N. 591, 599
Kirti Azad 601
Kirwan, J. H. 68
Kline, L. F. 434, 448, 449
Knapp, E. M. 123
Knight, A. E. 214, 216
Knight, B. R. 494
Knight, D. J. 374
Knight, G. T. 61
Knott, A. P. E. 489, 498, 502, 510, 513, 521, 534, 543, 549, 555, 563, 584
Knox, N. A. 227, 261
Kortright, C. J. 7, 184, 370
Kotze, J. J. 217, 230
Kourie, A. J. 591
Kruger, F. 133
Kruger, Paul 202
Kuruppu, D. S. P. B. 604

Lacey, F. E. 196, 268
Laker, J. C. 230, 397, 399, 404, 407, 409, 414, 415, 424, 427, 429, 433, 439, 440, 441, 572
Lamb, A. J. 592, 609, 621
Lambert, O. 422
Lambert, William 53, 55, 72, 517
Lander, B. R. 525
Lang, Andrew 7
Langley, G. R. A. 406
Langridge, James 331, 341
Langridge, J. G. 329, 341
Langridge, R. J. 465
Langton, A. B. C. 340, 367

Langtry, Lillie 155
Larwood, H. 297, 298, 304, 310, 314, 320, 321, 323, 324, 325, 326, 327, 333, 343, 370, 388, 396, 556
Laver, F. 173, 200, 223, 234, 236
Law, R. 559
Law, S. 147
Lawson, G. F. 583, 584, 596, 600, 618
Lawrence, C. 97, 105, 115
Lawry, W. M. 40, 452, 456, 457, 469, 471, 473, 480, 492, 494, 504, 509
Layne, O. H. 226
Leaney, E. 172
Leaney, J. 172
Learmond, G. C. 226
Leary, S. E. 446
Leatherbarrow, C. 369
Le Couteur, P. R. 240
Lee, F. 152
Lee, F. S. 343, 369, 445
Lee, H. W. 259, 369
Lee, I. S. 331
Lee, J. W. 369
Lee, R. 109
Leer, G. 29
Lees, W. K. 563, 603
Lees, W. S. 228
Legge, G. B. 363
Lenham, L. J. 465
Leno, Dan 205
Le Roux, G. S. 591
Leslie, C. F. H. 142
Lever, J. K. 552, 555, 573
Lever, P. 507, 539, 540
Leveson Gower, H. D. G. 238, 253
Levett, W. H. V. 339
Levick, T. H. C. 295
Lewis, A. R. 521
Lewis, D. J. 561
Lewis, R. V. 532
Leyland, M. 288, 304, 306, 323, 329, 334, 336, 339, 356, 362
Lightfoot, A. 437
Lillee, D. K. 7, 516, 518, 519, 520, 522, 524, 535, 537, 541, 542, 543, 547, 548, 551, 552, 553, 555, 556, 557, 568, 570, 574, 577, 584, 585, 589, 595, 607, 632
Lilley, A. F. A. 211, 214, 215, 216, 223
Lilley, B. 343
Lilley, Fred 88, 93
Lillywhite, F. W. (William) 61, 62, 66, 79, 82, 87, 91, 126
Lillywhite, James, jnr 105, 118, 125, 126, 127, 134, 137, 153, 158
Lillywhite, John 88, 93, 101, 118
Lincoln, Abraham 65
Lindbergh, Charles 271
Lindsay, D. T. 468, 478, 479, 487, 505
Lindwall, R. R. 379, 380, 387, 388, 389, 401, 406, 412, 419, 423, 428, 440, 460, 462, 625
Lister, J. 586
Livingston, L. (Jock) 418
Livingstone, D. A. 451
Livsey, W. H. 283
Llewellyn, C. B. 217, 235
Lloyd, C. H. 492, 499, 506, 527, 537, 538, 540, 541, 542, 545, 550, 575, 577, 589, 604, 608, 610
Lloyd, D. 500, 512, 533, 540
Lloyd, T. A. 608
Loader, P. J. 409, 419, 432, 441
Lock, G. A. R. 403, 404, 409, 414, 415, 417, 424, 425, 433, 436, 438, 446, 454, 455, 491, 492
Lockwood, E. 122, 132, 134, 145
Lockwood, W. H. 174, 209, 211
Lockyer, T. 88, 90, 93, 105
Lohmann, G. A. 157, 158, 164, 166, 167, 168, 174, 184, 191, 196

Long, A. 470
Long, W. H. 266
Lord, Thomas, 42, 53, 57, 61
Louden, G. M. 269
Love, James, 20
Low, David, 361
Lowe, W. W. 240
Lowry, T. C. 301
Lowry, W. C. 147
Loxton, S. J. E. 400
Lubbock, A. 105, 120
Lubbock, E. 120
Lucas, A. P. 131, 134, 148
Lucas, E. V. 30
Lucas, R. S. 183
Luckhurst, B. W. 506, 509, 513, 519, 534
Luty, A. 144
Lyons, Captain 57
Lyons, J. J. 160, 169
Lyttelton, A. 148, 149, 151
Lyttelton, E. 290

Macartney, C. G. 236, 248, 264, 268, 271, 274, 279, 280, 296, 333, 456, 628
Macartney, Clara 456
Macaulay, G. G. 288, 363
MacDonald, Ramsay 271
MacGregor, G. 163, 168, 205
Mackay, J. R. M. 225
Mackay, K. D. 411, 427, 439, 449, 450, 456
MacKinnon, F. A. 128, 131
Maclagan, Myrtle 337, 350
MacLaren, A. C. 180, 185, 187, 193, 194, 199, 207, 211, 214, 223, 227, 236, 247, 282, 285, 365
Maclean, J. A. 569
Macquarie, Governor Lachlan 58
Madan Lal 588, 601
Madugalle, R. S. 625
Mahmood Hussain 435
Mailey, A. A. 271, 274, 278, 279, 292, 294, 297, 299, 315, 333, 380, 413
Majid Khan 342, 490, 522
Makepeace, J. W. H. 276, 304
Malhotra, C. L. 430
Mallett, A. A. 522, 537
Maninder Singh 628, 634
Manjrekar, V. L. 408
Mankad, A. V. 538
Mankad, M. H. V. 385, 406, 410, 425, 498, 573
Mann, F. G. 391, 578, 592
Mann, F. T. 285
Mann, Sir Horatio 31, 37
Mann, Noah 29
Mann, N. B. F. 192
Mansoor Akhtar 549
Marcon, W. 81
Markham, N. E. 561
Marriott, C. S. 328
Marsden, T. 59, 72
Marsden-Smedley, G. 264
Marsh, G. R. 634
Marsh, J. 208
Marsh, R. W. 516, 522, 537, 549, 553, 555, 557, 570, 583, 584, 596, 607
Marsh, Roger 140
Marshal, A. 227
Marshall, Howard 374
Marshall, M. D. 566, 605, 608, 609, 615, 622, 623, 625
Marshall, R. E. 398, 436, 451
Marsham, C. H. B. 227
Martin, 'Bosser' 356
Martin, F. 165, 172
Martin, F. R. 304
Martin, G. 122
Martin, J. W. 442, 448
Martindale, E. A. 328, 369
Martingell, W. 76, 82, 88
Martyn, H. 227
Marx, W. F. E. 8, 276
Mary II, Queen 15
Mason, J. R. 193, 227, 237
Mason, Ronald 7

Mason, W. H. 87
Massie, H. H. 139, 140, 265
Massie, R. A. L. 518, 519, 583
Massie, R. J. A. 265
Matthews, A. D. G. 365, 367, 370
Matthews, G. R. J. 634
Matthews, T. G. 123
Matthews, T. J. 249
Maul, H. C. 131
Mayne, E. R. 274, 285
Mayne, L. C. 505
McAlister, P. A. 246
McCabe, S. J. 313, 314, 324, 335, 336, 342, 347, 354, 355, 357, 471
McCarthy, C. N. 408
McConnon, J. E. 419
McCool, C. L. 378, 379, 386
McCormick, E. L. 353, 355, 356
McCosker, R. B. 544, 555, 566, 600
McDermott, C. J. 618, 620
McDonald, C. C. 422, 434, 440, 448
McDonald, Donald 10
McDonald, E. A. 271, 276, 277, 281, 282, 312
McDonnell, P. S. 135, 138, 139, 142, 144, 146, 156, 160
McGilvray, Alan 378
McGlew, D. J. 412, 424, 434
McIlwraith, J. 156
McIntyre, A. J. W. 403, 404, 409
McIntyre, W. 116
McKechnie, B. J. 579
McKenzie, G. D. 450, 460, 467, 473, 496, 506, 510, 518
McKenzie, K. A. 591
McKibbin, T. R. 190, 191
McKinnon, A. H. 478
McLean, R. A. 412
McLeod, C. E. 194, 200, 223
McLeod, R. W. 177
McMaster, J. E. P. 162
McMillan, Q. 319
McNamee, R. L. A. 299
McNutt, H. 147
Mead, C. P. 239, 245, 269, 279, 285, 289, 303, 327, 431
Mead, W. 187
Meckiff, I. 440, 447, 467
Medlycott, K. T. 609
Meintjes, D. J. 291
Melville, A. 382
Mendis, L. R. D. 610, 625
Menzies, R. G. 365, 431
Mercer, J. 342
Merchant, V. M. 331, 344
Merritt, W. E. 301
Merry, C. A. 407
Middleton, J. 179, 184, 217
Midwinter, W. E. 113, 129, 137
Miers, Miss 331
Milburn, C. 483, 484, 494, 498, 499, 519, 628
Miles, R. F. 123
Miller, G. 564, 569, 597
Miller, K. R. 8, 372, 378, 379, 380, 388, 390, 397, 402, 406, 412, 414, 421, 422, 423, 427, 428, 611
Miller, L. S. M. 417
Milligan, F. W. 196
Mills, C. H. 179
Mills, E. 148
Mills, J. W. 301, 317, 524
Mills, R. 58
Milton, W. H. 162
Minshull, J. 31
Minter, E. J. 350
Misson, F. M. 442
Mistri, K. M. 243
Mitchell, A. 330, 331
Mitchell, B. 319, 340,

383, 384, 392
Mitchell, F. 196, 206, 217, 247
Mitchell, T. B. 334, 346
Mitford, Mary Russell 64
Mobey, G. S. 365
Modi, R. S. 371
Mohammad Idris Yusuf 346
Mohsin Khan 593, 604
Moir, A. M. 425
Mold, A. W. 204, 205
Moloney, D. A. R. 368
Molyneaux, Jan 487
Montgomery, Field Marshal Viscount 371
Moore, R. H. 348, 350
Morgan, W. C., jnr 147
Morland, George 42
Morley, F. 132, 134, 142
Moroney, J. 397
Morris, A. R. 364, 379, 380, 387, 388, 390, 402, 420, 422
Morrison, C. S. 226
Mortimore, J. B. 515
Mortlock, W. 88, 97
Moseley, H. R. 532
Moss, A. E. 425, 430, 445
Motz, R. C. 502
Moule, W. H. 135
Moxon, M. D. 630
Moyes, A. G. 265, 460
Moynihan, Sir Berkeley 279
Mudassar Nazar 562, 593, 595
Mudie, W. 97
Muhammad Ali 528
Mullagh, J. 115
Murdoch, W. L. 129, 131, 135, 139, 146, 148, 156, 172, 195, 218
Murray, A. R. A. 411, 412
Murray, B. A. G. 503
Murray, D. L. 465, 506, 538
Murray, J. T. 431, 452, 457, 477, 486, 487, 501, 598
Murray-Anderton, H. 167
Murrell, H. R. 269
Mushtaq Ali 331, 344, 406
Mushtaq Mohammad 438, 454, 506, 513, 523
Mussolini, Benito 361
Mutch, D. 586
Muybridge, Eadweard 153
Myers, S. B. 561
Mynn, A. 70, 71, 76, 79, 80, 82, 146

Nadkarni, R. G. 466
Naoomal Jeoomal 331
Napoleon 53
Nash, M. A. 493
Nayudu, C. K. 266, 300, 322, 331
Nayudu, C. S. 331, 370
Nazir Ali 331
Nelson, R. P. 363
Nettleton, C. 97
Newhall, C. A. 147
Newhall family 106
Newhall, R. S. 147
Newham, W. 158, 202
Newland, P. M. 223
Newland, Richard 17
Newman, J. A. 283, 289
Newton, A. E. 158, 167, 240
Nichol, M. 318, 332
Nicholls, D. 534
Nichols, B. 167
Nichols, M. S. 330, 331, 337, 343
Nicholson, A. G. 464
Nicholson, W. 111
Nicoll, H. R. 233
Nimbalkar, B. B. 390, 393
Nissar, Mahomed 322, 330
Noble, M. A. 200, 201, 209, 212, 214, 223, 235, 236
Noblet, G. 411
Noreiga, J. M. 511
Norris, Percy 616
Northington, Earl 33
Norton, J. E. 422

638

Nourse, A. D. 291, 342, 358, 373, 383, 391, 392, 397
Nourse, A. W. 238, 271, 285, 291
Nunes, R. K. 304
Nupen, E. P. 316
Nureyev, Rudolf 537
Nurse, S. M. 485, 499
Nyren, John 7, 40, 47, 61, 66
Nyren, Richard 17, 29, 30, 47

Oakman, A. S. M. 465
Oates, W. C. 185
O'Brien, T. C. 158
Ochse, A. E. 162
O'Connell, M. G. 515
O'Connor, J. 311, 343
O'Connor, J. D. A. 234
Odell, W. W. 262
O'Keeffe, F. A. 8, 283
O'Keeffe, K. J. 523
Old, C. M. 527, 533, 535, 564, 583, 584, 593
Oldfield, Ruth 326
Oldfield, W. A. S. 274, 294, 306, 323, 326, 335, 342, 357, 413, 468
Oldis, J. 333
Oldroyd, E. 288
O'Linn, S. 445, 446
Ollivierre, C. A. 218
Ollivierre, R. A. 226
O'Neill, N. C. 443, 447, 456, 458
O'Reilly, W. J. 325, 335, 336, 342, 355, 361, 374, 413, 578
O'Riordan, A. J. 501
Osbaldeston, G. 57
Oscroft, W. 116, 132, 134
O'Shaughnessy, S. J. 273, 601
Ottaway, C. J. 120
Owen-Smith, H. G. 318

Packer, Kerry 18, 512, 554, 557, 558, 559, 561, 563, 568, 570, 573
Padday, C. M. 259
Padgett, D. E. V. 489
Page, M. L. 317
Palairet, L. C. H. 167, 173, 213
Palairet, R. C. N. 167
Palmer, G. E. 135, 137, 139, 146, 156
Palmer, Olive 261
Pamensky, J. L. 561
Parfitt, P. H. 454, 476, 477, 519
Paris, C. G. A. 497
Parish, R. J. 578
Parkar, G. A. 587
Parker, C. W. L. 278, 290
Parker, H. 346
Parker, J. E. 226
Parker, J. F. 365, 381, 404
Parker, J. M. 576
Parkin, C. H. 280, 361
Parkin, D. C. 179
Parks, J. H. 351, 573
Parks, J. M. 424, 444, 446, 465, 473, 573
Parks, R. J. 573, 630
Parr, G. 82, 93, 94, 102, 104, 105, 106, 121
Parry, D. R. 566
Parsons, J. H. 244, 294
Pascoe, L. S. 557, 566, 577
Pataudi, Nawab of, jnr 453, 463, 487, 521, 604
Pataudi, Nawab of, snr 318, 320, 324, 334
Patel, J. M. 442
Patiala, Maharajah of 243, 266, 300, 331
Patil, S. M. 601
Patker, S. V. 430
Patterson, B. P. 623, 624
Pattisson, W. B. 128
Patton, T. 251
Paul, A. G. 187
Pawley, T. 245
Pawson, H. A. 348
Paynter, E. 312, 320, 326, 350, 354, 358, 369
Peach, H. A. 286
Pearce, T. N. 342
Pearson, F. A. 290
Peate, E. 137, 141, 144, 148, 151, 152

Peebles, I. A. R. 313, 314, 315, 317, 333
Peel, R. 158, 161, 164, 166, 168, 180, 181
Pegler, S. J. 249
Pell, O. 82
Pellew, C. E. 274, 277
Penn, F. 128, 131
Penny, E. 19
Penny, R. 238
Pepper, C. G. 372
Perkins, H. 192
Perks, R. T. D. 376
Perrin, P. A. 217
Peter 115
Petherick, P. J. 553
Petrie, E. C. 436
Pett, W. 27
Pettiford, J. 372
Philipson, H. 168
Phillip, N. 566
Phillips, H. 122
Phillips, J. 174, 204, 205
Phillips, W. B. 285, 607, 621
Phillipson, W. E. 365
Philpott, P. I. 435, 474
Pickering, F. P. U. 120
Pierre, L. R. 398
Pilch, F. 25, 65, 69, 76, 79, 80, 82, 87, 94
Pilling, R. 133, 134, 137, 158
Pinder, G. 122, 132
Pine, R. E. 31
Pithey, A. J. 468
Place, W. 369
Platts, J. T. B. D. 116
Pocock, P. I. 517, 614
Poidevin, L. O. S. 159
Pollard, J. 58
Pollard, R. 377, 389
Pollard, V. 477, 526
Pollock, P. M. 478, 479, 505, 506, 508
Pollock, R. G. 467, 468, 478, 479, 487, 504, 506, 507, 508, 547, 591, 600
Ponsford, W. H. 271, 285, 299, 302, 311, 312, 323, 333, 336, 578, 595
Ponsonby, Frederick 77, 79
Ponsonby Fane, Spencer 79
Ponsonby Staples, R. 155
Pooley, E. 115, 118, 124, 130, 134
Poore, R. M. 176, 184, 199, 202
Pope, A. V. 346
Pope, D. F. 321
Pope, G. H. 369
Pothecary, J. E. 403
Pougher, A. D. 158, 172, 189
Prasanna, E. A. S. 503, 522, 537
Prater, Ernest 64
Pratt Green, Charles 16
Preston, J. M. 144, 152, 158
Preston, K. C. 431
Price, J. S. E. 473, 484
Price, Walter 116
Price, W. F. F. 320, 362
Prideaux, R. M. 461
Priestley, A. 193
Procter, M. J. 205, 487, 505, 506, 507, 515, 517, 534, 563, 567, 572, 591
Prout, J. A. 233
Pullar, G. 446, 453, 474
Pullin, C. K. 123, 148
Purchase, R. 29
Pycroft, James 7, 84

Qasim Omar 618
Quaife, B. W. 284
Quaife, Walter 164
Quaife, W. G. 199, 244, 284
Quin, S. O. 331
Quinlan, L. 238
Quinn, N. A. 319

Radcliffe, O. G. 168
Radley, C. T. 564
Rae, A. F. 398, 399
Raju, Vikram 634
Ramadhin, S. 398, 406, 430, 432
Rameez Raja 634
Ranatunga, A. 610
Randall, D. W. 555, 556,

569, 570, 586, 592, 593, 606
Ranjitsinhji, K. S. 176, 190, 193, 194, 199, 200, 202, 204, 206, 210, 211, 231, 233, 266, 272, 284, 305, 315
Ransford, V. S. 236, 246
Ratcliffe, A. 318
Ratnayake, R. J. 625
Ravilious, Eric 354
Rawlin, J. T. 158, 174
Read, J. M. 158, 162, 168, 174
Read, W. W. 10, 142, 148, 151, 157, 172, 174
Red Cap 115
Reddy, S. J. 443
Redmond, R. E. 524, 528
Redpath, I. R. 480, 498, 509, 516, 523
Rees, W. 95
Reid, B. A. 634
Reid, J. R. 396, 454, 490
Reid, John R. (artist) 130
Relf, A. E. 214, 216, 218
Renneberg, D. A. 492
Reynolds, Frank 47, 286
Rhodes, H. J. 436, 482
Rhodes, W. 198, 206, 210, 211, 213, 214, 222, 223, 230, 238, 245, 275, 288, 297, 298, 311, 395, 431, 452
Rice, C. E. B. 551, 586, 591, 622
Rice, W. 21
Richards, B. A. 305, 495, 504, 505, 506, 507, 508, 567, 591
Richards, I. V. A. 305, 538, 541, 546, 547, 549, 552, 571, 581, 595, 610, 619, 620, 626, 629, 634
Richardson, A. W. 346
Richardson, H. 164
Richardson, P. E. 424, 430, 434, 440
Richardson, R. B. 616, 623
Richardson, T. 164, 174, 178, 181, 183, 184, 190, 191, 193, 209
Richardson, V. Y. 324, 326, 342, 378
Riches, N. V. H. 278
Richmond, 2nd Duke of 17
Richmond, 4th Duke of 43
Ricketts, E. W. C. 331
Ring, D. T. 386, 407
Ringrose, W. 288
'Rip' 203
Rippon, A. D. E. 252
Rippon, A. E. S. 252
Rippon, N. 251
Ritchie, G. M. 619, 621
Ritchie, John 94
Roach, C. A. 304
Roberts, A. M. E. 530, 532, 545, 548, 561, 605
Roberts, J. H. 162
Robertson, J. D. B. 370, 383, 387, 394
Robertson-Glasgow, R. C. 478
Robey, George 264
Robins, D. H. 543
Robins, R. W. V. 334, 344, 365, 368
Robins, T., jnr 147
Robinson, C. J. 167
Robinson, Emmott 288
Robinson, E. P. 367
Robinson, Ray 7, 421, 594
Robinson, R. D. 582
Robinson, R. T. 617
Robson, E. 240
Roe, W. N. 137, 153, 167
Roller, W. E. 155
Rommel, Marshal E. 371
Roope, G. R. J. 526, 562
Root, C. F. 295, 318
Rorke, G. F. 437, 440
Rose, Harry 115
Rose, W. M. 120
Rose-Innes, A. 162
Rossi, Henri 60
Routledge, T. W. 179, 184
Rowan, E. A. B. 360, 392, 405
Rowbotham, J. 122
Rowe, G. A. 179

Rowe, L. G. 516, 531, 549, 599
Rowlandson, Thomas 54
Roy, Ambar 503
Roy, Pankaj 406, 410, 425
Royle, V. P. F. A. 131
Rumsey, F. E. 481
Rushby, T. 278
Russell, A. C. 279, 280, 284
Rutherford, K. R. 633
Ryder, J. 274, 294, 299, 307

Sablet, J. F. 46
Sackville, Lord 28, 333
Sainsbury, P. J. 436, 451, 532
Salim Malik 627
Sampson, H. 72, 88, 103
Sandby, Paul 23
Sandham, A. 164, 256, 292, 294, 297, 301, 311, 332, 374, 531, 578
Sandhu, B. S. 601
Sang Hue, D. 568
Santall, S. 244
Sardesai, D. N. 511
Sarfraz Nawaz 566
Sarwate, C. T. 376
Saunders, J. V. 209, 212
Sawle, L. M. 435
Scaddon, R. 21
Schultz, S. S. 131
Schwarz, R. O. 217, 231, 238, 249, 267
Scott, H. J. H. 146, 148, 156
Scott, J. A. 147
Scott, Captain R. F. 279
Scott, S. W. 130
Scott, V. J. 374
Scotton, W. H. 137, 145, 148, 155
Sealy, J. E. D. 358, 359, 360
Seccull, A. W. 179
Seeff, L. 600
Selby, J. 125, 132, 134, 137, 145
Sellers, A. B. 323, 329
Sen, P. 406
Sewell, C. O. H. 179
Sewell, E. H. D. 261, 265
Sewell, T. 82, 97
Seymour, James 227, 237, 253, 273
Seymour, John 218
Shackleton, D. 423, 436, 451, 462
Shalders, W. A. 217
Sharp, J. C. 254
Sharpe, J. W. 168
Sharpe, P. J. 464, 470, 489, 501, 502
Shastri, R. J. 65, 601, 613, 617
Shaw, A. 116, 125, 126, 132, 134, 137, 145, 158, 168
Shaw, J. 116
Shaw, V. K. 128
Sheahan, A. P. 497
Sheffield, E. J. 317
Sheffield, Lord 8, 168, 170, 172
Shepard, E. H. 30
Shepheard, G. 44
Shepherd, B. K. 455
Shepherd, J. N. 515, 534
Sheppard, D. S. 398, 407, 433, 440
Shepstone, G. H. 217
Sherman, T. 88, 90
Sherwell, P. W. 225
Sherwin, M. 145, 164
Shields, Sir Douglas 352
Shivaramakrishnan, L. 614, 616
Shivlal Yadav 576
Shivnarine, S. 566
Shrewsbury, A. 132, 137, 145, 148, 151, 155, 157, 158, 164, 166, 174, 178, 187, 197, 199, 213, 235, 393
Shuter, J. 174
Shuttleworth, K. 500
Sibbles, F. M. 312, 345
Siedle, I. J. 340
Sikander Bakht 564
Silcock, F. 118
Silva, S. A. R. 610, 625
Simkins, W. V. 179

Simmons, J. 500, 569
Simon, Sir John 10
Simon, Robin 82
Simpson, R. B. 422, 434, 448, 455, 456, 458, 466, 468, 471, 492, 544, 561, 586
Simpson, R. T. 362, 402, 408, 419, 473
Simpson-Hayward, G. H. T. 238
Sims, A. 250, 251
Sims, J. M. 383
Sinclair, J. H. 184, 213, 217
Sismey, S. G. 372
Skinner, A. C. 162
Slade, Justice 570
Slater, K. N. 440
Slight, J. 135
Smailes, T. F. 362
Small, G. C. 590
Small, J. A. 304
Small, John 29, 30, 31, 38
Smith, A. C. 459
Smith, C. A. 158, 162, 284
Smith, C. I. J. 343, 349
Smith, C. L. 606
Smith, D. H. K. 501
Smith, D. M. 624
Smith, Ernest 206
Smith, E. J. 244, 245, 294, 295, 452
Smith, F. W. 162
Smith, H. 304
Smith, I. D. S. 603, 606
Smith, M. J. K. 444, 445, 473, 477, 480
Smith, N. 573
Smith, O. G. 431
Smith, S. G. 226, 254
Smith, Syd, jnr 246
Smith, T. P. B. 377, 452
Smith, V. I. 382
Smith, W. C. 239, 258
Smithson, G. A. 384
Snedden, M. C. 603
Snooke, S. J. 217
Snow, J. A. 465, 477, 485, 486, 490, 491, 510, 513, 520, 525
Snowball, Betty 350
Sobers, G. S. 65, 305, 417, 433, 435, 444, 447, 448, 464, 465, 483, 484, 485, 486, 490, 491, 493, 499, 506, 507, 508, 515, 516, 517, 523, 528, 531, 540, 587, 613
Sobers, M. 515
Solkar, E. D. 521, 533
Solomon, J. S. 430, 447, 462
Sondes children 27
Southerton, J. 118, 125, 129, 130, 132
Spencer, C. T. 436
Spencer, T. W. 528, 543
Spofforth, F. R. 104, 116, 128, 129, 135, 139, 140, 142, 146, 148, 149, 156, 191, 298, 585
Spooner, R. H. 214, 223, 243
Spring, A. W. 234
Sprot, E. M. 224
Squires, H. S. 367, 381
Srikkanth, K. 601, 628
Stackpole, K. R. 509, 515, 519, 523
Staples, A. 345
Statham, J. B. 406, 419, 420, 421, 423, 456, 458, 459, 462, 479
Stedman, J. 22
Steel, A. G. 134, 142, 148, 149, 151, 260
Steele, D. S. 543
Steele, J. F. 521
Steele, R. C. 578
Stephens, F. G. 244, 252
Stephens, G. W. 244, 252
Stephenson, E. 97
Stephenson, H. H. 93, 96, 97, 98, 457
Stephenson, H. W. 424
Stephenson, J. W. A. 363
Stevens, G. T. S. 268, 298, 368
Stevens, Edward

Simmons, J. 500, 569
'Lumpy' 9, 31, 38
Stevenson, G. B. 575
Stewart, M. J. 409, 430, 462, 464
Stewart, Peter 'Buck' 29
Stewart, R. B. 162
Stewart, W. J. 441
St Hill, E. L. 369
St Hill, W. H. 304
Stirling, D. A. 633
Stoddart, A. E. 9, 154, 158, 166, 168, 177, 180, 183, 193, 194, 260
Stoever, D. P. 147
Stollmeyer, J. B. 360, 398, 399, 406
Stollmeyer, V. H. 360
Storer, H. 346
Storer, W. 193, 200
Strachan, G. 129
Straw, T. 206
Streatfeild, E. C. 174
Street, J. 129
Stricker, L. A. 241
Strudwick, H. 164, 214, 242, 245, 258, 269, 291, 292, 298, 304
Strutt, J. 7, 12
Studd, C. T. 141, 142
Studd, G. B. 141, 142
Studd, J. E. K. 141
Subba Row, R. 437, 444, 450, 506
Sueter, T. 29, 30
Summers, G. 116, 439
Surridge, W. S. 409
Sutcliffe, B. 395, 417, 423, 482
Sutcliffe, H. 221, 271, 272, 288, 290, 292, 293, 298, 303, 310, 320, 321, 322, 323, 324, 325, 329, 334, 362, 374, 425, 474, 618
Sutcliffe, W. H. H. 424
Suttle, K. G. 441, 465
Swan, H. D. 295
Swanton, E. W. 7, 380
Swetman, R. 441, 444, 446

Taber, H. B. 498
Tahir Naqqash 593
Tallon, D. 357, 374, 379, 388, 391, 442
Tancred, A. B. 162
Tancred, L. J. 217
Tankerville, Earl 29, 38
Tarilton, P. H. 271
Tarpot 115
Tarrant, F. A. 260
Tarrant, G. 105, 116
Tate, F. W. 212
Tate, M. W. 212, 272, 285, 289, 291, 292, 298, 300, 304, 317, 320, 333, 399, 414
Tattersall, R. 402, 404, 405
Tavaré, C. J. 587, 597, 602, 610
Tayfield, H. J. 397, 411, 417, 428, 429
Tayler, A. Chevallier 227
Taylor, A. D. 286
Taylor, B. 521
Taylor, B. R. 477, 482, 524, 528
Taylor, C. G. 76
Taylor, D. J. S. 532
Taylor, H. W. 249, 251, 268, 285, 292, 319
Taylor, J. M. 274, 277
Taylor, K. 489
Taylor, L. B. 252
Taylor, M. L. 312
Taylor, M. N. S. 532
Taylor, R. W. 564, 570, 576, 593, 598, 630
Taylor, T. 29
Taylor, T. L. 206, 281
Taylor, W. T. 532
Tennyson, L. H. 279, 289, 295, 336, 351, 371
Teonge, Henry 16
Terry, V. P. 608
Thayer, J. B., jnr 147
Thewlis, J., snr 122
Thomas, J. G. 623
Thompson, A. W. 388
Thompson, Francis 133
Thompson, G. J. 219, 233
Thompson, J. 130

639

Thoms, R. A. 134, 156, 168
Thomson, A. A. 7
Thomson, A. L. 509
Thomson, H. S. 128
Thomson, J. R. 535, 536, 537, 541, 542, 543, 551, 557, 563, 566, 596, 597
Thomson, N. I. 465
Thornton, C. I. 113, 129, 160, 282
Tilak Raj 613
Timms, W. W. 282
Tinley, R. C. 102, 105
Titmus, F. J. 457, 466, 469, 471, 479, 491
Todd, L. J. 345, 365, 367
Tomkins 40
Toohey, P. M. 561
Toone, F. C. 7, 268, 292
Toshack, E. R. H. 378, 388
Townsend, C. L. 175, 199
Townsend, F. 123
Townsend, L. F. 330, 331, 346
Treanor, J. C. 422
Tredrea, Sharon 548
Tremlett, M. F. 436
Trestrail, K. B. 398
Trewineau, Mrs 48
Tribe, G. E. 377
Trim, J. E. 407
Trimble, S. C. 529
Trott, A. E. 182, 196, 199, 201, 204, 231, 256, 260, 285, 370
Trott, G. H. S. 160, 189
Troup, G. B. 576
Trueman, F. S. 393, 404, 408, 412, 415, 432, 438, 444, 446, 451, 452, 458, 464, 470, 471, 472, 489, 503, 545
Trumble, H. 176, 190, 200, 201, 209, 212, 213, 215, 584
Trumble, J. W. 156
Trumper, Anne 456
Trumper, V. T. 7, 199, 200, 209, 210, 211, 212, 214, 222, 223, 225, 241, 246, 250, 251, 260, 296, 305, 308, 365, 407, 456, 577, 628
Tunks, W. 77
Tunnicliffe, J. 197, 206, 322
Turnbull, M. J. L. 316, 371

Turner, A. 541, 543, 551
Turner, C. T. B. 138, 159, 160, 161, 177
Turner, G. M. 502, 516, 528, 531, 562, 571, 592
Turner, J. M. W. 46
Turner, Mary 18
Turner, S. 573
Turner (scorer) 152
Tyldesley, G. E. 269, 277, 296, 303, 304, 306, 312
Tyldesley, J. T. 196, 199, 211, 214, 216, 221, 223, 226, 227, 269, 296
Tyldesley, R. K. 290, 292, 312
Tylecote, E. F. S. 112, 142
Tyler, E. J. 167, 204
Tyson, C. 276
Tyson, F. H. 419, 420, 421, 423

Ufton, D. G. 450
Ullathorne, C. 122
Ulyett, G. 122, 125, 131, 132, 134, 137, 148, 151, 152, 158, 162, 164, 166
Umrigar, P. R. 406, 453
Underwood, D. L. 472, 485, 496, 502, 510, 524, 533, 534
Usman 546

Valentine, A. L. 398, 407, 426, 448
Valentine, B. H. 330, 339, 368
Valson, S. 601
van der Bijl, V. A. P. 591
van der Merwe, P. L. 468, 478
van Geloven, J. 441
van Ryneveld, C. B. 393
Varachia, M. R. 561
Veivers, T. R. 455, 470, 471, 481
Vengsarkar, D. B. 566, 588, 599, 601, 616, 628
Venkataraghavan, S. 504, 522
Venn, Henry 21
Verity, H. 321, 322, 323, 329, 331, 334, 335, 341, 344, 346, 360, 361, 362, 369
Vernon, G. F. 142, 158

Victoria, Queen 136
Viljoen, K. G. 384, 392
Vinall, J. 15
Vine, J. 218, 245
Vintcent, C. H. 162
Viswanath, G. R. 521, 546, 563, 587, 588, 593
Vivian, G. E. 318
Vivian, H. G. 318
Voce, W. 311, 312, 320, 321, 323, 324, 326, 336, 347, 377, 378, 381, 388, 452
Vogler, A. E. E. 231, 238, 241
Vorster, B. J. 496

Waddington, A. 288
Wade, W. W. 392
Wadekar, A. L. 492, 511, 514
Wadsworth, K. J. 516
Wahid Mirza 549
Wainwright, E. 193, 206
Wait, O. J. 404
Waite, J. H. B. 423, 429, 434, 445, 467
Walcott, C. L. 368, 398, 406, 418, 421, 422, 430, 433
Walcott, J. H. 417
Wale, S. 25
Walker, A. K. 428
Walker, C. W. 367
Walker, D. F. 365
Walker, H. 29
Walker, M. H. N. 537, 542, 555
Walker, P. M. 476
Walker, T. 29, 37, 40, 45, 61
Walker, V. E. 92, 113
Wall, T. W. 326, 335
Wallace, Boon 561
Wallace, W. M. 364
Wallach, B. 217
Wallis, J. 38
Walpole, Horace 27
Walsh, C. A. 635
Walsh, J. E. 408
Walters, C. F. 318, 330, 331, 332, 334, 336
Walters, K. D. 481, 492, 494, 498, 504, 505, 509, 523, 536, 544, 550, 555
Waqar Hassan 425
Ward, Alan 502, 509
Ward, Albert 180, 182, 183

Ward, T. A. 249
Ward, William 57, 61, 69
Wardill, B. J. 156, 193, 200
Wardle, J. H. 415, 419, 420, 423, 429
Warnapura, B. 590
Warner, P. F. 192, 196, 204, 214, 225, 236, 245, 265, 266, 268, 274, 323, 371, 384, 431, 461
Warner, R. S. A. 204
Warr, J. J. 400
Warren, A. 219
Warton, R. G. 162
Washbrook, C. 350, 365, 367, 377, 379, 392, 401, 403, 408, 412, 436
Wasim Bari 489, 576
Wass, T. G. 231, 235, 239
Wassell, A. 451
Watkin, Sir Edward 166
Watkins, A. J. 407, 424
Watmough, C. 548
Watson, C. 444
Watson, F. B. 295, 312
Watson, G. D. 480, 515
Watson, W. (Eng) 382, 413, 414, 417, 424
Watson, W. (NZ) 633
Watts, G. F. 65
Waugh, R. 31
Wazir Ali 331
Wazir Mohammad 438
Webb, Captain 171
Webb, P. N. 576
Webbe, A. J. 131, 134, 290
Webster, Tom 362
Weekes, E. D. 391, 398, 418, 430, 432, 508, 616
Weekes, K. H. 360
Weir, G. L. 364
Wellard, A. W. 337, 348, 370, 452, 620
Wellham, D. M. 585
Wellings, E. M. 380
Wellington, Duke of 53, 66
Wells, G. 97
Wells, H. G. 100
Wells, John 29, 45
Wells, Joseph 100
Wenman, E. G. 70, 87
Werner, Carl 84
Wessels, K. C. 566, 596, 619, 620
West, P. 465
Weston, G. N. 610

Wettimuny, Sidath 610, 611
Wheeler, W. C. 130
Whieldon, G. 79
White, A. A. 196
White, D. W. 451
White, G. C. 217, 231, 238, 267
White, J. C. 268, 278, 307, 309
White, John 152
White, R. A. 475
White, Thomas 29
Whitehead, G. W. E. 267
Whitehead, L. 206
Whitelaw, P. E. 346, 546
Whitington, R. S. 372, 380
Whittock, N. 86
Whysall, W. W. 292
Wickham, A. P. 167
Wight, C. V. 304
Wild, F. 116
Willes, J. 56, 61, 71
Willey, P. 577, 581, 624
William III, King 15
William IV, King 66
Williams, C. B. 398
Williams, W. 295
Willis, R. G. D. 509, 536, 552, 555, 564, 565, 570, 572, 577, 582, 583, 584, 585, 593, 594, 595, 596, 602, 607
Willoughby, J. T. 184
Wills, T. W. S. 115
Willsher, E. 101
Wilson, A. E. 370
Wilson, C. E. M. 196
Wilson, D. 465, 489
Wilson, E. R. 288
Wilson, G. 288
Wilson, J. T. 115
Wilson, J. V. 404, 419
Winchilsea, Earl 42, 45
Winlaw, R. de W. K. 365
Winter, G. 73
Wisden, J. 88, 93, 107, 111
Wodehouse, P. G. 261
Wood, A. 329
Wood, B. 500
Wood, C. J. B. 244
Wood children 43
Wood, G. E. C. 282, 290
Wood, G. M. 569, 577, 601, 619
Wood, H. 162, 172, 174
Woodfull, W. M. 299, 323, 324, 325, 335, 336

Woodhouse, W. H. 152
Woods, S. M. J. 163, 167, 171, 186, 333
Wooller, W. 389, 436
Woolley, F. E. 226, 234, 235, 237, 240, 245, 269, 271, 279, 287, 290, 292, 298, 303, 320, 322, 332, 338, 374, 376, 431, 452, 455, 461
Woolmer, R. A. 534, 544, 567
Wootton, G. 102, 116
Worrall, J. 160, 185
Worrell, F. M. M. 368, 398, 406, 407, 418, 430, 432, 443, 444, 448, 449, 453, 461, 462, 463, 465
Worsley, Sir William 474
Worthington, T. S. 344, 346
Woutersz, J. F. 600
Wright, Sir Allan 603
Wright, D. V. P. 354, 380, 385, 393, 401
Wright, H. 88
Wright, J. G. 576, 603, 606, 615, 633
Wright, Joseph 34, 43
Wright, W. 145, 164
Wyatt, R. E. S. 300, 311, 336, 339, 346, 367, 578
Wynyard, E. G. 199

'Yabba' 324
Yallop, G. N. 561, 570, 584, 585
Yardley, N. W. D. 369, 377, 384, 385, 404
Yardley, W. 116, 128
Yarnold, H. 405
Yashpal Sharma 588, 601
York, Duke of 43
Young, H. I. 452
Young, J. A. 383, 408
Young, R. A. 272
Younis Ahmed 501
Ypres, Earl 154
Yuile, B. W. 476

Zaheer Abbas 451, 513, 533, 535, 550, 565, 567, 595
Zoehrer, T. J. 634
Zoffany, Johan 27
Zulch, J. W. 271
Zulfiqar Ahmed 425

640